The Best Novels of the Nineties

To Nick and Justin
and
to Grif

The Best Novels of the Nineties

A Reader's Guide

by
LINDA PARENT LESHER

McFarland & Company, Inc., Publishers
Jefferson, North Carolina, and London

Acknowledgments: Having spent most of the 1990s immersed in the book reviewing literature of the English-speaking world, I can only marvel at my good fortune. Not only have I come away from this project convinced that the novel is very much alive and well at the end of the second millennium but I have also been struck by the overall quality (characterized by both intellectual generosity and reverence for craft) of late twentieth century literary criticism and commentary. It would be impossible to name all of the critics and commentators who have made the task of putting this guide together such a pleasure, but I am grateful to all of them for their insight, enthusiasm and clarity of expression.

Finally, it is with profound appreciation that I dedicate this guide to the 710 novelists whose work is featured herein and whose remarkable talent continues to enrich my life.

Library of Congress Cataloguing-in-Publication Data

Lesher, Linda Parent, 1947–
The best novels of the nineties : a reader's guide /
by Linda Parent Lesher.
p. cm.
Includes bibliography and indexes.
ISBN 0-7864-0742-5 (sewn softcover : 50# alkaline paper) ∞
1. English fiction — 20th century — Bibliography.   2. American
fiction — 20th century — Bibliography.   3. Commonwealth fiction
(English) — Bibliography.   4. Best books.   I. Title.   II. Title:
Best novels of the 90s.
Z2014.F4 L45   2000   [PR881]
016.823'91409 21 — dc21   99-44233   CIP

British Library Cataloguing-in-Publication data are available

Cover image ©1999 Eyewire

Manufactured in the United States of America

*McFarland & Company, Inc., Publishers
Box 611, Jefferson, North Carolina 28640
www.mcfarlandpub.com*

Contents

Introduction

"All books," wrote John Ruskin, "are divisible into two classes: the books of the hour and the books of all time."

Contemporary literary critics and avid readers of fiction would argue that there is a third class: novels which, while not necessarily destined to survive the age in which they are written, are set apart by their readability, felicities of style, successful experimentation, emotional resonance, thematic probity or narrative dexterity — novels, in short, which are capable of providing a great deal of pleasure to a wide range of readers.

That many of these titles are not better known to the general reading public is less a function of their inherent worthiness than of the nature of contemporary book selling and promotion. While there is no shortage of excellent novels published each year, only a handful will be given the push of a well-financed promotional campaign, and even those allotted prominent shelf space in the months immediately following publication will likely lose their high-visibility position once the new season's crop of novels arrives in the bookstores. All but a hardy few will wither in the competition with the "book of the hour," the sort of novel rewarded less for its innate qualities than for the simple fact that is exceedingly well known.

The Best Novels of the Nineties, presenting a thousand or so critically acclaimed works by approximately 700 contemporary novelists, hopes to introduce a wide range of readers to some of the best novels currently being published throughout the English-speaking world. Specifically, it is designed to

(1) celebrate the breadth and quality of fiction writing in the last decade of the twentieth century;

(2) bring a significant number of critically acclaimed titles to the attention of book professionals (particularly those whose job it is to make title recommendations), members of book groups (whose numbers are increasing exponentially), and the general fiction-reading public; and

(3) pique the interest of readers who read eclectically and widely as well as those with well-defined preferences.

Title Selection

The selection process was comprehensive without being exhaustive. All novels listed were published in English between 1990 and nearly the end of 1998. Titles were selected for inclusion by routinely consulting over 100 well-recognized sources of quality book reviews drawn from the entire English-speaking world. These include world-class newspapers (e.g., the *New York Times*, the *Chicago Tribune*, the *Los Angeles Times*, the *Washington Post*, the *London*

1

Times, the [London] *Guardian*, the [Melbourne] *Age*, the *Irish Times*, the *Christian Science Monitor*); respected literary journals (e.g., *Meanjin, Wasafiri, Yale Review, TLS, Sewanee Review, London Review of Books, New York Review of Books, Books in Canada, Australian Book Review, South African Review of Books,* the *Literary Review*); periodicals that devote significant space to book reviewing (e.g., the *New Yorker, Atlantic Monthly, The Spectator, New Statesman*), and book trade and library publications (e.g., *Booklist, Kirkus Reviews, Library Journal, Publishers Weekly*). On pages 3–4 is a list of all magazines and newspapers cited, along with the abbreviations used to cite them.

More than 1,000 recently published novels were selected for inclusion. Novels were deemed eligible for inclusion if they were reviewed in three or more recognized sources of book reviews, had obtained favorable evaluations from a preponderance of reviewers, or had been awarded a major literary prize.

Given the usual constraints of space, time and editorial judgment, not every title that fits this set of criteria was included in the guide. For example, titles were omitted if they had recently gone out of print or were published too late in 1998 to be included. Lastly, given the scope of this guide, one must assume that some worthy titles were inadvertently overlooked.

Format

Each title has been assigned a discrete entry number (from 1 to 1,033). Titles are organized under eight sections, each of which reflects a thematic or categorical focus (e.g., "1: The Ties That Bind," or "7: Humor"). Of course these categories are not always mutually exclusive; titles might belong in more than one section. To avoid repeating information, each book has only one "main" or primary entry, placed in the section deemed most appropriate; other sections will reflect author and title only, referring the reader to the main entry for full information. For example, an "experimental" novel with a historical setting would have a primary entry in the experimental fiction section ("3: The Innovators") with a cross reference in the section featuring historical fiction ("5: Time After Time").

Entries are arranged alphabetically by author within each section.

Individual title entries consist of a one-paragraph summary of the book and a one-paragraph selection of representative review excerpts. (Names of reviewers whose own novels are covered in this guide appear in **boldface** print.) These data are augmented with information regarding media adaptations (audiocassette recordings, television adaptations and film versions), literary prizes won and shortlisted for, and the availability of reading group guides.

A comprehensive listing of review citations is also included.

Three appendices follow the main text. These appendices list (1) books covered in this work that are available on audiocassettes; (2) books that have been adapted for films; and (3) books for which reading group guides are available.

Following the appendices, a Bio-Bibliography lists all fiction titles by each of the 710 novelists, along with brief biographical information.

In addition to an Author and Title Index, a detailed Subject Index has been provided. This Subject Index offers access to theme or topic (e.g., aging, child abuse, divorce, genetic engineering, religious fundamentalism, maternal abandonment, repressed memory), geographic and historical setting, historical personages and events, author nationality or ethnicity, fiction subgenres (e.g., academic satires, autobiographical fiction, black comedies, family sagas, "punk lit"), literary prize winners (by prize), debut novels, and more.

Review Media
and Abbreviations

ABR —*American Book Review*
Advocate — *The Advocate*
AfrAmRev —*African American Review*
Age — *The Age* (Melbourne, Australia)
Amer —*America*
AntR —*Antioch Review*
AtlM —*Atlantic Monthly*
AusB&P —*Australian Bookseller and Publisher*
AusBkRev —*Australian Book Review*
BBN —*British Book News*
BBR —*Boston Book Review*
BellesL —*Belles Lettres*
BksCan —*Books in Canada*
BL —*Booklist*
BlkSchlr —*Black Scholar*
BloomR —*Bloomsbury Review*
BosGlobe —*Boston Globe*
CanFor —*Canadian Forum*
CanLit —*Canadian Literature*
CCent —*Christian Century*
CF/BBT —*Contemporary Fiction* (British Book Trust)
ChiSun —*Chicago Sun-Times*
ChiTrib —*Chicago Tribune*
Civ —*Civilization*
ComW —*Commonweal*
CSM —*Christian Science Monitor*
Econ —*Economist*
EngJ —*English Journal*
Essence —*Essence*
Esq —*Esquire*
EW —*Entertainment Weekly*
FT —*Financial Times*

Guard — *The* (London) *Guardian*
GW —*Guardian Weekly* (London)
HarpBaz —*Harper Bazaar*
HartCour —*Hartford Courant*
Hisp —*Hispanic Review*
Independ — *The* (London) *Independent*
India Today —*India Today*
IrishT — *The Irish Times*
IrishRev —*Irish Review*
JNZL —*Journal of New Zealand Literature*
KR —*Kirkus Reviews*
Lancet — *The Lancet*
LAT —*Los Angeles Times*
LATBR —*L.A. Times Book Review*
Listener —*The Listener*
LitRev —*Literary Review*
LJ —*Library Journal*
LRB —*London Review of Books*
LST —*London Sunday Times*
LT —*London Times*
Meanj —*Meanjin*
MFSF/MF&SF —*Magazine of Fantasy and Science Fiction*
MontrG —*Montreal Gazette*
Ms —*Ms. Magazine*
MultCultR —*Multicultural Review*
Nation — *The Nation*
NatR —*National Review*
NewLeader —*New Leader*
NewR —*New Republic*
NewSci —*New Scientist*
NewsWk —*Newsweek*
NS —*New Statesman*

NS&S — *New Statesman & Society*
NY — *New Yorker*
NYMag — *New York Magazine*
NYRB — *New York Review of Books*
NYT — *New York Times*
NYTBR — *New York Times Book Review*
Obs — *London Observer*
PeopleW — *People Weekly Magazine*
PW — *Publishers Weekly*
Q&Q — *Quill & Quire*
QBR — *Quarterly Black Review*
RevCF — *Review of Contemporary Fiction*
Salon — *Salon Magazine*
SAROB — *South African Review of Books*
SatR — *Saturday Review*
Scotsman — *The Scotsman*
SeattleT — *Seattle Times*
Sewanee — *Sewanee*
SFCBR — *San Francisco Chronicle Book Review*

SFRB — *San Francisco Review of Books*
SLJ — *School Library Journal*
SMH — *Sydney Morning Herald*
SmPress — *Small Press Review*
SouthLiv — *Southern Living*
Spec — *The Spectator*
Time — *Time Magazine*
TLS — *Times Literary Supplement*
USA Today — *USA Today*
VFair — *Vanity Fair*
VLS — *Voice Literary Supplement*
VV — *Village Voice*
Wasafiri — *Wasafiri*
WLT — *World Literature Today*
WPBW — *Washington Post Book World*
WRB — *Women's Review of Books*
WSJ — *Wall Street Journal*
YaleRev — *Yale Review*

The Ties That Bind

The bedrock themes of love, friendship, family and community have long been the basis for resonant, deeply affecting works of fiction — works which refresh the soul, confirm one's humanity, or offer the fraternity of solace. In the pages of the following novels, hard won insights — and, occasionally, even joy — arise out of the most unpropitious circumstance; families from the benign to the pathological and amorous alliances from the sublime to the ridiculous — are explored in all their frustrating but wondrous complexity; and the power of belonging (to family, tribe, ethnic grouping, neighborhood) is tested and measured. Selected novels range from the modest (but highly regarded) works of such writers as Kathleen Cambor, Deborah Corey, and Paule Marshall to the latest offerings of established, much-honored novelists such as Saul Bellow, Alice McDermott, and Graham Swift. In settings as diverse as San Francisco, rural Montana, and the rust-belt of Upstate New York, the beautiful, if terrifying, dailiness of life, the shattering force of love, and the fascinating complexity of the human response are all explored with narrative skill and psychological insight

Adams, Alice (USA)

1 *Almost Perfect* (1993); Knopf 1993 (HC); Washington Sq 1998 (pbk)

When small, dark, "almost beautiful" Stella Blake (a San Francisco–based journalist and diffi-dent daughter of a minor celebrity) meets handsome, fair-haired Richard Fallon (a talented and wildly successful commercial artist), they begin a passionate affair. As Richard's behavior grows disturbingly erratic and their relationship lurches between violent confrontation and ecstatic reconciliation, it takes the smitten Stella much longer than the reader to realize that something is seriously amiss.

Publishers Weekly suggests that "Always an acute observer of people and relationships, Adams here writes convincingly and movingly of a passionate love affair, investing her controlled, analytical prose with remarkable depth and feeling" and calls the book "one of her best." In the view of the *Chicago Tribune*, "A lot goes on in the two-year span of the novel, and it's all marvelously well-told, full of revealing detail, smart dialogue and astute observation." Novelist **Lawrence Thornton** (*NYTBR*) observes that Ms. Adam's 12th work of fiction is "a fine and often very funny novel about "San Francisco's social hierarchies (the privileged as well as the working class, the straight and the gay)." The *L.A. Times Book Review* concludes that "*Almost Perfect* is an unflinching novel, the work of a wise and uncompromising mind. It resists easy resolutions, offers neither redemption nor revelation but leaves open the possibility of both."

RECOGNITION: *NYTBR* Notable Book of 1993; REVIEWS: *BellesL* Win '93/94; *BL* 4/15/93; *ChiTrib* 7/18/93; *KR* 4/15/93; *LATBR* 7/11/93; *NY* 8/2/93; *NYTBR* 7/11/93; *PW* 4/12/93; *WLT* Spr '94; *WPBW* 6/27/93; *WRB* 12/93; EDITOR'S NOTE: Ms. Adam's 13th work of fiction, *Medicine Men* (1997) was named a *NYTBR* Notable Book of 1997 and was praised by novelist **Francine Prose** for, while "not exactly breaking new ground," providing the reader with, like a "cup of one's favorite tea: something familiar, dependable, at once bracing and refreshing..." (*LATBR* 6/8/97).

Alvarez, Julia (USA)

2 *Yo!* (1997); Algonquin 1997 (HC); NAL-Dutton 1997 (pbk)

In her follow-up to *How the Garcia Girls Lost Their Accents*, Julia Alvarez features the oldest daughter Yolanda (affectionately known as "Yo"), now a sexy, highly successful novelist trailing a string of former lovers. As the story gets underway her best-selling novel, based as it is on the (sometimes intimate) details of the lives of friends and family members, has ruffled more than a few feathers. Actually, the unforgivably indiscreet Yo has thoroughly antagonized a whole raft of characters (including her sisters, mother, father, ex-boyfriends, former professors, best friends, childhood nanny, and Dominican cousins) and it is now **their** turn to reflect on her.

According to *Booklist*, "the cumulative effect ... results in a remarkably multifaceted portrait that will at once provoke, amuse, and warm readers." In its starred review, *Publishers Weekly* calls *Yo* "at once an evocation of a complex heroine and a wise and compassionate view of life's vicissitudes and the chances for redemption." Although *Kirkus Reviews* found the stories to be "sometimes puzzling and contradictory" it concluded that "the writing, as always, is animated and wonderfully imaginative; the characters jump off the page." As the *New Yorker* observes: "These high-spirited accounts indulge the pleasing fantasy that we are the heroes not only of our own lives but of everyone else's as well." *Ms. Magazine* concludes that Alvarez has "given us a stylish and accomplished novel about the often literal ranks of storytelling and imagination."

RECOGNITION: *LATBR* "Recommended Titles" 1997; REVIEWS: *AtlM* 2/97; *BL* 9/15/96; *ChiTrib* 3/30/97; *KR* 11/15/96; *LJ* 10/1/96; *Ms* 3-4/97; *NY* 5/12/97; *NYTBR* 2/9/97; *PW* 10/14/96; *Salon* 12/16-20/96; *WPBW* 1/19/97

Ansa, Tina McElroy (USA)

3 *The Hand I Fan With* (1996); Doubleday 1996 (HC); 1997 (pbk)

Tina McElroy Ansa's genial debut novel, *Baby of the Family* (1989), was a coming-of-age story featuring an African-American girl growing up in (fictional) Mullberry, a small town in rural Georgia. The youngster, Lena McPherson, was distinguished both by her powers of clairvoyance and by her ability to "talk with ghosts." In *The Hand I Fan With*, Lena is all grown up and is still communing with spirits who counsel her and allow her to peek into the future. Lena has parlayed her unusual gift into ownership of several profitable businesses and some very desirable riverfront property; she has also spread her good fortune throughout the community in the form of neighborhood projects and sponsorships. When Lena, whose ability to read

minds has frightened off more than one potential lover, discovers Herman (the ghost of a man dead for over a hundred years) she finally finds true love.

According to *Entertainment Weekly*, Ansa's "exuberant prose mixes Southern small-town realism with folk magic." In the opinion of the *New York Times Book Review* "Ansa writes believably of the spirit world" and the novel has "a strong sense of place and an engagingly eccentric cast of characters [which] keep the narrative moving — and ultimately bring Lena's two worlds together."

OTHER MEDIA: Audiocassette (Bantam /abr; Books-on-Tape/unabr); READING GROUP GUIDE; REVIEWS: *BL* 8/96; *Emerge* 10/96; *EW* 10/25/96; *KR* 8/1/96; *MultiCultR* 6/97; *NYTBR* 11/24/96; *PW* 8/5/96

Banks, Russell (USA)

4 *The Sweet Hereafter* (1991); HarBrace 1992 (pbk)

When the worst thing imaginable happens, who do you blame? In *The Sweet Hereafter*, Russell Banks sensitively explores the devastating impact on a small upstate New York town of a school bus accident which claims the lives of 14 children. The novel (part courtroom drama, part morality play) is structured around the personal accounts of four individuals intimately involved in the tragedy: sensible Molly Driscoll, the driver of the bus; Billy Ansell, the father of one of the dead children; Mitchell Stephens, Esqr., a negligence lawyer up from Manhattan; and Nichole Burnett, a popular, vivacious teenager, now paralyzed for life.

Instead of providing the reader with four unique (perhaps conflicting) perspectives on the event and its ramifications, Banks allows each of his narrators to tell a piece of the story, each one beginning where the previous one left off. Although some reviewers had critical reservations (e.g., the *Library Journal* found Mr. Banks' novel to be "uncharacteristically heavy-handed") the following assessment, offered by the *Christian Science Monitor*, was more typical: "*The Sweet Hereafter* is a work of wonderful tenderness and strength, told with the author's unique skill of keeping a fundamental philosophical question just below the surface of everyday events."

OTHER MEDIA: A film version was released in 1997 starring Ian Holm and Gabrielle Rose; RECOGNITION: *NYTBR* Notable Book of 1991; *Publishers Weekly* "Best Books" 1991; REVIEWS: *BL* 8/91; *ChiTrib* 9/15/91; *CSM* 9/24/91; *Econ* 10/19/91; *LitRev* 4/92; *LJ* 9/91; *Nation* 12/16/91; *NYTBR* 9/15/91; *Q&Q* 9/91; *TLS* 4/14/92

Bartlett, Neil (UK)

5 *Ready to Catch Him Should He Fall* (1990); Plume 1992 (pbk)

Neil Bartlett's debut novel, now considered a gay classic, is at heart a love story involving a young, innocent "beauty" and a strong, silent "older man." From the initial attraction, through the stirrings of romance, the flowering of passion maturing into love, leading, finally, to the exchange of marriage vows, the tale moves along conventional lines, except for the fact that the starry-eyed lovers are both men. The author has set *Ready to Catch Him* in "The Bar," a watering hole for a collection of regulars, gay Londoners who watch (with ever-increasing interest) the poignant story unfold. They are particularly fascinated (and heartened) by the pair's seemingly successful attempts to move out of the restrictive yet safe "gay" world and to join the world *out there*...

Kirkus Reviews notes that despite some "first novel tics — mostly self-conscious literariness and cutesiness — (the novel succeeds) as a celebration of homosexual love." According to the *Literary Review* this "is as good a novel as you are likely to read this year. Although gay London is its subject, Bartlett's writing is not camp, but disciplined, understated, innovative and gripping." English critic Valentine Cunningham, writing in the *British Book News*, observes that Bartlett's novel is an "extraordinarily magnetic portrait of a homosexual 'marriage' between two denizens of London's rootless gay underclass, perennially subject to awful murderous attacks from the conventional male community..." and concludes that the author's attempt to write this story "involves the rewriting of some famous homosexual texts — by Whitman, Wilde and Genet...."

REVIEWS: *Advocate* 10/8/91; *BBN* 12/90; *LitRev* 10/90; *NYTBR* 9/22/91; *PW* 8/9/91

Beattie, Ann (USA)

6 *My Life, Starring Dara Falcon* (1997); Knopf 1997 (HC); Vintage 1998 (pbk)

The "life" in Ann Beattie's title belongs to Jean Warner, a sweet, if unprepossessing, New Hampshire housewife who (orphaned while still a child) has married into a large and suffocatingly close-knit extended family. When Jean, acting totally out of character, develops an intense, almost devotional, friendship with the predatory Dara Falcon — a flamboyant, flirtatious newcomer with a talent for drama and pathological dissembling — she sets in motion a chain of events which will propel her in unforeseen directions. Jean "tells her story (set in the 1970s) from the safe distance of the 1990s and a happy second marriage" (*PW*).

In the view of the *Library Journal* "Beattie has crafted a fine study of obsessive relationships with her usual aplomb." Novelist and playwright **Jim Shepard** (*NYTBR*) observes that Ms. Beattie "is as good at acute observation as she ever was, and she's beautifully eloquent on both the quiet aggression within marriages and the pathos of families." According to *Publishers Weekly*, "What finally separates Jean from Dara ... is the ability to learn from her own failings. That ability makes this novel a comedy and something of a relief for readers who have always trusted Beattie to tell the truth about her generation's romantic troubles."

READING GROUP GUIDE: RECOGNITION: *NYTBR* Notable Book of 1997; REVIEWS: *BL* 3/15/97; *ChiTrib* 5/27/97; *EW* 6/20/97; *LJ* 5/15/97; *NYTBR* 5/11/97; *PW* 4/7/97; *WPBW* 6/22/97.

Begley, Louis (USA)

7 *About Schmidt* (1996); Random 1996 (HC); Fawcett 1997 (pbk)

The eponymous hero of *About Schmidt* — set in Manhattan and the Hamptons — is a self-absorbed, smugly intolerant corporate lawyer who, as the novel opens, is confronting early retirement, the death of a beloved wife, and estrangement from his only daughter. Schmidt — "Schmidtie" to his friends — is, in many respects, an anachronism: a WASP of the old-school for whom comfort, refinement, and "old money" are valued over conspicuous consumption and high-stakes capitalism. He, of course, considers himself too well-educated and broad-minded to harbor prejudices, but is having more than a little difficulty accepting his go-getter Jewish son-in-law-to-be. As he slips uncomfortably into retirement, Schmidtie is suffused with an unshakable melancholia until, that is, he is drawn into an unlikely (intensely liberating but vaguely threatening) sexual liaison with a Puerto Rican waitress. In his fourth novel, Begley has fashioned a highly sophisticated tale of self-deception.

Novelist **Francine Prose** (*WPBW*) observes that while the novel "offers us little in the way of coziness or consolation.... We do ... appreciate the elegant coolness and accuracy of Louis Begley's almost anthropological study of a dying breed.... His novel is tough, unsparing." *Kirkus Reviews* concludes that *About Schmidt* is a "sly, sharp portrait of an amoral but appealing figure, and of the declining world of privilege that has shaped him."

OTHER MEDIA: Audiocassette (recorded Bks/unabr); READING GROUP GUIDE; RECOGNITION: Nominated for the 1996 National Book Critics Circle Award; *NYTBR* Notable Book of 1996; *Publishers Weekly* "Best Books" 1996; REVIEWS: *BL* 8/96; *ChiTrib* 9/8/96; *EW* 10/4/96; *KR* 7/1/96; *LATBR* 9/15/96; *LJ* 6/15/96; *NYRB* 10/31/96; *NYTBR* 9/22/96; *PW* 6/17/96; *WPBW* 9/15/96; EDITOR'S NOTE: Begley's *Mistler's Exit* — about a New York advertising executive who has been diagnosed with cancer — was published in 1998 and was selected by the *New York Times Book Review* as one of its Notable Books of 1998.

Bellow, Saul (USA)

8   *The Actual* (1997); Viking 1997 (HC); Penguin 1998 (pbk)

Saul Bellow's latest novel, set in his beloved Chicago, is narrated by Harry Treliman, a sophisticated businessman in his middle fifties, a much-traveled importer who cannot loose the ties that bind him to the city of his birth. For forty years, he has been in love with Amy Wustrin, a former high school sweetheart disastrously married to (and eventually divorced from) his best friend Jay, a compulsive womanizer. Amy, a successful interior designer, re-enters Harry's life through the machinations of one of his business acquaintances, the wealthy Sigmund Adletsky, who has just purchased a luxury apartment with a spectacular view of Lake Michigan. The rest is up to Harry.

Michiko Kakutani (*NYT*) observes that Bellow's "language ... is somewhat more subdued than in the past, though Harry's own awareness of mortality, his awareness that the clock is ticking, lends his story an urgency all its own." In the view of novelist **Martin Amis** (*LATBR*), "Bellow's prose remains a source of constant pleasure because of its manifest immunity to all false consciousness." According to *Booklist* "The surface of the story carries few valleys and peaks, but beneath its outwardly uncomplex exterior pulsate reassuring emotions about permanence in the face of life's transience." The *New Statesman* concludes that "Bellow remains a masterful writer, tweaking *The Actual* into something compelling, succinct and, despite or because of its oddness, true."

RECOGNITION: *NYTBR* Notable Book of 1997; *LATBR* "Best Books" 1997; REVIEWS: *BL* 5/1/97; *ChiTrib* 8/17/97; *KR* 3/1/97; *LATBR* 12/14/97; *LST* 8/23/98; *MacL* 7/14/97; *NewsWk* 4/28/97; *NS* 8/29/97; *NYRB* 6/26/97; *NYT* 4/25/97; *NYTBR* 5/25/97; *PW* 3/24/97; *WPBW* 5/14/97; *WSJ* 5/21/97

Benitez, Sandra (Puerto Rico/USA)

9   *A Place Where the Sea Remembers* (1993); Coffee House Press 1993 (HC); Scribner 1995 (pbk)

In her debut novel, set in a small Mexican seaside town, Sandra Benitez presents us with an array of carefully drawn, often immensely appealing characters (a flower seller with a "cursed" pregnancy, a fisherman mourning the tragic death of his wife and children, an illiterate Indian girl carrying a child conceived by rape, etc.) each of whom is the focus of a separate chapter. In the background of each tale is the local healer or *curandera*, the town's "spiritual backbone" and keeper of secrets. The author brings all their stories together in a final linking chapter.

In the view of *Booklist*, the author "fills each page with small details that resonate with meaning, and her portrayal of what makes life worth living is breathtaking." *Publishers Weekly* suggests that "Benitez's unsparing vision into the stark realities of village residents' lives offers a poignant counterpoint to superficial vacation snapshots of Mexico." Novelist **Cristina Garcia** (*WPBW*), observes: Each tale possesses a quiet moral imparted as much in the language as in the silences of this seaside village and its inhabitants. Together they add up to a book of sparkling truths."

RECOGNITION: Winner of the Minnesota Book Award for Fiction, Winner of the Barnes & Noble Discover Award for Fiction; finalist *L.A. Times* Book Award; REVIEWS: *BL* 9/1/93; *Hisp* 4/94; *KR* 7/1/93; *LATBR* 9/11/94; *LJ* 9/1/93; *NYTBR* 10/31/93; *PW* 7/19/93; *SLJ* 4/94; *WPBW* 9/9/93

Bloom, Amy (USA)

10   *Love Invents Us* (1997); Random House 1997 (HC); Vintage 1998 (pbk)

In her debut novel, psychotherapist and award-winning short story writer Amy Bloom tells the tale of a young woman addicted to love. Elizabeth Taube, a plump and unassuming Jewish girl, has grown up in an affluent New York suburban household rich in all things except affection. As she moves into her teenage years the lonely youngster becomes "involved" with two much older men: Mr. Klein, the furrier, and Max Stone, her middle-aged English teacher. Elizabeth eventually falls in love with a young black man — with predictably traumatic results.

According to the *Library Journal* "Bloom's incredible talent lies in her ability to disturb, humor, and delight without ever becoming heavy handed or awkward." In the view of the *San Francisco Review of Books* "Elizabeth is sustained by her stoic, deadpan humor and the reader by Bloom's often astonishing writing." The *London Times* calls *Love Invents Us* "a perceptive often funny book with an offbeat slant on growing up and taking control, and as wonderful a description of falling in love as you are likely to find."

OTHER MEDIA: Audiocassette (Books-on-Tape/unabr); READING GROUP GUIDE: Vintage Books; RECOGNITION: *NYTBR* Notable Book of 1997; nominated for the National Book Award; REVIEWS: *BL* 12/15/96; *ChiTrib* 1/26/97; *KR* 12/01/96; *LATBR* 1/12/97; *LJ* 12/96; *LT* 4/5/98; *NYT* 5/29/97; *PW* 11/18/96; *Salon* 1/13–17/97; *SFR* 3-4/97; *TLS* 4/18/97; *WPBW* 2/23/97

Brookner, Anita (UK)

11   *The Visitors* (1997); Random House 1998 (HC)

Anita Brookner, in her 17th novel, examines age and loneliness in the person of Dorothea May a 70-year-old, determinedly self-sufficient widow who has lived alone in London since the death of her husband some 15 years previously. Dorothea has few friends or acquaintances, relying on her late husband's well-to-do female cousins and their spouses for infrequent socializing. When one of their (rather aggressive) granddaughters plans an unexpected London wedding, Dorothea is asked to put one of the out-of-town guests up for the week. He turns out to be an amiable, if self-obsessed, young American who has flown in to serve as Best Man. Dorothea reluctantly agrees and, not surprisingly, finds the experience unsettling.

In the view of *Entertainment Weekly* Ms. Brookner "proves her absolute mastery of the modern drawing-room novel … [replete with] minute epiphanies, exquisitely observed." *People Weekly* notes that Brookner's "triumph is subtle — not the stuff of great drama but quietly true to life." *Booklist* calls the book "a moving performance, the most positive tale [Brookner has] written in years."

RECOGNITION: *NYTBR* Notable Book of 1998; REVIEWS: *BL* 11/1/97; *ChiTrib* 2/22/98; *CSM* 2/18/98; *EW* 1/23/98; *KR* 12/1/97; *LJ* 11/1/97; *LT* 6/6/96; *NYTBR* 1/18/98; *PeopleW* 2/23/98; *PW* 11/17/97

12   *Altered States* (1996); Random House 1997 (HC); Vintage 1998 (pbk)

In *Altered States*, Anita Brookner tells the sobering story of Alan Sherwood — successful lawyer, sensible husband, and only-son of a genteel Englishwoman — whose orderly existence is turned completely upside down by his infatuation and brief affair with Sarah, an alluring (yet heartless) distant cousin. After Alan marries a very needy, deceptively mousy young woman, his cousin reenters his life. As usual, Ms. Brookner has divided the critics:

The *Literary Review* calls *Altered States* "powerful but bleak … brutally pessimistic, as ever, about the possibilities of romantic life… Brookner fans will just love it." In the view of *The* (London) *Independent* "Brookner excels at portrayals of extreme pain seeking refined expression. They are studied, understated, excruciating." According to *Booklist*, Sherwood's "altered states are all forms of loss and compromise, intrinsic aspects of life that Brookner analyzes with brilliant intensity and surprising suspense." *Kirkus Reviews* concludes that "Brookner remains our great poet of loneliness and loss." The *L.A. Times* reviewer says the book amounts to "a depressing portrait of a descent into 'contented mediocrity.' Her writing is as supple as ever, it's her subject that is tiresome." Novelist Michele Roberts, writing in the *London Times* notes that "Anita Brookner's novels remind me of the work of Jean Rhys, with its repeated insistence on the power of sex, or a badly chosen lover, to blight

a life for ever." *The Spectator* points to a "magnificent and gripping new twist in *Altered States*. The mouse gets her man, and turns out to be a monster."

OTHER MEDIA: Audiocassette (Dolphin/unabr); READING GROUP GUIDE; RECOGNITION: *NYTBR* Notable Book of 1997; REVIEWS: *BL* 11/1/96; *IrishT* 6/1/96; *KR* 11/1/96; *LATBR* 2/9/97; *LitRev* 6/96; *LJ* 12/96; *LT* 6/6/96; *NYTBR* 12/7/97; *PW* 11/11/96; *Spec* 6/15/96; *TLS* 7/24/96

13   *Incidents in the Rue Laugier* (1995); Random House 1995 (HC); Vintage 1997 (pbk)

In *Incidents in the Rue Laugier*, Anita Brookner explores the life-altering consequences of a young Frenchwoman's passionate, yet short-lived affair with a rakishly attractive Englishman. Married on the rebound, Maud Gonthier accompanies her new husband, a mild English bookseller, to London where she raises their only child and slips into a quiet, uneventful, vaguely melancholic life. The novel is narrated by her daughter who is attempting to piece together the strands of her mother's life, having little more to go on than a few cryptic entries in a journal now yellowed with age.

Prize-winning Anita Brookner (known for her preoccupation with loneliness and missed opportunity) is widely admired for her perspicacity and her lucid prose, and *Incidents in the Rue Laugier* was generally deemed to be one of her better efforts. *Publishers Weekly* notes that, despite its elegiac overtones, *Incidents* "… is a dazzling read in which every sentence seems clairvoyant. The reader turns pages compulsively." Long-time Brookner fan, Jonathan Yardley (*WPBW*), similarly observes "we may come to regard *Incidents in the Rue Laugier* as a small masterpiece…. To my mind it is the best book she has written and that to my mind is saying something." English novelist **Hilary Mantel** (*TLS*) is less admiring, suggesting that "For its first two-thirds, this sharp, sad book seems one of Ms. Brookner's best. But when the unsatisfactory marriage is described there is inevitably a loss of power."

OTHER MEDIA: Audiocassette (Chivers/unabr); REVIEWS: *BL* 11/1/95; *LATBR* 1/2/96; *LJ* 11/15/95; *LT* 6/8/95; *NYTBR* 1/14/96; *PW* 12/30/96; *TLS* 6/2/95; *WLT* Win '97; *WPBW* 1/7/96

Busia, Akosua (Ghana/USA)

14   *The Seasons of Beento Blackbird* (1996); Little, Brown 1996 (HC); PB 1997 (pbk)

In her debut novel, Akosua Busia, the Ghanaian actress who played Nettie in the movie version of *The Color Purple*, features Solomon Wilberforce a children's book author who (under the pen name Beento Blackbird) has made a name for himself in the area of multicultural literature. Solomon is handsome, charismatic and immensely successful, he is also a bigamist with a mature wife (Miriam) in the islands and a young wife (Ashia) in Ghana. All goes smoothly until....

Booklist applauds Busia for her ability to create "compelling characters ... are richly complex and realistically drawn" and calls *The Seasons of Beento Blackbird* "a highly ambitious first novel that [although] only partly successful ... clearly identifies Busia as a writer to watch." The *Washington Post Book World* found it to be a "beautifully crafted love story, filled with fantasy and lyricism."

OTHER MEDIA: Audiocassette (Brilliance/unabr); REVIEWS: *BL* 10/1/96; *LATBR* 4/13/97; *LJ* 9/15/96; *PW* 9/2/96; *WPBW* 9/29/96

Cambor, Kathleen (USA)

15 *The Book of Mercy* (1996); FS&G 1996 (HC); Harcourt Brace 1997 (pbk)

Kathleen Cambor's first novel, *The Book of Mercy*, tells the story of a father and daughter haunted by memories. When his children were still very young, Edmund Mueller's increasingly irresponsible and emotionally unstable young wife simply walked out of their lives. Edmund, a German immigrant and retired Pittsburgh Fireman looks for some meaning to life and finds it in his increasingly obsessive study of alchemy — based as it is on the "transformative" properties of fire. Meanwhile, his daughter, Anne, emotionally rootless and "unstable in love," pursues a career in medicine. Anne's older brother, Paul, has responded to maternal abandonment by turning inward. After entering a Dominican seminary at age 18 he becomes a much-traveled missionary. Although estranged throughout much of the book, Edmund, Ann and Paul (alchemist, psychiatrist and priest) begin to reconnect as the story progresses.

Kirkus Reviews calls *The Book of Mercy* "an old-fashioned, frequently moving always sweepingly readable tale." According to *Booklist* Ms. Cambor has produced "a [remarkable] study in psychological acuity and compassionate revelation about the destructive and transformative powers of family love." The *Library Journal* observes that Ms. Cambor "captures a Catholic childhood in ethnic Pittsburgh as effortlessly as she does late-night med-school dissections of Amelia, her practice corpse."

RECOGNITION: Nominated for the 1997 PEN/Faulkner Award; *NYTBR* Notable Book of 1996; REVIEWS: *BL* 5/1/96; *ChiTrib* 8/11/96; *CSM* 9/9/96; *LATBR* 8/25/96; *LJ* 6/1/96; *NYTBR* 7/28/96; *PW* 4/22/96

Cameron, Peter (USA)

16 *The Weekend* (1994); FS&G 1994 (HC); NAL-Dutton 1995 (pbk)

The "weekend" in question is a midsummer gathering — in a country house in rural New York state — of a sophisticated group of friends on the first anniversary of the death from AIDS of Tony, a man important to all but one of them. The house is owned by Tony's brother John and his wife Marian, and the couple is hosting Tony's former lover, Lyle (a middle-aged art critic) who has chosen to bring along his new friend (and prospective lover), Robert, a struggling artist. Completing the group is the couple's summer neighbor, an American woman who spends much of the year in Italy. Allusions to Shakespeare's *A Midsummer Night's Dream* abound.

The *London Times* calls *The Weekend* "two days of music, art, swimming and arguing in upstate New York" while *Booklist,* observes that Peter Cameron's "second novel is so easy to visualize, so full of articulate dialogue that reading it resembles watching a movie." The *Library Journal*, in its starred review, asserts that "tensions develop rapidly on all fronts: between the generations, between the new lovers, between the past and the present, between those with hope and those without ... " The *New York Times Book Review* notes that the novel occasionally calls to mind Woolf, Forster, Lawrence and Fitzgerald "whose brilliant narrative critiques of material culture open, again and again, to the metaphysical, to that dimension where the known world cedes to mystery." Novelist **Michael Dorris** (*LATBR*) concludes that Cameron has written a "fascinating literary page-turner ... [in which he demonstrates] the rare ability to take an ordinary event and invest it with heart and significance."

REVIEWS: *BL* 5/1/94; *LATBR* 7/28/94; *LJ* 7/94; *LST* 7/7/96; *LT* 5/18/96; *NY* 6/13/94; *NYTBR* 5/29/94; *PW* 3/14/94; *TLS* 6/14/96; *WPBW* 6/26/94

Canty, Kevin (USA)

17 *Into the Great Wide Open* (1996); Doubleday 1996 (HC)

In his debut novel, set in suburban Washington, D.C., Kevin Canty tells the carefully nuanced story of teenage love between two emotionally damaged youngsters from opposite ends of the socio-economic spectrum. Junie Williamson, the daughter of a successful career-absorbed couple (a lawyer and a pediatrician), lives in a house designed by Frank Lloyd Wright. Kenny Kolodny — whose mother is a patient at a state psychiatric hospital — lives in a run-down apartment building with his alcoholic father. When Kenny and Junie meet at a church-sponsored camp, they begin a passionate and intensely complicated relationship.

Publishers Weekly says Canty "evokes the bliss, uncertainty and pain of teenage love in an age of sexual freedom, drugs and parental irresponsibility." According to the *L.A. Times Book Review*, "*Into the Great Wide Open* is a stunning, sensual novel that brings adolescence to its highest state of grace." Called a "pleasure from start to finish" by *Entertainment Weekly*, Canty's novel was widely praised as a moving and original coming-of-age story.

RECOGNITION: *NYTBR* Notable Book of 1996; REVIEWS: *ChiTrib* 8/18/96; *EW* 8/16/96; *KR* 6/1/96; *LATBR* 10/6/96; *LJ* 9/1/96; *NYTBR* 9/8/96; *PW* 6/10/96; *Salon* 1996; *WPBW* 12/1/96

Casey, John (USA)

18   *The Half-Life of Happiness* (1998); Knopf 1998 (HC)

Set in Charlottesville (site of the University of Virginia where the author is a professor of English literature), John Casey's first novel since his National Book Award–winning *Spartina* (1989) explores the breakup of a marriage between Mike an attractively cerebral attorney and his equally attractive, engagingly temperamental wife, Joss, a talented filmmaker. The golden couple had been blessed with two bright, well-adjusted daughters (Edith and Nora) and a raft of amusing and accomplished friends drawn mostly from the University milieu. When Mike and Joss are introduced to Bonnie, a sexy new professor, it is Joss who loses her heart. The story is told — in large measure — through a series of reminiscences (serio-comic and frequently contradictory) as the now-grown daughters look back on their childhood.

Kirkus Reviews calls it "a moving work, and often in its portrait of intelligent people haplessly adrift, a convincing one." *Booklist* concludes that "Casey's rich novel offers many pleasures — witty dialogue, numerous literary references, brainy characters — but it is most notable for its generous vision." In the view of the *Chicago Tribune*, "John Casey is, as always, enormously readable, attuned to the large and small events that make up human experience. This is a novel for anyone who believes that fiction is a way of discovering the best and the worst in our selves and that our flawed lives can be redeemed in the long run." The *Washington Post Book World* concludes: "The overall diffuseness slows but does not stop the novel. Casey ... tracks the motions of the heart and frames his findings with epigrammatic grace."

RECOGNITION: NYTBR Notable Book of 1998; REVIEWS: *BL* 2/15/98; *ChiTrib* 4/19/98; *KR* 2/1/98; *LATBR* 4/13/98; *NYTBR* 4/5/98; *WPBW* 4/12/98

Chavez, Denise (USA)

19   *Face of an Angel* (1994); FS&S 1994 (HC); Warner 1995 (pbk)

Setting her debut novel in Agua Oscura, a fictional New Mexico town, Denise Chavez tells the story of Soveida Dosamantes, a once-divorced, once-widowed (through suicide) Mexican-American waitress who has spent her life in service to the Catholic church, to the men in her life, to her customers. Soveida's story is told partly through anecdotes, monologues, alternative histories and text-within-text (including excerpts from a handbook on waitresses which she has authored), and through the insertion of documents (e.g. letters from former husbands and college papers — complete with professors' comments).

Booklist calls *Face of an Angel* "a mesmerizing gem of a novel." According to *World Literature Today*, "When one thinks of Americans of Mexican descent, one does well to picture communities ordered by Catholicism and the family (its chief symptom). No surprise then to encounter Soveida, age twelve, ending her brief autobiography with a question worthy of Augustine: 'So what am I? Saint or sinner? Her answer, in the form of her life, is not conventional, and not very religious....'" *Publishers Weekly* observes that Chavez's "highly readable style effortlessly mixes Spanish and English in a way that won't jar the monolingual reader ('may — the Virgin Mary — spare you a drunken man ... smelling of frijoles and beer. Dios mío el gas!')."

REVIEWS: *BellesL* Spr '95; *BL* 9/15/94; *Hisp* 3/95; *KR* 7/1/94; *LAT* 11/24/94; *LJ* 8/94; *NYTBR* 9/25/94; *PW* 7/25/94; *WLT* Aut '95; *WP* 12/26/94

Chute, Carolyn (USA)

20   *Merry Men* (1994); HarBrace 1995 (pbk)

Carolyn Chute's *Merry Men* is the third volume of a trilogy (beginning with *The Beans of Egypt Maine* in 1985 and continuing with *Letournau's Used Auto Parts* in 1988) and is set, once again, in the rural town of Egypt, Maine. In this latest volume, Ms. Chute has created a larger-than-life figure whose sense of mission drives the plot. Lloyd Barrington, is college-educated and significantly under-employed. When the recession hits this part of New England, the woolen mill closes and the lay-offs have a disastrous ripple-effect throughout the community. Barrington, disgusted by the ever-increasing gulf between the local haves and have-nots, carries out a series of robberies designed to redress the imbalance.

According to the *Washington Post Book World*, "Chute's book is an epic cast as a tragedy.... She never condescends to sentimentalizing her characters, who for all their bitterness and despair and loss continue to do the one thing they have done all along: survive." Ann Hulbert (*NYTBR*) takes the opposite view: "This sprawling would-be epic in the end has the air of stale populist propaganda

... *Merry Men* may break new ground for its author, but it turns Egypt, Maine, into a surprisingly sentimental place." In the view of the *New Yorker*, Chute's "clear message is that you must stick with your class regardless and the final outcome of the book is uncompromising…. She certainly does not overstate the condition of poor people, for whom their heritage and their children may be all their treasure." Novelist **Madison Smartt Bell** (jacket notes) judges Ms. Chute's novel to be "one of the very few books from the end of our century which will be worth remembering."

RECOGNITION: *NYTBR* Notable Book of 1994; REVIEWS: *BL* 11/1/93; *KR* 10/1/93; *LATBR* 3/6/94; *NY* 2/14/94; *NYTBR* 2/6/94; *PW* 10/18/93; *WPBW* 2/6/94

Cisneros, Sandra (USA)

21 *The House on Mango Street* (1991); Knopf 1994 (HC); Vintage 1991 (pbk)

Sandra Cisnero's *The House on Mango Street*, an interconnected series of vignettes, traces the coming-of-age of Esperanza Cordero, a young girl growing up in Chicago's bleak, frequently violent Puerto Rican neighborhood where "families are always moving but never quite arrive" (*TLS*).

Judged "loving, playful and powerful" and "alive with the people that Esperanza—and Cisneros—left behind" by the *Times Literary Supplement*, *The House on Mango Street* was widely applauded upon publication. According to *Commonweal*, "Although the content is at times amateurish, the [novel], a composite of evocative snapshots that manages to passionately recreate the milieu of the poor quarters of Chicago, is a pleasurable read." In the view of the *Atlantic,* "Ms. Cisneros has compressed great force into this small, brilliant work."

OTHER MEDIA: Audiocassette (Random Audio/abr & unabr); stage adaptation 1992; REVIEWS: *AtlM* 6/91; *ComW* 9/13/91; *GW* 5/14/92; *LATBR* 5/12/91; *TLS* 5/15/92; *WPBW* 6/9/91

Corey, Deborah (Canada)

22 *Losing Eddie* (1993); Algonquin 1994 (pbk)

Losing Eddie, narrated by an unusually perceptive nine-year-old girl—already wise to the ways of the world—is set in the tiny Bible Belt settlement of New Temperance, Canada. It tells the story of one year in the life of a rural family struggling with poverty, mental illness, and a relentless string of calamitous events culminating with a death. Although Deborah Corey, in her debut effort, unflinchingly explores the darker aspects of family life, she has written a consistently upbeat, and frequently inspirational novel.

According to *Books in Canada* Corey's prize-winning novel "is a book of sudden and piercing truths, as when the child goes to visit her mother in a mental hospital, and discovers that 'Mama looks like someone I shouldn't talk to.' There are wonderful portraits of family members, of strange and disturbing neighbors, and Corey makes us sharply aware of how it is possible for daily life to go on in the presence of dreadful dangers." The *Quill & Quire* notes that the "overriding theme of the novel is love. Indeed, *Losing Eddie* could well stand as a cautionary tale to anyone accustomed to talking blithely—and dismissively—about 'dysfunctional families.' For, despite their bad fortune, the narrator and her family know a great deal more about love than many (seemingly well-adjusted) families."

RECOGNITION: Winner of the 1993 Smith Book/*Books in Canada* "First Novel" award; REVIEWS: *BellesL* Sum '94; *BksCan* 11/93, 4/94; *BL* 9/15/93; *KR* 8/1/93; *MacL* 4/11/94; *PW* 8/16/93; *Q&Q* 11/93

Delbanco, Nicholas (USA)

23 *Old Scores* (1997); Warner 1997 (HC)

Years later he would marvel at the ease of it, the ignorance, the blithe assumption on his part that there need be no damage. Years later he would ask himself how he could ever have imagined there would be no price to pay.

Nicholas Delbanco's bittersweet tale of love lost and love found opens in 1969 on the campus of a small Vermont college and features Elizabeth Sieverdsen, now a middle-aged woman, who, as a student, had fallen in love with Paul Ballard, an attractive 35-year-old professor. Their love affair had been intense but evanescent, having been cut short by a tragic accident which left Paul shattered and bitter. Though Elizabeth was pregnant at the time, she kept it a secret from Paul as she did the fact of the child's eventual birth and subsequent adoption. Elizabeth, soon after graduating, left the United States, married an Italian businessman and settled down in Tuscany where she raised a family. Once her children leave for college and her marriage loses it focus, Elizabeth returns to Vermont.

Kirkus Reviews calls *Old Scores* a "moving exploration of a believably passionate love, and of its subtle, powerful, persistent impact on the lives of two stubborn romantics." In the view of the *Washington Post Book World* "Delbanco has allowed his characters the uncertainties of failure, of thinning hair and sagging breasts. Love is deeper than flesh. It is the imprint one makes on another, and in the sure hands of Nicholas Delbanco, *Old Scores* is a lovely and honest retelling of how that imprint endures."

REVIEWS: *BL* 8/19/97; *KR* 6/1/97; *LJ* 7/97; *NYTBR* 8/24/97; *PW* 6/2/97; *WPBW* 9/4/97

Dixon, Melvin (USA)

24   *Trouble the Water* (1989); Fiction Collective 1989 (HC); PB 1992 (pbk)

In African-American poet Melvin Dixon's debut novel Jordan Henry, a professor of colonial history at a small New England college, returns to Pee Dee, North Carolina, for the funeral of his grandmother, "Mother Harriet," the strong-willed woman who raised him after his own mother died in childbirth. Jordan has not been "home" in sometime as his childhood memories are clouded by Mother Harriet's emotional instability and by her implacable hatred of Jordan's father.

According to noted scholar Henry Louis Gates (*ABR*), "Melvin Dixon is best known as a poet, and *Trouble the Water* is, as they say, a poet's novel: which means it's propelled by the lyricism of its language, carefully crafted imagery and a wealth of perceptual observation." Gates concludes, however, that "In the end ... Dixon may be betrayed by the generosity of his own vision...." The *New York Times Book Review* found: "On balance (some false notes aside), *Trouble the Water* is a success — primarily for its suspenseful, satisfying portrayal of Jordan Henry as he pursues grace in a fallen world." In the opinion of the *L.A. Times Book Review*, "The dualities and contradictions inherent in African-American life, in its folkloric background and its contrasting cosmopolitan sophistication, are superbly captured in a tale that has already won kudos for Dixon."

RECOGNITION: Winner of the 1989 Nilon Award; winner of the Excellence in Minority Fiction Award from the University of Colorado; REVIEWS: *ABR* 7-8/90; *LATBR* 10/1/89; *NYTBR* 9/24/89; *VLS* 5/90; *WPBW* 3/4/90

Donoghue, Emma (Ireland)

25   *Hood* (1995); HarperCollins 1995 (HC)

Emma Donoghue's second novel, an exploration of bereavement, is set once again in Dublin and tells the story of Cara and Penelope's fourteen-year love affair, from their initial meeting in a Catholic convent school until Penelope's death at age 30.

According to *Booklist*, "Although some may find it slow, others will consider this love story that well conveys the complexities and nuances of intimate relationships stately and elegiac." The *New York Times Book Review* observes that the novel's charm "and it is utterly charming — lies in its lack of political aggression, in its insouciant avoidance of the bandwagon...." The *Times Literary Supplement*, however, found *Hood* to be "formulaic" and suggests that the author is "Caught between an insistence on the particular bliss of female cohabitation and a compulsion to explain that lesbians have earth shattering sex."

RECOGNITION: Winner of the 1997 ALA Gay, Lesbian, Bisexual Books Award; REVIEWS: *BL* 3/1/96; *Guardian* 3/26/95; *KR* 1/15/96; *NYTBR* 3/24/96; *PW* 1/22/96; *TLS* 4/21/95

Dove, Rita (USA)

26   *Through the Ivory Gate* (1992); Vintage 1993 (pbk)

Pulitzer Prize–winning Poet Laureate Rita Dove's debut novel tells the story of a woman's return to her early childhood home and the poignant memories this evokes. Virginia, born in Ohio and raised in Arizona, is a musician and actress who has accepted the position of "Artist-in-Residence" at an elementary school in Akron, Ohio — the same school she attended briefly as a very young girl.

According to the *Christian Science Monitor*, "Dove skillfully interweaves Virginia's memories of the past with scenes from her present ... [and] demonstrates a strong grasp of the complexities of human character and interpersonal relationships: the kind of informed and realistic understanding so essential in producing a believable and affecting novel." The *Library Journal*, although suggesting that Dove's "prose could perhaps be tighter," concludes that "the emotions are always heartfelt and fresh and the passages on artistic creation everything you would expect from a poet of Dove's stature." Ms. Dove, in the view of the *Washington Post Book World*, "skillfully evokes the mood of the decade when social change seemed not only possible but imminent.... [Her] themes are important: she is an immensely gifted writer." The *Chicago Tribune* notes that Ms. Dove "continues her love affair with words in *Through the Ivory Gate*, a finely chiseled novel rich with graceful prose and informed by a poet's eye for detail."

REVIEWS: *BellesL* Spr '93; *BL* 9/15/92; *ChiTrib* 12/13/92; *CSM* 10/27/92; *LJ* 8/92; *NYTBR* 10/11/92; *WPBW* 10/11/92; *WRB* 3/93

Doyle, Roddy (Ireland)

27   *The Woman Who Walked Into Doors* (1996) Viking 1996 (HC); Penguin 1997 (pbk)

Set in contemporary Dublin, *The Woman Who Walked Into Doors* is an unsparing examination of a brutally abusive marriage. In Ireland "She walked into a door" is a common euphemism used to describe a woman beaten by her husband. Roddy Doyle, in his 5th novel, tells his story through the eyes of Paula Spencer, a 39-year-old battered wife and alcoholic mother of four. Doyle's novel opens one year after Paula has thrown Charlo, her handsome, chronically abusive, petty-thief of a husband, out of the house for good. The news that Charlo has been killed in an abortive bank-robbery triggers in Paula a series of flashbacks prompted by her desire to make some sense (and perhaps reclaim some part) of her life with a man she both deeply loved and greatly feared.

Irish novelist Aisling Foster in a review appearing in the *London Times*, found *The Woman Who Walked Into Doors* to be Doyle's "best work yet" and further insists that "he is one of those rare male authors who can bring women alive in fiction…." Novelist **James Hynes** *(WPBW)* argues that "Paula Spencer may be Doyle's most successful literary creation yet, a tour de force of literary ventriloquism that gives the lie to the old writing workshop canard that a man can't write from the point of view of a woman…." *The Economist* concludes: "Reading *The Woman Who Walked Into Doors*, which has no stylistic adornments whatsoever, is a sober experience. It is all the more affecting for that — and more true to life than any biography, encyclopedia or historical textbook."

OTHER MEDIA: Audiocassette (Penguin Audio/abr; Recorded Books/unabr); RECOGNITION: *NYTBR* Notable Book of 1996; *PW* Best Book of 1996; *L.A. Times* "Best Books" 1996; REVIEWS: *BL* 4/15/96; *Econ* 6/15/96; *LJ* 2/15/96; *LST* 4/7/96; *LT* 4/11/96; *NYTBR* 4/28/96; *PW* 1/22/96; *TLS* 4/12/96; *WPBW* 4/7/96

Dufresne, John (USA)

28   *Love Warps the Mind a Little* (1997); Norton 1997 (HC)

John Dufresne's second novel, a dark comedy about life, death and the urge to write, features Lafayette "Laf" Proulx, an exuberantly daft aspiring writer in search of a publisher. Laf has recently left his wife and, taking only his typewriter and his dog, has moved in with his reluctant mistress Judi, a psychotherapist. When Judi's chronic indigestion is diagnosed as ovarian cancer, Laf assumes the role of caregiver and learns much about the human heart.

According to the *New York Times Book Review* John Dufresne's "deeply affecting book" is not "your usual comic romp — even though at first glance, the life and times of its loopy narrator, Lafayette Proulx, seem safely hilarious." *Publishers Weekly*, in its starred review, observes that, although Dufresne's novel suffers a bit from "parochial preciousness" he manages to weave "a powerful spell, proving himself once again a writer of great energy and a big open heart." *Booklist* concludes that *Love Warps the Mind a Little* is a "breezy and egocentric narrative [that] propels a story that's very funny, quite sad, and occasionally tragic."

RECOGNITION: *NYTBR* Notable Book of 1997; REVIEWS: *BL* 12/15/96; *ChiTrib* 1/19/97; *NY* 1/27/97; *NYTBR* 2/16/97; *PeopleW* 4/21/97; *PW* 12/2/96; *WPBW* 2/9/97

Ephron, Delia (USA)

29   *Hanging Up* (1995); Putnam 1995 (HC); Ballantine 1996 (pbk)

Delia Ephron (sister of Nora Ephron) has written a wryly comic, semi-autobiographical novel about three sisters (Georgia, a successful magazine editor, Eve, mother of a teenager and owner of a party-planning company, and Maddy, a pregnant soap-opera actress) and their father, a senile, former alcoholic screenwriter who is slowly, inexorably dying of what the doctors call "the dwindles." The tale is narrated by Eve, the 44-year-old middle sister who has become her father's primary care-giver. *Hanging Up* skillfully tackles, among other subjects, sisterhood, impending death, and the assumption of responsibility.

According to *People Weekly*, *Hanging Up* "effectively conveys the sadness a family feels as it prepares for the passing of a troubled patriarch. Though the main characters have a bad habit of wisecracking their way through the tears, readers … will detect a true and touching humanity in this novel." Laura Shapiro (*Newsweek*) calls *Hanging Up* "a terrific debut novel" and observes that "a couple of hours with Ephron's dry, beautifully targeted witticisms would cheer up the most bedraggled victim of mid-life crises." *Booklist* found Ms. Ephron's novel to be "a funny, touching, often penetrating exploration of individual strengths and vulnerabilities."

REVIEWS: *BL* 7/95; *EW* 7/12/95; *LJ* 6/1/95; *LST* 4/14/96; *LT* 3/2/96; *NewsWk* 7/31/95; *NYTBR* 7/23/95; *PeopleW* 8/21/95; *PW* 5/22/95

Erdrich, Louise (USA)

30   *Tales of Burning Love* (1996); HarperCollins 1996 (HC); 1997 (pbk)

Jack Mauser, first introduced to readers of Louise Erdrich's debut novel (*Love Medicine*) as the casual lover who watches as June Morrisey walks into the certain death of a plains blizzard, is the focal character of Erdrich's sixth novel, *Tales of Burning Love*. The feckless Jack, in the intervening years, has been divorced three times and married four, he has also come, it now seems, to a bad end, the purported victim of a house fire. When Jack's widow and three former wives meet at his funeral and decide, on a whim, to travel back to the city together, they manage to drive themselves right smack into the great blizzard of 1995. The four women are forced to spend a long night together, stranded in a frigid car with the outside temperature dropping. To pass the time (and to keep from, quite possibly, freezing to death) the four tell each other stories, all of them having something to do with Jack and a lot to do with love and forgiveness.

In the view of the *Times Literary Supplement* the women's "dialogue … is finely balanced between naturalism and the kind of loaded reference that will draw the reader in." According to the *L.A. Times Book Review*, Ms Erdrich's ("almost reverentially sexual novel") is "completion, absolution, forgetfulness and memory all at once. *Tales of Burning Love*, like all of Erdrich's novels, is a book about recovering from the belief that you can stand alone."

RECOGNITION: Winner of the 1997 Minnesota Book Award for Fiction; *NYTBR* Notable Book of 1996; *L.A. Times* "Best Books" 1996; *Booklist* "Editors' Choice" 1996; REVIEWS: *AtlM* 2/97; *BL* 3/1/96; *ChiTrib* 4/21/96; *LATBR* 6/16/96; *NY* 7/8/96; *NYTBR* 5/12/96; *PW* 2/19/96; *Salon* 1996; *TLS* 2/14/97; *WPBW* 4/21/96

Ford, Richard (USA)

31   *Independence Day* (1995); Random House 1996 (pbk)

Pulitzer-prize winning novelist and short-story writer Richard Ford is known for his searing examination of late 20th century middle-class suburban malaise. His male protagonists, although beset by self-doubt, unrealized career goals, and emotional inadequacies, somehow manage to gamely (if wryly) "get on with" the quotidian business of living. In *Independence Day*, sequel to the widely praised *The Sportswriter* (1986), Frank Bascombe, a failed husband, father, teacher and writer is now a real estate agent in Haddam, New Jersey. Although the novel takes place entirely within the time frame of a 4th of July weekend, a series of important questions (regarding commitment, parental responsibility and the search for joy in living) are raised and explored.

According to *New Statesman and Society* no other "contemporary American writer ... has his finger so firmly on the jittery, apprehensive pulse of the American middle classes, and ... so understands their search for grace in a society that has lost its way. *Independence Day* is without question, a great American novel." The *Times Literary Supplement* suggests that although *Independence Day* "probes the losses time inflicts ... the reader is neither depressed nor amused, instead intrigued, page, after page ... " and concludes that "*Independence Day* is a book written in [the] exalted tradition of Scott Fitzgerald." Novelist **Charles Johnson** (*NYTBR*) says Ford writes with "a mastery second to none... and has created, and continues to develop in *Independence Day*, a character we know as well as we know our next-door neighbors" and concludes that "Frank Bascombe has earned himself a place beside Willy Loman and Harry Angstrom in our literary landscape, but he has done so with a wry wit and a *fin de siècle* wisdom that is very much his own."

OTHER MEDIA: Audiocassette (Recorded

Bks/unabr); READING GROUP GUIDE; Vintage Books; RECOGNITION: Winner of the 1996 Pulitzer Prize for Fiction; Winner of the 1996 PEN/Faulkner Award; nominated for the 1995 National Book Critics Circle Award; *NYTBR* "Editors' Choice" 1995; *PW* "Best Books" of 1995; REVIEWS: *ChiTrib* 6/25/95; *CSM* 7/3/95; *Guard* 6/30/95; *LATBR* 7/2/95; *LST* 7/16/95; *LT* 7/20/95; *NS&S* 7/4/95; *NYTBR* 6/18/95; *TLS* 7/14/94; *WPBW* 7/2/95

Frucht, Abby (USA)

32   *Are You Mine?* (1993); Grove/Atlantic 1994 (pbk)

In *Are You Mine?* (billed by its publishers as a "reproductive adventure") Cara and Douglas, a young couple faced with the prospect of an unplanned third pregnancy, begin to reassess their relationship, their expectations and their options.

The *New York Times Book Review* calls *Are You Mine?* "a rich and seamless work" and points out that "the reader is treated to just about every facet of human sexuality and its consequences, including the tragicomedy of a one-night stand, the physical as well as psychic pain and catharsis of childbirth and the staggering variety of choices open to a decidedly pro-choice couple." In the view of the *L.A. Times Book Review* "Abby Frucht is a writer of considerable warmth and charm, Cara and Douglas exude a sexy yet responsible glow, they are smart, serious and funny and can carry the story on personality alone. The abortion section, in particular, shows genuine insight into the psychology of a woman facing this painful choice."

RECOGNITION: *NYTBR* Notable Book of 1993; REVIEWS: *BL* 3/15/93; *KR* 2/15/93; *LATBR* 4/11/93; *LJ* 5/1/93; *NYTBR* 5/2/93; *PW* 3/1/93

Godwin, Gail (USA)

33   *The Good Husband* (1994); Ballantine 1995 (pbk)

The Good Husband, set in a fictional college town in upstate New York, weaves an affecting story around the dual realities of death and failed aspirations. Magda Danvers, a 58-year-old "celebrity" professor of literature, is dying of ovarian cancer. She is surrounded by her husband (who gave up the seminary to devote his life to her) and a small circle of friends all of whom are engaged in writerly pursuits. As the novel progresses, various members of this group experience career frustrations, marital breakups and, tragically, the death of an infant.

Despite the emphasis on loss and mortality *The Good Husband* is, according to *Booklist*, "remarkably laced with humor, thanks to Magda's enduring wit and the idiocies of her academic colleagues." In the view of the *Library Journal* "Godwin's intensely drawn characters are vividly portrayed during the most intimate times of love, marriage and death. The result is a winner."

OTHER MEDIA: Audiocassette (Random Audio/abr); RECOGNITION: *PW* "Best Books" 1994; *NYTBR* Notable Book of 1994; REVIEWS: *BL* 6/1/94; *ChiTrib* 8/28/94; *LJ* 6/1/94; *NYTBR* 9/4/94; *PW* 6/20/94; *Time* 9/26/94; *TLS* 9/26/94

34   *Father Melancholy's Daughter* (1991); Avon 1997 (pbk)

Gail Godwin's deeply nuanced novel is set within the confines of the small, southern, Episcopal Parish of St. Cuthbert. The "father" of the title is St. Cuthbert's rector, a profoundly idealistic man who has long-suffered from severe bouts of depression. He has also, to the utter astonishment of his congregation, single-handedly raised his only daughter, following his wife's abrupt departure (for New York City and self fulfillment in the world of avant-garde theater). Margaret, just six when her mother abandoned her, was always a serious, well-behaved child and has grown into a thoughtful and dutiful young woman with a significant role in the life of the parish. However, beneath her buttoned-up exterior, Margaret continues to burn with unanswered questions regarding her mother's behavior. When Margaret is 23 her father dies and she must confront the future by coming to terms with her past.

According to the *Library Journal*, Ms Godwin "has once again proven her masterful ability to weave an engaging story ... peopled with wonderful secondary characters whose foibles tenderly elucidate their dilemmas." The *Times Literary Supplement* calls *Father Melancholy's Daughter* "skillfully written, accessible, funny and discriminating," and concludes that "Ms. Godwin's novels are unusual in being readable **and** thoughtful." *Publishers Weekly* assents that "Godwin brings empathy, understanding and a 19th century sensibility to this novel of a young woman deeply committed to her father."

RECOGNITION: *NYTBR* Notable Book of 1991; REVIEWS: *BellesL* Sum '91; *LJ* 2/1/91; *NYTBR* 3/3/91; *PW* 2/3/92; *TLS* 5/24/91

Grimsley, Jim (USA)

35   *Dream Boy* (1995); B&N 1996 (pbk)

Award-winning author Jim Grimsley's second novel is set in the rural south and features Nathan, a high school sophomore with a history of abuse at the hands of his alcoholic father, a Christian fundamentalist with extremely rigid views regarding filial obedience. The "dream boy" of the title is Roy, a popular athlete (and high school senior) who lives next door and with whom Nathan finds himself powerfully, if inexplicably, attracted to.

The *Library Journal* observes that while "the plot is too subservient to atmosphere and theme" Grimsley's "Southern settings are evocative, and the dysfunctional family ... of young Nathan rings true, as does the violence that pervades [the novel]." The *San Francisco Review of Books* argues that Grimsley "succeeds in creating a complete world of fear, love, and sexual violence against a backdrop of a haunted past."

RECOGNITION: Winner of the 1996 ALA Gay, Lesbian & Bisexual Book Award; REVIEWS: *BL* 9/15/95; *LJ* 9/1/95; *PW* 7/10/95; *SFRB* 9-10/95; *SLJ* 3/96; *WPBW* 10/8/95

Haynes, David (USA)

36   *Somebody Else's Mama* (1995); Milkweed 1995 (HC); HarBrace 1996 (pbk)

Set in Missouri, in a small, predominantly African-American town, *Somebody Else's Mama* takes a bittersweet look at Midwestern family life. Paula and Al Johnson (schoolteacher and newspaper editor, respectively) are raising sons and are proving adept at juggling the growing demands of family and career. The Johnson's well-ordered, middle-class existence is sorely tested, however, when Al's aging, irascible mother, Miss Kezee, moves back from St. Paul to live with them. Her return to the very house where she raised Al and which (for her) is filled with unhappy memories of her much-hated first husband (Al's father), is not easy for anyone. The novel is narrated in alternating chapters by each of the major characters.

According to the *L.A. Times Book Review* "Hayne's ambitions here are refreshingly modest. He belongs to the old realist tradition that believes that everyday life, if truly rendered, is more than exciting enough ... Haynes is especially good with his women characters, and not just Miss Keezee; the give and take, compromises and evasions, love and exasperation between Paula and Al makes other fictional marriages look like cartoons." *Choice* notes that "Haynes explores a set of interconnected issues, including black class structure, politics, and gender relationships ... [while forging] a style that combines elements of literary and oral traditions" and concludes that Haynes is "a writer who should be read by anyone interested in the complexity of contemporary multicultural fiction." *Kirkus Reviews* concludes: "Interior monologues alternate with dialogue that sings off the page in this engrossing, endearing reach to the front line of middle age...."

RECOGNITION: David Haynes was named to *Granta* magazine's 1996 list of the twenty "Best Young American Novelists"; REVIEWS: *BL* 4/15/95; *Choice* 10/95; *Emerge* 5/95; *KR* 3/1/95; *LATBR* 9/24/95; *NYTBR* 6/18/95; *PW* 4/10/95; *WPBW* 4/21/95

Hearon, Shelby (USA)

37   *Footprints* (1996); Knopf 1996 (HC)

When Nan and Douglas Mayhall's beloved 22-year-old daughter is killed in an automobile accident, her untimely death drops a depth charge into the placid waters of the Mayhall's marriage. Douglas, obsessed with ensuring that some part of his daughter lives on through an organ donation, needs to reach out to the grateful recipient while, Nan, more conflicted, hangs back. As their relationship deteriorates, Douglas embarks on an affair with a younger woman and even contemplates having more children. Nan, who had given up a career in paleontology to devote herself to her academic husband's career and to raising her other children, is forced to re-engage with a life outside the family and to seek a "separate peace."

"Veteran writer Hearon brings the Mayhall's story to believable life (writes the *Library Journal*) through carefully wrought, affecting characterizations and accurately rendered details of place and custom." According to novelist Robb Forman Dew (*NYTBR*), "In fewer than 200 pages, *Footprints* takes on an extraordinary number of issues: the ethical and emotional implications of organ transplants, adultery and its effect on marriage, the compromises women make who sacrifice their own careers to their husbands', the relation of parents to children overall and in almost every permutation, the importance and complications of women's friendships, the dichotomy of mind versus heart, and more." Ms. Dew concludes that, in reading Ms. Hearon's book, we "are the beneficiaries of a clear-eyed view that catches the humor and poignancy of the evolution of a woman's life."

REVIEWS: *BL* 3/15/96; *ChiTrib* 3/31/96; *KR* 2/1/96; *LJ* 3/15/96; *NYTBR* 3/31/96; *PW* 1/22/96

38   *Life Estates* (1994); Knopf 1994 (HC); Random House 1995 (pbk)

Sarah and Harriet, casual friends since boarding school, have led oddly parallel lives: they both married bankers, are ensconced in large, comfortable homes, have raised two children, and are financially secure. When each is widowed at age 55, they renew their friendship. As it turns out, their individual responses to bereavement couldn't be more different: Sarah, the independent co-owner of a wallpaper shop, rejects her husband's legacy (a "life estate"), choosing, rather, to make her own way in the pleasant company, admittedly, of 70-year-old Dr. Will Perry (friend and lover); Harriet, blonde and still beautiful, appears paralyzed by her loss — and by the fact that she's lost her cherished role in society: wife. *Life Estates*, according to the critics, is characterized by an extraordinarily thoughtful look at marriage and friendship.

According to the *New York Times Book Review*, in *Life Estates* "Shelby Hearon has made it her busi-

ness to strip away the stereotype ... such lives have rarely been so thoroughly, honestly, yet lovingly evoked." The *L.A. Times* points out that "Sarah may be a bit over zealous as a feminist, a bit underinvolved as a mother, but she is altogether attractive — bright, caring, strong. It is, however, the funny/sad Harriet who touches the heart and stays in the head. Around these two ultimately heroic heroines, Hearon has woven yet another life-affirming novel which, while not profound, is profoundly readable and satisfying."

READING GROUP GUIDE; RECOGNITION: *NYTBR* Notable Book of 1994; REVIEWS: *BL* 1/15/94; *ChiTrib* 2/20/94; *KR* 12/15/93; *LATBR* 3/6/94; *LJ* 2/1/94; *NYTBR* 12/13/94; *PW* 12/13/93

Hegi, Ursula (USA)

39   *Salt Dancers* (1995); S&S 1997 (pbk)

Julia, a 41-year-old successful architect pregnant with her first child, journeys from her home in Vermont to her father's house in Washington state. She is at a critical juncture in her life: facing imminent motherhood, she must confront (and exorcise) her disturbing childhood memories.

According to *Booklist*, "In achingly beautiful prose that exacts a huge emotional toll, the author at once shatters and rebuilds the myth of the family unit." *Time* magazine asserts that the strength of Ms. Hegi's "forcefully written novel of child abuse and parental desertion" derives from the novel's "unfailing immediacy of language." Novelist **Abby Frucht** (*NYTBR*) suggests that "it is the peculiar authority of the narrative voice in Ursula Hegi's latest novel ... its refusal either to sentimentalize or sensationalize, its insistence on undulating intuitively through the various parts of the story — that makes *Salt Dancers* seem fresh. Perhaps it is also the adroitness with which the book shifts from the reality of daily life to the surreality of imagined or remembered moments that [also] makes it absorbing."

REVIEWS: *BL* 8/95; *LJ* 7/95; *NewsWk* 4/18/94; *NYTBR* 8/27/95; *PW* 5/22/95; *Time* 8/21/95; *WPBW* 9/10/95

Hellenga, Robert (USA)

40   *The Fall of a Sparrow* (1998); Scribner 1998 (HC)

Robert Hellenga sets much of his second novel (as he did his debut effort, *The Sixteen Pleasures*) in contemporary Italy. A Midwestern college professor has traveled to Bologna to bear witness at the trial of a group of Italian terrorists. Six years earlier one of his daughters, an exchange student, was killed in a bombing at an Italian train station, and his life has been in total disarray ever since starting with the breakup of his marriage.

According to *Kirkus Reviews*, "The primal power of family, and the limitations and blessing of the intellectual life, are unforgettably explored in a wrenching story that demonstrates precisely how 'it's not the great stories that give meaning to the little ones; it's the other way around.'" In the view of the *L.A. Times Book Review*, "the highest praise for a novel may be that it forced you to engage it, to argue, to confront it as you would a challenging but sometimes misguided lover. Robert Hellenga's *The Fall of a Sparrow* is such a novel." *Entertainment Weekly* concludes that *The Fall of the Sparrow* offers "autumnal prose, a playful intellectual curiosity, and a decent, disillusioned, all-embracing tenderness."

OTHER MEDIA: Audiocassette (Dove/abr); RECOGNITION: *LATBR* "Best Fiction of 1998"; *PW*'s Best '98 Fiction; REVIEWS: *ChiTrib* 6/14/98; *EW* 8/7/98; *KR* 5/11/98; *LATBR* 8/16/98; *LJ* 5/15/98; *NYTBR* 6/28/98; *PW* 4/6/98

Hijuelos, Oscar (USA)

41 *Mr. Ives' Christmas* (1995); Harper-Collins 1996 (pbk)

The eponymous Mr. Ives — a commercial artist employed by a Manhattan advertising company — associates his greatest joys and his deepest sorrows with the Christmas season: he was adopted from a foundling home at Christmas-time, he met his future wife at a Christmas party and, tragically, his seventeen-year-old son was murdered during the 1967 Christmas season. Mr. Ives, has never recovered from the death of his son and remains enveloped in an unshakable melancholia. Drawing on the Dickensian theme of regaining the true meaning of Christmas, Hijuelos has fashioned a story which — despite its emphasis on loss — celebrates the spiritual well-spring of this emotionally charged season..

The *New York Times Book Review* observes that "*Mr. Ives' Christmas* is Oscar Hijuelos's *Christmas Carol* for a crime-ridden, ethnically-divided urban America…. Mr. Hijuelos has told a tale of what theologians call final perseverance, a parable of good will lost and good will regained. [It is the] shortest of [the author's] recent novels [but] … both the deepest and the best." In the view of *Time* magazine, "Never didactic, *Mr. Ives' Christmas* is a spare, moving meditation on the spiritual life." According to Marie Arana-Ward (deputy editor of the *WPBW*) Hijuelos "offers no comfortably familiar morality tale, no easy lesson … nevertheless, [Hijuelos offers] … a powerful message about the spirit … [that] it is faith that ultimately frees a man, not because it brings him any closer to understanding the unknowable, but because it allows him to transcend it."

RECOGNITION: Nominated for the 1996 Pulitzer Prize for Fiction; REVIEWS: *BL* 10/1/95;

ChiTrib 12/24/95; *LATBR* 12/17/95; *LJ* 11/1/95; *LT* 12/7/95; *LST* 12/31/95; *NY* 8/21/95; *NYTBR* 12/3/95; *Time* 11/27/95; *TLS* 12/8/95; *WPBW* 12/10/95

Holleran, Andrew (USA)

42 *The Beauty of Men* (1996); Morrow 1996 (HC); B&N 1997 (pbk)

Mr. Lark, the protagonist of Andrew Holleran's latest novel, is a 47-year-old gay man who has moved to north central Florida to be near his paralyzed, wheelchair bound mother who is residing in a local nursing home. Lark once lived a discretely homosexual life in New York City, but left in 1983, the same year his first friend died from a perplexing new virus and his mother broke her neck. He now divides his time between his mother's bedside and the gay bars, baths and bush-shrouded or concrete-barriered rendezvous spots scattered about Gainesville.

Publishers Weekly, in its starred review, asserts that "Holleran's trademark prose — lush, carefully cadenced and keenly observed — creates a mesmerizingly claustrophobic world where the trapped elderly residents of Lark's mother's nursing home, the lonely men Lark encounters in his fruitless search for love and the overwhelming anonymity of suburban America have equal power to break the heart." The *Washington Post Book World* calls it "deeply despondent, soaked in sorrow, filled with erotic despair … an honest attempt to grapple with loneliness and aging without self-pity or sentimentality." English novelist, **Alan Hollinghurst** (*TLS*) observes: "To some [Lark's] world will seem alien, to others culpably negative; but it would be hard to read this novel, for all its exaggerations, without a sense that it describes something real, as much to heterosexuals as homosexuals: a modern atrophy of the spirit, and what I think Mr. Holleran wants to identify as a particularly American stupefaction and emptiness." According to *Booklist* Mr. Lark, "is pathetic, and only Holleran among gay novelists could make riveting reading out of an entire novel focused on him — which is precisely what Holleran, still a gorgeous writer, has done." The *London Times* concludes that Andrew Holleran "has woven a bleakly beautiful, compassionate elegy for life after AIDS."

RECOGNITION: Nominated for the 1997 ALA Gay, Lesbian Bisexual Books Award and the Lambda Book Award for Gay Fiction; *NYTBR* Notable Book 1996; REVIEWS: *LATBR* 7/28/96; *LJ* 1/97; *LST* 11/17/96; *LT* 2/28/98; *NYTBR* 6/30/96; *PW* 4/29/96; *TLS* 2/21/97; *WPBW* 6/9/96

Huneven, Michelle (USA)

43 *Round Rock* (1997); Knopf 1997 (HC)

Michelle Huneven has set her debut novel in

Rito, a small town in Santa Bernita, the citrus growing region of southern California and features Red Ray, a divorced former alcoholic (and one-time successful lawyer) who opens a "drunk farm" for recovering alcoholics, in his rambling old Victorian mansion. Plot complications include the arrival of a graduate student, Lewis Fletcher, with one too many alcohol-related arrests, and the presence of Libby Daw, an attractive trailer-dwelling divorcee who finds solace in the treatment center and in the arms of both Lewis and Ray.

According to *Kirkus Reviews*, *Round Rock* is "Long, slow, intelligent, and humane [and is] filled with high expertise about alcoholism." Novelist Valerie Miner (*LATBR*) notes that "Huneven is an audacious novelist, casting the narrative light evenly on various idiosyncratic characters" and concludes that "*Round Rock* is a textured drama of individual and cultural history, a promising debut from a writer of moral nerve, sharp wit and uncommon generosity." *Publishers Weekly*, in its starred review, observes: "There is nothing outwardly dazzling about [Huneven's] method, no breathtaking prose or startling wit, no perfectly tidy twisting to the plot, just a deep intelligent sympathy for people whose lives matter to the reader."

RECOGNITION: *NYTBR* Notable Book of 1997; *LATBR* "Best Books" 1997; REVIEWS: *KR* 5/15/97; *LATBR* 12/14/97; *NYTBR* 8/3/97; *PW* 6/30/97; *TLS* 10/31/97

Iida, Deborah (USA)

44 *Middle Son* (1996); Algonquin 1996 (HC); Berkley 1998 (pbk)

Set in "Japanese Row" in Wainoa, Maui — a settlement of transplanted Japanese-American sugar cane workers — Deborah Iida's debut novel tells the emotionally powerful story of a man's attempt to come to terms with a childhood tragedy which took the life of his older brother and for which he feels complicit. The novel is narrated by Stephen Fujii, the "middle son," and begins with his final journey home to confront his mother who is dying of cancer. The author makes liberal use of the pidgin dialect when she shifts the scene to the Fujii boys' childhood.

Kirkus Reviews observes that the author's "skill at balancing rhythmic pidgin with well-wrought description creates a small gem about a fascinating and strongly traditional way of life." The *Library Journal* describes *Middle Son* as "a delicate yet powerful work chronicling the ways in which birth order, traditional expectations, and custom affects three Hawaiian boys...." Says the *New York Times Book Review*, "Ms. Iida has mastered the difficult art of capturing the rhythms of hesitation and circumlocution, the ways in which characters talk about everything but the main thing on their mind."

RECOGNITION: Winner of Grand Prize from the Maui Writer's Guild; 1997 ALA Notable Book of the Year; New York Public Library 1997 "Books to Remember"; REVIEWS: *Choice* 6/96; *KR* 1/1/96; *LJ* 3/15/96; *NY* 6/24/96; *NYTBR* 6/2/96; *PW* 2/5/96; *W&I* 6/96

Irving, John (USA)

45 *A Widow for One Year* (1998); Random House 1998 (HC)

John Irving has created one of his most complex female characters in the person of Ruth Cole, the protagonist of his ninth novel. The story opens in 1958 on Long Island where Ruth's parents are in the final stages of a separation made inevitable by the deaths — in a car crash, five years previously — of their two, immensely talented, teenage sons. The four-year-old Ruth, who had been conceived, misguidedly, as a replacement for her dead brothers, has already absorbed the story of their luminous, tragically truncated lives. The story then shifts to New York City in 1990 where Ruth, a professional writer with four published novels to her credit, is leading a late–20th-century urban life characterized by serial marriage, type-A friends, vituperative critics, assorted stalkers, urban nut cases, and, finally, true love. Another chunk of the narrative is devoted to Ruth's European book tour including an extended episode in Amsterdam where she befriends a Dutch whore, witnesses a murder and is embroiled in a police investigation.

According to *Booklist* "As one excellently rendered scene follows another, each scene at once ribald, humorous, and tender, Irving achieves a nuanced depiction of overcoming familial and sexual dysfunction." *Kirkus Reviews* declares that "Irving's latest ... which portrays with seriocomic gusto the literary life and its impact on both writers and their families, is simultaneously one of his most intriguing books and one of his most self-indulgent and flaccid." The *Times Literary Supplement* calls *A Widow for One Year* "a seriofarce about loss and fidelity and the passage of time ... a fusion of *Love in the Time of Cholera* with something lewdly comic by Tom Sharp." Novelist **Stephen Amidon**, writing in the *London Sunday Times* argues that "Irving's fiction has always been notable for its scope. *A Widow for One Year*, spanning continents and decades, proves no exception. But whereas the best of his earlier novels were founded upon a single vivid character (e.g. Garp), here the heroine is too fragile a creation to allow for much emotional impact...." Michiko Kakutani (*NYT*) observes that although "*A Widow for One Year* is marred by some paint-by-number psychologizing and the heavy-handed use of coincidence, Irving's own storytelling has never been better."

OTHER MEDIA: Audiocassette (Random

Audio/unabr); READING GROUP GUIDE; RECOGNI-
TION: *LATBR* "Best Fiction of 1998"; *NYTBR* Notable Book of 1998; REVIEWS: *BL* 4/1/98; *ChiTrib*
5/31/98; *KR* 4/1/98; *LATBR* 7/12/98; *LT* 4/11/98;
NS 5/22/98; *NYT* 4/28/98; *NYTBR* 5/24/98; *TLS*
4/24/98; *WPBW* 7/26/98

Keller, Nora Okja (USA)

46 *Comfort Woman* (1997); Viking 1997
(HC); Penguin 1998 (pbk)

Nora Okja Keller's moving debut novel focuses on a mother and daughter living in Hawaii.
Beccah (an obituary writer) is the daughter of
Akido, a Korean-born spirit woman. Her father,
an American missionary, is long-since deceased.
Akido's traumatic experiences during World War II
(including forcible prostitution in a Japanese camp)
have left her with deep emotional scars. A third
character, a friend who calls herself "Auntie Reno"
adds a cheerfully vulgar note to a powerfully moving story about the strength of familial love. The
narration moves with great sensitivity between
mother and daughter.

Booklist notes that Ms. Keller "threads her
graceful narrative with themes of identity and the
search for self" and applauds the author for her
"deft and subtle use of humor ... and [for her] assured lyrical prose style." *Time* points out that
Comfort Women is really about pain, the kind that
haunts and is handed down like old, sad clothes"
and concludes that "this is a sturdy, eloquent book."
In the view of the *L.A. Times*, Keller's "impressive
debut" is "[s]trongly imagined, well-paced and
written with an eloquently restrained lyricism that
conveys the subtleties of feelings as well as the
harshness of facts."

RECOGNITION: *LATBR* "Best Books" 1997;
REVIEWS: *BL* 3/15/97; *KR* 2/1/97; *LATBR* 3/23/97;
LJ 1/97; *NYT* 3/25/97; *NYTBR* 8/31/97; *PW*
1/6/97; *Time* 5/5/97

Kingsolver, Barbara (USA)

47 *Pigs in Heaven* (1993); HarperCollins
1994 (pbk)

Pigs in Heaven, the sequel to Barbara Kingsolver's 1988 novel *The Bean Trees* (in which Taylor, a young white single woman, rescues — and
raises — a severely abused, abandoned Native
American toddler) picks up the story three years
later. Taylor and (the affectionately renamed) "Turtle" have set out on a sight-seeing tour of the American West. While visiting the Hoover Dam, a man
accidentally falls into a spillway, an event that is
witnessed only by six-year-old Turtle. The youngster's insistence that she has seen "a man fall" leads,
eventually, to the man's rescue. The ensuing media
exposure brings Turtle to the attention of a Native
American lawyer who is determined to see her re-

turned to her Cherokee relatives. Taylor and Turtle go underground.

According to the *Washington Post Book World*
"There is no one quite like Barbara Kingsolver in
contemporary literature. Her dialogue sparkles with
sassy wit and the earthy poetry of ordinary folks'
tales; her descriptions have a magical lyricism
rooted in daily life but also on familiar terms with
the eternal." *Newsweek* points out that in *Pigs in
Heaven* Ms. Kingsolver "challenges her own strong
60s-style politics by pitting its cultural correctness
against the boundless love between a mother and a
child. For all its political dimensions, this is no
polemic but a complex drama in which heroes and
villains play each other's parts and learn from
them." The *San Francisco Chronicle* concludes that
Ms. Kingsolver "makes you care about her characters to the point of tears: she is bitingly funny and
she writes like a dream."

OTHER MEDIA: Audiocassette (Harper
Audio/abr; Recorded Books/unabr); READING
GROUP GUIDE; RECOGNITION: Winner of the 1993
L.A. Times Book Award; *NYTBR* Notable Book of
1993; REVIEWS: *CSM* 8/9/93; *KR* 4/15/93; *LATBR*
7/4/93; *NewsWk* 7/11/93; *NYTBR* 6/27/93; *Time*
9/24/90; *WPBW* 11/11/93; EDITOR'S NOTE: Ms.
Kingsolver's latest novel, the extremely well-received *The Poisonwood Bible* (a NYTBR Editors'
Choice selection for 1998), features a missionary
family in the Congo in 1959.

48 *Animal Dreams* (1990); HarperCollins
1991 (pbk)

Barbara Kingsolver's second novel is set in
Grace, Arizona, hometown to Cosima (Codi) No-
line who has dropped out of medical school and,
at the loosest of ends, has returned home to be near
her aged father — the local doctor — who appears
to be in the incipient stages of Alzheimer's disease.
Codi takes a job as a biology teacher at the local
high school teaching a class which includes the
usual nature walks and water sampling expeditions.
It doesn't take long for Codi to realize that the local
river and orchards face a significant ecological threat
from the Black Mountain Mining Company. Codi
also slides into a relationship with a handsome, Native American train engineer, with whom she had
been briefly, and disastrously, involved while still in
high school.

The Nation observes that "like all good novels, *Animal Dreams* is a web of interlacing news. It
is dense and vivid, and makes ever tighter circles
around the question of what it means to be alive."
Novelist **Jane Smiley** (*NYTBR*) declares that "Barbara Kingsolver is one of an increasing number of
American novelists who are trying to rewrite the
political, cultural and spiritual relationships between our country's private and public spheres."
Novelist Ursula Le Guin (*WPBW*) found *Animal*

Dreams to be "Rich, complex and witty ... a sweet book, full of bitter pain; a beautiful weaving of the light and the dark." The *L.A. Times Book Review* notes that while Kingsolver's prose style may remind the reader of some Latin American writers (e.g. Juan Rulfo, Gabriel Garcia Marquez, Isabel Allende), "her concerns are rooted in 20th-century North America: the problems of rampant ecological destruction, sexual and other abuse issues, our responsibility towards the victims of U.S. foreign and domestic policies, and the grass-roots response to the terror rising about us as society comes apart at the seams." According to *Time* "To say everything is resolved happily would be misleading, but one hint may be allowed. Anyone who thinks a giant mining concern is any match for the Grace 'Stitch and Bitch' club has a lot to learn about eco-feminist novels."

OTHER MEDIA: Audiocassette (Recorded Books/unabr); READING GROUP GUIDE; RECOGNITION: Winner of the *L.A. Times* Book Prize for Fiction; *NYTBR* Notable Book of 1990; REVIEWS: *LATBR* 9/9/90; *LJ* 8/90; *Nation* 11/26/90; *NYTBR* 9/2/90; *Time* 9/24/90; *WPBW* 9/2/90

Lamb, Wally (USA)

49 *She's Come Undone* (1992); Washington Square 1996 (pbk)

Dolores Price is the wry, overweight, sensitive and cynical heroine of Wally Lamb's ambitious first novel. Lamb's harrowing tale follows Dolores's progress from her early shattered and repressed family life, through teenage cycles of sexual and food abuse, beyond periods of hospitalization in mental institutions, to her gradual recovery at the age of forty. Wally Lamb's novel was catapulted onto numerous best-seller lists when selected by Oprah Winfrey as one of her early Book Club of the Air selections.

Kirkus Reviews observes that "Dolores' career is a pleasure to follow, as she barrels through—with a killer mouth and the guts of a sea lion" and concludes that the book is a "warm-blooded, enveloping tale of survival, done up loose and cheering." According to *Publishers Weekly*, Wally Lamb "keenly evokes his protagonist's profound alienation and self-loathing, endowing Dolores with a bleak sense of humor that keeps readers rooting for her." Liza Schwarzbaum — commenting in *Entertainment Weekly* on the choice of *She's Come Undone* for Oprah Winfrey's Book Club — notes: "Some of the best female dialog ever to come from a male writer's head made Wally Lamb's [debut novel] an inspired choice."

OTHER MEDIA: Audiocassette (S&S/abr; Recorded Bks/unabr); RECOGNITION: *NYTBR* Notable Book of 1992; nominated for the *L.A. Times* Book Award 1992; Oprah Winfrey Book Club selection

REVIEWS: *BL* 8/92; *ChiTrib* 8/9/92; *EW* 3/21/97; *KR* 4/15/92; *LATBR* 9/13/92; *NYTBR* 8/23/92; *PW* 5/18/92; *LT* 10/11/97; *WSJ* 8/21/92

EDITOR'S NOTE: *I Know This Much Is True*, Lamb's most recent title, released in late 1998, was included in *Publishers Weekly*'s "Best of '98 Fiction" list.

Lamott, Anne (USA)

50 *Crooked Little Heart* (1997); Pantheon 1997 (HC)

Anne Lamott's 5th novel features Rosie Ferguson, a youngster who was first introduced to readers in the eponymous *Rosie* (1983). She now lives in California with her mother, who though happily married to James (a writer), is still mourning Rosie's dead father. Rosie, a scrawny, lanky thirteen-year-old, has developed into a formidable tennis player; she is, however, tormented by the usual range of early-teen insecurities and this is affecting her performance both on and off the courts. To make matters worse, her best friend, Simone, has already "blossomed." Lamott knows well of which she speaks — having been a nationally ranked doubles player herself as a teenager.

Calling *Crooked Little Heart* a "sweet, complex and compassionate tale" *Booklist* further observes that Lamott "is exquisitely sensitive to the confusion of emerging sexuality, the mix of fear and ambition involved in competitive sports, and the feeling of stunned helplessness in the face of birth and death." *People Weekly* found Lamott's portrayal of Rosie to be "eloquent, detailed [and] emotionally honest" and praises the author for "telling it like it is." *Entertainment Weekly* points out that "Humbert Humbert rhapsodized memorably about Lolita's elegant, if ineffectual, tennis game; something about this beautiful, warbling novel feels like that unfortunate kid's revenge." According to the *Chicago Tribune* Lamott "is a gifted chronicler of daily life. *Crooked Little Heart* is a bittersweet testament to the family, wherever we might find it, and to finding grace in the commonplace."

OTHER MEDIA: Audiocassette (Random Audio/abr); REVIEWS: *BL* 4/1/97; *ChiTrib* 4/20/97; *CSM* 4/24/97; *EW* 6/13/97; *LJ* 4/1/97; *NYTBR* 8/17/97; *PeopleW* 4/14/97; *PW* 2/17/97; *WPBW* 4/13/97

Leavitt, David (USA)

51 *Arkansas: Three Novellas* (1997); HM 1997 (HC); 1998 (pbk)

Praised as both deftly written and slyly comic, *Arkansas* is a collection of three novellas each exploring the dual themes of escape and exile. It is David Leavitt's first work of fiction since a literary scandal erupted following the publication of *While England Sleeps* (1993), a novel based on a Stephen

Spender–like character which was found to be invasive and offensively pornographic by Mr. Spender). Leavitt's latest offering takes its name from a quote attributed to Oscar Wilde: "I should like to flee like a wounded hart into Arkansas."

According to *Publishers Weekly*, "Leavitt has obviously decided to keep his distance from revered English poets with dicey sexual backgrounds. Here he presents three novellas about someone he can be reasonably sure won't sue — himself." *Kirkus Reviews* describes *Arkansas* as "Grim, disturbing explorations of the way in which lust and loneliness can destroy the possibility of love." The *L.A. Times Book Review* concludes: "This is classic Leavitt — writing with subtlety, maturity and compassion about the complexity and fragility of human relationships."

RECOGNITION: *LATBR* "Best Books" 1997; REVIEWS: *BL* 3/1/97; *KR* 2/1/97; *LATBR* 12/14/97; *LJ* 2/1/97; *NewsWk* 3/10/97; *NYT* 3/11/97; *NYTBR* 3/30/97; *PW* 1/27/97; *Time* 3/17/97; EDITOR'S NOTE: David Leavitt's most recent work of fiction *The Page Turner* (1998) features an 18-year-old aspiring musician who falls in love with the successful concert pianist who has hired him to "turn pages."

52   *Equal Affections* (1989); GroveAtlantic 1997 (pbk)

Leavitt has written perceptively about growing up gay in the American suburbs. In *Equal Affections* he tells an equally perceptive tale of a conflicted family headed by a dissatisfied, unfulfilled mother whose plight is exacerbated by a midlife diagnosis of cancer. Louise Cooper, mother of April and Danny is informed, while her children are still young, that she has breast cancer. She will live the rest of her life waiting for death (through twenty years of remission and relapse, to be exact). Her husband, through it all, is chronically unfaithful. Her daughter April grows up to become a feminist folk singer with a string of lesbian lovers while Danny pursues both a legal career and monogamy with his stable male lover in the California suburbs.

Michiko Kakutani (*NYT*) calls Leavitt "one of his generation's most gifted writers" and concludes: "When it comes to Louise and her relationship with Danny … Mr. Leavitt is able to demonstrate his full powers as a writer: his talent for empathy, his ability to write persuasively about highly emotional issues without resorting to sentimentality or irony, [and] his capacity for delineating the deeply felt currents of everyday life." According to the *Times Literary Supplement* "Leavitt has poached on the bourgeois preserve of the mini-series and the soap-opera and gives them a substance and harmony that transcends their episodic banalities.... [F]or gravity and elegance he has few rivals among younger American writers."

REVIEWS: *LATBR* 3/5/89; *LJ* 1/89; *NYT* 1/31/89; *NYTBR* 2/12/89; *PW* 11/17/89; *TLS* 6/9/89; *WPBW* 1/22/89

Lessing, Doris (UK)

53   *Love, Again* (1996); HarperCollins 1996 (HC); 1997 (pbk)

At the outset of Doris Lessing's latest novel, Sarah Durham, looking and feeling younger than her 65 years, has just secured funding for her newest play, an historical drama based on the life of Julie Vairon, a 19th-century French heroine. In a stroke of genius, the debut performance is to take place in the small town near Provence where Julie actually lived. The plot revolves around the (mostly amorous) activities of the cast and crew who have gathered in the French town to rehearse the play. When Sarah falls in love with the 26-year-old male lead and (shortly thereafter) with a 30-something American as well, she has ample cause to ruefully confront the unsettling reality of "an older woman in love." Lessing deals emotively and honestly with one of the last taboos and in so doing explores the larger issues of the meaning of love and desire.

Kirkus Reviews describes *Love, Again* as a "probing and provocative examination of the experience of love as the mind and body approach old age" and judges Lessing to be "a contemporary George Eliot, an intellectual whose imagination is firmly grounded in the sensual life and the natural world." The *New Statesman* calls Ms. Lessing's novel "a wholly compelling book, as vigorous and thought-provoking as anything she has ever written." *Publishers Weekly*, in its starred review, concludes that Lessing "wields a formidable analytic intelligence that makes this work provocative and often astonishingly beautiful."

REVIEWS: *BL* 2/15/96; *Econ* 6/15/96; *KR* 2/1/96; *LRB* 4/18/96; *NS&S* 4/12/96; *NY* 6/10/96; *NYRB* 4/18/96; *NYTBR* 4/21/96; *PW* 1/29/96; *TLS* 4/5/96

Lipsky, David (USA)

54   *The Art Fair* (1996); Doubleday 1996 (HC)

Richard Freely had spent the better part of his childhood shuttling between his divorced parents who live on opposite coasts. As a teenager, Richard opts for New York and settles down with his once-successful artist mother in Manhattan. Before long, he is engaged, full time, in an attempt to resurrect his mother's career. Described as the "anatomy of a tricky mother-and-son relationship" by *Booklist*, *The Art Fair* is set in New York City's bohemian art world of the 1970s. The story's aura of verisimilitude can be attributed to the fact that Mr. Lipsky is the son of Pat Lipsky Sutton, a painter whose work was shown at the Emmerich Gallery in the

1970s and whose work is now in the permanent collection of the Whitney Museum.

In the view of *Salon* magazine Lipsky has written a novel which, "with subtle strokes and sudden blasts of color ... brilliantly sends up the New York art scene." *The Art Fair* was called a "poised first novel" and "a deeply affecting ... portrayal of the ties between parent and child," by *People Weekly*. *Booklist*, found "the combination of Lipsky's unfailing psychological acumen and Seinfeld-like sensibility (minus the slapstick) makes for a distinctive and thoroughly enjoyable literary experience." The *Hartford Courant* observes that "Lipsky isn't adept simply at tweaking the Manhattan art world. His fictional autobiography expertly explores the deep, inexplicable bond between mother and son. His book brims with humor and thoughtful observation. It also is rich in the luminous joys and dark pains that color every family." *Kirkus Reviews* offers a different perspective: "Self described Gen-X writer Lipsky ... helps define a genre pioneered by Harold Brodkey and perfected by contemporaries David Leavitt and Michael Chabon — the tale of the disappointed Jewish prince; an upper–middle-class–whiner who feels cheated by life's difficulties and continues to exercise a puerile omnipotence over all those around him."

REVIEWS: *BL* 5/15/96; *ChiTrib* 5/12/96; *Hart-Cour* 8/18/98; *KR* 4/1/96; *LJ* 10/1/96; *NewsWk* 6/3/96; *NYTBR* 6/9/96; *PeopleW* 7/29/96; *PW* 4/8/96; *Salon* 5/96; *Vogue* 4/96

Lively, Penelope (UK)

55   *Heat Wave* (1996); HarperCollins 1996 (HC); HarperPerennial 1997 (pbk)

In the shimmering heat of an atypical English summer, Pauline, a 55-year-old freelance editor (hard at work "tidying up" a young Welsh writer's epic novel about knights and maidens) is making the best of the weather in her charming country cottage. Her 29-year-old daughter, Teresa (along with husband Maurice and infant son, Luke) are staying in the second of two cottages on Pauline's property. Maurice is a manipulative 44-year-old writer who reminds Pauline of her own ex-husband, a philandering academic now teaching at a University in California. As the summer progresses, it becomes obvious to Pauline that her daughter's marriage is in trouble — threatened both by the ebbing away of romantic love, and by Maurice's casual infidelities — and she yearns to protect her daughter from the painful breakup which appears inevitable.

Jonathan Yardley (*WPBW*) calls *Heat Wave* "witty, intelligent and understated ... [and far more complex] than first impressions would suggest." Irish novelist Aisling Foster (*TLS*) observes that it "is all about the power of love: protective maternal love, promiscuous sexual love, the nurturing love of mother nature and our love of animals and countryside which is both benign and exploitative...." Ms. Foster concludes that Lively has turned "a modern domestic drama into an enduring legend." According to the *New Yorker* "Wisdom tends to substitute for drama [in *Heat Wave*], yet you don't want to part company with these characters, who, time and again, elicit a sensation of intense familiarity." *Publishers Weekly*, in its starred review, notes that Ms. Lively "Creates a convincing picture of obsessive sexual love tainted by jealousy and misery, and of the kind of maternal love that carries its own implacable mandates."

OTHER MEDIA: Audiocassette (Books-on-Tape/unabr) RECOGNITION: *L.A. Times* "Best Books" 1996; *NYTBR* Notable Book of 1996; REVIEWS: *BL* 8/96; *LATBR* 12/29/96; *NY* 10/7/96; *PW* 7/1/96; *Spec* 5/25/96; *TLS* 5/24/96; *WPBW* 10/16/96

Long, David (USA)

56   *The Falling Boy* (1997); Scribner 1997 (HC); Penguin 1998 (pbk)

David Long's debut novel, set in Montana in the Eisenhower years, features Mark Singer, a young man who, following the death of his father and the subsequent disappearance of his mother, has been raised by his grandmother in the little town of Sperry. Mark is drawn to the Vagabond Cafe, a local watering hole run by Nick Stavros and his four daughters, for it is within the close-knit Greek-American Stavros clan that Mark finds the family he never had. Mark eventually (and quite expectedly) joins the Stavros family by marrying (sensible, serious) Olivia Stavros. As the story unfolds, Olivia's older sister Linny returns home from San Francisco (and its beatnik haunts), and Mark and Olivia's marriage will be sorely tested.

According to *Booklist* "Long is a writer of extraordinary sensitivity and grace. In examining the complex relationships of the close-knit Stavros sisters ... he provides myriad insights into the love and dependence that tie us together and the rivalries and obstinacies that isolate us." In the view of the *Library Journal* "Not since John Updike's *Merry Men* ... has there been such an honest and unflinching moral examination of marital infidelity." As the *Washington Post Book World* suggests: "The intricate world of human relations has often been considered women's domain, but [in *The Falling Boy*] ... Long enters it with nuance and razor-edge precision as he documents the marital decline of his protagonist, Mark Singer."

REVIEWS: *BL* 6/1/97; *LJ* 5/15/97; *Newsday* 7/6/97; *NYTBR* 9/28/97; *PW* 4/28/97; *WPBW* 9/14/97

Marshall, Paule (USA)

57 *Daughters* (1991); NAL-Dutton 1992 (pbk)

Paule Marshall's protagonist, Ursa Beatrice Mackenzie, lives and works in the United States but she was born on the (fictional) Caribbean island of Triunion where her father is a successful politician. Her American-born mother, Estelle, worried that her husband is about to make a fatal political mistake, asks Ursa to come home and talk "sense"to her formidable father.

In the view of *Publishers Weekly*, "This richly textured, intelligent, emotionally involving novel will add to Marshall's stature both as a prose writer and as a sensitive chronicler of lives of people of color." The *Women's Review of Books* calls Marshall's fourth novel "her most ambitious, mature and sharply political" yet. Novelist Susan Fromberg Schaeffer (*NYTBR*), found *Daughters* to be "Flawless in its sense of place and character, remarkable in its understanding of human nature ... [and] a triumph in every way." The *Chicago Tribune* notes that "*Daughters* is a work that has been mulled over and thought through; it is Marshall's most inclusive and sophisticated analysis of the intersection between personality, identity, family, politics, and culture, and an outstanding and important work and a fascinating novel." Novelist **Francine Prose** (*Washington Post Book World*) concludes "The narrative moves along so engagingly that, without any trace of ponderousness, Marshall is able to address a wide spectrum of serious subjects: race relations, female experience, and female friendship, history, loyalty, social responsibility, the legacy of memory and the necessity of forgiveness."

RECOGNITION: Winner of the 1991 *Booklist* Award for Best Adult Fiction; nominated for the 1992 *L.A. Times* Book Award; *NYTBR* Notable Book of 1991; REVIEWS: *ChiTrib* 10/6/91; *KR* 7/15/91; *LATBR* 10/6/91; *LJ* 11/1/91; *NYTBR* 10/27; *SFCBR* 11/10/91; *VLS* 11/91; *WLT* Sum '92; *WPBW* 9/22/91; *WRB* 11/91; *YaleRev* 4/92

McCauley, Stephen (USA)

58 *The Easy Way Out* (1992); Pocket Bks 1993 (pbk)

Stephen McCauley's second novel, referred to by more than one critic as a "sophisticated soap opera" is narrated by Patrick, a Boston-based travel agent in his mid '30s. It features a collection of offbeat, slightly out-of-sync middle-class Bostonians including Patrick's live in lover, Arthur, a successful immigration lawyer. The spark has long gone out of their relationship but Patrick can't quite muster the energy to end it. Sharon, Patrick's colleague at the travel agency ("Only Connect Travel"—which caters to eccentric Harvard professors, New Agers, and late-blooming, guiltily up-

wardly mobile types) continually badgers Patrick about pulling the plug with Arthur. Meanwhile, Patrick's older brother Ryan and younger brother Tony are both experiencing traumatic emotional difficulties of their own making.

Publishers Weekly, in its starred review calls McCauley's second novel a "beautifully written, heartbreaking book" and concludes that, though it lacks the "magnetism and spark" of the author's debut novel (*The Object of My Affection*), it "is an eloquent depiction of the compromises lovers and families make to keep relationships alive." The *NYTBR* concludes: "It's enormously difficult to write a successful novel about the decent souls of the middle class, people who are both too rich and not rich enough to do anything very dastardly or very heroic. The hugely talented Stephen Mc-Cauley has made it look easy." Novelist **Michael Dorris**, calls *The Easy Way Out* "an exhilarating, entertaining, smart novel. Vivid quirky characters leap off the page and sit at your table, already well into conversations describing the messy complications of their lives." The *L.A. Times* suggests that McCauley "seems to play the story for laughs entertaining the reader with witty dialogue and amusing scenes, yet something significant always seems to be going on just below the surface."

RECOGNITION: Nominated for the 1993 ALA Gay & Lesbian & Bisexual Book Award; REVIEWS: *LAT* 8/28/92; *LJ* 5/1/92; *NYTBR* 5/31/92; *PW* 3/16/92; *SFC* 7/5/92; *Time* 7/27/92; *WPBW* 8/8/93

McCracken, Elizabeth (USA)

59 *The Giant's House* (1996); Dial 1996 (HC); Avon 1997 (pbk)

In her debut novel, set in a small Cape Cod town in the 1950s, Elizabeth McCracken has fashioned an eerily compelling love story around two mismatched characters: Peggy, a petite, vaguely misanthropic 26-year-old librarian and James Carlson Sweatt, a sweet and graceful 12-year-old afflicted with an endocrinological disorder known as "gigantism." As James ages, his celebrity status grows along with his height until he becomes a kind of tourist attraction in his small, sea-side town. His mother tries, in her often ineffectual way, to provide her son with stability and comfort; but it is Peggy, a long-time family friend, who offers James unconditional and enduring love.

According to the *Times Literary Supplement*, "Where we might expect pathos or transformation, Elizabeth McCracken offers something far more individual and interesting. James is not a redemptive freak whose presence changes lives. The people around him are kind but ultimately untouched, except for Peggy, whose strength of feeling propels her into his life.... *The Giant's House* is a work of a writer who is as singular and astute as the characters she creates. Her book is funny, ambitious and precise." The *New Yorker* notes: "Because *The Giant's House* begins with a premise of freakishness (Peggy's as well as James's), it manages to surmount our postmodern wariness and, against all odds, make romance seem real — as real and inevitable as librarians or death. Who would have thought it — that you could take one overage virgin and one oversized boy and end up with a story that captures the feel of passion, its consuming hold?" The *Washington Post Book World* points out: "Needing James the way she does, Peggy brushes up against the cliché of the lonely librarian: desperately, quietly awaiting a rescuer, an excuse to forget about her own self. But the way she attaches herself to him makes her more psychopath than Cinderella" and concludes that "If *The Giant's House* is a romance, it's a Gothic one — which is of course what makes it interesting."

RECOGNITION: *NYTBR* Notable Book of 1996; nominated for the 1996 National Book Award; *PW* "Best Book" of 1996; *L.A. Times* "Best Books" 1996; *Salon Magazine* "Book of the Year" 1996; REVIEWS: *BL* 5/15/96; *LATBR* 12/29/96; *LJ* 7/96; *LST* 11/17/96; *LT* 11/29/96; *NY* 7/29/96; *NYTBR* 7/7/96; *PW* 1/22/96; *TLS* 11/29/96; *WPBW* 11/10/96; EDITOR'S NOTE: Ms. McCracken was named to *Granta* magazine's 1996 list of the twenty "Best Young American Novelists."

McDermott, Alice (USA)

60   *Charming Billy* (1998); FS&G 1998 (HC); Delta 1999 (pbk)

A young Irish-American woman looks back over the life of her father Dennis Lynch and his best friend (and cousin), the ebullient, engaging, alcoholic Billy. Billy Lynch has, for thirty years, carried a torch for his first love, Eva, who — so the story goes — died in Ireland before Billy could send money back home for her passage to New York. This tragic event has been long-used, by Billy and others, to explain his feckless ways. Ms. McDermott once again manages to paint a loving, authentic-feeling portrait of an urban Irish-American community.

Michiko Kakutani (*NYT*) observes: "Ms. McDermott writes about [the weight of familial wishes] with wisdom and grace, refusing to sentimentalize her characters, even as she forces us to recognize their decency and goodness." *Kirkus Review* calls *Charming Billy* a "softly resonant and nostalgic tale told so masterfully, so movingly, that it seems to distill a human essence on virtually every page." According to the *Chicago Sun-Times* this is "[a] classic McDermott novel, one that takes place on a small stage yet concerns epic themes … you needn't believe in the existence of an immortal soul to be deeply affected." Richard Eder (*LATBR*) con-

cludes that *Charming Billy* "is a powerful and moving book whose wit and intelligence never supersede the lovely unpredictable humanity of its characters."

OTHER MEDIA: Audiocassette (Books-on-Tape/unabr); READING GROUP GUIDE; RECOGNITION: Winner of the 1998 National Book Award; *LATBR* "Top Ten Books of 1998"; *NYTBR* Notable Book of 1998; *PW*'s Best '98 Fiction; REVIEWS: *BL* 12/15/97; *ChiSun* 3/29/98; *EW* 1/23/98; *KR* 11/1/97; *LATBR* 1/11/98; *LJ* 11/1/97; *NYT* 1/13/98; *NYTBR* 1/11/98; *PW* 10/6/97; *Time* 1/12/98

61   *At Weddings and Wakes* (1992); Bantam 1993 (pbk)

Alice McDermott's third novel explores both the approach of middle age and the dull ache of marital disappointment within the context of a close-knit, occasionally exasperating, extended family. The author tells the wryly (yet poignantly) observed story of an Irish American family through the eyes of three children, now grown. As the simple plot unfolds, attention is given to the middle-aged romance between one of the aunts (a former nun) and a sweetly diffident mailman.

The *Chicago Tribune* calls *At Weddings and Wakes* "a brilliant, highly complex, extraordinary piece of fiction and a triumph for its author." According to the *Library Journal* "Time circles backwards and forwards around a series of family rituals…. As they listen to oft-repeated stories about poverty, disease and early death, the children are solemn witnesses to the Irish immigrant experience in America." *Commonweal* observes that McDermott's novel contains "a complex narrative that beguiles with the strong rhythm of its prose and the almost liturgical movement of its story." The *Voice Literary Supplement* concludes that "Ms. McDermott is more than good. Not content with haunted characters, she insists on haunting you."

RECOGNITION: *NYTBR* Notable Book of 1992; *Chicago Tribune* "Outstanding Book of the Year" 1992; REVIEWS: *ChiTrib* 3/29/92; *ComW* 5/22/92; *LJ* 4/1/92; *NewsWk* 4/13/92; *NYTBR* 4/12/92; *SLJ* 9/92; *Time* 4/20/92; *VLS* 5/92

McKinney-Whetsone, Diane (USA)

62   *Tumbling* (1996); Morrow 1996 (HC); Scribner 1997 (pbk)

Set in "South Philly" in the 1940's and 1950's, Diane McKinney-Whetstone's debut novel is centered around the marriage of Herbie and Noon, a star-crossed pair who become the adoptive parents of two little girls abandoned on their doorstep. Noon, who had been brutally raped as a youngster, has great difficulty with physical intimacy; Herbie looks for physical release elsewhere and finds it in the arms of a jazz singer. Their lives are further complicated by the machinations of local officials who are intent on a redevelopment scheme that will lead inexorably to gentrification of their low-rent yet close-knit neighborhood.

According to the *New York Times Book Review*, "the story moves forward on the power of Ms. McKinney-Whetstone's characters. Herbie and Noon's neighbors — from the mean-spirited petty bureaucrat across the street ... to the well-intentioned but miscalculating local pastor ... are never merely props. Through these, and other deftly portrayed individuals ... [the author] captures the formidable struggle to protect both a community and a family." In the view of *Booklist*, "McKinney-Whetstone has written a powerful novel that is sure to launch her career among the great African American women writers." The *Washington Post Book World* concurs calling *Tumbling* "a remarkably skillful first effort."

REVIEWS: *BL* 4/15/96; *ChiTrib* 5/22/96; *KR* 3/15/96; *LATBR* 8/25/96; *LJ* 6/15/96; *NYTBR* 6/9/96; *PeopleW* 5/27/96; *PW* 4/8/96; *WPBW* 5/26/96

McManus, James (USA)

63   *Going to the Sun* (1996); HarperCollins 1996 (HC)

Penny Culligan, a stalled Ph.D. candidate, has decided to return to Alaska, the scene of a harrowing encounter with a grizzly bear seven years previously. A recreational hike with her boyfriend, David, had been brutally terminated when David was attacked and savagely mauled. The young man's injuries were massive: he lost his sight, his legs and his sexual organs. At David's pleading, Penny, who never left his side, had reluctantly administered a lethal dose of insulin. Since this traumatic event, Penny has been incapable of forming new attachments. Recognizing the importance of finally coming to terms with her memories, she decides to pedal her ten-speed from Iowa back to Alaska. The journey is grueling, dangerous, and redemptive.

According to the *Washington Post Book World*, "McManus takes big risks here ... the problems of a blocked Ph.D. candidate with diabetes are not guaranteed to get the heart racing. Yet, against the odds, he succeeds; his portrait of a gutsy lady dueling with death is both exhilarating and moving." *Entertainment Weekly* applauds McManus for crafting "a story that's both a rugged adventure and a mesmerizing inner monologue, a tale that finally becomes a love story, minus the mush." *Publishers Weekly*, in its starred review, observes that "Beckett, bicycling, basketball, bears and blood sugar are among the diverse interests of this meditative road novel told in the stunning voice of a diabetic, emotionally scarred young woman" and concludes that "Penny's narrative — by turns lyrical, pissed off and longing — is a triumph."

RECOGNITION: Winner of the Carl Sandberg Award and the Society of Midland Authors Award 1996; REVIEWS: *BL* 2/1/96; *EW* 2/23/96; *LJ* 1/96; *NYTBR* 2/18/96; *PW* 11/27/95; *WPBW* 6/2/96

Miller, Sue (USA)

64   *Distinguished Guest* (1995); HarperCollins 1996 (pbk)

Lily Maynard is a formidable woman. Long-divorced from a well-known, integrationist Chicago minister, Lily found literary fame at the age of 72 with the publication of her memoirs. As the novel opens, Lily, now ailing and in need of nursing care, has come to live — temporarily — with her architect son Alan, and Gaby his French-born wife. Alan has long-harbored resentment towards his mother whose rejection of his father and general lack of maternal warmth made for a problematic childhood. Linnett Baird, a free-lance journalist working on a magazine profile of Lily, has managed to gain access to the now-reclusive elderly woman and begins to ask probing, often unsettling, questions.

According to *Booklist* Ms. Miller "[w]ith a director's eye for movement and angles of perception ... unreels Lily's story like celluloid on screen." *Publishers Weekly* observes that Miller "subtly examines the themes of parental responsibility and failed communication in the context of a family attempting to hew to the highest religious principles..." and concludes that the author's "feel for detail and narrative pacing is impeccable, and her wisdom in understanding human relationships resonates with universal implications."

OTHER MEDIA: Audiocassette (Recorded Books/unabr); REVIEWS: *BL* 3/15/95; *ChiSun* 6/11/95; *ChiTrib* 4/16/95; *CSM* 5/9/95; *LATBR* 5/7/95; *NYTBR* 5/7/95; *PW* 2/27/95;

65   *For Love* (1993); Harper 1994 (pbk)

Charlotte "Lottie" Gardner has returned, following her mother's death, to the family home in Cambridge, Massachusetts, where she and her brother Cameron must ready the house for sale. Lottie is suffering from the knowledge that her second marriage to a widowed oncologist is coming apart.... Meanwhile, Cam finds himself attracted (once again) to Elizabeth (the former girl-next-door) who has returned home to temporarily escape her husband's philandering. Further complications include the tragic death of an au pair.

Entertainment Weekly calls it a "20th-century love story: ironical, disenchanted, and poignant." *Kirkus Reviews* points out that "Miller's special brand of intelligent emotionalism reaches its zenith here: it's deep, resonant, splendid." In the view of *Newsweek* "All Miller's gifts come to the fore at the end of the novel, when Lottie drives from New Haven back home to Chicago almost nonstop, dazed with pain killers for a raging toothache while her whole life seems to billow about the car. This long reverie is a tour de force by any standards, but more important, it gives the book an absolutely satisfying conclusion."

RECOGNITION: Nominated for the 1993 *L.A. Times* Book Award; *NYTBR* Notable Book of 1993; *Publishers Weekly* "Best Books" of 1993; REVIEWS: *BL* 1/20/93; *CSM* 6/17/93; *Econ* 4/17/93; *EW* 4/15/94; *KR* 1/1/93; *LATBR* 4/2/93; *LJ* 2/15/93; *NewsWk* 4/19/93; *NYT* 4/5/93; *WPBW* 4/4/93

Mitchard, Jacqueline (USA)

66   *The Deep End of the Ocean* (1996); Viking 1996 (HC); Signet 1997 (pbk)

In her debut novel, Jacqueline Mitchard, tells a riveting story of love and loss as she explores the effect on one family of the kidnapping of a three-year-old boy. The youngster, Ben Cappadora, disappears from a hotel lobby in Chicago after having been placed, momentarily, in the care of his seven-year-old brother Vincent. As the story progresses, the devastating impact of this event on the remaining family members in wrenchingly explored.

The *New York Times Book Review*, while criticizing Ms. Mitchard's improbable resolution, declares that "the first half of *The Deep End of the Ocean* is wonderfully written." According to *Booklist* "This is no check-out-line thriller; it is a meticulous and finely structured study of emotions under the extreme stress of long-term ambiguity and guilt.... Mitchard has made a spectacular fiction debut with this riveting and intelligent drama." *Publishers Weekly*, in its starred review, asserts that "Mitchard imbues her suspenseful plot with disturbingly candid psychological truths about motherhood and family relationships" and concludes that Mitchard "has a wise and compassionate heart and talent to spare."

OTHER MEDIA: Audiocassette (Penguin Audio/abr); RECOGNITION: Oprah Winfrey Book Club selection; *Publishers Weekly* Best Books of 1996; REVIEWS: *BL* 4/1/96; *ChiTrib* 9/2/96; *CSM* 9/9/96; *LJ* 4/15/96; *NewsWk* 6/3/96; *NYTBR* 8/18/96; *PW* 4/1/96

Morton, Brian (USA)

67   *Starting Out in the Evening* (1998); Crown 1998 (HC)

In his second novel, Brian Morton features an aging novelist, Leonard Schiller, whose much-admired-but-little-read (and sadly out of print) body of work is the subject of a young graduate student's Master's thesis. The student, Heather Wolfe, an ambitiously confidant 24-year-old,

hopes to stimulate renewed (but certainly not undeserved) interest in Schiller's novels, thereby advancing her own career. Heather, the scholar, is also determined to plumb the depths of Schiller's life to more fully understand the well-spring of his genius. Schiller's response is to fall in love.

Booklist observes: "In spare and elegant prose, Morton contemplates the value of art and ponders the ultimate meaning of a life devoted to the refinement of one's craft" and concludes that "Morton's affection and respect for the essential humanity of his conflicted characters are evident throughout." In the view of the *New Leader* "Brian Morton writes of complex, serious issues in a light and charming manner ... *Starting Out in the Evening* is a pleasure to read, a neat Jamesian tale told with an original modern touch." According to *Newsday* "You could say that [*Starting Out in the Evening* and Morton's first novel, *The Dylanist*] are meditations on people ... who are alive to the possibilities that the world offers for beauty and human connection.... There may be young novelists who are more daring, or work on a larger scale ... [but no one] who combines brains with tenderness the way Brian Morton does." The *New York Times Book Review* concludes: "As a piece of writing, it's nothing less than a triumph."

RECOGNITION: *PW*'s Best '98 Fiction; *NYTBR* Notable Book of 1998; REVIEWS: *BL* 1/1/98; *KR* 11/1/97; *LATBR* 1/25/98; *LJ* 10/1/97; *NewLeader* 12/29/97; *Newsday* 1/4/98; *NYTBR* 1/18/98; *PW* 9/29/97; *WSJ* 3/6/98

Mosley, Walter (USA)

68   *RL's Dream* (1995); WW Norton 1995 (HC); PB 1996 (pbk)

The first of Walter Mosley's books to drop the mystery format, *RL's Dream* is set in New York City and features Soupspoon Wise a down-and-out jazz guitarist from Mississippi with a recent diagnosis of terminal cancer. His unlikely champion is Kiki Waters, a foul-mouthed (formerly abused), red-haired, insurance company worker who hails from Arkansas.

According to *Publishers Weekly* "Mosley has always been a vivid writer, but here his work achieves a constant level of dark poetry: he flawlessly integrates Soupspoon's and Kiki's past harsh lives and memories with the keenly observed contemporary New York slum scene as the bittersweet blues constantly sound somber chords beneath." Novelist Tom de Haven (*EW*) calls *RL's Dream* "a beautiful little masterpiece ... a meditation on the history and meaning of the blues...." The *San Francisco Review of Books* concludes that *RL's Dream* "is, without doubt, the author's finest achievement to date, a rich literary gumbo with blues-tinged rhythms that make it a joy to read."

OTHER MEDIA: Audiocassette recording (AudioRenaissance/abr; Books-on-Tape/unabr; RECOGNITION: Winner of the ALA Black Caucus 1996 Literary Award for fiction; *NYTBR* Notable Book 1995; REVIEWS: *BL* 6/1/95; *ChiTrib* 9/17/95; *EW* 8/18/95; *LATBR* 8/6/95; *LJ* 9/15/95; *NYTBR* 8/13/95; *PW* 5/29/95; *SFRB* 9/95; *TLS* 9/22/95

Muske-Dukes, Carol (USA)

69 *Saving St. Germ* (1993); Penguin 1995 (pbk)

Carol Muske-Duke's second novel is a late '90s "mother/daughter" story which explores the bond between two highly gifted yet often intractable individuals: Esme Charbonneau a biochemist (the sort of person who mentally builds the chemical architecture of nicotine when she craves a cigarette) and her daughter, Ollie, who, while obviously very bright, has been diagnosed with an ill-defined "emotional dysfunction." When Esme and her husband (a film industry technician) who has a very different response to Ollie's "problem" separate, Esme must fight for custody of her child.

According to *Booklist, Saving St. Germ* "is an exquisite and wholly involving novel about the poetics of scientific creativity and the troublesome aspects of being a genius, especially if you are female." Novelist Tom de Haven (*NYTBR*) calls the novel " a truly original work of fiction ... (as it explores) a (scientific) subculture that's baffling, often intimidating to most of us, and usually ignored by American literary novelists." In the opinion of the *L.A. Times Book Review, Saving St. Germ* "isn't perfect ... (some of its characters) arrive straight out of central casting and some important plot strands are left loose at the end. Nonetheless, the story ... is mesmerizing." *N.Y. Newsday* concludes that *Saving St. Germ* is "a tragicomic tour de force ... (and) a prescient novel for the 1990s."

RECOGNITION: *NYTBR* Notable Book of 1993; REVIEWS: *BL* 12/1/94; *KR* 12/1/92; *LJ* 1/93; *NY* 4/26/93; *NYTBR* 4/11/93; *PW* 11/30/92

Nelson, Antonya (USA)

70 *Talking in Bed* (1996); HM 1996 (HC); S&S 1998 (pbk)

In her debut effort, called a "sharply observed novel of marital life" by the *Chicago Tribune*, Antonya Nelson explores the unpredictability of love and the painful impact of an adulterous affair on two families. As the novel opens, Evan Cole, a buttoned-up psychologist, and Paddy Limbach, the large, warm-hearted owner of a roofing company, meet in an intensive care emergency room. When Paddy's father dies, he grieves deeply; Evan's father, a disagreeable old man, lingers (until, that is, Evan finds a way to surreptitiously "pull the plug"). The serendipitous friendship formed in the hospital persists, the Coles invite the Limbachs over for dinner and, before long, Rachel, Evan's wife of 16 years, finds herself falling in love with Paddy. The ensuing emotional crisis — which threatens to ruin two families — is described from multiple perspectives including Evan and Rachel's two young sons.

According to novelist **Stephen McCauley** (*NYTBR*) *Talking in Bed* "is a satisfying serious novel. A portrait of decent people on the threshold of middle age, it watches intently as they try to keep their lives from spinning out of control by grasping — hopefully and doubtfully — at love." *Newsweek* observes that after Evan "snuffs his terminally ill dad" on page eight "things go to hell from there ... (but) so artfully that this sad tale of marriage and adultery feels triumphant." In the view of *Salon Magazine* the author "Like an archaeologist going through tons of rubble with a toothbrush then reconstructing the ruins ... has a patient, meticulous eye and her observations steadily build into an impressive whole." *Library Journal* points out that Nelson's novel "is about marital — and sexual — intimacy: what secrets lovers keep from each other and how these hidden thoughts can corrode a good relationship...."

RECOGNITION: Winner of the *Chicago Tribune's* Heartland Award for fiction; *NYTBR* Notable Book of 1996; REVIEWS: *BL* 4/1/96; *ChiTrib* 5/12/96; *KR* 3/1/96; *LATBR* 6/16/96; *LJ* 4/1/96; *NewsWk* 6/3/96; *NYTBR* 5/26/96; *Salon* 5/96

Oates, Joyc e Carol (USA)

71 *We Were the Mulvaneys* (1996); Dutton 1996 (HC); Plume 1997 (pbk)

Joyce Carol Oates' 26th novel, which chronicles the collapse of a large prosperous family living in semi-rural upstate New York, begins in the 1970s and spans some 25 years. The Mulvaneys (Mr. Mulvaney owned a profitable roofing company), had lived a comfortable, almost idyllic life at High Point Farm — a good-sized piece of property with a large, rambling old house, cow barns, corn fields and a duck pond. The Mulvaneys, as a couple were well liked, and their four talented children were popular being both good athletes and good sports. When Marianne Mulvaney (the only daughter) is sexually abused after a Valentine's Day dance, the incident leads to estrangement from the local community (many of whose families rally around the boy accused of raping Marianne) which leads, in turn, to a twenty-year slide in the family fortunes.

The *Washington Post Book World* notes thate while Oates is not "staking out new territory (in this) tempestuous family sagas ... her gift for broad, galloping narrative (has rarely) been this much on display." *Kirkus Reviews* declares that "Just when you think Oates has finally run dry, or is mired in mechanical self-repetition, she stuns you with another example of her essential kinship with the classic American realistic novelists" and concludes that "Dreiser would have understood and approved the passion and power of *We Were the Mulvaneys*." *Salon* calls it "a gracefully sprawling … modern family tragedy with a theme as painfully primal as 'Oedipus Rex.'" Novelist **Beverly Lowry** (*LATBR*) concludes that "Oates is a fearless writer. Where others tremble and falter, she plunges right in and does not look up or come to shore until the fullest telling of the tale … it is a book that, because it fulfills its promise to 'set down what is truth' will break your heart, heal it, then break it again every time you think about it."

RECOGNITION: *LATBR* "Best Books" 1996; *NYTBR* Notable Book of 1996; *Publishers Weekly* "Best Books" of 1996; REVIEWS: *BL* 8/96; *KR* 7/15/96; *LATBR* 12/29/96; *LJ* 8/96; *NYTBR* 9/15/96; *PW* 8/5/96; *WPBW* 9/22/96

72   *What I Lived For* (1994); Plume 1995 (pbk)

What I Lived for, set entirely during one Memorial Day Weekend in a mid-sized city in upstate New York, features Jerome "Corky" Corcoran a Democratic city councilman, abusive womanizer, failed husband, corrupt politician and "The nicest guy in Union City, New York." Corky is haunted by a premonition of his own mortality made worse by his frequent encounters with a strange character who is badgering him to contribute to the Union City Mausoleum for the Dead.

The *Times Literary Supplement* calls *What I Lived For* "an accomplished and companionable novel, whose irony towards its subject is characteristically feather-light." The *Washington Post Book World* notes that "By turns charming and deeply vulgar, passively racist and hideously misogynist Corky Corcoran is one of the most astonishing fictional creations in recent memory … (and despite being over-long by at least a hundred pages) *What I Lived For* is still one of the most compelling and important new books you will read this winter." *Kirkus Reviews* calls it a "pulsating portrait of the American fin-de-siecle, as immediate and unsettling as your morning newspaper, but more compulsively readable."

RECOGNITION: *NYTBR* Notable Book of 1994; *Publishers Weekly* "Best Books" of 1994; nominated for the PEN/Faulkner Award; REVIEWS: *BL* 7/94; *KR* 7/1/94; *LATBR* 12/18/94; *LJ* 8/94; *NYTBR* 10/16/94; *TLS* 12/22/95; *WPBW* 19/9/94

O'Donnell, Mark (USA)

73   *Getting Over Homer* (1996); Knopf 1996 (HC); Vintage 1997 (pbk)

A "coming of middle-age story" which encompasses an ill-fated love affair between two ill-suited men, *Getting Over Homer* is set primarily in Manhattan and is narrated by Blue Monahan, a pianist and song-writer with a string of unbought songs and an unsuccessful musical to his credit. The novel begins in a large, implacably Catholic household in Cleveland, Ohio with the birth of identical twins ("Hans Christian" and "Robert Louis"), nicknamed Blue and Red. The Monahan brothers eventually light out for opposite coasts. Free-spirited Red ends up in Hollywood, and is soon making a name for himself in a popular sitcom. Blue, a sensitive, persevering guy with a generous heart, loses and then finds himself in the gay "demimonde" of New York City.

According to *Kirkus Reviews* O'Donnell "has a golden ear for capturing the tones of New York's gay culture and concludes that "Blue's vulnerable heart, his grief and anger for his lost loves … is explored with great clarity." The *Library Journal*, in its starred review, observes that "Both gay and straight readers will easily identify with Blue as he heroically and humorously tries to cope with the vicissitudes of love, family, friendship, career, and aging in the 1990s." *Time* magazine calls *Getting Over Homer* "a bittersweet love story (and a) terrific (one at that)."

REVIEWS: *KR* 2/15/96; *LATBR* 6/16/96; *LJ* 3/1/96; *NY* 6/24/96; *NYT* 5/26/96; *NYTBR* 5/26/96; *PW* 3/11/96; *Time* 4/22/96

Parker, Gwendolyn (USA)

74   *These Same Long Bones* (1994); HM 1994 (HC); Plume 1995 (pbk)

Gwendolyn Parker's debut novel is set in the "colored" Hay-Ti section of Durham, North Carolina, and spans the years between the end of World War II and the Civil Rights Movement. It tells the story of Sirus McDougal, a light-skinned African American businessman, who must come to terms with the death of a beloved daughter, a deteriorating marriage, and a struggling business.

The *Washington Post Book World* applauds this "intensely moving portrait of a now-gone community" and concludes that Gwendolyn Parker is an "exquisitely" precise prose stylist. The *Times Literary Supplement* points out that "more attention has been paid in African-American literature to the horrors of the plantation and the hardships of the ghetto than to the experience of the black middle class. But it was a long journey from the cotton field to the anodyne semi-whiteness of the black middle class portrayed on *The Cosby Show*" and Ms. Parker helps to illuminate this progression." Called a "hauntingly beautiful portrayal of love and loss … peopled by exquisitely drawn characters" by the *Library Journal*, and "a tremendous achievement (which) heralds Parker as a novelist of note" by the *L.A. Times Book Review*, *These Same Long Bones* was widely viewed as one of the outstanding novels of 1994.

RECOGNITION: *NYTBR* Notable Book of 1994; *LJ* First Novel Award; REVIEWS: *BellesL* Spr '95; *BL* 5/1/94; *Econ* 6/3/95; *LATBR* 7/31/94; *LJ* 3/15/94; *NS&S* 3/3/95; *NYTBR* 7/17/94; *PW* 2/28/94; *TLS* 3/17/95; *WPBW* 7/12/94

Patchett, Ann (USA)

75   *The Magician's Assistant* (1997); Harcourt Brace 1997 (HC); Harvest 1998 (pbk)

Set in Los Angeles and the Midwest, Anne Patchett's third novel features Sabine, whose husband, Parsifal, an accomplished magician and rug merchant, has recently died. Parsifal, a loving husband, was also involved in a long-term homosexual relationship with Phan, his sweet-natured Vietnamese business partner. After Parsifal and Phan both die of AIDS, the grieving Sabine learns that her enigmatic husband (who claimed to be an orphan) actually has a mother and sister who are alive and well and living in Nebraska.

According to the *Times Literary Supplement* "There is ... an abundance of sweetness in Ann Patchett's highly readable third novel, *The Magician's Assistant.* So much so that, although the novel recounts some dark and violent acts, death by AIDS, death by aneurysm, patricide, child abuse, wife-beating, these somehow cast no shadow. Rather, as in a fairy-tale, everything is seen through a golden scrim. In the hands of a lesser writer, this might lead to the sentimental or the saccharine, but Patchett's witty sensibility creates a world that hovers just slightly above our own to exhilarating effect." The *L.A. Times Book Review* contends that a "family is love, pain, battle and bloodshed, and Sabine goes through it all." The *London Times* notes with interest that Ann Patchett is a new recruit to the ranks of that school of female American novelists whose writing is characterized by "a parade of domestic detail, fondness for whimsy [and] prose which scoops up cultural nuggets from the bran-tub" and concludes that — despite her tendency to "deal softly with some fearsome things ... she is a welcome one." The *Chicago Tribune* calls *The Magician's Assistant* "a captivating novel" that confronts "the ambiguities and conjuring involved in sex and gender, all without departing from the realism of literary fiction."

READING GROUP GUIDE: HarcourtBrace; RECOGNITION: *LATBR* "Recommended Titles" 1997; shortlisted for the 1998 Orange Prize; REVIEWS: *BL* 9/15/97; *ChiTrib* 11/16/97; *EW* 10/10/97; *KR* 8/1/97; *LATBR* 10/19/97; *LJ* 8/97; *LT* 2/7/98; *NYTBR* 11/16/97; *TLS* 2/6/98

Pate, Alexs D. (USA)

76   *Losing Absalom* (1994); CoffeeHouse 1994 (HC); Berkley 1995 (pbk)

Widely described as both "lyrical and moving" Alexs D. Pate's award-winning debut novel is set in Philadelphia's "inner city," and portrays an African American family in crisis. The patriarch, Absalom Goodman, a hard-working family man, is dying of brain cancer and his wife and two children have gathered around him. Absalom has struggled all his life to provide for his family, and now, on his death bed, must confront his failed dreams.

According to *Publishers Weekly* "Pate's restrained writing steers clear of the maudlin while gracefully illuminating both the contemporary and timeless aspects to his tale. Amid the realities of decay and dying can be glimpsed a brief, fragile vision of strength and hope." *Choice* observes: "Though stylistically a bit awkward at times, *Losing Absalom* is a carefully structured novel with compelling characters and an engaging plot." The *Multicultural Review* notes that "Fiction this brutally honest about human options chosen and ignored, this unflinching in the face of brittle-edged truths, is relatively rare; to find a work that so beautifully captures the everyday rhythms of contemporary urban life in prose so succinct and so extraordinarily well-written that it sparkles like cut crystal, is rarer still."

RECOGNITION: ALA Black Caucus 1994 Literary Award for First Novel; *Library Journal* First Novel Award; REVIEWS: *Choice* 10/94; *LATBR* 7/3/94; *LJ* 4/1/94; *MultiCultR* 9/94; *PW* 3/14/94; *VLS* 7-8/94; EDITOR'S NOTE: Alexs D. Pate wrote the film-to-book adaptation of Steven Spielberg's movie *Amistad* which is available through Signet Books.

Proulx, Annie (USA)

77   *The Shipping News* (1993); S&S 1993 (HC); 1994 (pbk)

Annie Proulx employs a pixilated frequently comic, narrative style in her story of the benighted Quoyle (a second-rate newspaper reporter) who, following the death of his unstable young wife and the nick-of-time rescue of his daughters (Bunny and Sunshine) from child pornographers, opts to start a new life for himself and his young family in a fog-shrouded Newfoundland fishing village called Killick Claw. When the physically awkward, big-hearted Quoyle secures a position on the town's quirky local newspaper, the *Gammy Bird*, he packs up Bunny, Sunshine, his elderly Aunt and her toothless dog Warren and moves them all into the family's long-deserted, cliff-top ancestral home. Ms. Proulx's modern-day *Pilgrim's Progress* is, characteristically, filled with inventive language and haunting images.

Booklist declares: "It is a testament to Proulx's unique storytelling skills that this tale of a miserable family opting to start life in a miserable Newfoundland fishing village has an enchanted, fairytale quality, despite its harrowing details of various abuses." The *Atlantic Monthly* notes that Ms. Proulx "blends Newfoundland argot, savage history, impressively diverse characters, fine descriptions of weather and scenery, and comic horseplay without ever lessening the reader's interest in Quoyle's progress from bumbling outsider to capable journalist." According to *World Literature Today* "It is language … which triumphs in Proulx's book … Its syllables urge and slice and spin the reader like a dervish wind. Salty, luscious, mindgrabbing, chewable words and phrases like *drenty*, *Nutbeem*, and the terrible *Nightmare Isles* energize the people and events."

OTHER MEDIA: Audiocassette (S&S/abr; Recorded Books/unabr); RECOGNITION: Winner: of the 1994 Pulitzer Prize for Literature, the 1993 National Book Award, the *Irish Times* International Fiction Prize; and the *Chicago Tribune*'s 1993 Heartland Award for fiction; nominated for the 1993 National Book Critics Circle Award; *NYTBR* Notable Book of 1993; REVIEWS: *AtlM* 4/93; *BL* 2/15/93; *ChiTrib* 3/21/93; *LATBR* 7/10/94; *LJ* 2/15/93; *NS&S* 12/3/93; *NYTBR* 4/4/93; *PW* 11/1/93; *Spec* 12/4/93; *TLS* 11/26/93; *WPBW* 8/1/93; *WLT* Spr '95

Quindlen, Anna (USA)

78   *Black and Blue* (1998); Random House 1998 (HC)

Pulitzer Prize–winning writer Anna Quindlen, in her fourth work of fiction, tackles the emotionally loaded subject of domestic violence. As the novel opens Fran Bendetto is nervously awaiting the train which will take her and her young son out of New York and into a new life. Fran, a nurse married to a New York City policeman (her handsome childhood sweetheart), has endured more than a decade's worth of beatings and broken bones at the hands of her increasingly violent and abusive husband. She is now, with the help of a battered wife support group, making a bid for freedom. The novel looks back over Fran's life before returning to the unsettling present as she attempts a fresh start. Meanwhile, Fran's increasingly desperate husband is looking for his wife and son.

Newsweek calls *Black and Blue* a "first rate new novel" about "a working class wife who has never looked very far around the corners of her life.…" According to *Booklist* "Quindlen's prose is precise and unrelenting as she refuses to gloss over the pain Fran learns somehow to live with, anguish that causes her to ask over and over again, 'What if?'" *Time* magazine argues: "If its moment should prove to be right (a long-shot to be sure), the novel is good enough to become to domestic violence what *Uncle Tom's Cabin* was to slavery — a morally crystallizing act of propaganda that works because it has the ring of truth."

OTHER MEDIA: Audiocassette (Random Audio/abr; Books-on-Tape/unabr); REVIEWS: *BL* 12/15/97; *ChiTrib* 1/25/98; *EW* 2/20/98; *LJ* 2/1/98; *NewsWk* 2/16/98; *NYTBR* 2/8/98; *Time* 2/23/98

79   *One True Thing* (1994); Wheeler 1994 (HC); Bantam 1997 (pbk)

In Anna Quindlen's deeply compelling third novel, Ellen Gulden first learns her mother Kate has cancer only after the disease is far advanced. Her father insists that Ellen, a recent Harvard graduate, quit her job and come home to care for her mother. Ellen has always been the special child in the family, the high achiever, her father's intellectual match, and the person caught in the middle between her parents. After her mother's death, Ellen is arrested on a charge of mercy killing.

According to *Publishers Weekly* Anna Quindlen "again examines delicate family dynamics with this resonating tale of a matriarch's illness and the tempest of emotion that swirls around her deterioration and death." In the view of the *Christian Science Monitor* "The beauty of this book is its long first section, when Kate and [her daughter] Ellen take tentative steps toward establishing a relationship. They spend their days reading together, discussing their past, and trying to live 'normally,' though both privately recognize that nothing will ever be normal again." *Kirkus Reviews* argues: "When Quindlen gets it right — which is often — she places herself in the league of Mary Gordon and Sue Miller." In the view of the *Times Literary Supplement* "*One True Thing* has no pretensions to being a great novel, but it is a good one, strengthened and enlivened by Quindlen's powers of observation. And its central story of a daughter's experience of her mother's agonizing passage into death is wrenchingly universal."

OTHER MEDIA: Audiocassette (S&S/abr); a film version was released in 1998 starring Meryl Streep and Renee Zellweger; RECOGNITION: *NYTBR* Notable Book of 1994; REVIEWS: *America* 12/17–24/94; *BL* 8/94; *CSM* 10/27/94; *KR* 7/15/94; *LJ* 9/15/94; *NYTBR* 9/11/94; *PW* 8/1/94; *Time* 9/12/94; *TLS* 3/31/95

Rainey, John Calvin (USA)

80   *The Thang That Ate My Grandaddy's Dog* (1997); Pineapple 1997 (HC& pbk)

John Calvin Rainey's first work of fiction is set in Boggy Bottom, an African American enclave in rural Florida on the edge of the Oklawha swamp, and is made up of a series of linked stories most of which are narrated by Johnny Woodside, a city boy whose mother has brought him home to his paternal grandparents while his father serves time in a New York City jail. Johnny's relatives have lived on this site since it was claimed (just after the Civil War) by Johnny's great-great-grandfather, an escaped slave.

In the view of the *Washington Post Book World*, "One is tempted to call this first novel an African American *Yearling*, and certainly young Johnny learns some of the same lessons as the boy in that beloved novel…. But Rainey *renders whole* men and women whom Marjorie Kinnan Rawlings left faceless and voiceless. A better comparison is to the novels and stories of Zora Neale Hurston, many of which were also set in Florida." *Booklist* calls *The Thang That Ate My Grandaddy's Dog* an "enchanting book" and observes that the "tales of growing up in Boggy … are funny, touching, and entertaining." According to *Publishers Weekly* "Rainey's first novel is a fine accomplishment, an exquisite balance of genuine humor and a feeling for the tenderness and tragedy of life."

RECOGNITION: Nominated for ALA Black Caucus 1998 Literary Award for Fiction; REVIEWS: *BL* 4/15/97; *LJ* 4/1/97; *PW* 4/21/97; *WPBW* 6/24/97

Raymond, Linda (USA)

81   *Rocking the Babies* (1994); Penguin 1995 (pbk)

Set in a neonatal, intensive-care nursery in a big-city hospital, Linda Raymond's debut novel features Martha and Nettie Lee, two African American women who work as volunteer grandmothers. The babies in their care are preemies and more than half of them were born addicted. Prim Martha and overweight and outspoken Nettie Lee have led very different lives and, though not particularly well-disposed to one another, are united in their love for these babies, particularly the one who had been abandoned in a port-a-potty. As the two women rock, they talk and share the stories of their lives, vividly elaborated stories which explore racism, poverty, loss and love.

Called a "tough and tender novel" by the *Library Journal*, *Rocking the Babies* was judged "warm and earthy" by the *New York Times Book Review* which concluded that the Raymond's message was clear: "even the most ordinary lives can contain tremendously powerful stories, whose retelling can link and sustain us." *Publishers Weekly* observes that with her "compelling, uncomplicated prose and imaginative, credible narrative" Raymond "moves gracefully between past and present and offers unusually accomplished characterizations."

RECOGNITION: Winner of the 1995 American Book Awaard; Nominated for the ALA Black Caucus 1995 Literary Award for Fiction; REVIEWS: *BL*

9/1/94; *KR* 7/1/94; *LABR* 1/7/96; *LJ* 9/1/94; *NYTBR* 1/1/95; *PW* 8/8/94; *WPBW* 12/25/94

Revoyr, Nina (USA)

82   *The Necessary Hunger* (1997); S&S 1997 (HC); St. Martin's 1998 (pbk)

Nina Revoyr sets her debut novel in South Central L.A. and features Nancy Takahiro, a shy six-foot tall Japanese-American high school basketball star. When Nancy's divorced father Wendell (a high-school math teacher and football coach) invites his girlfriend Claudia to move in with him, Claudia's teenage daughter, Raina — also an accomplished high school basketball player — moves in as well. To further complicate matters, both girls — who play for rival basketball teams — are lesbians and Nancy falls hard.

According to *Kirkus Reviews* "The familiar inner-city downers of racism, crime, family disintegration, and sports-as-salvation are handled with extraordinary intelligence and sensitivity in this episodic story. In the view of *Time* magazine Revoyr's novel "is the kind of irresistible read you start on the subway at 6 p.m. on the way home from work and keep plowing through until you've turned the last page at 3 a.m."

REVIEWS: *KR* 12/1/96; *LJ* 12/96; *PW* 1/3/97; *Time* 5/5/97

Rush, Norman (USA)

83   *Mating* (1991); Random 1992 (pbk)

Widely described as both stylistically clever and textually erotic, Norman Rush's first novel is set in the South African republic of Botswana and is narrated by an intelligent, wryly self-absorbed anthropologist whose doctoral thesis project has just evaporated. At loose ends, she meets and falls heavily for Nelson Denoon, a handsome, charismatic fellow-anthropologist, who is rumored to have established (somewhere in the Kalahari desert) a self-sustaining and vaguely utopian community for dispossessed and abused African women. Our narrator — who remains nameless — in an attempt to impress Denoon with her resourcefulness, sets out alone to find him and his fabled community. The remainder of the book (couched primarily in extended dialogue which is peppered with scientific jargon, French and Latin phrases, African words, Briticisms, and American slang) describes the intricacies of their deepening relationship.

Publishers Weekly notes: "In a wonderfully idiosyncratic voice [Rush's narrator] chronicles the progress of [her affair] in what amounts to a parody of an academic study" and concludes "Even readers who remember the luminous stories in [his] debut, *Whites*, may not be prepared for the cleverness, humor, insight into human nature and intellectual acuity demonstrated in this accomplished novel." According to playwright and novelist **Jim Shepard** (*NYTBR*) "Readers receive a palpable sense of having their education sternly tested — and expanded — by Mr. Rush's novel. Geography, history, political science, economics, literature, biology, popular culture and utter trivia — the narrator and her beloved Denoon hash everything out, and in doing so are encyclopedic in the extreme, segueing from bats to Boers to Borges to Botswana." In the view of *Newsweek*, *Mating* is "a novel that doesn't insult the intelligence of either its readers or its characters: a dryly comic love story about grown-up people who take the life of the mind seriously and know they sometimes sound silly … *Mating* is state-of-the-art artifice."

RECOGNITION: Winner of the 1991 National Book Award and the *Irish Times* — Aer Lingus International Fiction Award; finalist for the 1991 National Book Critics Circle Award; *NYTBR* "Editors' Choice" 1991; REVIEWS: *BL* 1/15/92; *ChiTrib* 9/1/91; *LitRev* 7/92; *NewsWk* 10/21/91; *NY* 10/21/91; *NYRB* 10/10/91; *NYTBR* 10/6/91; *PW* 6/21/91; *Time* 1/6/92; *TLS* 9/18/92

Russo, Richard (USA)

84   *Nobody's Fool* (1993); Random House 1994 (pbk)

Richard Russo sets his third novel in North Bath, a small ex-resort town (described as a "pretty, green grave") near Albany in upstate New York. Like his fictional Mohawk, North Bath — with its dwindling tax base, decreasing job prospects and an aging and increasingly eccentric population — is one of those "out of the way" places who's best years are behind them. Russo's protagonist is sixty-year-old Donald "Sully" Sullivan, a classic small-town underachiever with a painful past. Sully (for those who haven't seen the movie) lives alone in an apartment carved out of Miss Beryl Peeper's ramshackle mansion, and is quite content performing odd jobs and hanging out at Hattie's diner and the local bar. That is, until his octogenarian landlady's son decides to evict him, his arthritic knee starts acting up and his son — from a disastrously brief marriage — arrives unexpectedly with Sully's grandson in tow.

According to the *Library Journal* "Russo knows the small towns of upstate New York and the people who inhabit them [and] he writes [about them] with humor and compassion." The *San Francisco Chronicle* calls *Nobody's Fool* "a confident, assured" novel which, "simple as family love, yet nearly as complicated, … sweeps the reader up in the daily life of its characters." In the view of the *Times Literary Supplement* (which observed that Paramount lost no time in snapping up the movie rights), "Almost everything predictable about the novel — as well as its prime virtue, Sully's rich vein

of sarcasm — suggests a certain type of Hollywood feature. North Bath's decay is movie decay, certainly more picturesque than that of the towns of Russo's earlier novels.…"

OTHER MEDIA: A film version starring Paul Newman was released in 1994; Audiocassette (Random Audio/abr); READING GROUP GUIDE: Vintage Books; RECOGNITION: ALA Notable Book of 1993; REVIEWS: *ChiTrib* 5/30/93; *EW* 6/25/93; *LJ* 4/15/93; *NS&S* 7/30/93; *NY* 7/19/93; *NYTBR* 6/20/93; *PW* 3/29/93; *TLS* 7/2/93; *WPBW* 6/6/93

Schumacher, Julie (USA)

85   *The Body Is Water* (1995); Soho 1995 (HC); Avon 1997 (pbk)

Jane Haus, "casually" pregnant and in need of care and comfort, returns to her family's run-down seaside home. Dreamy and rudderless, she is still trying to overcome her childhood memories: her mother's lingering death from cancer intermingled with a series of ill-defined but distressing early experiences. Growing up near the ocean has given Jane a perception of the world as "boundless" lacking "finite events," where, in the character's words, "we didn't believe in starts, finishes, or death." Her eccentric father and quirky, brilliant sister are worried but supportive. The author relies on a series of flashbacks to punctuate and fuel the story.

Choice applauds Ms. Schumacher's writing which it calls "spare and haunting" and concludes: "Like flowing water, the novel moves. Just where is left uncertain." *Publishers Weekly* calls *The Body Is Water* an "expertly observed first novel" about an eccentric family which the reader "finishes … wishing it were just beginning." In the view of the *Washington Post Book World*, Schumacher "has a deft touch with dialogue and a clever way of limning characters."

RECOGNITION: ALA Notable Book of 1995; REVIEWS: *BL* 8/95; *Choice* 12/95; *KR* 7/1/95; *LJ* 8/95; *Ms* 9/95; *Newsday* 9/10/95; *PW* 7/10/95; *WPBW* 1/7/96

Smith, Faye McDonald (USA)

86   *Flight of the Blackbird* (1996); S&S 1996 (HC); Warner 1997 (pbk)

In her debut novel, Faye McDonald Smith tells the story of Atlanta-based Mel and "Builder" Burke an upwardly mobile black couple (he owns a thriving construction business, she works for the Chamber of Commerce) who are jolted first by Builder's business failure and then by Mel's job layoff. The resulting financial crisis has a devastating effect on their emotional well-being, their family, and their marriage. In a parallel development Mel's once-close relationship with her brother, a Harvard-educated lawyer, has been severely strained by his decision to represent drug dealers.

According to the *Publishers Weekly* "Smith's skill as a journalist and screenwriter are evident in the smooth dramatic pacing of her first novel ... (a) poignant and triumphant tale (told) with the ease of a natural storyteller." In the view of the *Library Journal* Ms. Smith's "impressive debut" is well-written and appropriately paced so that the story moves along without bogging down in unnecessary detail."

RECOGNITION: ALA Black Caucus Fiction "Honor' Book"; REVIEWS: *BL* 10/15/96; *CSM* 1/13/97; *Emerge* 11/96; *KR* 9/15/96; *LJ* 10/1/96; *PW* 10/7/96;

Stevens, April (USA)

87   *Angel Angel* (1995); Viking Penguin 1995 (HC); 1996 (pbk)

Called "intelligent and moving" by *Time* magazine and an "auspicious debut" by *Publishers Weekly*, *Angel Angel* is set in Connecticut and features the Irises, a seemingly typical suburban couple with two young-adult sons. When the patriarch, Gordie, flees to Europe with his mistress, his uncomprehending, emotionally devastated wife Augusta takes to her bed, for good. Matthew, a student at Harvard, is called home by his younger brother Henry who is having difficulty handling this family crisis. Matthew proves to be equally useless in rousing his mother and it is not until Henry's girlfriend, the "ethereal" bubble gum-chewing Bette, steps in that the situation rights itself. Ms. Stevens has been compared to both Alice Hoffman and Anne Tyler.

According to *Publishers Weekly*, "Stevens uses her characters' vivid dreams as well as Augusta's interior monologues to perceptively explore familial conflicts. Her touch is assured (and) her ear for vernacular dialogue marvelously sharp." In the view of *Time* magazine "It is a challenge to portray a forsaken woman in a way that evokes genuine sympathy, but Stevens manages, conveying Augusta's sadness with a knowing honesty reminiscent of Edna O'Brien. Augusta cannot bear thoughts of her husband existing in the world without her. 'It was the fact that he wasn't dead that worked me like a pin on a balloon,' she says, 'stabbing me and leaving me airless. Flat out.'"

REVIEWS: *BL* 2/1/95; *KR* 11/1/94; *LJ* 11/15/95; *NYTBR* 1/29/95; *PW* 11/21/94; *Time* 2/6/95

Swift, Graham (UK)

88   *Last Orders* (1996); Knopf 1996 (HC); Vintage 1997 (pbk)

Graham Swift's latest novel (his sixth) describes in minute and humorous detail an odyssey undertaken by the estranged son and three WW II buddies of Jack Dodd a crusty, recently deceased butcher. Their mission: to scatter Jack's ashes (his "last orders") off Margate Pier into the sea. Their journey from a rough working-class London neighborhood through the rich farmlands of Kent, to the cathedral town of Canterbury (long a destination of pilgrims), to the bracing English coast, parallels their inward journey through memory, catharsis and resolution.

According to the *New Yorker*, "As the day unfolds, we piece together (the four men's) private hopes and betrayals, but what moves us most is their tragicomic sense of ceremony as they make their way — drinking, remembering, fighting, praying — to the sea." Judged "A triumph" by *The* (London) *Times* and "inspired" by *The Guardian*, *Last Orders* garnered outstanding reviews on both sides of the Atlantic. Novelist and poet **Jay Parini** (*NYTBR*) observes, for example, that Swift's "ordinary working-class characters become oddly representative, almost mythic, as (the author) lifts them beyond the small circumference of their individual lives, underscoring the parts they play in inventing thatmost precious of things, a genuine community." *Kirkus Reviews* contends that Swift "listens closely to the lives that are his subject and creates a songbook of voices, part lyric, part epic, part working-class social realism — with, in all, the ring to it of the honest, human, and true." In the view of the *Washington Post Book World* "One reads a novel such as Graham Swift's *Last Orders* with a small, still sense of gratitude, somehow heartened that 'ordinary' lives have not been overlooked, small yearnings not gone unrecorded, final wishes not been dismissed." Irish novelist **John Banville** (*NYRB*) concludes that "Swift is quintessentially English in his convictions, as evidenced throughout his books that the family, not the individual, is the social unit which should be the essential concern of the novel. In this he is a direct heir of the great Victorians."

READING GROUP GUIDE: Vintage Books; RECOGNITION: Winner of the 1996 Booker Prize; nominated for the 1998 International IMPAC Dublin Literary Award; *The* (London) *Sunday Times* Notable Book of 1996; *NYTBR* Notable Book of 1996; *Publishers Weekly* "Best Books" 1996; REVIEWS: *BL* 7/96; *CSM* 2/27/97; *LJ* 4/1/96; *LATBR* 7/7/96; *LRB* 2/8/96; *LST* 1/7/96; *NY* 5/27/96; *NYRB* 4/4/96; *NYTBR* 5/5/96; *Spec* 1/27/96; *TLS* 1/19/96; *WPBW* 4/7/96; EDITOR'S NOTE: William Boyd was named to *Granta* magazine's 1983 list of the twenty "Best Young British Novelists"

Treuer, David (USA)

89   *Little* (1997) AMAZON etc; Greywolf 1995 (HC); Picador 1997 (pbk)

The eponymous "Little" of David Treuer's debut novel is a severely handicapped Native American boy whose tragic death and ensuing wake provide the framework on which is hung a story about the nature of family and paternity. Set in a section of a northern Minnesota reservation known as "Poverty," the novel spans approximately 15 years (from the mid-60s to 1980) and is characterized by multiple voices and shifting points of view. Principle characters include Jeanette, the matriarch who lives with her daughter Celia, and Celia's lover, a Vietnam veteran by the name of Sam. A foundling, called Donovan, and "Little" (Celia's son) round out this family group. Additional characters include Stan's sister, Violet, Violet's daughter, two elderly identical twins who are living in their Pontiac Catalina, and Father Paul, the well-meaning but naively ineffectual reservation priest. Treuer makes effective use of magical realist techniques in his vigorously told tale, a "full and subtle portrait of Indian life" (*WPBW*).

The *Washington Post Book World* further notest that "*Little* … has all the finish and polish we might expect from a writer of much larger accomplishments. His tale of life on a Minnesota reservation is a richly textured exploration of landscapes, memories, loss and old cars told in a wide range of closely observed and precisely modulated voices…." According to Scottish novelist **Margot Livesy** (*TLS*), Treuer, although easily compared with **Louise Erdrich**, "is very much his own writer, and frequently a dazzling one….With this debut he deserves our full [critical] vocabulary and earns our full attention." *Entertainment Weekly* calls *Little* "a passionate tale of place, race and human nature."

REVIEWS: *BL* 10/15/95; *EW* 2/7/97; *KR* 7/15/95; *LATBR* 12/10/95; *LJ* 10/1/95; *PW* 8/21/95; *TLS* 11/28/97; *WPBW* 4/4/96

Troy, Judy (USA)

90   *West of Venus* (1997); Random 1997 (HC)

Judy Troy sets her debut novel in the eponymous Venus, a small town in the heart of Kansas.

Her story features 36-year-old Holly Parker, a divorced waitress whose 16-year-old son is dating his former teacher, a woman twice his age. Although Troy's novel begins with a suicide and ends with a funeral, *West of Venus* is, at heart, a love story peopled with appealingly resilient characters who manage to cope with both disappointment and loss.

The *New York Times Book Review* calls *West of Venus* a "beguiling first novel … with an engaging cast of characters" and concludes that: Troy writes very simply and affectingly about emotional isolation and the courage it takes to seek connection." *Kirkus Reviews* notes that Ms. Troy has written a "Quietly genuine, light of touch, deftly amusing … [novel]. If only all tiny towns had such people in them, and so auspicious a writer as Troy to paint them for us."

RECOGNITION: *NYTBR* Notable Book of 1997; REVIEWS: *KR* 4/1/97; *LJ* 2/1/97; *NYTBR* 6/15/97; *PW* 4/14/97

Tyler, Ann (USA)

91   *A Patchwork Planet* (1998); Knopf 1998 (HC)

In her 14th novel Anne Tyler has created yet another hapless hero in the person of Barnaby Gaitlin who works for "Rent-a-Back," a company that specializes in doing odd jobs for the elderly. Barnaby is a failure: the grandson of a scion of Baltimore, he was raised in an upper–middle class family which had expected more from him than a life of manual labor. Barnaby's stasis can be traced back to a (perplexing) spate of teenage delinquency during which he broke into his neighbor's houses, read their mail and perused their photo albums.

According to *Booklist* "Things are still quirky, sweet, funny and wise in Tyler country, as once again, this always beguiling novelist portrays seemingly placid characters on the verge of abrupt metamorphosis." *Time* magazine observes that *A Patchwork Planet* "not only conforms to the familiar pattern the author has established in her fiction but does so in a fresh and engaging fashion." In the view of Irish novelist Aisling Foster, writing in the *London Times*, "Attention to detail combines with brilliant chiaroscuro to produce a modern classic. The picture is so rich and original that it will be revisited again and again." According to the *London Observer* "Ann Tyler has [compassion] in spades. No life is too ordinary, no existence too humdrum to be spared her penetrating gaze and gentle humor." The *Times Literary Supplement* offers a less laudatory view: "Aesthetically, Tyler seems never to challenge the limits of her formidable talent. It is as if, as a writer, she had internalized her novels' soothing moral: stay home, stay loved, stay safe. This is, in literary terms, a shame; because it is not truthful. And Tyler for all her astute perceptions and sharp details, disappoints. Her novels hymn the ordinary, but they play the same tune…." *Salon* notes that her "characters' wounds don't go very deep," and their "recoveries fail to inspire."

OTHER MEDIA: Audiocassette (Recorded Bks/unabr); READING GROUP GUIDE; RECOGNITION: *NYTBR* Notable Book of 1998; REVIEWS: *BL* 3/1/98; *CSM* 4/30/98; *LATBR* 4/19/98; *LJ* 4/15/98; *LT* 7/2/98; *NY* 7/13/98; *NYTBR* 4/19/98; *Obs* 6/7/98; *PW* 3/16/98; *Salon* 4/23/98; *Time* 4/27/98; *TLS* 6/19/98; *WPBW* 5/3/98; *WSJ* 4/23/98

92   *Ladder of Years* (1995); Knopf 1995 (HC); Fawcett 1996 (pbk)

One day, while sitting on a beach on the Maryland shore, middle-aged Delia Grimstead —

wife of a physician and mother of three teenage children — fed up with being taken for granted, simply picks up her towel and walks off the beach and out of her family's life.

According to *Booklist*, Anne Tyler is in "top form in *Ladder of Years*. Her seemingly effortless prose is, like silk, rich in subtle hues and sheeny with dancing light." The *New Yorker* suggests that "*Ladder of Years* feels, indeed, like the story of a woman who thought she could prune her life down to a short story, only to find it blooming, unexpectedly, into an Anne Tyler novel. There can be few more delightful revelations." *Belles Lettres* notes that *Ladder of Years* is "in large part, about family life and the compromises it requires, and no one depicts its frustrations and allures better than Anne Tyler." The *National Review* concludes that the author "has been seduced by her own generosity of spirit into taking on too banal a subject, unworthy of her powers. But her powers are still great, and they make even this book never less than readable."

OTHER MEDIA: Audiocassette (Random Audio/abr; Recorded Books/unabr); READING GROUP GUIDE: Vintage Books; RECOGNITION: *Booklist* Editors' Choice 1995; *NYTBR* Notable Book of 1995; Shortlisted for the Orange Fiction Prize; REVIEWS: *BellesL* 1/96; *BL* 3/15/95; *ComW* 6/16/95; *EW* 4/28/95; *LATBR* 5/7/95; *LJ* 4/1/95; *MacL* 6/12/95; *NewsWk* 4/24/95; *NY* 5/8/95; *NYTBR* 5/7/95; *PeopleW* 5/15/95; *PW* 2/27/95; *Time* 5/15/95; *WPBW* 4/16/95

93   *Saint Maybe* (1991); Ballantine 1996 (pbk re-issue)

Ian Bedloe is consumed by guilt after a series of family disasters for which he feels responsible. His brother (with whom he had just had a bitter argument) is killed in a car-accident and his grief-stricken widow, the "tiny-faced" Lucy, commits suicide soon after — leaving behind three orphaned children. Ian, finding the hope of forgiveness at the Church of the Second Chance, drops out of college and devotes himself to raising the three orphans. Fate, alas, has even more in store for the earnestly ascetic Ian.

According to novelist and critic, **Jay Parini** (*NYTBR*), *Saint Maybe* is "in many ways ... Anne Tyler's most sophisticated work, a realistic chronicle that celebrates family life without erasing the pain and boredom that families almost necessarily inflict upon their members." The *Times Literary Supplement* points out that "the narrative [in Ms. Tyler's novels] is always mediated through someone's point of view, so that there is no separate or superior voice doing the telling ... [that is what] makes her seem, for want of a better word, such a benevolent figure on the fictional scene. She plays the sort of God who's not, in the end, very interested in sitting in judgment." The *London Review of Books* observes that "*Saint Maybe* is told in an

artfully off-hand way which teases the reader into close engagement while suggesting that Tyler herself is only just this side of sarcasm." *Commonweal* concludes that "no one accords to children the seriousness and the fullness of treatment, the complexity and the humor, that Anne Tyler does, and it is her greatest strength...."

OTHER MEDIA: Audiocassette (Books-on-Tape/unabr; Chivers/unabr); adapted for TV 1998; RECOGNITION: *Publishers Weekly* "Best Books" of 1991; *NYTBR* Notable Book of 1995; REVIEWS: *ComW* 11/8/91; *CSM* 9/25/91; *KR* 6/1/91; *LJ* 6/1/91; *LRB* 3/12/92; *NS&S* 10/4/91; *NYRB* 1/16/92; *NYTBR* 8/25/91; *Q&Q* 8/91; *Time* 9/9/91; *TLS* 9/27/91; *WPBW* 8/18/91

Veciana-Suarez, Ana (USA)

94   *The Chin-Kiss King* (1997); FS&G 1997 (HC); Plume 1998 (pbk)

On the morning before the night Cuca's great-grandson came into this hard world, a mist thickened with the scent of honeysuckle seeped beneath her carved-oak front door, invaded the living room, saturated the kitchen, and impregnated her bedroom with a melancholy so deep and so impenetrable she awoke with a start.

"Llego," she said aloud, though there was no one else in the tiny, low-ceiling bedroom — no one that is, of this life.

Set in the lively, bodega-sprinkled Cuban section of Miami, *The Chin-Kiss King* features three generations of Cuban-American women: Cuca, the long-widowed, long-suffering, level-headed matriarch; Adela, her divorced — and rather flighty — cosmetologist daughter; and Maribel her granddaughter, recently abandoned by a drug-running husband. When Maribel gives birth to a severely handicapped infant, Cuca and Adela rally round.

The *New York Times Book Review* calls *The Chin Kiss Gang* "[a]s sweet and tart as the tropical fruits that are savored by the ebullient trio of Cuban-American women at is heart" and concludes that "rather than offering superficial bathos, [Ms. Veciana-Suarez] zooms in on the details of day-to-day existence that the arrival of a baby ... causes a family to reflect upon and appreciate anew." In the estimation of *Kirkus Reviews*, *The Chin-Kiss King* is a "three-hankie debut, luminously written, that is also a loving grace note to family and the human spirit." *Publishers Weekly* notes that "The musicality of her words, the mixture of familiar Latin American superstitions and the children's songs and the wisdom and naiveté she gives these three remarkable women offset the book's central tragedy. The tale is a tearjerker, but Veciana-Suarez tells it with frankness and delicacy."

REVIEWS: *KR* 5/15/97; *LJ* 4/15/97; *NYT* 7/30/97; *NYTBR* 9/7/97; *PW* 6/2/97

West, Dorothy (USA)

95   *The Wedding* (1995); Doubleday 1995 (HC); 1996 (pbk)

Set in a wealthy black enclave on Martha's Vinyard during the early 1950s, *The Wedding* focuses on the Coles, a family whose heritage of slavery has been thoroughly offset by a long line of successful preachers, teachers and doctors. As the novel opens, preparations are in full swing for the marriage of the Coles's youngest daughter Shelby to her intended, a white jazz musician named Meade Wyler. Tensions arise from multiple sources, and then tragedy strikes.

The *Library Journal*, in its starred review, observes that *The Wedding* was written by "the last surviving member of the Harlem Renaissance, the daughter of a former slave," and concludes that it is "a beautifully written and very moving story." According to *Publishers Weekly* "Through the ancestral histories of the Coles family, West subtly reveals the ways in which color can burden and codify behavior. The author makes her points with a delicate hand, maneuvering with confidence and ease through a sometimes incendiary subject."

OTHER MEDIA: Audiocassette (S&S/abr); REVIEWS: READING GROUP GUIDE; *BL* 12/1/94; *CSM* 2/2/95; *EW* 1/27/95; *LATBR* 2/26/95; *LJ* 12/94; *NYTBR* 2/12/95; *PW* 11/21/94

Winton, Tim (Australia)

96   *The Riders* (1994); Scribner 1996 (pbk)

Tim Winton's haunting sixth novel features a man desperately searching for his missing wife. Scully, a rough-hewn Australian carpenter, has come to Ireland where he has begun renovating a country cottage. The ramshackle house, which stands in the shadow of an ancient ruin, was bought on a whim at the end of a long sojourn in Europe with his wife, Jennifer, and precocious 7-year-old daughter, Billie. As the story begins he is alone, but expects to be joined by Jennifer and Billie, who have returned to Australia to put the family's affairs in order. When Billie alights from a plane at Shannon Airport alone, and the youngster has no idea where her mother is, Scully's life is turned violently upside down. Scully and the now-mute Billie (the shock of maternal abandonment has left her speechless) soon embark on a frantic European odyssey (retracing their earlier travels) in an attempt to track Jennifer down. More than one reviewer has commented on the rawness of Winton's language.

Novelist Nigel Krauth, writing in the *Australian Book Review* reports that *The Riders* "is a nightmare. It's hell.... It's the return ticket on all the paradigmatic journeys that make up the Australian male tradition. It's a transportation to the convict settlement of the male mind; it's an expedition to the dead male heart; it's a landing on the Gallipoli Aussi men have made of marriage...." Krauth concludes "It's a hell of a novel. It's probably a hell of an important novel. You find your own way through it." According to British novelist **Jonathan Coe** (*LRB*) *The Riders* "which is distinguished by its forceful engagement with the physical world, is also informed by a deep sense of the numinous; by a feeling which is probably best described — although Winton never spells it out in these terms — as religious." The *Library Journal* observes that *The Riders* "though action filled ... is primarily a study of the psychic price paid by an open-hearted man who loves deeply, if not wisely." The *Washington Post Book World* concludes that "Winton has written a psychological thriller that satisfies on every imaginable level...."

RECOGNITION: Shortlisted for the 1995 Booker Prize, the Victoria Premier's Literary Award, and the Australian Bookseller Association's Book of the Year Award; *PW* "Best Book" of 1995; REVIEWS: *AusBkRev* 9/94; *BL* 3/1/95; *LJ* 3/15/95; *LRB* 5/11/95; *LST* 2/26/95; *NYTBR* 11/19/95; *TLS* 2/17/95

Yamanaka, Lois-Ann (USA)

97   *Blu's Hanging* (1997); FS&G 1997 (HC)

Set in a lush Hawaiian village that belies the poverty of its inhabitants, *Blu's Hanging* is a tightly constructed, often painful story about the burden of duty. Thirteen-year-old Ivah Ogata is the oldest of three children and when her mother dies suddenly and her grief-ridden father begins a downward slide into substance abuse, she must personally hold the family together. Her feisty, overweight brother Blu would be a handful for any caregiver and her sister, Maisie, while of school-age, is barely able to speak English. All of the children appear to be vulnerable to sexual (and other forms of abuse) and predation. Eventually, Ivah is offered a scholarship to an island boarding school and she must choose between her family and her own best interests.

According to Filipino-American novelist **Jessica Hagedorn** (*Harpers Bazaar*), "Many of Hawaii's young writers, most notably Lois-Ann Yamanaka, explore cultural identity by working in pidgin English, long dismissed as a bastardized, substandard form but now becoming recognized as a source of cultural pride. In Hawaii, language carries the painful baggage of the Island's colonial history, and the choice to write in the creolized vernacular of the poor and uneducated plantation laborers is daring, both aesthetically and politically." The *Seattle Times* notes that the "force and inventiveness of Ivah's voice carries the novel. With a tenacious grace, she manages to tread between the adult world thrust upon her and the child's world in which she belongs." *Kirkus Reviews* concludes that *Blu's Hanging* with its "pungent mix of poetic observation and vulgar reality" is "further evidence that a literary Renaissance is brewing out in Hawaii...."

RECOGNITION: Assoc. for Asian American Studies (AAAS) Award for Fiction; REVIEWS: *BL* 2/24/97; *HarpBaz* 4/97; *KR* 2/1/97; *LJ* 3/1/97; *NYTBR* 5/4/97; *PW* 2/24/97; *SeattleT* 4/20/97; EDITOR'S NOTE: The AAAS recently voted to re-voke Ms. Yamanaka's Fiction Award in response to protestations from members of the Filipino community (a marginalized group in Hawaii) that her novel reinforced negative stereotypes regarding Filipino males. In Yamanaka's *Blu's Hanging*, a minor yet thoroughly despicable character — who is both a rapist and child sexual abuser — is identified as Filipino).

2

Unique Perspectives

Section 2 gathers together novels which illuminate the search for personal identity — particularly in the context of "otherness": the African-American experience forged in slavery and shaped by racial animosity and exclusion; the immigrant's experience of assimilation, which often includes generational discord and cultural free-fall; the attenuation — in many Native American communities — of the historically important mix of oral history and sacred ceremony and a concomitant cultural anomie; the barriers to full participation in society erected around notions of gender and sexual identity or religious affiliation; and, finally, the excruciating demands of orthodoxy in an increasingly secular world.

Abraham, Pearl (USA)

98 *The Romance Reader* (1995); Riverhead 1995 (HC); 1996 (pbk)

Pearl Abraham's poignant debut novel follows Rachel Benjamin, the rebellious oldest daughter of an ultra-conservative Jewish couple (her father is a Hasidic Rabbi and Holocaust survivor) from her 12th to her 19th year. Rachel wants nothing more than to be like the other girls in her upstate New York community: to speak English, have a library card, swim in a public pool, wear sheer stockings and sleeveless dresses, and choose her own husband. Rachel's parents are loving but unyielding.

According to *Booklist* "Abraham provides a great introduction to the Orthodox Jewish culture at the core of this work with her references to the common everyday practices and clash of growing up different in such a family." *Entertainment Weekly* applauds Abraham's ability to paint "a marvelously nuanced portrait of the family whose authority she rejects." According to the *San Francisco Chronicle Book Review*, "*The Romance Reader* is a good example of how suspense can arise simply from passionate characters. If the ending is a bit too ambiguous to satisfy us, that's in part because we don't want to leave Rachel without knowing everything that happens to her for the rest of her life."

REVIEWS: *BL* 8/95; *EW* 9/8/95; *LATBR* 10/13/96; *LJ* 7/95; *NYTBR* 10/29/95; *PW* 6/12/95; *SFCBR* 8/13/95

Alexander, Meena (India/USA)

99 *Manhattan Music* (1997); Mercury House 1997 (pbk)

Meena Alexander sets her second novel in New York City in the early 1990s (the time of Rajiv Ghandi's assassination, Desert Storm, and the World Trade Center bombing) and features Sandhya Rosenblum an Indian woman whose marriage to an American is being severely tested by her affair with a Manhattan-based Egyptian academic. Another character, Draupadi Dinkins, a performance artist of Indian, African, Japanese, Chinese, Filipino and European descent allows the author to explore notions of ethnicity and cultural identification.

According to *Kirkus Reviews,* "Examining the Indian Diaspora, Alexander focuses on one woman's attempt at American assimilation while holding onto her native identity." *Publishers Weekly* concludes that Meena Alexander "has produced another sophisticated novel reflecting the psychological realties of people coping with hyphenated identities, divided loyalties, fragmented dreams."

REVIEWS: *KR* 1/15/97; *LJ* 3/1/97; *Ms* 3/97; *PW* 2/10/97; *WPBW* 4/6/97

100 *Nampally Road* (1991); Mercury House 1991 (pbk)

Poet Meena Alexander's debut novel features Mira Kannadical, a young Indian academic (educated abroad) who has returned to her home in Hyderabad, India. While obtaining her Ph.D. in England, Mira has adopted a number of Western notions, not least of which is a self-assured feminism. Having accepted a teaching post at the Central University of Hyderabad, Mira anticipates a quiet, rather scholarly existence. Before long, however, she is drawn into the tumultuous political arena.

According to *World Literature Today*, *Nampally Road*, with its "cultural richness, psychological complexity, and sociopolitical — not to mention feminist — sophistication" makes a "major contribution to South Asian-American fiction." *Belles Lettres* calls *Nampally Road* "an absorbing, lyrical story about a 25-year-old who tentatively realizes that her poetic vision cannot accommodate the grim reality and chaos of daily life in Hyderabad." *Publishers Weekly* notes: "In quietly lyrical prose Alexander treats her protagonist's political awakening with engaging affection, and readers will enjoy the details of the Indian setting, from an apothecary's silver-plated Queen Victoria clock to the 300-pound servant Rani and her 'metaphysical urges,' fed by a steady diet of movies at the Sagar Talkies cinema."

REVIEWS: *BellesL* Fall '91; *LATBR* 1/27/91; *Newsday* 1/24/91; *PW* 12/14/90; *SFRB* Sum '91; *WLT* Spr '91

Alvarez, Julia (USA)

101   *How the Garcia Girls Lost Their Accents* (1991); Algonquin 1991 (HC); NAL-Dutton 1992 (pbk)

Julia Alvarez, in her semi-autobiographical debut novel, features four sisters who have been uprooted from their comfortable, almost languid, lives in the Dominican Republic and transplanted, not just to America, but to the noisy, tightly packed, trash-strewn neighborhoods of Queens. Given the setting (the 1960s and 1970s) the girls must negotiate their way through an urban culture characterized by experimental drug use, casual sex, and eroding "family values." Their bewilderment and enthusiastic, if initially awkward, attempts to make their individual ways in their adopted homeland are the focus of a series of linked stories.

The *New York Times Book Review* notes that Ms. Alvarez "to her great credit, beautifully captured the threshold experience of the new immigrant, where the past is not yet a memory and the future remains an anxious dream." In the view of the *School Library Journal*, "This unique coming-of-age tale is a feast of stories that will enchant and captivate readers." According to the *Women's Review of Books*, despite "bumps and curves in the narra-

tive that closer editing could have eliminated ... *How the Garcia Girls ... * is a noteworthy book, demanding our attention."

RECOGNITION: ALA Notable Book of 1991; *NYTBR* Notable Book of 1991; REVIEWS: *ComW* 4/10/92; *LJ* 5/1/91; *NewsWk* 4/20/92; *NYTBR* 10/6/91; *SLJ* 9/91; *TLS* 10/6/91; *WLT* Sum '96; *WP* 6/20/91; *WRB* 7/91

Boyd, Blanche McCray (USA)

102   *Terminal Velocity* (1997); Knopf 1997 (HC); Vintage 1998 (pbk)

Blanche Boyd has set *Terminal Velocity* (her first novel since *Revolution of Little Girls* 1991), in the early 1970s a time of widespread social experimentation. Boyd's story of sexual identification features Ellen, who, when we first meet her, is conventionally married to a nice young Harvard graduate and is working as an editor in a small Boston publishing house. Before long she meets Artemis Foote, a wealthy and physically entrancing artist, and is soon launched on a journey of self-discovery — this is, after all, the age of Aquarius:

In 1970 I realized that the sixties were passing me by. I had never even smoked a joint, or slept with anyone besides my husband. A year later I had left Nicky, changed my name from Ellen to Rain, and moved to a radical lesbian commune in California named Red Moon Rising, where I was playing the Ten of Hearts in an outdoor production of Alice in Wonderland *when two FBI agents arrived to arrest the Red Queen....*

According to *Kirkus Reviews*, Ms Boyd "leads her intriguing characters through complex psychological, sexual and philosophical mazes in this story of a clever southern belle turned radical lesbian." *KR* concludes that "Boyd's talent for creating convincingly tangled psychological webs is undeniable, but her novels are unshaped as life itself." The *New York Times Book Review* observes that "Boyd's story moves from comic high jinks through seduction, betrayal and finally violence with a speed that at times feels dizzying ... [and concludes that although] *Terminal Velocity* is not a novel for the squeamish ... [Boyd's] is a voice that never wavers in its authority or its fierce sexual politics." *Booklist*, in its starred review, asserts that "As Ellen/Rain suffers severe psychological disorder from the sheer velocity of the changes in her life, learning the hard way just how dangerous dabbling in lust, love, and radicalism can be, Boyd keeps her readers riveted with her incisive dialogue and revolutionary sex scenes."

RECOGNITION: Nominated for the 1998 Lambda Book Award; REVIEWS: *BL* 6/1/97; *KR* 5/15/97; *NYTBR* 8/24/97; *PW* 5/19/97; *VLS* Sum '97

Brown, Alan (USA)

103   *Audrey Hepburn's Neck* (1996); Pocket Books 1996 (HC); 1997 (pbk)

In *Audrey Hepburn's Neck*, Alan Brown (an American Fulbright Scholar who has lived in Japan for seven years) tells the artfully constructed coming-of-age story of Toshi, a young Japanese illustrator. Although he grew up in a small, isolated fishing village in northern Japan, Toshi has developed a fascination for all things American. As soon as he is of age, Toshi abandons his bleak, frequently silent, childhood home for the stimulation of Tokyo and a job as a cartoonist and quickly develops a circle of American expatriate friends. The easy chatter and confiding nature of the Americans (his best friend is the extroverted Paul, a gay advertising copywriter) contrasts sharply with his own upbringing. However, a disastrous affair with his English teacher, a seriously unstable young American woman, prompts Toshi to question his own identity and confront some disturbing childhood memories. Before the novel ends, Toshi will uncover the secrets of his own childhood, buried as they are in his parents' tragic past.

Salon magazine calls *Audrey Hepburn's Neck* "a disarmingly funny book, if one that shimmers with tragedy" and concludes that "this is outsider-lit without self-pity, a fresh tumble into the margins in which every moment of alienation is countered by understated observations about the clash, and occasional synchronicity, between all things American and Japanese." According to *Entertainment Weekly*, Alan Brown has given us "an honest and endearing host who [skillfully] guides [the reader] through ... an odd and terrible tale of betrayal and redemption." The much-traveled Pico Iyer (*Time*) applauds the author for his "meticulous style and sympathetic freshness" and his ability to capture the essence of contemporary Japan ... [evoking both] the sleek surrealism of Tokyo — where dogs are rented by the hour and people eat green-tea tiramisu cake — and the misty lyricism of rural Japan."

RECOGNITION: Winner of the 1996 Kiryama Pacific Rim Book Prize; REVIEWS: *BL* 2/15/96; *EW* 2/23/96; *LATBR* 3/24/96; *LJ* 8/96; *LST* 4/28/96; *LT* 3/9/96; *NYTBR* 4/28/96; *PW* 1/15/96; *Salon* 1996; *SLJ* 8/96; *Time* 2/5/96

Brown, Gita (USA)

104   *Be I Whole* (1995); MacMurray 1995 (HC)

Be I Whole tells the story of Papa Job — a former bell-hop and Detroit bar owner — who meets and marries Sizway, a mysterious young herbalist with roots in "Ki" an extended West Indian gypsy clan living in rural Ohio. The pair eventually returns to Sizway's family compound where their lives unfold in ways encompassing both sorrow and joy. Beneath it all lies the communal strength of Ki. Gita Brown's debut effort is characterized by the use of richly textured language and a fable-like structure.

According to *Publishers Weekly* Ms. Brown makes effective uses of some "wonderful West Indian proverbs" and (despite occasional pacing problems) provides her readers with a "crisply" narrated tale. In its starred review, the *Library Journal* observes: "What makes this 'parable' draw on our heartstrings are the numerous fables cleverly woven into the plot and the distinctive characters, who promise to remain with the reader long after the novel has been read." The *Hungry Mind Review* concludes "Brown has laden her novel with beautifully drawn moments full of cultural details."

REVIEWS: *Emerge* 12/95; *LJ* 11/1/95; *NYTBR* 12/24/95; *PW* 10/2/95; *WPBW* 12/31/95

Brown, Linda Beatrice (USA)

105   *Crossing Over Jordan* (1995); Ballantine 1995 (HC); 1996 (pbk)

Linda Brown's generational saga begins in 1873 and continues into the 21st century. Her story encompasses the lives of four generations of women in one family whose exposure to slavery, segregation and racial prejudice has shaped each of their lives. Story Temple, a resourceful yet emotionally damaged matriarch, dominates the tale.

According to the *Library Journal*, in her "entertaining and enlightening" novel, Ms. Brown has succeeded in imparting "a distinctive voice to each of her women characters ... [leading] readers to an understanding of the dilemmas and ambiguities of Story's relationship with both her daughter and her mother." In the view of *Publishers Weekly*, "Readers who get past the somewhat tedious first third of the novel will be rewarded with [a] pair of extraordinarily vibrant characters." The *School Library Journal* calls *Crossing Over Jordan* "a well crafted book" and concludes that the novel "sings with a sort of haunting clarity and honesty reminiscent of Toni Morrison's *Beloved*."

REVIEWS: *BL* 2/15/95; *LJ* 2/15/95; *MultiCultR* 6/95; *NYTBR* 2/19/95; *PW* 1/23/95; *SLJ* 9/95

Campbell, Bebe Moore (USA)

106   *Brothers and Sisters* (1994); Berkley 1994 (HC); 1996 (pbk)

Ms. Campbell's second novel — set in Los Angeles following the racially charged 1992 riots — features Esther Jackson, a hard-working bank manager and a number of her friends and colleagues including white co-worker, Mallory Post, and the seriously conflicted, albeit magnetic, "brother," Humphrey Boone. In *Brothers and Sisters* Ms.

Campbell has fashioned a subtly nuanced morality tale for the end of the millennium.

According to the *New York Times Book Review*, "What makes *Brothers and Sisters* different from the traditional pot-boiler is Ms. Campbell's genuine attempt to address the complexities of race in the modern age...." *Time* magazine calls Ms. Campbell's novel "captivating" and argues that the author "takes the notion of diversity and scrapes away all the myths and fears with which it has been encrusted ... [and] with wit and grace ... shows how all our stories — white, black, female — ultimately intertwine." In the view of *Belles Lettres* "Campbell's brilliance is not in the extraordinary but in the mundane. She takes the predictable, swirls it around in the batter of our realities, and bakes up a cake so rich with the stories of our lives that readers must close their eyes and say 'Lawdamercy, this book is good.'" Novelist and critic Carolyn See (*WPBW*) argues that "if this is a fair world, Bebe Moore Campbell will be remembered as the most important African American novelist of this century — except for maybe Ralph Ellison and James Baldwin. Her writing is clean and clear, her emotions run hot, but her most important characteristic is uncompromising intelligence coupled with a perfectionists eye for the detail."

OTHER MEDIA: Audiocassette (Audio Renaissance/abr; Books-on-Tape/unabr); REVIEWS: *BellesL* Spr '95; *BL* 6/1/94; *EW* 9/9/94; *KR* 6/1/94; *LJ* 8/94; *Ms* 9-10/94; *NYTBR* 10/16/94; *PW* 7/4/94; *SLJ* 2/95; *Time* 10/17/94; *WPBW* 9/4/94

Cao, Lan (Vietnam/USA)

107   *Monkey Bridge* (1997); Viking 1997 (HC); Penguin 1998 (pbk)

Lan Cao's debut novel tells the story of a Vietnamese widow and her daughter who, after fleeing Saigon during the U.S. military's chaotic disengagement, arrive in the United States unprepared for the shock of assimilation or the pull of the past. Mai, just 13 when she was airlifted from Saigon, soon begins to make the necessary adjustments to survive in her new community (a bustling neighborhood known as "Little Saigon" in suburban Washington, D.C.) and gradually begins to assume the dominant role in her relationship with her increasingly withdrawn mother.

According to *Booklist* "Not only is this Lan's first novel, it is one of the finest dramatizations of the experiences of Vietnamese refugees in the U.S. Lan herself was airlifted out of Saigon in 1975, and she has transformed her prismatic memories into a stunning and powerful drama." *Salon* magazine notes that "*Monkey Bridge*— which is being touted as the first novel by a Vietnamese-American about the immigrant experience — depicts generational angst worthy of an Amy Tan novel. Mai Nguyen,

Cao's buttoned-up adolescent narrator, shares the same preoccupations of the four daughters in *The Joy Luck Club*: making sense of a maddeningly enigmatic and strong-willed mother who's guarding an unsavory old-world secret." Michiko Kakutani (*NYT*) calls *Monkey Bridge* an "impressive debut ... [which] maps the state of exile and its elusive geography of loss and hope."

RECOGNITION: Shortlisted for the 1997 Kiriyama Pacific Rim Book Prize; REVIEWS: *BL* 6/1/97; *KR* 5/15/97; *LATBR* 9/14/97; *NYT* 8/19/97; *People W* 10/6/97; *PW* 5/26/97; *Salon* 7/8/97

Chao, Patricia (USA)

108   *Monkey King* (1997); HarperCollins 1997 (HC); 1998 (pbk)

According to Chinese legend, the *Monkey King* is a malicious schemer who makes dark mischief both in heaven and on earth. Patricia Chao, in her first novel, tells the story of Sally Wang, a 28-year-old Chinese-American woman and her 13-year-long nightmarish journey from despair and near madness to self acceptance and hope. Sally is a sophisticated, well-educated art director living in New York City, she is also, as the novel begins, a patient in a private psychiatric hospital where she is the object of a "round the clock" suicide watch. The victim of childhood sexual abuse, Sally must struggle to overcome both the legacy (self-mutilation, debilitating depression) and the memory of her father — the embodiment, in her mind, of the dark "Monkey King" of Chinese legend. In addition to Sally, Ms. Chao's cast of characters includes Nai Nai, the aristocratic matriarch, Sally's immigrant parents who continue to grapple with the price of assimilation, her loving Auntie Mabel and Uncle Richard, and her beautiful, emotionally distant sister Marty.

According to the *New York Times Book Review*, "Patricia Chao ... explores [a familiar fictional theme] ... with freshness and aplomb" and concludes that *Monkey King* is "a considerable achievement, the work of a writer worthy of serious attention." In the view of the *Chicago Tribune* Ms. Chao, using "cleanly understated prose and exquisite imagery ... skillfully laces past and present, China and America, into a compelling tale of one woman's fight for her life." The *Washington Post Book World* asserts: "What makes this a classy first novel is Chao's luminous prose, the evocations of the immigrant experience, and her intelligent sympathy for the frailties of her characters."

REVIEWS: *BL* 1/1/97; *ChiTrib* 3/23/97; *LJ* 12/96; *LST* 6/8/97; *NYTBR* 3/16/97; *People W* 2/24/97; *PW* 11/18/96; *Salon* 2/27/97; *Time* 5/5/97; *WPBW* 2/23/97

Chin, Frank (USA)

109   *Donald Duk: A Novel* (1991); Coffee House 1991 (HC); 1991 (pbk)

Chin's debut novel is set in San Francisco's Chinatown and features Donald Duk (son of King Duk and Daisy Duk), a disgruntled adolescent who is about to celebrate his twelfth birthday. As his special celebration (and the Chinese New Year) approaches, Donald is feeling more than a little out of sorts: he's irritated by his family's relentless ethnicity and is sick to death of his ridiculous name. As his relatives gather in his honor for a very special feast (Donald's father is a famous local chef), the youngster begins to take an interest in the stories that swirl about him, particularly those that recall the family's early years in America when many family members toiled for Central Pacific Railroad. Donald begins having extraordinarily realistic dreams featuring these ancestors and their often heroic railroad-building work. Donald is startled to learn that he is actually "dreaming history."

According to the *Library Journal*, Chin "uses a flip, clipped, present-tense narrative voice, slapstick dialog, and kinetic dreamscapes. The result is a tart social comment packed into a cartoon, with verbal energy verging on hyperactivity." *Publishers Weekly* observes: "The New Year's Festival in San Francisco's Chinatown becomes Donald's rite of passage and doorway to self-acceptance and respect; Donald and the reader find themselves on an odyssey that is at once stinging and seductive, reclaiming the exquisite myths of a beautiful and proud ancient civilization." Novelist Tom de Haven (*NYTBR*), suggests that although the "narrative [often] seems rushed, filled with first-draft bursts of staccato prose.... In dreams, Donald Duk and his eponymous novel come vigorously, even heroically alive." The *L.A. Times Book Review* notes that Frank Chin's *Donald Duk* is "a polemic with more than its share of humor" [and] "written in a prose that rings like gongs and pops like a string of firecrackers."

REVIEWS: *LATBR* 4/14/91; *LJ* 2/15/91; *NYTBR* 3/31/91; *PW* 2/8/91; *SFRB* Sum '91; *WLT* Aut '91

Choy, Wayson (Canada)

110   *Jade Peony* (1996); Picador 1997 (HC); 1998 (pbk)

Set in post World War II Vancouver, *Jade Peony* focuses on three siblings in an immigrant Chinese family: Jook-Liang (the eldest and the only daughter), an aspiring tap-dancer who lives (for a time) in a Hollywood-inspired daydream; Jung Sum, the handsome (adopted) middle child who becomes a boxer to offset his sense of powerlessness; and Sek-Lung, (the youngest), who develops a deeply rooted emotional strength in response to his family's perpetual struggles. Wayson Choy divides his debut novel into three sections narrated, in turn, by each of the siblings.

According to the *New York Time Book Review*, *The Jade Peony* "explores themes traditionally associated with novels about the immigrant experience: the promise and treachery to be found outside the matrix of the family, the burden of old ways, the necessity of learning new ones. But Choy ranges over this familiar territory with a fresh eye, disclosing universal themes in the particularities of the Asian-American life of half a century ago." *Publishers Weekly*, in its starred review, contends that "Choy, who teaches English at Humber College in Toronto, adds a heartfelt, beautifully expressed new voice to the growing literature of the Chinese immigrant experience." Canada's *Macleans* magazine observes that "*The Jade Peony* is one of the finest works of fiction yet to break the silence that surrounds so many of [Canada's] immigrant communities" *Kirkus Reviews* concludes that "Childhood lessons are quietly, powerfully drawn here, with Choy's evocation of harsh immigrant reality nothing short of masterful."

RECOGNITION: Winner of Canada's Trillium Award for fiction; nominated for the *Books in Canada* First Novel Award; REVIEWS: *CanFor* 5/96; *CSM* 5/6/97; *KR* 3/1/97; *LJ* 4/1/97; *MacL* 4/1/96; *NYTBR* 8/10/97; *PW* 3/24/97; *Q&Q* 1/96

Danticat, Edwidge (Haiti/USA)

111   *Breath, Eyes, Memory* (1994); Soho 1994 (HC); Random House 1995 (pbk)

Haitian-born, Edwidge Danticat's debut novel is a searing tale of poverty, rape, sexual abuse, and Third World political strife. Set in an impoverished Haitian village and in New York's Haitian community, *Breath, Eyes, Memory* tells the story of Sophie Caco, a young Haitian girl who is raised by her beloved "Tante Atie" while her mother works in America. Sophie eventually joins her mother in New York City but their reunion is marred by the fact that Sophie bears a strong resemblance to her father. Her mother cannot help but be painfully reminded of the brutal rape that resulted in Sophie's conception.

According to the *Women's Review of Books*, Danticat "has written a beautiful first novel, in brief, limpid sentences, about Haiti and the US, the pursuit of survival and the pursuit of happiness." The *New York Time Book Review* observes that, despite its subject matter, Ms. Danticat's "calm clarity of vision takes on the resonance of folk art ... [and] in the end, her book achieves emotional complexity that lifts it out of the realm of pot-boiler and into that of poetry." In the view of novelist **Bob Shacochis** (*WPBW*), "The writing in *Breath, Eyes, Memory* is loaded with folk wisdom and fairy tales, the imagery of fear and pain and an understated political subtext that makes this first novel much, much more than the elementary domestic story it might have been, were it not for the author's Haitianness."

READING GROUP GUIDE: RECOGNITION: Oprah Winfrey Book Club Selection; REVIEWS: *BellesL* Fall '94; *KR* 2/1/94; *LJ* 3/15/94; *Ms* 3/94; *NYTBR* 7/10/94; *WLT* Spr '95; *WPBW* 4/3/94; *WRB* 10/94; EDITOR'S NOTE: Ms. Danticat was named to *Granta* magazine's 1996 list of the twenty "Best Young American Novelists."

Divakaruni, Chitra Banerjee (India/USA)

112 *The Mistress of Spices* (1997); Anchor 1997 (HC) & 1998 (pbk)

Chitra Banerjee Divakaruni's first novel, called a mixture of "equal parts Isabel Allende and Laura Esquival" by the *L.A. Times Book Review*, follows her widely acclaimed short story collection *Arranged Marriages*. Ms. Divakaruni, drawing on Indian myth and fairy tales, tells a story which is at once lyrical and wryly engaging. Divakaruni's mistress of spices is Tilo, a clairvoyant and natural healer (of both the body and the spirit) who owns a small shop in a run-down section of Oakland, California, from which she routinely dispenses herbal remedies for a wide range of human ills (fenugreek to make a rejected wife desirable again, or cinnamon for "finding friends"). Tilo has lived (for more years than she cares to count) a somewhat monastic life in the service of her art. She eventually meets, and falls in love with, a handsome young Native American by the name of Raven.

According to *Booklist* "The story Divakaruni tells is transporting, but it is her gift for metaphor that makes this novel live and breathe." *People Weekly* observes that "This wry, sometimes elliptical novel charms with esoteric detail and inventive plot twists. But the heart of *Mistress of Spices* is Tilo, the ultimate outsider, and her dangerous romance that metaphorically retraces every newcomer's quest to shape an American identity." Indian novelist **Shashi Tharoor** (*LATBR*) concludes that *The Mistress of Spices* is an "often exquisite first novel that stirs magical realism into the new conventions of culinary fiction and the still-simmering caldron of Indian immigrant life in America."

OTHER MEDIA: Audiocassette (Bantam/abr); RECOGNITION: *L.A. Times* "Best Books" 1997; REVIEWS: *BL* 12/15/96; *EW* 3/21/97; *LATBR* 12/14/97; *LJ* 2/1/97; *NY* 6/23/97; *NYTBR* 4/13/97; *PeopleW* 6/9/97; *PW* 1/13/97; *SFRB* 3/97; TLS 3/21/97

Donaghue, Emma (Ireland)

113 *Stir Fry* (1994); HarperPerennial 1995 (pbk)

Emma Donaghue's debut novel, a coming-of-age-while-coming-out story, features Mariah an inexperienced college student newly arrived in Dublin. Mariah moves in with Jael and Ruth two "mature students" in their twenties and begins her university studies. Mariah surprises even herself when the usual search for identity ends with a realization that she prefers women to men.

According to *Booklist* Ms. Donaghue's descriptions of campus life "from women's group meetings to boozy theatrical shindigs" are "hilarious and wickedly" accurate and provide "a vivid backdrop to Maria's inner searchings." The *Christian Science Monitor* notes that "It is in the flatmates' conversations — earnest, irreverent, and extremely funny — that the true pleasure of the book resides." *Kirkus Review* concludes that "Donoghue deftly separates her novel from the usual coming-of-age fare with gentle language and a winning intelligent protagonist."

REVIEWS: *BL* 5/15/94; *KR* 4/1/94; *LJ* 5/15/94; *LRB* 3/24/94; *Ms* 5-6/94; *PW* 4/11/94; *TLS* 2/4/94

Erdrich, Louise (USA)

114 *The Bingo Palace* (1994); HarperCollins 1995 (pbk)

In *The Bingo Palace*, the fourth volume in a quartet of novels (*Love Medicine, The Beet Queen, Tracks*) spanning a full century and featuring the Chippewa Indians of North Dakota, Louise Erdrich reprises Lipsha Morrissey (a confused young man with the gift of healing) who, having failed to "make a go of it" in the wider world, has returned to the Chippewa reservation. There he meets and falls in love with the beautiful Shawnee Ray, a tribal dancer. Lipsha (whose father is serving time in a state prison) has been given a job in the local bingo hall owned by his uncle Lyman Lamartine, a savvy businessman who plans to build a gambling casino on reservation property. Lyman is also the father of Shawnee's illegitimate child and a romantic rivalry soon develops. Other Chippewa families (e.g., the Kashpaws, Nanapushes and Pillagers) featured in earlier novels, make return engagements here. Ms. Erdrich makes effective use of alternative voices and interjects a touch of magic realism into a story that concerns luck and hope in equal measure.

Novelist **Lawrence Thornton** (*NYTBR*) notes that "One of the dominant motifs in the fiction of American Indian writers is the 'vision' quest ... the integration of inner and outer being through knowledge gleaned from nature" and concludes that *The Bingo Palace* "shows us a place where love, fate and chance are woven together like a braid, a world where daily life is enriched by a powerful spiritual presence." Novelist **Claire Messud** (*TLS*) observes that Ms. Erdrich's quartet of novels is "an enterprise as absorbing, as whole, and as bold as Faulkner's Yoknapatawpha County, of Balzac's Comedie humaine … " and concludes that although "*The Bingo Palace* is less radiant, less intense a novel than its predecessors … Erdrich's prose is as full of marvels as ever…." The *Washington Post Book World* while pointing to an abundance of "good writing" argues that "there's something too familiar here, and a little too facile. It's as if old ground were being vigorously tilled, worked and furrowed diligently without producing the rich crop it once did."

READING GROUP GUIDE; RECOGNITION: *NYTBR* Notable Book of 1994; REVIEWS: *BL* 12/15/93; *CSM* 1/11/94; *LJ* 1/94; *NS&S* 6/10/94; *NYTBR* 1/16/94; *Q&Q* 5/94; *SFRB* Ap/May '94; *Time* 2/7/94; *TLS* 6/17/94; *WPBW* 2/6/94

Ganesan, Indira (India/USA)

115   *Inheritance* (1998); Knopf 1998 (HC)
Indira Ganesan sets her second novel on the fictional island of Pi, a tiny bit a of paradise floating in the Bay of Bengal, and features Sonil a fifteen-year-old girl Indian girl who, in the prolonged absences of her peripatetic mother, has been raised by her doting aunts. Sonil suffers from periodic bouts of bronchitis and has been sent to her grandmother's island home for the summer where it is hoped that the salubrious climate and unhurried pace will improve her health. As a special treat, Sonil's feckless (though much-loved) mother is also in residence. Sonil innocently whiles way the summer studying Italian with her eccentric uncle and lapping up her grandmother's kindnesses — until she meets and embarks on a passionate affair with an American hippy twice her age.

According to *Publishers Weekly* "In the atmosphere of ironic contrasts (Sonil's world contains both mutilated beggars and mystic healers) Ganesan fashions a witty portrait of a suffocating family set against a lush background that is a veritable naturalistic hymn to India." *Kirkus Reviews* points out that "Though writing about a nearly Edenic place, Ganesan takes care that Pi also comes across as not altogether unwordly. And so we meet a down-at-heels collection of cosmopolitan wanderers and odd locals, earthy yet only inches removed from myth." *Booklist* concludes that "Ganesan (who, like Arundhati Roy and Chitra Divakaruni, is part of a glorious flowering of contemporary Indian literature) accomplishes … much in this gracefully sensual tale, pondering questions of spirituality and forgiveness and taking the measure of just how much we inherit from our family, no matter how unconventional its configuration may be."

RECOGNITION: Named by *Granta* magazine as one of the "Best Young American Novelists"; REVIEWS: *BL* 1/1/98; *KR* 11/15/97; *LAT* 2/11/98; *LitRev*

9/97; *LT* 11/7/98 (pbk review); *NYTBR* 3/29/98; *PW* 11/10/97

Goldman, Francisco (USA)

116   *The Ordinary Seaman* (1997); Grove-Atlantic 1997 (HC); 1998 (pbk)
The idea for Francisco Goldman's second novel came from a newspaper account of a group of penniless Central American seamen who had been lured to New York City by the promise of a job. Expecting to join the crew of a merchant ship sailing out of Manhattan, they found instead a rusting, rat-infested junk (docked — literally — in the shadow of the Statue of Liberty), a bankrupt shipping company, no food or shelter (beyond the most rudimentary offered by the derelict vessel) and no provision for returning them to their homeland. Goldman takes these few facts and weaves together a compelling story of human resilience and courage featuring a nineteen-year-old former-guerrilla who becomes the leader of this collection of truly lost souls.

Publishers Weekly observes that "While this is surely a saga of betrayal and exploitation, Goldman maintains a note of cautious optimism about the resourcefulness of men pushed to the brink of despair, and about the determined search for both love and new life in a difficult new land." According to the *Guardian Weekly*, *The Ordinary Seaman* is "a wonderful book, particularly in its evocations of the condemned ship and the decayed docks…. Goldman seems set fair for an untroubled voyage as an exceptionally accomplished writer." The *Washington Post Book World* observes that Goldman "is crazy about his material and does a terrific job" and concludes that "*The Ordinary Seaman* does credit to the novelistic form, yielding up mysterious, vivid worlds, seldom seen but always there."

OTHER MEDIA: Audiocassette (Recorded Bks/unabr); RECOGNITION: Nominated for the 1997 PEN/Faulkner Literary Award; *Publishers Weekly* "Best Books" 1997; REVIEWS: *GW* 4/23/97; *KR* 12/1/96; *LATBR* 2/10/97; *NY* 3/31/97; *PW* 11/25/96; *WPBW* 2/7/97

Goodman, Allegra (USA)

117   *Kaaterskill Falls* (1998); Doubleday 1998 (HC)
Tiny, picturesque Kaaterskill Falls, a 200-year-old WASP enclave in upstate New York, is also — in the mid–1970s — the summer destination of a growing number of urbanites, many of them Jewish. In addition to the "secular" Jews who have started to put down seasonal roots, a small group of Orthodox Jewish families from Washington Heights arrive each June in the company of their venerable spiritual leader, the Rav Elijah Kirshner.

One of these seasonal visitors, Elizabeth Schulman (a devout follower of Kirshner), yearns to do something truly "her own." A capable, and increasingly confident, woman, Elizabeth manages, despite initial opposition, to open a store catering to the summer people. Her foray into the world of commerce will not be uneventful. Meanwhile Rabbi Kirshner, cognizant of his own mortality, is wrestling with the need to choose a replacement.

The *Washington Post Book World* notes that "Goodman's tale of the clash between Yankee year-rounders and the ultra Orthodox summer people … plunges the reader into a world where flesh and blood Jewish characters can have deeply held religious convictions as well as vulnerable human dimensions." *Kaaterskill Falls*, in the view of the *Wall Street Journal*, is "neither comic nor satirical, but a quietly appreciative, even reverent, portrait of a small, separatist, austerely devout Orthodox sect…." According to the *L.A. Times Book Review*, it is a different, surprising kind of Jewish novel for those weaned on Philip Roth and 'the classic Jewish neurotic experience' one that isn't afraid to both question and embrace Yiddiskeit and spirituality." Michiko Kakutani (*NYT*) calls Ms. Goodman a "gifted novelist" and observes that "So authoritative is her storytelling that she is able to move from one character's point of view to another without missing a beat…. At the same time … demonstrating an instinctive grasp of familial dynamics, the ways in which dreams and emotional habits are handed down and translated from generation to generation."

OTHER MEDIA: Audiocassette (Recorded Bks/unabr); RECOGNITION: Nominated for the 1998 National Book Award; *LATBR* "Best Fiction of 1998"; *NYTBR* Notable Book of 1998; REVIEWS: *BL* 7/19/98; *KR* 6/1/98; *LATBR* 8/23/98; *NYT* 8/21/98; *PW* 5/25/98; *WPBW* 8/16/98

Hagedorn, Jessica-Tarahata (Philippines/USA)

118 *The Gangster of Love* (1996); Houghton Mifflin 1996 (HC); Viking Penguin 1997 (pbk)

Jessica Hagedorn's second novel follows the escapades of Racquel (Rocky) Rivera and her increasingly unstable brother Voltaire. A pair of previously sheltered teenagers, they have accompanied their volatile mother, Milagros, from Manila to California where they eventually forge new identities within the flourishing 70s pop-music culture. Rocky becomes emotionally entangled with aspiring rocker Elvis Chang and, before long, she becomes the lead singer of a new band, the Gangsters of Love. The band moves to New York City where they almost make it and Rocky continues to live a flash, frenetic and always funky existence. Hagedorn uses flashbacks, dreams, and changes of voice to tell what is otherwise a fairly traditional story.

According to *Booklist* "As Hagedorn tracks Rocky's growth as an artist and a woman, she deftly conjures the reckless ambiance of that cocked-up, rock-and-roll, everyone's an artist era, then ups the ante by describing the alienation Rocky and company experience as Asian Americans." Novelist **Francine Prose** (*NYTBR*) observes that *The Gangster of Love* "wears its multiculturalism lightly. It asks serious questions about family, exile, identity, about the problems of learning to operate in another language…. Yet it never takes itself too seriously never preaches or moralizes." The *L.A. Times Book Review* suggests that "Nothing is more American than feeling alien. Nothing fits in quite like being a misfit, surrounded by assorted other misfits."

REVIEWS: *BL* 7/96; *LATBR* 10/28/96; *LJ* 7/96; *Ms* 9/10 '96; *Nation* 10/28/96; *NYTBR* 9/15/96; *Time* 9/16/96; *VLS* 9/96; *WPBW* 9/9/96

Hogan, Linda (USA)

119 *Power* (1998); WW Norton 1998 (HC)

In her third novel, Native-American writer Linda Hogan tells the story of Omishto Eaton, a 16-year-old Chickasaw Indian girl who, as a member of the (fictional) Taiga tribe, lives on the edge of the Florida Everglades. The young girl's adolescence has been significantly marred by the tragic death (by fire) of her older brother, her stepfather's abusive behavior and her mother's desperate attempts to lose herself in the larger "white" society. Omishto has chosen her tribe (particularly her friend and protector "Aunt Ama") and the everglades over life with her mother. The ritual killing of a panther (carried out in Omishto's presence by her aunt) lands the youngster in a cultural and legal quagmire. Because the panther is a protected species, Ama is charged with a Federal offense. As events unfold, Omishto is torn between the "Westernized" cultural values of her mother and those of her nearly extinct tribe.

Kirkus Reviews calls *Power* "an evocative coming-of-age saga" while the *Seattle Times* calls it "a mesmerizing meditation on survival, not just of cultures and creatures but of the planet itself." *Publishers Weekly* notes that "it is about two different ways of knowing the world and the problems that ensue when these ways come into conflict. Though slow at times, this in nonetheless a novel of gentle rewards."

REVIEWS: *KR* 5/1/98; *PW* 4/20/98; *SeattleT* 5/28/98; *SFCBR* 5/17/98; *WPBW* 8/16/98

120 *Solar Storms: A Novel* (1995); Scribner 1995 (HC); S&S 1997 (pbk)

The narrator of (Chickasaw poet, essayist and

novelist) Linda Hogan's second work of fiction is 17-year-old Angela Jensen, a troubled young Native-American woman with long red hair and what must once have been a beautiful face. The frightened yet resourceful teenager has left her foster home in Oklahoma and is making her way "home" to Adam's Rib, a poverty-ridden Indian village on a spit of land in the boundary waters between Minnesota and Canada. There Angela finds her great and great-great grandmothers, Agnes, and Dora-Rouge, she is also reunited with Bush the solitary woman who raised her from infancy. The four women join forces and embark on a canoe trip in search of Dora-Rouge's birthplace, which, as it turns out, has been chosen as the site of a major dam building project. Ms. Hogan's novel although full of sensuous imagery of the natural world, is unstinting in its depiction of rural poverty.

As the *L.A. Times Book Review* points out "Becoming human ... is the drama at the heart of this stunning book ... dazzling and heartbreaking because its vivid stories and characters make an eloquent case for the wisdom of a way of life that has been — and is still being — wiped out." The *Women's Review of Books* observes that "Angel's narration is mature and eloquent; her's is a survivor's voice." *Booklist* contends that *Solar Storms* is "exceptional in its voice, its story, and its intent," and concludes that "Hogan — magnetic, ardent, and sagacious — has created a universe within these pages that readers won't want to leave." In the view of *Publishers Weekly*, "Hogan's finely tuned descriptions of the land and its spiritual significance draw a parallel between the ravages suffered by the environment and those suffered by Angela's mother. And, as the land is transformed, so are the lives of the characters, often in deeply resonant ways."

RECOGNITION: Winner of the Colorado Book Award for Fiction; REVIEWS: *BellesL* 1/96; *BL* 9/15/95; *Choice* 2/96; *LATBR* 2/21/96; *LJ* 9/5/95; *NYTBR* 11/26/95; *PW* 8/28/95; *WRB* 2/96

Isler, Alan (UK/USA)

121   *The Bacon Fancier* (1997); Viking 1997 (HC); Viking Penguin 1998 (pbk)

The four novellas which make up Alan Isler's *The Bacon Fancier* all deal in some way with the Jewish experience in a dominant gentile world. Set, variously, in 17th century Venice, 18th century England, on a transatlantic crossing in the late 19th century, and in contemporary Manhattan, they feature a mix of characters drawn from literature, history and Isler's imagination: a Venetian moneylender, a Francis Bacon–spouting master violin maker in search of a wife, a wandering Jew who meets Oscar Wilde on shipboard, and a young actor with a professional interest in the Dreyfus Affair.

Publishers Weekly, in its starred review, observes that "Isler has an acute ear for dialogue, as well as dialects; the voices of his characters are distinctive and distinctly Jewish, though they emanate from different centuries, and brutally candid about their circumscribed lives.... (A)n intelligent and clever fabulist: his titles (*The Bacon Fancier*, *The Monster*, *The Crossing* and *The Affair*) are plays on words and each tale has a subtle connection to the one before it." According to *Kirkus Reviews* "Isler has a remarkable gift for catching the small telling details of a character and for creating intelligent, distinctive voices.... By turns angry, deeply inventive, and unsettling, these novellas are a penetrating and original meditation on the vexed question of identity and a pointed reminder that Isler is swiftly becoming a writer of very considerable powers." The *Washington Post Book World* calls Isler "one of our best comic novelists" and observes that "As Isler would have it, the relationships between art and commerce, illusion and reality, or Jew and Gentile are always fraught with tension. What often separates one story from another is how manifest these frictions are, and how much a given society is willing to act on its prejudices.... [In] the last analysis, Isler has serious, even wise, things to say about history and how individuals live uneasily within its folds." The *London Times* concludes that "Isler's mastery of voices from different periods is his most striking achievement in a work that manages to be funny rather than flippant." According to the *New Leader* "There is nothing overtly didactic here. The writer whizzes through history and while he does so dons and doffs literary styles with breathtaking ease."

RECOGNITION: *LATBR* "Recommended Title" 1997; REVIEWS: *KR* 4/1/97; *LJ* 6/1/97; *LT* 2/28/98; *NewLeader* 7/14/97; *NYT* 7/22/97; *NYTBR* 6/22/97; *PW* 5/5/97; *WPBW* 7/20/97

Jen, Gish (USA)

122   *Typical American* (1991); NAL-Dutton 1992 (pbk)

Gish Jen begins her debut novel in 1947 with the arrival in New York of Lai Fu Chang who has left his aging parents — and the social and economic chaos that followed the "Anti-Japan War" — to come to the U.S. where he plans to study engineering. Before long he has changed his name to Ralph, forgets to renew his visa, goes underground, finds a safe haven, gets married and continues to live his feckless — and incorrigibly impulsive — life in this baffling new world.

According to *Publishers Weekly* "The view of this country through the eyes of outsiders attempting to preserve their own language and traditions while tapping into the American dream of success and riches is the piquant motif that binds the novel — and underscores the protagonist's eventual disillusionment." Jonathan Yardley (*WPBW*), in a review of Ms. Jen's second novel *Mona in the Promised Land,* called *Typical American* "by any reasonable standard a rare accomplishment: mature, subtle, knowing, compassionate and, by no means least, funny" and concluded that it "was reviewed with the enthusiasm it deserved and sold modestly well, but was swamped — along with a number of other good books all dealing, in their different ways, with much the same subject — by the stupendous success of Amy Tan's *The Joy Luck Club*." Novelist **Jayne Anne Phillips** asserts that Ms. Jen's novel is "indeed an American story ... [it is also] immensely intelligent, thunderously funny [and] truly heartbreaking ... perhaps the best story of contemporary immigrant experience ever to grace our literature."

RECOGNITION: Nominated for the 1991 National Book Critics Circle Award; REVIEWS: *BellesL* Win '91; *LJ* 11/15/91; *LT* 5/23/98; *NYTBR* 3/31/91; *PW* 2/3/92; *WPBW* 5/12/96

Kim, Patti (USA)

123   *A Cab Called Reliable* (1997); St. Martins 1997 (HC); Griffin 1998 (pbk)

Ahn Joo, daughter of newly arrived Korean immigrants living in Arlington, Virginia, is only eight years old when her mother, youngest child in tow, abruptly abandons her husband and daughter and returns to Korea. The young mother's reckless act was precipitated by her husband's alcohol-fueled abusive behavior and, perhaps more definitively, by his apparent lack of ambition. Ahn Joo's last traumatic glimpse of her mother and brother — in the back seat of a taxi-cab with "Reliable" stenciled on its side — will haunt her for the rest of her life. The already precocious youngster, left to care for her father and "suffer" his feckless ways, grows up quickly.

Kirkus Reviews calls *A Cab Called Reliable* "memorable and moving" and observes that Patti Kim has written "an affecting if uneven debut in which a Korean girl, newly immigrated to the US, struggles to transcend the chaos of a strange land and of a violent and overstressed family." According *USA Today*: "Set behind the tourist scenes and out amid the town homes of its less individualized ... suburbs, this is both an angry story and a startlingly beautiful one.... *A Cab Called Reliable* takes us on no journey into greater darkness; rather it's a book shot through with bright illumination, as well as being a tale of fathers and forgiveness and a too-little-known but proud heritage in our midst."

REVIEWS: *KR* 5/1/97; *NYTBR* 9/14/97; *PW* 6/2/97; *USA Today* 7/3/97

King, Thomas (Canada)

124   *Green Grass Running Water* (1993); Houghton Mifflin 1993 (HC); Bantam 1994 (pbk)

In his second novel, which is set in Alberta, Canada, Thomas King weaves Blackfoot creation myths and tribal folklore into a complex tale of five contemporary "Indians" (the term Native American is assiduously avoided) and their search for a place in the world: Lionel Red Dog, an apathetic T.V. salesman; his sister Latisha, a restaurant-cum-tourist-trap owner; Uncle Eli Stands Alone, a former college professor and environmental activist; and Charlie Looking Bear, a lawyer who has sold out to a hydroelectric conglomerate. The plot is driven by the escape, from a mental institution, of four elderly Indians (survivors, it is said of a late 19th century Indian internment camp) who have broken out, periodically, for the past 60-odd years. This elderly quartet (known as Ishmael, Hawkeye, Robinson Crusoe and the Lone Ranger) have a mission and it appears to have something to do with a proposed man-made lake. The "Coyote Trickster" — familiar to readers of Native American stories and myths — plays a significant role in the story.

According to *Kirkus Reviews*, *Green Grass Running Water* is "Eloquent and outrageous: a richly rewarding saga from a first-rate talent." *Books in Canada* notes that "The narrative of the five realistic characters and of the four old men wind in and out of the plot, merging at times, their stories illuminating each other, their themes recurring ... " and concludes that "the effect is something like magic realism: an insight into a world-view lost long ago by those of us whose roots are in Anglo-Saxon Europe." The *Library Journal* observes that "Clever verbal motifs not only connect the stories but add fun visual themes, including missing cars and a ubiquitous Western movie" and concludes that Kim's novel is "Smart and entertaining ... [and] deserves a big audience."

REVIEWS: *BksCan* 4/93; *CSM* 3/31/93; *KR* 1/1/93; *LJ* 2/1/93; *NYTBR* 7/25/94; *PW* 1/25/93; *Q&Q* 5/94

Lamar, Jake (USA)

125   *The Last Integrationist* (1996); Random House 1997 (pbk)

Former *Time* reporter Jake Lamar's satirical novel about race relations in the near future is both compellingly written and disturbingly plausible. The America portrayed in *The Last Integrationist* is a racially polarized country where executions are televised live on pay-per-view and drug addicts are rounded up for deportation to special rehab camps.

Poet Jabari Asim, writing in the *Washington Post Book Review,* points out that "Lamar wisely offers no pat resolution to the conflicts he has introduced. By novel's end, race relations still teeter on the edge of violence, televised executions are ratings blockbusters, and the government is still energetically corrupt." Asim concludes, that "If the author's aim was to wrap complex questions in an entertaining package, he has more than succeeded." *Kirkus Reviews* notes that Lamar "expertly lays down a dystopian view of America's future, particularly in matters of race … " and concludes that he has produced "[a] compelling, controversial political thriller, part *A Clockwork Orange*, part *The Manchurian Candidate*." *Salon*, applauding Lamar's "empathy and a tough critical eye" concludes that *The Last Integrationist* is a "rare, intelligent, provocative novel on race in America." *Entertainment Weekly* calls Lamar "a fearless young talent to keep your eye on."

OTHER MEDIA: Audiocassette (Random Audio/abr); REVIEWS: *BL* 11/1/95; *EW* 2/23/95; *KR* 1/1/96; *PW* 11/6/95; *Salon* 1996; *WPBW* 3/10/96

Lee, Chang-Rae (USA)

126   *Native Speaker* (1995); Putnam 1995; Berkley 1995 (pbk)

Henry Park is not a native English speaker, he is a second-generation Korean-American with a facility for languages and a nearly flawless accent. Henry meets and marries Lelia (a speech therapist) with whom he has a son. Throughout the early years of his married life Henry works as an undercover investigator (a sort of white collar spy) in the employ of a company that specializes in "ethnic coverage." Henry will eventually confront both personal tragedy and professional soul-searching.

The *Times Literary Supplement* declares that Chang-Rae Lee's first novel, with its emphasis on the search for identity "is in the grand American tradition … from its opening quotation from Walt Whitman to its demure domestic conclusion." In the view of the *New Statesman* "language is the heroine of this novel: language spoken, written, stumbled over, learnt, misunderstood, found wanting. While plenty happens, the plot is really the vehicle for a thoughtful exploration of what it is like to take on a new language, to be the child of immigrants, to grow up with two cultures tussling within you." *Booklist* calls *Native Speaker* "lyrical, mysterious and nuanced" and observes that "the poignant moodiness of this first novel by a 28-year-old Korean American lingers long after the final page is turned." *Publishers Weekly* observes that "Writing in a precise yet freewheeling prose that takes us deep into Henry's head…. Lee packs this story, whose intrigue is well measured and compelling, with insights into both current political events and timeless questions of love, culture, family bonds and identity."

OTHER MEDIA: Audiocassette (Book cassette/unabr; Brilliance/abr); RECOGNITION: ALA Notable Book of 1995; REVIEWS: *BL* 2/15/95; *KR* 12/1/94; *LST* 7/4/98; *NS&S* 8/25/95; *NY* 7/10/95; *PeopleW* 6/5/95; *PW* 1/9/95; *TLS* 10/27/95

Lee, Gus (USA)

127   *Honor & Duty* (1994); Knopf 1994 (HC); Ivy 1995 (pbk)

Kai Ting, a first generation Chinese-American and the protagonist of Gus Lee's second novel, enrolls in West Point where he hopes to become a "real" American. The time is the mid 1960s and America's involvement in Vietnam is growing.

The *New York Times Book Review* notes that, despite its "unwieldy" size, Mr. Lee's "story of the formation of a young man, as he struggles to honor his Chinese inheritance in an American context, is an important one." The *Library Journal* observes that by "combining honest patriotism with Confucian values, Lee's novel defines the Chinese American male experience." In its starred review, *Publishers Weekly* concludes that Lee's "evocations of West Point's grandeur and of the ancient obligations of gahng and lun (bonds and relationships) at work in Chinese-American communities are enthralling."

OTHER MEDIA: Audiocassette (Random Audio/abr); REVIEWS: *BL* 1/1/94; *LATBR* 4/17/94; *LJ* 1/94; *NYTBR* 2/20/94; *PW* 1/3/94

128   *China Boy* (1991), NAL-Dutton 1993 (pbk)

Gus Lee has set his semi-autobiographical debut novel in San Francisco's Chinatown (a neighborhood with which he is intimately familiar) and features Kai Ting, who, as the novel begins, is only 7 years old. Before long Kai's mother, his only refuge, will die of cancer and his father will remarry an unfeeling Caucasian woman who takes such a dislike to her step-children that she takes to locking Kai and his sisters out of the house during the day.

Novelist Walter Dean Myers (*WPBW*) calls *China Boy* "a pure delight" and observes that as "the story of one small Chinese boy's adjustment to Western culture, to San Francisco's Chinatown and to the mean streets of urban America … it rings of truth, not only of the experiences of the youthful protagonists, but of larger, more important truths about our society." According to *Publishers Weekly* "This is the Chinese-American experience as Dickens might have described it, peopled by many rogues and a few saints … [Lee's] story is a primer on how to keep body and soul together in a world that is as gritty as the streets of his hero's neighborhood and seems dangerously out of control." The *Library Journal* notes that "*China Boy* resonates with strong characterizations, evocative descriptions of San Francisco in the 1950s, and the righteous indignation of abused innocence."

RECOGNITION: *NYTBR* Notable Book of 1991; REVIEWS: *LJ* 4/1/91; *NYTBR* 7/21/91; *PW* 7/13/992; *WPBW* 5/12/91

Liu, Aimee (USA)

129 *Face* (1994); Warner 1995 (pbk)

Face, Aimee Liu's debut novel, is narrated by Maibelle Chung, a red haired, green-eyed, mixed-race daughter of a half–Chinese father and a Caucasian mother, who grew up "different" in New York's Chinatown. Plagued by violent nightmares which cause her to awake screaming, Maibelle abandons New York (and a promising career) for a new life in California. When a photography assignment brings her back to Manhattan, she begins to confront her past.

*Kirkus Review*s observes that "The power of this enchanting debut novel lies in the evanescence of reality and the stealth of truth." The *London Sunday Times*, while arguing that "it seems implausible that Maibelle would 'forget' the kind of trauma she experienced" and pointing out that "Liu has an irritating habit of underlining the significance of every episode" concludes that what "the novel lacks in subtlety, it makes up for in passion. Liu may not be the first author to explore the Chinese American experience, but she is a welcome addition to the club." The *Los Angeles Times Book Review* notes that *Face* is a "story that is part psychological drama, part rite of passage, part literary exploration of being racially divided and part mystery" wherein a young woman of mixed race comes "to terms with the forces that made her."

REVIEWS: *LATBR* 1/8/95; *LJ* 8/94; *LT* 11/13/94; *PW* 8/8/94; *NYTBR* 10/9/94

Louis, Adrian C. (USA)

130 *Skins* (1995); Crown 1995 (HC)

Native American poet Adrian Louis's debut novel is set in South Dakota on the desolate Pine Ridge Indian Reservation and concerns two brothers, Rudy and Mogie Yellow Shirt. Rudy, volatile and self-loathing despite his college education, has joined the reservation police force; the less ambitious Mogie cannot escape familial -- and tribal — legacies of alcoholism. When Rudy falls and hits his head he suffers an unusual side-effect: a trickster spirit enters his psyche and releases his alter ego: the avenging warrior.

According to *Choice*, "Louis's unflinching portrait of reservation life ... makes a contribution to American literature that is reminiscent of Richard Wright's *Native Son* and John Steinback's *The Grapes of Wrath*." *Booklist* calls Louis's novel "Tremendously tragic and, unfortunately, highly realistic" and concludes that Louis examines "the many causes, including those self-induced and self-perpetuated, of the serious hardships facing American Indians today." In the view of *Publishers Weekly*, the author, by employing "an incisive blend of satire, fantasy and grim realism, and aided by a good eye for detail and an ear for natural dialogue ... presents a picture of contemporary Native American life that is often as funny and warm as it is disturbing."

REVIEWS: *BL* 7/95; *Choice* 12/95; *LJ* 6/1/95; *PW* 5/29/95

Major, Clarence (USA)

131 *Dirty Bird Blues* (1996); Mercury 1996 (HC); Berkley 1997 (pbk)

"Avant-garde" poet and novelist, Clarence Majors, sets *Dirty Bird Blues* — his first novel in eight years — in the gritty, racist Midwest of the 1950s and tells the story of blues musician Manfred Banks as he struggles to hold on to his dream of being a professional musician. Manfred, a gifted harmonica player and blues singer has trouble finding steady employment in Chicago's emerging jazz scene. His persistent weakness for alcohol (Old Crow Whiskey is the "dirty bird" of the title) is a complicating thread in a poignant tale of ambition thwarted and eventually regained.

Publishers Weekly, in its starred review, opines that Major "cleverly demonstrates the pervasive racism that's part of the black experience," and concludes that "the choices [his] flawed hero must make are compelling and weighty. The result is a novel that's moving — and highly enjoyable." According to *Booklist*, Major "thrills us with some of the wittiest, most melodious inner dialogue ever written and moves us with dramatic confrontations between loved ones that are remarkable for their sensitivity, authenticity, and significance." The *Library Journal* points out that *Dirty Bird Blues* "is marred only by an excess of blues lyrics, which seldom retain their power on the page" and concludes that "Major's vivid re-creation of postwar black America will appeal to fans of Walter Mosley."

REVIEWS: *BL* 5/15/96; *KR* 4/1/96; *LJ* 5/1/96; *PW* 5/27/96; *WPBW* 6/23/96

Meer, Ameena (India/USA)

132 *Bombay Talkie* (1994); Serpents Tail 1994 (pbk)

Sabah, a second generation Indian-American and a recent college graduate, has, at her parents urging, returned to India to soak up some heritage. There she falls in with a group of "Indibrats" with whom she wends her rather aimless way around Bombay. She also becomes immersed in the lives of a friend, now married to an Indian, and her movie-star uncle and his dysfunctional family. Tragedy lurks just off center stage left.

According to the *San Francisco Review of Books* "Meer offers an unsentimental view of Indian culture showing Indian identity from all sides: the Indian-American, the expatriate, the strong Indian woman, the public figure, and the traditional Indian. All of these facets are found within one family, as it struggles to reconcile Indian traditions with modern American liberties...." The *Times Literary Supplement* concludes that *Bombay Talkie* is an "honest, provocative study of an increasingly rootless generation...."

REVIEWS: *KR* 5/15/94; *LJ* 5/15/94; *NS&S* 7/28/95; *NYTBR* 1/1/95; *PW* 6/20/94; *TLS* 6/9/95

Min, Anchee (China/USA)

133 *Katherine* (1995); Berkley 1996 (pbk)

Anchee Min's debut novel (following her highly regarded memoir *Red Azalea*) is narrated by "Zebra" Wong a 29-year-old Chinese girl who, subjected to Mao's "thought reform through labor" program, has been forcibly returned to her home in Shanghai. Here she is required to work in a factory and learn English. Her language instructor is an American teacher, Katherine, who has come to China in search of adventure as well as thesis material. Katherine (with her Beatles tapes and freewheeling '60s sensibilities) has a profound effect on Zebra and her friends.

The *Times Literary Supplement* notes that "This is not a book of horrors, but it is certainly inspired by them. It is a pleasant surprise to reach a happy ending." *Entertainment Weekly* calls it "an English-teacher-in-Asia novel as seen through the looking glass" and concludes that "it's a fascinating view." According to the *Library Journal* Min "has written a little dewdrop of a work that is lyrical, to-the-point, and occasionally marred by writing that seems annoyingly childish but perhaps should be acknowledged as echoing the voice of a young woman painfully finding her way out of a terrible historical experiment."

OTHER MEDIA: Audiocassette (Dove/abr); REVIEWS: *BL* 4/1/95; *EW* 5/19/95; *NS&S* 8/25/95; *PW* 3/13/95; *TLS* 10/25/97

Mosley, Walter (USA)

134 *Always Outnumbered, Always Outgunned* (1997); W.W. Norton 1997 (HC); S&S 1998 (pbk)

Walter Mosley sets his second post–Easy Rawlins novel — comprised of a series of interlocking short stories — in contemporary L.A. and features Socrates Fortlow, a street-wise former convict who is grappling with the lure of violence: in the world at large and in himself.

The *L.A. Times Book Review* observes that in *Always Outnumbered, Always Outgunned* Mosley moves away from Easy Rawlins "to focus instead on the city today, a place where police helicopters prowl the night skies, where gunfire is never distant and where, most conspicuously, the black community is woefully divided among itself...." The *LATBR* concludes that Mosley's novel "is ultimately the picture of a black community struggling to take on the challenge of finding its own better life and — given the strength, moral questioning and willingness to break the rules — may, just, succeed." The *London Times* points out that Mosley while "skirting perilously close to sentimentality and Oprah-esque self-help ... is never insultingly glib. What he creates [here] is a profound fable for difficult times." *Booklist* notes that "These are often difficult stories to read; never sentimental, they are finally, one and all, about pain and how we live with it.... Hard-hitting, unrelenting, poignant short fiction."

OTHER MEDIA: A made-for-TV movie was released in 1998 starring Laurence Fishbourne; Audiocassette (Dove/abr); READING GROUP GUIDE: W.W. Norton; RECOGNITION: *LATBR* "Best Books" 1997; *Booklist* Editors' Choice 1997; REVIEWS: *BL* 8/97; *LATBR* 11/9/97; *LJ* 10/1/97; *LT* 10/17/98; *NYTBR* 11/9/97; *PeopleW* 11/3/97; *PW* 10/6/97; *Time* 1/12/98

Neihart, Ben (USA)

135 *Hey, Joe* (1996); S&S (HC); Berkley 1997 (pbk)

Ben Neihart's New Orleans–based debut novel is a coming-of-age-story featuring Joe Keith, a gutsy, gay 16-year-old, and his nocturnal adventures in that city's decadent French Quarter. Joe falls in with an intriguing assortment of urban denizens including Seth Michaels, a hustler; Welk, a "buzzhead" orphan; White Donna, a "faux teen" deejay; Black Chris, her Med School boyfriend; and music-shop owner, Kel. In a parallel plot, Rae Chipke, a psychotic orphanage administrator — accused of sexual abuse — has taken Joe's mother hostage.

The *New York Times Book Review* calls *Hey Joe* "a touching, even soothing affirmation of the magic wisdom of youth in the face of a mindless world." The *San Francisco Review of Books* asserts that although the "parade of odd folks leaves the reader a bit breathless.... Soon enough you learn to stop trying to figure out where the action is leading and appreciate the ride." *Salon* calls *Hey, Joe* "a breezy and individual debut" that "introduces a nasty cast of characters who seem like Southern cousins of Elmore Leonard's psychopaths." Novelist **Stephen Dixon** found it to be "funny and lyrical at times and always surprising, erratic, and hopping, with quiet mediations on the meanness and meaninglessness of some people's lives and the stupid reckless things they do to overcome their boredom and satisfy their appetites."

REVIEWS: *KR* 2/1/96; *LATBR* 5/5/96; *LJ* 4/1/96; *NYTBR* 4/21/96; *PW* 2/12/96; *SFRB* 5-6/96; *VV* 7/2/96

Ng, Fae Myenne (USA)

136 *Bone* (1993); Hyperion 1992 (HC); Harper 1994 (pbk)

Fae Myenne Ng, in her first novel, focuses on a Chinese-American family living in San Francisco and explores the profound difficulties posed by assimilation. The pivotal event in Ng's tale is the death (by accident or suicide) of the beautiful middle daughter of this conflicted immigrant family.

Novelist **Christina Garcia** (*WPBW*) observes that "there is much to savor in this novel: the cultural collisions and unlikely juxtapositions that claim all new immigrants: the growing sense of a new 'vocabulary of feeling' that is swelling and enriching the English language; the mysteries and rhythms of adaptation." Michiko Kakutani (*NYT*) calls it an "incantatory first novel" while the *Voice Literary Supplement* declares that its theme "the wondrous, inevitable, sorrow-inflicting powers which one's family is always endowed—won't go out of style for at least another millennium."

RECOGNITION: Nominated for the 1994 PEN/Faulkner Award; *NYTBR* Notable Book of 1993; REVIEWS: *BellesL* Spr '93; *BL* 9/15/92; *NYTBR* 12/5/93 & 1/16/94; *PW* 12/20/93; *VLS* 12/93; *WPBW* 1/10/93; EDITOR'S NOTE: Ms. Ng was named by *Granta* magazine to its 1996 list of the twenty "Best Young American Novelists."

Ng, Mei (USA)

137 *Eating Chinese Food Naked* (1998); Scribner 1998 (HC)

In her debut novel, Mei Ng tackles an increasingly familiar theme: generational conflict within immigrant families stemming from discrepancies in the pace of (or desire for) assimilation. Ng sets her novel in New York City and features a hard working Chinese-American immigrant couple, Franklin and Bell, and their daughter Ruby, a sophisticated college graduate whose sexual experimentation appears to be leading nowhere. Having just graduated from Columbia University and looking for her first real job, she has moved home temporarily as a cost-saving measure. The relationship between Ruby and her mother, Bell, is particularly well-delineated.

According to *Entertainment Weekly* Ng, using "taughtly written prose" skillfully captures the relationship between immigrant parents committed to the old ways and their children enamored of the new "without ever succumbing to sentimentality." In the view of *Booklist*, "*Eating Chinese Food Naked* is terrific. Ng writes in an earthy, rhythmic prose that captivates the reader.... [She] can write at any

level, expertly combining the explicit and sublime, humor and tragedy."

REVIEWS: *BL* 1/1/98; *EW* 1/23/98; *KR* 11/15/97; *LATBR* 1/11/98; *LJ* 12/97; *Ms* 1/98; *NYTBR* 3/1/98; *PW* 12/8/97

Obejas, Achy (USA)

138 *Memory Mambo* (1996); Cleis 1996 (pbk)

Memory Mambo, Achy Obejas' debut novel, is set in Chicago's Cuban exile community and features Juani Casas, a 24-year-old lesbian Cuban-American who runs the family laundry business.

Much of the novel's interest stems from Juani's attempts—in her search for self and heritage—to sort through the fascinating, if credulity-stretching, stories told by various members of her prodigiously extended, close-knit, quarrelsome and frequently violent clan. Oh, and then there's the little matter of being "gay" in a remorselessly macho culture.

Publishers Weekly says that "The power of and meaning of memory lie at the heart of Obeja's insightful and excellent second work of fiction" and concludes that *Memory Mambo* "is an evocative work that illuminates the delicate complexities of self-deception and self-respect, and the importance of love and family." The *Library Journal* points out that as she explores "the disturbing, at times cruel undertow of love and sex, Obejas's graphic scenes of violence are utterly compelling...." In the view of *Booklist*, Obejas with her "adept at stream-of-consciousness narrative ... mambos her way through this seamless, seductive, and ultimately, disturbing tale...."

RECOGNITION: Lambda Literary Award finalist for Lesbian Fiction; REVIEWS: *BL* 9/1/96; *LJ* 8/96; *Ms* 9-10/96; *WPBW* 12/15/96

Penn, W.S. (USA)

139 *The Absence of Angels* (1994); Permanent 1994 (HC); Univ. of Oklahoma 1995 (pbk)

In *The Absence of Angels* W.S. Penn—of mixed Native American and white ancestry—tells the affecting story of Albert (Alley) Hummingbird, a mixed-blood Indian who is attempting to both find his way in the world and reconcile his dual heritage. Albert was rescued at birth (literally from the jaws of death) by his grandfather who provides the young man with a conduit into his native culture—particularly into the afterlife region known as the "absence of angels." Meanwhile, "death" is assigned a walk-on role and pops up periodically as a comically mean and pathetic character.

Publishers Weekly notes that "skipping lyrically between his hero's childhood and young adulthood, Penn has produced a delightful work of magic realism reminiscent of John Nichol's *The Milagro*

Beanfield War" and concludes that "the author limns with insight the struggles of modern, urban, often mixed-blood Indians to forge a coherent identity." According to the *Library Journal, The Absence of Angels* has "all the usual pain-inducing ingredients identifiable with any bildungsroman … mixed together with the elements of Native American myth, a beautifully evoked Southwestern landscape, and humor." *Kirkus Reviews* calls it a "tender, compelling coming-of-age saga, with youthful alienation and family pride represented in a delicate, often uproarious combination."

RECOGNITION: 1994 North American Indian Prose Award — Univ. of Nebraska Press; REVIEWS: *KR* 12/15/93; *LJ* 1/94; *NYTBR* 10/29/95; *PW* 1/10/94

Pinckney, Darryl (USA)

140   *High Cotton* (1992); FS&G 1992 (HC); Viking-Penguin 1993 (pbk)

Darryl Pinckney's quasi-autobiographical debut novel features a young black man who has grown up in an upper-middle class black family founded by his revered grandfather Eustace — the first of many family members to attend an elite university and to reap the attendant professional rewards. The nameless narrator takes us from his formative years (a boyhood in the Midwest, matriculation at Columbia University, foreign travel) to his pursuit of a publishing career in New York city.

The *Yale Review* declares that "This is a bildungsroman in a special sense, by claiming for himself precisely the growing-up troubles (irritating relatives, nasty school friends, and so on) that are universally American rather than specifically black, Pinckney's narrator makes a subtle but powerful claim to cultural equality." According to *Kirkus Reviews, High Cotton* "delights in irreverence and irony [while] its politically incorrect narrator refuses to sacrifice his much-cultivated individuality for a ready-made racial identity." Novelist **Edmund White** (*WPBW*) concludes that "At a time in our history when a puerile 'political correctness' imposes hypocrisy on most writers dealing with sensitive topics, Darryl Pinckney has dared to treat his theme with excruciating honesty and the total freedom from restraint that Schiller said we find nowhere else but in authentic works of art."

RECOGNITION: Nominated for the 1992 *L.A. Times* First Fiction Award; REVIEWS: *CSM* 2/18/92; *KR* 11/15/91; *LATBR* 2/23/92; *LRB* 9/24/92; *LST* 8/23/92; *NS&S* 8/14/92; *NYTBR* 2/2/92; *NYTBR* 3/26/92; *PW* 12/6/91; *TLS* 8/14/92; *WPBW* 2/23/92; *YaleRev* 7/92

Sapphire (USA)

141   *Push* (1996); Knopf 1996 (HC); Vintage 1997 (pbk)

Described by the *Times Literary Supplement* as a novel "whose subject matter is inescapably shocking," *Push* tells the story of Precious Jones who is sixteen years old and pregnant for the second time. Precious has been sexually abused by her father from early childhood (he's the father of the child she is currently carrying as well as of the mentally retarded four-year-old she gave birth to at age 12), and her mother is totally unsympathetic. In fact, she blames her daughter for "stealing her man" and subjects her to additional abuse and punishing household servitude. In the only positive precipitating event of her life, Precious meets Ms. Blue Rain, an inspirational English teacher who encourages her to learn to read and write (Precious eventually begins making entries in a journal) and to leave her abusive home for the relative stability of a half-way house.

Booklist calls *Push* "an intense work, both heart-breaking and frightening." The *Times Literary Supplement* observes that "There are to be no fairy-tale endings for Precious who is HIV positive, save that her son has escaped the virus" and chillingly concludes that the author "a poet and performance artist who also has been a literacy teacher, notes that Precious's story is not an unusual one, but bears similarities to the lives of many of her former students." In the view of the *L.A. Times Book Review* "Although the right-wingers might dismiss the real-life Preciouses of this world as the Willie Hortons of Welfare, Sapphire gives the fictional Precious something that surveys and case studies do not — a mind, a heart, and a ferocious rage to survive."

OTHER MEDIA: Audiocassette (Random Audio/abr); READING GROUP GUIDE; RECOGNITION: *L.A. Times* "Best Books" 1996; Winner of 1997 ALA Black Caucus First Novel Award; REVIEWS: *BL* 5/1/96; *KR* 4/15/96; *LATBR* 12/29/96; *LJ* 6/1/96; *NYTBR* 6/14/96; *PW* 11/22/96; *TLS* 10/11/96

Sarris, Greg (USA)

142   *Grand Avenue* (1994); Hyperion 1994 (HC); Penguin 1995 (pbk)

Grand Avenue is the Native American ghetto of Santa Rosa, a small northern California coastal town. It's residents are Pomo Indians who, despite extreme poverty and dislocation, still find the remnants of community in a collection of tumble-down shacks and recycled army barracks. The author, who is himself the chief of the Coastal Miwok tribe, has fashioned a poignant, hard-hitting first novel from a series of interlocking stories. The nine narrators — mostly female voices — are all related in some way and include: an old woman who has reconnected with her family, a young woman reminiscing about her mother's seemingly wasted life, a mother coping with her daughter's leukemia, a father writing secret letters to a son he did not know he had.

According to *Kirkus Reviews* "The story cycle as a whole follows a subtle trajectory: It begins with hatred, rejection, and despair and ends with hope and belonging.... Sarris sets himself a difficult task and accomplishes it well." In the view of the *Times Literary Supplement,* "*Grand Avenue* is a skillful fictional account of the way the politics of dispossession deprive a culture of its self-esteem, ultimately depleting its moral sensibility." Novelist **Sherman Alexie** claims that Sarris has "made himself an exciting new part of the latest Native American literary renaissance." The late **Michael Dorris** noted in the *L.A. Times* that *Grand Avenue* "is not only one of the very best works of fiction by and about Native Americans, it's one of the most imaginative books of the year, period."

REVIEWS: *BL* 9/1/94; *HMR* Win '94; *KR* 7/1/94; *LATBR* 9/4/96; *LJ* 9/1/94; *PW* 8/8/94; *TLS* 2/3/95

Schulman, Sarah (USA)

143   *Rat Bohemia* (1995); Dutton 1995 (HC); 1996 (pbk)

Sarah Schulman's *Rat Bohemia* is a provocative story of a small group of homosexual friends who, abandoned by their families and unwelcome in the wider world, soldier on. The author's feisty heroine, lesbian Rita Mae Weems, is a rodent exterminator with the NYC Department of Health and it is her experiences (often in the company her best friend Killer), which drive this frequently witty yet always uncompromising tale of urban homosexual angst in the age of AIDS.

According to the *Washington Post Book World*, Rita's story is "both decadent and dead-on [and is] told with street-level accuracy and sardonic style." Novelist **Edmund White** (who is himself HIV positive) applauds *Rat Bohemia* for its "gimlet-eyed accuracy, its zero-degree honesty, [and] its charnel house humor." White concludes that the "force of [Schulman's] indignation is savage and has blown the traditional novel off its hinges. If she were contributing to the quilt project, her quilt would be on fire." The *Women's Review of Books* calls it "oddly moving ... it has the power to haunt long after the last page is turned." The *Library Journal* notes that "the novel is not only a poignant cry for understanding from a community that had to reinvent family in order to survive emotionally but also a dense and vital portrait of life on the fringes of society."

REVIEWS: *BL* 9/15/95; *LJ* 8/95; *NYTBR* 1/28/96; *WPBW* 10/13/96; *WRB* 2/96

Selvadurai, Shyam (Sri Lanka/Canada)

144   *Funny Boy* (1994); Morrow 1996 (HC); Harcourt Brace 1997 (pbk)

Set in Sri Lanka, this coming-of-age-in-a-troubled-paradise story features Arjie Chelvaratnam, a cheerfully mischievous young boy with a predilection for playing "dress-up" and a preference for girls as playmates. He is also a member of an upper-class Tamil family all of whose lives will soon be altered by civil war and ethnic violence.

Books in Canada calls Selvadurai's debut offering "warm , human, funny, moving, [the] kind of novel that, although set in another country, draws us into it with characters and families we can recognize in any culture." *Salon* magazine notes that the author "weaves a spider web of a narrative in *Funny Boy*, a delicate yet potent first novel that concerns itself with love, politics, gender, race, sexuality and terrorism." According to *Publishers Weekly, Funny Boy* "charts a boy's loss of innocence as he grapples with family conflict, political realities and his homosexuality." *Entertainment Weekly* notes that "British colonial holdovers (cricket, corporal punishment, and Latin poetry at the Queen Victoria Academy) enhance the atmosphere of madness masquerading as normalcy...."

RECOGNITION: Winner of *Books in Canada* "First Novel" Award 1994; nominated for the 1997 ALA Gay, Lesbian, Bisexual Books Award, the Lambda Book Award for Gay Fiction, and the 1994 Giller Prize; REVIEWS: *BL* 1/1/96; *BksCan* 4/95; *CanFor* 1-2/95; *EW* 3/8/96; *KR* 1/1/96; *Nation* 9/30/96; *NYTBR* 4/14/96; *PW* 11/6/95; *Salon* 1997

Shigekuni, Julie (USA)

145   *A Bridge Between Us* (1995); Doubleday 1996 (pbk)

In her debut novel, Julie Shigekuni tells the coming-of-age story of Nomi Hito a fourth generation Japanese-American teenager who shares a large house in San Francisco with her parents, her grandmother, Rio, and her great-grandmother, Reiko. While still a child, Reiko, the acerbic matriarch, had been abandoned by her mother (the daughter of a deposed princess) who simply up and returned to Japan. The beloved grandmother Rio carries with her the painful legacy of an abortive suicide attempt, while Nomi's mother Tomoe (Rio's daughter-in-law) is fastidiously tradition-bound. The story is narrated, in turn, by Reiko, Rio, Tomoe and Nomi, indomitable women all.

The *School Library Journal* observes that Shigekuni skillfully describes the bonds between the Hito women as "strands of love, duty, betrayal, revenge and hatred ... [which] can sustain, support, yet sometimes strangle." In the view of novelist **Lisa Shea** (*NYTBR*) "Nomi emerges most clearly from Ms. Shigekuni's meticulously drawn matriarchy: smart, skittish, full of secret sadness and, as we watch her drift out of childhood … sexually precocious." According to *Kirkus Reviews* "With this fluid debut novel, Shigekuni raises the emotional and artistic stakes in the burgeoning genre of the multi-generational ethnic saga."

REVIEWS: *BL* 1/1/95; *KR* 12/15/94; *LJ* 2/1/95; *Ms* 3-4/95; *NYTBR* 3/19/95; *SLJ* 8/95

Sidhwa, Bapsi (Pakistan/USA)

146   *An American Brat* (1993); Milkweed 1995 (pbk)

Bapsi Sidhwa's fourth novel is a continuation of sorts of the author's first novel *The Crow Eaters*. The brat of the title is sixteen-year-old Feroza Ginwalla a descendant of the Junglewalla clan featured in the earlier novel. Feroza' parents, Parsis from Lahore, Pakistan are concerned about the growing religious intolerance (and threat of violence) in the region, and have sent their daughter to live with a relative (Uncle Manek) a graduate student at MIT. Firoza's proposed three month visit turns into four years as (fascinated by the U.S.) she enrolls in an American college. The pain of cultural assimilation and romantic entanglements follow.

In the view of the *Washington Post Book World* "For many women born into societies with restrictive social and political codes … immigration may be the only real way to come of age. In *An American Brat* [Ms. Sidhwa] reveals with a humorous yet incisive eye the exhilarating freedom and profound sense of loss that make up the immigrant experience in America." According to *The Economist* "An attractive quality of this book is that Feroza is as often enchanted as she is appalled by the America and Americans she encounters. The pleasure she takes (and later her mother takes) in shopping malls, fast-food restaurants and modern kitchen appliances … illustrates how much the rest of the world longs for what most Americans take for granted."

RECOGNITION: NY Public Library "Best Books for the Teen Age"; REVIEWS: *Econ* 12/11/93; *LJ* 11/1/93; *NYTBR* 1/16/94; *PW* 8/30/93; *WPBW* 12/12/93

Sinclair, April (USA)

147   *Ain't Gonna Be the Same Fool Twice* (1996); Avon 1997 (pbk)

In her sequel to *Coffee Will Make You Black* (1994), April Sinclair continues the story of Jean "Stevie" Stevenson, a spunky young African-American girl who grew up on Chicago's South Side in the 1960s. In this second installment, Stevie has graduated from college and is newly arrived in San Francisco where she is looking for work in the field of broadcasting. It is now the late 1970s and Stevie is experimenting with, among other things, gay relationships, self-help groups, and feminist "events."

Entertainment Weekly notes that "Sinclair's affection for her feisty ingenue colors every page of this winning novel" while *Booklist* calls it "upbeat" and a "literary gem." According to *Publishers Weekly*, Stevie's "engaging enough, but the sunny earnestness of it all will make some readers long for at least some of the layered wit that Armistead Maupin brought to the me-generation San Francisco in *Tales of the City*." *Salon* calls Ms. Sinclair's novel "ripely funny, unpretentious, and sincere" and concludes that "Sinclair proves herself cunning by placing her curious heroine within a certain special interest group while slyly exposing their often foolish ideologies. Sisterhood is powerful, but a sense of humor is more so."

REVIEWS: *BL* 12/15/95; *EW* 1/26/96; *LJ* 12/95; *NY* 2/15/96; *PW* 11/20/95; *Salon* 1996

Syal, Meera (UK)

148   *Anita and Me* (1996); New Press 1996 (HC)

My mother would right now be standing in a haze of spicy steam, crowded by huge bubbling saucepans where onions and tomatoes simmered and spat, molehills of chopped vegetables and fresh herbs, jostling for space with bitter, bright heaps of turmeric, masala, cumin and coarse black pepper whilst a softly breathing mound of dough would be waiting in a china bowl, ready to be divided and flattened into round, grainy chapatti. And she, sweaty and absorbed, would move from one chaotic work surface to another, preparing the fresh, home-made meal that my father expected, needed like air, after a day at the office about which he never talked.

Set, in the 1970s, in the declining working class English town of Torrington, Ms. Syal tells the story of Meena Kumar, daughter of Punjabi immigrants, who is mischievously maneuvering her way through the cultural roadblocks thrown up by her parents and neighbors alike. Meena is befriended by the town's "tough-girl," Anita Rutter, much to the dismay of her parents, but this relationship is severely tested when Anita starts going out with a local skinhead with decidedly racism views.

The *Times Literary Supplement* calls Syal "a fine comic writer" and observes that "Unlike most first novels [*Anita and Me*] is not just the story of one person but the evocation of an era. Syal blends the yearning felt by every child, not to be different, with Meena's growing awareness of her brown skin in a white society…." According to *Kirkus Reviews* "Meena's loss of innocence, and her recognition of her heritage, coincides with her realization that her seemingly harmonious village also harbors violence, hatred and fear…. Far from just another coming-of-age saga, Syal's impressive debut offers a charming yet troubling evocation of recent times." *Salon* notes that "Syal's animated language pops off the page like a jeweled sari, making *Anita and Me* a great deal of fun to read."

RECOGNITION: Shortlisted for the 1996 Guardian Fiction Prize and the Betty Trask Literary Award; REVIEWS: *Guard* 4/6/96; *KR* 2/1/97; *LJ* 3/1/97; *LT* 4/6/94; *NYTBR* 8/10/97; *Salon* 4/14/97; *TLS* 4/5/96; *WPBW* 4/6/97; *WRB* 4/97; EDITOR'S NOTE: Meera Syal is well-known in the UK as an actress and screenwriter.

Tan, Amy (USA)

149 *The Hundred Secret Senses* (1995); Ballantine 1996 (pbk)

Prize-winning author Amy Tan's latest novel features San Francisco–born Olivia Yee a second generation Chinese-American who is caught between two cultures. An accomplished photographer, Olivia has carved out a successful career for herself. She cannot, however, fully escape the conflicting demands of her cultural heritage, particularly as they are embodied in the person of her older half sister Kwan Li. Kwan has played a significant role in Olivia's life since arriving in California to join her "American" family when Olivia was only 6. Kwan not only has the gift of second sight and can recall a previous life, she can also see and converse with spirits. In their shared bedroom Kwan had regaled Olivia with ghost stories and village tales. The adult Kwan convinces Olivia and her estranged photographer husband to accompany her to China to visit the town where she grew up.

Newsweek found Tan's latest novel to be "more finely nuanced than her previous two" while *Publishers Weekly*, in its starred review, declares that "no one will deny the pleasure of Tan's seductive prose and the skill with which she unfolds the many-layered narrative." On the other hand, novelist, **Claire Messud** (*NYTBR*), observes that "Olivia comes to believe not only in the spiritual truth of Kwan's visions but in their literal truth: hence her cringe-making exclamations about love, the soul and ghosts." Ms. Messud goes on to assert that "to accept the novel as anything more than a mildly entertaining and slightly ridiculous ghost story, the reader must also make this demanding leap of faith, turning a blind eye to rash improbabilities and a host of loose ends." According to the *Times Literary Supplement, The Hundred Secret Senses"* is fast-paced but ultimately aimless. We are shown versions, oppositions and differences that do not add up to the insights that Tan suggests she will impart ... [this] new novel is as troublingly fluent and vivid as its predecessors."

OTHER MEDIA: Audiocassette (Recorded Bks/unabr); RECOGNITION: Shortlisted for the Orange Fiction Prize; REVIEWS: *BL* 9/15/95; *EW* 11/29/96; *LJ* 5/15/96; *Ms* 11-12/95; *NYTBR* 10/29/95; *PW* 9/11/95; *SLJ* 7/96; *TLS* 2/16/96

Toibin, Colm (Ireland)

150 *The Story of the Night* (1996); Holt 1997 (HC); 1998 (pbk)

Richard/Ricardo is the only child of an Argentinean father and an English mother. Growing up bilingual and culturally bifurcated in Buenos Aires, he lacks a clear sense of identity. For, as he informs the reader, he "never had to be a fully formed person." Richard's homosexuality (which he hid from his mother and the world) further prevented him from achieving a sense of "belonging." Colm Toibin's latest novel (preoccupied with both the emergence of AIDS and the Falklands War) is set during the "time of the generals" when governmental opposition was ruthlessly crushed. It was a period of intrigue and duplicity and Richard was skilled at both. He eventually becomes involved with an American diplomatic couple who may or may not be working for the CIA.

According to *Salon* "This is a book about fear and the consequences of fear when it is pushed to the limits. That it turns out to be such a fierce and convincing affirmation of love as the only source of redemption is a tribute to the writer's courage in looking into the darkest of mirrors and to his consummate skill in describing what he sees there." The *London Times* notes that "What is good about this book is the ease, the fluidity, the economy, the precision of Toibin's ... prose, which makes this novel — despite much of the darkness it depicts — sheer pleasure to read." In the view of the *Times Literary Supplement* "Toibin's writing, a well-tuned engine, roars gloriously."

RECOGNITION: *NYTBR* Notable Book of 1997; REVIEWS: *BL* 5/15/97; *Guard* 9/12/96; *IrishT* 9/7/6; *LJ* 5/15/97; *LRB* 10/3/96; *LT* 9/12/96; *NS* 9/20/96; *NYTBR* 6/22/97; *PW* 4/14//97; *Salon* 6/5/97; *TLS* 9/13/96; *WPBW* 5/18/97

Trice, Dawn Turner (USA)

151 *Only Twice I've Wished for Heaven* (1997); Crown 1997 (HC); Anchor 1998 (pbk)

Chicago Tribune editor Dawn Trice's debut novel, a story of love, revenge and murder is set in Chicago in the mid-1970s and features two African American neighborhoods separated only by a fence: the decaying "35th Street," and Lakeland, a planned, upper-middle class enclave. *Only Twice I've Wished for Heaven* is narrated by both Tempestt Saville, an 11-year-old resident of Lakeland, and Miss Jonetta Goode, a long-time resident of Chicago's meaner streets. Tempestt, despite her parents' warnings, is drawn to the vibrant but dangerous world just over the fence.

Called "poignant and melodic" by the *Library Journal*, and "touching and memorable" by the *New York Times Book Review*, Ms. Trice's novel was widely admired. According to *Kirkus Reviews*, "Ms. Trice brings a light touch of magic realism to a tale of violence, urban squalor and upward mobility" and concludes that "Trice's greatest achievement may be how effortlessly [and modestly] she manages to mingle an original vision and real art."

RECOGNITION: Nominated for ALA's Black Caucus 1998 Award for Fiction; REVIEWS: *BL* 11/15/96; *Emerge* 3/97; *KR* 11/1/96; *LJ* 9/15/96; *NYTBR* 2/23/97; *PW* 9/15/96

Tyau, Kathleen (USA)

152   *A Little Too Much Is Enough* (1995); FS&G 1995 (HC)

Mahealani Wong is a Chinese American girl growing up in Hawaii in the post-war years. Her childhood and early adolescence, in the midst of a warm, tradition-bound family, are described in a series of linked stories. Ms. Tyau "uses pidgin dialect and some scrumptiously sensuous lyrical writing to evoke a rich collision of cultures: Chinese, Hawaiian, Japanese and American" (*Seattle Times*).

The *L.A. Times Book Review* says that *A Little Too Much Is Enough* "resembles a brightly colored painting that at first glance seems normal, until you notice that there in the corner an iridescent fish is leaping out of someone's head" and concludes that the novel is "unfailingly joyous, even when [Ms. Tyau's] characters are in pain." The *New York Times Book Review* found that Tyau's book "vividly recreates Honolulu after World War II," and observes that "when the author gets around to describing the brutal fields and canneries where Mahi and her brothers labor in the service of Hawaii's most famous fruit, its a revelation."

RECOGNITION: Winner of the Pacific NW Bookseller's Association Award for Fiction; REVIEWS: *BL* 7/95; *KR* 5/1/95; *LATBR* 6/4/95; *LJ* 6/1/95; *NYTBR* 10/15/95; *PW* 6/12/95; *SeattleT* 11/3/96; *WPBW* 7/28/95; *WRB* 7/96

Uyemoto, Holly (USA)

153   *Go* (1995); NAL-Dutton 1996 (pbk)

Holly Uyemoto sets her debut novel within the confines of a large Japanese extended family living in southern California. Her young, soul-searching and wryly amusing narrator, Wil, is inching back from the edge. She is recovering from a nervous breakdown (brought on by a broken love affair and a hurried abortion) and she's facing her twenty-first birthday — the harbinger of an adulthood that Wil is unprepared to assume. She's looking rather critically at the adults around her, many of whom seem, to her at least, to be selfish, unfeeling, neurotic or worse. What most of the adults in her family share is the experience of having been confined to an internment camp during WW II, an episode which appears to have left lasting scars.

According to *Ms.* "No other book captures so well, or with such acid humor, how the dysfunction of so many Japanese American families are a legacy of the camps.... " The *Library Journal* calls *Go* "an offbeat mix of *The Bell Jar* and the *Joy Luck Club*...." *Publishers Weekly* concludes that "This cathartic novel does not chart a typical journey to recovery, but its heroine's storytelling finally does allow her — and by extension, the reader — to accept her parents' cultural mores."

REVIEWS: *BL* 2/1/95; *KR* 12/1/94; *LATBR* 2/1/9/95; *LJ* 1/95; *Ms* 1-2/95; *PW* 1/9/95

Vilmure, Daniel (USA)

154 *Toby's Lie* (1995); HarperPerennial 1996 (pbk)

Seventeen-year-old Toby Sligh, a thoroughly disaffected teenager who refers to Dostoyevsky as "my main man," is picking his way through the emotional minefield of late adolescence. A senior in a Jesuit high school in Tampa, Toby hopes to "come out" by dancing with his boyfriend at the senior prom. Meanwhile his mother has confessed to some ambiguity regarding his parentage and his best friend, Juice, a drug dealer, seems to have gotten mixed up with the mob.

According to *Booklist*, although the novel does "strain to be more than its simple plotline can sustain," Vilmure's debut attempt is "light, humorous [and] effective." The novel's "real accomplishment" in the view of the *New York Times Book Review* is "in depicting the emotional life of a teen-ager in all its colorful confusion." *The Washington Post Book World* concludes that "Daniel Vilmure has a unique and powerful vision, and his novel is a significant contribution to the literature of the generation that came of age after the advent of AIDS."

REVIEWS: *BL* 4/15/95; *KR* 3/1/95; *NYTBR* 6/18/95; *PW* 4/17/95; *WPBW* 7/16/95

Walker, Alice (USA)

155 *Possessing the Secret of Joy* (1992); Pocket Books 1993 (pbk)

Possessing the Secret of Joy, Alice Walker's unsettling, often polemical 4th novel, features Tashi Johnson, an African woman who, after marrying an American missionary, has emigrated to the United States. While still a young girl, and in compliance with tribal custom, Tashi had submitted herself to the brutal yet culturally sanctioned custom of tribal initiation which consists of genital mutilation. This experience has left Tashi with such profound physical and emotional scars that her life is forever altered. After her arrival in the US, Tashi begins to suffer increasingly from psychotic episodes made much worse by the knowledge that the difficult birth of her brain-damaged son was a direct result of her mutilation. When the enormity of what has happened to her sinks in, Tashi returns to Africa seeking revenge. Readers were first introduced to Tashi in Walker's earlier novel *The Color Purple*.

According to the *Times Literary Supplement* "A significant silence has been broken, and as always when this happens you find yourself wincing, not wanting to know. Silence, though (Walker seems to say), is the torturer's ally, the silence and amnesia that have enabled generations of women to collude, and inflict their own agony on their daughters." *Kirkus Reviews* was less laudatory, calling *Possessing the Secret of Joy* a "pastiche of New Age mysticism, dubious history, and feminist ideology." The *Washington Post Book World*, however, concludes that "It's the suffering of children, the wholesale mutilation of little girls, that finally haunts us in Walker's daring novel." The *Literary Review* cautions "Those who are looking for a soothing read for the long winter nights ahead would be well advised to look elsewhere — this is strenuously, the stuff of nightmares."

OTHER MEDIA: Audiocassette (S&S/unabr); RECOGNITION: *NYTBR* Notable Book of 1992; REVIEWS: *BL* 4/15/92; *Essence* 7/92; *KR* 4/1/92; *LATBR* 7/5/92; *LitRev* 10/92; *LJ* 5/15/92; *NS&S* 10/9/92; *NYTBR* 6/28/92; *PW* 4/13/92; *WPBW* 7/5/92

Welch, James (USA)

156 *The Indian Lawyer* (1990); Viking Penguin 1991 (pbk)

On one level a gripping suspense thriller, on another a classic success story (complete with the requisite fall from grace), *The Indian Lawyer* tells of Sylvester Yellow Calf's rise from a Montana reservation to the (precarious) pinnacle of success in the white man's world. Sylvester Yellow Calf, although raised in extreme poverty on a Blackfeet reservation, has managed to obtain a law degree (from Stanford University), carve out a successful law practice in Helena and, as the novel opens, is being encouraged to run for Congress. A blackmailing scheme — initiated by a crafty convict hoping to exploit Yellow Calf's membership on the parole board — appears like a bolt out of the blue and, for the moment, all bets are off. Mr. Welch is widely acclaimed for his powerful portrayal of contemporary reservation life.

According to the *School Library Journal* "As events threaten Yellow Calf's security, a fascinating third world unfolds: the reservation childhood he has tried to leave behind. It is from his past that Yellow Calf eventually finds the truth about himself and the strength to do the right thing." *Publishers*

Weekly points out that "Sylvester's growing doubts about assimilation and his need to identify with his Native American roots are counterpoised to his realization that he may be deprived of the opportunity to make a contribution on a national scale." According to novelist **Reynolds Price** (*Civilization*) *The Indian Lawyer* "compels our interest ... [in contemporary Native Americans] both on the reservation and off, both resourceful and stalled, as they confront common problems of late 20th century America."

RECOGNITION: *NYTBR* Notable Book of 1991; REVIEWS: *Civ* Nov/Dec 1994; *KR* 8/1/90; *LATBR* 10/14/90; *Nation* 11/26/90; *NYT* 10/6/90; *NYTBR* 11/25/90; *PW* 8/10/90; *SLJ* 5/91; *WPBW* 12/30/90

Wong, Norman, (USA)

157 *Cultural Revolution* (1993); Persea 1993 (HC); Ballantine 1995 (pbk)

In a series of finely honed vignettes, Norman Wong chronicles the fortunes of the Lau family — beginning with its escape from mainland China — as it moves from Macao, to Hong Kong and finally, Hawaii. Using the device of linked stories or "snapshots," Wong charts the family's changing fortunes and the increasing westernization of its younger members. Most of the stories are set in Hawaii where Wei, the family patriarch, works hard but never attains his piece of the American dream (in his case, of owning his own restaurant). His wife Marie fares better in the process of assimilation while his children, Julia and Michael, grapple with the usual problems associated with adolescence, many of which are exacerbated by their immigrant status. As Michael, whose coming-of-age provides much of the book's momentum, becomes increasingly aware of his homosexuality, he plans his own escape.

The *Village Voice* calls *Cultural Revolution* a "moving collection by a gifted new writer with the wit and sympathy to make four generations of family experience all sound like his own...." As the *Multicultural Review* points out "Wong addresses a young man's acceptance of his homosexuality, a subject handled tastefully and without undue sensation, as he completes the circle in the title story, returning to a much-changed and hopelessly static homeland."

REVIEWS: *KR* 1/1/94; *LJ* 3/1/94; *MultiCultR* 6/94; *NYTBR* 3/27/94

Yamaguchi, Yoji (USA)

158 *Face of a Stranger* (1995); HarperCollins 1995 (HC)

Yoji Yamaguchi's debut novel is set in California in the early part of the 20th century and depicts a Japanese immigrant community awash in gambling dens, "strong men," and houses of prostitution. When two prostitutes, Kikue and Shino — each lured to America by an unscrupulous brothel owner using false offers of marriage — simultaneously recognize their "intended," a young man by the name of Arai Takashi, they vow to exact their revenge. Takashi, the handsome and feckless son of a wealthy merchant family (his scandalous behavior in Japan has led his family to banish him to the United States), had been persuaded — soon after arriving in California — to sell his photograph for ready cash. Unbeknownst to Takashi his picture was then used by the brothel owners in their bogus mail-order bride operation.

Booklist judges *The Face of a Stranger* to be a "clever, wonderfully crafted debut novel." The *Library Journal*, noting that Yamaguchi "interweaves Japanese myth and fairy tale into his characters' botched lives and longing for escape" concludes that though *Face of a Stranger* "may portray the diaspora at its grimmest and most cutthroat it is tempered by caring and humor." The *Washington Post Book World* calls it "an auspicious debut" and suggests that "Yamaguchi's first novel is a comic romp, with parallels — and more than a passing resemblance — to Shakespeare, specifically *Much Ado About Nothing*."

REVIEWS: *BL* 7/19/95; *KR* 4/15/95; *LJ* 7/95 & 12/95; *PW* 5/1/95; *WPBW* 10/8/95

Yamanaka, Lois-Ann (USA)

159 *Wild Meat and the Bully Burgers* (1996); FS&G 1995 (HC)

In a series of vignettes, the Japanese-Hawaiian writer Lois-Ann Yamanaka tells the story of Lovey Nariyoshi and her (painfully) humorous journey through adolescence. The daughter of an uneducated, blue-collar, Japanese-American couple from Hilo, Lovey suffers from low self-esteem and lower expectations. Yamanaka frequently uses a kind of Hawaiian Creole (or pidgin) dialect to emphasize the estrangement of Lovey's family from the wider American society.

In the view of the *New York Times Book Review*, although "the narrative becomes bogged down in adolescent angst" the book "delivers moments of stinging clarity, creating haunting images as [the author] sketches Lovey's search for a spiritual home." The *Library Journal* asserts that "By focusing on her own distinct culture, the author successfully uncovers the damaging restrictions of American culture at large" and concludes that "This commanding novel should delight and haunt every reader." *Publishers Weekly*, in its starred review, calls *Wild Meat and the Bully Burgers* "a starkly realistic debut novel" and concludes that "though Yamanaka pitilessly portrays the poverty of pocketbook, intellect and spirit in Lovey's environment, she also displays — especially in the moving denouement —

the bonds of love and understanding that can create poignant, epiphanic moments of reconciliation." *Salon* concludes that "In vivid and often violent vignettes, Ms. Yamanaka describes Lovey's defeats and triumphs as she learns to celebrate her origins and individuality."

REVIEWS: *BL* 12/1/95; *CSM* 1/10/96; *KR* 9/15/95; *LJ* 11/15/95; *NYTBR* 12/31/95; *PW* 10/2/95; *Salon* 1995

Yamashita, Karen Tei (USA)

160 *Brazil-Maru* (1992); Coffee House 1992 (HC); 1993 (pbk)

Karen Tei Yamashita's second novel (following the much-praised *Through the Arc of the Rain Forest*) is a multigenerational immigrant saga with a twist. In 1925, 600 Japanese (mostly contract laborers) made the oceanic voyage to Brazil, lured by promises of land, wealth and freedom. Traveling with them was a group of "educated Japanese Christians with socialist sentiments" who were hoping to start a utopian community — in the Brazilian jungle — founded on religious freedom. The historically documented trials and tribulations suffered by all of the newly arrived immigrants, and their heirs, drives Ms. Yamashita's dramatic tale. The reader would do well to remember that there are now a million Japanese living in Brazil.

Publishers Weekly notes that "This searching novel introduces Western readers to an unusual cultural experiment, and makes vivid a crucial chapter in Japanese assimilation the West." According to *Booklist*, "Yamashita's heightened sense of passion and absurdity, and respect for inevitability and personality, infuse this engrossing ... saga with energy, affection and humor."

The *Washington Post Book World* points out that, although lacking in a "unified thematic" thrust (primarily because of the use of multiple narrators), *Brazil Maru* is "warm, compassionate, engaging, and thought-provoking. An oddly angled view of immigrants elsewhere ... [Yamashita's novel] casts light into many of the darker corners of our own immigrant experience."

REVIEWS: *BL* 8/92; *KR* 7/1/92; *LATBR* 11/29/92; *LJ* 8/92; *PW* 7/6/92; *WPBW* 12/31/92

Young Bear, Ray A. (USA)

161 *Remnants of the First Earth* (1996); Grove/Atl 1996 (HC); 1998 (pbk)

Ray Young Bear, a member of the Mesquakie tribe, grew up on a reservation in Ohio. In *Remnants of the First Earth* (which follows his 1992 collection of stories *Black Eagle Child*) Young Bear draws on this experience to tell the story of Edgar Bearchild beginning with his 1950's childhood in the Black Eagle Child Settlement where White and Indian culture intermingled in curious ways.

Bearchild grows up to assume the role of Keeper of the sacred Journals of the Six Grandfathers — ancient documents filled with tribal history, native lore and religious prophecy. As the story moves into the present, a reservation murder investigation, mishandled by white policemen from the nearby town, draws Bearchild into a web of corruption that includes a powerful local shaman and the tribal casino industry.

In the view of the *Library Journal*, "Set against Edgar Bearchild's investigation into the murder of a childhood friend, noted poet Young Bear's first novel lyrically describes Bearchild's memories while detailing his tribe's suffering and its struggle to hold on to a fading tribal cultural." According to *Publishers Weekly* "Young Bear's prose pulses with lyrical ferocity, blending narrative, verse and tribal myth in a seamless web. He writes as one deeply familiar with Native tribal existence and committed to its survival, but he is unafraid to assault readers' senses and preconceptions." *Kirkus Reviews* concludes that "Out of an idiosyncratic mix of folk tales, rowdy adventures, and religious imagery, Young Bear has fashioned [in *Black Eagle Child* 1992 and *Remnants of the First Earth* 1997] a powerful, utterly distinctive, and unsettling portrait of Native American life."

REVIEWS: *KR* 12/01/96; *LJ* 1/97; *NYTBR* 5/25/97; *PW* 12/16/96

Youngblood, Shay (USA)

162 *Soul Kiss* (1997); Putnam 1997 (HC); Riverhead 1998 (pbk)

Poet and playwright Shay Youngblood's skillfully constructed debut novel is a coming-of-age story that explores erotic confusion and gender identification. Early in the tale, seven-year-old Mariah Santos is abandoned by her intensely physical, unstable, drug-dependent mother. The youngster is left in the care of Faith and Merleen, a pair of maiden "aunts" who are a bit old-fashioned but sensible and big-hearted. Mariah must adjust to the loss of her mother (to whom she remains utterly devoted), to the suffocatingly traditional, church-going ways of her gentle caregivers, and to the isolation of her new home in rural Georgia. As she grows to maturity — she is an excellent student and an accomplished cellist — Mariah feels emotionally complete only with other women. At fifteen, frustrated by her estrangement from her parents, Mariah sets out for Los Angeles in search of her father, an artist by the name of Matisse. There she is exposed to new varieties of attachment and erotic stimulation bordering on incest.

Publishers Weekly, in its starred review, points out that Youngblood has saturated "her writing with haunting eroticism, lyrical description and complex characterization, [and concludes that the author] gets inside the soul of an acutely isolated girl and takes the pulse of her desire to break out of that solitude." According to *Entertainment Weekly*, "The sensation of reading this shimmering novel is like savoring the taste of summer fruit on the tongue." The *London Times* observes that "Youngblood's control of her narrator's voice is sure and her intimate confessions are related with honesty and a sensitivity to the rich private fantasy world of childhood." In the view of *Salon* magazine, Youngblood's "deft manipulation of poetic devices seems particularly apt because *Soul Kiss* is also about language as a liberating force. Mariah accomplishes her troubled quest for self-knowledge primarily through her engagement with words and phrases."

REVIEWS: *BL* 4/15/97; *Emerge* 5/97; *EW* 8/15/97; *KR* 3/15/97; *LJ* 5/15/97; *LT* 7/28/98; *PW* 4/14/97; *Salon* 8/1/97; *WPBW* 5/25/97

The Innovators

At the end of the century which saw the birth of the modernist movement (most notably in the works of James Joyce and Samuel Beckett) there is certainly no shortage of stylistically inventive, anarchically playful, and generally provocative novels for the avid reader to choose from. Although reflecting a melange of modernist techniques and contemporary literary trends, what the following highly regarded novels all have in common is energy, intelligence, and a desire to "engage" the reader. While most are highly accessible some of these selections require a bit more effort on the part of the reader who is viewed by many contemporary authors and literary critics as playing a more symbiotic role in the creative process. For example, the well-known British academic and novelist Malcolm Bradbury, commenting on the popularity of Reading Groups, has suggested that all readers (from the most scholarly to the purely recreational) can be seen as "multipliers of meaning."

The demands made on the reader by the following titles ranges from the minimal (an open mind, a sense of the absurd) to the more strenuous (e.g., a willingness to piece together referential or allusive narrative elements). Keeping in mind that there is a great deal of fluidity in the definition of many of the literary terms associated with the modernists and postmodernists, Chapter 3 celebrates two categories of innovators:

those who push the boundaries, and those who can be said to step over the boundaries. First come the magical realists (Salman Rushdie, Jessica Hagedorn, Chitra Divakaruni and Rick Collignon), poet-novelists (Michael Ondaatje, Anne Michaels), self-reflexives (Harold Brodkey, John Barth), fabulists (Brooks Hansen, Cynthia Ozick, Steven Millhauser, John Hawkes), those who rely on "voices"—speaking at once on holding center stage—to drive the narrative (William Gaddis and Nicholson Baker), and the rest of the innovators who both continue to experiment with alternative notions of reality and to redraw the blueprints of narrative construction (Thomas Pynchon, Don DeLillo, Steven Dixon, Martin Amis, David Markson).

A separate section, "One Step Further," beginning on page 112, rounds up some of the current crop of "literary provocateurs"— mostly younger novelists (e.g., Dennis Cooper, W.T. Vollmann, Irvine Welsh) who are testing thematic and stylistic limits with even greater abandon.

As many novels which incorporate "modernist" elements have primary entries elsewhere in the guide, the reader with a particular interest in these titles should consult the Subject Index under the following headings: alternative histories/speculative fiction, deconstructionism, magical realism, post-modern thrillers, and "punk lit."

PUSHING THE BOUNDARIES

Abish, Walter (USA)

163   *Eclipse Fever* (1993); Godine 1995 (pbk)

Prize-winning novelist Walter Abish sets his first novel in thirteen years in a starkly drawn Mexico City in the year of a solar eclipse. A host of menacing, meticulously drawn characters (an American industrialist and his sexually frustrated wife, a nefarious pre–Columbian art dealer, and an assortment of Mexican writers and artists) all vie for the reader's attention as the decidedly non-linear plot unfolds. Called a "comedy of cultural imperialism" (*NYTBR*), Abish's story hinges on an American-financed restoration project (seemingly) dedicated to the repair and conservation of the Mayan pyramids.

World Literature Today calls *Eclipse Fever*: "Well crafted … carefully written [and full] of leavening irony," and concludes that it "is most assuredly not another baffling, multireferential, intertextual game of fiction. It is strangely realistic, and, as such, raises issues of two societies (North American and Mexican), of minority Indian culture, of the morals of intelligent and cultured elites, of historical consciousness…." Noted scholar, Harold Bloom (writing in the *Washington Post Book World*), calls *Eclipse Fever* Abish's "best novel [as well as] one of the handful of essential American works emanating from the decade preceding the end of the second millennium." The *Voice Literary Supplement* observes that "Abish's wit is as piercing as it is dry" and concludes that "he's crafted a sly humor from rigorous distance, the rarefied comedy of watching streetlife from a high window…. The somersault that is *Eclipse Fever* dazzles, even as it leaves you dizzy."

REVIEWS: *BL* 5/15/93; *LJ* 5/1/93; *NewR* 7/16/93; *NS&S* 7/16/93; *NYRB* 9/23/93; *NYTBR* 6/27/93; *PW* 3/1/93; *TLS* 7/9/93; *VLS* 5/93; *WLT* Win '95; *WPBW* 5/9/93

Alcala, Kathleen (USA)

164   *Spirits of the Ordinary: A Tale of Casas Grandes* (1997); Chronicle 1997 (HC)

Kathleen Alcala's debut novel, the first in a projected trilogy, opens in the small northern Mexican town of Saltillo. The year is 1870 and social unrest is on the rise: laborers in the local mines are in revolt, landless peasants and displaced Indians are restless, and, at the behest of the wealthy land owners, government troops are now stationed in the town. As the novel opens, Zacarias Carabajal, a dreamer of the first order, has just left his wife (Estela), his three children, a comfortable home and an assured income to take up prospecting in the nearby ore-rich mountains. A Jew who converted to Catholicism when he married, Zacarias appears to be driven more by inchoate spiritual longings than by the lure of gold. The story widens to include not only Zacarias's incident-fraught wanderings, but also his abandoned wife's newly aroused passion for an army doctor (she now considers herself a widow), the lives of Zacarias's parents ("closet" Jews of a mystical bent), and the return of Estela's androgynous twin siblings (an eerie pair who were taken into the desert as youngsters to become apprentices to a dowsing witch). Given her preoccupation with "intertwining themes of love, family and spirituality" (*WPBW*), Ms. Alcala has been compared to both Laura Esquivel and Isabel Allende.

Booklist observes that although Ms. Alcala "hasn't quite mastered the fluidity a novel requires … [she] has conjured a culturally and metaphysically complex world, animated by an irresistible cast of impassioned characters." According to the *New York Times Book Review*, "It is a testimony to Ms. Alcala's vivid talents as a storyteller, and to the mystical allure of the threads of magic realism that run through her narrative that we come to care about many of her characters, and to wonder what destinies await them in her next book." The *Washington Post Book Review* notes that: "she offers a poignant tale wrapped up in magic." As *Publishers Weekly* points out: "In the tradition of Latin American literary fabulism, Alcala's seductive writing mixes fatalism and hope, logic and fantasy, to create moral, emotional and political complexities. But her characterizations and plot sparkle with a freshness … [and her] multicultural vision [is] notable for its lack of preachiness." The *Library Journal* concludes that "Alcala embellishes straightforward prose with tinges of mysticism that will entice even the most spiritually disinterested."

REVIEWS: *BL* 2/1/97; *KR* 12/1/96; *LJ* 12/96; *MFSF* 9/97; *NYTBR* 5/4/97; *PW* 12/30/96; *WPBW* 2/13/97

Amis, Martin (UK)

165   *Night Train* (1997); Harmony 1998 (HC); See Section 6, #671

Time's Arrow (1991); Vintage 1992 (pbk)

Time is heading on now towards something. It pours past unpreventable, like the reflections on a windscreen as the car speeds through the city or forest. It's out there, and I'm in here.

Quite simply, *Time's Arrow* is the story of Odilo Unverdorben (alias Hamilton de Souza, alias John Young, alias Tod Friendly) an Auschwitz doctor turned fugitive. Martin Amis, in an impressive display of narrative command, has chosen to tell the doctor's story backwards, from death to birth.

In the opinion of the *Voice Literary Supplement*, *Time's Arrow* "seems to have been written with the term 'tour de force' in mind ... [as] Amis's radical rethinking of time ... brings the abomination of the Holocaust home to the jaded late 20th century reader in a way that few conventional novels could." The *London Review of Books* notes that "merely to turn the story backward would not have been enough: the other necessary trick was to make the vivid, cynically expressed detail, the coarse vigor of an Americanized prose, suggest the gentleness that can co-exist, perhaps only sporadically, with the apprehension of evil and with the natural dread of that fierce, ancient face." English novelist Adam Mars-Jones (*Literary Review*) suggests that "Martin Amis has devised a way of describing the Holocaust without a single word of explicit pity for its victims, so that the atrocious extinguishing of a race is rendered in celebratory terms as the making of a people from the weather, from thunder and lightning, with gas, electricity, shit and fire. This must be one of the most tasteless endeavors in literary history, but its tastelessness has a rigor. The reader must supply the pain to a representation that denies it...."

OTHER MEDIA: Audiocassette (David McKay/abr); RECOGNITION: Shortlisted for the 1991 Booker Prize; REVIEWS: *LitRev* 9/91; *LRB* 9/12/91; *NYTBR* 11/17/91; *TLS* 9/20/91; *VLS* 10/91; EDITOR'S NOTE: Mr. Amis was named by *Granta* magazine to its 1983 list of the twenty "Best Young British Novelists."

London Fields (1989); Random House 1991 (pbk); See Section 3, #290

Anderson, Alison (USA)

166   *Hidden Latitudes* (1996); Scribner 1996 (HC); Washington Square 1997 (pbk)

I can see a white sail on the horizon. There have not been many, these forty years; they stay out there on the intangible line where sea meets sky, well away from the dangers of reef and atoll. They continue on their way, to Tarawa or Butaritari, or further still, to Fiji or the Solomons; no one calls at this unnamed island. So I continue alone.

The circumstances surrounding the disappearance of Amelia Earhart as she attempted, in 1937 (along with co-pilot Fred Noonan), to fly around the world, remain an intriguing mystery. In Alison Anderson's highly imaginative debut novel, Earhart and Noonan crash land on an uncharted island and, having survived the crash, learn to eke out a satisfying if primitive existence. When, more than 40 years later, Robin and Lucy — an adventurous couple who have set out to navigate the globe in their 35-foot sailboat — become becalmed and develop engine trouble, they decide to "put in" on the nub of an island that has, fortuitously, appeared on the horizon. They, of course, assume the island to be uninhabited. What ensues is both "provocative" and "suspenseful."

Kirkus Reviews observes that *Hidden Latitudes* is "a novel about the secret life of Amelia Earhart after the crash [and] is beautifully written and controlled." According to the *Women's Review of Books Hidden Latitudes* is "a wise book. Anderson shows great insight into the psyche of a woman like Earhart, a celebrity suddenly alone, a woman of action suddenly forced into a life of waiting and contemplation, and she persuasively conveys how the natural rhythms of the island eventually change Earhart's perspective."

REVIEWS: *BL* 6/1/96; *KR* 5/1/96; *LATBR* 7/4/96; *LJ* 6/1/96; *NYTBR* 7/21/96; *PW* 5/1/96; *WRB* 7/96; EDITOR'S NOTE: Also see Jane Mendelsohn's *I Was Amelia Earhart* #272.

Antrim, Donald (USA)

167   *The Hundred Brothers* (1997); Crown 1997 (HC); 1998 (pbk)

Described variously as "blackly humorous" and a "hallucinatory" take on the Cain and Able story Donald Antrim's latest novel (the second part of a projected trilogy of short, surreal comic novels) does, indeed, feature a cast of 100 brothers all of whom have gathered, as the story opens, in the library of their crumbling ancestral estate. The brothers — personally introduced (by the narrator, a genealogist) in an opening paragraph which extends for eight pages — range in age from 25 to 93. They have more or less grouped themselves by a variety of characteristics (e.g. the young fathers, the homosexuals, various sets of twins, the infirm, the football players, etc.). The brothers have assembled to both honor the memory of their recently deceased father and to locate and bury the patriarch's ashes. During the course of a frequently ribald and increasingly chaotic evening, fights break out and what little order had heretofore been established is lost. By morning, calm descends....

The *Times Literary Supplement* observes that "Donald Antrim's text is full of forked, involving sentences, in which clauses multiply and adjectives pair rhythmically with nouns" and concludes that "[a]t its worst, *The Hundred Brothers* approaches what might be called slapstick, when events become subject to a crude farcical entropy; at is best, the comedy and image-making have a kind of skewed straight-facedness about them that makes the writing memorable." In the view of *Salon*, Antrim's novel is "full of dark Pynchonesque absurdities, as well as a whiff of apocalyptic dread that feels borrowed from Poe's classic short story 'The Masque of the Red Death.'" According to the *Library Journal*, Antrim "crafts a comic nightmare of a family reunion in which old hostilities renew themselves, cliques form and disintegrate with lightening speed, and the lines for the bar and buffet are so alarmingly long it's difficult to get a drink, let alone dinner...." The *London Sunday Times* concludes that "This is a richly entertaining comic novel that investigates how humanity uses social rituals to try to forget about the inevitability of death."

RECOGNITION: Nominated for the 1998 PEN/Faulkner Literary Award; REVIEWS: *BL* 1/1/97; *EW* 2/21/97; *KR* 12/15/96; *LJ* 1/97; *LST* 5/24/98; *NewsWk* 2/10/97; *NY* 1/27/97; *NYTBR* 3/30/97; *PW* 1/6/97; *Salon* 2/10/97; *Time* 4/1/97; *TLS* 5/30/97

Auster, Paul (USA)

168 *Mr. Vertigo* (1994); Viking 1995 (pbk)
Young Walter Rawley, life-hardened "ragamuffin," is rescued from the mean streets of St. Louis by the mysterious Master Yehudi a quasi-religious figure who "hails from Budapest via Brooklyn." Yehudi has spent his life searching for a youngster with Walter's potential (the ability — if so instructed — to levitate) and loses no time in exploiting the youngster's gift. Together they develop an act, take it on the road and become a national sensation. Auster's 8th novel opens in St. Louis in 1924, lingers in prohibition Chicago and concludes in rural Kansas in the postwar years.

The *New York Times Book Review*, writes appreciatively of *Mr. Vertigo*, observing that it "hovers gracefully between 'once upon a time' and the exact dates of realism, taking in a fair amount of the century's history...." It is also, the *NYTBR* continues, "witty, inventive in its language and invitingly playful with its metaphors." According to Jonathan Yardley (*WPBW*) "One hears America on every page of this novel, and sees it as well: *Mr. Vertigo* is both musical and visual. Indeed it's tempting to note what a wonderful movie it would make except the music and the pictures are all in Auster's words, and that's a form of magic the movies have yet to master." In the view of the *L.A. Times Book Review*, *Mr. Vertigo* US "A magical pertinent book ... gives us a bird's eye view of the strange, violent, paradoxical century behind us."

RECOGNITION: *NYTBR* Notable Book of 1994; REVIEWS: *BL* 5/15/94; *EW* 8/5/94; *KR* 5/15/94; *LATBR* 7/31/94; *LJ* 6/15/94; *NS&S* 4/8/94; *NYTBR* 8/28/94; *PW* 7/3/95; *Spec* 4/9/94; *Time* 9/5/94; *TLS* 4/8/94; *VV* 8/30/94; *WLT* Spr '95; *WPBW* 12/4/94

169 *Leviathan* (1992); Viking Penguin 1993 (pbk)
Early in Paul Auster's *Leviathan*, Benjamin Sachs, a crusty, intellectually belligerent writer, is blown to smithereens by a bomb (apparently of his own making). Deeply puzzled by Sachs's death,

Peter Aaron, one of his oldest friends begins to analyze the bizarre series of coincidences which led to this violent act. As the story progresses, Sachs's character is revealed through a series of remembered "confessions" which Peter replays and carefully examines. In a novel which mixes fictional lives with real ones, the elusiveness of truth is very much at issue.

Kirkus Reviews argues that "With each new work, Auster is quickly becoming our preeminent novelist of ideas — a postmodern fabulator who grounds his odd and challenging fictions in conventional and accessible narrative structures." In the view of the *Chicago Tribune* although it "sometimes seems as if [the narrator's] voice, and writerly control are at odds with the grandeur and terror seemingly promised by Sachs' vocation and by the title of the book ... the allure of Auster's elegant plotting, the play of his ideas, and the sensuous pleasure of his prose keeps us firmly hooked all the same." The *Wall Street Journal* judges Auster to be "a literary original who ... has reaffirmed the dignity of elegant, intricate plots." In the view of the *London Times* "The striking thing about Paul Auster is his ability to breathe life into a branch of fiction that looked as if rigor mortis had set in years ago. *Leviathan* may not have quite the weird zing of his brilliant 'New York Trilogy,' but Auster keeps the mind twisting, with his familiar compound of conceptual tricksiness, plotwise panache and cool, hard prose like beaten aluminum."

RECOGNITION: Winner of the French Medicis Prize for foreign literature; *NYTBR* Notable Book of 1992; REVIEWS: *BL* 6/15/92; *ChiTrib* 11/1/92; *KR* 6/15/92; *LJ* 7/92; *LRB* 12/17/92; *LT* 12/3/92; *NYRB* 12/3/92; *NYTBR* 9/20/92; *PW* 7/13/92; *TLS* 10/23/92; *VLS* 10/92; *WLT* Spr '93; *WPBW* 9/6/92; *WSJ* 9/15/92

170 *Music of Chance* (1990); Viking Penguin 1991 (pbk)
Paul Auster takes on some "big issues" (e.g. the nature of choice vs. chance) in a novel which has both dumbfounded and delighted the critics. The plot is easily summarized: a man by the name of Nashe wins a small fortune and determines to change his life. To this end, he leaves his daughter with a relative and hits the road. In his aimless travels across America he meets a young hustler by the name of Jack Pozzi. Nashe agrees to finance Pozzi in a bizarre poker match against a pair of reclusive oddballs — the results are unanticipated and highly unsettling.

According to *Entertainment Weekly*, "*The Music of Chance* tackles all those serious themes that American novelists aren't supposed to be good at: fate, loyalty, responsibility, the nature of evil, and the real meaning of freedom. Yet the story, so fast, so tricky and so fiendishly well-crafted, offers all the great guilty pleasures of popcorn fiction." The

NYRB observes that there "is pleasure to be had not only from Auster's prose but also from the odd mixture of detachment and suspense that the novel induces." The *London Review of Books* concludes that "*The Music of Chance* is a rare achievement: a novel of formal sophistication which is not consciously exquisite or ostentatiously ground-breaking."

OTHER MEDIA: A film adaptation starring James Spader and Mandy Patinkin was released in 1993; RECOGNITION: Nominated for the 1991 PEN/Faulkner Award; *NYTBR* Notable Book of 1991; REVIEWS: *EW* 11/2/90; *LJ* 9/1/90; *LRB* 5/9/91; *NS&S* 3/22/91; *NYRB* 1/17/91; *NYTBR* 11/4/90; *PW* 8/3/90; *TLS* 3/15/91.

Bail, Murray (Australia)

171   *Eucalyptus* (1997); FS&G 1998 (HC)
Murray Bail, a prize-winning Australian novelist, tells the story of a beautiful young woman whose father, in fine old fairy-tale fashion, has stipulated that the first suitor to correctly identify the more than 100 species of eucalyptus trees on his property may have her hand in marriage. After many failed attempts by a succession of suitors (sheep-shearers, commercial travelers, vagabonds) a middle-aged man named Mr. Cave arrives and (being a knowledgeable arborist) appears poised for success. Another man, both younger and infinitely more attractive, has also made an appearance and, though not adept at naming trees, is an enthralling story-teller. Set in New South Wales, Mr. Bail's third novel spins a fascinating tale which incorporates notions of feminine beauty, landscape, language, love and the power of narrative.

The *Times Literary Supplement* notes that "Bail sets his self-reflexive fantasy in a timeless rural Australia of the early 1960s, in a town 'west of Sydney, over the ranges and into the sun — about four hours in a Japanese car'." And concludes that "This phrase, with its offhand conflation of mythic and conversational tones, presents Bail's style at its most disarmingly effective." According to *Kirkus Reviews*, *Eucalyptus* is "[a] wonderfully written, melodic novel: Bail takes a simple idea and lifts it above the trees and beyond the horizon." The *London Sunday Times* suggests that "This is not only a highly sophisticated fairy tale, whose ancestors includes Ovid's metamorphoses and Scherezade, but also a satire on insularity, patriarchy and the competitive obsessions of men."

RECOGNITION: *NYTBR* Notable Book of 1998; REVIEWS: *KR* 8/1/98; *LST* 7/26/98; *NYTBR* 10/4/98; *TLS* 7/3/98; *WPBW* 11/22/98

Baker, Nicholson (USA)

172   *Fermata* (1994); Random House 1995 (pbk)
In a novel called an "X-rated sci-fi fantasy" by the *Seattle Times*, Arno Strine, an unassuming office temp, possesses the uncanny ability to stop time. Whenever he wishes, Arno can bring the universe to a halt — quite literally freezing the moment. What Arno chooses to do with this extraordinary talent (which, of course, has almost limitless applications) is to undress (and more) any woman he chooses. Baker has, it would appear, conjured up, and obsessively expanded upon, the ultimate male fantasy. *Fermata*, called "wildly comic [if] deeply disturbed" by *Newsweek*, was judged highly entertaining yet morally "confused" by more than one reviewer.

According to Michele Slung (writing in the *NYTBR*), Baker has created "a sort of boys' own horrid adventure of fondling the forbidden flesh of insensate maidens...." She concludes, however, that Baker's *Fermata* "seems ... more like a revenge of the girl-worshipping nerd than an offense against womankind." *Booklist* observes that "Were not the subject of Baker's first novel pornography, one would speak without hesitation of its delicious wit ... Baker can be very funny, and ... perverse or not, he certainly knows how to write." In the view of *Publishers Weekly* "many *Vox* readers will flock to this erudite smut even as Baker stalls in his campaign to eventually succeed Updike as America's most polished stylist."

OTHER MEDIA: Audiocassette (Random Audio/abr); REVIEWS: *BL* 1/1/94; *EW* 2/18/94; *KR* 12/1/93; *LJ* 1/94; *NY* 2/21; *NYRB* 4/7/94; *NYTBR* 2/13/94; *PW* 2/7/94; *Time* 2/28/94; *TLS* 2/18/94

173   *Vox* (1992); Random House 1993 (pbk)
Nicholson Baker again stretches the limits of the traditional novel in this tale of a sexual seduction conducted during a single, uninterrupted, erotically charged telephone conversation between two lonely people, who, though strangers and separated by hundreds of miles, are about as intimately involved with one another as it is possible to be.

According to *Kirkus Reviews*, *Vox* is a "mini epic of Big Chilled safe-sex: rambling stories that start out as aids to titillation but dry and crumble into homely and self-satisfied details ... the overturning of classical seduction theory [the telephone partners are using each other in precisely the same way]" ... combined with "lots of little snappy apercus and joshings [which] establish intellectual coziness." In the view of *Time* magazine *Vox* "illuminates the strange connections of modern life, how people achieve intimacy at a technological distance. Two hundred years ago, *Vox* would have been titled 'Lettres' and been an epistolary romance." The *NYRB* contends that *Vox* "Deserves to be read with full attention to what surrounds and lies between the sexually explicit moments." The *Times Literary Supplement* points out that, in a novel where "two people are supposedly involved in a scenario of swelling excitement, [the author's] tendency to meander and mull over [minutiae] constitutes a considerable barrier to credibility. So does the fact that [the telephone partners] sound vocally interchangeable."

REVIEWS: *Econ* 4/4/92; *KR* 12/1/91; *LitRev* 3/92; *LJ* 11/15/91; *LRB* 3/26/92; *NewsWk* 1/27/92; *NS&S* 3/6/92; *NYRB* 4/9/92; *NYTBR* 2/16/92; *NY* 3/9/92; *Time* 2/3/92; *TLS* 3/6/92; *WPBW* 2/9/92; EDITOR'S NOTE: Yes, this **is** the book — allegedly purchased by Monica Lewinsky at a Washington D.C. bookstore — that so interested Special Prosecutor Kenneth Starr.

174   *Room Temperature* (1990); Random House 1991 (pbk)

Employing a postmodernized stream-of-consciousness style reminiscent of his widely praised first novel (*The Mezzanine*), Nicholson Baker explores the consciousness of a young father (a part time writer and reviewer of TV advertisements) who "muses" as he feeds his infant daughter a bottle. By expanding on the free-association that characterizes human thought, the author successfully attempts to invest life's minutiae with deeper meaning.

According to the *London Sunday Times*: "The archness of *The Mezzanine* is abandoned in *Room Temperature* in favor of a questing, lucid inventiveness. It may have been done before, but unlike his predecessors in the game, Baker's playfully heuristic approach is not aridly cerebral, unlike Robbe-Grillet his disintegrated, digressional narrative does not aim to reveal the randomness which governs existence, but to bring order to chaos, to knit the skeins of disparate thoughts into a recognizable pattern." The *L.A. Times Book Review* concludes that although *Room Temperature* "has a smug *tour de force*-y quality to it ... it also includes some of the most tender, most delicate interaction between husband and wife, adult and infant, in modern fiction...." *Publishers Weekly* concludes: "This is a small masterpiece by an extraordinarily gifted young writer." In the view of the *Washington Post Book World*, "Less sharply innovative than its more clinical austere predecessor, *Room Temperature* is nevertheless a real charmer, a breath of fresh air, a show-stopping coloratura are made up of the quirks of memory and the quiddities of life."

REVIEWS: *AtlM* 7/90; *LATBR* 4/1/90; *LJ* 3/15/90; *LST* 4/15/90; *NS&S* 4/6/90; *NYTBR* 4/15/90; *NewsWk* 5/14/90; *TLS* 4/27/90; *VLS* 6/90; *WPBW* 5/7/90; EDITOR'S NOTE: *The Mezzanine*, Nicholson Baker's essentially plotless 1988 debut novel takes place completely within the consciousness of a young man riding the escalator to his office on the mezzanine floor of his building. He is returning from his lunch break and has just pur-

chased a pair of shoelaces and this simple act triggers a series of tangential musings (involving plastic straws, escalators, milk cartons, and the like) which, surprisingly, turn out to be exquisitely absorbing.

Bakis, Kirsten (USA)

Lives of the Monster Dogs (1997); FS&G 1997 (HC); See Section 6 #674

Banville, John (Ireland)

175   *Athena* (1995); Random House 1996 (pbk)

Athena is the third volume in a loose trilogy beginning with *The Book of Evidence* (1989) and continuing with *Ghosts* (1993). Each book is narrated by Freddie Montgomery, convicted murderer of a servant girl who surprised him in the act of stealing a valuable oil painting from an Irish country house. In *Athena*, Freddie "Morrow" (having served his time in prison and sporting a minor name change), is hired by a shady, black-market art dealer to authenticate some stolen paintings. Morrow also falls under the spell of a sexually voracious young woman identified only as A.

The *Times Literary Supplement* calls *Athena* "an astonishing new novel." Michael Gorra (writing in the *New York Times Book Review*) observes that "plot counts for nothing here ... mood becomes all — a mood sustained by a prose of idiosyncratic and appalling charm." In the view of the *London Sunday Times*, "There are some books, very few, whose opening pages impart to the reader a peculiar, and intensely pleasurable, comfort. John Banville's *Book of Evidence* was one such book. *Athena* is another. The comfort in question is an oxymoronic one. It co-exists with a sense of menace, with the anticipated possibility of horror and disorientation and with a blend of intellectual rigor and moral uncertainty which denies the reader rest." Novelist John Crowely (*WPBW*) notes that "Some American reviewers of *Ghosts* (the middle novel in Banville's trilogy) who read it without reference to the first novel ... were puzzled, understandably. For the three indeed are a series, as ambitious and original a series as Durrell's Alexandria Quartet, and better written." Crowley concludes that "Readers should begin at the beginning."

RECOGNITION: *NYTBR* Notable Book of 1995; REVIEWS: *BL* 5/15/95; *LJ* 5/1/95; *LST* 2/19/95; *NS&S* 2/17/95; *NYTBR* 5/21/95; *PW* 4/3/95; *SMH* 5/13/95; *TLS* 2/10/95; *WPBW* 7/9/95.

176   *Ghosts* (1993); Random House 1994 (pbk)

In *Ghosts,* the middle volume of John Banville's recent trilogy, convicted murderer Freddie Montgomery has been released from prison and is living in extreme isolation on an inhospitable island off the coast of Ireland. Freddie's solitude is interrupted when a boatload of "daytrippers" runs aground on the island's dangerous shoals.

Shifting in and out of fantasy, Banville has utilized the overarching structure of Shakespeare's *The Tempest* to shape his narrative. According to Eric Korn (*TLS*) "The *Tempest* theme is only one of the strands in the dense but never burdensome texture of reference: *Ghosts* is as much painterly as theatrical, and more dream than either. But Banville's tremendous adroitness ensures that the scholarship is not oppressive; and the wit, originality and resourcefulness of the diction are a constant pleasure...." According to *Publishers Weekly* "Banville has certainly developed into a writer of beautiful, sensuous prose ... his evocation of the island on which [*Ghosts*] is set ... is unforgettable ..." but concludes that "this novel is also elusive to a fault.... For most of its course ... *Ghosts* is beautiful but baffling." English novelist **Lawrence Norfolk** (*WPBW*) reports that "*Ghosts* is a strange and austere book. It is not an anti-novel in either the happy (Queneau) or unhappy (Robbe-Grillet) sense, but the outrageous evenness of its tone, the thoroughness of its self-inquisition, and the elaborate courtesy by which it exposes its own narrative machinery all betray a deep unease with its own 'novelishness.'" *World Literature Today* concludes that it is the "flawed narrator, at once sinister, self-deprecating, sly, witty, and wonderfully human, whose consistently realized voice gives unity to this beautifully written novel and is perhaps Banville's greatest achievement in it."

RECOGNITION: *NYTBR* Notable Book of 1993; REVIEWS: *BL* 11/15/93; *KR* 8/15/93; *LRB* 4/22/93; *LT* 3/26/94; *NS&S* 4/16/93; *NYTBR* 11/28/93; *PW* 8/23/93; *TLS* 4/9/93; *WLT* Sum '94; *WPBW* 12/12/93.

177   *The Book of Evidence* (1989); Warner 1991 (pbk)

John Banville's *The Book of Evidence*, is an intriguing blend of thriller, farce and tragedy. In a book-length dramatic monologue, Freddie Montgomery, bad husband, bad son, thief and convicted murderer, composes his prison confession in a narrative characterized by grim comedy and lacerating insights.

The *New York Times Book Review* calls *The Book of Evidence* "a disturbing little novel that might have been coughed up from hell." The *London Review of Books* observes that Banville's novel contains prose of "enviably luminous, ironic elegance ... " and concludes that *The Book of Evidence* "is at least seven-eighths of a minor masterpiece ..." The *Literary Review* notes that although there are books which are certainly "as cleverly constructed

as this one," few writers "can match Banville's technical brilliance. It is, in its cold, terrifying way ... a masterpiece." In the view of the *Christian Science Monitor* "Banville is one of Ireland's best writers. In his exploration of the negative space between fact and value, and the dangerous wobble between science and art, he belongs with Jonathan Swift. And like Joyce, Beckett, and Sean O'Faolain, turns the matter of Ireland into the soul of everyman."

OTHER MEDIA: Audiocassette (Books-on-Tape/unabr); RECOGNITION: Winner of the GPA Book Award; shortlisted for the 1989 Booker Prize; REVIEWS: *CSM* 5/17/90; *Lit Rev* 6/89; *LRB* 5/4/89; *NYTBR* 4/15/90; *TLS* 3/31/89; *WPBW* 4/8/90

Barnes, Julian (UK)

178   *A History of the World in 10½ Chapters* (1989); Random House 1990 (pbk)

Julian Barnes's kaleidoscopic *A History of the World ...* starts with a retelling of the biblical story of Noah and the Ark from the perspective of a woodworm, a heretofore "overlooked" stowaway. The chapters interlock and themes and motifs (of a generally maritime nature) are repeated throughout.

According to Michael Dirda (*WPBW*), readers of "this anatomy of the past will like some stories better than others ... [but] what really gives pleasure ... are the author's ventriloquism, his skillful narrative pacing, his waspish intelligence, the tight-lacing of the book's motifs and ironies." Novelist **Joyce Carol Oates**, writing in the *NYTBR*, suggests that "if the reader does not come to [Barnes's] book with the expectations of prose fiction ... [then *A History of the World ...* can be seen as] a playful, witty and entertaining gathering of conjectures by a man to whom ideas are quite clearly crucial: a quintessential humanist it would seem, of the pre–post-modernist species." In the view of *The New Statesman*, *A History of the World* "shapes up not only as Barnes's funniest novel but also his most richly cargoed and imaginatively designed."

OTHER MEDIA: Audiocassette (Dolphin/unabr); RECOGNITION: Shortlisted for the 1989 Booker Prize; REVIEWS: *CSM* 1/10/90; *LJ* 8/89; *LRB* 6/22/89; *NewR* 12/4/89; *NS&S* 6/23/89; *NYRB* 10/26/89; *NYTBR* 10/1/89; *Time* 10/30/89; *TLS* 6/30/89; *VLS* 11/89; *WPBW* 10/22/89

Barth, John (USA)

179   *Once Upon a Time* (1994); Little & Co. 1995 (pbk)

Award-winning novelist John Barth's 12th work of fiction, an operatic saga combining musical elements from both Verdi and Puccini (it opens with a "Program Note" and takes the form of a three-act opera), concerns a middle-aged writer by the name of John Barth and his wife/lover/editor/friend who, in celebration of the Columbus quincentenary, set sail on the Chesapeake Bay. They are soon blown off course by an unexpected tropical storm and find themselves deep in the Maryland tidal marshes, lost in a sort of Eastern shore equivalent of the Bermuda Triangle. While searching for a way out Barth stumbles upon "a threshold" which allows him to enter a "metaphysical zone" where he encounters scenes and characters from his earlier novels.

In *Once Upon a Time*, as *World Literature Today* points out, Barth "On the threshold of his sixtieth birthday, [and] beginning to contemplate an eventual, though preferably not proximous, decline and death as an inevitable but not altogether uninviting finale … performs a retrospective meditation on life's experiences…." According to the *Times Literary Supplement*, "*Once Upon a Time* tells its author's personal story, or parts of it, while at the same time admitting, by way of its title, that the true story is also a fairy-tale … [Barth] has produced a 'memoir' which recreates not only himself, but also a world. He sees all facts as fiction in so far as facts have mythic implications; and it is significant that Barth gives his 'true fiction' a musical context that overrides verbal meaning. In doing so he returns to his first published creation *The Floating Opera*, which made a fantasy world out of the riverboat musical shows popular during his provincial youth."

REVIEWS: *AtlM* 6/94; *BL* 2/15/94; *KR* 3/1/94; *LJ* 4/15/94; *NYTBR* 7/3/94; *Obs* 12/11/94; *PW* 3/7/94; *TLS* 11/25/94; *WLT* Sum '94; *WPBW* 5/8/94

180   *The Last Voyage of Somebody the Sailor* (1991); Doubleday 1996 (pbk)

A man falls overboard during a cruise retracing the voyage of Sinbad the Sailor and is rescued by sailors from Sinbad's world. In *The Last Voyage of Somebody the Sailor* Barth has constructed a postmodern tale which revels in time shifts, fancifully intermingled stories, and historical-cultural "revisionism."

In the view of the *London Sunday Times*, "John Barth is one of the few really original talents to emerge from the bleak landscape of contemporary American fiction. A virtuoso of stylistic pastiche, he makes inordinate demands on the reader [but in the end] fits the pieces of his schizophrenic double vision with unflagging gusto…." *Commonweal* calls *The Last Voyage* "clever as Scheherezade" and refers to Barth's hero as "variously exuberant, obnoxious, funny, self-conscious, and, not sober at all, but thoroughly intoxicated with sex, love, and story

telling, especially with their commingling." Novelist **Thomas Disch** (*Chicago Tribune*) points out that "While Barth's scheme [a double-stranded narration] makes for occasional tough sledding, there are corresponding rich rewards. Chief among them is a lapidary prose style that out-Nabokovs Nabokov, whether Barth is painting the scenery or caressing memories of erotic pleasure or evoking the Sensual Sublime." The *New York Review of Books* argues that the "voyages, sea fights, festivities, copulations, rapes, castrations, and intrigues are narrated with unflagging gusto. But after a while, tedium sets in …. "

OTHER MEDIA: Audiocassette (Dove/abr); REVIEWS: *ChiTrib* 2/3/91; *ComW* 5/17/91; *LJ* 12/90; *LST* 11/24/91; *NewR* 4/22/91; *NS&S* 1/17/92; *NYRB* 4/25/91; *NYTBR* 2/3/91; *TLS* 11/15/91; *WLT* Aut '92; *WPBW* 1/26/92

Berger, John (USA)

181   *To the Wedding* (1995); Pantheon 1995 (HC); Random House 1996 (pbk)

To the Wedding explores the power of love in the face of the most daunting of obstacles. In it, prize-winning English novelist John Berger tells the heart-breaking story of Ninon, a young French woman, who was "casually" infected with the AIDS virus through a brief, meaningless, teenage sexual encounter. When her fiancé, Gino, an Italian street vendor, learns of her illness, he refuses (despite her initial protests) to abandon their wedding plans. Wedding invitations are sent out and far-flung relatives begin to make their way to a small Italian village — Gorino, where the River Po reaches the open sea — for the ceremony. Although Berger employs a narrator (a Greek named Tsobarokos) he does not tell a linear tale, preferring to interweave memories, snatches of song and brief, almost cinematic, vignettes.

According to *Publishers Weekly* "Ritual and myth; technology and science; history both natural and human — each plays a crucial supporting role in [Berger's] novel." *Booklist* observes that Berger has "rendered this tale with the classic and devastating simplicity of a Greek tragedy … avoiding both melodrama and over-analysis." English novelist, **Louis de Bernieres** (*NYTBR*) assures us that *To the Wedding* "is far more than yet another sincere attempt to encompass the arbitrariness and injustice of AIDS, and infinitely more significant than a merely literary work. It is about the natural grandeur of human love." The *Times Literary Supplement* concludes that: "Shepherded along by a Greek narrator who maintains, along with an uncannily exact sense of the passing hours and minutes, a direct inspirational line to the universalities of classical tragedy, the brief narrative stanzas that compose this novel gather all history, all geography in their stately process."

READING GROUP GUIDE: REVIEWS: *BL* 5/2/95; *KR* 3/1/95; *LATBR* 7/16/95; *LJ* 5/1/95; *NY* 9/25/95; *NYTBR* 6/4/95; *PW* 3/6/95; *TLS* 9/29/95; *WPBW* 7/23/95

Blackburn, Julia (UK)

The Book of Color (1995); Vintage 1996 (pbk); See Section 6, #798

Brodkey, Harold (USA)

182   *Profane Friendship* (1994); Mercury House 1995 (pbk)

Profane Friendship (Brodkey's last novel before his untimely death from AIDS in 1996), was written in one year while the author was residing in Venice. Primarily a story about the power and constancy of love, it begins in the 1930s and concerns the 60-year friendship of two boys, Niles O'Hara and Giangiacomo Gallieni. Niles (Nino) has been brought to Venice by his father, an alcoholic expatriate American writer; Giangiacomo (Onni) is descended from a long line of Venetians. The boys are drawn to each other and develop a bond which, while not expressly sexual, certainly transcends ordinary friendship.

According to *Booklist*, "Lush, lyrical and haunting, *Profane Friendship* stands as one of the great novels of our time, its magnificence reminiscent of Henry James or Marcel Proust." English novelist **Alan Hollinghurst** (*WPBW*) draws our attention to Brodkey's "uncannily beautiful" descriptions of Venice: "the evocation of its light, color and sound are among the most haunting and attentive ever written and done wholly without art-historical stiffness. The city is brought to life as a dazzling compendium of sensations." The *New Statesman and Society* calls Brodky's second work a "bright novel with ambitions of its own [beyond its homage to Venice], and an honorable development on the contrary brilliance of *The Runaway Soul*." Irish novelist **Colm Toibin** (*London Review of Books*) concludes, however, that "*Profane Friendship* does not match up to *The Runaway Soul* in style or scope; it is too long and self-indulgent; some of it is only half-imagined. It is brave but it is not enough to make people turn and look at him."

RECOGNITION: *NYTBR* Notable Book of 1994; REVIEWS: *BL* 4/1/94; *KR* 1/1/94; *LATBR* 5/22/94; *LJ* 2/15/94; *LRB* 5/26/94; *NS&S* 4/8/94; *NY* 7/24/95; *NYTBR* 3/27/94; *Obs* 7/9/95; *PW* 1/17/94; *Spec* 4/9/94; *Time* 5/9/94; *TLS* 4/1/94; *WLT* Win '95; *WPBW* 3/6/94

183   *The Runaway Soul* (1991); FS&G 1991 (HC); H Holt 1997 (pbk)

In one of the most anticipated novels in American publishing history, protagonist Wiley Silenowicz, self-absorbed adopted son, looks back over his life. Brodkey employs a complicated narrative framework to tell his tale which encompasses the weighty themes of Jewishness, American-ness, sex and corruption. Described by most reviewers as "experimental" fiction, *The Runaway Soul* consists of long passages in italics, conversations with Self "A" and Self "B," buttressed by 100 pages devoted completely to one adolescent sexual encounter.

Upon its release in 1991, Brodkey's debut novel received mixed reviews. The *London Review of Books*, for example, found it to be "formless, plotless and graceless … " whereas the *New York Review of Books* applauded its "medley of Balkanized writings … various as a good minestrone … " and concluded that the reader "will find in it both tests of his adaptive powers and a rising sense of exhilaration." According to the *Library Journal:* "Brodkey's lush, carefully observed antidote to minimalism … will alternately enthrall and exasperate readers. The result? Brilliant, maddening, and essential for readers of good literature everywhere." *Kirkus Reviews*, while acknowledging that "many fans will fade early," suggests that we "[f]orget the Proust comparison, Brodkey is himself, and many pages here have the deep-rolling profound thrust, painterly originality, and lightning-bolt flash of great art."

REVIEWS: *KR* 8/15/91; *LJ* 11/1/91; *LRB* 11/21/91; *NewsWk* 11/18/91; *NS&S* 11/29/91; *NYTBR* 11/10/91; *PW* 8/30/91; *TLS* 11/15/91

Burgess, Anthony (UK)

184   *Byrne* (1995); Carroll & Graf 1997 (HC); 1998 (pbk)

Anthony Burgess's posthumously published novel, *Byrne*, is written in verse, a Byronic ottava rima (à la "Don Juan") to be precise, and is, by most accounts, surprisingly accessible and frequently engaging. The eponymous Byrne is a wild Irishman, an artist, failed composer and lover of wine and women in short "a lecherous, defective dreamer." Byrne becomes a cropper (a Nazi sympathizer in the end) but his descent is amusingly and imaginatively told. The second half of the novel (still in verse) is given over to some of Byrne's offspring who are busily at work rehabilitating their father's reputation.

The *Times Literary Supplement* observes that "It is hard to convey the full flavor of this great feast of a book, which (compelling both wonder and delight) is an abundant blend of Rabelesian bawdiness and Nabokovian complexity." Henry Kisor (*Chicago Sun-Times*) calls *Byrne* "mesmerizing" and observes that although "Burgess has never been easy … he is not at all impenetrable … [for] there has always been an infectious joy to his romps in the meadows of language. He could leap gaily from

Welsh to French to Malay to Yiddish in one breath." The *New York Times Book Review* observes that *Byrne* "is so fresh, funny and inventive that it ranks among his finest creations." *Kirkus Reviews* judged Burgess's last novel to be "one of the most delightful books of the decade" and must have caused Byron to roll "over in his grave. Laughing." *Publishers Weekly* concludes that *Byrne* "is an endlessly stimulating, cherishable memento from a writer [one of the most multitalented of the century] whose soaring imagination, capacious mind and Voltairian skepticism adorned his age."

RECOGNITION: *NYTBR* Notable Book of 1997; REVIEWS: *AtlM* 10/97; *BL* 9/1/97; *ChiSun* 8/24/97; *KR* 7/15/97; *LJ* 9/1/97; *LRB* 11/30/95; *NS&S* 10/20/95; *NYTBR* 11/30/97; *Obs* 10/22/95; *PW* 7/14/97; *Spec* 11/4/95; *TLS* 9/29/95; *WLT* Sum '96; *WPBW* 1/18/98

Butler, Robert Olen (USA)

185 *They Whisper* (1993); Holt 1993 (HC); Viking Penguin 1995 (pbk)

In his first novel since his award-winning collection of short stories (*A Good Scent from a Strange Mountain*) Robert Olen Butler explores the consciousness of a man whose entire life has been defined by his sexuality. Ira Holloway is a PR executive, a Vietnam veteran, son of a steelworker, husband to Fiona, and father of an eight-year-old. He is also obsessed with women, and, as he moves into middle age, is driven to examine this most defining feature of his life. Fiona, partly because of her fear of Ira's infidelities, has retreated into the safety of strict Catholicism.

As *Publishers Weekly* points out that "This is a literary novel about the physical chemistry of sensual love, told in lyrical prose via a sensitive narrator who venerates the memories of the many women with whom he has coupled, and who 'hears' the whispers of their voices, which are [eventually] interwoven into the text." Novelist Josephine Hart (*WPBW*) observes that "In literature, there are tales of singular passion — Emily Brontë's *Wuthering Heights*, Leo Tolstoy's *Anna Karenina*, Antoine Francois Prevost's *Manon Lescaut*. And then there are others, which tell of a multitude of amatory encounters — Molière's *Don Juan*, Cassanova's *Memoires* and Guy de Maupassant's *Bel-Ami*. Robert Olen Butler's *They Whisper* belongs to the latter category. It is a profound, disturbing and important book." According to Jane Smiley (*NYTBR*) *They Whisper* "fully partakes of the ambiguous nature of sexual politics in our time" and although finding herself "horrified" by some of Ira's fantasies" concedes that "it isn't hard to be seduced by Ira's voice which is also Mr. Butler's" and concludes that the novel "deserves a wide, if unavoidably ambivalent audience." *Newsweek* provides a less encour-

aging assessment: "a novel over stuffed with rhapsodic sex scenes — and sentences that run on and on to show how jeeped up the characters are." The *London Times* agrees, pointing out that "The problem with this book is that if one subtracts its lengthy descriptions of sexual acts, there is little in the way of plot, characterization or ideas to make it interesting."

REVIEWS: *BL* 11/1/93; *LATBR* 1/20/94; *LJ* 12/93; *LT* 3/24/94; *NewsWk* 2/14/94; *NYTBR* 2/13/94; *PW* 10/11/93; *Time* 2/21/94; *TLS* 3/18/94; *WPBW* 1/16/94

Cameron, Peter (USA)

Andorra (1996); FS&G 1996 (HC); Plume 1998 (pbk); See Section 6, #692

Carey, Peter (Australia/USA)

186 *The Unusual Life of Tristan Smith* (1994); Knopf 1995 (HC); Random House 1996 (pbk)

Tristan Smith, narrator and protagonist of Peter Carey's intricately structured 7th novel, is a grotesquely deformed young man, the son of Felicity Smith, a dissident actress who runs a theater company in Efica:

... a country so unimportant that you are already confusing the name with Ithaca or Africa, a name so unmemorable it could only have been born of a committee, although it remains, nonetheless, the home of nearly three million of the earth's people, and they, like you, have no small opinion of themselves, have artists and poets who are pleased to criticize its shortcomings and celebrate its charms, who return home to the eighteen little islands between the Tropic of Capricorn and the 30th parallel, convinced that their windswept coastline is the most beautiful on earth.

The Unusual Life of Tristan Smith is set in a parallel universe — specifically the countries of Voorstand (a colonial power), and Efica (a satellite state). The story follows Tristan from his ghastly early childhood, through his experiences with a radical theater company in Efica (where he becomes adept at costuming and disguise) to his journeys through Voorstand — a fully realized dystopia — in search of his father.

In the view of the *New York Review of Books*: "One of Carey's underlying conceits is that the far-flung provinces of the English-speaking world are engaged in permanent intramural competition. In the antipodes, the Australian team longs to win so it will be allowed to return home to England, where it knows itself to be despised. Meanwhile the Americans have outstripped their fellow former colonists by growing up to be an imperial power themselves, lording it about. In *The Unusual Life of Tristan Smith*'s fabulous version of this, the United States, complete with its macabre Disneyland culture, appears as the dreaded and envied nation of Voorstand...." Novelist **Carol Shields** (*NYTBR*) agrees, observing that Carey has written a "sustained meditation on the folly of imperialism ... [advancing the notion] that neither the weak nor the strong have been able to make themselves a safe home in the world." According to *Publishers Weekly*'s starred review, "Carey's novel approach to the narrative — the entire tale is in the form of Tristan's direct testimony to formal authorities of Voorstand culture — is brilliantly maintained throughout, and the fairy-tale quality of its figuration makes for a surpassingly rich feast of metaphors and mercurial meanings — George Orwell and Lewis Carroll wrapped into one." The *Australian Book Review* calls it a "dazzling book, a sprawling, sensual, rambunctious marvel of a novel [which] takes enormous risks, not least that of demanding our understanding for the monstrous." English novelist **Jonathan Coe** (*TLS*) suggests that "There's almost terminal bleakness in Carey's presentation of human relationship ... a disinclination for stylistic adornment [that makes] the process of entering his fictional worlds (both real and invented) a positively Spartan experience. There's the question, too, of his pronounced taste for the grotesque, which in this novel is taken to new extremes."

RECOGNITION: Winner of the 1994 *Age* "Book of the Year" Award and the Australian Book Seller's Association Book of the Year Award; *NYTBR* Notable Book of 1995; REVIEWS: *AusBkRev* 9/94; *LJ* 1/95; *LRB* 9/22/94; *NYTBR* 2/12/95; *NYRB* 6/22/95; *PW* 12/19/94; *TLS* 9/2/94

Castillo, Ana (USA)

187   *So Far from God* (1993); Norton 1993 (HC); NAL-Dutton 1994 (pbk)

Juggling resurrections, ectoplasmic hauntings, an industrial waste scandal, hermetic healing and much more, Ana Castillo's 3rd novel is set in Tome, a small town in southern New Mexico. *So Far from God* features the indomitable Sofia and her four daughters: La Loca (risen from the dead), Caridad (miraculously cured), Esperanza (a journalist assigned to Desert Storm), and Fe (exposed to toxic chemicals at her workplace). Life for these women is neither easy nor predictable and their intertwined stories are both ethereal and earthy and are permeated with the combination of faith and deep magic characteristic of their Mexican-American culture. The novel's structure conforms somewhat to a "telenova" the widely popular Spanish-language soap operas.

According to *Publishers Weekly*, "Castillo takes a page from the magical realist school of Latin American fiction, but one senses the North American component of this Chicana voice: in her work, occult phenomena are literal, not symbolic; life is

traumatic and brutal — as are men — but death is merely tentative...." The *Times Literary Supplement* notes that "Ana Castillo's *So Far from God* creates the illusion of a story told orally.... As in the best tradition of folk tales, an informal tone preserves the nuances of spoken narrative and a local flavour is added by a generous sprinkling of Latino-Hispanic words and local lore." The *Library Journal* concludes that "Although filled with tragic events, the narrative also offers hope in its portrayal of successful journeys towards wholeness by each of the five women."

RECOGNITION: *NYTBR* Notable Book of 1993; REVIEWS: *BellesL* Fall '93; *BL* 4/1/93; *Choice* 9/93; *ComW* 1/14/94; *LATBR* 5/16/93; *LJ* 7/93; *NYTBR* 12/5/93; *PW* 2/22/93; *TLS* 9/30/94; *WPBW* 5/14/95

Christopher, Nicholas (USA)

Veronica (1996); Doubleday 1996 (HC); See Section 6, #696

Coe, Jonathan (UK)

188   *House of Sleep* (1997); Knopf 1998 (HC)

Huge, grey and imposing, Ashdown stood on a headland, some twenty yards from the sheer face of the cliff, where it had stood for more than a hundred years. All day, the gulls wheeled around its spires and tourelles, keening themselves hoarse. All day, and all night, the waves threw themselves dementedly against their rocky barricade, sending an endless roar like heavy traffic through the glacial rooms and mazy, echoing corridors of the old house.

Jonathan Coe's atmospheric new novel is set in an imposing cliff-top manor on the English coast. Once a university residence, Ashdown has been transformed into a clinic specializing in the treatment of sleep disorders. Coincidentally, a number of the former student residents of the manor have been drawn back in search of remedies for their sleep-related maladies. Chief among them are Sarah, a narcoleptic who has trouble distinguishing between reality and dreams, and Terry, a film critic with chronic insomnia. The author employs an unusual structural device: the odd-numbered chapters of this novel are set mainly in the years 1983–1984; the even-numbered chapters are set in the last two weeks of June 1996.

The *Times Literary Supplement* calls *The House of Sleep* "a fiercely clever, witty novel" which "plunges us from romance to tragedy, from film noir to farce.... There are sublimely silly scenes, but there are also moments of exquisite pathos and beauty." According to the *New Statesman*, this is "a book of playful games and combinations, written with great brio.... It's also, as a worthy novel should be, a humane pleasure to read." The *L.A. Times*

Book Review observes that "*The House of Sleep* is put together with the compressed complexity of a watch movement: cogs and springs setting off other cogs and springs, movements and meanings doubled and reversed, coincidences that turn out to be precisely engineered, randomly emerging characters and events that, in fact, are fatefully linked." *Kirkus Reviews* calls Coe's book a "droll, ingenious novel, its satire nicely leavened by true romance," and observes that the "hectic plot provides [the author] with plenty of opportunities to satirize British medicine and the increasingly harsh, hustling nature of British society, as well as the confusions of modern love." According to *Salon* "For all the metaliterary touches Coe indulges in ... he's motivated primarily by rage and compassion. Margaret Thatcher and her legacy have provided him with as great a subject as the workhouses and orphanages did Dickens.... Coe is writing about a society suffering the aftereffects of an experiment intended to separate poor from rich, weak from strong, conducted for the simple pleasure of being able to exert such power."

RECOGNITION: *NYTBR* Notable Book of 1998; REVIEWS: *BL* 12/15/97; *Guard* 11/6/97; *KR* 1/1/98; *LATBR* 3/1/98; *LJ* 1/98; *LRB* 6/19/97; *LST* 5/25/97; *NS* 6/27/97; *NYTBR* 3/29/98; *Obs* 5/18/97; *PW* 2/9/98; *Salon* 4/2/98; *Spec* 5/24/97; *TLS* 5/23/97

Collignon, Rick (USA)

Perdido (1997); MacMurray & Beck 1997 (HC); See Section 6, #697

The Journal of Antonio Montoya (1996); MacMurray & Beck 1996 (HC); Avon 1997 (pbk); See Section 6, #698

Coover, Robert (USA)

Briar Rose (1997) Grove-Atlantic 1997 (HC) & 1998 (pbk); See Section 8, #999

189 *John's Wife* (1996); S&S 1996 (HC); 1997 (pbk)

John, a bullying, gregarious, amoral and highly successful developer wields considerable clout in the small Midwestern town he calls home. His wife, described by the author as "Coveted object, elusive mystery, beloved ideal, hated rival, princess, saint or social asset," commands her own share of attention. In Robert Coover's satirical take on contemporary life, no vulgarism is left unexplored or human weakness unplumbed.

According to *Kirkus Reviews* "Our most abrasive and challenging postmodernist writes at pretty nearly peak level in this mock-epic chronicle of the vagaries of sex, greed, and death in an unnamed Midwestern town whose inhabitants are all linked together by their admiration for — or friendship or obsession with — the opaque title character...." In the view of the *Los Angeles Times Book Review*, reading "Robert Coover's new novel about lewd, magical and mysterious happenings in a generic small American town is like being sucked down into a whirlpool. Is it all a bit too much? ... No doubt. Still Coover's skills are formidable ... and [*John's Wife*] has to be the one of the most ambitious novels of 1996, and one of the funniest." *Antioch Review* while acknowledging that Coover's novel has "an unsettling and almost nightmarish quality," calls it "a profoundly original work of fiction ... [which ranges] from farce to sadomasochism, alternating social criticism with Borgesian magic realism." The *Review* concludes that Coover's novel "is an altogether singular and memorable achievement by one of this country's most powerful voices." Novelist Brad Leithauser (*NYTBR*) takes a more jaundiced view of *John's Wife*, pointing out that its plot "is a rambling, reiterated and squalid affair. A not untypical paragraph opens with a flatulence contest, moves on to a forcible injection of hallucinogens administered by a mosquito spray gun, and concludes with group sex with a 14-year-old 'guttersnipe.'" The *San Francisco Chronicle Book Review* concludes that "once again, Coover ... proves himself the supreme chronicler of the unreality of American life."

RECOGNITION: *NYTBR* Notable Book of 1996; REVIEWS: *AntR* Sum '96; *BL* 4/15/96; *CSM* 4/5/96; *KR* 2/1/96; *LJ* 3/1/96; *NYRB* 10/17/96; *NYT* 4/1/96; *NYTBR* 4/7/96; *PW* 2/5/96; *SFCBR* 3/31/96; *WPBW* 3/31/96; *WSJ* 4/5/96

Pinocchio in Venice (1991); Grove-Atlantic 1997 (pbk); See Section 8, #1000

D'Aguiar, Fred

Dear Future (1996); Avon 1998 (pbk); See Section 4, #430

Darton, Eric (USA)

Free City (1996); W.W. Norton 1996 (HC); See Section 6, #807

Dawson, Carol (USA)

Meeting the Minotaur (1997); Algonquin 1997 (HC); See Section 8, #1002

de Bernieres, Louis (UK)

190 *The Troublesome Offspring of Cardinal Guzman* (1992); Morrow 1994 (HC); Vintage 1998 (pbk)

The Troublesome Offspring of Cardinal Guzman is the third novel by Louis de Bernieres to be set in the fictional Andean city of Cochadebajo de los Gatos. The colorfully eccentric and highly re-sourceful inhabitants of the city have (in earlier volumes) overthrown a repressive dictator and eliminated a powerful drug baron. They must now contend with a rigidly repressive church hierarchy which is determined to root out all forms of non-conformity and licentiousness, an objective that does not, safe to say, sit well with the notoriously pleasure-loving, "free-thinking" residents of Cochadebajo. Succinctly described by the *NYTBR* as a novel which "concerns good and evil and a clergyman who has his inner demons removed surgically," *The Troublesome Offspring* skillfully combines mordant humor and trenchant social commentary.

According to *Publishers Weekly*, "this deftly constructed novel pokes gentle fun at the well-mined genre of magical realism while providing an exuberant portrayal of a Latin America in which anything is possible." The *TLS* observes that *The Troublesome Offspring* ... "like its predecessors, is written in short episodes, from a giddily kaleido-scopic range of narrative view points, but always in a tightly controlled style, clipped yet archly aure-ate, which contrasts with the carnivalesque energy, vulgarity and violence of the subject matter." The *London Review of Books* argues that "for British readers steeped in the stabilities of the granny novel, the tales of Cochadebajo will be disturbing: broad sexual comedy (the President's exploits with his surgically enhanced penis, for instance) mixes with visionary flights of great beauty and graphic descriptions of the most nauseating tortures and rape." *Booklist* calls *The Troublesome Offspring of Cardinal Guzman* "wonderful ... by turns bawdy, uproarious, and tragic" and suggests that it "illuminates the tragedies which have [long] plagued Latin America ... bad government, drug lords, machismo that leads to mayhem, and, most important, the Catholic church."

REVIEWS: *AtlM* 3/94; *BL* 1/1/94; *LJ* 1/94; *LRB* 9/24/92; *NYTBR* 5/8/94; *PW* 12/20/93; *TLS* 8/21/92

191   *Señor Vivo and the Coca Lord* (1992); Vintage 1998 (pbk)

English novelist Louis de Bernieres' 2nd novel is set in an imaginary country (reminiscent of Colombia) where ancient shibboleths still hold sway, the supernatural is freely acknowledged, spirits walk the streets and the drug trade warps an entire society. *Señor Vivo and the Coca Lord* tells the story of a young South American philosophy teacher, Dionisio Vivo, who finds himself on a drug baron's hit list after writing letters of outrage to the local newspaper. When the townspeople begin to despair of ever breaking the grip of the drug lords, assistance comes from an unexpected quarter: Hec-

toro, a fierce soldier who died in a 1533 avalanche but who has been brought back to life by a sorcerer.

The *New York Times Book Reviewer* observes that *Señor Vivo and the Coca Lord* (dedicated as it is to the judge, Mariela Espinosa Arango, who was assassinated in Medellin in 1989) is a "deadly serious novel" and concludes that "As an imaginative denunciation of the cocaine trade and its human costs, [Mr. de Bernieres' novel] is amusing, terrifying and ultimately sobering." In the view of *Booklist*, "Praise can be expected for this tale of tragedy and triumph." According to the *Times Literary Supplement*, *Señor Vivo and the Coca Lord*, "following and improving on *The War of Don Emmanuel's Nether Parts* (1990), is magical realism much as E.P. Thompson's *The Sykaos Papers* is science fiction: both novels exploit genre to free a subjective moral voice whose keynote is a terrible anger. But where Thompson and Don Emmanuel often tell of anger, *Señor Vivo and the Coca Lord*, taking advantage of the archetypal country and wonderful characters of *Don Emmanuel*, shows it...."

REVIEWS: *BL* 8/92; *LJ* 7/92; *NYTBR* 9/13/92; *PW* 5/25/92; *TLS* 6/21/91; *WPBW* 8/17/92

192   *The War of Don Emmanuel's Nether Parts* (1990); Vintage 1998 (pbk)

When the haughty Dona Constanza diverts the village river to fill her swimming pool, the government, convinced that communist insurgents are to blame, dispatches the brutal Commander Figueras and his men to hunt them down. Don Emmanuel's "war" erupts when Figueras, hearing gunfire in a lowland village (it is actually the belch-ing of a malfunctioning bulldozer) orders his troops into action. One thing leads to many others (including ribald sex, torture, and supernatural events) in de Bernieres' serio-comic pastiche of magical realism.

In the view of the *Library Journal*, "a motley assortment of horrific or hilarious vignettes resolve themselves into an imaginative story set in a troubled fictional but familiar South American country." The *London Times* while pointing out that the novel does not lend itself to summarization, emphasizes that "what should be isolated and applauded is the fact that Mr. de Bernieres has the surest of narrative touches, an uplifting sense of the exotic and the easy-going wit which makes even the book's most brutal passages bearable...." According to the *Washington Post Book World* "Here is a wise, funny novel that nicely walks a precarious edge between slapstick and pathos, never once stumbling or losing its balance." The *New York Times Book Review* calls de Bernieres's debut novel a "mischievously brilliant ... romance" and concludes that "with his first book, Mr. de Bernieres joins a select group of British writers, including

David Lodge and A.S. Byatt, who have recently discovered marvelous new possibilities in this venerable genre." *Publishers Weekly*, in its starred review, argues that "De Bernieres, who taught in Colombia, captures the beauty, hope and desperation of Latin America as few other writers have done."

RECOGNITION: Winner of the Commonwealth Writer's Prize for Best First Fiction; *NYTBR* "Editors' Choice" 1992; REVIEWS: *AtlM* 3/92; *LJ* 7/92; *LT* 8/9/90; *NYTBR* 3/1/92; *PW* 12/6/91; *WPBW* 2/2/92

DeLillo, Don (USA)

193 *Underworld* (1997); Scribner 1997 (HC)

Don DeLillo's highly acclaimed 12th novel spans five decades and incorporates multiple voices to tell the story of America from the dawn of the nuclear age through the Cold War era. It is also the history of garbage: from rubble strewn urban lots to the nuclear waste dumps which dot the American southwest. And, finally, it's a love story. *Underworld* opens in 1951 — during the final game of the Giants-Dodgers pennant race — a game that was won (for the Giants) by Bobby Thomson's home run, referred to, in the following day's newspaper headlines, as "the Shot Heard Round the World." The other featured story that day was the chilling report that the Russians had successfully tested their own nuclear bomb. *Underworld*, although rife with minor characters, features two protagonists: Nick Shay, a waste analyst, and Klara Sax, an artist who, using decommissioned B-52s, has created a cold war monument in the American desert. A unifying thread in this sprawling, multi-limbed novel is the tracing back — from its current 1990's owner (Nick Shay) to its original owner (a Harlem resident who, as a 12-year-old caught the ball in the bleachers) — of the game-winning baseball from that 1951 pennant game.

Michael Dirda (*WPBW*) suggests that the reader should think of *Underworld* "as a great Victorian style panoramic novel — *The Way We Live Now*, say — or even as a 12-part miniseries, titled perhaps 'Cold War and Remembrance.' For DeLillo's masterpiece provides both a cultural history of America during the Bomb era and a suspenseful journey into the past." According to the *Times Literary Supplement* "With *Underworld*, DeLillo confirms himself in the select group of great American writers truly equal to the temper of very strange times. DeLillo claimed in 1982 that Thomas Pynchon and William Gaddis were the writers who 'set the standard.' In this he showed foresight, for the Bellow-Updike axis more favoured [in Great Britain] still belongs to an honorable tradition of classic realism — the problem is ... Amer-

ica no longer does." Michiko Kakutani (*NYT*) asserts that *Underworld* "is an amazing performance ... [in which the author showcases] his razzle-dazzle talents as a writer: his gift for surreal, dead-on dialogue, his jazzy, synthetic prose; and his cinematic ability to convey the simultaneity of existence." *Booklist* opines that "like novelists E.L. Doctorow and Thomas Pynchon ... [DeLillo] uses historical figures to great effect, but DeLillo is a far more emotive and spiritual writer, and *Underworld* is a ravishingly beautiful symphony of a novel." English novelist **Michael Dibdin**, writing in the *London Sunday Times*, suggests that while *Underworld* is marred by a touch of authorial "paranoia," what emerges is "a nostalgic elegy for a vanished sense of community and shared values, and a brilliantly crowded, stylized canvas similar to the Breughel paintings that are leitmotif in the text: naturalism with attitude." According to the *New York Review of Books* "Large thematic strokes may define [DeLillo's] architecture, but within lies continual surprise at the fluidity and resilience of the human conditions. All he wants you to see are the contradictions."

OTHER MEDIA: Audiocassette (Books-on-Tape/unabr); RECOGNITION: Nominated for the 1997 National Book Award and the National Book Critic Circle Award; nominated for the 1998 Pulitzer Prize for Fiction; *Time* magazine "Best Book" of 1997; *L.A. Times* "Best Books" 1997 (Top Ten); *Publishers Weekly* "Best Books" 1997; *NYTBR* Notable Book of 1997; *Booklist* Editors' Choice 1997; *Chicago Sun-Times* Best Books of 1997; REVIEWS: *BL* 8/19/97; *EW* 10/3/97; *KR* 7/1/97; *LATBR* 9/28/97; *LST* 1/4/98; *NewsWk* 9/22/97; *NY* 9/15/97; *NYRB* 11/6/97; *NYT* 9/1/97; *PW* 7/14/97; *Time* 9/29/97; *TLS* 12/26/97; *WPBW* 9/28/97

194 *Mao II* (1991); Viking Penguin 1992 (pbk)

Mao II — which opens at Yankee stadium where a mass marriage ceremony, involving 1,300 Moonies, is being conducted — offers a probing examination of some of the more disturbing trends in contemporary society: the displacement of traditional cultural arbiters by a sensation-seeking media, an increasing moral vacuum resulting from a widespread loss of faith, and the ever-more frenetic search for material gratification. Don DeLillo's 10th novel features Bill Gray a reclusive writer, unexpectedly blown into the world of political violence. Grey, for reasons which will become increasingly clear, is haunted by the intermingled spirits of such diverse figures as Andy Warhol, Mao Zedong, victims of the Hillsborough football disaster, and the Ayatollah Khomeini. As the *Library Journal* observes, Gray's "legend abounds while he slowly deteriorates from drinking, drugs, and depression" ... until, that is, he meets photojournalist Britta Nilsson.

According to the *Chicago Tribune* "Terrorists, Moonies, eccentric artists and reclusive writers, *Mao II* gathers them all in a world that is full of crowds but promises little more than the isolation of the homeless. DeLillo's genius, however, is to question rather than condemn — to ask.... 'When the old God leaves the world. What happens to all the expended faith?'" *Quill & Quire* notes that "In construction and style Don DeLillo's 10th novel is as sleekly elegant and starkly menacing as a razor blade. With deceptive simplicity he has sculpted a compact and compelling chronicle of the morally bankrupt times in which we live." In the view of the *New Statesman and Society,* "The book debates the degree to which the terrorist has replaced the writer as a shaper of consciousness in an age defined by the 'mass visual litter' of 24-hour history.... [DeLillo] refuses to lead the way out of this post-modern theme park, addressing himself to a vigorous examination of its functioning." The *San Francisco Chronicle* describes *Mao II* as "a beautifully readable, haunting tale that jolts along at its own unsettling pace." The *London Sunday Times* declares that "*Mao II* is a work of fiction not only astonishingly fitting for our times, but rich and rewarding for anyone wishing to understand them."

OTHER MEDIA: Audiocassette (NAL-Dutton/abr); RECOGNITION: Winner of the 1992 EN/Faulkner Award; *NYTBR* Notable Book of 1991; REVIEWS: *ChiTrib* 6/23/91; *Econ* 6/15/91; *LJ* 4/15/91; *LRB* 9/12/91; *LST* 9/8/91; *NewsWk* 6/3/91; *NS&S* 9/13/91; *NY* 6/24/91; *NYRB* 6/27/91; *NYTBR* 6/9/91; *PW* 4/12/91; *Q&Q* 7/91; *SFRB* Sum '91; *Time* 6/10/91; *TLS* 8/30/91; *WLT* Win '92

Denton, Bradley (USA)

Lunatics (1996); St. Martin's 1996 (HC); Bantam 1997 (pbk); See Section 7, #831

Divakaruni, Chitra

The Mistress of Spices (1997); Anchor 1997 (HC); 1998 (pbk); See Section 2, #112

Dixon, Stephen (USA)

195   *Gould: A Novel in Two Novels* (1997); H Holt 1997 (HC); 1998 (pbk)

Stephen Dixon's *Gould* features the eponymous Gould Bookbinder, a thoroughly self-absorbed college instructor and some-time book reviewer. Dixon, a well-regarded postmodernist, has constructed a work of fiction comprised of two novellas (each presenting a very different perspective) exploring one man's obsession with both sex and procreation. As the *L.A. Times Book Review* notes, there are 227 pages in *Gould* and only one paragraph.

According to *Publishers Weekly,* "*Gould* [is] more profound, if less flashy, than [the author's previous novel] *Interstate* ... its subject is human malleability ... [its] theme ... is that character — those consistencies of behavior and motive on which fiction traditionally stands — is an illusion." The *New York Times Book Review* observes that although "his [anti]hero starts the narrative as a repellent, sex-driven creep, Stephen Dixon has effected a strange turnaround by the close of this remarkable book: we may not like Gould Bookbinder, but after being privy to the minutest contortions of his interior life, we may at least feel stirrings of forgiveness, if not outright sympathy." *Kirkus Reviews* disagrees, calling *Gould* an "[e]xtremely readable and clever work [where] the pages don't add up to much except sex and more sex, described in clinical detail and with clinical dispassion, featuring a cast of characters who seem incapable of thinking about anything other than their bodies and their appetites."

REVIEWS: *BL* 2/15/97; *KR* 11/15/96; *LATBR* 2/23/97; *LJ* 1/97; *NYTBR* 4/20/97; *PW* 1/6/97

196   *Interstate* (1995); H Holt 1995 (HC); 1997 (pbk)

Stephen Dixon's 17th work of fiction, is a haunting, intricately structured novel that plumbs the depths of a father's love for his child. Consisting of eight chapters, each representing an alternative version of a horrific act of random violence, *Interstate* makes for difficult yet rewarding reading. As the book opens, a father and his two daughters are driving on a superhighway when they are shot at by two punks driving by in a van. Dixon's use of multiple versions has led to comparisons with such recognized modernists as Italo Calvino and Alain Robbe-Grillet.

According to the *Chicago Tribune* "The eight variations of this catastrophe give *Interstate* its special depth. The killing itself is powerful, but the world surrounding it is what makes Dixon's novel something more than a dramatized headline in the newspaper." The *Library Journal* calls *Interstate* a "timely, disturbing work" and observes that "Dixon's dense, plainspoken prose perfectly mirrors the chaotic workings of a mind riddled with rage and guilt." In the view of *Publishers Weekly,* "Dixon's crisis-mode narrative runs together in one seemingly jumbled, breathless rush, with evocative thoughts causing memories to surface not just in the minds of the narrators but in the reader's mind as well. Jarringly perceptive and darkly compelling, this novel will confirm Dixon as a writer of stature." The *L.A. Times Book Review* concludes that "in *Interstate* Dixon has honed his radical techniques to their finest sheen."

RECOGNITION: Nominated for the 1995 National Book Award; *Booklist:* "Editors' Choice" 1995; *PW*: "Best Book" 1995; REVIEWS: *BL* 6/1/95; *Chi Trib* 6/11/95; *KR* 3/1/95; *LATBR* 5/20/95; *LJ* 5/1/95; *NYTBR* 5/21/95; *PW* 4/3/95; *SFRB* 7/95

197   *Frog* (1991); H Holt 1997 (pbk)

Hailed by some critics as the *Finnigan's Wake* of our generation, Stephen Dixon's first novel, with its convoluted structure, light-hearted wordplay, and rhythmic prose, exhibits a distinctly Joycean quality. Conceived as a series of stories about Howard Tetch — a New York City–bred writer and academic, who is currently a member of the faculty of a major university located in Baltimore — Dixon's initially "diachronous" tale begins to cohere as the novel progresses.

Publishers Weekly observes that "opening portentously with the protagonist's trip to Kafka's grave…. Dixon's 860-page Joycean monolith deftly portrays the urban nightmare as cosmic candy…. Readers attuned to the author's run-on style may warm to a cunning, sexy, audacious performance; others will find this an arty bore." In the view of the *Library Journal*, "Dixon, best known as a gifted short story writer, demonstrates his mastery of the novel here, imaginatively expanding on a variety of themes, like a great jazz soloist." According to the *New York Times Book Review* "It is exasperating that [*Frog*] … which relies on the crude honesty of tom-tom prose in a freewheeling structure, should nevertheless be a work of undeniable resonance."

RECOGNITION: Nominated for the 1992 PEN/Faulkner Award and for the 1991 National Book Award; REVIEWS: *LJ* 1/92; *NYTBR* 11/17/91; *PW* 11/8/91; *WPBW* 1/19/92

Dobyns, Stephen (USA)

198   *The Wrestler's Cruel Study* (1993); WW Norton 1993 (HC); 1995 (pbk)

Stephen Dobyn's reality-bending novel is narrated by Michael Marmaduke, a professional wrestler known as "Marduk the Magnificent," whose fiancée, a gentle young woman by the name of Rose White, has been brutally kidnapped by a pair of thugs in gorilla suits. The bulk of Stephen Dobyn's decidedly postmodern novel is taken up with Marmaduke's search for his damsel in distress. Subplots straight out of the Brothers Grimm abound and minor characters include Violet, Rose's (possibly) evil twin, Primus Muldoon, Marmaduke's cerebral manager, and two detectives by the name of Brodsky and Gapsky.

Booklist calls *The Wrestler's Cruel Study* a "marvelous creation, rambunctious and clever" and observes that "Michael's quest, which involves both mayhem and mysticism, takes us, literally, down into New York City's bizarrely combative spiritual

underground, and metaphorically, deep into the age-old dispute over the origin and nature of good and evil…." *Kirkus Reviews* describes Marmaduke's search as "a kind of philosophical joyride that frequently invokes Nietzsche as it investigates such matters as dualism and causality" and concludes that "there are sluggish passages … notably those involving the hairsplitting Disputants, but only a churl would linger over defects in a work that is so stunningly imaginative, so liberating in its sense of possibilities in life and art, and so much fun." According to the *Washington Post Book World* "There are those who will say that this is not a novel and indeed, it bears about as much resemblance to the Novel as the theatrical event we call Professional Wrestling bears to the sport of the same name. But that's the gimmick and it works. Like its central metaphor, *The Wrestler's Cruel Study* puts on a lively show for those who are willing to set aside conventional literary expectations (morals and money and manners) and concentrate on less serious matters, such as the fall of man. Suspension of disbelief is more than a requirement for the reader, it is the very hair and bone of the story itself."

RECOGNITION: *NYTBR* Notable Book of 1993; REVIEWS: *BL* 7/93; *EW* 7/23/93; *KR* 6/1/93; *LATBR* 8/26/93; *LJ* 7/93; *NYTBR* 8/15/93; *PW* 6/21/93; *WPBW* 7/19/93

Duncker, Patricia (UK)

199   *Hallucinating Foucault* (1996); Ecco 1997 (HC)

I took my first degree at Cambridge. I studied French and German. In my last year I specialized in modern French, linguistics and literature. I also took a paper in modern French history. I ought to tell you that because it explains why I got so involved in the whole affair. It was already my chief interest, my intellectual passion if you like. It doesn't explain why it all became so personal. Or maybe it does. You see when I decided to go on with my studies and do a doctorate I was making a real commitment, not just to my writing, but to his. Writing a thesis is a lonely obsessive activity. You live inside your head, nowhere else. University libraries are like madhouses, full of people pursuing wraiths, hunches, obsessions. The person with whom you spend most of your time is the person you're writing about. Some people write about schools, groups of artists, historical trends or political tendencies. There were graduates doing that in my year, but usually one central figure emerges. In my case it was Paul Michel.

Patricia Duncker's engagingly cerebral debut novel concerns a British doctoral student's obsessive interest in a (fictional) writer, Paul Michel, the gay *infant terrible* of the contemporary French literary world. Michel, diagnosed as paranoid schizophrenic, has been incarcerated (since the death of the philosopher Foucault — a precipitating event in Michel's descent into madness) in an asylum for the "dangerously insane." The student, who remains nameless throughout the story, prompted by his ferociously intelligent live-in-lover, eventually travels to the asylum where he plans to liberate the writer in the name of artistic freedom. A bizarre, sexually charged triangle develops. Ms. Duncker skillfully weaves elements of French deconstuctionism (including the relationship of author to reader) and theories of mental illness into her academic romance.

According to the *New Statesman* "as a story about being burnt by language and its emotive properties, Duncker has brought complex critical ideas into the realms of drama — and love. As such, this is a compelling *tour de force* lit with both passion and verve." In the view of the *Times Literary Supplement* "Duncker never allows the elements of her story — sexual passion, madness, creativity — to overwhelm the calm tone of her narration. The reader's and the writer's voices are left to speak without interruption, and their hopeless situation is all the more affecting." *Publishers Weekly* observes that "Duncker's writing is oblique and thoughtful, a blend of playful narrative twists and meditations on the act of reading, the nature of fiction and homosexuality and the relationship between love and madness." The *Library Journal* concludes that "This is elegant and illuminating storytelling accessible to those who have never heard of Foucault and highly recommended to those who have philosophic interests in hermeneutics as well." The *Washington Post Book World* calls *Hallucinating Foucault* "a psychological mystery story that is at the same time a celebration of the reading act and a fitfully intriguing meditation on madness and artistic genius, sexual ambiguity, and the deeper legacies of art."

RECOGNITION: *LATBR* "Recommended Titles" 1997; REVIEWS: *BL* 2/1/97; *LATBR* 3/7/97; *LJ* 12/96; *NS&S* 3/1/96; *NYTBR* 2/16/97; *PW* 10/21/96; *Time* 3/3/97; *TLS* 3/22/96; *WPBW* 2/7/97

Dyja, Thomas (USA)

200   *Play for a Kingdom* (1997); Harcourt 1997 (HC)

When a decimated, battle weary company from Brooklyn loses its much loved and fiercely admired leader in one of the final skirmishes of the Civil War, the surviving troops are understandably despondent. At the tail end of their enlistment period — and nervously awaiting their final orders — they stumble upon a clearing and, in search of much-needed physical and emotional release, organize a game of baseball. Before long, a battalion of equally exhausted Confederate soldiers emerges

from the surrounding woods to challenge them to a "friendly" match. Even though both sets of soldiers will take part in the ensuing Battle of Spottsylvania, they will manage to play a series of five games described by the *Washington Post Book World* as "something of a covert between-the-fighting playoff series."

Booklist observes that "the games [which continue, intermittently ... squeezed between grisly, graphically described military engagements] begin to assume increased importance, representing a last desperate opportunity for redemption" and concludes that Thomas Dyja has written "an absolutely stunning narrative." According to *Kirkus Reviews, Play for a Kingdom* is "a sensitive, forceful, even breathtaking commingling of play and war, daydream and nightmare, the humane and the bestial, in which the human dimensions of warfare are unforgettably evoked." In the view of the *Christian Science Monitor*, "Baseball may allow the combatants to find virtue in their enemy as men, but Dyja and his characters give no metaphysical cast to the games.... Sometimes though, as Thomas Dyja proves with this impressive novel, peering into human desperation can produce insight and prose of unusual elegance."

REVIEWS: *BL* 8/97; *CSM* 8/18/97; *KR* 6/1/97; *LJ* 5/15/97; *PW* 6/23/97; *WPBW* 1/16/97

Echewa, T. Okinkaram (Nigeria)

I Saw the Sky Catch Fire (1992), Plume 1993 (pbk); See Section 4, #432

Erdrich, Louise (USA)

201   *The Antelope Wife* (1998); HarperCollins 1998 (HC)

Using an intricate string of native beads as her central metaphor, and drawing on the legends and sacred myths of the Ojibwa, Louise Erdrich tells the story of two fatefully intertwined families, the Roys and the Shawanos whose paths first cross when Scranton Roy, a soldier with the U.S. Cavalry, deserts his regiment during a brutal attack on an Ojibwa village. His objective: to "rescue" an Indian baby. Though eventually reclaimed by her mother, Blue Prairie Woman, the little girl, motherless once more, will be raised by antelopes before returning to the world of man. Generations later a young Native American woman is kidnapped from a pow wow.... Ms. Erdrich sets her tale, which moves back and forth in time, in and around Minneapolis, which was built on the site of the Ojibwa's sacred hunting ground.

Kirkus Reviews calls *The Antelope Wife* "a powerful and dauntingly elliptical tale of obsession and separation" and concludes that although "too many explanations are hastily knotted together at the end

... few readers will complain. This is realism at its most magical, in a novel as satisfying as any Erdrich has written." According to the *L.A. Times Book Review* Erdrich's writing is "[r]ichly cadenced, deeply textured ... [having] the luster and sheen of poetry, each sentence circling deeper into emotion, motivation and rationale, until love touches not eternity but death...."*Booklist* concludes that "Some readers may have difficulty with the narrative jumps and the rich overlay of magic realism, but for those willing to slowly immerse themselves in this nonlinear world as one soaks in a hot bath, the rewards are many."

RECOGNITION: *LATBR* "Best Fiction of 1998"; *NYTBR* Notable Book of 1998; REVIEWS: *BL* 3/1/98; *KR* 2/15/98; *LATBR* 5/17/98; *LJ* 3/15/98; *NYTBR* 4/12/98; *PeopleW* 4/13/98; *PW* 2/9/98; *Salon* 4/14/98; *WPBW* 5/17/98

Erickson, Steve (USA)

202 *Arc d'X* (1993); Holt 1997 (pbk)

Steve Erickson's post-modernist *Arc d'X* opens in Paris in 1789 and features (among others) Sally Hemmings, Thomas Jefferson's favorite slave, reputed mistress and, as recent DNA analysis indicates, the mother of at least one of Jefferson's children. *Arc d'X* concludes in the year 1999 and over the course of its 298 pages is transformed from a traditional historical novel into something much more challenging in terms of structure and sensibility. Mr. Erickson, by focusing on the inherent conflicts of the period [a pursuit of political freedom for some in the presence of officially sanctioned slavery for others] paints an ambiguous picture of both Thomas Jefferson and the country he championed. Tom Robbins, in an advance review of *Arc d'X*, called Steve Erickson "one of the two or three most exciting novelists in the world today."

According *Booklist*, the X in the title "refers to almost a year of days at the end of the millennium that (according to the text) have accumulated because of inaccuracies in the Western calendar. In the year X, time and history collapse, and actors from various times reenact Jefferson's dilemma." *Time* calls *Arc d'X* a "brilliant, desperate, sheet soaking nightmare of a novel" and concludes that Erickson is a "gifted sleight-of-hand artist [who works his] phantasmagorical effects ... without befuddling the reader." However, English novelist **Anthony Burgess** (*NYTBR*) found that Erickson had "jettisoned too many of the novel's traditional properties" for the book to be completely successful.

RECOGNITION: *NYTBR* Notable Book of 1993; REVIEWS: *BL* 3/15/93; *KR* 2/1/93; *LATBR* 5/19/96; *LJ* 3/15/93; *NYTBR* 5/2/93; *Time* 5/10/93; *VLS* 5/93; *WPBW* 5/9/93; *YaleRev* 10/93.

Eugenides, Jeffrey (USA)

203 *The Virgin Suicides* (1993); Warner Bks 1994 (pbk)

Called by Irish novelist **John Banville** "a *Catcher in the Rye* for the Nineties," *The Virgin Suicides* is a haunting tale of teenage angst. Set in a wealthy Midwestern suburb, Jeffrey Eugenides's first novel is centered around the suicides of the five (exceedingly attractive and highly protected) Lisbon sisters and the effect of their actions on the wider community. The tale is narrated by a former neighbor, now approaching middle-age, who (like many of the boys who knew the sisters) can neither understand nor, in some very fundamental way, yet overcome the impact of their deaths.

While concluding that Eugenides's "black, glittering novel ... won't be to everyone's taste ... " *Library Journal* asserts that the author's "engrossing writing style keeps one reading despite a creepy feeling that one shouldn't be enjoying it so much." The *London Review of Books* concludes that "Jeffrey Eugenides writes well; his fervent, richly-textured prose is funny, self-mocking, yet desperately serious and sad. Though we know the fate of the girls from the beginning, the novel never loses its tension, its air of expectancy; we keep hoping for one bit of information which will explain the suicides, which will comfort the boys and allow them to forget...." The *New York Review of Books* suggests that despite the novel's subject matter "reading [*The Virgin Suicides*] is ... a pleasurable melancholy experience." while further concluding that "Eugenides is a cocky performer, so seemingly at ease handling his dangerous material."

RECOGNITION: *NYTBR* Notable Book of 1993; REVIEWS: *BL* 4/1/93; *LitRev* 6/93; *LJ* 4/15/93; *LRB* 8/5/93; *NewsWk* 4/19/93; *NYRB* 6/10/93; *NYTBR* 4/25/93; *TLS* 6/18/93; *YaleRev* 10/93; EDITOR'S NOTE: Mr. Eugenides was named to *Granta* magazine's 1996 list of the twenty "Best Young American Novelists."

Everett, Percival (USA)

Frenzy (1997); Graywolf 1997 (HC & pbk); See Section 8, #1005

Ferre, Rosario (Puerto Rico/USA)

204 *Eccentric Neighborhood* (1997); FS&G 1997 (HC)

In her second English-language novel, Rosario Ferre returns to Puerto Rico and features an appealing heroine by the name of Elvira Vernet, a young woman who is related to two powerful, dynastic families: the Vernets, Cuban exiles who have made a name (and a sizable fortune) on their adopted island of Puerto Rico, and the Rivas de Santillanas, landed Puerto Rican gentry with deep historical roots. Narrated by Elvira, the story encompasses personal loss, romantic entanglement, betrayal, influence peddling and the unconscionable avarice of certain family members.

According to *Kirkus Reviews* "Moving like a firestorm, the novel throws off subsidiary characters and subplots with too-often confusing and occasionally reckless abandon.... Still one admires Ferre's ferocious ingenuity and energy as she depicts a society and century in flux. This most demanding of her novels is probably her best." In the view of *Time* magazine, "*Eccentric Neighborhoods* is nothing if not fertile, so dense with fables, anecdote, reminiscences and allegories that readers may find themselves wishing for machetes to cut away the fictional undergrowth." *Booklist* observes that "There is a minimal plot structured around Elvira's stormy relationship with her mother" but concludes that "the strength of this novel is in Ferre's finely wrought short chapters and the overall tapestry they create, with moods alternately funny, touching, lusty, and tragic, and with an underlying sensuousness."

REVIEWS: *BL* 12/15/97; *EW* 4/17/98; *KR* 12/1/97; *LJ* 12/97; *NYTBR* 2/22/98; *PeopleW* 3/23/98; *PW* 11/24/97; *Time* 3/16/98

205   *The House on the Lagoon* (1995); FS&G 1995 (HC)

Rosario Ferre's first novel to be written originally in English is set in Puerto Rico and takes the form of a multigenerational history of the Mendizabel family, as constructed by Isabel Montfort, wife of Quinten Aviles Mendizabel a prosperous importer. Quintin, a fifth-generation Mendizabel who sports a history degree from Colombia University and a well-developed sense of pride in his family's "illustrious" history, is shocked at the degree of poetic license employed by his wife in relating her tale. Quintin proceeds to make his own textual corrections in the margins of Isabel's manuscript. The story, therefore, moves forward on parallel tracks reflective of two very different interpretations of the same historical events.

Called a "fascinating work ... which is attempting to answer the question: What is a novel?" by the *Library Journal*, *The House on the Lagoon* was generally well-received by the critics. The *Washington Post Book World* called Ms. Ferre "one of Latin America's most gifted novelists" and found *The House on the Lagoon* to be an "absorbing, humorous and ironic novel." *Book World* also observes that it raises "troubling questions about troubling issues, including the political status of an island that has never enjoyed full independence and is in danger of losing its cultural identity to U.S. dominion." According to *The Nation*, Ms. Ferre has, with this novel, "consolidated her niche in a growing tradition of Latin American novelists ... capa-

ble of not only translating themselves but of creating original fictional universes in the English language."

RECOGNITION: Nominated for the National Book Award in 1995; REVIEWS: *KR* 7/15/95; *LJ* 8/95; *Nation* 11/20/95; *NY* 11/27/95; *NYTBR* 9/17/95; *PW* 7/3/95; *WPBW* 10/1/95; *WRB* 2/96

Forrest, Leon (USA)

206   *Divine Days* (1993); Norton 1993 (HC); 1995 (pbk)

Leon Forrest's highly inventive Chicago-based novel is narrated by Joubert Jones, a playwright who is intending to write a play about a mysterious (always elusive, now missing) mixed-blood Mississippian known as "Sugar-Grove." Jones' earlier efforts to write a play about a cult figure in the Father Divine/Jim Jones mold are similarly explored. Described by the *New York Times Book Review* as "an epic detective story ... [with] elements of the Gothic, the tall tale, parable, philosophical argument, the novel of ideas ... and the sort of close observation that Balzac, Mann and Hemingway would have admired," *Divine Days* is organized into 14 episodes that take place during a single week in 1966.

According to the *New Republic*, "*Divine Days* is unlike anything else in our recent literature. At once a comic opera and a metaphysical tract, this great wordy beast stamps and blinks in the glittering light of the market place like something kidnapped from a more expansive age." *Choice* points out that "Forrest develops his story by depicting many facets of African American life and the social impact they have during the turbulent 1960s" and concludes that *Divine Days* is "a landmark novel" that "is literarily and socially significant."

RECOGNITION: *NYTBR* Notable Book of 1993; REVIEWS: *AfrAmRev* Spr '95; *Choice* 2/94; *Emerge* 7-8/94; *NewR* 5/31/93; *NYTBR* 7/25/93

Frucht, Abby (USA)

207   *Life Before Death* (1997); Scribner 1997 (HC)

Abby Frucht's heroine, the 40-year-old, single, Isobel Albright, is a museum curator who is dealing with the aftermath of a destructive museum fire; she is also assimilating the news that she has metastatic breast cancer. Given only a 10 percent chance of survival even with aggressive chemotherapy, Isobel opts to forgo treatment and live her remaining months to their fullest. From this point on, Ms. Frucht's novel takes a definite post-modernist turn as Isobel manages to escape the normal boundaries of time and space to live, as it were, in an alternative reality filled with adopted babies, a young husband, intriguing travel, and the gift of aging, as her own life winds down.

According to the *Boston Globe* "With the help of sooty talismans salvaged from the museum fire … Isobel's imagination soars to a fantastic world, a place that flourishes with all she has planted in her rich, well-tended soul. In this fabulously imagined future, Isobel evolves into *'Bald Queen Butterfly,'* a cancer and chemotherapy survivor, a breastless, bejeweled, and (save for false eyelashes) hairless woman who Rollerblades to work. Meanwhile, in 'real time' Isobel is dying." *Kirkus Reviews* notes that "The experience of dying — of giving up what was and grieving for what might have been — is extraordinarily well captured in Frucht's sometimes whimsical, often luminous prose" and concludes that *Life Before Death* is a "unique and memorable work, marking a new level of artistry for the author." *Publishers Weekly*, in its starred review, asserts that "Frucht's high-spirited cleverness diverts attention from the devastating heart of the novel; the threat of Isobel's impending death; this cunning disarms the reader and lends a rare poignancy to a necessarily tragic ending and to its consolation: 'just because I was mortal didn't mean I wasn't alive.'"

RECOGNITION: *NYTBR* Notable Book of 1997; REVIEWS: *BL* 7/97; *BosGlobe* 8/17/97; *KR* 5/1/97; *NYTBR* 8/31/97; *PW* 6/2/97

Gaddis, William (USA)

208 *A Frolic of His Own* (1991); Simon & Schuster 1995 (pbk)

William Gaddis's fourth novel, a prize-winning commentary on our increasingly litigious society, exhibits all of the author's familiar trademarks: heft, a disdain for punctuation, a fondness for word games and jargon, and an almost "fiendish" cleverness. *A Frolic of His Own* begins with the hospitalization of Oscar Crease (a reclusive middle-aged college instructor, savant, and one-time playwright) following a run-in with his own car which he had been in the process of hotwiring. Despite being both victim and owner of the errant automobile, Crease is planning to sue the car's manufacturer for "pain and disfigurement." He is also in the process of suing a Hollywood producer for plagiarizing his play, *Once at Antietam,* which, though based on his grandfather's experiences in the Civil War, was itself borrowed from many sources, including, but not limited to: Eugene O'Neil, Plato, Rousseau, and Camus. Gaddis's plot is further enlivened by the addition of a free spirited (implant-challenged) girlfriend and an octogenarian father who happens to be a sitting Federal Court judge with a couple of outrageously frivolous suits of his own to contend with.

According to *World Literature Today* "William Gaddis writes as if he is using an Uzi instead of a typewriter. He writes, in fact, as no one has ever exactly written before. His characters and events are delineated not by narration but by dialogue, in staccato bursts of language — words, words, words. If the reader can persevere, Gaddis's novels reveal an articulately satiric view of a world Gaddis says he found 'wanting to be explored.'" The *London Review of Books*, while suggesting that Gaddis's novel reads "as if the Marx Brothers had rewritten *Bleak House…*," contends that "the ingenuity and the intelligence of the comment on the law, and the speed with which people talk and things happen, take us into something beyond satire." The *Times Literary Supplement* judges *A Frolic of One's Own* to be a "bleak, brilliant, exhausting novel."

RECOGNITION: Winner of the 1994 National Book Award; nominated for the 1994 National Book Critics Circle Award; *NYTBR* "Editors' Choice" 1994; REVIEWS: *BL* 11/15/93; *EW* 2/11/94; *KR* 11/1/93; *LATBR* 1/9/94; *LJ* 1/9/94; *LRB* 5/12/94; *Nation* 4/25/94; *NewR* 2/7/94; *NewsWk* 1/17/94; *NY* 1/31/94; *NYRB* 2/17/94; *NYT* 1/4/94; *NYTBR* 1/9/94; *PW* 6/21/9; *Spec* 7/23/94; *Time* 1/24/94; *TLS* 6/3/94; *WLT* Aut '94

Garcia, Christina (USA)

209 *The Aguero Sisters* (1997); Knopf 1997 (HC)

The Aguero sisters, Reina and Constancia, live on opposite sides of the political and economic divide that exists between the Cubans who fled Castro's regime and the Cubans who stayed behind. Constancia, and her husband Heberto, chose exile and, after a series of abortive attempts by Heberto to "make a go of it" in New York, eventually ended up in Key Biscayne, Florida, where Constancia operates a thriving cosmetics business. Constancia's sister, Reina, a beautiful, promiscuous, supremely self-confident "master engineer" — and champion of *la revolution* — chose to remain in Havana with her parents who were well-known intellectuals and naturalists. The tragic deaths of Reina and Constancia's parents (victims of an apparent murder/ suicide) have lasting repercussions for both sisters, and the slow unraveling of the mystery surrounding their parents' violent end propels the novel. When, after a thirty-year separation, Reina eventually makes her way to Florida, the sisters' reunion is freighted with long-buried secrets.

Publishers Weekly, in its starred review, calls *The Aguero Sisters* a "compelling and resonant story of thwarted relationships, intense, unslaked desires and family secrets" and concludes that it "surely confirms [the] promise [signaled in her first novel *Dreaming in Cuban*]." According to Michiko Kakutani (*NYT*) "As readers of *Dreaming in Cuban* will know, fantastic events are common in Ms. Garcia's fictional universe [e.g., a man is saved from the murderous wrath of his workers by a flock of tree ducks, another man is killed by a 'high velocity' avocado during a hurricane].... Blending the hallucinatory imagery of Gabriel Garcia Marquez with a homespun American idiom, Ms. Garcia uses such events to illumine the unpredictability of ordinary life...." *Kirkus Reviews* concludes that "As in many epics, we are presented with a bold and very richly detailed portrait that is here made the more comprehensible and vivid through the microcosm of family history. Fluid, graceful and extremely rewarding; a work of high seriousness and rich detail." In the view of the *London Sunday Times*, "The medley of voices can have a desultory effect on the narrative, yet it pulses with a heady imagination, finely limned characters and earthly passions." The *Washington Post Book World* found many similarities between Ms. Aguero's first novel *Dreaming in Cuban* but concludes that "*The Aguero Sisters* is undoubtedly the better novel of the two: denser, more focused, with a greater richness of language and of comic invention ... it's a case of practice makes perfect."

RECOGNITION: *NYTBR* Notable Book of 1997; REVIEWS: *BL* 5/1/97; *ChiTrib* 6/8/97; *Kirkus* 5/1/97; *LATBR* 6/8/97; *LJ* 3/15/97; *LST* 7/5/98; *NewsWk* 4/28/97; *NYT* 5/27/97; *NYTBR* 6/15/97; *PW* 3/10/97; *Salon* 5/12/97; *Time* 5/12/97; *TLS* 8/29/97; *WPBW* 7/13/97

210 *Dreaming in Cuban* (1992); Ballantine 1993 (pbk)

Cristina Garcia's debut novel, set in post–Revolutionary Havana, Brooklyn and the Cuban seaside during the 1970s and 1980s, tells the story of three generations of strong-willed del Pino women. Within the del Pino clan fierce — and divergent — loyalties abound: to Fidel, to counter-revolution, to art, to family. When various far-flung and long-estranged family members are eventually brought together by a devoted granddaughter, old wounds are healed and troubled souls are soothed. The nonlinear and often stylistically fragmented tale is told through monologues, letters, dreams, and even visions, as the matriarch, Celia del Pino, appears to have bequeathed her powers of clairvoyance to her female descendants.

According to the *Library Journal*, "Garcia tells [the story of the del Pino women] with an economy of words and a rich, tropical imagery, setting a brisk but comfortable pace." Michiko Kakutani, writing in the *New York Times*, calls *Dreaming in Cuban*: "Dazzling ... Remarkable ... Garcia stands revealed as a magical new writer."

RECOGNITION: Nominated for the National Book Award; REVIEWS: *BellesL* Fall '92; *GW* 12/6/92; *LATBR* 3/21/93; *LJ* 6/1/93; *NYT* 2/25/92; *NYTBR* 3/14/93; *Obs* 12/13/92; *PW* 11/2/92; *Time* 1/4/93; *TLS* 12/25/92; *WPBW* 3/1/92

Gass, William (USA)

211 *The Tunnel* (1995); Knopf 1995 (HC); HarperCollins 1996 (pbk)

In his latest novel, William Gass, "the dean of American prose modernists," (*PW*) features an obsessive-compulsive history professor at a Midwestern university who is both digging into his unsavory past **and** excavating a tunnel from his basement to "nowhere." Professor Frederick Kohler, a Nazi-apologist who grew up in Germany during World War II, has just completed his ponderous assessment of the period entitled *Guilt and Innocence in Hitler's Germany* and is attempting to write the book's introduction.

According to Christopher Lehmann-Haupt (*NYT*), Kohler finds that "he cannot proceed. Instead he starts writing an anti-introduction, a rambling, inexhaustible monologue that mixes memoir, confession, philosophical speculation, lectures on the meaning of history, philological rumination, pornographic verse, song lyrics, typographical tricks, puns, diagrams and comic drawings ... [which] while by no means as difficult to decipher, sounds many of the overtones of James Joyce's *Finnegan's Wake*." Critic John Leonard (*The Nation*) observes that Gass "with an obsessiveness bordering on Brodkey baroque ... has written a splendid, daunting, loathsome novel." The *New Republic* reaches a different conclusion, arguing that while some "may seize on [*The Tunnel*] as a postmodern masterpiece ... [it is actually] a bloated monster of a book ... [exhibiting both] moral and intellectual flatulence ... [while contributing to the] trivialization of the enormity of genocide, by absorbing it into the nickel-and-dime nastiness that people perpetrate in everyday life." *Booklist* notes that "Gass is known for his experimentation with the multiplicity of meanings and texture of words and syntax and has always been fascinated with creating a literary equivalent of the meanderings of the mind ... " and concludes that "Kohler's stream of consciousness carries both deep thoughts and sheer nonsense, and he is, by turns, funny, irritating, gross, poignant, and brilliant."

RECOGNITION: Nominated for the 1996 PEN/Faulkner Award; *NYTBR* Notable Book of 1995; REVIEWS: *AntR* Sum '95; *AtlM* 6/95; *BL* 1/1/95; *CSM* 3/6/95; *KR* 12/1/94; *LATBR* 3/19/95; *LJ* 1/95; *Nation* 3/20/95; *NatR* 5/1/95; *NewR* 3/27/95; *NYRB* 7/13/95; *NYT* 2/23/95; *NYTBR* 2/26/95; *PW* 1/2/95; *VLS* 2/95; *WPBW* 3/12/95; *YaleRev* 7/95

Gibson, William (Canada/USA)

212 *Idoru* (1996); Putnam 1996 (HC); Berkley 1997 (pbk)

Though often slotted, at least notionally, in

the sci fi category, William Gibson's work is considered by many to be both ground-breaking and boundary leaping. His debut novel, *Neuromancer* (in which he coined the term cyberspace), was widely praised as the harbinger of a new form of science fiction: an amalgamation of post-modern romanticism and tech-noir referred to as cyberpunk. *Idoru*, set primarily in 21st century Japan (which has recently suffered a major earthquake), explores the concept of virtual reality within the context of a post-millennial rock music scene. As the techno-thriller unfolds, Rez, a wildly popular member of the Seattle-based rock band Lo/Rez is rumored to have fallen in love with the Japanese Pop sensation Rei Toei, and may be planning to marry her. Rei is an "idoru" (Japanese-phonetic for "idol"), she's also a bloodless, virtual reality construct, "a sort of semi-sentient hologram" (*LJ*). Rez is followed to Japan by a staunch member his fan club, Chia Pet McKenzie, who is convinced Rez is making a terrible mistake. His bandmates have also hired a special "net runner" to look into a possible Russian Mafia connection.

According to the *New Statesman* "Gibson's work is powered by an unparalleled instinct for the metaphors through which technology reveals our own unconscious desires.... [And] though he rarely delves below the surface ... of his characters and their world ... we find ourselves [reflected in those surfaces]. Sometimes its not a pretty sight, but *Idoru* is always an exhilarating ride." In the view of the *Library Journal*, "Gibson's writing is thick with atmosphere, dislocating the reader with a future that is both familiar and unsettling." *Booklist* concludes that "Gibson remains on the cutting edge, but his vision does not now seem far-fetched ... [rather, it] resonates with startling realism as it presents a future not unlike the present, part hell and part paradise."

OTHER MEDIA: Audiocassette (Putnam/abr); REVIEWS: *BL* 8/96; *KR* 7/15/96; *LJ* 8/96; *Maclean's* 11/25/96; *MFSF* 2/97; *NS* 10/11/96; *NYTBR* 9/8/96; *PW* 8/5/96; *TLS* 9/27/96; *VV* 9/24/96; *WPBW* 10/27/96

Gilb, Dagoberto (USA)

213 *The Last Known Residence of Mickey Acuna* (1994); Grove-Atlantic 1995 (pbk)

Dagoberto Gilb sets his debut novel in contemporary El Paso and features Mickey, a wanderer who is living at the local "Y" and waiting for something to turn up. Gilb's novel (which is reminiscent of the work of such "post-colonial" writers as Alex La Guma) is peopled by a skillfully limned collection of misfits and no-hopers and offers gritty and affecting portrait of the Chicano underclass.

In the opinion of *World Literature Today*, "Before you read this book, have a generous splash of

your favorite liver-damaging liquid and prowl about the nearest dark, dank alleyway to set the mood, to capture the vibe of Dabogerto Gilb's first novel.... This is odd stuff, a heterosexually revised take on John Rechy's *City of Night* sans transvestites and wanderlust...." According to the *Library Journal* "Like the powerful stories in his 'The Magic of Blood,' Gilb's first novel evokes the heat and dust, poverty, lassitude, and passion of the urban southwest." The *New York Times Book Review* points out "At times Mickey's laconic fogginess has an almost generic quality.... And the lack of a plot, though it underscores a certain truth about Mickey's plotless life, becomes a bit wearying. Nonetheless, Mr. Gilb ... writes in a deft, ironic style that is all his own." The *L.A. Times Book Review* concludes that "As most readers know, good fiction is often like good conversation.... Dagoberto Gilb's novel *The Last Known Residence of Mickey Acuna* is good talk throughout. It feels like a beer-joint seance. Like a coffee klatch. Like two compadres across the picket fence tearing into mutual associates while hanging the wash."

RECOGNITION: *NYTBR* Notable Book of 1994; REVIEWS: *LATBR* 12/11/94; *LJ* 9/15/94; *NYTBR* 10/2/94; *PW* 8/8/94; *WLT* Aut '95

Gowdy, Barbara (Canada)

214 *Mister Sandman* (1996); Steerforth 1997 (HC)

Set in the 1950s and early 1960s, Barbara Gowdy's third novel (called a "curlicued, spangling Canadian Gothic" by the *New Yorker*) features a seemingly normal Canadian family: Doris and Gordon Canary and their three daughters. Upon closer inspection, however, the Canary clan (of which various members are engaged in all manner of illicit sexual liaisons both natural and unnatural) appears to be knee deep in dissimulation and outright deception. Clearly, the only truthful member of the family is Joan, the closet-dwelling, mute youngest sister who having been dropped on her head at birth was now, depending on one's perspective, either brain-damaged or a gifted savant.

According to *Entertainment Weekly* Barbara Gowdy leavens her prodigious doses of satire and eccentricity with compassion, making this one of the strangest — and most heartwarming — paeans to family ties you'll ever read." Novelist Katherine Dunn (*WPBW*) observes that Barbara Gowdy "cocks a snoot at conventions, both moral and literary, and [*Mister Sandman*] is so brilliantly crafted and flat-out fun to read that she makes jubilant sinners of us all." *Publishers Weekly*, in its starred review, observes that "This unidentifiably strange saga is related in beautifully polished prose shot through with witty asides, startlingly poetic images and a series of hilarious scenes that beg to be read aloud." The *New York Review of Books*, however, concludes that *Mister Sandman's* "comedy is dark, rooted in sad, alarming secrets and mysteries."

RECOGNITION: Short-listed for the 1995 Giller Prize (Canada); REVIEWS: *BL* 3/15/97; *EW* 4/18/97; *KR* 2/15/97; *LJ* 4/1/97; *NY* 8/11/97; *NYRB* 4/10/97; *NYTBR* 5/11/97; *PW* 1/6/97; *Salon* 4/1/97; *TLS* 6/21/96; *VLS* Spr '97; *WPBW* 3/30/97

Gray, Alasdair (UK-Scotland)

A History Maker (1996); Harcourt Brace 1996 (HC); See Section 7, #898

Poor Things (1992); Harcourt Brace 1993 (HC); HBK 1994 (pbk); See Section 7, #899

Hagedorn, Jessica (USA)

215   *Dogeaters*; Viking Penguin 1991 (pbk)
Jessica Hagedorn's debut novel is set in the Philippines during the reign of the Marcoses and is narrated retrospectively by Rio Gonzaga, a wealthy Filipino who, after immigrating to the U.S. with her family, looks back on her youth in Manila with a mixture of longing and horror.

According to *Publishers Weekly* "Hagedorn's unflinching view of Manila, encompassing child prostitution, the torture chambers and the slums, as well as the palatial quarters of the First Family, is leavened by ironic, often humorous observations." The *Library Journal* observes that the novel's "terrain is familiar from the writing of Gabriel Garcia Marquez and Manuel Puig: a lush, fantastical, overheated landscape, where the fractured lives of the poor are rendered palatable solely by dreams." The *Library Journal* concludes that *Dogeaters* "is exceptionally well written and emotionally wrenching." Australian novelist Blanche D'Alpuget (*NYTBR*) points out that the "exoticisms become tiresome, more a nervous tic than a desire to make connections across the gulf of culture. That said, *Dogeaters* remains a rich small feast of a book."

OTHER MEDIA: Audiocassette (American Audio/abr); RECOGNITION: Nominated for the 1990 National Book Award; REVIEWS: *BL* 3/1/90; *ComW* 3/91; *KR* 2/1/90; *LJ* 4/1/90; *PW* 2/9/90; *NY* 3/18/91; *NYTBR* 3/25/90; *TLS* 9/27/91; *WPBW* 4/8/90

Hall, Brian (USA)

216   *The Saskiad* (1996); HM 1996 (HC)
Brian Hall's unusual coming-of-age story features Saskia, a precociously bookish yet spirited 12-year-old who is growing up on a '60s style commune in upstate New York. A misfit at the local public school, she has developed a rich imaginative life in which she travels with both Odysseus and Marco Polo and hobnobs with Homer, Hornblower

and Tycho Brahe. Saskia's long-absent father, Thomas (an original founder of the commune), is currently living in Norway and Saskia's summer trip (in the company of Jane, her best friend) to visit him there occupies much of the book. Thomas is a particularly chilling example of the sort of charismatic yet fundamentally unstable and inherently exploitative personality that flourished in the heady days of the hippie movement.

According to the starred *Booklist* review "With this complex novel, Hall explores the dark side of the utopian ideal and tells an old, old story in utterly contemporary terms. Filled with passion and narrative drive, Hall's epic novel is simply riveting." *Publishers Weekly*, in its starred review, observes that *The Saskiad* is "a blend of mythical, literary and philosophical themes that flows easily between the concrete details of the heroine's contemporary life and the spinning worlds of her fantasies.... Despite Hall's many allusions to great works of literature, his prose tends more towards gentle humor and he doesn't belabor the obvious parallels...." In the view of *New Statesman, The Saskiad* "has a shape suggested by Cavafy's poem 'Ithaca: exile and return.' The value of an Ithaca is not what you find when you get there, but what you gain in your journey ... [Hall's novel] is about being human, and it's delightful."

REVIEWS: *BL* 12/1/96; *KR* 11/1/96; *LJ* 11/1/96; *NS* 10/18/96; *NY* 3/10/97; *NYTBR* 1/19/97; *Obs* 11/24/96; *PW* 10/28/96; *SLJ* 3/97; *TLS* 10/18/96; *WPBW* 2/9/97

Hansen, Brooks (USA)

217   *The Chess Garden* (1995); Berkley 1996 (pbk)
At the turn of the century, Gustav Uyterhoeven, a Dutch physician long-settled in Dayton, Ohio, sets off for South Africa where he offers his medical services to prisoners in the Boer War. While there, the good doctor undergoes a sort of spiritual rejuvenation and begins sending back to Dayton long letters full of grand tales and philosophical speculation. At approximately the same time, chess pieces and figurines — mentioned in the letters — begin appearing in the formal garden behind his Ohio residence. Dr. Uyterhoeven has gained entry into a parallel universe called the Antipodes where he acts out a series of adventures in the company of living chess pieces.

Although fanciful in construction, *The Chess Garden*, according to the *Times Literary Supplement*, "does not disappear altogether into some stratosphere of wooly philosophizing ... mostly ... the novel is a wonderfully bewitching compendium of stories, germinated in Arthurian Legend, Poe and Carroll ... told in pellucid prose and reminiscent, in its colorful muscularity, of such fabulists as

Borges and Calvino." Novelist and professor of literature, **Jay Parini** (*NYTBR*), calls the novel "an improbable, brilliant tale about the spiritual life of a 19th-century Dutch physician ... [which] becomes, by turns, a Bildungsroman, a novel of ideas, a love story and ... a spiritual guide." Parini concludes that "Comparisons to Nabokov and Calvino are doubtless in order.... But *The Chess Garden* stands by itself, a marvel of attention to the things of this world, and worlds beyond." According to the *Voice Literary Supplement* "Like Garcia Marquez, Borges, even Poe, Hansen crates a dangerous, enlightening new world.... He is a true inventor of fiction, and a protean, generous one at that."

RECOGNITION: *PW* "Best Book" of 1995; *NYTBR* Notable Book of 1995; REVIEWS: *LJ* 9/1/95; *NY* 1/8/96; *NYTBR* 9/24/95; *Obs* 1/14/96; *PW* 11/6/95; *TLS* 6/23/95; *VLS* 9/95

Harrington, Donald (USA)

Ekaterina (1993); Harcourt Brace 1993 (HC); 1994 (pbk); See Section 8, #1008

Harris, Wilson

Jonestown (1996); Faber & Faber 1997 (pbk); See Section 4, #441

Resurrection at Sorrow Hill (1993); Faber & Faber 1993 (HC); See Section 4, #441

Harrison, M. John (UK)

218   *Signs of Life* (1997); St. Martins 1997 (HC)

In his eighth novel, English novelist M. John Harrison tells a haunting, quirkily modern tale of obsession and desire. *Signs of Life* focuses on three characters: Isobel Avers, a beautiful Doc Martin-wearing, sometime-waitress who works in an aerodrome and dreams — each night — that she can fly; Isobel's lover, Mick "China" Rose, owner/operator of a disreputable air courier service (with a sideline in banned substances); and Mick's partner, the dark and dangerous Choe who appears to exercise on unnatural emotional hold over his associate. Through Choe (rhymes with Joey) Mick gets involved with some shady characters who deal in illegal dumping. Meanwhile, Isobel checks herself into a Miami clinic where she hopes to begin her winged transformation. Harrison's novel, although noirish in tone and secondary plot line, is essentially a love story.

In the view of the *Times Literary Supplement,* Harrison writes with "uncommon brilliance" especially "about love and loss, [and] about the sense of bereavement that follows the breakup of a relationship. But the most impressive feature of [*Signs*

of Life*] is ... the quality of the prose, which is intensely sensual and concrete, minutely attentive to textures, colours, odours." Novelist Elizabeth Hand (*WPBW*) found *Signs of Life* to be a "coup-de-théâtre which brings the curtain up on an adult tale of obsession, sexual and otherwise, and by novel's end lets it crash down onto all of late-century Europe.' Ms. Hand concludes that Harrison's novel is "an irresistible harbinger of the world we're entering, and an elegy for the one we've lost." According to *Kirkus Reviews*, *Signs of Life* is a "fascinating and terrible little tale, illuminated from unfamiliar perspectives in a spare and glowing prose."

REVIEWS: *KR* 8/1/97; *NewSci* 7/19/97; *PW* 7/7/97; *TLS* 5/30/97; *WPBW* 9/28/97

Hawkes, John (USA)

219   *An Irish Eye* (1997); Viking 1997 (HC); Penguin 1998 (pbk)

Called a "post-modern picaresque" by the *New York Times Book Review*, John Hawkes 16th novel is narrated by Dervla O'Shannon, a thirteen-year-old Irish orphan. Dervla — raised by the dour staff of the St. Martha's Home for Foundling Girls since she was left on their doorstep in a basket — meets, on an outing to Saint Clements Home for Old Soldiers, an old-timer by the name of Corporal Stark and falls madly in love. A series of madcap adventures featuring a riding accident, amnesia and a fabulous inheritance ensue.

According to *Kirkus Reviews*, *An Irish Eye* is a "bauble, really, and yet nevertheless — told in one long fine poetic unbroken Irish sigh — the bauble of a master indeed." Critic and novelist Carolyn See (*WPBW*) observes that "There's the obligatory Swiftian reference ... and more dirt, goo, mud, manure, slop and stench than can be imagined, but Dervla makes a story out of it.... Hawkes writes it with affection, and it's a pleasure to read." Liam Callanan (*NYTBR*) calls Hawkes' novel "an engaging blend of genres and literary traditions — from fairy tale to folk tale to farce to the epistolary novel." The *Library Journal* calls it "funny [and] ... fabulous (in the true sense of the word), with a sensuality not always suppressed and suspense to boot" and concludes that "it's great reading from a major author."

REVIEWS: *BL* 9/1/97; *KR* 6/15/97; *NYTBR* 9/21/97; *PW* 8/4/97; *WPBW* 9/20/97

220   *The Frog* (1996); Penguin 1997 (pbk)

John Hawkes 15th novel — which belong to a genre invented by Kafka known as the "false fable" — is set in France and tells the story of Pascal Gateau who has grown up — in the peaceful years preceding WWI — on a comfortable country estate where his mother was the cook and his father chief gardener. One fateful afternoon, while lazing about his favorite pond, Pascal inadvertently swallows a frog, and — not to put *too* fine a point on it — has his life irrevocably altered. Pascal, particularly in the beginning, suffers greatly from his amphibious parasite but, over time, comes to accept his fellow traveler, affectionately naming him "Armand." In compensation, Pascal develops unusual psycho-sexual powers.

Hawkes's novel was called "an elegant diversion" by the *Washington Post Book World* and "a valedictory for [the author's] eroticized landscapes" by the *Chicago Tribune*. According to *Library Journal*, *The Frog* is "[m]ore accessible than some of Hawkes's experimental narratives ... [and] is both funny and intellectually challenging." *Kirkus Reviews* observes that Hawkes's novel could be viewed as "a 'history' of French culture" and concludes that while the novel will likely be "most appealing to those with a taste for the luxuriantly decadent, it's served, in any case, under Hawkes' usual flawless, rich, smooth sauce of words."

REVIEWS: *AntR* Spr '97; *AtlM* 7/96; *ChiTrib* 7/28/96; *KR* 4/1/96; *LATBR* 9/8/96; *LJ* 6/15/96; *NYTBR* 12/22/96; *PW* 4/15/96; *WPBW* 8/23/96

Henry, Gordon (USA)

221   *The Light People: A Novel* (1995); Univ. of Oklahoma 1995 (HC)

At the heart of Gordon Henry's brief, stylistically inventive debut novel is Oskinaway, a young Anishinaabe boy who has been raised by his grandparents on the Fineday Reservation in northern Minnesota. Oskinaway is determined to locate his mother who has long since run off with a trader and "vanished on the powwow trail." The youngster's quest — fueled by his grandparent's recollections, the assistance of a tribal medicine man and a multitude of storytellers — will last for decades and will encompass "the dizzying complexity of rapidly changing tribal life" (*Booklist*).

Kirkus Reviews observes that by "[c]leverly nesting stories within stories and commingling literary forms [Henry] ... offers a complex, multifaceted view of contemporary Chippewa life." According to *World Literature Today*, the stories Henry weaves are important for the "moral, spiritual and historical lessons" they teach, "lessons which pertain to issues such as the suppression of native languages, the anthropological study of native cultures, and mixed-blood identity, to name only a few. But rest assured when Henry broaches such intense political, social, and philosophical issues, he does so with a keen sense of humor and creative play in the Vizenoresque vein of 'comic liberation.'" The *Library Journal* calls *The Light People* a "richly complex, multilayered, multiple-genre novel [in which] amazingly, the huge cast of characters and their snippets of stories manage to gel into a cohesive whole."

REVIEWS: *BL* 2/15/94; *KR* 1/1/94; *LJ* 2/1/94; *NYTBR* 7/3/94; *PW* 1/10/94; *WLT* Sum '94

Hospital, Janette Turner (Australia/Canada)

Oyster (1996); W.W. Norton 1998 (HC); See Section 6, #723

The Last Magician (1992); Ivy Books 1993 (pbk); See Section 6, #724

Howard, Maureen (USA)

222   *A Lover's Almanac* (1998); Viking 1998 (HC)

The story of a pair of star-crossed lovers, *A Lover's Almanac* takes place during the first three months of the 21st century. Louise Moffett, an artist, lives and works in Manhattan, a far cry from her childhood on a midwestern farm. Her computer-genius boyfriend Artie, however, is a New Yorker through and through. Raised by his grandparents — since the death of his young, single mother — he has an abiding interest in learning the identity of his father. As the story opens, Artie and Louise are attending an end of the millennium party where they engage in a drunken quarrel and break off their relationship.

Called a "funny, grouchy, madly non-linear love story" by *Time* magazine, *A Lover's Almanac*, in the view of *The Nation*, tells a story that "is both reunion journey and zodiac-managed time travel, for before Lou and Artie can join the march into the twenty-first century, they must first make peace with the twentieth." According to *Booklist*, as Artie and Lou "slowly realign, like heavenly bodies destined for a celestial event, Howard punctuates her affecting narrative with almanac-like entries about such subjects as ancient Egypt, Benjamin Franklin and Virginia Woolf, exploring, along the way, the often unexpected consequences of acts both creative and destructive." *Publishers Weekly,* in its starred review, concludes that sinewy prose that embraces the vernacular as well as expressing the profound is one of the pleasures of this provocative novel of ideas."

RECOGNITION: *NYTBR* Notable Book of 1998; REVIEWS: *BL* 1/1/98; *ChiTrib* 3/1/98; *Nation* 1/26/98; *NYRB* 7/16/98; *NYTBR* 1/18/98; *PW* 10/13/97; *Time* 2/9/98; EDITOR'S NOTE: *Natural History*, Ms. Howard's previous novel (widely described as "Joycean"), is both the historical account of one exceedingly hierarchical family (the Brays of Bridgeport, Connecticut) and a novelistic reverie that encompasses other Bridgeport notables such as P.T. Barnum, Robert Mitchum, and (Pogo-creator) Walter Kelly.

(*Natural History* was nominated for the 1993 PEN/Faulkner Award and was selected by *NYTBR* as a Notable Book of 1992 and *by PW* as a "Best Book" of 1992.)

Irwin, Robert (UK)

223 *Exquisite Corpse* (1995); Pantheon 1997 (HC)

In his third novel, Robert Irwin tackles the intellectual and aesthetic underpinnings of the "avant garde" art world which flourished in the first half of the 20th century. Set in England and Western Europe in the years surrounding WWII, *Exquisite Corpse* features a promising English surrealist painter by the name of Caspar and his love affair with Caroline, his "English rose." Caspar moves in a circle of self-absorbed bohemian intellectuals (some fictional, others not) who are involved in a wide range of artistic pursuits including the Theatre of Cruelty, the Chelsea Arts Ball, the Surrealist Exhibition and the notorious 1937 Nazi exhibit of "Entartete Kunst" (Degenerate Art). Caspar, unhinged by Caroline's abrupt disappearance, spends a few years in a psychiatric clinic. Discharged at the height of the Blitz, Caspar contributes to the war effort by drawing pictures of bomb damage for the British War Office. At the end of the war he is sent off to Bergen Belsen "to make an artistic record of a concentration camp the Nazi's had maintained there." He is led, therefore, into a world more decadent and surreal than even the most avant garde of his circle could imagine.

Entertainment Weekly calls *Exquisite Corpse* a "giddy, phantasmic portrait of the 1930s Surreal movement — complete with orgies, opium dens, and cameos by Andre Breton and Gala Dali." According to English novelist **A.S. Byatt**, writing in the *London Sunday Times*, it is a "splendidly intelligent ... surefooted" novel which "encompasses death and madness, the frivolous and the absurd. It [also] opens magic box inside magic box, with a conjurers panache. It is original and wholly successful." The *New York Times Book Review* observes that "Mr. Irwin's novel, in which fiction and reality are woven unobtrusively together, is consistently clever and inventive." The *Times Literary Supplement* similarly asserts that the "interplay of fact and fiction, what 'really' happened and how it was perceived and recorded, is at the heart of Irwin's intriguing book."

RECOGNITION: *NYTBR* Notable Book of 1997; REVIEWS: *EW* 6/27/97; *KR* 3/1/97; *LJ* 4/1/97; *LST* 4/7/96; *NS&S* 7/28/95; *NYTBR* 5/25/97; *PW* 3/3/97; *TLS* 3/24/95; *WPBW* 5/4/97

Ishiguro, Kazuo (UK)

224 *The Unconsoled* (1995); Knopf 1995 (HC); 1996 (pbk)

English novelist Kazuo Ishiguro's first novel since his Booker Prize–winning *Remains of the Day* is set in an unidentified, German-speaking city distinguished by its devotion to music. The narrator, an accomplished concert pianist, has come to the city to give a series of performances. He soon becomes enmeshed in a dream-like, free-associative procession of distractions, ranging from hotel managers with piano-playing sons, through love-besotted, one-legged conductors, to seriously unbalanced professional rivals.

Judged "deliberately disorienting, unpredictable and surreal ... [and] demanding of close reading" by *Publishers Weekly*, it was selected by that magazine for inclusion in its list of "Best Books" of 1995. The *New York Times Book Review* argues that "Far from being 'chaotic,' *The Unconsoled* is as tightly plotted as anything Ishiguro has written, with many interwoven narrative threads ... [none of which] are happily tied by the story's end" and concludes that, "with so many unresolved problems, the sadness is all the more overwhelming. Yet thanks to Ishiguro's impeccable timing, his ability to deploy the techniques of suspense thrillers and his hectic humor, what could have been a gloomy tale is a positive joy to read." Novelist and travel writer, Pico Iyer (*TLS*) judges *The Unconsoled* to be "a humane and grieving book, as well as one of the strangest novels in memory." According to the *New York Review of Books* "Ishiguro's deepest subject [is] not the sorrow of repression but the comedy and the pathos of the stories we tell ourselves to keep other stories away." *Time* contends that "Ishiguro has essentially created the world of *Alice and Wonderland*, but without the commonsensical presence of Alice." The *London Times* disagrees, calling *The Unconsoled* "a masterpiece, not only for the originality of its conception, the scope of its intentions, and the precision with which they are executed: it is above all a book devoted to the human heart, and as such is Ishiguro's greatest gift to us yet."

READING GROUP GUIDE; RECOGNITION: *NYTBR* Notable Book of 1995 *PW* "Best Books of 1995;" REVIEWS: *The Age* 5/20/95; *BL* 8/95; *CSM* 10/4/95; *Econ* 5/6/95; *KR* 8/1/95; *LATBR* 10/8/95; *LJ* 8/95; *LRB* 6/8/95; *LST* 5/14/95; *LT* 5/11/95; *NewR* 11/6/95; *NS&S* 5/12/95; *NY* 10/23/95; *NYRB* 12/21/95; *NYTBR* 11/6/95; *Obs* 11/26/95; *PW* 7/3/95; *Spec* 11/18/95; *Time* 10/2/95; *TLS* 4/28/95; *VLS* 10/95; *WPBW* 10/29/95; *WSJ* 10/11/95; EDITOR'S NOTE: Mr. Ishiguro was named to *Granta* magazine's 1983 **and** 1993 lists of the twenty "Best Young [i.e., under 40] British Novelists" (the only author to appear twice).

Jackson-Opoku, Sandra (USA)

225 *The River Where Blood Is Born* (1997); One World/Ballantine 1997 (HC)

Sandra Jackson-Opoku's debut novel is steeped in African legend. It begins with the tale of how Kwaku Ananse (a male) gains entry into the all-female village of ancestor spirits thereby gaining access to the souls and stories of unborn African women. Ms. Jackson-Opoku's tale ranges from the Gold Coast of the 18th century, through the horrific Middle Passage and antebellum Barbados, to 20th-century America where we meet smart, ambitious Alma and proud, feisty Cinnamon Brown.

Booklist calls *The River Where Blood Is Born* an "expansive tale that exquisitely melds mythical realms together with a ... family saga spanning centuries and continents" and concludes that Ms. Jackson-Opoku has created "a richly lyrical panoply of lives." The *Library Journal* notes that Jackson-Opoku's novel, "part folktale, part spiritual, part modern romance ... focuses on strong female characters [in search of] love fulfillment, justice, and ultimately, peace." According to the *Washington Post Book World*, the stories of Alma and Cinnamon "are the most conventional in the novel, and contain some of Jackson-Opoku's best and most engaging writing. These contemporary female characters are among the most interesting to be found in recent fiction."

READING GROUP GUIDE; RECOGNITION: Winner of ALA's Black Caucus 1998 Award for Fiction; REVIEWS: *BL* 9/1/97; *LJ* 8/97; *PW* 7/7/97; *WPBW* 10/16/97

Jones, Gayl (USA)

226   *The Healing* (1998); Beacon 1998 (HC)

In her first novel in over 20 years, Gayl Jones tells the story of Harlan Jane Eagleton — a race track habitué and former beautician turned rock star manager — who becomes an itinerant faith healer. Her story is told from back to front as the story prowls through the narrator's numerous incarnations moving restlessly towards the moment of her "first healing."

Called "a major literary event.... Surprising, romantic and wholly satisfying" by *Newsweek*, *The Healing*, in the view of *Publishers Weekly* "is prickly, frequently tendentious and occasionally brilliant." According to *Booklist* "Jones has a wonderful ear for dialogue; her characters sentences are filled with repetitions, abrupt changes of subject, and other quirks of everyday speech. The style of presentation ... with a carefully planned but seemingly reckless disregard for any linear narrative — takes some getting used to, but readers who persevere will find it is worth it." The *Washington Post Book World* observes that "The problem with the story is that Harlan is telling it. As a narrator, she is not as articulate, introspective or revealing as readers might wish her to be — or as we know Jones to be."

The *WPBW* concludes, however, that "*The Healing* marks the long-awaited return ... of a major literary talent ... an important, graceful writer who deserves readers' attention."

OTHER MEDIA: Audiocassette (Books-on-Tape/unabr); RECOGNITION: Nominated for the 1998 National Book Award; *NYTBR* Notable Book of 1998; REVIEWS: *BL* 2/1/98; *Guard* 11/6/98; *Essence* 2/98; *NYTBR* 5/10/98; *PW* 1/19/98; *WPBW* 3/1/98

Kurzweil, Allen (USA)

Case of Curiosities (1992); Ballantine 1993 (pbk); See Section 5, #594

Lethem, Jonathan (USA)

As She Climbed Across the Table (1997); Doubleday 1997 (HC); See Section 7, #921

227   *Amnesia Moon* (1995); St. Martin's 1996 (pbk)

Amnesia Moon, widely described as a "post-apocalyptic" vision of America, is firmly situated in a near future characterized by bomb-blasted cities, a mutated citizenry, sexual deviancy and the liberal use of psychotropic drugs as a means of social control. It is also a "Wizard of Oz–like road novel" featuring one man's odyssey from his mountain refuge (in the projection box of an abandoned multiplex in Hatfork, Wyoming) to the San Francisco of his pre-apocalyptic, dimly remembered youth. Like all of Lethem's work, *Amnesia Moon* is equal parts bizarre and equal parts hilarious.

In the view of *Publishers Weekly* "At its heart, [*Amnesia Moon*] remains a simple story — the search for identity, the search for family — but Lethem uses it successfully as a springboard for both a commentary on American culture and a convincing portrait of his main character." The *Library Journal* argues that Lethem" imbues his second novel with a breathtaking vision of a world in flux." *Newsweek* asserts that Lethem has delivered "a droll, downbeat vision that is both original and persuasive. After all, any writer who can make you hang onto every word of a conversation between a clock and a bonsai tree is an author to be reckoned with."

REVIEWS: *BL* 8/95; *KR* 7/1/95; *LJ* 8/95; *NewsWk* 10/2/95; *PW* 6/12/95; *WPBW* 11/26/95

Lightman, Alan (USA)

228   *Einstein's Dreams* (1993); Warner 1994 (pbk)

Alan Lightman, a professor of physics with an abiding interest in cosmology, has written what many have come to regard as a small literary masterpiece. *Einstein's Dreams*, Lightman's novella-length debut novel is set in Berne, Switzerland, in

1905 and purports to draw on the dreams of a young disheveled and distracted clerk employed by a Swiss Patent office. The result is a cycle of stories about the nature and, indeed, mystery of time.

According to *Booklist*, *Einstein's Dreams* "is a work of hypnotic perception, fluent intelligence, and consummate skill." *Publishers Weekly* observes that "Few endeavors are more beguiling than a grossly improbable conceit realized with subtlety and wit [a skill that] science writer Lightman appears to have mastered." The *Library Journal* concludes: "As a teacher of both physics and writing at M.I.T. Lightman offers provocative and elegantly wrought speculations on the nature of time." In the view of the *Times Literary Supplement*, "This excellent first novel is a double homage to Einstein and to Italo Calvino, whose *Invisible Cities* it imitates in form. All the cities portrayed by Calvino's Marco Polo are ways of looking at Venice; all the relationships between humanity and time dreamed by Lightman's Einstein are ways of looking at Berne."

OTHER MEDIA: Audiocassette (Books-on-Tape/unabr); READING GROUP GUIDE: "Reading Group Choices" 1998 (Paz & Associates); RECOGNITION: *NYTBR* Notable Book of 1993; REVIEWS: *BL* 11/15/93; *Econ* 1/16/93; *LJ* 11/15/92; *NewSci* 3/20/93; *NYTBR* 1/3/93; *PW* 1/24/94; *TLS* 1/22/93; *VLS* 4/93

Mailer, Norman (USA)

Oswald's Tale (1995); Ballantine 1996 (pbk); See Section 5, #605

Harlot's Ghost (1991); Random House 1991 (HC); Ballantine 1992 (pbk); See Section 5, #606

Malouf, David (Australia)

The Conversations at Curlow Creek (1997); Random House 1997 (pbk); See Section 4, #413

Remembering Babylon (1993); Vintage 1984 (pbk); See Section 4, #414

Markson, David (USA)

229 *Reader's Block* (1996); Dalkey 1996 (pbk)

In his 8th novel, David Markson features a writer named Reader who is attempting to write a novel about a character named Protagonist who lives either on a beach or in a cemetery. He finds it slow going as all manner of distracting thoughts jostle about in his consciousness including: quotations (many unattributed) from literature, arcana about literary personages, and personal memories and ruminations.

Publishers Weekly notes that "what Markson accomplishes [in his decidedly experimental novel] is an utterly fascinating document that in itself is a small education in the history of Western literature, seen through the eyes of a gravely impassioned literateur." According to *Kirkus Reviews* the "erudite" Markson has produced a "terse, modernist novel implying that history is over, the arts finished — yet offering extended, Beckett-like pleasures ... [drawn from] a lifetime of— well, reading...." Michael Dirda (*WPBW*) points out "Though death pervades, it never overwhelms the book's stoic and rueful gaiety.... Or the soul-satisfying pleasure of testing one's own literary connoisseurship. In these 200 pages the widely read reader will [notice] ... unattributed quotes from Beckett, Gertrude Stein, Flaubert, Valery, Dowson, Alexander Theroux, Melville, Paul Celine, Malory, a couple of Roman emperors, Goethe, Shakespeare scholar L.C. Knights and Wyndham Lewis...."

RECOGNITION: *Salon Magazine* "Book of the Year" 1996; REVIEWS: *KR* 9/15/96; *LJ* 10/15/96; *NYTBR* 1/12/97; *PW* 11/4/96; *WPBW* 11/3/96

Marlowe, Stephen (USA)

230 *Lighthouse at the End of the World* (1995); Plume 1996 (pbk)

Stephen Marlowe uses well-known biographical details associated with Edgar Allan Poe (his drunkenness, self-destructive behavior, and marriage to his 13-year-old cousin, and the fact that — in his 40th year — he vanished for several days before reappearing in a Baltimore hospital, fatally ill and suffering from partial amnesia) as a sort of literary springboard into a narrative with decidedly surreal overtones. Plot elements include doppelgangers, a sea-captain brother, a fateful journey to a remote South Sea island, mesmerism, and a native curse. Throughout the novel, characters from Poe's own fiction make appearances, including the French detective C. Auguste Dupin, and narrative time shifts — blurring distinctions between past, present and future — abound.

According to the *Washington Post Book World* "Marlowe, a noted historical novelist, attempts to fill in the gap in Poe's last days by examining dominant themes in the author's life and work." In the view of the *L.A. Times*, "Marlowe's [spellbinding] fictional exploration of Poe's life and creative vision is accomplished with great panache, providing fascinating insights into the nature of dreams and the workings of the imagination." *Booklist* observes that Marlowe's "premise is a fascinating one, and his writing is skillful and often engrossing. Whether readers will see this experimental novel as a brilliant work of art or a baffling maze, however, remains to be seen." *Entertainment Weekly* argues that *The*

Lighthouse at the End of the World "is exceedingly clever, but its elaborate structure and numerous twists never obscure the emotional heart of this story — that is, a life filled with frustration and sadness was transcended by dazzling acts of imagination." *Publishers Weekly* calls Marlowe "a historical novelist of the first rank, with a deliciously supple and fluid prose style," and concludes that (despite a very confusing plotline) he "makes Poe come alive in all his mad glory; and this is accomplishment enough to warrant applause."

REVIEWS: *BL* 10/1/95; *EW* 12/15/95; *LATBR* 2/4/96; *LJ* 9/1/95; *PW* 8/7/95; *WPBW* 11/17/96

Mawer, Simon (UK)

231   *Mendel's Dwarf* (1997); Crown 1998 (HC)

In his fourth novel, widely regarded as a *tour de force*, Simon Mawer elaborates a grand scientific adventure featuring Benedict Lambert, a world renowned geneticist who is the great-great-great nephew of Gregor Mendel, the Austrian monk credited with the discovery of genetics. The 38-year-old Lambert is also an achondroplastic dwarf and significantly misshapen to boot — the product of a genetic mutation and thereby uniquely motivated in his search for the "single letter spelling mistake in thirty-three billion" that results in dwarfism. Mawer's story is structured as a dual biography, a double helix of intertwined tales focusing both on the contemporary Lambert (and his struggle for love and acceptance) and on the historic Mendel who overcame a peasant background and strict religious constraints to conduct his seminal research. Although this is Mawer's fourth novel, it is his first to be published in the United States.

Washington Post Book World calls *Mendel's Dwarf* "a remarkable performance" and concludes that "Lambert's voice is distinctive, unique and often downright chilling; it grabs you by the throat and dares you to admit your own revulsion...." *Publishers Weekly*, in its starred review, observes that "Sophisticated, tortured and witty, Lambert is a character on the grand scale, a combination of erudition and cruelty reminiscent of Nabokov's Humbert Humbert." According to *Booklist* "Benedict, Mendel, and genetic science create a unique tension, with clever prose and the author's insight into human sadness turning it all into something truly profound." As *the London Sunday Times* points out, "the two men's lives are recounted in an overlapping narrative that is full of thought-provoking intelligence, moral insight and twisted human comedy."

RECOGNITION: *NYTBR* Notable Book of 1998; REVIEWS: *BL* 12/1/97; *KR* 1/1/98; *LJ* 11/15/97; *LST* 4/19/98; *NYTBR* 3/22/98; *PW* 11/3/98; *WPBW* 3/22/98

McCarthy, Cormac (USA)

232   *Cities of the Plain* (1998); Knopf 1998 (HC)

Cities of the Plain, volume three of McCarthy's "Border Trilogy" completes the cycle started in *All the Pretty Horses*. Here the author unites John Grady Cole from *All the Pretty Horses* and Billy Parham from *The Crossing*. These two young men who share painful, yet defining, experiences "south of the border," meet at the midpoint of this century, as cowhands on the Cross Fours ranch in New Mexico. Cole, the consummate horseman, is now eighteen; Parham, still nursing the tragic loss of his brother, is twenty-eight. Together they face a future which clearly has little use for the once-venerated virtues of a frontier life.

According to *Newsweek*, "Nobody living writes about friendship better than McCarthy, nobody writes better about animals, or the land, the desert especially. With each book, he expands the territory of American fiction." *Kirkus Reviews* observes that in *Cities of the Plain* (an essential component of a contemporary masterpiece) Cormac McCarthy once again "offers an unflinching depiction of the hard lives and complex fates of men ripped loose from the moorings of home and family, pursuing destinies that seem imposed upon them by external forces ... [The author's] magnificent descriptions of landscape, weather, and animals in their relationship to men, and the stripped-down dialogue that perfectly captures his characters' laconic fatalism are as impressive — and unusual — as ever." In the view of the *London Sunday Times* "McCarthy's border is the division between the workaday world and that which is hidden behind it — terrifying violence, political turmoil, sexual love. Crossing and re-crossing it in three fierce, desolate, beautiful novels, he has created a masterpiece, one that engages with tremendous questions of life and death and has the weight to take them on." The *Times Literary Supplement* points out that "The McCarthy who doesn't waste a word is present here, but so too is the McCarthy who glories in a recondite and *recherche* vocabulary, unfolding in long, rolling grammatically irregular sentences which are most commonly employed in descriptions of landscape and the seasons, thereby emphasizing the rhetorical in the midst of the ostensibly 'natural'...." According to the *New York Review of Books*, McCarthy's work is "part of a burgeoning popular literature of masculine sentimentality. His books fit neatly alongside — and share space on the best-seller lists with — novels like *Snow Falling on Cedars*, *Cold Mountain* and *The Horse Whisperer*. These books cannily mingle the conventions of the boy's adventure story with the ideological demands of the post-feminist men's movement. In them, manhood is at once the perpetual evasion of maturity and the achievement of a wisdom beyond measure."

OTHER MEDIA: Audiocassette (Random Audio/abr; Books-on-Tape/unabr); READING GROUP GUIDE; RECOGNITION: *LATBR* "Best Fiction of 1998'; *NYTBR* Notable Book of 1998; REVIEWS: *KR* 4/1/98; *LST* 6/7/98; *LT* 6/13/98; *NewsWk* 5/18/98; *NYRB* 9/24/98; *TLS* 6/19/98; *WPBW* 5/24/98

233 *The Crossing* (1994); Knopf 1994 (HC); Vintage 1995 (pbk)

The second volume of Cormac McCarthy's "Border Trilogy" once again features a young Westerner, a range-riding youngster by the name of Billy Parham. Billy lives in New Mexico, close to the border with Mexico which, in 1938, is still in the throes of revolution. Obsessed with a she-wolf that has wandered over the border and is now threatening livestock on his father's ranch, Billy manages to trap the animal, and, refusing to kill it, sets off to return it to its natural habitat in a Mexican mountain range. This is the first of three fateful border crossings that Billy will make, the second two being triggered by the murder of his parents and a search for his missing younger brother. Mexico, as in McCarthy's previous volume, is portrayed as archaic, anarchic and violent, a testing ground for the teenager's emerging manhood.

In the view of *World Literature Today*, "Cormac McCarthy is as good as a writer can be in his use of description, certainly better than any American now living and possibly even better than Faulkner or Melville. He uses this great talent to try to come to terms with the omnipresence of evil in man's nature, as he understands and presents it." *Kirkus Reviews* calls *The Crossing* "[r]elentless, frequently brutal, and ... because [McCarthy] is one of America's foremost literary craftsmen ... passionate and compelling" and concludes that "it will resonate for ages...." The *Times Literary Supplement* asserts "The elegiac lyricism which made *All the Pretty Horses* such exhilarating reading is not available to a novel in which sweet melancholy must make way for sheer sadness ... it seems Billy's wanderings have taken him beyond some limit of human sympathy and across some ultimate boundary which has left him outside the limits of God's grace ... [Billy's] scars are permanent, he cannot undo experience ... you can re-cross the border as often as you like, but you will never be able to uncross it."

OTHER MEDIA: Audiocassette (Random Audio/abr); READING GROUP GUIDE; RECOGNITION: *NYTBR* Notable Book of 1994; REVIEWS: *BL* 5/15/94; *EW* 6/17/94; *KR* 4/15/94; *LJ* 6/15/94; *NewsWk* 6/13/94; *NS&S* 8/19/94; *NY* 6/27/94; *PeopleW* 6/13/94; *PW* 4/25/94; *TLS* 9/2/94; *WLT* Win '95; *WPBW* 6/5/94

234 *All the Pretty Horses* (1992); Random House 1992 (HC); Vintage 1993 (pbk)

In *All the Pretty Horses* (Volume One of Cormac McCarthy's recently completed "Border Trilogy") John Grady Cole, a disaffected, horse-obsessed teenager who is reeling from the death of his grandfather and the imminent loss of his 18,000 acre Texas ranch, saddles up his beloved horse and — in the company of his best friend Rawlins — rides off into the early morning dawn. They soon meet up with another rootless teenager, the seriously unstable (13-year-old) Blevins. Forming a loose adventurer's alliance, the three ride south into Mexico. A stint on "La Purisima" a horse farm, a passionate affair with a haciendo's daughter, and incarceration in a casually brutal Mexican jail lay in wait for Cody who, by the end of the novel has achieved a measure of manhood and a well-honed code of ethics.

In the view of *Newsweek*, "This hymn to youth and times past is sweet-tempered, but never sentimental, accessible without compromise.... A modern-day Western, full of horses and gunplay and romance, it transcends the bounds of its genre with rambunctious, high-spirited, bottomless inventiveness." The *Library Journal* notes that "With its strong masculine point of view, lyric language, and thematic interplay of honor and survival [*All the Pretty Horses*], is often reminiscent of Hemingway." The *London Review of Books*, while observing that "McCarthy's novel is set about forty-five years ago, and his Mexico is satisfactorily primitive, impoverished, beautiful, at best ruggedly barbaric" concludes that this is "not a vision of Mexico that will please contemporary Mexicans. This 'Mexico' must exist as a place where a man can be a man: an American that is — the Mexican men are depicted as mostly cowardly or cruel." Novelist **Madison Smartt Bell** (*NYTBR*) argues that "The magnetic attraction of Mr. McCarthy's fiction comes ... from the extraordinary quality of his prose [which] difficult as it may sometimes be ... is also overwhelmingly seductive.... His diction and phrasing come from all over the evolutionary history of English and combine into a prose that seems to invent itself as it unfolds, resembling Elizabethan language in its flux of remarkable possibilities." Richard Eder (*LATBR*) declares that although the use of ornate syntax and "bilingual mannerisms" compromise McCarthy's work, it is, nonetheless, "a moving and often enthralling story, a compelling portrait of a young man's hungers" characterized by "a profound empathy for a different culture and a sweet skill in portraying it."

OTHER MEDIA: Audiocassette (RandomAudio/abr; Books-on-Tape/unabr); READING GROUP GUIDE; RECOGNITION: Winner of the 1992 National Book Award; Winner of the 1992 National

Book Critic's Circle Award; *Publishers Weekly* "Best Book" of 1992; *NYTBR* Notable Book 1993; RE- VIEWS: *ComW* 9/25/92; *CSM* 6/11/92; *LATBR* 5/17/92; *LJ* 5/15/92; *LRB* 12/16/93; *NewsWk* 5/18/92; *NYTBR* 5/17/92

Mendelsohn, Jane (USA)

235   *I Was Amelia Earhart* (1996); Knopf 1996 (HC); Random House 1997 (pbk)

This is the story of what happened to me when I died. It's also the story of my life. Destiny, the alchemy of fate and luck. I think about it sometimes, under a radiant sun. The tide laughs. The light swims. I watch the fish-skeleton shadows of the palm leaves on the sand. The clouds ripped to shreds.

Today when I think of my former life, I think of it as a dream. In the dream I am another person. In the dream I am the foremost aviatrix of my day, a heroine. I am Amelia Earhart.

Amelia Earhart the "goddess of flight" disap- peared on July 2, 1937, having lost all radio contact on a 'round-the-world solo flight. Jane Mendel- sohn's fictional tale of the famous aviatrix's final flight and its aftermath focuses on the stormy rela- tionship between Amelia and her near-sighted, al- coholic navigator, Fred Noonan and their (imag- ined) final days together on an uninhabited tropical island. The deceased Ms. Earhart narrates the tale.

According to the *Times Literary Supplement,* Mendelsohn "has used the few available facts of Earhart's life and final voyage to construct a vivid prose-poem, dazzling and as unresolved as that last flight." Francis Stead Sellers (*NYTBR*) argues that "if you can suspend disbelief and accept Earhart's self-conscious posthumous account, her story be- comes curiously compelling…. And while it is hard to feel much suspense over the fate of an already dead protagonist, you can't help admiring the bold- ness of a first novelist who would make fiction of a legend." In the view of *Publishers Weekly*, "The Earhart limned here is materialistic, glory-seeking, sexually hungry, outrageously self-absorbed and ut- terly charismatic." *Kirkus Reviews* calls *I Was Amelia Earhart* "Strange, slight, but wonderful: a modest portrait that manages to create some moments of exceptional intensity and power of feeling." Eng- lish novelist **Julia Blackburn** found it to be "a won- derfully mad, wild and lyrical book." The *LATBR* concludes that *I Was Amelia Earhart* "is a brief, brilliant study in redemption, a meditation on love and loneliness that steers far away from mawkish- ness."

OTHER MEDIA: Audiocassette (Random Audio/abr); READING GROUP GUIDE; RECOGNI- TION: Shortlisted for the 1997 Orange Fiction Prize; REVIEWS: *BL* 4/15/96; *Econ* 6/15/96; *EW* 4/26/96; *GW* 5/31/96; *KR* 2/15/96; *LATBR* 7/4/96; *LitRev* 7/96; *LJ* 4/1/96; *LT* 5/30/96; *Nation* 4/22/96; *NewR* 6/17/96; *NY* 5/20/96; *NYTBR* 5/12/96; *PW* 3/18/96; *SLJ* 10/96; *TLS* 6/14/96; *WRB* 7/96

Michaels, Anne (Canada)

236   *Fugitive Pieces* (1997); Knopf 1997 (HC); Vintage 1998 (pbk)

In her debut novel, Canadian poet Anne Michaels, tells the story of Jakob Beer, a Jewish poet who, as a child in WW II, was somehow over- looked by the Nazis as they rounded up every Jew in his Polish town. He was found, starving and di- sheveled, by Athos Roussos, a Greek geologist and scholar, midst the rubble of a blasted Polish village. The kind-hearted Athos manages to smuggle the child back to Greece (and a kind of precarious safety) and there he rears him as his son. The two eventually emigrate to Canada. The story is nar- rated by a 60-year-old Jakob who, at last, begins to commit his memories to paper. Throughout his life, Jakob has been haunted by memories of his family (all of whom died in the concentration camps), but especially of his sister Bella an accom- plished pianist. Jakob's diaries are eventually found by Ben, the son of two holocaust survivors.

According to *Booklist*, "stories of the Holo- caust keep surfacing in the minds of writers like bone fragments working their way through skin. Award-winning poet Michaels revisits that mon- strous time in her beautiful first novel, a work every bit as haunting as her fellow Canadian Michael On- daatje's celebrated *The English Patient*." *Maclean's* observes that *Fugitive Pieces* "forsakes linear story- telling for a poetic, multi-layered reminiscence. Most of the book's events … are recollections de- scribed in Jakob's notebooks. His journals inter- weave his own story of loss with survivors' accounts of Nazi-inflicted horrors and scraps of poetry and philosophy. Later, those notebooks offer spiritual redemption to Ben, whose life and marriage have become unmoored by the revelation of a long- buried secret from his parent's war experience." In the view of the *Christian Science Monitor* "Anne Michaels … offers a richly imagined portrait of Jakob's slow progress from reticence to poetic elo- quence and of the complex blend of memories, feel- ings, insights, and experiences that makes him the man he becomes." The *London Sunday Times* calls *Fugitive Pieces* both "beautiful and horrific, cele- bratory and threnodic; and as compassionate as it is cathartic [which] is all the more astonishing for being the author's first work of fiction."

OTHER MEDIA: Audiocassette recording (Chivers/unabr); READING GROUP GUIDE; RECOG- NITION: Winner of Britain's 1997 Orange and Guardian Prizes for fiction; shortlisted for the 1996 Giller Prize; *LATBR* "Recommended Title" 1997; *NYTBR* Notable Book of 1997; *Publishers Weekly* "Best Books" 1997; REVIEWS: *BL* 2/15/97; *CSM*

3/10/97; *LATBR* 3/10/97; *LJ* 3/1/97; *LST* 1/25/98; *Maclean's* 7/1/96; *Nation* 4/7/97; *NYT* 3/7/97; *NYTBR* 4/20/97; *PW* 12/30/96; *SLJ* 6/97; *Time* 3/3/97

Millhauser, Steven (USA)

237 *Martin Dressler: The Tale of an American Dreamer* (1996); Vintage 1997 (pbk)

Steven Millhauser's novel, a fable about genius, obsession and the pursuit of the American Dream, tells the story of New Yorker Martin Dressler and his bootstrap rise from humble beginnings (the son of a struggling tobacconist) to ownership of a string of luxury hotels. Alongside "sensual" period details "so palpable you can practically chew on them" (*WSJ*), Millhauser weaves a fascinating tale of the making of the consummate entrepreneur during a time when the creation of immense wealth was within the reach of men who dreamt large enough dreams.

According to *Booklist* "This *fin-de-siècle* allegory concerns the previous century and the mercurial play of a typical American entrepreneurial spirit." *Publishers Weekly* contends that "Taking its place alongside other fine tales of architectural symbology, from Poe to Ayn Rand, this enticing novel becomes at once a tale of life, a marriage and a creative imagination in crisis." English novelist **Claire Messud,** writing in the *London Sunday Times*, points out that "The resonance of this narrative far outstrips the simple historical tale: *Martin Dressler* is, in fact, a post-modern reflection upon the power, but also the limitations, of the imagination — and hence an exploration of the contradictions of fiction itself...." In *Time* magazine's view, *Martin Dressler* "is an urban fable about civilization and its discontents, the repression of instincts in the service of progress. Yet this commercial hero also represents a period of social history when ambition and new wealth outstripped utility and taste." The *Times Literary Supplement* observes that "Millhauser is a quintessentially 1960s writer, firmly placed alongside Donald Barthelme and John Barth. In other ways, his work is truly *sui generis.* For while his characters are obsessed with the magic of story-making, they are never reduced to mere pawns in some elaborate metafictional game." *TLS* concludes that "[Millhauser's] best of books have never been widely read, or even published much outside the United States. His newest and best novel, (the Pulitzer Prize–winning) *Martin Dressler,* has changed all that...." The *Washington Post Book World* concludes that this is a "most convincing [novel], well worth the wait since *Edwin Mullhouse.*"

OTHER MEDIA: Audiocassette (Recorded Bks/unabr); READING GROUP GUIDE; RECOGNITION: Winner of the 1997 Pulitzer Prize for Fiction;

nominated for the 1996 National Book Award; *NYTBR* Notable Book of 1996; *PW* "Best Books" 1996; REVIEWS: *BL* 4/1/96; *KR* 3/1/96; *LATBR* 5/26/96; *LJ* 4/15/96; *LT* 3/26/98; *Nation* 5/6/96; *NYTBR* 5/12/96; *PW* 3/25/96; *Time* 6/10/96; *TLS* 4/3/98; *WPBW* 4/28/96; *WSJ* 4/24/96

238 *Little Kingdoms* (1993); Random House 1998 (pbk)

Little Kingdoms is comprised of three novellas — "The Little Kingdom of J. Franklin Payne," "The Princess, the Dwarf, and the Dungeon," "Catalogue of the Exhibition: The Art of Edwin Moorash (1810-1846)." Each explores some aspect of the creative instinct and each takes place in a world a little to one side of, above, or below the "real" one. The stories feature a 1920's cartoonist who is on the verge of creating animation; a beautiful princess and a jealous prince, and a 19th century painter.

Kirkus Reviews notes that these "three novellas confirm Millhauser's status as a master fabulist" and concludes that "There's nothing overly academic about Millhauser's fictional inventions — for every bit of cleverness, there's the art of true passion." According to the *New York Times Book Review* "Mr. Millhauser's unfolding narrative of entanglements sexual and esthetic among the principals would have made Byron's heart leap and Poe's dance with dark recognition. Love requited and unrequited, and the torments and reprisals born of the triangles formed by the characters' love, verge ever so delicately on a parody of the Romantic territory of despair, incest, madness and the cult of death. But Stephen Millhauser circles back from the border of parody to plunge us into the very heartland of human complexity and folly." In the view of the *Chicago Tribune* "Millhauser has proved through the years to be an American writer of surpassing skill.... His books are learned and allusive, composed with wit and flair. Now in *Little Kingdoms* he continues to establish sovereignty in one corner of the fictional map: he chronicles obsession in three linked novellas and it's hard to imagine anyone doing it this way or this well."

REVIEWS: *ChiTrib* 10/3/93; *EW* 9/17/93; *KR* 7/1/93; *LJ* 4/15/96; *NY* 2/7/94; *NYTBR* 10/3/93; *PW* 7/12/93; *WPBW* 9/5/93

Moody, Rick (USA)

239 *Purple America* (1997); Little, Brown 1997 (HC); 1998 (pbk)

Rick Moody sets his latest novel in the "Gothic underside of Connecticut's privileged suburbs" (*Kirkus*) and features the following principles: Billie Raitliffe, a strong-minded woman in late middle-age who suffers from a degenerative disease and is therefore confined to a wheelchair;

her second husband, Lou Sloane, a director of the local nuclear power plant (which is teetering on the edge of crisis); and her alcoholic, thirty-something son Dexter ("Hex") who, learning that Sloane has just walked out on his mother, has dutifully returned home for the weekend to fill the breach. All the events of *Purple America* occur during just one highly charged 24-hour period in the life of this troubled family.

Called a "transfixing experience" by *Booklist*, *Purple America*, in the view of *Publishers Weekly*, "catalogues the detritus that fills" the thoughts of the three protagonists: Billy, Lou and Hex. *Kirkus Reviews* observes that "The language has a jazzy punch and freshness, flawlessly catching the ebb and flow of thought and the way in which fear adds an edge of frenzy to even the smallest events. The sad climax is predictable, yet is nonetheless powerful and moving." According to the *Chicago Tribune* "Self consciously artful but rarely obtrusive, Moody's prose dazzles with labyrinthine sentences of Faulknerian length. Its opening passage rings with biblical cadences, into the middle of which he tosses a Zen koan, all describing Hex giving his mother a bath. So rich in fact, is the book, that it demands to be read twice." The *Times Literary Supplement* concludes that *Purple America* "further establishes [Moody] as part of a gifted generation of American writers—writers like David Foster Wallace, Jonathan Franzen, and fellow Brown alumni, Jeffrey Eugenides and Donald Antrim, concerned with crises of masculinity and modernity."

READING GROUP GUIDE: "Reading Group Choices" 1998 (Paz & Associates); RECOGNITION: *NYTBR* Notable Book of 1997; *LATBR* "Recommended Title" 1997; *Publishers Weekly* "Best Books" 1997; *Booklist* Editors' Choice 1997; REVIEWS: *BL* 3/15/97; *ChiTrib* 5/11/97; *KR* 2/1/97; *LATBR* 4/20/97; *NewsWk* 4/28/97; *NYTBR* 4/27/97; *SFCBR* 3/30/97; *Time* 4/14/97; *TLS* 2/27/98; *WPBW* 4/8/97

240   *The Ice Storm* (1994); Little Brown 1994 (IIC); Warner 1995 (pbk)
Set in New England in the 1970s, Rick Moody's *Ice Storm* captures a low point in American social history. The Hoods are an upper–middle-class suburban family adrift in the decade that brought us pet rocks, leisure suits, shag carpets, wife-swapping, and the fall of Saigon. Benjamin Hood is an alcoholic securities analyst given to compulsive philandering, his wife Elena is too disillusioned and self-absorbed to provide adequate parenting to her son Paul who suffers from low self-esteem or her daughter Wendy who's preoccupied with alcohol and sex. Benjamin is actively pursuing his neighbor, Janey Williams, mother to another pair of dysfunctional teenagers.

As the *L.A. Times Book Review* points out

"This is not so much a novel as an excavation — of that nearly but not quite extinct entity, the nuclear family as it was in the those dark ages, the 1970s. The argot, the foibles, the fads and the artifacts: they're all here, meticulously catalogued and historically framed with discussions of the design, politics and groping psychology of the period." According to *Time*, "While the problems of the Hoods are unrelenting, Moody recounts them with a detachment that sets the novel apart from those darker chronicles of New England suburban misery, the works of John Cheever and Richard Yates." *Publishers Weekly*, while finding the cultural references a bit thick on the ground, contends that Moody's "depiction of these families ... is insightful and convincing.... And the central tragedy of the tale remains resonant...." In the view of *The London Guardian*, "*The Ice Storm* is one of the wittiest books about family life ... ever written. In synchronizing public and private crises it demonstrates mesmerically, the historicity of these heedless, wasteful lives."

OTHER MEDIA: A film version directed by Ang Lee was released in 1997 starring Kevin Kline and Sigourney Weaver; REVIEWS: *ChiTrib* 5/29/94; *Econ* 6/18/94; *Guard* 7/12/94; *KR* 3/1/94; *LATBR* 8/7/94; *LST* 8/28/94; *PW* 3/14/94; *Time* 5/30/94; *TLS* 8/5/94

Morley, John David (USA)

Feast of Fools (1994); St. Martin's 1995 (pbk); See Section 8, #1018

Morrison, Toni (USA)

241   *Paradise*; Knopf 1998 (HC)
Set in the mid-1970s, Toni Morrison's new novel centers on four young women who are brutally attacked at a women's center (located in an old mansion now referred to as "the convent") located just outside the all-black town of Ruby, Oklahoma. The building, once a school for Native American girls, has long-functioned as a refuge for abused women. It has also now been targeted by the men of Ruby as a place where "evil" things (e.g., abortions, witchcraft) are allowed to thrive. The stories of the "convent" women are told in individual chapters intermingled with a history of the town and its founding families.

Richard Eder (*LATBR*) calls *Paradise* "a fascinating story, wonderfully detailed" and concludes that the town she has imagined becomes "the stage for a profound and provocative debate — always personified and always searching — about black identity and destiny in American's past and present." The *Times Literary Supplement* points out that Morrison's "supple and unconventional handling of time is strong here. For the women of the Convent, present time is replete with flashes of future and past, which go well beyond memory." According to the *New York Review of Books*, "*Paradise* pulls off a rare and stunning feat: it is a novel with a double life, a serious work of fiction which also functions as a parable, a novel that is, effectively and ironically, also a work of literary criticism. *Paradise*, perhaps more directly than any of Toni Morrison's other novels, draws [the] black presence forward from the margins of imagination to the center of American literature and history." Michiko Kakutani (*NYT*) offers a dissenting opinion in asserting that "*Paradise* is everything that *Beloved* (her 1989 Pulitzer Prize–winning novel) was not: it's a heavy-handed schematic piece of writing, thoroughly lacking in the novelistic magic Ms. Morrison has wielded so effortlessly in the past. It's a contrived and formulaic book that mechanically pits men against women, old against young, the past against the present."

OTHER MEDIA: Audiocassette (Random Audio/abr); READING GROUP GUIDE; RECOGNITION: *LATBR* "Top Ten Books of 1998"; *NYTBR* Notable Book of 1998; REVIEWS: *KR* 11/15/97; *LATBR* 1/11/98; *NYRB* 6/11/98; *NYT* 1/6/98; *NYTBR* 1/11/98; *TLS* 3/27/98; *WPBW* 1/11/98

Mosley, Nicholas (UK)

242 *Hopeful Monsters* (1990); Dalkey Archive 1991 (HC); Vintage 1993 (pbk)

Nicholas Mosley's prize-winning novel, *Hopeful Monsters* begins in Weimar, Germany, in 1929 and encompasses the major events, philosophical preoccupations and scientific discoveries of the first half of the 20th century. Max a young English physicist/philosopher/cyberneticist, and Eleanor a German-Jewish anthropologist/philosopher/psychologist meet at a performance of Faust and fall in love at political demonstration punctuated by a violent clash between the newly formed Hitler Youth and a collection of young communists. Mosley employs a dense, non-linear narrative style which is shaped by Eleanor and Max's correspondence and shared memories. The *Chicago Tribune* reviewer points out that this is the "culminating volume in a series of five fictions called 'Catastrophe Practice' that (in this reviewer's opinion) may be one of the most important extended literary projects of this century, on a level with the multivolume universes created by Proust, Anthony Powell, Laurence Durrell and John Updike."

Publishers Weekly calls *Hopeful Monsters* a perfectly realized exposition of notions integral to the Western mind" and observes that Max and Eleanor's "intellectual and emotional journeys are sustained by the ambiguities of the modern era — [for example] the pursuit of the bomb for peaceful ends" In the view of the *Library Journal* Mosley's

book is "[d]ense but accessible ... a work of major import that belongs in all collections of serious fiction." According to the *New Statesman and Society* there "is an intellectual engagement here, a devouring determination to investigate, to refrain from judgment while never abandoning moral convictions, that is rare among British novelists — or, for that matter, among novelists of any nationality." The *Christian Science Monitor* (although drawing attention to the novel's weaknesses) points out that "the achievement of *Hopeful Monsters* ... is that it so convincingly conveys the hopes and anguishes of those mercurial decades. To render the confusion of the times, Nicholas Mosley banishes the advantage of hindsight. He adopts a journal form through which he is better able to represent the mental life of those who could only suspect the roaring apocalypse awaiting them in the fall of 1939." The *Washington Post Book World* reviewer notes that Mosley's "book seems ... so copiously right in its range and understanding: He has got more of our [century's] reality into language than any other contemporary novelist I know of. *Hopeful Monsters* is an amazing achievement — and a hopeful one."

RECOGNITION: Winner of the Whitbread Literary Award; REVIEWS: *ChiTrib* 12/22/91; *CSM* 1/29/92; *KR* 12/2/91; *LATBR* 12/15/91; *LJ* 10/1/91; *LST* 6/3/90; *NYT* 12/26/91; *PW* 9/20/91; *WPBW* 11/10/91

Murdoch, Iris (UK)

243 *Jackson's Dilemma* (1996); Viking 1996 (HC)

In her latest metaphysical comedy of manners, Dame Iris tells the story of an imperiled love affair between a sensitive would-be poet by the name of Edward Lannion and his lovely neighbor, Miss Marian Fox. The primary action takes place at adjoining country houses: Hattling Hall, an aging structure which Edward — a heretofore confirmed Londoner — has just inherited and Penndean Hall which belongs to Edward's rather fastidious friend, Benet. On the day before his wedding, however, Edward receives a note from Marian — who, it appears, has disappeared — informing him that the marriage is off. The note reads, quite simply "I am very sorry, I cannot marry you." Through the combined musings and observations (fully aired) of each of their friends, the situation is eventually clarified, new romantic pairings are made, fortunes are found and inheritance secured. Dramatis personae include the usual (Murdochian) circle of brainy-eccentric friends with the addition of Jackson, a Caliban-like figure in the employ of Benet.

Novelist Valerie Miner (*The Nation*) observes that "Iris Murdoch has choreographed her twenty-sixth novel with characteristically witty gender-bending, genre-bending acrobatics. The Philoso-pher-novelist pits Spirit against Will.... If any-thing, *Jackson's Dilemma* is typical Murdoch fiction, only more so: tense with dichotomy, teased by in-tellectual puzzling, rich in allusion." According to *Booklist* Murdoch "has decided to have fun, so her twenty-sixth is a romp as well as a homage to that master of convoluted comedy, Shakespeare. Mur-doch has adopted a syncopated, slightly seeking tone, and many scenes have a distinctly theatrical air." *Salon* calls *Jackson's Dilemma* a "freewheeling novel of ideas, in which philosophical positions are happily subordinated to the quirks and tics of human nature."

RECOGNITION: *NYTBR* Notable Book of 1996; REVIEWS: *BL* 10/15/95; *ChiTrib* 1/28/96; *EW* 1/12/96; *LATBR* 2/25/96; *LJ* 11/1/95; *Nation* 1/8/96; *NY* 4/15/96; *NYTBR* 1/7/96; *PW* 10/23/95; *Salon* 1996; *WPBW* 2/4/96

The Green Knight (1993); Viking 1994 (pbk); See Section 8, #1019

Naylor, Gloria (USA)

244   *Bailey's Cafe* (1992); Vintage 1993 (pbk)
Bailey's cafe is a magical diner, a port-in-the-storm for a colorful collection of characters living in a Brooklyn neighborhood in the late 1940s. Bai-ley, the proprietor, mans the grill while his wife, Nadine, presides over the cash register. The food is unexceptional but the place is always crowded with patrons (pilgrims?) who come for a different sort of sustenance: acceptance, understanding and an op-portunity to share their life stories. In her fourth novel Gloria Naylor effectively incorporates alle-gory (along with dollops of the supernatural) into her often dreamy depiction of a modern-day Tabard Inn.

According to the *Women's Review of Books*, *Bailey's Cafe* is Naylor's "finest novel to date. Her rendering of life in a New York alley reflects the city's magic, its jazz, its violent stories, its street-lamp sparks of hope." Richard Eder *(LATBR)* calls Ms. Naylor's novel "an unforgettable successor to Ellison's metaphor of the invisible man, and as incandescent." *Belles Lettres* concludes that "Nay-lor's expansive vision of humanity moves beyond racial, gender, and ethnic boundaries as she affirms miracles, life, survival, wholeness, and redemp-tion."

OTHER MEDIA: Audiocassette (Brilliance/unabr); REVIEWS: *BL* 7/92; *BellesL* Spr '93; *KR* 6/15/92; *LATBR* 8/30/92; *LJ* 9/1/92; *NYTBR* 10/4/92; *PW* 6/15/92; *TLS* 7/17/92; *WRB* 2/93

Noon, Jeff (UK)

Automated Alice (1996); Crown 1996 (HC); See Section 8, #1021

245   *Pollen* (1995); Crown 1996 (HC)
The sequel to Jeff Noon's prize-winning, cy-berpunk novel *Vurt* has been described variously as: dystopian satire, surrealistic fiction, and "genre-transcending" Sci-Fi. Whatever its label, *Pollen* is set in post-millennial England, in a northern city, where the widespread use of fertility pills has cre-ated a strain of mutants, where the citizenry is kept docile through the ingestion of a recreational drug called vurt and the countryside is littered with post-industrial detritus. The plot, such as it is, is jump-started by a series of murders linked by the discov-ery — near each body — of a sweet-scented pollen. The chief of police gives the investigation over to a telepathic "shadow cop," Sybil Jones, who is ca-pable of gaining access to the final thoughts of mur-der victims. As the pollen proliferates, and menac-ingly luxuriant plants begin to sprout around the city, an epidemic of fatal hay fever sweeps through the populace. Policewoman Jones and her teenage daughter, both curiously immune to the effects of the pollen, take it upon themselves to find the source of the epidemic.

Kirkus Reviews notes that *Pollen* is that "wel-come rarity, a sequel that surpasses its original" and concludes that the novel is "intriguingly textured, reliably witty and inventive: Noon's whirling pur-poseful insanity packs quite a wallop." Called "weird as it is wonderful" by the *London Times*, "good subversive fun" by the *L.A. Times* and "phan-tasmogic and pulpish" by *Salon*, it has already achieved cult status. In the view of the *Times Lit-erary Supplement*, Jeff Noon is "energetic and un-conventional.... A counter-culture adventurer" a view shared by *Booklist* which asserts that "Noon's blend of quirky ideas, striking prose, and imagina-tive characterizations establishes him as one of the most original new voices in imaginative fiction."

REVIEWS: *BL* 12/15/95; *EW* 3/8/96; *KR* 12/1/95; *LATBR* 5/6/95; *LJ* 1/96; *Obs* 12/31/95; *PW* 12/4/95; *TLS* 5/19/95

246   *Vurt* (1994); St. Martin's 1996 (pbk)
Jeff Noon's prize-winning novel *Vurt* has been widely compared to, among other works, *Alice in Wonderland A Clockwork Orange, Neuromancer* and *Naked Lunch*. Set in a futuristic northern English city peopled by a curious mixture of mutants, ro-bots, and retro-humans, *Vurt's* plot revolves around the mythical quest of a brother (Scribble) for his missing kid sister (Desdemona). Noon's story is played out against a background of urban violence and the availability of feathers (black feathers, pink pornovurt feathers, glorious yellow feathers) which allow the user to experience a virtual reality state known as "the Vurt." When Desdemona (who is also Scribble's lover) fails to return from an excur-sion propelled by the particularly powerful feather

labeled "English Voodoo," Scribble sets off in hot pursuit.

According to the *Library Journal*, *Vurt* is "humorous, horrific, and wildly original ... [in short] an imaginative triumph." The *New Yorker* suggests that "While [*Vurt*] observes most of the conventions of cyberpunk fiction, its imagery is insistently organic, and owes more to the underground pharmacology of the rave scene than to the world of hardwired chips and user interface...." The *New Statesman and Society* notes that Noon's novel contains "the streetwise cynicism of Kurt Vonnegut at his best..." and concludes that "It may be too harsh for hippies, too beautiful for bikers; but its spikiness should appeal to the punks, and its obsession with danger and death should grab the goths." *Time* magazine asserts that *Vurt* "is a good try at great nonsense, and if someone doesn't use it as the basis for Son of Blade Runner, Hollywood isn't paying attention."

OTHER MEDIA: Audiocassette (S&S Audio/ abr); RECOGNITION: Winner of the 1994 Arthur C. Clark Award; REVIEWS: *BL* 12/1/94; *EW* 2/10/95; *KR* 10/15/94; *LJ* 11/28/94; *NS&S* 1/21/94; *NY* 2/13/95; *NYTBR* 2/5/95; *PW* 11/28/94; *Time* 2/20/95; *WPBW* 2/26/95

Norfolk, Lawrence (UK)

The Pope's Rhinoceros (1996); Henry Holt 1997 (pbk); See Section 5, #631

Ondaatje, Michael (Sri Lanka/Canada)

247   *The English Patient* (1992); Vintage 1996 (pbk)

Michael Ondaatje opens his Booker Prize–winning novel in a ruined Italian villa in the months just prior to the end of World War II. Here, in the hills overlooking Florence, he has gathered four (of his five) major characters: Hana, a 20-year-old Canadian nurse; Kip, a Sikh, whose expertise is defusing bombs; Caravaggio, a Canadian thief-turned military spy; and the English patient, burnt beyond recognition. As the German soldiers retreat, they have left behind a landscape dotted with land mines. Against this immediate scenario, Ondaatje gradually reveals — through a series of often dream-like flashbacks to the Libyan desert of the 1930s — the story of a painfully intense love affair between the English patient and the beautiful wife of a British archaeologist and flyer.

According to noted literary critic Lorna Sage (*TLS*) "Michael Ondaatje's special gift as a novelist is to keep all the elements of a story in suspension, up in the air, seeming still yet buzzing with life, like a juggler's dinner-service.... It's a dazzling performance...." The *London Review of Books* concludes that *The English Patient* "is an exceptional book, and perhaps it could only have acquired its special character through the self-involvement of the author. The good here is part and parcel of the bad. A humbler spirit would have taken fewer risks and achieved less...." *Books in Canada* argues that "There are books that change the shape of literature. Each new book does in a way, of course, but with some you can feel the ground shift.... *The English Patient* ... is such a book. It represents the work of an exceptionally gifted writer at the peak of his powers." *Booklist* notes that "Ondaatje seems to whisper, even confess each scene to his reader, handling them gingerly like shards of shattered glass."

OTHER MEDIA: Academy Award–winning film adaptation released in 1996 starring Ralph Fiennes and Kristin Scott Thomas; audiocassette (Random Audio/abr); READING GROUP GUIDE; RECOGNITION: Co-Winner of the 1992 Booker Prize; Winner of the (Canadian) Governor General's Literary Award; *Booklist* "Editors' Choice" 1992; *NYTBR* "Editors' Choice" 1992; *TLS* International Book of the Year 1992; REVIEWS: *BksCan* 11/92; *BL* 9/5/93; *CanFor* 1/93; *EW* 11/20/92; *LitRev* 9/92; *LRB* 11/24/92; *NYTBR* 11/1/92; *Q&Q* 7/92; *TLS* 9/11/92; *WLT* Sum '93

248   *In the Skin of a Lion* (1987); Vintage 1997 (pbk)

In the Skin of the Lion is set in Canada in the 1920s and features Patrick Lewis, a resourceful young man new to Toronto who was hired by a group of disgruntled investors to search for Ambrose Small, a vanished millionaire. Throwing himself into political organizing, Patrick moves easily among the army of laborers who were then transforming sleepy Toronto into a great city: tunnelers, bridge builders, "high-wire" construction workers, and the like. A number of characters featured in *The English Patient* make their first fictional appearance here. *In the Skin of a Lion* is constructed out of the rich language and vivid imagery so associated with Ondaatje the poet.

According to the *New Statesman* "Ondaatje leaps beyond the contemporary preoccupation with a man 'finding' himself: his central character does not monopolize center stage. Patrick's story is also the story of Canada — particularly of the building of Toronto — and is juxtaposed with the stories of his contemporaries: schemers, dreamers, actresses, immigrant workers, Nicholas the dare-devil bridge builder, Caravaggio the thief. The novel turns on how Patrick the outsider finally becomes part of something, a piece of the mural." In the view of the *L.A. Times Book Review*, "Ondaatje's complex design draws together a vivid romance, a political fable and a celebration of the wonder and harshness of constructing a modern country in a wilderness. The story can seem arbitrary, and it can get out of hand ... and there is a marginal surplus of unanchored mysterics.... But the freshness and the inventiveness of the writing overcome most of the difficulties. If the pattern is impracticably ambitious at times, the fabric is splendid." The *Times Literary Supplement* concludes that in this novel Michael Ondaatje "maps high society and the sub culture of underprivilege in Toronto in the 1920s and 1930s, and in the process does for Toronto what Joyce did for Dublin...."

OTHER MEDIA: Audiocassette (American Audio/abr); REVIEWS: *BksCan* 9/96; *LATBR* 10/4/87; *LitRev* 9/87; *LJ* 1/88; *LRB* 10/1/87; *NY* 1/25/88; *WPBW* 11/1/87

Ozick, Cynthia (USA)

249   *The Puttermesser Papers* (1997); Knopf 1997 (HC)

Ruth Puttermesser, attorney and polymath, has appeared in a number of Cynthia Ozick's stories since first being introduced in 1981's *Levitation: Five Fictions*. In *The Puttermesser Papers*, the author has collected previously published stories and interwoven them with some new episodes in the life of this exquisitely cerebral — yet romantically inclined — woman as she makes her way from a blueblood Manhattan law firm, through the office of Mayor of New York City, to fulfillment in paradise. "Along the way, she [accidentally] manufactures a golem, serves as mayor of New York, becomes George Eliot's alter ego, goes to heaven and finds that it disappoints" (*LATBR*).

According to *Booklist*, "Ozick is fascinated by the allure of mysticism, the intoxication of intellectual pursuits, the narcosis of romance, and the chill of disillusion. All [of which] come into play in her first novel in many years." The *Library Journal*, in its starred review, notes that Ozick a "master stylist with a powerful command of the English language ... has created a revealing portrait of a complex woman, as well as a dark satire of government bureaucracy." *Kirkus Reviews* declares that "despite its slapdash structure ... this is one of Ozick's most appealing books: a witty, precisely written, enjoyably sympathetic depiction of a worldly woman ... a thinker who has learned that 'it was possible for brains to break the heart' and that it's also possible to muddle through, and maybe even endure." Richard Bernstein (*NYT*) observes that "Cynthia Ozick's fanciful, poignant, elegant new novel is a kind of Jewish magical realism brought to the normally earthbound spiritual territory of the Bronx and Manhattan." Richard Eder (*LATBR*) points out that Ruth Puttermesser "is an intellectual and a romantic; her monsters are truths that dwindle to facts ... Cynthia Ozick's novel is as galumphing as her heroine, as endearing and twice as smart."

RECOGNITION: *NYTBR* "Editors' Choice" (1997); nominated for the 1997 National Book Award *L.A. Times* "Best Books" 1997 (Top Ten); *Publishers Weekly* "Best Books" 1997; *Booklist* Editors' Choice 1997; *Chicago Sun-Times* Best Books of 1997; REVIEWS: *BL* 5/15/97; *EW* 7/18/97; *KR* 4/15/97; *LATBR* 12/14/97; *LJ* 5/15/97; *NYT* 6/11/97; *NYTBR* 6/15/97; *PW* 4/21/97; *Spec* 11/15/97; *WPBW* 7/20/97; *WSJ* 6/20/97

Palliser, Charles (USA/UK)

250   *Betrayals* (1994); Ballantine 1996 (pbk)

Oft-described as a puzzle within a puzzle, *Betrayals* (by an American novelist living in London) combines elements of cerebral, metafictional postmodernism with old-fashioned suspense. Composed of 10 mystery stories linked by a common theme of rivalry, double-cross and murderous revenge, Palliser's 3rd novel (following *Quincunx* in 1989 and *The Sensationist* in 1991) uses parody and pastiche to some very clever ends.

According to the *Washington Post Book World* "*Betrayals* is a thought-provoking and wonderful novel that establishes numerous expectations, fulfills some and thwarts most and does so playfully and seriously." *Publishers Weekly*, in its starred review, contends that Palliser has produced an "enthralling work" in which his "sure-handedness ... allows him to maintain suspense even while poking fun at the technical trickery that makes it possible." In the view of *Booklist*, "Palliser once again demonstrates that he is ingenious, witty, brilliant, and immensely talented." *Kirkus Reviews* points out that, in the course of the novel "Palliser deftly parodies deconstructionist criticism, the middlebrow style of Jeffrey Archer, three different pulp genres, perhaps the most obtuse serial killer's diary in fiction, countless historical takes on Jack the Ripper — and inevitably, his own professional anxieties, as dramatized by (among others) Cyril Pattison, the fictional author of the fictional novels *Quintessence* and *The Sensation Seekers*."

REVIEWS: *BL* 1/15/95; *KR* 11/1/94; *LJ* 11/4/94; *LRB* 5/12/94; *LST* 3/13/94; *NYTBR* 3/5/95; *PW* 11/7/94; *TLS* 2/25/94; *WPBW* 3/5/95

Paul, Jim (USA)

251   *Medieval in L.A.* (1996); Counterpoint 1996 (HC); Harcourt Brace 1997 (pbk)

A friend of mine jokes about parking karma. Live a certain way, think the right thoughts, and you can get a space to materialize right in front of your destination, as if virtue could give you an edge on city traffic. When my friend speaks of this, he talks half-seriously, though I can tell some part of him — his medieval part — believes. Irony is good for talking about parking karma, allowing you to cling to the magic and still be modern.

Jim Paul's intellectual collage of a novel follows a mild-mannered historian named Jim as (in the company of a female friend named Les) he muses his way through a weekend spent visiting friends in L.A. The result is nothing more nor less than a playfully presented capsule history of Western thought.

According to *Booklist*, Paul — in his debut novel — uses the framework of an ordinary weekend to "consider the slow evolution of thought and how such influential figures as Moses, William of Ockham, Gallileo, John Cage, and Bertolt Brecht have invigorated human consciousness." In the view of *Kirkus Reviews Medieval in L.A.* is a "weekend book that's penetrating and pleasant at once — a humanities refresher equally at home on coffee table or in any student's scruffiest backpack."

The *Los Angeles Times Book Review* notes that the question "How does the way I see the world affect the way I live?" can be answered with brevity and humor "as Jim Paul proves. It can just be a weekend in L.A."

REVIEWS: *BL* 6/1/96; *KR* 3/1/96; *LATBR* 5/10/96; *NY* 9/9/96; *PW* 4/8/96

Peck, Dale (USA)

252 *The Law of Enclosures* (1995); FS&G 1995 (HC)

Structured as a kind of double-helix, Dale Peck tells the story of two married couples, the twenty-something Henry and Beatrice and the sixty-something Hank and Bea. Peck moves back and forth between their stories which, though equally disturbing, are not exactly continuous.

The Nation notes that "The source of Henry-and-Beatrice, Hank-and-Bea, lies in the marital scenes whose shocks and mysteries pounded the writer's childhood like an endless Kansas dust storm of malice and violence on display." According to the *London Observer*, "This autobiographical memoir forms the center panel of a triptych. On either side are the split halves of a fictional anatomy of a marriage. You see Bea and Henry, John's parents from the first novel, falling in youthful love in a race against time.... Suddenly the lovers have turned into those freaks from David Lynch's Eraserhead, vacant figures stumbling through the domestic shadows in a slow-motion daze." English novelist **Stephen Amidon**, writing in *The London Times*, points out that Peck's first novel "was a sporadically brilliant, yet ultimately callow work. Here, the author has made a significant leap forward, using his stylistic daring to bolster equally risky subject-matter. In doing so, he has breathed fresh life into that most glorious of oxymorons, 'honest fiction,' creating a beautiful concoction which tells

us more about this brave writer than the boldest of novels or frankest of memoirs ever could." The *Washington Post Book World* calls The *Law of Enclosures* "more pretentious in its concept, and if possible, more virtuosic in its execution (than its predecessor)" and concludes that Peck's first novel "typically turns up in the 'Gay Fiction' of bookshops, where most readers don't venture. *The Law of Enclosures*, out-of-place ruminations on blood ties and all, belongs on the shelves under the 'Literature' sign."

RECOGNITION: Nominated for the 1997 Lambda Book Award for Gay Fiction; REVIEWS: *BL* 12/15/95; *LRB* 5/23/96; *LST* 3/3/96; *Nation* 1/29/96; *NY* 1/15/96; *NYTBR* 1/14/96; *Obs* 3/3/96; *PW* 10/16/95; *TLS* 2/16/96; *WPBW* 2/18/96; *Editor's Note*: Dale Peck's 1998 offering *Now It's Time to Say Goodbye* (which appears on the *LATBR*'s end of year list of the "Best Fiction of 1998") concludes a loose trilogy of novels which began with *Martin & John* in 1992 and continued with *The Law of Enclosures* (1995).

253 *Martin & John* (1992); FS&G 1992 (HC)

Dale Peck's debut novel is structured around a series of nested stories featuring John a gay man coping with the death of his lover Martin from AIDS. Each also includes a mother named Beatrice and an abusive father named Henry. As the novel progresses, it becomes clear to the reader that the author is constructing a series of "alternative realities" where, although the names Martin and John, Beatrice and Henry never change, the characters' identities and life experiences do.

Publishers Weekly, in its starred review, observes that "Peck's operatic intensity and lyric grief come tumbling out in these pages ... [and concludes that] though the symbolism is often obvious and, and the writing so pitched that it would seem excessive in less talented hands, the narrative plunges forward on a wildly romantic course." Calling Peck a "brave and talented writer" The *New York Times Book Review* notes that "by breaking the story line and blurring the identity of his characters and the hard boundaries between the stories [the author] succeeds in exploring the experience of being gay with a remarkable complexity and depth of feeling." In the view of the *Library Journal*, "This kind of structural complexity would be enough to sink most novels, but Peck writes so splendidly that it is a pleasure just to keep on reading. By themselves, some of these stories are among the most powerful representations of gay life written."

RECOGNITION: *NYTBR* Notable Book of 1993; REVIEWS: *LitRev* 3/93; *LJ* 11/15/92; *Nation* 3/15/93; *NYTBR* 2/28/93; *NewsWk* 5/10/93; *PW* 11/9/92; *SFRB* 3-4/93; *VLS* 2/93

Pollack, Rachel (USA)

254   *Temporary Agency* (1994); Overlook 1995 (pbk)

When I was fourteen, a cousin of mine angered a malignant One. It was a big case, a genuine scandal. Maybe you remember it. At the time, when it ended, I just wanted to forget the whole thing. But a couple of years have passed and maybe it's time to think about it again.

Described by *Booklist* as a "two-part story of intrigue, double-crosses, and political deal making" *Temporary Agency* begins with a tale of demonic possession and adolescent crushes and ends with a slam-bang, all-out global confrontation between the forces of good and evil. That each segment features Ellen Pierson (14 when we first meet her in Part I; an attractive lesbian in her late 20s when we are reintroduced in Part II) in a significant role makes the tale all the more intriguing.

According to *Library Journal*, "Pollack's latest novel features a determined heroine whose faith in her own convictions becomes her most formidable weapon." *Booklist* points out that Ms. Pollack's novel "combines magical realism, science fiction, and surrealism, in a gripping drama of conspiracy at the highest level of power." The *Women's Review of Books* observes that "having grown up searching for a book that would show how people like me — women, that is — could help save the world, I couldn't ask for a better ending." *Kirkus Reviews* calls *Temporary Agency* "Brilliant, original, funny, and fascinating" and concludes that "Pollack turns the world on its spiritual head, offering an alternative view of the matters in which the government, however spiritualized, is still not to be trusted."

REVIEWS: *ASF&F* 5/95; *BL* 8/94; *KR* 6/1/94; *LJ* 8/94; *PW* 7/25/94; *WLB* 3/95; *WRB* 7/95

255   *Unquenchable Fire* (1992); Overlook 1992 (HC); 1994 (pbk)

Rachel Pollack sets her award-winning novel in an alternative version of New York's Hudson Valley 87 years after the successful takeover of the U.S. government by a coalition of eco-feminists. In this brave new world where magic and modernism co-exist, Jennifer Mazden a young divorcee receives a "visitation." She doesn't want to be a mother.

According to *Kirkus Reviews*, *Unquenchable Fire* is "an intricate feminist/New Age fantasy set in the near future [which] throws an ordinary young woman into the center of a mythic drama." The *Library Journal* observes that Pollack "the author of numerous books on the Tarot ... has crafted a powerful — and powerfully funny — vision of a mystical yet modern world. Enlightened and knowledgeable in tone, this recent winner of the Arthur C. Clark Award for speculative fiction is both a cautionary tale and a paean to the New Age." *Publish-*ers *Weekly* notes that "Spinning her tale from strands of the commonplace and themes and rituals of many religions, Pollack develops a new mythology for her skewed, strangely familiar society."

RECOGNITION: Winner of the Arthur C. Clark Award for speculative fiction; REVIEWS: *KR* 4/1/92; *LJ* 4/15/92; *PW* 3/23/92; *WPBW* 4/26/92

Power, Susan (USA)

256   *The Grass Dancer* (1994); Berkley 1997 (pbk)

Susan Power, a member of the Standing Rock Sioux tribe, sets her debut novel on a North Dakota reservation and tells a powerful, resonant story that begins in 1981 with a tragic car accident. Power's tale, incorporating elements of magic realism and non-linear story-telling, "reassembles the history of the Sioux Indians" (*TLS*). The narrative moves back and forth in time and space, touching down in 1864 (with a fully elaborated description of a tragic encounter between Sioux Indians and a group of missionaries), the 1930s and 1961. Each segment is precisely narrated and contributes in some way to the reader's understanding of the tragic events outlined in the prologue. The contemporary story features Harley Wind Soldier, whose father was killed in the pivotal accident, his traumatized mother (mute since her husband's death), Pumpkin, a red-haired Menominee dancer of Irish/Native American ancestry, and Anna Thunder and her mother Mercury who, through use of witchcraft, can ensnare young men.

According to the *New York Times Book Review*, "The reader responds to the narrative as if it were a series of photographs ranging from the crisp images of a Nikon to the grainy daguerreotypes spotted with age. But Ms. Power's method has thematic as well as technical brio for it also replicates the tribal sense of time and connectedness, reifying a world where ancestors are continually present in everyday life as spirits, memories and dreams." The *TLS* observes out that "The lure of white society fails to impress Power's Sioux characters: their culture rolls on, adapting prevailing modes to express a Sioux vision," and concludes that Power's "scrupulously wrought novel, deftly fusing traditional story-telling with the forms of contemporary fiction, provides a sparkling demonstration of that culture's continued vitality." In the view of the *Irish Times*, Power's narrative "is less flamboyant than [fellow Native-American novelist Louise] Erdrich's, her prose is as richly lyrical, her metaphors harder and stronger." The *Library Journal* calls *The Grass Dancer* "a stunning book, [filled with] some of the most beautiful writing to be found in any recent novel.... a classic, to be read over and over."

OTHER MEDIA: Audiocassette (Brilliance/ unabr); REVIEWS: *BellesL* Sum '95; *BL* 8/94; *LJ* 10/1/94; *NYTBR* 8/21/94; *PW* 6/6/94; *SLJ* 5/95; *TLS* 12/2/94; *WPBW* 7/24/94; *WRB* 1/95

Powers, Richard (USA)

Galatea 2.2 (1995); FS&G1995 (HC); See Section 8, #1023

257   *Operation Wandering Soul* (1993); HarperCollins 1994 (pbk)

Operation Wandering Soul with its near-future setting in Angel City, California, features Richard Kraft, a surgical resident assigned to the children's ward of a large public hospital. He works closely with Linda Espera (a child therapist) as together they attempt to heal — or at least relieve the suffering of— the seriously ill youngsters entrusted to their care. Powers, known for his stylistic virtuosity seamlessly interweaves historical events (e.g. the Children's Crusade, the evacuation of children from London during the blitz, etc.) with discussions of pop culture, contemporary literature, folklore and medicine. Dr. Kraft eventually embarks on a contemporary odyssey with his young patients in tow.

The *Washington Post Book World* calls Powers "the most unjustly neglected" novelist of his generation, and argues that *Operation Wandering Soul* "represents another bravura display of [his] dazzling talent ... [one that] might be described as sophistication's tribute to innocence." The *Library Journal* observes that "Beneath its cover story — and this novel plumbs great depths — this is nothing less than the story of humankind, with the Pied Piper as a central metaphor." *Choice* praises Powers ability to write in a way that "no previous American writer has attempted" while concluding that *Operation Wandering Soul* is "clearly among the most brilliant and significant novels of the last 50 years."

OTHER MEDIA: Audiocassette (Books-on-Tape/unabr); RECOGNITION: nominated for the 1993 National Book Award; REVIEW: *Choice* 9/93; *LJ* 5/1/93; *NYTBR* 7/3/94; *WPBW* 6/13/93

Pynchon, Thomas (USA)

258   *Mason & Dixon* (1997); H Holt 1997 (HC)

In his fifth novel Thomas Pynchon tells a playful, quirky (quintessentially American) story featuring British astronomer Charles Mason and his partner, a surveyor by the name of Jeremiah Dixon. Initially brought together when appointed by the British Royal Society to chart — in appropriately perilous 18th century fashion — the 1761 Transit of Venus, the pair was subsequently charged with establishing the boundary between the colonies of Maryland and Pennsylvania. This endeavor is relayed in highly picaresque (i.e., Pynchonesque) fashion. Pynchon has not, of course, written a conventional work of historical fiction, rather he presents the reader with an 800 page phantasmagorical reverie on the meaning of exploration and subjugation.

Michael Dirda (*WPBW*) observes that *Mason & Dixon* "proves a dazzling work of imaginative recreation, a marvel-filled historical novel.... In its pages Pynchon sets the reader down in a bustling world where bewigged men of science believe in ghosts and magic, where geometry may butt up against ancient myth where dogs talk and Golems stride through the wilderness and Jesuit agents are masters of guile and disguise." According to the *Wall Street Journal* "Astronomy, gastronomy, morphology, ethnography, pornography — these subjects and many more cascade, in the manner of a Cole Porter catalog song, through the dense but boisterous pages of Thomas Pynchon's brand-new 18th-century novel." The *L.A. Times Book Review* calls the book "a masterpiece" and concludes that "it is the vision itself that one takes away from this remarkable book: a wilderness America, peopled as much by European hopes and longings as by the interlocking kingdoms of the indigenous; a virgin, undivided land. Until, one morning, two ordinary men appear, charged with cutting a perfectly straight line, eight yards wide, westward into its heart." Henry Kisor (*Chicago Sun-Times*) while pointing out that *Mason & Dixon* contains much "prose [which] is very funny" often sounding like "a cross between Henry Fielding and Monty Python" concludes that "Much of [the novel] ... will be impenetrable to all but the chiefly academic Pynchon coterie, which is noisily enthusiastic out of all proportion to its numbers." John Updike, in his *New Yorker* review suggests that "Pynchon is furiously clever, but more crucial, and I suspect more durable, in his anatomy of melancholy, his conjuring of a doleful burlesque. He offers readers a trip as long and full of yearning as that of his heroes."

OTHER MEDIA: Audiocassette (Books-on-Tape/unabr); RECOGNITION: *NYTBR* "Editors' Choice" 1997; *LATBR* "Best Books" 1997 (Top Ten); *Publishers Weekly* "Best Books" 1997; *Time* Best Books of 1997; *Salon Magazine* "Book of the Year" 1997; REVIEWS: *ChiSun* 4/27/97; *LATBR* 5/11/97; *NY* 5/12/97; *PW* 4/14/97; *Time* 5/5/97; *WPBW* 4/27/97; *WSJ* 5/2/97

259   *Vineland* (1990); Penguin 1997 (pbk)

Thomas Pynchon's 4th novel (his first since *Gravity's Rainbow* in 1973) is set, in 1984, in a California community reminiscent of the "counterculutural" communes of the 1960s. Vineland is peopled with a collection of feckless misfits, dropouts from, among other things, Reagonomics, self-re-straint and a boob-tube–driven culture. One day, in 1984, Zoyd Wheeler and his daughter Prairie arrive looking for Prairie's mother, missing since the late sixties when she ran off with a narcotics agent…

In the view of Jonathan Yardley (*WPBW*) "Reduced to its barest essentials, *Vineland* is a celebration of the '60s revolution and a lament for what Pynchon sees as its destruction from without and its betrayal from within. Its heroic figures are the innocent and idealistic, its villains are the destructive and cynical; however much of its prose may bristle and clang, at its core it mourns "a people's miracle, an army of loving friends." Novelist Brad Leithauser writing in the *New York Review of Books* observes that "*Vineland* is the work of a man of quick intelligence and quirky invention. Many of its episodes flicker with an appealingly far-flung humor. And Pynchon displays throughout what might be called an internal loyalty: he keeps the faith with the generally feckless and almost invariably inarticulate misfits he assembles, tracking their looping thoughts and indecisive actions with a patience that seems grounded in affection." In the view of the *New Statesman*, "The Pynchon unveiled here is a wise child who speaks, like Whitman or Kerouac, of paradise lost and paradise regained. At the core of his yearning stands the tragi-comedy of the American left: forever panting, forever young."

REVIEWS: *BL* 1/15/90; *LRB* 2/8/90; *NS&S* 1/26/90; *NY* 2/19/90; *NYRB* 3/15/90; *NYTBR* 1/14/90; *VLS* 2/90; *WLT* Win '91; *WPBW* 1/7/90

Reuss, Frederick (USA)

260   *Horace Afoot* (1997); MacMurray 1997 (HC)

A contemplative, reclusive man by the name of Horace moves to a small (intensely parochial) Midwestern town appropriately named Oblivion. Horace has a fondness for walking and the local residents (who walk neither for exercise nor for pleasure) find his mere presence disturbing, but are particularly suspicious of his habit of solitary peregrinations. When, while strolling through a corn field on the outskirts of town, Horace stumbles upon a naked woman who is both bleeding and unconscious, community suspicions turn to outright hostility.

According to the *New York Times Book Review*, Reuss has created a "sly satire of Midwestern life and a restrained account of how a closed heart comes to be unlocked." *Kirkus Reviews* observes that "Reuss, in a spare, precise prose, does a deft job of catching, without overdoing, the quirks, obsessions, and longings of his characters" and concludes that the author's "voice lingers, as do many of the scenes in this terse, moving exploration of modern

anomie and the longing for—and fear of—intimacy." In the view of Michael Dirda (*WPBW*), "Question of identity … meditations on the nature of the world, the growing tugs of love and hate and fear all contribute to the appeal of this quietly entertaining, thought-filled novel. The narrative voice is particularly congenial — cool without being laugh-out-loud funny, particularly when Horace reacts to and tries to interpret events around him."

RECOGNITION: *NYTBR* Notable Book of 1998; REVIEWS: *BL* 10/15/97; *LJ* 10/1/97; *NYTBR* 2/28/97; *PW* 9/15/97; *WPBW* 10/12/97

Roth, Philip (USA)

261   *Operation Shylock* (1993); Random House 1994 (pbk)

In *Operation Shylock* Philip Roth tells the story of a well-known novelist by the name of Philip Roth who, while in Israel during the trial of John Demjanjuk, meets his doppelganger a man who not only bears a striking resemblance to him but has also appropriated his name. The second Philip Roth, a Jewish detective from Chicago who has been diagnosed with cancer, has come to Israel to promote a scheme (a sort of second Diaspora) designed to return Jews to Europe.

According to *Time* magazine "The increasingly frenzied and farcical minuet between the two Philips takes place against a complex background of contemporary scenes and questions: the evolution of Israel and Zionism, the grievances of displaced Palestinians, the lacerating choices that must be made between group solidarity and individual freedom." Novelist **D.M. Thomas** (*NYTBR*) notes that "Despite the seriousness of its theme, the book carries the feeling of creative joy. One feels that Mr. Roth feels that he's let rip." Harold Bloom (*NYRB*) argues that "though his context tends to remain stubbornly Jewish, he has developed fresh ways of opening out universal perspectives from Jewish dilemmas, whether they are American, Israeli, or European." The *London Review of Books* argues that "Roth, even in his most slapdash and disappointing books, has the intimacy to reach a reader's heart, the force to bounce around and about the world outside the text. Roth in other words, has *voice*." In the view of novelist **John Updike** (*New Yorker*), Roth's "Dostoyevskian phantasmagoria is an impressive reassertion of artistic energy, and a brave expansion of Roth's 'densely overstocked little store of concerns' into the global market place. It should be read by anyone who cares about (1) Israel and its repercussions; (2) the development of the postmodern novel; (3) Philip Roth."

RECOGNITION: Winner of the 1994 PEN/Faulkner Award; *NYTBR* Notable Book of 1993; REVIEWS: *BL* 3/1/93; *CSM* 4/29/93; *LJ* 4/15/93;

LRB 5/13/93; *NewsWk* 3/8/93; *NY* 3/15/93; *NYRB* 4/22/93; *NYTBR* 3/7/93; *Time* 3/8/93; *TLS* 3/26/93; *WPBW* 3/14/93

Rushdie, Salman (India/UK)

262   *The Moor's Last Sigh* (1995); Pantheon 1996 (HC); 1997 (pbk)

Salman Rushdie, in his first novel since the imposition of the infamous 1989 fatwa, tells the story of the rise and fall of three generations of the de Gama–Zogoibys, a Christian/Jewish Portuguese merchant family. The tale spans the years from the late 1800s to the mid 1990s and is narrated, for the most part, by Moraes Zagoiby ("the Moor") the blighted, asthmatic son of Aurora de Gama, a beautiful "demonically" talented artist of some repute and the ruthless Abraham Zagoiby, once a mere clerk in the de Gama family's spice conglomerate, who now controls the family business and dabbles in a profitable sideline: drugs and child prostitution. The action shifts from the family estate on Cabral Island in Cochin to Malabar Hill the poshest suburb of Bombay. The novel embraces a huge cast of supporting characters including: a beautiful (possibly vampiric) woman, an Indian who changes his name to Jimmy Cash and travels to Nashville (he's got a "country and eastern" band), and Nadia Wadia (Miss World) "who has a walk like a warrior and a voice like a dirty phone call." And then, of course, there's Rushdie's trademark use of language: allusive, playful, cultured, slangy and hip.

According to novelist **Norman Rush** (*NYTBR*) *The Moor's Last Sigh* "is a triumph, an intricate and deceptive one … [and one that will undoubtedly expose] its author to a new range of potential antagonisms." *Booklist* observes that "The plot does not unfold — it floods like a river gone over its banks, exploding with incredible events and larger-than-life characters, and to be carried along is to ride beautiful prose through the colliding and conjoining of races and religions that have gone into the making of the fabric of Indian history and culture." *Publishers Weekly*, in its starred review, notes that "Rushdie's moral rigor has not faltered. Where *Midnight's Children* heralded the birth pains of modern India, *The Moor's Last Sigh* charts a nation's troubled middle passage." English novelist **Malcolm Bradbury**, writing in *The London Times*, argues that "At times [Rushdie's] invention wanders a little, the palimpsest has too much random detail; we can occasionally feel the lapses in the driving verbal and imaginative energy which makes Rushdie, quite simply, a great writer." Mr. Bradbury concludes however, that *The Moor's Last Sigh* is still a wonderful book. Its characters spring to life with comic energy and allegorical power. It accepts the disorder of the world and its implications for art."

OTHER MEDIA: Audiocassette (Random Audio/abr); READING GROUP GUIDE; RECOGNITION: Winner of the 1995 Whitbread Award for Fiction; Shortlisted for the 1995 Booker Prize; *Booklist* "Editors' Choice" 1996; *Salon Magazine* "Book of the Year" 1996; REVIEWS: *BL* 11/1/95; *LRB* 9/7/95; *LST* 9/3/95; *LT* 8/31/95; *Maclean's* 10/9/95; *NYRB* 3/21/96; *NYTBR* 1/14/96; *PW* 10/2/95; *WPBW* 1/7/96; EDITOR'S NOTE: Mr. Rushdie was named by *Granta* magazine to its 1983 list of the twenty "Best Young British Novelists."

263   *The Satanic Verses* (1988); Holt 1997 (pbk re-issue)

As the novel opens, a jumbo jet explodes over the English Channel; two of it's passengers float down from the sky and are later washed up on a beach, miraculously unscathed. Saladin and Gibreel, as the survivors are called, have been spared for a reason: as the human embodiment of Good and Evil they will continue the eternal wrestling match between the forces of darkness and light. Using the traditional "epic" form and a large dose of magic realism (liberally seeded with other postmodern devices), Salman Rushdie explores — in addition to the fundamental theme of the existence of good and evil — a number of big issues, particularly the nature of faith, personal freedom, and cultural identity. The author, despite the seriousness of his themes, employs a particularly irreverent, bawdy, fantastical narrative style. The *Satanic Verses* was banned in Pakistan soon after publication and the author was condemned to death by Iran's Ayatollah Ruhollah Kohmeini for the alleged anti–Muslim sentiments contained therein.

According to the *New York Times Book Review*, *The Satanic Verses* "In its entirety … resembles only itself [but, for the sake of the Western reader unfamiliar with Rushdie's work, resemblances to a number of Western authors can be pointed out]: to Sterne, for one, in the joys of digression; to Swift in scathingness of political satire; to the fairy and folk tales of the Brothers Grimm, to Ovid's 'Metamorphoses', 'The Arabian Nights,' Thomas Mann's 'Transposed Heads' and the work of Gabriel Garcia Marquez, Gunter Grass, Thomas Pynchon, John Barth, Italo Calvino, 'Saturday Night Live' and Douglas Adams' 'Hitchhikers Guide to the Galaxy' to name a few…." Novelist **Bharati Mukherjee** (*VLS*) observes that "*The Satanic Verses* [while bloated with] … too many tangential subplots, too much undramatized narration, and too many pages where the major characters simply are not present … is swollen with irritated life … and completes a trilogy that must be swallowed whole, python-style, hair, horns, hoofs and all." Jonathan Yardley (*WPBW*) argues that "As is so often true of fiction that aches with ambition,

The Satanic Verses reaches for more than is within its grasp. It is smart, energetic, protean and clamorous, but its diverse elements never merge ... and it never engages the reader in the lives and hearts of its characters; for all the feeling that Rushdie expresses through these characters, the novel remains cold and distant, more an exercise in pyrotechnical fiction than a recreation of human life in its individuality and community."

RECOGNITION: *NYTBR* Notable Book of 1989; REVIEWS: *BL* 11/1/88; *Econ* 8/5/89; *LATBR* 2/12/89; *NY* 5/15/89; *NYRB* 3/2/89; *NYT* 1/27/89; *NYTBR* 1/29/89; *PW* 1/29/89; *TLS* 12/2/88; *WPBW* 1/29/89

Ryman, Geoff (UK)

Was (1992); Penguin 1993 (pbk); See Section 8, #1025

Shange, Ntzoke (US)

264   *Liliane: Resurrection of the Daughter* (1995); St. Martin's 1995 (pbk)

Ntzoke Shange, author of the critically acclaimed play *For Coloured Girls Who Have Considered Suicide/When the Rainbow is Enuf*, has created, in the talented young African American artist, Liliane Lincoln, an intriguing multi-faceted protagonist. The eponymous Liliane, concerned with her grasp on reality, is being treated by a psychiatrist who encourages her to examine her past. Within this framework, Ms. Shange uses Liliane's memories, dreams, and expectations to paint a portrait of a brilliant yet conflicted woman. By interweaving the voices of Liliane and her analyst with monologues from friends and lovers, a complex story begins to unfold, one which reaches back into Liliane's childhood and includes encounters with the last moments of legal segregation in Mississippi, the nascent Civil Rights Movement and the beginnings of class warfare within the black community of Queens.

According to the *Times Literary Supplement* "In *Liliane*, Shange's third novel, rhythm, mood and a collage of voices predominate over linear narrative. It is a flamboyant and demanding novel." In the view of *Entertainment Weekly*, Shange has written a funny, seductive and seditious book ... [and, along the way has created] complex, provocative black female characters." In the view of the *Library Journal*, *Liliane* is "musical, erotic, and scathingly reactive to racial history." *World Literature Today* concludes that "*Liliane* joyfully celebrates the complexity of sexual relationships, the dynamics of family and friendship, and the emerging multicultural ethos that is America." The *L.A. Times Book Review* calls *Liliane* "risky and stylish" and suggests that "of 'memories and pictures,' 'memories and

stories,' she has made a novel that takes its place on the ... shelves of exciting contemporary black writers."

REVIEWS: *BL* 9/1/94; *EW* 3/10/95; *LATBR* 12/18/94; *LJ* 10/15/94; *NS&S* 5/19/95; *NYTBR* 1/1/95; *TLS* 6/2/95; *WLT* Sum '95; *WPBW* 2/5/95

Sherman, Charlotte Watson (USA)

265   *One Dark Body* (1993); HarperPerennial 1994 (pbk)

Twelve-year-old Septeema Barnett, abandoned by her mother shortly after birth, is being raised by a midwife in an African American community in the Pacific Northwest. Nicknamed "Raisin," because of her oddly wrinkled skin (a consequence of her mother's botched abortion attempt) Septeema is a precocious youngster who can, among other things, communicate with spirits; her best friend, Sin Sin, is a fourteen-year-old boy who has been befriended by a shaman named Blue. When her birth mother, Nola, arrives unexpectedly from Chicago, Raisin's life becomes infinitely more complicated. The introduction of Spirit women, Night People (the ghosts of slaves who roam the near-by woods) and the ghost of her father El, a suicide, lends a magical-realist air to Charlotte Sherman's debut novel.

The *Library Journal* calls *One Dark Body* "a tapestry interwoven with stories about ancestry and blood and underknit with mysticism and magic." The *Women's Review of Books* observes that although her novel is not without flaws (the introduction of spirits and soul catchers "muddies" her message), Ms. Sherman "has undertaken important work in *One Dark Body*. She has tried to convey the timely message that even the deepest wounds can be healed if we draw on our African cultural and spiritual traditions." According to *Publishers Weekly* the novel "offers a convincing portrayal of the spirituality that shelters these African Americans against racist and sexist oppression." The *School Library Journal* concludes that it is a novel "rich in characterization, language, and meaning, and a thoroughly joyful read."

REVIEWS: *BellesL* Sum '93; *BL* 2/15/93; *LJ* 1/93; *PW* 11/23/92; *SLJ* 6/93; *WRB* 7/93

Silko, Leslie Marmon (USA)

266   *The Almanac of the Dead* (1991); Viking 1992 (pbk)

Leslie Marmon Silko's *The Almanac of the Dead* features, among *many* other characters a Native American clairvoyant who teams up with the ex-mistress of a cocaine wholesaler, Alsakan villagers sharing a communal TV, sundry witches and shamans and, more centrally, a pair of sixty-year-old (gun-running) twin sisters of Mexican and

American Indian lineage who are holed up on their heavily fortified ranch on the outskirts of Tucson. The myriad plotlines include an ancient manuscript that foretells the second coming, a plot to blow up the Glen Canyon Dam, and a corrupt U.S. judicial system. Ms. Silko's publisher suggests that the author has undertaken to "re-create the moral history of the Americas, told from the point of view of the conquered, not the conquerors."

In the view of *Time* magazine Silko's "sentences have a drive and a sting to them. But the receptacle of her crowded, raging, enormously long book swirls with half-digested revulsion, half-explained characters and, a white elitist might add, more than a little self-righteousness." Meredith Tax, writing in the *Voice Literary Supplement* opines: "When I was a girl, writers — mainly Norman Mailer — used to talk about the 'Great American Novel,' and wonder which of them would master her.... What a joke on all those big-mouthed New York guys. This one was written by a woman, and a Native American one at that." Sven Birkerts, writing in the *New Republic* suggests that the "tragedy and the rage at tragedy that underwrite *Almanac of the Dead* are very real. They have spawned in Silko's mind an epic of collapse and retribution — and implied regeneration. Unfortunately, her narrative proliferation, at which she excels, forces her to extremes of resolution." In the opinion of the *New York Times Book Review*, "Appearing on the eve of the quincentennial of Columbus's arrival in the Americas.... (*The Almanac of the Dead*) burns at an apocalyptic pitch — passionate indictment, defiant augury, bravura storytelling." *Kirkus Reviews* calls Silko's novel: "Fantastic and colorful in the fine detail, even if belabored and unwieldy as a whole. All in all, a chillingly dark vision of corruption, despair and chaos in the Americas, where a Native new world order appears ready to begin."

RECOGNITION: *NYTBR* Notable Book of 1992; REVIEWS: *Choice* 9/92; *CSM* 2/3/92; *EW* 12/13/91; *KR* 8/15/91; *LJ* 10/15/91; *NewR* 11/4/91; *NewsWk* 11/18/91; *NYTBR* 12/22/91; *PW* 9/6/91; *VLS* 11/91; *WPBW* 11/26/91

Sinclair, Iain (UK)

267 *Downriver: Or the Vessels of wrath* (1991); Random House 1993 (pbk)

In his second novel, Iain Sinclair, using a first person narrative structure, spins a strange and obsessive tale about the hidden life of the Thames river as it flows through East London and on to the North Sea. Sinclair's novel, according to the *Library Journal* "is ostensibly the story of a crew of writers and filmmakers who try to document the passing of a way of life in the gentrified Thames basin, the history they uncover, their attempts to

develop a way to record it, and the problems Sinclair (who is both author and character) encounters in writing the script and the novel itself."

As the *Times Literary Supplement* observes: "All is grist to Sinclair's watermill. *Four Quartets* and *Krazy Kat*, W.H. Hodgson and Monty Python.... The resulting loaf is tasty if unwholesome.... As the pace quickens, the book begins to recycle itself. Later episodes concern projected or fantasized television films based on the early scenes. Names that appear on the dust wrapper, praising the contents, reappear as part of the content. The book draws on itself so vigorously that the fainthearted reader may stand back for fear of catching his fingers in it when it implodes. But the faint-hearted reader has long ago given up. And is the poorer for it." English novelist Angela Carter (*London Review of Books*) observes that "as Sinclair walks round London, he reinvents it, and remembered pain will always dance like heat in the air above the spot where the Ripper struck down poor Lizzie Stride. The singing that turned to screaming continues to impress itself on the water where the *Princess Alice* went down. Listen, you can hear it on the slapping tide." *The Spectator* argues that *Downriver* "should attract not only Dracula's dentist and aging friends of Nicholas Moore, but those delighting less in plot than the plottings of a mind obsessed by language, myth, the shadowy cities within a city." *Publishers Weekly*, in its starred review concludes that "Filled with the ghosts and wrecks of London history, inhabited by grubby barflies and Cockney wharf-rats, this teeming novel seems as rich, fecund and ultimately mesmerizing as the muddy Thames." Michael Dirda (*WPBW*) argues that "As often perverse as brilliant, *Downriver* is like an engaging but impossible acquaintance who insists on being taken on his own terms."

RECOGNITION: Winner of the James Tait Black award; Winner of the Encore Prize for "Best Second Novel of 1991"; REVIEWS: *BL* 5/1/93; *LJ* 4/15/93; *LRB* 3/7/91; *NYTBR* 8/15/93; *PW* 3/1/93; *Spec* 3/6/91; *TLS* 4/5/91; *WPBW* 8/29/93

Skibell, Joseph (USA)

268 *Blessing on the Moon* (1997); Algonquin 1997 (HC)

Joseph Skibell the son of a Holocaust survivor who had lost most of his immediate family to death squads and concentration camps, tells the wrenching, yet magical and, at times even humorous, story of the after-death journey of Chaim Skibelski, a 60-year-old businessman who (along with his family and fellow Jewish townsmen) had been shot, killed and dumped in a mass grave on the outskirts of his Polish town of Mintz. When Chaim climbs out of the corpse-laden ditch — into which he had fallen when the Nazi bullets pierced his skull and torso — he has difficulty accepting the fact that he is actually quite dead. As the novel progresses, Chaim, though dead, is able to eat, drink (copiously), communicate with animals, and generally cause mischief. He also encounters more of the living dead, including a rabbi transmogrified into a crow. Chaim eventually stumbles upon a group of Jewish scholars who have managed to avoid capture and who have spent the war years employing their arcane talents in the service of restoring the moon to its (now empty) place in the sky.

According to the *Washington Post Book World*, "For a dead man Skibleski is a lively narrative presence, given to flights of language so delicate [however incongruous] that they make the heart crack. For the first generation of Holocaust writers, breaking the silence about what had happened to them required a rigorous attention to facts that seemed to defy description, much less meaning. Skibell, by contrast, has found a new way to prove the very essence of the horror; his radical inventions ... promise to change the very definition of writing about catastrophe." *Kirkus Reviews* calls *A Blessing on the Moon* "a haunting novel, intensely imagined, and — if less successfully plotted and paced — redeemed by Skibell's gifts for vivid imagery ... and robust gallows humor" and concludes that it is "a fine debut novel, manifestly infused with deep familial and cultural feelings, and a significant contribution to the ongoing literature of the Holocaust." The *New York Times Book Review* observes that Skibell's debut novel is "Daring in its haunting, often painful honesty, dense in thoughtful observation and unsparing incident ... at the same time proving itself an unlikely page-turner ... a confirmation that no subject is beyond the grasp of a gifted, committed imagination."

READING GROUP GUIDE; "Reading Group Choices" 1998 (Paz & Associates); RECOGNITION: Publishers Weekly "Best Books" 1997; REVIEWS: *BL* 9/1/97; *KR* 8/15/97; *LJ* 9/1/97; *NYTBR* 1/28/97; *PW* 7/14/97; *WPBW* 12/4/97

Sontag, Susan (USA)

269   *Volcano Lover* (1992); FS&G 1992 (HC); Anchor 1993 (pbk)

With *The Volcano Lover* Susan Sontag has chosen to tell the intriguing and tragically intertwined stories of Sir William Hamilton (ambassador to the Kingdom of Two Sicilies), his wife Emma (a notorious beauty from the "lower classes") and Lord Nelson, the greatest naval hero of his time.

The *Literary Review* observes that "This is the story of the queen, the envoy, his wife and her lover. It is also a book about history, sex, aesthetics, modernism, the Portland vase and how to repair it, what to wear when disguising pregnancy, Goethe, architectural follies along the grand tour, Don Juan,

Pygmalion, melancholy and, of course, volcanoes. You can really say it's about these things with impunity, because Sontag never troubles to disguise the essays inserted in her novel as fiction of any sort." *Kirkus Reviews* observes that, at first, *The Volcano Lover* "seems little more than the Vivien Leigh [Hollywood] melodrama.... But Sontag adds such historical texture to her saga of sexual intrigue that it all comes to sordid life, full of passion and politics. Her warts-and-all version of history relies on a profound imagining of each character's point of view." According to the *Times Literary Supplement*, Ms. Sontag "favours the mode initiated by John Fowles in *The French Lieutenant's Woman* ... whereby the writer acts as interpreter, offering the occasional gloss on the quirks and foibles of the age evoked and keeping the reader carefully alienated by means of a post-modern tricksiness with tenses and spasmodic references to events still to happen or to concepts yet unhatched." English novelist **A.S. Byatt** concludes that *The Volcano Lover* "is a slippery, intelligent, provocative and gripping book, and a very good one."

REVIEWS: *BellesL* Spr '93; *EW* 8/21/92; *KR* 5/15/92; *LitRev* 10/92; *LRB* 12/3/92; *NYTBR* 7/18/93; *TLS* 9/25/92; *WPBW* 8/16/92

Theroux, Paul (USA/UK)

My Other Life (1996) Houghton Mifflin 1997 (pbk); See Section 5, #652

Thomas, D.M. (USA/UK)

270   *Eating Pavlova* (1994); Carroll & Graf 1995 (pbk)

In *Eating Pavlova* D. H. Thomas posits a scenario where Sigmund Freud, in reviewing his life shortly before his death in 1939, imparts to his daughter Anna a series of (sometimes shocking) adventures both amorous and otherwise.

The *New York Times Book Review* observes that "In his brilliant new novel ... Mr. Thomas grabs Freud just in time ... and snatches for us these final imaginary memories: the dreams, recollections, hallucinations, fictions and elaborates lies of the most devious and tragically generous Freud ever envisioned...." According to *Publishers Weekly*, "Thomas, whose best known, if not best, book remains *The White Hotel*, is his haunting, obsessive self in this *tour de force* that combines two of his passionate interests: the dark corners of psychiatry and the ironies of history." *Booklist* calls *Eating Pavlova* "an engaging, many-layered novel." *Kirkus Reviews* argues that Thomas "slips further down the greasy pole toward literary ignominy in this trashy account of Sigmund Freud's last days." The *Times Literary Supplement* concludes that "As its title suggests, *Eating Pavlova* is gross and elegant at once. Easy to recoil from, hard to forget."

RECOGNITION: *NYTBR* Notable Book of 1994; REVIEWS: *BL* 9/15/94; *KR* 7/15/94; *NYTBR* 10/23/94; *PW* 4/22/94; *TLS* 4/22/94

271 *Pictures at an Exhibition* (1993); Carroll & Graf 1994 (pbk)

Fifty years after the Holocaust a group of survivors gathers in London. They are about to enact a baroque Freudian masquerade with backdrops of Munich and music by Mahler. Thomas's challenging novel tackles moral ambiguity as well as the use of sex as an instrument of domination and degradation.

The *Library Journal* observes that "organized around an exhibit of Edvard Munch paintings portraying love, jealousy, despair, and death, Thomas's novel is a stunning commentary on the effects of the Holocaust on society today." According to the *Washington Post Book World*, *Pictures at an Exhibition* "is a fiercely intelligent book, and a shattering experience to read." In the view of novelist **Frederich Busch** (*NYTBR*), however, *Pictures* is lumbered with a plot that "is tied together in an unconvincing Freudian bundle." The *Times Literary Supplement* reviewer concurs: "Thomas seems to believe that the right formula of Freud for beginners, Nazism, sadistic sex and historical revisionism will sell anything. I dearly hope that he is proved wrong." *Publishers Weekly*, on the other hand, concludes that "there is no mistaking the stark compassion of Thomas's world, his mastery of the modern psyche and his ability to draw the reader into the darker corners of the human heart."

REVIEWS: *KR* 9/1/93; *LJ* 10/15/93; *NYTBR* 10/31/93; *PW* 9/13/93; *TLS* 1/29/93; *WPBW* 10/3/93

Thomson, Rupert (UK)

272 *Air & Fire* (1994); Random House 1995 (pbk)

Set in 1890, Rupert Thomson's "oddly lyrical" novel explores the quixotic attempt by Theophile Valence a (fictional) disciple of Gustave Eiffel to build a steel cathedral in a remote town in Baja, California. Valence arrives in Santa Sofia, an exotic outpost of the civilized world, with 2,348 pieces of metal ready for assembly and a beautiful young wife, Suzanne. The narrative also features a feckless yet courageous young American prospector, Wilson Pharoah.

According to novelist Carolyn See (*WPBW*), Thomson "has constructed a wonderful landscape that resembles the Mexico of B. Traven's lesser-known novels and Celine's nightmare Africa…. This world is utterly engaging, full of adventure and excess, and 130 degrees in the shade." According to the *London Review of Books*: "The narrative (which in places is characteristically hallucinatory) is anchored to a series of pedantic reports from Valence to Eiffel, describing the progress (of the cathedral) which is, of course, doomed … [and] as Valence discovers, the difficulty is not with technology but with 'the human problems that abound.'" David Murray (*NYTBR*) suggests that "This often surreal, evanescent story takes careful reading, but the effort is well worth it." Michael Kerrigan (*TLS*), on the other hand, finds Thomson's "abundance and extravagance of imagery" to be "merely inchoate."

REVIEWS: *KR* 11/1/93; *LJ* 11/15/93; *LRB* 7/8/93; *NYTBR* 3/13/94; *TLS* 4/9/93; *WPBW* 1/21/94

Thornton, Lawrence (USA)

273 *Tales from the Blue Archives* (1997); Doubleday 1997 (HC)

Described by *Kirkus Reviews* as a "richly, evocatively told, blood-is-thicker-than-blood melodrama" that employs a number of "eerie, magical realist touches," *Tales from the Blue Archives* is the final volume in Lawrence Thornton's Argentinean trilogy. The novel is set in modern day Argentina during and immediately following the years of the infamous "Dirty War." Key players in Thornton's third installment include: Dolores Masson, a grandmother (who, along with hundreds of wives, mothers and grandmothers, has taken to demonstrating in Buenos Aires' great square in the memory of the Disappeared); Carlos Ruedos, a psychic, and his daughter Teresa. The plot is driven by Dolores's search for her twin grandsons (now teenagers) and by her growing suspicion that they have been adopted by a former member of the — now-deposed — junta's death squad.

According to *Kirkus Reviews* "For all its operatic pomp, Thornton's vision of beyond-the-grave revenge and retribution comes off as heartwrenchingly sincere." The *New York Times Book Review* observes that even though "Thornton seems to feel the need to use speechmaking, obvious dreams and heavily loaded, unnatural conversations as crutches for a story that is perfectly capable of carrying its own weight … he closes his trilogy with a novel that occupies the same turf as did *Imagining Argentina*. The high ground is firmly his, and he has earned it."

REVIEWS: *BL* 10/15/97; *KR* 10/1/97; *LJ* 10/1/97; *NYTBR* 12/7/97; *PW* 9/22/97; *WPBW* 1/11/97

274 *Naming the Spirits* (1995); Bantam Doubleday Dell 1995 (pbk)

As *Naming the Spirits* opens, a young girl by the name of Teresa has, miraculously escaped death at the hands of an Argentinean death squad. After wandering across the pampas she finally arrives, filthy, incoherent, memoryless and bearing the scar of a bullet would, in Buenos Aires where she is taken in by the Christianis whose only daughter never returned home from a student led anti-government demonstration. Teresa's extraordinary story is narrated by the ghostly voices of eleven of Teresa's compatriots who, when gunned down by government soldiers on the lonely edge of the pampas, joined the swelling ranks of the *Desaparecidos*: Argentineans of all ages and walks of life who "disappeared" during Argentina's "Dirty War" for expressing even the mildest form of government opposition. *Naming the Spirits* is a sequel to Mr. Thornton's 1978 novel *Imagining Argentina*.

According to the *Library Journal* "this new novel employs a restrained but highly effective version of magic realism. Thornton surprises the reader with carefully rational doses of fantasy in an otherwise straightforward narrative." *The Nation* observes that: "Nearly fifteen years after the departure of the generals, it still seems impossible to understand the implosion of Argentine civilization … that was the Dirty War. So it is with all the dictators of South America, the Strossners, the Pinochets, the Banzers, these generals who, using the wider cold war as only the flimsiest pretext, devised a twisted recipe of Catholicism, anti-communism, patriarchy and bourgeois paranoia to nourish their various dreams of national purity…. The generals imagined their Argentina and imagined it with torture and lies and Falcons. And silence. Thornton's novel … fills that emptiness with names and stories and a promise never to forget." *Hispanic* argues that "Thornton's direct, empathetic writing shows how the power of imagination, of desire, and of the spiritual world can outlive any oppressive political control."

REVIEWS: *BL* 7/95; *Hisp* 4/95; *LJ* 7/95; *Nation* 9/25/95; *NYTBR* 9/17/95; *PW* 5/29/95; *SFCBR* 10/8/95

Tuck, Lily (USA)

275   *The Woman Who Walked on Water* (1996); Riverhead 1997 (pbk)

In her second novel, Lily Tuck tells the spare, impeccably crafted story of the enigmatic Adele and her search for spiritual fulfillment. Set in the 1970s, *The Woman Who Walked on Water* explores one woman's intense pursuit of "higher meaning," and personal enlightenment. Adele is a vivacious, attractive young wife and mother who, after meeting a guru while vacationing in France, follows him to his Asram in India. Profoundly changed by this experience, Adele repairs to a Caribbean island to reflect on what she has learned at the feet of her uncompromising spiritual guide and to explore her desire to abandon both her wealthy husband and her two children . Her story is narrated by a woman who after meeting Adele at the island resort, has be-

come her confidant. Like the other guests, the unnamed narrator is amazed at Adele's fearless ability to swim far out into the sea before returning to the beach to sit in silent meditation.

According to *Booklist* "this compelling and enigmatic tales is not unlike a Zen koan, a paradox fashioned to inspire sustained, even circular meditation." *Kirkus Reviews* calls *The Woman Who Walked on Water* "an exquisite, gem-like treatise on the nature of illumination — a case study of metamorphosis" and observes that the novel is broken into "76 slim, self-contained, dreamlike chapters … [which gradually paint] an engrossing portrait of Adele — a shining star of a woman…." *Salon* suggests that "Layering subtle allegory and ancient wisdom with sharp-edged characterization, this enigmatic book portrays a thoroughly believable and memorable quest for a life that transcends even its charmed beginnings."

REVIEWS: *BL* 2/15/96; *LJ* 3/1/96; *NYTBR* 4/28/96; *PW* 1/8/96

Updike, John (USA)

276   *Toward the End of Time* (1997); Knopf 1997 (HC); Fawcett 1998 (pbk)

John Updike's 18th novel, a dystopian romance, is set in the year 2020, in an America still recovering from the effects of a nuclear war with China. Some aspects of late–20th-century society (at least as Updike's older characters must surely have known it), have disappeared, along with a national currency, and a centralized government. Opportunistic crime is rife and protection money must be paid to ensure neighborhood and personal security. Ben Turnbull, a retired investment banker, lives in a relatively undisturbed plush North Shore community from which he occasionally commutes into Boston. His younger, second wife, is an "energetic scold." The novel takes the form of Ben's journal — maintained over the course of a year — which is filled both with the everydayness of his life (scuffles with his wife, visits to and from grandchildren, assignations with Deirdre his favorite prostitute, etc.) and with general ruminations on the meaning of life, the laws of physics and the mysteries of the natural world.

According to the *Atlantic Monthly*, Ben Turnbul "is a fascinating, amusing, eloquent companion, and one feels genuine regret when the year, his journal, and with them Mr. Updike's novel comes to an end." Richard Eder (*LATBR*) observes that "stripped of vitality and power, the failing protagonist makes a final grab for command by using the loopy metaphors of physics to declare reality for the cloudiness of his mind and desires. In his rage against the 'dying of the light' he elevates the imminent end of his particular time into the astrophysical hypothesis of the End of Time." *Publish-*

ers *Weekly* argues that "as Ben confronts the looming certainty that time is running out for him and for the universe, the narrative sweeps to a bittersweet conclusion befitting a book that has all the hallmarks of a classic." Novelist **Gore Vidal**, writing in the *Times Literary Supplement* concludes that "like all Updike's work, *Toward the End of Time* is a novel of narcissism."

RECOGNITION: *LATBR* "Recommended Title" 1997; *NYTBR* "Editors' Choice" 1997; *Publishers Weekly* "Best Books" 1997; REVIEWS: *AtlM* 10/97; *BL* 8/19/97; *EW* 10/17/97; *KR* 8/1/97; *LATBR* 10/5/97; *LJ* 9/15/97; *NYTBR* 10/12/97; *TLS* 2/6/98; *WPBW* 11/2/97

Urquhart, Jane (Canada)

Away (1994); Penguin 1995 (pbk); See Section 5, #658

Vanderhaeghe, Guy (Canada)

The Englishman's Boy (1997); Picador 1997 (HC); See Section 5, #659

Vea, Alfredo (USA)

277   *The Silver Cloud Cafe* (1996); Dutton 1996 (HC)

Set both in the California migrant worker camps of the 1950s and in contemporary San Francisco's seedy Mission District, *The Silver Cloud Cafe* features a magical cantina, which acts as a magnet for a collection of troubled souls. These include: a Mexican priest pursued by personal demons; a philosopher midget still nursing a broken heart; a gay Filipino; a washed up black former prizefighter; and an improbable assassin. The tale incorporates two murders — occurring forty years apart — and plot tributaries which wend their way back to the Mexican Revolution of the 1920s. It also explores the powerful role of religion and superstition in the lives of an extended family of immigrants.

The *San Francisco Chronicle* points out that in his "(b)ig hearted ... magical" novel Alfredo Vea blends "Garcia Marquez with Raymond Chandler." *Kirkus Reviews* is also reminded of Gabriel Garcia Marquez (as well as John Steinbeck) and concludes that Vea's "crowded" novel is "a highly original work ... equally concerned with religion and the oppressed." The *Los Angeles Times* reviewer asserts "If I were a murder suspect and had my choice of literary lawyers to represent me, Alfredo Vea would be the one."

REVIEWS: *KR* 8/15/96; *LAT* 9/30/96; *LJ* 9/1/96; *PW* 8/5/96; EDITOR'S NOTE: See Gloria Naylor's *Baily's Cafe*, #224.

Vidal, Gore (USA)

Live from Golgotha (1992); Penguin 1993 (pbk); See Section 7, #971

Vollmann, William T. (USA)

278   *The Rifles* (1994?); Viking 1995 (pbk)

The Rifles, volume three in William T. Vollmann's proposed seven-volume history of the European conquest of North America, is subtitled: *Seven Dreams About Our Continent in the Days of the Riflemen ... Whose Heroes Smoothbored the Northwest Passage, Checked the Rampages of Whales, Relocated the Esquimaux, etc.* Set primarily in the mid-1800s, it focuses on the intense interest in — and energy expended towards — the discovery of a Northwest passage. The story leads, inevitably, to the Canadian north where contemporary Inuit elders mourn the loss of their culture while their grandsons are consumed with anomie.

According to the *Times Literary Supplement*, "Vollmann, for all his stylistic quirkiness, is the master of his material. His tale is cunningly placed: like its shamanic myths and deities, the Arctic habitat plays tricks on its prisoners. Land that appears to be solid splits suddenly to reveal the polar sea...." The *San Francisco Chronicle* notes that in "everything he writes, Vollmann adamantly refuses to lie to himself or us. In an era saturated with political and commercial dishonesty and Disneyesque sentimentality, it is a quality as precious as diamonds." In the opinion of the *Yale Review*, *The Rifles* is a "much more courageous and successful work than, say, Cormac McCarthy's prizewinning (and rather too nostalgic) *All the Pretty Horses*." The *Washington Post Book World* concludes that *The Rifles*, like all of Vollmann's books, exhibits "enormous range, huge ambition, stylistic daring, wide learning, audacious innovation and sardonic wit."

RECOGNITION: Nominated for the 1994 *L.A. Times* Book Award; *NYTBR* Notable Book of 1994; REVIEWS: *BL* 1/1/94; *KR* 12/1/93; *LJ* 12/93; *Nation* 3/21/94; *NYTBR* 2/27/94; *Time* 3/28/94; *TLS* 6/10/94; *WPBW* 2/13/94; *YaleR* 4/94

279   *Fathers and Crows: Seven Dreams: A Book of North American Landscapes* (1992); Penguin 1993 (pbk)

In volume two of his fictional history of the exploration and settlement of North America — W.T. Vollmann concentrates on the violent clashes between native and European cultures characteristic of in the 1600s. Using the story of the 17th-century Iroquois saint (Catherine Tekakwitha) as a point of departure, Vollmann begins his myth-laden story incorporating the exploits of the *voyageurs*, e.g., Champlain and the Jesuit missionaries who played a significant role in the subjugation of the native peoples of Canada.

According to the *Times Literary Supplement*, Vollmann's "language moves interestingly between contemporary colloquial, Hollywood historical, Middle High Tolkientalk, and a quirky and enjoyable poetry ... [and is] never less than vigorous and inventive.' The *Washington Post Book World* observes that Vollmann looks capable of "filling the seven-league boots of John Barth, William Gaddis, and Thomas Pynchon," and concludes that *"Fathers and Crows* is a richly imaginative and boldly innovative achievement." *The* (London) *Guardian* argues that "Vollmann's imagination is so explosively — almost blindingly, you might say — vivid, so virile, so conjurous and enabling, that his 'symbolic' or poetic history burns with a fire no historian should ever want to put out." The *L.A. Times Book Review* concludes that *Fathers and Crows* "is a novel that is worth every word, a work of such elegant structure and uncompromising intelligence that it will change the way you think about the opening of the New World — indeed, the way you think about all of history, and what it means."

RECOGNITION: *NYTBR* Notable Book of 1992; REVIEWS: *BL* 9/1/92; *Guard* 10/8/92; *KR* 6/1/92; *LATBR* 8/23/92; *NYTBR* 9/6/92; *PW* 6/15/92; *Spec* 10/24/92; *TLS* 10/23/92; *WPBW* 8/2/92

280   *The Ice Shirt* (1990); Penguin 1993 (pbk)

The Ice Shirt, the first volume in W.T. Vollmann's projected seven-volume fictional history of the settlement of North America, is characterized by highly inventive prose and an intermingling of Norse mythology, fictionally elaborated character studies, and historical records. It begins with the arrival in the New World of Norse seafarers, fully 500 years before Columbus, and concentrates on their bloody wars, exploratory voyages in search of plunder, and family sagas steeped in fratricide, violence, and treachery. The author mixes flights of poetic fancy with ordinary slang while periodically interrupting the narrative with conflicting, contemporary versions of historical events.

According to *Newsday, The Ice Shirt* is "a recklessly ambitious amalgam of James Joyce and Thomas Pynchon which proposes to tell us the story of our [country's] bloody origins," The *New York Times* describes Vollmann's work as "a performance of Wagner's 'Ring' cycle directed by Sam Peckinpah with a new libretto by J.R.R.Tolkien and occasional music by Aaron Copland" and concludes that it is "an ambitious, often enthralling novel." The *London Times* calls *The Ice Shirt* a "Nordic saga, a dream-book, a vast pastiche, a travelogue: it crosses genre-boundaries like a virus crossing frontiers" and concludes that it is "[f]ull of enticements but many more frustrations, it is remarkable, rudely inventive, drunkenly daring, and, finally, intolerable."

REVIEWS: *KR* 10/1/90; *LJ* 10/1/90; *LT* 5/31/90; *NS&S* 6/8/90; *Newsday* 5/24/93; *NYTBR* 10/14/90; *PW* 8/3/90

Wagner, Bruce (USA)

I'm Losing You (1996); Random House 1996 (HC); See Section 7, #973

Wallace, David Foster (USA)

281   *Infinite Jest* (1996); Little Brown 1997 (pbk)

Weighing in at over 1,000 pages, *Infinite Jest*, with its post-modern narrative quirkiness, may yet join the ranks of contemporary novels which are more talked about than read. Wallace is being widely compared with the post-modern American masters (e.g., John Barth, Don DeLillo, Thomas Pynchon, William Buroughs, William Gaddis et al.) with whom he shares a penchant for both philosophical satire and allegorical constructs. *Infinite Jest* is set in the near future (2014, to be exact), and the plot, such as it is, revolves around the intertwined destinies of the habitués of two institutions — situated side-by-side in a non-descript Boston suburb — a halfway house and a tennis academy.

Publishers Weekly argues that "With its baroque subplots, zany political satire, morbid, cerebral humor and astonishing range of cultural references, Wallace's brilliant but somewhat bloated dirigible of a second novel will appeal to steadfast readers of Pynchon and Gaddis." According to *Time* magazine, David Foster Wallace's "marathon send-up of humanism at the end of its tether is worth the effort. There is generous intelligence and authentic passion on every page, even the overwritten ones in which the author seems to have had a fit of graphomania." In the view of the *Times Literary Supplement*, "The stylistic idiosyncrasies of the novel, while producing many striking effects, do not always convince us that they could only have been written as they were, or that the choice at any one point is especially pertinent: the old circularity about 'doing justice to confusion' only holds up to a point. It remains to be seen if *Infinite Jest* heralds a return to popular experimental novels in the United States." The *Library Journal* calls Wallace's book "[d]istinct, idiomatic, wild and crazy" and concludes it "is destined to have a cult following."

RECOGNITION: *L.A. Times* "Best Books" 1996; *NYTBR* Notable Book of 1996; *Salon Magazine* "Book of the Year" 1996; REVIEWS: *AllM* 2/96; *ChiTrib* 2/16/97; *LATBR* 12/29/96; *LJ* 1/96; *NatR* 6/17/96; *NYMag* 2/12/96; *NYTBR* 3/3/96; *PW* 11/27/95; *TLS* 6/28/96; *WPBW* 3/24/96

West, Paul (UK/USA)

282   *Sporting with Amaryllis* (1996); Overlook 1997 (pbk)

Even at their wettest, his eyes could be surly, and when the heavy upper lids slid down he had sealed you

away, unworthy of further insult. He was only seventeen, but Chappell his tutor scolded him for not being
sleek enough, for not adapting himself to the whims
of his elders. Smart, gifted, busy, retentive, but somewhat brash, he let his emotions get the better of him,
complaining (as if there could be any changing of it)
about the dryrot curriculum that represented the
human creature at its deadest and most barren.... His
father had schooled him in music, his school, St.
Paul's, had equipped him with Latin, Greek and He-
brew; and private tutors had seeded him with French
and Italian. Where else should such a little monster
go but Cambridge? Later centuries would have dubbed
him a swot, which is to say studies with obvious tedium. He heard the music of humanity all right, but
not in the programs of Scholastic logic designed to
ready him for becoming a clergyman.

In his 17th novel, Paul West conjures up an
audacious account of the early life of John Milton,
the eminent 17th century man of letters. In *Sporting with Amaryllis*, Milton is depicted as a greedily
sensual young "rube" who, at 16 and on holiday
from his studies at Cambridge, falls under the sway
of a mysterious black prostitute (by the name of
Amaryllis) who initiates him into the pleasures of
unbridled sex — eventually becoming his creative
muse.

According to *Booklist* "Amaryllis, an unearthly
but decidedly earthy being, initiates her charge into
the realms of sex and poetry and West regales us
with a heady blend of lewdness and aesthetics as he
surrealistically and provocatively ponders the mysteries of art, eroticism, myth, paradox, and
suffering." As *Publishers Weekly* observes "The real
protagonist here is arguably language itself, and the
sheer gorgeousness and texture with which West
delineates both the artistic and the sensual supplies
abundant rewards." Novelist and critic Carolyn See
(WPBW) concludes that "To anyone who says, 'Isn't
John Milton that *Paradise Lost* guy? — or to people
who deplore the idea of women as muses ... or to
people who couldn't care less about how English
poetry has continued through the centuries — I'd
say avoid this novel like, the, umm, plague. But the
learned, the witty, the horny, the goofy just might
be charmed by this little book."
REVIEWS: *BL* 11/1/96; *KR* 10/1/96; *LJ* 11/15/96;
PW 10/7/96; *WPBW* 1/10/97

Wideman, John Edgar (USA)
283 *The Cattle Killing* (1996); Houghton
Mifflin 1996 (HC); 1997 (pbk)
John Edgar Wideman's eighth novel is set in
Philadelphia in 1793. A plague-like illness is sweeping through the city and racial animosities are
heightened by rumors that the sickness is spread by
Negroes who are themselves immune. The tale is
told mostly through the interior monologues of

three characters: a 20th-century author looking
back in time, an aged griot (African storyteller),
and a young mixed-race itinerant preacher whose
search for a Haitian woman — glimpsed carrying
an apparently dead infant in her arms — brings him
to Philadelphia where he is plunged into a nightmare world. Underpinning the novel is the author's
recounting of the fable of the South African Xhosa
people who — in heeding a false prophecy — killed
their precious cattle in hopes of ridding their land
of the rapacious white men. Throughout the novel,
Wideman makes frequent use of myth and
metaphor.

According to *Booklist*, "It has been said that
Wideman is a novelist who is 'capable of reinventing the form.' He does not quite reinvent the form
with this work, but it is not due to lack of trying.
This novel is multistoried and must be read more
than once to appreciate its inventiveness." The *New
York Times Book Review* observes that "Mr. Wideman may have ventured beyond his readers this
time out. Whereas figurative elements traditionally
serve narrative interests, here things are the other
way around. Filaments of story, of precious sense,
are woven like bits of rag into a rug of shimmering
but also perplexing suggestiveness ... if there were
a statute of restriction on narrative proliferation,
John Edgar Wideman would be flagrantly, brilliantly — in violation." According to the *New York
Review of Books*, "no contemporary writer, with the
possible exception of John Barth, is more riskily
self-referential. The dangers of such a preoccupation with the self are obvious, yet there are rewards
as well, for the gradual accretion of biographical
fact establishes the reader as an intimate of the
writer's, familiar with both the life and the work."

OTHER MEDIA: Audiocassette (Books-on-
Tape/unabr); RECOGNITION: *PW* "Best Book"
1996; REVIEWS: *BL* 8/96; *KR* 8/1/96; *LJ* 7/96; *Nation* 10/28/96; *NYTBR* 11/3/96; *PW* 8/12/96;
WPBW 9/29/96

284 *Philadelphia Fire* (1990); Vintage 1991
(pbk)
Philadelphia Fire is based on an actual police
action which culminated in the fire-bombing of the
headquarters of a Philadelphia-based Afro-centric
cult. Ordered by the mayor, the 1985 bombing of
an inhabited building (in a densely populated
neighborhood of row-houses) led to numerous
deaths and the eventual destruction of the entire
block. The novel is structured around the return to
Philadelphia of a novelist by the name of Cudjoe
who has come in the hopes of researching a book
about the tragic event. The final section of the book
is a reworking, in a black urban vernacular, of
Shakespeare's *Tempest* wherein the conflagration assumes the role of Prospero's storm.

According to *Publishers Weekly*, "In incantatory lyrical, naturalistic and inventive prose, Wideman writes of sex and race and life in the city, with all the beauty, profane humor and literary complexity of Joyce writing about Dublin." In the view of the *New Statesman & Society:* "What we get [in *Philadelphia Fire*] ... is a rehash of Ralph Ellison, Richard Wright and George Lamming, decorated with a magpie selection of classical and contemporary allusions." The *Christian Science Monitor* concludes that "Wideman asks us to unlearn our assumptions, and he writes an un-novel. All this fracturing of literary convention does not make for a smooth, easy read, but as one of Wideman's characters says, 'Technique, technique is truth, bucko.'"

RECOGNITION: Winner of the 1991 PEN/Faulkner Award; *NYTBR* Notable Book of 1990; REVIEWS: *CSM* 10/23/90; *NewsWk* 10/1/90; *NS&S* 2/1/91; *NYTBR* 9/30/90; *PW* 8/17/90

Willis, Connie (USA)

To Say Nothing of the Dog (1998); Bantam Books 1998 (HC); See Section 7, #981

Winterson, Jeannette (UK)

285   *Gut Symmetries* (1997); Knopf 1997 (HC); Vintage 1998 (pbk)

Giovanni Rosetti, an Italian American physicist, is traveling from Southampton, England, to New York on the QE2 where he has agreed to give a series of lectures about Paracelsus and the "new Physics." Also on board is a young English physicist by the name of Alice Fairfax. In short order Giovanni (Jove) and Alice begin a torrid affair. Once arriving in New York City, Jove introduces Alice to Stella, a poet and his wife of 24 years. Alice and Stella, immediately attracted to one another, begin a passionate affair. All does not end well on a yacht near Capri.

According to *Kirkus Reviews*, Winterson "[a]lways a narrative daredevil and linguistic voluptuary ... sustains a level of writing here that's at once incantatory, discursive, and passionate: a breath-taking Joycean romp that explores the mysteries of love in a world freed from common sense by the wonders of modern math and physics." *Booklist* concludes that "Winterson, ever innovative and unnerving even as she is enchanting, dives to remarkable emotional depths as she moves toward the revelation that 'total beauty' is what makes life worth living." *Gut Symmetries* is, in the words of the *London Sunday Times* "Erudite, erotic and rarely less than enchanting ... a modern *ménage à trois* [by a writer] near the peak of her formidable powers."

REVIEWS: *BL* 4/1/97; *KR* 2/15/97; *LATBR* 4/13/97; *LJ* 4/15/97; *LST* 1/25/98; *NewR* 4/7/97; *NS* 1/10/97; *NYTBR* 5/11/97; *TLS* 1/13/97; EDI-TOR'S NOTE: Ms. Winterson was named by *Granta* magazine to its 1993 list of the twenty "Best Young British Novelists."

286   *Art & Lies* (1994); Knopf 1995 (HC)

As the novel opens, three passengers board a train which appears to be carrying a cargo of light: Handel, a failed priest who works as a doctor; Picasso, a woman artist tormented by memories of incest; and Sappho the reincarnated form of the Greek lyric poet. In her relentlessly esoteric, aggressively non-linear fifth novel, Ms. Winterson attacks patriarchy and social repression and (often explicitly) explores the interconnections between art and eros.

According to the *Washington Post Book World* "it seems that Winterson has done no less than create a fin-de-siècle retort to the fourth-century philosopher Boethius, who, while imprisoned for conspiracy, wrote *The Consolation of Philosophy.* From the prison of our post-modern world, where books are entering the ranks of endangered species, Winterson gives us the 'Consolation of Literature.' Poignant, breathtaking, humorous and erotic ... and a real page-turner, the surreal rail passage of *Art & Lies* is not to be missed." *Booklist,* in its starred review, observes that "As Winterson spins the intriguing, dramatic and significant tales of each of her characters, she satisfies our craving for story but accomplishes so much more, articulating the meaning of time, art, passion, and hypocrisy in prose charged with the pulse and imagery of poetry." The *L.A. Times Book Review* concludes, however, that "[a] curious paradox is sustained throughout *Art & Lies* and clearly unintentionally. In the name of liberty and fearless experiment, the novel is strait jacketed by issues that matter — when it is not pushed over the top into silliness."

REVIEWS: *BL* 2/15/95; *LATBR* 4/22/95; *LJ* 3/1/95; *LRB* 7/7/94; *MFSF* 4/95; *NS&S* 7/1/94; *NYTBR* 3/26/95; *PW* 2/20/95; *TLS* 6/17/94; *WPBW* 3/19/95

287   *Written on the Body* (1992); Vintage 1994 (pbk)

In her fifth novel Jeannette Wilson tells the story of an intense love affair between beautiful, red-headed Louise, a married woman (who has recently been diagnosed with cancer), and the narrator, a subversive Lothario, whose gender is never revealed.

According to *The Atlantic*, "Winterson has toned down her penchant for magic realism and has turned her feminist fairy stories into shaggy-dog tales of domestic life. These temper the narrator's passion for Louise with a dry humor, making the story all the stronger for it. The issue of gender has been refined as well — right out of the text, in fact. The non issue of the narrator's sex quietly asks the unsettling question What does it matter? and then lets the story go on its lovely way...." The *New York Review of Books* argues that the narrator of *Written on the Body*, compared with earlier Winterson characters "is more plaintive and given to self-pity, more sententious and preachy. Winterson's inbred missionary fervor is employed to put across the gospel of sexual freedom, but there is not much forgiveness.... All this may be irrelevant to the literary merit of the new novel, but it makes it harder to like, which is a pity, because Winterson has a lot of talent." The *Washington Post Book World* concludes that "*Written on the Body* is a very, very special book. The vision of love it offers is revolutionary, and it is sorely needed."

RECOGNITION: *NYTBR* Notable Book of 1993; nominated for the 1993 ALA Gay & Lesbian & Bisexual Book Award and the Lambda Book Award; REVIEWS: *AtlM* 2/93; *BL* 2/15/93; *EW* 2/26/93; *LitRev* 9/92; *LRB* 9/24/92; *NNYMag* 1/25/93; *NS&S* 9/18/92; *NYRB* 3/4/93; *NYTBR* 2/14/93; *PeopleW* 3/8/93; *PW* 12/7/92; *TLS* 9/4/92; *WPBW* 2/14/93; *YaleR* 10/93

ONE STEP FURTHER

Acker, Kathy (USA)

288   *Pussy, King of the Pirates* (1996); Grove-Atlantic 1996 (HC); 1997 (pbk)

Kathy Acker, ever the literary extremist, has fashioned a provocative, sexually explicit tale of swashbuckling and unbuckling. Drawing heavily on Robert Louis Stevenson's *Treasure Island*, Acker's story revolves around a treasure map, a band of girl pirates, a search for a desert island, and a lost city...

According to the *Library Journal*, *Pussy King* is "heavily influenced by pulp fiction, social satire, religious allegory, and picaresque novels. Acker give readers a lot to chew on here...." The *American Book Review* calls Acker's novel "part detective novel, part fairy tale from hell, part Dr. Seuss gone mad, part Greek tragedy" and concludes that "Acker's prose has never been more poetic, surprising, inimitable, her acidic humor never more quirkily funny." The *New York Times Book Review* was considerably less enamored of Ms. Acker's 13th novel: "the reader must endure a string of adventures that take place in China, Alexandria and everywhere else, most of which have something to do with sex and nothing to do with sense.... One of [Acker's] favorite subjects here is the importance of self-stimulation — appropriately enough, because in this book she has raised literary masturbation to an anti-art form." *Publishers Weekly* concludes that "Like Acker's other works, this campy and enigmatic novel is self-consciously provocative as she

detonates her battery of literary and sexual references in order to illuminate themes of masochism and rebellion — but it's also often funny and invariably intelligent."

REVIEWS: *ABR* 2-3/96; *KR* 11/1/95; *LJ* 1/96; *NYTBR* 3/3/96; *PW* 10/16/95; *SFCBR* 1/21/96

289   *My Mother: Demonology* (1994); Grove-Atlantic 1994 (pbk)

In *My Mother: Demonology*, a writer is attempting to understand her crippling vulnerability by coming to terms with a series of traumatic events that occurred while she was growing up. The author uses a variety of literary techniques (from aphorisms to prose fragments) in her aggressively post-modern exploration of the psychological underpinnings of memory.

Written in a highly confrontational "punk" style, Kathy Acker's 12th novel was described by the *New York Times Book Review* as "a wild motorcycle ride through a nightmare landscape awash in bodily fluids and excrement, a rotting America where sexual politics and political sexuality clash as people do their best to create an identity — a language — out of memory and desire...." According to the *Library Journal*, Acker's "formidable talented hand gives the cacophonous materials compelling poetic rhythm and balance." Kathy Acker was referred to as the "Marquis de Sade for mindless headbangers" by *Kirkus Reviews*, which goes on to deplore "her endless stream of ranting about sex, politics, and the pain of childhood."

REVIEWS: *ABR* 2/94; *KR* 5/15/93; *LATBR* 10/10/93; *LJ* 7/93; *NYTBR* 11/21/93

Amis, Martin (UK)

290   *London Fields* (1989); Random House 1991 (pbk)

This is a true story but I can't believe it's really happening. It's a murder story, too. I can't believe my luck. And a love story (I think), of all strange things, so late in the century, so late in the goddamed day.

This is the story of a murder. It hasn't happened yet. But it will. (It had better.) I know the murderer, I know the murderee. I know the time, I know the place. I know the motive (her motive) and I know the means. I know who will be the foil, the fool, the poor foal, also utterly destroyed. And I couldn't stop them I don't think, even if I wanted to. The girl will die. It's what she always wanted. You can't stop people, once they start creating.

London Fields, Martin Amis's "millennium" novel, is a darkly realized (often grotesquely funny) tale of murder and decadence. Narrated by Sam, an American writer with a mysterious, terminal illness, it is set in London which — during the waning months of 1999 — has fallen into decadence and decay as a result of a creeping eco-disaster. Nicola

Six, an actress who prefers real life to the stage, enters a pub one afternoon and recognizes her future murderer.

According to *The New Statesman*, Martin Amis is "the only English writer of his generation to kick his way out of the reticent, genteel language of the contemporary novel into a modern idiom which manages to be both coarse and eloquent, demotic and cerebral." The *New York Times Book Review* argues that *"London Fields* is not a safe book; it is controlled and moved not by the plot but by the density of its language. The author freely offends sensibilities. Indeed, it's difficult to think of anything he spares us when it comes to the concerns of the flesh. But his language is demonically alive." The *Times Literary Supplement* observes that *London Fields'* "construction ... is both solid and intricate ... so that even [or especially] the most incidental dialogue will allude to other strands of the novel to establish an exhaustive, punning coherence." The *London Review of Books* concludes that despite its self-indulgent humor "this [is] the most intellectually interesting fiction of the year, and a work beyond the reach of any British contemporary."

REVIEWS: *CSM* 4/11/90; *LJ* 3/1/90; *LRB* 9/28/89; *Nation* 4/23/90; *NewsWk* 3/5/90; *NS&S* 9/22/89; *NYTBR* 3/4/90; *Q&Q* 11/89; *Time* 2/26/90; *TLS* 9/29/89; *WLT* Win '91; *WPBW* 2/18/90; EDITOR'S NOTE: Martin Amis was named to *Granta* magazine's 1983 list of the twenty "Best Young British Novelists."

Banks, Ian (UK-Scotland)

291   *The Wasp Factory* (1984); S&S 1998 (pbk re-issue)

Ian Banks' 1984 sinister, over-the-top (and, some would argue, wildly comic) cult classic, is set on an isolated Scottish island. It tells the unexpurgated story of Frank Cauldhame, an emotionally isolated youth — abandoned by his mother at birth, mauled by a dog at three and a sociopath at eight — who experiments with life and death, with some very nasty results. Frank and his father live in "a state of partial derangement": Frank patrols his island fastness checking his "Sacrifice Poles" (totems, erected as warnings, which are decorated with the severed heads of animals) while his father (the feckless son of a laird and disgraced former don) rarely emerges from his secret tower laboratory. Despite the widespread outrage (mixed with critical acclaim) *The Wasp Factory* inspired upon publication, Banks' debut novel was chosen in a recent British survey as one of the most important books of the 20th century.

According to English critic Lorna Sage (*BBT*) "This novel, Iain Banks' first, caused a great fuss in (appropriately enough) 1984, when it was denounced as degenerate, hailed as savagely surreal, and generally taken as a belated manifesto of the punk generation. In fact it's a witty Scots variation on the venerable tradition of island allegories." The London *Financial Times* reviewer called Banks' novel "a Gothic horror story of quite exceptional quality. It is macabre, bizarre and — toward the end — impossible to put down. There is control and sensitivity in the book, and originality rare in established writers twice the author's age." The *Times Literary Supplement*, on the other hand, judged *The Wasp Factory* to be "a literary equivalent of the nastiest brand of juvenile delinquency." The *Washington Post Book World* suggests that while "Banks indulges too often in imagery and insight beyond the years of his young narrator, and the humor of the book seems suddenly discarded in the straight-faced severity of its ironic conclusion ... *The Wasp Factory* is ... a compelling and refreshingly bold fiction." The *WPBW* further concludes that "One is tempted to offer the caveat, 'not for the squeamish' ... but perhaps *The Wasp Factory* is the very book for the squeamish — a literate, penetrating examination of the nature of violence and the dwindling value of life in the modern world."

REVIEWS: *CF/BBT 1990*; *FT* 2/25/84; *NS* 2/17/84; *TLS* 3/16/84; *WPBW* 9/9/84; EDITOR'S NOTE: Ian Banks' 1986 novel *The Bridge* (reissued by HarperCollins in 1998) — a mysteriously structured novel that features a car crash and its aftermath — was described by *Publishers Weekly* as a "Pynchonesque ... satire ... [which] target[s] ... the British Isles' equivalent of American 'yuppies'."

Cohn, Nik (UK)

292   *Need* (1997); Knopf 1997 (HC)

Nik Cohn sets his end-of-the-millennium novel in New York City during a record-breaking "bad moon" heat wave. Cohn's fourth novel features four misfits whose common point of reference is Ferdousine's Zoo an Upper West Side pet shop: Katie Root, a knife-throwing psychic who tends the shop; Anna Crow, a belly dancer who lives upstairs; Willie D, who dreams of opening a topless carwash in the Bronx; and John Joe McGuire, a lost soul (accepted by some as the authentic voice of doom). The plot is enlivened by the presence of the "Black Swans" a cult inspired by a 16th century slave whose adherents have gathered in New York's underground to await the end of the world.

Booklist calls *Need* "a strangely exalted tale of improvised, end-of-the-millennium survival." and concludes that Nik Cohn though "born in London ... [is] an inveterate New Yorker ... jazzed by the city's maniacal, even apocalyptic energy." According to *Kirkus Reviews*, *Need* is a "[r]affish, neo-expressionist novel in low-life slang, set in Manhattan but with a strong flow of London guttertalk."

The *Times Literary Supplement* observes that "Nik Cohn's prose is terse, vivid and darkly humorous, the story a cry from the heart of the quintessential urban jungle ... it is keen observation of estranged commonality." The *Literary Review* observes that Cohn "has a dazzling verbal facility and a free-rolling style right up there with Martin Amis...."

REVIEWS: *BL* 2/1/97; *KR* 12/15/96; *LitRev* 7/96; *LJ* 3/1/97; *NYTBR* 3/9/97; *NS* 7/12/96; *TLS* 7/12/96

Cooper, Dennis (USA)

293 *Guide* (1997); Grove-Atlantic 1997 (HC); 1998 (pbk)

Dennis Cooper sets his latest novel (compared, by more than one critic, to the work of William Burroughs) in L.A.'s gay urban demi-monde and features a frequently disturbing assemblage of teenage hustlers, runaways and drug addicts.

The *Library Journal* calls Cooper "a master (like Jean Genet) of his own disenfranchised generation" and observes that though *Guide* is "as compelling as it is perverse, Cooper purposefully overrides it with an innovative style and raw, truthful character studies." According to the *Nation,* Dennis Cooper "is often mistaken as the postmodern disciple of Sade and Genet (from whom, unquestionably, he has learned), but the daring of *Guide* is how clearly he shows his interests in extremity to be a way of getting at the precariousness of living through language stripped down to its most vulnerable, tender and sweet." In the view of novelist Gary Indiana (*LATBR*) *Guide* "is the most seductively frightening, best-written novel of contemporary urban life that anyone has attempted in a long time; it's the funniest, too, and does for Clinton America what *The Tin Drum* did for postwar Germany." *Salon* calls it "a sub-zero nihilist investigation ... loose, hallucinatory and grounded in pop idiom" and concludes that Cooper is "one of the few serious writers working in the literary tradition of subversion." The *London Times* suggests that *Guide* "which makes *American Psycho* and *Lolita* seem budgie-safe ... is not cheap erotica" and argues that Cooper "has written a brilliantly base tale of human self-destruction for the brave." *Kirkus Reviews* asserts that *Guide* is "[a]s offensive in its aimlessness as it is in its perversity. Cooper should be ashamed of himself."

RECOGNITION: *LATBR* "Best Books" 1997; REVIEWS: *KR* 4/1/97; *LATBR* 6/8/97; *LJ* 5/1/97; *LT* 3/21/98; *Nation* 6/16/97; *NYTBR* 8/3/97; *PW* 5/5/97; *Salon* 9/19/97

294 *Try* (1994); Grove-Atlantic 1995 (pbk)

In *Try*, teenage Ziggy has suffered a panoply of physical and sexual abuse at the hands of those family members who haven't actually abandoned him. Dennis Cooper's 8th novel is an uncompromising portrait of a young man who, in the face of extreme sexual predation and a drug saturated milieu, manages to retain his humanity.

The *New York Times Book Review*, calls *Try* "high risk literature," further asserting that "it takes enormous courage for a writer to explore ... the extreme boundaries of human behavior and amorality, right to the abyss where desire and lust topple into death. It also takes courage — not to mention a strong stomach — for the reader to follow the author in his ... journey into hell." According to the *NS&S* "Cooper's antecedents are clear; from Nietzsche and Sade through Bataille, Burroughs and contemporary cultural theory ... [His] triumph ... is to be able to write about extreme experience and even recover a redemptive vocabulary without relying on ironic strategies or the easy collapse into satire." *Kirkus Reviews* points out that "Caveats often accompany reviews of Cooper's work, and its not hard to see why. His novels (including this one) depict a nasty, brutish kind of gay sex, shadowed by violence and exploitation, yet they also have an inescapable power."

REVIEWS: *KR* 12/15/93; *LJ* 1/94; *NatR* 6/17/96; *NS&S* 9/30/94; *NY* 5/16/94; *NYTBR* 3/20/94; *PW* 12/13/93.

Gifford, Barry (USA)

295 *Baby Cat-Face* (1995); Harcourt Brace 1995 (HC); Harvest 1997 (pbk)

Set in and around New Orleans, Barry Gifford's seventh novel featuring Sailor and Lula concerns a young creole, Esquerita Reyna aka "Baby Cat-Face," who having led a violence-prone, drug-fueled life for just a little too long, is now looking for some peace. She thinks she's found it in Mother Bizco's Temple of the Few Washed Pure by Her Blood. Further plot developments include a car chase through "the backwaters of fundamentalist Christianity" and an encounter with a serial killer who thinks of herself as an "insect goddess." The novel is awash in physical and sexual violence.

The *Washington Post Book World* observes that in *Baby Cat-Face* "the author of *Wild at Heart* takes episodic excursions into a strangely familiar subculture of eroticized violence and perfervid religiosity" and concludes that the novel is actually "a string of wondrously inventive narrative diversions, and Gifford has a marvelous time spinning them." *Publishers Weekly* takes a more jaundiced view, suggesting that, while *Baby Cat-Face* is "often great fun," the author as he "takes his brand of trash–Americana through three generations of Christian fundamentalism and conspiracy theory ... remains disinterested in anything resembling sustained drama or characterization, content to rely on mo-

mentum, funky phrasing and the idiosyncrasies of his hyperthyroid world."
REVIEWS: *BL* 9/1/95; *LJ* 8/95; *NYTBR* 10/15/95; *PW* 6/19/95; *WPBW* 11/19/95

Harrison, Jim (USA)

296   *Julip* (1994); Washington Sq. 1995 (pbk)

Jim Harrison's *Julip* is a compilation of three novella-length and loosely linked stories that revolve around sex, animals and escape; each advances the view that men are really no match for women.

Publishers Weekly calls the three novellas which make up *Julip* "rambunctious, spirited chases through emotional territory," and judges Harrison to be a "protean writer ... [whose] humor tests the borders of the socially acceptable and the extremes of what is tolerable ... and concludes that "there is pleasure to be had in this recklessness." Alexander Harrison (*TLS*) observes that "The novella is an unfashionable and indeterminate form; is it a short novel or a long short story? What can a writer do with it that cannot be achieved more concisely or completely in its shorter or longer cousin? The answer, in Jim Harrison's *Julip*, is a tremendous amount." According to *Booklist* "In each of these ingenious, funny, and absorbing tales, Harrison muses over the fact that while other people can be veritable quagmires for our souls, their odd, selfish little behavior can also be, perversely enough, a genuine elixir."

REVIEWS: *BL* 3/1/94; *KR* 2/15/94; *LATBR* 8/14/94; *NYTBR* 5/22/94; *PW* 2/28/94; *TLS* 11/25/94

Homes, A.M. (USA)

297   *The End of Alice* (1996); S&S 1996 (HC); 1997 (pbk)

In A.M. Homes highly provocative novel, the narration is shared between a Princeton-educated pedophile serving a 23-year sentence for child molestation and murder, and a young female college student with decidedly abnormal sexual proclivities.

In the words of the *L.A. Times Book Review*: "Beware gentle reader, the soothing aspects of life as we know it are about to be profoundly disturbed. Crack the back of *The End of Alice* and a visceral nerve will be laid open, exposed for the quick pen of A.M. Homes to tease out of its mind. With all the cunning and control of a brilliant love, she takes us to places we dare not go alone...." According to British novelist **Margot Livesy** (*TLS*), "When it was published in America last year, A.M. Homes's novel was both widely reviled and widely admired. Some reviewers claimed to be deeply shocked,

while others argued that *The End of Alice* was performing the traditional functions of the novel: to raise deep moral questions, and to make us think about the Other. That it was written by a woman only added fuel to the fire." The *Library Journal* calls it "deliberately shocking and confrontational" suggesting further that the author's objective "seems to be to force the reader into a kind of Dostoevskian identification with the blackest and most perverse elements of human nature." The *New York Times Book Review*, concludes that Homes is "concerned with the fluid nature of identity, with the permeable boundaries that divide an overly deranged consciousness from a smugly socialized one.... To the extent that each of us believes the normal is both obvious and ours alone to define, Ms. Homes's novel comes as a powerful and disturbing antidote."

REVIEWS: *Advocate* 2/20/96; *EW* 3/8/96; *LATBR* 5/26/96; *LJ* 12/95; *LRB* 5/9/96; *NewsWk* 3/4/96; *NYTBR* 3/24/96; *PW* 12/11/95; *Time* 3/18/96; *TLS* 10/31/97

Maso, Carole (USA)

298   *The American Woman in the Chinese Hat* (1994); Dalkey 1994 (HC); NAL-Dutton 1995 (pbk)

Set on the French Riviera, *The American Woman in the Chinese Hat* is narrated (in both the 1st and 3rd person) by Catherine, a bisexual novelist who, recently jilted and in the throes of romantic despair, assuages her pain in casual sex and in reinventing herself in the pages of her notebook. Carol Maso's 4th novel explores the nature of creativity, high risk love and unchecked desire.

According to *Publishers Weekly*, "Maso's enchanting fourth novel unfolds in a fragmented, poetic prose that is exciting, delicious and lucid." In the view of the *Library Journal* "Like Maso's [previous novels] this book may shock the genteel reader, but others will be enthralled." The *L.A. Times Book Review* notes that *The American Woman* is "a book that begins and ends in a flash of light, with a clatter of voices that are speaking French. In between is silence, a glass of wine, a knife, a dark room, and a lot of passion." Ms. Maso's work was described by the *San Francisco Chronicle* as a "brilliant puzzle ... that uses the blazing primary colors of the French Riviera and its heat, thirst and public passion."

REVIEWS: *BellesL* Sum '94; *KR* 3/1/94; *Lamb-BkRev* 9/94; *LATBR* 7/31/94; *LJ* 2/1/94; *NYTBR* 5/15/94; *PW* 3/28/94; *SFCBR* 7/3/94

McEwan, Ian (UK)

299   *The Cement Garden* (1978); Random House 1993 (pbk re-issue)

Exploring themes of adolescent sexuality,

incest and childhood transvestitism, Ian McEwan's debut novel is narrated by an adolescent named Jack who, when his mother dies, orphaning him and his three siblings, opts to bury her body in the basement rather than be remanded into the care of the local authorities. The four siblings assume new roles to accommodate their new "family." *The Cement Garden*, upon publication, was widely compared to William Golding's *The Lord of the Flies*.

Doris Grumbach (*Saturday Review*) argues that "Huck Finn spoke authentically to his 19th century readers, Holden Caulfield served the adolescent boy in the middle century. Now meet Jack, Julia and Julia's sly snooker-playing friend, Derek. Who knows? These young people may well be speaking nastily for the youth at the end of the century." Novelist **Anne Tyler** (*NYTBR*) disagrees pointing out that "what makes the book difficult is that these children are … so consistently unlikable, and bitter that we can't believe in them … and we certainly can't identify with them." The *Times Literary Supplement* notes that *The Cement Garden* (wherein the) "morally extraordinary is made ordinary by the indifference of the telling … should consolidate Ian McEwan's reputation as one of the best young writers in Britain today." *The Cement Garden*, was called "just about perfect" by the London-based *Spectator*.

OTHER MEDIA: A film version was released in 1993; REVIEWS: *BL* 9/1/78; *KR* 8/1/78; *LJ* 10/1/78; *NS* 9/29/78; *NYTBR* 11/26/78; *PW* 9/4/78; *SatRev* 10/14/78; *Time* 11/27/78; *TLS* 9/29/78; *WPBW* 10/29/78; EDITOR'S NOTE: Ian McEwan was named to *Granta* magazine's 1983 list of the twenty "Best Young British Novelists."

Palahniuk, Chuck (USA)

300 *Fight Club* (1996); WW Norton 1996 (HC); Holt 1997 (pbk)

Chuck Palahniuk's debut novel is set in an apocalyptic urban future and is narrated by a depressed insurance adjuster who attends cancer support group meetings to boost his own self-esteem. It also features Tyler Durden, projectionist, waiter, self-styled nihilist, and the originator of a secret society called the Fight Club. The "club" provides young "Type A" professionals with an opportunity to let off steam through vicious, bare-knuckle combat in which literally "anything" goes. As the club's popularity grows (and spin-offs begin appearing throughout the country) Durden devises a thoroughly twisted scheme to harness this pent-up rage. *Kirkus Reviews* calls *The Fight Club* "brutal and relentless … a creepy, dystopic, confrontational novel that's also cynically smart and sharply written" and concludes that this "dangerously compelling" book "takes anarcho–S&M chic to a whole new level." *Booklist* calls it a "dark and disturbing

book … a powerful, and possibly brilliant, first novel" and concludes that "Every generation frightens and unnerves its parents, and Palahniuk's first novel is Gen X's most articulate assault yet on baby-boomer sensibilities." According to *Entertainment Weekly*, Palahniuk's "crackling irony skewers modern life … while high-lighting the unraveling of an apocalypse-obsessed mind." *Publishers Weekly*, in its starred review, notes that "Caustic, outrageous, bleakly funny, violent and always unsettling, Palahniuk's utterly original creation will make even the most jaded reader sit up and take notice."

OTHER MEDIA: A film version starring Brad Pitt was released in 1999; REVIEWS: *BL* 7/96; *EW* 9/6/96; *KR* 6/1/96; *LATBR* 8/18/96; *NY* 12/23/96; *PW* 6/3/96; *WPBW* 12/1/96

Robson, Ruthan (USA)

301 *a/k/a* (1997); St. Martin's 1998 (HC); 1999 (pbk)

Ruthan Robson's *a/k/a* features two women, both lesbians, who have lived with so many situationally driven aliases that they appear to have lost touch with their true selves. Margaret is a law student and lesbian prostitute whose name changes to suit her varied clientele (among whom she lists a minister's wife); BJ is a soap opera star who's attempts to "come out" have been frustrated by her producer.

Booklist notes that "Slowly, tantalizingly, this well-crafted novel weaves the threads of these women's lives together, divulging a bit more background here, a chance encounter there" and concludes that "Only when this otherwise fascinating book becomes something of a soaper itself does it strain credulity, but lesbian and other readers alike will keep turning the pages." According to *Kirkus Reviews, a/k/a* "is a potentially intriguing meditation on lesbian identity, but [is] episodic and too gratuitously weird to have much impact." *Publishers Weekly* observes that although *a/k/a* gives off "an antiseptic whiff of agitprop … Robson weaves intrigue, mystery and romance into a compelling tale."

RECOGNITION: Nominated for the 1998 Lambda Book Award; REVIEWS: *BL* 9/15/97; *KR* 7/1/97; *LJ* 9/15/97; *PW* 7/28/97

Self, Will (UK)

302 *Great Apes* (1997); Grove 1997 (HC)

Simon Dykes, a fashionable painter and protagonist of Will Self's latest novel of extremes, is caught up in a nightmare of shifting reality. Prone to overindulgence of every kind (he is a frequent user of recreational drugs and long-time habitué of the "young and debauched" London nightclub scene) he manages to keep things reasonably under control until the morning he awakes to find his girl-friend has metamorphosed into a chimp. Soon he finds that the wider "everyday" world is also populated by chimpanzees and is eventually hospitalized for "delusions of humanity." Many critics indicated that a "strong stomach" was essential to enjoyment of Self's novel.

In the view of *Booklist* "Self creates a fully realized chimp world with this Kafkaesque, or Swiftian, satire that hypnotizes with its comic romps, existential posturings, and Shakespearean intrigues." According to the *New York Times Book Review, Great Apes* is Will Self's "most satisfying book so far ... [and with it, the author] establishes himself as an alpha male in the English literary hierarchy." The *Economist* observes that "Will Self has brought off his elaborate conceit with audacity, verbal panache and much ribaldry." The *Washington Post Book World*, on the other hand, argues that Self, "never previously hesitant to skewer his fellow humans to their faces ... only attenuates his usual justifiable savagery by clothing his victims in fur."

RECOGNITION: *NYTBR* Notable Book of 1997; *Booklist* Editors' Choice 1997; REVIEWS: *BL* 8/19/97; *Econ* 5/10/97; *KR* 7/1/97; *PW* 7/14/97; *TLS* 5/9/97; *WPBW* 8/31/97

303   *My Idea of Fun* (1993); Random House 1995 (pbk)
Will Self's outrageous, frighteningly dark first novel, tells the story of Ian Wharton a very ordinary young man who has grown up in a trailer park on the Sussex coast where he has been taken under the insalubrious wing of a "seaside-retiree" known as Mr. Broadhurst (aka the Fat Controller). Ian shows up at University sporting a newly acquired photographic memory and, after a bout or two with telekinesis and teleportation, he seeks help from the resident psychiatrist, Dr. Gyggle. Self's postmodern take on the Faustian legend will not be to every reader's taste.

According to the *New Statesman Society & Society* "The least charitable reading of this novel would be that Self is no more than an up-market Clive Barker who has stippled his Faustian horror show with intellectual credibility. Shades of Proust, Nietzsche, Bulgakov, Jonathan Carroll and other restless ghosts twist uneasily in the slipstream of his turbo-charged imagination ... [however] we certainly find ourselves cheek-to-cheek with some very rough magic." English novelist James Buchan (*The Spectator*) observes that in *My Idea of Fun*, Self "introduces that stock figure of Anglo-American male highbrow fiction, the yuppie psychopath" and concludes: "the book's mixture of affectation, solemnity, offal and narrative indiscipline [described in the publisher's blurb as 'dirty magical realism'] ... does not flatter his talent." The *Guardian*

Weekly, on the other hand, finds Self's debut novel to be (although "somewhat rickety") "an antidote to the genteel proficiency of current British fiction...." George Stade (*NYTBR*) praises *My Idea of Fun* for "intelligence and ambition, for inventiveness, comedy, heartbreak and ferocity." Literary critic Jonathan Yardley (*WPBW*) finds "nothing beneath its flash and dazzle except vast emptiness."

RECOGNITION: Will Self was named one of the "Best of Young British Novelists" by *Granta* magazine; REVIEWS: *GW* 1/15/95; *LJ* 2/1/94; *LRB* 10/7/93; *NS&S* 9/10/93; *NY* 4/11/94; *NYT* 6/3/94; *NYTBR* 4/24/94; *PW* 2/7/94; *SFRB* 4-5/94; *Spec* 9/18/93; *TLS* 1/9/93; *WPBW* 4/3/94

304   *Cock & Bull* (1992); Grove/Atlantic 1993 (HC); Vintage 1994 (pbk)
Made up of two novella-length companion pieces, one the mirror image of the other, *Cock & Bull* features a woman who inexplicably grows a penis and a man who develops a vagina on the back of his leg.

The *London Times* describes *Cock & Bull* as "a film of Kafka's 'Metamorphosis,' scripted by William Burroughs and shot by David Cronenberg." The *London Review of Books* observes that "for all its singularity, the experience of *Cock & Bull* fades very quickly: not so much a mediation of gender politics as a bizarre and calculatedly repellent party-turn." The *Times Literary Supplement* judged *Cock and Bull* to be "a minor disaster." American reviewers were, on the whole, more laudatory. It was called "deliciously funny" by *New York* magazine, and "brilliant, gender-bending, surreal ... " by *Newsday*. According to *Publishers Weekly* "Self relates [his] Kafkaesque fables with an acerbic wit and a narrative mastery that makes the absurd seem credible and the commonplace absurd." *Esquire* concludes that "Feminists, Iron Johns, and anyone without a polymorphous perverse sense of humor will probably be offended by the ever-odder couplings, but that's the way sexual satire out to be: a Swiftian kick in the you-know-what."

REVIEWS: *BL* 4/1/93; *Esquire* 5/93; *LJ* 3/1/93; *LRB* 1/7/93; *LT* 11/1/92; *Newsday* 5/19/93; *PW* 2/22/93; *TLS* 10/9/92

Thomas, D.M. (USA/UK)

305   *The White Hotel* (1981); Penguin 1993 (pbk re-issue)
D.M. Thomas's provocative 3rd novel is an account of a fictitious patient of Sigmund Freud, Lisa Erdman, who suffers from unremitting pains in her breast and ovary for which no physical cause can be found. Five of the novel's seven parts are concerned with Ms. Erdman's psychoanalysis, which dredges up vivid sexual fantasies and a fear of death.

According to the *New York Times Book Review* "What *The White Hotel* sets out to perform, clearly, is the diagnosis of our epoch through the experience of an individual; and the highest praise I can give it is that for some time it comes close to achieving that goal." The *New Republic* observes that "the richness of this book is reminiscent of a painstakingly woven tapestry; one can focus on the details but must be absorbed by the whole." However, a number of reviewers found aspects of *The White Hotel* significantly off-putting. For example, *New Statesman & Society* argues that "there is no doubt that the accounts of Lisa's stay at the White Hotel with Freud's son are pornographic…. The moral: if you write pornography that is what it is and no amount of fumbling with artistic devices and excuses makes it any different."

RECOGNITION: Cheltenham Prize 1981; Silver Pen Award; REVIEWS: *BksCan* 10/81; *Harper* 4/81; *LJ* 2/1/81; *LRB* 8/16/90; *Nation* 5/2/81; *NewR* 3/28/81; *NewsWk* 3/10/81; *NS* 1/16/81; *NYRB* 5/28/91; *NYTBR* 3/13/81; *Q&Q* 6/81; *SatR* 3/81

Vollmann, William T. (USA)

306 *The Atlas* (1996); Penguin 1997 (pbk)
Described by the author as a "palindrome" of 53 interconnected stories, W.T. Vollmann's novel *The Atlas* (actually a semi-autobiographical memoir) ranges from Phnom Penh to Sarajevo, from Jerusalem to New York. Vollmann has been called the heir to Thomas Pynchon and William Burroughs, and in this volume it is easy to see why. In the course of the novel — the protagonist — among other things — pays to go on a Walrus hunt with an old Inuit and his grandsons, walks out of a kick boxing match in Bangkok when the sport's brutality overwhelms him, ingratiates himself with urban aborigines in Sydney by plying them with beer, and has unprotected sex with Cambodian prostitutes.

According to *Booklist* "Vollmann has gained cult status in the writing world, which, by definition, means his work is not for tradition-bound, and certainly not timid, readers." In the view of the *NY Observer*, "at his best, Mr. Vollmann is both lucid and lush, like sunlight in a wet forest…. a witness and a talker and a frightenly close and violent visionary." Novelist **Jim Paul** (*Salon*) calls *The Atlas* "a tour de force [formally and otherwise]" and observes that "Wherever the setting, the place is hell. Its residents live in torment, and Vollmann's own character is as vulnerable and wounded as anyone." *Publishers Weekly* concludes, however, that "Vollmann never manages to escape his own obsessions. Whether he is discoursing on drinking beer or shooting heroin or smoking crack or chewing khat in San Francisco, Bangkok or Kenya, the reader is treated to the same lovelorn teddy-bear pining after a devastated whoredom, as if the world

can be reduced to a rainy afternoon in a bug-infested hotel room."

REVIEWS: *BL* 2/1/96; *EW* 3/29/96; *KR* 1/15/96; *LJ* 3/1/96; *Nation* 5/6/96; *NY* 4/8/96; *PW* 1/15/96; *WPBW* 5/26/96

307 *Butterfly Stories: A Novel* (1993); Grove/Atlantic 1994 (pbk)
Not (as above) for readers faint of heart, *Butterfly Stories* offers another dark look at the sexual cesspools of the third world. Reminiscent of the more extreme work of William Burroughs and Henry Miller, it features a journalist, who, despite his penchant for irresponsible and opportunistic behavior, is redeemed by his gentleness and his protectiveness towards women and girls. The journalist is on assignment in Thailand and Cambodia in the months following the downfall of the Khmer Rouge — and the costs of this brutal regime, in human terms, are everywhere. He is working on a story about the growing numbers of young Asian girls who are being sold into a life of prostitution by unscrupulous relatives and so-called labor contractors. The journalist becomes caught up in the seedier side of his research, and develops a penchant for "sexual roulette" (i.e., he sleeps with prostitutes, many of whom are infected with the AIDS virus). When he actually falls in love with one of the Cambodian "girls" he turns his life upside down in an effort to save her.

According to *Booklist* "There is [despite his excesses] … great tenderness in Vollmann, and wit, and he seems to know his settings intimately; in *Butterfly Stories*, one enters a vast, introverted, nearly psychotic mind, and the effect is hypnotic." The *New Statesman and Society* argues that "Vollmann is a man out of time, squatting miserably at the wrong end of the wrong century, sniffing wearily at the diseased state of things. You worry that this disgusted whimsy could be the front end of a bandwagon. The New Dandyism: authors who write like angels but talk dirty, delighting in 'bad taste.'" The *L.A. Times Book Review* calls *Butterfly Stories* a rewarding, albeit "scary and a difficult book" and concludes that Vollmann's writing "has its own bright, lethal rhythm like a cut that pulses blood with every heartbeat. Instead of being gratuitous, the graphic sex and violence are completely organic to the story, which turns liquid and contradicts itself on a moment's notice."

RECOGNITION: *NYTBR* Notable Book of 1993; REVIEWS: *BL* 9/15/93; *KR* 9/1/93; *LATBR* 1/9/94; *NS&S* 11/19/93; *NYTBR* 11/14/93; *TLS* 11/5/93

Warner, Alan (UK-Scotland)

308 *These Demented Lands* (1997); Anchor 1998 (pbk)

Warner is certainly one of the freshest voices in Scottish fiction, with many critics rating his debut novel *Morvern Caller* as among the best of recent years. Morvern, the off-beat, thoroughly irreverent, rock-and-roll–obsessed protagonist of Alan Warner's eponymous debut, is back from the rave clubs and beaches of Spain. In fact Morvern has (literally) washed up on a cold, gray island off the coast of Scotland — the result of a boating accident. The wind-whipped isle is populated by an odd assortment of home grown lunatics and imported eccentrics including New Age travelers who are camped out in the hills and whelk hunters who trawl the midnight beaches. Morvern has put up at the Drome Hotel — a dreary establishment catering to "economizing Honeymooners" — run by John Brotherhood, a vaguely sinister fellow with a secret. Morvern, aware that all is not as it seems at this establishment, hooks up with the Argonaut — a young man purporting to be an air-crash investigator — who spends his days busily assembling the metallic remains of a ten-year-old crash. Meanwhile, a Scottish DJ is attempting to organize a "rave to end all raves" on the hotel's airstrip.

The Scotsman (searching for analogies) suggests that *These Demented Lands* reflects "the inventiveness of an **Iain Banks** hilted to the weird lens of a David Lynch, with a soundtrack from Verde and Bob Dylan" and concludes that it is fiction "on the Outer Rim of Everything." According to *Booklist* "Warner's novel, with its powerfully realized setting, evokes *The Road Warrior* with an alternative-rock soundtrack. Although those unfamiliar with the first novel might feel a bit lost, Warner's inventive prose and intriguing characters ... are the hooks here and ample evidence of the author's large talent." The *London Times* observes that "Warner's latest novel is a tricksy work, structured not as one text but many: letters, diary entries, posters, press releases ... " most written by the shipwrecked Morvern ... who, though "rough, reckless and certainly unhinged" achieves a certain "grandeur" for her "rejection of the mores of conventional society." The *Times* concludes that there "is unlikely to be a more original, or hysterically imagined, book published this year."

RECOGNITION: *London Times* "Books of the Year" 1997; REVIEWS: *BL* 3/15/98; *KR* 3/15/98; *LST* 3/23/97; *LT* 3/22/97; *NS* 4/25/97; *PW* 2/23/98; *TLS* 4/4/97

309 *Morvern Callar* (1996); Anchor 1997 (pbk)

In his debut novel, Alan Warner, one of the new "Scottish Beat" writers — frequently compared with Irvine Welsh of *Trainspotting* fame — explores the occasionally exhilarating yet frequently grotesque and dangerous world of the tripped out "rave generation." Morvern Callar (her name in Scottish means "quieter silence") is a produce-stacker in an economically depressed Scottish town whose only industry is a desultory tourist trade. Morvern's interests are limited to drugs and music, specifically the rave scene. One morning Morvern wakes up to find her boyfriend dead on the kitchen floor, an apparent suicide. One thing leads to another as Morvern looks for a quick way of disposing of the body. Morvern Callar pulls the reader along with her in a hip, first-person narrative couched in an aggressive punk–Scots vernacular.

The *London Review of Books* call *Morvern Callar* the "first great rave novel" while the *Times Literary Supplement* points out that a "novelist who kills his principal male character on the first page and has the heroine stub out her cigarette in a pool of his blood on page three is hardly unwilling to take chances. Alan Warner delivers nasty surprises like these on almost every page of his first novel ... but he writes with enough excitement and confidence to get away with it." The *Library Journal* observes that while the "story (occasionally) stretches the believable ... Morvern and the supporting cast are compelling enough characters for the reader to accept a few inconsistencies" and concludes that "this novel may well trigger a young, cult following." *Kirkus Reviews* argues that "Morvern is the raw, resilient voice of a generation, and if this not-quite-ironic tale of redemption and Irvine Welsh's *Trainspotting* are any indication, the Scottish Beats are already strong contenders for world-class literary status."

OTHER MEDIA: A film version was recently released by the BBC; RECOGNITION: Winner of the 1995 Somerset Maugham Award; *Times Literary Supplement* "International Book of the Year" 1995; REVIEWS: *BL* 2/15/97; *Econ* 4/26/97; *GW* 3/5/95; *KR* 1/1/97; *LJ* 2/1/97; *LRB* 11/2/95; *NS&S* 3/10/95; *NYTBR* 5/18/97; *PW* 1/27/97; *TLS* 3/31/95

Welsh, Irvine (UK-Scotland)

310 *Marabou Stork Nightmare* (1995); WW Norton 1997 (pbk)

The world we live in is not run by cuddly, strong bears, graceful, sleek cats or loyal friendly dogs. Marabous Storks run this place, and they are known to be nasty bastards.

In his second novel (and third work of fiction), Scottish Beat writer Irvine Welsh introduces Roy Strang, soccer hooligan and product of an all-too-typical dysfunctional working-class family. He is also a man obsessed with the eradication of the Marabou stork — an utterly repellent bird species which is reportedly driving the flamingos from Lake Torto in Africa. This obsession is played out in a hallucinatory state for Roy is in the hospital lying in a deep coma where his "hallucinations of swashbuckling, Technicolor African safaris (in pursuit of the sadistic marabou stork) merge with memories of his depraved childhood in Edinburgh's slums and among Johannesburg's white supremacists" (*EW*). Told in a voice which alternates between "plummy" Englishman and a nearly indecipherable, yet spectacularly vulgar, Scots dialect, *Marabou Stork Nightmare* makes, in the words of *Booklist*, for "compelling reading but nae fir the faint of heart."

According to the *Washington Post Book World*, "Much of *Marabou Stork Nightmare* is told in Scottish dialect, and though at times grasping it can be difficult, the narrative is most often a music of real beauty and pain that stays with you and sings and stings in your head. Roy Strang is one of the most brutal and memorable narrators to come along in years." As English novelist **Tibor Fischer** observes in the *London Times*: "Many writers reach for the gore in the way that some actresses get their kit off: it may be gratuitous but it gets you noticed. Welsh is exceptional in showing, à la *Clockwork Orange*, the lure of violence, of letting the demon within off the leash, but also the nauseating results that can accompany such surrender." *Library Journal* points out that "Welsh writes in the rough gutter-slang of Edinburgh, Scotland, and his phonetic transliterations take some deciphering but this work is well worth the effort." *Publishers Weekly*, in its starred review, argues that "With as good an ear for Scotch as James Kelman and as twisted an imagination as Will Self, Welsh makes his novelist's debut stateside with a darkly hilarious, deeply disturbing but ultimately compassionate book."

REVIEWS: *EW* 1/19/96; *LJ* 1/96; *LT* 5/11/95; *NS&S* 4/28/95; *NYTBR* 2/11/96; *PW* 12/11/95; *Salon* 1996; *TLS* 4/28/95; *WPBW* 4/14/96

311 *Trainspotting* (1993); Norton 1996 (pbk)
Irvine Welsh's jarring, frequently shocking, fragmented ride through the seedy proletarian underbelly of Scotland's major city, leavened as it is with a particularly mordant humor, will not be to every reader's taste. *Trainspotting*, the episodic story of a group of "no-hopers," mates who share alcohol, drugs and a nihilistic view of life (typified by position that if they *choose* to waste their lives on drugs, they should be allowed to so) has an undeniable raw power and manic charm which won it critical accolades in Britain and the United States.

The *New York Times Book Review* argues that the book is "worth ... the effort [even if one has already seen movie] not merely because relatively few writers have rummaged through this particular enclave of British youth culture, but because even fewer have dug there so deeply." *The London Sunday Times* calls *Trainspotting* "the voice of punk grown up, grown wiser and grown eloquent" and concludes that "Welsh's prose is dazzlingly and self-assured." The *Times Literary Supplement*, although finding the novel marred to a certain extent by what

it calls its "knowingness" observes that *Trainspotting* is "extremely readable, in part because of Welsh's comic talent ... the dialogue is frequently hilarious."

REVIEWS: *LATBR* 8/18/96; *LST* 8/15/93; *NewR* 9/2/96; *NYTBR* 7/28/96; *TLS* 10/1/93; *WPBW* 9/8/96; EDITOR'S NOTE: Welsh's title is taken from the British pastime (compared by some to birdwatching) which consists of hanging about train stations in order to keep a record of the engines passing through — the objective being to "spot" all of the engines in the British Rail fleet. In other words, a socially acceptable waste of one's time.

Womack, Jack (USA)

312 *Random Acts of Senseless Violence* (1994); Grove-Atlantic 1995 (pbk)
Womack's 1994 novel — which reads as a sort of prequel to two earlier titles (*Ambient* and *Elvissey*) is set in Manhattan in the near-but-hardly bright future. *Random Acts* is narrated — in the form of diary entries — by a precocious 12-year-old, by the name of Lola Hart, whose parents, in economic free-fall, have been forced to move to a particularly rough part of an increasingly lethal city. Lola, once the privileged resident of a Park Avenue apartment, must now negotiate street gangs, urban riots and martial law. Meanwhile, the social fabric, such as it is, continues to unravel.

In the view of (cyber)novelist **William Gibson** (*Vanity Fair*): "If you dropped the characters from *Neuromancer* into Womack's Manhattan, they'd fall down screaming and have nervous breakdowns." According to *Publishers Weekly* "with street-slick future-speak worthy of *A Clockwork Orange* and an unflinching eye for the degeneration of our cities, Womack portrays a relentlessly convincing tomorrow that will leave no reader unmoved." The *San Francisco Chronicle Book Review* notes that "*Senseless Acts of Random Violence* is shocking all right — but never gratuitous. Instead Womack, by taking you right inside his heroine's life and mind makes her journey from a world of privilege to one of predation as harrowing and poignant as they come." *Entertainment Weekly* concludes that "Womack performs feats of brilliance on many levels here. He succeeds in balancing blistering social commentary with shrewd literary experimentation in a heartrending coming-of-age story."

REVIEWS: *BL* 7/19/94; *EW* 10/7/94; *KR* 6/15/94; *LJ* 7/94; *NYTBR* 10/30/94; *PW* 8/8/94; *SFCBR* 9/30/94

Wright, Stephen (USA)

313 *Going Native: A Novel*; FS&G 1994 (HC)

Stephen Wright's chilling third novel, begins with a routine dinner party in an upscale Chicago suburb given by Rho and Wylie Jones for their friends Gerri and Tom Hanna. Before the night is over, Wylie ("he was such a quiet guy ... the sweetest man imaginable") has walked out the back door, commandeered a neighbor's Ford Galaxy, and lit out for parts unknown. Before Wright's decidedly post-modern road novel is over, the reader — in a series of linked vignettes — will encounter: a serial murderer, a Hollywood couple pursing "authenticity" in the jungles of Borneo, a lesbian couple who run a Las Vegas wedding chapel, assorted suburban crackheads, a souvenir shop owner flogging in his screenplay about aliens, and last but not least, heavy metal Satanists and psycho hitchhikers. Each narrative segment is related in the style of a different "genre" (e.g., neo–Updike, urban noir, postmodern pornography, etc.).

According to *Kirkus Reviews* "Wright is assembling a portrait of a culture irredeemably passive, tacky and corrupt, whose influence has girdled the world. The former headhunters of Borneo watch their treasured Batman video as intently as do the crackheads back in Chicago." *Booklist* observes that "In each setting, whether it is a porno playhouse in Colorado, a marriage chapel in Las Vegas, or the jungles of Borneo, we watch people take the concepts of 'going native...' to the ultimate extremes. This is, indeed, a nihilistic and chilling tale, told with tremendous artistry and intensity." The *Library Journal* notes that "The novel plays out like a 1990s version of *On the Road*, but Kerouac's life-affirming rebels have been replaced by characters who express an angry hunger for something that no longer seems to exist" and concludes that *Going Native* is "highly recommended, but not for the faint of heart." The *L.A. Times Book Review* argues that *Going Native* stands out in "the crowded fictional field of postmodern American nightmare" and concludes that "Wright has produced a witty, prodigal and desolate novel of virtual reality." According to the *New Yorker*, Wright's "dark [sophisticated, literary] style is a boat up a river in his very own jungle, headed for an outpost deep in the tangle of the mind."

RECOGNITION: *NYTBR* Notable Books of 1994; REVIEWS: *AntR* Spr '94; *BL* 12/15/93; *KR* 10/15/93; *LATBR* 1/30/94; *LJ* 11/1/93; *NY* 1/17/94; *NYT* 1/7/94; *NYTBR* 1/23/94; *PW* 10/25/93; *SFRB* 7-8/95

Geographical Identification

Geographic identification (regional, national, post-colonial, etc.) often plays a defining role in the formation of a writer's literary sensibilities. Section 4 is in three parts — the American South; Britain and Ireland; and nations that were once part of the British Empire or Commonwealth.

THE AMERICAN SOUTH

American Southern writers have long been admired not only for their facility with language but also for the tangible sense of place in their works. Well known novelists like Reynolds Price, Shirley Ann Grau, Wendell Berry and Peter Taylor rub shoulders with such representatives of the New South as Larry Brown, Lewis Nordan, Clyde Edgerton and Jill McCorkle.

Allison, Dorothy (USA)

314 *Cavedweller* (1998); Dutton 1998 (HC)

In her second work of fiction, Dorothy Allison, whose autobiographical debut novel *Bastard Out of Carolina* won both critical and popular acclaim, tells the story of Delia Byrd, a young woman from Cayro, Georgia who, fed up with her life, simply walks away from it. Leaving behind an abusive husband and two young daughters, Delia strikes out for California where, intent on a singing career, she eventually links up with a musician by the name of Randall. The two form a band (the Mud Dogs) and eke out a reasonably comfortable living on the margins of the West Coast music "scene." Delia and Randall have a daughter, Cissy,

but Delia is haunted by the memory of the little girls she left behind in Georgia. When Randall dies in a motorcycle accident, Delia decides to return home to Cayro with Cissy in tow. Known as "that bitch who ran off and left her babies," Delia is not exactly welcomed back with open arms.

According to *Booklist*, "Cissy, the cavedweller of the title ... is at the molten core of this mystical tale of blood ties and friendship, madness and love, hard work and grace, and she is something to behold." *Time* magazine notes that "allegorists as well as just plain readers should feel at home in *Cavedweller*, a mix of down-home authenticity, old-time religion and neo-paganism." In the view of *Salon* this novel "isn't as taut and as sharply focused as its predecessor.... But given the tale's extraordinary vitality and wisdom that is a small price to pay."

OTHER MEDIA: Audiocassette (Nova/abr; Bookcassette/unabr); READING GROUP GUIDE: Plume; RECOGNITION: *NYTBR* Notable Book of 1998; REVIEWS: *BL* 2/1/98; *ChiTrib* 4/12/98; *KR* 1/15/98; *LATBR* 3/15/98; *LJ* 3/1/98; *NYTBR* 3/15/98; *PW* 1/19/98; *Salon* 3/98; *Time* 4/13/98

315 *Bastard Out of Carolina* (1992); Dutton 1992 (HC); Plume 1993 (pbk)

The disreputable Boatwright clan consists of pugnacious, hard-drinking, "no-account" males and their feisty, if long-suffering, women. Early in Dorothy Allison's debut novel, Anney Boatwright — a twenty-year-old unwed mother of a five-year-old daughter ("Bone") — meets and marries Glen, a young man from a "good family," and hopes to shake off the Boatwright legacy. What Anney hadn't counted on was her husband's inability to hold a job, his weakness for alcohol or his quick temper. To makes matters worse, Anney's rapidly maturing daughter is becoming the object of "Daddy" Glen's increasingly abusive behavior.

According to the *Times Literary Supplement*, Dorothy Allison "grew up in a large, poor, haphazardly supportive family.... But if *Bastard Out of Carolina* is rooted in autobiography, it never takes on the obsessive tone of a confessional or the crusading fervor of an exposé." The *Library Journal* observes that Allison, in her debut novel, "creates a rich sense of family and portrays the psychology of a sexually abused child with sensitivity and insight." Novelist **George Garrett** (*NYTBR*) asserts that Allison's "technical skill ... so gracefully executed as to be always at the service of the story and its characters and thus almost invisible, is simply stunning, about as close to flawless as a reader could hope for...." The *L.A. Times Book Review* concludes that *Bastard Out of Carolina* is an "enviably assured first novel, tough, plain-spoken and thoroughly unsentimental."

OTHER MEDIA: Audiocassette (Brilliance Audio/abr; Penguin Audio/abr; Bookcassette/ unabr); made-for-TV movie adaptation 1996; RECOGNITION: *NYTBR* Notable Book of 1992; *Booklist* Editors' Choice 1992; nominated for the 1992 NATIONAL BOOK AWARD; REVIEWS: *BL* 3/15/92; *EW* 10/30/92; *KR* 2/1/92; *LATBR* 8/16/92; *LJ* 3/1/92; *NYTBR* 7/5/92; *PW* 1/27/92; *TLS* 8/14/92; *VLS* 6/92; *WPBW* 5/3/92; *WRB* 7/92

Baldwin, William (USA)

The Fennel Family Papers (1995); Algonquin 1995 (HC); See Section 7, #859

The Hard to Catch Mercy (1993); Algonquin 1993 (HC); Fawcett 1995 (pbk); See Section 6, #795

Berry, Wendell (USA)

316 *A World Lost* (1996); Counterpoint 1996 (HC); 1997 (pbk)

In his fifth novel (and ninth work of fiction), Wendell Berry tells — in the form of an extended reminiscence — the story of a young man's life-altering experience: the violent shooting death of his beloved uncle Andrew. The facts are simple. In 1944, in Port William, Kentucky, a man by the name of Andrew Catlett was shot, on a clear summer day, by a man who, given the presence of "mitigating circumstances," was sentenced to only two years in prison for the crime. The victim was deeply mourned by his family, particularly by his adoring nine-year-old nephew, Andy, for whom life would never hold quite the same promise. Berry's novel opens some fifty-one years later as Andy, now approaching sixty, begins to try to piece together what happened (and why) on that fateful summer day.

According to the *Library Journal* "This gentle tale deals with big issues: grief, love, truth and loss and their effects on a young mind." *Publishers Weekly* observes that in his "simple soul satisfying" tale Berry "shows us the psychic costs of misplaced

family pride and social rigidity and yet he also celebrates the benevolent benefits of familial love." The *Atlantic Monthly* concludes that "Mr. Berry writes elegantly, effortlessly balancing tragedy and a quiet, sly humor."

REVIEWS: *AtlM* 11/96; *BL* 9/15/96; *KR* 8/15/96; *LJ* 2/1/97; *NYTBR* 11/3/96; *PW* 9/2/96

317 *Souls Raised from the Dead* (1994); Scribner 1995 (pbk)

Souls Raised from the Dead revolves around a young girl with a terminal illness. Mary Grace Thompson, an energetic, wise-mouthed youngster with a passion for horses is thirteen when she is diagnosed with a rare kidney disease. Mary's father, a North Carolina state trooper, has raised her single-handedly since his wife, a self-absorbed cosmetic company sales manager, walked out on the two of them more than three years earlier. The youngster needs a kidney but her father only has one...

The *Washington Post Book World* calls Doris Betts's new novel "a gift for critics who bemoan the loss of a Southern literary sensibility, who grieve the passing of the South of Faulkner, Welty and O'Connor" and concludes that "Betts shares with these [writers] the particular gifts of a keen ear for dialogue, a sharp eye for the absurd, a sense of history as gene pool and an ability to make the reader feel as though he or she is hearing (rather than reading) the story told on a front porch, against a whoosh of fans waving away the heat of a sticky summer night." According to *Booklist*, "This isn't ... [a] melodramatic story about a dying child ... it's about Mary Grace's relationship with her father ... and what that relationship has to go through as Mary Grace sickens.... Sustained by Betts's rich, Southern voice [*Souls Raised from the Dead* is] an effecting, exacting ... tale of true family values."

REVIEWS: *BL* 2/15/94; *ChiTrib* 4/26/94; *KR* 2/15/94; *LJ* 3/1/94; *Ms* 5-6/94; *NYTBR* 4/17/94; *WRB* 7/94; *WPBW* 5/15/94

Brown, John Gregory (USA)

318 *The Wrecked, Blessed Body of Shelton Lafleur* (1996); HM 1996 (HC); Avon 1997 (pbk)

In John Gregory Brown's absorbing second novel, Shelton Lafleur, a successful African American folk artist, looks back over the defining moments in his life beginning with a fall from a tree, at the age of eight, which left him both crippled and orphaned. After a particularly harrowing stint in an orphanage, Shelton is befriended by a canny street artist by the name of Minou who encourages the young man to develop the skills which will eventually lead to his success. The aged artist's earliest, most perplexing, memories (dreams?), however, are of a life of ease in the company of his sweet, bed-ridden "white" mother. The narration slides smoothly between the voice of an old man and that of a young boy's.

According to *Kirkus Reviews*, "Brown's second novel (an example of "Retro southern fiction: Faulkner by way of the creative writing department") returns to the hot house milieu of his first: a New Orleans full of familial tragedy and racial strife." *Library Journal* observes that the author's "style is sometimes beautiful, sometimes grandiose … [and recommends it] for … the good writing, the imaginative force, and the author's promising future." The *Washington Post Book World* calls it a "lyrical and thoughtful second novel" and concludes that although "what makes Brown stand out among young literary novelists—is the power and rhythm of his prose, he [also] has an enthusiasm for plot that is rarer than it should be among serious novelists of any age." The *L.A. Times Book Review* argues that "If William Faulkner and Flannery O'-Connor were around to read [this novel] they would say that Brown has honored their legacy."

REVIEWS: *BL* 3/1/96; *ChiTrib* 3/17/96; *KR* 1/15/96; *LATBR* 4/7/96; *LJ* 4/1/96; *NYTBR* 8/18/96; *PW* 1/22/96; *TLS* 10/14/96; *WPBW* 7/7/96

319   *Decorations in a Ruined Cemetery* (1993); Avon 1995 (pbk)

John Gregory Brown's debut novel opens in New Orleans in 1965 but moves back and forth between the 1930s and the 1960s encompassing multiple generations of Eagens, a mixed race family from New Orleans. Key characters include a doctor by the name of Thomas Eagen (the son of a white man and a light-skinned black woman) and his daughter, Meredith, whose white mother died in childbirth. The novel is driven by Meredith's attempts to understand her family's complex and tragic history, shaped as it was by racial identity and personal betrayal.

Novelist Ann Arensberg (*NYTBR*) asserts that "John Gregory Brown's compassionate vision of human destiny is one that contains both suffering and the possibility of deliverance … " and concludes that "his novel teeters for an instant under the expository burden of uncovering so many mysteries, [but] the narrative balance is restored as quickly by his transporting prose." In the view of *Booklist* "each facet of this bittersweet drama reflects the hideous tangle of racism and desire that has long warped and distorted relationships between whites and blacks…. Brown explores this sensitive subject with consummate delicacy and eloquent intensity…." The *Washington Post Book World* observes that "In its Southern-ness, Brown's novel … has an antique quality worth admiring and conserving. His Southerners take care in speaking to each other. The conversations between black

Southerners and whites are sometimes of necessity wary and vigilant, but the characters are listening to each other…." *Book World* concludes that "Brown's stretches of careful and melodious writing make his first novel something much better than the proverbial promising debut."

REVIEWS: *BL* 12/1/93; *KR* 11/1/93; *NYTBR* 1/30/94; *WPBW* 2/20/9

Brown, Larry (USA)

320   *Father and Son* (1996); Algonquin 1996 (HC); Holt 1997 (pbk)

Larry Brown, in his darkly nuanced, heart-stoppingly suspenseful second novel, has crafted a story with Oedipal and biblical overtones. Set in rural Mississippi in the late 1960s, *Father and Son* concerns two half-brothers — one fatally twisted, the other, upright and fair-minded — who have some serious scores to settle. Glen Davis, a recently released convict, has just returned to his home town near Oxford, Mississippi, where his stepbrother, Bobby Blanchard (the local sheriff) is bracing himself for what he knows must come. Bobby was not only the arresting officer when Glen, recklessly drunk, killed a youngster in a traffic accident, he has also fallen in love with Jewel, his stepbrother's former girlfriend. Glen's shiftless, alcoholic father, Virgil, is even less enthusiastic about Glen's return, as Glen has vowed to "blow his head off" for a whole litany of fatherly failings. The relentless, hardscrabble existence of many of the peripheral characters punctuates the basic story.

According to the *Voice Literary Supplement*, "Brown paints his portrait in a series of meticulous and clean strokes; his eye is photographic, the pictures here so finely and judiciously drawn that for the most part his readers are trusted to come to conclusions for themselves." The *Library Journal* concludes that *Father and Son* is "filled with the gritty, working-class realism of one of Bruce Springsteen's darker songs and resonates back to Cain and Abel and Jacob and Esau." The *Times Literary Supplement* notes that though a number of critics have compared Brown with Faulkner, "*Father and Son* recalls Erskine Caldwell's white-trash world, with its grotesque and Gothic prominences, rather than Faulkner's faded aristocratic realm. Brown is a much better writer though than Caldwell…. He doesn't simply turn loose a crowd of cartoon country folk, but creates characters of flesh and blood — even if the flesh is weak and the blood always close to spattering."

OTHER MEDIA: Audiocassette (Recorded-Books/unabr); READING GROUP GUIDE RECOGNITION: Winner of the Southern Book Critics 1997 Book Award for Fiction; REVIEWS: *BBR* 9/96; *BL* 7/19/96; *ChiTrib* 10/9/96; *KR* 7/15/96; *LJ* 8/96; *NYTBR* 9/22/96; *TLS* 4/10/98; *VLS* 9/96

321   *Joe* (1991); Algonquin 1991 (HC); Warner 1992 (pbk)

In his debut novel, set in the backwoods and small towns of Northern Mississippi, Larry Brown features ex-con Joe Ransome, a forestry crew foreman and failed father with a predilection for gambling, alcohol, and women. Joe has recently hired Gary Jones, a hard-working teenager (and much-abused son of a depraved migrant worker) to fill in on his deforestation crew. Young Gary finds much to admire in his tough-but-fair new boss, a man frankly unused to (but ultimately deserving of) such unqualified admiration.

According to *Booklist* "The authenticity of Brown's voice and the seamless world he creates are breathtaking. His theme of love and redemption, hope and dignity, weakness and strength are universal, and the telling is mercilessly compelling." *Kirkus Reviews* observes that "this is white trash, lumpen fiction with a vengeance … a gritty novel that ranks with the best hard-knocks, down-and-out work of Jim Thompson and Harry Crews. It's lean, mean and original." The *Washington Post Book World* noting Brown's "starkly poetic" prose and "darkly comic [but] always … convincing," characterizations" concludes that "Larry Brown has slapped his own fresh tattoo on the big right arm of Southern Lit."

RECOGNITION: Winner of the Southern Book Critics 1991 Book Award for Fiction; *Publishers Weekly* Best Book of 1991; *Booklist* Editors' Choice 1991; REVIEWS: *BL* 7/19/96; *ChiTrib* 9/29/91; *KR* 7/15/96; *NYRB* 1/16/92; *NYTBR* 11/10/91; *PW* 10/11/92; *Time* 10/28/91; *WPBW* 10/20/91

Chappell, Fred (USA)

322   *Farewell, I'm Bound to Leave You* (1996); Picador 1996 (HC); Picador 1997 (pbk)

In a series of linked stories Fred Chappell creates a perfectly realized time and place: the Carolina Hill Country in the early part of the twentieth-century. As the story opens, a young man sits with his father in a mountain home while his mother attends to his grandmother in the next room. The old woman is dying and her imminent death prompts the young man to remember the deeply textured stories — featuring Hill Country folk — that she had so loved to tell. The stories run the gamut from boisterous, to slightly chilling, to lyrically romantic.

Kirkus Reviews opines that "Chappell, like most regionalists, is attempting to re-create an entire society, and the success with which he does so gives his characters an uncommon depth and texture." In the view of *Entertainment Weekly*, "Chappell revels in the contradictions and embroideries of oral history … and writes piercingly about a way of life teeming with folk wisdom." Novelist

Howard Frank Mosher (*WPBW*) observes that what "elevates the stories in *Farewell I'm Bound to Leave You* from folklore to literature is the author's passionate affection for his characters, combined with his sorrow over their passing" and concludes that from "the legacy of their lives [Chappell] has created the most affecting work of fiction about place and love that I have read since *A River Runs Through It*." *Publishers Weekly*, in its starred review, advances the idea that "a genuine patience distinguishes Chappell from the vast herd of writers — especially Southern writers — who mistake languid melancholy for lyricism' and concludes that "he writes with a feel for emotional timing that is as acute as his sense of style."

OTHER MEDIA: Audiocassette (Recorded Books/unabr); REVIEWS: *BL* 9/1/96; *EW* 9/6/96; *KR* 7/15/96; *LJ* 8/96; *NYTBR* 12/15/96; *PW* 7/15/96; *WPBW* 10/13/96

Childress, Mark (USA)

Crazy in Alabama (1993); Ballantine 1994 (pbk); See Section 6, #694

Daugharty, Janice (USA)

323   *Earl in the Yellow Shirt* (1997); HarperCollins 1997 (HC); 1998 (pbk)

Janice Daugharty's fourth novel set, once again, in Cornerville, Georgia, in the piney woods of Swanoochee County, features the impoverished Scurvy clan. As the story opens the family is grappling with the tragic death (following the delivery of her fifth baby) of Louella Scurvy. Her daughter, Loujean, a capable teenager, has taken over the responsibility of caring for her infant sister, but the most immediate (and seemingly insoluble) problem facing the family is coming up with the money for mama's funeral. Papa, alcoholic and shiftless, subsides further into his twin vices while Loujean's grown-up brothers Buck and Pee Wee bank on a risky moonshine scheme to produce some cash. Earl, a neighbor who is definitely "soft" on Loujean, comes up with a better solution.

Kirkus Reviews calls *Earl in the Yellow Shirt* an "audacious novel, hilarious and moving by turns, offering some sharp and startling variations on southern themes" and concludes that it is another "strong, highly original work from one of our most promising, and idiosyncratic, authors." *Booklist* suggests that "city folk may need to concentrate to catch the drift of this rotating-narrators novel's backwoods talk (and some will find its use of the n-word troubling)." In the view of *Library Journal*, "Daugharty's brilliant fourth novel, which recalls Faulkner's *As I Lay Dying*, shows that there is good and evil in every family."

REVIEWS: *BL* 4/15/97; *KR* 3/1/97; *LJ* 5/15/97; *PW* 3/17/97

324 *The Paw-Paw Patch* (1996); Harper-Collins 1997 (pbk)

In her third novel, Janice Daugharty explores the theme of racial prejudice in a small southern town through the perspective of Chanell Foster, the sassy proprietor of Cornerville's most popular beauty salon. When someone starts a rumor about Chanell's (heretofore unacknowledged) Creole blood, her business dries up and she finds herself shunned by former customers and friends alike. Chanell fights back.

According to the *St. Louis Post-Dispatch* "Faulkner-like, Janice Daugharty sets her work in a place all her own, the mythic small town with minds to match...." In the opinion of *Kirkus Reviews* "The enduring prejudices, resentment, and regrets boiling away just beneath the surface of small-town life are given a thorough (and salutary) airing in Southern writer Daugharty's provocative new work." *Publishers Weekly* call the *Paw Paw Patch* a novel "about the power of secrets shared and secrets kept" and concludes that Daugharty "invests her Southern setting with a richly textured, visceral reality." The *New York Times Book Review* concludes that "Swirling with details that become more disturbing the closer you look, Ms. Daugharty's portrait of Cornerville is both intimate and unsettling."

REVIEWS: *KR* 2/16/96; *LJ* 4/15/96; *NYTBR* 6/23/96; *PW* 3/4/96; *St. Louis Post-Disp* 6/2/96

Dufresne, J. (USA)

Louisiana Power and Light (1994); Norton 1994 (HC); Dutton 1995 (pbk); See Section 6, #706

Edgerton, Clyde (USA)

325 *Where Trouble Sleeps* (1997); Algonquin 1997 (HC); Ballantine 1998 (pbk)

Clyde Edgerton's 7th novel is set, once again, in his fictional North Carolina town deep in the seemingly somnambulant 1950s. Edgerton's story is composed, initially, of a series of loosely linked short stories that feature a number of amiable, eccentric townspeople. However, when the residents of the town begin to take notice of a stranger in their midst — Jack Umstead, a disturbingly dapper young man with a (stolen) Buick Eighty-eight and a suitcase full of dirty movies — the authorial focus shifts and the pace accelerates.

According to *Booklist* the "reader immediately knows what the town does not know, that Jack is up to no good, that he's here for his own benefit.... But it doesn't take long for the town to learn this, too, and in the process, we have been treated to a delightful tale of innocence and betrayal." Novelist **Mark Childress** (*NYTBR*) observes that Edger-

ton has set seven novels "mostly in and around the town of Listre, the fictional stand-in for his hometown of Bethesda, N.C." adding that "each of these books is in its own way, thoroughly appealing." *Kirkus Reviews* concludes that in his "charming" seventh novel Edgerton "brings together his usual cast of drunks, church-going Baptists, and southern eccentrics, all of whom encounter the Devil in the form of a traveling ne'er-do-well."

READING GROUP GUIDE; RECOGNITION: *NYTBR* Notable Book of 1997; REVIEWS: *BL* 7/19/97; *EW* 12/97; *KR* 6/15/97; *NYTBR* 9/28/97; *PW* 6/23/97

326 *In Memory of Junior* (1992); Algonquin 1992 (HC); Ballantine 1996 (pbk)

Edgerton sets his morbidly comic tale in Summerlin, North Carolina, where an elderly couple, one of whom has children from a previous marriage, are lingering near death. Depending on who "goes" first, different sets of offspring will inherit the family property. Local residents are not above placing a wager or two.

Publishers Weekly notes that Edgerton has produced another "prime example of entertaining, down-home Southern fiction" distinguished by a "mastery of dialogue, irony and characterization." According to *Booklist* "Readers won't be surprised that the family in this funny and moving novel ends up with too many graves and too few tombstones." *Library Journal*, while pointing to a" complicated ... often morbid" plot concludes that "Edgerton is the new master of Southern family tales."

OTHER MEDIA: Audiocassette (Recorded Bks/unabr); REVIEWS: *BL* 8/92; *Chi Trib* 10/6/92; *KR* 7/15/92; *LJ* 9/1/92; *NYTBR* 9/28/97; *PW* 6/23/97

Fowler, Connie May (USA)

327 *Before Women Had Wings* (1996); Putnam 1996 (HC)

Nine-year-old Avocet Abigail Jackson, better known as "Bird," has seen only the dark, destructive side of family life. The daughter of a dirt-poor couple with country-music aspirations, Bird — along with her sister Phoenix (the sisters have been named, more poignantly than whimsically, after birds) — has, from infancy, been on the receiving end of her father's alcohol-fueled rages and her mother's heavy hand. Her father's eventual suicide leads to a move to Tampa where Bird's mother, Glory Marie, finds work (and a "home" for her family) at the Travelers Motel. The habitual abuse continues. Bird finds hope and comfort from two quarters: her faith in Jesus (on whom she has a romantic "crush") and her friendship with Miss Zora, a kindly black woman who lives in a cabin at the motel.

According to novelist Elizabeth Buchan, in a

review appearing in the *London Times*, the "American Deep South has gestated instantly recognizable and darkly Gothic literature which feeds on the fallout from heat, poverty, racial oppression and violence. The title ... of Connie May Fowler's third novel hoists this flag and also adds on a feminist stripe." The *Chicago Tribune* calls *Before Women Had Wings* a "thing of heart-rending beauty, a moving exploration of love and loss, violence and grief, forgiveness and redemption" and concludes that while "Fowler overdoes the bird symbolism [she] otherwise she gets everyone and everything right." *Booklist* concludes that "Fowler may well be Florida's most lyrical novelist, and once again the wild beauty of that state shapes her fiction."

OTHER MEDIA: Made-for-TV movie starring Oprah Winfrey; READING GROUP GUIDE; REVIEWS: *BL* 6/1/96; *ChiTrib* 5/28/96; *KR* 3/15/96; *LT* 7/5/97; *NYTBR* 7/21/96; *PW* 3/11/96

Gibbons, Kaye   (USA)

328   *Sights Unseen* (1995); Avon 1997 (pbk)
Sights Unseen, set in the author's native South Carolina, is the frequently powerful story of a family dominated by the charming and beautiful Maggie Barnes a wife and mother whose mental instability causes much pain in those closest to her. The story is narrated by Maggie's daughter, Hattie, who longed throughout her childhood for the sort of maternal love and nurturance that her mother (eventually diagnosed as a manic-depressive) was incapable of providing. Maggie's disorder, characterized by extreme swings of mood and personality, went largely untreated throughout most of her life making normal emotional attachments all but impossible.

According to *Booklist*, "Hattie is a quiet yet powerful narrator—calm, lucid, trustworthy, and, most importantly, forgiving. Almost dismissive of her own suffering both as a frightened, lonely child and as a grieving adult ... Hattie chronicles her mother's dramatic battle with her demons in stark, indelible detail." Novelist **Jacqueline Carey** (*NYTBR*) observes that "Hattie's sights are always set at a delicate intersection of the ordinary and the horrific ... [providing numerous examples] of how Maggie's illness seeps into the very fiber of the household." *Belles Lettres* applauded Gibbons' skill as a writer ("every sentence is unerringly polished and interesting") while suggesting that had the author "provided more narrative concerning the eventual reconciliation between Hattie and Maggie, readers might be able to develop greater affection and sympathy for the mother." According to the *Chicago Tribune* "Gibbons has "an eye that is remarkable—both deadly cold and deeply moving." The *London Times* concludes that Gibbons "writes movingly of the damage madness can inflict, even

on a family as close-knit as this. Her account is all the more intense because it is seen from a child's perspective, so that painful and disturbing episodes acquire a surreal humor."

OTHER MEDIA: Audiocassette (S&S/abr); REVIEWS: *BellesL* 1/96; *BL* 6/1/95; *ChiTrib* 8/20/95; *EW* 8/4/95; *LJ* 6/15/95; *LT* 6/15/96; *NYTBR* 9/24/95; *PW* 6/5/95

329   *Charms for the Easy Life* (1993); Putnam 1993 (HC); Avon 1995 (pbk)
Kaye Gibbons' fourth novel is narrated by the bookish Margaret who looks back over her childhood and adolescence (encompassing the Great Depression and World War II) which she spent in the company of her beloved mother and grandmother, a pair of accomplished and exceedingly independent women. Their feminine household (husbands and fathers had a way of dying or disappearing early on) was headed by her grandmother, "Charlie Kate" Birch, a well-respected midwife and doctor of homeopathic medicine. Charlie Kate was, throughout Margaret's childhood, ably assisted by Margaret's mother, the high-spirited, happily widowed Sophia.

According to Stephen McCauley (*NYTBR*) the "evocative and gracious" *Charms for the Easy Life* "is about the lives of strong, indomitable women ... armed with fierce survival instincts and folk wisdom passed down from one generation to the next." *Publishers Weekly* observes that "related with the simple, tart economy of a folktale, the narrative brims with wisdom and superstition, with Southern manners and insights into human nature." In the view of *Time* magazine Gibbons "paints ... [Charlie Kate] in colors as pungent as mashed garlic, as invigorating as sarsaparilla, and as soothing as lemon-balm tea. The charm for the reader is that there is still such a thriving population of Southern women left in the author's well-healed imagination." *Booklist* concludes that "Gibbons's humor is sly and her handling of period detail deft, while her unabashed delight in telling a good, old-fashioned, heart-warming story is refreshing and welcome."

OTHER MEDIA: Audiocassette (S&S Audio/abr); RECOGNITION: *NYTBR* Notable Book of 1993; REVIEWS: *BL* 1/15/94; *KR* 1/1/93; *LJ* 2/15/93; *NYTBR* 4/11/93; *PW* 3/14/94; *Time* 4/12/93

Gilchrist, Ellen   (USA)

330   *Starcarbon: A Meditation on Love* (1994); Little Brown 1994 (HC); 1995 (pbk)
A sequel to *I Cannot Get You Close Enough* (1990), *Starcarbon* once again features the Hands, a family with deep North Carolina roots. As the story opens, Olivia de Havilland Hand, Daniel Hand's illegitimate daughter, has returned to her

Native American family in Tahlequah Oklahoma where she hopes both to learn more about her Cherokee legacy and to renew her relationship with (former) boyfriend) Bobby Tree. Meanwhile, Olivia's half-sister is coping with new-motherhood in Louisiana her aunt is heavily involved with a poet in Boston and her father is coping badly with his family's peripatetic ways. At the heart of Ms. Gilchrist's generally upbeat story is the recognition of the limits of family: of the burdens of unconditional love, of the need to look beyond to find oneself, and of the price of allegiance.

According to the *Chicago Tribune* it "is the summer of 1991, the eruption of Mt. Pinatubo is creating beautiful sunsets, the Soviet Union is about to unravel and tornadoes are going to rumble through Oklahoma. A portentous time, indeed, but the Hands have other things on their minds — namely love in kaleidoscopic variety." The *New York Times Book Review* observes that *Starcarbon* is filled with voices as the Hands (scattered from North Carolina to New Orleans, with outposts in Oklahoma and Boston) are a garrulous lot who "talk to one another, to their psychiatrists, to themselves" and concludes that Ms. Gilchrist "has blended these resolutely individual voices to create a richly textured family fugue." In the view of *Publishers Weekly* Ms. Gilchrist "writes with a distinctively Southern toughness about people who are selfish, demanding and often cruel to those closest to them, but who invariably gain the reader's sympathy with their total honesty and fierce need for love."

OTHER MEDIA: Audiocassette (Books-on-Tape/unabr); REVIEWS: *BL* 1/15/94; *ChiTrib* 3/21/93; *LJ* 3/1/94; *NYTBR* 6/19/94; *PW* 1/31/94; *TLS* 7/1/94

Grau, Shirley Ann (USA)

331 *Roadwalkers* (1994); Knopf 1994 (HC)
Shirley Ann Grau, who won the Pulitzer Prize for fiction in 1965 for *The Keeper of the House*, sets her latest novel in the deep South in the dark days of the Great Depression. In it she tells the story of "Baby" a homeless black child who — like many other destitute children of this period was forced to "walk" the back roads of the rural south searching for scraps, begging and, when all else failed, stealing what food she could get her hands on. The youngster was eventually "captured" and placed in an orphanage and the evolution of Baby from "feral" child to accomplished seamstress and successful business woman is skillfully recounted.

According to the *Library Journal* this "is quintessential Grau: the vivid descriptions of the South, the multiple perspectives, the unblinking lack of sentimentality, and the strong female characters, whose amazing inner strength allows them to rise above the most dreadful and degrading experi-

ences." In the view of novelist Sandra Scofield, (*NYTBR*) *Roadwalkers* seduces us with its vigorous prose, enthralls us with its narrative — and disquiets us with its defiance of our expectations."

REVIEWS: *BellesL* Spr '95; *BL* 6/1/94; *ChiTrib* 10/13/94; *CSM* 8/1/94; *LATBR* 7/31/94; *LJ* 6/15/94; *NYTBR* 7/31/94

Grimsley, Jim (USA)

332 *My Drowning* (1997); Algonquin 1997 (HC); S&S 1998 (pbk)
Set — for the most part — in the North Carolina hill country during WW II, Jim Grimsley's third novel describes, in a series of disturbingly realistic flashbacks, the brutal existence of a poor white family headed by an abusive, alcoholic, tenant-farmer. One of the children, Ellen Tote, is now in her sixties and is still plagued by recurring nightmares rooted in her early homelife. A particularly disturbing dream features her mother, a loving, well-meaning woman (worn to the bone by poverty, cruelty and multiple pregnancies), as she "surrenders herself" to a dark, swollen river. As Ellen becomes ever-more determined to unlock the mystery of this dream, she must force herself to relive her memories — some of which, surprisingly, are coloured by love and affection.

Kirkus Reviews observes that the "gradual sorting out of [Ellen's] childhood [engendered by] the dream ... is as credible and rich as the world that contains it" and concludes that *My Drowning* is "[m]oving, vivid, and very real: a work of tremendous, quiet intensity." According to the *Library Journal* "Readers will find [the novel as] harsh, and as haunting, as an old woman's dreams." The *New York Times Book Review* concludes that "Ellen is an appealing narrator, and ... [her] recollection of stolen moments of love provide welcome relief from the viciousness all around her."

REVIEWS: *BL* 11/15/96; *KR* 11/1/96; *LJ* 11/1/96; *NYTBR* 2/2/97

333 *Winter Birds* (1994); Algonquin 1994 (HC); S&S 1995 (pbk)
Eight-year-old Danny Crill and his baby brother are hemophiliacs in need of special care and attention. They find precious little of either in a household consisting of a physically abusive father and a loving mother rendered powerless through fear. *Winter Birds*, Jim Grimsley's (at times) appallingly graphic debut novel, is set in rural North Carolina on a snowy Thanksgiving day. Danny's father, Bobjay, fueled by alcohol, begins a deadly argument with Danny's beloved mother, Ellen. The children watch in growing terror. The author, by utilizing the second person, allows the older Danny to actually tell the story to his younger self.

Booklist calls *Winter Birds* a "remarkable first

novel" and concludes that Grimsley has created "a harrowing Southern gothic world, reminiscent of Faulkner or Caldwell." According to the *Library Journal*, this "grimly violent first novel would seem unbelievable if not largely autobiographical...." The *New Yorker* concludes that the "violence ... is just half the story. The other half is the poetry that infuses *Winter Birds*, and it only intensifies the terror."

RECOGNITION: Winner of the Sue Kaufman Award for Fiction; nominated for the PEN/ Hemingway Award; REVIEWS: *BL* 8/94; *KR* 7/1/94; *LJ* 8/94; *NY* 10/24/94; *PW* 8/1/94

Haines, Carol (USA)

Touched (1996); Plume 1997 (pbk); See Section 6, #815

Hazelgrove, W E (USA)

Tobacco Sticks (1995); Pantonne Press 1995 (HC); See Section 6, #818

Humphreys, Josephine (USA)

334   *The Fireman's Fair* (1991); Viking 1991 (HC); Penguin 1992 (pbk)

The Fireman's Fair opens in 1989 on a barrier island off the coast of Charleston, S.C., in the aftermath of Hurricane Hugo. Acts of God and the pull of the heart conspire to complicate 32-year-old Rob Wyatt's life. Rob, a "likable, passive, hopelessly romantic, bird-watching quasi lawyer" (*NYT*) who firmly rejects the philandering ways of his father, falls in love twice in the course of Josephine Humphrey's gently romantic novel.

In the view of *Time* magazine, "Humphrey's seemingly effortless sense of character and place comes from a life-long association with the Low Country and its ways. Like summer heat lightening, her style is subdued and swiftly illuminating...." The *Times Literary Supplement* observes that the book "casts a powerful spell" and concludes that "All is drawn tightly together by a fine use of metaphor, in particular the recurrent sea-related images...."

REVIEWS: *ChiTrib* 5/19/91; *LJ* 4/1/91; *NS&S* 11/1/91; *NYTBR* 5/19/91; *Time* 5/27/91; *TLS* 11/29/91

Lowry, Beverly (USA)

335   *The Track of Real Desires* (1994); Knopf 1994 (HC)

Beverly Lowry's 6th novel is set in Eunola, Mississippi, and is structured around a dinner party thrown in honor of Leland Standard, a native Eunolan, who has returned (in the company of her adult son of undisclosed paternity) for a brief visit. Baker Farrish, one of the old high school gang is hosting the event and has invited a dozen of Le-

land's oldest friends. Unbeknownst to the partygoers (or their host), Leland is carrying a heavy burden, the knowledge of her son's positive HIV status and her own breast cancer. As the evening progresses, it becomes clear that all of the guests have bitter secrets of their own ... as well as dreams.

The *New York Times Book Review* observes that *The Track of Real Desire* is "deceptively simple, comic without slipping into burlesque, poignant without veering into sentimentality" and concludes that it is "a fine, funny, altogether admirable novel." According to *Booklist* "Lowry walks a fine line here as she deftly prevents her characters concerns from degenerating into a collective whine; instead, she invokes with skill and compassion the great southern theme of endurance." The *Library Journal* concludes that "Lowry's skillful use of humor and well-paced irony elevates her sad theme just enough to make it bearable."

RECOGNITION: *NYTBR* Notable Book of 1994; REVIEWS: *BL* 4/15/94; *CSM* 6/14/94; *EW* 4/22/94; *LJ* 5/1/94; *NYTBR* 5/8/94; *PW* 3/7/94; *WRB* 7/94

Mason, Bobbie Ann (USA)

Feather Crowns (1993); HarperCollins 1994 (pbk); See Section 5, #613

McCorkle, Jill (USA)

Carolina Moon (1996); Algonquin 1996 (HC); Fawcett 1997 (pbk); See Section 6, #742

336   *Ferris Beach* (1990); Algonquin 1990 (HC); Fawcett 1997 (pbk)

Ferris Beach, a strip of ocean-front playland (highly suggestive of Myrtle Beach) on the South Carolina coast, holds a special fascination for Katie Tennyson Burns. Its blue collar tawdriness appeals to the youngster who is growing up in a predictable, oh-so-respectable middle-class household dominated by her socially fastidious mother. Katie is painfully shy, attributable, in large measure, to a prominent facial birthmark. Before the story ends, McCorkle's young heroine will fall under the spell of her beautiful, dare-devil cousin, experience romance (with a boy from the "wrong side of the tracks") and otherwise test the more rigid boundaries of her world.

Called "whimsically entertaining and dramatically compelling" by the *Boston Globe*, Ms. McCorkle's "coming-of-age" story was judged "special" by the *School Library Journal* which went on to observe that "The humor, tenderness, sharply defined characters, and a feeling of 'being there' make the 1970s come alive in the small southern community depicted." The *Chicago Tribune* points out that "McCorkle is not inclined to mind her manners, [and] her writing is marked by a relentless, clear-eyed bluntness." *Publishers Weekly* concludes that "Whether portraying the love/hate relationship of best friends, the pangs of an ungainly girl during adolescence or the insult-laden repartee of teenagers attracted to one another, McCorkle illuminates character with ironic humor and empathetic insight."

OTHER MEDIA: Audiocassette (Books-on-Tape/unabr); RECOGNITION: *NYTBR* Notable Books of the Year 1990; REVIEWS: *BL* 9/1/90; *BosGlobe* 9/26/90; *ChiTrib* 10/28/90; *KR* 7/15/90; *NYTBR* 10/7/90; *PW* 8/3/90; *SLJ* 2/91; EDITOR'S NOTE: In the view of the *Chicago Tribune* "Jill McCorkle belongs to an exclusive organization for women. With her Southern sisters Bobbie Ann Mason, Lee Smith, Josephine Humphreys and Kaye Gibbons, McCorkle is part of a talented circle of feisty youngish writers who are trying to makes sense of the contradictions that characterize the New South" (*ChiTrib* 10/28/90).

McLaurin, Tim (USA)

337 *The Last Great Snake Show* (1997); Putnam 1997 (HC)

In his fourth novel, Tim McLaurin follows a rag-tag troupe of performers (former employees of the "House of Joy") as they wend their frequently surreal way from North Carolina to the coast of Oregon. They have embarked on this journey with one objective in mind: to bring their much-loved former boss (Darlene, a retired topless dancer) back to her home town for burial. Darlene had run the (lively if disreputable) House of Joy until it was destroyed, and she herself was tragically killed in a powerful hurricane. In the storm's bitter wake, this little band of modern pilgrims (consisting of Gloria, an "exotic" dancer; Jubal Lee, a snake handler; and Cappy, a cantankerous Vietnam vet cum doorman/bouncer) is working its way Westward in the discomfort of an old school bus. To support themselves, the "pilgrims" put on "hoochie-coochie" shows in the small towns along the way.

According to *Kirkus Reviews* McLaurin's novel is "a disarmingly sweet tale of love and courage ... [a] Southern Wizard of Oz, celebrating kindness and character and the way that—sometimes—they can be bonded together." The *New York Times Book Review* observes that "McLaurin clearly endorses the wholesome view of his story, contrasting the camaraderie and honesty of the performers with the hypocrisy, racism and greed of the people they entertain. What works is the Southern dialogue, brash with and pride of place." In the view of the *Washington Post Book World, The Last Great Snake Show* is "an occasionally poignant but mostly sentimental tale of displacement and redemption."

REVIEWS: *KR* 6/1/97; *LJ* 6/15/97; *NYTBR* 11/23/97; *PW* 6/9/97; *WPBW* 8/31/97

Morgan, Robert (USA)

The Truest Pleasure (1995); Algonquin 1995 (HC); 1996 (pbk); See Section 5, #623

Naumauf, Lawrence (USA)

338 *Silk Hope* (1994); Harcourt Brace 1994 (HC)

Sisters Frannie and Natalie have inherited the family farm — a rambling property graced by a fine old farmhouse — on the outskirts of Silk Hope, North Carolina. As the reader soon learns, the family homestead has been passed along for generations through the female side of the family. This rather unusual legacy was consciously put in place by a family matriarch who (recognizing the precariousness of a woman's lot in life) wished to ensure that her female descendants "will always have their own place no matter what the men in their life did or didn't do...." The difficulties which arise when the sisters find themselves in disagreement over their inheritance form the basis of Lawrence Naumoff's "darkly funny and deeply reflective" (*NYTBR*) fourth novel. Natalie, the serious sister, is engaged to a man who "understands money" and together they have decided that it makes the most (economic) sense to sell the place and divide the profits. Frannie, the heretofore wildly irresponsible and mildly promiscuous sister, is determined to keep the farm — for its emotional and historic value **and** for the sense of purpose it has given her. Additional plot elements include spectacular run-ins with pigs (of the two-footed and four-footed varieties) and a litigious televangelist.

According to *Kirkus Reviews*, "Naumoff is an interesting combination, a progressive champion of women's rights and a conservative wedded to the land and fearful of development.... The excitement in Naumoff's story comes from watching his endearing heroine, a funny-sad clown, fighting for the farmhouse (and her life) and slowly turning the tide." The *Library Journal* observes that Mr. Naumoff "carefully delineates the confusions and cruelties of the little community of Silk Hope" and concludes that "His harsh portrait of humanity is balanced with sudden bursts of laughter and understanding." In the view of the *Washington Post Book World*, "Naumoff (in this slip of a novel) invests his slip of a girl with enough personal spunk and inspirational family history to propel her through a gauntlet of creeps to a happy ending. The tale is southern and modern, comic and cautionary, told partly for fun and partly to get in some punches at the sorry state of American values."

REVIEWS: *BL* 5/15/94; *ChiTrib* 8/14/94; *KR* 4/15/94; *LATBR* 8/21/94; *LJ* 5/15/94; *NYTBR* 7/24/94; *PW* 4/18/94; *WPBW* 6/5/94

Nordan, Lewis (USA)

339 *Lightning Song* (1997); Algonquin 1997 (HC); Algonquin 1998 (pbk)

Set on a backwoods Mississippi farm and narrated by 12-year-old Leroy Dearman, Nordan's frequently off-beat coming-of-age tale focuses particularly on the youngster's growing sexual awareness. Leroy's oddball parents (his father is a one-armed llama rancher nicknamed Swami Don; his mother, mercurial at the best of times, is curiously obsessed with the kidnapping of Aldo Moro) are having marital difficulties — a situation which is not improved by a visit from Leroy's good looking, freeloading paternal uncle Harris. Leroy's narrative voice is, in the view of the *New York Times Book Review*, "Southern, boyish and goofy."

According to *Kirkus Reviews* "Odd sexual doings and outpourings of desire and need are particularly amusing when seen through the eyes of Leroy Dearman, an awkward boy given to inappropriate outbursts and off-the-wall commentary.... Hardly sentimental, Nordan's idiosyncratic fiction delights in its ragged edges — the tall tales, the wacky set pieces, the flat-out bizarre behavior." In the view the *Library Journal*, "Nordan handles this coming-of-age novel with grace, charm, and humor, its 'American-ness' may remind readers of the work of Wallace Stegner." *Entertainment Weekly* concludes that "Nordan's sense of life's not-so-ordinary events makes [*Lightning Song*] flow evenly." *Booklist* argues that this is a "novel of character over plot that is a sidesplitting, wonderfully ingratiating story that makes you feel good about good writing."

RECOGNITION: *NYTBR* Notable Book of 1997; *LATBR* "Recommended Title" 1997; REVIEWS: *BL* 3/1/97; *EW* 5/23/97; *KR* 4/1/97; *LATBR* 7/30/97; *LJ* 4/1/97; *NYTBR* 5/25/97; *PW* 3/10/97

Owen, Howard (USA)

340 *The Measured Man* (1997); Harper-Collins 1997 (HC)

Howard Owen sets his latest novel in St. Andrews, North Carolina, a typical Southern town of strict racially defined boundaries and long-simmering racial animosities. The "measured" man of the title is Walker Fann, the editor of an influential local newspaper which has been owned by his family for three generations. Walker, in the wake of his young wife's tragic death, has moved himself and his two children back to the ancestral home still occupied by his father, the paper's current owner. Once re-ensconced, Walker drinks too much, broods and drifts. Soon after, a movement to establish a slavery museum in the old slave market in Cottondale (the "black" section of town) emerges in the face of significant local opposition from the white community. When Walker's father nixes his son's pro-museum editorial (written, it appears, in an alcoholic haze) in favor of one in opposition, Walker meekly acquiesces and withdraws his piece. When the museum proposal is defeated at the ballot box and race riots erupt, Walker feels in some way responsible.

According to the *New York Times Book Review*, Howard Owen (himself a Southern newspaper editor) "has written a nicely plotted novel inhabited by real people living in a real — and thus complex — world." *Kirkus Reviews* observes that Owen "movingly details the moral education of a 40ish white male as he finally tries to do the right thing in his racially divided hometown." *Publishers Weekly* points out that "Owen's achievement here is in provoking without soapboxing" and concludes that "He invites readers to hold up a yardstick to their own lives to calculate how far their adult behavior has strayed from the idealism of their youth."

RECOGNITION: *LATBR* "Recommended Titles" 1997; REVIEWS: *BL* 2/15/97; *KR* 12/1/96; *LJ* 2/1/97; *NYTBR* 4/27/97; *PW* 12/9/96

341 *Answers to Lucky* (1996); Harper-Collins 1996 (HC); 1997 (pbk)

In *Answers to Lucky* Howard Owen tells the story of a sibling rivalry fueled by a combination of fate and a father's ambition. The novel is set in North Carolina and features the Sweatt family. When twin sons are born — in the mid 1940s — to a "no-account," truck driver by the name of Tommy Sweatt, he vows that they will be the engine of the family's changing fortunes. Both boys (Thomas Edison Sweatt and John Dempsey "Lucky" Sweatt) are exhorted — almost from birth — to excel in everything they do. However, when the ironically named "Lucky" contracts polio, his father loses interest in his now-crippled son and focuses exclusively on his brother, Tom. The two brothers grow apart (Lucky — the adoptive father of two Vietnamese children and one black child — becomes ever-more liberal, while Tom's reflexive consevatism becomes increasingly entrenched) but are eventually reunited for Tom's gubernatorial race.

According to *Publishers Weekly* "Lucky's search for emotional closure as he confronts his good ole boy brother and their distant father gains emotional resonance in Owen's sure evocation of Southern life." *Kirkus Reviews* observes that "In a rich regional diction, and with flights of satiric darts aimed at hometown politicking.... [Owen tells] a completely engaging story about the family ties that bind — tight — and the ego-pricking legacy of growing up poor." In the view of the *Atlanta Journal and Constitution*, "What makes *Answers to Lucky* more than just a novel of Southern politics are the tangled, familial subtext and Owen's powers of observation — [it's] that rare political novel that transcends its genre!"

REVIEWS: *BL* 3/1/96; *KR* 1/1/96; *NYTBR* 5/5/96; *PW* 1/1/96

Pearson, T.R. (USA)

Cry Me a River (1993); H Holt 1994 (pbk); See Section 6, #766

Phillips, Jayne Ann (USA)

Shelter (1994); Delta 1995 (pbk);See Section 6, #837

Powell, Padgett (USA)

342 *Edisto Revisited* (1996); H Holt 1997 (pbk)

Padget Powell's follow-up to *Edisto* (1984) again features Simons Manigault a young man who, despite his long-held desire to pursue a writing career (and mostly to appease his cheerfully complacent, "country squire" sort of daddy), has just completed his architecture degree. A brief stay in his beautiful, mildly alcoholic mother's oceanfront cottage in the company of his older, dangerously attractive first cousin Patricia, convinces Simons (who in the words of the *L.A. Times* "is swaying temporarily in the crack between college, out to avoid commitment and none too desperate for that first paycheck") to hit the road. The conflicted Simons makes his way to the Louisiana bayous in search of Taurus, one of his earliest mentors (and one of his mother's former lovers), who is now eking out a bare-bones living as a game warden. It is here that Simons is shown what "lies at the absolute end of the road of dalliance."

People Weekly observes that "while the plot runs thin, [Powell's] humor and sense of character once more prevail, deftly capturing that time of life when the pressure to be someone can be overwhelming." *Publishers Weekly*, in its starred review, applauds Powell's "brilliantly discursive and often hilarious narrative style and consistently elegant prose" which is put to excellent use in a sophisticated "tightly told coming-of-age tale." Novelist **Valerie Sayers** (*WPBW*) concludes that "*Edisto Revisited* is frustrating and exhilarating, dark and light, willful and mysterious. I wish there were more of it … [Simons Manigault's] story is only just beginning."

REVIEWS: *BL* 2/15/96; *ChiTrib* 3/31/96; *KR* 1/15/96; *LATBR* 4/28/96; *LJ* 4/1/96; *NYTBR* 3/31/96; *PeopleW* 4/29/96; *PW* 1/15/96; *WPBW* 3/24/96

Price, Reynolds (USA)

343 *Roxanna Slade* (1998); Scribner 1998 (HC)

Reynolds Price, in *Roxanna Slade*, has chosen to concentrate on the life of an ordinary Southern woman and by doing so has essentially told the story of the evolution of "the American South." The eponymous heroine was born in rural North Carolina in 1900, but her tale begins on her twentieth birthday, the day she falls in love with a young man who tragically drowns later that same day. Roxanna eventually marries the young man's older brother, raises a family and generally goes on about the quotidian business of an "ordinary" life.

In the view of Richard Bernstein (*NYT*) "Roxanna's free-spirited, leisurely [it may test your patience] account of an unexceptional life is well told, and Price shows a great gift for occupying the mind of a woman facing her 10th decade with a kind of lonely, elegiac resignation." According to *Booklist* "Roxanna recounts the contents of her long decades on earth; she took some pretty hard knocks [the death before her eyes of her first love, the infidelity of her husband, etc.] but her true grit served her well…. Roxanna has great respect for the life she has led. And the reader once more comes away from a Price novel with great respect for his ability to fashion full and credible characters and tell their quietly heroic stories with the greatest of empathy." The *Chicago Tribune* concludes that at "all times we are aware that this is the tale of a singular, indomitable woman, trying to understand herself as she struggles to make sense of the world and God's design."

Recognition: *NYTBR* Notable Book of 1998; Reviews: *BL* 2/15/98; *ChiTrib* 7/19/98; *CSM* 7/23/98; *KR* 4/1/98; *NYT* 5/4/98; *NYTBR* 7/12/98; *WPBW* 6/11/98

344 *The Promise of Rest* (1995); S&S 1995 (HC); Scribner 1996 (pbk)

With this story of love and loss, Reynolds Price completes a trilogy begun with *The Surface of Earth* (1975) and continued in *The Source of Light* (1982). Wade Mayfield, an architect who contracted AIDS soon after moving to New York City nine years ago, has been brought home to North Carolina by his father, Hutch Mayfield. Hutch, a sixty-year-old college professor, finds in his son's courage — as he faces a painful and lingering death — the impetus to reconnect with other family members from whom he has been long-estranged.

Booklist calls *The Promise of Rest* a "rich, difficult, but nonetheless beautiful novel" which "speaks eloquently, even soaringly, about reconciliation and closure, awareness and awakening, and life's mysterious but inexorable cycles and patterns." According to the *Library Journal* the author, with his "crystalline, lyric prose … evokes the poetry of need and passion that animates the soul and the grace and gratefulness that responds to such needs." *Time* magazine calls it "a turbulent crossgrained story … that leads back to the earlier novels" and concludes that "Price's dour trilogy is rich not bleak, a satisfying accomplishment by a fine artist." Novelist Sandra Scofield (*Chicago Tribune*) observes that "Part of the accomplishment of the book is that it reminds the reader how much extends beyond a single man's life or death, a single family's sin and redemption. A poet has to believe this … because a poet stands on the edge of the world and declares it. Reynolds Price has done so for thirty years."

OTHER MEDIA: Audiocassette (S&S/abr); READING GROUP GUIDE; REVIEWS: *BL* 3/15/95; *ChiTrib* 6/11/95; *LATBR* 7/16/95; *LJ* 4/1/95; *NYTBR* 5/14/95; *Time* 5/22/95; *WLT* Win '96

Reynolds, Sheri (USA)

345   *A Gracious Plenty* (1997); Crown 1997 (HC)

Set in a small Southern town, Sheri Reynold's third novel tells a bittersweet story of rejection and redemption. At the age of four Finch Noble was badly burned in kitchen accident, leaving her with scars over much of her face and upper body. Rejected or pitied by the other children and stared at by one and all, Finch rarely ventures outside her parents farm and, after they pass on, easily settles into the life of a recluse, becoming, in fact, the local outcast (children call her "witch" and "Ughlee"). Finch busies herself with her back-country chores which includes tending to the local cemetery — one of her father's responsibilities — which adjoins her family's property. And it is here that she finds community, for the dead have begun to speak to Finch. The plot revolves around the mystery surrounding the death of the Mayor's baby — dead and buried before the age of two — and Finch's attempts to comfort the tiny, speechless spirit.

In the view of *Publishers Weekly*, "Reynold's lyricism and the gentle voice of her heroine carry this poignant but redemptive story of an emotionally and physically scarred woman who finds her way out of the land of the dead and into the land of the living." According to *Kirkus Reviews* this is "A Southern tearjerker with some nice surprises…."

OTHER MEDIA: Audiocassette (Crown/abr; Books-on-Tape/unabr); READING GROUP GUIDE; REVIEWS: *BL* 6/1/97; *ChiTrib* 10/29/97; *EW* 9/5/97; *KR* 6/1/97; *NYTBR* 10/5/97; *PW* 7/7/97

346   *The Rapture of Canaan* (1996); Putnam 1995 (HC); Berkley 1997 (pbk)

Sheri Reynolds's second novel is narrated by fourteen-year-old Ninah Huff, a life-long member of a restrictive religious community founded by her preacher grandfather, Herman Langton. Having survived a brutal wartime experience, he had come home to devote himself to God by leading a penitential sect he has named the Church of Fire and Brimstone and God's Almighty Baptizing Wind. Herman's God is a vengeful God and his community is a place where punishments — for even the most unintended "transgressions" — are handed out with great regularity. Instructed by her grandfather to focus her thoughts on the great hereafter, Ninah much prefers the company of her grandmother Leila whose view of life is considerable less harsh. When Ninah is matched with the fifteen-year-old James, as a "prayer partner," she begins to experience feelings she ascribes to the will of God.

According to the *L.A. Times Book Review*, "We know what to expect of a "fresh new Southern voice," as Sheri Reynolds has been called, and she delivers: a certain folksy lyricism. Overt homage to storytelling tradition. A strong maternal figure … [and a] powerful, puffing male…." According to *Booklist*, "Reynold's second assured novel … is also a devastating portrayal of organized religion as illogical, intolerant, and cruel but still unable to extinguish the spark of the human spirit." *Publishers Weekly* concludes that Ms. Reynolds "once again showcases a compelling narrative voice that's simultaneously harsh and lyrical."

OTHER MEDIA: Audiocassette (Books-on-Tape/unabr); RECOGNITION: Oprah Winfrey's Book Club selection; REVIEWS: *BL* 1/1/96; *ChiTrib* 2/23/96; *LATBR* 2/11/96; *LJ* 12/95; *NYTBR* 3/31/96; *PW* 11/6/95; *WPBW* 1/7/96

Sayers, Valerie (USA)

347   *Brain Fever* (1996); Doubleday 1996 (HC)

Valerie Sayer's story of a middle-aged parttime college professor and former boy-wonder (he'd been admitted to Columbia University at the tender age of 16) by the name of Tim "Looney" Rooney, begins as a deceptively frothy, almost madcap Southern comedy. As the novel opens Looney, in a great whosh of manic intention leaves both the Carolina lowlands ("where even the poverty is picturesque") and his fiancée, Mary Faith Rapple, and heads for the Big Apple. He is traveling with $15,000 hidden in his shoes and is in search of his first wife, now a well-respected professor at NYU, to whom he had been married — for all of 6 days — in the early 1970s. Looney, diagnosed variously as "schizophrenic, neurotic, manic-depressive and alcoholic" is off his medication and is slowly going mad. Or is he?

According to the *New York Times Book Review*, Ms. Sayers presents the reader "with so many notions of sanity and insanity, and of tenderness and mercy, that this 40-day-long diary of a madman, with echoes of Christ's 40 days in the desert, is as much a case study as a lesson in faith through the eyes of an on-again, off-again Catholic and those of his jilted fiancée [an atheist and former Baptist]. Both have appeared before in [the author's] work, as have these themes of fidelity, apostasy and salvation." The *Times* reviewer concludes that Ms. Sayers uses "graceful prose" to create a novel of "large ambition, compassion and psychological depth."

RECOGNITION: *NYTBR* Notable Book of 1996; REVIEWS: *BL* 2/1/96; *ComW* 6/1/96; *KR* 12/1/95; *LJ* 12/95; *NYTBR* 3/17/96; *PW* 12/18/95

Shivers, Louise (USA)

Whistling Woman (1993); Longstreet 1993 (HC); See Section 6, #840

Skinner, Margaret (USA)

348 *Molly Flangan and the Holy Ghost* (1995); Algonquin 1995 (HC)

Twelve-year-old Molly Flanagan is an engaging youngster who has the dubious distinction of having been born Catholic in the middle of the Bible-belt. She was also born with a "wandering eye" a condition that affords her a unique, if distorted, view of the world. Molly is growing up in a middle-class family in Memphis, Tennessee — in the sleepy Eisenhower '50s. As Molly's polar-opposite grandmothers vie for her soul, she struggles with the everyday challenges of adolescence (piano recitals, friendships, a prodigiously talented older sibling, adult mysteries, her father's near-fatal accident) by putting her faith, at least initially, in the Holy Ghost. By the end of her leisurely paced story, Molly has glimpsed self-knowledge and achieved a deeper understanding of her place in the world.

According to *Booklist, Molly Flanagan and the Holy Ghost* is a "tender and warmhearted coming-of-age story from a talented southern writer, who manages to capture and communicate the residual angst and the fascinating contradictions that characterize her native region." The *Washington Post Book World* calls the novel a "valuable period piece" which skillfully describes a time and a place where "everyone believes in the melting pot and everybody knows their place. There are Catholics and non–Catholics. Negroes sit at the back of the bus. 'There was some rule about this,' Molly vaguely registers…. People eat their own kind of food and take their religious proscriptions seriously." *Publishers Weekly*, in its starred review, asserts that "[a]lthough this affecting novel takes its time arriving at its particularly poignant climax, Skinner's rich, lyrical prose and fresh insights into

human relationships make the wait well worth while."

REVIEWS: *BL* 3/1/95; *ChiTrib* 3/27/95; *KR* 12/15/94; *PW* 1/23/95; *WPBW* 7/30/95

Smith, Lee (USA)

349 *Saving Grace* (1995); Putnam 1995 (HC); Ballantine 1996 (pbk)

Lee Smith's immensely readable and (at times) darkly comic novel tells the story of Florida Grace Shepherd ("Florida for the state I was born in, Grace for the Grace of God"), the 11th child of an itinerant, snake-handling, womanizing preacher and a devout, long-suffering mother. Grace, worn out by sleeping in tents and drafty backwoods cabins and by the constant movement (she has endured more miles than she cares to remember in a seat-sprung school bus), dreams of escaping into a more normal life with a permanent address, everyday playmates and store-bought toys. Denied this childhood dream, Grace eventually grows up and marries a young preacher (more easy-going and mainstream than her father), but she is ill-suited for a life of domesticity. Ms. Smith has written 10 other books that explore small town life in the American South.

According to *Booklist* the much-admired Lee Smith "sweeps readers in with her fascinating portrayal of a bizarre, arcane religious cult … the scenes depicting religious ecstasy are [particularly] mesmerizing." The *Boston Sunday Globe* concurs claiming Smith provides her readers with a "compelling journey into all that matters, Southern and spiritual." The *Washington Post Book World* argues that *Saving Grace* "has a grand and singular purpose, to clothe the spirit with flesh" and concludes that the novel is "lucid in execution, breathtaking in scope and heart-rending in effect [in short]—a redemptive work of art." The *Chicago Tribune* observes that, in her 11th work of fiction, Smith's style is characteristically "lilting, resonant with the rhythm and accent of Appalachia" and concludes that she continues to construct "compelling plots in which innocence is often over shadowed by circumstances that are at once humorous and harrowing."

REVIEWS: *BL* 4/1/95; *ChiTrib* 7/16/95; *LATBR* 5/28/95; *Newsday* 8/23/96; *NYTBR* 7/9/95; *PW* 2/27/95; *SLJ* 1/96; *WPBW* 5/28/95

Taylor, Peter (USA)

350 *In the Tennessee Country* (1994); Picador 1995 (pbk)

In his last novel, published the year he died, Pulitzer Prize–winning author Peter Taylor tells the story of a middle-aged man's obsession with an enigmatic fellow, known to him since childhood as

"Uncle Aubrey," a distant relative who seemed to be present (if only on the margins) at all the crucial events in his family's life. The story begins in 1916, on the funeral train which is bringing the narrator's grandfather, a U.S. Senator, home for burial in Tennessee and ends some 60 years later in a Virginia suburb.

Booklist calls *In the Tennessee Country* "a novel about the old-fashioned times ... told in Taylor's characteristic limpid style, and with a nostalgia for a bygone, genteel Old South." Jonathan Yardley (*WPBW*) observes that Taylor's latest novel "moves at the unruffled pace of a lazy evening's front-porch story-telling...." Novelist Mary Flanagan (*NYTBR*) concludes that Taylor's novel is "so graceful and lucid, one has the impression that it just happened, dropping from the heavens onto the page."

RECOGNITION: *NYTBR* Notable Book of 1994; REVIEWS: *BL* 6/19/94; *ChiTrib* 9/11/94; *KR* 6/1/94; *LRB* 1/12/95; *NYTBR* 9/24/95; *PW* 8/7/95; *WPBW* 12/4/94

Warlick, Ashley (USA)

351   *The Distance from the Heart of Things* (1996); HM 1996 (HC); 1997 (pbk)

Ashley Warlick (the youngest-ever recipient of the Houghton Mifflin Literary Fellowship) sets her debut novel in South Carolina and features Mavis Black a recent college graduate who has returned to her grandfather's prosperous vineyard, and by extension, to the whole of her decidedly eccentric southern family. As Mavis settles into her job as vineyard bookkeeper (a role she had been summoned home to assume) she is caught up in a number of family celebrations, entanglements and contretemps.

Calling *The Distance from the Heart of Things* "a marvelous first novel" novelist **Frank Mosher** (*WPBW*) further points out that it is a "character-driven novel galloping along with laugh-out-loud humor and great good fun." *Booklist* observes that although "[n]othing much happens ... readers will not miss a strong storyline, because they will be mesmerized by Mavis's distinctive voice: languorous, self-assured, and wise beyond her years." Ms. Warlick's debut effort was called "uncommonly good" by the *Newsday* reviewer who went on to point out that "[w]hat's most impressive about the novel is Warlick's fluid almost instinctive use of language." The *Library Journal* concurs pointing out that her "writing is lyrical and sensual, evocative of the South, full of smells, tastes and sensations."

READING GROUP GUIDE: "Reading Group Choices" 1998 (Paz & Associates); REVIEWS: *BL* 3/1/96; *ChiTrib* 5/19/96; *KR* 2/1/96; *LJ* 3/1/96; *Newsday* 8/23/96; *NYTBR* 9/22/96; *PW* 1/15/96

Wells, Rebecca (USA)

352   *Divine Secrets of the Ya-Ya Sisterhood* (1996); HarperCollins 1996 (HC); 1997 (pbk)

A serious mother/daughter rift, sparked by an interview in which a successful young Seattle-based theater director (by the name of Siddalee Walker), suggests that her mother, Vivi, was (in the slyly distorted words of the sleek *New York Times* reporter) a "tap-dancing child abuser" sets the stage for a redemptive, retrospective journey. Vivi, enraged by the article, has disowned her ungrateful "self-centered liar" of a daughter and the much-chastened Sidda is desperate to make amends. Into the breach jump her mother's three life-long pals (collectively known as the "Ya Yas") who persuade Vivi to send Sidda a scrapbook — dubbed the "Divine Secrets of the Ya Ya Sisterhood" — filled with mementos from their exuberantly irreverent girlhood in a small central Louisiana town. Sidda repairs to a remote cabin where she immerses herself in her mother's early life. (*Divine Sisters* continues the story of Sidda Walker first introduced to readers in 1992 in *Little Altars Everywhere*.)

In the view of *Booklist*, *The Divine Secrets* is "a wonderfully irreverent look at life in small town Louisiana from the thirties up to the present through the eyes of the Ya Yas, a gang of merry, smart, brave, poignant, and unforgettable princesses." Wells's second — wildly popular — novel was described by the *Washington Post Book World* as a "very entertaining and, ultimately, deeply moving novel about the complex bonds between mother and daughter." *Publishers Weekly* is more critical, arguing that although Wells' "ambition is admirable and her talent undeniable" her "attempts to wed a folksy homespun tale to a soul-searching examination of conscience" never quite works.

OTHER MEDIA: Audiocassette (Harper Audio/abr); REVIEWS: *BL* 6/1/96; *LJ* 5/1/96; *NewsWk* 7/6/98; *PW* 4/8/96; *WPBW* 6/10/96

Woodrell, Daniel

Give Us a Kiss: a country noir (1996); H. Holt 1996 (HC); PB 1998 (pbk); See Section 6, #790

BRITAIN AND IRELAND

This part celebrates those novelists from the British Isles and Ireland whose work, while more than capable of holding its own in the international literary arena, draws clear inspiration from the historical forces and cultural trends reflective of this region. English novelists such as Alice Thomas Ellis, Jane Gardam, and Tim Pears; Scottish novelists such as Janice Galloway and Jeff Torrington; and Irish novelists such as Sebastian Barry, Roddy Doyle and Robert McLian Wilson are writing — with great skill and insight — from within one of the most venerable of all literary traditions.

Barry, Sebastian (Ireland)

353   *The Whereabouts of Eneas McNulty* (1998); Viking 1998 (HC)

Sebastian Barry, a successful Irish playwright, has put his obvious command of the lively Sligo vernacular to effective use in his latest novel. Barry's wryly comic story begins in Ireland during the early decades of the 20th century and features the hapless Eneas McNulty who — just as his countrymen are wresting independence from the British — makes a fateful decision to join the Royal Irish Constabulary. He will, forever after, be branded a traitor, a transgression which carries the ultimate penalty. To make matters worse, a former childhood friend has been selected to carry out the sentence. McNulty becomes a sort of fugitive Everyman.

The *Washington Post Book World* observes that "Although *The Whereabouts of Eneas McNulty* begins slowly with more lyricism than plot, once Sebastian Barry puts Eneas on the path of exile, he tells a powerful tale of longing, loss and redemption." In the view of the *Irish Times* "Sebastian Barry has created in the character of wandering Eneas McNulty, a figure who is both imaginatively singular and universally emblematic, and in this novel, a funny, tender poignant portrayal of a life thwarted by an absence of guile." The *Christian Science Monitor* concludes that Barry, in "prose that's stunningly poignant ... has produced a novel about a most unusual plight. But he delves so deeply into Eneas's peculiar fate and redemption that it speaks for us all."

REVIEWS: *ChiTrib* 10/12/98; *CSM* 8/13/98; *Econ* 6/13/98; *IrishT* 2/28/98; *LST* 3/1/98; *PW* 6/8/98; *TLS* 2/20/98; *WPBW* 10/29/98; *WSJ* 7/24/98

Connaughton, Shane (Ireland)

354   *The Run of the Country* (1991); St. Martin's 1995 (pbk)

Shane Connaughton's debut novel is set in the 1950s on the Cavan-Fermanagh border (the dividing line between Northern Ireland and the Irish Republic) and features the rebellious teenage son of a harshly authoritarian police officer. *The Run of the Country* describes the boy's 17th year, beginning with the death of his mother. Having lost his loving ally (the only buffer he had ever known be-

tween himself and his father's fists) the young man runs away from home. On his own, he falls in love for the first time and is quickly initiated into the ways of a violent agrarian community — made more so by the tensions peculiar to a border region. In time, the runaway falls seriously afoul of his father.

According to the *Times Literary Supplement*, "An orgy of killing accompanies (the protagonist's) initiation into adulthood, what with visits to the knackers yard, cock fighting ... pigs at the mercy of cars along the road, decapitated bodies along the railway line, duck for shooting, hares for hunting ... vermin to be exterminated with an old boot, and finally a terrible accident with a tractor in a bog. This is Irish country life at its bloodiest, and the novel is written in a rather livid style to match." In the view of the *London Times*, *The Run of the Country* "is a bloody tale about a bloody area, but the occasional stabs of passion and understanding strike home like the bayonets stuck in the ground as goal posts, when the Irish lads play football with the local police." *Booklist* concludes that, aside from a tendency towards overwriting, "Connaughton is overloaded with talent and keen powers of observation ... and demands, at least, to be watched." *Publishers Weekly*, in its starred review, contends that "In this extraordinary first novel, the realms of tragedy and comedy are deftly balanced by a writer whose authority is matched by his love of language."

REVIEWS: *BL* 3/15/92; *LJ* 2/15/92; *LT* 10/24/91; *NYTBR* 4/12/92; *PW* 1/1/92; *TLS* 10/11/91

Deane, Seamus (Ireland)

355   *Reading in the Dark* (1996); Knopf 1997 (HC); Vintage 1998 (pbk)

Seamus Deane's debut novel is a fictionalized account of a Derry childhood set in post–World War II Northern Ireland. Incorporating much autobiographical material, Deane tells a story fraught with mystery, the weight of unspoken family secrets and the imperatives of a violent and complex national history. When published in England in 1997, *Reading in the Dark* attracted significant attention on the literary prize front, winning the *Guardian* Fiction Prize as well as being shortlisted for both the Booker Prize and the Whitbread First Novel Award.

According to the *New Statesman*, a "colonial culture is a culture of secrecy" and "Seamus Deane's superb first novel, set in the Derry Bogside of the 1940s and 1950s, is all about who knows what in a place awash with rumors, hauntings, metamorphoses and misinformation." *Booklist* while observing that Deane "relishes the sensual beauty of language and the power of stories and draws deeply from the wellspring of Irish literature" concludes that "his rendering of the supple mind of this young hero is wholly original, expressing as it does a rich blend of curiosity, romance, fear, and stoicism." Richard Eder (*LATBR*) contends that the "beauty of Dean's lament ... is that it is not told as such. The narrator speaks with all the vitality, the appetite for life and discovery and the pleasurable distractibility of his age." According to the *Washington Post Book World*, "Dean's narrative seems artless [at first] ... But gradually the random remarks, anecdotes and bits of memory begin to fit together: betrayal of comrades, a false accusation, a family feud, a traitor's escape, and a wide conspiracy of silence — remorse, torment and always tears." Irish novelist **Edna O'Brien** (*TLS*) offers a somewhat different view. Although praising the novel's realism and intelligence and pointing to "beautifully told passages" Ms. O'Brien concludes that "our collusion with the story is interrupted a little too often by authorial nudges, inviting us to savour yet another artful effect."

OTHER MEDIA: Audiocassette (Chivers/unabr); READING GROUP GUIDE; RECOGNITION: Winner of the 1997 *Guardian* Fiction Prize; shortlisted for the 1997 Booker Prize and the Whitbread First Novel Award; *NYTBR* Notable Book of 1997; *L.A. Times* "Best Books" 1997 (Top Ten); *Publishers Weekly* "Best Books" 1997; REVIEWS: *BL* 4/1/97; *KR* 3/1/97; *LATBR* 5/11/97; *LJ* 3/15/97; *LRB* 9/5/96; *LST* 5/11/97; *NewR* 5/19/97; *NewsWk* 5/12/97; *NS* 8/30/97; *NYTBR* 5/4/97; *PW* 3/3/97; *TLS* 9/27/96; *WPBW* 6/15/97

Doyle, Roddy (Ireland)

The Woman Who Walked Into Doors (1996); Viking 1996 (HC); Penguin 1997 (pbk); See Section 1, #27

356 *Paddy Clark Ha Ha Ha* (1993); Penguin 1995 (pbk)

Set in the late 1960s, *Paddy Clark Ha Ha Ha* is the coming-of-age story of an Irish boy growing up in a working-class neighborhood in Dublin. His eager exploration and boisterous enjoyment of his own little corner of the world is particularly remarkable given his troubled home-life and limited expectations.

According to the *New York Times Book Review*, "Roddy Doyle's strength as a novelist has been his capacity to construct and animate a world out of speech alone. But unlike *The Commitments* and *The Snapper*, works that resound with the amiable, anarchic babble of Dublin voices, *Paddy Clark Ha Ha* ... is narrated by a single voice, that of a 10-year-old boy." The *Times Literary Supplement* observes that "Skillfully enough, Doyle resurrects 1960s Ireland. But his book's real feat is its uncannily immediate bringing back to life of the re-

sponses and routines of a boy in that place and period. Paddy's headlong enthusiasms whoop and bounce across the pages...." The *TLS* concludes that *Paddy Clark Ha Ha Ha* "in its feisty comedy, unsentimental nostalgia and vivid realizing of a young boy's take on life ... makes an impressive and likable addition to a line of Irish writing that got memorably underway with Joyce's *Portrait of the Artist as a Young Man* and was recently given a macabre twist in Patrick McCabe's *The Butcher Boy*." According to the *New Statesman & Society* "the obvious parallel is with [James] Kelman ... the only other contemporary writer who can inhabit a non-ironic consciousness so absolutely and convincingly. There is, though, none of Mr. Kelman's sandbagging proletarianism."

OTHER MEDIA: Audiocassette (Penguin Audio/abr; Chivers/unabr); RECOGNITION: Winner of the 1993 Booker Prize; *NYTBR* Notable Book of 1994; REVIEWS: *ChiTrib* 3/3/94; *EW* 1/14/94; *LitRev* 6/93; *NS&S* 6/18/93; *NY* 1/24/94; *NYRB* 2/3/94; *NYTBR* 1/2/94; *PW* 11/15/93; *Time* 12/6/93; *WLT* Aut '94; EDITOR'S NOTE: Each volume of Roddy Doyle's much-praised Barrytown trilogy consisting of *The Van*, *The Snapper* and *The Commitments* has been made into a motion picture; the trilogy was published in a single volume by Penguin in 1995.

Ellis, Alice Thomas (UK)

357 *Fairy Tale* (1996); Moyer Bell 1998 (HC)

As Alice Thomas Ellis's latest "witch's brew" of a novel opens, teenage Eloise and her boyfriend Simon have fled London (and promising jobs) for a little red cottage in rural Wales. They have come to the country in search of a life more in harmony with the "natural" world. Simon now goes off each morning to his job as a woodworker while Eloise, an accomplished seamstress, stays home tending the hearth and working on the exquisite undergarments she crafts for expensive London shops. Eloise's mother, a sophisticated urbanite and middle-aged divorcee, is not at all pleased with this turn of events. When Simon — who is himself growing concerned — alerts her to the fact that Eloise is now talking about having a baby, she persuades her long-time friend, Miriam, to journey up to Wales in order to talk some sense into her. It soon becomes apparent that Eloise is beyond reaching; has, in fact, become even dreamier and more distracted than usual. Eloise's newly acquired habit of walking in the woods by herself heightens everyone's anxiety, as does the appearance of four strange, nearly silent, "religious" men particularly in conjunction with the unnerving stories (about a convicted sex offender recently returned from prison) told by the local gamekeeper. When Eloise returns from one of her solitary walks with a baby in her arms, the plot takes a decidedly supernatural turn.

According to the *London Sunday Times*, "Alice Thomas Ellis (in her latest novel) casts a devilishly clever and lingeringly eerie spell, sprinkling her writing with cabalistic magic, swiping at pseudo-spirituality and scoring points for her Puckish merrymaking." *Kirkus Reviews* calls *Fairy Tale* "perfectly toned social satire [that] unfailingly holds its own" further observing that it is "[b]right, thoughtful fiction that clips along, having both its say and its fun." The *Times Literary Supplement* observes that in her latest novel Ms. Ellis, employing "her usual brevity and levity … [expertly] picks her way through the thickets of magic, mythology and its up-to-date application, through the toils and delusions of contemporary mores, and the comedies and contretemps … peculiar to domestic life" and concludes that she "is a writer to cherish; irreverence makes her entertaining, while perspicacity keeps her observations shrewd."

REVIEWS: *BL* 3/15/98; *KR* 2/1/98; *LJ* 3/1/98; *LST* 10/12/97; *NYTBR* 4/26/98; *PW* 3/2/98; *TLS* 9/13/96; EDITOR'S NOTE: Ms. Ellis's debut novel *The Sin Eater* (1977) — published for the first time in the United States by Moyer Bell (1998) — was described by the *New York Times Book Review* as "a sly novel of [bad] manners" which is set in Wales and which "examines a contentious family that's fetched up for a long weekend in a house outside the village of Llanelys to see whether the ailing patriarch, identified only as the Captain, is going to die."

358 *The Summer House: A Trilogy* (1987–1989); Viking Penguin 1994 (pbk)

Alice Thomas Ellis's trilogy of novellas: "The Fly in the Ointment" (1989), "The Skeleton in the Cupboard" (1988) and "The Clothes in the Wardrobe" (1987) were issued collectively in the United States in 1994 as *The Summer House*. Each is set mostly in the London suburb of Croydon (with interludes in Egypt) during what appears to be the late 1950s and each provides a unique view of a single event, the up-coming marriage of a dreamy young woman (Margaret, aged nineteen) to her much older next-door-neighbor, Syl Monro, a crass solicitor (and unappealing womanizer) still living with his gimlet-eyed mother. The bride-to-be has recently returned from a traumatic stay in Egypt and appears to be sleep walking her way towards the wedding. Alternative, contemporaneous views on the events leading up to the wedding are provided by: Margaret ("The Clothes in the Wardrobe"); Syl's curmudgeonly mother, Mrs. Monro ("The Skeleton in the Cupboard"); and Lili, a decidedly flamboyant (half–English, half–Egyptian) friend of Margaret's all-too-conventional mother ("The Fly in the Ointment").

In the view of novelist **Francine Prose**

(*NYTBR*) "Alice Thomas Ellis's wry trilogy … is a work of astonishing illumination and delight … Old and young, the women here are tough (even when they are passive), funny, imaginative and quite brilliant at turning a phrase. They are capable of philosophical, moral and religious theorizing without being boring, pompous or pious…. Modest, unassuming, entertaining, *The Summerhouse* poses a challenge to much of what our culture appears to consider essential for serious fiction: grand emotions, important events, big ideas, heavy breathing." According to the *London Review of Books*, "The Fly in the Ointment" "concludes a trilogy of novels which has wittily laid bare some of the least comforting aspects of human existence…. For all its glitter and flippancy … it is a sober exploration of the nature of sin and the possibility of pardon."

OTHER MEDIA: A film version directed by Waris Hussein starring Jeanne Moreau and Joan Plowright was released in 1994; RECOGNITION: *NYTBR* Notable Book of 1994; REVIEWS: *FT* 10/8/88, 11/7/87; *LATBR* 12/1/89; *LitRev* 10/88, 11/87; *LRB* 10/13/88, 12/1/89; *NS&S* 12/1/89; *NYTBR* 4/24/94; *Spec* 11/4/89; *TLS* 10/16/87; 11/10/89

Galloway, Janice (UK)

359 *Foreign Parts* (1994); Dalkey Archives 1995 (pbk)

In her second novel, called "Scotland's answer to *Thelma and Louise*" by the *New York Times Book Review*, Janice Galloway features two friends, Cassie and Rona, Scotswomen in their late thirties, on a driving holiday in northern France. They are both single, a status which neither woman particularly enjoys, but though they "fancy men" they don't actually like them very much, which does tend to get in the way of finding a mate. Of course, neither Cassie nor Rona would say no to a knight on a white charger…

According to the *New York Times Book Review*, Ms. Galloway "offers readers a carefully observed, caustic portrait of two opposites — one prickly, one plodding — and their troublesome but enduring friendship." The *Times Literary Supplement* concludes that "in *Foreign Parts*, Janice Galloway has ventured further into her established territory of language, gender, power and dependency. That this enjoyable novel wears its complexity and depth so lightly is an indication of her ambition, control and remarkable craft." The *New Statesman and Society* argues that "Janice Galloway is way up with the best of the Glaswegian wits…. The exchanges between Rona and Cassie — right at the edge and yet so laconic, so funny — just shine from the page."

RECOGNITION: Winner of the 1994 McVittie Prize: Scottish Writer of the Year; REVIEWS: *LJ*

10/15/95; *LST* 5/3/95; *NS&S* 4/29/94; *NYTBR* 10/1/95; *PW* 7/24/95; *TLS* 5/6/94

Gardam, Jane (UK)

360   *Queen of the Tambourine* (1991); Picador 1996 (pbk)

In her sixth novel, Jane Gardam tells the wryly comic story of Eliza Peabody — the childless, middle-aged wife of an upper level British bureaucrat — whose grip on reality, strained by years of suburban isolation, slips dramatically when her husband announces his intention of leaving her. For most of her married life, Eliza — bright, imaginative and a consummate busybody — has had no meaningful occupation beyond "good works" (e.g., volunteering at a local hospice), and no reliable companionship beyond the family dog. Inexplicably, Eliza begins to write letters to a neighbor, Joan, who has recently (it is assumed) abandoned her own family and "run off" to Asia. Eliza, we begin to suspect, might not actually be posting these letters and is probably working her way through a full-blown nervous breakdown.

According to *Booklist*, "Jane Gardam, recipient of two Whitbread Awards, strikes an unusual balance between wit and sweetness, creating a smart but gentle novel that seems to be from a far less explicit era than our own." English novelist **Anita Brookner** (*Spectator*) concludes that "The tone is unified throughout; manic delusions were never so persuasive. And it is very moving when it is not being exceedingly funny." The *L.A. Times* asks: "How can the classical British comedy of eccentricity be played out against a background in which young men die of AIDS, the Shah of Iran's firing squads echo in the night and babies might drown. Like mystery fans flipping back to find the clues they missed, we will be tempted to reread this novel just to see how Gardam did it." The *London Times* concludes that *Queen of the Tambourine* is "a marvelously subtle and moving novel which combines wit with gentle understanding of the human condition."

RECOGNITION: Winner of the 1991 Whitbread Book of the Year Award; REVIEWS: *BL* 8/95; *LATBR* 10/23/95; *Lit Rev* 4/91; *LJ* 7/95; *LST* 4/21/91; *LT* 6/13/92; *NS&S* 11/29/91; *NYTBR* 8/27/95; *PW* 6/19/95; *Spec* 4/13/91; *TLS* 5/3/91; *WPBW* 8/23/95

Gray, Alasdair (UK)

A History Maker (1994); Harcourt Brace 1996 (HC); See Section 7, #898

Greig, Andrew (UK)

361   *Electric Brae* (1993); Trafalgar Square 1993 (HC); Canongate 1998 (pbk)

The debut fictional offering of Scottish poet Andrew Greig is narrated by Jimmy Renilson an engineer with a North Sea Oil company and an avid mountaineer. A thirty-something Scot, Jimmy, while not exactly a "new man," is certainly a bit more reflective (sensitive, even, on occasion) than his peers. As the story opens, Jimmy is living with a volatile artist by the name of Kim. Along with his best friend Graeme and Graeme's bi-sexual girlfriend, Lesley, they form a spirited, if uneasy, foursome. In a series of flashbacks, Jimmy tries to make sense of it all. The author (himself an experienced "climber") has written two extremely successful non-fiction books about Himalayan expeditions.

According to the *London Times* Greig's novel "offers an earnest naturalistic portrait of Bohemian Scotland in the Eighties." The *Times Literary Supplement* calls *Electric Brae* "insightful" and "lyrical" with "a highly involuted narrative, containing many neatly plotted, eyes-down-for-the-last paragraph mysteries." *Publishers Weekly* observes that Greig's "characterizations are honest and complex ... [enhanced by his] sparing, pungent use of Scots dialect" and concludes that "Greig will win new admirers ... with this probing tale of contemporary Scotland, into which he has woven the age-old themes of love, death and madness."

REVIEWS: *GlasgHerald* 11/26/92; *LT* 12/26/92; *PW* 7/5/93; *TLS* 1/1/93

Hamilton, Hugo (Ireland)

The Last Shot (1992); FS&G 1992; See Section 6, #816

Haverty, Anne (Ireland)

362   *One Day as a Tiger* (1997); Ecco 1998 (HC)

According to a Tibetan proverb "It is better to have lived one day as a tiger than a thousand years as a sheep." Irish poet and screenwriter, Anne Haverty, has written an oddly plotted, tragi-comic tale that hinges on an Irishman's love for his sister-in-law and his odd preoccupation with a genetically altered sheep named Missy. Abandoning a promising academic career, Martin Hawkins has returned to the family farm after the accidental death of his parents. Haverty's plot includes a scheme to deliver Missy to Bridgett Bardot's animal sanctuary in the south of France.

One Day as a Tiger was called the "best first novel of the season" by the *Economist* which concluded that Haverty's "elegantly written" story "is a marvelously engaging portrait of the suffocating qualities of rural life in Tiperrary." *Kirkus Reviews* observes that "The plot dances along at a brisk clip as Haverty's precise language beautifully captures her eccentric, isolated cast of rural characters." The *London Times* notes that "Haverty's undeniably strange plot, alongside her skillful depiction of misfits in a time-locked community, leaves the reader with a powerful sense of dislocation." According to the *Literary Review*, "*Lolita* crossed with [Chatwin's] *On the Black Hill* with a dash of Molly Keane and J.R. Ackerly thrown in is what a Hollywood mogul might say about this book if Hollywood moguls talked about books the way they talk about films."

REVIEWS: *Econ* 4/19/97; *KR* 1/1/98; *LitRev* 3/97; *LJ* 1/98; *LT* 3/7/98; *PW* 11/24/97; *NS* 3/14/97; *SFCBR* 2/15/98; *WPBW* 4/19/98

Healy, Dermot (Ireland)

363   *A Goat's Song* (1994); Viking 1995 (HC)

In *A Goat's Song*, set in modern Ireland, Dermot Healy tells the story of a doomed love affair between Catherine Adams, a Protestant actress from the North and Jack Ferris, a boozy Catholic playwright from the South. Their relationship is buffeted by all the expected complications, and then some. When they first meet, Jack tells Catherine that he "writes 'billy tunes,' 'goat songs' ... 'Tragedies. Tragos — goat. Oide — song. From the Greek." She is charmed....

According to *Publishers Weekly*, *A Goat's Song* is "Effectively the story of the breakup of the relationship between Catholic playwright Jack Ferris and Protestant actress Catherine Adams — The novel opens in Donegal, in the west of Ireland, as Jack slowly realizes that a combination of cultural misunderstandings and his own alcoholism have driven his lover from him...." The *Times Literary Supplement* observes that "Though Healy tells a bleak tale, he hasn't written a bleak book" and concludes that "[p]sychological acuteness and social immediacy, fresh responsiveness to the natural world and seasoned revulsion from a nightmarish political one all make *A Goat's Song* well worth attending to." *Booklist* argues that given "its finely drawn and complex characters, this is a memorable portrayal of a country and its people by one of its notable writers."

REVIEWS: *BL* 11/1/95; *LRB* 6/23/94; *LST* 6/8/97 (pbk rev); *NYTBR* 11/12/95; *PW* 9/4/95; *TLS* 4/22/94

Jordan, Neil (Ireland)

364   *Nightlines* (1995); Random House 1995 (HC)

Neil Jordan, better known in the United States as the director of *Mona Lisa* and *The Crying Game* is also an accomplished novelist and short story writer. Some of his earlier works — such as *Nights in Tunisia* (short stories) and his novel *The Dream of the Beast* — have moved into the ranks of post-

modern classics. His latest novel, *Nightlines* (published in England as *Sunrise with Sea Monster*) is narrated by Donal Gore an Irishman who, as the novel opens, is waiting to be executed by a Spanish firing squad. The story of how Donal came to be in a Spanish jail ("of all courses of action I could have taken it was the only one I knew with certainty that my father would have disapproved of") is less important, however, than the price he will be made to pay for his release. Franco's victory, was, after all, secured with the assistance of the newly empowered Third Reich and Nazi officers were thick on the ground.

The *Library Journal* calls *Nightlines* "a classic tale of Irish angst replete with themes of betrayal, rebellion, and reconciliation." According to *Publishers Weekly* Jordan's novel which raises significant historical issues such as Ireland's ambiguous neutrality during WW II and in the Spanish Civil War "is essentially a love triangle with a peculiar twist: two of the participants are father and son." The *New York Times Book Review* observes that by "the end [of the novel] Mr. Jordan has achieved precisely the sort of fabular tone for which his films so often strive unsuccessfully, doomed by the camera's literalism" and concludes that he "should set his imagination free in fiction more often." The *London Sunday Times* concludes that the "value of this novel ... lies ... in the singular beauty of its prose and the eloquence of its imagery."

RECOGNITION: *L.A. Times* "Top 10" Books of 1995; REVIEWS: *BL* 9/1/95; *KR* 7/15/95; *LJ* 9/1/95; *LST* 1/15/95; *NS&S* 1/13/95; *NYTBR* 10/15/95; *Obs* 1/8/95; *PW* 7/31/95; *Spec* 12/31/94; *TLS* 1/13/95

Keane, John (Ireland)

365   *Ram of God* (1996); Roberts Rinehart 1996 (HC)

In *Ram of God* John Keane tells the bittersweet story of Eddie Drannaghy, a young seminarian whose life is dramatically altered when, in a moment of weakness, he succumbs to the wiles of his seductive American cousin. Observed in "the act" by his twin brothers, news of his transgression spreads, and eventually makes its way back to the head of his seminary. The devout young man is, of course, summarily expelled. Denied the possibility of ever becoming a priest, Eddie resolves to lead an exemplary life.

According to *Kirkus Reviews* "Playwright-novelist Keane movingly evokes the pervasive pettiness and prejudice of Irish rural life, blighting dreams and love, in the story of a young man who's destined for the priesthood but is nearly destroyed by gossip, family greed, and his own stubbornness." *Publishers Weekly* conclude that "Pervaded with a strong dramatic, even cinematic quality, this is a solid melodrama propelled by the lilt of musical language and honest scenes of Irish country life."

REVIEWS: *KR* 6/1/96; *LJ* 7/96; *PW* 6/24/96

Kearney, Colbert (Ireland)

366   *The Consequence* (1993); Dufour 1994 (pbk)

Colbert Kearney's *The Consequence*— a comic tale with postmodern overtones — tells the story of an English professor by the name of Fintan Kearney, who's writing a book about writing a book. What he's actually hoping to do is make amends for a book titled *Gone the Time* which, though attributed to him (and unquestionably autobiographical) he cannot, in all honesty, remember writing. To make matters worse, the book — complete with thinly veiled, and highly unflattering, references to colleagues and various Irish authors — has not only become a bestseller, but is being hailed as a modern classic.

The *London Sunday Times* suggests that "Kearney has hit on a refreshingly original concept for his first novel, and he carries it off with style and panache." *Publishers Weekly* observes that *The Consequence* is "[w]ritten with warm sensitivity to the rhythms of Irish humor and speech" and concludes that "this brilliantly structured and executed metafictional novel is essentially comic, but its playful aspect frames a more serious exploration of the hazy links between fiction and reality." According to the *New Statesman*, Kearney "takes a playful approach to the shaping of fiction — and of myth or moonshine, come to that. The parts don't quite cohere and it has moments of pretentiousness. Once he gets into his stride, though, Kearney shows himself to be inventive and fluent…. *The Consequence* is a very accomplished performance."

REVIEWS: *Irish Literary Supplement* Fall '94; *LST* 11/93; *NS&S* 12/3/93; *PW* 9/5/94

Kelman, James (UK)

367   *How Late It Was, How Late* (1994); Norton 1994 (HC); Dell 1996 (pbk)

James Kelman's brutally realistic novel about being down and out in Glasgow caused a rift in the Booker Prize panel (one member called it "completely inaccessible" and a "disgrace") when it won that most prestigious of literary prizes in 1994. Using a militantly working-class Scottish vernacular (liberally laced with profanity), Kelman's protagonist, Sammy, an unemployed Glaswegian suffering from chronic alcoholism and temporary blindness (brought on by the blow of a billy club), describes his journey through the "netherworld" of the Scottish welfare system. Though feckless and not above breaking the law, Sammy is portrayed with great sensitivity and affection. However, its episodic structure, reliance on interior monologue, and frequent use of expletives, particularly the "f" and "c" words, will make the novel rough going for some readers.

In the view of the *London Sunday Times* "even by the criterion of gripping readability [Kelman's novel], is a roaring success. And it really is superbly well-written. Quite simply, *How Late It Was, How Late* is, to use one of its key phrases, out of sight." In the view of the *London Review of Books*, "James Kelman's most effective political act was, and is, his singular adaptation of the prose sentence to meet the demands of place and speech and, to a limited extent, economic reality on the west coast of Scotland. That's what he does best. At his worst, he indulges a series of paranoid fantasies — vague generalities which draw credibility from cases of negligence, fraud, mis-diagnosis, censorship and the like, all of which have firm bases in reality, but no relation to each other. He brings together any number of these institutional horror stories and fuck-ups, and banalizes them to death." According to novelist **Richard Bausch** (*NYTBR*) Kelman's novel "is a work of marvelous vibrancy and richness of character … deserv[ing of] every accolade it gets."

RECOGNITION: Winner of the 1994 Booker Prize; REVIEWS: *ChiTrib* 1/1/95; *GW* 4/3/94; *LRB* 5/26/94; *LST* 3/27/94; *NS&S* 3/18/94; *NYTBR* 2/5/95; *Spec* 4/2/94; *TLS* 4/1/94; *WPBW* 1/24/95

Lively, Penelope (UK)

368   *Passing On* (1989); HarperCollins 1991 (pbk)

In her 8th novel — set in a small English town called Spaxton — prize-winning English author Penelope Lively tells the story of a brother and sister, middle-aged and unmarried, who have always lived in the shadow of their selfish, overbearing mother. The tale opens soon after her death, as the siblings struggle with their conflicted emotions and with the difficult business of reclaiming their lives. As the story progresses, the sister suffers the pains of unrequited affection, and the brother, a diffident schoolmaster, appears to have placed his beloved career in jeopardy.

The *Literary Review* points out that Ms. Lively "makes us concerned about these people and the things that threaten them…. Skillfully she encompasses within her tale almost imperceptible hints of many possible disasters, mirroring the range of anxieties that hover over humanity" and concludes that *Passing On* is "good in every part. Dialogue, description, detail, emotions, place — she seems to get it all right." *Publishers Weekly* applauds the "subtle plot … one that does well with Lively's gently assured style. By revealing developments through small details … she delicately delineates the impact of love, scandal and turmoil." The *Library Journal* observes that "Lively has already proven herself to be one of Britain's finest authors. *Passing On* simply burnishes this reputation."

OTHER MEDIA: Audiocassette (Dolphin/unabr); REVIEWS: *ChiTrib* 3/4/90; *LitRev* 4/89; *LJ* 3/1/90; *LRB* 4/20/89; *NYT* 2/2/90; *NYTBR* 2/11/90; *PW* 12/1/89; *Q&Q* 11/89; *TLS* 4/7/89

MacKay, Shena (UK)

369   *The Orchard on Fire* (1996); Moyer Bell 1996 (HC); Harcourt Brace 1997 (pbk)

Shena MacKay's seventh novel is a finely drawn tale of the joys and pains of an English childhood. Set in the 1950s, *The Orchard on Fire* is a poignant, occasionally comic, coming-of-age story which explores the deeply felt friendship between two schoolgirls: Ruby Richards, the daughter of Pub owners Lex (fleshy and brutish) and Gloria (beetle-browed and ill-tempered) and April Harlency whose parents, though loving and hardworking, are incapable of protecting her from harm — or, to be more precise, from the evily ingratiating Mr. Greenridge.

According to the *Times Literary Supplement*, the book's "triumph is in capturing the sense of grief for a friendship untimely ripped apart almost half a century ago and the evocation of the magical intensity with which childhood cloaks landscape — the sadness and treachery of those 'blue remembered hills.'" *Booklist* found *The Orchard on Fire* to be "filled with the enchantment and wonder of childhood, as well as its terror and fear." The *New York Times Book Review* observes that *The Orchard on Fire* is "an intensely domestic novel" but concludes that the book's "touching and somber drama arises from much larger elements: love, loyalty, courage, sex, fear and oppression ... [and] Ms. MacKay explores them all with clarity, elegance and power."

RECOGNITION: Shortlisted for 1966 Booker Prize; *NYTBR* Notable Book of 1996; *Publishers Weekly* "Best Books" of 1996; REVIEWS: *BL* 9/15/96; *ChiTrib* 11/29/96; *LJ* 10/1/96; *NS* 6/21/96; *NYTBR* 11/3/96; *PW* 8/12/96; *TLS* 6/14/96

MacLaverty, Bernard (Ireland)

370   *Grace Notes* (1997); WW Norton 1997 (HC); 1998 (pbk)

In his first novel in 14 years, Bernard MacLaverty tells the story of Catherine McKenna, a talented young pianist/composer, as she struggles towards emotional **and** artistic fulfillment. Summoned home to Northern Ireland for her father's funeral, Catherine finds herself contemplating her unsatisfactory life: her difficult relationship with her parents, her alcoholic lover (by whom she has a baby), and the welter of tangled, destructive emotions within which she feels hopelessly trapped.

According to *Kirkus Reviews*, *Grace Notes* is "a lyric novel about music and motherhood ... [in which the author] has tried to suggest the interior life of an artist trying to balance the urgent demands of creating and the equally pressing demands of life." The *London Times* calls it "a magical, disturbing novel" and suggests that it is quite an achievement to "so fully realize a female character." *Booklist* concludes that "Impeccable in both psychology and structure, the latest novel by this first-rate Northern Irish fiction writer is an admirably graceful character study."

OTHER MEDIA: Audiocassette (Sterling/unabr); RECOGNITION: Shortlisted for the 1997 Booker Prize; *Booklist* Editors' Choice 1997; REVIEWS: *BL* 9/15/97; *ChiTrib* 11/16/97; *KR* 8/1/97; *LJ* 9/15/97; *LT* 5/16/98; *NYTBR* 9/28/97; *PW* 8/11/97; *TLS* 7/4/97; *WPBW* 10/5/97; EDITOR'S NOTE: Roddy Doyle and William Boyd have also won praise for their ability to write from a woman's perspective.

McCabe, Patrick (Ireland)

The Dead School (1995); Dell 1996 (pbk); See Section 6, #741

The Butcher Boy (1992); Doubleday 1994 (pbk); See Section 6, #826

371   *Carn* (1989); Delta 1996 (pbk)

Patrick McCabe's second novel is set in the small Irish border town of Carn and spans the years from the early 1960s through the late 1980s, a period characterized by economic and social revitalization followed by recession. As the novel opens, a well-financed Irish-American has just returned to his (economically depressed) home town to start a meat-processing plant. Local hopes are quickly raised, and almost as quickly met, at least for a time. McCabe follows a group of villagers as they grapple not only with the vagaries of the business cycle but also with sexual hypocrisy, incest, commercial exploitation, and border-related terrorism and violence. Mr. McCabe's use of lively regional vernacular draws the reader further into this world.

According to the *London Review of Books* McCabe's "skillfully intertwined" stories point up the "dangerous energies of rumour, romanticism, spoilt religion, and a sexuality not so much repressed as viciously rerouted." The *Washington Post Book World* observes that "rather than a predictable tale of boom-and-boost, much less a mechanical variation on the theme of *plus ça change* ... and concludes that "*Carn* is a disturbing, dramatic, and affecting treatment of emotional and social vulnerability ... which confirms Patrick McCabe as one of the more significant contemporary Irish novelists. "

OTHER MEDIA: Audiocassette (Books-on-Tape/unabr); REVIEWS: *BL* 2/1/97; *IrishRev* Aut' 88; *LJ* 2/1/97; *LRB* 5/4/89; *NYTBR* 2/9/97; *PW* 12/9/96; *TLS* 5/19/89; *WPBW* 1/26/97

McGahern, John (Ireland)

372   *Amongst Women* (1990); Penguin 1995 (pbk)

In this brief but luminous novel, widely considered his most accomplished, John McGahern tells the story of an Irish family, the Morans of "Great Meadow." The family patriarch, "Moran" to one and all, is a former member of the IRA — and although long-returned to farm and family — has been a lifelong patriot, an upstanding member of his rural community and a devout Catholic. In the course of the novel, Moran, a widower for many years, is courted by — and eventually marries — the sweetly sensible Rose who raises his three daughters and youngest son with love and understanding. Moran, though charming in his way, is a pillar of the old order and a daunting patriarch. McGahern very specifically grounds his story in the rural west of Ireland with its small farms, church encircled villages, and leafy country lanes.

According to *The Listener* "John McGahern is the quiet heavyweight of contemporary Irish literature. He is also, without question, the foremost arbiter of rural Irish life at work today, as he has an unerring eye for is compatriots' tribal rituals, their astringent use of language, and their profound emotional hesitancy." The *London Times* observes that "In a mere 184 pages, McGahern fuses past and present, repression and individuality, aspiration and conflict in a seamless narrative of extraordinary tension and effect" and concludes that "*Amongst Women* is much more than a good book, it is an overwhelming experience."

RECOGNITION: Shortlisted for the 1990 Booker Prize and the *IrishTimes* 1991 Book of the Year; REVIEWS: *ChiTrib* 9/2/90; *Listener* 5/24/90; *LJ* 8/90; *LRB* 5/24/90; *LT* 5/10/90; *NS&S* 5/11/90; *NYRB* 12/6/90; *NYTBR* 9/9/90; *Spec* 6/2/90; *TLS* 5/18/90

McIlvanney, William (UK)

373   *Strange Loyalties* (1991); Harcourt Brace 1993 (pbk)

When Jack Laidlaw's brother is killed in a road accident, the maverick Glasgow inspector wants to find out for himself what happened — not, at first, because he suspected foul play, but because he had the impression that all had not been well with his brother in the weeks leading up to his death.

According to *Publishers Weekly*, McIlvanney's

"extraordinary and beautifully written" novel is animated by Jack Laidlaw's investigation into his brother's untimely death, which, in turn, leads to "much larger questions about the nature of pain and injustice and — not least of all — about the meaning of his own life and how it encompasses the impending failure of his relationship with the woman he loves. Trying to piece together the events of his brother's final days, Laidlaw embarks upon a journey into moral darkness." In the view of the *Times Literary Supplement* "The task [McIlvanney] sets for himself is to reconstruct his brother's life, to clarify his values and illuminate the forces which drove him to death. He frets over loneliness, he deplores the fading of love, he agonizes about the conditions of men and women condemned to life on the margins of society, he searches for explanations of crime in the wider injustice which certain people suffer daily. This is a thriller born of pain." KR concludes: "structurally a detective story with more solution than mystery, but really a grimly effective novel like Chandler's *The Long Goodbye*, about the detectives loyalty to the dead."

REVIEWS: *KR* 3/15/92; *LATBR* 6/14/92; *NYTBR* 5/24/92; *PW* 4/26/93; *Spec* 11/30/91; *TLS* 8/16/91; *WPBW* 5/24/92

McNamee, Eoin (Ireland)

374   *The Last of Deeds & Love in History* (1996); Picador 1996 (HC); 1997 (pbk)

Eoin MacNamee in *The Last of Deeds and Love in History* presents two novellas dealing with love and longing in times of acute societal stress. The first, "The Last of Deeds" (shortlisted for the *Irish Times*/Aer-Lingus Irish Literature Award) features a group of male friends living in Northern Ireland and explores the difficulties which result when one of their number falls in love with a woman of the wrong religion. The second, "Love in History," is set during the last months of WWII and revolves around the presence of a US Air Force base situated near Belfast and the action of a "mad" priest who is obsessed with protecting his female parishioners from the American airman and sailors.

In the view of Frank McCourt (*LATBR*) "McNamee's craft gleams on every page.... If it's a tight tale of the back streets of Northern Ireland or a look behind the front lines of a world war that you're looking for, these two novellas will stay with you forever." According to *Booklist* "Death seems to lurk in the background of much of McNamee's fiction, making his characters' efforts to connect all the more poignant."

RECOGNITION: *LATBR* "Best Books" 1996; shortlisted for the *Irish Times*/Aer-Lingus Award for Irish Literature; REVIEWS: *BL* 11/15/96; *LATBR* 11/24/96; *NYTBR* 11/17/96; *PW* 9/30/96

Resurrection Man (1995); Saint Martin's 1996 (pbk); See Section 6, #747

Messud, Claire (US/UK)

375 *When the World Was Steady* (1995); Granta/Penguin 1995 (HC); Granta 1996 (pbk)

Set variously in the British Isles, Australia and Indonesia, book critic Claire Messud's debut novel features two sisters who have taken significantly divergent life paths. Emmy — after her 27 year marriage to an Australian ends in divorce — seeks adventure in Bali; her older, deeply religious unmarried sister Virginia (their irascible mother's dutiful companion and caregiver) accompanies her mother to the Isle of Skye in search of the elderly woman's "roots." What each woman (eventually, if painfully) finds is a modicum of self-knowledge.

According to the *New York Times Book Review*, Claire Messud "in her assured and engaging debut [creates characters] who fail to get what they want [from life, and, though we] may not admire this trio of sad-sack searchers ... Ms. Messud makes us eager to see them get their rare shot at bliss." English novelist **Penelope Fitzgerald** (*LRB*) concludes that "Messud is a deeply interesting young writer who has the perception to write about middle age." In the view of the *Library Journal*, Messud develops her female characters "with wryly humorous albeit sad undertones, thus making them believable."

RECOGNITION: Nominated for the 1996 PEN/Faulkner Award; REVIEWS: *LJ* 8/95; *LRB* 10/6/94; *NYTBR* 9/24/95; *PW* 6/12/95; *TLS* 7/22/94; *WPBW* 8/18/95

Morrissy, Mary (Ireland)

376 *Mother of Pearl* (1995); S&S 1995 (HC)

In her debut novel, Mary Morrissy tells the heartbreaking story of Irene Rivers, an Irish woman, who after years spent in a sanitarium recovering from TB, marries a good, kind man with whom she hopes to create the family she has never had. Irene's husband proves impotent and, driven to extremes by her desire for a child, Irene manages to steal a newborn baby from a local hospital, and for four years raised it as her own. The book is divided into three sections. The first focuses on Irene's life in the sanitarium and immediately after; the second features the couple (Rita and Mel Golden) whose (admittedly "unwanted") baby has been stolen, the third puts the reader inside the mind of Pearl (now returned to Rita Golden and re-named Mary), as she tries to reconcile her early memories with her present life.

Belles Lettres calls Morrissy's debut novel "a painfully deep exploration of the power of mem-ory — particularly childhood memory — to color and define a life." *Publishers Weekly* observes that *Mother of Pearl* is a "lushly lyrical portrait of women wrestling with their inner demons (obsession, betrayal, neurosis and lost innocence)" and concludes that "Morrissy's writing gives off sparks of feminist insights and gimlet humor." The *Times Literary Supplement* calls it a "lyrical and poignant debut novel" and concludes that "Morrissy's central idea of a single life as a piece of fiction either successfully or unsuccessfully achieved is thoroughly convincing."

REVIEWS: *BellesL* Win '96; *BL* 7/95; *KR* 4/15/95; *LATBR* 9/24/95; *NS&S* 1/12/96; *NYTBR* 7/9/95; *PW* 5/8/95; *TLS* 1/12/96; *WLT* Spr '96; *WPBW* 7/9/95

O'Brien, Edna (Ireland)

377 *Down by the River* (1997); FS&G 1997 (HC); Plume 1998 (pbk)

Down by the River is *à roman à thèse* which grew out of the actual (and widely reported) case of a 14-year-old Irish girl — raped and impregnated by her father — who was forcibly returned to Ireland from England where she had fled (with a sympathetic neighbor) in search of a legal abortion. Throughout her ordeal, the youngster (called Mary MacNamara in Ms. O'Brien's chilling version), while admitting to being raped, refuses to name the perpetrator. This reticence, of course, only adds to Mary's vulnerability, as it is assumed by many in her staunchly Catholic rural community that she has only herself to blame. Ms. O'Brien's novel amounts to a ferocious attack on contemporary Irish life and culture.

According to *Booklist* "The reader ... is left with heart in throat to consider a tale that is difficult on two levels: the intense pathos of the story and O'Brien's harshly poetic style" and concludes that O'Brien's "legion of fans will find this a stunning work." English novelist **Hilary Mantel** calls *Down by the River* "a forlorn, unsparing and consciously exquisite novel of rural despair." *Kirkus Reviews* observes that the "panorama of characters who wander into and around the controversy — including judges, journalists, schoolgirls, transvestites, and madwomen — give a rich background to the story" but concludes that "the book's angry impact is diminished ... through a presentation that is relentlessly partisan." The *L.A. Times Book Review* concludes that "in this moving addition to O'Brien's impressive body of work, fatalism is edged with genuine glimmers of hope, and the reader discovers, despite evidence to the contrary, that there is goodness in the world." The *Literary Review* concludes that "[d]espite lingering suspicion that Edna O'Brien has jumped on the child-abuse bandwagon, there is no denying the impact of her vivid and terrible tale."

RECOGNITION: *NYTBR* Notable Book of 1997; *Booklist* Editors' Choice 1997; REVIEWS: *BL* 3/1/97; *KR* 2/15/97; *LATBR* 6/8/97; *LitRev* 9/96; *NS* 8/30/96; *NYTBR* 5/25/97; *PW* 3/3/97; *TLS* 9/27/96

378   *The House of Splendid Isolation* (1994); FS&G 1994 (HC); NAL-Dutton 1995 (pbk)

Edna O'Brien's 18th work of fiction is set on the outskirts of a remote Irish village, home to Josie O'Meara, an elderly widow who lives by herself in a beautiful old farmhouse set well back from the road. When McGreevy, an escaped IRA gunman spots the O'Meara property, he decides to use it as a temporary hideout. Holding Josie O'Meara hostage, McGreevy attempts to sort out his options. Hostage and hostage-taker eventually develop a wary understanding of each other. Interspersed with the contemporary tale, is the story of Josie's tragically unhappy life as the wife of farmer O'Meara.

Irish novelist Aisling Foster, in a review appearing in the *London Times*, observes that Edna O'Brien "has written a philosophical novel, looking deep into the Irish conscience, north and south, their ambivalent feelings about Ulster and one another. Whether she finally succeeds may depend on the reader's preference for the rule of the head or of the heart...." Novelist John L'Heureux (*NYTBR*) observes that "Ms. O'Brien has gone behind the newspaper headlines of bombings, atrocities and midnight murders and finds there only good intentions, blind devotion, stalemate and ruin. All of it sadly human." L'Heureux concludes that "This is a brave book, and if it does not altogether succeed, the attempt nonetheless merits praise. Edna O'Brien has shown that all wars begin at home." *Booklist* calls *The House of Splendid Isolation* "a splendid novel by a superb writer."

OTHER MEDIA: Audiocassette (Chivers/ unabr); RECOGNITION: *NYTBR* Notable Book of 1994; REVIEWS: *BL* 4/1/94; *CSM* 7/1/94; *LJ* 4/1/94; *LT* 4/16/94; *NS&S* 4/15/94; *NYTBR* 6/26/94; *PW* 4/25/94; *TLS* 4/22/94; *WLT* Win '95; *WPBW* 8/21/94

Pears, Tim (UK)

379   *In the Place of Fallen Leaves* (1993); Fine 1995 (HC); 1996 (pbk)

Set in a tiny, hillside village near Dartmoor — remote and, even in 1984, scarcely touched by the late 20th century — *In the Place of Fallen Leaves* is centered around an English summer of record-breaking, near-hallucinatory heat. In his debut novel (described as "piercingly beautiful and "fiercely lyrical" by *PW*), Tim Pears tells the story of thirteen-year-old Alison, a farmer's daughter suspended between childhood and adolescence.

The youngster must confront two, as-yet unfamiliar, facets of life: death and sex.

According to the *London Times*, Tim Pears has "taken an ordinary coming of age story [and] transformed [it] into something fresh and original." The *New York Time Book Review* calls Tim Pears "a gifted storyteller, steeped in country lore and the beauty of ordinary events. Like Thomas Hardy, whose kindred spirit quietly animates these pages, he is concerned with the dignity of farm work, the force of destiny and the consequences of human passion." Novelist **Jane Smiley** (*WPBW*) finds that "Pears's seemingly idle and desultory narrative almost invisibly builds both suspense and insight. His technique of pausing here and there to discourse on one character or another seems like country gossip and proves to be a deft interweaving of character and fate." *Publishers Weekly*, in its starred review, concludes that "Pears evokes unspoken bonds of love, a sense of community, organic connectedness to nature in a remarkable debut, a work shot through with moments of great tenderness, beauty and emotional power."

RECOGNITION: Winner of the 1994 Hawthornden Prize for literature; REVIEWS: *AtlM* 3/95; *BL* 1/15/95; *CSM* 3/30/95; *KR* 11/15/94; *LT* 3/26/94; *NYTBR* 2/5/95; *PW* 12/12/94; *TLS* 4/16/93; *WPBW* 3/5/95

Ridgway, Keith (Ireland)

380   *The Long Falling* (1998); Houghton Mifflin 1998 (HC)

In his debut novel, Keith Ridgway tells the powerful story of Grace Quinn, a long-suffering Englishwoman married to an abusive Irishman. Early in their marriage, Grace's husband, while driving home drunk from the local pub, caused an accident which killed a young woman. The Quinns had been ostracized within their small town from that day forward. When her husband is killed under suspicious circumstances, Grace moves to Dublin to be with her son, a homosexual estranged from his father since childhood. She and her son reconnect but Grace soon finds herself pursued by the police and the media.

According to the *London Sunday Times* "Ridgway's Dublin is an ambivalent city, full of hostile homeless people, drenched in constant rain, yet mapped with loving almost Joycean care. It forms a poignant backdrop to this story of quiet familial nemesis." *Booklist* observes that "Ridgway evokes place and mood beautifully, with shimmering description, and the reader *feels* Grace's 'long falling....'" *Booklist* concludes that "this is a domestic tragedy featuring a firm sense of place and an expertly drawn portrait of alienation and loss." In the view of English novelist **Penelope Fitzgerald** (book jacket) *The Long Falling* is not a "comfortable novel to read, but it was a hundred times worth reading." The *Times Literary Supplement* points out that Keith Ridgway has set his novel in the "new" Dublin, one of "cafes, gay bars and jet-setting middle-class youth, at the centre of a progressive Europe...." and concludes that Ridgway's novel "is a powerful exposure of the new, reforming, optimistic Irish, in the same way as its predecessors have been honest about the failings of the past."

RECOGNITION: *NYTBR* Notable Book of 1998; REVIEWS: *BL* 3/1/98; *ChiTrib* 9/6/98; *LJ* 2/15/98; *LST* 3/25/98; *LT* 2/28/98; *NYTBR* 9/13/98; *PW* 6/26/98; *TLS* 2/20/98

Rogers, Jane (UK)

381   *Promised Lands* (1995); Overlook 1997 (HC); Penguin 1998 (pbk)

Stephen Beech, a disillusioned secondary school teacher with utopian yearnings, is writing a book about English astronomer, William Dawes, a participant in the first British settlement at Sidney Cove, Australia. Dawes's dream that a "new order" could be established in this new world is soon dashed as the realities of life in a harsh and primitive environment—with a population comprised of soldiers, convicts and aborigines—assert themselves. The novel is divided into three segments and two time periods. The first segment is set in the late 1700s and describes Dawes's experiences as a member of the Sidney Cove colony. The second, consisting of a third-person narrative belonging to Stephen Beech, is set in the 1980s and explores Stephen's abortive attempts to reform certain aspects of the British school system. The third, which is also set in the 1980s, is narrated by Stephen's wife who, after a series of miscarriages, has given birth to a severely brain-damaged infant.

In the view of the *Library Journal,* "Rogers's superbly crafted narrative immerses the reader in the harsh choices and conditions of colonial life and in a political and philosophical exploration of utopias...." The *Times Literary Supplement* observes that "Jane Rogers's novel is ambitious, brave and beautifully crafted. It is plainly anxious to avoid being reduced to such ready-made categories as the historical novel, self-referential fiction or women's writing." The *TLS* concludes however that "at moments, a certain strain arises when it seems to want to be all three."

REVIEWS: *BL* 4/15/97; *KR* 4/1/97; *LJ* 4/1/97; *LST* 8/20/96; *NYTBR* 9/21/97; *PW* 3/10/97; *TLS* 9/15/95

Ryan, Hugh Fitzgerald (Ireland)

382   *Ancestral Voices* (1994); Vandamere 1994 (HC)

The ancestral "voices" featured in Hugh Fitzgerald Ryan's first novel to be published in the United States belong to participants in the doomed Wexford Rising of 1798 wherein a group of Irish Catholic peasants fought to prevent a Protestant-dominated government from seeking union with England. Ryan's protagonist, Jack Dempsy, is a contemporary Dublin-based antiques dealer who, influenced by his father-in-law, a Wexford farmer, becomes obsessed with uncovering the role played by his wife's relatives in this historic event. Determined to write a book about the uprising, Dempsy quits his job and moves his family to a seaside cottage in Wexford where he throws himself into research and writing. Jack, disillusioned by the cruelty perpetrated by both factions (e.g., a chapel full of Quakers burned to the ground, and 77 prisoners thrown from a cliff), and suffering from a severe case of writer's block, begins to regret having started the project, a feeling which increases 100 fold when his wife leaves him.

According to *Publishers Weekly* "Irish author Ryan uses a novel-within-a-novel framework to link the events of 1798 to the present and to Jack's personal life—for example to the acrimony between his parents, who stand at opposite poles politically." *Kirkus Reviews* observes that "At times beautifully written, dense with striations of setting, time, and meaning, this thickly layered tale of one man's struggle with his heritage reads like Ian McEwan crossed with W.B. Yeats." The *Irish Times* reviewer observes that "along the way substantial delights are provided by the author's powers of invention, his erudition and his wit, marred only by the occasionally fit of whimsy."

REVIEWS: *IrishT* 12/17/94; *KR* 11/1/94; *LJ* 3/15/95; *PW* 11/7/94; *TLS* 12/16/94

Sweeney, Eamonn (Ireland)

383   *Waiting for the Healer* (1997); St. Martin's 1998 (HC); Picador 1999 (pbk)

I did everything for the best. Everyone does everything for the best. You do it and you think the best way is how it's going to turn out. That's how you mean it to turn out. But it just turns out like it wants to. That's how it is.

So begins Eamonn Sweeney's debut novel, described by Irish novelist **Colm Toibin** as a cross between *Angela's Ashes* and Cormac McCarthy. *Waiting for the Healer* (the title refers to an alcoholic's first drink of the day), is a darkly comic exploration of the ties of family and the pull of history which features London pub-owner Paul Kelly, a widower with a four-year-old daughter and a fondness for drink. When Paul hears of his brother's savage murder, he returns to his family's home in Ireland bent on revenge. In the company of an old friend, Paul soon finds himself back on Rathbawn's meaner streets in search of the killer.

As the *Times Literary Supplement* points out: "This is a new Ireland, somewhere between Roddy Doyle and Quentin Tarantino, post–Catholic, as much in the absence of Sacred Heart pictures and authoritarian clergy as in the absence of social convention; an Ireland without a sense of national identity." According to *Entertainment Weekly*, "Sweeney's language fuses residual Gaelic lilt with staccato rapster rhythms and obscenities. The MTV generation takes over the Irish novel and makes it startlingly new." In the view of *Publishers Weekly* "The conclusion, which tells of Paul's spiritual transcendence, is neither trite nor typical. It's a fitting end to this bold and exhilarating gallop through the dark side of Irish life."

REVIEWS: *ChiTrib* 4/12/98; *EW* 3/13/98; *LJ* 2/1/98; *NYTBR* 5/24/98; *Obs* 3/23/97; *PW* 12/13/97; *TLS* 4/4/97

Swift, Graham (UK)

Last Orders (1996); Knopf 1996 (HC); See Section 1, #88

Toibin, Colm (Ireland)

384   *The Heather Blazing* (1992); Penguin 1994 (pbk)

Colm Toibin's second novel, a subtle yet poignant assessment of one man's life, features Irish High Court Judge Eamonn Redmond, son (and grandson) of patriots active in Ireland's historic struggle for independence. Eamonn's Ireland is a very different place and he is of the generation whose job it is to "put the djinn of nationalist feeling back into the bottle" (*TLS*) so as to get on with the everyday business of nation-building. Toibin sets his novel on the Irish coast where Eamonn spends his summers lost, with greater and greater frequency, in reverie.

Novelist **Alice McDermott** (*WPBW*) observes that Toibin's novel "proceeds with stately grace, from past to present, incident to incident, slowly forming, as it moves, the full shape of a man's public and private life ... And ... manages to discover in him a depth of feeling that is as frightening and as beautiful as the relentless sea." In the view of Irish novelist Julia O'Faolain (*TLS*), "Fiction glorifies outcasts, but societies consist of those within; Redmonds rather than Daedluses. Though the sobriety with which Toibin rightly presents his pillar of the community makes this a less seductive novel than [his debut novel] *The South*, it has more to tell about today's hidden Ireland." The *Christian Science Monitor* concludes that "Toibin, who is rapidly emerging as a principal Irish writer, writes with a good deal of humor. The book laughs at it-

self." The *Voice Literary Supplement* was similarly impressed, pointing out that "One of the book's surprises is its subtle humor, its awareness of small ironies."

RECOGNITION: *NYTBR* Notable Book of 1993; REVIEWS: *BL* 1/15/93; *CSM* 3/17/93; *KR* 11/15/92; *LATBR* 6/13/93; *LJ* 2/1/93; *NYTBR* 3/14/93; *PW* 11/23/92; *TLS* 9/4/92; *VLS* 2/93; *WPBW* 1/31/93

385   *The South* (1990); Viking 1992 (pbk)

In his debut novel Colm Toibin tells the story of Katherine Proctor, a wealthy Irishwoman who, consumed with a desire to pursue the unfettered life of an artist (far from the particular constrictions of 1950s Ireland), flees to Barcelona leaving her husband, her child, and her country behind. Katherine's flight is universally perceived to be the act of a madwoman. While in Spain, Katherine meets and falls in love with a Catalan anarchist, a veteran of the Civil War. She also falls into a relationship with Michael Graves, a Catholic Irishman from the wrong side of the tracks.

The *London Review of Books* points out that the "story is told with spare, simple elegance, from Katherine's point of view. She certainly has a painter's eye, but she is not one to discuss motivation or to make connections — between Ireland and Spain, for instance, with their civil wars: the reader must do that." According to the *Washington Post Book World*, Toibin's "talent is amazing. His skilled short hand technique for turning Spain into Ireland and Ireland into Spain, has birthed a stunning, and very particular novel." The *Library Journal,* in its starred review, calls it an "exceptional novel [which] has the unusual quality of taking Irish material, allegedly unique, and making it European, a matter of significance on the brink of the '92 European Community."

RECOGNITION: Winner of the *Irish Times* Aer-Lingus Literature Prize 1991; REVIEWS: *ChiTrib* 10/20/91; *IrishT* 9/7/91; *KR* 6/15/91; *LJ* 7/91; *LRB* 10/11/90; *NYTBR* 9/15/91; *PW* 7/5/91; *WPBW* 9/22/91

Torrington, Jeff (UK)

386   *Swing Hammer, Swing* (1992); Harcourt Brace 1995 pbk)

Jeff Torrington's Whitbread Prize–winning debut novel (which takes place during the span of one week in 1969) is set in "the Gorbals" a working-class neighborhood in Glasgow and features slum-dwelling Tam Clay, an unemployed, would-be novelist whose first child is on the way. Tam is fast approaching meltdown, and the fact that there are bulldozers parked in the street below, waiting to demolish his apartment block (his neighborhood has been designated a "redevelopment area" by the city government) doesn't help matters. Meanwhile, someone is moving about the city passing himself off as Clay and making ominous inquiries. Jeff Torrington worked on this novel for thirty years before finally publishing it to widespread acclaim.

According to *Publishers Weekly* "Here a new landscape stamps itself indelibly onto the literary map: the infamous Glasgow slum called the Gorbals, in whose ripe decaying airs Torrington's intoxicated and intoxicating debut is steeped…." The *Library Journal* observes that "What plot exists is subservient to vignette, but, in the tradition of Joyce, the language is rich and colorful" and further points out that this book is "not for the average U.S. fiction reader, especially with its heavy use of regionalisms." Michael Dirda (*WPBW*) suggests that *Swing Hammer Swing* "is probably too odd a book, too male and too Glaswegian, to achieve best-sellerdom in this country [as it did in Great Britain]" but states he would be unsurprised "if it became a kind of cult, admired and quoted and reread to pieces." *Booklist* argues that "Torrington [like Joyce, Pynchon and Rushdie] has a beautifully barbed wit and a fabulous ear for language…. Writers this good, writing in the English language, can almost be counted on the fingers of one hand."

RECOGNITION: Winner of the 1992 Whitbread First Novel Award and the Scottish Arts Council Award; REVIEWS: *BL* 4/15/94; *LJ* 3/1/94; *LRB* 7/8/93; *NS&S* 8/14/92; *NYTBR* 5/1/94; *Obs* 1/31/93; *PW* 3/28/94; *TLS* 1/1/93; *WPBW* 5/22/94

Trapido, Barbara (UK)

387   *Temples of Delight* (1990); Grove/Atlantic 1992 (pbk)

In her 3rd novel (judged a "delightful reading experience" by the *Library Journal*), Barbara Trapido tells the story of the friendship between quiet, well-bred Alice Piling and Jem McCrail, a gifted free-spirit and the product of a family in perpetual emotional and financial disarray. They meet when Jem is enrolled, at mid-term, in Alice's characteristically stuffy English girl's school. Alice is immediately drawn to the delightfully mendacious Jem whose coping mechanisms include the ability to filter the mundane on painful elements of life through a finely chiseled romantic prism. The heretofore sheltered Alice soon learns the "joys of unconventionality" which, while enriching her life, complicate it as well. When the feckless Jem disappears, Alice is determined to find her, if not today, than surely tomorrow. Thematic elements from Mozart's *The Magic Flute* are sprinkled throughout the narrative.

The *New York Times Book Review* observes that *The Temples of Delight* is "written with an authority and ease that verge on casualness" and concludes that Ms. Trapido's novel "celebrates imagi-

nation in fiction and in life." According to the *Times Literary Supplement*, Ms. Trapido's novel "gives no comfort to those for whom her elegant combination of social comedy and implied morality-play has always given off a faint whiff of bad faith … The plot involves not one, but four independent major pieces of forgery — not so much a post-modern gesture towards problems of textuality as much as a demonstration of the subtle working of Grace. That whiff of bad faith is almost disguised by the incense: Trapido seems to be saying, in this entertaining dance of the amoral and the pietistic, that happiness can only be achieved through elegant lies." In the view of the *L.A. Times Book Review*, "As tricky as a master composer, Trapido has taken us on a spiritual journal right through the dark forest of lost friendships and broken hearts, out into the sunshine of renewal. It is, Jem would say, 'Very deeply to do with the nature of your being.'" *Kirkus Reviews* concludes that *Temples of Delight* is "One of those amiably literate British novels, with modest intellectual pretensions, vivid characters, and a creaky, but engaging plot … an eminently satisfying read."

REVIEWS: *KR* 8/15/91; *LATBR* 10/20/91; *LJ* 9/15/91; *LRB* 9/90; *NYTBR* 12/29/91; *PW* 8/16/91; *TLS* 11/9/90

Trevor, William (UK/Ireland)

388   *Two Lives* (1991); Viking Penguin 1997 (pbk re-issue)

Two Lives is made up of two novellas: "Reading Turgenev," the story of a woman driven mad by the absence of love in her marriage and "My House in Umbria" which concerns an overweight "romance" writer living in Umbria who becomes entangled with the survivors of a terrible accident in which she was also involved.

According to novelist Julia O'Faolain (*TLS*) *Two Lives* is "the umbrella title for a brace of novellas which turn on a common theme: fantasy filtering into a woman's life to replace, and perhaps redeem it. The lives are harsh and the dream-doses powerful. Side-effects wreak havoc and the women end up a little mad. The question left simmering is whether this is a mercy." In the opinion of Michael Gorra (*WPBW*), "*My House in Umbria* is not as successful on its own terms as *Reading Turgenev*; Mrs. Delahunty's rage for order is perhaps too easily seen through, though that is also the source of its pathos. But the echoes between these two long tales makes *Two Lives* as a whole stronger than either would have been on its own, and one of this great writer's best books."

RECOGNITION: Shortlisted for the 1991 Booker Prize and the *London Sunday Express* Book of the Year; *NYTBR* "Editors' Choice" 1991; *Publishers Weekly* "Best Books" of 1991; REVIEWS: *ChiTrib*

9/15/91; *IrishT* 6/1/91; *LitRev* 5/91; *NYTBR* 9/8/91; *TLS* 5/31/91; *WPBW* 8/18/91

Trollope, Joanna (UK)

389   *A Spanish Lover* (1993); Random House 1997 (HC); Berkley 1998 (pbk)

In Joanna Trollope's 12th novel, set in both England and Spain, twin sisters come to grips with the declining fortunes of one and the emotional ascendancy of the other. The decidedly soapy plot features Frances — the single twin, and owner of a small travel agency who has long-envied her sister Lizzie's happy marriage, large family and successful antique business. Frances, on a trip to Seville, meets and falls in love with a married Spaniard, and, stimulated by their affair, begins to blossom. Meanwhile, Lizzie and her husband suffer severe financial reversals.

According to *Publishers Weekly* "Stepping away from her usual provinces and into more cosmopolitan territory, Trollope delivers an insightful and thoroughly engrossing story of 39-year-old twin sisters whose lives and fortunes change dramatically in the course of a year…. With sparkling dialogue Trollope manages to bring all her characters, adults and children, to full life while managing to bestow unforgettable glimpses of Spain in all its melancholy and magnificence." The *London Sunday Times* suggests that "the *Spanish Lover* while it does not break the pattern of paunchy chauvinistic heroes and quietly rebellious women, is a highly enjoyable book to read, full of perceptive observations and imbued with a refreshing irony." *A Spanish Lover* was recommended "with enthusiasm" by *WPBW* columnist, Jonathan Yardley, in his year-end review.

RECOGNITION: *LATBR* "Recommended Title" 1997; nominated for the *London Express* "Book of the Year" (a book prize which celebrates "readability"); REVIEWS: *BL* 2/1/97; *ChiTrib* 2/23/97; *KR* 11/1/96; *LATBR* 3/3/97; *LitRev* 5/93; *LJ* 12/96; *LST* 5/30/93; *LT* 7/19/93; *NS&S* 7/9/93; *PeopleW* 2/10/97; *PW* 12/9/96; *WPBW* 1/22/97

390   *The Men and the Girls* (1992); Avon 1995 (pbk)

Joanna Trollope sets *The Men and the Girls* in Oxford where two long-time friends (both in their early 60s) live with their much-younger wives. As the novel opens, James Mallow, a journalist, is happily married to Kate, while his old friend Hugh, a handsome TV personality, lives nearby with his wife Julia and his two young sons. Into this blissful circle comes the irascible Beatrice Batchelor who sets the wives to thinking about their personal "accommodations."

Publishers Weekly points out that "Underlying the novel's richly orchestrated movement of leave-takings and homecomings is the view that a loving, cozy home life — whether rowdy or serene — is a blessing to be trifled with at one's peril." *Kirkus Reviews* concludes that Ms. Trollope has written "One of those rare novels that can claim the high middle-ground where wisdom, wit, and literate characters meet to tell an entertaining — and all-around fulfilling — story." In the view of Jonathan Yardley (*WPBW*), Ms. Trollope "is, as you may well have hoped, Trollopian … in sensitivity to social nuance and in strength of characterization. If she has a bit of penchant for the soap-operatics, well, so too did her distant kinsman; she neutralizes it, though, with a touch of the irreverent and by simply being very good." The *Chicago Tribune* concludes that "The author has a wonderful knack for authenticity. It's no small feat to make the rarefied atmosphere of Oxford ring true without sounding brittle or elitist."

OTHER MEDIA: Audiocassette (Chivers/ unabr); REVIEWS: *BL* 10/1/93; *ChiTrib* 10/24/93; *KR* 7/15/93; *LATBR* 10/15/93; *LST* 4/26/92; *LT* 4/25/92; *NY* 9/27/93; *NYTBR* 10/17/93; *PW* 8/9/93; *WPBW* 10/6/93

Welch, Robert (Ireland)

391   *Groundwork* (1998); Dufour 1998 (HC)

Poet and critic Robert Welch has constructed an affecting family saga around two Irish families, the Condons and the O'Dwyers who are, it would seem, born to struggle. The author weaves his multi-threaded story through four centuries, with the bulk of the narrative taking place in the early half of the 20th. His themes incorporate the epic conflict between the Irish and their British "masters" as well as the personal pursuit of love and happiness.

Booklist calls *Groundwork* "literature of the first rank, revealing a fiction born of the clash between history and legend" and concludes that the book's "ultimate power is derived from the chorus of narrative voices: most of the characters like true Irish bards, step forward and tell stories of their lives that shaped them as men and women, and incidentally, connect them to the larger histories of their families and country." According to the *New York Times Book Review* "Robert Welch intends nothing less than to distill into 200 pages of fiction the essence of the Irish experience over the past 400 years … and has succeeded brilliantly." The *Irish Times* concludes that *Groundwork* "which is so aware of history as a certain blend of personal, tribal and national narratives, provides us with the opportunity to blend these narratives in our own ways while also providing us with a few strong characters who create their own histories."

RECOGNITION: *NYTBR* Notable Book of

1998; REVIEWS: *BL* 4/1/98; *IrishT* 10/10/98; *KR* 3/1/98; *NYTBR* 6/7/98; *PW* 2/23/98

Williams, Niall (Ireland)

392 *The Four Letters of Love* (1997); FS&G 1997 (HC); Little Brown 1998 (pbk)

In his debut novel, Niall Williams tells two loosely intertwined stories. The first features William Coughlin, a Dublin Civil Servant who, quite unexpectedly, announces to his family that he is quitting his job in the city and moving to an isolated spot on the West Coast of Ireland to become an artist. Within a few years, the family is destitute and William's despondent wife (who has been left in Dublin with her young son Nicholas) commits suicide. The second story features Isobel Gore, an innocent young woman who lives on a remote island near Galway Bay. Her father, Muiris Gore, is a school teacher and frustrated poet whose own family has suffered greatly due to an accident which has left his son, Sean, in a near-coma. Isabel, who had been with her brother at the time of the accident, still feels responsible many years later. The two families are linked through the agency of one of William Coughlin's painting (his only successful work), which had been awarded to Muiris Gore, first-place winner in a regional poetry contest. Coughlin eventually commits suicide by burning down his home and studio, and all of his paintings are destroyed, except, of course, for his masterpiece which is still in the possession of the Gore family. William's son, Nicholas, hoping to buy the painting back, sets off for the Gore's island home. Upon his arrival, he meets Isabel, recently married but already deeply unhappy. Nicholas's presence on the island has an unsettling but, in the end, salubrious effect on one and all.

The *Library Journal*, in its starred review, observes that, in *Four Letter of Love*, "the two stories meet and blend beautifully." According to *Kirkus Reviews* Williams "spellbinding" and "brilliant" novel offers "a powerful portrait of tragedy and of the redemptive power of love." The *Christian Science Monitor*, while pointing out that towards "the end ... Williams' mysticism goes into overdrive" concludes that "there are many lovely and truthful things in this novel that far outweigh its mildly irritating mannerisms." Richard Eder, Book Editor of the *L.A. Times*, would agree, arguing further that "Williams uses language, as he does his miracles, to adorn a story which, had he trusted it more, might have had more resonance." *The* (London) *Guardian* call it "lyrical and passionate" and "strangely old-fashioned" and ultimately "a brave, flawed debut."

OTHER MEDIA: Audiocassette (Books-on-Tape/unabr); RECOGNITION: Shortlisted for the 1997 Booker Prize; *NYTBR* Notable Book of 1997;

Publishers Weekly "Best Books" of 1997; REVIEWS: *ChiTrib* 10/27/97; *ComW* 12/19/97; *CSM* 2/11/98; *Guard* 9/21/97; *KR* 7/1/97; *LATBR* 9/14/97; *LJ* 7/97; *LST* 8/17/97; *NYTBR* 11/9/97; *PW* 6/23/97; *TLS* 9/5/97

Wilson, Robert McLiam (Ireland)

393 *Eureka Street* (1996); Arcade 1997 (pbk)

In his third novel, the first to be set primarily in Ireland, Robert McLiam Wilson tells the story of Jake Jackson, a Catholic and a former bouncer who is looking to both improve himself and (with any luck) find a new girlfriend. Jake's story intersects with that of Chuckie Lurgan's — a Protestant from Eureka Street and Jake's best friend, who is also on the make, but much more successfully so. Wilson's story is set in the months preceding and immediately following Belfast's first (and therefore grandly historic) IRA cease-fire.

Publishers Weekly observes that Wilson demonstrates "a satirical sensibility that favors broadness over poignancy" and concludes that the author's "sheer exuberance saves this winning story of two men and a community at odds with itself." According to *Kirkus Reviews* the "plot twists are over the top at times, but the characters are genuine, often funny, and Wilson's evident love for the long-suffering city itself is an inspired thread that binds the story gloriously together." The *Times Literary Supplement* calls "*Eureka Street* a "sprawling, exuberant novel [which] empathizes with [Belfast's] vulnerable mass of people" and concludes that the author "has created a novel of ambitious scope and compelling power ... marking a new level of accomplishment in an already formidable writer."

REVIEWS: *KR* 8/15/97; *LJ* 9/1/97; *NS* 8/23//96; *NYTBR* 12/14/97; *PW* 9/1/96; *Spec* 11/16/96; *TLS* 8/23/96

THE FORMER BRITISH EMPIRE OR COMMONWEALTH

This third part of Section 4 gathers novelists from the far-flung reaches of the former British Empire: from Australia and New Zealand, where indigenous and colonial literatures have evolved vigorous new ways of describing and interpreting the world (Peter Carey, Alan Duff, Thomas Keneally, David Malouf); from English-speaking Africa (Simi Bedford, Mark Behr, Abdulrazak Gurnah, Ben Okri) and the Carribbean (Dionne Brand, Jamaica Kincaid, Wilson

Harris); and from post-colonial India, Pakistan and Sri Lanka (Vikram Chandra, Anita Desai, Romesh Gunesekera, Salman Rushdie) where English is often a second or even third language, but where writers are creating new forms of English expression startling in their power and beauty.

AUSTRALIA AND NEW ZEALAND

Adams, Glenda (Australia/New Zealand)

394   *The Tempest of Clemenza* (1995); Faber & Faber 1996 (HC)

In her fourth novel, award-winning Australian author Glenda Adams tells the gothic-tinged story of a mother and her terminally ill 13-year-old daughter who, as the story opens, are ensconced in a cabin on a lake in Vermont. The pair (Abel and Clemenza) has fled their native Australia, for reasons which will be revealed later in the tale. One night, as a violent storm roils the lake waters and rattles their windows, a strange woman bursts into their cabin demanding to know if they are in possession of a certain manuscript. They plead ignorance and the intruder departs, leaving Abel and Clemenza thoroughly mystified. Soon after, Abel finds a manuscript — the 1956 diary of a young Australian by the name of Cordelia Benn — at the bottom of a pile of recently purchased used books. Intrigued and delighted by this discovery, Clemenza asks her mother to read it to her. Interleaved within the diary — which is filled with descriptions of a happy adolescence in Australia — is a mystery/adventure yarn authored by the young diarist. Into this unusual narrative mix, Adams inserts a series of flashbacks: to Abel's disastrous marriage, Clemenza's unhappy childhood and a the shocking events which explain their flight from Australia. Described by more than one reviewer as having a structure like "nesting Russian dolls," Ms. Adam's artful story unfolds in a series of interlocking vignettes.

Kirkus Reviews calls *The Tempest of Clemenza* "a haunting and compelling work" in which the narrative threads "move [together] seamlessly ... foreshadowing the events of Abel's life until Abel and Clemenza's own unhappy story is finally told." According to the *Library Journal* this is an "absorbing and moody novel which opens to reveal succeeding layers of finely detailed prose." The *Australian Book Review* concludes that "the most appealing sections of [Adams'] new novel are the extended episodes set in the Sydney of 1956, that recent, very ordinary world which seems to grow more and more exotic with the passing of each year.... A particular strength of these pages is that

they steer a confident path between the ever-present dangers of nostalgia and condescension."

RECOGNITION: Winner of the 1996 Miles Franklin Award for Fiction; REVIEWS: *AusBkRev* 4/96; *Econ* 11/16/96; *KR* 8/1/96; *LJ* 9/15/96; *PW* 8/12/96

395   *Longleg* (1990); Cane Hill 1992 (pbk)

It took William Badger some time to understand that he was going to be left behind, deliberately abandoned, what seemed like a thousand miles from home. His mother had simply asked if he would like a nice seaside holiday and he had said yes.

So begins Glenda Adams third novel, a moving story of maternal abandonment, self discovery and, finally, emotional healing. The story opens in Australia in the late 1940s, when William's mother "the youngest, prettiest mother in the world" returned, without warning or farewell, to England, leaving him in the care of his embittered, middle-aged father. *Longleg* follows the solemn, over-anxious little boy as he matures into a repressed, well-meaning young man and finally into an adult capable of love.

Kirkus Reviews, while pointing out that there may be one too many "coincidences and predictable revelations," concludes that *Longleg* "is probably Adams' most successful book thanks to brisk, vivid prose, and the sort of bumbling yet valiant hero that readers love to root for." Novelist John Crowley (*NYTBR*) while observing that there "is little in *Longleg* that sounds unfamiliar in summary: an unusually sensitive, unassertive child, whose sensitivity is heightened unbearably by the unintelligible cruelties of adults" concludes that the "delightful quality of the novel ... lies in the telling." The *Australian Book Review* suggests that *Longleg* "doesn't have the exuberance or so much of the wickedly barbed wit of [some of Ms. Adams earlier works] but it shares [with them] an unerring sense of time and [particularly Australian] place."

RECOGNITION: Winner of the 1991 Australian Age Book of the Year Award and the National Council Award; REVIEWS: *Age* 9/15/90; *AusBkRev* 9/90; *CSM* 8/26/92; *KR* 5/1/92; *NYTBR* 9/3/92; *PW* 6/15/92

Anderson, Barbara (New Zealand)

396   *Portrait of the Artist's Wife* (1992); WW Norton 1993 (HC)

The artist of the title is Jack Macalaster, a charming, philandering, critically acclaimed novelist married for more than forty years to Sarah Tandy a fiercely independent and accomplished artist. The story opens in the late 1980s with Sarah delivering a eulogy for her late husband at a gathering in honor of his last, posthumously published work. The story then moves back in time to the late 1940s, a period when (particularly in New

Zealand) "men did the work and women had the babies." Childhood friends and then lovers, Jack and Sarah find themselves (given Sarah's accidental pregnancy) facing a marriage for which neither is particularly desirous of or prepared for. Equally strong-willed and ambitious, they vow to continue with his writing and her painting, no matter what.

Belles Lettres observes that the author "concentrates our attention across the years on these two artists bonded by birth, accident, design of codependence ... [and their] tension and triumph are fascinating to witness." According to the *Times Literary Supplement* the "myths implicit in this narrative ... are well-known: growing up, the young country, the integrity of art, having babies versus painting pictures, the wisdom of the old world. [However, what] Anderson does with them is quite original." *Publishers Weekly* concludes that "Anderson weaves together events of several decades in a seamless, succinct narrative that captures both the simplicity and the complexity of the character's life."

RECOGNITION: Winner of the 1992 Wattie Award; REVIEWS: *BellesL* Fall 1993; *KR* 2/15/93; *LRB* 8/6/92; *Obs* 7/14/92; *PW* 3/15/93; *TLS* 6/12/92

Astley, Thea (Australia)

397   *Coda* (1993); Putnam 1994 (HC)
Kathleen Hackendorf, an elderly woman who's been pushed to the brink by uncaring, manipulative children — her daughter, who leans on her for childcare, wants to install her in a retirement villa called "Passing Downs" — and by the indignities of the aging process itself, has time on her hands and she spends much of it pondering her options. Kathleen may be getting a bit foggy ("rooting about for words in that old handbag of her years"), but she's sure of one thing, she's sick to death of being patronized and she will not, under any circumstances, be "corpsed at in the local retirement community." Kathleen, homeless by choice, takes to wandering among the malls and coffee shops, a "feral grandmother" with no intention of going quietly into that dark night.

As *Booklist* observes "Astley's high regard in her native Australia is understandable after reading this taut, compelling new novel about a strong-minded widow not yet ready to concede defeat and bow to the realities of her fading memory and the physical limitations of an aging body." According to the *Washington Post Book World* "like Muriel Spark's *Memento Mori*, *Coda* casts a ruthlessly unsentimental, satiric eye on the ravages of mortality." *Kirkus Reviews* calls *Coda* "A spare, sharp-boned bird of a novel, whose song is wrenchingly sad yet full of indomitable spirit" and concludes that "Ashley is a marvelous writer and a hilarious, merciless,

and poignant truth-teller." Novelist Beverly Lowry (*NYTBR*) referring to Kathleen's final stand, concludes that "It's a terrifically satisfying victory, one that the redoubtable Thea Astley pulls off with characteristic skill and compassion."

RECOGNITION: Nominated for the 1993 *Age* Book of the Year Award; *NYTBR* Notable Book of 1994; REVIEWS: *AusBkRev* 2-3/94; *BL* 10/1/94; *KR* 8/1/94; *NYTBR* 10/2/94; *PW* 8/15/94; *WPBW* 10/2/94

Bail, Murray (Australia)

Eucalyptus (1998); FS&G 1998 (HC); See Section 3, #171

Brett, Lily (Germany/Australia)

398   *What God Wants* (1991); Birch Lane 1993 (HC)
Lily Brett was born in Germany but has long made her home in Australia which is where she has set her second work of fiction, a collection of interlocking stories featuring the children of Holocaust survivors. Revolving around the themes of family, sex, love, and what it means to be Jewish, the stories paint a colorful portrait of a Jewish community in contemporary Melbourne, Australia. The Birch Lane edition is illustrated by the author's husband David Rankin.

In the view of *Publishers Weekly* the women "in these [wryly comic] tales shine with originality and strength.... Each has her own individual problems [often created by the man in her life] but they share subtle self-imposed barriers: each stifles her anger, distrusts the consequences of happiness and feels an overwhelming need to keep the family together" According to the *Library Journal* Ms. Brett's "storytelling is skillful, the scenarios are raunchy, and the Jewish community is portrayed as less than exemplary." The *Australian Book Review* asserts that "Brett is a serious comic. Her surgical bent, her dissection of superficially well-ordered, mundane suburban life and the pedestrians that make their way through it, is tempered by an eye for the absurd and for the plain funny."

RECOGNITION: Winner of Australia's 1992 National Steel Award; REVIEWS: *AusBkRev* 10/91; *KR* 7/1/93; *LJ* 8/93; *PW* 7/19/93

Carey, Peter (Australia)

Jack Maggs (1997); Knopf 998 (HC); See Section 8, #995

The Unusual Life of Tristan Smith (1994); Vintage 1996 (pbk); See Section 3, #186

399   *The Tax Inspector* (1991); Vintage 1993 (pbk)
The day Benny Catchprice was fired from the

spare-parts department of Catchprice Motors by his Aunt Cathy was also the day that tax inspector Maria Takis arrived to begin her over-due audit of the family business. Peter Cary sets his wry and violent story (with overtones of incest and abuse) in a Sydney suburb in the late 1940s.

According to *Booklist*, "That this remarkable novel is both harrowing and funny, and that we come to care deeply about what happens to the Catchprices, is all the more striking for its being set in this cramped, oily space." As the *Literary Review* observes "You don't expect her to be pretty, Greek, eight months pregnant, sexy *and* a tax inspector. She — her name is Maria Takis — does not expect, when she visits Catchprice Motors ... to be exposed to almost everything about the Catchprice family apart from their accounts ... [However, in] Peter Carey's original, outstanding ... novel, expectation is constantly overthrown." In the view of novelist Edmund White (*TLS*) "Carey's triumph is that he doesn't ever turn his eccentrics into grotesques. We experience everything so intimately from several points of view that we scarcely judge any one at all.... This suspension of moral discrimination is brought to our appalled attention only at the end of the book."

RECOGNITION: "Best of Books" Australian Book Scene 1989; REVIEWS. *AusBkRev* 8/91; *BL* 1/15/92; *LATBR* 12/29/91; *LitRev* 9/91; *LRB* 9/12/91; *NYRB* 6/25/92; *NYT* 1/16/92; *NYTBR* 1/12/92; *TLS* 8/30/91; *WPBW* 2/2/92

400   *Oscar & Lucinda* (1988); Harper-Collins 1989 (pbk)

In Peter Carey's Booker Prize–wining novel, an Oxford seminarian (and passionate gambler) meets a Sydney glassworks heiress (with a similar predilection) on a boat to Australia. The story — set for the most part in late 19th-century Australia — concerns the transportation of a glass church through the wilds of Australia, and features Oscar (a compulsive red-headed, hydrophobic, man-of-the-cloth) and Lucinda (a highly intelligent and head-strong young woman) is told with Carey's characteristic ebullience and off-beat artistry. Peter Carey has been called by many reviewers the finest Australian novelist since Patrick White.

According to the *Spectator* "As a piece of historic reconstruction, the novel is impressive.... As a piece of writing, the novel is no less impressive. It has a Dickensian amplitude; and the energy of its writing — similes and metaphors jostle one another, giving off a baleful phosphorescence, like the Medusas of the Indian Ocean about the ship on its way to Australia — is also Dickensian." In the view of the *New Statesman*, *Oscar & Lucinda* "takes pride in its limitless powers of incidental accumulation ... the short chapters begin midway through a scene and gradually, like someone walking back up a

down escalator, make their way back to the beginning." The *London Sunday Times* observes that *Oscar & Lucinda* bursts "with informed gusto, freewheeling comedy, pauses of pathos and moments of surreal poetry ... [a veritable] explosion of delight at life's wayward, diverse plentifulness."

OTHER MEDIA: A film version starring Ralph Fiennes was released in 1997; Audio cassette recording (Random Audio/abr); RECOGNITION: Winner of the 1988 Booker Prize and the Miles Franklin Award; REVIEWS: *ChiTrib* 6/19/88; *LitRev* 4/88; *LRB* 4/21/88; *LST* 5/10/88; *NS* 4/1/88; *NYTBR* 5/29/88; *Spec* 4/2/88

401   *Bliss* (1981); Vintage 1996 (pbk reissue)

Bliss, Peter Carey's much-lauded (recently reissued) early comic novel, tells the fable-like tale of Harry Joy, a successful businessman and complacently happy husband and father. While mowing his lawn on a sunny weekend afternoon, he suffers a sudden heart attack, complete with a heart-stopping, near-death experience. While his temporarily un-moored spirit floats free of his body, Harry glimpses "the worlds of pleasure and worlds of pain, bliss and punishment, Heaven and Hell." When he regains consciousness he finds his life strangely altered.

The *British Book News* calls *Bliss* a "rich, rewarding novel, crisply written, daringly conceived [and] brilliantly achieved." The *Quill & Quire* observes that "Carey uses coarse elements of farce — elephants that sit on cars, funny waiters, or wives and lovers caught *flagrante delicto* ... with a stylish insouciance." The *Spectator* concludes that "in all its misery and happiness and in the profundity of his insight into moral dilemmas, Mr. Carey makes the works of most of our "promising" young and not so young novelists seem tinselly and trivial."

RECOGNITION: Winner of the Miles Franklin Literary Award, the National Book Council Award and the New South Wales Premier's Award; nominated for the 1981 *Age* Book of the Year Award; REVIEWS: *LJ* 2/15/82; *NewsWk* 4/19/82; *NS* 11/20/81; *NY* 8/23/82; *Q&Q* 7/82; *Spec* 12/12/81; *TLS* 5/3/85; *VLS* 2/82; *WPBW* 5/2/82

Davison, Liam (Australia)

402   *The White Woman* (1994); UQP 1995 (pbk)

In 1846, Melbourne newspapers headlined the story of a private expedition which — with much hoopla and fanfare — was heading off into the bush to rescue a white woman rumored to be held by a group of aborigines. The "brave adventurers" under the command of Christian De Villiers (recently resigned from the notorious native police) were propelled by the need to save this unknown woman from the "horror of captivity." Liam Davison, using actual events as a springboard, constructs a haunting and profoundly disturbing novel about the nature of civilization, the fear of the unknown, racism and the imperatives of power.

According to *The* (Melbourne) *Age* owning up to "the dark side of the history of settlement, the 'things that couldn't be uttered ,' is another process of reclamation for European Australians.... [And with this novel] Davison seems to be reminding us all that the 'past is never dead; it's not even past.'" The *Australian Book Review* observes that *The White Woman* "is meant to be more than a story, meant to move us away from where we are to some poetic destination, away from the fixed, the definable, the literal and to touch deeper resonances."

RECOGNITION: Nominated for the *Age* Book of the Year Award; REVIEWS: *AusB&P* 8/94; *AusBkRev* 10/94; *The Age* 10/1/94

Drewe, Robert (Australia)

403 *The Drowner* (1997); St. Martin's 1997 (HC)

In his fifth novel, Robert Drewe tells the story of Will Dance, a young Englishman with an affinity for water. The son of a famous "drowner" (who made his living creating dewponds and meadowlands) Will, naturally enough, has embarked on a career as a water engineer. While still a young man, he meets — in the regenerative baths at Bath — and falls in love with, Angelica Lord, an aspiring actress with a troubled childhood. They marry and soon move to Australia where Will has been hired to construct a water pipeline to feed the newly discovered goldfields.

According to the *Times Literary Supplement The Drowner* "is an ambitious piece of work, by turns a love story, something of a *Boys Own* adventure, a meditation on the various powers and properties of water and an examination of the 'elemental' qualities that distinguish the sexes." *Kirkus Reviews* observes that "Will and Angelica, their life riven by undercurrents ... have to face their demons by bringing water to the desert" and concludes that Drewe's novel is "Clever, informative, exquisite in sensibility but cool in sentiment." In the view of the *London Times.* "This is not an easy read. Robert Drewe's style is as elusive as it is fluid, but it is worth the effort. Evocative and moving, *The Drowner* is spellbinding."

REVIEWS: *KR* 8/1/97; *LJ* 10/1/97; *LST* 6/15/97; *LT* 7/11/98 (pbk review); *PW* 9/8/97; *TLS* 7/4/97

Duff, Alan (New Zealand)

404 *One Night Out Stealing* (1992); Univ. of Hawaii 1995 (pbk)

Alan Duff's second novel takes a raw look at New Zealand's underclass — heavily weighted with individuals of Maori descent — which has been mired for decades in a culture of poverty and violence. Duff's story is centered around Sonny, a substance-abusing, part–Maori teenager with an alcoholic mother and a brutal father. Sonny, a fairly gentle soul despite his history of abuse, has drifted in and out of prison as he half-heartedly pursues a life of petty crime. When he joins forces with Jube, a particularly vicious white boy with a pathological hatred of women, things go from awful to tragic.

According to the *Australian Bookseller*, Alan Duff "has written a forceful book but one which is almost unredeemably ugly, perhaps because he chooses to spend so much time on Jube and explicit rape scenes which tip nastily towards the voyeuristic. However, as in his first book, there is a compelling plot and the feeling that Duff is offering a grimly authentic look at a miserable world." *World Literature Today* calls *One Night Out Stealing* "a frankly harrowing ... engrossing saga of two criminals, Sonny and Jube, mired in a hopeless cycle of abuse, petty crime, drink, drugs, and lovelessness" and concludes that in it Duff offers a "harrowing exegesis of what it means to fester in the crude savagery of a social and racial, criminal lumpen proletariat some see as a creation of recent New Right political philosophy."

REVIEWS: *AusB&P* 10/92; *NYTBR* 12/7/95; *PW* 10/30/91; *WLT* Sum '93

405 *Once Were Warriors* (1990); Vintage Books 1995 (pbk)

Alan Duff's debut novel — when published in New Zealand in 1990 — raised some very troubling issues, chief among them was the proposition that the Maoris who, as a group, occupy the lowest rung of New Zealand society, were, to some degree, responsible for their plight. *Once Were Warriors* focuses on the Hekes's a Maori family consisting of Jake and Beth and their three children. They have lived for as long as any of them can remember, in a squalid urban housing project where their lives have been blighted by alcohol, gang violence, and despair. Beth in particular has had a rough go of it as she is the victim of Jake's frequent, and unspeakably brutal, alcohol-inspired rages. Duff, eschewing sentimenatlity, does a particuarly effective job of portraying the "double oppression" of the female members of this materially and spiritually impoverished segment of New Zealand society.

According to *Publishers Weekly*, the author's "staccato prose style is ideally suited to a world of not-quite-so-quiet desperation. Regardless of one's position on the [author's controversial perspective], the half–Pakeha/half–Maori Duff provides a compelling and insightful glimpse into the overwhelming struggles faced by the disenfranchised poor of any urban society — including America's own inner cities." *World Literature Today* observes that in *Once Were Warriors* "Duff has encountered head-on, the ineluctable problems besetting colonized cultures. The colonized thirst for identity and an explanation of their predicament, hence a way out. If Duff is proposing any strategies against the cultural, political-economic juggernaut grinding his characters, when set against the horror and cruelty of their predicament, one wonders what strategy would ever suffice." The *Library Journal* concludes that *Once Were Warriors* "written in broken dialect and sprinkled liberally with coarse language allows readers to experience the raw reality of [New Zealand's Maori] society."

OTHER MEDIA: A film version starring Temeura Morrison was released in 1994; audiocassette (AudioLit/abr); RECOGNITION: Winner of the New Zealand/PEN First Book Award; REVIEWS: *KR* 5/1/94; *LJ* 6/15/94; *PW* 6/27/94; *WLT* Win '95; *WPBW* 3/26/5

Grenville, Kate (Australia)

406   *Albion's Story* (1994); HBJ 1994 (HC)
Originally published in Australia as *Dark Places*, Kate Grenville's 4th novel is a companion volume to her powerful 1984 novel, *Lilian's Story*, which was based on the life of a well-known Sydney eccentric Bea Miles. It appears that Bea, after being raped by her father while still a young girl, had been committed to a mental institution — from which she did not soon emerge. In *Albion's Story*, which is set in late 19th-century Australia, Ms. Grenville gives us Bea/Lilian's father's version, a chilling saga filled with lust and loathing.

Kirkus Reviews observes that "Australian Grenville triumphantly returns to the setting of her memorable debut novel ... to trace the development of Lilian's [appalling] father — a turn-of-the-century bourgeois whose public arrogance and private terrors wreak havoc on those he should have loved" and concludes that Grenville's "masterful, sharp-tongued portrait of an individual and an age ... is impossible to put down." The *Australian Bookseller and Publisher* calls Grenville's writing "assured, her timing impeccable and her humor all-pervading" and concludes that with this second installment of Lilian's story, she will certainly attract "a new legion of followers." According to the Australian literary journal, *Meanjin*, *Albion's Story* "is a bleak, rather nasty book, and its plentiful jokes are not pretty. It will not go down well with women who have done their best to forgive heavy-handed fathers or with men who are weak and cruel, but ... this is a powerfully conceived novel and the unspeakable matters it rehearses are made into a painful and riveting drama." The *Times Literary*

Supplement observes that *Albion's Story* "conveys the tone and attitudes of nineteenth-century repression with twentieth-century acuity" and concludes that Grenville "has not just confronted a taboo, but entered into it ... [making her novel] as disturbing as it is impressive."

RECOGNITION: Nominated for the 1995 *LATBR* Book of the Year Award; REVIEWS: *AusB&P* 5/94; *AusBkRev*7/94; *BL* 10/15/94; *KR* 8/15/94; *Meanj* Spr '94; *PW* 8/29/94; *TLS* 9/2/94

Hall, Rodney (Australia)

407   *The Grisly Wife* (1993); FS&G 1995 (pbk re-issue as *The Yandilli Trilogy*)
The Grisly Wife, the second volume (although third-published) in Rodney Hall's *Yandilli Trilogy*, is a messianic tale of delusion and faith and a shattering exploration of Australian history. The novel is narrated by Catherine, a 19th century missionary who, thirty years before the story opens, had moved from England to Australia with her husband, the dangerously unbalanced, self-styled prophet, Muley Molloch.

According to novelist Beverly Lowry (*NYTBR*), the books in the *Yandilli Trilogy* "don't depend on one another for completion or to make sense, but each one certainly adds fire, subtext and liveliness to the others. Rodney Hall is a thrillingly smart and juicy writer. It's hard to imagine not hearing him out until he finishes revealing his own catalogue of secrets too huge for indiscriminate telling." In the view of *Booklist* "this final link in the [trilogy's] chain ... displays the complexity and power of Hall's historical vision and the elegance of his composition's structure." *Publishers Weekly* asserts that "Those familiar with ... [Hall's] earlier novels ... will recognize [the author's ...] distinctive combination of magical realism, psychological penetration and astute social observation." The *Times Literary Supplement* concludes that "Hall's novel follows a trend in recent Australian fiction ... (see Carey & Malouf) which brings a magical realist imagination to bear on colonial history."

RECOGNITION: Winner of the 1994 Miles Franklin Literary Award; nominated for the 1994 Banjo Award for Fiction; *NYTBR* Notable Book of 1993; REVIEWS: *AusBkRev* 7/94; *BL* 9/15/93; *NYTBR* 9/26/93; *PW* 6/21/93; *TLS* 9/24/93

408   *The Second Bridegroom* (1991); FS&G 1995 (pbk re-issue of the *Yandilli Trilogy*)
The Second Bridegroom, the third volume (but second-published) of Rodney Hall's *Yandilli Trilogy*, is narrated by a young man from the Isle of Man who, at the age of nineteen, after being tried and (falsely) convicted of forgery, has been shipped off to the penal colony of New South Wales. The time is the 1830s — towards the end of Australia's

period of "convict transportation." When the ship is finally within sight of the shore, the young convict — opting for escape — manages to free himself, jump ship and literally swim to "freedom" in the Australian bush.

According to the *Australian Book Review* "The central figure ... is an unlikely pathfinder.... He is undersized, near-sighted, pert, convicted of what was more a prank than a crime.... Arriving in a place where nothing he knows can help him, he surrenders himself myopically to a blur of chaos ... and slips happily out of the old world into the dangerous, endangered new one." The *Times Literary Supplement* observes that "the convict's mental confusion provides the link between story and theme. Torn between two worlds, the old familiarity of English civilization, and the new familiarity of the bush, he is forced to reflect on the two, and Hall is free to introduce the manifold variations of his basic juxtaposition, chaos and order, natures and civilization, Australia and England." Calling Hall's work a "historical novel with mythic dimension" the *Australian* further observes that "Hall gives us a way of seeing the land and the clash between the traditional bush culture and the punitive convict culture with fresh eyes."

RECOGNITION: *NYTBR* Notable Book of 1991; REVIEWS: *AusBkRev* 11/91; *Australian* 5/2/91; *BL* 8/91; *LRB* 9/12/91; *NYTBR* 9/1/91; *TLS* 9/6/91; *WPBW* 9/15/91

409 *Captivity Captive* (1987); FS&G 1995 (pbk re-issue of the *Yandilli Trilogy*)

Part One of Rodney Hall's *Yandilli Trilogy*, *Captivity Captive* is based on a fragment of historical information — a brutal unsolved triple murder which occured in New South Wales at the turn of the century. According to the record of the time, Mary and Daniel Murphy lived with their ten children on an isolated farm called, ironically, "Paradise." On Boxing Day in 1898 police were summoned to the Murphy's farm where they found the murdered bodies of three siblings: 29-year-old Michael, 27-year-old Mary, and 18-year-old Ellen. The female bodies had also been violated. The behavior of the taciturn Murphys (who apparently showed neither shock nor grief) was particularly unsettling to the public, as was the fact that the case was never solved and no one was ever brought to justice. Hall has taken the few known facts and weaves around them a "blackly mesmerizing thriller" (*WPBW*). Hall's story is narrated by Patrick Murphy, brother of the victims and self-appointed family historian.

According to the *Literary Review* Hall's "writing is authentic and almost entirely convincing ... [it is also] masterful.... Lawrentian yet controlled ... " In the view of the *London Sunday Times* "*Captivity Captive* carries the momentum of a thriller,

not only from speculation about the murder, but from the complex, throttled intensity of this ravaged family, which makes the outside world, however raw, remote and innocent." Richard Eder (*LATBR*) calls Hall's writing "brilliant" and concludes that its "descriptions of the bitter and beautiful landscape, and of the shocking burden of physical labor ... are unforgettable.... Hall burns to make us see and we do see; and from time to time, our eyes fill with smoke from his unruly fire."

RECOGNITION: Winner of the Victoria Premier's Literary Award and the Vance Palmer Prize for Fiction; REVIEWS: *LATBR* 1/24/88; *Lit Rev* 3/88; *LST* 3/27/88; *NYT* 1/20/88; *NYTBR* 2/14/88; *TLS* 5/27/88; *WPBW* 4/23/89

Hospital, Janette Turner (Australia)

The Last Magician (1992); Ivy Books 1993 (pbk); See Section 6, #724

Jennings, Kate (Australia)

410 *Snake* (1996); Ecco 1997 (HC)

Australian writer and feminist Kate Jennings' first novel to be published in the United States is the story of a spectacularly bad marriage played out against the parched landscape and stifling provinciality of the post-war Australian outback. Describing life on the land in the 50s and 60s, *Snake* features Irene, the bitterly discontented and chronically unfaithful wife of Rex an almost pathologically laconic, "buttoned-up" war hero. This mismatched pair live with their children "Boy" and "Girlie" on the outskirts of a town called Progress.

The *Australian Book Review* asks: "How often do you find a book that seizes you and doesn't let go until it has finished its assault? *Snake* does that ... quite painfully and beautifully ... while teasing our fictional appetite at every turn." The *LATBR* concludes that "It's hard to believe a full-blown family tragedy can be told so wholly and so well in such small, deft snatches, but then rarely has a poet's skill at compaction been put to better use in prose."

RECOGNITION: *NYTBR* Notable Book of 1997; REVIEWS: *AusBkRev* 8/96; *BL* 4/1/97; *LATBR* 7/27/97; *LJ* 4/1/97; *NYTBR* 5/11/97; *PW* 3/10/97

Jones, Rod (Australia)

Billy Sunday (1995); H Holt 1996 (pbk); See Section 5, #587

Keneally, Thomas (Australia)

411 *A River Town* (1995); Plume 1996 (pbk)

Thomas Keneally's 21st novel is set in Kempsey, a small river town on the "lush and humid north coast of New South Wales" approximately 300 miles from Sydney. The story opens in

1898 — at the tail end of the Victorian era and shortly before Australia's Unification — as the local inhabitants prepare themselves for nationhood and a new century. Featured players include: Tim Shea, a well-meaning but blundering Irish immigrant and proprietor of the local general store; Bandy Habesh, the town's Punjabi hawker, Ernie Malcolm, an unctuous, ambitious accountant (and Shea's nemesis); Lucy (a wild child, cynical and prescient) orphaned in a tragic surrey accident on New Year's Day 1900; and the spirit of "Missy," an unidentified victim of a botched abortion whose severed head is trundled around Kempsey by police as they try to learn her identity.

According to *Booklist A River Town* is both "[r]ich in context and psychologically elegant ... a beautifully rendered tale that gains potency in reflection." *New York Times Book* calls it a "finely told novel ... fired with the passion and hidden poetry that only a sure and experienced novelist can bring to fiction." In the view of Australian novelist Janette Turner Hospital (*London Review of Books*) Keneally's orphan, Lucy is so well drawn that only "in Henry James does one encounter another such riveting portrait of cursed innocence, and Keneally's Lucy is a more vibrantly warm flesh-and-blood waif than any of the little lost souls in James." The *Australian Book Review* found Keneally's book to be "racy, informal, highly colloquial, full of oaths and swear words ... enormously energetic ... [and] a very good read."

RECOGNITION: *NYTBR* Notable Book of 1995; REVIEWS: *AusBkRev* 5/95; *BL* 3/15/95; *ChiTrib* 5/12/95; *LRB* 55/25/95; *NYTBR* 5/14/95; *TLS* 3/24/95

412   *A Woman of the Inner Sea* (1992); Plume 1994 (pbk)

The setting of Thomas Keneally's 20th novel — which purports to tell a tragic tale based in fact — ranges from Sydney's affluent Double Bay to the tiny outback town of Myambagh. *A Woman of the Inner Sea* incorporates elements of the thriller and Australian mythology within a post-modern narrative structure. Keneally teasingly provides the outline for the story on the first page:

Stricken young woman, favoured by nature and fortune, absorbs an absolutely frightful event, becomes demented, seeks vengeance and left-handedly achieves it— together with a kind of salvation and then lives on.

The "reader" to whom Mr. Keneally makes frequent asides, is then asked to collaborate with him in fleshing out the story. Additional plot elements not mentioned in the author's synopsis include: flight to the outback, a stint as a barmaid, pursuit by lawyers with divorce papers, a cataclysmic flood, and escape in the company of a peaceful, long-suffering kangaroo and his equally gentle owner.

According to the *Washington Post Book World* "Loss, retreat, and rebirth in the wilderness are plot elements as old as Biblical tradition, often so predictable that they are worn threadbare as a result. Not in Keneally's book. His story is rich, dense, sad, terrible, rowdy and improbable as Australia's own.... Keneally obviously took great pleasure in his tale and so will the reader." *Entertainment Weekly* points out that "only the wealthy young woman who told Keneally the tale of her tragic marriage and self-imposed exile in the wilds of the Australian outback could possibly know how much of the story is pure invention. For the rest of us, the sheer delight of the novel's witty and disarmingly off hand narration of an increasingly horrifying tale about cruelty, deception, and greed will have to suffice." The *Library Journal*, while acknowledging that Keneally's tale "is rich in detail," points out that "the writing can be maddeningly elliptical." The *Australian Book Review* concludes that "Within this beguiling tale, peopled with memorable characters, Keneally has achieved an amazing blend: an inquiry into the blurred territory between good and evil and a celebration of Australia hovering between past and present."

RECOGNITION: *NYTBR* Notable Book of 1992; REVIEWS: *Age* 6/20/92; *AusBkRev* 6/92; *BL* 1/15/93; *EW* 3/19/93; *KR* 1/1/93; *LATBR* 5/16/93; *LJ* 2/15/93; *NYTBR* 4/10/93; *PW* 1/18/93; *Time* 5/3/93; *TLS* 6/26/92; *WPBW* 2/28/93

Koch, Christopher J. (Australia)

Highways to a War (1994); Viking 1995 (HC); Penguin 1996 (pbk); See Section 5, #592

Malouf, David (Australia)

413   *Conversations at Curlow Creek* (1997); Setting; 19th Century New South Wales

David Malouf's 8th novel is set in the bleak highlands of western Australia in 1827. Two men are waiting for the dawn: Daniel Carney, an illiterate Irishman who has been convicted of fomenting rebellion among the native population and sentenced to death and Michael Adair, the soldier in charge of his execution. The two men share an Irish childhood but come from very different social strata. As they talk, Michael begins to suspect that the dead leader of Daniel's rebel group, may be a beloved boyhood friend. Daniel and Michael's conversation is wide ranging and lasts all night.

Publishers Weekly, in its starred review, observes that "Malouf ... raises existential question about moral order and justice, depicts the contrast between rich and poor in Ireland and Australia and lyrically describes the landscapes of both countries and the spirits that abide there." According to *Li-*

brary Journal, "As usual Malouf's breathtaking prose — both daring and absolutely apt — gets right to the heart of things." In the view of the *Times Literary Supplement*, "One of the most impressive things about [Malouf's novel] is the way the primary philosophical interests are incorporated into the events; it is like Hemingway rewritten by Proust." Australian novelist, Janette Turner Hospital (*London Review of Books*) concludes that "despite [a certain] softness at its core, the novel exerts such poetic power and such pleasures of form and such potency in the final scene at Curlow Creek ... that one must consider the work a flawed triumph."

RECOGNITION: Winner of the International IMPAC Dublin Literary Award; *LATBR* "Recommended Reading" 1997; REVIEWS: *BL* 12/1/96; *Econ* 11/16/96; *LJ* 11/15/96; *LRB* 12/12/96; *NYT* 1/22/97; *NYTBR* 1/19/97; *PW* 11/4/96; *Salon* 1/13/97; *TLS* 9/13/96; *WPBW* 3/16/97

414 *Remembering Babylon* (1993); Random House 1994 (pbk)

David Malouf sets his 7th novel in the mid-nineteenth century Australian outback. Essentially the story of a young man caught between two worlds, Gemmy, a shipwrecked British cabin boy, adopted by Australian Aborigines, is reunited with "his kind" when he wanders into a white settlement and is discovered by a group of children. The product of a horrifically deprived childhood, Gemmy had adapted easily to life with the peaceful Aborigines. His subsequent re-entry into "civilized" society, after sixteen years with "the blacks" proves more problematic. When the "in-between" creature is adopted by the McIvor's, for example, they are ostracized by the community which is repelled by this mixture of "monstrous strangeness and unwelcome likeness."

The *Times Literary Supplement* calls Malouf's prose style and narrative voice "as attractive as those of anyone writing fiction at present" and concludes that *Remembering Babylon* ... (some "inconsitencies of presentation" aside) is an "intelligent" and "distinctive" work of contemporary fiction. In view of the *Australian Book Review*, Malouf's novel is "an astonishing, horrifying, and yet finally uplifting masterpiece."

READING GROUP GUIDE; RECOGNITION: Winner of the NSW Literary Award; shortlisted for the 1993 Booker Prize and the 1994 Banjo Award for Fiction; *NYTBR* Notable Book of 1993; REVIEWS: *Age* 4/23/93; *AusBkRev* 5/93; *LRB* 6/10/93; *NS&S* 5/7/93; *NYTBR* 10/17/93; *PW* 8/9/93; *TLS* 5/7/93; *WLT* Aut '94

The Great World (1990); Random House 1993 (pbk); See Section 5, #610

McGahan, Andrew (Australia)

415 *1988* (1996); St. Martin's 1996 (HC)

1988 Andrew McGahan's second novel (following his 1993 Vogel and Commonwealth Prize-winning *Praise*) is set in Australia's Bicentennial Year, and features two rather loopy young men: Gordon, a would-be-writer looking desperately for a change of scene, and Wayne, a frustrated artist who has just landed a job with the Australian Weather Service. Wayne offers to share his new posting with Gordon and the two set off (with backpacks full of painting supplies and notebooks) for one of the remotest corners on the continent. The journey out includes a six-day drive north to Darwin followed by short, choppy flight to Cape Don, on the Cobourg Peninsula. Needless to say, six months in a ramshackle lighthouse perched on the edge of a crocodile-infested swamp with only a handful of (none-too-pleased) aborigines for company, is not exactly the best solution to writer's block.

According to the *Australian Book Review*, *1988* "with its pared down, colloquial prose ... looks at myths of masculinity in the year of the Bicentennial, the 'Celebration of a nation' — a strangely appropriate context for [the protagonist's] six months of Northern exposure, of isolation, desolation, revelation and boils." The *New York Times Book Review* argues that McGahan's "triumph ... is in having brilliantly managed to avoid the cliché of the brutally realistic novel of boredom: the my-generation-is-missing-a-soul-thus-my-novel-is-missing-a-plot conceit" and concludes that "Unlike his ultra-realist contemporaries who thumb their noses at Chekov's famous dictum and leave the revolver glimpsed in the desk drawer during Act I sitting there, stubbornly unused, through Act III, Mr. McGahan ... is much more likely to have his bored hero stumble across the weapon somewhere in the middle of Act II, take it outside for recreational target practice, accidentally perforate the siding on someone's porch, do a reasonable job of repairing the damage and forget about the whole matter."

REVIEWS: *AusBkRev* 10/95; *BL* 1/97; *KR* 11/15/96; *LJ* 1/97; *NYTBR* 2/23/97; *PW* 12/2/96

Moorhouse, Frank (Australia)

Grand Days (1993); Books Britain 1994 (HC); See Section 5, #621

Porter, Dorothy (Australia)

The Monkey's Mask (1994); Serpents Tail 1997 (pbk); See Section 6, #767

Reidy, Sue (New Zealand)

416 *The Visitation* (1997); Scribner 1997 (HC)

Sue Reidy's off-beat and decidedly irreverent comedy features the Flynn sisters (Theresa and Catherine: two little Catholics girls who are growing up fervently immersed in the mysteries of their faith) who are "visited" by the Virgin Mary in their suburban New Zealand backyard. Mary, it appears, is on a mission to encourage the use of contraceptives. Needless to say, Theresa and Catherine's devout father is far from pleased.

Called a "wonderfully offbeat, coming of age novel" by *Booklist, The Visitation* was described by *Kirkus Reviews* as "a wickedly funny, laugh-out-loud novel … [and an] offbeat, surprisingly entertaining look at a Catholic girlhood, by a writer with a predator's eye for comic detail." *Publishers Weekly* concludes that "Reidy's *joie de vivre* and infectious sense of humor keep her portrait of Catholic childhood at once funny, affectionate and eminently entertaining."

REVIEWS: *BL* 9/15/97; *KR* 9/15/97; *LJ* 10/15/97; *PW* 9/29/97

Shadbolt, Maurice (New Zealand)

417   *Monday's Warriors* (1990); Godine 1992 (HC)

The second novel in Maurice Shadbolt's factually based historical trilogy about New Zealand's Maori Wars is a full-steam ahead adventure tale featuring the legendary Kimball Bent of Sodom Docks, Maine, an unlikely spy and strategist for the ferocious Maori warriors who managed, at least for a time, to forestall the British juggernaut. The story begins in 1858, when, in a drunken haze, Bent signed up with a British Navy whose primary purpose in the mid 19th century was to subdue native peoples in far flung reaches of the emerging British Empire. After six years (of thankless labor, unpalatable military actions and frequent floggings) Bent, on patrol in a New Zealand rain forest, deserts – eventually allying himself with the Maoris in their doomed struggle against the European invaders.

According to the *Library Journal* there "is not a dull moment in this comic romp, which offers the best historical fiction to come along since E.S. Forrester." Novelist Ivan Doig (*NYTBR*) observes that "Shadbolt's maximalist, when-in-doubt-be-vivid style capaciously suits *Monday's Warriors* … for his characters, caught up in a struggle that scorched the earth they fought over, it was a maximal time…. All in all, the novelist manages a legerdemain that keeps his tale simultaneously winsome and gory." According to the *Literary Review, Monday's Warriors* "is a novel suffused with the old-fashioned virtues of honor in battle and glorious death, but Shadbolt's wry voice achieves precisely the right degree of detachment from these values, and his comic touch is always sure." *Publishers*

Weekly, in its starred review, calls Maurice Shadbolt "an accomplished raconteur" and observes that the "narrative is propelled mainly through dialogue, much of it hilarious, as Bent struggles to puzzle out Maori habits and the tribesmen cope with his foreign ways—and fecund profanity."

REVIEWS: *BL* 3/15/92; *JNZL* 12/94; *KR* 12/15/91; *LitRev* 8/90; *LJ* 2/15/92; *NYT* 3/26/92; *NYTBR* 5/3/92; *PW* 12/20/91

Stead, C.K. (New Zealand)

The Death of the Body (1986); HarperCollins 1992 (pbk reissue); See Section 7, #965

Wilkins, Damien (New Zealand)

418   *Little Masters* (1997); Holt 1997 (HC)

Damien Wilkins' second novel and third work of fiction explores the theme of alienation as it follows two young New Zealand expatriates who have arrived in London through disparate but equally circuitous routes.

According to the *Times Literary Supplement, Little Masters* is "a rich and enjoyable study of such varieties of foolishness as love, ambition and forward planning." *Publishers Weekly*, in its starred review, calls Wilkins "a young novelist of extraordinary promise" and observes that his second novel "stretching across a handful of countries and featuring characters from a wide variety of nations and backgrounds … offers an abundant display of his remarkable talent for setting scenes and sketching characters." In the view of *Booklist*, Wilkins "deepens his portrait of alienation with clever and colorful allegories and metaphors. *Little Masters* only suffers from being too rich at times." Richard Eder (*LATBR*) calls *Litttle Masters* "a novel that enchants and irritates" and goes on to conclude that "Wilkins writes whole sequences of scenes that are by turns comic, tender and achingly inspired."

REVIEWS: *BL* 6/1/97; *KR* 5/1/97; *LATBR* 6/29/97; *LJ* 1/94; *NYTBR* 10/5/97; *PW* 5/12/97; *TLS* 8/1/97

Winton, Tim (Australia)

The Riders (1994); Scribner 1996 (pbk); See Section 1, #96

419   *Cloudstreet* (1991); Graywolf 1993 (pbk)

Tim Winton's 6th novel features two country families who move to the city and end up sharing a tumble-down mansion at Number 1, Cloud Street in the city of Perth, Australia. Key characters include the hapless, shiftless Pickles (Sam Pickles a gambling, one-armed former guano collector and Dolly his alcoholic and unfaithful wife) and the industrious Lambs (including their son Fish, brain-damaged since childhood when he was saved from drowning) who keep the place afloat by selling ice cream out of the front parlour. The cast is rounded out by a talking pig.

According to *Kirkus Reviews* this "marvelous postmodern novel of family life by best-selling Australian writer Winton ... celebrates all the great traditional values in writing that is emphatically contemporary." The *New York Times Book Review* observes that "a novel like *Cloudstreet* may strain at first to wow a reader with its maverick originality. It may begin unsteadily, like a dinghy drifting among the huge familiar barges of familiar literature; but slowly it edges past the danger of collision to make its way into the mainstream realm of elegies for working-class life." Australian novelist Marion Halligan (*AusBkRev*) calls it a "long sprawling book" which has "plenty of sex and violence and a dwelling on masculine pursuits" and concludes that it "is crammed full of excellent things, and some odd ones, and each reader will decide for herself what it is they all amount to, and how much to admire its large achievement."

RECOGNITION: Winner of the 1992 Miles Franklin Literary Award, the Banjo Award and the Deo Gloria Prize; REVIEWS: *AusBkRev* 4/91; *BL* 3/15/92; *KR* 2/1/92; *NYTBR* 8/23/92

AFRICA AND THE CARIBBEAN

Aidoo, Ama Ata (Ghana)

420 *Changes: A Love Story* (1993); Feminist Press 1993 (HC)

Ms. Aidoo's third work of fiction is set in a rapidly modernizing Ghana and reflects the author's feminist orientation. Her protagonist, Esi Sekyi, is a well-educated African woman who, though dismissive of many traditional African social conventions, particularly those that prevent women from full social and economic participation, agrees to become the second wife of a charismatic businessman in a polygamous arrangement.

Publishers Weekly, in its starred review, asserts that Ms. Aidoo "writes with intense power in a novel that, in examining the role of women in modern African society, also sheds light on women's problems around the globe." According to *Belles Lettres*, in *Changes* "the dilemmas facing a well-educated, modern West African woman share center stage with the continent's post-independence needs. Entering into a polygamous marriage for very non-traditional reasons ... Esi 'was thinking that the whole thing sounded so *contemporary African* that she would save her sanity probably by not trying to understand it'." The *Library Journal* concludes that the "prize-winning Ghanaian-born author Aidoo [has taken] a satir-

ical look at modern women and points out similarities in their lives — whether in Africa or anywhere else."

RECOGNITION: Winner of the Commonwealth Writers' Prize; REVIEWS: *BellesL* Fall '93; *KR* 10/15/93; *LJ* 11/5/93; *Ms* 7-8/93; *PW* 10/25/93

Antoni, Robert (Trinidad)

421 *Blessed Is the Fruit* (1997); H Holt 1997 (HC)

Robert Antoni's second novel is set on a decaying estate in the post–Colonial Trinidad of the late 1940s and tells the tale of two West Indian women: Lilla Woodward and Velma Bootman. Lilla, the white owner of the plantation house, is the daughter of an Englishman and a pious — yet alcoholic — Creole heiress. Vel, a single, black woman whose life has been shaped by extreme poverty (she's lost four children to disease and malnutrition) has worked for Lilla for the past ten years and is the only servant left on the failing estate. Both women are thirty-three years old. The novel opens with Vel's failed abortion attempt and Lilla's life-saving intervention. As the two women lay beside each other on the large bed in Lilla's master bedroom they each tell their life stories to the as yet unborn child.

According to *Booklist*, "The lilting patois of the islands, both Lilla's white colonial and Vel's 'local,' offers the reader not a language barrier, but a bridge ... a language of the heart that's as direct and infectious as a calypso beat." *Kirkus Reviews*, in a dissenting view, calls Antoni's novel "a Caribbean gothic with literary pretensions" that is "drenched to soddenness with lush language and symbolism." The *Library Journal* concludes that "Literate and intricately crafted, this novel is an interesting exploration of a time when different races led very different lives." The *New York Times Book Review* argues that "even when the tale becomes wildly overcooked, Antoni's lyrical, incantatory prose vividly evokes a world of soul crippling repression and forbidden desires."

REVIEWS: *BL* 3/15/97; *KR* 2/1/97; *LJ* 3/1/97; *NYTBR* 7/20/97; *PW* 2/10/97

422 *Divina Trace* (1991); Overlook 1993 (pbk)

In his debut novel Robert Antoni draws on the complex cultural history of the Caribbean in spinning a myth-drenched tale set on the fictitious island nation of Corpus Christi. Antoni employs multiple spirits and voices from the past to advance his story which originates with Old Granny Myrna, who, on her deathbed, tells her grandson Johnny Domingo the tale of Magdelena the nun who gives birth to a half-man/half-frog. And then there is the monkey god....

According to *Publishers Weekly*, "Seven spell-binding storytellers, each speaking in a distinctive, lilting, often ribald patois, propel this imaginative first novel about a mysterious 'frog-child' who has become a legend on the island...." *Booklist* observes that Antoni "overlays the legends of the Domingo family of the island of Corps Christi with myth, religion and history, as each of [the] narrators recounts his or her version of the Ramayana and the monkey god's story at its center." The *Washington Post Book World* concludes that *Divina Trace* "is magical realism with an avant garde twist, as if Garcia Marquez and Joyce had themselves engaged in unholy cohabitation."

RECOGNITION: Winner of the Commonwealth Writers Prize: First Novel Award (Canada & Caribbean Region); REVIEWS: *BL* 2/1/92; *KR* 12/1/91; *PW* 4/26/93; *TLS* 11/22/91; *WPBW* 2/2/92

Bedford, Simi (Nigeria)

423   *Yoruba Girl Dancing* (1991); Penguin 1994 (pbk)

Taken from her wealthy family in tropical Lagos to attend a British boarding school in the damp Sussex countryside, six-year-old Remi (whose entire life up until that time had been spent within an airy family compound surrounded by loving family members, devoted servants, and happy-go-lucky playmates) must learn to cope with (in addition to a heartbreakingly wrenching separation from her family): inhospitable classmates, drafty dormitories and unspeakably bland English food. The time is the early 1950s, Nigeria is still a British colony but has been promised full independence by the end of the decade. Remi's father, one of the richest men in Lagos, has decided that at least one of his children must be prepared to take an active role in the soon-to-be-born modern state of Nigeria. Remi's assimilation into the alien British culture is neither rapid nor easy, it is also not without its comic aspects.

Booklist observes that Ms. Bedford "imbues her magnanimous and charming first novel with the tingle of suppressed laughter and the power of triumph over adversity," and concludes that "Remi grows up savvy, wise, and proud of both her African heritage and her English education." In the view of novelist Francine Prose (*WPBW*), "what saves (*Yoruba Girl Dancing*) from being a mere comic send-up of a culture with odd customs and unappetizing dietary tastes is the depth of Remi's vision, and the brightness of her voice. Her quick judgments are razor-sharp, yet she is never simply judgmental — or in any case is always even-handed and forgiving...." *Kirkus Review* observes that "Remi is vibrant, no victim, but her experiences still break the reader's heart: upon seeing her father and her uncle for the first time in five years, Remi puts out her hand and with her best English manners asks, 'How do you do, which one of you is my father?'" *Belles Lettres* concludes that "While (*Yoruba Girl Dancing*) is not the politically conscious, feminist, anti-colonial novel that some might expect from an African Woman writer, it charms and delights the reader with its portrayal of a spirited, self-confident protagonist determined to hold fast to an Africa that few Europeans acknowledge."

REVIEWS: *BellesL* Spr '93; *BL* 10/1/92; *KR* 7/15/92; *LJ* 9/1/92; *LST* 4/14/91; *PW* 7/27/92; *TLS* 2/22/91; *WPBW* 9/27/92

Behr, Mark (South Africa)

424   *The Smell of Apples* (1995); St. Martin's 1995 (HC); Picador 1997 (pbk)

Mark Behr's debut novel is set in Cape Town in the waning years of apartheid and is narrated by a 12-year-old Afrikaner boy by the name of Marnus Erasmus. Marnus's handsome father is a military man whose affectionate manner within the family belies his role as an official representative (and enforcer) of a repressive state. His beautiful mother — a former opera singer — is devoted to her husband and children. As the novel unfolds, Marnus, displaying the simple, unadorned perceptions of a child, describes life in a society literally rotten to its core.

According to the *London Times*, Behr's "Apartheid is nowhere mentioned by name in the text, but it is present on almost every page. Behr's characters tell us how it quickened, deadened or shaped the lives and instincts of all South Africans." *Booklist* points out that "Behr shows that the political and the personal are one." In the view of novelist Claire Messud (*WPBW*), "Mr. Behr has created a portrait of Afrikaner society in the mid 1970s as vivid and powerful as it is chilling." The *Los Angeles Times* observes that "Behr makes good use of Marnus' naive voice. He believes that he is having a nice, normal childhood, but we see him slowly being fed the poison of apartheid in sugar-coated pills. That some of the niceness is genuine only compounds the tragedy...."

RECOGNITION: Winner of the Eugene Marais Prize, the CNA Literary Debut Prize and the Betty Trask Award for Best First Novel Published in England; 1996 *L.A. Times* Book Award (First Fiction); REVIEWS: *BL* 9/1/95; *ChiTrib* 11/7/95; *Econ* 12/16/95; *KR* 7/1/95; *LATBR* 9/24/95; *LJ* 3/15/96; *NYTBR* 9/10/95; *PW* 7/17/95; *WLT* Win '96; *WPBW* 9/10/95

Brand, Dionne (Trinidad/Canada)

425   *In Another Place, Not Here* (1997); Grove/Atlantic 1997 (HC)

In her debut novel, poet, essayist and filmmaker Dionne Brand features two West Indian women: one island-bound, the other an educated young woman who has returned to the island of her birth from her new home in Canada. Elizete is a sugar cane worker on an unnamed Caribbean island, Verlia is an idealist who has come "home" to help raise the consciousness of the island's agricultural workers. They meet and fall passionately in love.

According to Canadian novelist Catherine Bush (*NYTBR*), "in its attention to emotional nuance and visual detail, *In Another Place* weds beauty and a fierce intelligence in a work that offers a syncretic and multiple sense of place." The *Women's Review of Books* observes that "[t]he narrative is not linear but moves in a see-saw motion, or like the waves of the sea, according to the logic of exile with its restless contradictions — the impossible longing for flight, for stasis, for escape, for homecoming. The opening chapters also account — in a series of lovely riffs — for the whole of Caribbean history since the first slaves were brought over, four hundred years ago." The *Washington Post Book World* suggests that "Brand's novel is a remarkable meditation on city versus island life, the material and spiritual poverty of the colonized, and the inner struggle of women attempting to define themselves within these environments." *Kirkus Review* concludes that *In Another Place* contains "Luminous prose and some on-target insights into the immigrant experience, but the polemic and the passion seem more contrived, however artfully dressed, than fresh and persuasive."

RECOGNITION: *NYTBR* Notable Book of 1998; REVIEWS: *KR* 8/1/97; *NYTBR* 1/4/98; *WPBW* 2/1/98; *WRB* 4/98

Brink, Andre (South Africa)

426 *Imaginings of Sand* (1996); Harcourt Brace 1996 (HC)

Kristien Muller, an expatriate South African living in London, has returned home after 11 years at the request of her grandmother, Ouma, who is dying and wants to reconnect the young woman to her family and her past. More than one reviewer has noted that the novel advances an aggressive feminist perspective.

Booklist observes that "as in his earlier novels, Brink fuses politics with family intimacy " and concludes that "American readers will be caught by the parallels with this country in a story of strong women on a frontier shaped by men." According to the *Library Journal* Kristien's grandmother tells her "magical stories of strong women, with enough truth and enough mystery to enchant the reader." *Publishers Weekly*, in its starred review, observes that Brink's "profoundly moving" novel has "two overwhelming climaxes, an election-day scene that joy-

fully captures the spirit of a nation turning itself around, and a multiple murder as grimly terrifying as anything in American crime fiction."

RECOGNITION: Nominated for the 1998 IMPAC Dublin Literary Award; REVIEWS: *BL* 10/1/96; *KR* 9/1/96; *LJ* 9/14/96; *NS&S* 2/23/96; *NYTBR* 12/1/96; *PW* 8/26/96; *TLS* 2/9/96; *WSJ* 11/8/96

Buffong, Jean (Grenada)

427 *Under the Silk Cotton Tree* (1993); Interlink 1993 (HC); 1997 (pbk)

Buffong's debut novel features Flora and her growth to maturity in a close-knit Grenadian village. Her tale is filled with stories of her family and neighbors and is told in a rich Grenadian patois.

In the view of *Publishers Weekly*, "Set in a small village on her native island, Grenadian author Buffong's debut novel vividly captures the rhythm of daily life there and the musical speech of the inhabitants." According to *Kirkus Reviews*, *Under the Silk Cotton Tree* takes place "against a background of strong religious sentiment, local superstition, and a culture shaped as much by its African origins as the island's own traditions. A wonderfully evocative portrait of growing up on an island where 'news travels faster than African drums....'" The *Library Journal* points out that "Flora's youthful remembrances highlight the fears and half-understanding of childhood while emphasizing the importance of otherworldly forces, family, and community."

REVIEWS: *KR* 10/1/93; *LJ* 11/15/93; *Ms* 1/94; *PW* 11/1/93

Cartwright, Justin (South Africa/UK)

428 *Masai Dreaming* (1995); Random House 1995 (HC)

Set in East Africa, *Masai Dreaming* has been likened to Joseph Conrad's *Heart of Darkness* in its exploration of the clash between native and colonial cultures, and its trenchant exploration of good and evil. Justin Cartwright's 6th novel features a journalist (Tim Curtiz) who arrives in Kenya to research a screenplay he has been commissioned to write concerning the life of Claudia Cohn-Casson. Ms. Cohn-Casson was a Jewish anthropologist working with the Masai before and during WW II who, towards the end of the war, made a fateful trip back to France.

The *Times Literary Supplement* observes that "Cartwright's novel draws together two strands of narrative; one chronicling the dissolution of Masai culture in east Africa, the other telling of the destruction of a family of French Jews in the final months of the Second World War." According to *Booklist*, *Masai Dreaming* is a "fascinating, multi-textured novel" which inserts the story of Ms.

Cohn-Casson [a saga of "deception, misunderstanding and betrayal over cataclysmic moral issues"] into a tale of the modern-day machinations of a conflicted Hollywood producer who is bankrolling the proposed film of the anthropologist's life."

REVIEWS: *BL* 6/1/95; *KR* 4/15/96; *LATBR* 6/18/95; *LJ* 5/15/95; *NS&S* 8/27/93; *NYTBR* 6/18/95; *Obs* 10/30/94; *Time* 7/3/95; *TLS* 8/20/93

Coetzee, J.M. (South Africa)

The Master of Petersburg (1994); Penguin 1995 (pbk); See Section 6, #805

429   *Age of Iron* (1990); Vintage Penguin 1998 (pbk re-issue)

Life-long Cape Town resident, Elizabeth Curren, a retired Classics teacher, is dying of cancer. The year is 1986 and social unrest, always a part of South African life, is on the rise. A white vagrant, by the name of Mr. Vercueil, has moved into a shed at the bottom of her garden. Meanwhile, Bheki the activist son of her black housemaid has arrived on her doorstep seeking sanctuary. Coetzee employs the letter-diary format to advance his story.

According to the *London Review of Books* "Though it is less a realist novel than an allegorical tale about contemporary South Africa, *Age of Iron* suggests the extent to which Nadine Gordimer's writings have set an agenda for her younger compatriots. The imminent death of white society and the problem of inheritance overshadows a novel which ... centres on what may be called illicit relationships." In the view of the *Times Literary Supplement* "even though Coetzee reduces the action, setting and number of characters to a bare minimum (a few days in Cape Town recording the progress of a dying old lady, her black domestic and a drunk tramp), Coetzee, nonetheless manages to address the large issues of life, love death, South Africa and the internecine political intractability." The *Library Journal* concludes that "Less allegorical than Coetzee's previous novels, [*The Age of Iron*] is still richly metaphoric ... [and is a] brilliant chilling look at the spiritual costs of apartheid." The *Washington Post Book World* argues that "Mr. Coetzee has created a superbly realized novel whose truths cut to the bone."

REVIEWS: *CSM* 2/6/91; *LATBR* 9/27/90; *LitRev* 9/90; *LJ* 8/90; *LRB* 9/13/90; *NS&S* 9/21/90; *NYTBR* 9/23/90; *Spec* 9/29/90; *TLS* 9/28/90; *WPBW* 9/23/90

D'Aguiar, Fred (Guyana/USA)

430   *Dear Future* (1996); Avon 1998 (pbk)

In his second novel, Fred D'Aguiar tells the story of "Red Head" a young man whose sobriquet results from a wound to the head administered by an ax-wielding uncle. Since the accident Red Head has heard voices. Red Head's new-found visionary gift — and his family's reaction to it — forms the framework for D'Aguiar's latest novel.

Kirkus Reviews observes that D'Aguiar has written a "poetic and often moving tale of a broken up Caribbean family ... [in which] life, laughter, and sorrow [are] woven into a thing of beauty by a gifted writer." The *London Review of Books* argues that there "is a suspicion that the tale may have taken over from the teller, which may account for the feeling that this bold, funny and sensuous book is shadowed at several points ... by a larger, as yet unwritten and probably more conventionally realistic book." According to the *New Statesman & Society*, Fred D'Aguiar "is shaping into a crafty storyteller who challenges his readers to think" and, in *Dear Future* reminds us "that magic realism is as much at home in the Anglophone world as in the Latin countries."

REVIEWS: *BL* 8/96; *KR* 8/19/96; *LRB* 7/6/96; *Nation* 1/13/97; *NS&S* 3/22/96; *NYTBR* 11/10/96; *Obs* 2/18/96; *PW* 7/15/96; *TLS* 3/16/96; *WLT* Win '97; EDITOR'S NOTE: D'Aguiar's recently published third novel *Feeding the Ghosts* (1998) is set in 1780 and concerns the actions of the captain of the slave ship Zong in the face of a transatlantic outbreak of disease among the human cargo.

431   *The Longest Memory* (1994); Pantheon Bks 1994 (HC); Avon 1996 (pbk)

The Longest Memory tells, in an unsettling, matter-of-fact manner, the searing tale of "Whitechapel" an elderly slave on the Whitechapel plantation in 19th century Virginia, who has made numerous (albeit embittering) accommodations to ensure his own survival. It is also the story of Whitechapel's son, "Chapel," a rebellious slave, who attempts escape and pays the ultimate price.

Publishers Weekly points out that Fred D'Aguiar powerfully "explores the conflict among African American slaves between obedient, stoic survivalists and defiant rebels, adding resonance to his haunting tale." African novelist Abdulrazak Gurnah (*TLS*) asserts that in the figure of Whitechapel, D'Aguiar "effectively demonstrates the inevitable intimacies between oppressor and oppressed." *Kirkus Reviews* calls *The Longest Memory* "a small book with the emotional impact of a widescreen blockbuster, the reasoned progress of a play, and the painful beauty of poetry." *Booklist* concludes that "The inhumanity of slavery has not been so achingly understood or expressed so beautifully since Toni Morrison's very disturbing *Beloved*."

RECOGNITION: Winner of the 1994 Whitbread and David Higham Awards; REVIEWS: *BL* 12/15/94; *KR* 11/1/94; *LJ* 12/94; *NS&S* 9/2/94; *NYTBR* 5/7/95; *PW* 11/21/94; *TLS* 7/15/94

Danticat, Edwidge (Haiti/US)

Breath, Eyes, Memory (1994); Soho 1994 (HC); Vintage 1995 (pbk); See Section 2, #111

Echewa, T. Obinkaram (Nigeria)

432 *I Saw the Sky Catch Fire* (1992); Plume 1993; (pbk)

T.O. Echewa's third novel is set in modern-day Nigeria and is narrated by Ajuzia, a young man who is about to leave for America where he will begin his university studies. On the eve of his departure his grandmother, Nne-nne, regales him with the "stories" of her life and, by extension, of his own African heritage. One story has to do with her own participation in the 1929 "Tax Revolt" when a white woman, Elizabeth Ashley-Jones (an anthropologist who had recently arrived to do ethnographic field work), was held hostage by the women of the village. Echewa includes excerpts from the anthropologist's diary in his narrative.

According to *Booklist*, Echewa's novel is so "[d]ensely atmospheric ... so rich in metaphor, myth, and telling moments that it's best savored in small leisurely samplings." *Publishers Weekly* observes that "The struggle of women lies at the heart of Echewa's remarkable new novel, a work that demonstrates the author's exceptional sensitivity to feminist issues...." Novelist Connie Porter (*NYTBR*) concludes that in *I Saw the Sky Catch Fire*, "Mr. Echewa's various narrative techniques — the use of Ajuzia's consciousness, Mrs. Ashby-Jones's journal and, most of all, the powerful and beautiful voice of Nne-nne — combine to transport us to a world rich with tradition, myth and magic."

REVIEWS: *BL* 1/15/92; *LATBR* 2/9/92; *NYTBR* 5/10/92; *PW* 11/15/92; *SFRB* 2/92

Farah, Nuruddin (Somalia)

433 *Secrets* (1998); Arcade 1998 (HC)

Set in Somalia on the eve that country's civil war, *Secrets* focuses on two childhood friends whose lives have reconnected after many years. Kalaman, at thirty-three, is the owner of a computer company in Mogadishu and, much to the despair of his mother, Damac, is still single and childless. Sholoongo, the "older" girl with whom he had had an intense, sexually charged relationship while still an adolescent, has recently returned to Somalia from the United States. Sholoongo has immersed herself in African magic, and, much to Kalaman's chagrin, has acquired the skills of a shapeshifter, or, more precisely, a witch. Sholoongo wants Kalaman to father her child. The novel opens in the small village where Kalaman is growing up under the tutelage of his grandfather, Nonno, a man possessed of great wisdom. The story is told in the "daring, lush, urbane voice of the author..." (*NYTBR*).

According to *Kirkus Reviews*, *Secrets* is a "densely written ... [and] enthralling psychodrama [incorporating] a tale of a vengeful elephant stalking a man, a stolen birth certificate, a 'secret marriage,' and other shadowy matters ... [which result in] the inextricable entwining of the personal and the political." *Booklist* call Farah's novel "[p]aranoiac and voyeuristic, sexually charged and profoundly sinister" and concludes that it "compellingly limns the social and biological structure of a family and the ways in which truth and lies both support that structure." *L.A. Times Book Review* concludes that its "plot is rich, the language is superb, exciting and consciousness-expanding...."

RECOGNITION: Winner of the 1997 Neustadt International Prize for Literature; *LATBR* "Best Fiction of 1998"; REVIEWS: *BL* 5/15/98; *KR* 4/1/98; *LJ* 5/1/98; *Newsday* 5/3/98; *NYTBR* 7/19/98; *PW* 3/30/98; EDITOR'S NOTE: Mr. Farah's highly praised trilogy (*Sweet & Sour Milk*, *Sardines* and *Close Sesame* which explore the twin evils of colonialism and dictatorship, first published in England between 1979 and 1983) were reissued by Graywolf Press in 1992.

Foster, Cecil (Barbados)

434 *No Man in the House* (1992); Ballantine 1992 (pbk)

Cecil Foster's debut novel (called a "celebration of the human spirit" by M.G. Vassanji) is set on the island of Barbados in the 1960s — during the Barabadian struggle for independence from Britain — and concerns Howard Prescod, a ten-year-old boy who has been left in the care of his grandmother by his parents who have gone to England seeking work. In Howard's highly circumscribed world poverty is the norm but his circumstances are more dire than most. When the new headmaster of his school singles Howard out for some special attention, the youngster begins to dream of the possibility of a better life.

Kirkus Reviews calls *No Man in the House* a "remarkable debut" novel which depicts "poverty in all its wrenching detail" but concludes that "it is Howard and his grandmother who touch the heart with all the splendor of their boundless courage." According to the *Boston Globe* "the beleaguered grandmother, Howard's young aunts, and the other village women are vividly drawn; their angry, loving voices are riches in an impoverished world."

REVIEWS: *BlkSchlr* Spr '94; *BosGlobe* 10/19/92; *KR* 8/1/92; *LATBR* 11/8/92; *LJ* 10/15/92; *PW* 8/24/92

Gordimer, Nadine (South Africa)

The House Gun (1998); FS&G 1998 (HC); See Section 6, #715

435 *None to Accompany Me* (1994); FS&G 1994 (HC); Penguin 1995 (pbk)

Nadine Gordimer's 11th novel, set in that "tremulous" period between the release of Nelson Mandela and the first democratic elections, features Vera Stark, a competent, committed lawyer who has devoted a good chunk of her 60 or so years to the cause of racial equality in South Africa. Vera has just started to confront the fact that while her life has been admirably spent in a societal sense, she has often failed those closest to her.

According to the *Washington Post Book World* "Gordimer's exquisitely rendered fiction of the complexities of contemporary South Africa and the sacrifices exacted from its people — black and white — is a triumph of reality no factual account can rival." In the view of *Publishers Weekly*, *None to Accompany Me* "begins rather slowly, but it includes so many brilliant moves of plot and character, and such emotionally rending scenes and moments, that by the end a reader understands again what a novel can do, and why other genres can't do it." The *London Times* observes that *None to Accompany Me* "vividly documents ... the expectations and tensions of a metamorphic nation" and concludes that "desolate and hopeful, this is more than just a chronicle of a political era."

RECOGNITION: *NYTBR* Notable Book of 1994; REVIEWS: *BL* 8/19/94; *KR* 7/1/94; *LT* 7/22/95; *NYTBR* 9/25/94; *PW* 7/11/94; *WPBW* 10/2/94

436 *My Son's Story* (1990); Penguin 1991 (pbk)

In *My Son's Story*, Will, a colored South African schoolboy playing hooky one afternoon, runs into his father, Sonny, leaving a movie theater. The most disturbing thing about the totally unexpected encounter is the fact that his father is arm and arm with a young white woman. Will's father — a former schoolteacher from one of the segregated townships — is a leading member of an influential anti-apartheid group and a well-known "freedom fighter." The mysterious woman, Hannah by name, is an anti-government activist who first met Will's father while he was serving time in prison for his political activities. Their relationship, nourished as it was by simple attraction and dedication to a common cause, persisted both in spite of, and because of, the risks involved.

According to the *South African Review of Books*, Nadine Gordimer here "continues her engagement with the complexities and conflicts of a racially-divided South Africa. As in her earlier novels she concentrates on a cross-racial relationship in order to focus upon the strains and inhumanities which such a system entails." Novelist Bharati Mukherjee (*WPBW*) observes that the "shameful injustices and the brutal apparatus of apartheid are, this time, merely the context for Gordimer's relentless scrutiny of our capacity for self-deception." The *Literary Review* suggests that *My Son's Story*, structured as it is around the "twin themes of trust and betrayal contains the following message: 'even within a close family, there is exclusion. Everyone is outside somebody's else's story.'" The *Times Literary Supplement* argues that in *My Son's Story* Ms. Gordimer "takes up a substantial challenge by making a coloured teenage boy her narrator, and perhaps did not entirely intend the sullen, Oedipal youth who emerges."

REVIEWS: *LitRev* 9/90; *NS&S* 9/21/90; *SAROB* 1-2/91; *TLS* 9/28/90; *WPBW* 11/11/90

Gurnah, Abdulrazak (Zanzibar/UK)

437 *Admiring Silence* (1996); New Press 1996 (HC)

Abdulrazak Gurnah, in his fifth novel, tells the story of a man moving uneasily between two worlds. The unnamed narrator has lived in England for more than 20 years, having fled the island nation of Zanzibar shortly after it was granted independence. Although the man's family has lived in Zanzibar for centuries, they are descended from Arab merchants and slavers and are therefore looked upon with some suspicion by the newly enfranchised Zanzibarans. To further complicate matters, the narrator has had a long-term (recently ended) relationship with an English woman with whom he has a daughter. A return trip to post–Colonial Zanzibar (around which he has spun romanticized memories) only re-inforces the narrator's sense of alienation.

Kirkus Reviews calls *Admiring Silence* "a beautifully calibrated story of a wrenching search for a home, for the heart and soul in an age of immigrants and exiles" and concludes that Gurnah "poignantly redefines the colonial experience as he details the 'disappointed love' that an exile feels for both the colonial mother, England, and his now independent homeland." The *Times Literary Supplement* argues that "infected [as it appears to be] by his narrator's enervation and disquiet, Gurnah's writing is not always assured ... [and] the narrative voice lacks not only the lyricism but also the elegance which distinguished the poetic diction and rhythms of its compelling predecessor, *Paradise*." The *New York Time Book Review* concludes that "Mr. Gurnah gracefully depicts the agony of a man caught between two cultures, each of which would disown him for his links to the other.... We may not like the narrator, but his torment is all too real."

REVIEWS: *BL* 10/1/96; *KR* 8/15/96; *LJ* 10/1/96; *NYTBR* 10/20/96; *TLS* 9/20/96; *WLT* Win '95

438 *Paradise* (1994); New Press 1995 (pbk)
Abdulrazak Gurnah's fourth novel is set in East and North Africa in the early years of European colonization. *Paradise* features Yusef, who, at age twelve, has been given to a rich trader in exchange for one of his father's debts. The trader "Uncle" Aziz, takes Yusef from his small mountain village to his own comfortable home on the coast where the boy is given a job in his shop and is welcomed into the family. Yusef is eventually asked to accompany Aziz on a trade safari into the untamed interior. On this trip the young man learns much about the ways of the world as he discovers child slavery, fierce tribal animosities, rampant superstition, mosquito-infested swamps and a host of tropical diseases. The plot combines elements of the travel adventure, social documentary and doomed love story.

According to the *Library Journal*, Gurnah's novel "melds a fascinating coming-of-age story and an indictment of the European colonization of Africa...." The *London Sunday Times* points out that the "East Africa that Gurnah describes is one where slavery at its crudest [the blatant trafficking in shackled human beings] is officially over. But now, more subtle forms of subservience, are taking its place. Aziz uses economic bonds as an updated substitute for leg-irons. And he is himself increasingly fettered by colonial constraints.... The main tale [Gurnah] tells is of [Yusef's] growing ... awareness of his trapped plight." The *Times Literary Supplement* observes that Gurnah's "finely written novel is a journey in many senses, a far-reaching exploration of an intricate culture in East Africa, where a frontier of the nostratic world hardly known to Europeans confronts the heart of darkness. As in the best of Conrad ... the encounter and the ravishment reveals man's complex vulnerability and the power of economic forces." *World Literature Today* observes that what "Achebe did for the Igbo and Vassanji for the Asians of East Africa, Gurnah has done for the Arabs of that region who are now remembered only as slave traders" and concludes that "*Paradise* is an absorbing story, and a balanced testimony to a now-vanished way of life."

RECOGNITION: Shortlisted for the 1994 Booker Prize; REVIEWS: *LJ* 3/15/94; *LST* 3/7/94; *NS&S* 3/4/94; *NYTBR* 12/18/94; *PW* 2/29/94; *Spec* 3/94; *TLS* 3/11/94; *WLT* Win '95

Guy, Rosa (Haiti/US)

439 *The Sun, The Sea, a Touch of the Wind* (1995); Plume 1996 (pbk)
Rosa Guy's latest novel is set in Haiti in the 1970s and features Jonnie Dash a successful African-American artist who has come to the island nation to re-invigorate her mind and her spirit. She achieves neither as she gradually becomes more and more caught up with a group of fast-living expatriates devoted to the pursuit of pleasure among the island's elite. When she encounters an orphaned street beggar by the name of Lucknair, she begins to reassess her situation.

According to *Ms. Magazine* "Guy, a Trinidad native and founding member of the Harlem Writers' Guild, places Dash within the harsh world of Haitian politics and social class not only to illuminate Dash's own need to redefine herself and her relationships, but to shed light on the distinct class lines and politics she left behind in the United States. *Booklist* observes that Ms. Guy "adroitly meshes historical fact with emotional truths" and, in so doing, "lives up to her reputation as a lyrical interpreter of human relationships, both personal and political." The *Multicultural Review* concludes that "Guy has created a strong, memorable protagonist, and she successfully evokes her setting from the eyes of an outsider who desperately wants to fit in."

REVIEWS: *BL* 8/95; *KR* 8/1/92; *Ms* 9-10/95; *MultiCultR* 3/96

Harris, Wilson (Guyana)

440 *Jonestown* (1996); Faber & Faber 1997 (pbk)
Inspired by the infamous Jonestown massacre that occurred in a remote Guyana forest in 1978, Harris pens a fictional reconstruction of the events which led up to the tragedy. Narrated by a "survivor" by the name of Francisco Bone, the story is told through a decidedly magical realist perspective as it strives to incorporate the author's musings about the rise and abrupt demise of the pre–Colombian Mayan civilization.

The *New Statesman* observes that Harris "transforms the banner headline of Jonestown into something rich and strange, weaving a new pattern from ancient and contemporary threads" and concludes that "[a]lthough the dialectics of Harris's novel are not simple, his imagery is compulsive." According to novelist Abdulrazak Gurnah, writing in the *Times Literary Supplement*, "Francisco Bone and his companion, Mr. Mageye, 'Magus-Jester of History,' travel back and forth across times as they debate the proliferating matters that interest them ... [and are assisted in their journey by] ... a Celestial Camera, which can provide clips of the past as required." The *Literary Review* argues that "For readers who are prepared to make the effort to grapple with [Harris's] hermeticsm, the reward is an initiation into one of the most original minds writing today. For others, there is still the magical mystery tour through his kaleidoscopic use of language and imagery."

REVIEWS: *LitRev* 7/96; *NS* 7/12/96; *Obs* 9/1/96; *TLS* 7/5/96; *VLS* 7/96

441   *Resurrection at Sorrow Hill* (1993);
Faber & Faber 1993 (HC)

In his 20th novel, noted Guyanese author Wilson Harris uses a perilous up-river journey as the framing device in a story that incorporates myth and fable and includes madness, violent death, and a dangerous love triangle. The story begins, deep in the Guyanese rain forest, at a run-down meteorological station named Sorrow Hill.

Publishers Weekly calls Harris's work "[u]ncompromisingly visionary [and] often inscrutable" and concludes that Harris's latest offering "makes daunting demands of even the most alert and sensitive reader." The *Times Literary Supplement* concurs, pointing out that "Harris's metaphors come heavily laden, and his narrative, though full of striking images and phrases, is constructed from a language that is obstinate and difficult." The *New Statesman* observes that rarely has Harris "used the Christian underpinning so boldly [as in *Resurrection*] where "the voyage upstream into the uncharted hinterland [represents a search for] the mythic unconscious." *World Literature Today*, in an attempt to define the art of Wilson Harris, argues that "His is a mind split open and spewing its contents like the maddest of lunatics and the greatest of innovative geniuses."

REVIEWS: *Independ* 12/2/93; *NS&S* 11/12/93; *PW* 2/7/94; *TLS* 11/12/93; *WLT* Spr '94

Heath, Roy (Guyana/UK)

442   *The Ministry of Hope* (1997); Marion Boyars 1997 (HC)

The Ministry of Hope, a sequel to *Kwaku*, Roy Heath's 1982 novel about a Guyanese simpleton with an agenda, catches up with Kwaku who is now down on his luck and ill-treated by his sons. In his latest (darkly humorous) novel Heath explores the role ambition in a thoroughly corrupt society.

According to novelist Mark Childress (*NYTBR*), "Kwaku comes from a long line of literary buffoons who manage to triumph over the 'intelligent' people around them. The language Mr. Heath employs to describe this process is luxurious and densely baroque in places, sweetly comic in others." The *Library Journal* observes that although "[b]illed as a comic novel, this is really a dark, psychological study of the ways corruption, prejudice, and superstition infect all layers of society." *Kirkus Reviews* calls *The Ministry of Hope* a "dramatic display of character in action that has seldom been matched by any contemporary novelist" and concludes that "On all counts, [it's] a triumph."

REVIEWS: *BL* 3/1/97; *KR* 12/1/96; *LJ* 11/15/96; *NYTBR* 5/11/97; *PW* 11/18/96; *TLS* 6/27/97; EDITOR'S NOTE: The publication of *Ministry of Hope* coincides with the American publication of Heath's 1982 novel *Kwaku: or the Man Who Could Not Keep His Mouth Shut* (see #444).

443   *The Shadow Bride* (1991); Persea 1996 (HC — reprint)

Roy Heath's 8th novel is set in the 1920s in Guyana's East-Indian community and tells the tale of Betta Singh, who has returned to his homeland after receiving a medical degree in Dublin. The community to which Betta returns is a series of villages and plantations which lie along Guyana's mosquito coast, a flat, marshy estuary characterized by high humidity and mosquito-borne diseases. The Indian residents are, for the most part, impoverished second-generation indentured laborers — descendants of a labor force which was imported in the late 19th century to replace African slave labor. Drawn from throughout the subcontinent, these "Indians" are not at all homogenous, speaking many different dialects and practicing Hindu, Muslim or (more recently) Christian faiths. The "shadow" bride of the title is Betta's mother, a fiercely controlling and over-protective matriarch who, when deciding to send Betta off to receive an education overseas, did not anticipate his growing spirit of independence.

The *Washington Post Book World* calls *The Shadow Bride* "a brooding, politically grounded vision of cultural displacement, spiritual striving and material poverty in colonial Guyana ... [and] a splendidly achieved, hauntingly tragic, unsentimental vision of a people's past." *Booklist* observes that its narrative "power grows as the story progresses, as Heath explores the effects of imperialism, the role of women in East Indian society, and the simmering antagonism of Hindus and Muslims in Guyana." According to the *New York Times Book Review*: "If the conflict between Betta and Mrs. Singh is the engine that powers the novel, the fuel for that engine is an entire fragmentation of culture ... Betta's mother is rooted in the society of a country Betta has never seen.... [H]e is Muslim but his closest confidant is Creole and Christian. His education is European, but he frequently finds it useless in tropical Guyana. His language is 'proper' English, which sets him apart from his Hindi- and pidgin–English speaking countrymen, but he is considered 'black' by the white colonists. Who is he? Which country, which language, which culture is truly his? The answer, Mr. Heath implies ... is to be found in himself and his family, or in his simple participation in the process of human life." *Publishers Weekly* concludes that "Heath's modest, unpretentious style undergirds a powerful realism as his subtle analysis of family conflicts builds to a tragic and moving climax."

RECOGNITION: Shortlisted for the 1991 Booker Prize; REVIEWS: *BL* 11/15/95; *NYTBR* 1/21/96; *PW* 8/28/95; *WPBW* 2/18/96

444 *Kwaku: Or the Man Who Could Not Keep His Mouth Shut* (1982); Marion Boyars 1997 (pbk)

Roy Heath's almost Dickensian tale revolves around Kwaku Cholmondeley, described by the author as a man "who was reduced to a state of idiocy by intelligent men, but made a spontaneous recovery." The Pickwickian Kwaku, in search of happiness and material success (including marriage to the formidable Miss Gwendolyn and a seat-of-his-pants "career" as a natural healer) leads a serendipitously adventurous life, rife with odd and intriguing characters.

According to *Kirkus Reviews*, Heath's story of Kwaku's "fortunes is both a delicious episodic picaresque and a tightly structured narrative that consistently reveals and develops characters as it traces a whirlwind path through … Kwaku's variously successful and disastrous enterprises." In the view of *Booklist*, "Readers will laugh at Kwaku's misadventures, even as they wince at the futility of his dreams." Novelist Mark Childress (*NYTBR*) points out that "Kwaku is no ordinary idiot: he has big dreams and never doubts that he will have a wonderful life…. All that stands in his way is his disconcerting tendency to say and do exactly the wrong thing."

RECOGNITION: Winner of the *Guardian* fiction prize; REVIEWS: *BL* 4/1/97; *KR* 2/15/97; *LJ* 4/1/97; *NYTBR* 5/11/97; *Obs* 10/31/82

Hope, Christopher (South Africa/UK?)

Darkest England (1996); Norton 1996 (HC); See Section 7, #906

Kincaid, Jamaica (Antigua/USA)

445 *The Autobiography of My Mother* (1996); Plume 1997 (pbk)

Jamaica Kincaid's latest novel is narrated by a 70-year-old West Indian (by the name of Xuela) who looks back over her — often harrowing — life. When Xuela's Carib Indian mother died in childbirth, her Scottish-African father gave her to the washer woman to be raised … as "casually as if he were dropping off his dirty laundry." Xuela was brought up without love or affection and as she reaches school age realizes that her schoolmates and teachers (all of whom are "of the African people") look down on her because of her Carib-African mixture. Xuela, is raped at fifteen, aborts her own pregnancy (thereby rendering herself sterile) and eventually enters into a loveless marriage. Xuela never learns to love, never establishes an emotionally fulfilling relationship and manages to live her whole life wrapped in a cocoon of hatred and resentment. Miss Kincaid was born and raised on the West Indian island of Antigua but now lives in Manhattan — where she has carved out a career for herself as a brilliant young writer.

Time magazine calls Ms. Kincaid "the most personal of writers" and concludes that "by now most readers will [recognize her] primal theme, repeated well past the point of obsession … [an] abiding resentment of her mother." Novelist Darryl Pinckney (NYRB) argues that "Kincaid's rhythms and the circularity of her thought patterns in language bring Gertrude Stein to mind. She is an eccentric and altogether impressive descendant." Novelist Cathleen Schine (*NYTBR*) while observing that *Autobiography of My Mother* "is pure and overwhelming, a brilliant fable of willed nihilism" concludes that "chilling as it is, there is also something dull and unconvincing about Xuela's anguish. For as personal as Xuela's account is … [she remains] a symbol, an abstraction of an entire people's suffering and degradation." Richard Eder (*L.A. Times Book Review*) takes a somewhat different view, pointing out that "Here, taken to an extreme, is a woman's retort to sexual, racial and historical oppression on a West Indian island, and perhaps elsewhere. It is not that the argument necessarily convinces. Kincaid does not say that Xuela is right. She says that you will nor forget her. And she is right."

OTHER MEDIA: Audiocassette (Airplay/unabr); RECOGNITION: *L.A. Times* "Best Books" 1996 (Top Ten); nominated for the 1997 PEN/Faulkner Award; nominated for the 1996 National Book Critics Circle Award; nominated for the 1998 IMPAC Dublin Literary Award; REVIEWS: *EW* 1/17/97; *LATBR* 1/14/96; *LRB* 2/6/97; *NS* 10/11/96; *NYRB* 3/21/96; *NYTBR* 2/4/96; *Obs* 9/29/96; *Time* 2/5/96; *TLS* 9/20/96; *WLT* Win '97

Lovelace, Earl (Trinidad)

446 *Salt: A Novel* (1997); Persea 1997 (HC)

Earl Lovelace sets his 5th novel (and first since 1982) in tiny Trinidadian community and tells the story of two men: Alford George, son of a poor farm worker, who becomes — through dint of much hard work — a school teacher and later an activist with political aspirations; and Bango Durity, an untutored craftsman with a philosophical bent, who organizes a neighborhood children's drill team, a source of community pride. Lovelace begins his story with a recounting of the fable of Guinea John, a Trinidadian who flew back to Africa using a pair of corncobs for wings. His descendants, too heavy to fly because they have learned to eat salt, must remain on the island and make the best of their fate.

Publishers Weekly observes that, in using "language that's as lush as the foliage of Trinidad and dialogue as vivid as the Caribbean, Lovelace creates a parable that applies to any nation struggling to free themselves from their past." *Booklist* concludes that "Lovelace is an astute political satirist, but it is his benevolent delight in humanity that makes this tender and funny novel sing."

RECOGNITION: Winner of the 1997 Commonwealth Writers' Prize for Fiction; nominated for the 1998 IMPAC Dublin Literary Award; REVIEWS: *BL* 2/15/97; *KR* 1/1/97; *NS* 9/27/96; *NYTBR* 4/20/97; *Obs* 8/25/96; *PW* 1/27/97; *TLS* 9/20/96; *WPBW* 3/30/97

447   *The Dragon Can't Dance* (1979); Persea 1998 (HC)

In *The Dragon Can't Dance* Trinidadian novelist Earl Lovelace uses the imagery of *Carnival* to illuminate his modern fable set in a recently independent Caribbean island nation. Lovelace looks at how a small impoverished island community prepares for its annual Mardis Gras–like celebration and how the dynamics of that event spill over into violent anti-government activity. Lovelace focuses most specifically on the activities of Aldrick Prospect, a young, unemployed islander who, looking for both diversion and "affirmation" is busily working on his dragon costume. It isn't long before Aldrick realizes that the traditional bands and dancers are attracting commercial sponsors and that the money men are calling the shots.

According to *Publishers Weekly* the "lilting, metallic harmonies of steel drums and the musical rhythm of Trinidadian Creole patois are elegantly rendered" in *The Dragon Can't Dance* which portrays "West Indian men and women [struggling, in the face of dehumanizing living conditions] to find their individual identities ... and to resist cultural assimilation." In the view of *Booklist* Lovelace "masterfully choreographs the dance of each of his finely drawn characters ... [revealing] the conundrums not only of Caribbean life but of the human condition itself." *Publishers Weekly* concludes that "[k]aleidoscopically colorful characters and a faithful ear help make this quest for personhood one of Lovelace's best works."

REVIEWS: *BL* 2/15/98; *KR* 2/1/98; *LT* 7/6/90; *PW* 2/2/98; *TLS* 5/15/98

Maraire, J. Nozipo (Zimbabwe/USA)

448   *Zenzele* (1996); Crown 1996 (HC)

J. Nozipo Maraire, a neurosurgeon and writer who divides her time between New Haven and Zimbabwe has written a first novel consisting of letters from a mother to her daughter. The eponymous Zenzele is a young African woman studying at an elite American university who receives frequent letters from her mother, Shiri, the wife of a Zimbabwean lawyer involved in the struggle for independence. The letters, which often take the form of stories, are designed to remind and instruct and

touch on a whole range of subjects from the importance of love and faith and heritage to the casual yet pervasive racism that infects the West.

According to the *Washington Post Book World* the "picture of Africa and Africans Shiri gives her daughter is rich with a sense of community and entwined destinies under threat from the homogenizing impact of Western commercial values.... Maraire ... [also] includes bits of mother-daughter advice ... [as well as some] generational angst ... [and it is this mix] that makes *Zenzele* for much of its length a spectacular achievement." English novelist Penelope Lively (*NYTBR*), while finding the epistolary form somewhat constricting, observes that the novel offers "plenty of rewards [including] a rich impression of the warmth and color of Zimbabwean family life, a view of the traumas of the struggle for independence ... and, above all, a sense of the mother's passionate conviction that 'Africa needs the hearts and minds of its sons and daughters.'"

RECOGNITION: *NYTBR* Notable Book of 1996; REVIEWS: *Ms* 9/96; *NYTBR* 3/3/96; *PW* 4/14/97; *WLT* Win '97; *WPBW* 6/16/96

Melville, Pauline (Guyana/UK)

449   *The Ventriloquist's Tale* (1997); Bloomsbury 1998 (HC)

London-based Pauline Melville sets her decade-spanning novel, in Guyana, a former British colony. In her prize-winning (and fervently admired) debut effort, Ms Melville skillfully intertwines two stories: the long-ago incestuous relationship between a mixed-race brother and sister (the offspring of Alexander McKinnon—a Scotsman who arrived in Guyana at the turn of the century—and one of his two Wapisiana Indian wives), and the contemporary (adulterous) love affair between a British literary critic and a Guyanese descendant of the original McKinnon clan. In the late 1990s, Rosa Mendelson, an Englishwoman, has come to Guyana to research an article, tentatively entitled: "Evelyn Waugh—a Post Colonial Perspective," about that writer's experience in the colonies in the early decades of the 20th-century. Chofy McKinnon has also come to Georgetown, to seek work and to assist his Aunt Wilfreda who is in desperate need of an eye operation. Wilfreda, it turns out, had once met Evelyn Waugh and it is through her that Chofy and Rosa meet. The narrative is framed by a prologue and epilogue in the voice of "the Ventriloquist" who remains nameless but appears to be the product of the afore-mentioned incestuous union. Melville explores both the deep chasm of misunderstanding that exists between Western and aboriginal cultures and the lasting impact of colonialism on one family.

The *New York Times Book Review* calls "*The*

Ventriloquist's Tale "both a sensuous evocation of the sun-blistered savannas and rain-drenched forests of Guyana and a celebration of its [often intruded upon] ancestral way of life" and concludes that "in this magnificent novel Melville shows herself to be a discerning observer and a gifted satirist, the kind who takes no prisoners." *Kirkus Reviews* calls it a "[r]ich, penetrating, idiosyncratic work from a new, uniquely gifted storyteller" while the the *London Times* judged it to be "Hypnotically brilliant." The *Washington Post Book World* argues that by "focusing on a single family precariously balanced on the fault line between wilderness and technology, Christianity and indigenous religion, Melville creates her own myth" and concludes that Ms. Melville's novel "is as contemporary as this morning's news [and] as eternal as the Indian legends she so lovingly evokes." According to the *Times Literary Supplement* "[w]ithin the beautiful cadences and luminous writing of the novel, the voice of the Ventriloquist offers itself as the voice of the colonial Other — the analytic, compromised, but radiant voice of South America, as it survives in the distorting mirror of a Western fiction."

RECOGNITION: Winner of the 1997 Whitbread First Novel Award; *NYTBR* Notable Book of 1998; REVIEWS: *KR* 6/15/98; *LST* 4/12/98; *LT* 4/11/98; *NYTBR* 10/11/98; *PW* 7/6/98; *TLS* 6/6/97; *WPBW* 11/29/98

Naipaul, V.S. (Trinidad/UK)

450 *A Way in the World* (1994); Knopf 1994 (HC); Vintage 1995 (pbk)

V.S. Naipaul, in *A Way in the World*, ranges across the centuries and the oceans in a series of linked stories that reflect on the notion of exploration, be it in the service of empire-building, artistic creation or self-knowledge. The collection include a recreation of Sir Walter Raleigh's doomed expedition to the Orinoco, the down-at-heel literary London of the 1950s, and Miranda's disastrous invasion of South America.

According to *Booklist* "Naipaul has redefined the genre of historical fiction in this curiously old-fashioned, matter-of-fact, yet utterly eviscerating sequence of linked stories [which explore] ... the betrayals and follies that have wreaked havoc in the nations of the Caribbean and Africa." *Kirkus Reviews* observes that the "theme that repeats throughout [the novel] is the shifting nature of reality as it is refracted through the eyes and thoughts of those who shaped Trinidadian and South American colonial history [as well as those who fumble for identity in its aftermath]" and concludes that "Naipaul reveals [the] human roots [of colonialism]: the restless search for identity, for a sense of completion, that drove conquerors and conquered alike." *Publishers Weekly*, in its starred review, as-

serts that "Naipaul's mastery of his material is absolute, and his seemingly effortless, beautifully wrought prose carries the reader to the heart of the mysteries of human destiny." The *New Statesman and Society* concludes that "Naipaul's ability to locate a profound and elusive truth in eloquent, simple language is still unmatched."

REVIEWS: *BL* 4/1/94; *LJ* 5/1/94; *NatR* 8/29/94; *NewR* 6/13/94; *NewsWk* 6/13/94; *NS&S* 5/13/94; *NYRB* 5/12/94; *NYTBR* 5/22/94; *PW* 4/4/94; *Time* 5/30/94; *WLT* Win '95

Okri, Ben (Nigeria/UK)

451 *Songs of Enchantment* (1993); Doubleday 1994 (pbk)

Ben Okri's sixth work of fiction is a sequel to his Booker Prize–winning novel *The Famished Road* but reads more like a collection of short stories or folk tales than a traditional novel. The work again features Azaro, the spirit child who refuses to die, as well as other members of his family, including: his mother who has been bewitched by the mysterious, demonic tavern-owner Madame Koto and his father, Black Tyger, who is in thrall to a beautiful beggar girl. Okri, once again, draws his readers into a violent provincial world aswarm with malevolent magical spirits who continually trick and test the hapless, often unsuspecting humans. The novel is set in a Nigerian slum on the eve of a election characterized by corruption and thuggery

The *Times Literary Supplement* observes that Okri's current novel, much like his previous work, is "carried along by verbal energy and novelty of incident rather than narrative line." *Kirkus Reviews* calls the novel "stunning [if ocassionally repetitive]" and concludes that Okri continues to "conjure up the fabulous with the same ease as he affectingly details the ways of the human spirit in a lovingly evoked African setting teeming with life — both real and mythic." The *Washington Post Book World*, more critical of this later work, pointed out that the "primary colors that gave the sharp savor to *The Famished Road* now seem crude, unsubtle; the accumulation of sensory details that once seemed thrilling and original, now reads like the agglomeration of disjointed experiences — sound and fury, signifying nothing."

REVIEWS: *BL* 10/1/93; *KR* 7/15/93; *NYTBR* 10/10/93; *PW* 8/16/93; *TLS* 3/12/93; *Wasafiri* Aut '93; *WPBW* 10/3/93; EDITOR'S NOTE: Ben Okri was named by *Granta* magazine to its 1993 list of the twenty "Best Young British Novelists."

452 *The Famished Road* (1991); Anchor 1993 (pbk)

Ben Okri's Booker Prize–winning fifth novel is a particularly accomplished example of African magical realism. *The Famished Road* takes place in Nigeria on the eve of Independence, it also takes place in the hallucinatory mind of Azaro, a "spirit child" who is condemned to die and be reborn endlessly. Azaro is drawn to a tavern frequented by spirits and which acts as a portal into their world. As the *New Statesman and Society* points out, "By opening *The Famished Road* you are not so much reading a story as entering a different definition of mental space."

According to Henry Louis Gates, Jr. (*NYTBR*), "Ben Okri, by plumbing the depths of Yoruba mythology, has created a political fable about the crisis of democracy in African and throughout the modern world. More than that, he has ushered the African novel into its own post-modern era through a compelling extension of traditional oral forms that uncovered the future in the past." The *New Statesman* notes that "Whether you are reading it for its prose styles, for its vision, or to get a look-in at the sorts of tragedies … comedies … calumnies and kindnesses this author sees as making up the corner of Nigeria he grew up in, the way Okri explodes it all together is overwhelming." Novelist Charles Johnson (*TLS*) points out that at 500 pages "it is too long, and it is padded out with descriptive passages that slow it down. Yet Ben Okri is, if not yet a careful craftsman, a gifted poet of the African experience; his characters are excitingly drawn, and his imagination is as rich as the continent he writes about." Michael Dirda (*WPBW*) calls it "a strikingly original piece of writing and a delicately nuanced picture of love between a child and his parents." The *London Times* concludes that "Not even a cynic would describe *The Famished* as a good read. It is difficult read, a brilliant read, unlike anything you have ever read before."

RECOGNITION: Winner of the 1991 Booker Prize; REVIEWS: *CSM* 7/10/92; *KR* 4/1/92; *LJ* 6/1/92; *LT* 10/24/91; *NYTBR* 6/28/92; *PW* 3/30/92; *Time* 6/8/92; *TLS* 4/19/91; *WPBW* 5/24/92

Phillips, Caryl (St Kitts/UK/US)

453 *The Nature of Blood* (1997); Knopf 1997 (HC)

In his sixth novel Caryl Phillips writes about fragmented lives: a Jewish woman who survives a Nazi concentration camp but whose family, and therefore, identity is destroyed; 15th-century Jews living in the Italian city of Portobufole who are accused of ritual murder in the wake of a child's death; and an Othello-like African general hired to command the Doge's armies. Their narratives weave and overlap across time and space exploring the twin themes of "foreignness" and the roots of bigotry. Throughout, the dominant voice is that of Eva Stern the young Holocaust survivor.

According to *Publishers Weekly* Phillips, who has frequently "experimented with voice to convey the dislocations of slavery, colonialism and post-colonialism … [here] deals with unexpected subject matter: the Holocaust. This, *PW* continues, allows Phillips to "boldly challenge notions of essential ethnic identity by turning from the experience of slavery to that of the German concentration camps, from pan–African nationalism to Zionism." The *New York Times Book Review* observes that "in writing much of the novel in the voice of a white Jewish woman, Mr. Phillips (black, West Indian, Oxford-educated) also challenges the current literary tribalism" and concludes that despite "a certain flatness of style" and some "shaky narrative control" *The Nature of Blood* is "an extraordinarily perceptive and intelligent novel, and a haunting one."

RECOGNITION: Winner of the 1998 Fisk Fiction Prize (*Boston Book Review*); REVIEWS: *BL* 3/15/97; *KR* 4/15/97; *LJ* 4/15/97; *LRB* 3/20/97; *NYTBR* 5/25/97; *PW* 3/24/97; *Spec* 2/15/97; *TLS* 1/31/97; EDITOR'S NOTE: Caryl Phillips was named by *Granta* magazine to its 1993 list of the twenty "Best Young British Novelists."

454 *Crossing the River* (1994); Vintage 1995 (pbk)

The African Diaspora is the focus of *Crossing the River* Caryl Phillips century-spanning fifth novel. It begins with the heartbreaking story of a man who sold his own children into slavery.

As *Kirkus Reviews* points out, Caryl Phillips' 5th novel "like a work of sacred music, combines a 'many-tongued chorus' limning the pervasive legacy of slavery with an eloquent celebration of survival — of arrival 'on the far bank of the river.'" According to *New Statesman & Society*, "Caryl Phillips's exploration of the relations between black and white is nuanced, humane and sympathetic. And his deep awareness of the historical process is combined with an exceptionally intelligent prose style — clear, unencumbered and compassionate." The *Library Journal* calls it a "grand novel of ideas … [b]old in its design, beautiful in its language, [and] compelling because of its characters."

RECOGNITION: Shortlisted for the 1994 Booker Prize; *NYTBR* Notable Book of 1994; REVIEWS: *AusBkRev* 11/93; *BL* 2/15/94; *CSM* 2/10/94; *KR* 11/15/93; *LJ* 1/94; *LRB* 9/23/93; *NS&S* 5/21/93; *NYTBR* 1/30/94; *PW* 11/22/93

455 *Cambridge* (1991); Vintage 1993 (pbk)

The eponymous Cambridge is a devoutly Christian slave, born Olumide, who belongs to a West Indian sugar grower. Emily Cartwright is a genteel young Englishwoman who has been sent out to the islands to inspect her father's sugar plantations. In his 4th "exquisitely crafted" (*TLS*) novel, West Indian writer Caryl Phillips tells — in their own voices — their interlocking stories.

In the view of novelist George Garrett (*NYTBR*) "Caryl Phillips is fascinated by the ways and means of storytelling and he is especially concerned with the creation of memorable characters. In *Cambridge* there is action aplenty—sex, violence, beatings, madness, murder—as, separately and equally the Englishwoman and the displaced African find their way towards sad endings. Events and ideas matter in this fictional world, but not as much as the humanity, with all its depths and nuances, of the characters." The *Times Literary Supplement* observes that "Through its multiple ironies and fertile ambiguity (*Cambridge*) offers a startling anatomy of the age of slavery, and of the prejudices that were necessary to sustain it." Novelist Clarence Major (*WPBW*) argues that, "One of the many remarkable things about [Phillips' novel] is the creation of Emily Cartwright ... [whose] 19th-century white racist mentality becomes a black author's allegorical and ironic means of making one of the subtlest, but most insistent, statements ever about the troubled and urgent relationships between a particular past and the present, Africa and Europe, justice and injustice, cruelty and compassion."

RECOGNITION: *NYTBR* Notable Book of 1992; REVIEWS: *BL* 1/1/92; *KR* 12/1/91; *LitRev* 3/91; *LJ* 2/1/92; *NYTBR* 2/16/92; *PW* 1/11/93; *TLS* 3/15/91; *WPBW* 2/9/92

Vassanji, M.G. (Tanzania/Canada)
456 *The Book of Secrets* (1994); Picador 1997 (pbk)

M.G. Vassanji's prize-winning novel is set in East Africa and uses the discovery of a decades-old diary as a framing device. Begun in 1913 by Alfred Corbin—at the time a minor bureaucrat in the British Colonial Service—it was subsequently stolen and secreted away only to be found (and read—apparently for the first time) some 75 years later. As the novel opens, a retired Tanzanian school teacher by the name of Pius Fernandes (actually a Goan who had immigrated to East Africa) has been asked to look at the tattered diary and to assess its value as a historical document. Corbin, it transpires, had gone on to carve out a distinguished career for himself within the Colonial Service, ending up as the governor general of Uganda. As Pius delves into the diary he is impressed by the writer's sensibilities and intrigued by the coded mysteries that lie therein. Because the diary was maintained during the volatile years leading up to and including World War I, the story Pius uncovers is studded with references to wartime spies, community upheaval and, perhaps even more fascinating, forbidden liaisons, some with modern-day implications.

According to *Booklist* "this richly atmospheric tale of lives and events in a faraway place and time tackles the big subjects—love, death, war, intrigue—while supplying a wonderful overview of the ragout of cultures that come together in the shadows of Mt. Killaminjaro." In the view of novelist David Willis McCullough (*NYTBR*), Vassanji's novel is "a testament to the almost mystical power of written words ... Pius Fernandes's search for the truth is also a celebration of storytelling, of how gossip and fact and legend and myth become mixed in everyday conversation and then—half remembered, half forgotten—are passed on as they undergo still other ravages of memory, invention and repetition." The *London Sunday Times* found Vassanji's tale to be "by turns detective story, family saga, national history, and analysis of the decline and fall of the British Empire."

RECOGNITION: Winner of the 1994 Giller Prize; REVIEWS: *BL* 2/1/96; *CanFor* 9/94; *LJ* 8/96; *LST* 7/2/95; *NYTBR* 3/10/96; *PW* 12/11/95; *WLT* Win '95

INDIA, PAKISTAN AND SRI LANKA

Appachana, Anjana (India/USA)
457 *Listening Now* (1998); Random House 1998

Anjana Appachana, in her debut novel, tells the story of Padma, a young, free-thinking woman of modern India who meets and falls in love with another college student by the name of Karan. They become lovers and plan to marry but are thwarted by parental intervention. When Padma's father finds out she is pregnant she is ostracized. Padma moves to Delhi where she passes herself off as a widow and pursues a career as a college professor. Padma's story is told in conjunction with those of six other Indian women (including Padma's estranged mother, her sensitive young daughter, an unhappily married sister, and a small circle of colleague/friends) all of whom harbor buried secrets (a forbidden love affair, abortion, abuse, illness) as well as broken dreams. Ms. Appachana—who was born in India but currently lives in Arizona—won a NEA fellowship based on excerpts from this novel.

According to the *New York Times Book Review*, Appachana "convincingly portrays the strains on women in modern India—confined by their extended families [and] diminished and betrayed by the men they look to for security." *Booklist* suggests that although *Listening Now* "is centered on Indian culture, it holds resounding truths for all women. Appachana intimately portrays relationships between and within families and friends and shows how women build strong friendships and lives for themselves, despite disappointment in marriage and the limitations of career."

REVIEWS: *BL* 3/1/98; *BosGlobe* 5/3/98; *KR* 3/98; *NYTBR* 4/19/98; *PW* 1/19/98

Bhattacharya, Keron (India)

458 *Pearls of Coromandel* (1996); St. Martin's 1996 (HC)

When John Sugden, an idealistic young Oxford-graduate, joins the British Civil Service in the final decades of the British Raj, he is immediately dispatched to India. With his arrival, a chain of events is set in motion that will lead to tragedy. India was, at that time, a hotbed of nationalistic fervor, it was also riven by Hindu-Muslim animosity. When a young Hindu woman, the daughter of Sugden's Hindu assistant, is raped by a Muslim, she is rejected by both her husband and her family as "unclean." Sugden takes pity on the beautiful young woman and gives her shelter. They fall in love and, because they have flaunted conventions of every segment of Indian society — including the British — must flee for their lives.

Kirkus Reviews calls *Pearls of Coromandel* a "moving and refreshingly intelligent story of love across the racial divide " and concludes that "the lucidly detailed history and the unusual lovers remarkable both for their smarts and their virtues, make for an accomplished debut." According to *Publishers Weekly* "While Bhattacharya's prose is merely serviceable and the novel's climax soap-operatic, the author evokes clearly the delicate social, religious and political issues at stake. His background detailing gives density to an intelligent story whose characters play out their fates while buffeted by the winds of change."

REVIEWS: *KR* 4/1/96; *PW* 5/20/96; *WPBW* 7/14/96

Chandra, Vikram (India)

459 *Red Earth and Pouring Rain* (1995); Little Brown 1997 (pbk)

Vikram Chandra's debut novel, richly imagined and complexly structured, incorporates Indian myths, competing interpretations of history, and a contemporary college student's road trip in search of America. Despite its fluid, shifting time frame, the novel is set, for the most part, in the late 18th and early 19th centuries. The novel begins simply enough. Abhay, a young Indian has returned from the United States (where he is a college student) to visit his parents. One afternoon he notices a white faced monkey stealing his blue jeans from the wash line and, irritable from jet lag and cultural re-entry, Abhay takes a pot shot at it with an old toy pistol. The god of death soon arrives to collect the fatally wounded monkey's soul, but the mon-

key, seizing a nearby typewriter begins to type out his story. The monkey, it turns out, is the reincarnation of a famous 19th century poet named Sanjay. As the monkey types, the story gains momentum attracting first children and then a crowd of neighbors.

According to the *Washington Post Book World*, *Red Earth and Pouring Rain* by the "latest young heavyweight storyteller out of India ... often reads like a Generation X version of [Salman Rushdie's] *Midnight's Children*." According to the *London Sunday Times*, "Chandra is not so much Rushdie's imitator as a writer who belongs, like him, in a tradition of storytellers stretching back in the east to Scheherazade, and in the west to the poets of the medieval romances, a tradition in which the mundane and the fabulous, the bawdy and the sublime are all allowed room." *Booklist* observes that "as each story leads to another, Chandra's multifaceted narrative spins and whirls as hectically and alluringly as a kaleidoscope, leaving us a bit dazed if impressed." *Publishers Weekly*, in its starred review, finds that "Chandra has built a powerful, moving saga that explores colonialism, death and suffering, ephemeral pleasure and the search for the meaning of life." The *Guardian* concludes that "This is a book that requires not a review but a dissertation, a doctorate, a deconstruction. Chandra's writing-tender, funny, incandescent — so animates his subjects that it becomes possible to see through other eyes, to sense another culture and to shed for a while the dead flesh of European objectivism."

REVIEWS: *BL* 7/19/95; *GW* 7/95; *LJ* 7/95; *LRB* 8/3/95; *LST* 6/11/95; *Guard* 7/9/95; *NYTBR* 9/10/95; *PW* 5/29/95; *WPBW* 8/24//95

Desai, Anita (India/USA)

460 *Journey to Ithaca* (1995); Knopf 1995 (HC); Penguin 1996 (pbk)

Anita Desai's novel explores the oft-noticed tendency of some Westerners to view India through excessively romantic eyes — particularly when it comes to issues of spirituality and enlightenment. In *A Journey to Ithaca* a privileged, young, recently married couple (Sophie is German, Matteo is Italian) set out for India in search of the exotic and the "true." It is the early 1970s — and the "hippie trail" is crowded with fellow seekers. Matteo eventually falls under the sway of a charismatic guru and Sophie must confront hard truths about personal history and the quest for spiritual meaning.

According to the *London Sunday Times*, *A Journey to Ithaca*, though it leaves far too many questions unanswered and can hardly "bear the spiritual weight" placed on it is, nonetheless, "a riveting and romantic novel with flashes of Desai's expected brilliance." Novelist **Kathryn Harrison** (*WPBW*), argues that as Desai "is too sophisticated a writer to offer unambiguous answers to eternal questions ... all that is properly mysterious remains so, and it is testimony to the author's clear vision and her pungent, exact prose that arguments about the nature of divinity or meaning can capture and hold the reader, that they seem as much issues of life and death as the carnal manipulations of more pedestrian fiction." The *Library Journal* concludes that an "ambiguous denouement reiterates the haunting questions about sacred and profane love that echo throughout the book."

REVIEWS: *LJ* 8/95; *LST* 6/18/95; *NYRB* 5/23/96; *NYTBR* 9/17/95; *Time* 8/21/95; *TLS* 6/2/95; *WPBW* 9/17/95; *WSJ* 8/24/95

461 *In Custody* (1984); Penguin 1994 (pbk re-issue)

Deven, an impecunious scholar living in a small town in the north of India, longs for intellectual excitement and career advancement. When he is given a commission to interview Nur, India's greatest Urdu poet, the meeting has a result quite different from the one Deven imagined.

According to the *Spectator* "Although [Anita Desai's] voice is quiet, it is wholly distinctive; and though what that voice says may, at a careless hearing, seem unremarkable, it contains all kinds of cross-currents of meaning." The *Times Literary Supplement* calls *In Custody* "[though "bleak" in tone] Anita Desai's most subtle and mature work to date" and concludes that it is "handled with her familiar elegance ... demonstrating an unforced and powerful ease in conveying the colour and sounds and sensations of Indian life." The *New Republic* concludes that Desai's India "for all the cosmopolitan literary skill she brings to it is an India that very few foreigners have ever penetrated, the India that is Indian."

OTHER MEDIA: Film version (an Ivory/Merchant production) released in 1994; Audiocassette (Isis/unabr); RECOGNITION: Shortlisted for the 1984 Booker Prize; REVIEWS: *LJ* 2/15/85; *NewR* 3/18/85; *NS* 10/12/84; *NYTBR* 3/3/85; *Spec* 10/20/84; *TLS* 10/19/84

Desai, Kiran (India/USA)

462 *Hullabaloo in the Guava Orchard* (1998); Grove-Atlantic 1998 (HC)

Kiran Desai, daughter of the much-admired novelist Anita Desai, has produced a contemporary fable — sprinkled with sly allusions to Salman Rushdie's *Midnight's Children* — set in the Indian village of Shakhot. It features an appealing young man by the name of Sampath Chawla, failed postal worker and feckless son of an eccentric family. Sampath, seeking a bit of uninterrupted contemplation after being fired from his job, takes up residence in a guava tree, and soon finds himself elevated to the rank of holy man: "the Hermit of Shakhot." His knowledge of the villagers private lives (gleaned, of course, through his prior habit of reading their mail) authenticates his status. A group of monkeys takes up residence in the nearby trees and all is well until they discover the pleasures of alcohol. In the words of the *London Times*, "How the town authorities attempt to remove the monkeys without shooting them — which would provoke a riot — makes for a hullabaloo ... with ... a beautiful, genuinely mystical twist."

According to *Kirkus Reviews* "It's a pleasure to report that this particular fruit of a distinguished literary lineage, having fallen rather far from the tree, is producing bountiful and delicious results." The *Wall Street Journal* calls *Hullabaloo* "a sprightly first novel" and concludes that with it, Kiran Desai "takes her place among the pack of gifted young Indian writers now tracking a society where stock scandals have begun to steal the spotlight from gurus." The *Atlantic Monthly* calls Ms. Desai "a delightfully funny, amiable satirist, with [a] Puckish view..." and points out that in her outstanding debut effort Ms. Desai effectively "mocks [among other things] pious enthusiasm, official incompetence, domestic confusion, young love, marriage customs, and sacred monkeys."

RECOGNITION: *NYTBR* Notable Book of 1998; REVIEWS: *AtlM* 6/98; *ChiTrib* 5/17/98; *IndiaToday* 3/9/98; *KR* 5/11/98; *LJ* 5/1/98; *LST* 6/28/98; *LT* 5/2/98; *NYT* 6/12/98; *NYTBR* 7/19/98; *WSJ* 5/1/98

Ganesan, Indira (India/USA)

Inheritance (1998); Knopf 1998 (HC); See Section 2, #115

Ghosh, Amitav (India)

463 *The Calcutta Chromosome* (1995); Avon 1997 (HC); Bard 1998 (pbk)

The Calcutta Chromosome — subtitled *A Novel of Fevers, Deleriums and Discovery* — by anthropologist and novelist Amitav Ghosh opens in a decaying 21st Century Manhattan and features Antar, an Egyptian-born computer technician. Antar's job consists of monitoring the endless data streams (mostly electronic detritus collected from the atmosphere) flickering across his computer screen and noting — for further investigation — whenever the computer finds something it cannot catalog. As the story opens, a string of computer anomalies has lead Antar to discover the identity card of a man named Murugan (coincidentally, a former friend and fellow immigrant) who disappeared in Calcutta some years back while investigating a scientist involved in malaria research. Antar is soon drawn into a mystery that involves, among other things, a 1902

Calcutta cabal wherein chromosomes are being manipulated by unscrupulous scientists. Ghosh's novel embraces a very shifty time frame: from futuristic Manhattan, to Calcutta in the 1990s (presented as the recent past) to the past of a century ago (when pioneering malarial research was being conducted). The author animates an intriguing cast of characters.

According to the *New York Times Book Review*, "Genetic engineering, precognition, shape-shifting, ancient Egyptian mysticism and global mind control are combined here in a strange plot that's worthy of *The X-files*." According to the *New Statesman*, Ghosh's latest "with its dazzling and haunting mix of science fiction, the history of malaria research, thriller, ghost story and post-colonial allegory ... is — like [the author's] previous work — wonderfully clever as well as a good read." *The Lancet* (a highly regarded British medical journal) observes that "details, both mystical and medical, loop around the facts of malaria research" and concludes that non-specialist "readers of *The Calcutta Chromosome* will learn more about mosquitoes than they ever would need to know, while physicians and scientist will enjoy the plot's twists on the familiar." *The* (London) *Times* concludes that "ingeniously shuttling between near-future New York City and India under the Raj, (Ghosh's novel) offers a marvelous mix of scientific burlesque, gothic ghost story and post-colonial comedy." *Booklist*, while noting that "Ghosh resorts to too many long-winded pseudoscientific explanations," contends that "most scenes are crisp and suspenseful, and his characters, especially the impetuous reporter Urmila, are great fun." *Publishers Weekly* concludes that "Like Pynchon, Ghosh ... creates a world in which conspiracies, big conspiracies, lurk everywhere and the people who stagger into the complex plot known as History are inevitably swallowed whole."

RECOGNITION: *The* (London) *SundayTimes* Notable Book of 1995; REVIEWS: *BL* 9/15/97; *CSM* 1/8/98; *KR* 8/15/97; *Lancet* 12/21/96; *LATBR* 9/21/97; *LJ* 9/15/97; *LST* 8/25/96; *LT* 9/12/96; *NS* 9/6/96; *NYTBR* 9/14/97; *PW* 8/11/97

Gunesekera, Romesh (Sri Lanka)

464   *Reef* (1994); New Press 1994 (HC); Riverhead 1996 (pbk)

Romesh Gunesekera's debut novel (following his well-received short story collection *Monkfish Moon*) is set in Sri Lanka — before and during the period of intense civil unrest of the 1980s — and London. Gunesekera tells the story of Triton, a servant in the employ of Mr. Selgado, a wealthy Sri-Lankan intellectual with an interest in Marine Biology. Triton's passage from idealistic young houseboy, through accomplished cook and confi-

dant, to London restaurateur has (according to the *Atlantic Monthly*) "a touch of magic in it."

Called "sensuous" and "incessantly pleasurable to read" by *The* (London) *Times*, *Reef* was widely praised when published in 1994. *Booklist* observes that "it is easy to see why this flawless (exquisitely rendered)book was short-listed for the Booker Prize" and concludes that it "signals a writer to be closely watched." The *New York Times Book Review* comparing *Reef* to Michael Ondaatje's reminiscences of his Sri Lankan childhood *(Running in the Family)* concludes that "both are peopled with colorful, memorable characters." *Kirkus Reviews* notes that the "simple pleasures of domestic arts well done become the stuff of metaphor in this wise and poignant tale of loss, both political and personal." and concludes that *Reef* represents "An extraordinarily accomplished mix of the sensual and the cerebral in beautifully detailed settings."

RECOGNITION: Winner of the *Yorkshire Post* Best First Work Award; shortlisted for the Booker Prize and the *Guardian* Fiction Award; REVIEWS: *AtlM* 3/95; *BL* 1/15/95; *KR* 12/15/94; *LJ* 2/1/95; *LT* 3/7/98; *NS&S* 9/2/94; *NYTBR* 5/26/95; *PW* 12/19/94; *Guard* 5/7/95; *TLS* 6/24/94

Gupta, Sunetra (India)

465   *Memories of Rain* (1992); Grove Press 1993 (pbk)

Sunetra Gupta's debut novel explores the notions of "nostalgia, exile and belonging" (*TLS*) in its finely limned depiction of the disastrous marriage of Moni, an intelligent, yet naively romantic young Indian woman and, Anthony, the handsome young Englishman brought home for a visit by her brother in the midst of a monsoon. Moni moves with Anthony to England where the greyness of the London climate and the stiffness of its inhabitants causes her to withdraw. Anthony, in time, looks elsewhere for stimulation and companionship.

Kirkus Reviews calls *Memories of Rain* a "stunning, luminous debut (and a shimmering dream of a book) ... by a young, true heir to Virginia Woolf" and concludes that "Moni's sensibility — formed by the poetry (both English and Bengali) of anguished passion, darkness, and death — is the basis for gorgeous prose that flickers between romantic longing and exquisite detail." In the view of *Belles Lettres* Gupta's novel is an "introspective, poetic and surreal journey through Moni's mind" written in prose that is "rich in detail and with a fervor reminiscent of (Wuthering Heights)." Indian novelist Shashi Tharoor (*WPBW*) concludes that *Memories of Rain* "marks the triumphant debut of a gifted and compelling voice."

REVIEWS: *BL* 4/1/92; *BellesL* Wint '92/93; *KR* 1/1/92; *LATBR* 5/10/92; *Ms* 5/92; *WLT* Spr '93; *WPBW* 3/29/92

Jhabvala, Ruth Prawer (India/USA)

466 *Shards of Memory* (1995); Doubleday 1995 (HC); Anchor 1996 (pbk)

Ruth Prawer Jhabvala's 12th novel is set primarily in New York with occasional forays to London and the odd Delhi flashback. It spans the 20th century and features five generations in one family beginning with an American, Elsa Kopf who, while in London seeking a guru known as the Master, meets and marries an Indian poet by the name of Hormusji ("Kavi")Bilimoria. In time they have a child (referred to throughout the novel only as "Baby") but the marriage does not last and Kavi and Baby move in with Elsa's Jewish mother in New York while Elsa returns to London (still in search of the Master) and moves into a lesbian collective. Baby grows up, marries and produces Renata who visits her grandmother in London where she meets Carl, an idealistic young German with whom she has a child, Henry. In a parallel story, Madame Richter, a Russian immigrant piano teacher ensconced in a run-down apartment on Manhattan's West Side, is living a largely uneventful life. However, later in the novel we learn that Madame Richter's daughter, Sonia, was fathered by a key player in the Elsa/Kavi drama ... and so it goes.

In the view of the *London Sunday Times* in *Shards of Memory*, "Jhabvala's observations are sharp but her judgments are gentle, and she uses the English language with such subtle wit as to bring off the miracle of being simultaneously satirical and forgiving." The *Wall Street Journal*, equally appreciative of this quality, notes that Jhabvala "is one of those rare writers who manages to mock without sneering, to be simultaneously caustic and loving with her creations." According to the *New York Times* the "best part of [Ms. Jhabvala's novel] and the noblest, is the explicit acknowledgment that any configuration of human beings, however unlikely, may be called a family if among or between them there is love — even if it is a kind of love that can only be described but cannot be comprehended by those outside that family's magic circle."

REVIEWS: *BL* 9/1/95; *KR* 7/1/95; *LATBR* 10/1/95; *LJ* 10/1/95; *LRB* 11/30/95; *LST* 7/9/95; *NYTBR* 9/17/95; *PW* 5/20/96; *TLS* 7/21/95; *WPBW* 11/12/95; *WSJ* 8/24/96

467 *Poet and Dancer* (1992); Anchor 1994 (pbk)

Poet and Dancer is a bittersweet tale set within an extended family living in Manhattan. Angel, a plain, studious, serious young girl much loved by her family develops a passionate attachment to her beautiful, artistic cousin Lara while they are still children. When grown, Angel renews her all-consuming relationship with her cousin who, it is clear to all except Angel, is dangerously unbalanced. In her 11th novel, Ms. Jhabvala has created a haunting tale of the dangers of obsessive attachment.

According to the *New Statesman & Society Poet and Dancer* is "the story of family love: of an uncle who sleeps with his niece, cousins who feed on each other's weaknesses and a daughter for whom the outside world, epitomized by a Manhattan of glass towers crowding out cozy brownstones, is so flawed, so terrifyingly indifferent that she cannot bear to leave her mother." In the view of *Kirkus Reviews*, Ms. Jhabvala, a writer "of remarkably acute sensitivity and perception" has produced "a quiet horror-tale of a relationship in which innocence willingly pays the price evil demands." Novelist Francine Prose (*WPBW*) suggests that when reading *Poet and Dancer* "one thinks often of fairy tales — (not the Disney version) but **real** ones, scary fragments from the vernacular, or the darker narratives of Anderson or Grimm, stories that lull us with a charming plot or a tone of wry bemusement and then neatly administer a series of nasty, chilling little shocks."

REVIEWS: *BL* 1/1/93; *ChiTrib* 8/20/94; *KR* 12/15/92; *LT* 4/16/94; *NS&S* 4/9/93; *NYTBR* 3/28/93; *TLS* 4/16/93; *WPBW* 2/21/93

Kesavan, Mukul (India)

468 *Looking Through Glass* (1995); FS&G 1995 (HC)

As Mukul Kesavan's debut novel opens, the narrator, a young ambitious photographer is on his way to the Ganges river in order to scatter his grandmother's ashes. When he reaches the railroad bridge at Lucknow he stops to take a picture and, as he raises the camera to his eye, he sees, through his zoom lens, a man looking at him through a telescope. Our hero loses his balance and falls both into the river and into temporary oblivion. When he awakens, he finds he has fallen back in time — to the year 1942. After some futile attempts to find a way back to the present he accepts his "timelessness" and devotes himself to constructing some kind of history for himself, for, although he has plenty of "general" history, he has, of course, no verifiable history of his own. His solution is to convince the Muslim Gangoo family who rescued him from the river that he is suffering from amnesia. As he bonds with the Gangoos he grows increasingly fearful about their future, knowing that they may be slaughtered in the bloodbath that will accompany partition in 1946 — unless, of course, they choose to leave for Pakistan before that crucial year.

According to the *Guardian* the novel's "serious and hilarious aspects are indivisible. Mukul Kesavan describes, with delightful comedy, jelabies fried up as verses of the Koran, a man who tries to sell canned water from the Ganges forgetting that it is holy and therefore cannot go bad, a would-be porn star who becomes a human cannonball, rape, mutilation and burning: by embracing what is ordinary and ridiculous, he also grasps what is loaded and terrible." The *Times Literary Supplement* observes that "Kesavan is not always in complete command of the picaresque form that he has selected to subvert an epic view of history, and at points the novel races spectacularly out of control ... [something] that is more than made up for by the sheer inventiveness of the story, which includes some accomplished pieces of magic realism." *Publishers Weekly* concludes that *Looking Through Glass* is an "unusual first novel that blends vivid realism, fantasy, raunchy sexual comedy and political commentary." English novelist Ian Buruma (*Economist*) argues that "This is serio-cum-comic writing of a high order indeed — the kind that both instructs and entertains."

REVIEWS: *Econ* 3/25/95; *Guard* 3/5/95; *LJ* 6/15/95; *NS&S* 3/3/95; *NYTBR* 7/2/95; *PW* 4/24/95; *TLS* 3/3/95

Mehta, Gita (India/UK)

469   *A River Sutra* (1993); Vintage 1994 (pbk)

In her second work of fiction, author/filmmaker Gita Mehta presents a series of interlocking stories narrated by a retired civil servant who has given up his urban existence to manage a government rest house on the leafy banks of the Narmada, the holiest river in India. The retiree had been looking forward to his new life as a vanaprasthi "someone who has retired to the forest to reflect" but finds instead a constant stream of pilgrims — each, it seems, with an intriguing story to relate.

Booklist (in its starred review) notes that "As our innkeeper converses with [the] troubled travelers, he becomes as immersed in their startling stories as if he'd dived into the babbling river and was carried away by the current. Each person he meets, whether Hindu, Muslim or Jain, reveals a different aspect of India's fervent soul and endless quest for enlightenment." The *London Times* calls *A River Sutra* "a beautiful, uplifting book, heightened by the inescapable romance and spiritual otherness of India." Novelist **Francine Prose** (*WPBW*) argues that "At its best [Ms. Mehta's novel] evokes the Indian landscape so sharply that we can practically smell the night-blooming jasmine and provides some of the rewards that we are more accustomed to finding in poetry: the sense that things are richer and more meaningful than they seem, that life is both clear and mysterious, that the beauty and horror of the world is irreducible and inexplicable, that everything is interconnected, imminent — and just beyond our grasp." The *New York Times Book Review* concludes that *A River Sutra* "takes place in a fabled land of the romantic imagination, drawing on timeless literary traditions. Told with skill and sensitivity, Gita Mehta's tales are a delight to read, bringing to Western readers the mystery and drama or a rich cultural heritage."

OTHER MEDIA: Audiocassette (Random Audio/abr); RECOGNITION: *NYTBR* Notable Book of 1993; REVIEWS: *BL* 5/15/93; *CSM* 7/2/93; *KR* 3/15/93; *LATBR* 7/11/93; *LT* 6/20/93; *NYTBR* 6/20/93; *Spec* 6/5/93; *TLS* 6/4/93; *WPBW* 5/30/93

470   *Raj* (1989); Fawcett 1991 (pbk)

Gita Mehta's debut novel (referred to more than once as "Roots in a turban") is set in "Princely India," that portion of the subcontinent that never passed under direct British control. The story features Jaya, daughter of a Maharaja who ruled over Balmer, a small independent princely state in northern India. *Raj* begins at the turn of the century and ends in 1950, the year Jaya registers as a Parliamentary candidate in independent India. As the story progresses, a detailed and historically accurate picture of a now-vanished society emerges.

The *Washington Post Book World* notes "Painted elephants, a concubine who dances on their trunks, tiger hunts, cobras loose in the house, paranoid eunuchs, harem girls swinging on opium and a heroine who goes from purdah to polo to Parliament are just some of the high spots in this endlessly fascinating first novel about India from Queen Victoria's Diamond Jubilee to the bloody civil wars of post–Mountbatten independence." According to the *Times Literary Supplement* "like most of her characters Mehta has been overwhelmed by conflicting aims. Her serious attention to her theme (the disintegration of India as seen through the initially restricted eyes of a woman) saves the book from being a mere block-buster yarn or historical romance; but she knows how difficult it is to combine epic sweep with an exploration of one individual's 'dharma.'" The *New York Review of Books* found Mehta's novel to be "important because, for once, it deals with the Raj without nostalgia or bitterness..." and notes that the author "is at her best when describing the twisted human relations in a colonial society."

OTHER MEDIA: Audiocassette (Blackstone/unabr); REVIEWS: *LATBR* 5/18/89; *LRB* 3/8/90; *NS&S NYRB* 5/18/89; *TLS* 7/7/89; *WPBW* 3/21/89

Mistry, Rohinton (India/Canada)

471   *A Fine Balance* (1996); Knopf 1996 (HC); Vintage 1997 (pbk)

Rohinton Mistry's second novel opens in an unnamed Indian city (suggestive of Bombay or Cal-

4 472–474 *India, Pakistan...* 178

cutta) in 1975 — the year Indira Ghandi ordered the "State of Emergency" that significantly curtailed human rights in India. Mistry chooses to focus on four individuals caught up in the ever-widening social unrest: Dina Dalal, a widow who, out of financial necessity, has taken in a border; Maneck, the border (a college-student son of one of Dina's more prosperous childhood friends), and two untouchables (Ishvar and Om) who have known extreme privation in their lives and are now employed by Ms. Dalal in a modest tailoring business.

According to the *Library Journal*, in Mistry's "unforgettable book" one "first learns the characters' separate, compelling histories of brief joys and abiding sorrows, then watches as barriers of class, suspicion, and politeness are gradually dissolved." In the view of *Macleans'* "the reader's attention never strays from Mistry's narrative.... *A Fine Balance* is an intricately stitched, lovingly crafted tale that gives warmth but does not deny the coldness outside." *Kirkus Reviews* observes that Mistry's novel is "a sweeping story, in a thoroughly Indian setting, that combines Dickens's vivid sympathy for the poor with Solzhenitsyn's controlled outrage, celebrating both the resilience of the human spirit and the searing heartbreak of failed dreams."

OTHER MEDIA: Audiocassette (Stoddart/abr); READING GROUP GUIDE: "Reading Group Choices" 1998 (Paz & Associates); RECOGNITION: Giller Award for Fiction (Canada); 1996 *LA Times* Book Prize; *NYTBR* Notable Book of 1996; REVIEWS: *ChiTrib* 6/9/96; *KR* 2/1/96; *LJ* 4/1/96; *Maclean's* 10/23/95; *NYTBR* 6/23/96; *WPBW* 4/21/96

472 *Such a Long Journey* (1991); Vintage 1992 (pbk)

Rohinton Mistry has set his debut novel in Bombay during Indira Ghandi's administration — a time of rampant political corruption and regional tension including the Bangladesh war. *Such a Long Journey* tells the story of the Nobles, a Parsi family consisting of Gustad Noble (bank clerk and family patriarch), his gentle wife (who is dabbling in witchcraft), an estranged son and a sickly daughter, all of whom are residents of an apartment complex known as the Khodadad Building. In addition to the day to day struggle to provide for his family, Gustav inadvertently becomes mixed up in a government spy scandal.

According to *Publishers Weekly*, throughout Mistry's "Byzantine scenario, [he] demonstrates empathy for and deep understanding of his characters. His novel evokes Rushdie in its denser, florid moments, and T. Coraghessan Boyle in its more madcap flights." The *New Statesman and Society*" calls *Such a Long Journey* "utterly unpretentious and brilliantly perceptive" and applauds its "emotional depth, [and] sympathetic" central characters. The *Atlantic Monthly* concludes that "Mr. Mistry pro-

vides variety, action, comedy, and tragedy with Dickensian generosity. His basic themes of loss and change are melancholy, but they are presented in lavishly entertaining terms."

OTHER MEDIA: Audiocassette (Stoddart/abr); RECOGNITION: Winner of the Governor General's Award, Commonwealth Writers Prize for Fiction; Smith Books/Books in Canada First Novel Award; REVIEWS: *AtlM* 5/91; *BksCan* 3/92&4/92; *LRB* 4/4/91; *NS&S* 3/22/91; *NYTBR* 7/12/1992; *PW* 5/18/92; *TLS* 3/1/91; *WPBW* 6/28/92

Naipaul, V.S. (Trinidad)
A Way in the World (1994); Vintage 1995 (pbk); See Section 4, #450

Nigam, Sanjay (India/USA)
473 *The Snake Charmer: A Novel* (1998); William Morrow 1998 (HC)

In his debut novel, Sanjay Nigam (a Harvard-based research scientist who was born in India and raised in Arizona) tells the serio-comic tale of Sonalal — the most talented snake-charmer in all of India — who, in a moment of blind rage triggered by a bite from his prized cobra, bites his snake back, severing the snake in two.

According to Richard Bernstein (*NYT*), "Mr. Nigam spins an engaging light-as-feather tale of a comically stubborn struggle for both moral absolution and a few dollops of worldly pleasure ... [and] while his story of the Delhi streets zips along like a bicycle rickshaw, it passes through what is actually some pretty serious cultural and intellectual traffic." In the view of the *Washington Post Book World*, "Sanjay Nigam's *The Snake Charmer* bids fair to join [the] select company of [Roy's *The God of Small Things* and Chandra's *Red Earth and Pouring Rain*].... Nigam's style is sparer but not for that reason less intense or less effective. The story partly is an allegory, but it is not fantastic. Because he is not given to verbal pyrotechnics or to adventitious tricks of style, he does not build barriers between himself and his reading public." *Kirkus Reviews* concludes that *The Snake Charmer* is "A small gem of a story that entertains, moves — and naturally, charms."

REVIEWS: *BL* 4/15/98; *KR* 4/15/98; *NYT* 7/6/98; *WPBW* 5/31/98

Roy, Arundhati (India)
474 *The God of Small Things* (1997); Random House 1997 (HC); HarperCollins 1998 (pbk)

Arundhati Roy's Booker Prize–winning debut novel, a lushly rendered family saga, is set largely in Kerala, India, in both the late 1960s and the present time, and begins with the tragic death of a child by the name of Sophie Mol. Among the mourners gathered at her funeral are her twin cousins Rahel and Estha children who, in the wake of their mother's wrenching divorce, have been living with their wealthy and eccentric relatives at the family's homestead in southern India. With their arrival in Kerala, an ineluctable series of events — with profoundly tragic ramifications — has been set in motion.

Michiko Kakutani (*NYT*) notes that in *The God of Small Things* Ms. Roy "creates a richly layered story of familial betrayal and thwarted romantic passion by cutting back and forth between time present and time past. Set in southern India against a backdrop of traditional religious and caste taboos, her story depicts the tragic confluence of events — both personal and political, private and public — that bring about the murder of an innocent man and the dissolution of a family." *Kirkus Reviews* observes that Roy's "brilliantly constructed first novel" is "in part a perfectly paced mystery story, in part an Indian Wuthering Heights: a gorgeous and seductive fever dream of a novel, and a truly spectacular debut." *Publishers Weekly*, in its starred review, argues that "With sensuous prose, a dreamlike style infused with breathtakingly beautiful images and keen insight into human nature, Roy's debut novel charts fresh territory in the genre of magical, prismatic literature." The *Times Literary Supplement* (while critical of Ms. Roy's "tendency to overwrite") suggests that the author's "finest touches spring from her skill at registering the unsayable terrors lodged below the surface of everyday things, in particular the terrors which take hold of children." Richard Eder (*LATBR*) observes that "Among the appealing elements [in this novel] are a wit that is sardonic and whimsical by turns, a portrait of social change in rural India in mid-century and both sympathy and harsh judgment for a doomed small-town upper-class. Above all, Roy evokes the promontory pain of the two children through whose eyes the story is told...." Mr. Eder concludes, however, that "Roy has dressed much of her book in an ambitious gorgeousness that she often lacks the dexterity to manage..."

OTHER MEDIA: Audiocassette (Harper Audio/abr; Books-on-Tape/unabr); RECOGNITION: Winner of the 1997 Booker Prize; *Publishers Weekly* "Best Books" 1997; *NYTBR* Notable Book of 1997; *Booklist* Editors' Choice 1997; REVIEWS: *BL* 5/1/97; *EW* 5/26/97; *LATBR* 6/1/97; *LJ* 4/15/97; *LST* 6/15/97; *LT* 6/7/97; *NewsWk* 5/26/97; *NY* 6/23/97; *NYT* 6/3/97; *NYTBR* 5/25/97; *PW* 3/3/97; *TLS* 5/30/97; *WPBW* 6/22/97

Rushdie, Salman (India/UK)

The Moor's Last Sigh (1995); Pantheon 1997 (pbk); See Section 3, #299

The Satanic Verses (1988); Holt 1997 (pbk reissue); See Section 3, #300

475   *Midnight's Children* (1981); Penguin 1995 (pbk reissue)

Salman Rushdie's Booker Prize–winning novel adroitly mixes Indian history, satire, autobiography and pure imagination to tell the story of Saleem Sinai, born on the stroke of midnight, August 15, 1947, the exact hour of India's Independence. Saleem, the illegitimate son of a low-caste Hindu woman and a British colonist, was switched at birth and has been raised by an unsuspecting, well-to-do Muslim couple. Shiva, the Muslim child, winds up in the care of a poor Hindu street performer. Saleem represents modern India (with its passionate, often irrational, dichotomies based on religion, class and station) and Saleem's life has a way of sympathetically coinciding with the critical events of the fledgling Indian nation, and, in some instances, of actually instigating them. Shiva, on the other hand, is destined to become India's most honored war hero.

According to Lorna Sage (*CF/BBT*), *Midnight's Children* is a book that "encompasses the rich contradiction of imperialism's legacy. Inheritance and its ramifications (legitimacy, authority, dynastic ambition) are at the center of the plot which converges on the accident-prone and unheroic person of the narrator Salem ... tied as if by an extra umbilical cord to the sub-continent's quarrelsome destiny." In the view of *The New York Times*, *Midnight's Children* is "a Bombay book, which is to say, a big-city book, [it] is coarse, knowing, comfortable with Indian pop culture and, above all, aggressive...."

RECOGNITION: Winner of the 1981 Booker Prize; REVIEWS: *CF/BBT* 1990; *NS&S* 7/30/82; *NYTBR* 3/28/82; *PW* 3/5/82; *WLT* Win '86

Sahgal, Nayantara (India)

476   *Mistaken Identity* (1988); New Directions 1992 (pbk)

Prize-winning Indian author Nayantara Sahgal's 9th novel is set in India in 1929 — a year characterized by extreme social and political unrest. Officials of the British Raj are nervous — the winds of nationalism and revolution are setting flags flapping all over the world. As the novel opens, Bhushan Singh, the feckless son of a minor Raj, has just returned to India from a brief sojourn in Europe. As he travels by train from Bombay to his ancestral village of Vijargarh, he is awakened in his sleeping compartment, arrested, mistakenly charged with treason and thrown into jail. As months and then years pass while Bhushan awaits trial, he assumes the role of Scheherezade, regaling his cellmates (National Congress Party members, communists, anarchists, and the like) with stories of his formerly privileged life. Women figure prominently in his stories, particularly his mother, assorted ayahs and his very modern Parsee girlfriend. In due time, the story of his relationship with a Muslim girl and the murderous riots which resulted are also revealed. Suspense builds as the stories move towards an unforeseen climax.

In the opinion of the *London Review of Books*: "For the actors in Nayantara Sahgal's *Mistaken Identity*, the agonies of Partition have yet to be; nevertheless, the story anticipates them. This is an elegant, adroitly constructed, mordantly witty book, in which the general image of and particular manifestation of our glamorous Raj is a garrulously over-populated prison cell." According to the *Times Literary Supplement* "Bhushan, a poet and aesthete, relates in half-exploratory, half humorous tones the ways of his world to his communist cell-mates. Many levels of meaning are unfolded — not least the questionable role of the rajas; through it all, Sahgal sustains the note of suspense while clearly suggesting the contrast between cultural synthesis [which characterized the 11th century arrival of Islam in India] and the divide-and-rule of recent, fractured times." The *L.A. Times Book Review* observes that Sahgal "offers an offbeat look at the early days of the Indian Independence Movement in this chatty novel" and concludes that "Sahgal's tale of one individual's reluctant politicization offers Western readers an unusual view of the struggle to end the Raj."

REVIEWS: *BellesL* Sum '89; *Books* 4/88; *KR* 3/1/89; *LATBR* 6/28/92; *LRB* 9/15/88; *NYTBR* 7/9/89; *TLS* 4/7/88; *WLT* Win '90

477 *Rich Like Us* (1986); New Directions 1990 (pbk)

Nayantara Sahgal has set her 8th novel in Delhi during the 1975 State of Emergency, a critical period in modern Indian history when many civil rights were substantially curtailed. *Rich Like Us* features Sonali, a senior Administration Officer, who fights for the rule of law, and Rose, a cockney ex-pat who fell in love with India and although married to an Indian for 40 years, brings her outsider's perspective to bear on the ramifications of post-Independence Indian politics.

The *New York Times Book Review* observes that Ms. Sahgal has produced a "fervent and ambitious" novel that "explores the complacency, hypocrisy and venality of several highly placed New Delhi families as observed by two women who, through chance rather than through heroism, find themselves outside the new regime's conspiracy of silence." The *Times Literary Supplement* observes that "some of the ignominious aspects of this time (e.g., the 1975 'Emergency') form the background to parts of *Midnight's Children*, and both Sahgal and Salman Rushdie use this material to illustrate

the confrontation between liberal traditions, and technological imperatives, a severely stratified society and the masses seeking to break these constraints...." *Publishers Weekly* further points out that *Rich Like Us* "which teems with the actualities of life in India [including] corruption, injustice, bureaucratic finagling, is wonderfully set apart by a fine, clear, disenchanted eye and an acerbic moral intelligence that is devastating without ever raising its voice."

RECOGNITION: Winner of England's Sinclair Prize for Literature; REVIEWS: *KR* 3/1/86; *LJ* 4/1/86; *NYTBR* 7/6/86; *PW* 2/28/86; *TLS* 7/85; *WLT* Spr '86

Selvadurai, Shyam (Sri Lanka)

Funny Boy (1995); Morrow 1996 (HC); See Section 2, #144

Seth, Vikram (India/USA)

478 *A Suitable Boy* (1993); Harper 1994 (pbk)

Vikram Seth's second novel (following — by seven years — his novel in verse *The Golden Gate*) is set in the post–Colonial India of the 1950s. At over 1,300 pages in length, *A Suitable Boy* is a sprawling family saga with a prodigious cast of characters and a dizzying array of plots and subplots. The basic story revolves around four families, the Mehras, Kapoors, Chatterjis and Khans whose domestic and financial crises reflect the historical and social events of that era. Much of the action takes place in the fictitious town of Brahmpur, a provincial backwater in the northern state of Purva Pradesh. As the tale progresses, mothers are pitted against daughters, fathers against sons, Hindus against Muslims, rich landowners against subsistence farmers. And through it all, the search for the "suitable boy" (a husband for Lata Mehra) continues...

According to the *New York Times Book Review*, *A Suitable Boy* "begins with a lavishly detailed set piece devoted to a Hindu wedding and, more than 1,300 pages later, ends with another. One might well see the book in terms of a coupling (an odd one), for Mr. Seth ... has joined an essentially tidy Jane Austen–like main plot with an attempt to re-create the multitudinous life of post–British India on a scale unequaled since Salman Rushdie's *Midnight's Children*." In the view of the *Montreal Gazette*, "What makes *A Suitable Boy* such a remarkable novel is Seth's extraordinary skill in drawing characters and his control over a story that meanders like the Ganges. All this at a time when the literary trend favors undermining narrative and character." The *Guardian* calls *A Suitable Boy* a "huge testament to human comedy, lightly told but not lacking the depth of understanding we should demand from novelists." According to Tunku Varadarajan of the *London Times*, "In its sweep, the book reminds one of a Bombay — or 'Bollywood' — cinematic blockbuster. But unlike 'Bollywood' it works, genuinely, at more than one level. Of course it is soap operatic, but it is also epic.... It is this intriguing schizophrenia that readers have lapped up, and paid wads of notes for.... His Indian readers, furthermore, are at ease with the book, and it has not generated the sort of polemic 'back home' which modern Indo-Anglian literature so often does."

RECOGNITION: Winner of the W.H. Smith Award, nominated for the *Guardian* Fiction Prize; *NYTBR* Notable Book of 1993; REVIEWS: *ChiTrib* 5/23/93; *Guard* 4/10/94; *KR* 3/15/93; *LT* 3/5/93; *MontrG* 5/1/93; *NS&S* 3/19/93; *NYTBR* 5/9/93; *TLS* 3/19/93

Sidhwa, Bapsi (Pakistan/USA)

An American Brat (1993); Milkweed 1995 (pbk); See Section 2, #146

479   *Cracking India* (1991); Milkweed 1992 (pbk)

Bapsi Sidhwa sets *Cracking India* in the Punjab during India's violent 1947 "partition," which took the lives of more than a million people and displaced 13 million more. One of the most disturbing aspects of this event was the ferocity of the violence, particularly in the Punjab where Sikhs, Muslims and Hindus — with breathtaking cruelty — acted out their ancient communal hatreds. Ms. Sidhwa's tale is told exclusively from a child's perspective, that of Lenny, the seven-year-old, crippled yet privileged daughter of a wealthy Parsi family. Lenny's world is dominated by her ayah, a beautiful young Punjabi girl with numerous suitors — each of whom is drawn from a different segment of Punjabi society. Lenny's lack of social differentiation (i.e., she does not categorize the people in her world by age, caste, or religion) throws the events of the time into sharp relief.

According to the *Washington Post Book World*, most fictions "deal in therapeutic falsehoods, but in *Cracking India* Bapsi Sidhwa has written an emphatically historical novel bout a child who cannot lie to save a life. More than that: she has told a sweet and amusing tale filled with the worst atrocities imaginable; she has concocted a girlishly romantic love story which is driven by the most militant feminism; above all she has turned her gaze upon the domestic comedy of a Pakistani family in the 1940s and somehow managed to evoke the great political upheavals of the age." The *Literary Review* found Ms. Sidhwa's "Rabelesian language and humor [to be] enormously refreshing, especially in the context of modern Indian fiction, which has

tended towards the prim and stilted ... [and concludes that] as a portrait of an Indian childhood at a critical time, it is ... a small jewel." Indian novelist **Shashi Tharoor** (*NYTBR*) calls this a novel "in which heartbreak coexists with slapstick, where awful jokes ... give way to lines of glowing beauty" and concludes that even though Ms. Sidhwa doesn't handle politics well, has "given us ... a memorable book, one that confirms her reputation as Pakistan's finest English-language novelist." *Belles Lettres*, while observing that "Some readers may find that Sidhwa tends occasionally to pander to Western tastes, or reinforces communal stereotypes and biases while seeking to inject relief via farcical scenes replete with sexual imagery, bathroom humor, and profanity" concludes that "Sidhwa's novel provides a fascinating cross-cultural vignette of how broken lives triumph when the past is forgiven, even if fate cannot be undone."

OTHER MEDIA: a film version will be released in 1999; RECOGNITION: *NYTBR* Notable Book of 1991, ALA Notable Book; NY Public Library "Books for Young Readers" Literature Prize for Fiction; REVIEWS: *BellesL* Fall '91; *LitRev* 3/88; *LRB* 9/15/88; *NS* 2/26/88; *NYTBR* 10/6//91; *WPBW* 11/24/91; EDITOR'S NOTE: *Cracking India* was originally published in 1988 in the UK under the title *Ice Candy Man*.

480   *The Crow Eaters* (1982); Milkwood 1992 (pbk reissue)

In her debut novel Bapsi Sidhwa takes a satirical look at the lives of one Parsee family in the early years of the 20th-century. When Faredoon (Freddy) Junglewalla decides to load his pregnant wife, infant daughter and widowed mother-in-law onto a bullock cart and leave his ancestral village for the bustling city of Lahore, he sets in motion a series of events which will culminate in the family's rise to prominence and prosperity. Freddy's ongoing antagonistic relationship with Jerbanoo, his intransigent mother-in-law, provides the grist for the author's comic mill.

According to the *Washington Post Book World*, *The Crow Eaters* "is best read as a series of wonderfully comic episodes, to be enjoyed for their wit and absurdity. Although the author has written more eloquently in subsequent books, this is a welcome reissue of a lively and entertaining first novel by a talented writer." The *Bloomsbury Review* found Ms. Sidhwa's novel to be "a good-humored satirical miracle of one Parsee family." The *Library Journal* concludes that *The Crow Eaters* is a "comic novel stuffed with rich, spicy characters. Sidhwa makes every step of Faredoon's journey through time and culture a joy to read."

REVIEWS: *BloomR* 10/85; *KR* 1/1/82; *LJ* 1/15/82; *NYTBR* 1/10/93; *PW* 1/15/92; *WPBW* 11/24/92

Syal, Meera (Indo-British)

Anita & Me (1997); New Press 1997 (HC); 1999 (pbk); See Section 2, #148

Tharoor, Shashi (India)

481 *Show Business: A Novel* (1992); Arcade 1992 (HC); 1993 (pbk)

Set in "Bollywood" Bombay's version of Hollywood, Shashi Tharoor's second novel takes a humorous look at the colorful, conniving, irrepressible world of Indian filmmaking. Tharoor tells the story of Ashok Banjara, a venal, philandering mega-star in the Indian film industry pantheon. When Ashok, in search of a new challenge, decides to run for Parliament (after all, politicians are just actors in a different medium, aren't they?) trouble — in the form of blackmail, a frame-up, declining screen popularity and a near-fatal accident — soon follows.

According to *Booklist*, *Show Business* is "an animated and deliciously satirical critique of the Bombay film industry ... an effervescent and thoroughly satisfying rendition of the human comedy." In the view of English novelist **William Boyd** (*NYTBR*), "What makes *Show Business* particularly impressive and accomplished is its elaborate structure, a mix of first-person narration, synopses of Ashok's dreadful Hindi films and resentful and accusatory monologues by the supporting cast. The effect is to fragment and rearrange the chronology of the rise, fall and rise again of Ashok Banjara in a way that replicates the crazy razzle-dazzle of the Hindi film world, but that also permits Mr. Tharoor to comment, with telling irony and insight, on the curious parallels between India's unique film culture and the swarming, baffling and beguiling variety — the vivacity and corruption, the serenity and chaos, the sophistication and naive self-delusion — of India itself." Jonathan Yardley (*WPBW*) notes that "Eschewing the temptations of magical realism to which other Indian writers have succumbed, he has written a witty, ironic novel in which Indian film — and India itself— is seen from any number of revealing angles." English novelist **Jonathan Coe**, writing in the *London Sunday Times*, concludes that "Tharoor has succeeded in pulling off a substantial literary coup by writing an enormously funny and enjoyable novel which has never for a moment been frivolous."

REVIEWS: *BL* 6/15/92; *KR* 4/1/92; *LATBR* 8/29/93; *LST* 6/26/94; *NYTBR* 9/27/92; *PW* 3/16/92; *TLS* 6/94; *WPBW* 9/27/92

The Great Indian Novel (1989); Arcade 1992 (pbk); See Section 8, #1031

Vakil, Ardashir (India)

482 *Beach Boy* (1997); S&S 1998 (HC)

Ardashir Vakil's debut novel is a coming-of-age story set in 1972 in a comfortable suburb of Bombay, India. The narrator, Cyrus Readymoney, is a precocious (sexually inquisitive) eight-year-old whose loving but self-absorbed parents are in perpetual marital turmoil. Cyrus looks for connection elsewhere — particularly among his eclectic group of neighbors.

Publishers Weekly observes that in "[m]arrying a universal story (an adolescent boy's coming of age) with a specific locale (India in the 1970s), Indian writer Vakil has produced a charming and agreeable first novel distinguished by vivid detail, wry humor and charismatic characters." According to the *Times Literary Supplement Beach Boy* "is a rich portrait, with telling insights into the characteristics of the different communities which make up the modern Indian middle-class.... The descriptions of food are numerous and memorable." The *L.A. Times Book Review* notes that "From the spectacular imagery of Hindi cinema to the exquisitely prepared and presented traditional foods, Vakil mirrors a sensuality almost spiritual in its intensity, thus sharpening the irony reflected in the surname he gives his protagonist."

RECOGNITION: Winner of the 1997 Betty Trask Award for Fiction; nominated for the Whitbread Prize for First Fiction; *LATBR* "Best Fiction of 1998"; REVIEWS: *Guard* 5/23/98; *KR* 7/1/98; *LATBR* 8/9/98; *LST* 6/15/97; *LT* 5/24/97; *Obs* 6/1/97; *PW* 6/15/98; *TLS* 3/30/97; *WPBW* 9/27/98

5

Time After Time

Section 5 features well-crafted novels incorporating historical figures (e.g., Glyn Hughes's *Bronte*, C.S. Godshalk's *Kalimantaan*, Jay Parini's *Benjamin's Crossing*) or historical events (e.g., Charles Frazier's *Cold Mountain*, Beryl Bainbridge's *Master Georgie*, Christopher Koch's *Highways to a War*). It also includes novels whose historical settings are integral to the narrative (e.g., A.S. Byatt's *Babel Tower*, Philip Roth's *American Pastoral*, Andrea Barrett's *Voyage of the Narwhal*). Century-spanning family sagas and fictional memoirs (from such writers as Michael Cunningham, Micheal Dorris, Mark Helprin, and Elizabeth Jane Howard) are also well represented. What they all have in common is an ability to capture a sense of lives lived within a wholly believable historical context.

Ackroyd, Peter (UK)

483   *Milton in America* (1996); Doubleday 1997 (HC); SETTING: Puritan America in 1660

Peter Ackroyd, in his ninth novel, spins a highly speculative tale around the (fictitious) proposition that John Milton — in the early days of the English Restoration — had fled to the colonies to escape the wrath of the newly reinstated Charles II. Milton had, indeed, assisted the (now deposed) Oliver Cromwell by writing inflammatory pamphlets in support of Puritan causes, and was briefly imprisoned in 1660. In the end, however, he was saved from a traitor's death through the intercession of Royalist friends. In Peter Ackroyd's version of the story, an already-blind Milton, fearful for his life, sails for the new world in the company of a young well-educated scribe, nicknamed Goosequill, and eventually takes up residence in a Puritan settlement by the name of New Tiverton (subsequently renamed New Milton). Ackroyd's novelistic conceit is to imagine what Milton (who, as the historical record suggests, could be harsh and vitriolic), might have gotten up to if his prodigious energies and creative genius were engaged in social engineering rather than in the writing of his masterpiece, *Paradise Lost*. The author's verdict is not flattering. When a group of Catholic settlers arrives with plans to establish themselves in a community across the river, they soon learn that the Puritans are prepared to go to great lengths to prevent this incursion of unbelievers.

Had Milton actually shipped out to the colonies, "How (in the words of the *London Times*) would he have fared out there, and what would he have done?" This is the question that Peter Ackroyd addresses in an altogether splendid and visionary conjuration of Puritan New England, with Milton taking a hand in its politics and religion." The *L.A. Times Book Review* notes that "Ackroyd's vision ... rings uncannily true ... [further suggesting that Ackroyd's "thought-provoking" novel] should be set alongside the most recent in a long line of Milton biographies." In the view of the *Times Literary Supplement* this "is not a perfect novel ... [Ackroyd] mixes dream sequence with chronicle, epistle, journal, first- and third-person narrative, dialogue, and dialogue within dialogue, until the punctuation looks like Morse-code and the reader begs for mercy. Milton's arch-enemies, too, are unevenly drawn." The *TLS* concludes, however, that "Milton himself is a wonderful creation: as exasperating and exhilarating as we have come to expect of an Ackroyd hero." *Booklist* echoes this observation, concluding that the reader's "perseverance is worth it; Ackroyd's Milton is an extraordinary character whose voice rings out long after the book is closed." The *London Sunday Times* observing that Peter

Ackroyd "is keen to explore the dark side of Protestantism and what he obviously sees as a fanatical strain in Milton's Puritanism (turning him into a half-mad bigot who gets up to something mysteriously untoward in the woods)" concludes that Ackroyd "handles [the story] with his usual flair."

OTHER MEDIA: Audiocassette (Books-on-Tape/unabr); RECOGNITION: *Booklist* Editors' Choice 1997; REVIEWS: *BL* 3/15/97; *KR* 2/15/97; *LATBR* 4/27/97; *LJ* 4/1/97; *LST* 10/12/97; *LT* 8/29/96; *NewL* 5/5/97; *NS* 9/27/96; *NYT* 5/14/97; *NYTBR* 4/6/97; *PW* 2/24/97; *TLS* 8/30/96; *WPBW* 6/15/97

Adams, Alice (USA)

484 *A Southern Exposure* (1995); Knopf 1995 (HC); Columbine 1996 (pbk); SETTING: The fictional college town of Pinehill, North Carolina, in the years preceding World War II.

On a fine blue summer afternoon, in the distant 30s, one of those brief and hopeful years between the Depression and the War, a once-grand wood-paneled station wagon heads south, down all those winding white concrete miles, in flight from Connecticut....

So begins *A Southern Exposure*, Alice Adams's 12th work of fiction. The Bairds (long-established New Englanders) have decided to pull up their patrician roots and replant themselves in a small, picturesque college town in North Carolina. They are drawn by the lure of gracious living, by an understanding that the "depression dollar" goes farther the farther one goes south, and by the promise of a gentle, languid climate. They are searching for the elusive fresh start — an opportunity to rejuvenate both their fortune and their marriage....

Novelist **Doris Betts** (*WPBW*) observes that "Alice Adams is a novelist of manners, alert to what Lionel Trilling called 'a culture's hum and buzz,' and in (*A Southern Exposure*) she shrewdly not only selects the noises she has heard with her own ears but detects that first change in the standard rhythm that signaled in the late 1930s that America, and especially Southern, mores were about to change." The *New Yorker* critic found *A Southern Exposure* to be "a smart, immensely readable novel about lives unraveling in a Southern college town where there is an urgent conspiracy to keep things as they are." In the view of the *L.A. Times Book Review*, "*Southern Exposure* succeeds as an intricate, often surprising portrait of cultural collision." The *New York Times Book Review*, while noting Ms. Adams's use of an occasionally "sudsy" plotline (strong on amorous intrigue), praises the author's "wistful lyricism [which] perfectly captures this lovely place and golden time."

RECOGNITION: *NYTBR* "Notable Book" of 1995; REVIEW: *BL* 8/95; *ChiTrib* 11/26/95; *EW* 10/21/95; *KR* 8/1/95; *LATBR* 1/3/96; *LJ* 9/1/95; *NYTBR* 10/8/95; *NY* 1/22/96; *PW* 7/31/95; *WPBW* 11/19/95

Alvarez, Julia (USA)

485 *In the Time of the Butterflies* (1994); Algonquin 1994 (HC); NAL-Dutton 1995 (pbk); SETTING: Dominican Republic 1930s–1960s

She remembers a clear moonlit night before the future began. They are sitting in the cool darkness under the anacahuita tree in the front yard, in the rockers, telling stories, drinking guanabana juice. Good for the nerves, Mama always says.

They're all there, Mama, Papa, Patria–Minerva–Dede. Bang, Bang, Bang, their father likes to joke, aiming a finger pistol at each one, as if he were shooting them, not boasting about having sired them. Three girls, each born within a year of the other! And then, nine years later, Maria Teresa, his final, desperate attempt at a boy misfiring.

Julia Alvarez sets her second novel in the Dominican Republic during the Trujillo dictatorship and tells the fictionalized story of the four Mirabal sisters, three of whom, along with their husbands, were members of an underground resistance movement dedicated to the overthrow of Trujillo's regime. Their code names were Mariposa I, II and III — the "butterflies." Dede, the one apolitical sister, narrates the story. Ms. Alvarez imagines the lives of these women from girlhood, through young adulthood and marriage and, finally, to their final hours in the resistance movement.

According to *Belles Lettres*: "The story is related through first-person accounts of each sister, resulting in multiple perspectives of central events. It is embellished with Maria Teresa's diary entries and sketches, as well as bits of poetry and song...." *Booklist* calls *In the Time of the Butterflies* "a statement about politics and history told in very human terms and, as importantly, told not with outrage, but with self-possession." *Hispanic* observes that "The last quarter of the book covers the events leading up to the day that the three sisters ... make the treacherous journey over the mountains to visit their husbands in jail. The reader knows what is going to happen, but now those everyday details build the suspense and keep the pages turning." *World Literature Today* deems Ms. Alvarez's fictional account "a superb, heartrending story" and concludes that she has "again displayed her fine talent as a novelist. Especially noteworthy is her ability to maintain an equilibrium between the political and the human, the tragic and the lyrical."

RECOGNITION: Nominated for the 1994 National Book Critics Circle Award; REVIEWS: *BL* 7/94; *BellesL* Spr '95; *ChiTrib* 10/24/94; *Hisp* 12/94; *LJ* 8/94; *Ms* 9-10/94; *Nation* 11/7/94; *NewsWk* 10/17/94; *NYTBR* 12/18/94; *WLT* Aut '95; *WPBW* 11/27/94

Ansa, Tina McElroy (USA)

486   *Baby of the Family* (1989); Harcourt-Brace 1991 (pbk); African American Images 1996 (pbk); SETTING: Small-town Georgia in the 1950s

In her first novel, Tina McElroy Ansa tells a poignant and life-affirming tale of a black girl's coming-of-age in a small Southern town in the 1950s. Lena McPherson, daughter of Nellie and Jonah, was born in a private "blacks only" rural hospital. From the moment of her birth Lena was marked out as special, arriving as she did with a fetal membrane known as a "caul" covering her face. It surprises no one that Lena possesses special powers which include both second sight *and* an ability to communicate with spirits. While the supernatural element adds spice, Ms. Ansa focuses primarily on Lena's every-day experiences (parental tensions, a grandmother's death, etc.) growing up in a comfortable, middle-class black family in the pre–Civil Rights era.

According to critic and novelist **Valerie Sayers** (*NYTBR*) "Tina McElroy Ansa tells a good story, and she tells it with humor, grace and respect for the powers of the particular." *Publishers Weekly* observes that "Despite her extraordinary talent, Lena is most memorable for the ordinariness of her everyday life. Following Lena's first friendships, her years at school, her observations of her parents sometimes stormy relationship, her grief at her grandmother's death, Ansa beautifully renders Lena's stable well-off world." The *School Library Journal* says that "Ansa's dialogue is realistic, and her characters are colorful" and concludes that "The supernatural elements are well-blended into the novel, adding to the richness of the fiction." The *Chicago Tribune* notes that "*Baby of the Family* [which is both delicate and enveloping] gives a sense of black life in America that is both healthy and unaffected by racial tension" and concludes that it is "a book that creeps up on the reader, conveying wisdom as subtly as experience conveys wisdom to Lena."

RECOGNITION: *NYTBR* Notable Book of 1990; REVIEWS: *BL* 11/1/89; *ChiTrib* 12/24/89; *Essence* 3/90; *KR* 9/1/89; *Newsday* 11/5/89; *NYTBR* 11/26/89; *PW* 9/8/89; *SLJ* 6/90; *VLS* 5/90

Askew, Rilla (USA)

487   *The Mercy Seat* (1997); Viking 1997; Viking Penguin 1998 (pbk); SETTING: Kentucky, Arkansas & the Oklahoma Indian Territory — late 1880s

In her debut novel, a Cain-and-Abel story transposed to Arkansas and the Oklahoma Indian Territory in the final decades of the 19th century, Rilla Aksew (herself an Oklahoma native) tells of John and Fayette Lodi who, in the aftermath of a business deal gone sour, flee Kentucky for the unbridled promise of the newly opened western territories. It soon becomes clear that the brothers, although inseparable, are polar opposites: John is stoical and forbearing while Fayette ("Fate") is feckless and opportunistic. During their arduous westward trek, John's wife dies, and 10-year-old Mattie, John's oldest daughter, must assume her mother's role.

According to *Publishers Weekly*, "Among the many triumphs of this story ... none surpass its depiction of time and place: Oklahoma in the late 1800s, a gritty epoch of guns, whiskey and horses.... Askew's prose is mesmerizing, saturated with the rhythms of the prophets and patriarchs (as heard by Faulkner rather than Steinbeck)." *Booklist* observes that "the novel [told mostly in the voice of John's eldest daughter], is bleak, dark, and moving, peopled with vivid characters and filled with compelling details and poetically rendered narrative." *Kirkus Reviews* argues that "Mattie is simply one of the most engaging and heartbreaking characters in contemporary fiction" and concludes that *The Mercy Seat* is "a magnificent debut novel."

RECOGNITION: Nominated for the PEN/Faulkner Award; REVIEWS: *BL* 8/19/97; *KR* 6/1/97; *LJ* 7/97; *NYTBR* 10/12/97; *PW* 6/23/97

Bahr, Howard (USA)

488   *The Black Flower* (1997); Aviation Press 1997 (HC); SETTING: Franklin, Tennessee — 1864

The Black Flower, a poignant and harrowing drama set during the American Civil War, was exceedingly well-received when published by a small press in 1997. Set during a period of 48 hours in 1864, Bahr's novel follows a group of Mississippi soldiers at the Battle of Franklin, Tennessee. Under orders to attack a regiment of fresh Union soldiers, the battle-weary men of the storied 21st marched across an open field into the oncoming fusillade.

The *Chicago Tribune* calls *The Black Flower* "a [powerful and elegiac] novel of the blighted world that belies the romance of the Lost Cause" and concludes that in its pages, Bahr "has collapsed the whole fury of a battle onto a tiny stage — the fields of a small Tennessee farm, and with players no more numerous than a few members of a Mississippi regiment and the family in the farmhouse." *Publishers Weekly*, in its starred review, argues that "Amidst all the powerful Civil War historical fiction of recent years, Bahr's first novel stands as a memorable story of war at its most emotional and painful." The *New York Times Book Review* concludes that the author captures "the malignity of war ... with post–Vietnam graphic ferocity."

RECOGNITION: *NYTBR* Notable Book of

1998; REVIEWS: *BL* 4/15/97; *ChiTrib* 3/20/98; *KR* 2/1/97; *NYTBR* 8/2/98; *PW* 3/10/97

Bainbridge, Beryl (UK)

489 *Master Georgie* (1998); Carroll & Graf 1998 (HC); SETTING: England & the Crimea in the mid–1800s

Beryl Bainbridge punctuates her sixteenth novel — which begins in Liverpool in 1846 and moves to the Crimea during the ill-fated British military campaign — with a succession of photographs taken by (the fictional) George Hardy, a medical student and amateur photographer who has volunteered for military duty. Little understood at the time (although enthusiastically supported on the home front), the Crimean War was characterized by the kind of gross incompetence and misadventure which results in unconscionably heavy casualties. Ms. Bainbridge, ignoring the War's most well-known figures (Florence Nightingale, Lord Cardigan, William Howard Russell), follows the enigmatic young George Hardy and his circle of intimates (the devoted Myrtle, a foundling raised as Georgie's sister; Pompey Jones, George's technical assistant and sometime lover; and George's brother-in-law, the brilliant, lascivious, Dr. Potter) as they make their way from Liverpool, to Constantinople and finally to the killing fields of Sevastopol.

Kirkus Reviews calls *Master Georgie* an "exemplary work from one of Britain's finest writers [and] a triumph of imaginative empathy. "To describe [the novel] as historical fiction would be" in the view of the *Times Literary Supplement* "to deprive it of its individuality. What Bainbridge has achieved is a form of realism which makes its historical setting as immediate and vivid, and as chaotic, as anything set in the present." Novelist **Francine Prose** (*NYTBR*) observes that "Beryl Bainbridge … places little stock in the ability of good intentions and common sense to dampen our natural appetite for duplicity, cruelty and violence, or to defeat the threatening, disruptive force of haphazard actions" and concludes that "For these reasons, *Master Georgie* is hardly a feel-good book — unless you're a reader whose spirits are lifted by the prospect of a writer so original and so firmly in control of her art."

RECOGNITION: Shortlisted for the 1998 Booker Prize; *LATBR* "Best Fiction of 1998"; *NYTBR* Notable Book of 1998; *PW*'s Best '98 Fiction; REVIEWS: *BL* 11/1/98; *KR* 8/15/98; *LT* 4/24/98; *LST* 4/19/98; *NYTBR* 11/29/97; *TLS* 4/24/98; *WPBW* 11/15/98

490 *Every Man for Himself* (1996); Carroll & Graf 1996 (HC); 1997 (pbk); SETTING: Maiden voyage of the *Titanic* — The North Atlantic, 1912

The sinking of the *Titanic*, one of the more poignant catastrophes of the newly emergent 20th century, has yet to lose its capacity to appall and enthrall. In her 15th novel, English novelist Beryl Bainbridge uses the *Titanic* disaster as an effective framing device for her tragi-comic depiction of pleasure-seeking, class-bound Edwardian society teetering on the edge of an historical abyss. Her story is narrated by Morgan, a 21-year-old adopted nephew of J.P. Morgan who owns the *Titanic*, an appealing, if rather superficial, young man who discovers his true self as the tragic scenario unfolds.

Every Man for Himself, shortlisted for the prestigious Booker Prize, has garnered widespread critical approval. For example, The *New York Times Book Review* argues that given the surfeit of recent treatments "it is difficult to imagine a more engrossing account of the famous shipwreck than this one." According to the *L.A. Times Book Review*: "Joining the throng of Titania is a fast-paced novel that blends known facts with fiction into a coming-of-age tale that also captures a social moment. For acclaimed British novelist Beryl Bainbridge, tragic death is only part of it. What interests her are the thorny moral questions — of fate versus human intervention, of compassionate acts versus an individual's responsibility for himself." *Booklist* notes that Ms. Bainbridge "seamlessly interweaves real people and invented characters with the actual events of the sinking ship [thereby using] life aboard the *Titanic* as a metaphor for the years immediately preceding World War I…." The *New Statesman* praises the novel's pace, wit and "complex characters who engage first the reader's curiosity, then affection," further noting that the "elegiac theme extends far beyond the historical event." *Publishers Weekly* argues that "Bainbridge's swift economical novel tell us more about an era and the ways in which its people inhabit it than volumes of social history." The *Washington Post Book World* concludes that "*Every Man for Himself* is a paradigm of precision. In a time of narrative sprawl, when many novels seem sold for weight rather than content, Bainbridge recounts as epic in slightly more than 200 pages."

OTHER MEDIA: Audiocassette (Sterling Audio/ unabr); RECOGNITION: Winner of the Whitbred Prize for Literature; Shortlisted for the 1996 Booker Prize; *London Sunday Times* Notable Book of 1996; REVIEWS: *AtlM* 12/96; *BL* 11/1/96; *LATBR* 11/24/ 96; *LJ* 9/1/96; *LRB* 10/17/96; *NS* 9/13/96; *NY* 10/14/96; *NYTBR* 12/22/96; *PW* 8/26/96; *TLS* 9/6/98; *WPBW* 11/24/96; *WSJ* 1/15/96; EDITOR'S NOTE: Ms. Bainbridge's 1992 novel *The Birthday Boys* is woven around Robert Scott's ill-fated expedition to the South Pole. Scott is one of five personalities brought to life in Beryl Bainbridge's powerful story of courage, endurance and folly in one of the least forgiving spots on the face of the earth. The story centers around the five men of the expedition who, during their three years together, celebrate their birthdays in a variety of locations, physical conditions and states of mind.

Baker, Larry (USA)

491   *The Flamingo Rising* (1997); Knopf 1997 (HC); Ballantine 1998 (pbk); SETTING: North Florida in the late '50s and early '60s

Larry Baker's debut novel, a coming-of-age story—which owes more than a nod to William Shakespeare—is a curious mixture of late 1950s Florida kitsch, tender young love, and domestic tragedy. The narrator, Abraham Isaac Lee, is the son of Hubert Lee, the owner of a drive-in theater featuring the world's largest outdoor screen. Mr. Lee has chosen to build his dream project on the beach between Jacksonville and St. Augustine, right smack on top of—so to speak—a stately funeral home owned by Turner West the local mortician. An extremely unhealthy rivalry develops between these two men and, in the meantime, Abe falls desperately in love with Mr. Turner's daughter, Grace. The story is liberally larded with the antics of a large cast of southern eccentrics.

The *L.A. Times Book Review* calls *Flamingo Rising* a debut novel that "dares to mix the Icarus, Oedipus and Earhart myths, risks a Romeo and Juliet update, plunders Dante, references the Bible, rewrites movie history and inside-outs the American past." According to *Entertainment Weekly*, Larry Baker's novel "resonates with good humor, adolescent lust, complex love, and heartrending loss." The *New Yorker* notes that "Larry Baker is writing for adults, but he remembers how it felt not to be one, and renders the experience in unforced, unshowy prose, neither folksy nor formal."

OTHER MEDIA: Audiocassette (Random Audio/ unabr); Reading Group Guide; RECOGNITION: *LATBR* "Best Books" 1997; REVIEWS: *BL* 8/97; *ChiTrib* 9/19/97; *EW* 10/31/97; *KR* 7/15/97; *LATBR* 10/5/97; *NY* 9/15/97; *NYTBR* 9/28/97; *PW* 8/4/97; *WPBW* 9/11/97

Banks, Russell (USA)

492   *Cloudsplitter* (1998); HarperCollins 1998 (HC); 1999 (pbk); SETTING: Harpers Ferry, Virginia, in 1859

Russell Banks uses the voice of Owen Brown, son of the famous abolitionist, freedom fighter, and religious fanatic, John Brown, to narrate his prodigiously researched, 700-page novel. The story is told through a series of letters written by Owen (40 years after his father's execution) to an academic who is planning to write a biography of the anti-

slavery crusader. *Cloudsplitter*, which is written in a sober 19th century expository style (no post-modern playfulness here) explores the twin issues of racism and religious commitment in pre–Civil War America.

Banks novel was called "monolithic and masterly" by *Time* magazine which further argues that "Nobody who reads the first chapters ... can doubt that [the author] has found his big subject. It is surely his best novel, a furious, sprawling drama that commands attention like thunder heard from just over the horizon." According to Michiko Kakutani (*NYT*) "While *Cloudsplitter* plays fast and loose with the facts, it does two things very well: it gives us a vivid, emotionally tactile portrait of John Brown the man, a portrait quite in keeping, overall, with the work of Brown biographers ... and it leaves us with equally potent understanding of the passions animating the anti-slavery movement during the 1840s and '50s." As noted in the *New York Times Book Review*, Banks's novel is "shaped like an explosive with an exceedingly long and winding fuse ... [and while] here and there the writing grows slow and solemn ... the book has an underlying tidal flow that rolls the story inevitably forward." The *L.A. Times Book Review* calls *Cloudsplitter* "a vibrant, outsized, mesmerizing portrait of the mercurial Brown that reveals his charm as well as his piety, his compassion as well as his demonic wrath, his intellect as well as his willfulness."

OTHER MEDIA: Audiocassette (Audio Literature/abr; Books-on-Tape/unabr); RECOGNITION: *LATBR* "Best Fiction of 1998"; *NYTBR* "Editors' Choice" 1998; *PW's* Best '98 Fiction; REVIEWS: *BL* 12/1/97; *ChiTrib* 3/15/98; *KR* 1/1/98; *LATBR* 3/8/98; *NY* 4/6/98; *NYT* 2/17/98; *NYTBR* 2/ 22/98; *PW* 12/1/97; *Time* 3/2/98; *WPBW* 4/7/98

Barker, Pat (UK)

493   *The Ghost Road* (1995); Dutton 1995 (HC); Viking Penguin 1996 (pbk); SETTING: W.W.I England and France

The Ghost Road completes Pat Barker's powerful, prize-winning W.W.I Regeneration Trilogy. The third volume again features Dr. M.H.R. Rivers (based on the real-life psychologist) whose job it is to rehabilitate—with a goal to returning them to active, front-line duty—the shell-shocked officers assigned to his care. In *The Ghost Road*, Dr. Rivers experiences a bout of influenza which triggers vivid fever-induced memories of his early anthropological work in Melanesia where he lived with a tribe of former headhunters. These memories now color the doctor's analysis of so-called "civilized" warfare. Lieutenant Billy Prior, a profoundly war-damaged, bisexual, working-class officer, also makes an encore appearance.

The *Washington Post Book World* observes that

in her trilogy's final volume "Barker's shell-shocked lieutenant returns to France and her noble psychologist to his past — both perilous terrains" and concludes that *The Ghost Road* mixes "the single-bullet understatement of the best war fiction with a bottomless grasp of its tragic ironies." The *New Yorker* notes that Barker has rescued M.H.R. Rivers from historical obscurity by inventing "a consciousness for [him] — a deep-flowing and somewhat turbulent one. And she also invents a patient for him: [tough, libidinous] Billy Prior … Pat Barker respects Rivers, but she loves Prior. His energy, particularly his sexual energy, is what makes this trilogy more than mere historical fiction. Through him, Pat Barker presents the First World War as the test tube of the modern spirit." *Publisher Weekly*, in its starred review, concludes that "The whole trilogy, which in its entirety is only equivalent to one blockbuster serial killer frenzy, is a triumph of an imagination at once poetic and practical." The *Times Literary Supplement* calls *The Ghost Road* "a startlingly good novel in its own right" and concludes that with "the other two volumes of the trilogy, it forms one of the richest and most rewarding works of fiction of recent times. Intricately plotted, beautifully written, skillfully assembled, tender, horrifying and funny, it lives on in the imagination, like the war it so imaginatively and so intelligently explores."

OTHER MEDIA: Audiocassette (Chivers/unabr; Recorded Books/unabr); RECOGNITION: Winner of the 1995 Booker Prize; *NYTBR* Notable Book of 1996; *WPBW* "Best Books of 1996"; nominated for the 1996 *L.A. Times* Book Prize; REVIEWS: *BL* 2/1/96; *ChiTrib* 4/5/96; *Econ* 10/21/95; *LJ* 2/15/96; *LRB* 10/15/95; *NewR* 4/29/96; *NS&S* 2/29/95; *NY* 1/22/96; *NYRB* 2/15/96; *NYTBR* 12/31/95; *OS* 11/26/95; *PW* 11/27/95; *Salon* 12/2/95; *TLS* 9/8/95; *WPBW* 12/10/95; *WSJ* 12/18/95; EDITOR'S NOTE: Ms. Barker was named by *Granta* magazine to its 1983 list of the twenty "Best Young British Novelists"

494   *Eye in the Door* (1993); Dutton 1995 (pbk); SETTING: WWI England

Shortly after the outbreak of war, Miss Burton's little dog had gone missing. Miss Burton was a spinster who haunted the parish church, arranged flowers, sorted jumble, cherished a hopeless love for the vicar — how hopeless probably only Prior knew. He'd been home at the time, waiting for orders to join his regiment, and he'd help her search for the dog. They found it tied by a wire to the railway fence, in a buzzing cloud of black flies, disemboweled. It was a daschound. One of the enemy.

The *Eye in the Door* is the second volume of Pat Barker's award-winning World War I trilogy. The "eye" in the door of the title refers to the intrusive interest of British officialdom in the sexual pro-

clivities of its citizenry and the novel is inspired, in part, by a specific historical incident, the Pemberton Billings libel trial, in which all of Britain's military troubles were laid at the feet of homosexuals. Once again, Ms. Barker provides a brilliant examination of the doctor/patient relationship.

The *London Review of Books* refers to *The Eye in the Door* as "a continuation, and enrichment, of *Regeneration*," further noting that as "a novel of formidable energy and integrity … it confirms Barker's status as one of the most rewarding writers to have emerged in recent years." Novelist and playwright **Jim Shepard** (*NYTBR*) says it "succeeds both as historical novel and as sequel" and concludes that "Ms. Barker memorably renders the pride and fierce shame, bewilderment, humiliation, fear and icy self-disgust of those young men who, raised to venerate a concept of honor based on self-control, nevertheless broke down under the lunatic horror of trench warfare." *New Statesman & Society* concludes that *The Eye in the Door* "is shockingly good: as powerful an indictment of the first world war as the earlier novel, and further reaching in its analysis of the social and psychological forces that created and sustained the catastrophe." Irish novelist Julia O'Faolain (*TLS*) argues that *The Eye in the Door*, has "as much scope … and greater buoyancy [than *Regeneration*] … [and] is exhilaratingly readable; an original and impressive achievement."

OTHER MEDIA: Audiocassette (Chivers/unabr; Recorded Books/unabr); RECOGNITION: **Winner** of the *Guardian* Fiction Prize; *NYTBR* Notable Book of 1994; *Chicago Tribune* "Year's Best" 1994; REVIEWS: *BL* 5/1/94; *ChiTrib* 5/22/94; *LRB* 10/21/93; *NS&S* 9/10/93; *NYTBR* 5/15/94; *PW* 3/14/94; *Spec* 11/27/93; *TLS* 9/10/93; *WPBW* 5/21/95

495   *Regeneration* (1991); Dutton 1993 (pbk); SETTING: WWI England

Burns. Rivers had become adept at finding bearable aspects to unbearable experiences, but Burns defeated him. What had happened to him was so vile, so disgusting, that Rivers could find no redeeming feature. He'd been thrown into the air by the explosion of a shell and had landed, head-first, on a German corpse, whose gas-filled belly had ruptured on impact. Before Burns lost consciousness, he'd had time to realize that what filled his nose and mouth was decomposing human flesh. Now, whenever he tried to eat, that taste and smell recurred. Nightly he relived the experience, and from every nightmare he awoke vomiting. Burns on his knees, as Rivers has often seen him, retching up the last ounce of bile, hardly looked like a human being at all. His body seemed to have become merely the skin-and-bone casing for a tormented alimentary canal. His suffering was without purpose or dignity, and yes, Rivers knew exactly what Burns meant when he said it was a joke.

One of the many heartbreaking aspects of World War I was the practice of sending shell-shocked soldiers (particularly officers) to special psychiatric hospitals with the sole purpose of restoring enough of their sanity to make them eligible, once more, for active duty. In *Regeneration*—which draws heavily on the historical record and freely intermingles real and fictional characters—Siegfried Sassoon, poet and officer, publishes his declaration of protest against the conduct of the war. Although the young soldier's actions would normally have led to a military trial and a possible sentence of death, the authorities decide to have him declared mentally unstable and send him instead to Craiglockhart Hospital where he meets the conflicted military psychologist, Dr. W.H.R. Rivers.

Kirkus Reviews notes that "At the center [of *Regeneration*] is Rivers, a model therapist, whose unstinting support may give even the wretched Burns a chance at a normal life ... but the heart of the work, where the big fish swim, is River's consciousness, his insights into front-line behavior enriched by his anthropological training." The *New York Times Book Review* calls Ms. Barker's book "an anti-war novel ... in a tradition that is by now an established one, though it tells a part of the whole story of war that is not often told—how war may batter and break men's minds—and so makes the madness of war more than a metaphor, and more awful." The *Times Literary Supplement* concludes that "*Regeneration* is so much more than the excellent historical novel other writers might have settled for. It is one of the most impressive novels to have appeared in recent years."

OTHER MEDIA: Audiocassette (Chivers/unabr; Recorded Books/unabr); a film version was released in 1997; RECOGNITION: *NYTBR* "Editors' Choice" 1992; REVIEWS: *BL* 4/15/92; *KR* 2/1/92; *LJ* 3/1/92; *LRB* 6/27/91; *NS&S* 5/31/91; *NY* 8/10/92; *NYTBR* 12/6/92; *TLS* 5/24/91; *WPBW* 4/3/92

Barrett, Andrea (USA)

496   *Voyage of the Narwhal* (1998); Norton 1998 (HC); SETTING: Philadelphia and the Arctic in the mid–1800s

Andrea Barrett sets her first novel in the 1850s, a period of intense interest in exploration and discovery. In it she tells the fictional story of the Arctic voyage of the Narwhal, an ocean-going vessel which sailed from Philadelphia in 1855 in search of the lost expedition of Sir John Franklin. In 1845, Sir John, along with two ships (the *Erebus* and the *Terror*) and 129 crewmen, disappeared while attempting to find the coveted Northwest Passage. Barrett's focus rests primarily on two characters: Zeke Voorhees, the seriously flawed, flamboyantly

intrepid young commander of the expedition, and his soon-to-be bother-in-law, Erasmus Darwin Wells, a bookish-yet-experienced naturalist cut from more measured cloth. The narrative is fueled by the physical reality of such a journey including atrocious weather, faulty maps, frostbite, scurvy, polar bears, suspicious Esquimau and, always, the treacherous ice and the heaving sea.

According to *Publishers Weekly*, "Barrett balances meticulous observation of the natural world with similarly acute insight into the vagaries of human nature." *Newsday* suggests that the *Voyage of the Narwhal* is "an astonishingly good book by a writer we must now declare as major." *Booklist* calls the novel: "Authoritative and imaginative on all fronts" and concludes that Barrett "tells a gripping story shaped by masterful interpretations of the paradigms of science and the volatile nature of the mind, a wilderness every bit as challenging as the forbidding Arctic." *Entertainment Weekly* argues that "Despite the disappointingly pat finale, Barrett masterfully navigates the waters of envy and egotism." The *New York Times Book Review* concludes that "Barrett's marvelous achievement is to have re-imagined so graphically that cusp of time when Victorian certainty began to question whether it could encompass the world with its outward-bound enthusiasm alone—when it started to glimpse the dark ballast beneath the iceberg's dazzling tip."

OTHER MEDIA: Audiocassette (Recorded Books/unabr) RECOGNITION: *PW*'s Best '98 Fiction; *NYTBR* Notable Book of 1998; REVIEWS: *EW* 10/9/98; *LJ* 9/1/98; *NYT* 9/4/98; *NYTBR* 9/13/98; *Newsday* 9/10/98; *PW* 6/15/98; *Time* 10/19/98

Bartlett, Neil (UK)

497   *The House on Brooke Street* (1996); Dutton 1997 (HC); SETTING: UK 1920s–1950s

England in the mid–1950s was a singularly inhospitable place for homosexuals. Gay men were actively pursued and sodomy arrests, and subsequent prosecutions, routinely made the headlines. Neil Bartlett's second novel opens on Christmas Eve in 1956 in the small flat belonging to Mr. Page, a middle-aged store manager who is just putting pen to paper. His memoirs span three decades and describe—in sometimes feverish detail—his dangerous, illicit, and, ultimately, obsessive relationship with the wealthy and glamorous Mr. Clive, heir to a famous mansion on Brooke Street.

Kirkus Reviews notes that in Bartlett's second novel (after the well-received *Ready to Catch Him Should He Fall*, 1991) the author's "storytelling gifts are amply confirmed ... thanks to expertly voiced narration ... and to a masterly evocation of time and place, with the house on Brooke Street an effective symbol of Victorian values in disarray." *Booklist* concludes that Bartlett's novel is "a lush, sumptuous tapestry of mood and memory...."

RECOGNITION: Nominated for the 1998 Lambda Book Award; REVIEWS: *LJ* 1/97; *LST* 4/28/96; *NYTBR* 2/23/97; *PW* 12/2/96; *TLS* 3/29/96

Bauer, Douglas (USA)

498   *The Book of Famous Iowans* (1997); Holt 1997 (HC); Owl 1998 (pbk); SETTING: 1950s Iowa

Called a "boy's elegy for his lost mother" (*People*) The *Book of Famous Iowans* is a thoughtful story about one man's life-long attempts to understand and forgive his mother's act of abandonment. Douglas Bauer sets his pivotal story in the somnambulant Midwest of the 1950s, and focuses on the character of LeAnne Vaughan, a small-town girl from Wyoming who thought the world would offer her more than the circumscribed life of a farmer's wife. Torn between maternal love and the need to escape from a world that was sapping her spirit, she chose to leave. The story is told retrospectively by her son, Will Vaughn.

According to Michiko Kakutani (*NYT*) "Mr. Bauer has written a moving coming-of-age story, and in doing so he has taken a time honored American theme — the tension between domesticity and independence, stability and freedom — and re-examined it ... from the perspective of a child. He has also taken a much used, melodramatic plot and given it an emotional shape and heft." In the view of the *Washington Post Book World*, *The Book of Famous Iowans* "despite [the excruciating drama of a family's dissolution at its core] is not so much about that [event] as it is about the lifelong emotional wrestling match [it] guarantees for its victims."

RECOGNITION: *NYTBR* Notable Book of 1997; *LATBR* "Recommended Title" 1997; REVIEWS: *ChiTrib* 10/12/97; *KR* 7/1/97; *LJ* 8/97; *NYT* 9/9/97; *NYTBR* 9/28/97; *PW* 7/14/97; *WPBW* 11/16/97

499   *The Very Air* (1993); Morrow 1993 (HC); Holt 1997 (pbk); SETTING: American Southwest 1905–1933

Douglas Bauer's second novel traces the life of one Luther Mathias (orphaned in the Texas Panhandle in 1905) as he makes his roughshod way through the early decades of the American century. His experiences encompass a number of the less admirable aspects of unbridled capitalism (e.g., the peddling of fake syphilis cures to men frightened of sex and its consequences). Luther, armed with a newly acquired mail-order medical degree, begins specializing in male impotency — an activity that leads him to southern California via his "clinical"

relationship with silent movie actor Billy Boswell. Bauer's novel is strongly evocative of the freewheeling atmosphere of the old Southwest and the early days of Hollywood.

The *New York Times Book Review* calls *The Very Air* "a good story, if a touch improbable, with all the right elements in place: the rise of that quintessential American hero, the salesman; the ending of Hollywood's golden age; the birth of broadcasting" and concludes that it "is material in which Mr. Bauer justifiably delights, and, when he is at his best, is more than a match for." According to the *Washington Post Book World* "Bauer [much praised for his first novel, *Dexterity*] consolidates his reputation with this masterfully crafted tale, which combines an intensely focused narrative of one man's range with a broad-based social panorama that shows the protagonist tapping into a national malaise." *Kirkus Reviews* notes that *The Very Air*, an "engaging and episodic romp through the first half of the 20th century, is lighter, more accessible, and far more commercial than Bauer's lyrically intense debut" and concludes that it is a "rough and tumble fiction that exults in its inventiveness and seems written with an eye to the big screen."

REVIEWS: *BL* 9/1/93; *ChiTrib* 10/7/93; *KR* 7/1/93; *LJ* 8/93; *NYTBR* 10/17/93; *PW* 7/5/93; *WPBW* 9/5/93

Bausch, Richard (USA)

500   *Good Evening Mr. and Mrs. America and All the Ships at Sea* (1996); HarperCollins 1996 (HC); HarperPerennial 1997 (pbk); SETTING: Washington D.C. — 1964

Richard Bausch's wryly comic tale of innocence lost features nineteen-year-old Walter Marshall, a naive and idealistic (even by mid–1960's standards) young man who is studying broadcast journalism at the (failing) D'Alessandro School of Broadcasting in Washington, D.C. It is late 1964 and Walter is still recovering from the assassination of his idol, JFK, the previous autumn. It has recently occurred to Walter that while he might not be destined to follow in the footsteps of Edward R. Murrow, the White House (with adequate preparation, of course) might not be completely out of his reach. Plot complications — having to do with Walter's love life (he has managed to become engaged to two girls simultaneously) and a plot to save the D'Alessandro school — propel the story.

Publishers Weekly, in its starred review, says "Bausch holds a mirror up to 1960s America, whose vague dreams of Camelot were soon to sour in the debacle of Vietnam and the ensuing political scandals" and concludes that "Walter's slide from idealism to disillusionment is revealed through brilliant passages of mundane (but revealing) conversations, hilarious comic moments and characters' poignant attempts to communicate with one another." In the view of the *Library Journal*, Bausch "vividly evokes Washington in 1964 and has created a wonderful cast of characters." According to *Booklist* "Bausch's shrewd and supple fiction has garnered an impressive list of awards, and happily, his newest work confirms the validity of his sterling reputation. In [this] charmingly humorous and keenly insightful novel.... Bausch explores the 'What Planet are you from?' motif within a constellation of quirky relationships."

RECOGNITION: *PW* "Best Books" 1996; REVIEWS: *BL* 8/96; *KR* 7/1/96; *LJ* 8/96; *NYTBR* 10/27/96; *PW* 7/15/96; *WPBW* 11/1/96

501   *Rebel Powers* (1993); Random House 1994 (pbk); SETTING: Wyoming in the late 1960s

In *Rebel Powers*, Richard Bausch explores the painful process of memory and understanding as an introspective, bookish man in his 40s attempts to come to terms with a tragic episode in his family's history. In 1967 his father, a career Air Force man and former POW, was arrested for theft and given a military court martial. When he is sent to prison in Wyoming, his mother relocates nearby with her two young sons. Given the growing opposition to the war in Vietnam, the story is played out against a background of civil unrest and national tension.

According to Phoebe-Lou Adams (*AtlM*), Bausch's "admirable" novel presents an "always interesting study of the distortion inflicted on ordinary people by the conflicting pressures of circumstance and character." *Booklist* applauds *Rebel Powers*' "precise and steady detail" and concludes that Bausch's "first rate" novel "reveals a family and a nation trying painfully, desperately to find themselves again."

RECOGNITION: *NYTBR* Notable Book of 1993; REVIEWS: *AtlM* 5/93; *BL* 4/15/93; *LJ* 4/1/93; *NYTBR* 5/16/93; *PW* 2/15/93; *WPBW* 4/11/93

Begley, Louis (USA)

502   *Wartime Lies* (1991); Ivy Books 1993 (pbk); SETTING: Poland during World War II

Louis Begley's debut novel is a tale of survival through deception. Set in W.W.II Poland, *Wartime Lies* is narrated by Maciek, a young Jewish boy whose mother died in childbirth and whose father (once a prosperous physician), has been forcibly absorbed into the Russian Army. Maciek's Aunt Tania assumes responsibility for him and manages to resettle them both in a nearby town; they pose as Roman Catholics thereby avoiding deportation to a concentration camp. Aunt Tania enhances their prospects (of survival) by becoming the mistress of a German officer.

Called "readable to a fault" by the *London Review of Books*, *Wartime Lies* was widely praised

when first published in 1991. According to the *New York Review of Books* "In the relationship of the boy and the aunt we see a kind of distorting mirror image of the relationship of the Jew and the Nazi. Although the aunt is 'good,' her methods have a heart-freezing Teutonic efficiency, and the boy's abject dependence on her has a chilling pathos. Embedded in Begley's narrative of the boy's ambivalence toward his too powerful and too desirable protectress ... is a meditation on authoritarianism of great subtlety and originality." The *New York Times Book Review* observes that the "testimony of young children who have survived extremes of persecution and cruelty carries an authority that is all the stronger because they are not yet able to judge the offenses committed against them. It is this kind of unguarded authority — as if the appalling events spoke for themselves — that compels us in the voice of 'polite little Maciek,' the narrator of Louis Begley's masterly first novel."

RECOGNITION: Winner of the 1991 *Irish Times*-Aer Lingus International Fiction Prize and the Hemingway Prize for Fiction; nominated for the 1991 National Book Award and the 1991 National Book Critics Circle Award; *NYTBR* "Editors' Choice" 1991; REVIEWS: *ChiTrib* 11/19/91; *LJ* 5/1/91; *LRB* 11/19/92; *NewsWk* 9/29/91; *NYRR* 6/13/91; *NYTBR* 6/13/91; *Time* 5/27/91; *TLS* 8/16/91; *WPBW* 11/4/91

Bell, Madison Smartt (USA)

503   *All Souls Rising* (1995); Random House 1995 (HC); Viking Penguin 1996 (pbk); SETTING: 18th-century French Colonial Haiti

All Souls Rising is a fictional account of the Haitian Revolution wherein former slaves, led by the charismatic military strategist Toussaint l'Ouverture, by defeating experienced soldiers from the major European powers, managed to end French colonial rule on the island of Haiti. The story is played out against the backdrop of extremes: opulence and personal license on the one hand, bone-grinding poverty, disease and the world's harshest punitive system on the other.

Publishers Weekly, in its starred review, argues that *All Souls Rising* is "an astonishing novel of epic scope [which follows] ... the lives of a handful of characters from radically different social strata during the period of Haiti's struggle for independence" and concludes that "after more than 500 wrenching pages of rapes and massacres and fetuses impaled on pikes, there can be no question of a winner of the battle for Haitian liberation. Surviving it was feat enough." The *Washington Post Book World* calls Bell's novel "a big, morally intricate book that grows, deepens and shifts as the narrative progresses. At more than 500 pages, too, *All Souls Rising* ... sits lightly on the lap. It is that increasing rarity: a serious historical novel that reads like a dream." The *New York Times Book Review* applaudes its power and intelligence and concludes that it is "refreshingly ambitious ... takes enormous chances, and consequently will haunt readers long after plenty of flawless books have found their little slots on their narrow shelves."

RECOGNITION: Nominated for the 1995 National Book Award; *NYTBR* Notable Book of 1995; REVIEWS: *BL* 9/1/95; *ChiTrib* 10/22/95; *LJ* 10/1/95; *LST* 1/21/96; *NS&S* 2/9/96; *NYTBR* 10/29/95; *PW* 8/28/95; *QBR* 1995; *TLS* 2/9/96; *WPBW* 11/5/95

Benitez, Sandra (Puerto Rico/USA)

504 *Bitter Grounds* (1997); Hyperion 1997 (HC); St. Martin's 1998 (pbk); SETTING: Central America 1930s–1990s

Sandra Benitez's second novel — which draws on her own childhood memories — is a multigenerational tale set in El Salvador that begins in the 1930s and extends to the present day. It is, essentially, the story of three generations of mothers and daughters (representative of both the peasant and upper classes) whose lives are inextricably linked. Ms. Benitez's novel begins with the infamous massacre of 1932 and continues through a violence-plagued 20th century.

Bitter Grounds, called a "delicate, domestic look at violent history" by *Entertainment Weekly*, is written by a Puerto Rican author who, according to the *Washington Post Book World*, "has spent part of her youth in El Salvador [and] demonstrates a convincing feel for the Salvadoran culture, topography and idiom." *Publishers Weekly* points out that Benitez's Spanish-sprinkled, elegant prose is mesmerizing in its simplicity and frankness." *Kirkus* observes that, in Benitez's "luminously rendered" novel "memorable pairs of mothers and daughters, caught up in the violence of recent Salvadoran history, live, love, and die for their passions" and concludes that *Bitter Grounds*, although "sometimes schematic" is an "always vivid chronicle of strong women facing the challenges of living in sad and violent times." *Booklist* suggests that "A gentle infusion of Spanish words and phrases — always translated — adds to the enjoyment of Benitez's fluid style."

RECOGNITION: Winner of the 1998 American Book Award; nominated for the 1998 Minnesota Book Award for fiction; REVIEWS: *BL* 9/15/97; *ChiTrib* 10/20/97; *EW* 10/31/97; *KR* 8/1/97; *LJ* 9/1/97; *PW* 8/11/97; *WPBW* 8/25/97

Berry, Wendell (USA)

A World Lost (1996); Counterpoint 1996 (HC); 1997 (pbk); SETTING: Port William, Kentucky, 1944; See Section 4, #316

Binstock, R. (USA)

505 *Tree of Heaven* (1995); Soho 1995 (HC); 1996 (pbk); SETTING: China: 1938 — shortly after the Japanese invasion.

The Japanese invasion of China just prior to World War II is the initiating event in R. Binstock's tender war-time love story. When Capt. Kuroda, the Japanese officer in charge of a remote Chinese outpost, observes an unruly mob of Japanese soldiers in pursuit of a young Chinese woman, he quickly intervenes. Impressed with Li's courage and her ability to speak Japanese, he offers her a position in his household. Despite extreme personal risk they eventually become lovers.

According to *Booklist*, Binstock "acclaimed author of *The Light of Home* (1992), has written an exquisitely restrained and deeply affecting tale of love under duress. Its reigning metaphor is the tree of heaven, which flourishes in the harshest environments." Novelist **John David Morley** (*NYTBR*) found *The Tree of Heaven* to be a "subtle and moving story, leavened with a redemptive touch of love."

REVIEWS: *BL* 8/95; *LJ* 10/1/9; *NYTBR* 9/3/95; *PW* 6/5/95; *SLJ* 10/95

Bishop, James, Jr. (USA)

506 *Brittle Innings* (1994); Bantam 1995 (pbk); SETTING: Georgia — 1943

Back at the "homefront" during World War II, there was precious little in the way of amusement for the average American and baseball — be it major league or bush league — played a key role in helping to relieve the anxieties of the period. In his recent novel, James Bishop spins a "baseball fantasy" which he sets in Georgia in 1943 and peoples with an engagingly eccentric cast of characters. *Brittle Innings* is narrated by Danny Boles, a talented shortstop who, leaving Tenkiller, Oklahoma behind, joins the Hellbridge Hellbenders, a Class C farm club in Georgia's Chattahoochee Valley League. Boles, however, was so traumatized by a brutal encounter on the train east that he has lost the ability to speak. Undaunted, the Hellbenders' manager rooms him with first baseman Henry "Jumbo" Clerval, an endearing misfit and near-giant, with a strange gait, strange accent and even stranger scars. A pennant race, complete with last minute injuries, inopportune trades and un-sportsmanlike behavior, fuels the plot.

According to *Booklist* "this elaborate mix of fantasy and inspirational baseball story somehow holds together; it's schmaltzy, it's absurd, but it's got a terrific narrative drive — like mixing John R. Tunis and Edgar Rice Burroughs." *Kirkus* concludes that *Brittle Innings* is "resonantly evocative of time and place, with a splendid gallery of characters in a beautifully reticulated plot."

REVIEWS: *BL* 4/15/94; *KR* 3/1/94; *LJ* 3/15/94; *NYTBR* 4/10/94; *PW* 3/7/94; *WPBW* 7/19/94

Bowering, George (Canada)

507   *Shoot!* (1995); St Martin 1995 (HC); SETTING: British Columbia, Canada — late 1800s

Replete with thundering hooves and blazing six guns, George Bowering's *Shoot* is a fictional retelling of the escapades of "the McLiams," Canada's answer to the Jesse James Gang. The McLiam gang, comprised of three half-breed brothers (aged 24, 17 & 15) and a 16-year-old friend (Alex Hare), robbed, rustled and generally terrorized Canada's Western provinces in the late 1880s. Rejected by both the White and Indian worlds, the McLiams were hellbent on wreaking revenge.

Quill & Quire, notes that, in George Bowering's latest novel "we see the tragic collision of white and native cultures in British Columbia in the middle years of the 19th century" and concludes that "Bowering offers us a revisionist western in a language that is tough, laconic, and satirical, but which also reaches the elemental power of fable." *Publishers Weekly* offers a similar observation: "With powerful imagery and crisp narration, Bowering delivers a stinging commentary on the desperation of racism in the harsh environment of the Canadian West." *Booklist* argues that "It isn't much of a stretch to find a lesson for our times in this fine, remarkably empathetic historical novel, which portrays four youngsters who turned to crime because they had nowhere else to go and no one else with whom to socialize but other outcasts."

REVIEWS: *BksCan* 12/94; *BL* 1/1/96; *NYTBR* 2/4/96; *PW* 11/13/95; *Q&Q* 1/95.

Boyle, T. Coraghessan (USA)

508   *Riven Rock* (1998); Viking 1998; Viking Penguin 1999 (pbk); SETTING: A California estate — early decades of the 20th century

"*'The important thing,' he said, or rather whispered in the narcotic tones he used on his charges, 'is Mrs. McCormick. The sooner we're able to move the patient and establish him in the proper way in California, the better it will be for all concerned. Especially the patient. What he needs, above all, is a tranquil environment, with all the stresses that led to his blocking removed. Only then can we hope to—' He faltered. Mrs. McCormick had cleared her throat— that was all: cleared her throat— and that stopped him cold.*"

T.C. Boyle's 8th novel (widely described as an inventive black comedy with serious intent) is based on the true-life story of Stanley McCormack, the "neuresthenic" youngest son of the Chicago inventor/millionaire. Stanley appears to have suffered from a form of sexual dementia triggered by female contact. He married Katherine Dexter, the first female graduate of M.I.T. but, before they could consummate their union, Stanley had a complete breakdown. The title is taken from the name of the California estate to which young McCormack was sent, and where he lived his life — "in a world without women" under the watchful supervision of a psychiatric nurse, a handsome young Irishman by the name of Eddie O'Kane. Stanley's wife, Katherine — who went on to become an outspoken member of the Women's Suffrage movement — never abandoned hope of her husband's recovery. In Boyle's version, we follow Stanley's unusual incarceration — in a luxurious *cordon sanitaire*— through the perspective of nurse O'Kane who was witness to the stream of maladroit professionals who grappled with his patient's perplexing disorder.

According to *Kirkus Reviews* the "issues that divide the emergent [20th] century and the gulf that separates the sexes ... frame, and memorably echo, this big novel's narrative and emotional core: the craziest love story imaginable, but a love story nevertheless — one that chills the bones as you read." The *L.A. Times Book Review* points out that had "Stanley not been a Chicago-born, Princeton-educated heir, he would likely enough, in turn-of-the-century America, have landed in the Boston lunatic asylum, along with some of the weirder illustrations from Krafft-Ebbing's recently published 'Psychopathia Sexualis'" and concludes that T.C. Boyle "writes with the muscle of a collegiate fullback ripping the OED in two just for fun." *Salon* notes that "T. Coraghessan Boyle has taken the depressing story of Stanley R. McCormick ... and turned it into a thrilling, romantic, careening tale of love, redemption and the rewards of the faithful heart." According to the *London Sunday Times* Boyle once again "proves himself a master satirist of that distinctly American hunger for a psychic Eden in which natural human corruption is replaced by an idealized wellness that usually destroys what it seeks to purify." The *New Yorker* concludes that "In Boyle's assured hands, this odd American tale turns into a bracing examination of misogyny, mental illness, and the shadowy side of love."

OTHER MEDIA: Audiocassette (Books-on-Tape/unabr); RECOGNITION: *LATBR* "Best Fiction of 1998"; *NYTBR* Notable Book of 1998; REVIEWS: *KR* 11/15/97; *LATBR* 2/22/98; *LST* 6/14/98; *NYT* 1/20/98; *NYTBR* 2/8/98; *PW* 11/24/97; *Salon* 1/28/98; *WPBW* 1/20/98

509   *The Road to Welville* (1993); Penguin 1994 (pbk); SETTING: Battle Creek, Michigan — 1907

The Road to Wellville, is a cheerful, cheeky tale of fanaticism, gullibility and the (peculiarly American) "religion" of healthy living taken to extremes. Boyle, who sets his novel in Battle Creek, Michigan, in 1907 and bases it, somewhat loosely, on the life of Doctor Kellogg, inventor of Kellogg flakes and founder of the breakfast cereal empire, takes obvious pleasure in satirizing the doctor's devotion to inner cleanliness, yogurt, enemas and celibacy.

In his fifth novel, T. Coraghessan Boyle, "one of America's most exuberant satirists takes on the national obsession with health and nutritional fads [and] it's a perfect fit." (*Kirkus Reviews*). Jane Smiley (*NYTBR*) while judging *The Road to Wellville* to be Boyle's "lightest, least fierce novel," reassures those readers who "have savored the sharpness, complexity and bitterness of his previous works" that "the animals still bite, the fecal matter still flies and foolishness is still on ample display." According to *Newsweek*, Boyle's "funny, thoughtful, immaculately written novel ... eviscerates the gullible pilgrims and conniving hucksters who rubbed shoulders in turn of the century Battle Creek." The *Washington Post Book World* argues that while *The Road to Wellville* is written with Boyle's "customary zest," the novel's put downs of food-faddists and flim-flammers come down to variations on the old joke about patients running the sanitarium...."

OTHER MEDIA: Audiocassette (Books-on-Tape/unabr); RECOGNITION: *NYTBR* Notable Book of 1995; REVIEWS: *BL* 3/15/93; *KR* 2/1/93; *LJ* 3/15/93; *LT* 2/2/95; *NewR* 10/4/93; *NS&S* 10/22/93; *NewsWk* 4/19/93; *NYTBR* 4/25/93; *PW* 4/4/94; *SLJ* 10/93; *Time* 5/10/93; *TLS* 10/15/93; *WPBW* 5/9/93

Brady, Joan (USA/UK)

510   *Theory of War* (1993); Fawcett 1994 (pbk); SETTING: America in mid–19th century

Theory of War (by an American writer who has lived in England for much of her life) focuses on a little-known historical phenomenon, "white-on-white" slavery, which was practiced in 19th century America in the years immediately following the Civil War. Joan Brady's often searing novel is narrated by the grandson of a man who, at the age of four, was sold — by his own father — to a farmer in a practice commonly known as "bounding over." The youngster, Jonathan Carrick by name, was immediately "broken" for labor, a process which included frequent beatings, the withholding of education, and a work day which stretched from dawn until dusk. For twelve years, Jonathan was relentlessly and maliciously mistreated, finding particular torment at the hands of the farmer's son, a boy of his own age. When Jonathan finally managed to escape he had trouble with even rudimentary speech, for all of his teeth had been extracted (and sold by the farmer to a maker of false teeth). Although Jonathan manages to educate himself, becomes a preacher and marries a loving woman, he cannot escape the legacy of pure hatred (and the white hot desire for revenge) that he carries inside

him, nor, apparently, can his progeny. Joan Brady's novel is based on the experiences of her own grandfather, about whom she writes in her author's note: "The slave's life my grandfather led until he ran away at 16 so scarred him that no one who came near him afterwards could escape the effects of it: four of his seven children — including my father — ended up suicides."

According to *The Spectator*, "*Theory of War* is like a backhanded slap in the face of the American ideal, delivered with all the power of a thwarted lover. It will be interesting whether in the longer term the novel can establish a genuine foothold on its home ground. Perhaps, amongst the American reading public who seem to take to heart such slush as *Love Story* and *The Bridges of Madison County*, there is room in some corner for this magnificent and excoriating novel." *Kirkus Reviews* points out that while Ms. Brady's novel suffers somewhat from an "awkward format, [an] awkward fact/fiction straddle ... [and a] hokey showdown" this "deliberately rough-edged work does command respect for its blistering anger at the poison of slavery in the bloodstream of the Carricks ... and America." The *London Review of Books* notes that "when we read about the little boy whose charming spirit is destroyed, we cannot help but think of generations of black slaves whose stories Jonathan's repeats" and concludes that "Through Jonathan the reader may feel what it means to lose one's bearings, to be made less than human."

RECOGNITION: Winner of the 1993 Whitbread Award for Fiction; nominated for the *Guardian* Fiction Prize; REVIEWS: *BL* 4/1/93; *ChiTrib* 5/16/93; *KR* 2/15/93; *LJ* 4/15/93; *LRB* 8/5/93; *PW* 3/1/93; *Time* 4/19/93

Bram, Christopher (USA)

511   *Almost History* (1992); Plume 1993 (pbk); SETTING: 1950s–1980s

Christopher Bram's fourth work of fiction covers 35 years in the life of a US career diplomat. Jim Goodall, an instinctually reserved, sexually ambiguous young man, joins the Foreign Service in the early 1950s — a time when even suspected homosexuals were purged immediately from the State Department. His career takes him through succeeding decades of profound change and postings to some of the hottest spots in a diplomatically perilous world: Vietnam, Thailand and the Marcos-era Philippines. Most of his on-the-job perils pale, however, in the light of his eventual decision (reached in his mid-40s) to "come out of the closet." Bram creates a beloved "tomboyish" niece (an avid listener/sounding board) for Goodall, ensuring narrative cohesion.

According to *Kirkus Reviews*, Bram has produced "an authoritative, very readable [and mostly mainstream] novel ... [wherein he] convincingly recreates a historical moment from a gay perspective." The *Library Journal* points out that "Bram has described himself as 'a gay novelist' ... who tries to treat gayness as just one strand in a life that has more similarities with 'mainstream' life than dissimilarities ... [In *Almost History* his coming-out] is not the main thrust. Rather, Bram is concerned with the moral and political complications inherent in diplomatic life...."

REVIEWS: *BL* 4/15/92; *KR* 2/15/92; *LJ* 3/1/92; *PW* 2/10/92

Brink, Andre (South Africa)

Imaginings of Sand (1996); Harcourt Brace 1996 (HC); SETTING: South Africa during Apartheid; See Section 4, #425

Brown, Wesley (USA)

512 *Darktown Strutters* (1994); Cane Hill Press 1994 (pbk); SETTING: American South — mid 1800s

Jim Crow, a highly talented former slave-turned-minstrel dancer is featured in Wesley Brown's second novel. Set in the American south in the years surrounding the Civil War, *Darktown Strutters* tells Jim's story as he progresses from minstrel shows in which whites performed in blackface (and to which he had once been "leased") to participation in a black owned vaudeville show launched during the Reconstruction period. In the volatile post-war years, racially inspired violence was omnipresent.

According to *Publishers Weekly* "This compelling and imaginative historical novel takes off from a 19th-century incident that gave birth to the term 'Jim Crow': a white actor named Tom Rice gained fame performing in blackface a dance he learned from a slave named Jim Crow." The *Library Journal* observes that "Written in hot, jazzy language and filled with lively characters ... [*Darktown Strutters*] is dynamite. It is the second recent attempt by an African American author to rewrite black history in a manner reminiscent of Herman Melville's 'Confidence Man.' [The other is **Charles Johnson**'s *Middle Passage*.] Like Melville, Brown tells a good story, but he is also a moralist of considerable power." The *New York Times Book Review* argues that "as Jim Crow disappears into history, the primary images of *Darktown Strutters* remain powerful and ominous. Combining the simple prose of a folk tale with the meta-psychology of a philosopher, Wesley Brown has created a vivid, disturbing work of the historical imagination."

RECOGNITION: *NYTBR* Notable Book of 1994; REVIEWS: *KR* 12/15/93; *LJ* 12/1/93; *NYTBR* 3/6/94; *PW* 12/93

Burgess, Anthony (UK)

513 *A Dead Man in Deptford* (1993); Carroll & Graf 1995 (HC); 1996 (pbk); SETTING: Elizabethan England

The dead man in Anthony Burgess's last novel is Christopher Marlowe (aka Kit Morley) poet, playwright, atheist, likely homosexual and (as some would have it) a secret agent of the crown. The rakish Marlowe was killed in suspicious circumstances in a tavern brawl in Deptford 400 years ago and numerous theories (from a simple misadventure involving alcohol and argument, to political assassination) have been put forward to explain his untimely death. In *A Dead Man in Deptford* Burgess offers persuasive answers to a whole range of questions posed by literary historians while managing to produce a thoroughly involving narrative that, as Suzanne Keen points out in *Commonweal*, "puts the flesh back on Christopher Marlowe."

According to Michael Dirda (*WPBW*) "One needn't be an expert on this swashbuckling period to enjoy *A Dead Man in Deptford*, but — as always with Burgess — one may need to stretch a little to enjoy his allusions, lip-smacking vocabulary and quicksilver style.... Anthony Burgess died shortly after completing *A Dead Man in Deptford*, and so this fine novel should serve as a memorial not only to a great poet but also to a distinguished, consistently surprising modern writer." In the view of *Booklist*, Mr. Burgess's posthumously published novel is "a splendidly atmospheric re-creation of the life of ... [an] eminent Elizabethan playwright ... [and a] delicious engagement with the past...." *New Statesman & Society* assures us that Burgess's "grasp of the age and its angsts is profound, and his portrait of Marlowe, sympathetic, critical and brilliantly imagined all at once. The rich, deft handling of language is a joy." *Publishers Weekly*, in its starred review, declares "Burgess's command of his material [to be] absolute" and points out that Burgess "brings a lifetime's linguistic and fictional gifts to this headlong, shining, cruel portrait of a terrifying — but posthumously glorious — age."

REVIEWS: *BL* 2/1/95; *ChiTrib* 7/16/95; *ComW* 2/11/94; *LJ* 3/15/95; *NS&S* 4/23/93; *NYTBR* 5/28/95; *PW* 3/6/95; *TLS* 4/30/93; *WPBW* 5/28/95; *WSJ* 4/28/95

Byatt, A.S. (UK)

514 *Babel Tower* (1996); Random House 1996 (HC); Vintage 1997 (pbk); SETTING: England in the 1960s

Babel Tower, third volume in a projected quartet which includes *The Virgin in the Garden* (1979) and *Still Life* (1985), finds Frederica regretting her marriage to Nigel who over time has become vehemently dismissive of her clever Cambridge friends.

When his intolerance escalates into physical abuse, Frederica takes her young son and moves to London where the sixties are beginning to "swing" in earnest. There she resumes the sort of cerebral life for which she is well-suited, dividing her time between teaching and an editorial position with a forward-looking publisher. The "Babel Tower" of he title is derived from a "de Sade-like" (arguably pornographic) book entitled *Babbletower* which Frederica is in the process of editing.

According to *Booklist*, *Babel Tower* is "Extravagantly clever, Byatt entertains on a grand, even maddening scale, but her prose is both impeccable and sexy, her perspicacity astonishing." South African novelist, **J.M. Coetzee** (*NYRB*) calls *Babel Tower* "a novel of ideas ... [which often brings] to life the intellectual excitement of the mid-1960s...." *Kirkus Reviews*, while judging Byatt's novel to be "an ambitious, intelligent work ... with moments of wit and insight" concludes that it is "a somewhat lumbering dance to the music of time." *Publishers Weekly*, in its starred review, notes that "This is a book about language, and how it is used to conceal and reveal" and concludes that it's also a book that "*employs* language, brilliantly, to create a large cast of characters whose struggles, anxieties and small triumphs are at once specific to a time and place, and universal."

OTHER MEDIA: Audiocassette (Random Audio/abr); READING GROUP GUIDE: RECOGNITION: *NYTBR* Notable Book of 1996; REVIEWS: *BL* 3/15/96; *ChiTrib* 6/2/96; *Econ* 6/15/976; *KR* 3/1/96; *LJ* 5/1/96; *LATBR* 6/16/96; *NYRB* 6/6/96; *NYTBR* 6/9/96; *PW* 3/25/96; *Time* 5/20/96; *TLS* 5/10/96; *WPBW* 5/12/96

Campbell, Bebe Moore (USA)

515   *Your Blues Ain't Like Mine* (1992); Ballantine 1993 (pbk); SETTING: Mississippi—1950s

In *Your Blues Ain't Like Mine*, Armstrong Todd, fifteen-years-old and Chicago-born, is brutally beaten for speaking to a white woman in a small Mississippi town in the 1950s. This act will dramatically change the lives of two families — one black, one white. Bebe Moore Campbell's debut novel is loosely based on an actual historical event, the 1955 vigilante-style murder of Emmet Till, a black teenager, for the "crime" of whistling at a white woman.

According to the *Library Journal*, "Campbell ably reveals the complex relationships among townspeople in this multilayered Southern community ... all have compromises to make and grief, shame, and responsibility to bear or share." *Booklist* applauds Ms. Campbell's ability to write with "incredible power and insight about the private wars sparked by integration." Novelist **Clyde Edgerton** (*NYTBR*) observes that "Much of the

power of this novel results from Ms. Campbell's subtle and seamless shifting of point of view" and concludes that " She wears the skin and holds in her chest the heart of each of her characters one after another, regardless of the character's race or sex, response to fear and hate, or need for pity, grace, punishment or peace...." The *School Library Journal* concludes that "Powerful in emotion ... [and] propelled by unstoppable forces, [*Your Blues Ain't Like Mine*] is compelling reading."

OTHER MEDIA: Audiocassette (Warner/abr); RECOGNITION: NAACP Image Award for Best Literary Fiction; REVIEWS: *BellesL* Spr'93; *BL* 8/92; *LATBR* 9/6/92; *LJ* 7/92; *NYTBR* 9/20/92; *PeopleW* 11/21/94; *PW* 6/22/96; *SLJ* 1/93; *WPBW* 10/10/92

Carey, Jacqueline (USA)

516   *The Other Family* (1996); Random House 1996 (HC); SETTING: Massachusetts and New York City in 1968

In her debut novel, Jacqueline Carey tells a very "late '60s" story featuring fourteen-year-old Joan Toolan who lives with her eccentric father in Western Massachusetts but visits (each July) her mother who has abandoned everyday motherhood for a new "counter-cultural" life in New York City. On these visits Joan (along with her 12-year-old brother Hugh) is also immersed in her Aunt Iris's comfortable Brooklyn Heights household within whose magnetic field Joan's mother is serenely orbiting. Iris (an accomplished woman with political aspirations) presides over a seemingly secure world — one that includes a psychiatrist husband, two well-bred daughters (Polly and Budge) and an efficient Austrian nanny. The scales, as they say, soon fall from Joan's eyes.

In the view of novelist Karen Karbo (*NYTBR*) "Part of the deep delight of Jacqueline Carey's first novel ... is the freshness with which she captures the flavor of the years between the Summer of Love and the summer of Watergate...." Ms. Karbo further observes that the Brooklyn Heights family (full of money and secrets) are "the modern descendants of Edith Wharton's New Yorkers" and concludes that "Ms. Carey's talents lie less in plotting than in fashioning a subtext that's at once witty, poignant and foreboding." According to *Booklist*, even though Ms. Carey "seems to be dealing with intensely personal material that she has not fully processed, her novel contains many powerful scenes ... [and Joan's] hard-won insights will cut you to the quick."

RECOGNITION: *NYTBR* Notable Book of 1996; REVIEWS: *BL* 8/19/96; *CSM* 9/9/96; *KR* 6/15/96; *LATBR* 11/17/96; *NY* 12/23/96; *NYTBR* 9/8/96

Cary, Lorene (USA)

517 *The Price of a Child* (1995); Knopf 1995 (HC); SETTING: New York and Philadelphia—1855

Lorene Cary's debut novel is a heartbreaking story of an escaped slave whose freedom came at a terrible price. In 1855, Ginny, a slave belonging to a Virginian who has been appointed Ambassador to Nicaragua, has been taken (along with two of her three children) to New York where they are to board a ship bound for Central America. While in New York, Ginny and her children manage (with the assistance of a local abolitionist group) to escape via the underground railway. Underpinning this act, is the appalling fact that she will never see her youngest child, left behind in Virginia, again.

According to the *Library Journal* "Cary has drawn a vivid portrait of survival and struggle for self-worth against a backdrop of one of the bleakest periods in American history." Novelist **Fernanda Eberstadt** (*NYTBR*) calls Cary "a powerful storyteller, frankly sensual, mortally funny, gifted with an ear for the pounce and ragged inconsequentiality of real speech and an eye for the shifts and subterfuges by which ordinary people get by." The *School Library Journal* found Ms. Cary's novel to be a "wonderful, moving, and truthful account of a slave woman's walk away from her master and toward freedom."

REVIEWS: *BlkSchlr* Sum'95; *Essence* 7/95; *LJ* 4/15/95; *NYTBR* 6/30/96; *PW* 8/29/96; *SLJ* 12/95; *WPBW* 5/31/95

Castedo, Elena (USA)

518 *Paradise* (1990); Grove/Atlantic 1995 (pbk); SETTING: Chile—1930s

The theme of exile suffuses Elena Castedo's debut novel which is set in Chile during the late 1930s. The story (called a "classic coming-of-age novel" by the *Christian Science Monitor*) is told through the eyes of Solita, an intelligent nine-year-old who has been brought to South America by her parents, Spanish Republicans who were forced to flee their own country as Franco assumed control. They have taken temporary refuge in a large country estate, "El Topaz" owned by her mother's rich Chilean friends. Solita takes an immediate dislike to the household's privileged inhabitants.

The *New York Times Book Review* notes that although *Paradise* lacks "resonance" it is "filled with rich descriptions and vivid scenes. Ms Castedo's language is exuberant, and she's extraordinary when it comes to rendering the mixture of religious invocations and superstitions that flavor the speech of the campesinos...." According to the *Christian Science Monitor*, "Castedo whose own family fled Spain for Chile ... has done a brilliant job of showing us the world through the eyes of an intelligent child ... [and although] it contains elements of social satire, *Paradise* also retains the emotional intensity of the youthful experience it describes." In the view of the *Atlantic Monthly*, "Ms. Castedo has brought off, with acid wit, the far from easy task of revealing folly, injustice, and debauchery through the eyes of an observer who does not know what those qualities are."

RECOGNITION: Included in *500 Great Books by Women;* REVIEWS: *AtlM* 3/90; *BL* 1/15/90; *CSM* 7/18/90; *KR* 12/15/89; *NYTBR* 12/7/95; *NYTBR* 4/1/90 *PW* 12/22/89

Cheong, Fiona (Singapore)

519 *The Scent of the Gods* (1991); Norton 1993 (pbk); SETTING: Singapore—1965

Fiona Cheong's debut novel—set in Singapore in 1965, shortly after that country gained its independence from Great Britain—features an 11-year-old orphan by the name of Su Yen. The youngster lives with her grandmother, assorted aunts and cousins in her family's modest yet comfortable compound and is a student at the near-by mission school, the Convent of St. Catherine of Sienna. As Su Yen matures, she begins to ponder life as it is lived in that corner of a rapidly developing Asia. Ethnic tensions (particularly between the Malayan Muslims and the Chinese), the bonds of ancestry, and political violence color this coming-of-age story. The perspective of childhood also lends an air of mystery to the tumultuous external events described.

Kirkus Reviews applauds Ms Cheong's "memorable characters" and her ability "to evoke not only the political friction but also a family history built from equal parts of mythology, tradition, and rebellion" and concludes that *The Scent of the Gods* is a skillful first novel "which deserves a wide readership." Described as "The first book to represent life in Singapore in its full spectrum" by the *Library Journal*, The *New York Times Book Review* notes that "Ms Cheong, who grew up in Singapore, has managed to convey with great immediacy what it was like to live there in a dangerous time, protected by a close, but fearful family." *Publishers Weekly* asserts that Ms. Cheong's story "is exquisitely poised between the explicit and the mythic, delicately narrated and profoundly resonant."

REVIEWS: *BellesL* Fall'91; *KR* 8/1/91; *LJ* 5/1/92; *LATBR* 7/18/93; *NYTBR* 7/4/93; *PW* 8/9/91; *SLJ* 3/92

Clair, Maxine (USA)

520 *Rattlebone* (1994); FS&G 1994 (HC); 1995 (pbk); SETTING: American South—1950s

Set in the pre–Civil Rights 1950s, Maxine

Claire's debut novel is structured around a series of interrelated stories, each of which takes place in a fictional African-American community — located just north of Kansas City — known as Rattlebone. Dominating these stories is Irene "Reenie" Wilson, who is followed, in a series of vignettes, from childhood through her high school years. Other stories feature Reenie's parents, and her best friend and rival, Wanda.

According to *Belles Lettres* "The dominant voice [fresh, sassy, inventive] is Irene's as she makes her passage from grade school to high school graduation. But the most affecting voices are those of the adults who speak of losses Irene has not grown old enough to experience." In the view of *Entertainment Weekly* "Clair's fiction debut leaps and hums like fine gospel harmony, heralding the arrival of a distinctive new literary voice." The *NYTBR* called *Rattlebone* "extraordinary" and concluded that "There is magic dust sprinkled over each and every page."

RECOGNITION: Winner of the *Chicago Tribune* Heartland Award; Winner the ALA Black Caucus 1995 Literary Award for Fiction; REVIEWS: *BellesL* Fall'94; *EW* 7/22/94; *NYTBR* 1/8/95; *PW* 4/18/94; *SLJ* 2/95

Cowan, James (USA)

521 *A Mapmakers Dream* (1996); Random House 1996 (HC); Warner 1997 (pbk); SETTING: Venice during the Renaissance

In his debut novel, James Cowan tells the story of Fra Mauro, a 16th-century Venetian cartographer, whose goal it is — without ever leaving his monastic cell — to construct a "perfect" map of the world using first-hand information from the merchants, explorers and ambassadors of his age. The curious monk floats, understandably, between opposing poles of medieval dogmatism and a more "modern" appreciation for the new and unexplained.

In the view of the *Library Journal*, "Each tale falls like a tiny gem in the reader's lap, and the atmosphere is at once dreamy and sharply detailed." *Kirkus Reviews* found less to like, calling *The Mapmaker's Dream* "A potential feast for thought, but in a novelistic equivalent of talking heads." *Booklist* concludes, however, that "This journal-cum-novel is marvelous not only at capturing time and place but also at *recapturing* the mentality of its milieu." In the view of *The London Times* James Cowan "has created [in Mauro] an endearing and sympathetic vessel who counter-balances [the author's] self-consciously clever introduction, footnotes and notes to readers." Novelist and physicist **Alan Lightman** (*LATBR*) concludes that "We are enchanted — wrapped in that magic and strangeness that comes of a journey far from our own time."

RECOGNITION: *L.A. Times* "Best Books" 1996; REVIEWS: *AusBkRev* 2/97; *BL* 9/15/96; *KR* 8/1/96; *LATBR* 12/29/96; *LJ* 9/15/96; *LT* 8/8/98 (pbk review); *NYTBR* 12/15/96; *PW* 8/5/96; *TLS* 7/11/97

Crace, Jim (UK)

522 *Quarantine* (1997); FS&G 1998 (HC); Picador 1999 (pbk); SETTING: Palestine in roughly 5 BC

Prize-winning English novelist Jim Crace, in his latest novel (called a "literary miracle" by *USA Today*), reimagines the two thousand-year-old story of Christ's forty days in the desert. In Mr. Crace's version five pilgrims enter the desolate Judean desert for the purpose of performing the ritual 40 days of fasting and prayer: a handsome, self-absorbed ascetic; an elderly Jew who is gravely ill; an unassuming peasant; and a wealthy but sadly barren woman. Bringing up the rear, is a young barefoot man from Galilee. Meanwhile, a rapacious merchant by the name of Musa has fallen ill shortly after entering the desert with his caravan. Comatose, he is being half-heartedly nursed by his pregnant wife Miri who, frankly, looks forward to his death. When the fifth pilgrim approaches her campsite, Miri offers him a gourd of water from which he drinks. Before moving on, he sprinkles water on her husband and pronounces the traditional words of comfort "So, here, be well again." Musa awakes the next morning fully recovered. Being a man of particularly base and grasping instincts, he claims the surrounding land as his and extorts money from the four pilgrims living in the nearby caves. He also sets off in pursuit of the young Galilean — who he credits with his miraculous recovery — wanting to shower him with gifts of food and wine. The young man manages to resist the merchant's blandishments.

According to *Booklist* "Crace's humanist recasting of Jesus's 40 days in the desert — Musa and the others have become the tempting demons to the hallucinating Jesus — raises new issues of theology, ethics, biblical narrative, and cause and effect." The (London) *Sunday Times* observes that "Patches of this sun-seared narrative shimmer into a heated blur, and there are some plodding stretches in the interactions between its characters. But, as a feat of fictional archaeology, this is a novel of scorching distinction. Crace knows his chosen terrain down to the last swag fly and star lizard" and concludes that "Far more than the resuscitation of Musa, Crace's uncannily sure-handed exhumation of a long-gone world constitutes his novel's real miracle of resurrection." **John Updike**, writing in *The New Yorker* concludes that "Crace is a writer of hallucinatory skill and considerable cruelty. The beatings and thievery of the ancient world, its intimate murderous commerce with animals, and its bestial treatment of women are not stinted, nor is the compromised quality of religious experiences, or the deadly beauty of desert mountains...." *Time* contends that "Crace ... is not the first writer to take fictional liberties with Scripture. He won't be the last. But his new effort proves to be one of the more successful reimaginings."

RECOGNITION: Winner of the 1997 Whitbread Novel of the Year Award; Shortlisted for the 1997 Booker Prize; *PW*'s Best '98 Fiction; *NYTBR* Notable Book of 1998; REVIEWS: *BL* 3/1/98; *LRB* 7/3/97; *LST* 6/15/97; *NY* 5/12/97; *NYTBR* 4/12/98; *PW* 1/12/98; *Salon* 4/10/98; *Spec* 6/14/97; *Time* 4/20/98; *TLS* 6/13/97

523   *Signals of Distress* (1994); FS&G 1995 (HC); Ecco 1997 (pbk); SETTING: A small port on the English Channel—1836

Jim Crace's fourth novel begins with a storm-tossed night and a shipwreck. An American sailing ship (The Belle of Wilmington), having just crossed the Atlantic ocean from Montreal, wrecks on a sandbar near the coastal village of Wherrytown. The cargo, a herd of Canadian cattle, manage to swim to shore and the crew are rescued by local fishermen. The isolated community offers what hospitality it can to the crew, but the Americans prove to be a disturbing presence. Another boat, a "steamer" called the "Ha 'Porth of Tar," has also found safe harbor at Wherrytown and its only passenger, the forward-thinking Aymer Smith is sharing Wherrytown's single inn with the American sailors who count an escaped slave among their number. As the novel progresses, the large cast of disparate characters (entrepreneur, sailors, merchants, emigrants, former slave, etc.) who have been thrown together because of the storm, find their lives to be inextricably linked.

Called a "brilliant, unsettling novel" by the *Washington Post Book World*, *Signals of Distress* was widely admired. The *Times Literary Supplement*, for example, pointed out that Crace had set his "intriguing work" at a key transitional point of society, one in which the fiercely modern technology of the steam ships was beginning to supplant the infinitely more graceful but much less efficient wind-driven variety ... with profound ramifications. *Kirkus Reviews* declared that in its pages "Human nature in all its tangled glory is quietly but powerfully evoked along with a tangy, lasting impression of the intricate life of those who dwell between land and sea."

REVIEWS: *The Age* 10/1/94; *KR* 7/15/95; *NewR* 5/6/96; *NYTBR* 9/24/95; *TLS* 9/2/94; *WPBW* 2/4/96.

Cunningham, Michael (USA)

524   *Flesh and Blood* (1995); FS&G 1995 (HC); 1996 (pbk); SETTING: Europe and the United States 1900s—1980s

Flesh and Blood follows the Stassos family through four generations as it is transformed by ambition, love, violence and accumulated history. Constantine Stassos, a Greek immigrant, amasses a fortune, marries Mary Cuccio, an Italian-American girl, and sires three star-crossed children: Susan, oppressed by her beauty and her father's affection; Billy, brilliant and gay; and Zoe, a wild, heedless visionary. As the years pass, their lives unfold in ways that compel them and their parents to meet even greater challenges.

According to *Booklist*, *Flesh and Blood* is an "empathetic and searing family drama (in which) the haphazardness of genetics and fate plays in mocking counterpart to the predictability of heartache." *Publishers Weekly*, in its starred review, observes that "Cunningham's portraits are so honest and sensitive that we can see into their souls. His prose is both restrained and mesmerizing: individual scenes—such as one of teenagers in a car wreck—become incandescent images." The *London Review of Books* points out that "Cunningham's narrative is compelling—it seems to consume time rather than merely surrender to it—but it is in small circumstances that he prefers to linger. Decorating a cake can be revelatory, climbing a tree, religious; and every sentence, no matter how mundane its subject, a literary event. Such ostentatiousness could go disastrously wrong in a less gifted stylist or less perceptive observer, and for much of *Flesh and Blood* I waited uneasily for Cunningham to slip up. But he doesn't...."

OTHER MEDIA: Audiocassette (S&S Audio/abr); RECOGNITION: *NYTBR* Notable Book of 1995; Winner of the 1996 Lambda Award for Gay Men's fiction; REVIEWS: *BL* 1/15/95; *EW* 5/10/96; *LJ* 4/15/95; *LRB* 2/22/96; *NY* 4/10/95; *NYTBR* 4/16/95; *PW* 1/23/95; *TLS* 8/11/95; *VFair* 5/95

Davies, Robertson (Canada)

525   *The Cunning man* (1995); Viking 1995 (HC); Viking Penguin 1996 (pbk); SETTING: Canada—1920s to 1980s

The Cunning Man, the last novel by one of Canada's most revered men of letters, is narrated by an unorthodox Toronto physician who, in 1985, looks back over the past 60-odd years spent, primarily, in his beloved city of Toronto. Dr. Jonathan Hullah's reminiscences have been stimulated by the probing questions of a young reporter who is preparing a story about the "old Toronto." She has, in the course of her research, stumbled upon an unresolved mystery stretching back to 1951: the death, on the high altar of Toronto's venerable St. Aidan's (at the most solemn point of the liturgical calendar) of a priest by the name of Father Hobbes. Dr. Hulllah had known the zealous Father Hobbes since they were boys together at a Toronto boarding school in the early years of the 20th century. The tenacious young reporter is determined to shed some modern light on Father Hullah's dramatic end.

According to *The* (London) *Sunday Times,* "A tone of robust irony ripples over the novel's lively cavalcade of changing Canadian life and customs…. Cerebral gusto and humane enjoyment make this novel irresistible." English novelist Isabel Colegate (*WPBW*) found *The Cunning Man* to be "wise, humane and consistently entertaining" and concluded that it is one of Mr. Davies "most entertaining and satisfying books." The *TLS* notes that in his last "entertaining … [and] magnificently written novel, " Davies's "chosen affinities are with Chaucer and Goethe and his book combines the earthy worldliness of the one — the Miller's Tale features a couple of times — with the 'humanism' of the other…." *Kirkus Reviews* concludes that "Ideas, aphorisms, and wit are as evident as Davies's more teleological concerns, which all makes for a splendid intellectual romp as well as an absorbingly literate novel."

OTHER MEDIA: Audiocassette (Blackstone/ unabr); RECOGNITION: *NYTBR* Notable Book of 1995; REVIEWS: *BL* 11/15/94; *KR* 11/1/94; *LATBR* 3/26/95; *LJ* 12/94; *LST* 4/2/95; *NYTBR* 2/5/95; *PW* 12/5/94; *TLS* 4/7/95; *WBPW* 1/22/95; *WLT* Aut'95

526   *Murther & Walking Spirits* (1991); Viking Penguin 1992 (pbk); SETTING: North America 18th–20th centuries

I was never so amazed in my life as when the Sniffer drew his concealed weapon from its case and struck me to the ground, stone dead.

How did I know that I was dead? As it seemed to me, I recovered consciousness in an instant after the blow, and heard the Sniffer saying, in a quavering voice: "He's dead! My God, I've Killed him!" My wife was kneeling by my side, feeling my pulse, her ear to my heart; she said, with what I thought was remarkable self-possession in the circumstances, "Yes, you've killed him."

Robertson Davies' 10th novel is narrated by the ghost of Conor "Gil" Gilmartin who, at the novel's outset, is murdered by a newspaper colleague not-so-affectionately referred to as "the Sniffer." Gil was struck dead when, returning home early from the office, he found his wife and the Sniffer "in flagrante." The novel's primary conceit is that Gil — in his new ghostly state — is not only aware of the details of his own death, but must now linger on, consigned to an afterlife that appears to consist of accompanying his killer to a film festival. "But," according to *Books in Canada,* "what

the ghostly Gil sees is 'cinema verite' with a vengeance. While 'the Sniffer' watches such archival masterpieces as *The Spirit of '76'* and *Shadows of Our Forgotten Ancestors,* Gil watches the stories of his own ancestors unfold on screen."

Booklist observes that "Davies has great fun, giving full rein to his sense of drama, love of gritty, historical detail, and delight in satire" and concludes that *Murther & Walking Spirits* is "A sage and witty interpretation of the afterlife that asks 'Do we die and learn?' We do, in any case, certainly enjoy Davies' humor, warmth, and wisdom." In the view of English novelist, Adam Mars-Jones (*TLS*), *Murther* "is finely written and [is] always entertaining. Even a minor character, like the ineffectual medium Mrs. Selenius, gets the benefit of some first-rate phrase-making: she speaks English in a 'quiet, regretful voice, the voice, as it were, of Garbo, speaking through a mouthful of chocolate.' " According to *Entertainment Weekly, Murther* "has all the usual Davies ingredients — irascible wisdom, mischievous humor, and the stubborn individuality of both characters and the author. The difference is that it's a more personal book." The *Financial Times* of London points out that "When an Ackroyd or a Byatt forays into the past, it is as if giant earth moving machines were burrowing into humus. Davies, on the other hand, with Welsh wizardry in his veins, simply dances." Richard Eder, Book Editor of the *L.A. Times,* concludes that "In an epic journey that stretches from pre-industrial Wales to Revolutionary America to contemporary Canada, Davies takes you on a time trip through his own colorful past. And he's never been more wicked or wonderful."

RECOGNITION: *NYTBR* Notable Book of 1991; REVIEWS: *BksCan* 11/91; *BL* 9/15/91; *FTimes* 12/7/91; *LATBR* 11/14/91; *LitRev* 10/91; *LRB* 8/6/92; *NY* 2/10/92; *NYTBR* 11/17/91; *PW* 9/6/91; *Q&Q* 8/91; *Spec* 10/5/91; *TLS* 9/27/91; *WPBW* 11/10/91

Davis, Thulani (USA)

527   *1959* (1991); HarperCollins 1993 (pbk); SETTING: Virginia — 1959

Thulani Davis's novel is set in Virginia at the dawn of the civil rights movement and features Willie Tarrant, a black youngster who will be catapulted into the newly emerging struggle for racial equality. Willie lives in Turner, a former slave-built enclave that had evolved into a typical, segregated southern town. Her father, Dixon Tarrant watches apprehensively as Willie meets Martin Luther King, participates in lunch counter sit-ins and is recruited to help integrate the near-by white high school.

According to the *New York Times Book Review,* "Ms. Davis has a masterly sense of time and place, using the history of the town and Willie's aunt's diary to create a raw and moving testament to the power that rests within a community." *Newsweek* observes that Davis has "combined a coming- of-age story with an evocative portrait of a segregated community on the cusp of the 1960s. What happens when the blacks of Tuner, Virginia, get fed up with their lot can be read as micro-history of the civil rights movement, and even a grimly prophetic emblem of the entire African-American experience." In the view of the *Womens Review of Books*, "*1959* is an affirmation. It embodies the spirit which sparked that historic period and which will sustain the future...."

RECOGNITION: Nominated for the 1992 *L.A. Times* First Fiction Award; REVIEWS: *EW* 2/19/93; *NYTBR* 3/15/92; *NS&S* 6/5/92; *NewsWk* 3/9/92; *PW* 12/6/91; *TLS* 5/29/92; *VLS* 3/92; *WRB* 5/92

de Bernieres, Louis (UK)

528   *Corelli's Mandolin* (1994); Pantheon 1994 (HC); SETTING: Cephallonia (Crete), Greece, during W.W.II

After setting his first three novels in a quasi-Marquesean South America, Englishman Louis de Bernieres turns his novelistic attention to Europe. His much-admired fourth novel, *Corelli's Mandolin*, is set on the peaceful, tradition-bound Greek island of "Cephallonia" (i.e., Crete). Although de Bernieres' story begins in the early 1940s and spans a full 50 years, the central action takes place during the Italian and subsequent German occupations in the waning years of W.W.II. During these years, a communist-led insurgency skirmished half-heartedly with the generally empathetic Italian soldiers, a situation which changed dramatically with the arrival of the Germans. Against this historical background, de Bernieres has fashioned an exuberant, at times heart-breaking, love story featuring Captain Corelli (a charming, mandolin-playing and exceedingly reluctant officer attached to the Italian occupying forces), Pelagra, the lovely, patriotic and fiery daughter of the local doctor, and a sensitive young fisherman-turned-insurgent.

According to English novelist **A.S. Byatt**, *Corelli's Mandolin* "is so good it will last...." The *Washington Post Book World* calls *Corelli's Mandolin* "a good old-fashioned sort of novel ... [which] brims with all the grand topics of literature, or at least literature of the pre-modern era -love and death, heroism and skulduggery, humor and pathos, not to mention art and religion, the practice of general medicine, and the proper method of cooking snails." In its starred review, *Publishers Weekly* concludes that *Corelli's Mandolin* "Swinging between antic ribaldry and criminal horror, between corrosive satire and infinite sorrow ... glows with a wise humanity that is rare in contemporary fiction."

OTHER MEDIA: Audiocassettes (Chivers/unabr); READING GROUP GUIDE; RECOGNITION: *NYTBR* Notable Book of 1994; *PW* "Best Book" 1994; *TLS* :International Book of the Year"; REVIEWS: *BL* 9/15/94; *LJ* 7/94; *LST* 5/15/94; *LT* 4/11/94; *NS&S* 4/22/94; *NYTBR* 11/13/94; *PW* 6/27/94; *Spec* 4/16/94; *TLS* 4/8/94; *WPBW* 9/18/94; EDITOR'S NOTE: Mr. de Bernieres was named to *Granta* magazine is 1993 list of the twenty "Best Young British Novelists"

DeLillo, Don (USA)

Underworld (1997) See under *Pushing the boundaries* #230; S&S 1997 (HC); 1998 (pbk); SETTING: Post-war America

529   *Libra* (1988); Viking Penguin 1991 (pbk); SETTING: 1960s US & Soviet Union

Don DeLillo, in *Libra*, attempts a fictional reconstruction of one of the defining moments in American history: the assassination, on November 22, 1963, of President John F. Kennedy. DeLillo uses the conventions of the thriller to tell his story, throughout which he intermingles real and imagined characters including CIA agents, Cuban immigrants, Mafia dons, police officers, politicos and bystanders. Overshadowing all others, of course, is the author's portrait of Lee Harvey Oswald, the ultimate outsider.

According to *Publishers Weekly* "DeLillo's ninth novel takes it title from Lee Harvey Oswald's zodiac sign, the symbol of 'balance.' And, as in all his fiction.... DeLillo's perfectly realized aim is to balance plot theme and structure so that the novel he builds around Oswald ... provokes the reader with its clever use of history, its dramatic pacing and its immaculate and detailed construction." The *Library Journal* notes that "what haunts the reader most is the image of Oswald as a confused young man searching for an identity and accidentally caught up in something bigger than himself." In the view of the *Chicago Tribune*, "The long-standing unresolved questions about Kennedy's assassination make the perfect subject for DeLillo's obsessive imagination ... Mixing fact and fiction, DeLillo has created a thriller of the most profound sort, because we know the ending, we become attentive to the slowly accumulating, utterly convincing detail. Jonathan Yardley (*WPBW*) argues that *Libra* uncharacteristically is "notable for its lack of interesting prose, its deficiency of wit and — this, perhaps, most surprising of all — its failure of the imagination; in *Libra* that is to say, DeLillo offers no pleasures or surprises to compensate for the tedious predictability of his politics."

OTHER MEDIA: Audiocassette (Books-on-Tape/unabr); RECOGNITION: Nominated for the 1988 National Book Award; REVIEWS: *ChiTrib*

7/31/98; *Guard* 1/2/92; *LJ* 4/15/91; *NYTBR* 7/24/88; *PW* 4/12/91; *WPBW* 7/31/98

Dickey, James (USA)

530   *To the White Sea;* HM 1993 (HC); Dell 1994 (pbk); SETTING: Wartime Japan (1945)

James Dickey (author of the highly successful 1970 novel *Deliverance*) has chosen in his third novel to tell the story of an American tail gunner on the run in war-torn Japan. Airman Muldrew has been forced to parachute into enemy territory from his burning B52 which was shot down during a bombing raid over the Tokyo docks. Having grown up in the wilderness of Alaska, he has complete confidence in his survival skills and (once making his way out of the Japanese port city) instinctively heads north toward the sparsely inhabited island of Hokkaido. The result is a bone-chilling, violence-strewn odyssey in the company of a consummate predator. The climax is appropriately Dickey-esque.

Publishers Weekly, in its starred review, observes that "As a poetic novel that offers thrilling language and profound insights into man and nature, *White Sea* is enthralling." *Kirkus Reviews* suggests that "the prose of the 70-year-old poet slices down to the bone of things like an immaculate knife..." and concludes that *To the White Sea* is a "ruthless adventure of body and soul by a writer of mature — even awesome — powers." Novelist Leon Rooke (*NYTBR*) was less enamored of Dickey's novel, pointing out that "In quick succession, (Muldrew) kills one unlucky Japanese for his clothes, another for his shoes and a third to shut her mouth. You get the idea he likes it. He prefers the knife to the pistol, dwells at length on the quality of one blade over another and lets us know what he favors is slicing a carefully honed blade 'up through the gut' [and concludes] Muldrew is not a soldier trying to survive; he's a psychopath [and] it will be hard for most readers to view this misdirected novel as a significant morality tale."

OTHER MEDIA: Audiocassette (Brilliance/abr; Bookcassette/unabr); RECOGNITION: *Booklist* Editors' Choice 1993; REVIEWS: *BL* 7/93; *KR* 6/15/93; *LJ* 8/93; *NYTBR* 9/19/93; *PW* 6/21/93; *TLS* 2/11/94; *WLT* Aut'94

Dillard, Annie (USA)

531   *The Living* (1992); HarperCollins 1993 (pbk); SETTING: American Northwest — 19th century

In her debut novel, set in and around the 19th century Pacific Northwest community of Bellingham Bay, Annie Dillard skillfully delineates the shifting fortunes of a diverse group of settlers (resourceful frontiersmen, pathological misfits, and others) and the Native Americans with whom they come into inevitable contact.

According to the *Library Journal*, *The Living* a "compelling portrait" of a very specific time and place "is unflinching in its delineations of pioneer life at its worst and best — racism and brutality on the one hand and optimism and charity on the other." Novelist **Barbara Kingsolver**, writing in *The Nation*, points out that even though this is Annie Dillard's first novel, it differs very little from her works of non-fiction, observing that "it most closely resembles *Pilgrim at Tinker's Creek* (1974), whose every paragraph yields stunning revelations but whose whole does not move forward along any single path...." *Publishers Weekly* similarly concludes that Ms. Dillard's saga, "a tapestry woven in deep relief, is held together less by a single narrative thread than by [the author's] superb evocation of the implacable, no-nonsense relationship of these people to their surroundings...."

OTHER MEDIA: Audiocassette (Blackstone/unabr); RECOGNITION: *NYTBR* Notable Book of 1992; *BL* "Editors' Choice" 1992; REVIEWS: *Atl* 6/92; *CSM* 5/22/92; *LJ* 3/15/92; *Nation* 5/25/92; *New Leader* 8/10/92; *NewsWk* 6/8/92; *NYTBR* 5/3/92; *PW* 2/21/92; *YaleR* 10/92

Doane, Michael (USA)

532   *Bullet Heart* (1994); Knopf 1994 (HC); Berkley 1995 (pbk); SETTING: South Dakota Indian Reservation in 1970s

Michael Doane's *Bullet Heart* is based on a real event, the exhumation of a pioneer grave (on land being developed as a golf course) and the unequal treatment accorded the skeletal remains found at the site. The bones of the white settlers were re-interred, those of a young Native American were sent to the State House where they were displayed as artifacts. This culturally insensitive act triggered what came to be known as the "Bone Wars" a series of skirmishes between the Oglala Sioux and the F.B.I.

In the view of *Booklist*, "Doane effectively captures, occasionally with haunting insight, more than a dozen voices and relates how a community with intricate and indelible ties based on blood, land, age, and heritage erupts into chaos and violence." According to novelist **Lesley Craig** (*NYTBR*) *Bullet Heart* is "a moving story of survival, of keeping family and community together after devastating loss ... [one which] invites the reader to consider the long struggle [of Native Americans] for acceptance and equality. Mr. Doane's vision of the journey is brilliant and haunting." *Kirkus Reviews* concludes that *Bullet Heart* is "Derring-do mixed with personal drama, sometimes bogged down by a crowded chorus."

REVIEWS: *BL* 6/19/94; *KR* 4/15/94; *LATBR* 7/24/94; *LJ* 6/1/94; *NYTBR* 8/21/94; *PW* 5/16/94; *WPBW* 7/3/94

Doctorow, E.L. (USA)

533   *Billy Bathgate* (1989); HarperCollins 1994 (pbk); SETTING: NYC in the 1930s.

The eponymous Billy Bathgate, Bronx born and bred, is being personally groomed for a leadership role in the crime syndicate by Dutch Schultz a powerful Depression-era gangster. When Billy falls for Dutch's latest girlfriend he begins to take a more critical look at the "the mob" and its ethos.

According to novelist **Anne Tyler** (*NYTBR*), *Billy Bathgate* is "Mr. Doctorow's shapeliest piece of work: a richly detailed report of a 15-year-old boy's journey from childhood to adulthood, with plenty of cliff-hanging adventures along the way ... [Billy is] Huck Finn and Tom Sawyer with more poetry, Holden Caulfield with more zest and spirit — a wonderful new addition to the ranks of American boy heroes." In *Newsweek*'s opinion, "Doctorow brings a nice sense of moral ambiguity and creates characters who develop or deteriorate at an appropriate pace. His fecund run-on sentences are a joy to read. It all adds up to that rarity: a formal literary work that's also hugely entertaining." Richard Eder (*L.A. Times Book Review*) observes that "Billy tells the story in vivid cinematic scenes, related with a mix of rich detail, ironic tension and a nervy, darting reflectiveness that keeps taking us in unexpected directions." Novelist and columnist **Pete Hamill** (*WPBW*) concludes that "Once more [Doctorow] has explored our popular nostalgias, embracing them while revising them. The result is that rarity, the grand entertainment that is also a triumphant work of art."

OTHER MEDIA: Audiocassette (Blackstone/unabr); a film version starring Dustin Hoffman was released in 1991; RECOGNITION: Winner of the 1990 PEN/Faulkner Award 1990; Winner of the 1989 National Book Critics Circle Award; nominated for the National Book Award; *Booklist* "Editors' Choice" 1989; REVIEWS: *LATBR* 3/12/89; *LJ* 2/15/89; *NY* 3/27/89; *NYTBR* 2/26/89; *NewsWk* 2/13/89; *Time* 2/27/89; *WPBW* 2/19/89

Dorris, Michael (USA)

534   *Cloud Chamber* (1997); Scribner 1997 (HC); S&S 1998 (pbk); SETTING: Ireland — 19th century & American South and West — 20th century

Michael Dorris's five-generational family saga expands on the story begun in *A Yellow Raft in Blue Water* and continues to focus on the descendants (some of them mixed-race) of a feisty Irish woman by the name of Rose Mannion. Rayona Taylor, the part black, part Native American teenager featured in *A Yellow Raft in Blue Water* appears at the end of Dorris's last novel, where she meets, Marcella, her white paternal grandmother who is the granddaughter of Rose Mannion. Having contracted TB from her father as a child, Marcella was confined for extended periods in a sanitarium where she met, and later married, a young black man. The product of this brief union was Elgin, Rayona's feckless father.

Publishers Weekly, in its starred review, applauds the author's "evocative prose [that] gathers strength and clarity" as the tale progresses and concludes that "Dorris provides a moving and persuasive image of reconciliation for which America still yearns." According to *Time* magazine, "Dorris, whose own ancestry is Irish, French and Madoc Indian, writes that 'the past ruled the present with unsympathetic dominion.' And until Rayona, this is true, with her, the future is April going on May. Her reappearance at the end of this intricate and brooding second novel cools like a spring breeze." The *L.A. Times Book Review* concludes that "In *Cloud Chamber*, Dorris tells the American story of hard people leading difficult lives with as much courage, insight and allowance for complexity as anyone writing today."

RECOGNITION: *NYTBR* Notable Book of 1997; *L.A. Times* "Best Books" 1997; REVIEWS: *BL* 10/15/96; *LATBR* 12/14/97; *LJ* 11/15/96; *NYTBR* 2/9/97; *PW* 11/11/96; *Time* 2/17/97; *WPBW* 1/12/97

Duffy, Bruce (USA)

535   *Last Comes the Egg* (1997); S&S 1997 (HC); SETTING: Washington, D.C. and the American south — 1960s

Bruce Duffy's second novel (called a "beguiling serio-comic tale" by *Kirkus*) is set, primarily, in and around the Maryland suburbs of Washington DC. 12-year-old Frank Daugherty's mother has recently died and his relationship with his father, not good even in the best of times, is further fractured by his father's apparent interest in another woman. Frank takes refuge in his friendship with Alvy Loomis, an altar boy with a guilty secret (and a talent for hot-wiring cars). Eventually, the two conflicted adolescents hook up with Sheppy an older African American boy with his own set of issues. When the three boys, powered by a stolen car, hit the runaway trail they run smack into a series of sobering and enlightening experiences.

In the view of the *New York Times Book Review*, *Last Comes the Egg* is a "disturbing and original [novel] of suburban adolescents on the run in the 1960's [which] uncovers the scars beneath the optimism of postwar America." According to *Booklist* "Duffy's prose style won't be to everyone's taste.... Yet if you can step up and buy in, you'll be rewarded by a heartbreaking, pathetic, and painfully funny novel." *The* (London) *Times* notes that the author "presents a beguiling world of children's thinking as a way separate from adults. What sets them apart from most of their English counterparts is [his] use of language *as it is spoken* and the creative possibilities within that." *Kirkus Reviews* observes that "the novel hums along agreeably, powered by Frank's high-energy, ribald, plaintive voice (he's telling the story in retrospect, almost 25 years later, addressing it to his dead mother) and by several adroit variations Duffy plays on the controlling (title) metaphor; which describes the process of thinking oneself inside unfamiliar situations or other people's skins and making yourself understand them."

RECOGNITION: *NYTBR* Notable Book of 1997; REVIEWS: *BL* 1/1/97; *KR* 11/15/96; *LATBR* 3/9/97; *LJ* 12/96; *LT* 2/5/98; *Nation* 3/24/97; *NYTBR* 3/9/97; *PW* 12/2/96

Edgerton, Clyde (USA)

Where Trouble Sleeps (1997); Algonquin 1997 (HC); Ballantine 1998 (pbk); SETTING: North Carolina—1950s; See Section 4, #325

536 *Redeye* (1995); Algonquin 1995 (HC); Viking Penguin 1996 (pbk); SETTING: Colorado in the 1890s

Clyde Edgerton's wild and wooly Western satire is set in southern Colorado in the 1890s and includes within its colorful cast of characters P.J. Copeland, a recent graduate of the Darless Mortuary Science College. It also features, in addition to a passel of cowboys, Indians, and eccentric Englishmen, a "steel-jawed, single-minded" pitbull (the eponymous "Redeye") who belongs to Cobb Pittman, a bounty hunter hell-bent on revenge. The frenetic plot is driven by, among other events, an attempt to seek retribution for the (Mormon-initiated) Mt. Meadows, Utah massacre of 1857, and the discovery and eventual exploitation of prehistoric cliff dwellings on Mesa Largo.

Novelist **Tim Sandlin**, in a review appearing in the *New York Times Book Review*, suggests that "a Hollywood pitchman might call *Redeye* Eudora Welty meets Mark Twain. An admirer of good fiction might say that Clyde Edgerton has created a small gem of a novel." *Publishers Weekly* calls it simply "fun from start to finish." In the view of *Booklist*, Edgerton's "many fans, accustomed to the rural North Carolina setting of Edgerton's previous five novels, may be a bit startled by this book's move west, but they'll stick around for the ride anyway."

REVIEWS: *America* 11/44/95; *BL* 3/15/95; *LJ* 4/15/95; *NYTBR* 4/30/95; *PW* 3/20/95.

Elegant, Simon

537 *A Floating Life* (1997); Ecco Press 1997 (HC); SETTING: 8th-century China

Simon Elegant — editor of the *Far Eastern Economic Review* and long-time resident of Hong Kong — tells the story of the great Chinese poet Li Po who is known to have lived a roisterously creative life in the first half of the Eighth Century. Li Po, while unknown to most Westerners, is a literary legend in China and Mr. Elegant brings him to ribald life in his debut novel. Mr. Elegant's novel is constructed as a mock autobiography dictated by Li Po to a young provincial scholar as they travel together up the Yangtse River.

In the view of the *Atlantic Monthly*, "Mr. Elegant's fictionalized life of Li Po is a swashbuckling picaresque tale ... [in which Po's] complaints about that old bore Confucius, phony scholarship, court etiquette, and the straightjacket rules of Mandarin verse ring true." According to *Kirkus Reviews* "The structural looseness of Elegant's historical re-creation is appropriate to the picaresque genre, and yet a certain lack of depth in the author's portrayal of his protagonist does limit the book's impact and imaginative reach." Novelist **John Derbyshire** (*WPBW*) points out that Li Po was possessed of a contradictory personality: "For all his faults, Li Po seems to have been one of those people — like William Blake — whose genius shines from their eyes ... this kind of charisma is hard to capture, especially across cultures, but I think Elegant has done a very creditable job of it, deploying his own translations of Li's poems to great effect. *A Floating Life* is a charming story, skillfully told."

REVIEWS: *AtlM* 11/97; *KR* 8/1/97; *LJ* 9/1/97; *NYTBR* 3/8/98; *PW* 8/11/97; *WPBW* 9/21/97

Epstein, Leslie (USA)

538 *Pandaemonium* (1997); St Martin's 1997 (HC); 1998 (pbk); SETTING: Europe in 1938 and Hollywood during W.W.II

John Milton hovers a bit over Leslie Epstein's wildly inventive new novel about the "old" Hollywood and its movie moguls, wisecracking screenwriters and feckless actors. Milton's *Pandaemonium* was the seat of Satan, the capital of Hell. Epstein's Pandaemonium is set primarily in Europe on the verge of World War II. Described by *Publishers Weekly* as a "comic fantasia about Hollywood and nazis, power and imagination," *Pandaemonium* is narrated first by a fictionalized Peter Lorre and then by the Hollywood gossip-columnist, Louella Parsons. The novel opens in Austria at the world famous Salzburg Music Festival. It is 1938 and the legendary director Rudolph von Beckmann, fresh from Hollywood, is mounting a production of "Antigone" starring Peter Lorre (born Laszlo

Loewenstein) and international beauty Magdalena Mezaray. Almost without warning, Hitler annexes Austria and various members of the production find themselves "at considerable risk." The action eventually switches to California and Nevada during the war years.

According to *Publishers Weekly*, Epstein (the son of Philip Epstein, who with his twin brother Julius, wrote the screenplays for such Hollywood classics as *Casablanca* and *Arsenic and Old Lace*) piles "his narrative high with Hollywood knowledge and bracing portrayals of real personalities ... [and] delivers his tale on a grand if somewhat unwieldy scale that shuttles bumpily between broad humor and moral seriousness." In the view of the *Los Angeles Times Book Review*, *Pandaemonium* "is a novel about the ways in which movie reality and historical reality get mixed, causing public confusion and large scale disaster.... The mood is sustained hysteria; the mode is sex, murder, image-mongering and what might be called control of the final cut. The visuals Epstein rolls forth are colossal in conception, surprisingly haunting, even beautiful. Let all who think 'image is everything' read this book."

RECOGNITION: *NYTBR* Notable Book of 1997; *LATBR* "Best Books" 1997; REVIEWS: *KR* 4/1/97; *LATBR* 12/14/97; *LJ* 4/15/97; *NYT* 6/2/97; *NYTBR* 6/22/97; *PW* 3/24/97

Faulks, Sebastian (UK)

539   *Birdsong* (1993); Random House 1993 (HC); Vintage 1997 (pbk); SETTING: France 1910–1918

A best-seller in Britain, *Birdsong*, Sebastian Faulks' third novel, is both a love story and a searing chronicle of war. The story begins in 1910 and features Stephen Wraysford, a moody young Englishman who has been sent — by his guardian — to Amiens, France where he is to be "apprenticed" to a French factory owner by the name of Rene Azaire. Stephen moves into the Azaire home and falls promptly, passionately and, of course, adulterously in love with Rene's beautiful young wife, Isabelle. Stephen and Isabelle eventually run off together and experience a few stolen years of happiness. With the outbreak of World War I, Stephen, still in France, he joins the British Army and is quickly exposed to the horrors of trench warfare. In the late 1970s, Stephen's grand-daughter, Elizabeth, delves into her grandfather's past.

Novelist *Penelope Lively* (*Spectator*) calls *Birdsong* "an extremely good novel, and a considerable addition to the fin-de-siecle flowering of first world war literature." Michael Gorra (*NYTBR*) applauds Faulk's "spare and precise prose" observing that trench warfare "has scarcely ever been presented in such unrelenting and dispassionate detail." "It is,"

concludes Mr. Gorra, "as if Mr. Faulks has bled his own prose white, draining it of emotion in order to capture the endless enervating slog of war." Regarding the earlier, romantic sections, Gorra writes that Stephen and Isabelle "seem plausible as characters willing to stake everything on passion. Their sex scenes, while always decorous in language, are some of the most satisfyingly graphic this side of **Nicholson Baker**." Novelist **George Garrett** (*LATBR*) notes that "The accounts of combat both above and below ground, ringing with credibility and authenticity, are among the finest I have ever read. The sensuous, affective surfaces, the details, the fully imagined physicality of life and death are so powerful as to be almost unbearable." The *New Statesman & Society* asserts that *Birdsong* "remains an impressive achievement as a new hybrid creation: the literary-blockbuster, Bovary-and-bonking."

OTHER MEDIA: Audiocassette (Chivers/unabr); READING GROUP GUIDE: "Reading Group Choices" 1998 (Paz & Associates); RECOGNITION: *L.A. Times* "Best Books" 1996; *NYTBR* Notable Book of 1996; REVIEWS: *GW* 10/31/93; *KR* 12/1/95; *LATBR* 12/29/96; *LST* 9/19/93; *LT* 9/9/93; *NS&S* 9/7/93; *NY* 4/1/96; *NYTBR* 2/11/96; *PW* 12/11/95; *Spec* 9/18/93; *TLS* 9/10/93; *WPBW* 2/18/96

Fell, Alison (UK)

540   *The Pillow Boy of the Lady Onogoro* (1996); HarcourtBrace 1996 (HC); SETTING: Japan — 11th century

The Pillow Boy of the Lady Onogoro skillfully combines a richly detailed (and undeniably exotic) historical setting with lushly rendered descriptions of erotica. The Lady Onogoro, the young, beautiful and talented (she's a poet) mistress to the rather lumbering and insensitive General Motosuko lives in 11th century Japan, at the royal court of Kyoto. Given her need to achieve the degree of arousal expected of a concubine of this period, the lady has instructed her servant Oyu (a blind stable boy) to act as "pillow boy" and, from a hiding place behind the bed, recite into her ear specially chosen erotic tales.

The *Washington Post Book World* observes that "Fell constructs her imaginary pillow book in an artful manner, complete with an academic forward detailing its supposed reconstruction. But more to the point, she gives it a modern sensibility without jarring the ancient setting." The *New Statesman* notes that "It is rare to come across a book that offers quite so many pleasures, all very different. The language alone is a treat for connoisseurs of the highest quality of prose. Most intriguing, though, is the effect that language has on the direction of the narrative itself. For Oyu's silver-tongued tales do not merely bring Onogoro to fulfillment. They also prompt her to see herself more clearly.... This is a book about the power of language ... which makes its point with wisdom, wit and a charming lightness of touch." In the view of *The* (London*) Sunday Times The Pillow Boy* is a "skillfully wrought ... mischievous novel ... in which the pleasures of sex and the glamour of times past are cleverly combined." *Booklist* concludes that "in spite of its historical trappings, this funny and titillating romp is a thoroughly modern tale about the frustrations of a woman writer in a man's world."

REVIEWS: *BL* 2/1/96; *KR* 12/1/95; *LATBR* 2/25/96; *LJ* 1/96; *LT* 7/7/94; *NS&S* 6/3/94; *NYTBR* 3/3/96; *PW* 10/23/95; *TLS* 7/22/94; *WPBW* 6/16/96

Fitzgerald, Penelope (UK)

541   *The Blue Flower* (1995); HM 1997 (pbk); Wheeler 1998 (HC); SETTING: 18th century Saxony

Penelope Fitzgerald, who published her first work of fiction at the age of 60, has — as of 1998 — written nine novels. Her second, *Offshore*, won the 1979 Booker Prize (Britain's most influential literary award), while *The Bookshop* (1978), *The Beginning of Spring* (1988), and *The Gate of Angels* (1990) all made the Booker shortlist in subsequent years. Her most recent novel *The Blue Flower*— which appeared on more British end-of-year "Best Book" lists than any other title published in 1995 — is a superbly imagined work of fiction based on the life of the great German Romantic poet Frederick von Hardenberg, known to his readers as "Novalis." Frederick (Fritz to his family), was one of five children of an impoverished Saxon nobleman and his loving but chronically distracted wife. While still a youngster, Fritz was sent to an austere Brethren's boarding school from which the unusually introspective (and stubborn) young man was eventually expelled for arguing that "the body is not flesh, but the same stuff as the soul." Fritz returned to his chaotically lively and much-loved family where he remained until gaining admittance to the renowned University of Jena. There he was immediately embraced by an impassioned group of young intellectuals. In her brief yet fully realized novel, Ms Fitzgerald tells the story of Fritz's early years and his grand (albeit impossibly romantic) passion for, and subsequent engagement to, Sophie, a sweetly uncomplicated adolescent girl with an undeveloped intellect and weak lungs.

Richard Eder (*LATBR*) calls Penelope Fitzgerald "the finest English writer alive" and suggests that *The Blue Flower* while "deceptively small in size ... is a fictional evocation of the Romantic movement that revolutionized Europe's sensibility at the beginning of the 19th century." Elder concludes that "Fitzgerald is the most cosmopolitan of English writers.... Like any excellent writer she creates a world, but like only a very few — Milan Kundera and Italo Calvino come to mind — she creates a metaphysics as well." According to the *Times Literary Supplement The Blue Flower* "is fastidious, funny, sad, clever, and very engaging. The tragic tale is told with a dryness that has humor built into it, as though Jane Austen instead of Mrs. Gaskell were writing about the Brontës." Frank Kermode (*LRB*) observes that Ms. Fitzgerald's use of detail "expertly dabbed in, provides in the end a substantial background for the story of a poet which, it is subtly suggested, is also the story of a remarkable moment in the history of civilization...." Kermode concludes that it "is hard to see how the hopes and defeats of Romanticism, or the relation between inspiration and common life, between genius and mere worthiness, could be more deftly rendered than they are in this admirable novel." *Publishers Weekly*, in its starred review, argues that "history aside, (*The Blue Flower*) is a smart novel. Fitzgerald is alternately witty and poignant, especially in her portrayal of the intelligent, capable women who are too often taken for granted by the oblivious poets" and concludes that "Fitzgerald has created an alternately biting and touching exploration of the nature of Romanticism — capital "R" and small." In the view of Michael Dirda (*WPBW*), "It is quite astonishing how much Penelope Fitzgerald packs into a little more than 200 pages. It is even more astonishing to realize that she is, past 80, writing better than ever. Perhaps such masterpieces as this, serene with wry wisdom, can only be achieved in later life. So seek *The Blue Flower*, and when you find it, rejoice. After a while, you'll want to go out and look for *The Beginning of Spring, Innocence*, and *The Gate of Angels*."

RECOGNITION: Winner of the 1997 NBCCA; *TLS* International Book of the Year 1995; *NYTBR* "Editors' Choice" 1997; *L.A. Times* "Best Books" 1997 (Top Ten); *WPBW* Readers' Pick 1997; *Publishers Weekly* "Best Books" 1997; REVIEWS: *KR* 2/15/97; *LATBR* 4/13/97; *LRB* 5/10/95; *NYTBR* 4/14/97; *PW* 3/10/97; *TLS* 9/15/95; *WPBW* 4/6/97

542   *The Gate of Angels* (1990); Houghton Mifflin 1998 (pbk); SETTING: Cambridge, England—1912

How could the wind be so strong, so far inland, that cyclists coming into the town in the late afternoon looked more like sailors in peril? This was the way in to Cambridge, up Mill Road past the cemetery and the workhouse. On the open ground to the left the willow-trees had been blown, driven and cracked until their branches gave way and lay about the drenched grass, jerking convulsively and trailing cataracts of twigs. The cows had gone mad, tossing up the silvery weep-

ing leaves which were suddenly, quite contrary to all their experience, everywhere within reach. Their horns were festooned with willow boughs. Not being able to see properly, they tripped and fell. Two or three of them were wallowing on their backs, idiotically, exhibiting vast pale bellies intended by nature to be always hidden. They were still munching. A scene of disorder, tree-tops on the earth, legs in the air, in a university city devoted to logic and reason.

With these opening lines, Penelope Fitzgerald establishes the tone of her 7th novel, a romantic, historical tale of ideas — set in Cambridge, England in 1912 — in which (following a bicycle collision) Fred a young experimental physicist (and parson's son) falls in love with Daisy, a failed student nurse raised in a South London slum. It is also a story about the birth of atomic physics and, somewhat more tangentially, women's suffrage. Just to complicate matters, Fred is a Junior Fellow at one of Cambridge's most ancient and "eccentrically ordered" colleges. It does not admit women to its premises and forbids its Fellows to marry.

The *Times Literary Supplement* notes that when Fred Fairly exclaims, early in the novel, that "These are wonderful years in Cambridge he "can hardly be grudged his enthusiasm [for this] ... was indeed a time when the reputation of Cambridge science ... was at a peak" and concludes that "In the course of her charming parable, Ms. Fitzgerald sets about undermining the exciting certainties of the nuclear physicists, and more generally, the closed-in male rationality that engendered them." As the *Literary Review* points out, "Just toward the end of Penelope Fitzgerald's brilliant new novel, the reader is treated to a ghost-story in the manner of M.R. James.... [Her] pastiche daintily sets all you nerves individually on end, and then knocks them down like dominoes, so that a wave of panic sweeps up your back to the top of your head. The fact that the horror story sits comfortably in a novel ostensibly dealing with more mundane matters ... is an indication ... that this is a novel about the power of the unconscious mind, and the knowledge that goes deeper than response to observable fact." In the view of the *New York Review of Books*, "Penelope Fitzgerald is not only an artist of high order but one of immense originality, wholly her own woman. She composes with an innocent certainty which avoids any suggestion that she might have a feminist moral in mind, or a dig against science, or a Christian apologetic. The translucent little tale keeps quite clear of such matter, and yet it is certainly about goodness...." *The* (London) *Observer* argues that *The Gate of Angels* "contains more wit, intelligence, and feeling than many novels two or three times its length."

OTHER MEDIA: Audiocassette (Chivers/

unabr); RECOGNITION: Shortlisted for the 1990 Booker Prize; REVIEWS: KR 10/15/91; LitRev 8/90; LRB 9/13/90; NYRB 4f/9/92; *NYTBR* 3/1/92; Obs 9/7/91 (?); TLS 9/24/90

543   *The Bookshop* (1977); HM 1997 (pbk — reissue); SETTING: East Anglia—1959

In 1959 Florence Green occasionally passed a night when she was not absolutely sure whether she had slept or not. This was partly because of her worries as to whether to purchase a small property, the Old House, with its own warehouse on the foreshore, and to open the only bookshop in Hardborough. The uncertainty probably kept her awake. She had once seen a heron flying across the estuary and trying, while it was on the wing, to swallow an eel which it had caught. The eel, in turn, was struggling to escape from the gullet of the Heron and appeared a quarter, a half, or occasionally three-quarters of the way out. The indecision expressed by both creatures was pitiable. They had taken on too much. Florence felt that if she hadn't slept at all — and people often said this when they mean nothing of the kind — she must have been kept awake by thinking of the heron.

So begins Penelope Fitzgerald's spare yet exquisitely limned tale of Florence Green, an unassuming, yet resourceful widow with a small inheritance, who has decided to purchase "Old House," a vacant 500-year-old property in the center of Hardborough. She has decided, after much soul searching — and in the face of some stiff local opposition (both from the local banker and wealthy Mrs. Gamart, the local arts doyenne, who has designs on the same building) — to open a bookshop. It being 1959, Mrs. Green's decision is widely regarded as a very bold move; after all, modern amenities, not to mention *amusements*, had not yet made their way to this tiny East Anglian town untouched by fish 'n' chips shops, launderettes, or even a weekly cinema. Once opened, Mrs. Green's bookshop (despite periodic warehouse floodings, general dampness and a spectral presence) gets off to a successful start, helped in no small measure by her decision to stock Vladimir Nabokov's new novel *Lolita* and by the perspicacity of her fourteen-year-old assistant. Mrs. Green's good fortunes, however, are far from assured.

New York Times Book Review calls *The Bookshop* a "psychological and moral map of awful English provincial life in 1959" in which "the protagonist, a widow trying to run a bookshop, is undone by upper-class twits." In the view of English novelist **A.S. Byatt** "Fitzgerald writes with a mysterious clarity nobody else approaches." The *Washington Post Book World* suggests that "Where some writers like to build effects slowly, Fitzgerald prefers a quicksilver economy ... [and the results are] [v]ivid ... elegant ... astonishing." The *Spectator* concludes that *The Bookshop* is a "solid and satisfying bit of life.... Every action in it matters, however small."

READING GROUP GUIDE: "Reading Group Choices" 1998 (Paz & Associates); RECOGNITION: *NYTBR* Notable Book of 1997; LATBR "Recommended Title" 1997; shortlisted for the 1978 Booker Prize; REVIEWS: BL 5/15/79; KR 2/1/79; LJ 4/1/79; NS 10/7/77; *NYTBR* 12/7/97; Spec 10/14/77; TLS 10/7/77

Flanagan, Thomas (USA)

544   *End of the Hunt* (1994); Warner 1995 (pbk); SETTING: Ireland 1919–1923 (Civil War)

With *The End of the Hunt*, Thomas Flanagan completes his Irish trilogy that began with the award-winning *The year of the French* (1979) and continued with *The Tenants of Time* (1988). The latest volume continues his story of Ireland's struggle to free itself from British domination and features (among others) Janice Nugent (a gentlewoman from a Catholic land-owning family whose husband was killed at Gallipoli) her lover, Christopher Blake (a historian and Sin Fein leader), and the ruthless, Virgil-reading military genius Frank Lacy. Intermingled with these fictional characters are the redoubtable Michael Collins, Eamon de Valera (the villain of the piece), and (in more minor roles) Winston Churchill (a wily, heavy-drinking member of Lloyd George's cabinet), and Lloyd George himself. Set in the turbulent 1920s it encompasses the creation of the Irish Free State and the brutal Civil War which followed.

According to *Booklist* "Flanagan continues to expand the chronological dimensions of his splendid rendering of Ireland's long climb to self-determination in the face of parental England's infuriation." *Kirkus Reviews* notes that Flanagan "deftly describes — with enough details to satisfy those who prefer their history lightly spritzed with fiction — a nasty little war with even nastier consequences." The *Washington Post Book World* concludes that "Irish history to this day is a continuing lesson in the extreme difficulty of negotiating the end of fighting. Each of Flanagan's novels illustrates how easily the frail underpinnings of peace can be destroyed, how quickly the streets can be filled with soldiers. It is not only in Ireland past that love of nation or tribes, mixed with a sense of holy mission, and fueled by centuries of grievance can destroy civil order."

RECOGNITION: *NYTBR* Notable Book of 1994; REVIEWS: *BL* 1/15/94; *ComW* 9/23/94; *KR* 2/1/94; *LJ* 2/15/94; *NS&S* 4/14/95; *NYTBR* 4/3/94; *Time* 5/23/94; *WPBW* 4/3/94; EDITOR'S NOTE: The two earlier volumes in Flanagan's trilogy: *The Year of the French* and *The Tenants of Time* are still widely available

Fleming, John Henry (USA)

545   *The Legend of the Barefoot Mailman* (1996); Faber & Faber 1996 (HC); SETTING: late 19th century Florida

John Henry Fleming's debut novel tells the tragi-comic tale of Josef Steinmetz who is drafted into the fledgling Florida state Postal Service by Earl Stank, an ambitious small-town Post-master. The setting is post-Civil War America, when Florida, a sparsely settled and relatively undiscovered state, was poised for rapid development. Mail delivery was not a service taken for granted in the isolated ocean-front community of Figulus, Florida, and, until the arrival of Stank (and the subsequent hiring of Steinmetz) the local inhabitants had to walk 60 miles of beach to retrieve their mail. Steinmetz, once persuaded to take the job, faces a daunting array of occupational hazards in the form of hungry alligators, suspicious Seminoles, heat stroke and sunburn. When a series of mishaps and misunderstandings brings the "barefoot" mailman to the attention of an enterprising reporter, he is unwittingly propelled into the public arena as a genuine folk hero.

According to the *Christian Science Monitor*, *The Legend of the Barefoot Mailman* "is filled with action packed scenes involving fistfights, scavengers, shipwrecks, Seminole Indians, and rescues, deftly narrated in a wry, tongue-in-cheek style reminiscent of Mark Twain or Ambrose Bierce." *Booklist* observes that "Fleming's insights into mythmaking are keen, and his narrative skills and humor, finely honed" and concludes that the author has produced a "marvelously inventive, thoroughly enjoyable tale about our capacity for self-invention, adaptability, and perseverance." In the view of *The Southern Quarterly The Legend of the Barefoot Mailman* "flirts steadily with the opportunity of becoming a southern classic."

REVIEWS: *BL* 1/1/96; *CSM* 1/10/96; *LJ* 12/90; *NYTBR* 2/25/96; *PW* 11/20/95

Flowers, A.R. (USA)

546   *Another Good Lovin Blues* (1993); Ballantine 1994 (pbk); SETTING: American South — 1920s

Set in the 1920's in Arkansas, Mississippi and Tennessee, *Another Good Lovin Blues* features Lucas Bodeen, piano-playing bluesman "extraordinaire" and his longtime lover, the "conjure woman," Melvira Dupree. Flower's tale revolves around love lost (and regained) and a search for a missing mother — all set against the background of a dangerously racist American South.

According to the *New York Times Book Review*, *Another Good Lovin Blues* "is a provocative novel in which Mr. Flowers seamlessly blends the rich rhythms of the blues and a Deep South patois in a lyrical, literate style, while skillfully interlacing his high-spirited story with flashes of painful insight...." In the view of *The* (London) *Times* "This is a journey of the 'conjurwoman' Melvira Dupree and her lover Lucas Bodeen who has given his heart to playing the blues. The passing miles and years chart the trials and growth of their relationship as they learn to adopt to the changing face of the American deep South between the wars. The story has the weight and compass of an odyssey...." The *Library Journal* applauds a style that "flows as smoothly as the music that forms its core," and concludes that Flowers (himself a native Memphis blues singer) "has woven a fable of the South that captures the heart of the blues musician as few others have done before."

REVIEWS: *BL* 1/15/93; *LJ* 1/3; *LT* 10/11/93; *Newsday* 2/16/93; *NYTBR* 3/7/93; *WPBW* 3/7/93

Forster, Margaret (USA)

547   *Lady's Maid* (1990); Ivy 1996 (pbk reissue); SETTING: Mid–19th century England and Europe

Margaret Forster, biographer of Elizabeth Barrett Browning has, in *Lady's Maid*, provided readers with a fresh perspective on the rarefied literary world of the Barrett-Brownings and their celebrated romance. Ms. Forster's 1990 novel is narrated by "Wilson," Elizabeth's maid whose devotion to her mistress, in the face of her own relatively powerless position, casts a sharp light on the inequities of the rigid class system of that era. The novel is constructed around a series of chatty, colloquial and unfailingly perceptive letters written by Wilson to her mother in the North Country.

Publishers Weekly calls *Lady's Maid* "top-drawer historical fiction" and suggests that "Wilson's ambivalence about Miss Elizabeth, whom she loves and resents, is the most interesting aspect of the novel." According to the *Library Journal*, "Forster brilliantly explores the uneasy intimacy between mistress and servant, working-class girl and educated lady of leisure to produce a compelling character study and an engrossing novel of the colorful Browning menage." In the opinion of the *Literary Review* "Forster has a fine sense of the way in which emotional blackmail operates, and her exploration of the relationship between mistress and maid is nicely handled, but the inherent sentimentality of the story makes *Lady's Maid* feel like Georgette Hyer with guts...." The *Times Literary Supplement* observes that Wilson's "story is thoroughly imagined, socially illustrative and psychologically individual" and concludes that "The narrative structure, a hybrid of the old and the new, is ingenious."

RECOGNITION: *NYTBR* Notable Book of 1991;

REVIEWS: *LitRev* 7/90; *LJ* 1/91; *LRB* 9/27/90; *NYTBR* 3/17/91; *PW* 1/11/91; *TLS* 7/20/90

Fowler, Karen Joy (USA)

548   *The Sweetheart Season* (1996); H Holt 1996 (HC); Ballantine 1998 (pbk); SETTING: Magrit, Minnesota—1947

The Sweetheart Season, told retrospectively, chronicles the formation of an all-girl baseball team (the Sweetwheat Sweethearts) sponsored by the local cereal mill. The mill—located in the seriously male-depleted town of Magrit, Minnesota—has been a major source of employment for young women during and immediately following World War II. Its owner, attempting to both publicize his new cereal brand and assist his employees in locating husbands, throws his enthusiastic support behind the team.

Novelist Deirdre McNamera (*NYTBR*), applauds Ms. Fowler's "willingness to take detours, her unapologetic delight in the odd historical fact, her shadowy humor and the elegant unruliness of her language," which, she concludes, "all elevate her story from the picaresque to the grand." According to *Publishers Weekly*'s starred review, "The now-adult daughter of a Sweetheart recalls the team's history in a wry, witty voice that balances our revisionist present with the romanticized past.... With fictional Magrit, Fowler depicts our nation's past as more surreal than real, while at the same time slamming her novel out of the ballpark." Richard Eder (*LATBR*) suggests that "What gives *The Sweetheart Season* its distinction is the delicate comedy with which Fowler creates her townspeople...." The *Washington Post Book World* concludes that Ms. Fowler's novel is "Smart, wry, and just this side of insane."

RECOGNITION: *NYTBR* Notable Book of 1996; REVIEWS: *KR* 8/1/96; *LATBR* 9/29/96; *NYTBR* 10/13/96; *PW* 7/22/96; *WRB* 3/97

549   *Sarah Canary* (1991); Ballantine 1998 (pbk); SETTING: Pacific NW in the 1870s

Karen Joy Fowler's debut novel combines fact and fiction in telling the story of Chin Ah Kin, a Chinese railway worker whose life is altered by a mysterious "wild woman" in a dirty black dress. As the novel opens, the woman has taken up residence on the edge of a Chinese Railway workers' camp where her disheveled appearance and strange warbling language has perplexed (and unsettled) the men. Chin's uncle, mindful of the woman's potential for stirring trouble in this all-male environment, orders him to escort the woman back to an insane asylum (located clear across the Washington territory) from which it is assumed she has escaped. Their journey together is fraught with peril and near-escapes as it becomes clear that the woman is being pursued by (among others) an itinerant lecturer on women's sexual freedom and a carnival freak-hunter.

Publishers Weekly asks: "Is Sarah Canary, the mute, misshapen object of Chin's confused affections, a vampire, an apparition, a shape-shifter, a feral child, a murderess?" and concludes that "these are just a few of the intriguing questions that will keep readers turning the pages of this buoyant first novel set in and around the Washington territories of 1973." According to the *New York Times Book Review, Sarah Canary* "is [although not without faults] an extraordinarily strong first novel." The *American Book Review* asserts that *Sarah Canary* "swells with elaborately subtle and unobtrusive situational ironies and puns.... Call it 'magical new historicism' or 'magical multi-culturalism,' and be assured that no clunky label does justice to the wonderful strangeness Fowler discovers in the gaps our national mythologies — both historical and literary." *Kirkus Reviews* observes that "To Chin, Sarah is an ever-elusive mystery, captivating in her very unresponsiveness to other mortals and in her determination to remain free ... " and concludes that *Sarah Canary* is "a fascinating romp, in which actual events are so cleverly intertwined with the author's fanciful inventions that the reader grows unsure which to disbelieve." Richard Eder (*LATBR*) points out that "The history that Fowler lifts to myth ... is that of oppression , the boot heel of progress. She sets her story in the 1870s and the headlong westward expansion that followed the Civil War. Her characters are the victims: The Chinese brought in to build railroads, the Indians, the wildlife, the landscape, the misfits and, above all, the women." Mr. Eder further observes that "Victims" "is partly misleading. Fowler gives them an exuberant and raffish voice, in their innocence, they will rise again with a power of dream. Fowler's book has its own dreamlike power; it is part ghost story, part picaresque adventure, and partly a carnival of sad and comic extremes."

READING GROUP GUIDE; RECOGNITION: *NYTBR* Notable Book of 1991; REVIEWS: *ABR* 4-5/91; *BellesL* Wint'91; *KR* 8/1/91; *LATBR* 10/21/91; *LJ* 5/1/92; *NY* 11/18/91; *NYTBR* 10/10/91; *PW* 8/23/91

Frazier, Charles (USA)

550 *Cold Mountain* (1997); AtlM 1997 (HC); Vintage 1998 (pbk); SETTING: The American South at the end of the Civil War.

Set in the final months of the Civil War, Charles Frazier's debut novel describes the 300 mile journey home of Inman, a deeply disillusioned Confederate soldier who, languishing in a military hospital with a neck wound, decides to pick himself up and head back to Cold Mountain in the hills of North Carolina. His act of desertion is fueled by his revulsion at the carnage (and increasing futility) of the war and by an overwhelming desire to be reunited with Ada, the woman he loves. The story of Inman's often hair-raising trip through a war-devastated south is counterpointed with the story of Ada, a minister's daughter raised in Charleston, and "educated beyond the point considered wise for females" as, after her father's death and throughout the war, she fights to keep body and soul together on her family's hill-top retreat. Frazier's novel is based, at least partly, on his own great-great-grandfather's experiences as a Confederate soldier.

In the view of *Entertainment Weekly, Cold Mountain* contains "enough weapon clanging to satisfy all but the most thirsty Civil War buffs, yet Frazier lavishes equal narrative weight on Ada's trials and ravaged psyche as she watches and waits, struggling to tend her dead father's farm." Alfred Kazin, writing in the *New York Review of Books* asserts that Frazier "has written an astonishing first novel, if that is what it is.... The prose is so silky and arch in capturing the stiff speech of the period that the book must have had much unpublished work behind it." Novelist, **Claire Messud**, writing in the *Washington Post Book World* points out that "Frazier has adopted an antiquated style to authenticate the 19th-century Southern world. His locutions sound unnatural to the contemporary ear ... and his vocabulary thrills in its oddity." Ms. Messud concludes that "*Cold Mountain* delights above all, as an exceedingly free natural history, in which Frazier's characters learn and live by their surroundings."

OTHER MEDIA: Audiocassette (Random Audio/abr; Random Audio/unabr); READING GROUP GUIDE; RECOGNITION: Winner of the 1997 National Book Award; *NYTBR* Notable Book of 1997; *LATBR* "Recommended Titles" 1997; nominated for the National Book Critics Circle Award *Publishers Weekly* "Best Books" 1997; *Salon Magazine* "Book of the Year" 1997; *Booklist* Editors' Choice 1997; REVIEWS: *BL* 6/1/97; *ChiTrib* 8/17/97; *CSM* 7/14/97; *EW* 7/18/97; *KR* 4/1/97; *LJ* 5/15/97; *LT* 4/19/98; *NewsWk* 6/23/97; *NYTBR* 7/13/97; *PeopleW* 7/21/97; *PW* 5/5/97; *WPBW* 7/6/97

Freed, Lynn (South Africa)

551 *The Mirror* (1997); Random House 1997 (HC); SETTING: South Africa —1920 onward

And then, one day, the old man sent up a mirror for my room, and I stood it across one corner. It was tall and oval, and fixed to a frame so that I could change the angle of it by a screw on either side. And for the first time ever I could look at myself all at once, and there I was, tall and beautiful, and there I took to standing on a Saturday afternoon, naked in the heat, shamelessly before myself and the Lord.

Lynn Freed, in her third novel, tells the story of Agnes La Grange a working class English girl who, in 1920 — at the age of seventeen — emigrates to South Africa with the intention of making something of her life. Her first job is as a housekeeper for a wealthy Jewish man and his dying wife. Before long, however, she discovers the power of her innate sexuality which she usees to her very great advantage. The book is formatted to look like a small diary complete with photographs tucked into each chapter.

According to *Kirkus Reviews*: "Candor, passion and love of life put Agnes on a par with the Wife of Bath, while Freed adds the treats of succulent place and period flavor." In the view of *Entertainment Weekly* "Agnes is Moll Flanders without excuses — an enchanting and infuriating heroine, both admirable and wrongheaded in her commitment to honesty and her pursuit of adventure." *The New York Times Book Review* concludes that "Like so many of the best books, *The Mirror* makes us laugh while packing, finally, a punch in which life's sadness prevails over its consolatory moments of humor."

READING GROUP GUIDE; RECOGNITION: *NYTBR* Notable Book of 1997; REVIEWS: BL 9/1/97; EW 9/12/97; KR 7/1/97; LJ 8/97; *NYTBR* 9/21/97; PW 6/23/97

Freeman, David (UK)

552   *One of Us* (1997); Carroll & Graf 1997 (HC); 1998 (pbk); SETTING: Egypt — 1930s

David Freeman sets *One of Us* in Egypt, a former British Protectorate, during the turbulent decade leading up to WW II. Sir Malcolm Cheney, the British High Commissioner, has taken a keen interest in young Prince Farouk, a pampered, yet engaging, youngster who will eventually assume the Egyptian throne. Looking to insure a future pro-English regime, Cheney has taken it upon himself to supervise Farouk's education in the early years includes a British tutor (one Jimmy Peel the first of several narrators) followed by, at the age of fifteen, enrollment in an elite British boarding school. When Sir Malcolm — a widower with two daughters — remarries, his beautiful, independent-minded young second wife immediately becomes a favorite of the thoroughly anglicized Farouk who (at his father's death) has returned to Egypt to assume the throne. Complications arise.

According to the *New York Times Book Review*, *One of Us* is an "engaging historical novel, set in a grand colonial Egypt, where an ambassador's effort to Anglicize the young King Farouk evokes a personal and political bedroom revenge." *Kirkus Reviews*, calling the novel a "stylish, startlingly inventive evocation of a pre-Nasser Egypt [and] a

classy, exciting entertainment" observes that David Freeman, "against a deadly mix of cultures … [skillfully] plays out the farcical-to-tragic consequence of an unlikely triangle" Richard Bernstein (*NYT*) found *One of Us* to be "a delicious novel, full of understated eroticism and intellect and able to make you feel a vicarious nostalgia for a world that has been swept away." *Booklist* points out that "Some writers — **Beryl Bainbridge** is perhaps the leading example — write historical novels that are so firmly rooted in their time and place that the authors' imaginative version of what happened becomes more 'real' to us than the version we read about in history books. Add Freeman to that short list."

RECOGNITION: *NYTBR* Notable Book of 1997; REVIEWS: BL 10/1/97; KR 8/1/97; LJ 8/97; *NYTBR* 11/23/97; PW 8/11/97

French, Albert (USA)

553   *Holly* (1994); Penguin 1996 (pbk); SETTING: North Carolina — 1940s

Holly, a young white woman living a hardscrabble existence in Supply, a tiny North Carolina town during World War II, has in the aftermath of the combat death of her fiancé, fallen in love with Elias Owens, an injured black veteran. The couple will pay dearly for their societal "transgression."

According to the *Quarterly Black Review*, Albert French "writes in a terse, revealing style, like Pete Dexter working in dialect, wasting few words or scenes … [and has created] an estimable work of all-too-real fiction." Called "beautifully written" by the *Library Journal*, *Booklist* contends that, although the tone of French's second novel is "far more languorous and diffuse [than his highly successful first novel *Billy*, the author's] provocative power … is undeniable." The *Washington Post Book World* notes that "French beautifully sketches Holly's tale, painting characters rich enough to demand sympathy even as they react with unthinking racism."

REVIEWS: BL 4/15/95; LJ 4/15/95; *NYTBR* 6/4/95; QBR 1995; WPBW 8/6/95

554   *Billy* (1993); Penguin 1995 (pbk); SETTING: Mississippi — 1937

Albert French's debut novel is set in rural Mississippi in 1937 and tells the story of Billy a young black boy who is tried and convicted for the murder of Jenny, a white teenager. The tale begins on a hot and sultry day when Billy and his best-friend Gumpy decide to make their way across the railroad tracks for a quick (albeit "forbidden") dip in a pond belonging to Jenny's family.

Novelist **Michael Dorris** (*NYTBR*) observes that *Billy* "once in motion, gathers momentum like a landslide" and concludes that the novel is a "tragedy in the classical mode, mythic in the sense that instead of surprise, the twists of plot we might discover in a more typical contemporary novel, here we are confirmed in our worst dreads as destiny immutably and shockingly unfolds." *The Chicago Tribune* praised the book, especially the author's "ear for language and his eye for detail [which bring all the people in the book] to vibrant life." *Booklist* contends that "This is an American tragedy, stark and resonant, told in a voice as unwavering as the August sun and as timeless as sorrow." In the opinion of the *Quarterly Black Review*, *Billy* "is a haunting book, but not in the ethereal sense. It hooks onto you like a cocklebur, startling you awake in the middle of the night with visions of myriad cruelties, both personal and societal, and of the permeation of evil."

RECOGNITION: *NYTBR* Notable Book of 1994; REVIEWS: *BL* 10/1/93; *ChiTrib* 12/14/93; *LJ* 10/1/93; *NYTBR* 12/19/93; *QBR* 1995

Freud, Esther (UK)

555   *Summer at Gaglow* (1997); Ecco 1998 (HC); SETTING: Germany early 1900s through W.W.I & Contemporary London

In her third novel, Esther Freud (actress/novelist, sister of designer Bella, daughter of artist Lucien and great-granddaughter of Sigmund) tells the story of the Belgards a German-Jewish family, by focusing on Eva, the youngest of three sisters. Ms. Freud employs a dual narrative which alternates between World War I Germany (moving from the family's opulent residence in Berlin to their sprawling country house, Gaglow) and contemporary London. Ms Freud's finely realized novel depicts a way of life that will soon come to a decisive, inescapably violent end. In a parallel story, Eva Belgard's granddaughter, Sarah Linder, a young single mother, is just beginning to piece her family's history together.

According to *The* (London*) Sunday Times*, "This is a sad elegiac book of broken dreams and private betrayals. The cool aestheticising style may sometimes seem a little pretentious, but the atmosphere is well sustained." In the view of the *Library Journal* "Freud cleverly juxtaposes the world of Gaglow as it was and the myths of the inhabitants of Gaglow as they are told in family stories. Freud's prose is lyrical, her characters remarkable and her story compelling." *Kirkus Reviews* argues that Freud has constructed a "shrewdly observant, emotionally astute postmodern version of a family saga ... [which] focuses more on individual episodes than on continuity."

RECOGNITION: *NYTBR* Notable Book of 1998; REVIEWS: *KR* 3/15/98; *LJ* 2/15/98; *LST* 5/11/97; *NYTBR* 5/17/98; *PW* 2/9/98; *TLS* 5/2/97; *WPBW* 11/1/98; EDITOR'S NOTE: Ms. Freud was named *to Granta* Magazine's 1993 list of the twenty "Best Young British Novelists"

556   *Peerless Flats* (1993); Ecco 1998 (pbk); SETTING: London —1970s

In her second novel Esther Freud tells the story of a girl's adolescence within the context of her dysfunctional and decidedly "counter cultural" family in the London of the early 1970s. Placed in temporary apartments for the homeless (called "Peerless Flats") with her mother and young brother, sixteen-year-old Lisa is exposed to the twin sirens of ready drugs and easy sex.

The *Library Journal* points out that "Freud's prose is graphic, her dialog, concise. The story jumps from adventure to adventure, with Lisa the thread that sews the pieces together." According to *Publishers Weekly*, "With barely a nod to conventionally linear narrative structure, this unusual book is like a beautiful, disturbing painting that renders, on an intuitive level, a troubled young girl's soul." The *Literary Review* concludes that "Esther Freud is such an accomplished writer that [one] can't help hoping she ventures beyond the autobiographical daughters — mother triangle; but even as book three ends up being about an actress-turned-writer, her willful dress-designer sister, and their stuck-in-the-sixties mother, it's bound to be a treat."

REVIEWS: *KR* 2/1/93; *LitRev* 2/93; *LJ* 11/15/93; *NS&S* 3/5/93; *NY* 5/31/93; *NYTBR* 6/20/93; *PW* 2/22/93

557   *Hideous Kinky* (1992); Ecco 1998 (pbk); SETTING: North Africa —1960s

Esther Freud (great-granddaughter of Sigmund Freud), in her debut novel, tells the loosely autobiographical story of a feckless young "hippie" mother, who, with her two young daughters, her boyfriend (with his strangely passive wife in tow), sets off for Morocco. It is, of course, the psychedelic '60s. The boyfriend's wife refuses to speak. "Hideous" and "kinky" are the only words anyone remembers hearing her say, and the guileless youngsters turn the two words into a kind of chant. Upon their arrival in Marrakech, Mum immerses herself in the Sufi religion, and the children begin to rebel: 7-year-old Bea insists on going to school, while the 5-year-old narrator dreams of mashed potatoes.

According to the *Times Literary Supplement*, Ms Freud's book "has a delightful lightness of being. It springs from the child's acceptance of whatever comes.... Beggars, shepherds, innkeepers, idiots, dubious Moroccan and eccentric European ladies are funny and appealing and seen with affection and so are Mum and determined, tyrannical Bea." The *New York Times Book Review* points out that, *Hideous Kinky* "evocatively renders the breathless static of vagabond life, and the way a quest for meaning can become an escape from freedom." The *London Review of Books* concludes that "the handling of the narrative is a tour-de-force of artfulness...."

OTHER MEDIA: A film version starring Kate Winslet was released in 1998; REVIEWS: *KR* 11/1/92; *LRB* 3/12/92; *NYTBR* 5/31/92; *TLS* 1/31/92; *VLS* 1/31/92

Gaines, Ernest (USA)

558   *A Lesson Before Dying* (1993); Vintage 1994 (pbk); SETTING: Louisiana — 1940s

Ernest Gaines's award-winning novel — set in a fictional Louisiana town in the 1940s — tells the achingly poignant tale of Grant Wiggins, a black school teacher, and his relationship with Jefferson, a semi-literate young black man who has been wrongly sentenced to death. The condemned man's mother has asked Wiggins to teach her son how to "die like a man."

According to the *Christian Science Monitor* "Gaines has a gift for evoking the tenor of life in a bygone era and making it seem as vivid and immediate as something that happened only yesterday.... [The author's] craftsmanship and conviction in writing about this world transforms what might have been a moralizing tale into a convincing moral drama." The *New York Times Book Review* asserts that "Despite the novel's gallow's humor and an atmosphere of pervasively harsh racism, the characters, black and white, are humanly complex.... Gaines has written a moving and truthful work of fiction." *Time* magazine concludes that few writers have Gaines's "dramatic instinct for conveying the malevolence of racism and injustice without the usual accompanying self-righteousness."

OTHER MEDIA: Audiocassette (Random Audio/abr & Books-on-Tape/unabr); READING GROUP GUIDE; RECOGNITION: Winner of the 1993 National Book Award, the 1993 National Book Critics Circle Award, and the ALA Black Caucus 1994 Literary Award for Fiction; REVIEWS: *BL* 2/15/93; *Choice* 10/93; *CSM* 4/13/93; *LJ* 4/1/93; *NYTBR* 8/8/93; *PW* 3/1/93; *SLJ* 7/93; *Time* 3/29/93

Garrett, George (USA)

559   *Entered from the Sun* (1990); Harcourt Brace 1991 (pbk); SETTING: Elizabethan England

The 16th century poet and dramatist, Christopher "Kit" Marlowe, is the subject of George Garret's final novel in his Elizabethan cycle begun with the publication of *Death of the Fox*. The mystery surrounding Marlowe's untimely and, many would argue, suspicious death in a tavern brawl is the subject of Garrett's tale. Two fictional characters, an actor by the name of Joseph Hunnyman and Captain Barfoot, an aging soldier, join forces in an attempt to solve the mystery.

According to the *Sewanee Review,* "Everything works here: the characters are splendidly angular and energetic; the dialogue is a perfect mixture of ancient and modern usage: it achieves an antique flavor without deflecting the reader's comprehension or calling attention to itself. Even when the stuff of the story is inherently unattractive.... Garrett's rendering of person and scene gives ugliness and pain a kind of beauty." The *Washington Post Book World* calls *Entered from the Sun* "a happy symbiosis of learning and art." The *L.A. Times Book Review* found Garrett's novel to be: "A sprightly deft narrative in which you can smell and feel the rambunctious London of the 1500s with all of its bawdiness and its endless political and religious intrigues."

RECOGNITION: *NYTBR* Notable Book of 1990; REVIEWS: *BL* 9/1/90; *LATBR* 9/16/90; *LJ* 9/1/90; *NYTBR* 9/16/90; *PW* 7/6/90; *Sewanee* Wint '91; *WPBW* 9/9/90

Giardina, Denise (USA)

560   *Saints and Villains* (1997); Norton 1998 (HC); SETTING: Europe and the United States — 1920s through WW II

Denise Giardina, in her 4th novel, tells the fictionalized story of Dietrich Bonhoeffer, the outspoken German theologian whose courageous opposition to the Nazi regime cost him his life. The novel begins with Bonhoeffer's privileged German boyhood, and continues with his theological studies at the Union Theological Seminary in New York City (where he is first exposed to overt racism), continues with his life as a pastor a in England and Germany and concludes with a fascinating account of his wartime experiences as a member of the German Military Intelligence — where he worked to subvert the Nazi regime. Ms Giardina makes the "moral imperative," the choice of good over evil, the primary focus of her story.

Publishers Weekly, in its starred review, observes that "Dietrich Bonhoeffer is one of the most moving figures in the pantheon of Germans who resisted Hitler, and this novelized version of the pastor's life by Giardina manages the extremely difficult task of giving a known story genuine tension and spiritual resonance." *Booklist* notes that "Giardina does not draw a simple lesson from Bonhoeffer's story, which she has altered slightly for greater narrative coherence, but instead illumines the web of moral decisions within which we all exist" and concludes that the author has "with passion, understanding, and eloquence ... [written a] compelling, frightening, yet beautiful novel." *Kirkus Reviews* says that Ms. Giardina "has the gift of making intellectual argument excitingly dramatic, this time with a dozen or more passionate exchanges in which the fate of civilization and the responsibilities of citizens are memorably debated. A big novel in every sense of the word, and a triumphant portrayal of one of the century's authentic heroes."

READING GROUP GUIDE; REVIEWS: *BL* 2/15/98; *KR* 1/1/98; *NYTBR* 4/19/98; *PW* 1/22/97; *WPBW* 4/16/98

Glancy, Diane (USA)

561 *Pushing the Bear*: A Novel of the Trail of Tears (1996); Harcourt Brace 1998 (pbk); SETTING: North Carolina, Alabama, Georgia, Tennessee and Oklahoma —1838

Diane Glancy, poet, dramatist and short-story writer, has, reimagined in *Pushing the Bear* the forced 1838 eviction of 13,000 Cherokee Indians from their lands in North Carolina, Alabama, Georgia and Tennessee. Their unspeakably grueling and heartbreaking 900-mile forced march (through the dead of winter) to a reservation in Oklahoma was in every way a trail of tears.

According to *Booklist*, "Using the voices of both the captive Cherokee and the white soldiers, and subtly incorporating her extensive research on the subject, Glancy provides a moving firsthand account of a terrible moment in U.S. history." In the view of the *Publishers Weekly* "At times, the novel proceeds as slowly as the march itself, but it rewards the reader with a visceral, honest presentation of the Cherokee conception of story as the indestructible chain linking people, earth and ancestry, a link that becomes, if not unmitigated salvation, then certainly a salve to the spirit." *The L.A. Times* calls "*The Trail of Tears* ... a slow, grinding tragedy ... (in which) old people and children die of pneumonia, wagons full of the sick plunge through Ohio River ice, bare feet leave bloody footprints in the snow" and concludes that Glancy's "restraint and evenhandedness make it a powerful witness to one of the most shameful episodes in American history." *Kirkus Reviews* observes that "The voices that comprise the narrative are vigorous, and the period details convincing but not obtrusive" and concludes that *Pushing the Bear* is a "distinctly original and haunting work of historical fiction."

RECOGNITION: Nominated for the 1997 Minnesota Book Award for fiction; REVIEWS: *BL* 8/96; *KR* 6/15/96; *LATBR* 9/2/96; *LJ* 7/96; *MS* 7/96; *PW* 6/17/96; *WPBW* 10/6/96; *WRB* 1/97

Glendinning, Victoria (UK)

562 *Electricity* (1995); Doubleday 1997 (HC); Picador (pbk); SETTING: England —1880s

Award-winning English-biographer Victoria Glendinning sets her second novel in the 1880s a decade characterized by numerous scientific advances, when, in fact, (in the words of the *London Times*) "human progress was high theatre." Ms. Glendinning features a "plucky" young woman by the name of Charlotte Mortimer who marries a talented electrical engineer by the name of Peter Fisher. Peter is soon hired to "electrify" a grand house in the country, and the young couple eagerly moves into a guest cottage on the grounds of the estate. The story is told through a series of diary entries made by Charlotte as she is introduced to (but not necessarily accepted by) "high" society, loses herself in a passionate affair, is widowed and, finally, dabbles in spiritualism.

According to the *Times Literary Supplement*, the subject of *Electricity* "is England in the 1880s, as the old world of gas lamps, fallen women and the landed aristocracy gives way to the bright new future of electric lighting, women's suffrage and a meritocracy of professionals. The material texture of the period is carefully evoked in accounts of fashions and furnishings ... and in a minute detailing of class barriers creaking but still managing to hold firm." In the view of *The* (London) *Times*, Ms. Glendinning's "excellent, intelligent" novel is a story of "20th-century hearts in Victorian bodies."

OTHER MEDIA: Audiocassette (Chivers/unabr); REVIEWS: *BL* 8/95; *EW* 10/13/95; *LJ* 7/95; *LST* 4/23/95; *NS&S* 4/14/95; *NYRB* 4/8/93; *NYTBR* 10/22/95; *PW* 7/17/95; *TLS* 4/7/95; *WPBW* 11/20/95;

Godshalk, C.S. (USA)

563 *Kalimantaan* (1998); Holt1998 (HC); SETTING: Far East (particularly Borneo) mid 18th-century

C.S. Godshalk's debut novel, twenty years in the making and based, at least loosely, in fact, tells the little-known story of Gideon Barr, a British explorer who, in the mid 1800s, set himself up as the ruler (rajah, actually) of a private kingdom (known as Sarawak) on the island of Borneo. As the novel progresses, Barr, the consummate Englishman and his wife, a good Victorian helpmate, attempt to create a little England — complete with chintz furnishings and garden parties on the lawn — in the midst of this jungle outpost — a hellish spot with debilitating humidity, rampant disease, lethal weather, aggressive wildlife, unscrupulous opium traders, incessantly warring Dyak tribesmen, and last but certainly not least, the blackest of magic. Josef Conrad's powerful novel *Lord Jim* is thought to have based on the near-legendary exploits of Gideon Barr.

The L.A. Times Book Review calls Godshalk's novel a "brilliant historical chronicle" while *Booklist* deems it a "tour de force ... one of the finest examples of literary historical fiction anywhere." In the view of *The* (London) *Times*, Godshalk, by "[v]ividly evoking the humid tropics as well as the authentic mixture of imperial arrogance, innocence, anxiety, dejection, irony, recklessness and cold courage that one finds in so many contemporaneous accounts ... carries one deep into the lost world of the Victorian British Diaspora, especially the female half." According to the *Washington Post Book World*, "This is no languorous journey through the outposts of the East. Godshalk lived for 20 years in Southeast Asia, and the damp heat, the smell of frangipani and rank vegetation rise from these pages. So do the sense of fear, the spouts of blood, the blackened skulls swinging from long-house rafters. Godshalk's novel is compounded of such beauty and horror in equal measure." *Entertainment Weekly* notes that "Godshalk accretes a chilling portrait of Barr's megalomania: his systematic execution of the native Dyaks and his acceptance of their gruesome currency, human heads ... " and concludes that "in prose as lush and febrile as the rain-forest setting, [the author] evinces the violent 'dichotomy' between colonialism and civilization ... and between hubris and love." The *New York Times Book Review* observes that "*Kalimantaan* is the work of a born storyteller" and concludes that "C.S. Godshalk's knowledge that this is a human, not just a colonial, predicament amplified the narrative from a highly accomplished novel of the contradictions of empire to a brilliantly subtle panorama of life forces played out in the face of death."

RECOGNITION: *LATBR* "Best Fiction of 1998"; *NYTBR* Notable Book of 1998; *PW*'s Best '98 Fiction; REVIEWS: *BL* 3/15/98; *EW* 4/17/98; *LATBR* 12/13/98; *LST* 6/26/98; *LT* 8/6/98; *NYTBR* 4/26/98; *WPBW* 7/6/98

Golden, Arthur (USA)

564 *Memoirs of a Geisha* (1997); Knopf 1997 (HC); Vintage 1999 (pbk); SETTING: Pre-WW II Japan

In his debut novel, called a "bold act of ventriloquism" by the *New York Times Book Review*, Arthur Golden has chosen to tell the fascinating tale of a young Japanese woman's journey from child slave to one of Japan's most celebrated Geisha. Sayuri, born in 1920 to an impoverished fisherman, was sold, at the age of nine, to a geisha "house" in Kyoto's famous Gion district. An exquisitely attractive child, Sayuri's path from servant to apprentice to full-fledged geisha is fraught with danger as her beauty marks her as a potential rival for even the most established geisha. Setting his story in the decadent heart of 1930s Kyoto, the author (who holds degrees in Japanese art and history from Harvard and Columbia) provides the reader with a fascinating glimpse into both pre-war Japanese culture and the esoteric world of the geisha.

In the view of the *New Yorker*, Arthur Golden "has brought to [the writing of this novel] a prodigious trove of research ... and an uncanny degree of empathy for a woman usually regarded in the

West as either caricature or museum piece.... Rarely has a world so closed and foreign been evoked with such natural assurance...." *Newsweek* calls *Memoirs of a Geisha* "a faux autobiography 10 years and 2,300 pages in the making ... a captivating, minutely imagined Cinderella story ... that is full of cliffhangers, great and small, a novel that is never out of one's possession, a novel that refuses to stay shut." According to *Entertainment Weekly*, "The arcane lore fascinates: What does a Geisha wear beneath her kimono? Who may remove it and what will it cost him? Golden, a Japanese scholar, offsets the detail with high-toned prose." The *LA Times Book Review* observes that "the subject of geisha, like prostitutes, is a natural attention-grabber, arousing easy prurient interests" and concludes that it was a "delight, then, to find the subject treated with intelligent forthrightness and delicacy in this day of no-holds-barred lasciviousness ... it is a remarkable achievement for any writer, but especially for a white male from a markedly different culture."

OTHER MEDIA: Audiocassette (Knopf/abr; Random Audio/unabr; Books-on-Tape/unabr); Electronic book; READING GROUP GUIDE; RECOGNITION: *NYTBR* Notable Book of 1997; *LA Times* "Best Books" 1997; *Booklist* Editors' Choice 1997; REVIEWS: *BL* 9/1/97; *EW* 9/97; *KR* 8/15/97; *LATBR* 11/30/97; *LJ* 8/97; *New Leader* 11/3/97; *NewsWk* 10/13/97; *NY* 9/29/97; *NYT* 10/14/97; *NYTBR* 10/5/97; *PeopleW* 12/1/97; *PW* 7/28/97; *Salon* 10/29/97; *TLS* 12/12/27; *WPBW* 9/21/97

Goldstein, Rebecca (USA)

565 *Mazel* (1995); Viking 1995 (HC); Penguin 1996 (pbk); SETTING: Pre-war Poland & Contemporary New York and New Jersey

Rebecca Goldstein's multigenerational saga begins in prewar Europe and features Sasha, a young Jewish girl who moves with her family from a "shetel" in rural Poland to Warsaw, a cosmopolitan city with a large population of "enlightened," and highly accomplished Jews. Sasha eventually takes up acting and joins a Yiddish theater company where she finds love and professional success. The scene then shifts to present-day New Jersey where Sasha (a grand-matriarch and wise New York grandmother) is attending the wedding of her granddaughter Phoebe, a physicist who, despite the secularism of both her grandmother and mother (the latter is a "free-thinking" professor of Classics at Columbia University) has embraced the orthodox lifestyle of her in-laws.

In the view of *Booklist*, "Sasha's vivid story dominates this heartbreakingly tender and devilishly funny drama, an ebullient, folktale-like novel that celebrates the passion of the old Jewish ways, the resiliency of women and our capacity for joy."

The *New York Times Book Review*, although it found the early scenes (set in Sasha's 1920s world) to be "overly familiar and written, perversely … like a pastiche of Sholem Aleichem and I.B. Singer" concluded that "framing Sasha's story is a hilarious sendup of suburban Jewish life." The *Library Journal* opines that while the "retelling of all these lives may be a bit cloying for some, [many] others will find it good reading." The *New Yorker* review was more effusive, noting that *Mazel* "shimmers with humor and intelligence."

RECOGNITION: Winner of the National Jewish Book Award; REVIEWS: *BL* 9/15/95; *LJ* 8/95; *NY* 1/15/96; *NYTBR* 10/29/95; *PW* 8/7/95

Gooch, Brad (USA)

566 *The Golden Age of Promiscuity* (1996); Knopf 1996 (HC); Masquerade 1997 (pbk); SETTING: Manhattan — 1970s

Set in Manhattan's gay club scene of the 1970s, Gooch's novel (his first since *Scary Kisses* in 1988) captures the zeitgeist of a vanished era. Narrated by Sean Devlin, a Columbia University dropout with filmmaking aspirations, the novel trains a knowing eye on a cityscape of raw ambition, drugs and sexual abandon.

Kirkus Reviews notes that Gooch (the biographer of poet Frank O'Hara) "here tells us everything we ever wanted to know about the dark and decadent gay subculture in Manhattan before AIDS altered the landscape" and concludes that he has produced a "well written and intelligent novel that's of more than sociological or historical interest." In the view of the *San Francisco Chronicle*, "Gooch's detailed description and provocative observations make The *Golden Age of Promiscuity* the next best thing to taking a time-machine trip to grovel in the glorious '70s gutter."

REVIEWS: *Advocate* 6/11/96; *ChiTrib* 7/28/96; *EW* 7/19/96; *KR* 4/1/96; *LJ* 6/1/96; *NYTBR* 7/14/96

Goodman, Allegra (USA)

567 *The Family Markowitz* (1996); FS&G 1996 (HC); Washington Square 1997 (pbk); SETTING: USA — mid to late twentieth-century

In this series of linked stories, Allegra Goodman explores the theme of family within the context of an extended Jewish-American clan headed up by a formidable matriarch by the name of Rose Markowitz. With sensitivity and humor, the author follows three generations of the Markowitz family as they make their various ways in the world. Punctuated by the usual life events and warmed by the warp and woof of intricately-woven family life, *The Family Markowitz* provides an intimate portrait of lives that never seem less than real. Many of the book's chapters were originally published, as short stories, in the *New Yorker* magazine.

According to *Booklist*, "Newly widowed, Rose is complicated and adept at complicating the lives of her two sons. Henry an art dealer discreet about his homosexuality, lives in California. Ed is an expert on terrorism at Georgetown University and the father of four. As Goodman profiles each Markowitz and tracks the course of their familial relationships, she evinces great sensitivity to the paradoxes of personality." As *Salon* Magazine points out "Goodman has a gift that's inherent in many comic writers — the ability to pull together an intimate but far-flung group of people (in this case, a family of failed intellectuals, cranky matriarchs and religiously obsessive children) and stand back while they annoy the hell out of each other. What's refreshing about Goodman, however, is that she doesn't settle for easy riffs and cheap ironies."

RECOGNITION: *Salon Magazine* "Book of the Year" 1996; REVIEWS: *BL* 9/15/96; *KR* 7/15/96; *NYTBR* 11/3/96; *Salon* 11/96

Gottlieb, Eli (USA)

568 *The Boy Who Went Away* (1997); St Martin's 1997 (HC); Anchor 1998 (pbk); SETTING: 1960s America

Eli Gottleib's skillful debut novel, set during the summer of 1967, features Danny Graubart, a self-described "highly skilled domestic intelligence operative." He is, more accurately, the family sneak. Danny's diligent "intelligence gathering" (he listens in on telephone calls, hovers at closed doors, steams opens letters…) has convinced him that his mother is having an affair and that his father is a closet alcoholic. In actuality, Danny's family is in crisis: his autistic older brother, James, has grown increasingly uncooperative and his parents have just about run through all of the traditional (as well as a number of alternative) therapies currently on offer. His mother, Harta (desperate to keep her son out of an institution), is waging a battle with the state in an effort to continue his home care. Danny, quite clearly, has gotten very lost in the family's emotional quaqmire. Meanwhile, the Vietnam war rages across the family's television screen.

According to *Kirkus Reviews The Boy Who Went Away* is a "first novel about dysfunctional family life and coming of age in suburbia that relies on careful writing and a sly wit to distinguish itself from other narratives in this most contemporary of genres." *Publishers Weekly*, in its starred review, observes that Gottlieb "records the utterly confounding and inevitable plunge into adulthood with bold clarity. He depicts the spoken and unspoken language of cruelty and love in a family with confidence and poetry." The *Washington Post Book World* concludes that "there is much here that is authentic and deeply felt ... [*The Boy Who Went Away*] is filled with the confusion and pain of a boy's coming of age alone among the strangers who had formerly been his family."

RECOGNITION: Winner of the McKittrick Prize; *NYTBR* Notable Book of 1997; REVIEWS: *BL* 12/15/96; *KR* 11/1/96; *LJ* 12/96; *NYTBR* 2/16/97; *PW* 11/18/96; *SLJ* 5/97; *WPBW* 2/16/97

Graver, Elizabeth (USA)

569 *Unraveling* (1997); Hyperion 1997 (HC); SETTING: Massachusetts and New Hampshire in the middle 1800s

Elizabeth Graver has set her first novel (which follows her award-winning short-story collection, *Have You Seen Me?*) in mid-19th Century New England. *Unraveling* tells the story of Aimee Slater, a lively, determined young woman who, after growing up on a farm in New Hampshire, convinces her parents to allow her to move to Lowell, Massachusetts to take a job in the fabric mills. Before long, Aimee is swept off her feet by a charming "rotter" and soon finds herself pregnant and abandoned. Given the options and mores of the day, Aimee has no recourse but to return home in disgrace. Her mother offers her nothing but reproach, her father, a 12-by-12-foot bogside cabin on the edge of his property. The story, at heart an examination of forgiveness, is compellingly narrated in Aimee's indomitable voice.

Publishers Weekly, in its starred review, asserts that Ms Graver "conjures up the sensory environment of Aimee's world with great skill ... its depiction of the dissonance between what Aimee's heart tells her and what her world expects of her is genuinely haunting." According to *Booklist* Graver "holds us in Aimee's heart and mind. It is a scary place, so full of need.... Occasionally Aimee's voice sounds a bit too modern, and incest, pregnancy out of wedlock, and mental and physical disabilities are sometimes cast in ways that seem too 20th-Century, but Graver's mastery of emotional resonance carries the reader along." The *New York Times Book Review* concludes that "As its heroine battles bitterness, taking revenge on public cruelty by scouring her private life clean of meanness, *Unraveling* creates a home-on-the-margins beyond cant — a kind of exiles' utopia, intensely imagined, right-valued, memorable."

RECOGNITION: *NYTBR* Notable Book of 1997; REVIEWS: *BL* 7/19/97; *KR* 6/15/97; *LJ* 7/97; *NYTBR* 8/17/97; *PW* 6/23/97

Gurganus, Allan (USA)

570 *Plays Well With Others* (1997); Knopf 1997 (HC); SETTING: Manhattan '70s & '80s

Allan Gurganus, who achieved literary recog-

nition with his mainstream, prize-winning novel *The Oldest Living Confederate Widow* (1989) has chosen, in *Plays Well with Others*, to tell the story of the rise and fall of the unbridled, aggressively artistic gay culture that flourished in pre-AIDS Manhattan during the '70s and '80s. The author focuses primarily on a trio of transplanted New Yorkers: Hartley Mims a writer from North Carolina (and narrator of the tale), Robert Gustafson, a talented composer (and the "prettiest boy in New York"), and their "gal-pal" — the no-nonsense, heterosexual painter (and former debutante) Angelina "Alabama" Byrnes. A number of reviewers have pointed out the similarities between this novel and Daniel Defoe's "A Journal of the Plague Year" a mixture of fact and fiction which described the great plague that decimated London in 1664. Gurganus actually sprinkles his text with Defoe quotes.

The *Times Literary Supplement* calls *Plays Well with Others* "the best novel yet to be written about AIDS and certainly the funniest." *Salon* magazine concurs noting that "This is a wickedly funny novel, unsentimental, free of self-exculpation and determined to keep a bright face on things despite the subject matter." Michiko Kakutani (*NYT*) concludes that *Plays Well* is "Vexing, uneven, powerful...."

OTHER MEDIA: Audiocassette (Random Audio/abr; Books-on-Tape/unabr); RECOGNITION: *NYTBR* Notable Book of 1997; *LATBR* "Recommended Title" 1997; nominated for the 1998 Lambda Book Award; *Booklist* Editors Choice 1997; REVIEWS: *KR* 10/1/97; *LATBR* 11/9/97; *NYT* 11/4/97; *Salon* 11/10/97; *TLS* 2/6/98

571 *Oldest Living Confederate Widow* (1989); Fawcett 1996 (pbk); SETTING: American South mid 19th-century to present

Allan Gurganus's debut novel is an epic tale of love and war, an absorbing family saga, and a complex love story, featuring the (chronologically-challenged) recollections of a 99-year-old Southern belle by the name of Lucy Marsden, the resident of a charity "rest home" in Falls, North Carolina. Born in 1855 (and married at fifteen to a 50-year-old former Confederate Captain with whom she bore nine children) Lucy has been a witness to history on both a grand and local scale. In the view of the *New Republic*, "American history is Gurganus's subject, specifically the history of the South.... He has addressed this with a cleverly conceived and imaginatively sustained narrative strategy — summed up in his title — which allows him to bring his considerable linguistic resources into play." According Christopher Lehman-Haupt (*NYT*) "Lucy Marsden is ... a superb, if somewhat long-winded, storyteller. If she tells you more than you want to know about herself, she's skilled at milking every drop of drama from her narrative...." Mr. Lehman-Haupt concludes that despite some weaknesses

"*Oldest Living Confederate Widow Tells All* is an overwhelming performance. Some of its set pieces will take your breath away."

OTHER MEDIA: Audiocassette (Random House/abr & Books-on-Tape/unabr); RECOGNITION: *NYTBR* Notable Book of 1989; REVIEWS: *LJ* 5/1/89; *LRB* 11/23/89; *NewsWk* 9/25/89; *NewR* 10/30/89; *NS&S* 11/10/89; *NYT* 8/10/89; *NYTBR* 8/13/89

Hamill, Pete (USA)

572 *Snow in August* (1997); Little, Brown 1997 (HC); Warner 1998 (pbk); SETTING: Brooklyn—1947

Pete Hamill's 8th novel, a coming-of-age tale, is set in a working-class Brooklyn neighborhood in 1947. The story features two characters: Michael Devlin, an 11-year-old Irish Catholic altar boy whose father had been killed at the Battle of the Bulge, and Rabbi Judah Hirsh, a lonely refugee from Prague. After meeting one Saturday morning in a freak summer snowstorm (the rabbi asks Michael to turn on a light for him in the synagogue, for, as he explains to the boy, he is not allowed to do labor of any kind on Shabbos) they develop an unlikely friendship wherein Michael (a thoughtful, intellectually curious boy) is introduced to the world of Judaism, including Jewish folklore, while Rabbi Hirsh has the intricacies of American culture, particularly baseball, explained to him. Anti-Semitism is alive and well in Michael's neighborhood and in due time the youngster is threatened by local thugs. In Mr. Hamill's fanciful ending, Michael conjures up a figure from Jewish folklore, the golem, to defeat his enemies.

As the *New York Times Book Review* points out "Somewhere between the Brooklyns of Chaim Potok and Spike Lee lies Pete Hamill's brawling, brokenhearted borough, as gritty, sentimental and ultimately optimistic as its creator." According to *Booklist, Snow in August* is an "intelligent, heartfelt, and ironically charming novel." *Publishers Weekly,* in its starred review, observes that "Hamill, in this beautifully woven tale, captures perfectly the daily working-class world of postwar Brooklyn. Sounding religious overtones that will thrill believers and make non-believers pause, he examines with a cool head and a big heart the vulnerabilities and inevitable oneness of humankind." *Library Journal* notes that Hamill "Serves up a coming-of-age tale with a hearty dose of magical realism mixed in."

OTHER MEDIA: Audiocassette (Books-on-Tape/unabr); RECOGNITION: *LATBR*; "Recommended Title" 1997; *Booklist* Editors Choice 1997; REVIEWS: *BL* 3/10/97; *KR* 3/1/97; *LATBR* 7/3/97; *NYT* 5/1/97; *NYTBR* 5/4/97; *PW* 3/17/97; Hamilton-Paterson, James (UK)

573 *Gerontius* (1989); Soho 1991 (HC); Sophia 1992 (pbk); SETTING: England and South America 1923

James Hamilton-Paterson has constructed his "wonderfully readable, wonderfully insightful first novel" (*NYTBR*) around an actual—but largely undocumented—event in the composer Sir Edward Elgar's life: a six week cruise to Brazil and up the Amazon as far as Manaus. This nautical adventure was undertaken in 1923, the year Elgar, who was no longer composing, turned sixty-six. Hamilton-Paterson explores a number of poignant themes including the waning of creativity and post-war disillusionment.

According to the *Times Literary Supplement* "The idea of imposing informed inventions on the thoughts, feelings, dreams, creative processes and speech of the composer at this shadowy period of his career is a fascinating and exciting one. The obvious pitfalls (over- simplification or caricature, conversational absurdity, wild surmise concerning inspiration and lost musical scores) are, for the most part, avoided. Wrong notes are rare ... and are outweighed by many convincing representations of what may be going on within a musical mind." The *Christian Science Monitor* suggests that "Readers willing to indulge the novel its formal conceits will be rewarded with alert and sensitive verbal descriptions that roam with facility over the suggestive configurations of jungle flora and land, with an occasionally soft whack, on the theatricality of Victorian etiquette." Novelist John Crowley (*WPBW*) observes that "Hamilton-Paterson's writing has many of the qualities of English music: sweet fluency, clarity and feel for natural beauty, and modesty.... His story has the poignancy of exactness, a willingness to picture incompletion and loss without mitigation, and with a nice eye for the muddled comedy of living. It is [Mr. Crowley concludes] absolutely convincing."

RECOGNITION: Winner of the 1989 Whitbread Prize for fiction; REVIEWS: *CSM* 5/14/91; *LJ* 4/1/91; *LRB* 5/4/89; *NYTBR* 6/30/91; *TLS* 3/24/89; *WPBW* 5/5/91

Harrison, Kathryn (USA)

574 *Poison* (1995); Random House 1995 (HC); Avon 1996 (pbk); SETTING: 17th century Spain

Kathryn Harrison utilizes a background of the Spanish Inquisition to great effect in her strange, frequently disturbing and ultimately feminist tale of two 17th century women born on the same day: Francesca, daughter of a failed silk grower, who has been labeled a witch and therefore subject to routine torture for having had a sexual liaison with a priest; and Marie-Louise de Bourbon the French-born wife of the impotent King Carlos who **must** produce an heir if she values her life.

In *Poison* Ms Harrison has, according to *People Weekly*, "abandoned the themes of her earlier works — the weird psychosexual underbelly of contemporary life. Instead, she examines the weird psychosexual under-belly of life during the Spanish Inquisition." The *Times Literary Supplement* notes that "In her first venture into historical fiction.... [Harrison] has avoided the traps of costume romance and dry-as-dust factual accuracy; revivifying her history with audacious feats of imagination, she triumphantly justifies her ambitious narrative project. In its unrelenting piling up of images of horror this rich and complex novel is both harrowing and compelling, but it disturbs most of all in its insistence that cruelty is intimately related to beauty." According to *Publishers Weekly*, "Harrison is totally in command of her tragic narrative which proceeds with the stately, mesmerizing pace of a pavane, stepping to one side to look behind, to the other to look ahead." In the view of *New Statesman & Society*, *Poison* "is a highly decorative novel ... of a society of passion, decadent luxury and colourful poverty in which the depraved, pathetic Carlos II, the Bewitched, lies curled like a worm in an apple. Francesca and Maria share a sort of flippant gaiety that makes them grand."

REVIEWS: *BL* 5/1/95; *EW* 5/26/95; *LJ* 4/1/95; *LST* 7/9/95; *NS&S* 7/28/95; *NYTBR* 5/14/95; *PeopleW* 5/29/95; *PW* 3/6/95; *Time* 5/29/95; *TLS* 6/23/95; EDITOR'S NOTE: Ms. Harrison's novel was published in Great Britain as *A Thousand Orange Trees*

Hazelgrove, W.E. (USA)

Tobacco Sticks (1995); Pantonne 1995 (HC); SETTING: Richmond, Virginia — 1945; See Section 6, #818

Hegi, Ursula (USA)

575   *Stones from the River* (1994); S&S 1997 (pbk);   SETTING: Germany 1915–1951

Ursula Hegi's story of life in the rural town of Burgdorf, Germany — as told from the perspective of Trudi Montag, dwarf, librarian, and town gossip — is played out against the background of World War II. Trudi's outsider status allows her to empathize with Germany's persecuted Jewry.

The *New York Times Book Review* observes that "Through Trudi's intimate ordeals, Ms. Hegi's novel ... explores the way private grief can break out as political madness" and concludes that "This moving, elegiac novel commands our compassion and respect for the wisdom and courage to be found in unlikely places at unlikely times." In the view of Michael Dorris (*LATBR*) *Stones from the River* is "[w]hat a novel is supposed to be: epic, daring,

magnificent, the product of a defining and mesmerizing vision ... in a word, remarkable." *Newsweek* concludes that "At the end of this wonderful novel, it's not just Fascism that a reader thinks back upon, it's the sheer dizzying abundance of life itself."

OTHER MEDIA: Audiocassette (Pocket Books/ abr); RECOGNITION: *NYTBR* Notable Book of 1994; nominated for the 1995 PEN/Faulkner Award; REVIEWS: *BL* 3/15/94; *CCent* 8/10/94; *EW* 3/21/97; *KR* 1/1/94; *LATBR* 3/20/94; *LJ* 1/94; *NewsWk* 4/18/94; *NYTBR* 3/20/94; *PW* 1/17/94; *WPBW* 4/10/94

Helprin, Mark (USA)

576   *Memoirs from an Antproof Case* (1995); HarBrace 1995 (HC); Avon 1996 (pbk); SETTING: Europe & South America — 1st half of the 20th-Century

Mark Helprin's fourth novel is a fictionalized autobiography which manages to shed a very satirical light on the entire 20th century. Its title is derived from the extraordinarily well-made trunk (impervious to even the tiniest insect) wherein the coffee-phobic, octogenarian (and former fighter pilot/investment banker/and insane asylum inmate) narrator has entrusted his memoirs. His saga is a long and winding one ranging from fin-de-siecle Europe to the sensual beaches of post-World War II Brazil.

Called "An action-packed story of obsession and revenge" by the *LA Times Book Review*, *Memoirs from an Antproof Case* was judged: "An engaging blend of fantasy and realism that makes the book compulsively readable." According to *Publishers Weekly*, "Helprin's narrator writes his 'memoir' as an old man reviewing an extravagant and occasionally perilous life spanning many of the major events of the 20th century." *Booklist* calls *Memoirs from an Antproof Case* "a magical and transcendent story [told to us by] a veritable Scheherazade, spinning one mesmerizing but highly unlikely tale after another," and concludes that Helprin "has a great gift for meaningful, dazzlingly detailed description as well as a nimble sense of humor...." In the view of Richard Bernstein (*NYT*) "Mr. Helprin's work is in the tradition of grand, cerebral, picaresque storytelling, but with a modernist edge of self-parody."

RECOGNITION: *NYTBR* Notable Book of 1995; REVIEWS: *BL* 1/15/95; *EW* 4/7/95; *KR* 1/1/95; *LATBR* 5/14/95 *LJ* 2/15/95; *NYT* 4/20/95; *NYTBR* 4/9/95; *PW* 1/30/95; *WSJ* 4/4/95

577   *A Soldier of the Great War* (1991); Harcourt Brace 1991 (HC); Avon 1996 (pbk); SETTING: Italy's Austrian front — W.W.I

As the novel opens, a well-dressed elderly man

alights from a streetcar in the company of a boy who has just been refused a seat because he has insufficient lira for the fare. The older man, Alessandro Guiliani, has decided, on principle, to accompany the youngster as he makes his way, on foot, to a distant village. As they walk, Guiliani tells the boy about his experience in the Great War which encompass trench warfare, desertion, imprisonment, hard labor, re-assigment and heroism, in more or less that order.

Indian novelist **Shashi Tharoor** (*WPBW*) observes that Helprin and has created "an abiding depiction of the war's trials, torments and tragic triumphs that is fit to stand alongside the works of Erich Maria Remarque and, yes, Hemingway's *A Farewell to Arms*." According to the *Christian Science Monitor*, "As a writer, Helprin has few handicaps. He excels at natural descriptions, at suspense, at battle scenes, at moral observation. Occasionally a sentence goes soft, or an intrusive voice points out something to the nodding reader. Helprin knows the important things, how to pace a big book, how to relieve moral symbolism with fantasy and even frank absurdity...." *Time* magazine calls *A Soldier of the Great War* "about four-fifths of a marvel" and concludes that with this novel he "has simplified his language, though he still works up a good head of rhetorical steam, and he has moderated his enthusiasm for phantasmagoria set pieces. He has also picked themes — war and loss, youth and age — that suit a large elaborate style...."

REVIEWS: *CSM* 6/3/91; *LJ* 4/15/91; *NYRB* 8/15/91; *NYTBR* 5/5/91; *Nation* 6/10/91; *WPBW* 5/5/91

Hijuelos, Oscar (USA)

578 *The Fourteen Sisters of Emilio Montez O'Brien* (1993); FS&G 1993 (HC); HarperCollins 1996 (pbk); SETTING: United States from turn of century to present day

In his third novel, Oscar Hijuelos charts the fortunes and misfortunes of the astonishingly prolific Montez O'Briens, an immigrant stew of a family. In 1898, the family patriarch Nelson O'Brien — an enterprising young Irishman — travels to Cuba as a photographer during the Spanish-American War. While there he meets, courts and marries the beautiful, young (and decidedly aristocratic) Mariela Montez. Their first daughter, Margarita, is born on a steamer en route to America. The Montez O'Briens, after settling in a small Pennsylvania town, produce thirteen more daughters and, finally, a son.

Called "Exuberantly, richly detailed" by the New Yorker, *The Fourteen Sisters of Emilio Montez O'Brien* enjoyed somewhat more popular than critical success. *Time* magazine observes that "Hijue-

los creates a series of vibrant snapshots from the lives of different members of the Montez O'Brien clan, all rendered in the writer's exquisitely sensuous prose..." and concludes that "Reading *The Fourteen Sisters of Emilio Montez O'Brien* is like leafing through the pages of a treasured family album. Many of the pictures evoke warm memories, but some, alas, are faded and out of date." English novelist, **Nick Hornby** (*TLS*) calls *The Fourteen Sisters* "at all times readable and diverting" but argues that only "occasionally [does] Hijuelos manages to transcend the middle-brow saga format with which he has landed himself to create an attractive atmosphere of yearning and disappointment, of lives half-fulfilled and of loves half-lost."

OTHER MEDIA: Audiocassette (Dove/abr); RECOGNITION: *NYTBR* Notable Book of 1993; REVIEWS: *BL* 2/1/93; *LJ* 3/1/93; *LRB* 9/23/93; *NS&S* 7/30/93; *NYTBR* 3/7/93; *Time* 3/29/93; *TLS* 8/6/93

579 *The Mambo Kings Play Songs of Love* (1989); FS&G 1989 (HC); HarperCollins 1990 (pbk); SETTING: NYC 1940s onward

Oscar Hijuelos's second novel is the story of Cuban immigrant Cesar Castillo who — shortly after arriving in New York City in 1949 — forms a band, with his brother Nestor, called "The Mambo Kings." In time, the brothers achieve a modest degree of success and are a popular attraction at clubs and dancehalls all up and down the East Coast. After a tragic automobile accident, however, the hard-living, hard-drinking, sexually voracious Cesar can no longer find the inner spark necessary to animate his music. The novel is told retrospectively in a series of flashbacks, memories and dreams.

Called a "vibrant tragicomic novel" by *Newsweek*, *The Mambo Kings Play Songs of Love* was awarded the Pulitzer Prize in 1990. According to *Time* magazine, Cesar "may have urgent appetites and simple tastes, but he gives as much pleasure as he receives. In addition, his story strikes resonant chords when told against the rich cultural fusion of postwar New York." Michiko Kakutani (*NYT*) calls Hijuelos's novel "By turns street smart and lyrical, impassioned and reflective" and concludes that "it is a rich and provocative book — a moving portrait of a man, his family, a community and a time."

OTHER MEDIA: Audiocassette (Dove/abr); a film version starring Antonio Banderas and Amand Assante was released in 1992; RECOGNITION: Winner of 1990 Pulitzer Prize, *Booklist* Editors' Choice 1989; REVIEWS: *Age* 8/25/90; *LRB* 9/23/93; *NewsWk* 8/21/89; *NYT* 8/4/89; *NYTBR* 8/27/89; *Q&Q* 9/89; *Time* 8/14/89; *WPBW* 12/3/89

Howard, Elizabeth Jane (UK)

580   *Casting Off : Vol IV of the Cazalet Chronicles* (1995); S&S 1996 (HC); PB 1995 (pbk); SETTING: England—1937 to 1947

Elizabeth Jane Howard's four-part Cazalet Chronicles—which follows the members of an extended English family from 1937 to 1947—was launched in 1990 with publication of *The Light Years* which opened against a backdrop of growing concern over German aggression. As war becomes more likely, various Cazalets move, with their families, to the patriarchal country estate in Sussex where (most of) the women and children remain ensconced throughout the war years. The ordinary wear and tear of family life with parents, children, servants and lovers is magnified by an undercurrent of growing anxiety which is soon replaced by the harsh reality of a nation at war. *Marking Time* and *Confusion* take the Cazalet clan through the darkest days of the war years and focus more on the younger members of the family as they come to maturity. The final volume, *Casting Off* (1995), is set in the years immediately following D-Day—from the Labour landslide victory in 1945 to Indian Independence—and explores the physical and emotional toll exacted by the war on various members of the family.

Ms. Howard's series has been called "lush, sprawling escapist fiction of the first order" by *Publishers Weekly* and "charming, poignant [and] quite irresistible" by *The (London) Times*. The *Times Literary Supplement* concludes that "the creation and development of the Cazalet Chronicle has been an ambitious project undertaken in an unfashionable form ... the hazards of writing serially about so many characters ... are obvious, but in the essential matter of making her characters distinct from each other without caricature, Howard succeeds well.... The narrative winds from one viewpoint to another, with overlaps and slight jumps forward and backward to allow different strands of story to merge or be suggested at remove.... [The author] ends her quartet on a celebratory note, but not a conclusive one, and it is a tribute to her skills as a novelist that the characters seem likely to persist, even though there is no further book to house them." *The* (London) *Independent* concludes that *Casting Off* is "beautifully written, with the deceptive ease of a fine novelist completely in charge of her material."

OTHER MEDIA: Audiocassette (Chivers/unabr)—for each volume in the series; REVIEWS: *FTimes* 11/25/95; *Independent* 12/9/95; *LST* 12/3/95; *LT* 11/4/95; *SeattleT* 9/22/96; *TLS* 11/10/95; *WSJ* 8/2/96; EDITOR'S NOTE: [Other titles include: The *Light Years* (1990); *Marking Time* (1991); *Confusion* (1993); See the following citations for reviews of earlier volumes in the series: *BL* 6/15/92; *CSM* 7/1/94; *LJ* 7/92; *LST* 12/3/95; *LT* 11/7/91; *NS&S* 12/3/93; *NYTBR* 7/19/92, 9/16/90; *PW* 2/28/94, 6/15/92; *Spec* 11/16/91; *TLS* 10/29/93, 11/8/91, 8/2/90]

Hughes, Glyn (UK)

581   *Brontë* (1996); St Martin's 1996 (HC); SETTING: Yorkshire, England—1840s

Yorkshire novelist Glyn Hughes (author of the well-regarded *Rape of the Rose* 1987) sets his fifth novel in mid 19th-century England and tells the story of one of English literature's most intriguing families. Charlotte, Emily and Ann Brontë lived (for most of their relatively short lives) in a dank and drafty Yorkshire parsonage with their austere father, the Reverend Patrick Brontë, and dissipated brother, Branwell. They also managed to produce some of the most enduring fiction of the 19th century.

In the view of the *Times Literary Supplement* "Hughes has written an enjoyable novel, ambitious in scope and absorbing in detail, about the lives of one of Britain's most important literary communities...." According to *Kirkus Reviews*, "A gifted Yorkshire novelist tackles his region's most famous literary family, illuminating their inner lives and the sources of their creativity. Hughes lives within 20 miles from Haworth, staging ground for the Brontë's short, tragic lives, and he ably captures the harsh natural beauty and even harsher human attitudes that informed the sibling's writings." The *Washington Post Book World* notes that "This is a quietly told but dramatic story of unrivaled geniuses living and dying" and concludes that "Oddly, by fictionalizing the Brontes, Glyn Hughes has succeeded in bringing them out of the realms of fiction and back to the true astonishment of their lives and achievements."

REVIEWS: *KR* 7/15/96; *LJ* 9/15/96; *NYTBR* 11/10/96; *PW* 8/5/96; *TLS* 7/19/96; *WPBW* 10/24/96

Huth, Angela (UK)

582   *Land Girls* (1994); St Martin's 1996 (HC); 1998 (pbk); SETTING: England during WWII

English writer Angela Huth's second novel is set in rural England during the second World War and features three young women who have volunteered to work as "land girls" thereby freeing up young male farmhands for the military. Drawn from different regions and social classes, vivacious Prue, shy Agatha and dreamy Stella form a close-knit family as the war drags on and the Battle of Britain begins in earnest.

According to the *Christian Science Monitor*, Ms. Huth "manages to capture the nostalgic glow of this wartime pastoral interlude without softening its hardships or descending into mere sentimentality." The *Times Literary Supplement* concludes that "Despite occasional lapses, this is a good story, told with wit and a keen observation of detail." *Kirkus Reviews* observes that "If the ending seems a bit of a letdown, with too many events compressed into too few paragraphs, it's only because we, like the land girls themselves, would have been content for those farm days to go on and on" and concludes that *Land Girls* is: "Engaging on all fronts."

OTHER MEDIA: Film adaptation 1998; Audiocassette (Recorded Books/unabr); RECOGNITION: *NYTBR* Notable Book of 1996; REVIEWS: *CSM* 6/27/96; *LJ* 5/1/96; *NYTBR* 6/16/96; *PW* 4/29/96; *SLJ* 10/96; *TLS* 3/25/94

Isler, Alan (UK/USA)

The Bacon Fancier (1997); Viking 1997 (HC); Penguin 1998 (pbk); SETTING: 17th & 18th century Europe & Contemporary New York; See Section 2, #121

Jackson, Mick (UK)

583 *The Underground Man* (1997) William & Morrow 1997 (HC); Penguin 1998 (pbk); SETTING: Nottinghamshire, England — mid 19th century

Mick Jackson's debut novel is based on the life of William John Cavendish Bentinck-Scott the Duke of Portland, one of the more eccentric residents of a country that has raised eccentricity to an art form: The Duke (who died in 1879) spent most of his life on his estate in Nottinghamshire, England, and it is here that he oversaw the construction of eight underground tunnels — twenty miles worth, to be exact — which were outfitted with skylights and were large enough to drive a team of horses through. The Duke was known to indulge in a rich fantasy life, and the impetus for his monumental project appears to be (a complexly rooted) desire for secrecy. The Duke of Portland was also an obsessional hypochondriac who, in the end, performed brain surgery on himself in an abortive effort to find relief. Along the way, Mick Jackson provides the reader with intriguing glimpses into the Victorian world.

According to *The* (London*)Sunday Times,* filmmaker Mick Jackson's debut novel "is soaked through and through with originality and is expertly written: tragi-comic fiction with the most endearingly sympathetic of anti-heroes." As *Kirkus Review* observes, Jackson's "portrait, through the Duke's eyes, of an age poised between credulity and science is shrewd and fascinating" and concludes that although "a little of the Duke goes a long way ... there's enough vigor and imagination here to

suggest the emergence of a lively new talent." The *New York Times Book Review* contends that "Jackson has produced a marvelous study of human foibles."

RECOGNITION: Shortlisted for the 1997 Booker Prize; REVIEWS: *BL* 6/1/97; *KR* 5/1/97; *LJ* 6/1/97; *LST* 2/9/97; *NYTBR* 7/20/97; *PW* 5/5/97; Spec 1/25/97; *TLS* 1/31/97

Johnson, Charles Richard (USA)

584 *Dreamer* (1998); Scribner 1998 (HC); SETTING: USA—1960s

Charles Johnson's fictionalized treatment of the final years in the life of Martin Luther King, Jr., is also the story of a fictional character by the name of Chaym Smith — a young man who bears such a close physical resemblance to King that he has been hired to act as his "stand-in." The deeply philosophical tale is narrated by Matthew Bishop, one of King's devoted followers.

Jabari Asim, assistant editor of the *Washington Post Book World*, points out that "Although *Dreamer* takes as its subject the extraordinary life of Martin Luther King Jr., it is hardly a straightforward fictional recreation. Charles Johnson's novel ... only indirectly examines the historical King." Mr. Asim concludes that Johnson "has produced an important and engaging meditation on the vagaries of motivation and identity, one with answers which lead only to other, equally intriguing questions. His *Dreamer* is what we've come to expect from Johnson: a tale that's complex, richly told and open-ended enough to inspire readers to launch their own imaginative explorations." In the view of *The* (London) *Times*, "Johnson is a deeply sensitive and erudite writer; his prose is rich with historical perspective, weighty with study, and profound in its compassion ... [and] if the novel's plot [involving the parallel lives of King and his young double, Chaym Smith] is not much more than a cipher to allow Johnson to investigate individual identity in a culture that denies the identity of whole races, it hardly matters ... *Dreamer* may be a flawed novel, but it is a vital one, in both senses of the word." Novelist **Dennis McFarland** (*NYTBR*) observes that "the greatest victory of *Dreamer* is the light it shines on the life work of Martin Luther King Jr. as a ministry — the way the strategies, designs, disappointments, choices, challenges and sacrifices endemic to his leadership are brought back to a context of truthseeking and spiritual practice." *The* (London) *Guardian* concludes that "Like a skiff exploring history's more hidden currents, Johnson's poetic language drifts with care over the moiling currents of King's intellect, leaving in its wake a wonderful prismatic novel, exhorting and testifying but never preaching."

OTHER MEDIA: Audiocassette (S&S Audio/

abr); RECOGNITION: *NYTBR* Notable Book of 1998; REVIEWS: *ChiTrib* 4/7/98 & 4/26/98; *Guard* 10/31/98; *KR* 2/15/98; *LJ* 4/1/98; *LT* 10/17/98; *NYTBR* 4/8/98; *WPBW* 4/12/98

585   *Middle Passage* (1990); NAL-Dutton 1991 (pbk); Scribner 1998 (pbk re-issue); SETTING: Louisiana & the High Seas —1830s

In his third novel, Charles Johnson builds a picaresque story around Rutherford Calhoun a puckish, recently freed slave from Illinois who, in an attempt to elude — among other things — the tentacles of marriage, smuggles himself aboard the *Republic* anchored in the harbor at New Orleans. The year is 1830 and the vessel turns out to be a slaver. Before long, the ship, under the command of a high-strung dwarf named Captain Falcon, sets sail, bound for the Gulf of Guinea. Stopping in the coastal trading post at Bangalang, Captain Falcon takes on a cargo of Allmuseri tribesmen who are highly valued for their fortitude and physical prowess, they are also a dangerous cargo, skilled as they are in a particularly lethal form of unarmed combat. Also loaded into the *Republic*'s hold is a crate containing the Allmuseri's "god" a malevolent talisman which "churns" below deck. Rutherford Calhoun, the manumitted slave, senses the danger emanating from this source.

According to the *Library Journal* "The horrors of the voyage are chronicled in grotesque detail in Calhoun's journal, and his outlook on life undergoes a radical alteration as a result of the trip." *Publishers Weekly* observes that "Blending confessional, ship's log and adventure, the narrative interweaves a disquisition on slavery, poverty, race relations and an African world view at odds with Western materialism. In luxuriant, intoxicating prose Johnson makes the agonized past a prism looking onto a tense present." Charles Johnson's award-winning novel was called "Highly readable" by the *L.A. Times* which goes on to observe that it "by turns mimics historical romance, slave narrative, picaresque tale, parable, and sea yarn, [and is] indebted to Swift, Coleridge, Melville, and Conrad."

RECOGNITION: Winner of the 1990 National Book Award; nominated for the 1990 National Book Critics Circle Award; REVIEWS: *Choice* 1/91; *LATBR* 6/24/90; *LJ* 5/1/90; *NS&S* 6/14/91; *NYRB* 1/17/91; *NYTBR* 7/1/90; *PW* 4/6/90; *TLS* 6/7/91

Jones, Madison (USA)

586   *Nashville 1864: The Dying of the Light* (1997); J.S. Sanders 1997 (HC); SETTING: American South during the Civil War

Simply plotted, Madison Jones' 10th novel tells the story of a 12-year-old boy who — in the waning months of the Civil War — sets off to find his father, an officer in the Confederate army. He is accompanied by his friend and contemporary, a slave named Dink. The boys don't know exactly where they are going or what exactly they will do once they get there, but they travel bravely northwards, moving inexorably towards the waiting carnage.

In the view of novelist **George Garrett** "In a year of Civil War novels, including a couple of enormously successful ones, this one is, for my money, the best of the lot." *Kirkus Reviews* observes that many scenes "have a raw power and harsh originality that set them apart from most recent fiction about the War ... " but concludes that "the narrative ... suffers by seeming so entirely partisan [and the] grown Stephen's rhapsodic celebration of the Confederate soldier, and his defense of slavery — while perfectly believable in this character — diminish the book's power somewhat." The *School Library Journal* notes that "Jones writes with a tender and understated simplicity to convey the confusion and tragedy the boys experience as they muddle through fog, smoke, and cannon and gun fire" and concludes that this novel is "an important addition to Civil War literature." Jonathan Yardley (*WPBW*) argues that "It will be a terrible pity if reviewers and readers in 1997 allow [the fact that the protagonist defends the institution of slavery] to color their response to [Jones's novel]." He concludes that "brief though it is, *Nashville 1864* is populated by a large cast of thoroughly believable characters, it moves forward with irresistible narrative force, and it is written in prose of the utmost elegance. It is, in all respects, a splendid piece of work."

REVIEWS: *BL* 5/15/97; *KR* 3/15/97; *PW* 4/14/97; *SLJ* 1/98; *WPBW* 5/28/97 & 12/7/97

Jones, Rod (Australia)

587   *Billy Sunday* (1995); H Holt 1996 (pbk); SETTING: Wisconsin —1892

Set in the backwoods of Wisconsin in the 1892, Rod Jones' third novel features an intriguing cast of characters: American historian Frederick Jackson Turner, a youngster by the name of Billy Sunday (who would one day be widely known for his evangelical fervor), the famous 19th century photographer Charles van Schaick, and Pauline L'Allemande (soprano and former prostitute). Jones's Wisconsin is deep-wooded lake country, "sacred" Indian ground, a place for fishing and dreaming and losing one's self. When the body of a dead girl is discovered in the woods beside a lake, disturbing questions must be asked. A curious mixture of ghost story, murder mystery and gothic romance, *Billy Sunday* is essentially a novel of ideas, chief being is an exploration of Turner's famous "frontier thesis" which validated much of the American drive for expansion during the 19th century.

Booklist points out that in 1893 the seminal

historian Frederick Turner argued that "In the crucible of the frontier the [European] immigrants were Americanized, liberated and fused into a mixed race." *Booklist* further points out that "In this challenging and ambitious novel, Australian author Jones explores the genesis of this thesis, using the lives of real people ... as springboards for a richly metaphoric north woods allegory." The *Australian Book Review* found *Billy Sunday* to be "fully imagined ... and fully realized: the Ringling Brothers Circus ... a Pinkerton detective, a diva fallen on hard times, her crippled, violin-playing, homicidal son, trout fishing in America ... the metaphysics of sex, the writing or imagining of history — all these are among the threads of Rod Jones's rich postlapserian tapestry." The *Washington Post Book World* contends that *Billy Sunday* "is an audacious work, unafraid of excess, rampant with sentiment and philosophical speculation.... The language is mannered, the narrative circular and repetitious as a dream. Yet the result is a book that sits stubbornly in the mind long after you've closed it, surely one criterion of art."

RECOGNITION: Winner of the 1996 Australian C.U.B. Banjo Award for Fiction; REVIEWS: *AusBkRev* 6/95; *BL* 5/15/96; *LATBR* 6/23/96; *PW* 5/6/96; *WPBW* 6/2/96; *YaleRev* 1/97; EDITOR'S NOTE: Van Schaick's photographs were memorably reproduced in Michael Lesy's *Wisconsin Death Trip*)

Jose, Nicholas (Australia)

588   *The Rose Crossing* (1994); Overlook 1997 (HC); 1997 (pbk); SETTING: Island in the Indian Ocean — 17th century

Edward Popple, a 17th-century horticulturist and his (stowaway) daughter, tired of the conventions of England, set off on a voyage to the Indian Ocean. When the crew mutinies they are set ashore on an uncharted but marvelously fertile island. Father and daughter enjoy a rather idyllic period of research and exploration (marred somewhat by Popple's unnatural interest in his beautiful daughter) interrupted by the unexpected arrival of a Chinese junk carrying an elderly eunuch and the young pretender to the Chinese throne.

According to *Booklist*: "Eastern and Western cultures meet face to face in a small place in this luminous historical novel by an obviously talented Australian who writes about a disparate grouping of people stranded on an island in the Indian Ocean in the seventeenth century." *Kirkus Reviews* notes that "Jose's evocation of his island, and of the conflicting worldviews of two utterly different civilizations in collision, is rich, often witty and startling" and concludes that Jose "fumbles only in imposing too abrupt and mechanical an end on his odd, engaging characters."

RECOGNITION: *Booklist* "Editors' Choice"

1996; REVIEWS: *Age* 5/7/95; *AusBkRev* 10/94; *BL* 5/1/96; *CanLit* Spr'96; *KR* 4/15/96; *LJ* 2/9/95; *LT* 2/9/95; *PW* 5/20/96; *TLS* 1/6/95

Just, Ward (USA)

589   *Echo House* (1997); Houghton Mifflin 1997 (HC); 1997 (pbk); SETTING: Washington, D.C., 1920s to present

Ward Just's multigenerational saga (his 12th novel) features the Behls, an influential Washington family who have successfully pursued power and its fringe benefits. The author focuses primarily on the men of the family, sleek operators all, who not only understand power-broking, but accept it as their birthright. As marriages fall apart, presidents come and go, and capital is amassed, the Behls continue to do what they do best. Ward Just, a foreign correspondent and member of the staff of the *Washington Post*, certainly knows the milieu of the "insider's" Washington.

Booklist suggests that "Just's brilliantly orchestrated tale of several generations of Washington, D.C. insiders may very well be the break-out book for this wrongfully neglected writer...." and concludes that Ward Just "who writes of love as astutely as he interprets political clout, proves that even a world as controlled and controlling as Washington is vulnerable to the inexplicable, a force of nature he boldly, and convincingly, associates with women." *Time* magazine observes that "Just is a sharp-eyed observer and acerbic commentator, but he is also a bighearted host to all the has-beens and will-bes gathered in this roomy and inviting novel." *The New Leader* asserts that "Ward Just knows the score and he gives it to us with great insight and muscularity. *Echo House* is a fine book, beautifully written. It projects a strong light on the shadows." The *Washington Post Book World* notes that Ward Just "is first and foremost a teller of tales. In *Echo House*, he creates a fascinating if ultimately painful fairy tale, complete with haunted houses, enchanted castles, witches and wizards, and a family curse." *Publishers Weekly*, in its starred review, concludes that "Just's writing has weight, texture and subtlety, gravity, intelligence and wit. The result is a political novel par excellence that takes the reader through eight decades of U.S. history, offering ironic and resonating insights into the culture of power and into the minds of the men who attain and manipulate it."

RECOGNITION: *NYTBR* Notable Book of 1997; nominated for the 1997 National Book Award; *Publishers Weekly* "Best Books" 1997; *Booklist* Editors' Choice 1997; REVIEWS: *BL* 4/15/97; *LATBR* 7/27/97; *LJ* 3/1/97; *NewLeader* 6/30/97; *NewsWk* 5/12/97; *NYT* 5/8/97; *NYTBR* 5/18/97; *PW* 2/17/97; *Salon* 5/21/97; *Time* 5/19/97; *WPBW* 5/22/97

Kennedy, William (USA)

590   *The Flaming Corsage* (1996); Viking 1996 (HC); Penguin 1997 (pbk); SETTING: Albany, New York (1884 and 1912)

The seventh novel in William Kennedy's "Albany Cycle" is set in turn-of-the-century New York and concerns the explosive "mixed" marriage between beautiful, melancholic Katrina, a high-born WASP, and Edward Daugherty, a charismatic young playwright from a working-class, Irish-American family. As the story progresses, Edward's fame as a playwright grows but his marriage begins to deteriorate under the strain of his habitual philandering and his wife's headstrong nature. Edward's pivotal role in a 1908 society scandal (a lightly fictionalized version of the infamous "Love Nest Killing") doesn't help matters.

In the view of the *New Yorker*, the author "forgoes the subtler emotions of his finest Albany novels in favor of an array of richly imagined spectacles and assignations, which include a visit to a makeshift brothel at the State Fair, a ruinous fire at the Delavan hotel, and Grover Cleveland's 1884 victory parade." According to *Kirkus Reviews*, "Filled [as it is] with precise details of Albany's vanished life, narrated in a prose both salty and exact, catching the vigorous cadence of spoken English, this is the most impressive entry in the Albany Cycle since *Ironweed*." *Booklist* argues that "At first, we feel as though we're sitting in a cozy parlor, sipping tea and listening to a clever romance. Then, suddenly, the walls give way, winds howl, and we find ourselves at the center of a great conflagration, a blossoming of blood and flame. But there is such beauty in Kennedy's prose and dialogue, such astuteness in his portrayals, that we are enchanted and even renewed by his contemplation of death in life, by the paradox of a flaming corsage."

OTHER MEDIA: Audiocassette (Penguin Audio/abr); RECOGNITION: *Booklist* "Editors' Choice" 1996; *NYTBR* Notable Book 1996; REVIEWS: *BL* 3/1/96; *KR* 2/1/96; *LATBR* 7/14/96; *LJ* 4/15/96; *NY* 5/27/96; *NYTBR* 5/19/96; *PW* 3/4/96; *Time* 5/13/96; *WPBW* 4/26/96

591   *Very Old Bones* (1992); Penguin 1993 (pbk); SETTING: Albany—1958

The Phelan family saga continues in the form a "mock-memoir" written — in the late 1950s — by Orson Purcell, the 34-year-old illegitimate son of Francis Phelan's brother, Peter, a painter with deep roots in New York's Greenwich Village

In the view of novelist **Maureen Howard** (*NYTBR*) "Few Irish-American writers have produced more haunting portraits of their ancestors or the ghosts that possessed them than Mr. Kennedy has in *Very Old Bones*." According to the *Times Literary Supplement*, "*Very Old Bones* will sustain Kennedy's reputation and will keep his readers on the hook for the subsequent narratives which will, presumably, bring the Phelan saga to the present day. But the form of this latest novel is not entirely successful. The interior monologue encourages flights of artificially literary writing. One misses the racy dialogue and picaresque adventures which propel *Ironweed*...." *Kirkus Reviews* concudes, however, that "Kennedy's achievement is to place [all of the Phelan goings-on] into a comic structure that is, in the end, elegiac and celebratory."

RECOGNITION: *NYTBR* Notable Book of 1992; *Booklist* Editors' Choice 1992; REVIEWS: *BL* 2/15/92; *CSM* 5/12/92; *KR* 2/1/92; *LATBR* 4/26/92; *LitRev* 8/92; *NYRB* 8/13/92; *NYT* 4/23/92; *NYTBR* 5/10/92; *PW* 2/3/92; *Spec* 7/25/92; *TLS* 8/21/92; *WPBW* 5/10/92

Kinsella, W.P. (Canada/USA)

Box Socials (1992); Ballantine 1993 (pbk); SETTING: Rural Canada—1940s; See Section 7, #916

Koch, Christopher J. (Australia)

592   *Highways to a War* (1995); Viking 1995 (HC); Penguin 1996 (pbk); SETTING: S.E. Asia—1960s and 1970s

Christopher J. Koch's 5th novel (part thriller, part heroic epic) features Mike Langford, a popular semi-legendary war photographer who disappears into the jungles of Cambodia in 1976, a year after the Khmer Rouge began their reign of terror. The story is told from a variety of perspectives including that of Raymond Barton, an old friend (to whom Mike had been mailing taped diaries since 1965), a number of Langford's correspondent and photographer buddies interviewed by Barton, and the tapes themselves. The plot is driven by Barton's courageous-but-risky decision to search for his missing friend himself.

According to the *New York Time Book Review*: "As Barton's research mounts up, no one can quite believe that the magnetic Langford won't some day saunter into a hotel bar, order a round and tell his latest tale — an undercurrent that adds even more tension to a remarkably resonant and haunting story." The *Australian Book Review*, while finding one too many "oriental femmes fatales" praised the author for achieving the sort of "elegiac tone [appropriate] for this excursion into the past, into a legendary war, and the doomed life of one adventuresome Australian." The *Christian Science Monitor* concludes that "It takes a remarkable novelist to pull far enough away to see the big picture while not losing track of the details that make a book worth reading. But Koch does it — writing a novel with fresh images, dialogue, and technique."

RECOGNITION: Winner of the 1996 Miles Franklin Literary Award; REVIEWS: *Age* 7/8/95; *AusBkRev* 8/95; *CSM* 12/26/95; *KR* 4/1/95; *LJ* 4/15/95; *NYTBR* 8/6/95; *PW* 5/1/95

Korman, Keith (USA)

593   *Secret Dreams* (1995); Arcade 1995 (HC); SETTING: Pre–World War II Europe

Secret Dreams, a historical novel exploring the origins of psychoanalysis, is set — for the most part — in the Burgholszli Institute in Zurich, Switzerland, in the early decades of the 20th Century. Korman's story is constructed around the treatment and eventual recovery of Fraulein S, a fictional character loosely based on Carl Jung's celebrated patient Sabina Spielrein. When Fraulein S first arrived at the Swiss Institute in a profoundly psychotic state little was expected in the way of cure. The innovative Carl Jung, with the assistance of his mentor Sigmund Freud did eventually find the key to S's recovery, and Jung — at least in Korman's version — fell in love with his newly-cured patient. *Secret Dreams* (which incorporates memories, dreams and reveries) opens thirty years after S's dramatic recovery. Sigmund Freud, is now near death, and, a psychoanalyst herself, S is prompted to revisit that period in her life when, but for the interventions of two of history's most celebrated psychiatrists, she might never have recovered her sanity. Korman also explores the relationship of eroticism and the art of psychoanalysis.

According to *Booklist* "Korman's impassioned reconstruction ... travels back in time to Fraulein Schanderein's eventual emergence from mental illness and to a vivid portrayal of her progressively erotic relationship with Jung." *Publishers Weekly*, in its starred review, calls *Secret Dreams* "a captivating fictionalized account of Jung's early work" and concludes that "While this account won't win over critics of psychoanalysis — and may be a little too pat even for its advocates — its depictions of the field's pioneers and its evocation of the mind's mysteries are engaging and memorable." The *New York Times Book Review* concludes that "Mr. Korman takes some wild imaginative flights as he explores the wobbly baby steps of psychoanalysis, particularly in his portrayal of Jung's emotional life and of Freud as a raging old man racked with cancer, sitting alone in his office with a 'little tribe of gargoyles' set upon his desk."

REVIEWS: *BL* 5/1/95; *KR* 4/1/95; *LJ* 5/15/95; *NYTBR* 8/13/1995; *PW* 5/1/95;

Kurzweil, Allen (USA)

594   *A Case of Curiosities* (1992); Ballantine 1993 (pbk); SETTING: France — 18th century

The "case" of the title dates from the 18th-century and turns up (worn and battered) at a late 20th-century Paris auction. The contents, as the purchaser/narrator discovers, represent the *memento hominen* of a French clockmaker by the name of Claude Page, an inventor possessed of extraordinary mechanical understanding and dexterity. Kurzweil's tale follows the Frenchman in his energetic, eventful and often ribald life's journey from apprentice to genius and, in so doing, effectively portrays both the spirit and the historical reality of the "age of enlightenment."

According to *New Statesman & Society*, "Without any hint of heavy-handed literalism, Kurzweil makes it clear that he has soaked up the intellectual spirit of the 18th century.... The most triumphant of Kurzweil's conceits is the choice of watch-making as the central metaphor for a story all about turning back the clock and revivifying the past." In the view of novelist and critic **Malcolm Bradbury** (*WPBW*) "this is a brilliantly bookish book — and why not? Mr. Kurzweil has a formidable instinct for history. However, this is not history as wars, revolution or bodice-ripping. Rather, it is an exotic account of the ideas, images, mental quests and artistic preoccupations of a discovering and mentally lively age." The *New York Review of Books* calls *A Case of Curiosities* "a remarkable historical novel ... laden with antiquarian lore and descriptive set pieces ... " and concludes that "what the reader retains ... is a series of extraordinarily vivid images, beautifully composed, and the pleasurable illusion of having been allowed to visit an authentic landscape of the past." *Entertainment Weekly* judged it "brilliant ... witty, learned, ingenious, sly, and bawdy." The *London Review of Books* notes that "Allen Kurzweil combines immense imaginative exuberance with an irritating archness of style. Most of the dialogue sounds as if it has been literally translated from the French. which may of course be another of the author's jokes" and concludes that "even such near-terminal playfulness may be forgiven in an author who conducts his *Three Musketeers*-type narrative with such irrepressible high spirits."

Recognition: *NYTBR* Notable Book of 1992; REVIEWS: *EW* 1/31/92; *LitRev* 5/92; *LJ* 11/11/91; LRB 5/28/92; *NS&S* 3/27/92; *NYRB* 4/9/92; *NYTBR* 1/26/92; *TLS* 3/20/92; *WPBW* 1/26/92

Ladd, Florence (USA)

595   *Sarah's Psalm* (1996); S&S 1996 (HC); Scribner 1997 (pbk); SETTING: US and Africa early 1960s

Florence Ladd, director of the Bunting Institute at Radcliffe, has, in her first novel, chosen to tell the story of Sarah Stewart, a young African-American graduate student, who, while working on her Harvard doctoral dissertation, meets and falls in love with Ibrahim Mangane, a famous Senegalese poet. The year is 1962 and Sarah returns to Boston where she promptly divorces her husband Lincoln, an up-and-coming lawyer and member of the growing civil rights movement. Sarah, immersed in her studies, remains apolitical. When Mangane's wife dies, Sarah, who has recently received her Ph.D., travels back to Senegal where she marries Mangane, moves into his large and beautifully appointed home, bears him a son and (in the words of *Kirkus Reviews*) "leads the fairy-tale of an African princess." Although she acts as her husband's muse and assistant, Sarah's own career is put, decidedly, on hold.

Kirkus Reviews observes that *Sarah's Psalm* is "an elegantly written first novel [which] offers a feminist journey toward self-discovery, drawing its strength from it unique insight into the Pan-African consciousness of the post-colonial era ... " but concludes that, although "intermittently persuasive ... [it] seems at times uncomfortably like Afrocentric chic with a heavy dollop of conventional romance." In the view of *Booklist*, "This first novel suffers from stilted prose and improbable plot devices, but the story moves briskly and the diverse cultures and settings add unusual richness and substance." The *Library Journal* concludes that "Although Ladd's didactic tone sometimes stops the narrative flow, the mixture of ideology and romance is nicely reminiscent of Doris Lessing."

RECOGNITION: Winner of the ALA Black Caucus Literary Award for Fiction; REVIEWS: *BL* 7/1/96; *KR* 6/15/96; *LJ* 7/96; *PW* 7/8/96

Lawrence, Starling (USA)

596   *Montenegro* (1997); FS&G 1997 (HC); Berkley 1998 (pbk); SETTING: Serbo-Croatia circa 1908

Starling Lawrence — an editor-in-chief at Norton Books — sets his first novel in the Balkans, a perennial geo-political tinderbox, in the period just prior to World War I. *Montenegro*, a novel of historical adventure, political intrigue and international romance, features Englishman Auberon Harwell, an industrial spy posing as a botanist. In the employ of the (decidedly shady) Lord Cosgrove, Harwell has been sent to Montenegro to collect information for powerful British interests who stand to profit from further destabilization in the region. As the story unfolds, the English "botanist" makes his perilous way from the Adriatic to the Montenegrin mountain fastness. Once there, he encounters partisans, falls in love, survives an earthquake, and is drawn, inexorably, into fierce nationalistic conflicts.

In its starred review, the *Library Journal* suggests that "At first, we are seduced by the wonderful storytelling, but eventually we are humbled by the story's moral dimensions." *Publishers Weekly*, in its starred review, observes "This is adventure writing at a lofty pitch, exquisitely calibrated to its period and filled with superb evocations of landscape, tender penetration of personality and unflinching scenes of sex and violence." *Kirkus Reviews* concludes that *Montenegro* is a "lush, middlebrow drama that's perfect for the big screen — and could easily become the next *English Patient*, given the right director." In the view of the *Washington Post Book World*, "The real test of a historical novel is whether is evokes the period and whether it tells us about the present too. The answer is positive. The book is incisive. The warrior mentality of Serb peasants is described well, as are the harmful manipulations of empires that can't bear to leave a people to their own devices."

RECOGNITION: *LATBR* "Recommended Title" 1997; REVIEWS: *BL* 8/19/97; *KR* 6/15/97; *LATBR* 9/14/97; *LJ* 5/15/97; *NYTBR* 11/9/97; *PW* 6/2/97; *WPBW* 8/20/97

Law-Yone, Wendy (Burma/USA)

597   *Irrawaddy Tango* (1994); Knopf 1994 (HC); SETTING: S.E. Asia and US — late 1940s to present

Nights in Irrawaddy had a bloom, a hum, a pulse so tantalizing it seemed a shame to go to sleep. It wasn't just the flowers that released their perfumes only after dark, or the orange flames that blossomed in the kerosene lamps lit throughout the huts along the river, or the budding of the stars all across the black soil of the sky. It wasn't just the chorus of cicadas and bullfrogs and night birds, the rollicking breezes that fanned down the heat of the day. At the right season, on the right days, whole lives, whole dramas, unfolded at night.

Wendy Law-Yone has set her second novel in the fictional Asian country of Daya — which is patterned quite obviously after Myanmar (formerly Burma), the author's birthplace — and features a lively and beautiful young woman by the name of Tango. Born into a rural backwater in the period immediately following WW II, the once self-absorbed, dreamy little girl blossoms under the influence of a fellow villager who, having spent some time in Argentina, has learned to dance the Tango. Before long, the young girl masters the intricate dance steps, wins dance contests (assumes the name "Tango") and finally comes to the attention of "Supremo," one of Daya's most powerful military leaders. They marry; he takes over the country and enforces a repressive regime; she eventually rebels and pays a terrible price.

According to the *New York Times Book Review*, "Tango, the heroine of Wendy Lay-Yone's second novel *Irrawaddy Tango*, is sexy, savvy, sardonic and scattered. Which is not surprising since her story encompasses almost five decades, three countries and two husbands, as well as violence, torture, captivity and madness." In the view of Indian novelist **Shashi Tharoor** (*WPBW*), *Irrawaddy Tango*, despite some problems with pace and plotting "remains a book to savor. Law-Yone's intimate evocations of place and mood convey a palpable sense of experience relived. Her Tango — street-smart, opportunistic yet manipulative, sensitive, and ultimately despairing — is a striking creation, deformed but not defined by the successions of men whose patronage she accepts and loses (or discards)."

REVIEWS: *BellesL* Vol.9.No.4; *BL* 2/1/94; *NYTBR* 2/20/94; *WPBW* 1/16/94

Leavitt, David (USA)

598   *While England Sleeps* (1993); Viking 1993 (HC); HM 1995 (pbk); SETTING: England and Spain —1930s

Shortly after *While England Sleeps* was published in 1993, a literary scandal erupted, fueled by British poet Stephen Spender's accusations that Mr. Leavitt had actually plagiarized parts of Spender's 1951 autobiography *World Within World*, and that Leavitt's protagonist, Brian Botsford, could only be viewed as a thinly disguised version of Spender himself. To further complicate matters, Spender (a homosexual whose own sensibilities were forged in an earlier age) found *While England Sleeps* to be obscene. Set *entre deux guerres*, *While England Sleeps* tells the story of a young upper class Englishman, a homosexual writer, who meets and falls in love with a young subway worker from a decidedly working-class background. When the relationship falters, Brian, a man of the left, heads off to Republican Spain to join the ill-fated anti-fascist fight.

According to *Booklist*, Leavitt's controversial novel "is a historical romance in the purest sense.... The novel's action is compelling, its language beautiful. Its story lingers as movingly in the reader's memory as in its narrator's." English novelist **Penelope Lively** (*NYTBR*) observes that Leavitt "has given us a narrative that for the most part rings true" but concludes that "the reader ends up with a feeling of respect for the assiduous research that has been undertaken, rather than with any sense of deep involvement with the characters." In the view of *Publishers Weekly*, "Leavitt captures his protagonist's youthful ardor — both amatory and political — with an understated style that carries the reader as the story builds in intensity."

RECOGNITION: *NYTBR* Notable Book of 1993; REVIEWS: *LJ* 8/93; *NewR* 1/8/93; *NS&S* 11/12/93; *NYTBR* 9/12/93; *PW* 8/9/93; *TLS* 10/29/93; *WPBW* 9/12/93

Lee, Helen Elaine (USA)

599   *The Serpent's Gift* (1994); S&S 1994 (HC); 1995 (pbk); SETTING: Midwest —1910 to 1990

Helen Lee's first novel begins in 1910 and spans 80 tumultuous years in the lives of two Midwestern African-American families: the Smalls and the Staples. Their fates are intertwined when Ruby Staples opens her door (and her heart) to Eula Small, battered wife and mother of two small children.

According to the *Library Journal*, *The Serpent's Gift* is a "much-above-average first novel [in which] Lee has portrayed both pain and happiness and woven together incredibly imaginative stories ... while staying firmly rooted in the African American experience." *Booklist* calls *The Serpent's Gift* a "confident debut-novel" and observes that "Through several generations of births and deaths, isolation and intimacy, [and] painful but essential memories ... the Smalls and Staples share secrets, sorrows, and always stories, with each family member finding a way to survive." The *School Library Journal* finds Helen Lee's "skill with language" to be "extraordinary," and concludes that "she captures the cadence of the region, creating profound sympathy for the people about whom she writes." *Belles Lettres* concludes that "Lee's writing resembles a natural creek, at once fluid and earthy, meandering a bit towards the end...."

RECOGNITION: Winner of the ALA Black Caucus Literary Award for First Novel; REVIEWS: *BellesL* Vol.9.No.4; *BL* 3/15/94; *LJ* 3/1/94; *MultiCultR* 9/94; *NYTBR* 11/13/94; *SLJ* 4/95; *WRB* 9/94

Lesley, Craig (USA)

600   *The Sky Fisherman* (1995); HM 1995 (HC); Picador 1996 (pbk); SETTING: Rural Central Oregon in the 1950s

Craig Leslie weaves a low-key, likable tale featuring Culver, a young man growing up in a small town in Central Oregon where the principle industries are a lumber mill and tourism centered around salmon fishing. As the novel opens, Culver's mother (widowed after only a few years of marriage) has just left her unstable second husband (Culver's stepfather) and has returned to the town where she grew up and near where her first husband drowned in a canoe accident. Culver is soon taken under the expansive and exuberant wing of his uncle Jake, proprietor of a fish and tackle shop–cum–sporting goods store, and a widely respected river guide. All is well until Culver discovers that his uncle knows more than he is willing to divulge regarding his father's fatal accident.

Booklist suggests that Leslie has "a real feel for the way the intimacy and pettiness of small-town life push and pull both young and old," while concluding that *The Sky Fisherman* further established the author as "a major force in the fiction of the American West." *Publishers Weekly* found Culver to be an "unusually appealing character, and when the novel's close toes a maudlin line, it feels almost earned." The *L.A. Times Book Review* concludes that "Lesley wisely refuses to wrap everything up in a neat package, leaving some of Gateway's mysteries unsolved."

OTHER MEDIA: Audiocassette (Recorded Bks/unabr); RECOGNITION: Winner of the 1995 Pacific NW Book Award; REVIEWS: *BL* 9/15/95; *KR* 7/1/95; *LATBR* 11/17/96; *LJ* 6/1/95; *PW* 5/29/95

Liu, Aimee (USA)

601   *Cloud Mountain* (1997); Warner Books 1997 (HC); 1998 (pbk); SETTING: 20th century America and China

Aimee Liu's sweeping, occasionally melodramatic, historical novel tells the story of a Chinese-American mixed marriage. An obvious labor of love, it is based on the lives of the author's white American grandmother, Hope, and her Chinese grandfather, Paul. Hope (an English tutor) was engaged to an American professor when she met and fell in love with Paul, one of her private English students. Paul, a charismatic young man, is committed to bringing democracy to China. They marry in 1901 (a time when mixed-race marriages were actually illegal in most states of the United States) and forge a life together that takes them from turn-of-the-century California to revolutionary China.

According to the *Library Journal*, Ms. Liu's "prose has a haunting, lyrical quality and an aura of authenticity." *Publishers Weekly*, points out that although the somewhat "whiney" Hope is a "difficult character to sympathize with ... her attitude improves towards the book's end, and she bears up well under some truly frightening experiences." *Kirkus Reviews* found *Cloud Mountain* to be both "Riveting and bittersweet.... A Moving tale of true love, besieged by politics and prejudice." *Booklist* concludes that "The story of [Hope and Paul's] strong love for each other, set against a backdrop of revolution and mayhem, two world wars, bigotry, and personal tragedy, is exciting and beautifully written."

OTHER MEDIA: Audiocassette (Time-Warner/abr); REVIEWS: *BL* 6/1/97; *KR* 5/1/97; *LJ* 5/15/97; *PW* 5/12/97

Long, David (USA)

The Falling Boy (1997); Scribner 1997 (HC); SETTING: Montana in the 1950s; See Section 1, #56

Lord, Bette Bao (China/USA)

602   *The Middle Heart* (1996); Knopf 1996 (HC); Fawcett 1997 (pbk); SETTING: China: 1930s–1980s

Bette Bao Lord's first novel in the fifteen years since her best-selling *Spring Moon* is set in China and spans the tumultuous decades from the 1930s to the late 1980s. *The Middle Heart* follows three friends from their first meeting during the 1932 Japanese Conquest of Manchuria, through the turbulent years of Civil War, the Cultural Revolution, and, eventually, Tienanmen Square.

According to *the New York Times Book Review*, "Bette Bao Lord, the Chinese-born wife of a former United States Ambassador to China, has carved out an interesting career by bringing China and the lives of the Chinese to American readers in a variety of forms.... *The Middle Heart* is a compelling and admirably accurate history of China over the last 75 years, lightly disguised as a conventional multigenerational love story." *Booklist* concurs while observing that Ms. Lord "is as adept at dramatizing cultural upheaval as she is at depicting affairs of the heart as she relates all the adventures, catastrophes, and bitter ironies that rule the lives of her protagonists...." The *Library Journal* notes that "Much like Pearl S. Buck, Lord has the ability to reveal the soul of China through her characters."

OTHER MEDIA: Audiocassette (Books-on-Tape/unabr); RECOGNITION: *NYTBR* Notable Book of 1996; REVIEWS: *BL* 12/15/95; *LJ* 2/1/96; *NYTBR* 2/11/96; *PW* 12/4/95; *SLJ* 7/96

MacDonald, Ann-Marie (Canada)

603   *Fall on Your Knees* (1996); S&S 1997 (HC); Scribner 1998 (pbk); SETTING: Cape Breton Island, Canada—1st half of the 20th-century

Here's a picture of the town where they lived. New Waterford. It's a night bright with the moon. Imagine you are looking down from the height of a church steeple, onto the vivid gradations of light and shadow that make the picture. A small mining town near cutaway cliffs that curve over narrow rock beaches below, where the silver sea rolls and rolls, flattering the moon. Not many trees, thin grass.... The silhouette of a colliery, iron towers against a slim pewter sky with cables and supports sloping at forty-five-degree angles to the ground. Railway tracks that stretch only a short distance from the base of a gorgeous high slant of glinting coal, toward an archway in the earth where the tracks slope in and down and disappear. And spreading away from the collieries and coal heaps are the peaked roofs of the miners' houses built row on row by the coal company. Company houses. Company town.

Look down over the street where they lived. Water street. An avenue of packed dust and scattered stones that leads out past the edge of town to where the

wide, keeling graveyard overlooks the ocean. That sighing sound is just the sea.

Family secrets loom large in Ann-Marie Mac-Donald's debut novel, a multi-generational tale of the Piper family, James (a Scotsman) and his Lebanese child bride, who, in the early years of the 20th century, made their home — and raised four daughters — on the storm-washed coast of Cape Breton Island.

According to the *Library Journal*, "This gorgeously realized family saga shot to the top of Canada's best-seller list shortly after its release [and] … deserves no less attention in the US." *Fall on Your Knees* was called: "A plate piled dangerously high with calamities" by *Kirkus Reviews* which concluded that "the time, place, and people — especially the children — all ring clear and true, making for an accomplished, considerably affecting saga." *Booklist* found MacDonald to be "a talented storyteller with a crisp yet lilting prose style that captures equally well the atmospheres of World War I trenches and Harlem jazz clubs." The *Washington Post Book World* notes that "Like the Brontes, MacDonald does not shy from the shadowy recesses of conscious and subconscious desire [both of which] form the toxic chemistry fueling this novel."

RECOGNITION: Winner of the 1997 Commonwealth Writer's Prize for Best First Book; nominated for the 1996 Giller Prize; REVIEWS: *BksCan* 11/95; *BL* 4/1/97; *KR* 1/15/97; *LJ* 3/1/97; *LST* 11/10/96; *Maclean's* 6/17/96; *NYTBR* 5/11/97; *PW* 2/24/97; *TLS* 10/11/96; *WPBW* 8/3/97

MacKay, Shena (UK)

The Orchard on Fire (1996); Moyer Bell 1996 (HC); Harcourt Brace 1997 (pbk); SETTING: Rural England in the 1950s; See Section 4, #369

Mailer, Norman (USA)

604   *The Gospel According to the Son* (1997); Random House 1997 (HC); Ballantine 1998 (pbk); SETTING: Judea — 1st Century

Essentially the life of Jesus told by Himself, *The Gospel According to the Son* is variously, a "profoundly heretical 'Gnostic' gospel" (*LJ*), "partially a failure … [but] a great and profoundly moving one that is also a triumph," (*PW*), or a "sincere — and thoroughly unexceptional" exploration of Jesus's mission (*KR*).

According to the *Washington Post Book World*, *The Gospel According to the Son* "purports to be Jesus's autobiography. Unsatisfied with the exaggerated accounts given in the gospels and apocrypha, which he has read, Jesus decides to tell his own story. But what follows is basically the synoptic gospels retold in the first person, with a few de-

tails borrowed from John. Mailer's version reads like a simplified novelization for grade-school children, or for adults who find the New Testament tough going…." *Publishers Weekly*, in its starred review, suggests that "Its penetration into Jesus's heart rivals Dostoyevsky for depth and insight. Its recreation of the world through which Jesus walked is as real as blood. Ultimately Mailer convinces, more than any other writer before him, that for Jesus the man it could have been just like this, in itself, some sort of literary miracle." *Booklist* concludes that "Students of the Bible will find food for thought; fiction readers, particularly Mailer's fans, will discover a provocatively imagined historical novel." John Updike, writing in *The New Yorker*, observes that Mailer's "gospel is written in a direct, rather relaxed English that yet has an eerie, neo-Biblical dignity. Some of his sentences may be a bit too simple … and some not simple enough … but the tone as a whole is quietly penetrating."

OTHER MEDIA: Audiocassette (Dove/abr); REVIEWS: *BL* 4/15/97; *EW* 5/97; *KR* 3/15/97; *LATBR* 5/4/97; *LJ* 5/15/97; *NY* 5/12/97; *NYT* 4/14/97; *NYTBR* 5/4/97; *PW* 3/31/97; *TLS* 9/12/97; *WPBW* 4/27/97; *WSJ* 4/18/97

605   *Oswald's Tale*: *An American Mystery* (1995); Random House 1995 (HC); Ballantine 1996 (pbk); SETTING: Soviet Union 1950s, and USA 1960s

In *Oswald's Tale* Norman Mailer paints a fascinating fictional portrait of the ex-marine and consummate American misfit Lee Harvey Oswald. Mailer's exploration of the psyche of Kennedy's assassin revisits and, ultimately, rejects a melange of conspiracy theories—finally concluding that "Lee … probably did it alone."

According to *Booklist* "Mailer's latest book pulls readers back into the JFK assassination mess, but even those most opposed to yet another airing of that topic will quickly surrender to the pull of Mailer's compelling account." The *Maclean's* reviewer quotes Mailer: "The difficulty with closing the case on Oswald is that every time one shuts the door, a crack opens in the wall" and concludes that "As if to proves the point, Mailer's fascinating but infuriating book succeeds in turning the crack into a gaping crevasse." *Entertainment Weekly* suggests that Mailer is "good at getting a sense of quirky individuals and the societies that spawned them — in this case, the Khrushchev-era USSR and an America that, with one push from a neurotic, lonely man, was starting to come apart." The *Times Literary Supplement* observes that *Oswald's Tale* "contains … a thoroughly convincing account of the feel of life in a provincial Soviet city in the 1950s…."

OTHER MEDIA: Audiocassette (Random Audio/abr); REVIEWS: *AtlM* 5/95; *BL* 4/1/95; *Econ*

6/10/95; *EW* 5/19/95; *LJ* 4/15/5; *Maclean* 6/5/95; *NewR* 7/17/95; *NYRB* 6/22/95; *NYTBR* 4/30/95; *PW* 3/20/95; *TLS* 9/12/97

606   *Harlot's Ghost* (1991); Random House 1991 (HC); Ballantine 1992 (pbk); SETTING: USA & Europe & Latin America 1955–1963

Harlot's Ghost features Harry Hubbard, a CIA operative with family connections. Both his father and godfather, Hugh Montague (code name: Harlot), are seasoned operatives who have worked their way into the organization's upper-echelons. We follow the brainy, eager young Harry from his initiation into the agency in 1955, through his postings in Berlin (working in the world's most advanced subterranean listening post) and Uruguay (under Howard Hunt), and then through a stint back in Washington during the Bay of Pigs fiasco. The story is told, retrospectively, by an older, wiser Harry as he looks back over his career and partly through an exchange of letters between Harry and Harlot's beautiful wife, Kittredge.

The *Times Literary Supplement* notes that Mailer's "partly true, heavily fictionalized novel about the CIA ... has a narrative momentum which makes it feel too short at over 1,100 pages ... [and features] a narrator through whom the extraordinary could be made credible...." In the words of the *Library Journal* "To call Mailer's CIA novel a spy story would be like calling Moby Dick a whaling story ... for Mailer's true purpose is to define that part of the American psyche that has spawned and sustains [it]." According to *Publishers Weekly*, *Harlot's Ghost* "is an utterly convincing portrait of that strange, snobbish, macho, autocratic collection of brainy misfits who have played so large and often tragic a role in American history." The *New York Times Book Review* observes that "Mailer here espouses just about all known and several unknown forms of fiction: Bildungsroman, epistolary novel, diary novel, phone-call novel, gossip-column novel, philosophico-political novel, pornographic novel and adventure story rotate into our field of vision. He comes closest to another highly gifted, overexuberant ex-Harvard man, Thomas Wolfe.... What he lacks is his editor."

OTHER MEDIA: Audiocassette (Random Audio/abr); RECOGNITION: *NYTBR* Notable Books of 1991; *PW* Best Books' 1991; *Booklist* "Editors' Choice" 1991; REVIEWS: *CSM* 10/15/91; *Econ* 10/26/91; *EW* 10/18/91; *KR* 8/1/91; *LJ* 9/1/91; *LRB* 11/7/91; *NewsWk* 9/30/91; *NY* 11/4/91; *NYRB* 12/5/91; *NYTBR* 9/29/91; *PW* 8/16/91; *Time* 9/30/91; *TLS* 10/18/91; *VLS* 10/91

Mallon, Thomas (USA)

607   *Dewey Defeats Truman* (1997); Pantheon 1997 (HC); St Martins 1997 (pbk); SETTING: Owosso, Michigan, in 1948

Thomas Mallon's 4th novel, a romantic comedy whose title is derived from the *Chicago Tribune*'s erroneous election-night headline, is set in presidential candidate Thomas E. Dewey's home town of Owosso, Michigan. The main action takes place in the months leading up to the election and features Anne MacMurray, a bookstore clerk and aspiring novelist, and her suitors: a handsome Republican lawyer and an earnest young union organizer.

As novelist **Jay Parini** (*NYTBR*) points out, "Amorous configurations and public events are tightly linked in this novel, persuasively located in Dewey's Michigan hometown on the eve of the 1948 election." According to the *L.A. Times Book Review*, "The key to this amiable story is not shock, even among Owosso's staunchest Republicans ... but the sensation of awakening confusedly from an agreeable hallucination." According to *Entertainment Weekly*, *Dewey Defeats Truman* "is a warm, touching, and richly textured novel; a classic American movie filmed in glorious prose deluxe The *Times Literary Supplement*, concludes that Mallon's "small-town pastoral has been, from the start, a profound comedy, not merely of reversals, but of renewal and resurrection."

RECOGNITION: *NYTBR* Notable Book of 1997; *Publishers Weekly* "Best Books" 1997; REVIEWS: *BL* 11/15/96; *EW* 2/21/97; *LJ* 11/15/96; *NYT* 1/16/97; *NYTBR* 2/2/97; *PW* 10/28/96; *TLS* 7/25/97; *WSJ* 1/15/97.

608   *Henry & Clara* (1994); Ticknor & Fields 1994 (HC); St Martin 1995 (pbk); SETTING: US and Europe 1845–1911

Thomas Mallon's 3rd novel, a "harrowing psychological tragedy" (*TLS*) incorporating both insanity and murder, features Major Henry Rathbone and Miss Clara Harris. This unlucky pair, acquainted since childhood and recently engaged, were the guests of Mr. and Mrs. Lincoln at Ford's Theater on the night the President was assassinated. Henry was badly wounded by Booth's knife, but Clara, unaware of Henry's condition, abandoned him to care for Mrs. Lincoln. Henry and Clara eventually marry but carry with them the emotional and psychological "fall-out" from their proximity to this horrific event. Both harbor intense feelings of guilt; Henry, in particular, suffers greatly from his belief that he should have been able to stop the assassin. The Rathbones eventually move to Europe where their relationship deteriorates further.

In the view of novelist **George Garrett** (*WPBW*) Mallon's "powerful story is superbly told .... You can't ask for much more from historical fiction." *Publishers Weekly* points out that "It is a wonder that the story of Colonel and Mrs. Henry Rathbone is not etched like a fable in the American consciousness.... Mallon outdoes himself in this re-creation, which raises the private consequences of history to what seems their deserved status—legend." John Updike, writing in the *New Yorker*, observes that Thomas Mallon who "has shown himself to be, at the age of forty-three, one of the most interesting American novelists at work" has, in his third novel, "done an amazing, somewhat sinister thing. He has found tucked into the crevices of the glaringly lit assassination of Abraham Lincoln, two close witnesses and eventual victims of the event, and he has enlarged them into movingly star-crossed figures."

RECOGNITION: *NYTBR* Notable Book of 1994; *PW* "Best Books" 1994; REVIEWS: *BL* 7/94; *EW* 8/19/94; *LATBR* 9/21/94; *LJ* 8/94; *NatR* 9/26/94; *NY* 9/5/94; *NYTBR* 8/28/94; *PW* 6/20/94; *WPBW* 8/14/94:

609 *Aurora 7* (1991); W.W. Norton 1992 (pbk); SETTING: May 24, 1962

Thomas Mallon uses Scott Carpenter's historic 1962 planetary orl it as the jumping off place for a novel steeped in the zeitgeist of the period. Although character-filled (including walk-ons by JFK, Walter Cronkite and LBJ) the novel features young Gregory Noonan, a fifth grader who, playing hooky from school, has joined the crowd at Grand Central Station gathered in front of the huge TV monitors. *Aurora 7* takes place in the space of a single day, May 24, 1962, the day that American astronaut Scott Carpenter flew his space craft three times around the planet earth ... and the whole world watched and waited.

According to the *Washington Post Book World*, "It was a flamboyant mission that nearly ended in failure. Most of what Thomas Mallon observes happens in the lives of the ordinary grounded folks, people who are quietly risking their dreams while the world holds its breath for the safety of one astronaut." *Publishers Weekly* points out that "Using an omniscient narrative voice, novelist Mallon interweaves other lives—those of a highly sexed young priest, a snooty writer who has just dumped her husband, a Puerto Rican high school dropout desperately seeking a job, a New York cabbie, etc.—to show what effect Carpenter's historic flight has—or does not have—on each personal trajectory." In the view of the *LATBR* "*Aurora 7* is a book ... that risks interpreting the heavenly design for a single day, revealing bits and pieces of the divine plan. Mallon even gives the reader the opportunity to try omniscience and omnipotence on for size...."

REVIEWS: *ChiTrib* 2/3/91; *PW* 12/7/90; *LATBR* 2/3/91; *WPBW* 2/17/9

Malouf, David (Australia)

Conversations at Curlow Creek (1997); Ran-

dom House 1997 (pbk); SETTING: New South Wales—19th-century; See Section 4, #413

Remembering Babylon (1993); Random House 1994 (pbk); SETTING: Australian outback—mid 19th-century; See Section 4, #414

610 *The Great World* (1990); Random House 1993 (pbk); SETTING: Asia—WW II

David Malouf's 6th novel grapples both with the terrible reality of war and the mitigating quality of "mateship." Set during World War II and after, it features Victor Curran and Digger Kean—as unlikely a pair of friends as existed in any man's army. The two soldiers are brought together as prisoners of war following the surrender of Singapore to the Japanese Army in 1942. Vic is aggressive, impetuous, virile, while Digger is cerebral, passive, and sensitive; their relationship is crucial to their mutual survival and absolutely pivotal in the full context of their lives.

The *Sydney Morning Herald* advances the view that *The Great World*, "an ample and generously paced tale of the fortunes of two men thrown together by the fall of Singapore" is "quite simply ... a masterly novel, a deeply satisfying work of literary art." The *Library Journal* notes that "Malouf, who is being touted as the successor of the great Patrick White, has written a wonderfully constructed, beautifully phrased novel that transcends its geography and its time to give us the dramatic interactions between human beings and history."

RECOGNITION: Winner of the 1991 Miles Franklin Literary Award; *LJ* "Best Books" 1991; REVIEWS: *LJ* 3/1/91; *LRB* 4/19/90; *NYRB* 7/19/90; *NYTBR* 3/31/91; *PW* 1/25/91; *SMH* 2/17/90; *TLS* 4/6/90; *WPBW* 3/24/91

Marius, Richard (USA)

611 *After the War* (1992); Rutledge Hill 1994 (pbk); SETTING: Bourbonville, Tenn.—immediately following WW I

In 1918, a Belgian-educated Greek refugee in search of his father arrives in the backwater, quintessentially Southern, town of Bourbon, Tennessee. *After the War*, Richard Marius's third novel, is comprised of a series of stories told by members of a community stewing in xenophobia and racial hatred but also steeped in a powerful, occasionally redeeming, oral tradition.

According to the *New York Times Book Review* "Mr. Marius has written an old-fashioned blockbuster chock full of wildness and enough excitement [of the type that keeps you up reading all night] for three novels...." In the view of the *Library Journal*, Marius has constructed a "resonant, if at times somewhat melodramatic, tale that marvelously captures the sense of time and place."

Kirkus Reviews calls it "an unusual, compelling immigrant's tale, vibrant in mingling present and past and redolent with personal and social history." *KR* concludes that "the dramatic peaks are masterful and memorable even if the fires burn low in the end."

Recognition: *NYTBR* "Notable Book of 1992"; Reviews: *America* 12/5/92; *KR* 3/15/92; *LJ* 5/1/92; *NYTBR* 6/21/92

Mason, Anita (UK)

612   *Reich Angel* (1995); Soho 1996 (HC); 1997 (pbk); Setting: Germany—1930s and 1940s

In pre–Nazi Germany, Frederika ("Freddie") Kurtz, the brilliant tomboyish daughter of a physician, pursues her dream of flight. Giving up her medical studies, Hanna earns her wings on glider planes (eventually becoming an Olympic glider pilot) and once Germany begins preparing for war, learns to fly military planes. Through sheer grit (she volunteers for the most hazardous flights) Freddie becomes the only woman in the Luftwaffe, eventually rising to the position of Germany's top test pilot. Freddie's commitment has, throughout, been to her career as an aviator, not to the military regime she finds herself serving. When, having been assigned to a squadron stationed at the Russian front, Hanna witnesses—first hand—unspeakable Nazi atrocities, she renounces flying and returns to Berlin to drive an ambulance. Before the war ends, Freddie falls deeply in love with a woman whose Communist father was killed in a Nazi prison camp. Ms. Mason's novel is based on the life of Hanna Reitsch, a Third Reich heroine who died in 1979.

Booklist points out that Mason "writes novels as rich and complex as good red wine" and concludes that in this "taut and penetrating tale" she "refuses to resolve the moral ambiguity at [its] center … leaving us somewhat dissatisfied but respectful of the reality her honesty reveals." According to *Publishers Weekly*, *Reich Angel* is "an incisive analysis of a woman caught up in evil … [and] a viscerally realistic novel about a Nazi test pilot.…"

Reviews: *BL* 6/1/95; *KR* 6/15/95; *LJ* 6/15/95; *NYTBR* 7/16/95; *PW* 5/1/95

Mason, Bobbie Ann (USA)

613   *Feather Crowns* (1993); HarperCollins 1994 (pbk); Setting: Hopewell, Kentucky, 1900 onward

In her third novel, which begins in Kentucky in 1900, Bobbie Ann Mason tells the fictional "life story" of Christianna Wilburn "Chrissie" Wheeler, the young, uneducated wife of a tobacco farmer, who gives birth to America's first recorded quintu-

plets. Before long, the Wheelers' farm is invaded by a steady stream of curious on-lookers and their lives are changed irrevocably. Although characterized in the popular press as provincial folk (Mason's story is loosely based on a real-life occurrence), the Wheelers, particularly "Chrissie," are far from ignorant.

According to novelist **Pinckney Benedict** (*WPBW*), *Feather Crowns* "careens from absurdity to tragedy and back again, through adventures too numerous and too astonishing to diminish by brief description, without ever losing sight of the fragility and appealing humanity of its characters." The *Library Journal* observes that Ms. Mason "possesses a keen ear for the cadences and tropes of everyday speech, transforming prose into another kind of poetry." *World Literature Today* concludes that "*Feather Crowns* is a superbly written and richly peopled novel. Mason evokes the economic and physical problems or rural existence not far removed from the American frontier." In the view of the *L.A. Times Book Review*, Bobbie Ann Mason has crafted a "stunning morality tale and wonderfully told story."

Recognition: *NYTBR* "Notable Book of 1993"; *Publishers Weekly* "Best Books" 1993; nominated for the 1993 National Book Critics Circle Award; Reviews: *KR* 7/15/93; *LATBR* 10/24/93; *LJ* 11/1/93; *NYT* 9/24/93; *NYTBR* 9/26/93; *PW* 11/1/93; *TLS* 10/15/93; *WLT* Sum'94; *WPBW* 9/5/93

McDermott, Alice (USA)

At Weddings and Wakes (1992); FS&G 1992 (HC); Dell 1993 (pbk); Setting: NYC and its suburbs in the 1960s; See Section 1, #61

McGrail, Anna (UK)

614   *Mrs. Einstein* (1998); Norton 1998 (HC); Setting: Europe—1902 to the 1950s

In her debut novel, Anna McGrail draws on the historical fact that in 1902 Albert Einstein and Mileva Maric had an illegitimate daughter—named Lieserl—whom they promptly gave up for adoption. (Albert and Mileva eventually married and produced two sons). Although it is assumed that Lieserl died of Scarlet fever in infancy, Ms. McGrail has imagined a life for her and it is a fascinating one, involving the pursuit of science (she has inherited her father's genius), the horror of the holocaust, and—because she believes her father to be a pacifist—a (spiteful) role in the development of the ultimate weapon.

As the *New Statesman* observes "Lieserl's compulsion, fueled by fury, holds the potentially chaotic tale together like one of her own elusive theories of matter. Her narrative voice has enough irony to take the edge off her self-regarding excesses." *Kirkus Reviews* suggests that "McGrail's formidably intelligent novel presents with perfect clarity intimidating scientific matter and offers unusually thought-provoking ideas about the energies liberated by women's or at least this woman's resentment of male myopia and condescension." According to poet and novelist **Jay Parini** (*WPBW*) McGrail's "ample knowledge of modern physics, including the race to discover the atomic bomb, is evident here; indeed, she makes the quest for scientific knowledge absorbing as she imagines a course Lieserl's life might have taken beginning with her restrictive childhood on a remote Hungarian farm." Parini concludes that "Anna McGrail's mythic telling represents all that has gone wrong in this unhappy century." In the view of the *Times Literary Supplement*, "This beautifully written but unselfconscious novel [an intimate history of atomic power, a gripping and enlightening adventure into scientific ideas, a fusion of poetry and physics] captures the functional poetry of modern science, but it trails no allusions to an ambition or a tradition. Instead, it is full of splendid symmetries...." *Entertainment Weekly* concludes that "Atomic rage is a most attractive — and original — trait."

REVIEWS: *EW* 7/24/98; *KR* 5/15/98; *LJ* 6/15/98; *NS* 1/16/98; *NYTBR* 7/12/98; *PW* 6/15/98; *TLS* 2/13/98; *WPBW* 7/26/98

McPhee, Martha (USA)

615   *Bright Angel Time* (1970s); Random 1997 (HC); Harvest 1999 (pbk); SETTING: America—1970s

Martha McPhee's debut novel is narrated by Kate, a thoughtful eight-year-old girl who, until 1969, had been living a secure and stable life with her parents and two sisters in a leafy New Jersey suburb. When her father decides to abandon his wife and children (he chooses, symbolically, the day of the first moon walk) Kate's mother, the beautiful Eve, is thrown into a deep depression. When she emerges from her emotional funk, Eve meets — and becomes infatuated with — Anton, a charismatic ex-priest who is now peddling Gestalt therapy and communal living. Desirous of the sort of free-spirited, adventuresome life denied her while married, Eve piles her three daughters into Anton's VW camper (already filled with Anton's five hippie kids) and sets off for (where else?) California.

In the view of *The (*London*)Times* "This intensely felt, vividly written autobiographical novel is a memorable account of a bizarre episode in the evolution of a family and in the life of a young girl." Michiko Kakutani (*NYT*) observes that the author "shares her father John McPhee's gift for fine lapidary prose, and in this novel, her carefully controlled language is the perfect counterpoint to her

story of divorce and dissolution." Ms. KatKutani concludes that Ms. McPhee "is a gifted novelist with the ability to surprise and move us." According to *Kirkus Reviews*: "The new extended family wanders aimlessly through deserts and semi-abandoned towns, sneaking into unoccupied motel rooms for showers, dropping in on Indian settlements and millionaires' resorts, and absorbing various hitchhikers into their fold, while the children bicker and the adults preach free love." *Booklist* asserts that McPhee "writes skillfully about love, loyalty, hope, disillusionment, and survival, while relentlessly, and at times with exquisite subtlety, holding the tension of conflicting emotions."

RECOGNITION: *NYTBR* Notable Book of 1997; REVIEWS: *BL* 6/1/97; *KR* 3/15/97; *LJ* 1/97; *LST* 6/15/97; *LT* 9/6/98; *PW* 4/7/97; *TLS* 6/20/97; EDITOR'S NOTE: See Esther Freud's *Hideous Kinky* & James Hamilton-Paterson's *That Time in Malomba*

Merlis, Mark (USA)

616   *American Studies* (1994); HM 1994 (HC); Penguin 1996 (pbk); SETTING: Washington, D.C.—1940s and 1950s

As the novel opens, Reeve, a 62-year-old gay bureaucrat, is lying in a hospital bed recovering from a particularly brutal encounter with some "rough trade." Enforced inactivity gives rise to reminiscences of his life as a closet homosexual in Washington, D.C., during the '40s and '50s. Reeve's friendship with Tom Slater, a well-respected literary critic who had taken his own life as a result of McCarthy-led "witch hunts," dominates his memories. In his debut novel, Mark Merlis has constructed a darkly comic, exceedingly well-written account of gay life in this century.

According to *Kirkus Reviews*, "Reeve slowly recounts his friendship with Slater (based loosely on Harvard Professor F.O. Matthiessen, who virtually created the field of American Studies in the 1940s), his own ambivalent coming to terms with his gayness, and the events that led to Slater's suicide.... All of the events are retold with a bitter, wry humor that leads gradually to a surprising and thoroughly satisfying denouement." In the view of the *Times Literary Supplement*, Reeve (in this "fine novel") looks back "on fifty years of sexual life with a voice that seems fully Audenesque, bitchy and resonant, at once resourceful, self-deprecating and alive to the ironies of history." The *Library Journal* concludes that "Merlis's novel belongs to the best of contemporary literature, gay or other."

REVIEWS: *KR* 8/1/94; *LJ* 8/94; *NY* 10/24/94; *PW* 6/27/94; *TLS* 11/10/95

Michaels, Anne (Canada)

Fugitive Pieces (1997); Knopf 1997 (HC); SETTING: WW II; See Section 3, #236

Miller, Andrew (UK)

617 *Ingenious Pain* (1997); Harcourt Brace 1997 (HC); Harvest 1998 (pbk); SETTING: 18th Century Devonshire

Andrew Miller's debut novel describes the unusual life of James Dyer, a fictional 18th century surgeon with a "genius for the knife," a skill attributed to his inability to feel pain. Orphaned at 11, James was — so the local story goes — conceived on ice, the result of a bizarre sexual encounter between his mother and a stranger she had met while skating on a frozen river. Early in Miller's tale, the youngster falls into the hands of Marley Gummer, an itinerant huckster who uses the child's strange gift as a way of selling bogus pain relievers. After surviving a series of exploitative relationships, James finds his true calling as a ship's surgeon where he quickly develops a reputation for his ability to deal effectively with the most gruesome injuries including the administration of painful, yet life-saving, remedies. Dyer's ambitions grow along with his reputation and when Catherine, the Empress of Russia, announces a desire to be inoculated against smallpox, he mounts an expedition to the frozen city of St Petersburg. It is in Russia that Dyer meets the "witch-woman" who gives him an extraordinary gift.

According to English novelist **Patrick McGrath** (*NYTBR*), Andrew Miller's "extraordinary" debut effort is "entirely its own creature, a mature novel of ideas soaked in the sensory detail of its turbulent times. Working at that moment when "the secret arts of the old world" still clung on, even as the West trembled before the bright future promised in the emerging age of reason, the novel displays a sort of inverted image of the present." Indian novelist **Shashi Tharoor** (*WPBW*) found *Ingenious Pain* to be "a curious, compelling and disturbing book." Tharoor further observes that Miller's novel "offers a panoply of purely literary pleasures: a storyline that keeps the pages turning, and a command of style and nuance that most writers would envy." The *Journal of the American Medical Association* (*JAMA*) concludes that *Ingenious Pain* "is a sweeping story tackling issues of human worth, empathy, alienation, redemption, and salvation. It asks the reader what he or she would most like to extract from life." In the view of *Literary Review*, *Ingenious Pain* is "strange, unsettling, sad, beautiful, and profound. You can't ask for more than that."

RECOGNITION: *NYTBR* Notable Book of 1997; REVIEWS: *BL* 3/1/97; *JAMA* 12/24/97; *KR* 1/15/97; *Lit Rev* 2/97; *NYTBR* 4/13/97; *PW* 1/20/97; *TLS* 2/28/97; *WPBW* 7/27/97; *WSJ* 7/29/97

Millhauser, Steven (USA)

Martin Dressler (1996); Vintage 1997 (pbk); SETTING: New York City at the turn of the last century; See Section 3, #237

Minot, Susan (USA)

618 *Folly* (1992); Washington Square Press 1994 (pbk); SETTING: Boston 1917–1937

Susan Minot's third novel *Folly* is set in the "upper register" world of Boston's social elite. Lillian Eliot is eighteen, well-connected and attractive and, at the novel's outset, is chafing ever so slightly under the constraints of family and social expectations. She eventually falls in love with a cad but marries a decent, if flawed, young man thereby setting in motion a painful emotional triangle.

In the view of the *Christian Science Monitor*, Minot, "Like the British novelist Anita Brookner ... explores the interiorized, Henry Jamesian territory lying concealed in the heart. But where Brookner's passive heroines seem hobbled by oddities of temperament an character, Minot has made her heroine a victim of time and place." According to the *Times Literary Supplement*, Susan Minot "does what many writers have done before, and what a great many more have failed to achieve: she floats a delicious social comedy on an ocean of private pain and desolation.... One imagines Edith Wharton would recognize gratefully such a gifted and elegant young descendent." *Kirkus Reviews*, while pointing out that the author's work is derivative (in concept and execution) concludes that Minot's "eye for the acute detail is flawless, period flavor is impeccable, character is drawn with conciseness, and style is repeatedly lovely, with seldom a clumsy step. Rich with pleasures from start to finish if you don't mind them being second hand."

REVIEWS: *CSM* 11/10/92; *KR* 10/15/92; *LJ* 9/15/92; *NY* 11/2/92; *NYTBR* 10/18/92; *PW* 8/31/92; *TLS* 4/23/93; *VLS* 11/92; *WPBW* 10/11/92

Mistry, Rohinton (India/Canada)

Such a Long Journey (1991); Vintage 1992 (pbk); SETTING: India (1960s and 1970s); See Section 4, #472

Moore, Brian (Ireland/Canada/USA)

619 *No Other Life* (1993); Plume 1997 (pbk); SETTING: Caribbean mid to late 20th-Century

In *No Other Life*, set on the fictional Caribbean island of Ganae, Father Paul Michel, a Canadian missionary, rescues a local boy, Jean Pierre Cantave, from illiteracy and abject poverty and later assists the young man in his pursuit of the priesthood. Jean Pierre is ordained abroad but soon returns to his island nation determined to preach (and live) a form of "liberation theology." The charismatic, avowedly revolutionary priest (blessed with a keen intellect and great oratorical skills) speaks out against the avaricious light-skinned elite, the corrupt military and the repressive ruling junta. Although expelled from his religious order, Jean Pierre is eventually elected to the presidency of his country. Moore's story is clearly modeled on recent 20th-Century Haitian history.

According to novelist Henry Louis Gates, Jr. (*NYTBR*), *No Other Life* "is a brilliant meditation on spiritual indeterminacy, on the struggle between religious and temporal faith — on the question of how (or even whether) religious belief should be expressed in the political realm." *Kirkus Reviews* concludes that "Moore's gift for framing volatile political and religious questions in terms of particular human experience has never been taken to such extraordinary lengths as in this brief, ambitious, deeply unsettling novel." According to *Quill & Quire*, *No Other Life* is "vivid in the telling, stitchlessly plotted, and suspenseful." Irish novelist John Banville (*TLS*) calls Mr. Moore's book "an exciting, superbly paced and extremely alarming novel" and concludes that "The theme of religious failure, of despair and eschatological terror, which Moore insinuates so delicately into his fast-paced narrative, confers the ineluctable, subversive aura of a nightmare on what would otherwise have been no more than a straightforward, if murky, story of Third World politics."

RECOGNITION: *NYTBR* Notable Book of 1993; REVIEWS: *BL* 10/1/93; *Econ* 3/13/93; *KR* 6/15/93; *LJ* 8/93; *LRB* 4/8/93; *NS&S* 2/1/9/93; *NYTBR* 12/5/93; *PW* 11/1/93; *Q&Q* 4/93; *TLS* 2/10/93

Moore, Lorrie (USA)

620   *Who Will Run the Frog Hospital?* (1994); Warner 1995 (pbk); SETTING: Upstate NY — 1972

In Lorrie Moore's 3rd novel, Berie Carr, a middle-aged woman vacationing in France with her increasingly distant husband, looks back to her fifteenth year and the fateful summer spent in the company of her best friend Silsby Chause. They both had jobs at Storyland, a theme park in upstate New York, where Silsby (Sils) was required to dress as Cinderella (and pose in her papier-mache pumpkin) and Berie manned the ticket booth. Berie, still skinny and awkward, idolized her physically precocious, incurably sassy, and immensely big-hearted friend. When Sils' first love affair leads to pregnancy, Berie risks much to save her.

Booklist observes that "Berie narrates in a voice that reaches directly into the part of your brain that cradles your own memories of youth's fierce convictions and wild naiveté." As *Belles Lettres* points

out, "If you have ever been driving a car on that first warm day of spring — a day when summer once again seems possible — and heard a song that immediately propels you into a moment from the past richly suggestive of the future, you'll understand the poignancy and brilliance of Moore's novel." *The* (London) *Sunday Times* concludes that "This is an elegant, beautifully written novel, and there is much in Lorrie Moore's account of an adolescent friendship that everyone will recognize."

READING GROUP GUIDE: "Reading Group Choices" 1998 (Paz & Associates); RECOGNITION: *NYTBR* Notable Book of 1994; REVIEWS: *BellesL* 1/96; *BL* 9/1/94; *LJ* 9/15/94; *LST* 7/16/95; *NY* 10/10/94; *NYT* 9/23/94; *NYTBR* 10/9/94; *PW* 8/15/94; *TLS* 11/4/94

Moorhouse, Frank (Australia)

621   *Grand Days* (1993); Books Britain 1994 (HC & pbk); SETTING: Europe (principally Geneva, Switzerland) in the 1920s

Frank Moorhouse's latest novel — set in the years immediately following World War I — is a comedy of manners full of sex, wit and seriousness featuring the young, game-for-anything Edith Campbell. The story opens in 1920, as Edith, a junior member of the Australian delegation to the just-formed League of Nations, begins her journey to Geneva. Through Edith's eyes the reader is invited "behind the scenes" to witness the formal dance of diplomacy, the politicking of bureaucrats, and the occasional (official and unofficial) lunacy that characterized the early days of the abortive attempt to form the first world body. Based on extensive historical research, *Grand Days* appears to be the first in a proposed series of novels about the early days of the League of Nations.

English novelist **Penelope Fitzgerald** (*WPBW*) points out that Frank Moorhouse, "Known for his sardonic fiction, often featuring a wry look at American influences Down Under ... has not been much noted outside his native Australia. Now he has undertaken a very long, very detailed and very engrossing novel of the early years of the League of Nations which promises to make him celebrated." According to *Publishers Weekly*, *Grand Days* "after a very arch beginning, turns into a vastly beguiling character study set against a fascinating and little-known background. Edith Campbell Berry, the adventurous daughter of a free-thinking Australian family who comes to the fledgling League of Nations in Geneva in the early 1920s ... is one of the most winning women in contemporary fiction." In the view of *Meanjin*, "*Grand Days* is a comedy of manners, ending, as the genre requires with marriage; the heroine identifies the right partner for her after being misled by a charming bounder who is more and less than a man. But, unlike the conventional comedy of manners Edith is also her own hero: she takes action, she initiates, she decides — she, not Fate, drives the plot through its bizarre and incredible turns." The *Australian Book Review* concludes that "Moorhouse has for a long time been one of the most original and professional of Australian writers in the world of literature in English. *Grand Days* all 500 pages of it, is the summit of this achievement."

RECOGNITION: Winner of the South Australia Festival Award for Literature; nominated for the 1994 Banjo Award and the New South Wales State Literary Award; REVIEWS: *AusBkRev* 11/93; *KR* 1/1/94; *Meanjin* Aut '94; *PW* 2/14/94; *TLS* 9/24/93; *WPBW* 3/27/94

Mordden, Ethan (USA)

622   *How Long Has This Been Going On?* (1995); St Martin's 1997 (pbk); SETTING: New York City, 1950s–1990s

Ethan Mordden, a frequent *New Yorker* contributor and long-time chronicler of New York's gay subculture, has, in his fifth novel, written a saga which encompasses the entirety of gay and lesbian experience in contemporary America. *How Long Has This Been Going On?* begins in the firmly "closeted" fifties and ends with a Gay Pride march in 1991 and ranges from New York to L.A and from San Francisco to the Bible Belt.

The *Times Literary Review* observes that Mordden's style is "a mixture of reportage, polemic, soft porn and witty asides," and concludes that "what redeems [the novel] over and over again is Mordden's affection for his characters, even the losers." *Publishers Weekly* observes that "this singular work chronicles the emerging gay consciousness with trenchant humor, editorial observations tinged with a soupcon of cynicism and scenes of often devastating emotional impact." The *London Review of Books* concludes that "The idea that one's 'identity' — be it ethnic, religious, sexual or otherwise — places one in perpetual conflict with a more powerful Other is a classic American trope in both politics and literature; but a novel which aspires to social criticism ought to depict the society it criticizes. There's only so much you can learn about homophobia by looking at gay people. Eventually you have to examine the homophobes, and that means looking at straight people ... and Mordden gives straight folk short shrift...."

REVIEWS: *KR* 4/15/95; *LATBR* 6/25/95; *LRB* 2/22/96; *NYTBR* 7/15/95; PW 4/14/95; *TLS* 5/17/96 *WPBW* 6/18/95

Morgan, Robert (USA)

623   *The Truest Pleasure* (1995); Algonquin 1995 (HC); 1996 (pbk); SETTING: North Carolina early 1900s

Set in the North Carolina mountains at the turn of the century, Robert Morgan tells the story of Tom and Ginny and their marriage of convenience which, despite tremendous odds, develops into a loving union. Ginny Peace, the narrator, is well on her way to spinsterhood when she meets, marries and brings home to her family's farm Tom Powell, a man who grew up in an orphanage and has a burning desire to be rooted. Ginny, a Pentecostal "holy roller," cannot fathom her husband's distrust of religious fervor. Tom's religion is hard work, pure and simple, with little room for joy or celebration.

The *Washington Post Book World* observes that "Robert Morgan's second novel juxtaposes religious zeal with love for the land" and concludes that "through its exquisite detail and resonant images, this book creates a nuanced portrait of love and loss." According to *Booklist*, he has "succeeded in a most difficult endeavor, writing a thoroughly entertaining and even moving novel about a time, place and people that most contemporary Americans know only as cartoons ... [without resorting to] hillbilly stereotypes...."

OTHER MEDIA: Audiocassette (Chivers/unabr); RECOGNITION: *Publishers Weekly* "Best Books" of 1995; REVIEWS: *BL* 9/1/95; *KR* 8/1/95; *NYTBR* 10/29/95; *PW* 7/24/95; *WPBW* 2/4/96

Morris, Bill (USA)

624   *All Soul's Day* (1997); Avon 1997 (HC); Bard 1998 (pbk); SETTING: Thailand and Saigon — 1963

Bill Morris has set his second novel in Saigon and Thailand in 1963, the year of the US-sponsored assassination of Ngo Dinh Diem, South Vietnam's corrupt prime minister. Sam Mallory, a former Navy frogman (with bitter memories of some horrific secret missions in Vietnam) has settled in Bangkok and wants nothing more than to run a hotel and rent out his imported fleet of 1954 neon-colored Buicks. When Sam falls in love with Anne Sinclair, who's on leave from her duties as a purveyor of misinformation for the US Information Service, his life becomes significantly more complicated. Fueled by Anne's growing disgust over the duplicity of the US Military, the pair attempts to subvert the assassination attempt. Cameo appearances by such real-life figures as Marlon Brando, JFK and David Halberstam abound.

Kirkus Reviews calls *All Soul's Day* "An ... ingenious blend of fact and fiction about the early stages of the war in Vietnam" and concludes that "Morris's version of the moment when America out of duplicity and arrogance, became tragically enmeshed in Vietnam, is deeply moving, a persuasive vision of the greatest tragedy in our recent past." *Booklist* applauded *All Soul's Day*, calling Bill Morris "an engaging writer who knows how to tell a story."

REVIEWS: *BL* 6/1/97; *EW* 6/27/97; *KR* 4/1/97; *PW* 4//21/97

Morrison, Toni (USA)

625 *Jazz* (1992); David McKay 1992; NAL-Dutton 1993 (pbk); SETTING: Harlem — 1920s

Toni Morrison's powerful sixth novel begins in Harlem in 1926. A young woman by the name of Dorcas has been shot to death by Joe Trace, a 50-ish traveling salesman and her lover of three months. At her funeral, Joe's wife, a woman grown increasingly volatile over the years since she and Joe first moved up from Virginia, tries to mutilate the young woman's body.

The *Library Journal* notes that "The vision of Morrison's nameless narrator frames this love story, and this anonymous voice slowly draws readers into the rhythm of the city, specifically Harlem, where jazz casts bewitching spells on people's psyches...." According to Merle Rubin (*CSM*) "It's a book I found myself reading aloud ... just for the sheer pleasure of hearing the musical, yet perfectly natural and colloquial, sound of the never-to-be-identified voice that narrates the story." Novelist Jane Mendelsohn (*VLS*) found *Jazz* "at times almost painfully exciting to read" and concluded that although it "can also be disjointed, unconvincing, even irritatingly repetitive ... the poetry of the book stays in the mind, while the rest drifts into the background like incidental music."

OTHER MEDIA: Audiocassette (Random Audio/abr); RECOGNITION: Winner of the Nobel Prize for Literature in 1993; *NYTBR* "Editors' Choice" 1992; REVIEWS: *CSM* 4/17/92; *KR* 2/15/92; *LitRev* 4/92; *LJ* 5/1/92; *NS&S* 5/1/92; *NYTBR* 4/5/92; *TLS* 5/8/92; *VLS* 5/92

Morrow, Bradford (USA)

626 *Trinity Fields* (1995); Viking 1995 (HC); SETTING: Los Alamos, N.M. New York City, Laos, Vietnam (1944–1994)

Bradford Morrow's third novel begins in 1944 with the birth of Kip and Bruce, the sons of two nuclear scientists engaged in the furious, top-secret race to create an atom bomb. The boys become friends, growing up together in the secluded high-tech desert environment of Los Alamos, New Mexico. However, Kip and Bruce share more than the usual childhood memories, they are both burdened by feelings of guilt and anger over the contribution their fathers made to the dawning age of nuclear warfare and the attendant risk of total annihilation. As they reach their teenage years, their paths diverge dramatically: Bruce, a student at Columbia University throws himself into the anti-war movement while Kip signs on for a tour of duty in Vietnam.

According to *Booklist* "Everyone working on the atomic bomb at Los Alamos understood that creating the most fearful form of destruction ever to stun the earth had profound moral and spiritual implications. Recognition of this endlessly repercussive reality is the impetus behind Morrow's powerfully lyrical and philosophical novel...." The *New York Times Book Review* applauds the "formal unity and dramatic intensity" achieved by Bradford Morrow in his novel's "long march toward self-discovery" and concludes that the author's "assiduous probing of the intricacies of moral choice hits us where we live — or ought to live." *Kirkus Reviews* notes that "Morrow situates a fragile story of friendship within an imposing political conflict to create a classic American tale of epic proportions."

RECOGNITION: Nominated for the 1995 *LATBR* Book of the Year Award; REVIEWS: *BL* 2/1/95; *CCent* 5/24-31/95; *KR* 12/15/94; *LJ* 1/95; *NYTBR* 7/9/95

Mosher, Howard F. (USA)

627 *Northern Borders;* Dell 1995 (Pbk); SETTING: Rural Vermont — 1948

Northern Borders is the story of six-year-old Austen Kittredge who had been sent — by his widowed father — to his grandparents' Vermont farm in Lost Nation Hollow "just" for the summer. Austen ends up living with his loving but irascible and headstrong grandparents (their marriage is referred to as the Forty Years War') for the next twelve years.

According to *Publishers Weekly*, "Haunting pastoral images and odd, unforgettable characters pervade this spellbinding tale of rural northern Vermont in the late 1940s and 1950s." The *Library Journal* observes that "This thoughtful coming-of-age tale ... contains memorable characters, excellent writing, and even a little wisdom." The *L.A. Times Book Review* calls *Northern Borders* "A contemporary classic ... a complex, yet idyllic story of childhood...." The *Chicago Sun-Times* concludes that "It's hard to imagine a better novel to let fall into the hands of an adventurous young reader."

RECOGNITION: *NYTBR* Notable Book of 1994; REVIEWS: *ChiSun* 11/30/94; *LATBR* 9/27/94; *LJ* 9/1/94; *NYTBR* 12/4/94; *PW* 8/15/94; *SLJ* 2/95; *WPBW* 11/15/94

Murphy, Yannick (China/USA)

628 *The Sea of Trees* (1997); HM 1997 (HC); SETTING: Indochina — 1930s and 1940s

Yannick Murphy, in her debut novel, tells the poignant story of Tian, the once-privileged daughter of French mother and a Chinese father who, after the invasion of China, spends most of the war years in a Japanese internment camp in Indochina. When the family is reunited in Shanghai in 1945, their beloved city is in ruins and the Communists are in power.

According to the *Times Literary Supplement The Sea of Trees* "is much more than a beautifully written account of atrocity. The lyricism is never sentimental or simplistic. Even after the family's flight to France, there can be no return to normality." *Booklist* points out that "Tian's experiences are related in a stoic monotone, almost matter-of-factly, as befits a little girl who is determined to survive despite being forced into adulthood by the brutalities of war." *Kirkus Reviews* concludes that Ms. Murphy has crafted "An indefatigably forward-going if often poetic story of girlhood and family amid war, terror, loss — and sometimes luck."

RECOGNITION: *NYTBR* Notable Book of 1997; REVIEWS: *BL* 4/15/97; *KR* 3/1/97; *NYTBR* 8/17/97; *PW* 3/10/97; *TLS* 1/23/98

Murray, Albert (USA)

629   *The Seven League Boots* (1995); Pantheon 1996 (HC); Knopf 1997 (pbk); SETTING: America and Europe 1920s and beyond

This is the concluding volume in Albert Murray's decade-spanning trilogy about the coming to maturity of Scooter, a black musician in 20th-century America. Divided into three segments, the story encompasses Scooter's experiences (he has now acquired the nickname "Schoolboy" on account of his college degree) while traveling with a jazz band, his stint in Hollywood composing for the movie studios, and an extended musical sojourn in Europe.

Booklist calls Murray "An overlooked genius" who is "at his scintillating best" in *The Seven League Boots* which is "infused with the elegant energy of jazz, the sonority of history, and the spirituality of art." According to *Publishers Weekly*, "Keenly observant and intensely curious, Schoolboy makes an engaging narrator, completing a story that, after three volumes, is as vital as the period in black American history that it evokes so well." *Newsweek* concludes that *The Seven League Boots* is "Murray's most singular achievement".

REVIEWS: *BL* 2/15/96; *LJ* 12/95; *NewsWk* 2/5/96; *NYTBR* 3/10/96; *PW* 12/18/95

630   *The Spyglass Tree* (1991); Random 1992 (pbk); SETTING: American South —1930s

A sequel to *Train Whistle Guitar* (1974), *The Spyglass Tree* is set in the depths of the Great Depression and features Scooter, a young black man from Gasoline Point, Alabama, who is now enrolled at a segregated college (clearly based on Tuskegee, the author's alma mater). Scooter's education which began in a country schoolhouse in a black town on the outskirts of Mobile — continues on both the academic and cultural fronts.

The *Washington Post Book World* observes that "*The Spyglass Tree* can certainly be read with pleasure in its own right, but to appreciate its nuances, it is really necessary to know *Train Whistle Guitar* and to understand something of Murray's ideas about tradition, heroism and the South." In the view of the *New Republic*, "Murray's tale is essentially an autobiographical examination of "horizons of aspirations" as they existed for poor blacks in the south during the Depression." *Newsweek* observes that "In shimmering, loosey-goosey language that flirts with post-Faulknerian trance talk without ever succumbing.... Albert Murray evokes the Tuskegee Institute as it was 50 years ago" and concludes that "Precocious and impressionable, Scooter maps the territory precisely and evocatively...." The *New York Times Book Review* argues that while *The Spyglass Tree* is short on plot "what drives the narrative is our deepening interest in Scooter's Stephen Dedalus-like growth and the stories he brings us, which strike a perfect balance between the black folk tradition and Faulknerian rumination."

REVIEWS: *Nation* 3/25/96; *NewR* 2/3/92; *NewsWk* 12/9/91; *NYT* 11/22/91; *NYTBR* 3/1/92; *WPBW* 11/3/91

Norfolk, Lawrence (England)

631   *The Pope's Rhinoceros* (1996); Henry Holt 1997 (pbk); SETTING: Late 16th century Europe

The Pope's Rhinoceros is a post-modern makeover, in the spirit of William Vollmann or Thomas Pynchon, of an old-fashioned genre: the historical double-decker. Judged a "swollen behemoth of a narrative" by novelist and noted literary critic **Jay Parini**, Norfolk's second novel is set in motion when a group of monks, in grave need of Papal guidance, decide to leave their crumbling monastery on the Baltic Sea and journey to Rome. In a separate plot line, the Portuguese, feuding with Spain and anxious to curry favor with Pope Leo X, have financed a naval expedition to Africa to capture a rare rhinoceros as a gift for the jaded pontiff. As multiple plot lines converge, what results is a magical mystery tour of sixteenth century Europe — and its denizens — with a stop in the rain forests of West Africa.

Kirkus Reviews observes that "the long voyage out and back is the story's centerpoint, [but] it's only one part of Norfolk's considerable canvas, which also includes a peculiar, isolated order of monks, the plots and counterplots of two intemperate empires, and a wonderful portrait of a decrepit but nonetheless vivid Rome." The *Washington Post Book World* points out that "Norfolk displays an encyclopedic knowledge of every setting he uses, from arcane aspects of shipwrighting and canon law to the ecology of West African rain forests. Like the Pope, he too has a penchant for marvels and prodigies and enlivens his prose with bold, flamboyant descriptions and some daring personification (e.g. observations from the point of view of animals)…" and concludes "All of this is both admirable and exhausting, overwhelming the narrative at times and stunning the reader by the amount of research Norfolk must have done."

RECOGNITION: Nominated for the 1998 IMPAC Dublin Literary Award; REVIEWS: *BL* 9/15/96; *KR* 7/15/96; *LJ* 7/96; *LST* 4/28/96; *NTYBR* 11/10/96; *PW* 6/24/96; *TLS* 4/26/96; *WPBW* 9/15/96; EDITOR'S NOTE: Mr. Norfolk was named by *Granta* magazine to its 1993 list of the twenty "Best Young British Novelists"

Norman, Philip (England)

632   *Everyone's Gone to the Moon* (1996); Random House 1996 (HC); SETTING: London — Swinging '60s

Philip Norman's 6th novel is set in London during the swinging sixties and concerns itself primarily with London's indigenous rock scene. Norman, having published non-fiction books about both the Beatles and the Rolling Stones, knows his subject matter inside out and in his latest novel manages to create an authentic-feeling cast of characters and period milieu. The protagonist, a talented young writer who has snagged a "plummy" job with a quality newspaper, appears to be modeled on the author himself.

According to *Entertainment Weekly*, "Philip Norman's cheerfully rambling, preening *roman a clef* takes the measure of London during the swinging late '60s and finds it a time of cheery inventiveness, indulgence, and backstabbing." Normans's novel was called a "mischievous and entirely delicious send-up of big-time journalism" by Jonathan Yardley (*WPBW*) who suggests that "no immense stretch of the imagination is required to believe that readers of all sorts and conditions will find [*Everyone's Gone to the Moon*] funny, wicked, entertaining and — by no means least — principled." In its starred review, *Publishers Weekly* calls it "a wicked portrait of an era and a screamingly good read" and notes that "Norman's prose positively reels with a distinctly British humor and sharp satirical edge, and his large roster of deftly rendered characters [with some real celebrities thrown in] remains engaged in furious action without a moment of letdown."

REVIEWS: *EW* 5/10/96; *KR* 3/15/96; *LJ* 5/15/96; *NYTBR* 5/26/96; *PW* 4/8/96; *WPBW* 5/15/96

Olds, Bruce (USA)

633   *Raising Holy Hell* (1995); H Holt 1995 (HC); penguin 1997 (pbk); SETTING: Pre–Civil War Virginia

Raising Holy Hell explores the life of abolitionist John Brown, a little-understood yet pivotal figure in American history. Bruce Olds's fictional biography covers the years from Brown's childhood, through his involvement with free soil settlers who periodically skirmished with slaveholders to his fatal attempt to lead a massive slave uprising. Olds is clearly interested in illuminating the social and psychological influences which led Brown to assume the mantle of liberator.

According to Susan Dodd (*WPBW*), *Raising Holy Hell* is "an extravagant book. One senses from start to finish its determination to hold nothing back. Even its most muted and strictly factual passages are opulent with nuance…. 'History-as-received' here is dreadful with vitality, and the John Brown who seizes that history is not a shade, but a palpable physical presence." The *New Statesman* concludes that Olds's "ambitious combination of fractured narrative and dazzling montage [drawn from historical records] could have resulted in sprawling confusion. Instead we have a vibrant, triumphant portrait of a complex and troubled man who found in the cracks of history a version of himself he could live with and, when the time came, die for." The *Library Journal* concludes that *Raising Holy Hell* "is one of the more interesting novels published [in 1995]." *Booklist* observes that Olds's novel "…forces the reader to confront John Brown's unique brand of passion." The *Times Literary Supplement* concludes that "This ambitious novel raises questions about how a life can be represented in writing, and argues for fiction's place alongside conventional biography."

Recognition: *Booklist* "Editors' Choice" 1995; REVIEWS: *BL* 8/95; *LJ* 7/95; *NS* 10/25/96; *NYTBR* 8/27/95; *PW* 6/5/95; *TLS* 10/11/96; *WPBW* 10/1/95.

Ondaatje, Michael (Sri Lanka/Canada)

The English Patient (1992); Vintage 1996 (pbk); SETTING: North Africa and Italy immediately preceding and during WW II; See Section 3, #247

O'Nan, Stewart (USA)

634   *A World Away* (1998); Holt 1998 (HC); SETTING: Long Island mid 1940s

Set on the homefront during WW II, *A World Away* features the Langers, a family grappling with more than war shortages and family dislocations. James and Anne Langer, a middle-aged couple, have moved into the family's run-down beachfront homestead on Long Island in order to care for James' father, the recent victim of a debilitating stroke. Their marriage has been severely tested by James' recent infidelity (involving one of his teenage students) and by Anne's retaliatory affair with a solider. They are both also deeply disturbed by their older son Rennie's passage through the war years. A conscientious objector who becomes a Navy medic, he is now missing in action in the Pacific theater. Jay, the youngest Langer, looks in vain for stability and solace.

According to the *Washington Post Book World* "In *A World Away* O'Nan has constructed a literary novel with the grip of a page-turner ... the plot line continues to push ahead and the reader, caught up in the anxiety of the Langer family as a whole and individual pathologies that drive each member, is invested entirely in Rennie's fate." *Publishers Weekly* calls it "a compassionate, acutely observant and deftly understated novel that evokes the longings that tug at one's heart as it unfurls in elegant prose."

RECOGNITION: *NYTBR* Notable Book of 1998; *PW* Best '98 Fiction; REVIEWS: *BL* 5/1/98; *KR* 4/1/98; *LATBR* 7/12/98; *LJ* 5/1/98; *NYTBR* 6/21/98; *PW* 4/13/98

Parini, Jay (USA)

635   *Benjamin's Crossing* (1997); Holt 1997 (HC); 1998 (pbk); SETTING: Europe—1940

In his fifth novel, Jay Parini tells the moving story of the tragically abbreviated life of the noted 20th century German-Jewish scholar, Walter Benjamin. Although touching on his intellectually precocious student years in Berlin and his emergence as a brilliant young philosopher (counting Hannah Arendt and Bertolt Brecht among his friends), Parini focuses primarily on Benjamin's final year. The author intersperses the tale of Benjamin's valiant yet futile attempt to elude the German SS in 1940 with episodes from his intensely cerebral life, including his long stay in Paris where—despite his intense absorption in the writing of his magnum opus (a never-to-be-completed study of 19th century Paris)—he mingled with the leading intellectuals of Europe. The story is narrated primarily through the (fictional) recollections of a number of historical figures who were close to Benjamin. They include: Gershom Scholemm, a good friend and fellow Jewish scholar; Lisa Fittko, an intrepid young anti-fascist (who was instrumental in leading a number of political and religious refugees over the Pyrennes mountains to safety); and the Marxist intellectual Asja Lacis, Benjamin's great, unrequited love. The novel opens in 1950 at a grave site in a mountain-top village in Spain where Gershom Scholemm has come to mourn the loss of his friend. How Benjamin came to be buried in this lonely spot is the subject of Mr. Parini's book.

Novelist **Robert Grudin** (*NYTBR*) calls *Benjamin's Crossing* "at once painstakingly researched and dramatically recounted. It locates Benjamin's mystifying traits in a vivid and believable psychology. And it has something important to tell us, not just about Benjamin but about the role of the intellectual in modern Western society." *Kirkus Reviews* notes that "Parini's portrait of an entire generation of intellectuals overwhelmed by revolution and war, and of their desperate attempts to make sense of their world, is resonant, convincing and deeply sad." The *Times Literary Supplement* observes that *Benjamin's Crossing* "engages convincingly with its subject and has been not only carefully researched but also, more importantly, thoroughly imagined." In the view of *The* (London) *Sunday Times* "the friends who recall Benjamin come across as vivid individuals.... But [it is] Benjamin [himself who] dominates the book and he is wonderfully, infuriatingly alive, an intellectual hopelessly out of touch with his ailing body, curiously and tragically blind to the Europe disintegrating around him." *Publishers Weekly* concludes that "Parini ... is able both to expose the blind spots of the highbrow European mind, which is easy, and to dramatize and summarize highbrow ideas, which is difficult. His novel is not so much a tragedy as it is a eulogy—not just for Walter Benjamin, but for an entire cosmopolitan European intellectual tradition." Richard Bernstein (*NYT*) observes that the Walter Benjamin "who emerges from these pages is far from the hero worshipped these days in English and Art History departments.... [He is portrayed as] a selfishly improvident, politically myopic, sexually unfaithful figure. But he is also brilliant, startlingly original and possessed of a redeeming gift for irony."

RECOGNITION: *NYTBR* Notable Book of 1997; *LATBR* "Recommended Title" 1997; REVIEWS: *BL* 5/15/97; *KR* 3/15/97; *LST* 6/14/98; *NYT* 7/2/97; *NYTBR* 6/29/97; *PW* 3/31/97; *TLS* 6/20/97; *WPBW* 5/18/97

Park, Jacqueline (USA)

636   *Secret Book of Grazia dei Rossi* (1997); Simon & Schuster 1997 (HC); Scribner 1998 (pbk); SETTING: Italy—16th century

Jacqueline Park's debut novel is written from an unusual vantage point, that of Grazia dei Rossi, an educated Jewish female—heiress to a banking dynasty—living in 16th-Century Florence. When Grazia falls in love with a Christian nobleman, she must choose between her love and her faith. Grazia's story is set against a background of religious persecution and Byzantine papal politics. The author is a professor emeriti in the NYU dramatic-writing program.

According to the *Library Journal*, "Two letters from the court of Isabella d'Este found in an attic and published in an obscure Italian journal provide the inspiration for this historical novel ... [which] deftly mixes romance, historical details, memorable characters and drama." *Publishers Weekly*, in its starred review, suggests that "Through Grazia [the author] elucidates the intricate and perilous world of Italian Jews during the Renaissance, telling her spellbinding story with honesty and humor and meticulous historical accuracy." According to the *New York Times Book Review*, "There is much to be learned from the story of Grazia's family; at the mercy of Christian fanaticism and political intrigues disguised as religious righteousness, they are forced to move from one city to the next as they try to spare themselves from annihilation."

REVIEWS: *KR* 6/15/97; *LJ* 8/12/97; *NYTBR* 12/19/97; *PW* 9/18/97; *WPBW* 12/28/97

Peery, Janet (USA)

637   *River Beyond the World* (1996); St Martin's 1996 (HC); Picardy 1997 (pbk); SETTING: Mexico and Southwest Texas, 1944–present

In her first novel, Janet Peery tells the story of two women — from very different cultures and economic classes — whose lives are closely intertwined for more than fifty years. Luisa Solis has grown up in a Sierra Madre mountain village where she had been impregnated following an ancient fertility ritual. Pregnant and terrified of what will happen next, Luisa leaves her village and heads towards the Texas border where she is picked up by Thomas Hatch, a kindly farmer, who brings her home and gives her a job in his orchard groves. Before long, Luisa comes to the attention of his bored and dissatisfied wife, Edwina (Eddie), a former "Southern belle" from a well-to-do Virginia family, who appropriates her as a personal maid. When Eddie (who has been fooling around) becomes pregnant soon after Luisa's arrival in the Hatch household, the two women give birth and raise their children in tandem.

According to *Kirkus Reviews*, "*River Beyond the World* "is a lyrical, dramatic first novel [which] traces the passages and passions of womens' lives with an ardent empathy that will remind many of the fiction of Barbara Kingsolver." *Booklist* observes that "As the years pass, [Luisa's and Eddie's] respective life choices cause them to reevaluate their connection to love, legacy, and each other. Peery's prose has a touch of magical realism and is rich with poetic and philosophical description." Ms. Peery's "penetrating wit," concludes the *New York Times Book Review*, "is focused on [Eddie] ... whose story alternates in languorous, satisfying stretches with Luisa's more earnest one."

RECOGNITION: Nominated for the 1996 National Book Award; Peery was selected as one of the Best of Young American novelists by *Granta* magazine; REVIEWS: *BL* 10/1/96; *KR* 8/15/96; *LJ* 3/15/97; *NYTBR* 11/10/96; *PW* 8/19/96

Picano, Felice (USA)

638   *Like People in History* (1995); Viking 1995 (HC); Penguin 1996 (pbk); SETTING: Manhattan and environs, 1950–present

Hailed as a gay *Gone with the Wind* by Edmund White, *Like People in History* follows two cousins, Roger Sansarc and Alistair Dodge, from their childhoods through to Dodge's death in his forties from AIDS. As Picano endows both men with talent, ambition and good connections, they experience much of the "good life" before it all begins to sour.

As the *London Review of Books* points out *Like People in History* is "split into two interwoven parts: one very long night in 1991— a birthday party, an AIDS demonstration, a stint in jail, a midnight quarrel in Central Park an attempted suicide, a fistfight, an ambulance ride, a fallen crane, a traffic pile-up and, finally, a death — and the 36 years of acquaintance between Roger Sansarc, the novel's narrator, and his cousin Alistair Dodge, which lead up to that night." Called a "beach book" by *Booklist*, which goes on to observe that "being both gay and an epic (i.e. it's campy and it's long), it succeeds as a story that doesn't take itself too seriously and will be much in demand...." In the view of *Publishers Weekly*, Picano [best-selling author and founder of the first gay publishing house in New York] has created "memorable characters ... and wonderfully dishy dialogue [that] evoke changing gay sensibilities with affecting measures of both tragedy and comedy."

REVIEWS: *BL* 7/95; *LJ* 6/15/95; *LRB* 2/22/96; *NYTBR* 7/15/95; *PW* 6/19/95

Ping, Wang (China/USA)

639   *Foreign Devil* (1996); Coffee House 1996 (HC); SETTING: Shanghai, 1960s–present

Ni Bing, female protagonist of Wang Ping's autobiographical novel, *Foreign Devil*, was born in Shanghai and grew up during the harshest years of Mao's Communist Regime. The daughter of a naval officer and a harshly domineering mother, Ni Bing is determined to obtain a college education and to eventually study abroad. However, given the fanatical dictates of the Cultural Revolution, Li Bing is forced to spend eight years (from age 15 to 22) in an isolated village undergoing "re-education." To complicate matters, Ni Bing's parents have always been ominously secretive regarding her own birth and these secrets have weighed heavily on the young girl's mind. Before her story is through, Ni Bing will confront a public shaming, a dangerously jealous lover and enforced prostitution as punishment for consorting with foreigners.

According to the *Library Journal*, "Even without focusing on arduous interactions with the [Communist] 'Party,' Ni Bing's story would be a wonderful narrative, showing as it does her indomitable spirit in the face of abusive treatment from her family and male companion." *Publishers Weekly* observes that, despite the occasional "awkward flashback," the author has produced a moving testament and that "scenes depicting the brutality of China's repressive society are as searing as those in Anchee Min's *Red Azalea*." *Publishers Weekly* concludes that "Ping writes with compelling candor about an authoritative regime where the experiences of victim and torturer are often inescapable."

REVIEWS: *BL* 9/1/96; *LJ* 7/96; *Ms*.11-12/96; *PW* 7/15/96

Proulx, Annie E. (USA)

640   *Accordion Crimes* (1996); S&S 1996 (HC); Scribner 1997 (pbk); SETTING: America 1891–1991

The "epic" saga of an instrument and its successive owners, the green button accordion of the title was constructed in Sicily and arrived in the US in the early 1890s where it is passed from one working-class owner to the next over the next 100 odd years. What Ms. Proulx manages to create is an alternative history (one that features primarily "hyphenated" Americans) of the United States in the 20th century.

According to Michael Dirda (*WPBW*) "Though *Accordion Crimes* may at times seem like North American magic realism, the book, with its admixture of representative types, gallows humor and overt symbolism, actually belongs to the under-appreciated tradition of naturalism…. And in its grand ambition to portray the immigrant experience in this country, Proulx's novel might almost be a condensed American version of Zola's Rougon-Macquart cycle [for] like Zola, Proulx knows life's extravagant bounty and wastefulness [and] loves a melodramatic flourish." The *Times Literary Supplement* found *Accordion Crimes* to be, for the most part, "a grim and funny story, running on the powerful fuel of continuous invention," concluding that Ms Proulx's novel is a "sprint from start to finish, with never a longueur or more than a flash of a digression; more, in the end, than one can say for most epics." However, the *New York Times Book Review* contends that "Horrific moments arrive every few pages in *Accordion Crimes*, with a regularity that at first is disconcerting but soon grows numbing and finally ludicrous…. Ms. Proulx

wrings glorious language from her characters' agony, yet in the end the spectacle is both repellent and trivial."

OTHER MEDIA: Audiocassette (S&S/abr; Books on Tape/unabr); RECOGNITION: Booklist "Editors' Choice" 1996; nominated for the 1997 "Orange" Fiction Prize; REVIEWS: *NS* 10/18/96; *NY* 7/15/96; *NYTBR* 6/23/96; *TLS* 10/4/96; *WPBW* 6/16/96

Pye, Michael (UK)

641   *The Drowning Room* (1995); Viking 1996 (HC); Penguin 1997 (pbk); SETTING: 17th century New Amsterdam

Gretje Reyniers, an actual 17th century inhabitant of New Amsterdam about whom little is actually known, has been rescued from historical obscurity by historian-turned-novelist Michael Pye. Gretje was born in The Netherlands and, in Pye's version of her life, arrived in New Amsterdam in 1624 in pursuit of her husband; her name occasionally appears in historical court records of lawsuits involving debt and slander. Pye's Gretje is the "first whore of New York" an engaging young woman who, in addition to harlotry, made her living in various other ways such as household service, money lending, fur dealing, and fishmongering. When her husband, the "Turk" dies suddenly, the tavern tongues begin to wag.

The *Times Literary Supplement* notes that Gretje "the daughter of a pikeman and an army whore … [finds the new world] scarcely more accommodating than the old" and concludes that "Acceptance of the crude actuality, simply because she can hardly run away from it, gives Gretje a plausible heroism." Richard Bernstein (*NYT*) points out that "In the background to *The Drowning Room* are the East India Company and earliest Manhattan and Long Island; there is a prim, hypocritical colonial governor; there are sailors, notaries, midwives and Indians who kill whales from their canoes. Most of all, however, Gretje Reyniers dominates Pye's pages. She is amoral, opportunistic, fragile, unyielding, disillusioned, ungodly, manipulative, harsh, licentious and admirable — an American ancestor."

RECOGNITION: *NYTBR* Notable Book of 1996; REVIEWS: *BL* 12/15/95; *EW* 1/12/96; *LJ* 11/1/95; *NS&S* 7/28/95; *NYT* 1/3/96; *NYTBR* 1/7/96; *PW* 10/9/95; *TLS* 6/23/95

Pynchon, Thomas (USA)

Mason & Dixon (1997); Holt 1997 (HC); SETTING: Maryland & Pennsylvania—mid 18th century; See Section 3, #258

Ricci, Nino (Canada)

642   *Where She Has Gone* (1998); St. Martin's 1998 (HC); SETTING: Toronto and Italy 1960s onward

The third volume of Nino Ricci's highly acclaimed trilogy is set in Toronto and in Valle del Sole the Italian village of his protagonist's (Vittorio Innocente) birth. In the first volume (*The Book of Saints*) Vittorio was forced to grapple with his mother's fall from grace (she conceives a child after her husband had left postwar Italy to find work in Canada), her subsequent ostracism by the community, and, her tragic death in childbirth). In volume two, *In a Glass House*, Vittorio journeys to Canada, along with his half-sister Rita, to live with his emotionally distant father, now a vegetable grower in Ontario. Rita is eventually given up for adoption. In volume three, *Where She Has Gone*, Vittorio is briefly reunited with Rita in Toronto; they are both unnerved by the power of their mutual attraction, and Rita leaves Canada for Europe in pursuit of her biological father. Vittorio eventually makes his way back to Valle del Sole where he learns the truth about Rita's paternity and confronts the power of the past.

The *Times Literary Supplement* calls *Where She Has Gone* an "outstanding novel" and argues that its "force ... lies equally in the suggestive accretion of details, the small observations, involuted dreams and delicate encounters from which Ricci constructs a kind of fraught meditation about the power and fragility of family and home and the past." *Publishers Weekly* notes: "Ricci's poetic prose and fluid plot create a tense and beautiful story whose sad ironies achieve resolution in a haunting conclusion." In the view of *Time* magazine, "For those who surrender to the spell, Ricci has spun out a delicate and soulful novel...."

RECOGNITION: Winner of (Canada's) Governor General's Award; REVIEWS: *BksCan* 12/97; *KR* 5/15/98; *LATBR* 6/10/98; *LJ* 6/15/98; *Maclean's* 10/20/97; *NYTBR* 9/27/98; *PW* 5/18/98; *Q&Q* 8/97; *Time* 8/10/98; *TLS* 3/20/98

Rogers, Jane (UK)

Promised Land (1997); Overlook 1997 (HC); Penguin 1998 (pbk); SETTING: Australia in 1788 and Contemporary England; See Section 4, #381

Roth, Henry (USA)

643   *Requiem for Harlem* (1998); St. Martin's 1998 (HC); SETTING: NYC—1920s and 1930s

Requiem for Harlem is the concluding volume to a quartet of autobiographical novels that make up Henry Roth's highly praised series "Mercy of a Rude Stream." According to Allegra Goodman (*NYTBR*), "Each volume of the series recounts a phase of Roth's early life: his childhood in *A Star Shines over Mt. Morris Park*" (his family immigrated to the US when he was three), his school days at Stuyvesant High School in *A Diving Rock on the Hudson*, his adolescence in *From Bondage*, and in *Requiem for Harlem*, his years at City College. These novels are rich with details of immigrant life in Harlem in the 1920s: The Yiddish spoken at home, the school fights and friendships, the calls of the street vendors.... In *Requiem for Harlem*, the story of Ira as a college student attending CCNY is told both contemporaneously, in the voice of the young man, and retrospectively, as the now aged Ira conducts a rueful dialogue with his computer. Ira eventually falls in love with Edith Welles, one of his professors, suffers over his sordid relationship with a cousin and resolves to leave Harlem. (An editorial endnote included in this volume alerts the reader to the existence of two more—as yet unpublished—volumes in this series.)

According to *Booklist*, "As Roth traces the traumatic events that instigate Ira's departure from his parents' Harlem apartment for Edith's book-filled Greenwhich Village apartment, he elevates the mean facts of his hero's existence to the plane of classical tragedy, depicting the storm of Ira's mind and the 'labyrinthian implications' of his predicaments in prose that roars, roils and foams within the confines of the page like rapids surging against a river bank." *Kirkus Reviews* concludes that "This brilliantly talky story ends with Ira's escape from home, possessed by what he persuades himself is a 'vibrant new vision ... of liberation, of independence' ... Whatever more we're fated to learn of Ira Stigman and Henry Roth, in finished form or not, will be well worth waiting for." According to *World Literature Today* "In that 'rude stream' which carried Roth through a childhood in New York tenements and an adulthood of economic depression and war, Roth finds mercy in his family's emigration from Europe at the beginning of this century, in his marriage to 'M' (his wise companion and support through a painful and debilitating illness), and in his return to writing fiction so late in life ... *Mercy of a Rude Stream* should be recognized as one of the finest autobiographical fictions of our time. With uncompromising integrity as an artist, Roth seeks to understand and to communicate the intricacy of identity, of aging and illness, and finally of an unexpected mercy discovered in autobiographical writing."

REVIEWS: *BL* 1/1/98; *KR* 1/1/98; *NYTBR* 4/5/98; *WLT* Aut '94; *WPBW* 3/15/98

Roth, Philip (USA)

644   *American Pastoral* 1997); HM 1996 (HC); Vintage 1998 (pbk); SETTING: America—1940s–1970s

American Pastoral is Philip Roth's 18th novel

and the 5th to include the character of Nathan Zuckerman. The redoubtable Zuckerman plays only a very minor role in Roth's latest outing, as Roth trains his authorial attention on Seymour Levov (nicknamed "Swede" for his blonde good looks) and his daughter Merry Levov. Swede had been a classmate of Zuckerman's in high school (his hero, actually); he was a popular, confidant student, the type generally voted "most likely to succeed." Spared active duty in World War II to play baseball, Swede, at the end of the war, married a former beauty queen (Miss New Jersey 1949) and assumed control of his father's thriving glove factory. A successful life, by most people's standards, until, that is, his 16-year-old, much-pampered daughter, Merry, joins the "Weatherman," a group of student radicals dedicated to the overthrow of the society Swede cherishes. When Merry is implicated in a terrorist bombing in which innocent people died, Merry goes underground and Swede's "perfect" life disintegrates.

According to *Kirkus Reviews* "...passion seethes through the novel's pages ... [which] contain some of the best pure writing Roth has done. And Swede Levov's anguished cry 'What the hell is wrong with doing things right?' may be remembered as one of the classic utterances in American fiction." Michiko Kakutani (*NYT*) calls *American Pastoral* "one of Roth's most powerful novels ever, a big, rough-hewn work built on a grand design, a book that is as moving, generous and ambitious as his last novel, *Sabbath's Theater*, was sour, solipsistic and narrow." In the view of *Booklist*, "Roth [in his latest novel] vents his bitterness with America and himself. Once again, no one escapes the misery that personifies modern America." Richard Eder (*LATBR*) observes that *American Pastoral* "scintillates with more Rothian wit, paradox, eloquent tantrums and absurd pratfalls placed at the exit of each irresistible argument than can be counted. In embattlement and the old matrix of persecution, he strikes a vivid blaze.... Yet [Eder continues] Roth's recent books, for all their ingenious fever, are growing a leaden shell. The battling is increasingly forced and overtaken by time. *American Pastoral*, set mainly from the '40s to the '70s, is not an opening but a closing. It is Zuckerman, fighting his Great War at his one-man veteran's reunion."

OTHER MEDIA: Audiocassette (Dove/unabr); READING GROUP GUIDE; RECOGNITION: Winner of the 1998 Pulitzer Prize for Literature; *LATBR* "Recommended Titles" 1997; *NYTBR* Editors' Choice 1997; nominated for the National Book Critics Circle Award; *Publishers Weekly* "Best Books" 1997; REVIEWS: *BL* 2/15/97; *EW* 5/16/97; *LATBR* 5/4/97; *LJ* 2/15/97; *NYT* 4/15/97; *NYTBR* 4/20/97; *PW* 2/10/97; *WSJ* 4/22/97

Sanders, Dori (USA)

645   *Her Own Place*: A Novel (1993); Random House 1997 (pbk); SETTING: North Carolina, '40s–'90s

Dori Sanders' family saga begins during WW II and is set in Tally County, North Carolina. Her story revolves around an indomitable matriarch, Mae Lee Jones, daughter of a tenant farmer, war bride and single mother of five who, through sheer perseverance, not only acquires a small farm, but makes a very successful "go" of it, all the while raising her children to be successful, responsible members of society. Mae Lee eventually finds a respected role for herself in the wider community as well.

According to *Kirkus Reviews*, Dori Sanders has created a finely written "life story that seems to hum along so simply it takes a while to notice that it resonates as powerfully as an old hymn.... Small, sharp truths and day-to-day details add up to a story that's larger than life." *Booklist* contends that "Fully and lovingly realized characters mark this quiet yet glowing novel that has the taste of the salt of the earth." The *Library Journal* concludes that *Her Own Place* is "A salute to the extraordinary in ordinary lives and a delightful reading experience."

REVIEWS: *AfrAmRev* Spr '95; *BL* 2/15/93; *CSM* 6/24/93; *KR* 3/1/93; *LJ* 3/15/93; *SLJ* 3/15/93

Shadbolt, Maurice (New Zealand)

Monday's Warriors (1990); Godine 1992 (HC); SETTING: NZ "Maori Wars"—1860s; See Section 4, #417

Shepard, Jim (USA)

646   *Nosferatu* (1998); Knopf 1998 (HC); SETTING: Germany 1907–1920s

Jim Shepard's fictionalized biography of the German filmmaker F.W. Murnau (born Friedrich Wilhelm Plumpe into a stolid Westphalian family) is based on a short story which appeared in his 1996 collection *Batting Against Castro*. Shepard, in creating his fascinating portrait of a complex genius (best known for his now-classic vampire film *Nosferatu*), focuses on such salient details of Murnau's life as the tragic loss of his first love, Hans, in World War I, and his pivotal role in the newly emergent European film industry. Shepard's technique—most of Murnau's story is told through the medium of an "unedited production diary" allows him (in the view of the *Times Literary Supplement*) to "smoothly ... present us with a good deal of technical information about this most heroic period in the history of cinema, while offering, as it were, a long close-up on the director's troubled spirit."

In the view of novelist **Leslie Epstein** (*NYTBR*), "Jim Shepard's unusual new novel is an imaginative reconstruction of the life and work of

... the greatest of all German film directors and one of the two or three real masters of the silent screen." According to *Entertainment Weekly*, "Shepard captures the cut-and-paste excitement of early filmmaking, and he keeps Murnau's heart, broken and sad, quietly beating in our imagination." *The* (London) *Sunday Times* calls *Nosferatu* "an atmospheric picture of an era as well as a sensitive evocation of a man." The *Times Literary Supplement* observes that "One simple virtue of this novel is that it makes one want to go and see *Nosferatu* [the movie] again. The prodigious inventiveness of filmmakers like Murnau, their mixture of visual daring and practical resourcefulness, most of all their awareness of the need to fashion the discoveries of [this fledgling medium] ... into something that would function as art ... cannot be praised too highly, particularly in a period when the big movies seem to be about special effects and nothing else."

RECOGNITION: *NYTBR* Notable Book of 1998; *LATBR* "Best Fiction of 1998"; REVIEWS: *BL* 3/1/98; *EW* 4/17/98; *KR* 1/15/98; *LATBR* 12/13/98; *LST* 6/14/98; *NYT* 4/12/98; *NYTBR* 4/12/98; *PW* 1/26/98; *TLS* 6/5/98

Sherwood, Frances

647 *Vindication* (1993); FS&G 1993 (HC); Penguin 1994 (pbk); SETTING: 18th century England

Frances Sherwood's debut novel is loosely based on the life of Mary Wollstonecraft, the 18th Century feminist writer, friend of Thomas Paine and witness to the French Reign of Terror. Ms. Sherwood's story begins with Mary's impoverished childhood (overshadowed by an abusive father), continues with her intellectual development and subsequent acceptance among London's intellectuals, and concludes with her passionate but disastrous love affairs.

Publishers Weekly, in its starred review, calls *Vindication,* both "arresting and convincing" and observes that "In meticulously rendered background detail, Sherwood describes the brutal realities of the 18th century: public hangings, maimed children, abused women ... [as well as] the excesses of the French Revolution...." In the view of English novelist **Hilary Mantel** (*TLS*), "Frances Sherwood has used [Mary] Wollstonecraft's career as the starting point for an imaginative exploration of the London of William Blake and the Paris of Dr. Guillotin. She handles ideas deftly, and emotions with conviction; her tone is arch and funny, slightly throw-away, and quite free from cramping reverence." According to the *Library Journal*, "What's most remarkable about this fictional biography is that it manages to touch upon so many trendy topics — child abuse, mental illness, homosexuality, and drug addiction — without departing from the basic facts."

RECOGNITION: Nominated for the 1993 National Book Critics Circle Award; *NYTBR* Notable Book of 1993; REVIEWS: *KR* 2/15/93; *LATBR* 9/3/95; *NS&S* 6/4/93; *NYTBR* 7/11/93; *PW* 3/1/93; *TLS* 5/21/93

Shields, Carol (USA/Canada)

648 *Larry's Party* (1997); Viking 1997 (HC); Penguin 1998 (pbk); SETTING: Canada — 2nd half of 20th century

Carol Shields, in her eighth novel, describes the life of Larry Weller, a successful garden maze-designer with blue collar origins. In the words of the author "The evidence is in. Whether the cause is genetic or accidental, he knows himself doomed to live inside the hackneyed parentheses of predictability, a walking, head-scratching cliché: first the dreamy child, next the miserable adolescent, followed closely by the baffled young husband, and now, too suddenly, a settled 40-year-old white male professional who chafes at that number 40." The question that Ms. Shield adroitly tries to answer in her latest novel is "What is it like being a man in the closing years of the 20th-century?"

In the view of Michael Dirda (*WPBW*), "To say that a novel is extremely enjoyable may seem like faint praise, but *Larry's Party* is, before anything else, just that: a book that page after page offers a great deal of pleasure." According to Michiko Kakutani (*NYT*), although "Ms. Shields occasionally tries too hard to make him into a representative man.... Larry Weller emerges from this novel as a remarkably sympathetic, idiosyncratic human being, a male counterpart to the Everywoman Ms. Shields created in her Pulitzer Prize–winning novel *The Stone Diaries*." The *Times Literary Supplement* observes that "If there is a problem with [*Larry's Party*] it is to do with the very richness of Shield's central conceit, a metaphor so complex and sappy that its multiple philosophical possibilities occasionally threaten to overwhelm her no-nonsense hero...." *Kirkus Reviews* concludes that Ms. Shields "writes with the rare self-assurance of one who from the first knows where her characters are going and what will become of them once they arrive, and rarer still manages not to bend them out of shape along the way." *Larry's Party* was called "truly brilliant" by *The* (London) *Times* which goes on to observe that "Shield's touch is light but sure; funny, adroit and with a canny grasp of the zeitgeist of the past three decades." The *L.A. Times Book Review* concludes that "Shields' provocative hero offers her readers an excellent conversation piece for dinner parties. *Larry's Party* is a curiously unsettling comedy of our time." As *The* (London) *Sunday Times* notes: "Bitterly funny at times, sometimes poignant, this is a vibrant portrait of a most admirable life."

OTHER MEDIA: Audiocassette (Penguin Audio/abr; Books-on-Tape/unabr); RECOGNITION: Shortlisted for the 1997 Booker Prize, the Orange Prize and the 1997 Giller Prize; *NYTBR* Notable Book of 1997; *Publishers Weekly* "Best Books" 1997; REVIEWS: *BL* 7/97; *EW* 9/19/97; *KR* 6/1/97; *LATBR* 10/5/97; *LJ* 8/97; *LST* 6/21/98; *LT* 5/16/98; *NewsWk* 10/6/97; *NS* 9/12/97; *NYT* 8/26/97; *NYTBR* 9/7/97; *PW* 8/11/97; *Time* 9/29/97; *TLS* 8/22/97; *WPBW* 9/14/97

649   *The Stone Diaries* (1993); Viking 1994 (HC); Penguin 1995 (pbk); SETTING: Canada and the USA 1905–1980s

Daisy Goodwill Flett, an "unremarkable" Canadian woman born in 1905, is the subject of Carol Shields' award-winning novel *The Stone Diaries*. Throughout the story of her life, which is long and not exactly uneventful (she is married twice, raises children, and turns her love of gardening into a mini-career before subsiding into old age), Daisy tries to understand where she "fits" in the grand scheme of things.

According to *Books in Canada*, "Shields has audaciously created a heroine who 'is crowded out of her own life' by relations and friends who are generally more interesting than she, and [has] produced a book that is richly detailed, engrossing, unsentimental, and wise…." **Jay Parini**, writing in the *New York Times Book Review*, asserts that "Carol Shields has explored the mysteries of life with abandon, taking unusual risks along the way. *The Stone Diaries* reminds us again why literature matters." In the view of the *New Statesman*, *The Stone Diaries* is "as great a treat as any of [Shields'] earlier novels. Like them, it is a miraculous meeting of intellectual rigour and imaginative flow. On the one hand, it's a sharp-as-tacks investigation into the limits of the autobiographical form, on the other, a novel of effortless pleasure and sensuality." *Kirkus Reviews* concludes that "Shields, who began as a miniaturist, has come full bloom with this latest exploration of domestic plenitude and paucity; she's entered a mature, luminous period, devising a style that develops an earlier whimsical fabulism into a hard-edged lyricism perfect for the ambitious bicultural exploration she undertakes here."

OTHER MEDIA: Audiocassette (Recorded Books/unabr); RECOGNITION: Winner of the 1995 Pulitzer Prize for Literature and the 1994 National Book Circle Critics' Award; shortlisted for the 1993 Booker Prize; *NYTBR* Notable Book of 1994; REVIEWS: *BksCan* 10/93; *KR* 12/15/93; *LST* 8/27/93; *NS&S* 8/20/93; *NYTBR* 3/27/84; *TLS* 8/27/93

Sontag, Susan (USA)

Volcano Lover (1992); FS&G 1992 (HC); SETTING: Naples —1772; See Section 3, #269

Strong, Albertine (USA)

650   *Deluge* (1997); Harmony 1997 (HC); SETTING: Minnesota 1907–late 1980s

Albertine Strong's affectionately told multigenerational tale is narrated by Aja Sharrett, a part-Chippewa teacher who grew up on a reservation in northern Minnesota. However, since going East to college, she has lived exclusively in the "white world." Her story features her grandfather Peke Oshogay, a college-educated Chippewa, her Swedish grandmother Isabel Olson and her mother, the ambitious, conflicted Nina. The many layered plot, incorporating Chippewa lore (especially as it relates to Wenebojo — the Trickster) and family history is unified by the emotional pull of the Ojibiwa tribe. Ms. Strong, a Minnesota native, grew up in Minneapolis and St. Paul and on the White Earth and Red Lake reservations. Ms. Strong has been widely compared to fellow Chippewa writer Louise Erdrich.

According to the *New York Times Book Review*, "the vigor with which Strong explores the complex history and conflicted hopes of Aja's family gives the novel a distinctive, if fitful force. And her evocation of three generations of tough, idiosyncratic, resourceful women lingers in the reader's mind, as does her lively portrait of Wenebojo, the unseen but irrepressible immortal." The *Library Journal* notes that "Strong explores the importance of family, the dangers of too much and too little pride, and coming to terms with one's personal history." *Publishers Weekly* applauds Ms. Strong's "easy grace and subtle eye for the details of Native existence" and as well as her ability to "seamlessly" combine "scenes of beauty, violence, grimness and humor."

RECOGNITION: *NYTBR* Notable Book of 1997; REVIEWS: *BL* 9/1/97; *KR* 7/1/97; *LJ* 7/97; *NYTBR* 12/7/97; *PW* 7/7/97

Swick, Marly (USA)

651   *Paper Wings* (1996); HarperCollins 1996 (HC); 1997 (pbk); SETTING: 1960s America

In her debut novel, set in Madison, Wisconsin, in the 1960s, Marly Swick tells the coming-of-age story of Suzanne Keller, whose adolescence coincides with her mother's deepening bouts of depression. When President Kennedy, Mrs. Keller's idol, is shot in 1963, her condition worsens, and as she plunges into dark moods and begins exhibiting eccentric behavior, the entire family suffers. Suzanne's journey back to her mother's hometown in Nebraska unlocks the past and helps explain the present.

As *Booklist* observes "Swick, author of [the short story collection] *The Summer Before the Summer of Love* has made the leap from short story to the novel without diluting her deep tenderness or gift for detail." According to *Kirkus Reviews*, Ms. Swick "renders the stuttering momentum of family dynamics with equally warm emotion and relentless clarity." The *New York Times Book Review* observes that *Paper Wings* "becomes a moving elegy to that era that, like John Updike's mythical '50s, still looks to many like the 'last happy time.'" *Booklist* concludes that *Paper Wings* "evokes a sweet, uniquely American nostalgia as it follows Suzanne through the years, dissecting a family's — and a country's — innocence lost." *Publishers Weekly*, in its starred review, concludes that "Beautifully composed and controlled, and steeped in the small details that produce emotional veracity, [*Paper Wings*] again shows Swick ... [to be] a writer of mature insights and impressive gifts."

Reviews: *BL* 6/1/96; *EW* 8/2/96; *KR* 5/1/96; *LJ* 7/96; *NYTBR* 9/8/1/96; *PW* 5/27/96; *SLJ* 5/97; *TLS* 3/28/97

Taylor, Peter (USA)

In the Tennessee Country (1994); Picador 1995 (pbk); See Section 4, #350

Theroux, Paul

652 *My Other Life* (1996); Houghton Mifflin 1996 (HC); 1997 (pbk); SETTING: US. Asia & UK 1950s–1990s

In his aptly named, loosely autobiographical novel, *My Other Life*, Paul Theroux uses the rough outlines of his life as a framework for telling an altogether different story. His protagonist, "Paul Theroux," starts off life in Massachusetts, has a defining Peace Corps experience in Africa, lives, loves and teaches in Singapore, and makes a permanent move to England. Interspersed are descriptions of marriage, children, divorce and much exotic travel. The story is enlivened by vivid encounters with a clutch of famous personages including: Anthony Burgess, Queen Elizabeth, and Nathan Leopold.

According to the *Library Journal*, "The narrator of this book certainly resembles the famous writer of the same name, but in an introductory note Theroux insists that this is an imaginary memoir a 'what if' fantasy.... This is autobiography in the postmodern mode, very much like Kosinski's outrageous *Hermit of Sixty Ninth Street*." As the (London) *Independent* observes, "Theroux invites us to speculate about the dividing line between the veracious and the invented.... The self-portrait here is ruthless. He is a man who, having merged with his fictive self, did not attend properly to the very things that gave his life ballast. He finally shows us that he too bleeds." The *Chicago Tribune* finds in *My Other Life* (which contains "some of the best, indeed most beautiful pages the author

has ever written") a "new depth of Theroux honesty."

OTHER MEDIA: Audiocassette (Dove/abr & Dove/unabr); RECOGNITION: *NYTBR* Notable Book of 1996; REVIEWS: *BL* 7/19/96; *ChiTrib* 9/1/9; *KR* 7/15/96; *LJ* 8/96; *NYTBR* 9/15/96; *TLS* 7/5/96; *WPBW* 9/22/96

Tilghman, Christopher (USA)

653 *Mason's Retreat* (1996); Random House 1996 (HC); Pica Books 1997 (pbk); SETTING: Eastern Shore Maryland — late 1930s, early 1940s

In the Depression years immediately preceding World War II, an American businessman, Edward Mason, has left his failing factory (in the North of England) in the hands of an assistant and has returned with his wife, Edith, and two young sons (Sebastien and Simon) to America. The family takes up residence at "The Retreat" a once-prosperous 1,000-acre family farm located on the wooded Eastern shore of the Chesapeake, which Edward has recently inherited this property from his aunt. Although he is an indifferent farmer and the Victorian mansion has fallen into extreme disrepair, his wife and sons, particularly the elder, Sebastian, are happier here than they were in England. When intimations of war begin to revive the industrial sector, Edward returns England to run his now-profitable factory. His family stays behind in Maryland. Edith and her two sons appear to thrive in the absence of the family patriarch, until Edith meets the handsome Tom Hazelton. The story ends, possibly as it must, in tragedy.

According to *Booklist*, "Tilghman's thoughtful pacing and talent for setting the scene reward the reader with a satisfying and memorable understanding of a complex family." *Kirkus Reviews* observes that Tilghman's novel (despite its flaws) resonates "with echoes of *The Great Gatsby*, William Styron's *Lie Down in Darkness*, O'Neill and Faulkner ... [and is] a stunning individual achievement." Novelist **Thomas Mallon** (*NYTBR*) concludes that "*Mason's Retreat* is a stately, absorbing tragedy whose catastrophe arises less from a hasty exercise of personal passion than a civilized effort to accommodate the passions of others...."

Other Media: Audiocassette (Recorded Books/unabr); Recognition: *NYTBR* Notable Book of 1996; PW "Best Books" 1996; REVIEWS: *BL* 4/15/96; *KR* 2/15/96; *NYTBR* 4/28/96; *TLS* 7/5/96; *WPBW* 4/7/96

Tremain, Rose (UK)

654 *Sacred Country* (1992); Washington Sq 1995 (pbk); SETTING: England and USA mid to late 20th-century

Sacred Country begins in rural Suffolk, in 1952, and tells the story of Mary Ward, who at the age of six is acutely aware of being trapped in the wrong body. The tale follows a number of small-town English characters (friends and relatives of Mary) in the tumultuous postwar years, but most especially Mary who evolves (via a sex-change operation) into Martin and moves to Nashville where she embarks on a musical career.

According to *Kirkus Reviews*, Rose Tremain (whose previous novel, *Restoration*, was set in the 17th century) "returns triumphantly to the 20th ... sketching the outwardly stunted postwar lives of a dozen small-town characters in rural Suffolk — people whose inner lives, however, are surprising, colorful, sometimes tragic, and drive many of them to a bittersweet, affecting end." The *Literary Review* points out that "Rose Tremain writes comedy that breaks your heart. She also has a taste for melancholy which teeters on the brink of farce. The balancing point is where she situates her fiction — poised, lucid and inventive ... "what Tremain is writing about is destiny — recognizing your nature, finding a place in the world, being true to yourself. Novelist **Penelope Fitzgerald**, writing in the *Times Literary Supplement*, observes that Ms. Tremain "has written a strong, complex, unsentimental novel, luscious in some passages, wonderfully restrained in others." Novelist **Lynn Freed** (*WPBW*) observes that "The writing ... is sheer delight. It is skilled, intelligent storytelling at its best."

OTHER MEDIA: Audiocassette (Isis/unabr); RECOGNITION: *NYTBR* Notable Book of 1993; REVIEWS: *KR* 2/1/93; *LitRev* 9/92; *LRB* 10/8/92; *NYTBR* 4/11/93; *PW* 1/10/93; *TLS* 9/4/92;

655 *Restoration: A novel of 17th century England* (1989); Penguin 1991 (pbk); SETTING: England (17th-century)

Rose Tremain, in her sixth novel, tells the frequently ribald story of Robert Merivel, the son of a glove-maker, a lapsed physician who finds favor with the King (by curing one of this dogs) and becomes — for a time — a favorite at the Royal court. Kingly favor comes and goes and Merivel is eventually sent away (to a substantial estate in Norfolk) where he alternatively broods and makes (raucous, uncouth) "merry." Persuaded by Pearce, an old Quaker friend, that he is wasting his life, he joins the staff of an insane asylum located in the Fens. Merivel later brings his medical skills back to a plague-ridden London.

In the view of the *New Statesman*, *Restoration* is "a tour de force.... It dissects the deepest questions: loneliness and change, poverty and madness, art and science; and perhaps especially the furies of unrequited love — on both sides, giving and receiving. And it ends both hopefully and darkly." According to the *Times Literary Supplement* "This is an anti-historical novel, eschewing the usual effects and local colouring associated with the genre.... The power of the vision lies in its oddity, and it is the hero's skewed sense of the world, rather than the novelist's sense of period that lingers in our mind." Angeline Goreau, writing in the *Washington Post Book World*, points out that "Rose Tremain has chosen to write a novel set in the Restoration ... because (perhaps) in one important sense at least it offers a powerful metaphor for the present: As Pearce tells Merivel, 'This age suffers from a woeful moral blindness.'" Ms. Goreau concludes that "Whether or not one chooses to read [*Restoration*] as analogy, [it] offers a brilliantly written, originally conceived exploration of what it means to live in concert with one's own time — or outside of it."

OTHER MEDIA: Audiocassette (Chivers/unabr); a film version starring Robert Downey, Jr., was released in 1995; RECOGNITION: (London) *Sunday Express* "Book of the Year" 1989; Shortlisted for the 1989 Booker Prize; *NYTBR* Notable Book of 1990; REVIEWS: *LitRev* 9/89; *LRB* 11/9/89; *NS&S* 9/29/89; *NYTBR* 4/15/90; *TLS* 9/29/89; *WPBW* 4/22/90

Updike, John (USA)

656 *In the Beauty of the Lilies* (1996); Fawcett 1997 (pbk); SETTING: America 1910–1990s

John Updike's seventeenth novel takes the form of a family saga that begins in New Jersey in 1910 and continues to the present day. Updike focuses on various members of the Wilmott family, whose patriarch, Clarence Wilmot, a Presbyterian clergyman, lost his faith and became an encyclopedia salesman. Through four generations the Wilmots will remain obsessed with religion and with another fundamental American institution: Hollywood.

Publishers Weekly, in its starred review, points out that "Charting the spiritual malaise of four generations of one family, [Updike] explores changing religious and ethical standards as influenced by social upheaval, scientific and industrial progress and the currents of American history. It's an absorbing story with an unusual, timely resonance." The *London Review of Books* notes that, "Underneath the busy surface there is Updike's permanent preoccupation with the vagaries of the spirit in ex-Puritan America. The careful abundance of the writing testifies to his love and admiration for the daily beauties and oddities of American life, past and present, but the deep structure suggests sadness and disappointment." George Steiner, in a review appearing in the *New Yorker*, informs us that "John Updike's genius, his place beside Hawthorne and Nabokov have never been more assured, or chilling. One puts down this novel with the intimation that America is, very near its center, the saddest country on earth. As Updike puts it, repeatedly, 'have mercy.' " Novelist and essayist **Gore Vidal**, writing in the *Times Literary Supplement* comments: "Although I've never taken Updike seriously as a writer, I now find him the unexpectedly relevant laureate of the way we would like to live now, if we have the money, the credentials and the sort of faith in our country and its big God that passes all understanding. Finally, according to the mainline American press, Updike has got it all together, and no less an authority than the *New Yorker's* George Steiner (so different from Europe's one) assures us that Updike now stands alongside Hawthorne and Nabokov, when, surely, he means John P. Marquand and John O'Hara."

RECOGNITION: *The* (London) *Sunday Times* Notable Book of 1996; *NYTBR* Notable Book of 1996; *PW* "Best Books" 1996; *Booklist* "Editors' Choice" 1996; REVIEWS: *BL* 11/15/95; *CSM* 2/29/96; *LJ* 12/95; *LRB* 3/21/96; *Nation* 2/12/96; *NY* 3/11/96; *NYTBR* 1/28/96; *PW* 11/13/95; *Time* 1/29/96; *TLS* 4/26/96; *WPBW* 2/4/96

Urquhart, Jane (Canada)

657 *The Underpainter* (1997); Viking 1997 (HC); Penguin 1998 (pbk); SETTING: America & Canada — spanning most of the 20th century

As Jane Urquhart's fourth novel opens, an elderly minimalist painter, by the name of Austin Fraser, is working on a new series of paintings. Receiving news of a woman who for many years had been his model and his muse, he falls into an extended reverie drawing on the events of more than seven decades. Beginning in Rochester, New York, in the early part of the 20th century, Ms. Urquhart's novel wends its way to contemporary Manhattan with intermediary stops in France (including the battlefields of WW I), Toronto, and the northern shores of Lake Superior.

Publishers Weekly declares that "Urquhart here offers a brilliantly imagined exploration of an artist's personality and the world in which he lives" and concludes that "Such is [the author's] mastery of language and subtlety of construction that the book carries the tension of an unresolved love story, the surprising revelation of tragic secrets, the visceral shock of war's terrible suffering and the heartbreak found in the recognition of finality and loss." According to *Kirkus Reviews* "Few stories have brought artistic narcissism to light so powerfully or thoroughly, but this is a painterly masterwork also in its own right, poignant in each of its several landscapes and subtle in tracing the mingled nuances of love and pain." In the view of *Booklist*, "If Urquhart ... worked with line and light rather than language, she would be a landscape painter, so

acute is her identification with the rugged beauty of the Great Lakes region, a place divided by an international border, and the sharp contrast between brief and glorious summer and the long snowy spell of winter."

RECOGNITION: Winner of the 1997 (Canadian) Governor General's Award; REVIEWS: *BL* 9/15/97; *KR* 8/15/97; *NYTBR* 11/23/97; *PW* 8/4/97; *TLS* 11/28/97

658 *Away* (1994); Penguin 1995 (pbk); SETTING: Ireland and Canada mid 19th-century through mid 20th-century

In her third novel, Canadian author Jane Urquhart tells the lyrical, passionate story of an Irish family in thrall both to the "fairies" and "the cause." The tale — which begins in Ireland in the 1840s (during the potato famine) and moves to the Canadian wilderness — features, among other family members, Mary who falls in love with a dying sailor (actually, a demon-fairy) on a beach in County Antrim, and her daughter Eileen who, many years later, falls in love with an Irish revolutionary.

According to *Quill & Quire*, "Urquhart's book juggles an ambitious sweep of history, myth and geography, from County Antrim to the environs of Belleville and Port Hope [in what is now Ontario] in the early years of the Canadian union ... [And, with its] unerring sense of place and enduring portraits of Irish-Canadians ... [makes an effective] case for respect for the land and its myths, whether they be Celtic or Ojibiway, or best of all, a blending of the two." Irish novelist Aisling Foster (*TLS*) observes that "Urquhart writes with clear, sensuous poetry, locating her imagery in the watery Irish coastline, the wilderness forests of upper Canada and a developing urban sprawl on the banks of Lake Ontario." In the view of *The* (London) *Times*, Ms. Urquhart "tells the story of the generations of her family who struggled against adversity to forge a future in a new land but also how they never forgot the rhythms and cadences of the old." The *Library Journal*, in its starred review, contends that "Urquhart beguiles the reader with a cast of lovable eccentric characters in a wonderfully surreal world that includes a talking crow and a man who can charm skunks 'away.'" *World Literature Today* notes that "Earlier in the novel, one of Urquhart's characters bemoans the tyranny of the English over the Irish — their repression of the Irish language, of Irish voices and stories. In one sense *Away* can be read as an answer to his lament, for in writing it, Urquhart retrieves, in her daring, beautiful fashion, some of the poetry, voices and stories he has feared cast from his people."

REVIEWS: *BL* 6/1/94; *KR* 3/15/94; *LJ* 6/1/94; *LT* 4/11/94; *NYTBR* 6/26/94; *Q&Q* 8/93; *TLS* 4/22/94; *WLT* Win '95; *WPBW* 6/26/94

Vanderhaeghe, Guy (Canada)

659   *The Englishman's Boy;* Picador 1997 (HC); St. Martin's 1998 (pbk); SETTING: USA and Canada, 1870s and 1920s

In *The Englishman's Boy,* Canadian writer Guy Vanderhaeghe tells two interlocking stories. The first is set in the Canadian West of the 1870s and features a young drifter who has joined up with a group of wolf hunters pursuing a band of Indian horse thieves. The trail leads to Saskatchewan where a terrible vengeance is exacted. Also involved in the incident is Shorty McAdoo, a Scotsman whose "failure to act" in the face of unspeakable savagery, will haunt him for the rest of his life. The second narrative is set in the 1920s and concerns Harry Vincent, a crippled young Hollywood scenarist who is working on a monumental movie about the "transcendent" American West. For background, he seeks out McAdoo, known to many old timers as the "cowboy's cowboy." A brutal betrayal pulls the two stories together.

According to *Entertainment Weekly,* "The power of the movies to rewrite history is the fascinating theme fueling this trenchant novel.... Vanderhaeghe's masterful storytelling plays irony against idealism while vividly animating two ruthless American frontiers." In the view of *Maclean's* magazine *The Englishman's Boy* is quite unlike anything else Vanderhaeghe has written: "Until now, the author has preferred a dark, almost claustrophobic focus on the conflicts of friendship and family life. But [this novel, with its "thriller-like momentum"] has a clean, exhilarating expansiveness, as if a prairie wind were blowing through its pages." In the view of *The* (London) *Sunday Times* "Grimly authentic and intensely cinematic, [*The Englishman's Boy*] is a novel that rides tall in the saddle." *The L.A. Times Book Review* calls *The Englishman's Boy*: "An epic tale that brings together the American West before the turn of the century with the Hollywood of the 1920s ... and though far from perfect, is nearly a great [North] American novel."

RECOGNITION: Winner of the (Canadian) Governor's General Award; nominated for the 1996 Giller Prize; nominated for the 1998 International IMPAC Dublin Literary Award; REVIEWS: *CanForum* 3/97; *EW* 9/31/97; *KR* 7/15/97; *LATBR* 9/28/97; *LJ* 9/1/97; *LST* 3/8/98; *Maclean's* 9/23/96; *NYTBR* 10/5/97; *PW* 6/16/97; *Q&Q* 9/96; *TLS* 8/29/97

Vassanji, M.G. (Canada/Africa)

The Book of Secrets (1994) See under *The Empire Writes Back* #456; Picador 1997 (pbk); SETTING: North Africa early 20th-century

Vollmann, William T. (USA)

The Ice-shirt (1990); Penguin 1993 (pbk); SETTING: North America—10th century; See Section 3, #280

Welch, Robert (Ireland)

Groundwork (1998); Dufour 1998 (HC); SETTING: Ireland—16th through 20th centuries; See Section 4, #391

Wesley, Mary (England)

660   *Part of the Furniture* (1997); Viking 1997 (HC); Penguin 1998 (pbk); SETTING: England—WW II

Mary Wesley sets her latest novel in England during World War II and features 17-year-old Juno Marlowe who (after a night of not-quite-consensual sex) has just put her two (no longer virginal) handsome young cousins, Jonty and Francis, on a train back to the front. Juno has been besotted with both Jonty and Francis for as long as she can remember—she has, after all grown up almost next-door to them—but they have always treated her (until the previous night) as if she were just "part of the furniture." London during the blitz is risky, at best, and Juno is caught in an air raid before she can leave the city. She is given shelter by a kindly though mortally ill stranger and in gratitude, agrees to the young man's final request: that she take a letter to his father who lives in Cornwall. The increasingly resourceful Juno eventually arrives at Mr. Robert Copplestone's estate and her life is changed forever.

In the view of the *Spectator,* Wesley's latest novel "will give a lot of pleasure, featuring as it does a beautiful young girl, a nostalgic glance at the English country, teenage sex, the war, a gay gardener, a nosy neighbor, a question of paternity, and—finally—romance." Called a "tart and persuasive portrait of an uncertain young woman's discovery of her heart's true needs" by *Kirkus Reviews, Part of the Furniture* was judged "a real heartwarmer" by *Booklist.* According to the *Library Journal* Ms. Wesley's latest fictional offering contains a "beautiful, ironic, utterly winning story ... one of [her] best." The *Times Literary Supplement* concludes that "One of the refreshing aspects of Mary Wesley's work is the way she has transformed the traditional love story. Not for her the 'innocent' heroine carefully guarding her virtue until someone offers unconditional love and a lifetime of paid bills."

OTHER MEDIA: Audiocassette (Chivers/uabr); REVIEWS: *BL* 3/1/97; *LJ* 3/1/97; *NYTBR* 4/13/97; *NS* 2/14/97; *Spec* 2/8/97; *TLS* 2/21/97

West, Paul (UK/USA)

661   *The Tent of Orange Mist* (1995); Overlook 1997 (pbk); SETTING: 1930s China (Assault of Nanking)

In *The Tent of Orange Mist* Paul West tells the harrowing story of Scald Ibis, a 16-year-old Chinese girl who must make enormous personal sacrifices to protect her father during the invasion (and subsequent occupation) of China by the Japanese army in the late 1930s. The plight of Chinese intellectuals at the hands of the Japanese invaders is particularly well-delineated as is the enforced prostitution of young Chinese girls unfortunate enough to have survived the initial "Rape of Nanking."

According to *Booklist,* West "expresses grim humor as well as scorching insights into the consequences of evil. The narrative thread wears thin in spots, but West is a tremendous stylist, fashioning phrases of mind-stopping clarity and power." *Publishers Weekly,* in its starred review, concludes that "Through meticulous prose and stylistic daring, he cultivates subtle cultural insights while making his wrenching, affecting tale credible on both historical and psychological levels."

RECOGNITION: Nominated for the 1995 National Book Critics Circle Award; REVIEWS: *BL* 8/95; *KR* 6/15/96; *LJ* 8/95; *NYTBR* 9/3/95; *PW* 7/3/95; EDITOR'S NOTE: See also R.C. Binstock's novel (*Tree of Heaven* #505).

White, Edmund (USA)

662   *The Farewell Symphony* (1997); Knopf 1997 (HC); Vintage 1998 (pbk); SETTING: USA (1950s and 1960s)

The Farewell Symphony is the third volume of White's autobiographical novel sequence which began in 1983 with *A Boy's Own Story* and continued with the 1988 release of *The Beautiful Room Is Empty.* Set primarily in New York and Paris, this third volume covers, in the form of a fictional memoir, the narrator's adult life from the 1960s to the 1990s.

In the view of the *L.A. Times Book Review,* Edmund White's "ambitious and elegiac new novel ... is a literary hybrid, a vivid and variegated. Part confession, part memoir, part social and sexual history of the last three decades of Gay life in America...." *The Farewell Symphony* was called "Proust on poppers" by *The* (London) *Times,* which went on to suggest that "the purple passages which clogged [White's] earlier work have been discarded in favor of a poetic, honest prose that manages both raunchy sex and deathbed scenes, as one by one, [the author's] friends and lovers succumb to AIDS." According to *Kirkus Reviews* "White's unmatched ability to communicate the tension between asserting one's right to be 'different' and yearning to be accepted as 'normal' is brilliantly displayed again. Nothing human is alien to him, and none of his alienated souls is anything less than achingly human." *Booklist* points out that "Some have found [White's] work emotionally cold or discomfiting because of his unapologetic snobbery and preoccupation with physical beauty. But others gladly steep themselves in the bittersweet pool of emotion beneath the polished surface of his prose." The *Economist* observes that in his latest volume White includes "real people" such as Peggy Guggenheim, Michel Foucault, Herve Guibert and Gore Vidal "and since the book is admittedly autobiographical, he gets them about right. But the story, howsoever dressed up, remains banal. The narrator who, as early as page ten, celebrated having had sex with his first (sic) 1,000 men is disinclined to slow down during the next 400 odd pages."

RECOGNITION: *LATBR* "Best Books" 1997; *NYTBR* Notable Book of 1997: nominated for the 1998 Lambda Book Award; REVIEWS: *BL* 9/15/97; *Econ* 11/15/97; *LATBR* 8/31/97; *LJ* 9/15/97; *LT* 6/6/98; *Nation* 10/20/97; *NY* 12/1/97; *NYTBR* 9/14/97; *PW* 8/11/97; *TLS* 5/2/97; *WPBW* 9/7/97

Winegardner, Mark (USA)

663   *The Veracruz Blues* (1996); Viking 1996 (HC); Penguin 1997 (pbk); SETTING: Mexico 1946

Mark Winegardner, in his debut novel set in post–WW II America, tells the fascinating story of how Jorge Pasquel, a powerful Mexican entrepreneur, attempted to lift the Mexican baseball league into the ranks of Major League Baseball by luring (with extremely generous salaries) talented American players (of all races) south of the border. The league, made up of teams with a mix of white and black Americans and Latin Americans from all over the region, particularly Cuba, was, in retrospect, significantly ahead of its time. The story is narrated by Frank Bullinger, Jr., a fictional sportswriter from St. Louis who, in the novel's concluding section, is retired and living in Veracruz and still working on his great baseball novel. Occasional chapters are given over to other characters, however, including: Thoelic "Fireball" Smith, a feisty black pitcher from the Negro League; Robert Ortiz, a Cuban with one of the hottest bats in North or South America; and Danny Gardella, a first baseman from the Bronx. Although a work of fiction, *The Veracruz Blues* draws heavily on historical fact.

According to the *Washington Post Book World,* Mark Winegardner's "beguiling story illuminates the racism that existed in the pre–Jackie Robinson majors and, more subtle but no less damning, this country's alternately paternalistic and bellicose attitude toward Mexico.... Add to this a swirl of characters that includes a drunken Ernest Hemingway, an arrogant Babe Ruth, a wary Gene Tunney, an agreeable Cantinflas, a promiscuous Frida Kahlo, and a fanciful Diego Rivera ... and Mark Winegardner's spirited novel covers the field like dew on a spring-training morning." *Publishers Weekly*, in its starred review, observes that "In Bullinger, a frustrated novelist ... he's created a narrator who sounds like Damon Runyon or Ring Lardner at their Bourbon-soaked best. The novel invites comparisons to other baseball books, but Winegardner does something special here: he writes about both baseball and the past with a nostalgia that isn't cloying, always aware of how the ridiculous cohabits with the sublime." The *Library Journal* concludes that Winegardner "hits a home run with this first novel."

RECOGNITION: *NYTBR* Notable Book of 1996; *LATBR* "1st Novel Award" 1996; REVIEWS: *CSM* 3/15/96; *LATBR* 3/31/96; *LJ* 12/95; *NYTBR* 4/7/96; *PW* 11/6/95; *WPBW* 2/18/96

Youmans, Marly (USA)

664   *Catherwood* (1996); FS&G 1996 (HC); Avon 1997 (pbk); SETTING: 17th century Colonial America

Marly Youman's second novel, set in the early Colonial period, begins in England in the mid 1600s as Catherwood, a street urchin, is sold to a gentleman who intends to make a gift of the child to his mother, a wealthy woman devastated by the death of her three young daughters. Catherwood finds a loving home at Grevell Hall and, in time, an upstanding young man for a husband. In 1676 Catherwood Lyte and her husband Gabriel set sail for the New World. Upon landing at "Neue York," the young couple make their way to a wilderness settlement (near what is now Albany) where they build a home and start a family. Catherwood, a resourceful young woman, readily adapts to colonial life and all goes well — until the day the young woman, carrying her infant daughter, decides to set off through the dense forest to visit one of her neighbors. On her way home, she becomes hopelessly lost, and the short walk through the woods becomes a tragic, months-long ordeal.

In the view of the *Washington Post Book World*, "Marly Youmans has created a work of great lyrical beauty and spiritual grace.... *Catherwood* ... is a historical romance graced with the archetypal power of myth." *Booklist* notes that "The psychology of fear and grief is immaculately played out against a wonderfully created backdrop of threatening wilderness." According to the *Library Journal* "the 17th-century English dialect used in the dialog, in Catherwood's letters back to England, and in the epilog, adds an almost overwhelming sense of authenticity." The *New York Times Book Review* observes that Ms. Youmans' "prodigious powers of description render with acuity both small moments and large: the sea crossing, a childbirth, snowfalls, the slitting of a fawn's throat, the 'rammish' stench of a trapper" and concludes that she has "written a subtle, intelligent novel."

REVIEWS: *BL* 5/15/96; *KR* 3/1/96; *LJ* 3/1/96; *NYTBR* 5/26/96; *PW* 3/4/96; *WPBW* 9/14/97

6

More Than
Meets the Eye

Part one of this section is contemporary. An interesting trend in such fiction writing is the incorporation of elements from traditional "genre" fiction (e.g. classic mystery stories, techno-thrillers, neo-gothic chillers) into more "serious" or literary works of fiction. Examples abound: Martin Amis's "captivatingly noir" mystery *Night Train*, Richard Dooling's new cyber-thriller-cum-social-satire, *Brain Storm*, or James Hynes's "hauntingly gothic," smoothly cerebral *Publish and Perish*. Also included in this chapter are highly regarded mystery/thriller titles that have been judged to "transcend" their genres (e.g., Craig Nova's modern thriller *The Universal Donor* described as "Dostoevskyan and pulpish at the same time," Native American Louis Owen's "darkly irresistible" *Nightland* and T.R. Pearson's "wickedly witty" *Cry Me a River*).

In part two, "Historical Settings," the focus is on works of fiction of the type described above which are further characterized by a deft use of period detail: Joseph Kanon's *Los Alamos*, a literary thriller set in New Mexico during WW II which gets the "atmospherics exactly right"; Margaret Atwood's prize-winning *Alias Grace*, about a celebrated 19th-century Canadian murderess; E.L. Doctorow's "stylish whodunit" *The*

Waterworks set in a "corrupt but hideously exciting" 19th-century Manhattan; and Iain Pears' erudite period mystery, *An Instance of the Finger Post*, which brings to exhilarating life a 17th-century Oxford "treacherous as quicksand."

Readers interested in more specific classifications (e.g., gothics — neo-, Southern-, or California — mystery/comedy hybrids, Native American mysteries, postmodern thrillers, etc.) should consult the Index.

CONTEMPORARY SETTINGS

Ackroyd, Peter (UK)
665 *First Light* (1989); Grove-Atlantic 1996 (pbk)

In *First Light* Peter Ackroyd offers up a strange, multilayered tale that includes the ongoing archaeological excavation of a decidedly eerie Neolithic grave site, the oddly mysterious behavior of a group of scientists stationed at a nearby astrological observatory, and the secretive (possibly corrupt) practices of a group of local farmers. Add to this a clutch of eccentric characters (including a lesbian government official, a reclusive farmer and his idiot savant son, and a drink-addled antiquarian) and you have a strange brew indeed.

Although novelist **Thomas M. Disch** *(WPBW)* declared *First Light* to be "the worst novel *ever* by a novelist of certifiable distinction," most reviewers took a more positive view of Mr. Ackroyd's book. The *Times Literary Supplement* promised readers "comic suspense of almost Hitchcockian precision." Other assessments include *Time Magazine*'s: "suspenseful, eerie, entertaining" and the *New Republic*'s: "a performance of much skill and ingenuity.... [Peter Ackroyd] is a writer of highly intelligent entertainments." The *Library Journal* concludes that *First Light* is "a tasty, expertly crafted novel that challenges as it entertains."

OTHER MEDIA: Audiocassette (Books-on-Tape/unabr); REVIEWS: *CSM* 1/10/90; *LitRev* 4/89; *LJ* 7/89; *LRB* 5/18/89; *NatR* 10/13/89; *NewR* 9/4/89; *NS&S* 4/21/89; *NYTBR* 9/17/89; *Time* 9/18/89; *TLS* 4/28/89; *VLS* 9/89; *WPBW* 9/10/89

Akst, Daniel (USA)

666   *St. Burl's Obituary* (1996) McMurray & Beck 1996 (HC); HB&J 1997 (pbk)

L.A. Times reporter Daniel Akst's debut novel, an off-beat, darkly comic excursion into thriller territory, is jump-started when lead character Burl Bennet, an overweight obituary writer for the *New York Times*, enters his favorite restaurant and stumbles into a Mafia execution. Targeted as a witness, Burl takes to the road where he finds himself confronting the "verities" of American life.

According to Charles Monaghan (*WPBW*), Akst's novel is "a map of the contemporary world, a black comedy that carries Burl, fearfully fleeing the Mafia, into the belly of the American beast ... [it is] ingenious and thought-provoking ... [without being] difficult reading.... [In fact,] it goes down as easily as cotton candy, one of the few foods that Burl Bennett does not down in this epic of consumption." *Publishers Weekly*, in its starred review, applauds Akst for his ability to handle "labyrinthine plot twists deftly" and for his style "that is at once literate and funny as he explores contemporary links among food, sex, identity and death."

READING GROUP GUIDE; RECOGNITION: Nominated for the 1996 *L.A. Times* Book Prize and the 1997 PEN/Faulkner Prize; REVIEWS: *AtlM* 6/96; *BloomR* 7/96; *LATBR* 8/11/96l; *LJ* 2/1/96; *PW* 4/1/96; *SmPress* 7–8/96; *WPBW* 5/26/96

Alcorn, Alfred (USA)

667   *Murder in the Museum of Man* (1997); Zoland 1997 (HC); 1998 (pbk)

Alfred Alcorn's astringently comic murder/ mystery is set in a museum of natural history and features cannibalism, a bevy of fraudulent scientists and a narrator committed to preserving the venerable (and rather sadly outdated) Museum of Man. The museum, located in the British village of Seabord and known affectionately as "the MOM," has been the recent scene of some rather perplexing goings-on. For a start, Dean Cranston Fessy, assigned to look into the museum's financial affairs, has been found murdered, and the state of his

corpse suggests that he might actually have been partially eaten. Mr. Alcorn, a member of the staff of Harvard University's Museum of Culture and Natural History, brings a knowing, if somewhat jaundiced, eye to the proceedings.

According to Nina Auerbach (*NYTBR*) "While *Murder in the Museum of Man* is an imperfect detective novel, it is never a dull or formulaic one: even its self-indulgent passages are permeated with a sophisticated intelligence.... Mr. Alcorn ... brings the setting to life with such wisdom that it transcends the rough patches of his novel." *Publishers Weekly* calls it: "Sly and spicy from start to finish" and concludes that "Alcorn's unexpected hybrid blends academic spoofery, cannibalism, and a murder mystery, serving it up with a just right balance of innocence, subtle malevolence and cheeky irony."

REVIEWS: *BL* 4/15/97; *LJ* 4/1/97; *NYTBR* 4/27/97; *PW* 3/31/97

Alexie, Sherman (USA)

668   *Indian Killer* (1996); Atl Monthly 1996 (HC); Warner 1998 (pbk)

In Sherman Alexie's second novel, a serial killer is on the loose in Seattle and, because bodies of white men are turning up scalped, it is widely assumed that the killer must be an Indian. Tension mounts and reciprocal "White-on-Indian" violence erupts on Seattle's meaner streets. Alexie, a Spokane/Coeur d'Alene Indian, presents his readers with a cast of well-drawn character/suspects including: John Smith, a disaffected Indian adopted at birth by a well-meaning but culturally obtuse white couple; Prof. Clarence Mather, a white, wanabe-Indian writer; Marie Polatkin, a "militant" Indian enrolled at a local university and her cousin, Reggie, a half-breed with "tainted" blood.

The *Christian Science Monitor* observes that "in spare, unflinching scenes ... [Alexie] takes a metaphorical knife to the heart of American racism and, like the Indian killer, he does so to redeem his Indian brethren." According to the *Washington Post Book World*, the author has "laid claim to a very special piece of territory. Scorning whites and scorning mixed-bloods even more, he writes for full-blooded native Americans. He writes very well." *Booklist* points out that Alexie's novel is "populated almost completely by angry people. There is not even much black humor to ease the pain of a world gone wrong. But the anger and the fear smell so real, so shockingly familiar, that we resist the temptation to turn away. *Indian Killer* is a difficult pill to swallow, but Alexie compels us to take our medicine." *Kirkus Reviews* concludes that *Indian Killer* is "Both a splendidly constructed and wonderfully readable thriller — and a haunting, challenging articulation of the plight and the pride of contemporary Native Americans."

OTHER MEDIA: Audiocassette (Audio Lit/abr); RECOGNITION: *NYTBR* Notable Book of 1996; REVIEWS: *BL* 9/1/96; *CSM* 1/6/97; *Kirkus* 8/1/96; *LJ* 2/1/97; *NYTBR* 11/24/96; *PW* 7/29/96; *WPBW* 10/18/96

Amidon, Stephen (USA/UK)

669 *The Primitive* (1995); Ecco Press 1995 (HC)

Stephen Amidon's *The Primitive* is a literary thriller that skillfully explores the dual themes of obsession and betrayal. The plot hinges on a simple act of kindness: a happily married man offers assistance to an accident victim, a beautiful, temporarily disoriented young woman—an artist, as it turns out—thereby setting in motion a harrowing sequence of events. Amidon's storyline is fueled throughout by desire, unsavory secrets and compulsive indiscretion.

The (London) *Times* found *The Primitive*'s plot to be "highly compelling" while Steven Poole, writing in the *Times Literary Supplement*, applauds Amidon for producing a "fluid, snaky thriller of great momentum." A similar assessment was offered by *Publishers Weekly* which noted that "there is something fascinating in the mixture of lust, ennui and good intentions that pushes [Amidon's] protagonist to act with such unaccustomed abandon."

Reviews: *LT* 4/9/95; *NYTBR* 8/13/95; *PW* 6/19/95; *TLS* 3/17/95

670 *Thirst* (1991); Ecco Press 1993 (HC)

A man's sudden death on a transatlantic flight from New York to London triggers in his estranged son—an expatriate American actor living in England—a furious search for truth and inheritance. What he finds—when he accompanies his father's body to Arizona—is Lindy, his young, attractive, mildly alcoholic step-mother and a deeply troubled step-brother. Stephen Amidon's southwestern setting is exploited fully in a quasi-thriller plot which includes environmental exploitation, drained liquefers, Native American tribal law, and unscrupulous developers.

According to the *Guardian Weekly*, "Amidon is good at the ordinary, unretained mess of life, the incompetence, the dead ends, the dust filled creases and sweat-sticky surfaces of this hell-zone. To make this kind of ordinariness work for the narrative is no easy thing. And there is something else that makes *Thirst* a gifted, subtle piece of fiction, Amidon is not shy of irrigating the novel with themes." The *Times Literary Supplement* points out that although Amidon can be "morbid, mordant and just plain silly ... *Thirst* is a brilliant novel and true to its title, it leaves you crying for more." In the view of *Publishers Weekly* "Amidon is a gifted stylist and a writer to watch. He turns the stark desert into a semi-surreal landscape pregnant with telling details in a sizzling parable about finding a moral fulcrum in a throwaway society."

REVIEWS: *BL* 6/1/93; *GW* 4/9/92; *KR* 4/15/93; *Lit Rev* 3/92; *NYTBR* 9/19/93; *PW* 4/26/93; *TLS* 4/3/92

Amis, Martin (UK)

671 *Night Train* (1997); Harmony 1998 (HC); Random House 1999 (pbk)

Wildly described as a gritty, captivatingly "noir" mystery, *Night Train* is told in an "almost" faultless American idiom and features big-city homicide detective Mike Hoolihan, a strapping, boozy-voiced, "tough-guy" kind of cop, who just happens to be a woman. As the novel opens, Mike has been summoned to the scene of what appears to be a homicide and quickly recognizes the victim: Jennifer Rockwell, the highly accomplished daughter of the Chief of Police. As the investigation proceeds—and the Police Chief is baying for blood—Mike has the unenviable job of ruling out what looks suspiciously like suicide.

According to English novelist **John Lanchester** (*New Yorker*), *Night Train* "draws its energies equally from the linguistic pyrotechnics of Nabokov and the human immensities of Bellow.... It sounds unlikely—indeed it *is* unlikely—but the outcome is sentence after sentence that nobody else could have written." Michiko Kakutani (*NYT*) calls Amis's novel "a deliciously readable, highly polished diversion, a testament to its author's Nabokovian love of language and games, and his utter ease in delineating the seamy underside of modern life." *Time* magazine notes that *Night Train* in "paying homage to the American tough-guy novelists of yore [e.g. Hammet and Chandler] ... pushes the boundaries of noir almost to the edge of darkness" and concludes that even though the "experiment does not always work ... this little book never gets boring." In the view of the *Wall Street Journal*, "*Night Train* [a metaphor here for suicide ...] is a virtuoso performance by Mr. Amis, who proves he can do autopsies as clinically as Patricia Cornwell and female detectives as convincingly as Linda La Plante."

OTHER MEDIA: Audiocassette (Dove Audio/abr); RECOGNITION: *NYTBR* Notable Book of 1998; REVIEWS: *BL* 11/15/97; *KR* 11/1/97; *GW* 7/29/97; *LATBR* 1/25/98; *NS* 11/14/97; *NY* 2/1/98; *NYT* 1/27/98; *PW* 10/27/97; *Salon* 1/26/98; *Time* 2/16/98; *TLS* 9/19/97; *WSJ* 1/29/98

Anaya, Rudolfo, A. (USA)

672 *Zia Summer* (1995); Warner Books 1995 (HC); 1996 (pbk)

Rudolfo Anaya, a well-respected Mexican-

American writer, sets *Zia Summer*, his first murder mystery, in Albuquerque, New Mexico, and features the handsome amateur P.I., Sonny Baca. When Sonny's cousin, Gloria Dominic, is found murdered (with a Zia sun symbol carved into her stomach), he immediately suspects witchcraft but, in time, uncovers a lot more than he bargained for.

According to *World Literature Today*, "Anaya skillfully transforms the traditional detective novel into a novel that addresses the broader question of Mexican-American identity." *Booklist* observes that "Though satisfying purely as a mystery, the novel sacrifices none of Anaya's trademark spirituality — a connectedness to the earth and a deep-seated respect for the traditions of a people and a culture" and concludes that one should read "this multidimensional novel for its rich language and full-bodied characters. Anaya is one of our greatest storytellers."

REVIEWS: *BL* 5/15/95; *NYTBR* 7/2/95; *WLT* Spr '96

Anshaw, Carol (USA)

673   *Seven Moves* (1996); HM 1996 (HC); 1997 (pbk)

Carole Anshaw's protagonist, Christine Snow, is a Chicago-based therapist whose live-in, lesbian lover, Taylor, a professional photographer, has abruptly disappeared. Christine is, at first, hurt, bewildered and disoriented by her companion's inexplicable departure. However, after stumbling upon a series of clues found in Taylor's darkroom, she resolves to get to the bottom of her friend's (possibly sinister) disappearance, and embarks on a quest which leads her to Morocco, one of Taylor's frequent photography-shoot destinations. In this exotic and vaguely threatening locale, Christine must confront a series of hard truths.

According to the *Library Journal*, Anshaw has created "a heady mix of suspense and humor, edgy urban ambiance, and down-to-earth, touching characters." The *Boston Book Review* notes that "With [its] warm but hip sensibility and cock-eyed humor, comparisons to the work of Anne Tyler or Stephen Macauley are inevitable ... [she] has that kind of comforting authority." *Booklist* concludes that "Anshaw's present-tense narrative is witty and intimate, and her story is peopled with remarkably sympathetic, three-dimensional characters." In the view of the *Washington Post Book World*, *Seven Moves* "is less a detective story than a study of loss and discovery.... This is writing of a high order where sexuality has less to do with the meshing of limbs than the discoveries of the heart."

READING GROUP GUIDE; RECOGNITION: Nominated for the 1997 Lambda Literary Award for Lesbian Fiction; REVIEWS: *BL* 9/15/96; *BBR* 11/12/96; *LJ* 9/15/96; *NYTBR* 11/10/96; *PW* 9/3/96; *WPBW* 11/17/96

Bakis, Kirsten (USA)

674   *Lives of the Monster Dogs* (1997); FS&G 1997 (HC); 1998 (pbk)

Kristen Bakis's "tragic and philosophical" (*LJ*) debut novel is set in New York City in the year 2008 and concerns the abrupt appearance of a group of formally dressed, six-foot-tall dogs who walk upright, have been fitted with prosthetic hands, and speak with the help of an electronic voice box. The "monster" dogs (actually man/dog hybrids) were engineered, it transpires, in the late 20th century by the followers of a 19th century Prussian madman by the name of Augustus Rank. Electing to leave the isolated Canadian village of their "birth," they have made their way to New York, a city known for its free-wheeling, assimilative nature. Flush with cash, the superintelligent canines take up residence at the Plaza Hotel and quickly become celebrities. However, whatever their past, it soon becomes evident that the "monster" dogs face a frightening future.

Publishers Weekly, in its starred review, asserts that Ms. Bakis has produced an "audacious, intriguing and ultimately haunting debut." Called an "effective fantasy in the tradition of Robert Louis Stevenson and Mary Shelley by the *Wall Street Journal*, *The Lives of the Monster Dogs* was judged "a dazzling, unforgettable meditation on what it means to be human" by the *New York Times Book Review*. In the opinion of *Kirkus Reviews* Ms. Bakis's "wry variation on the shaggy dog story ... [is a] vivid parable that manages to amuse even as it perplexes and intrigues." *Entertainment Weekly* directs our attention to the "melancholy ending of this memorable book" and suggests that "Bakis deserves praise so high only dogs can hear it."

OTHER MEDIA: Audiocassette (Audio Lit/abr); RECOGNITION: Winner of the 1998 Bram Stoker Award for Horror; shortlisted for the 1998 Orange Prize; *NYTBR* Notable Book of 1997; REVIEWS: *BL* 1/1/97; *KR* 11/15/96; *LATBR* 2/16/97; *LJ* 1/97; *LT* 6/14/97; *NY* 6/16/97; *NYTBR* 3/9/97; *People* 4/21/97; *PW* 12/16/96; *Salon* 2/6/97; *Time* 3/3/97; *TLS* 6/20/97; *WSJ* 3/3/97

Banks, Iain (UK)

675   *Complicity* (1993); Bantam 1996 (pbk)

Iain Banks's aggressively postmodern Scottish thriller is a chilling story of accountability in a morally bankrupt world. Its protagonist, Cameron Colley, is a self-styled gonzo reporter who is covering a series of horrifically brutal, vigilante-style killings wherein the victims are all highly unsavory characters. Colley is a late–20th Century variant on the traditional newspaper hack — cynical, hard-bitten, but also drug-abusing and addicted to S&M. While investigating the murders, Colley becomes enmeshed in a series of scandals having to do with the local nuclear submarine base and the criminal adulteration of that most sacred of all Scottish exports: Scotch whiskey.

A best-seller in Great Britain, *Complicity* is not, suggests the *Literary Review* "a book to be read by those of a nervous or squeamish disposition ... [although] the violence [while] horrifying [is], strangely, not gratuitous." The *Guardian* found *Complicity* to be "as daring and brilliant as [Bank's] third novel, *The Bridge*" and concludes "For verve and pace, it's his best yet." *Booklist*, calls Bank's novel "Dark, cynical, shocking, but immensely satisfying ... " Novelist **Donald Westlake** found *Complicity* to be "Banks at his absolute best. It isn't that you can't put this book down; it's that you don't dare put this book down."

REVIEWS: *BL* 1/15/95; *LitRrv* 9/93; *LJ* 2/1/95; *LRB* 11/18/93; *Guard* 10/31/93; *NYTBR* 2/19/95; *PW* 2/19/95; *WPBW* 2/19/95; EDITOR'S NOTE: Mr. Banks was named to *Granta* magazine's 1993 list of the twenty "Best Young British Novelists"

Banks, Russell (USA)

676 *Rule of the Bone* (1995); HarperCollins 1996 (pbk)

Rule of the Bone is a darkly comic story of a homeless teenager living on the edge of society. Growing up neglected in the rust-belt of upstate New York, 14-year-old Chappie looks for "connection" in drugs, truancy and gang allegiance. After being kicked out of his trailer park home (for stealing and flunking out of school), he joins the growing ranks of rootless, homeless adolescents who eke out a marginal, peer-driven existence on the fringes of urban America. In one of his first acts of independence, Chappie acquires a skull and bone tattoo which provides him with his new road name, "Bone." Chappie/Bone is both achingly vulnerable and dangerously unstable and he's going nowhere fast. Until, that is, he meets I-Man, an exiled Rastafarian, with whom Bone travels to Jamaica in search of his real father.

The *Chicago Tribune* calls *The Rule of the Bone* "brilliantly funny and heartfelt" and concludes that Bone is "believably young, with all the raw freshness, resiliency an sense of adventure that implies." The *New Statesman* argues that it "has an insistent, buttonholing quality even at its most neutral. But when it inhabits the coolly wised-up consciousness of Chappie aka 'Bone', it's harder to get away from than a Big Issue ambush.... This is the book that promotes Banks to the premier division of U.S. novelists." The *Times Literary Supplement* calls it "unfailingly readable' and observes that "Bone's sharp and funny comments bring an unfooled, Holden Caulfield-ish distaste to white self-loathing, and Banks offers wry, lacerating descrip-

tions of blue-collar white America, whether in the mall, at Christmas, or on packaged tours."

OTHER MEDIA: Audiocassette (Harper Audio/abr); RECOGNITION: *NYTBR* Notable Book of 1995; REVIEWS: *BL* 1/1/96; *ChiTrib* 6/11/95; *EW* 5/3/96; *LATBR* 6/23/96; *NYTBR* 12/3/95; *SLJ* 12/95; *TLS* 6/30/95

Banville, John (Ireland)

Athena (1995); Knopf 1995 (HC); Vintage 1996 (pbk); See Section 3, #175

Ghosts (1993); Random House 1994 (pbk); See Section 3, #176

The Book of Evidence (1989); Warner 1991 (pbk); See Section 3, #177

Baratham, Gopal (Singapore)

677 *Moonrise, Sunset* (1996); Serpents Tail 1996 (pbk)

Singapore surgeon Gopal Baratham has constructed a chilling, frequently offbeat tale around the investigation of a series of murders committed in a public park in central Singapore. Gratuitous homicide (robbery and/or sexual assault had been ruled out), while not unheard of, is a relative rarity in this Asian city-state with its penchant for law-and-order predicated on excessive (by Western standards, at least) physical punishment. As the novel opens, Ho Kum Menon, a young man of Chinese and Malay extraction, wakes up in a secluded area of a park to find his fiancée (Vanita Sundram) dead of a vicious knife wound. Ho Kum is, of course, the prime suspect until other bodies start turning up in the same park, murdered with the same knife that killed Vanita. The plot is enlivened by a dogged Chief Inspector by the name of Ozzie D'Cruz and by a cast of comically sinister characters including a wacky FBI behavioral scientist (on loan from the US) whose specialty is serial killers, and an over-the-top psychic with interests in seances and polygraphs.

According to *Booklist*, "This novel is engaging primarily because of its setting. Singapore, one of the world's busiest ports, is a seemingly orderly metropolis.... Yet it's also home to an incredible array of ethnicities, and the differences between races, cultures and religions, along with the inevitable conflicts between haves and have-nots, ensure that the city is filled with intrigues, friction, and corruption." *Publishers Weekly* observes that "Baratham takes the traditional mystery format apart piece by piece, then puts it together again to create a mystical and cerebral novel." *PW* concludes that "Even more impressive than the sharp characterization is Menon's measured narration. Strong, controlled writing full of concrete images keeps the ethereal subject matter in check and carries the plot along with just the right amount of skepticism."

REVIEWS: *BL* 3/1/96; *KR* 2/1/96; *PW* 2/19/96

Barnhardt, Wilton (USA)

678   *Gospel* (1993); Picador 1995 (pbk)

Wilton Barnhardt's *Gospel* is both a serious novel about faith and its ramifications and an intricate international thriller. It features Patrick O'Hanrahan, a disgraced University of Chicago professor who is hot on the trail of a "lost" gospel supposedly authored by the disciple Mathias. When O'Hanrahn abruptly disappears, Lucy Denton, a graduate student from his department, is sent to Oxford to track him down. They eventually join forces in an increasingly puzzling search which takes them to Rome, Greece, Palestine and Africa.

According to *Publishers Weekly*, "Bernhardt's massive, erudite novel turns on a trans-continental search for a lost, biblical gospel." In the view of the *Times Literary Supplement,* "What is admirable in this book is the extent to which it makes the spiritual preoccupations of its central characters emotionally credible.... [For example] Lucy's experiences ... are so particularized and concrete that we trust her spiritual life as well." *Booklist* observes that "Barnhardt has some very big metaphysical points to make, and readers willing to persevere to the fascinating conclusion will see how every thread of the multifaceted story is necessary to complete the tapestry." "A splendid novel on all counts" (*NYTBR*).

OTHER MEDIA: Audiocassette (Audio Renaissance/abr); REVIEWS: *BL* 1/15/93; *CCent* 10/12/94; *ComWl* 10/8/93; *EngJ* 11/96; *EW* 4/16/93; *LJ* 3/1/93; *NYTBR* 12/19/93; *PW* 2/1/93; *TLS* 8/4/95

Bedford, Martyn (UK)

679   *Acts of Revision: A Novel* (1996); Doubleday 1996 (HC); Bantam 1998 (pbk)

My Name is Gregory Lynn. I am thirty-five years old. I am an orphan, a bachelor, an only child from the age of four and a half. My feet are size 12, I am six feet two inches tall and weigh 263 pounds. I am not clumsy, it's just that my body sometimes misinterprets the signals emitted by my brain. I have one brown eye and one green.

Martyn Bedford's first novel tells the chilling—often blackly humorous—story of a psychopath who, having suffered significantly at the hands of his elementary-school teachers—pedagogues who seemed to enjoy humiliating him and who asked repeatedly for "revisions" of his inferior school work—decides to seek out and "revise" these tormentors from his past.

According to the *Times Literary Supplement* "On the surface, the novel is a chillingly clever variation, compellingly written and impressively structured, on the theme of revenge. Beneath that, it is a complex psychological portrait painted with a subtle and instinctive hand." *Kirkus Reviews* notes that "Thoroughly unsettling, this tale forcefully presents the workings of a deranged mind in all its complexity while retaining the page-turning pleasures of a genuine thriller." *Salon* calls *Acts of Revision* "a book about schoolboy humiliation and long-simmering revenge that should rank among the year's best and brainiest psychological thrillers."

REVIEWS: *BL* 7/19/96; *KR* 5/15/96; *LJ* 6/15/96; *NS&S* 3/8/96; *NYTBR* 9/1/96; *Salon* 1996; *TLS* 3/1/96

Benabib, Kim (USA)

680   *Obscene Bodies* (1996); HarperCollins 1996 (HC)

Kim Benabib, the son of an artist **and** an art dealer, has set his debut novel in the cynical Manhattan art world and manages to combine both satirical and thriller elements to interesting effect. *Obscene Bodies* features Stuart Finley, a young, idealistic art historian and assistant curator of Old Masters at the Metropolitan Museum of Art, and tells the story of his disillusioning plunge into the depths of New York's Soho district with its struggling artists, PR flaks, rapacious dealers and high-living low-lifes. When Stuart witnesses a murder, more than his assumptions are tested. Benabib's novel (the title of which is slang for "overhyped paintings") is filled with *roman à clef* characters.

Newsweek calls *Obscene Bodies* an "oddly affecting ... cautionary tale." The *Washington Post Book World* argues that, although Benabib's first novel is not without faults [e.g. an occasional lack of subtlety and over-reliance on flash-back narrative techniques], it is a "slick satire of the Soho art scene ... [that] rises above the jaded universe it inhabits." The *Christian Science Monitor* observes that *Obscene Bodies* is both "Keenly observant and elegantly written" and concludes that "it is perhaps a little dazzled by its own stylishness and a little chilly in its zeal to be 'cool,' but a scintillating read nonetheless." *Kirkus Reviews* calls it a "[g]entle but on-target satire [which is] buttressed by Benabib's copious and clearheaded knowledge of the world he portrays."

REVIEWS: *CSM* 11/13/96; *KR* 7/15/96; *LJ* 8/96; *NewsWk* 8/19/96; *NYTBR* 9/29/96; *WPBW* 12/1/96

Benedict, Pinckney (USA)

681   *Dogs of God* (1994); Doubleday 1994 (HC); Plume 1995 (pbk)

Pinckney Benedict's debut novel is set in and around a West Virginia drug ranch run by Tannhauser, a 12 fingered backwoodsman turned drug lord, whose main cash crop is marijuana. The Mafia has a controlling interest in the operation and, when it suspects some local hanky-panky, it sends Bodo and Toma, a couple of "louche and dandy" Mafiosi to look into the matter. Additional local (and imported) characters play supporting roles: a corrupt sheriff, a severely unbalanced loner, assorted gun-runners and petty criminals, federal agents, and Goody, an amateur boxer.

According to the *Washington Post Book World* "the setting is a sinister version of West Virginia, where every drive ends in an accident, every canebrake hides a corpse, vicious packs of dogs prey on the vulnerable, and marijuana is king." The *Times Literary Supplement* calls *Dogs of God* "a savage and philosophical novel" further pointing out that "against a brutal and beautiful landscape, a deep backwoods in which the dark ages and the twentieth century meet ... people become both animals and beasts, and the calm, ambiguous tone of Benedict's writing poses questions, not only about his characters but about the wider world from which they seem so cut off." *Kirkus Reviews* argues that "Too many of Benedict's oddball secondary characters are drawn too broadly and disappear with a stroke. Which is particularly annoying in a novel that nevertheless manages to suck you into its wild intrigue." *Publishers Weekly* notes that *Dogs of God* is "a taut, muscular thriller [which] ... hurtles the reader toward a chillingly apocalyptic climax replete with high-tech weaponry and old-fashion treachery" and concludes that "this is an ambitious and skillful literary thriller, not to mention a rip-roaring read."

OTHER MEDIA: Audiocassette (Chivers/ unabr); REVIEWS: *BL* 10/1/93; *KR* 11/1/93; *NS&S* 7/1/94; *NewYork* 1/3/94; *NY* 4/11/94; *NYTBR* 2/6/94; *PW* 10/11/93; *TLS* 7/1/94; *WPBW* 3/6/94

Berger, Thomas (USA)

682 *Suspects* (1996); William Morrow 1996 (HC)

On a normal day in a typical small town, Mary Jane Jones, perplexed by her neighbor's failure to answer her phone or her doorbell, finally gets up enough nerve to try the back door, and, finding it unlocked, goes in to have a look. Thomas Berger, an acknowledged master of black comedy and absurdist humor, has, in his 20th novel used the murder mystery format to tell a deeper, darker tale of family and friendship in contemporary American society.

According to the *Washington Post Book World* "From the very first pages, when an elderly widow discovers the slashed bodies of gorgeous Donna Holland and little Amanda, the story-telling grips the reader and never lets go.... In plot *Suspects* recalls a classic police procedural — who killed the Hollands and why? — and it deftly reproduces the lingo of law officers and psychiatrists and nut cases; yet the overall tone remains slightly Olympian, irony tempered by wistfulness: gin and bitters." In the opinion of the *Library Journal*, Berger "takes on the 'detective story' with all its situational clichés and hackneyed language. The joy of it is that he does it with such a straight face...." *Kirkus Reviews* calls the novel a "deadpan deconstruction" and concludes that "fans of the genre under dissection are more likely to be bemused than enlightened."

RECOGNITION: *NYTBR* Notable Book of 1996; REVIEWS: *BL* 5/1/96; *KR* 6/1/96; *LJ* 7/96; *NYT* 9/29/96; *PW* 7/1/96; *WPBW* 9/29/96

Binstock, R.C. (USA)

683 *The Soldier* (1996); Soho 1996 (HC)

R.C. Binstock's second novel, a "subtly gothic" psychological drama set in rural New Hampshire, features a spurned lover, an ill-advised romantic entanglement, and a ghostly presence. Philip, a middle-aged writer, has taken up residence in an old house (inherited from a distant relative) in order to devote himself to finishing his latest novel, an historical tragedy involving a Civil War soldier. Quite unexpectedly, his young, beautiful and decidedly enigmatic niece arrives seeking refuge.

According to the *Boston Book Review*, "Any character's inner life is a vast and strange landscape; Binstock has here recorded a set of precise geographics, set against a difficult moral plot. Most disturbing is the sense of fate-and-not-fate, the idea that events are both inexorable and preventable." *Booklist* notes that the reader is "seduced by this contemplative tale's quiet intensity [even as he becomes] increasingly aware of a dark, foreboding force...." The *New York Times Book Review* found *The Soldier* to be "an ambitious, evocative novel with a shocking denouement that is a satisfying example of poetic justice."

REVIEWS: *BBR* 5/1/96; *BL* 5/1/96; *KR* 3/1/96; *LJ* 5/1/96; *NYTBR* 8/18/96; *PW* 4/1/96

Bowen, Peter (USA)

684 *Notches* (1996); St. Martin's 1996 (HC); 1998 (pbk)

The fourth volume in Peter Bowen's Montana-based mystery series features his Metis detective Gabriel Du Pre. In the latest installment, Bowen's fiddle-playing, part-time deputy (of mixed Cree, Chippewa and French mountain-man descent) uses his "instinctual, hunter-like approach" (*BL*) to outwit a serial killer who has been burying the bodies of young women in the remote Montana sagebrush. Gabe is "assisted" by a host of intriguing characters: FBI agents Harvey "Weasel Fat" Wallace (a culturally conflicted Blackfoot) and Anna Pidgeon (a pistol-packing psychologist), long-distance trucker, Rolly Challis, and local would-be seer Young-Man-Who-Has-No-Name. Although generally reviewed as genre mysteries, *Notches* and the earlier titles - *Wolf, No Wolf* (1996), *Specimen Song* (1995) and *Coyote Wind* (1994) — are regularly applauded for their colorful and exceptionally well-realized characters, effective use of Metis speech patterns, and the delineation of a Montana "so alive" as to function almost as an extra character.

Publishers Weekly calls *Notches* "an absorbing tale of vengeance," while *Entertainment Weekly* judges it: "A haunting tale, punched out in arresting rhythms of speech powerful as a tribal drummer." According to *Booklist*, "Flowing around the case are the supporting characters and atmospheric elements that Du Pre fans have come to love," and concludes that Bowen's series "is on the verge of major commercial success."

REVIEWS: *BL* 3/15/97; *EW* 2/21/97; *KR* 12/15/96; *PW* 12/2/96; *NYTBR* 3/2/97

Boyd, William (UK)

685   *Armadillo* (1998); Random House 1998 (HC)

William Boyd's 7th novel, a darkly comic quasi-thriller set in contemporary London, features a young, attractive insurance adjuster (born Milomre Blocj to Romanian-Hungarian parents) who has reinvented himself in his adopted London. Lorimer Black, as he now calls himself, heads up the loss-adjusting office of Fortress Sure, a powerful insurance conglomerate. As the story opens Lorimer's reasonably well-ordered existence appears to be fraying somewhat and the discovery of a client, Mr. Dupree, hanging from a rafter in his burnt out factory, certainly doesn't help.

According to the *Times Literary Supplement*, Boyd's "extremely enjoyable" novel, in addition to being "a London comedy ... is also in some senses a thriller. It hints continually at a dimension of menace, though its exponents take a while to give Lorimer their full attention — not as long, however, as it takes Lorimer to work out that conspiracy and concealment may amount not merely to an attitude but will have consequences for him, unless he takes steps to save his neck." The *London Times* observes that "*Armadillo* purports to be a literary comedy but sits somewhere between the two stools. Yet what Boyd lacks in psychological depth he makes up for with story-telling prowess." *Booklist* calls Boyd "a deft craftsman" who, in his latest novel "continues to explore his frequent themes of iden-

tity, insecurity, and the fragility of life...." English novelist **Geoff Nicholson** (*WPBW*) found it: "Everything good fiction should be ... it begins with a jolt ... and then goes on to become even better."

RECOGNITION: *LATBR* "Best Fiction of 1998"; *NYTBR* Notable Book of 1998; REVIEWS: *Econ* 3/14/98; *LST* 2/15/98; *LT* 2/19/98; *NS* 3/6/98; *NYTBR* 11/22/98; *Obs* 2/15/98; *TLS* 2/20/98; EDITOR'S NOTE: Mr. Boyd was named to *Granta* magazine's 1983 list of the twenty "Best Young British Novelists."

Bradfield, Scott (USA)

686   *What's Wrong with America* (1994); St. Martin's 1994 (HC); 1995 (pbk)

Set in southern California and widely described as an example of "California gothic," Bradfield's second novel takes steady aim at an array of peculiarly American preoccupations. Purporting to be the journal of Emma O'Hallahan (to be read by her "progeny" after her death), it tells the story of Emma's unusual approach to personal liberation — beginning with the murder and backyard burial of Marvin O'Hallahan, her husband of 45 years.

According to the *Library Journal*, *What's Wrong with America* targets "suburban consumerism, dysfunctional families, New Age cults, and popular psycho-babble." John Sutherland, writing in the *London Review of Books* suggests that Bradfield's California is "America squared ... the place where you go to find more America than you ever thought possible." *Booklist*, concludes that Bradfield's novel is a "fast, funny skewering of the fads and foibles of middle-class 'life in these United States' in the late twentieth century."

REVIEWS: *BL* 8/94; *KR* 6/15/94; *LJ* 8/94; *LRB* 4/7/94; *LST* 1/23/94; *NS&S* 4/8/94; *NYTBR* 10/2/94; *PW* 7/11/94; *TLS* 2/11/94

687   *The History of Luminous Motion* (1990); St. Martin's 1996 (pbk)

Scott Bradfield's debut novel explores with "ferocious humor" (*TLS*) the disturbed psyche of an eight-year-old boy with an Oedipal complex the size of California. Philip Davis and his mother are drifters, moving from town to town, from one seedy motel to another — and Philip likes their rootless freedom just fine. When his mother finally decides to get married and "stay put," Philip's reaction is, to say the least, deadly.

According to the *New York Times Book Review*, *The History of Luminous Motion* "is a dizzying journey into one boy's very complicated interior life ... [and is] both a gripping tale of a haunted young mind and a penetrating, frightening symbolic look at the state of childhood in America." The *Times Literary Supplement* found Bradfield's

book to be "a powerful whimsy of a first novel …
a revenge for the helplessness of childhood" and
concludes that "Its force comes from the shear
venom with which Mr. Bradfield's unnaturally precocious eight-year-old protagonist views the adult
world." In the view of novelist **Andrew Klavan**,
"Bradfield captures Philip's doomed battle against
conformity with compassion and dark wit…. *The
History of Luminous Motion* is a coming-of-age
novel in which childhood is a grand madness and
maturity an inevitable death"

REVIEWS: *LATBR* 10/22/89; 9/9/90; *LJ* 9/1/89;
NYT 8/18/89; *NYTBR* 8/19/90; *PW* 6/22/90; *TLS*
12/8/89; *VLS* 9/89; *WPBW* 9/24/89

Bram, Christopher (USA)

688 *Gossip* (1997); NAL-Dutton 1997
(HC);1998 (pbk)

Set variously in New York City's East Village
and Washington, D.C., Christopher Bram's sixth
novel, is a tautly-paced story of sexual and political intrigue. Its narrator, Ralph Eckhart, an insouciant, liberal-minded, gay bookstore employee,
meets Bill O'Connor (a Washington, D.C.–based
journalist) in a homosexual chat room and is intrigued enough to make a visit to the capital city.
When Ralph discovers Bill's ultra-conservative
affiliations (he's about to bring out a book trashing
the Democratic president's activist wife), the relationship sours. No one is more shocked than Ralph
to learn of Bill's murder.

Booklist observes that "Bram's musings about
gay love are relentlessly smart, hip and sunny" and
concludes that, although Ralph becomes a touch
whiny by the end of the novel, Bram "maintains wit
and suspense all the way through the crackerjack
surprise ending." *Kirkus Review* calls *Gossip* "a
closely-wrought psychological portrait of both a
decent man and the sharply divided gay world he
inhabits." Novelist Robert Plunkett (*NYTBR*) describes *Gossip* as "a wonderfully told tale of human
misadventure" and concludes that "A final twist
deepens the plot considerably … [and what starts
as] a superior piece of literary entertainment …
[becomes] in its final chapter … something much
more — an examination of some hard truths about
politics, homosexuality and the sort of family values that to straight back to Sophocles." In the view
of the *Washington Post Book World*:"This isn't the
stuff of great literature. But it does make for very
entertaining fiction."

RECOGNITION: Nominated for the 1997
Lambda Book Award; REVIEWS: *Advocate* 5/2/95;
BL 3/1/97; *KR* 2/1/97; *NYTBR* 6/1/97; *PW* 2/10/97;
WPBW 6/8/97

Brown, Rosellen (USA)

689 *Before and After* (1992); FS&G 1992
(HC); Dell 1993 (pbk)

The Reisers, a modern, city-bred couple, have
put down roots in a picturesque New Hampshire
town. Carolyn, a pediatrician, and Ben, an artist
and stay-at-home father, have created a comfortable if, by local standards, somewhat unconventional life for themselves and their two children.
Competent, cerebral Carolyn, the family's primary
income-provider, is happy in her small-town practice, while Ben revels in his dual role. As the novel
begins, Dr. Reiser has been called to the emergency
room of the local hospital where a teenager's blood-
ied and battered body has just been brought. When
the Reisers' teenage son, Jacob (who had been dating the girl), is accused of her murder, they are
forced to confront the unthinkable and, ultimately,
to choose between the urge to protect one's child
and the dispassionate pursuit of justice.

According to the *Times Literary Supplement*,
"Rosellen Brown, an American poet and novelist,
has written a profound novel about a family which
has to find out about itself. Witnesses, clues, evidence, the grand finale in the courtroom, these are
the periphery of this story, as the sickening sequence of suspicion and knowledge is reversed."
The *Library Journal* notes that "Deep questions of
loyalty, honesty, and love are forced to the surface
in this psychologically riveting tale."

OTHER MEDIA: Audiocassette (S&S Audio/
abr; Recorded Bks/unabr); a film version starring
Meryl Streep and Liam Neeson was released in
1995; REVIEWS: *AtlM* 10/92; *LJ* 9/1/92; *Nation*
9/28/92; *NewR* 11/2/92; *NewsW*k 8/31/92; *NYRB*
1/14/93; *NYTBR* 8/23/92; *TLS* 3/5/93; *VLS* 9/92;
WRB 11/92; EDITOR'S NOTE: See Nadine Gordimer's
The House Gun #715

Bryers, Paul (UK)

In a Pig's Ear (1996); FS&G 1996 (HC); See
Section 8, #994

Busch, Frederick (USA)

690 *Girls* (1997); Harmony 1997 (HC);
Fawcett 1998 (pbk)

Frederick Busch's 18th work of fiction combines a tautly organized thriller plot with a sensitively drawn character study. Jack — a 44-year-old
Vietnam veteran and lifelong resident of a climat-
ically-challenged town in Upstate New York — is a
security guard at an exclusive liberal arts college regarded by many locals as little more than a play-
ground for the sons and daughters of the upper
middle class. Over the years, Jack has rescued his
share of coeds from the usual range of adolescent
excess. Traumatized by the recent death of his infant daughter, Jack has begun to see all females as
inherently vulnerable. When the 14-year-old
daughter of a local minister is abducted he becomes
obsessed with her rescue.

Donna Rifkind (*WPBW*) praises *Girls* for its "pitch perfect dialogue, skillfully contrived plot and authentically wintry atmosphere" and notes that she was quite unprepared "for the seductive beauty of this very disturbing book." In the view of the *Chicago Tribune*, *Girls*, which is based on the author's short story "Ralph the Duck" "does not achieve the same high level of synthesis [as the shorter version but] is still a painful pleasure. The protagonist is a prickly and worthy creature, and Frederick Busch is a superb writer. The second chapter alone is worth the price of admission."

READING GROUP GUIDE; RECOGNITION: *NYTBR* Notable Book of 1997; *LATBR* "Recommended Title" 1997; *PW* "Best Books" 1997; REVIEWS: *BL* 1/1/97; *ChiTrib* 3/16/97; *LJ* 2/1/97; *NYTBR* 3/16/97; *PW* 11/25/96; *WPBW* 3/9/97; *WSJ* 3/20/97

Byatt, A.S. (UK)

691   *Possession* (1990); Random House 1991 (pbk)

Widely praised both here and in England (where it won the prestigious Booker Prize in 1990), *Possession* explores the tragic romance between two 19th century poets (Randolph Henry Ash and Christabel Lamotte) and the parallel relationship of their biographers (young British academicians, Maud Bailey and Roland Mitchell). The novel is fueled initially by the benign (albeit competitive) scholarly interest which consumes both Maud and Roland as they begin to tease out the details of what appears to be an intriguing (possibly illicit?) relationship between two major Victorian writers. However, the tantalizing nature of the early clues attracts a wider circle of eager (bordering on rapacious) academics, and, as the possibility of a literary "coup" looms large, the pursuit intensifies.

In the view of *The* (London) *Times*, Byatt "combines the drive of the thriller with the measured exploration of human nature more normally associated with the 19th century novel." English novelist **Anita Brookner**, writing in *The Spectator*, found *Possession* to be "teeming with more ideas than a year's worth of ordinary novels…. A brilliant start to the publishing season and one which it will be very difficult to overtake." According to the *Women's Review of Books* "the most satisfying aspect of this novel is the intricacy of its structure. Although the notion of scholarly sleuths unraveling the mystery of a past relationship is common enough, Byatt's achievement is to make the Victorian protagonists … every bit as alive as their modern counterparts. Soon we too are searching for answers: how did the relationship between LaMotte and Ash ultimately manifest itself, we wonder, as we piece together the jigsaw puzzle of suicides and seances, distrust, distress and disappearance…."

OTHER MEDIA: Audiocassette (Recorded Bks/unabr); READING GROUP GUIDE; Vintage Books; RECOGNITION: Winner of the 1990 Booker Prize and the *Irish Times* Literary Award; REVIEWS: *CSM* 11/16/90; *LATBR* 10/28/90; *LRB* 3/8/90; *LT* 3/1/90; *NS&S* 5/16/90; *NY* 11/19/90; *NYRB* 3/28/91; *NYT* 10/25/90; *NYTBR* 10/21/90; *PW* 8/24/90; *Spec* 3/3/90; *TLS* 3/2/90; *WRB* 5/91

Cameron, Peter (USA)

692   *Andorra* (1996); FS&G 1996 (HC); Plume 1998 (pbk)

Set in a highly fictionalized version of the European country of the same name, Peter Cameron's third novel is narrated by a handsome, enigmatic former antiquarian bookseller by the name of Alexander Fox. A recent arrival, via the night-train from Paris, to Andorra's capital city of La Plata, Fox is fleeing a painful personal tragedy which appears to have resulted in the death of his wife and daughter. He admits to having chosen Andorra as a destination because it has "haunted" him ever since first encountering Rose Macaulay's description of it in her satirical 1926 novel *Crewe Train*. Fox is soon adopted by a number of eccentric, yet well-connected, local denizens (including a bi-sexual Australian couple and a kayaking doyenne) who are distinguished as much by what they keep to themselves as by what they reveal to our narrator. On the day of Fox's arrival in Andorra, the body of a young man is found floating in the harbor.

According to the *Washington Post Book World*, "What may sound pulpily melodramatic in outline is adroit and disturbing in the telling." Scottish novelist **Margot Livesey** (*NYTBR*) calls *Andorra* a "wonderful" novel and further observes "Like so many good novels, *Andorra* ends badly for the characters but well for the reader. Mr. Cameron steers us through the final, fantastical events of Alex's story with an unfaltering hand. In the real world, we might pause to question the rapid denouement. In the world of *Andorra*, we know better." In the view of novelist **Scott Bradfield** (*TLS*), this is a "compelling novel" in which "the voices of his characters are always utterly engaging, even when the subjects they discuss [the mystery of identity, the nature of loneliness, etc.] don't seem especially original or profound. Perhaps this is because those same voices continually reverberate with a sense of what they're not saying."

RECOGNITION: *NYTBR* Notable Book of 1997; REVIEWS: *AtlM* 2/97; *BL* 1/1/97; *KR* 1/97; *LJ* 11/15/96; *NYTBR* 12/29/96; *PW* 11/11/96; *TLS* 2/14/97; *WPBW* 1/26/97

Carr, A.A. (USA)

693   *Eye Killers* (1995); Univ. of Oklahoma 1995 (HC); 1996 (pbk)

In his debut novel, set in eastern New Mexico, Navajo/Pueblo filmmaker A.A. Carr mixes elements of Native American oral tradition and mythology with standard components of the gothic thriller. Walking to school, Melissa Roanhorse, a rebellious Navajo teenager, encounters Falke, a 1,000-year-old European vampire who has been roused from his centuries-long slumber in a nearby cave. When Melissa subsequently disappears (after causing a disturbance at school) her grandfather — a Navajo sheepherder armed with potent tribal chants and a deep knowledge of the spirit world — sets off in search of her. He is joined in his quest by Melissa's teacher, Diana Logan, an earnest young Irish American who is ill-prepared for what lies ahead.

According to the *New York Times Book Review*, "If you think this sounds like Dracula- meets-Geronimo, think again ... A.A. Carr's novel is much better than that. The grandfather and the English teacher are very well-drawn characters, the satisfying solitude of the one playing off nicely against the anxiety-ridden loneliness of the other." *Publishers Weekly* observes that Carr "delivers a fast-paced novel that will grab readers by the jugular," and concludes that the book, which "sizzles with erotic excitement ... makes a fine addition to the publisher's American Indian Literature and Critical Studies series."

REVIEWS: *BL* 3/1/95; *BloomR* 5/95; *KR* 1/1/95; *NTRBR* 4/30/95; *PW* 2/20/95

Carroll, Jonathan (USA/Vienna)

694 *Kissing the Beehive* (1998); Doubleday 1998 (HC)

In Jonathan Carroll's "adroit entertainment" (*LT*), a thrice-divorced thriller writer, suffering from a severe case of writer's block, is drawn back to the unsolved murder of Pauline Ostrava, a beautiful, headstrong teenage girl he knew 30 years ago in high school. He returns to his hometown of Crane's View, New York, where his digging into the past is viewed by someone as especially threatening. Before long a string of new murders must be solved to make sense out of the 30-year-old crime.

According to the *Library Journal*, "Carroll's book is strung like a piano wire whose surprising final note only sounds on the last page. Stephen King has aptly compared Carroll to Alfred Hitchcock." *Kirkus Reviews* observes that *Kissing the Beehive* is a "gripping and often quite amusing literary thriller ... [with] a smashing and surprising climax" and concludes that "If this be Carroll's attempt to enter the commercial mainstream, more power to him. With this terrifically entertaining tale, he has improved the quality of the water." The *L.A. Times* points out that "Jonathan Carroll's

fiction seduces you.... He's a movie generation virtuoso with the literary sensibility of a metaphysical eccentric." *USA Today* argues that "the best reason to read *Beehive* is to know throughout that if you like this even a little, you will love the rest of Carroll's canon."

REVIEWS: *KR* 11/1/97; *LT* 6/13/98; *LJ* 12/97; *NYTBR* 3/29/98; *USA Today* 2/26/98; *WPBW* 1/1/98; EDITOR'S NOTE: Jonathan Carroll, the son of a successful screen writer and a famous Broadway actress, has been considered something of a "cult novelist" since the publication of his first novel *The Land of Laughs*. He lives and writes in Vienna.

Childress, Mark (USA)

695 *Crazy in Alabama* (1993); Ballantine 1994 (pbk)

Mark Childress's *Crazy in Alabama* tells the intertwined stories of young Peejoe Bullis and his "wacky" Aunt Lucille. It is the summer of 1965 and 12-year-old Peejoe has been sent to Industry, Alabama, to live with his uncle, a small-town mortician and county coroner. Peejoe, a thoughtful, broad-minded sort of fellow, soon finds himself caught up in a series of racial disturbances triggered by the integration of the town's swimming pool. Meanwhile, across town, Aunt Lucille has murdered her abusive husband, abandoned her six "bratty kids" and lit out for California in a stolen Cadillac. On the seat beside her is her husband's severed head ... in a Tupperware lettuce keeper.

According to novelist Robert Plunkett (*NYTBR*), Mr. Childress has "managed to confront every [southern Gothic] cliché, every convention of the genre head on and pound it into submission, so that his novel seems not only fresh and original but also positively inspired." The *Library Journal* reviewer was impressed by Childress's ability to construct a "funny, insightful and poignant tale with full-blooded, passionate characters [that] ... captures the essence of our memories of the middle sixties." *Kirkus Reviews* concludes that "Flames of passion and rebellion confront the darkness of intolerance in Alabama, with many a macabre twist in Childress's latest southern-fried coming-of-age tale."

RECOGNITION: *NYTBR* Notable Book of 1993; REVIEWS: *BL* 6/1-15/93; *EW* 8/6/93; *KR* 5/13/93; *LJ* 6/1/93; *NYTBR* 8/22/93; *NS&S* 11/19/93; *PW* 5/31/93; *TLS* 10/29/93

Christopher, Nicholas (USA)

696 *Veronica* (1996); Doubleday 1996 (HC); Avon 1997 (pbk)

On a snowy night in February in lower Manhattan, Leo, a photographer, meets a mysterious woman, and his life is totally altered. Veronica is a woman like no other Leo has ever met: although corporeal she is effectively weightless, appears to have no trouble reading Leo's mind, and keeps a Tibetan Guard dog by her side. Nicholas Christopher, a highly regarded poet, grounds his debut effort (called a phantasmagorical "page-turner" by more than one reviewer) in a version of contemporary Manhattan. Before his tale is fully told, the author incorporates time travel, a missing father, magic, sadistic villains and disappearing stairways.

According to the *Library Journal* "Christopher has unlocked a rich fantasy world, that despite being dangerous, is extremely enticing." *The New Statesman* found Christopher's novel to be "written in beautifully simple prose ... a joy from first page to last." *Publishers Weekly*, in its starred review, concludes that "This darkly seductive tale maintains a dreamy urgency that keeps the reader intrigued until its poignant, hypnotic conclusion."

READING GROUP GUIDE; REVIEWS: *BL* 12/15/95; *LATBR* 3/3/96; *LJ* 1/96; *NS&S* 4/19/96; *NYTBR* 2/11/96; *PW* 11/6/95; *WPBW* 4/14/96; EDITOR'S NOTE: Nicholas Christopher, an accomplished and widely published poet, was born, and currently lives, in New York City where he is affiliated with a number of universities. A graduate of Harvard University, he is a past winner of the prestigious Guggenheim Fellowship.

Coe, Jonathan (UK)

House of Sleep (1997); Knopf 1998 (HC); Vintage 1999 (pbk); See Section 3, #188

Collignon, Rick (USA)

697   *Perdido* (1997); MacMurray & Beck 1997 (HC); Avon 1999 (pbk)

Perdido is a postmodern mystery with more than a touch of irresolution in its climax. Set (as was his first novel) in the fictional New Mexican town of Guadalupe, it features Will Sawyer, a relative "new-comer" (he'd lived in Guadalupe for a mere 20 years) who gradually becomes obsessed with the mysterious (unresolved) death of a young girl found hanging from a local bridge in 1968. Will angers most of the town (including his girlfriend Lisa) in his relentless search for answers.

The *Library Journal* observes that Collignon "describes tense relationships between ethnic and racial groups while delving into the concept of identity and providing subtle touches of magical realism." *Booklist* suggests that "those who don't mind a little mystery in their literary fiction ... will discover a well-written novel, whose simple and direct narrative contrasts ironically with the multitude of secrets that burden the lives of its well-drawn characters." The *New York Times Book*

Review concludes that "*Perdido* is a one-sitting read, a novel that captivates and surprises all the way to its chilling end."

REVIEWS: *AtlM* 8/97; *BL* 7/19/97; *LJ* 1/15/97; *NYTBR* 8/25/96; *PW* 6/16/97

698   *The Journal of Antonio Montoya* (1996); MacMurray & Beck 1996 (HC); Avon 1997 (pbk)

Rick Collignon has set his debut novel in the tiny New Mexican town of Guadalupe and tells the story of a Ramona Montoya, a 44-year-old artist, who has returned to the dusty backwater town of her ancestors to paint in peace. Soon after settling in, her brother and sister-in-law are killed in a bizarre car accident (involving a wayward cow) and she brings their son Jose home to live with her. Ramona soon realizes that she and the youngster are "not alone." In fact, the pair appear to be sharing the house with a whole passel of dead relatives who routinely help themselves to food and occasionally borrow the car. When one of them gives her the faded 1924 diary of Antonio Montoya, an illustrious forbear, standard concepts of time are challenged as historical events elucidated in the diary become interwoven with events in the present.

The *Library Journal* observes that *The Journal of Antonio Montoya* is: "Strongly reminiscent of ... Garcia Marquez" and concludes that "this is an enchanting work by a new writer." The *Atlantic Monthly* points out that "Mr. Collignon's novel interweaves intriguing ideas on the relation between art and religion and between family history and family solidarity, doing this obliquely through a story in which half the characters are charming, amiably meddlesome ghosts." According to the *Times Literary Supplement The Journal* "is a novel of dialogues: between the traditional and the modern; between Spanish and English; between the ghostly imaginings of magical realism and the clear-sighted imagery of early Hemingway. It is by such dialogues that Rick Collignon negotiates the world of the border. One hopes it is a world he will continue to explore."

REVIEWS: *AtlM* 9/96; *LJ* 5/1/96; *NYTBR* 8/25/96; *PW* 4/28/96; *TLS* 9/19/97

Crews, Harry (USA)

Mulching of America (1995); S&S 1995 (HC); Scribner 1996 (pbk); See Section 7, #876

Davis, Thulani (USA)

699   *Maker of Saints* (1996); Scribner 1996 (HC); Viking 1997 (pbk)

Thulani Davis's second novel, a story of murder and revenge, is set in the "edgy" New York City art community. Alex Decatur, a young and beautiful black artist, is found dead outside the apartment she shares with Cynthia "Bird" Kincaid and, although suspicion is immediately trained on Alex's white boyfriend, a skeptical Bird embarks on a campaign to find out exactly who killed Alex and why. Along the way she discovers a series of video tapes (featuring Alex) which raise troubling doubts about how well she knew her friend. Ms. Davis's novel appears to be based on the 1985 death of Ana Mendieta, a New York–based artist. Although her husband, a sculptor, was the prime suspect, he was never convicted of the crime.

According to *Publishers Weekly*, *Maker of Saints* is "a riveting crime story that enters some of the darker corners of the artistic soul...." The *Washington Post Book World* describes *Maker of Saints* as "an intelligent, ambitious stew of friendship, jealousy, the crossroads of myth and lies, the nature of woman's creative expression and the ennui-riddled world of certain postmodern African Americans." *Booklist* observes that *Maker of Saints* "combines cultural elements from African American and Spanish traditions, including mystical and spiritual conventions...." and concludes that "Davis has written a book quite removed from the contemporary homegirl variety."

REVIEWS: *BL* 9/15/96; *LJ* 9/1/96; *NYTBR* 11/17/96; *PW* 8/26/96; *WPBW* 12/30/96.

Dawson, Carol (USA)

700 *Body of Knowledge* (1994); Algonquin 1994 (HC); Washington Square 1996 (pbk)

Carol Dawson's prickly, multigenerational second novel, called an "intellectual bodice ripper ... [complete with] Southern gentility, irresistible passion, and revenge" by the *Times Literary Supplement*, is narrated by the 500-pound Veronica Grace Ransom, the last of the Ransom dynasty. Veronica, whose hypothalamus was thought to be damaged following a childhood bout with measles, has rarely left the family mansion since her birth in 1947. She has long-occupied herself with the family's history, mostly passed along — in the grand old Southern tradition — by the compassionate and selfless Viola, the Ransom's black housekeeper. Veronica, over time, has become the repository of the whole bloody history of the Ransom clan, and what a history.

According to *Booklist*, "Dawson's dialogue is sly, her scandals irresistible, and her subtext on the danger of repression provocative." *Publishers Weekly* notes that Dawson's "labyrinthine plot — a 'potboiler' in the grandest sense — is transformed by a dark vision and poetic language into a work of the highest literary caliber." The *Times Literary Supplement* concludes that "It ought to matter that we cannot [in Dawson's latest novel] distinguish between fiction and allegory; that we cannot tell whether Dawson's writing is ironic, or in earnest. Strangely, these things don't matter: cloudy, almost

Spenserian under analysis, *Body of Knowledge* is a gripping story."

REVIEWS: *BL* 8/94; *LJ* 8/94; *NS&S* 8/4/95; *PW* 7/18/94; *TLS* 7/14/95

701 *The Waking Spell* (1992); Algonquin 1992 (HC)

Set in the author's native Texas in 1959, *The Waking Spell* features Sarah Grissom, an engaging youngster who, during her annual visit to her grandmother Northgate's rambling old home (at the age of seven), first becomes aware of a malignant spirit which has haunted the lives of Northgate women since the turn of the century.

In the view of *Kirkus Reviews*, *The Waking Spell* is a "nearly perfect" debut novel "that explores the simmering rage passed through four generations of emotionally stunted southern 'ladies'— an unusually confident and original debut that unveils the spiritual anesthetization behind the gracious feminine smile ... courageous, revelatory, and, in the end, deeply moving." Described by the *Library Journal* as an "extended feminist history, *Waking Spell*, according to *Publishers Weekly*, is "a book to be savored and shared" for "Dawson's evocative powers and poetic eye make the long, hot days and twilights of a Texas Summer come alive."

REVIEWS: *KR* 8/1/92; *LJ* 9/15/92; *NYTBR* 12/27/92; *PW* 8/17/92

Dibdin, Michael (UK)

702 *Così Fan Tutte* (1997); Pantheon 1997 (HC); Random House 1998 (pbk)

In his genre-stretching crime novels, Michael Dibdin often features Venetian-born, Rome-based detective Aurelio Zen, a phlegmatic fellow who is not above bending the law to suit his needs. In *Così Fan Tutte*—wherein Dibdin borrows freely from the opera buffa tradition — Zen has taken a posting in Naples, a Mafia stronghold, where he attempts to help a wealthy woman (the widow of a prominent Mafioso) snatch her daughters from the amorous clutches of a pair of "lowlifes." Meanwhile a sinister garbage truck has been seen in the vicinity of some high-profile Mafia assassinations.

Publishers Weekly observes that "In his spry new mystery constructed along comically operatic lines, Italian copper Aurelio Zen finds that his quest for the simpler life leads to a new beat in Naples and to a series of convoluted criminal conundrums" and concludes that the "richly talented" Dibdin is "able to fashion the mystery into an endless series of deft variations ... " In the view of *Kirkus Reviews* "As in the best farces, practically everybody, including Zen, turns out to be in disguise — the outrageous variety of masquerades ranges far beyond anything Mozart ever thought of." *Booklist* contends that "what this multileveled, wildly entertaining novel is all about [is] Aurelio Zen's life, [which, if] twisted just a few degrees moves from [Roman Polanski's] Chinatown to opera buffa." *BL* concludes that "The same thing could be said of all our lives, and it is that tantalizing prospect that gives this unique story its zest — and its appeal to lovers of Mozart, Italy, crime fiction, and the joys of the absurd."

REVIEWS: *BL* 4/15/97; *KR* 5/1/97; *LJ* 5/1/97; *NYTBR* 5/11/97; *PW* 4/7/97

Didion, Joan (USA)

703   *The Last Thing He Wanted* (1996); Knopf 1996 (HC); Vintage 1997 (pbk)

Joan Didion's first novel in 12 years, a foray into thriller territory, is an intricate, fast-moving tale of international arms dealers, conspiracies and assassinations. It is set, for the most part, in the midst of covert US operations in Central America. The narrator of this "chronicle of unease" attempts to unravel the mystery of how and why the pampered wife of a powerful Californian came to be involved in a dangerous undercover operation violently played out on a Caribbean island.

The *New York Times Book Review* points out that *The Last Thing He Wanted* shares with (other) Didion novels "a marvelous notation of disaffection and despair...." Maria Arana-Ward (*WPBW*) points to Didion's ability in this new novel "to knit together north south history, politics and an irresistible story line: woman sets out to understand her father and wanders into hell instead." The *L.A. Times Book Review* contends that "Didion has created a menacing world where the reader is held hostage." *Booklist* notes that Didion's "narrative voice has never been edgier or more cryptic and full of pain, and her irony and suspense have never been sharper" and concludes that "[a]s this tale of evil for evil's sake unfolds ... we recognize Didion's genius for portraying the type of slippery, behind-the-scenes people who actually shape history."

OTHER MEDIA: Audiocassette (Random Audio/abr); RECOGNITION: *Booklist* "Editors' Choice" 1996; *NYTBR* Notable Book of 1996; *L.A. Times* "Best Books" 1997 (Top Ten); REVIEWS: *BL* 7/96; *LATBR* 8/25/96; *LJ* 7/96; *LRB* 10/31/96; *NYRB* 10/31/96; *NYTBR* 9/8/96; *NewR* 10/14/96; *NY* 9/16/96; *Time* 9/9/96; *WPBW* 9/8/96; *WRB* 12/96

Disch, Thomas M (USA)

704   *The Priest* (1995); Knopf 1995 (HC)

Thomas M. Disch's provocative novel *The Priest* is subtitled "A Gothic Romance" and is patterned (albeit loosely) after that most famous of all 18th century gothic romances: Matthew Lewis's *The Monk*. Set in Minneapolis, Disch's story revolves around Father Pat Bryce, the pastor of St. Bernadine. Father Bryce, an "activist" priest who has thrown his support firmly behind the local anti-abortion forces, is also a pedophile. The Pastor's unfortunate predilection leads to a number of plot complications including blackmail and eventually (while undergoing torture) the exchange of personalities with a 13th century bishop charged with rooting out heresy. Throughout the novel, Disch mercilessly satirizes the "institutional hypocrisies" of the Catholic Church and advances the idea that the "right-to-lifers" insistence on dominating other people's bodies is a form of rape.

Booklist observes that Disch "weaves murder, bizarre anti-abortion conspiracies, the Shroud of Turin and the Inquisition into a tight fabric of preternatural horror and blackest comedy" and concludes that he is "becoming deservedly more widely known for his tales of evil amidst the mundane." According to the *Times Literary Supplement* "little of the literary subtlety and complexity [present in] some of Disch's earlier novels" can be found in this work, however, it does contain "considerable moral complexity." Novelist Tom de Haven calls the novel "by turns creepy and darkly funny." The *Yale Review* calls Disch's series of "gothic" novels (of which *The Priest* appears to be the last) "a large achievement."

REVIEWS: *BL* 3/15/95; *LJ* 3/15/95; *NYTBR* 4/23/95; *TLS* 11/11/94; *WPBW* 4/27/95; *Yale R* 4/95; EDITOR'S NOTE: *The Priest* is the third in a series of novels "that are at once comprehensible within a genre and have aesthetic and perhaps other ambitions well beyond the usual scope of such books...." (*Yale Review*). The first was *The Businessman: A Tale of Terror* (1984) in which Disch "exposed the terror of rampant commerce and masculinity" (*TLS*); the second was *The M.D.: A Horror Story* (1991) in which he "dwelt on oppressive medical omniscience and greed" (*TLS*).

Dobyns, Stephen (USA)

705   *The Church of Dead Girls* (1997); Henry Holt 1997 (HC); 1998 (pbk)

In the sleepy town of Aurelius a psychopath has murdered — and severed the hand of — the town floozy. Soon after, young girls begin disappearing "without a trace" except, most disturbingly, for a bundle of their clothing. By the time the third teenager disappears, the town (an economically depressed upstate New York community), begins experiencing a sort of social meltdown as suspicion is trained on those members of the community who are in any way "out of step." Suspects include the gay hairdresser, the Algerian teacher at the local college (plus the small quirky knot of "Marxist" academics' he has attracted), and a supercilious high school biology teacher. As the police investigation progresses, disturbing intimations of nymphomania and schizophrenia begin to surface; and, as the investigation drags on, there are many within the town who would prefer to take matters into their own hands. Stephen Dobyns, a poet who also writes genre mysteries has, in *The Church of Dead Girls*, written a contemplative, cerebral thriller which transcends genre boundaries.

According to *Booklist*, Dobyns "is not as interested in the pathology of the serial killer in their midst as he is in the pathology that exists within us all." The *Times Literary Supplement* observes that "subject matter of Dobyns' books may repel, but he knows the value of careful construction, good writing and characterization, and that for inducing fear, less is more."

OTHER MEDIA: A film version was released by HBO in 1998; REVIEWS: *BL* 4/15/97; *KR* 4/1/97; *TLS* 10/31/97; *WPBW* 6/8/97

Dooling, Richard (USA)

706 *Brain Storm* (1998); Random House 1998 (HC); Picador 1999 (pbk)

Richard Dooling's foray into the "cyberthriller" arena explores — in pacy, absurdist fashion — a number of contemporary issues: the American obsession with sex, "hate crimes" and the excesses of the legal profession. *Brain Storm* is set in St Louis, in an all-too-recognizable near future, and features a cantankerous judge by the name of Stang and a "Webhead" lawyer by the name of Joe Watson. Watson has been coerced by Stang into representing a rotter by the name of James Whitlow, an avowed white supremacist accused of murdering a deaf black poet. *Brain Storm* intermingles biting social satire with an off-beat murder mystery, throwing in libidinous monkeys, brain researchers and "yuppie moms from hell."

According to columnist George Will (*WPBW*) *Brain Storm* "is a hilarious novel about hate ... [and] a serious novel of ideas, including Dooling's idea that laws mandating enhanced penalties for hate crimes creates, in effect, thought crimes." Novelist Colin Harrison (*NYTBR*) suggests that Dooling's "narrative Niagara probably requires caffeine or some other smart drug for maximum enjoyment. To read [it] ... is like cramming for an exam, yet deeply pleasurable; great swaths of biological and legal abstraction are shoehorned into the reader's head in a hopped-up frenzy that neither distracts from the seriousness of the dialectic nor diminishes the reader's astonishment at the info-rich, logic-switchbacking, jargon juxtaposing riffs machine-gunned out of the characters's mouths." *Kirkus Reviews* concludes that "Dooling has such a gorgeously rampaging take on brain chemistry, hate-crime law, and the grounds for con-

tempt of court that you may find yourself, like Joe Watson, losing sight of the brilliantly overinflated conflict at the heart of this postmodern fable."

OTHER MEDIA: Audiocassette (Books-on-Tape/unabr); RECOGNITION: *NYTBR* Notable Book of 1998; REVIEWS: *KR* 1/1/98; *NYT* 4/24/98; *NYTBR* 4/19/98; *PW* 2/23/98; *WPBW* 6/4/98

Dufresne, John (USA)

707 *Louisiana Power & Light* (1994); Norton 1994 (HC); NAL-Dutton 1995 (pbk)

John Dufresne's second novel is set in the bayou community of Monroe, Louisiana, and features Billy Wayne, hapless yet curiously optimistic member of the cursed Fontana clan, "the most executed white family in the history of Louisiana." When young Billy, the last of his line, is consigned to a Catholic orphanage, his neighbors are relieved. Some think Billy Wayne may yet escape his familial destiny. Others are less optimistic. Dufresne's style has been likened (more than once) to a combination of Faulkner and Barry Gifford.

According to novelist **Jill McCorkle** (*NYTBR*), Dufresne "offers a plot line as complex as the network of backwoods roads these people and their ancestors have committed to memory." The *Library Journal* points appreciatively to the author's ability to "distill high comedy from intense pain, philosophical insight from bayou murkiness."

RECOGNITION: *NYTBR* Notable Book of 1994; REVIEWS: *BL* 7/94; *KR* 5/1/94; *LJ* 6/1/94; *NYTBR* 7/31/94; *PW* 5/2/94

Dunmore, Helen (UK)

708 *Talking to the Dead* (1996); Little Brown 1997 (HC); 1998 (pbk)

British novelist Helen Dunmore's *Talking to the Dead* is a chilling tale of sibling rivalry and sudden infant death. Nina, an uninhibited London-based photographer, travels down to Sussex to assist her more domesticated sister Isabel who has just had her first baby. Before long, the reader becomes acutely aware that the sisters, unusually close throughout their lives, are grappling with disturbing childhood memories of a brother who died in infancy.

In the opinion of *Kirkus Reviews*, *Talking to the Dead* "combines the suspense of a Hitchcock thriller with a captivating family drama" to produce a debut novel that is "Sophisticated, sensual, frightening and remarkably visual...."According to *Booklist*, "Dunmore is a deeply sensual writer: heat and shimmer, food and water, texture and scent are beautifully realized." The *Washington Post Book World* observes that Helen Dunmore "takes a tale that could drive a thriller and weaves her linguistic spell around it. The result is brilliant and terrifying, an unbeatable combination." The *New States-*

man concludes that Ms. Dunmore's fourth novel "is a beautifully crafted, delightfully tense novel exploring rich themes of sisterhood and maternal conflict."

RECOGNITION: Winner of the first Orange Prize (a major British literary prize awarded exclusively to female novelists); REVIEWS: *BL* 5/1/97; *KR* 4/1/97; *LitRev* 7/96; *LST* 6/8/97; *NS* 7/19/96; *NY* 8/11/97; *NYTBR* 6/1/97; *PW* 5/5/97; *TLS* 7/12/96; *WPBW* 8/10/97

Ellis, Alice Thomas (UK)

Fairy Tale (1996); Moyer Bell 1998 (HC); See Section 4, #357

Forbes, Leslie (Canada/UK)

709   *Bombay Ice* (1998); FS&G 1998 (HC)

Roz Bengal (born Rosalind Benegal to a Scottish father and Indian mother) is a London-based radio journalist who specializes in "true crime." As the novel opens, Ms. Bengal is drawn back to her native India by an unsettling letter from her sister, the wife of a prominent Bombay film director, who has reason to believe that her husband has killed his first wife, an aging actress. In the course of the novel it becomes clear that Roz is a rather unlikely heroine (she drinks too much, for a start) who has found herself, on more than one occasion, submitting to (maybe even provoking) sexual abuse.

Entertainment Weekly found the novel's "strange brew of arcana, erotica and violence" to be "heady" and concluded that "*Bombay Ice* manages to be both a brainy thriller and a psychological striptease." In the view of *Kirkus Reviews*, Forbes "keeps [her story] humming, in a lively narrative whose really rather formidable intellectual content (including, among other subjects, meteorology, alchemy, forensic pathology and at least three kinds of forgery) is agreeably leavened by good old melodramatic standbys like a looming monsoon, a cobra poised to strike, and numerous hairbreadth escapes." The *Times Literary Supplement* notes that "Forbes has a gift for well-paced, well-blocked flurries of violent action and for moments of terrified stillness" and concludes that "Her heroine is a memorable creation, all the more attractive for being flawed."

OTHER MEDIA: Audiocassette (Soundelux Audio/abr); REVIEWS: *EW* 8/7/98; *KR* 6/1/98; *LATBR* 7/10/98; *LT* 1/20/98; *NYT* 7/23/98; *NYTBR* 7/23/98; *PW* 4/27/98; *TLS* 4/3/98; *WPBW* 7/5/98

Gifford, Barry (USA)

Baby Cat-Face (1995); Harcourt Brace 1995 (HC); Harvest 1997 (pbk); See Section 3, #295

Girardi, Robert (USA)

710   *Vaporetto 13* (1997); Delacorte 1997 (HC); Dell 1998 (pbk)

Vaporetto 13, Robert Girardi's third novel, a ghost story set in a contemporary Venice, is redolent of both high finance and the reek and rot of history. Jack Squire, a trader in international currencies, has been sent to Venice to check out the political scene preparatory to a buy-up of lira. While there, Jack meets a mysterious woman, Caterina Vendramin, who feeds stray cats in a deserted square while most of Venice sleeps. The beautiful, ethereal Caterina will profoundly change Jack's life.

According to *Kirkus Reviews*, *Vaporetto 13* "is an erotically charged, dreamlike novel ... [that] is both exquisite and eerie." The *New York Times Book Review* observes that "With this artful novel, he invites us to put aside our rational skepticism and enter a world where the past is still hauntingly present." Novelist **Jonathan Carroll** observes that *Vaporetto 13* is "easily the most evocative and disorienting Venetian tale since *Don't Look Now*." According to the *Times Literary Supplement* "There are moments of closely imagined strangeness — a barge of dead cats chugs past, and Caterina is oddly talented at roulette. And the weirdness is balanced by the quotidian Venice of Jack's colleagues, a bourgeois city of baptisms and adultery." The *Washington Post Book World* concludes that in *Vaporetto 13* Girardi "has written a slick, fast-paced and subtly erotic novel to tell an ancient truth: It is not until a man makes love with death that he discovers his soul."

REVIEWS: *KR* 8/15/97; *NYTBR* 11/30/97; *PW* 7/28/97; *TLS* 3/6/98; *WPBW* 10/13/97

711   *The Pirate's Daughter* (1996); Delacorte 1996 (HC); Delta 1997 (pbk)

Robert Girardi's second novel is a fast-paced tale of modern piracy and the slave trade and features Wilson Landers who, in thrall to a copper-haired enigmatic beauty by the name of Cricket, abandons his long-term girlfriend and signs on as a cook on a billionaire's yacht. When the yacht is captured off the cost of Africa by a pirate gang — led, surprisingly enough, by Cricket's father — Wilson realizes he's in for some rough sailing.

According to *Publishers Weekly*, *The Pirate's Daughter* is "a sinister and lusty romantic adventure propelled by a fluid narrative style laced with disturbing undertones ... a clever and intriguing balancing act, a fantasy with enough real world roots to make it all seem horribly plausible...." In the view of *The (London) Times*, Girardi's novel is "Thrilling and imaginative...." *Kirkus Reviews* concludes that "Riding high on the widespread raves for his delightful debut, *Madeleine's Ghost* (1995), Girardi offers up a tale of modern pirates and the slave trade that is not without its charm, though falling far short of the mark left by its predecessor."

OTHER MEDIA: Audiocassette (Audio Renaissance/abr; Books-on-Tape/unabr); REVIEWS: *KR* 10/15/96; *LST* 4/6/97; *LT* 3/22/97; *NYTBR* 2/16/97; *PW* 10/28/96; *WPBW* 3/29/97

712 *Madeleine's Ghost* (1995); Delacorte 1995 (HC); Dell 1996 (pbk)

Ned Conti, a graduate student living in a rent-controlled and apparently haunted apartment in one of New York city's meaner neighborhoods, needs a stipend to complete his doctoral studies in history. Father Rose, pastor of St. Basil's church in Brooklyn, needs an historian to review a mountain of moldy documents that may lead to the canonization of Sister Januarius, a saintly, little-known nun who died in St. Basil's parish in 1919. God knows, Brooklyn could certainly use a saint.... A parallel love story, set in and around a sensual and steamy New Orleans, features Ned's one-time lover, the beautiful, dangerously unstable Antoinnete.

Madeleine's Ghost—called an "enchanting debut novel" by the *Washington Post Book World*, and "a ghost story with an inexhaustible panoply of sensational effects" by *Newsday*—impressed a wide range of reviewers. *Booklist* noted that "Girardi's tightly written tale unfolds with an intriguing cast of characters ... and achieves a near flawless rhythm" as the narrative builds. The *L.A. Times Book Review* calls Conti's first novel "part love story, part ghost story, [and] always absorbing."

OTHER MEDIA: audiocassette (Recorded Bks/unabr); REVIEWS: *BL* 6/1/95; *LATBR* 8/6/95; *LJ* 4/15/95; *Newsday* 7/8/95; *NYT*BR 8/6/95; *PW* 5/15/95; *WPBW* 10/29/95

Godden, Rumer (UK)

713 *Cromartie V. the God Shiva: Acting Through the Government of India* (1997); William Morrow 1997 (HC); 1998 (pbk)

In her latest novel Rumer Godden returns to India and weaves a story around an actual event, the theft of a statue of the god Shiva and the resulting lawsuit in which the god Shiva, acting through the Government of India, became the plaintiff. Michael Dean, the young British attorney who is assigned to the case meets (while staying at Patna Hall, a seaside hotel in south India), and falls in love with Artemis, an archaeologist with a hidden agenda. The tale incorporates a number of fictive elements including art, religion, love, class, race and greed.

According to the *Times Literary Supplement* "'If you've been in a country as a child, it is, as it were, in your bones', is the explanation given in this novel of a rising young British barrister's attachment to India. It could equally apply to Rumer

Godden, who, at the age of ninety, here returns to the land of her birth and the setting of some of her most popular earlier tales." According to *Kirkus Reviews*, Ms. Godden's latest is "a delight for Godden's many followers, one encompassing the experience of the beauties and traditions of India, the richness of its religions, and Godden's own essential dash of gallantry and grand gesture." The *London Sunday Times* concludes that Ms. Godden's novel is "a graceful fable, as brief as its title ... is prolonged."

REVIEWS: *BL* 9/15/97; *KR* 9/1/97; *LJ* 10/1/97; *LST* 1/11/98; *LT* 11/27/97; *PW* 9/15/97; *TLS* 2/13/98

Goldman, Francisco (USA)

714 *Long Night of the White Chicken* (1992); Atlantic-Grove 1998 (pbk)

In his debut novel, Francisco Goldman tells a suspenseful tale involving the sort of human rights abuses that have become commonplace in many Latin-American countries. Set partly in Boston and Guatemala, Goldman's story focuses on the death, at the hands of terrorists, of Flor de Mayo Puac—a young woman who (after having spent part of her life in Boston) had returned to Guatemala to run an orphanage in Guatemala City—and the subsequent investigation mounted by her lover Luis Moya Martinez, an investigative reporter, and Roger Graetze, an American friend with Guatemalan family connections.

In the view of the *Christian Science Monitor*, Goldman "captures with great skill and poetic beauty the history of Guatemala, the corruption caused by its military rule, and the terror resulting from human rights abuses committed there." According to the *Library Journal* "Flor is an appealing character whom the author uses successfully to ignite our curiosity about Guatemalan culture and reflections on our own private lives." The *Times Literary Supplement* suggests that Goldman's use of Roger Graetze, a "rambling, incompetent narrator [who is] ... plainly out of his depth ... allows Guatemala itself to occupy the emotional center of the novel" and concludes that "There is a great vitality about the country that emerges in this remarkable novel."

RECOGNITION: Winner of the 1993 Sue Kaufman Award; nominated for the 1993 PEN/Faulkner Award; REVIEWS: *Choice* 1/93; *CSM* 1/8/93; *LitRev* 3/93; *LJ* 6/1/92; *LRB* 3/11//93; *NYTBR* 8/16/92; *PW* 4/13/92; *TLS* 1/15/93

Gordimer, Nadine (South Africa)

715 *The House Gun* (1998); FS&G 1998 (HC); Penguin 1999 (pbk)

In her thirteenth novel Pulitzer Prize–winning novelist Nadine Gordimer appears to be exploring — among other issues — the question of parental responsibility and parental loyalty. When the Lindgards, a white, upper-middle class South African couple discover that their son has committed a murder (a *crime passionnel*), using a loaded gun which has been kept, for all the usual security reasons, in the house that he shared with a group of 20-something professionals, they are forced to grapple with their own complicity. How have they failed their son? How has South African society, which has become inured to violence, contributed to the crime?

Kirkus Reviews calls Ms. Gordimer's most recent novel a "passionately schematic moral anatomy of a murder." British novelist **Margaret Forster** (*Literary Review*) argues that "This is fiction as it should be, serious in intent and execution and yet gripping and deeply satisfying." Michiko Kakutani (*NYT*) disagrees, pointing out that "Whereas Ms. Gordimer's earlier novels tended to open into subtle examinations of the relationship between individuals and society, society and history, *The House Gun* is little more than a courtroom thriller, dressed up with some clumsy allusions to apartheid's legacy of violence and the uses and misuses of freedom." The *Library Journal* notes that this is a "novel of ideas that investigates troubling issues of race and gender ... [and] a subtle character study that avoids easy stereotypes."

RECOGNITION: *NYTBR* Notable Book of 1998; REVIEWS: *BL* 10/15/97; *KR* 1/98; *LATBR* 1/18/98; *LitRev* 2/98; *LJ* 11/1/97; *NYT* 1/16/98; *PW* 10/20/97; *TLS* 2/13/98; *WSJ* 1/20/98

Hamilton-Paterson, James (UK)

716   *Ghosts of Manila* (1994); FS&G 1994 (HC)

James Hamilton-Paterson's seventh novel is set in a Philippines awash in the worst excesses of a "copy cat" third world culture. "The Spanish Inquisition taking place in a Dunkin Donuts" is how principle character John Prideaux, a middle-aged filmmaker-turned-anthropology student doing "field work" in the barrios of Manila, describes it. In furtherance of his thesis on transcultural psychopathology, Prideaux is investigating the local concept of "amok," the state of near frenzy reached, apparently, when one is pushed "too far." Additional plot elements include an outbreak of vampirism in a local shantytown, a "fake" priest dispensing morally uplifting advice, and a Chinese drug baroness operating out of her family's mausoleum.

The *Library Journal*, in its starred review, observes that in Manila "role-playing and deception are part of the national fabric. As an ex-American protectorate, the country's entire administrative structure is simply a copy or 'ghost' of the American system [and Hamilton-Paterson] plays a daz-

zling set of variations on the ghost metaphor." *Commonweal* observes that "The novel wears its considerable learning lightly, offering us archaeological snippets of ancient Chinese settlement and trade, the mad history of Imelda Marcos's 'edifice complex,' the seedy and violent underworld of Manila, and accounts of savage anti-terrorist conflicts 'in the south'.... The spectral call for social justice, for some sort of response not so much to the hand of God or to fate but to 'the hand of man which beats you to a pulp' is the preoccupation of this [haunting] book."

REVIEWS: *BL* 10/15/94; *ComW* 4/21/95; *KR* 8/1/94; *LJ* 10/1/94; *NYTBR* 11/27/94; *WPBW* 12/30/94

Hansen, Ron (USA)

717   *Atticus* (1995); HarperCollins 1997 (pbk)

Early on in Ron Hansen's fourth novel, Colorado rancher Atticus Cody receives word that his youngest son, Scott, has committed suicide in the seedy little seaside Mexican town of Resureccion. Scott — as a teenager — had been responsible for the death of his mother in a car accident, and has never recovered from the pain and guilt, and, despite considerable talent as an artist, has led a bohemian's life in various out-of-the-way-spots in the US and Mexico. Atticus makes the painful journey to Mexico to reclaim Scott's body and, while waiting for permission to fly the body home for burial, stays at his son's home in Resureccion and meets a number of his friends and acquaintances. Atticus begins to suspect that his son has actually been murdered. Hansen tells his story from the perspectives of both the father and the son.

According to *Kirkus Reviews, Atticus* "succeeds as both a mystery and as a story of deep love and misunderstanding between a father and son." In the view of Joseph J. Feeney, writing in *America*, "In *Aspects of the Novel* the most sensible book I have ever read about fiction, E.M. Forster writes that 'the final test' of a novel will be our affection for it. I have great affection for Hansen's *Atticus*." The *Nation* observes that "With terse dialogue and canny understatement, Hansen impresses an indelible image of father and son, and dramatizes the issues that caused the breach between them...." *Booklist* claims that "*Atticus* is a wonderful novel, and taken together with the earlier *Mariette in Ecstasy* (1991), clearly establishes Hansen as a major talent."

OTHER MEDIA: Audiocassette (Recorded Bks/unabr); RECOGNITION: Nominated for the 1997 PEN/Faulkner Award and the 1996 National Book Award; *Booklist* "Editors' Choice" 1996; *NYTBR* Notable Book of 1996; REVIEWS: *America* 5/25/96; *BL* 12/1/95; *KR* 12/1/95; *Nation* 4/15/96; *NYTBR* 2/18/96; *PW* 12/11/95

Hitchcock, Jane (USA)

718 *Trick of the Eye* (1992); NAL-Dutton 1993 (pbk)

Jane Stanton Hitchcock's debut novel is a spine tingling tale featuring a fabulously wealthy widow, an opulent Long Island estate, a long-ago murdered daughter and a "spinsterish" trompe l'oeil artist. Faith Crowell). Faith has been hired to paint a series of murals on the wall of the estate's ballroom. Before long, she begins to realize that she bears an unusual resemblance to the daughter whose gruesome death has never been solved.

According to the *New York Times Book Review*, *Trick of the Eye* "hums briskly along, thanks to Faith's lucid, flexible voice.... Jane Stanton Hitchcock, who has had four plays produced off Broadway, knows how to write crackling dialogue that expresses character while steadily, stealthily advancing the plot." *Library Journal* observes that Hitchcock's "first work of fiction is distinctly dramatic. While paced to the rhythm of performance, this nouveau gothic tale of deceit is studded with descriptive gems." *Publishers Weekly* concludes that "Dramatist Stanton's first novel is a thoroughly satisfying thriller — simultaneously luscious and ladylike as it traces the cast-and-mouse relationship between a wealthy old New York dowager and the solitary artist she hires to help re-create her past."

RECOGNITION: Nominated for an Edgar Award; REVIEWS: *LJ* 7/93; *NYTBR* 10/18/92; *PW* 8/92; *TLS* 3/5/93; *WPBW* 9/6/92

Hoffman, Alice (USA)

719 *Practical Magic* (1995); Berkley 1996 (pbk)

Gillian and Sally, descendants of a 17th century ancestress who narrowly missed being burned at the stake, are being raised by their maiden aunts in a spooky old house on Magnolia Street. A decidedly matriarchal family, there have been Owenses in this small New England town since colonial times. In fact, Owens women have practiced their "inheritance" here for more than 200 years. Specializing in love potions, the aunts have frequent night visitors — desperate women seeking remedies for broken dreams and romantic failure. The girls, once grown, are understandably eager to escape their inheritance.

According to *Entertainment Weekly*, in Hoffman's latest novel, "Spells are cast, a dead criminal causes the rampant bloom of lilacs, and the two main characters ... have latent powers that allow them to see ghosts and inspire undying love." Novelist **Mark Childress** (*NYTBR*) found Hoffman's tale to be "charmingly told and a great deal of fun. Dark comedy and a light touch carry the story along to a truly gothic climax, complete with heaving skies and witchery on the lawn...." In (*TLS* reviewer) Lorna Sage's opinion, *Practical Magic* is "a particularly arch and dexterous example of [Hoffman's] narrative powers. You don't even have to be charmed to find it an intriguing act — not 'magic realism', though it's sometimes billed that way, more, Erica Jong meets Garrison Keillor, and they live happily ever after...."

OTHER MEDIA: Audiocassette (S&S Audio/ abr; Recorded Bks/unabr); a film version was released in 1998; RECOGNITION: *NYTBR* Notable Book of 1995; REVIEWS: *BL* 3/15/95; *EW* 6/9/95; *LJ* 5/15/95; *NewsWk* 7/17/95; *NYTBR* 6/25/95; *PW* 3/20/95; *SLJ* 11/95; *TLS* 7/5/96

720 *Turtle Moon* (1992); Berkley 1993 (pbk)

Alice Hoffman's *Turtle Moon* is a steamy Southern mystery with overtones of magical realism. The story is set in Verity, Florida, a town known for its wilting humidity and for the annual migration of sea turtles who periodically mistake Verity's street lamps for the moon. On one particularly oppressive night, a woman is murdered as she does her laundry and her baby (who was asleep in a laundry basket) is kidnapped. Two life-hardened characters, local cop Julian Cash and Lucy Rosen, a transplanted New Yorker with a juvenile delinquent for a son, join forces to solve the murder.

British novelist **Shena MacKay** (*TLS*) notes that "Sometimes the writing slips into slickness and is a little on the sentimental side, but overall its acute observation set in bizarre, lush imagery makes it a pleasure to read" and concludes that *Turtle Moon* "celebrates makeshift happiness tinged by melancholy and cautious redemption with a rare generosity of spirit." Novelist **Frederick Busch** (*NYTBR*) observes that "Ms. Hoffman writes quite wonderfully about the magic in our own lives and in the battered, indifferent world" and concludes that *Turtle Moon* contains "a magnificent examination of a troubled child about whom the readers will care enormously." The *London Review of Books* argues that "This material for a Faulknerian comedy is made into sticky romantic mush.... The writing remains stylish, but mush is mush."

OTHER MEDIA: Audiocassette (Brilliance/ unabr & abr); RECOGNITION: *NYTBR* Notable Book of 1992; REVIEWS: *BL* 3/15/93; *EW* 7/9/92; *LitRev* 7/92; *LJ* 2/15/92; *LRB* 8/6/92; *NYTBR* 4/26/92; *TLS* 6/19/92

Hogan, Linda (USA)

721 *Mean Spirit* (1990); Ivy 1991 (pbk)

Native American poet and essayist Linda Hogan's debut novel is set on an Osage reservation in the 1920s at the dawn of the Oklahoma oil boom. The plot is driven by a series of violent deaths widely assumed to be the work of a group of white men who are trying to frighten the Indians from their once worthless, but now seemingly oil-rich, land. As the novel opens, Nora Blanket has just witnessed the murder of her mother.

According to the *Library Journal*, Linda Hogan "writing in a spare, compact style ... sketches the bewilderment, hope, greed, and ultimate tragedy brought on by sudden (mis)fortune in this fine, sad first novel." The *School Library Journal* claims that "Young Adults will enjoy the suspense and unexpected twists of the storyline, but will also find it thought-provoking and unsettling." *Publishers Weekly* concludes that Ms. Hogan "mines a rich vein of Indian customs and rituals, and approaches her characters with reverence, bringing them to life with quick, spare phrases. Her absorbing novel pays elegiac tribute to the slow and irrevocable breakup of centuries of culture." Barbara Kingsolver (*LATBR*) argues that "although the history of Native Americans since colonization is a fairly predictable story of betrayal and land theft, this chapter is a particular shocker. Only a poet could have made it both shocking and beautiful to read."

REVIEWS: *LATBR* 11/4/90; *LJ* 11/1/90; *NYTBR* 2/24/91; *PW* 11/90; *SLJ* 4/91; *WRB* 4/91; *WLT* Win '91

Homes, A.M. (USA)

The End of Alice (1996); Scribner 1997 (pbk); See Section 3, #297

722 *In a Country of Mothers* (1993); Vintage 1994 (pbk)

A.M. Homes, chronicler of urban life *in extremis*, has crafted a psychological thriller which explores the fine line between sanity and obsession. When therapist Claire Roth becomes convinced that her new patient, Judy Goodman, is actually her daughter given up for adoption at birth, she uses her professional status to probe Judy's past.

According to the *New York Times Book Review*, "half the book is devoted to Claire (who doesn't) seem to have an inner life independent of her obsession.... [However] emotional dependency is like that.... And so, in spite of the questions readers may ask themselves, the entanglement at the center of *In a Country of Mothers* keeps accumulating power as the narrative rushes to a surprising, fitting conclusion." Although judging Ms. Homes' novel an "intriguing if ultimately disappointing debut" *Kirkus Reviews* observes that *In a Country of Mothers* is characterized by "[s]nappy dialogue, [a] transparently clear style, and characters handled with just the right amounts of secrecy and acerbity."

RECOGNITION: *NYTBR* Notable Book of 1993; REVIEWS: *BL* 4/15/93; *KR* 3/1/93; *LJ* 8/93; *NYTBR* 5/23/93; *PW* 3/15/93

Hospital, Janette Turner (Australia/Canada)

723 *Oyster* (1996); W.W. Norton 1998 (HC); 1999 (pbk)

Janette Turner Hospital's seventh novel is set in the Australian outback in the opal mining town of Outer Maroo where the "locals" are a hardy, intransigent lot: gun-toting, hard-working, xenophobic, scripture-reading, and government-wary." When the mysterious and charismatic Oyster arrives on the scene and establishes a commune referred to as "Oyster's reef" on the outskirts of town (to which many of the more disaffected members of the community are drawn), the stage is set for disaster. Although Oyster appears to be employing what amounts to slave labor in his cult-controlled opal mines, the townspeople are, by and large, accepting of the local guru and the questionable goings on at the "reef." One day, two parents searching for their missing children arrive in Outer Maroo and the march toward Armageddon begins in earnest.

According to *New Statesman and Society*, *Oyster*, a novel about "demagoguery, mass hysteria and the closed societies in which they flourish ... is cunningly constructed: told from different view points, it moves forward and backward in time. Its tight plotting and ventriloquial characterization give it the grip of a thriller...." *Booklist* calls *Oyster* a "genuinely hypnotic novel," in which Ms. Hospital "writes of the lure of cults not with the outraged eyes of a moralist but with an artist's sensitivity to mood and character." *Kirkus Reviews* observes that "Echoes of Waco, Heaven's Gate and Jonestown combine with intimations of apocalypse in a stunningly evocative story of life in a remote Australian hell-hole — a place where evil is as pervasive as the heat, goodness as rare as rain" and concludes that *Oyster* is a "deep and harrowing journey ... into the recesses of the soul and then back into the light, all recorded in luminous prose." According to *Publishers Weekly*, Hospital has created "her most powerful and dazzling novel to date. In sensuous prose, feverish with the cadences of mystery and doom, sometimes hallucinatory but always meticulously controlled, she spins a story eerie in its timeliness and credibility." The *New York Times Book Review* calls *Oyster* a "half-surreal novel set in a dreamscape Australia, populated by frontiersmen and cultists whose consciousness, warped by extreme conditions ignites a combustive disaster."

RECOGNITION: *PW*'s Best '98 Fiction; *NYTBR* Notable Book of 1998; REVIEWS: *BL* 3/15/98; *Econ*

7/11/98; *KR* 1/15/98; *NYTBR* 3/22/98 & 12/6/98; *PeopleW* 3/30/98; *PW* 1/12/98; *Time* 4/6/98

724 *The Last Magician* (1992); Ivy Books 1993 (pbk)

Janette Turner Hospital's sixth novel features a group of former friends who grew up together in Brisbane, Australia, and who share a terrible secret. The group includes: Cathie, a successful television producer; Charlie, a Chinese-Australian photographer; Robbie, a judge; and Cat, a dangerously self-destructive resident of "the quarry" a ragged, crime-riddled Sydney neighborhood. Although long-separated, the four have been drawn back together at mid-life, unable to escape the traumatic event that binds them.

According to the *Australian Book Review*, Janette Turner Hospital, in the *Last Magician*, "takes us into Dante's dark wood and down into his inferno." *Publishers Weekly* observes that thus is "a mesmerizing study of the effects of a dark secret on the people who must live with it.... [Ms. Hospital] proves herself a magician with words and narrative structure." In the view of novelist Edward Hower (*NYTBR*), "The real magic at work [in *The Last Magician*] is, of course, the writer's ... [Ms. Hospital] knows how to cast a spell that makes us as eager as her narrator to uncover the truth.... She fills her novel with evocative settings, characters we care deeply about and language that is entrancingly lyrical. *The Last Magician* is an ambitious, intense and satisfying book."

REVIEWS: *AusBkRev* 6/92; *Age* 5/2/92; *BL* 9/1/92; *GW* 8/2/92; *LRB* 9/24/92; *NYTBR* 9/13/92; *PW* 6/29/92

Hustvedt, Siri (USA)

725 *Enchantment of Lily Dahl* (1996); Holt 1996 (HC); 1997 (pbk)

Set in a darkly realized rural Minnesota town, Siri Hustvedt's second novel features Lily, a dreamy nineteen-year-old waitress (she works the early morning shift at the Ideal Cafe) and aspiring actress. Lily plans to move to New York City but, in the meantime, she has landed a role in a summer production of *A Midsummer's Night Dream*. She also manages to fall obsessively in love with a recently arrived painter who, in intriguing all-night sessions, is painting the more eccentric residents of the town. When, in rapid succession, Lily becomes the object of one of her customer's menacing attentions and "Lily-like" apparitions begin appearing around town, she is forced to plant her feet more firmly on the ground.

In the view of *Publishers Weekly*, Hustvedt has written a "coming of age story with Kafka-esque trappings and a mystery veneer ... [and, in addi-

tion] has created a charming and scrappy heroine." According to *Entertainment Weekly*, *The Enchantment of Lily Dahl* "works as a ghost tale, romance, and coming-of-age story, but it goes deeper. Hustvedt uses images of twinning to explore themes of age and youth, art and life, and truth and fiction with exquisite subtlety and control." The *Washington Post Book World* calls *The Enchantment of Lily Dahl* "archly gothic" and a "dark and brooding and sinister version of Garrison Keillor's Lake Wobegon." *Kirkus Reviews* was less enthusiastic, pointing out that the novel contains "[m]ystery, murder, and provincial caricatures, all in a readable but curiously dusty mix from a writer whose aims seemed higher the first time around."

OTHER MEDIA: Audiocassette (Airplay/abr); REVIEWS: *EW* 11/22/96; *KR* 7/1/96; *LJ* 9/1/96; *LT* 11/21/96; *NYTBR* 10/20/96; *PW* 7/1/96; *TLS* 11/29/96; *WPBW* 10/31/96

726 *The Blindfold* (1992); W.W. Norton 1993 (pbk)

Siri Hustvedt's debut novel — set in a decidedly off-kilter and disturbingly sinister New York City — is neatly divided into four sections. In the first, Iris, the narrator (a graduate student at Columbia University) lands a job which consists of cataloging the objects that once belonged to a murdered woman. In the final three sections, Iris is confronted with her boyfriend's possible homosexuality, is hospitalized for debilitating migraines and has an affair with one of her professors.

As the *Literary Review* observes "Hustvedt, a Minnesotan, lives in New York, and the city, particularly downtown Manhattan, leaves its neurotic, soiled imprint all over the novel, her first. This is a New York shared with such as Mary Gaitskil and Hustvedt's husband Paul Auster. Modernist themes — alienation, troubled identity, the irrational — are given contemporary trappings and fixed in the collapsing city." According to novelist David Plante (*Yale Review*), *The Blindfold* "is about evil, but, more, it is about identity, or the fragmenting of identity ... [and this preoccupation] in all its obviousness is like a sharply cut crystal that reflects the space around it: a very deep and frightening darkness." As *Belles Lettres* points out "[t]hings happen to Iris, not the other way around, and, although she approaches life with intelligence and even fearful pleasure, one has the distinct sense that if she lets herself go in this inscrutable world ... there will be nothing left of her." The *Library Journal* concludes that "Hustvedt's powerful metaphors and haunting descriptions combine to make this a striking first novel that deserves public attention."

REVIEWS: *BellesL* Win '93/94; *KR* 2/1/92; *LitRev* 2/93; *LJ* 3/15/92; *NS&S* 3/12/93; *NYTBR* 6/27/93; *TLS* 2/19/93; *YaleR* 10/92

Hynes, James (USA)

727   *Publish and Perish: Three Tales of Tenure and Terror* (1997); Picador 1997 (HC); 1998 (pbk)

The three tales included in James Hynes' second work of fiction display the author's firm grasp of the elements of classic horror fiction; the fact that they are all set in academic environments makes them more intriguing still. "Queen of the Jungle" features Paul and Elizabeth who have settled into a "tenure track" marriage which requires Elizabeth to commute four days a week to Chicago. In her absence, Paul falls into a dalliance which he will most certainly regret. In "99" ("a classic innocents-abroad tale" according to *Kirkus*) a cultural anthropologist travels to a small town in rural England where he learns considerably more about pagan rituals than he had bargained for. "Casting the Runes" introduces Virginia Dunning, an academic who, fed up with a colleague's plagiarisms, forces a confrontation and finds herself face-to-face with witchcraft and sorcery.

According to *Kirkus Reviews*, "Hynes creates pungent satires of academic life while at the same time infusing them with genuine suspense and real terror." Novelist **Cathleen Schine** (*NYTBR*) concludes that *Publish and Perish* (in which "the playfulness of post-modernism keeps house with cliffhanging narrative") is "a genre book for those who don't really like genre books — pure entertainment that is not a waste of time." In the view of Michele Slung (*WPBW*) "this trio of novellas exuberantly weaves together academic satire and the dark menace of the supernatural. Concluding with a brilliant re-working of one of M.R. James's most celebrated stories 'Casting the Runes', Hynes's tour de force reminds us how much sheer *fun* a clever, creepy book can provide." *Publish and Perish* was deemed "chillingly amusing" and was recommended "with enthusiasm" by *Washington Post Book World* editor, Jonathan Yardley.

RECOGNITION: *NYTBR* Notable Book of 1997; *Publishers Weekly* Best Books (Sci Fi & Fantasy) 1997; REVIEWS: *KR* 4/15/97; *LJ* 4/15/97; *NYTBR* 8/3/97; *PW* 5/5/97; *WPBW* 6/11/97; 12/7/97; EDITOR'S NOTE: See Penelope Fitzgerald's *Gate of Angels* #542 and Andrew Klavan's *The Uncanny* #731 for additional M.R. James influences.

Irving, John (USA)

728   *A Son of the Circus* (1994); Ballantine 1997 (pbk)

John Irving's eighth novel is set in India and features Dr. Farrokh Daruwalla, a circus-loving Canadian/Indian orthopedic surgeon who not only finds time to pursue his avocation (the genetic study of dwarfs) but also writes screenplays for a widely popular series of films featuring the sneering "Inspector Dhar." Before long, the multi-talented doctor, a Swiss film star, twins separated at birth and an American hippie come together in search of a serial killer.

According to *The Economist*, Mr. Irving "is at the peak of his powers in [*Son of the Circus*]. He plunges the reader into one sensual or grotesque scene after another with cheerful vigour and a madcap tenderness for life." *Booklist* suggests that "Irving's nimble humor springs from compassionate insights into cultural and sexual confusion and alienation, baffling questions of faith and purpose and the kind of hope that thrives in even the most jaded atmosphere."

OTHER MEDIA: Audiocassette (Brilliance/abr; Bookcassette/unabr); RECOGNITION: *NYTBR* Notable Book of 1994; REVIEWS: *BL* 7/94; *Econ* 10/13/94; *KR* 7/1/94; *LJ* 9/15/94; *NS&S* 9/23/94; *NYTBR* 9/4/94; *Time* 9/12/94; *TLS* 9/2/94

Jacobs, Mark (USA)

729   *Stone Cowboy* (1997); Soho 1997 (HC); 1998 (pbk)

Mark Jacobs, an American Foreign Service Officer currently stationed in Madrid, has set his debut novel in Bolivia and features the unlikely pairing of Roger, an American drop-out and sometime drug-dealer (the "stone cowboy" of the title), and Agnes, a prim young social worker. Agnes has come to South America in pursuit of her brother, Jonathan, an idealistic young magician/adventurer who, in search of "real" magic, has fallen under the influence of a local drug lord.

"What follows" observes the *Washington Post Book World* "is a hallucinatory journey, as [wounded spirits] Roger and Agnes (like a drug-addled Bogart and a slightly neurotic Hepburn) board ramshackle buses [all named the "Bolivian Queen" and] set out after Jonathan...." *Book World* concludes that "This is a remarkable debut from a writer of great promise." *Salon* magazine observes that "Our diplomat ... knows his James M. Cain pacing, his Graham Greene jungle milieu, his Raymond Chandler similes. Furthermore, Jacobs makes the familiar unique with a magic realism that owes more to Carlos Castenada than Garcia Marquez." According to *Kirkus Reviews*, *Stone Cowboy* "is an impressive debut.... As if 'The African Queen' were mixed with 'Panic in Needle Park'."

REVIEWS: *KR* 7/15/97; *LJ* 9/1/97; *PW* 8/4/97; *Salon* 10/10/97; *WPBW* 9/30/97

Johnson, Denis (USA)

730   *Already Dead* (1997); HarperCollins 1997 (HC); HarperFlamingo 1998 (pbk)

Denis Johnson's sixth novel, aptly subtitled "A

California Gothic," features 30-something Nelson Fairchild, Jr., the disenfranchised heir to a substantial California logging fortune. Fairchild is a classic "screw up": intemperate, unreliable, imprudent, unscrupulous and lazy. He's also married to a woman he would like to see dead. Chronically short of ready cash, Fairchild is banking on a thriving marijuana plantation tucked away on his family's property. He's also managed to get himself involved in a cocaine smuggling scheme with a group of particularly nasty individuals, which, in retrospective, even he wishes he had left well enough alone. Meanwhile, the severely depressed Carl Van Ness, a man "already dead," rolls into town, presenting Fairchild with a solution literally honed in hell.

According to *Booklist*, "Johnson's northern California is a gothic land peopled by the emotionally damaged, the walking wounded veterans of wars and drugs and drug deals gone bad; it is a coast inhabited by real spirits and lost souls, madmen and hitmen." *L.A. Times Book Review* notes that "Johnson is a crafty writer, alternating between internal monologues and omniscient third-person narratives" and concludes that "His characters cross-pollinate the novel with human emotions and inclinations, from the mystical to the criminal, the addictive to the predictive...." Novelist David Gates (*NYTBR*) suggests that "it is up to the reader whether to take *Already Dead* as a superior genre entertainment, a sort of Stephen King novel for highbrows, or to take it seriously and suspend the secularist disbelief in gaga demonology" and concludes that, either way "once Johnson gets his hooks into you — it takes about two sentences — it's not so easy to maintain your bemusement and pretty much impossible to stop reading." *Salon Magazine* observes that "for the most part Johnson handles this tale, and its High Seriousness (there are allusions to Emerson, Wittgenstein, the Talmud, Whitman), with genuine aplomb. The fact that he's a wicked stylist, and a very funny one, helps." *Salon* further observes that "*Already Dead* succeeds as a chilling exploration of evil ... " and concludes that "It's a novel that leaves you feeling, as one character memorably puts it, that 'We are lost.... We are scrotally alone in this universe'."

RECOGNITION: *NYTBR* Notable Book of 1997; *LATBR* "Recommended Title" 1997; REVIEWS: *BL* 8/19/97; *KR* 6/15/97; *LATBR* 9/28/97; *NYTBR* 8/31/97; *Salon* 7/28/97

Judd, Alan (UK)

The Devil's Own Work (1991); Vintage 1995 (pbk); See Section 8, #1013

Klavan, Andrew (USA)

731 *The Uncanny* (1998); Crown 1998 (HC); Dell 1998 (pbk)

Richard Storm, a successful Hollywood producer — he has more than twenty horror films to his credit — is still reeling from a recent diagnosis of inoperable brain cancer when he abruptly abandons Los Angeles for London and a position with a small British journal devoted to parapsychology. At a free-wheeling London party, Richard is asked to read "Black Annie," (the short story upon which he based his first horror film) a goose-bump inducing tale in the style of M.R. James. During the reading Sophia Enderling, one of the other party-goers, faints when it becomes obvious to her that she has actually "lived" certain parts of Richard's story. Richard is immediately and powerfully drawn to the beautiful young woman. Additional characters include: Sophia's father, Sir Michael, the wealthy owner of an art gallery, Richard's new colleague Harper Albright (who smokes a death's-head meerschaum pipe); her gay, computer obsessed son Bernard; and Bernard's sinister father "Saint Iago."

In the view of *Publishers Weekly*, "Klavan pulls out all the stops, repeatedly blindsiding the reader with shifts in plot, tone and point of view, peopling his tale with wild eccentrics and wilder settings, winking at the genre but honoring it too, right through the over-the-top climax set in a ruined abbey on a dark and stormy night." According to the *New York Times Book Review*, "Mr. Klavan, who has a perfect sense of timing, delivers all the cliffhangers and hair pin turns that you want from a beat-the-clock suspense thriller." He also delivers characters, continues the *Book Review*, who are "so deeply human that there is nothing cheap or manipulative about their desperate maneuvers to escape the relentless second hand of fate." The *Chicago Tribune* concludes that Klavan has written a "gripping" modern ghost story.

OTHER MEDIA: Audiocassette (Brilliance Audio/unabr); REVIEWS: *BL* 10/15/97; *ChiTrib* 3/8/98; *KR* 11/1/97; *LJ* 10/15/97; *PW* 12/1/97

Lamar, Alexander

The Last Integrationist (1996); Crown 1996 (HC); Random House 1997 (pbk); See Section 2, #125

Lambkin, David (South Africa)

732 *The Hanging Tree* (1996); Counterpoint 1996 (HC); 1998 (pbk)

Kathryn Widd, a South African paleontologist (specializing in violence) has been called to Nykia Desert of Kenya to investigate a skull found at an active archaeological site and ends up investigating a murder that may, or may not, be four million years old. Ms. Widd's investigation soon begins to take on the disturbing characteristics of an ill-fated 1908 expedition to the same spot. Lambkin incorporates a brooding African veld ambiance, forensics, quantum physics, bush magic, sexual intrigue, J.S. Bach, and philosophical observations on the origins of human violence in a complex, thought-provoking literary whodunit.

In the view of the *Chicago Tribune*, "Science, passion, past and present all mingle in David Lambkin's compelling novel ... Part mystery, part meditation, Lambkin's story works on several levels." According to *Kirkus Reviews*, "Lambkin is extremely skilled in evoking the raw malevolence of backcountry Kenya. [*The Hanging Tree* is] *Heart of Darkness* from a woman's point of view." *Publishers Weekly* concludes that "Magic and science, past and present, collide in Lambkin's ... page-turning puzzler filled with suspense and a richly evoked sense of the African landscape."

REVIEWS: *ChiTrib* 10/21/96; *KR* 8/1/96; *LT* 7/18/96; *PW* 8/26/96; EDITOR'S NOTE: William Boyd's 1993 novel *Brazzaville Beach* covers similar terrain in equally intriguing fashion.

Lanchester, John (UK)

733   *The Debt to Pleasure* (1996); McClellan & Stewart 1996 (HC); H. Holt 1997 (pbk)

John Lanchester's debut novel *The Debt to Pleasure* is on its surface an account of food writer Tarquin Winot's gustatory travels through the south of France, complete with digressive essays and the occasional recipe. Described on its jacket as "Peter Mayle meets P.D. James," most readers will be alive to the (increasingly pointed) authorial hints that deeper, more sinister currents run beneath the surface of this novel.

According to Richard Bernstein (*NYT*), "Lanchester's novel is a glittering performance that, aside from its very smart conceit, provides the pleasure that comes from good writing. *The Debt to Pleasure* is Nabokovian in its wryness and delight with words, Tarquin Winot reminding us at times of another literati-sensualist, Humbert Humbert, the narrator of *Lolita*." *New Statesman* is also reminded of Nabokov: "Cocksure, obtuse, increasingly sinister, Tarquin Winot is a brilliant creation — as compelling an unreliable narrator as we have had since Nabokov set the gold standard with Charles Kinbote in *Pale Fire*." *Publishers Weekly*, in its starred review, concludes that "For those who appreciate linguistic virtuosity and light-fingered irony, who enjoy constructing a jigsaw puzzle out of tantalizing clues, this novel will be a lagniappe, fit for connoisseurs of fine food and writing."

OTHER MEDIA: Audiocassette (Audio Lit/abr); READING GROUP GUIDE; RECOGNITION: *NYTBR* Notable Book of 1996; Winner of 1996 Whitbread First Novel Award and the Betty Trask Award; REVIEWS: *BL* 2/15/96; *LJ* 6/1/96; *LRB* 3/15/96; *Nation* 5/6/96; *NS&S* 3/15/96; *NYT* 5/8/96; *NYTBR*

4/21/96; *PW* 1/29/96; *TLS* 3/16/96; *WPBW* 5/26/96

Lee, Gus (USA)

734   *Tiger's Tale* (1996); Knopf 1996 (HC); Ivy 1997 (pbk)

In the waning days of the Nixon administration, Jackson Kan, a second generation Chinese-American military lawyer, is asked to take on a sensitive top secret mission: to investigate a series of troubling occurrences (involving, among other things, the disappearance of a former colleague) at a remote military base in Korea. Kan agrees to accept the assignment even though his departure will surely jeopardize a newly formed romantic attachment. In the course of his investigation, Kan encounters a number of suspicious characters, including the base's senior legal officer, Frederick LeBlanc (aka "The Wizard"), Magrip, a highly unstable Vietnam veteran, and Levine, a "feminist nuclear weapons expert." Before long, our hero uncovers a sinister plot fueled both by megalomania and a pathological hatred of communism.

According to *Booklist*, *Tiger's Tale* is an "odd, quixotic book" that "mixes outrageous humor and larger-than-life characters with piteous victims and situations designed to tug at the heartstrings," and concludes that "Lee's latest is compelling, charming [despite the violence], and captivating." The *Library Journal* observes that *Tiger's Tale* "is a gripping, literate military thriller with appeal to genre fans and readers of serious fiction alike." *Publishers Weekly*, in its starred review, agrees that Lee's characters tend to "wear white or black hats" but suggests that "through vigorous prose ... his vision — daring deep and unflaggingly moral — comes to vibrant life as [the author] takes Kan on a tense and moving journey toward redemption."

OTHER MEDIA: Audiocassette (Audioscope/abr); REVIEWS: *BL* 2/1/96; *KR* 2/1/96; *LJ* 3/15/96; *NYTBR* 4/21/96; *PW* 1/29/96; *WPBW* 4/7/96

Lethem, Jonathan (USA)

735   *Gun with Occasional Music* (1994); Tor Books 1995 (pbk)

Jonathan Lethem's debut novel — called a "brilliant postmodern romp" by novelist **James Morrow** — is a hard-boiled detective story (of the "California-noir" variety) with a twist: it is set in Oakland in the near (and highly dystopian) future. The narrator, a tough-talking private eye named Conrad Metcalf — a new age gumshoe who is running out of the "karma points" that keep him out of the "state-ordained deep-freeze" has been called into a case involving a murdered urologist, an "evolved" baby and an assortment of (often interchangeable) policemen and gangsters. Lethem's publisher provides an intriguing synopsis of his novel: Twenty-first century P.I. Conrad Metcalf has problems — a monkey on his back, a rabbit in his waiting room, and a trigger-happy kangaroo on his tail — not to mention a murder.

Booklist found *Gun with Occasional Music* to be "a sparkling pastiche of Chandleresque detective fiction displaced to an almost comical postmodern landscape" and an "outstanding debut for a welcome new voice." Malcolm Jones, Jr. (*Newsweek*), calls Lethem's first novel a "dazzling debut" and argues that although "[n]ovelists and movie-makers have fused sci-fi with detective stories for a long time ... nobody has every done it this well." *Kirkus Reviews* points out that *Gun with Occasional Music* "whose mix of genres and voices ('Tell him next time he wants to talk to me, don't send a marsupial') comically focuses a nightmare hash of yesterday, today, and tomorrow." The *Library Journal* concludes that "this first novel imparts a new meaning to the word mystery."

REVIEWS: *BL* 2/15/94; *GW* 2/5/95; *KR* 1/1/94; *LJ* 2/15/94; *NewsWk* 4/18/94; *NYTBR* 5/14/95 *PW* 1/17/94; *SFRB* 6-7/94

Livesey, Margot (UK)

736 *Criminals* (1995); Knopf 1995 (HC); Penguin 1997 (pbk)

Margot Livesey's increasingly unsettling second novel — which ranges from Scotland to America and thence to Italy — concerns the fate of an abandoned baby inadvertently "rescued" by an appealing young banker journeying from London to his sister's remote country house in Scotland. His sister, Mollie, he assumes, will know what to do. However, when Mollie (an undiagnosed paranoid-schizophrenic) absconds with the foundling the story deepens and darkens.

According to the *New York Times Book Review*, readers of the "thoroughly engrossing" *Criminals* will become "enmeshed in the complex windings of Ms. Livesey's plot, a web of criminal circumstance and mortal consequences that conveys the awful randomness of life even as it offers the abiding pleasures of artfully constructed fiction." *The Washington Post Book World* found *Criminals* to be: [a]t times quirky and charming, at others as starkly disturbing and bleak as its landscape." *Book World* further concludes that Livesey's second novel "is a resounding success, deceptively simple in its exploration of the moral ambiguities inherent in contemporary life." In the view of *Booklist*, *Criminals* is "Beautifully written ... [a] remarkably inventive fiction [which] satisfies on all counts." *Publishers Weekly*, in its starred review, claims that "Livesey [has produced a fascinating narrative in which she] maintains, a low-key style

that perfectly matches the way ordinary lives can slip into chaos."

REVIEWS: *BL* 1/1/96; *LJ* 1/96; *NYTBR* 3/31/96; *PW* 12/11/95; *TLS* 8/16/96; *WPBW* 8/11/96

Maitland, Sara (UK)

737 *Ancestral Truths* (1994); Holt 1995 (pbk)

Clare Kerslake — on the recommendation of her doctors and the wishes of her stepmother — is spending the summer at her family's ancestral home in the Scottish highlands. She is there to recover from a recent, unspeakably traumatic, event that occurred on the slopes of Mount Nyangani in Zimbabwe. When found by rescue workers, Clare had been holding the bleeding stump of her right wrist from which her hand had been, unaccountably, severed. She was also mumbling that she had killed her hiking companion and long-time boyfriend, David whose body has yet to be found. Clare can neither recall the circumstances which led to David's (presumed) death nor the cause of her own injury. To make matters even worse, Clare, in the months leading up to their African trip, had begun to withdraw from David (always a psychological bully) because of his increasingly distasteful demands for "perverse" sex. Clare has been fitted with a prosthesis to which she is slowly adjusting, but her traumatic amnesia has not yielded to therapy. The family vacation, it is hoped, will help to restore her memory. The assembled family, in addition to a controlling matriarch, includes (among assorted siblings and their offspring) Ben, a recently disgraced gay Anglican priest; Anni, a brilliant mathematician and outspoken feminist; and Felicity, a devoted wife and mother to a profoundly deaf child. Family conversations range far and wide, including discussions of chaos theory, Mandelbrot equations and Southern African history and mythology.

Ancestral Truths was called a "fascinating tale that explores more than just the mystery surrounding David's death" by *Booklist* and a "splendid novel" by the *New York Times Book Review*. According to the *L.A. Times*, *Ancestral Truths* "is truly accomplished and thoroughly literate storytelling, accessible yet intricate, comical yet contemplative, shrewd yet deeply empathetic." The *Times Literary Supplement* points out that if Maitland "errs on the side of doggedness ... her understanding of the dynamics of self-deception and moral cowardice justifies her [methods]. Violence, especially repressed violence, is best approached with extreme caution." Novelist Carolyn See (*WPBW*) suggests that Maitland's book (with its wide-ranging and often trendy interests in things such as kinky sex) could be called a "kitchen-sink novel ... [one that's] old-fashioned in a nice sense. You ... spend a pious afternoon [reading it] flaked out on the couch with hints of chaos theory, bondage sex and a house so organized that the Virgin Mary is honored on the Feast of the Assumption and the trout are arranged according to length and weight. You know it's blatant escapism, but when you need to escape, there's nothing else that so effectively hits the spot."

RECOGNITION: *NYTBR* Notable Book 1994; REVIEWS: *BL* 2/15/94; *KR* 12/15/93; *LATBR* 3/27/94; *NYTBR* 3/13/94; *PW* 1/10/94; *TLS* 4/23/93; *WPBW* 1/28/94; EDITOR'S NOTE: *Ancestral Truths* was originally published in London in 1993 as *Home Truths*

Malone, Michael (USA)

738 *Time's Witness* (1989); Washington Square 1994 (pbk)

Southern writer Michael Malone sets his sixth novel in Hillston, North Carolina (familiar to readers of *Uncivil Seasons*), and features Police Chief Cuddy Magnum and his sardonic assistant, Justin Savile V (the product of a "fine old southern family"). As the novel opens, the state of North Carolina has just granted death row inmate), George Hall, a black man convicted of killing a white cop, a stay of execution. Before a new trial can be brought, however, Hall's younger brother, an active campaigner on his behalf, is found murdered. Magnum, who had also filed an appeal on Hall's behalf, takes on the murder investigation.

As the *Chicago Tribune* notes "There is a lot to savor in *Time's Witness*. Malone's portrait of his corner of the New South is detailed, thoughtful and appealing with none of the smirking cynicism that often passes for analysis of that region's prosperity and character." In the view of novelist **Valerie Sayers** (*NYTBR*) the character of Magnum "the lonely police chief— deserted by his first wife, tangled in a guilty adulterous affair, stalked by a former cop — offers moral vision ... [for the lawman] is after far bigger game than anything Philip Marlowe or Sam Spade ever tried to bring down ... the relationship between racism and capital punishment."

REVIEWS: *BL* 3/15/89; *ChiTrib* 4/24/89; *KR* 3/1/89; *NYTBR* 4/23/89; *PW* 3/10/89; *WPBW* 5/21/89

Mantel, Hilary (UK)

An Experiment in Love (1995); H Holt 1997 (pbk); SETTING: England in the 1960s; See Section 6, #824

A Change in Climate (1994); Holt 1997 (pbk); SETTING: South Africa & Botswana — mid '60s and '70s and Norfolk, England '80s; See Section 6, #825

739 *Eight Months on Ghazzah Street* (1988); Holt 1997 (pbk)

Frances Shore, a British cartographer, has accompanied her engineer husband to Saudi Arabia where he has taken a lucrative position with an international construction company located in the Red Sea port of Jidda. Not wishing to live surrounded exclusively by other Britons, Frances and her husband take up residence (on Ghazzah Street) in one of the Muslim sections of the city. However, the intellectually curious Francis encounters nothing but polite indifference from her Saudi neighbors, and soon becomes bored. She also finds herself at odds — at least philosophically — with the Saudi culture, especially its restrictive, sexist legal code. To counteract her growing frustrations, Frances connects (reluctantly) with the chummy, ever-so-social expatriate community. She also begins to keep a journal, and begins to indulge her mildly voyeuristic interest in her Muslim neighbors. Before long, the disturbing sounds of a woman sobbing somewhere in her apartment building begin to wake her each night and, when she encounters a shadowy figure with a gun in the building's hallway, Frances becomes increasingly apprehensive.

Eight Months on Ghazzah Street, called an "expatriate horror story" by the *Washington Post Book World*, is, in the opinion of the *Wall Street Journal* "a tautly written tale of suspense that makes brilliant use of monotony and claustrophobia to heighten [its] heroine's growing sense of danger." *Publishers Weekly* says that "Mantel's relentless pounding away at Francis's stultifying life offers a bit of misdirection, enabling the mystery to sneak towards its conclusion with disconcerting stealth. With marvelously understated wit, Mantel chronicles a world of teas and dinner parties that eventually coalesce into a sinister story of horror just beyond a veil." According to the *L.A. Times Book Review* Mantel's "blend of dark and light comedy and tragedy, heart-in-the-mouth narrative, and a slow-working analysis of the human condition, is nowhere more successfully displayed than in *Eight Months on Ghazzah Street*..." which made its American debut in 1997.

RECOGNITION: Winner of the 1988 *Sunday Express* "Book of the Year"; *LATBR* "Recommended Title" 1997; *Publishers Weekly* "Best Books" 1997; REVIEWS: *LitRev* 4/88; *LATBR* 9/14/97; *NYTBR* 7/20/97; *PW* 7/14/97; *WPBW* 7/27/97; *WSJ* 9/24/97

Martin, Valerie (USA)

740 *The Great Divorce* (1994); Bantam 1995 (pbk)

The Great Divorce is set in Louisiana and explores the lives of three women: Elizabeth Boyer

Schlaeger who was hanged in 1848 for the murder of her husband; Ellen a thirty-something wife, mother and large-animal veterinarian who is confronting a deadly virus that threatens the "big cat" population at the New Orleans City Zoo; and Camille an awkward, alienated young woman who works at the city zoo as the "keeper of the cats." Each woman is faced with an emotional crisis: Ellen is struggling with the knowledge that her husband has taken a lover, the affection-starved Camille cannot extricate herself from an abusive relationship, and Elizabeth has been driven nearly mad by a bullying, controlling husband. Ms. Martin draws on the 19th century myth of the "cat woman" as a thematic and unifying device and makes skillful use of the exotic, over-ripe atmosphere of New Orleans to add piquancy to a novel that is both chilling and thought-provoking.

According to novelist Tom de Haven (*Entertainment Weekly*) *The Great Divorce* is both a "carefully calibrated blend of gothic horror and psychological drama" and "an extraordinary and endlessly mysterious work of fiction." Novelist **Francine Prose** (*LATBR*) observes that "Ellen's meditations on our progressively attenuated relationship to the natural world provide a unifying philosophic dimension to these cautionary tales of women pushed to the point at which the thin cloak of civilization drops, with dire results, from their shoulders." The *New Statesman* concludes that *The Great Divorce* "emerges as a balanced, truthful and compelling book."

REVIEWS: *EW* 4/8/94; *LATBR* 5/27/94; *NS&S* 8/8/94; *PW* 1/3/94; *WPBW* 3/13/94

Mawer, Simon (UK)

Mendel's Dwarf (1997); Harmony 1998 (pbk); See Section 3, #231

McCabe, Patrick (Ireland)

741 *The Dead School* (1995); Dell 1996 (pbk)

Patrick McCabe sets his fourth novel within the confines of St. Anthony's School for Boys (a prestigious private academy located in Dublin) and tells the converging stories of two academics with diametrically opposed views of life. Raphael Bell, the school's Headmaster, was born in 1913 at the height of the struggle for Irish independence. While still a youngster, he was made to watch as his father, a member of the fledgling IRA, was executed by the Black and Tan. Bell has ruled St. Anthony's with iron-fisted discipline for the better part of forty years. Malachy Dudgeon, a barely competent first-year teacher with little use for "tradition" (at least of the more oppressive sort that is enshrined at St. Anthony's) is forty years younger than Bell and is the product of a very different historical pe-

riod (the permissive sixties) and paternal heritage (his father committed suicide in the wake of his mother's chronic infidelities). The two men clash, a power struggle ensues and a horrific denouement appears inevitable. As in his previous work, McCabe combines fatalism, mordant humor and a penchant for the macabre.

According to the *Times Literary Supplement*: "Cornered by the author's insinuating tones ... most readers will find it hard to resist hearing his dreadful and sometimes appallingly funny story out. To say this is not to give anything away. The fascination of *The Dead School* lies in the details of the characters' destruction — roughly speaking, at the hands of modernity — and the ease with which McCabe incorporates historical and cultural dimensions into the tale." Irish novelist Michael Collins (*NYTBR*) argues McCabe "employs a deft cinematic sensibility combined with a virtuoso use of dialect to capture the splintering of Irish society. *The Dead School* is a timely novel, coming during the current Northern Ireland negotiations. And on the heels of recent biographies of Michael Collins and Eamonn de Valera, founders of modern Ireland, [it] is a fictional complement, tracing the turbulent emergence of Ireland from colonial possession to postcolonial nation." The *Library Journal* observes that *The Dead School* "is a more complex and ambitious work than McCabe's award-winning novel *The Butcher Boy*, but it is just as pitiless in its depiction of Irish life." Denis Donoghue, writing in the *New York Review of Books*, assumes that although somewhat laborious in execution, what "McCabe has in mind is a social novel, broad in scale, contrasting the Ireland of John MacCormack with the Ireland of Pink Floyd, Horslips, skinheads, secularization, and the IRA."

READING GROUP GUIDE; REVIEWS: *KR* 4/26/95; *LATBR* 5/28/95; *LJ* 4/15/95; *LST* 6/18/95; *NYRB* 6/8/95; *NYTBR* 5/28/95; *PW* 2/27/95; *TLS* 5/26/95

McCorkle, Jill (USA)

742 *Carolina Moon: A Novel;* Algonquin 1996 (HC); Fawcett 1997 (pbk)

By combining the trappings of suspense (unsigned letters referring to an ancient affair, a woman in a coma, a piece torn out of a suicide note, a missing person, etc.) with a peculiarly southern comic sensibility, Jill McCorkle has produced a novel with multiple plot lines that snake their invariably intriguing ways towards resolution. The cast of characters is headed up by Quee Purdy, a 60-something, former masseuse, seamstress, cake decorator, therapist, and incorrigible cupid, who has recently opened a smoke-enders clinic whose motto is "Put out your butt and bring your butt in."

Kirkus Reviews calls *Carolina Moon* "a narrative gem that emanates dramatic heat, southern Gothic light, and an uncanny emotional wisdom." Novelist **Jayne Anne Phillips** (*Harper's Bazaar*) observes that "From the moment the corpse of a local philanderer/frat boy turns up in fresh garden mulch delivered to a proper southern matron, *Carolina Moon* unfolds in user-friendly prose that is slap-your-thigh funny, yet lyrically honest and unfailingly incisive." Ms. Philips concludes that McCorkle's 6th book is "also a suspenseful honest-to-God detective story whose myriad details fall into place as neatly as a row of dominoes. Yet McCorkle deftly delineates the mysterious patterns of time itself: Generations and events overlap, secrets evolve into stories. *Carolina Moon* resonates long after the pages are turned." The *Library Journal* notes that "The razor-sharp humorous portrayals of the disintegration of a small town is reminiscent of McCorkle's best early work."

OTHER MEDIA: Audiocassette (Books-on-Tape/unabr); RECOGNITION: *Booklist* "Editors' Choice" 1996; REVIEWS: *BL* 8/96; *EW* 9/27/96; *HarpBaz* 9/96; *LJ* 11/1/96; *NYTBR* 12/15/96; *PeopleW* 11/18/96; *PW* 7/8/96; *SLJ* 1/97; *SouthLiv* 10/96

McCrum, Robert (UK)

743   *Suspicion* (1997); W.H. Norton 1997 (HC)

Robert McCrum, a former editor with the publishing house of Faber & Faber (and currently the literary editor of the *London Observer*), has written a stylish, literate thriller which tells the story of a comfortable, upper-middle class family's response to the disturbing arrival of a long-absent maverick older brother (an old-style Marxist) and his exotic, East German wife. Before long, deeply submerged family passions will surface, along with a growing sense that something "rather nasty" is in the offing. *Suspicion*, an intriguing blend of mayhem and civility, is narrated by Julian Whyte, barrister, bachelor and respected resident of the tiny village of Mansfield, England.

The *Times Literary Supplement* found *Suspicion* to be "an elegantly crafted tale of betrayal ... [and] an engrossing study of English bourgeois manners." The *L.A. Times Book Review* concludes that Robert McCrum has constructed a "riveting, complex tapestry of sibling rivalry, love and hate ... [wherein] violence, building like a summer thunderstorm ... erupts in unforeseen directions with tragic results." In the opinion of *Entertainment Weekly*, "London publishing bigwig McCrum gives literate underpinnings to [what is at heart] a trashy psychological thriller...."

OTHER MEDIA: Audiocassette (Sterling Audio/unabr); RECOGNITION: *LATBR* "Best Books" 1997; REVIEWS: *EW* 4/25/97; *KR* 1/1/97; *LATBR* 4/13/97;

LJ 2/15/97; *LST* 6/2/96; *LT* 6/1/96; *NS* 6/14/96; *NYTBR* 4/16/97; *TLS* 6/14/96

McEwan, Ian (UK)

744   *Enduring Love* (1997); Doubleday 1998 (HC); Anchor 1998 (pbk)

Ian McEwan has long been known for his cerebral-yet-macabre sensibilities and for his novelistic explorations of deviant sexuality. In *Enduring Love* McEwan explores the phenomenon of homoerotic religious obsession as he tells the story of a 40-something couple, Joe and Melissa Rose who, as a result of Joe's involvement in a freak accident, find their lives turned upside down. As the story opens, Joe and Melissa—to take advantage of a beautiful, if windy day—have taken themselves and a picnic basket to a rural area outside London. While eating, they are disturbed by shouts, and it soon becomes clear that a hot-air balloon—with a youngster in its basket—is dangerously out of control. Joe and a number of other onlookers rush to help. They grab the dangling ropes and try to bring the balloon to earth, but, during the rescue attempt, a man is killed. The group is profoundly affected by this experience, none more so than Jed Parry, a devout Christian, who, inexplicably, becomes obsessed with Joe (he professes love) and in "bringing God" into Joe's life. Ed, a science writer trained in the rational method of scientific inquiry, can only look at "the facts" both of the traumatic event and of Jed's increasingly disturbing behavior. Clarissa provides yet another perspective, casting doubt on Joe's perception of events.

In the view of *Entertainment Weekly Enduring Love* "offers eerie, slow-paced suspense worth its weight in caffeine for keeping you up all night." The *Wall Street Journal* calls it "a thriller that satisfies the intelligent reader's hunger for strong characters, emotional depth and artistic symmetry" and concludes that "Mr. McEwan is a consummate professional, and for erudition, slickness (in the best sense of the word) and just plain smarts, he has few peers." According to Christopher Lehman-Haupt (*NYT*) "How the story plays out is too exciting to be spoiled by revealing what happens. Not only suspenseful, it is also thematically rich, opposing as it does Joe's scientific view of the world with that of Clarissa, a Keatsian scholar who believes, as the poet did, that science is robbing the world of wonder." *Kirkus Reviews* notes that "McEwan's terse, lucid prose and sure grasp of character give resonance to this superb anatomy of obsession and exploration of the mind under extreme circumstances" and concludes that this is a "Painful and powerful work by one of England's best novelists."

OTHER MEDIA: Audiocassette (Recorded Bks/unabr); RECOGNITION: *PW's* Best '98 Fiction;

NYTBR Notable Book of 1998; Amazon.Com Editors' Choice "Top Ten Books of 1998"; REVIEWS: *EW* 2/13/98; *KR* 11/15/97; *LATBR* 1/25/98; *NYT* 1/15/98; *TLS* 9/12/97; *WSJ* 1/23/98

McFarland, Dennis (USA)

745 *A Face at the Window* (1997); Broadway 1997 (HC); Bantam 1998 (pbk)

Dennis McFarland's spine tingling third novel features Cookson ("Cook") Selway, a recovering alcoholic and former drug dealer (now "clean") who has accompanied his mystery-writer wife to England where she plans to soak up some local color for her next novel. After settling their much-loved daughter in a boarding school, the Selways take up residence on the top floor of the Willerton, a charming London hotel. (Unbeknownst to Cookson and his wife, their flat was the site of a 50-year-old murder-suicide.) Cook soon begins to hear music that no one else seems to be able to hear and to see figures visible only to himself. To the consternation of his long-suffering wife, he becomes increasingly (and dangerously) obsessed with these ghostly manifestations.

According to *Booklist* "McFarland's three-dimensional characters weave an involving spell." English novelist Isabel Colegate (*NYTBR*) observes that McFarland "has a most beguiling narrative style: he is sometimes funny and sometimes moving; in descriptions of the haunting he is so exact that it is easy to suspend disbelief, and in his ulterior purposes he is persuasive." Ms. Colegate further concludes that "the whole makes for a thoroughly satisfying novel." According to *Publishers Weekly* "To describe McFarland's subtly plotted, eerily plausible third novel as a sophisticated ghost story does it an injustice, because it is as securely based in the real world as any well-written narrative whose characters contemplate existential questions."

RECOGNITION: *NYTBR* Notable Book of 1997; REVIEWS: *BL* 2/15/97; *LJ* 1/97; *NY* 5/12/97; *NYT* 3/14/97; *NYTBR* 3/16/97; *PeopleW* 3/24/97; *PW* 11/25/96; *WSJ* 3/20/97

746 *School for the Blind* (1994); HM 1994 (HC); Ivy 1995 (pbk)

In his second novel, which is set on the Gulf Coast of Florida, Dennis McFarland features a pair of septuagenarian siblings who have lived most of their lives apart from one another. Francis Brimm — a (much-honored) photo-journalist who has spent most of his adult life traveling about the world — has recently returned to his hometown of Pines, Florida, and has taken up residence just down the street from his sister, Muriel Brimm, who has spent her entire (highly circumscribed) life in the very home she was born in. When the elderly pair discover the skeletal remains of two young girls (students from the local school for the blind who had been abducted, murdered and dismembered) while walking on a local golf course, both Muriel and Francis experience the return of long-buried childhood memories of physical and sexual abuse which both of them had long suppressed. To complicate matters Muriel receives a sinister phone call (from a man claiming to be the murderer) and is drawn, inexorably, into the investigation. Francis, meanwhile, is dying.

Novelist **Karl Ackerman** (*WPBW*) observes that "McFarland explores Muriel's memory of sexual abuse without cliché, brilliantly capturing her fearful skittishness and 'the bottomless sense of betrayal peculiar to a person running from the truth.'" According to *Booklist* "Once again, McFarland traces the shadows of childhood as they darken the psyche well into adulthood ... [and concludes that the author] has retained the lyricism and generosity of spirit that distinguished his first novel while extending the range with humor, suspense, and a bracingly clear-eyed consideration of death." The *Times Literary Supplement* offers a dissenting view: "Although [the] affirmative conclusion features some impressive writing — notably an account of the purgatorial, afterlife gradually conceived by Francis — it fails to come off. Not because McFarland eschews fashionable gloom, but because everything is too neat, too Hollywood."

OTHER MEDIA: Audiocassette (Publishing Mills/abr); RECOGNITION: *NYTBR* Notable Book of 1994; REVIEWS: *BL* 5/1/94; *ChiTrib* 6/5/94; *GW* 9/4/94; *KR* 3/15/94; *LATBR* 5/15/94; *NYTBR* 5/22/94; *PW* 3/14/94; *TLS* 8/26/94; *WPBW* 6/19/94; *WSJ* 5/18/94

McNamee, Eoin (Ireland)

747 *Resurrection Man* (1994); St. Martin's 1996 (HC); Picador 1996 (pbk)

McNamee's sparely written debut novel, set in a gritty, violence-ridden Belfast, features Victor Kelly a loyalist Protestant hit man "disabled at birth by having what is perceived to be a 'Catholic' surname" (*TLS*). Victor, an utterly conscienceless killer — he mutilates his victims before he kills them — is spiraling ever deeper into the culture of violence, stimulated by the fear he inspires. While McNamee develops his plot with a thriller-writer's attention to pace and readability, he attempts and, according to the critics, achieves much more.

English novelist **Jonathan Coe**, in a review appearing in the *London Review of Books*, calls *Resurrection Man* "relentlessly dark and grisly ... and more about serial killing than it is about terrorism" but concludes that "it lunges without fear or compromise through very dangerous territory [and] ... is an impressively confident book." According to the *Times Literary Supplement*, McNamee's novel is well observed, and although at times the author strives just a little too hard for effect, the clever stuff succeeds much more often than it fails." *Booklist* concludes that "McNamee produces a powerful, claustrophobic vision of a world in which Victor Kelly's psychopathology is both inevitable and necessary. An intense journey into the heart of darkness." *The* (London)*Times* argues that "McNamee's novel offers no redemptive answers. It does, however, serve as a stark and disturbing warning about what happens when primitive hatreds stir the stagnant waters of society, and makes you ponder even now ... whether in a Belfast backstreet some rough beast waits, its hour come at last."

RECOGNITION: *Publishers Weekly* "Best Book" of 1995; REVIEWS: *BL* 9/1/95; *LRB* 3/24/94; *LT* 3/12/94; *NYTBR* 10/1/95; *PW* 7/17/95; *Time* 10/2/95; *TLS* 5/27/94

Mitchard, Jacqueline (USA)

The Deep End of the Ocean (1996); Viking 1996 (HC); Signet 1997 (pbk); See Section 1, #66

Moore, Brian (Ireland/Canada/USA)

748   *The Statement* (1996); Plume 1997 (pbk)

Brian Moore's 18th novel, an intellectual thriller set in contemporary France, delves into the (still unresolved) ethical dilemmas which arose as a result of official French collaboration with the Nazis during WW II. Moore's story focuses on Pierre Brossard, a 70-year-old Frenchman who—following the war—had been tried and convicted "in absentia" for the murder of 14 Jews at Dombey, France, in 1944. Brossard was immediately given "sanctuary" by ultra-conservative groups within the French Roman Catholic church (with the backing of influential members of the French government), and has therefore managed to elude capture for more than 50 years. As the novel opens—Brossard, targeted for assassination by a Jewish organization dedicated to exacting revenge—has just survived an attempt on his life.

Kirkus Reviews notes that Moore has produced "A superlative political novel that, like its immediate predecessors, *Lies of Silence* (1990) and *No Other Life* (1993) blends the visceral appeal of a beautifully plotted thriller with the more complex pleasures of a thoughtful exploration of conflicting and long-lingering moral quandaries.... They don't write them any better than this." According to Christopher Lehmann-Haupt (*NYT*), *The Statement* "is above all a clever thriller, so not only can't its resolution be hinted at, but one also can't spell out what the source of its suspense turns out to be." Lehmann-Haupt concludes by pointing out that "What certainly can be revealed is that the ending of *The Statement* is a surprising shock. And that the waves of that shock wash over all the complex moral nuances of the story and leaves in their paths the sense that history as an instrument of justice is at best extremely crude." The *Times Literary Supplement* found *The Statement* to be "the most boldly conceived [of Moore's novels]. Breathless in execution, plotted like a cinematic thriller, it provides hardly more than the exoskeleton of a conventional novel." The *TLS* concludes that its "most powerful passages ... [are the extensive] monologues of the virulent anti-Semitic murderer Brossard [characterized by a childlike, narcissistic love of the Roman Catholic Church and by a rabid French patriotism], who reveals himself to the reader, but rarely to himself."

OTHER MEDIA: Audiocassette (Chivers/ unabr); RECOGNITION: *NYTBR* Notable Book of 1996; *Publishers Weekly* "Best Books" 1996; REVIEWS: *Econ* 10/28/95; *LATBR* 1/23/96; *LJ* 5/1/96; *Maclean's* 9/25/95; *NY* 7/15/96; *NYTBR* 6/30/96; *PW* 4/22/96; *TLS* 9/12/97; *WPBW* 6/30/96

Moore, Susanna (USA)

749   *In the Cut* (1995); Knopf 1995 (HC); Onyx 1996 (pbk)

Susanna Moore's heroine/narrator, Frannie Thornstein, is a 34-year-old creative writing teacher who lives and works in lower Manhattan. A street smart urbanite, Frannie is currently writing a book on urban slang and regional dialects. When she is both precipitously and inadvertently drawn into a sordid sex-related murder (as an innocent yet "identifiable" witness) she finds herself involved—in more ways than one—with a member of the NYPD investigative team assigned to the case.

The *New York Times Book Review* calls *In the Cut* "a ferociously uninhibited erotic thriller whose sex and savagery are all the more disturbing for being rendered in a stylish prose that simmers along with wit and erudition." Novelist **Joyce Carol Oates** (*NYRB*), while expressing reservations regarding some "inconsistencies of voice" and a "frequently mechanical ... genre-driven plot" concludes that Ms. Moore's novel is "powerful, shameless (or fearless) in its depiction of female passivity in the face of male aggression ... a repudiation in a sense not merely of adult womanhood but of personhood itself, with its obligations of personal responsibility and integrity." *Time* magazine which found the "language and the sex scenes [to be] blunt, graphic and definitely not to everyone's taste" also concluded that the novel "poses questions—about the irrational, the perverse—that tap fiction's deepest potential." *Publishers Weekly*, in its starred review, contends that "Moore's control of her material is impressive: as she sweeps toward a knockout ending, she employs the gritty vernacular, red-herring clues and cold-blooded brutality of a bona-fide thriller without sacrificing the integrity of her narrative." In the view of the *Times Literary Supplement*, "As in all good thrillers, the suspense is pumped up to just this side of cardiac arrest in a series of ingeniously perverse formal and psychological twists which recall Henry James's *The Turn of the Screw*. Both stories are obsessed with the interpretation of chaos and haunted by disturbing sexual desires. Both blur the boundaries between memory, fantasy, nightmare and reality. Moore can admit the murkiness neurotically denied by James's governess. But as Detective Molloy so aptly points out, 'Knowing doesn't mean shit.' "

RECOGNITION: *NYTBR* Notable Book of 1995; REVIEWS: *BL* 10/1/95; *LJ* 9/1/95; *NYRB* 11/16/95; *NYTBR* 11/12/95; *PW* 8/28/95; *Time* 11/20/95; *TLS* 4/19/96

Morley, John David

Feast of Fools (1994); St. Martin's 1995 (pbk;) See Section 8, #1018

Mortimer, John (UK)

750 *Felix in the Underworld* (1997); Viking 1997 (HC); Overlook 1998 (pbk)

Felix Morsom is a gentle soul, a respected author (described, not particularly accurately, by his publisher as "the Chekhov of Coldsand-on-Sea") who has been nominated for a major literary prize. Felix is soon wrenched from his slight celebrity and mildly melancholic seaside life first by the appearance of a hitherto unknown ten-year-old son (sporting a claim for child support), and then by an accusation of murder — an accusation made all the more alarming by the fact that Felix has seen the dead woman several times since she supposedly met her brutal end. Mortimer's decidedly literate mystery features a cast of English eccentrics: an outrageously camp solicitor, a ghastly female author of raunchy novels, and a host of London down-and-outs.

According to *Kirkus Reviews* Mortimer's latest is a "diverting mixture of murder mystery, character study, and social comedy ... [and] Top-drawer escapist fare...." Richard Bernstein (*NYT*) says that *Felix in the Underworld* is a delight ... [set as it is] in the same modestly absurd arena as most of Mr. Mortimer's work, a place where ordinary good sense and the desire for a sanely predictable and quiet world smash headlong into blind fate and odd people." Mr. Bernstein concludes that *Felix in the Underworld* is "[s]omewhere between P.D. James and a British after-dinner speech ... [a novel] whose

surprises keep coming right up to the very end ... [and] a charming and worthy addition to the Mortimer oeuvre." In the view of *Entertainment Weekly*, "Mortimer has smirky fun throwing middle- aged novelist Felix Morsom — author of sensitive, hopelessly unsexy books about life in his English seaside village — into a wellspring of mayhem."

OTHER MEDIA: Audiocassette (Viking Audio/ abr); RECOGNITION: *NYTBR* Notable Book of 1997; REVIEWS: *BL* 9/1/97; *EW* 1/9/98; *KR* 11/97; *LJ* 11/1/97; *LST* 7/6/97; *NS* 7/25/97; *NYT* 12/10/97; *NYTBR* 11/16/97; *PW* 8/25/97; *Spec* 6/28/97; *TLS* 8/1/97; *WPBW* 11/6/97

751 *Summer's Lease* (1988); Penguin 1991 (pbk)

A holiday villa in Tuscany becomes the setting for an astringently comic tale of mystery and detection. The Pargeters (husband, wife, father-in-law and two children) have temporarily exchanged their gloomy London row-house for a sun-struck villa in "Chianti-shire," They soon find themselves up to their sun-glasses in scandal, sexual and otherwise. John Mortimer, known for his sympathetic take on the human condition, has produced a light, consistently entertaining domestic comedy with foul play as an agreeable subtext.

According to the *L.A. Times Book Review*: "Though the mystery itself may seem a bit mild and predictable to the jaded aficionados of the genre, the deft characterization of the Pargeters and the tart portraits of their less winsome fellow countrymen are supremely diverting. The accurate information on the various charms of the Tuscan countryside is an added bonus; the cultural clash between the naive, no-nonsense Brits and the shrewd *dolce far niente* villagers lending even more brio to the concoction." The *Literary Review*, which found *Summer's Lease* to be "funny and gripping and, above all, fresh," further concludes that Mortimer must have "chuckled aloud as he was writing it: you can almost hear the laughter as you read." The *New York Times* notes that "the well-known effects of Italy on English visitors of a certain disposition are much in evidence in John Mortimer's highly entertaining new novel. " The *Atlantic Monthly* concludes that "There's mystery here as well as humor. In fact, mystery is piled so tantalizingly on mystery that we keep reading, even though [a number of the] characters are rather unpleasant."

OTHER MEDIA: Audiocassette (Chivers/ unabr); adapted for British Television; REVIEWS: *CSM* 8/23/88; *LATBR* 8/19/88; *LitRev* 4/88; *NYT* 7/27/88; *NYTBR* 7/31/88; *TLS* 4/29/88; *WPBW* 7/24/88

Mukherjee, Bharati (India/USA)

752 *Leave It to Me* (1997); Knopf 1997 (HC); Fawcett 1998 (pbk)

Leave It to Me features a young woman who, abandoned at birth in India by her hippie American mother and her dangerously unstable, yet charismatic, Eurasian father, was adopted, while still a toddler, by the Martinos, a solid, middle-class family from upstate New York. Debby Martino grows up "different," an exotic flower in a rather humdrum garden. A disastrous affair with her Chinese-American boss — she burns down his Saratoga mansion after he dumps her — convinces Debby that she has inherited some pretty scary genes. Debby sets out in search of her biological parents, a search which leads the increasingly violent young woman to California where she changes her name to Devi Dee, meets her mother, the wealthy proprietor of a Bay Area escort service, and continues to wreak havoc.

Booklist points out that "With poignancy and wit, Mukherjee makes present-day San Francisco the setting for the age-old story of the foundling in search of her parents and herself" and concludes that "What may hold readers is the laid-back first-person narrative as ... Devi Dee finds a life between the homeless and the high-rollers and learns about karma from a burger muncher at McDonalds." *Kirkus Reviews* notes that "Mukherjee probes the origins of violence and the nature of identity in this grim tale of a young woman whose need to know her past leaves corpses from Sarasota to Sausalito.... The mythic overtones keep this bloody saga engaging as its Electra proves worthy of the zeitgeist that created her." Noted English critic Lorna Sage, writing in the *New York Times Book Review*, calls Devi "a brilliant creation — hilarious, horribly knowing and even more horribly oblivious — through whom Bharati Mukherjee, with characteristic and shameless ingenuity, is laying claim to speak for an America that isn't 'other' at all."

READING GROUP GUIDE; RECOGNITION: *NYTBR* Notable Book of 1997; REVIEW: *BL* 4/15/97; *KR* 4/15/97; *LJ* 6/15/97; *LST* 9/13/98; *Maclean's* 7/21/97; *NY* 6/23/97; *NYT* 6/24/97; *NYTBR* 7/20/97; *TLS* 7/18/97; *WPBW* 8/10/97

Nelson, Antonya (USA)

753   *Nobody's Girl* (1998); Scribner 1998 (HC); 1999 (pbk)

Antonya Nelson's second novel *Nobody's Girl* features Birdy Stone, a thirty-year-old high school English teacher, a Chicagoan, who has taken a teaching position in rural New Mexico. Birdy (reeling from her mother's death and her father's precipitous remarriage) has come west seeking solitude and to this end has settled herself into trailer home in the little town of Pinetop. She divides her time between the local high school (where she half-heartedly attempts to turn her students on to liter-ature) and her tin can of a home where she gets stoned and watches endless videos with a homosexual colleague by the name of Jesus Morales. When Isadora Anthony, the mother of one of her students, asks for Birdie's editorial assistance with a rambling — but intriguing — family history, Birdie is drawn into a 10-year-old mystery involving the deaths (at an ancient Anasazi ruin in the cliffs outside of town) of Isadora's husband and daughter. She is also drawn into a reckless, passionate love affair with Mrs. Anthony's 17-year-old son.

According to *Booklist*, "One of the many pleasures of Nelson's finely crafted and deeply felt novels ... is her bright humor, and she has never been funnier, shrewder, or more magnetic than she is here.... This resonant novel has the power of the best of Ellen Gilchrist and Lorrie Moore and deserves a wide readership." The *Chicago Tribune* notes that Antonya Nelson "is an every-word-counts kind of novelist ... [and] she is very funny, albeit in a wry, offhanded manner." In the view of *Publishers Weekly* "The easy rhythms of her prose, her eye for telling detail and evocative description, the zesty candor of her humor and her rueful but compassionate assessment of the ironies of the human condition make her second novel ... a delight to read."

RECOGNITION: *NYTBR* Notable Book of 1998; REVIEWS: *BL* 2/1/98; *ChiTrib* 3/1/98; *LJ* 12/97; *NYTBR* 3/1/98; *PW* 12/15/97; EDITOR'S NOTE: See Cathline Schine's novel *The Love Letter* (#958) for another depiction of a sexual relationship between a young man and an older woman.

Nicholson, Geoff (UK)

Bleeding London (1997); Overlook 1997 (HC); Penguin 1998 (pbk); See Section 7, #938

Nordan, Lewis (USA)

754   *The Sharpshooter Blues* (1995); Algonquin 1995 (HC); 1997 (pbk)

In *The Sharpshooter Blues* — set in the sleepy Mississippi Delta town of Arrow Catcher — Lewis Nordan tells the languidly cadenced yet riveting story of a robbery-gone-wrong. Hydro Rainey, a sweet, "simple" (mentally retarded), 20-year-old swamp-loving country boy works part time at the William Tell grocery store. When a pair of teenagers are killed attempting to hold up the store, the town immediately assumes that a local character by the name of The Sharpshooter is responsible. After all, gentle Hydro couldn't have done it. The only witness to the killing is a 10-year-old boy whose dissembling leads to tragedy.

According to the *Washington Post Book World*, "Norman's seductive prose suggests that his tale is a piece of folklore, another yarn that the citizens of Arrow Catcher spin. The plot emerges through a series of 'tragic consequences, as almost all actions do.'" The *New York Times Book Review* notes that "In this steamy, swampy backwater, the sometime quite mad people of Arrow Catcher coexist in a kind of timeless mythic wonderland, a world of outrageous Southern Gothic storytelling ... people shoot watermelons and refrigerators.... They do it to relax; they do it to prove who they are. But most of all they do it to prove they are real." The *Voice Literary Supplement* says that although "much of the book's strengths arise from the tragic and grotesque.... Nordan exposes something new and wholly unexpected in his characters — a seemingly boundless capacity for love and acceptance." *Booklist* declares that, as always, Nordan "charms the reader's pants off with his storytelling skills."

REVIEWS: *BL* 7/95; *LJ* 8/95; *NYTBR* 11/5/95; *PeopleW* 1/15/96; *PW* 7/10/95; *VLS* 10/95; *WPBW* 2/14/96

Nova, Craig (USA)

755　*The Universal Donor* (1997); HM 1997 (HC); W.W. Norton 1998 (pbk)

Terry McKechnie — a young doctor working the E.R. graveyard shift at the Los Angeles city hospital — is rapidly approaching emotional and professional burnout. When he meets up with an old friend from medical school and is introduced to his fiancée, a herpetologist by the name of Virginia, he falls precipitously in love. The reader soon learns that Virginia's research brings her into daily contact with some of the world's most poisonous reptiles. After being bitten by a particularly deadly snake, Virginia (now married to his friend) rushes to Terry for medical assistance. Terry soon realizes that without a blood transfusion, she will die. To complicate matters, the young woman has an extremely rare blood type. When a possible donor is identified, Terry throws himself into tracking the man down, a search which is complicated by the fact that the man is a psychopath on the run from the LAPD. Meanwhile, Terry must somehow come to terms with Virginia's (understandably distraught) husband.

In the view of Christopher Lehmann-Haupt (*NYT*), *The Universal Donor* "works well as both a thriller and a literary artifice. And if at times its plot grows too contrived, the worst thing that you can say is that at certain crucial moments a story that has gripped you completely turns back into a novel that you find yourself reading enjoyably." Novelist Gary Indiana (*LATBR*) while deploring the "camera-ready" quality of Nova's novel, suggests that parts of it "cut deep into the shadowland murk associated with the best noir: Dostoeveskyan and pulpish at the same time." Indiana concludes that "It's a pity Nova doesn't run to the end of the night with his manifest talent for terror,

opting instead for a tidy middle-class morality tale." *Kirkus Reviews* contends that the novel's "overuse of coincidence" and "slight tendency towards melodrama ... [is counteracted by the author's] spare lyricism and philosophical manner [which combine to make the novel] absorbing, original and moving." *The Universal Donor* was recommended "with enthusiasm" by *Washington Post Book World* columnist Jonathan Yardley in his year-end review.

RECOGNITION: *NYTBR* Notable Book of 1997; REVIEWS: *BL* 6/1/97; *KR* 4/1/97; *LATBR* 10/19/97; *NYT* 6/29/97; *NYTBR* 7/28/97; *PW* 3/31/97; *WPBW* 6/15/97

Oates, Joyce Carol (USA)

756　*Man Crazy* (1997); NAL/Dutton 1997 (HC); Penguin 1998 (pbk)

Set in the near-gothic northern reaches of upstate New York, Joyce Carol Oates's 27th novel features Ingrid, a disturbed young woman, and Chloe, her sluttish, alcoholic mother, who are holed up in a depressing lodge on the darkly sinister Wolf's Head Lake. Ever since Chloe's husband, the handsome, former fighter pilot with a violent temper, deserted her and their daughter, the two have led a precarious existence. Ingrid, severely lacking in self esteem, grows up emulating both her mother's overt sexuality and her neediness. In high school she is known as "doll girl" because she's willing to do most anything to please the boys. Before the sordid tale is concluded, Ingrid will fall under the sway of Enoch Skaggs, a malevolent, messianic biker and the leader of a Satanic cult. Powerless to resist him, she becomes Skaggs' "dog-girl," his personal slave.

In the view of the *Library Journal*, *Man Crazy* is an "ugly tale told by a master of evocative misery, but to what purpose?" According to the *Washington Post Book World*: "There are things [one] probably [doesn't] have to say about Joyce Carol Oates's latest novel ... : that it is a lyrical and violent book; that its voice is hypnotic and powerful; that it tells the story of a woman, who curtailed by circumstances, seems destined to come to a bad end. [One doesn't] have to say these things because they were true of Oates's last novel, as well, and the one before that, and the one before that. Oates's themes are as established her voice as recognizable as those of any American writer living." Michiko Kakutani (*NYT*) calls it a "gratuitously lurid story — an embarrassing performance, particularly for a writer of Ms. Oates's experience and talents." *Kirkus Reviews*, on the other hand, concludes that "Oates shows us the paradoxical resilience that sustains people who endure more than we can imagine, and somehow hang on. Her boldly drawn grotesques reach out to us, making us believe in them and care about their fates."

RECOGNITION: *NYTBR* Notable Book of 1997; REVIEWS: *BL* 7/97; *EW* 9/26/97; *LJ* 7/97; *KR* 7/1/97; *LT* 9/6/98; *NYT* 8/29/97; *NYTBR* 9/21/97; *PeopleW* 9/22/97; *PW* 6/16/97; *Salon* 8/15/97; *WPBW* 9/21/97

757   *Zombie* (1995); Plume 1996 (pbk)

Joyce Carol Oates's 26th novel is a "riveting" (if not always completely successful) gothic thriller featuring Quentin "P," a 31-year-old sex offender, serial killer and son of a college professor. The hopelessly psychotic Quentin is out on parole and has taken an apartment in his father's university town; to make matters worse, Quentin is obsessed with the idea of creating a "zombie" and is always on the lookout for raw material.

According to *Booklist*, "Oates repeatedly exhibits the unwavering ability to depict the shadowy, at times malignant aspects of human nature. Her latest endeavor is perhaps her most chilling novel to date, a diary with the eerie familiarity of yesterday's headlines." The *New York Times Book Review*, while praising Ms. Oates ability to "transform what is excruciatingly painful, awful to imagine and difficult to contemplate into rapid, fluent and easy-to-read prose," notes that "the idea of this narrative — that the uncaught serial killer is somehow particularly representative of our current condition — is more interesting than its execution ... which is neither convincing ... nor successfully dramatized as fiction." The *Library Journal* disagrees with this assessment, concluding that "What gives *Zombie* its awesome power is Oates's ability to convince us that Quentin might be anyone: a casual acquaintance, a friend, or a brother."

RECOGNITION: Winner of the 1996 Bram Stoker Award for Horror; *NYTBR* Notable Book of 1995; REVIEWS: *BL* 9/1/95; *EW* 10/20/95; *LATBR* 10/22/95; *LJ* 8/95; *NYTBR* 10/8/95; *PW* 7/17/95

Offutt, Chris (USA)

758   *The Good Brother* (1997); S&S 1997 (HC); Scribner 1998 (pbk)

Dusk was short, Kentucky nights began on the ground, in the hollows and in the woods, moving upwards to join the sky.

In his first novel, Chris Offutt tells the chilling story of a man ensnared by a tradition of violence. Virgil Caudill has grown up in the hills of Kentucky, in an Appalachian culture known for clan feuding and for its logical outcome: revenge. When Virgil's hot-headed older brother, Boyd, is murdered, Virgil is expected (even by the local police authorities) to avenge him. A reluctant Virgil complies, but, to break the cycle (and save himself from a similar fate) he flees to Montana, where he begins a new life under an assumed name. Before long, Virgil inadvertently falls in with a group of "patriots," modern militiamen who have declared war on the U.S. government.

The *New York Times Book Review* calls *The Good Brother* a "poignant first novel ... [which] vividly evokes the moral complexity of the hill people, however alien their conclusions." In the view of *People* "the sound of regional voices — flat and spare in the Rockies, baroque in the Appalachians — makes the idea of community as real to the reader as it does to Virgil Caudill." *Kirkus Reviews* found the "apocalyptic ending ... [to be] bloody, sad and convincing" and concludes that "As a portrait of a good man's life shattered by violence, and as a meditation on the persistent attraction of violence in American society, Offutt's first fiction is persuasive, original and disturbing." The *Times Literary Supplement* notes that "One step further, and *The Good Brother* would be a parody of American Gothic; there are family trees that don't fork, mutterings in post offices about retribution, pathological insularity.... But Virgil's reaction to his brother's death — rather than his reaction to the pressure from the amoral majority of Blizzard to kill Boyd's murderer, whose identity all consider to be beyond question — is worth taking seriously as the basis of the novel."

RECOGNITION: *NYTBR* Notable Book of 1997; Chris Offutt was named one of the "Best Young American Fiction Writers" by *Granta* magazine; REVIEWS: *KR* 4/15/97; *LJ* 6/1/97; *NYTBR* 6/22/97 & 12/7/97; *PeopleW* 7/14/97; *PW* 5/5/97; *Time* 6/9/97; *TLS* 2/27/98; *WPBW* 8/31/97

O'Nan, Stewart (USA)

759   *The Speed Queen* (1997); Doubleday 1997 (HC); Ballantine 1998 (pbk)

The "Speed Queen" of the title is Marjorie Standiford, a convicted murderer and drug addict with a penchant for fast cars. O'Nan's novel opens on the eve of her execution and takes the form of Marjorie's first-person, death-row confession. A Stephen King–like author has, it transpires, purchased the rights to her story and she is answering a series of pre-submitted questions ranging from "What were you wearing?" to "Why did you do it?"

The *Washington Post Book World* calls *The Speed Queen* "literature on fast forward: truncated, fragmented, edgy, reveling in its manic momentum. Rumour has it that [O'Nan] wrote it while living along Route 66, and, indeed, it reads like a feverish tour of the Midwestern psyche on, well, speed." *Booklist* concludes that Marjorie's "tragic road trip through America's quiet towns and highways lulls us into detachment, and innocence redefined." Stewart O'Nan's novel, in the view of *The* (London) *Times*, "runs the risk of being clever-clever, toying self-referentially with one of the most routine of genres. It's just as well he's so good."

RECOGNITION: *LATBR* "Recommended Titles" 1997; REVIEWS: *BL* 4/1/97; *EW* 4/25/97; *KR* 1/15/97; *LJ* 2/1/97; *LT* 8/8/98; *NYTBR* 5/11/97; *PeopleW* 5/5/97; *PW* 1/20/97; *WPBW* 7/27/97

760 *Names of the Dead* (1996); Doubleday 1996 (HC); Penguin 1997 (pbk)

Stewart O'Nan's second novel is set (with time-shifts to Vietnam during the war years) in Ithaca, New York, and explores the disintegrating world of Larry Markham, a former Army medic who can't seem to lay the ghosts of Vietnam to rest. As the novel opens, he is sleepwalking his way through a dead-end job as a delivery man, his wife has just walked out on him, his father has been diagnosed with Alzheimer's disease, and, to cap it all off, he is being stalked by an ex–CIA assassin from his support group. The escalating stress in Larry's life triggers increasingly frequent flashbacks from the war.

According to the *Washington Post Book World* "Larry Markham's life before, during and after his participation in Vietnam is the subject of O'Nan's exceptionally well-crafted, dense novel, the author's second. At times, especially in the Vietnam sequences, the details of Larry's life are painful to read. But in O'Nan's hands, *The Names of the Dead* is compelling, propelled by a fast-moving plot, crisply realistic dialogue, vivid evocations of place and sharp insights in to the protagonist's psyche." *The Names of the Dead* was described as a "Heart-rattling melodrama set against a thriller background" by *Publishers Weekly* which goes on to conclude that the novel "while not as seamless as O'Nan's first [*Snow Angels*] ... offers a confident, gripping narrative, as well as some of the most searing wartime storytelling in recent memory." *Booklist* insists that O'Nan (who) "rightfully refuses to pander to our desire for easy answers," has taken "a now overworked subject — a Vietnam veteran's troubles — and [has come] up with a real winner of a book."

RECOGNITION: *Granta* magazine selected O'Nan as one of its "Best of Young American Novelists" in 1996; REVIEWS: *BL* 1/1/96; *LJ* 3/1/96; *Nation* 4/22/96; *NYTBR* 4/7/96; *PW* 1/22/96; *WPBW* 4/21/96.

761 *Snow Angels* (1994); Penguin 1995 (pbk)

We have all worked very hard this year, he (the band teacher) said, and paused, breathing steam ... and then we heard what I immediately identified (from my own .22, my father's Mossberg, the nightly news from Vietnam) as gunshots. A clump of them. They crackled like fireworks, echoed over the bare trees on the other side of the highway. They were close. The band turned towards them in unison, something Mr. Chervenick never could get us to do.

Snow Angels, Stewart O'Nan's debut novel, is set in a small, depressed western Pennsylvania town in the late 1960s. It is actually two stories: the first is the coming-of-age tale narrated by an appealing 15-year-old boy coping with raging hormones, divorcing parents, and family disintegration; the other is a poignantly narrated, deeply affecting story of mental illness and murder.

Booklist calls *Snow Angels* "a beautifully composed and deeply felt tale of domestic tragedy ... [told] without a shred of sensationalism." The *Library Journal* applauds O'Nan's ability to shift "the focus among characters he wishes to make the reader care about." The *L.A. Times Book Review* concludes that Snow Angels "has a strangely beautiful, desolate appeal."

RECOGNITION: Nominated for the ALA Book of the Year Award; REVIEWS: *BL* 10/15/94; *LATBR* 12/8/94; *LJ* 10/15/94; *NYTBR* 1/8/95; *PW* 9/12/94; *Time* 11/14/94; *WPBW* 1/29/95

Owens, Louis (USA)

762 *Nightland* (1996); Dutton 1996 (HC); Signet 1997 (pbk)

Louis Owens sets his third Native American thriller in rural New Mexico and features two Anglo-Cherokee half-breeds, Will and Billy, a pair of long-time hunting buddies and hardscrabble ranchers. As the story gets underway, the two friends, in the midst of a tumultuous thunderstorm, stumble upon a corpse impaled on a treetop. When Will and Billy also find a suitcase containing close to a million dollars in cash, they are understandably (if temporarily) gratified. Not long after, Billy's grandfather (a village elder) receives a ghostly visitor with whom he plays checkers (and goes for an automobile ride), Will's estranged wife Jace (now a successful big-city lawyer) makes an unexpected appearance, followed by the beautiful, yet sinister, Odessa Nighthawk (who seems to have her eye on Billy). When a local drug dealer — with his foul-mouthed moll in tow — comes looking for the money — things get even more interesting for Will and Billy.

According to *Booklist,* "It's amazing that Owens can transform the tired theme of stolen drug money into such a galvanizing and magical tale, but he does so by virtue of great characters (including a sexy and ruthless villainess), eloquent outrage, and candescent lyricism." *Kirkus Reviews* concludes that "Owens skillfully blends together deadpan comedy, Indian legend and superstition, and stringent criticism of White American injustice ... in a swiftly paced tale that's as thoughtful and provocative as it is irresistibly entertaining." The *Library Journal* was similarly impressed with the book's "unique combination of literary style, strong story and American Indian culture."

REVIEWS: *BL* 8/96; *KR* 6/15/96; *LJ* 7/96; *PW* 6/24/96; *WPBW* 10/6/96

763   *Bone Game: A Novel* (1994); Un of Oklahoma 1994 (HC); 1996 (pbk)

Called a "metaphysical mystery" by the *New York Times Book Review*, *Bone Game*, a sequel to *The Sharpest Sight* (1993), again features Cole McCurtain, a mixed blood Native-American. Owens's Choctaw-Cherokee-Irish-Cajun protagonist is now a professor of English literature at the University of California at Santa Cruz, the site of a centuries-old (possibly haunted) Spanish mission. Santa Cruz is also, as the novel opens, the provenance of a brutal serial killer. Prof. McCurtain finds himself dreaming of a malevolent Indian whose body is painted half black and half white and to his horror begins to suspect a link between his personal haunting and the malignant spirit animating the local sociopath. Owens' intriguing and frequently macabre tale includes the employment of ancient wisdom (brought to McCurtain in the person of various family members who, sensing Cole's plight, make the long trek out to California) and is enlivened by a colorful cast of supporting characters such as Cole's prescient daughter, Abby, and his wise-cracking, cross-dressing Navajo friend Alex Yazzie. In this prize-winning second novel, Louis Owens also manages to combine chilling suspense with humor and a generous dollop of sex.

The *New York Times Book Review* found *Bone Game* to be "eerie enough to be read aloud around a campfire" and concludes that the insertion of Cole's relatives (shrewd tribal elders) "keep the dialogue tart and save the story from its more pretentious inclinations." *World Literature Today* observes that "the text's richness lies in its addressing [both the question 'whodunit?' and] the more pressing ... psychological mystery of the contemporary mixed-blood Native American: the internal conflicts of 'who am I?' Neither question is easily answered; rather, the dual mysteries' inextricable relationship sustains *Bone Game*'s narrative and creates a much more complex text than the term 'mystery' connotes." *Kirkus Reviews* asserts that "Owens writes about what he knows and does so with a sure hand—from the simultaneous fascination and repulsion of the dominant culture with Indians to the little stupidities of academia. A neat blend of elements of fantasy, mystery and Native tradition." *Publishers Weekly* concludes that "Owens expertly mixes genres and blends in generous amounts of Native American history. To his credit, he also leavens his grim but gripping tale with substantial humor."

RECOGNITION: Winner of the Julian J. Rothbaum Prize for the best book published by the University of Oklahoma Press in 1994; REVIEWS: *BL* 10/1/94; *KR* 8/1/94; *LATBR* 2/26/95; *LJ* 9/1/94;

NYTBR 10/23/94; *PW* 8/22/94; *VV* 11/1/04; *WLT* Spr '95

764   *The Sharpest Sight* (1992); Un of Oklahoma 1995 (pbk)

Described by *Kirkus Reviews* as "part murder mystery and part Indian vision-quest," Louis Owens' debut novel is set variously in Amarga, a dusty little California town (nestled in the Big Sur hills between the Pacific and the Salinas River valley), and in a hair-raising Mississippi swamp. Attis McCurtain, a "mixed-blood" Vietnam veteran, goes missing and then turns up dead, an apparent suicide. His best friend Mundo Morales (a Chicano cop) and his great uncle know differently, for they have both dreamed of his murder. Mundo, with steely-eyed determination, devotes himself to apprehending his friend's murderer. Meanwhile, Attis's younger brother, Cole, is summoned by his uncle, a Choctaw wise man, to a swamp in Mississippi where (to quiet his brother's restless spirit) he must find and then bury Attis's bones.

The *Library Journal* (which called *The Sharpest Sight* "a fine inaugural novel for an important new series") notes that "Ghosts and Choctaw soul eaters move throughout this novel as matter-of-factly as do the living characters ... leading each man deeper into his own roots." *Choice* notes that Owens' "lyrical prose evokes the classic American writers of this century: Stevens, Williams, Crane," and concludes that "this is a graceful literary production ... [although] feminists may object to attacks on women as a central plotting device." The *American Book Review* observes that "Despite the moral lessons, we still have a serious murder mystery, written by a clever, entertaining writer with magic in his metaphors." According to the *L.A. Times Book Review*, "The metaphor of searching—for a body, for identity, for revenge, for understanding—gives the book more strength than a simple whodunit. Other images interact and reverberate throughout the story, as the Indian characters struggle to define and reclaim an identity that had been lost and distorted by the dominant culture."

RECOGNITION: Co-winner of the Josephine Miles, PEN Oakland Award for 1993 and the 1995 Roman Noir Award (the French equivalent of the Edgar Award); REVIEWS: *ABR* Apr/May '93; *Choice* 6/92; *KR* 12/15/91; *LATBR* 6/21/92; *LJ* 1/92; *PW* 12/20/91

Palliser, Charles (USA/UK)

Betrayals (1995); Ballantine 1996 (pbk); See Section 3, #250

Parks, Tim (UK)

765   *Shear* (**1993**); Grove 1995 (pbk)

In the aftermath of a fatal construction accident in Australia, Peter Nicholson, a 40-year-old British consulting geologist, is sent to a Mediterranean island to inspect the quarry which supplied the stone. Peter, throwing caution and fidelity to the wind, has brought along his mistress and has pushed his wife and family to the back of his mind. When the mother of the dead construction worker arrives on the scene she has revenge uppermost in her mind.

According to Jonathan Yardley (*WPBW*), "literary" novelist Tim Parks has given *Shear* "a genuinely arresting, suspenseful story without in any way compromising the integrity of the work." Yardley concludes that Park's novel "can be read purely as entertainment, though ... there is far more to it than that." The *London Review of Books* concludes that "What is most impressive about this novel is that it expertly mixes genres — the sort of thriller that flourishes lots of technical detail, the detective story, the sex story — yet is also an 'experimental' novel in that it does unusual things with prose." The *New York Times Book Review* found *Shear* to be an "eerie, engrossing and beautifully written suspense novel."

RECOGNITION: *NYTBR* Notable Book of 1994; REVIEWS: *BL* 7/19/94; *KR* 5/1/94; *LRB* 11/4/93; *NYTBR* 7/31/94; *PW* 5/16/94; *WPBW* 7/10/94

Pearson, T.R. (USA)

766   *Cry Me a River* (1993); Owlet 1994 (pbk)

T.R. Pearson's sixth novel is a tale of doomed love, murder, and the things small-town people do to stave off boredom. The novel's inciting event is the brutal murder of a policeman. A fellow officer, with little more to go on than a pornographic Polaroid print of a woman "not his wife," pursues the official investigation through the bars, brothels and back streets of a small southern town. Along the way we learn much about the community at large and through Pearson's rambling narrative we are told "the whole story but not the whole truth" (*TLS*).

According to novelist **William T. Vollmann** (*NYTBR*), "Beneath its whodunit disguise, *Cry Me a River* is a minor *Middlemarch* in its vivid delineation of a large gallery of complex, driven figures. Although Mr. Pearson has bowed so far as to give us a perfunctory, obligatory denouement, you'll find no suspense, no burning gunpowder narrative trail to get you there. I would say this novel is about two-thirds digressions by weight, and the digressions are delicious." *Kirkus Reviews* makes a similar observation: "Pearson's latest comedy of bad manners confirms his status as a master storyteller.... Something of a murder mystery, this raucously funny novel is more focused than the usual Pearson narrative. But even this intrigue allows for his characteristic digressions, his elegant variations,

and his ability to transform the vulgar into the sublime." The *Times Literary Supplement* calls Pearson "a very funny writer" and concludes that "the account of how a policeman was caught by a passing liberal tourist, dangling a car-thief off the bridge, the descriptions of various murders from the narrator's past and of the uncomfortable Christmas he spends with his brother's family, have a dry laconic absurdity, achieved with a minimum of means."

OTHER MEDIA: Audiocassette (Recorded Bks/unabr); RECOGNITION: *NYTBR* Notable Book of 1993; REVIEWS: *KR* 11/1/92; *LJ* 12/92; *NY* 3/22/93; *NYTBR* 4/11/93; *PW* 11/2/92; *TLS* 11/15/93; *WPBW* 1/17/93

Porter, Dorothy (Australia)

767   *The Monkey's Mask: An Erotic Murder Mystery* (1994); Arcade 1995 (HC); Serpents Tail 1997 (pbk)

Dorothy Porter has, in *Monkey's Mask*, created a unique literary hybrid: A lesbian crime thriller in verse. Featuring Jill Fitzpatrick, a street smart, wise-cracking P.I., and set variously in the fog-chilled Blue Mountains and the Sydney urban poetry "scene" (where the would-be intelligentsia hold sway), Dorothy Porter's debut novel is about obsession, love and the desire for power — and the sexual underpinning of all three.

According to the *Library Journal*, Porter "writes short verse in a staccato, telegraphic style accented by salty language and graphic Australian slang, for which she provide a delightful glossary." In the view of the *Australian Bookseller*, "No one else springs to mind who writes so aptly about female sexuality. A book to rave about, to gasp at the daring, the beauty — and the wit." The *Australian Book Review* notes that "There are murders and betrayals and red herrings and a number of nefarious characters and the plot races along at breakneck speed as the words race down the page. Porter's language is lean, colloquial, raw, yet rich in imagery and that sensuousness for which she is renowned." *The Age* argues that "Those who get suspicious about literary gushing, particularly where poetry is concerned, can be reassured when it comes to the *Monkey Mask*. This detective novel in verse from poet Dorothy Porter has sent the literati scuttling for their Thesauruses for new superlatives. Hype notwithstanding, this is a terrific read."

RECOGNITION: Shortlisted for the Australian Bookseller's Association Book of the Year Award; REVIEWS: *Age* 10/22/94; *AusB&P* 6/94; *AusBkRev* 10/94; *LitRev* 1/98; *LJ* 11/1/95

Powers, Charles T. (USA)

768   *In the Memory of the Forest* (1997); Scribner 1997 (HC); Penguin 1998 (pbk)

The late Charles T. Powers — a journalist for the *L.A. Times* for more than 20 years and the former chief of the Eastern European bureau, has crafted a deeply felt and fully realized tale of wartime complicity and moral cowardice. The novel opens in a small Polish village soon after the collapse of the Soviet Union and features Leszek, a young farmer, who begins to ask troubling questions regarding the death of a childhood friend. Although his murdered body was found in a nearby forest but no one (neither the police or civic leaders) seems to be particularly interested in getting to the bottom of the crime.

Publishers Weekly calls *In the Memory of the Forest* a "searching exploration of the social, moral and personal impact of communism's collapse in Poland." According to the *Atlantic Monthly*, "Mr. Powers's novel starts in the shape of an amateur-detective thriller ... with Leszek and the victim's father [starting] their own investigation.... [But] becomes an exploration of the guilt, fear, and corruption that underlie the history of the town, where nothing is ever said about the disappearance of the once large Jewish population or the network of bribery and smuggling that supplanted normal business under the Communists." The *New York Times Book Review* calls it an "acutely moral novel ... that manages to extract hope from post-Communist chaos and from a village's huge investment in disremembering the 80 percent of its prewar population who were Jews" and concludes, "In this mystery novel the central mystery is the past, which shimmers, liquid and iridescent, determining identity and destiny." The *L.A. Times* found "Charles Powers' sense of place [to be] astounding. His knowledge of Poland fills *In the Memory of the Forest* with details that bring the novel alive."

RECOGNITION: *NYTBR* Notable Book of 1997 *L.A. Times* "Best Books" 1997; REVIEWS: *AtlM* 4/97; *LATBR* 12/14/97; *NYTBR* 4/13/97 & 12/7/97; *PW* 12/9/96

Read, Piers Paul (UK)

769   *The Patriot* (1995); Random House 1996 (HC)

American Art Historian Francesca McDermott, an expert on Russian dissident artists, is in Berlin to organize an exhibition of Russian experimental art, much of which had been long-suppressed by the Soviets. McDermott is excited by what she perceives to be the new "openness" in the former Soviet Union. Working with her is the mysterious Serotkin, an arrogant young Russian expert with whom she becomes emotionally involved. Meanwhile, a KGB lieutenant by the name of Nikolai Gerasimov is hot on the trail of a fellow KGB officer (Andrei Orlov) who had been assigned to investigate an illegal, and highly profitable, icon-

smuggling operation. Orlov, it appears, has absconded with the smugglers' profits.

According to Christopher Lehman-Haupt (*NYT*), *The Patriot* (originally published in London as *A Patriot in Berlin*) "represents a new level of achievement for Read [and is] an impressive blending of atmosphere, characters and ideas." The *Times Literary Supplement* observes that Read has "plotted a tense and tortuous thriller exposing the failure of post-Gorbachev Russia and probing guilt and deception in Berlin after the Wall." The *TLS* concludes that in *A Patriot in Berlin* "the tension is not simply between icons and abstract art, not even between patriotism and self-expression: the crux appears to be the imposition yet again, as in 1917 (this time by international capitalists rather than Marxists), of Western-inspired dogma on a population which remained resolutely in the Middle Ages for a millennium too long." English novelist Philip Kerr, writing in *The* (London) *Sunday Times* argues that "In *A Patriot in Berlin*, Read has produced not merely an engrossing and plausible thriller, but also a thoughtful and elegantly written novel — perhaps his best yet."

REVIEWS: *BL* 2/1/96; *Econ* 10/28/95; *LJ* 2/1/96; *LST* 9/3/95; *NS&S* 9/22/95; *NYT* 2/22/96; *NYTBR* 3/10/96; *PW* 12/11/95; *TLS* 9/8/95

Reuss, Frederick (USA)

Horace Afoot (1997); Vintage 1999 (pbk); See Section 3, #260

Schwiedel, David (USA)

770   *Confidence of the Heart* (1995); Milkweed Editions 1995 (pbk)

A young, "hot-shot" anthropologist by the name of Patrick ('Spoon') McGuffin is determined to avoid the conveyor belt to Yuppie-dom. Fieldwork in Guatemala has resulted in a love affair — capped by a proposal of marriage — with the daughter of a wealthy coffee grower. The wedding will, of course, take place in Guatemala and Spoon has convinced Armando, an old college friend (of a much more philosophical bent than Spoon) to fly down to act as best man. The ultra-liberal Spoon has begun to organize the Indian workers on the coffee baron's plantation and is soon at odds with his father-in-law-to-be. Meanwhile, Armand, during a short trip into the countryside, is captured by guerrillas and the novel turns ever darker.

Publishers Weekly observes that "Schweidel's prize-winning first novel ... ventures deep into the dark heart of friendship and identity amid the post-civil war chaos of Guatemala" and concludes that "With an ambiguous ending appropriate to its shadowy tone, *Confidence of the Heart* provides a powerful illustration of the uncharted boundaries of friendship." In the view of *Booklist*: "This novel works surprisingly well, hooking the reader with its grim but gripping story line while relentlessly making the point that America's quality of life depends upon the blood and sweat of the Third World."

RECOGNITION: Winner of the 1995 Milkweed Fiction Award; REVIEWS: *BL* 5/1/95; *KR* 3/15/95; *LJ* 5/15/95; *NYTBR* 11/5/95; *PW* 4/10/95

Shacochis, Bob (USA)

771 *Swimming in the Volcano* (1993); Penguin 1994 (pbk)

Swimming in the Volcano is set on the fictional Caribbean island of St. Catherine and features an American economist by the name of Mitchell Wilson. Mitchell has come to the island to work for its Minister of Agriculture, and his former lover Johanna (Johnnie) has just made a reappearance in his life. The plot is fueled by island intrigue of a political nature as well as by a sinister dollop of drug running.

In the view of the *Times Literary Supplement,* "Shacochis catches brilliantly the teeming sensuality of the island, in a prose so purple that one can get lost in the intricate mazes of his sentences...." Called "the finest novel I have read in many years" by William O'Rourke writing in the *Chicago Tribune, Swimming in the Volcano* was judged to be a "splendid first novel" by the *Library Journal* which goes on to point out that it "may sound like a fast-paced thriller, but though there's a mystery to crack at the heart of this richly detailed novel, Shacochis in fact offers a chilling evocation of the misunderstandings that arise between feckless Americans and struggling islanders for whom St. Catherine's is no paradise." The *New York Times Book Review* suggests that "each of *Swimming in the Volcano*'s many scenes is expertly wrought, and the sum of the parts is greater than the whole." In the view of the *L.A. Times Book Review* Shacochis's novel "is rich in incident and sense of place. And rich in detail. Thanks to his vivid, unblinking depiction, St. Catherine emerges as real as, and perhaps more real than, any existing Antilles isle...." *The* (London) *Sunday Times* calls it "a serious richly nuanced work, a bold voyage into waters once piloted by Conrad or Greene."

RECOGNITION: Nominated for the 1993 National Book Award; *NYTBR* Notable Book of 1993; REVIEWS: *BL* 3/1/93; *ChiTrib* 4/25/93; *LATBR* 5/16/93; *LST* 12/5/93; *LT* 11/15/93; *NYTBR* 5/2/93; *PW* 2/8/93; *TLS* 2/18/94; *WPBW* 6/13/93

Shakespeare, Nicholas (UK)

772 *The Dancer Upstairs* (1995); Doubleday 1996 (HC)

In Nicholas Shakespeare's second novel (after his award-winning *The Vision of Elena Silves* 1990), the author returns to South America and weaves a compelling story around the murky reality of Peru's violent Marxist guerrilla movement. The Shining Path, a fanatical Maoist organization which operated as much like a religious sect as a revolutionary movement, held sway in Peru for a good ten years until its charismatic leader, Chairman Guzman, a philosophy professor from Ayucucho, was captured. Shakespeare's fictionalized account — utilizing the form of a political thriller — is narrated by Colonel Augustin Rejas, the arresting officer who is, in turn, being interviewed by John Dyer, a British journalist. Using the few known facts regarding the pursuit and capture of "the Chairman" Shakespeare creates a context for a tension-filled tale featuring a love triangle comprised of a hunted man, his pursuer and a beautiful ballet teacher.

According to *Publishers Weekly,* Nicholas Shakespeare "has written a gripping literary thriller in which a detective's pursuit of a terrorist leader expands into a many-layered tale of politics and love.... Shakespeare delivers an unusually powerful examination of what animates the souls of those who choose — or are forced — to play even small parts upon the stage of history." The *Times Literary Supplement* notes that "Shakespeare is a good writer ... and [concludes] if he hasn't yet moved into the Graham Greene class, he is surely slowly getting there...." The *New Statesman & Society* observes that "in addition to being a satisfyingly rich tale of romance (the Conradian terms are unavoidable) this is a highly intelligent examination of Peruvian — and South American — reality."

OTHER MEDIA: John Malkovich has, according to *Booklist,* bought the film rights to this novel; RECOGNITION: *Booklist* Editors' Choice 1997; REVIEWS: *BL* 1/1/97; *KR* 12/1/96; *LJ* 1/97; *NS&S* 9/22/95; *NYTBR* 3/16/97; *PW* 12/9/96; *TLS* 9/22/95; EDITOR'S NOTE: Mr. Shakespeare was named by *Granta* magazine to its 1993 list of the twenty "Best Young British Novelists."

Shea, Lisa (USA)

773 *Hula* (1993); H.H. Norton 1993 (HC); Dell 1995 (pbk)

In her critically-acclaimed debut novel set in the early 1960s, Lisa Shea focuses on two sisters whose violently unstable and abusive father (a retired soldier with a metal plate in his skull) has thoroughly blighted their childhoods. As their mother, a former dance instructor, is too cowed by her husband to adequately protect her daughters, the girls must rely on each other. *Hula* takes place — almost exclusively — in the girls' suburban Virginia backyard, a place of refuge and elaborate fantasy play which, over time, grows ever darker as their games are influenced more and more by their nascent sexuality. Matters come to a head one shocking summer.

According to *Booklist* "The family members remain nameless in this claustrophobic and often cryptic tale, an anonymity that lends a certain mythic terror to events and personalities." In the view of the *New Yorker*: "The tenacity of the narrator [the younger of the two sisters] and the imaginative resources she brings to bear on her day-to-day survival literally make you ache." *Publishers Weekly* concludes that "The nameless terrors in their home life counterpoint the irrepressible optimism that is native to childhood and that, Shea implies, can see children safely through the grimmest of circumstances, such as the searing climax of this quiet, expertly told novel."

REVIEWS: *BL* 11/15/93; *LATBR* 1/27/94; *LJ* 11/15/93; *LT* 4/20/95; *NY* 2/21/94; *NYTBR* 1/16/94; *PW* 11/1/93; *WRB* 7/94

Shields, Carol (USA/Canada)

774   *Mary Swann* (1987); Penguin 1990 (pbk)

In Carol Shield's fourth novel, the eponymous *Mary Swann*, a uneducated, impoverished farmer's wife, who is also a talented though little-known young poet, is brutally murdered. The tale is narrated by four disparate individuals (an earnest feminist scholar, a pompous literary biographer, a sheltered, small-town librarian and a feisty retired newspaper editor) who, while generally admiring of her talents, perceive Mary Swann in very different ways. Within the framework of a detective story, Ms. Shields skillfully explores the distortions inherent in biography and memory.

According to the *London Review of Books*, *Mary Swann* "is a very good novel, alive in every sense; formally ingenious and inventive, strikingly evocative of place [rural Canada], of character, of the world of things, capable of both comedy and tenderness, and above all beautifully, pleasurably written." Christopher Lehman-Haupt (*NYT*) observes that the author "takes aim at everything from feminism to academic scholarship to Canadian provincial life and its aspirations to culture...." *Booklist* calls *Mary Swann* "an odd but affecting novel" and concludes that it "alternately skewers the literary world and makes some moving, perceptive comments about the nature of identity." Canadian poet and novelist **Margaret Atwood** found Carol Shields's novel to be "deft, funny, poignant, surprising and beautifully shaped."

OTHER MEDIA: Adapted for film in 1996 (starring Miranda Richardson); REVIEWS: *BL* 5/15/89; *CSM* 8/11/89; *KR* 4/15/89; *LATBR* 8/20/89; *LRB* 9/27/90; *NYT* 7/17/89; *PW* 5/12/89; *TLS* 11/16/90; *WPBW* 7/30/89

Shreve, Anita (USA)

775   *The Weight of Water* (1997); Little, Brown 1997 (HC); 1998 (pbk)

Jean, a newspaper photographer, has been assigned to take pictures at an old weather-beaten house on Smuttynose Island, an unprepossessing expanse of rock and marsh off the coast of Portsmouth, New Hampshire. The long-abandoned property was, it appears, the scene of a grisly mid-19th century double murder and Jean's paper (prompted by the widespread interest in the O.J. Simpson story) plans to run a story on this piece of bloody local lore. According to the historical record, in 1873 two female residents — recent immigrants from Norway — of the island were brutally hacked to death and a third woman had been found huddled in a shoreline cave. The women's husbands, fishermen all, were away at sea during the time of the murders and a Prussian itinerant worker was eventually hanged for the ghastly crime. Jean, engaging in a bit of background research in the local newspaper's morgue, unearths a box of yellowed papers related to the case. As Jean reads on, it becomes obvious that what she has found is the confession of Maren, the "third woman." From this point on, Jean's story is intercut with that of Maren's tragic tale ... a particularly dark one that includes brother-sister incest and pathological jealousy. In the contemporary portion of the story, Jean's marriage to a well-known poet, precarious at best, is deteriorating rapidly, occasioned in large measure by her husband's interest in her brother's new girlfriend. Meanwhile Jean, wanting a bit of company during the picture shoot (and responding to what appears to be the pull of history), persuades her husband, son, and brother (with girlfriend in tow) to go over to the island with her. The day ends in tragedy.

Kirkus Reviews declares that *The Weight of Water* is a "highly readable yarn and a complex, convincing exploration of the ramifications of jealousy." The *L.A. Times Book Review* notes that "Anita Shreve is fascinated by crimes of passion ... [and] once again, in her fifth novel (a stunning ... inquiry into the ravages of love) heinous crimes — including murder most foul — are presented in such a way as to heighten our sympathy for the perpetrator and make us question our moral certitudes." *The* (London) *Times* concludes that Ms. Shreve's " beautifully crafted" novel "is [also] a cuticle destroying thriller."

READING GROUP GUIDE: "Reading Group Choices" 1998 (Paz & Associates); RECOGNITION: *LATBR* "Recommended Titles" 1997; shortlisted for the 1998 Orange Prize; REVIEWS: *BL* 1/1/97; *KR* 10/15/96; *LATBR* 11/19/97; *LJ* 10/15/96; *LT* 6/7/98; *NYTBR* 1/19/97; *PW* 10/14/96

Smith, Dinitia (USA)

776 *The Illusionist* (1997); Scribner 1997 (HC); 1999 (pbk)

Dinitia Smith, a reporter for the *New York Times*, bases her third novel on a sensational Midwestern murder case involving a transsexual. Ms. Smith sets her story in Sparta, a dreary upstate New York town, and features three women, each of whom falls in love with a newcomer by the name of Dean Lily. Dean is a magician who gives impromptu performances in a local bar. He's also an adrogyne. The women (a part-time college student with limited prospects, a frazzled single-mother employed in a nursing home, and the local beauty queen) either do not notice, or simply do not care, that he is, anatomically speaking, a woman. The men of Sparta, of course, have no illusions with regard to Dean Lily.

According to *Kirkus Reviews, The Illusionist* a "dark, meditative tale of a transsexual murder in upstate New York," offers a "harsh but deadly accurate evocation of late-20th-century rural life" as it plumbs the "unfathomable mysteries of sexual identity and charisma...." In the view of novelist Carolyn See (*WPBW*), "We have always had prevailing myths about small-town America. Many of them have to do with boredom and dullness and ennui. We're always surprised when it turns out that drugs and sex and inexplicable strangeness permeate those lonesome side roads.... We're always surprised when love and longing lead to murder as much in the countryside as in the city. Smith has taken this 'true' story and given its characters introspection and sad dignity. It's a peculiarly American tragedy. Smith has made us see both the America part and the tragic part.... It's another sad document about the failure of the American dream."

RECOGNITION: *NYTBR* Notable Book of 1997; REVIEWS: *BL* 9/15/97; *KR* 9/1/97; *LJ* 9/1/97; *NYTBR* 11/2/97; *WPBW* 11/2/97

Stone, Robert (USA)

777 *Damascus Gate* (1998); HM 1998 (HC); Scribner 1999 (pbk)

Robert Stone sets his sixth novel in Jerusalem, a city which vibrates with religious, cultural and historical tensions. A free-lance journalist — half Jewish, half Catholic but practicing neither — by the name of Christopher Lucas has drifted to the Holy City in search of material for a story. While there he agrees to co-author — with an Israeli psychiatrist — a book about the "Jerusalem syndrome" (the well-documented exacerbating effect the city appears to have on religious extremists). Lucas, professionally rootless and spiritually unmoored, is also in search of spiritual renewal. In the course of his research, Lucas eventually stumbles upon a terrorist plot (involving Jerusalem's venerable Temple Mount) spearheaded by an unholy alliance of Christian zealots and Jewish radicals.

Richard Eder of the *L.A. Times* calls *Damascus Gate* "A novel of springy action, a witty political thriller, an artfully lighted labyrinth of conspiracy and deception and a testing of Israel's edges" *The* (London) *Sunday Times* says it's a "millennial blockbuster" featuring "an extraordinary treatment of Jerusalem itself, as a multi-level labyrinth that is fascinating and horrifying by turns." According to the *New Yorker* it "brims over with plots, subplots, and an impressive array of incisively drawn characters." *Booklist* concludes that the "story line is skillfully developed, engendering considerable suspense, but the heart of the book lies in its characters' tormented inner lives, as a handful of Jews, Christians, Arabs, and combinations of each struggle with the idea of God and the nature of belief."

OTHER MEDIA: Audiocassette (Recorded Bks/unabr); RECOGNITION: Nominated for the 1998 National Book Award; *LATBR* "Top Ten Books of 1998"; *NYTBR* Notable Book of 1998; *PW*'s Best '98 Fiction; REVIEWS: *BL* 2/15/98; *ChiTrib* 5/3/98; *KR* 5/11/98; *LATBR* 5/17/98; *LST* 10/18/98; *NY* 4/13/98; *NYT* 4/14/98; *NYTBR* 4/26/98; *PW* 2/16/98

Straight, Susan (USA)

778 *The Gettin Place* (1996); Hyperion 1996 (HC); Doubleday 1997 (pbk)

In her third novel, Susan Straight describes a disturbing episode in the life of the Thompsons, an African-American family living in the fictional southern California town of Rio Seco. The enterprising Thompson clan own and run a number of family businesses including a towing and car repair outfit, a rib joint and a small olive orchard. When a burning car containing two dead white women turns up on Hosea Thompson's property, the 74-year-old patriarch is doubly troubled for, as he awaits the arrival of the homicide squad, the smell of burning flesh reminds him of the vicious race riots that occurred while he was growing up in Tulsa and which led to the burning of that city's black neighborhoods. One thing leads to another in this racially-charged thriller which features five generations of an African-American family.

Novelist **Francine Prose** (*WPBW*) argues that "Few authors in America manage (with the sort of easy confidence that makes the writing of fiction seem effortless) to do anything more difficult or (given the currently intense suspicion of anyone daring to write across the lines of race, gender, class) more nervy and brave." According to *Publishers Weekly*, "Although *The Gettin Place* does suffer from a surplus of characters and plot twists...

[Straight's] imagined Rio Seco is surely among the richest soils worked by an American novelist today." In the view of the *L.A. Times*, Ms. Straight "as she has done in all her books ... opens up a whole world, which good writers do. In her case, however, it happens to be a world that many of us don't really want to go to, a place where children get raped and see other children being murdered, where good people who try to raise themselves up get sucked back in because they are tired of fighting, or because there is no hand on the other side to pull them out and up. It is a world where the language is often not lush but hard and rough as concrete." *Kirkus Reviews* found *The Gettin Place* to be an "ambitious and engrossing portrayal of a black family under siege in white America" and concludes that "Straight has contrived a fascinating mystery, whose credible and fascinating solution contains a stunning climactic irony."

REVIEWS: *AtlM* 9/96; *KR* 4/15/96; *LATBR* 9/6/96; *LJ* 5/1/96; *Nation* 7/15/96; *PW* 5/6/96; *WPBW* 7/21/96

Swan, Susan (Canada)

779   *Wives of Bath* (1993); Random House (Canada) 1993 (HC)

In *The Wives of Bath* Canadian writer Susan Swan tells the story of one year in the lives of two 13-year-old girls, boarding students at Bath Ladies College, an Anglican girls school housed in a mock–Norman castle on the outskirts of Toronto. Ms. Swan's frequently gothic and sexually-charged coming-of-age story features Mary "Mouse" Bradford and her roommate and kindred spirit Pauline Sykes. Pauline, convinced that boys definitely have a "better deal," spends half her time dressed as a boy pretending to be her own invented brother "Lewis."

The *Literary Review* observes that "From Charlotte Brontë's *Jane Eyre* to Lillian Hellman's *The Children's Hour* and Muriel Spark's *The Prime of Miss Jean Brodie*, girls' schools (bristling with demonic matrons, petty tyrants and unfulfilled desires) have lent themselves to gothic horror.... And now the Canadian author Susan Swan adds another classic to the genre with her riveting new novel, *The Wives of Bath*." Calling *The Wives of Bath* a "well-wrought novel," *Booklist* points out that "[c]ompetition between character and experience graduates into a grisly climax of murder and mutilation, an end that unites fluid emphases on spooky descriptions, the psychological insights of a girl's Bildungsroman, and the clues of a crime mystery." *Publishers Weekly* judges *The Wives of Bath* to be "touching, suspenseful [and] often hilarious."

RECOGNITION: Shortlisted for the *Guardian* Fiction Prize and Ontario's Trillium Prize; REVIEWS: *BellesL*: Vol 9 No. 3; *BL* 9/15/93; *KR* 7/1/93;

LJ 9/1/93; *LRB* 12/2/93; *NS&S* 10/15/93; *PW* 7/19/93; *Q&Q* 8/93

Sweeney, Eamonn (Ireland)

Waiting for the Healer (1997); St. Martin's 1998; Picador 1999 (pbk); See Section 4, #383

Tartt, Donna (USA)

780   *The Secret History* (1992); Ballantine 1996 (pbk)

In Donna Tartt's debut novel, a young man, Richard Papen, recounts (from a vantage point some years later) a series of highly disturbing events to which he was a witness while a student at a small, progressive liberal arts college located in the verdant hills of Vermont. Richard, a Californian, had been drawn into a highly charged circle of student "aesthetes" who were fascinated by arcane knowledge and dedicated to the pursuit of the Dionysian "ideal." Contemptuous of their fellow undergraduates, they spent much time in the company of a professor of Classics who encouraged their growing sense of moral and intellectual superiority. When they inadvertently (yet cavalierly) cause the death of a local farmer, their undergraduate "game" appears to be up.

The *Washington Post Book World* calls *The Secret History* a "mellifluous, ambitious first novel, while the *New York Times Book Review* observes that "There are echoes here of William Harrison's sinister *In a Wild Sanctuary* and of the complex psychologies so carefully examined by John Casey in *An American Romance*, yet the strengths of this accomplished, sometimes annoying and eminently readable first novel are clearly Donna Tartt's alone." According to *Time* "What Donna Tartt has attempted — and largely brought off — is a challenging combination of a mystery ... an exploration of evil, both banal and bizarre, and a generous slice of the world as seen by the author, a brainy graduate of Bennington [College].…" The *London Review of Books* notes that while it is "about the nature of evil, [it is also] full of wonder and romance — the romance of money, class, intelligence and beauty. It is swoonily compulsive, like listening to your own heartbeat.…" The *Literary Review* argues that (an occasional slide into pretentiousness aside) Donna Tartt's first novel "is utterly brilliant. It's funny, clever, frightening, quite disgusting, absolutely impossible to put down."

OTHER MEDIA: Audiocassette (Random Audio/abr); REVIEWS: *KR* 7/1/92; *LitRev* 10/92; *LRB* 11/19/92; *NatR* 10/5/92; *NewR* 10/19/92; *NewsWk* 9/7/92; *NYTBR* 9/13/92; *PW* 6/29/92; *Time* 8/31/92; *WPBW* 6/29/92; EDITOR'S NOTE:

For another novel which paints a fictionalized portrait of life at Bennington College see Nicholas Delbanco's *Old Scores #23*.

Theroux, Paul (USA/UK)

781 *Kowloon Tong* (1997); Houghton Mifflin 1997 (HC); Chapters 1998 (pbk)

Paul Theroux' mordant satire is set in Hong Kong in the months immediately preceding its hand-over to the People's Republic of China and features Neville "Bunt" Mullard, a "quintessential Englishman," his indomitable mother, Betty, and the sinister Mr. Hung, a business representative from the People's Republic of China.

According to the *Wall Street Journal*, Theroux "who has made a name for himself satirizing the follies of British colonialism in other novels, finds a natural target in the arrogant Betty but an even bigger one in the ruthless Mr. Hung. Bunt is skewered as well, but we are made to feel considerable pity for him, caught between the irresistible force of China's menacing emissary and the immovable object that is his mother." In the view of Richard Bernstein (*NYT*), "Mr. Theroux's novel is a tingly, spicy, melancholy story reminiscent of the novels of Graham Greene, and its most salient feature is the spiritual smallness, the plain bad taste of its characters." The (London) *Times* found *Kowloon Tong* to be "a perceptive, engaging thriller; Theroux at his best." *Booklist* argues that "Theroux's taut and suspenseful unraveling of Bunt's little world is absolutely riveting, capturing, as it does, the haunting sound of the last nail being pounded in the coffin of the British Empire." The *Library Journal* concludes that "this chilling little tale must be read to the end to catch the full extent of Bunt's breathtaking weakness."

OTHER MEDIA: Audiocassette (Dove/unabr); REVIEWS: *BL* 3/1/97; *KR* 4/1/97; *LJ* 3/1/97; *LT* 3/28/98; *NYT* 6/13/97; *WSJ* 5/21/97

Thomson, Rupert (UK)

782 *The Insult* (1996); Knopf 1996 (HC); Vintage 1997 (pbk)

Martin Blom, while carrying groceries across a parking lot, is struck in the head by a stray bullet. He regains consciousness in a hospital where his neurosurgeon informs him that he has been permanently blinded. He soon discovers, however, that he can actually see in the dark. His doctor assures him that he is suffering from delusions. After breaking off all ties with family, fiancée and friends, the increasingly disturbed young man begins an exhilaratingly furtive nocturnal existence. He eventually meets Nina, a supremely uninhibited young woman, only to lose her when she realizes he is not totally blind. Martin begins to suspect that whatever is going on in his head and behind his eyes has something to do with a clandestine medical experiment.

The London *Guardian* judges *The Insult* to be "a gripping and cerebral novel" and asks "How can people say that fiction is in a bad way when stuff like this is being written." According to the *Library Journal*, "Thomson proved himself a master of the surreal in *Air & Fire*— this one should confirm him as one of England's best young writers." The *Times Literary Supplement* observes that "Rupert Thomson has a pitiless humor about human confusion; his prose maintains a high tension between fragile polished ironies and Brando-esque spunkiness" and concludes that "*The Insult* is the most irresistible of his books; its resolution comes in a series of brutal and bleak surprises which will leave readers feeling incriminated by their own stupidity and weak-kneed of comfortable solutions."

RECOGNITION: Shortlisted for the 1996 *Guardian* Fiction Prize; REVIEWS: *Guard* 9/15/96; *KR* 6/1/96; *LJ* 7/96; *PW* 6/3/96; *TLS* 3/8/96; *WPBW* 8/30/96; EDITOR'S NOTE: Thomson's latest novel, *Soft* (Knopf 1998) was described by *Publishers Weekly* as "A sophisticated literary thriller of dazzling velocity" and was named to that publication's "Best '98 Fiction" list.

Tremain, Rose (UK)

783 *The Way I Found Her* (1998); FS&G 1998 (HC); Washington Sq. Press 1999 (pbk)

Rose Tremain has constructed a serio-comic romantic thriller around a precocious young boy's fascination with a much older woman. The protagonist —13-year-old Lewis Little— is spending the summer in Paris at the home of a best-selling Russian emigre writer whose novels are being translated into English by Lewis's beautiful, talented mother. Left almost exclusively to his own devices by his mother who has taken a French lover, Lewis wiles away his vacation discussing philosophy with an existentialist roofer, confiding to his journal, fraternizing with the household help, and fantasizing about the exotic Russian novelist. When the latter mysteriously disappears, the besotted and indomitable Philip sets off in hot — and ultimately tragic — pursuit.

In the view of English critic Amanda Craig (*New Statesman*) "Every book Tremain writes is different, yet what remains astonishing is her style. Most good prose unfolds along predictable lines, its satisfaction lying partly in being able to anticipate what comes next; very few writers learn what Nabokov called "the Knight's move" of unexpectedness. Combined with her ability to project herself inside the skin of beings as diverse as a transsexual and a 17th-century doctor, her moral intelligence and her narrative skill, Tremain has become, alongside Hilary Mantel, the major writer of her generation." Novelist Carolyn See (*WPBW*), observes that "This is a literary puzzle where every sentence counts as a mystery" and concludes that "I can't think of a better novel to read this summer."

OTHER MEDIA: Audiocassette (Sterling Audio/unabr); RECOGNITION: *NYTBR* Notable Book of 1998; *PW*'s "Best '98 Fiction"; REVIEWS: *EW* 8/21/98; *KR* 5/15/98; *LJ* 5/15/98; *NS* 5/30/97; *NYTBR* 8/2/98 & 12/6/98; *PW* 4/27/98; *WPBW* 7/10/98; EDITOR'S NOTE: Ms. Tremain was named by *Granta* magazine to its 1983 list of the twenty "Best Young British Novelists"

Trevor, William (Ireland)

784   *Felicia's Journey* (1994); Viking 1994 (HC); Penguin 1995 (pbk)

Felicia, a young Irish-Catholic girl from rural Ireland, finding herself pregnant, journeys to England in search of her lover, Johnny, who is reportedly working for a lawn mower factory in the English Midlands. Disoriented by the strange English accents, rootless, and increasingly fearful, Felicia is befriended by an older man. Mr. Hilditch, a jovial, overweight foodservice manager, is unexpectedly kind and when Felicia loses her wallet, he offers her a place to stay.

According to *The* (London) *Times* "Hilditch is a sinister prowler, brilliantly evoked by Trevor, who conveys the scent of evil and corruption that surrounds him. Yet Trevor is endlessly empathetic — his work is full of true depths, of hells whose inhabitants do not know where they are." The *Library Journal*, in its starred review, asserts that Mr. Trevor "has written a taut psychological thriller with an unusually effective surprise ending...." *Publishers Weekly* notes that "What happens to Mr. Hilditch, in the brilliantly evoked setting of dank cafes and pubs, homeless wanderers, revivalists and bus trips to stately homes, is the stuff of nightmare; not cynically created, but one born of deep understanding and piercing truth. This is a thriller lifted to the level of high art...." According to Michiko Kakutani (*NYT*), "Mr. Trevor is able to turn the stuff of lurid, tabloid headlines into a sad and oddly moving tale of lost opportunities and misplaced hopes." In the view of novelist **Francine Prose** (*WPBW*), "One hopes that tens of thousands people will buy *Felicia's Journey*. Let them read it for the plot — and something else will get through: the depth, the bravery, the felicities of language, style, narrative economy and psychological insight."

OTHER MEDIA: Audiocassette (Chivers/unabr); RECOGNITION: Winner of 1994 Whitbread Award and the (London) *Sunday Express* 1994 Book of the Year; *NYTBR* Notable Book of 1995; nominated for the *L.A. Times* Book of the Year; RE-

VIEWS: *BL* 11/1/94; *CSM* 1/10/95; *EW* 1/13/95; *KR* 10/1/94; *LJ* 12/94; LST 8/28/94; *NS&S* 8/19/94; *NYT* 1/3/95; *NYTBR* 1/8/95; *PW* 10/31/94; *Time* 1/16/95; *TLS* 8/26/94; *WLT* Sum '95; *WPBW* 1/22/95; *WSJ* 1/26/95; EDITOR'S NOTE: Trevor's latest novel *Death in Summer* (1998) was described by *Publishers Weekly* as a "chilling" story about the "capriciousness of fate, the randomness of death and the tragedy of downtrodden lives." It appears on *PW*'s "Best '98 Fiction" list and on the *New York Time Book Review*'s list of Notable Books of 1998.

Unsworth, Barry (UK)

785   *After Hannibal* (1996); Doubleday 1997 (HC); W W Norton 1998 (pbk)

The are called "strade vicinale," neighborhood roads. They are not intended to join places, only to give access to scattered houses. Dusty in summer, muddy in winter, there are thousands of miles of them wandering over the face of rural Italy. When such a road has reached your door it has no necessary further existence; it may straggle along somewhere else or it may not. You can trace their courses on the survey maps kept in the offices of the local "comune"; but no map will tell you what you most need to know about them: whether they are passable or ruinous or have ceased altogether to exist in any sense but the notional. Their upkeep falls to those who depend on them, a fact that often leads to quarrels. The important thing, really, about roads like this, is not where they end but the lives they touch on the way.

So we are introduced to the lay of Barry Unsworth's particular land in his darkly comic ensemble piece set in modern Umbria near the site where the elephant-riding Hannibal and his invading band of Carthaginians ambushed and slaughtered a Roman legion 22 centuries ago. The aptly-named *After Hannibal* features a group of British, American and German expatriates (modern invaders, certainly) whose presence leads to local disputes, rivalries, avariciousness, and a good deal of honest treachery.

Kirkus Reviews notes that "Following his grim, medieval *Morality Play* (1995) with a more delicate modern work, Unsworth makes the most both of his Booker Prize-winning talents and the Italian countryside he now calls home to offer an homage to Umbria and a skewering of the motley multinational crew who've taken up residence there." Richard Eder (*L.A. Times Book Review)* observes that "Barry Unsworth weaves history, art and custom into his sinuous and mordant account of five hopeless attempts, ranging from comic to touching, to possess the beauty of an old civilization without paying a portion of the blood price upon which it was built" and concludes that the result is "entirely beguiling." *The* (London) *Sunday Times*, concludes that "In keeping with the novel's blend of disenchantment and enchantment, the figure linking the various plots is a lawyer who combines worldly irony with openness to life's wider aesthetic and moral horizons. Part-amused, part-melancholy, humane, sophisticated, suavely resourceful, he encapsulates the spirit of this appealing book with its highly civilized look at savagery."

RECOGNITION: *L.A. Times* "Best Books" 1997 (Top Ten); REVIEWS: *BL* 2/1/97; *KR* 12/15/96; *LATBR* 3/9/97; *LST* 8/25/96; *LT* 8/29/96; *WPBW* 3/20/97; *WSJ* 2/21/97

Walsh, Jill Paton (UK)

786 *The Serpentine Cave* (1997); St. Martin's 1997 (HC)

Jill Paton Walsh sets her latest novel on England's Cornish coast and features Marian Eaton, the troubled middle-aged daughter of a well-known artist. Marian has returned to Cornwall — where she spent much of her childhood — with her grown children (Alice a musician and Toby a stockbroker — both with troubles of their own) in tow. Marian hopes to unravel a mystery — tied to a 1939 lifeboat disaster — which she is convinced will reveal the identity of her father, something her strong-willed and temperamental mother had managed to keep from her for more than 40 years. But now, in the wake of her 84-year-old mother's death, Marian is determined to uncover long-buried family secrets and retrieve her past.

In the view of *Entertainment Weekly*, *The Serpentine Cave* "is not always a subtle psychological study, but it is affectingly done." The *(London) Times* observes that it is "a compelling tale with an oddly period quality although it opens in the present on a dark morning in Addensbrook hospital...." *The Washington Post Book World* suggests that "Although facts contribute to Marian's solving of the mystery, it is the emergence of suppressed memories and the rediscovery of a natural environment that gives *The Serpentine Cave* its particular poignancy and beauty." *Kirkus Reviews* concludes: "Pleasant sleuthing, likable people, fine Cornish seascapes, lots of St. Ivesian charm, and plenty of sensible, outright interesting talk about art. Top Walsh, all around."

REVIEWS: *EW* 12/97; *KR* 8/15/97; *LST* 1/12/97; *LT* 1/2/97; *TLS* 1/31/97; *WPBW* 1/5/98

Weldon, Fay (UK)

787 *Worst Fears* (1996); AtlM 1996 (HC); 1997 (pbk)

Fay Weldon's 21st novel, "a snappy whodunit of the heart" (*NYTBR*) features Alexandra Ludd, a successful — typically self-absorbed — West End actress who splits her time between London and the country house which she shares with her husband (Ned), her appealing three-year-old son (Sasha), and an ill-tempered Labrador named Diamond. When Alexandra learns of her husband's sudden death, she rushes home to the comforting circle of her "country" friends. Never one for focusing on the minutiae of everyday life, it takes the actress quite a while to realize that all is not as it seems, least of all her "divine" marriage to Ned.

According to the *Times Literary Supplement*, Ms. Weldon has produced an "expanded cautionary tale, the vehicle for a simple message about complacency, envy, and how truth both corrodes and liberates." *Entertainment Weekly* applauds Ms. Weldon's "bristly British wit" and concludes that *Worst Fears* is "a studied tour-de-force on the unsanctity of marriage and the treacherous nature of womanhood." The *LATBR* notes that "the closest that American writers have come to [Weldon's characteristic] fearlessness was the acidulous and bibulous Dorothy Parker, or Anita Loos, whom H.L. Mencken once told in envy and dismay that she had broken the American taboo of making fun of sex, Fay Weldon breaks taboos like the tape at a marathon, and she hasn't stopped running yet." *Booklist* declares that *Worst Fears* "unfolds in straightforward fashion, without the giddily complex plot twists that characterize much of Weldon's work, but her fans can rest assured that her acerbic wit and ruthless insight are present in full force."

OTHER MEDIA: Audiocassette (Recorded Bks/unabr); RECOGNITION: *NYTBR* Notable Book of 1996; REVIEWS: *BL* 5/1/96; *EW* 7/12/96; *KR* 4/15/96; *LATBR* 6/30/96; *NYTBR* 6/9/96; *TLS* 11/1/96; *WPBW* 6/28/96

Weller, Anthony (USA)

788 *Garden of the Peacocks* (1996); Marlowe 1996 (HC); Shooting Star 1998 (pbk)

In his debut novel, Anthony Weller weaves a mysterious tale around an aging Cuban-born sculptor (by the name of Cristobal de la Torra) who once hobnobbed with Picasso and other luminaries. A tormented Cristobal has faked his own death and retired to a Caribbean island, where, with his right-hand man Scully, he is building a memorial to his wife, who took her own life many years earlier. Cristobal hopes to win back the affection of their daughter, Esther, from whom he has long-been estranged. In due course Esther arrives on the island followed by a young American photographer, Thomas Simmons, with whom she has had a recent affair. Weller weaves the themes of artistic genius, expatriation and mortality into a very modern tale set variously in Havana, New York City, Barcelona and the Bahamas.

According to *Booklist*, "Anthony Weller has thrown all but the kitchen sink into his first novel. *Peacocks* includes the drama of a mystery novel and the passion of a romance tale, while capturing the beauty of its setting, a remote island in the Bahamas that has become the fortress of solitude for Cuban sculptor Cristobal de la Torre." *Kirkus Reviews* calls it an "intellectually ambitious first novel about a woman whose happiness is threatened by a family legacy mingling tragedy and genius." The *Library Journal* concludes that "The author's rich style complements his spirited characters and engrossing plot."

REVIEWS: *BL* 10/1/96; *KR* 8/1/96; *LJ* 9/1/96; *NYTBR* 10/27/96; *PW* 9/2/96

Westlake, Donald E. (USA)

789   *The Ax* (1997); Mysterious Press 1997 (HC); Warner 1998 (pbk)

Called a "chilling little fable for the end of the millennium" by Christopher Lehman-Haupt (*NYTBR*), *The Ax* is the aggrieved first-person narrative of one Burke Devore, a 51-year-old mid-level executive who has lost his job as product manager at the Halcyon Mills paper company as a result of downsizing. His response? He identifies a suitable replacement job (for which he is qualified — but by no means assured of being hired — for), and hatches a plot to eliminate all likely competitors.

According to *Booklist*: "Bypassing satire and heading straight for horror, Westlake offers an ingenious depiction of the perfect nineties employee — a cold-blooded assassin whose only loyalty is to himself and his family. This cold, clever novel is bolstered by Westlakes's inventive plotting, his meticulous use of abundant, credible details, and his burning anger over corporate tactics." *Publishers Weekly* observes that "[t]he suspense is tight as a steel coil, the background sociology is impeccably developed and the book should have upper level downsizers trembling in their Gucchis at the thought of the hideous anguish they are unleashing in the land."

RECOGNITION: *NYTBR* Notable Book of 1997; *LATBR* "Recommended Title" 1997; REVIEWS: *BL* 4/15/97; *KR* 5/15/97; *NYTBR* 6/29/97; *PeopleW* 7/4/97; *PW* 4/21/97; *WSJ* 6/30/97; EDITOR'S NOTE: Mr. Westlake's 1998 novel *Comeback* (published under the pseudonym of Richard Stark) appears on the *LATBR*'s "Best Fiction of 1998" list.

Winton, Tim

The Riders (1994); Scribner 1996 (pbk); See Section 1, #96;

Woodrell, Daniel (USA)

790   *Give Us a Kiss: A Country Noir* (1996); H. Holt 1996 (HC); PB 1998 (pbk)

Daniel Woodrell's fifth novel features Doyle Redman, a mildly successful, college-educated Cal-ifornia writer who, giving up his trendy West Coast life, returns to what passes for reality in the Ozark mountains he still calls home. *Give Us a Kiss* is a darkly comic novel about marijuana farms, blood feuds and gun-toting grandpas.

In the view of *Salon* magazine *Give Us a Kiss* is "a fast-talking white trash libretto about the eternal two-step between genes and karma ... [and] is charmingly (and terrifyingly) good, dirty fun." Richard Eder (*LATBR*) observes that "Woodrell does for the Ozarks what Chandler did for Los Angeles or Elmore Leonard did for Florida." The *New York Times Book Review* called it "a slick, sparkling and stylized" crime novel that (although it "transcends" its genre) contains "fast action, a great deal of mayhem and a soupcon of sex" and concluded that "Readers who prefer Jamesian character exploration or Tolstoyan sweep won't get it from this writer.... What they *will* get (as its subtitle makes plain) is a 'country noir' — and a first-rate one too."

RECOGNITION: *NYTBR* Notable Book of 1996; REVIEWS: *BL* 2/15/96; *KR* 11/15/95; *LATBR* 2/25/96; *LJ* 12/95; *NYTBR* 3/10/96; *Salon* 1996

HISTORICAL SETTINGS

Ackroyd, Peter (UK)

791   *The Trial of Elizabeth Cree: A Novel of the Limehouse Murders* (1994); Doubleday 1995 (pbk); SETTING: London — Victorian era

The Trial of Elizabeth Cree, an elaborately conceived transvestite murder mystery, features Dan Leno, a famous 19th century music hall artist. According to the historical record, Elizabeth Cree, a protege of Dan Leno, was hanged in London in 1881 for the murder of her husband. At roughly the same time, a series of gruesome murders were committed in the Limehouse section of the city. Given their extraoridnary "fiendishness" these murders were widely attributed to a supernatural force known as "the golem," a sort of Jewish vampire. Historical coincidences abound and numerous suspects are interviewed during the course of Ackroyd's frequently macabre and always inventive novel including: Karl Marx, Oscar Wilde, George Bernard Shaw and George Gissing — all habitués of the Reading Room of the British Library.

According to the *Library Journal*, Ackroyd has fashioned an "intellectually stimulating, if grisly, historical thriller." The *Times Literary Supplement* observes that "Dialectical materialism and Literary Realism are busily searching for truth in the streets of London, but they haven't the faintest notion of how to deal with the Golem.... Only Dan Leno, with the intuition of the dramatic artist, glimpses the truth, and even for him it is nothing but a shadow. Or is it?...." In the view of *New Statesman and Society,* "Ackroyd's obsession with London murderers and the vulgar brilliance of music-hall are fruitful here. His magpie way with relevant texts becomes more forgivable when real documents in the case are laid bare alongside his created ones. Research becomes the sibling of invention."

OTHER MEDIA: Audiocassette (Recorded Bks/unabr); RECOGNITION: *NYTBR* Notable Book of 1995; REVIEWS: *BL* 5/1/95; *LJ* 5/1/95; *NS&S* 9/9/94; *NYRB* 9/21/95; *NYTBR* 4/16/95; *Time* 5/29/95; *TLS* 9/9/94

Amis, Kingsley (UK)

792 *The Green Man* (1969); Acad Chi Press 1997 (pbk re-issue); SETTING: Sussex, England — lubricious 1960s

The late Kingsley Amis's re-issued novel *The Green Man* is regarded by many as a particularly fine example of the "literary" ghost story. Amis's benighted protagonist, Maurice Allingham, is the philandering, self-indulgent proprietor of "The Green Man," a prosperous pub — once a medieval coaching inn — with a nasty secret: it is haunted by the ghost of a 17th-century parson rumored to have been a sexual deviant and a particularly malevolent practitioner of the black arts.

As the *New Statesman* points out the narrator "Maurice Allingham, owner of the 'The Green Man' neglects his daughter, ignores his second wife and despises his mistress — although he spends what energy he can spare from drinking and ghost-hunting in trying to get the ignored and despised into bed with him at the same time.... The whole thing is hugely enjoyable...." The *Times Literary Supplement* observes that Amis is "offering the reader at least three genres of novel in one. There is a straight, spooky ghost story; there is a moral fable ... and there is a display of (his) distinctive style of comic preaching...." The *New York Times Book Review* calls *The Green Man* "a splendid chiller in the uncomplicated old fashioned sense.... The dialogue is filled with humor and a chilling strangeness. Indeed, the success of this short novel depends very much upon the balance that Amis maintains between laughter and fear." In the view of the *Philadelphia Inquirer* "Amis crafts a post–H.P. Lovecraft, pre–Stephen King chiller at a degree of sophistication considerably higher than either."

OTHER MEDIA: Adapted for British TV (starring Albert Finney); Audiocassette (Books on Tape/unabr); REVIEWS: *NS&S* 10/10/69; *NYT* 8/17/70; *NYTBR* 8/23/70; *TLS* 10/9/69

Atwood, Margaret (Canada)

793 *Alias Grace* (1996); Doubleday 1996 (HC); 1997 (pbk); SETTING: Toronto, Canada — mid-19th century

Margaret Atwood's latest novel — an adroit literary thriller which explores issues of gender and privilege in mid 19th-century North America — is based on the widely publicized murder trial of Grace Marks, Canada's answer to Lizzie Borden. In 1843, Miss Marks, a sixteen-year-old chamber maid, was tried, convicted and sentenced to life imprisonment for the murder of her employer, Thomas Kinnear, and his housekeeper (and mistress) Nancy Montgomery. Although Grace had initially confessed to the crime, she later claimed to have no memory of the event. It remains unclear whether Grace Marks was an innocent dupe or an evil manipulator. In Ms. Atwood's version, a young New England doctor interested in the fledgling field of mental health is brought in, sixteen years after Grace was imprisoned, to attempt to get to the bottom of her amnesia.

The *New Statesman* observes that Margaret Atwood "turns her attention to the past in this new *tour de force*.... Retelling the story of an 1840s murder scandal that dished up to newspaper readers all the delights of sexy working-class girls killing off their betters, the book makes voyeurs of us all." Richard Eder (*LATBR*) notes that Atwood's novel "evokes the society of the time in ironic and richly diverting detail" and concludes that "It portrays an astonishing heroine — Grace, the woman servant — so as to make her utterly present and unfathomable." According to the *Times Literary Supplement, Alias Grace* "... has its perverse aspects.... The effect is stunning and vaguely horrible, like rolling in a scented heap of someone else's laundry." The *Nation* calls it "criminally seductive" and concludes that it's "the novel Margaret Atwood has been preparing to write since she crossed the border and studied Victorian literature at Harvard in the sixties...." *Booklist* observes that "Atwood's humor has never been slier, her command of complex material more adept, her eroticism franker, or her descriptive passages more lyrical" and concludes that *Alias Grace* "is a stupendous performance." Judged "brilliantly accomplished" by *The* (London) *Sunday Times* and "irresistible ... a time machine of impeccable design" by *Entertainment Weekly, Alias Grace* was included on numerous year-end lists of outstanding books.

OTHER MEDIA: Audiocassette (BDD/abr); RECOGNITION: READING GROUP GUIDE; Winner of the 1996 Giller Prize; *L.A. Times* "Best Books" 1997 (*Top Ten*); *NYTBR* Notable Book of 1997; *PW* "Best Books" 1997; shortlisted for the 1996 Booker and Orange Prizes; shortlisted for the 1998 International IMPAC Dublin Literary Award; *Salon Magazine* "Book of the Year" 1997; REVIEWS: *BL* 9/15/96; *CanFor* Jan-Feb '97; *EW* 11/29/96; *LATBR* 12/15/96; *LJ* 11/1/96; *LST* 9/8/96; *Ms.* Jan-Feb '97; *Nation* 12/9/96; *NS* 10/4/96; *NYRB* 12/19/96;

NYTBR 12/29/96; *PeopleW* 1/27/97; *PW* 10/7/96; *Time* 12/16/96; *TLS* 9/13/96

Bainbridge, Beryl (UK)

794   *An Awfully Big Adventure* (1990); Carroll & Graf 1995 (pbk); SETTING: London —1950s

An Awfully Big Adventure, set in the London Theater world of the 1950s, is the bleakly humorous, increasingly disturbing tale of Stella an aspiring young actress who joins a theatrical company as an unpaid assistant stage manager. Stella is rapidly absorbed into the circumscribed, vaguely claustrophobic life of the company (deep in rehearsals for a holiday production of "Peter Pan") and becomes both a sharer of secrets and a catalyst for emotional mayhem.

Novelist **Francine Prose** (*Women's Review of Books*), praises Bainbridge's numerous gifts particularly "her terse wit, her precision, her economy of style and, above all, the absolutely unique sensibility with which she observes and records the unjust, upsetting, clumsy and terribly moving comedy of errors that we call human relations." In the view of the *New Statesman*, "the novel, with its ear for provincial manners, its undercurrents of violence, unlovely sexual encounters and increasingly brittle theatrical dialogues, tells a sinister story of emotional abuse." According to the *Washington Post Book World* the "matter-of-fact way in which Beryl Bainbridge presents [her characters], the dexterity with which she weaves the minute subtleties of the British class system into the narrative ... are all reasons why this is precisely the kind of well-told tale in modern novel form for which the British have the mold that no one else is able to replicate."

MEDIA: A film version starring Hugh Grant, Georgina Cates and Alan Rickman was released in 1994; RECOGNITION: Shortlisted for the 1990 Booker Prize; REVIEWS: *LitRev* 2/90; *LJ* 2/1/91; *LRB* 1/25/90; *LT* 4/8/95; *NS&S* 1/5/90; *NYTBR* 3/17/91; *TES* 1/5/90; *TLS* 12/15/89; *WPBW* 9/3/90; *WRB* 7/91

Baldwin, William (USA)

795   *The Hard to Catch Mercy* (1993); Fawcett 1995 (pbk); SETTING: Cedar Point, South Carolina —1916

A wry combination of southern history, family lore, race relations, myth and mystery, William Baldwin's debut novel is set in Cedar Point, South Carolina, in 1916. *The Hard to Catch Mercy*, narrated by 14-year-old Willie T. Allson, encompasses two fateful years in the young man's extended family. It begins with the stranding of a cow in a local swamp, continues with the arrival of energetic Uncle Jimmy and his subsequent infatuation with Amy Mercy (sister to the fearsome "Hard to Catch," a well-known animal trapper), and ends with the cataclysmic impact of World War I. Additional plot elements include a pair of tragic deaths, a treasure hunt, the unearthing of long-interred family secrets and the arrival, from Paris, of Willie's mysterious, flamboyant Aunt Lydia — a thoroughly modern woman — who is of the opinion that "the Negro in the South was much maligned" (a notion so troubling and foreign to the Allson clan that young Willie couldn't help but take notice).

Publishers Weekly, in its starred review, refers to Baldwin as a "devil of a storyteller" and calls *The Hard to Catch Mercy* a "rambunctious debut ... a sly but loving send-up of Deep South gothic mythology [which] plays fast and loose with nearly every Southern stereotype, including wounded Civil War heroes, loyal black servants, a dowry lost when it was hidden from the Yankees, and the charred remains of a family mansion." According to *Booklist*, Baldwin's narrator, fourteen-year-old Willie T. Allson, is "looking back to the eventful year of 1916, when adulthood first hit him square in the face" and recounts a story "that winds its way around and around like a mouse-hunting black snake through the barnlot, and with a back-porchy tone reminiscent of a grandpa relating one outrageous event after another."

RECOGNITION: Winner of the Lilliane Smith Award for Fiction; REVIEWS: *BL* 6/1/93; *KR* 4/15/93; *LJ* 11/1/93; *PW* 4/26/93

Banville, John (Ireland)

796   *The Untouchable* (1997); Knopf 1997 (HC); Mac Lib 1998 (pbk); SETTING: England — 1930s through 1960s

Set in Cambridge and London from the early 1930s to the 1960s, *The Untouchable* blends historical fact with the author's own artistic preoccupation with authenticity, guilt and redemption. Banville's "untouchable" is Victor Maskell, a character clearly based on Anthony Blunt, a Cambridge-educated aesthete, director of London's prestigious Courtauld Museum, art advisor to the Queen, and secret homosexual. Blunt was also, for roughly thirty years, a spy for the Soviet Union, the famous "4th man" in the infamous Burgess, Kilby and MacLean spy ring.

According to English novelist **Patrick McGrath** (*NYTBR*), *The Untouchable* is "an extraordinary book containing prose of a glorious verve and originality, in the service of a richly painted portrait of a man and a period and a society and a political order — the whole governed by an exquisite thematic design. Contemporary fiction gets no better than this." *Publishers Weekly*, in its starred review, assures us that "It is seldom one encounters as keen a literary intelligence as Banville's embarked upon as compulsively entertaining and thought-provoking a tale as this." Novelist **James Hynes**, writing in the *Washington Post Book World*, calls Victor Maskell "one of the great characters in recent fiction, a masterpiece of literary ventriloquism. He is by turns charming and self-pitying, lubricious and puritanical, heart-breakingly vulnerable and infuriatingly arch. The ultimate unreliable narrator, he is a brilliant and sophisticated man who devotes his life to lies and betrayals, only to realize much too late just whom he is betraying." The *New York Review of Books* concludes that "In an age when conventional pieties and a standardized 'seriousness' have tended to rob the novel of its lightness.... Banville's books are not only an illumination to read—for they are always packed with information and learning—but a joyful and durable source of aesthetic satisfaction."

RECOGNITION: *NYTBR* Notable Book of 1997; *LATBR* "Recommended Titles" 1997; *Publishers Weekly* "Best Books" 1997; REVIEWS: *BL* 4/15/97; *ChiTrib* 6/17/97; *ComW* 6/20/97; *KR* 4/15/93; *LATBR* 4/20/97; *LJ* 4/15/97; *LT* 5/11/97; *LST* 5/11/97; *NewsWk* 5/12/97; *NS* 5/16/97; *NYRB* 5/29/97; *NYTBR* 6/8/97; *PeopleW* 7/21/97; *PW* 4/14/97; *Salon* 4/9/97; *TLS* 5/9/97; *WPBW* 5/4/97

Berne, Suzanne (USA)

797 *A Crime in the Neighborhood* (1997); Algonquin 1997 (HC); H. Holt 1998 (pbk); SETTING: Washington, D.C., suburbs—1973

Suzanne Berne's deftly limned first novel, set in the fictional Washington D.C. suburb of Spring Hill during the summer of 1973, combines classic mystery elements with the psychological insight associated with successful coming-of-age novels. *A Crime in the Neighborhood* is narrated by thirty-five-year-old Marsha Eberhard as she looks back—over a quarter century—to the summer when she was ten years old ... the summer her father ran off with her mother's favorite sister, her older siblings began acting out in dangerous ways, a young neighborhood boy was raped and murdered and, as the drama of "Watergate" unfolded. A summer, in other words, when even the president of the United States stood accused of illegal behavior.

According to *Salon* magazine the "concentric circles of lawlessness—adultery inside the local terror inside the cheating heart of national politics—play nicely off one another and save this from being yet another child-of-divorce" tale. *Booklist* notes that "Berne is equally skillful at both capturing nuances of family life and detailing the potentially devastating effects of one person's actions on others in this impressive literary debut." *Kirkus Reviews* observes that "Berne's skill with language and her talent for evoking believable, all-too-human characters add to this fascinating story of evil and fear, and the unexpected consequences they engender." *Publishers Weekly* concludes that "Through

seamless narrative structure, an extraordinary sense of lightness and suspense and a deeply affecting conclusion, Berne's debut delivers a resonant portrait of a girl's community and a country's loss of innocence."

RECOGNITION: Winner of the 1999 Orange Prize; *NYTBR* Notable Book of 1997; REVIEWS: *BL* 4/15/97; *KR* 3/15/97; *LJ* 4/1/97; *NYTBR* 7/20/97; *PW* 3/3/97; *Salon* 9/4/97

Blackburn, Julia (UK)

798 *The Book of Colour*; Pantheon 1995 (HC); Vintage 1996 (pbk); SETTING: Seychelles Islands—19th Century onward

In her debut novel, Julia Blackburn, daughter of the English poet Thomas Blackburn, employs more than a hint of magical realism in telling the story of her family's ill-fated association with Mauritius, an island in the Seychelles. The story begins in the 1880s with the arrival "in paradise" of Ms. Blackburn's forebear, a missionary who has come both to bring the word of God and to eradicate sexual license. The ensuing culture clash would have disastrous far-reaching ramifications for the Blackburn family. The author serves up a "tropical cocktail of themes relating to race, dementia, sorcery and Victorian venery" (*NYTBR*) as she explores four generations of Blackburns.

As the *Washington Post Book World* points out, "A history irrevocably affected by race and a distant islander's curse could easily degenerate into a Gothic page-turner or a tendentious polemic, but it is a measure of Blackburn's sensibility and talent that the story she tells is, rather, a profoundly subtle exploration of prejudice as well as a poignant threnody for the dead...." The *Times Literary Supplement* finds the theme of "the stifling repression and racism of the English ... in the colonies and elsewhere [to be] not entirely original" but concludes that Blackburn, "with her talent for shrouding a story in a kind of chimerical vision, has created an intense brooding atmosphere which sticks long after the book itself has been put down." Michiko Kakutani (*NYT*) concurs, calling *A Book of Color* "a dense, poetic tale of a family's inheritance."

RECOGNITION: *TLS* "International Book of the Year"; shortlisted for the 1996 Orange Fiction Prize; REVIEWS: *KR* 6/15/95; *LJ* 7/95; *NYT* 9/20/95; *NYTBR* 10/1/95; *PW* 7/10/95; *TLS* 8/25/95; *WPBW* 11/5/95

Boyd, William (UK)

799 *The Blue Afternoon* (1993); Vintage 1997 (pbk); SETTING: 1930s L.A. & Manila in 1901

The Blue Afternoon, William Boyd's story of passion, lost love, and colonial intrigue is set, for the most part, during the period just following the conclusion of the Spanish-American War. Boyd's turn-of-the century Manila is a stagnant colonial city of drenching rain, staggering humidity and seething malcontent. When the bodies of mutilated American soldiers begin turning up in the old trench lines surrounding the city, the American governor, William Howard Taft, threatens reprisals. The ensuing police investigation is intertwined with the story of an illicit love affair between a young mestizo surgeon and the wife of an American Army officer. Boyd was widely praised for balancing the elements of historical romance, murder mystery, and political thriller.

According to Australian novelist **Thomas Keneally** (*NYTBR*), Boyd "writes novels in a grand, old-time way with complex plots and sweeping historical backdrops, exotic settings and casts of thousands...." In the view of the *L.A. Times Book Review*, *The Blue Afternoon* "ranges over the burgeoning disciplines and theories of architecture, surgery and aviation. Chronicling political unrest and weaving a murder mystery, it also ... studies seduction and enchantment." *Time* magazine calls *The Blue Afternoon* a "superior piece of fiction ... with unusual, mostly immoral characters, plenty of suspense and a truly ghoulish surprise.... In all, typical Boyd — satisfying and baffling at once."

OTHER MEDIA: Audiocassette (Chivers/unabr); RECOGNITION: Winner of the *L.A. Times Book Review* 16th Annual Book Prize; *Sunday Express* (London) Book of the Year; *NYTBR* Notable Book of 1995; REVIEWS: *BL* 2/1/95; *GW* 9/19/93; *LATBR* 12/10/95; *LJ* 2/1/95; *LRB* 9/23/93; *LT* 9/17/94; *NS&S* 9/24/93; *NYTBR* 4/2/95; *Time* 2/6/95; *TLS* 9/10/93; *WPBW* 2/19/95

Byatt, A.S. (UK)

800   *Angels & Insects* (1992); Random House 1994 (pbk); SETTING: Mid 19th century England

Angels & Insects consists of two novellas: "The Conjugal Angel" and "Morpho Eugenia." The first is a philosophical ghost story based on Tennyson's poem "In Memoriam" that revolves around two women who have been bereaved: a widow, Lilias Papagay, now a medium, and her client Emily Tennyson Jesse, whose fiancé, poet Arthur Hallam, died before they had a chance to marry. The second novella, "Morpho Eugenia," is a gothic fable (with a deceptively idyllic setting) about the parallels between insect and human society. William Adamson, a naturalist recently returned from ten years in the Brazilian rainforest where he has been studying social insects, has been invited to the home of his benefactor, a wealthy amateur biologist and collector. Here he meets and falls in love with his host's eldest daughter, Eugenia.

According to English novelist **Lawrence Norfolk** (*WPBW*), *Angels and Insects* "offers two brief visions of a world that Byatt understands well: 19th century England and the men and women who shaped it. Taken separately, either tale could stand as a perfectly formed, but essentially minor, work. Together they form something rather more complex and substantial...." In the view of the *Christian Science Monitor*, Byatt's "lushly descriptive prose has a Pre-Raphaelite vividness of color and detail." The *Times Literary Supplement* suggests that *Angels and Insects* is "[m]ore fully assured and satisfying than *Possession* ... and must be her best work to date." The *Literary Review* concludes that "*Angels and Insects* is the most voluptuously intelligent book this year."

OTHER MEDIA: An (Oscar-winning) film version was released in 1995 starring Mark Rylance and Kristin Scott Thomas; REVIEWS: *AtlM* 5/93; *BL* 3/15/93; *CSM* 5/25/93; *LitRev* 10/92; *LJ* 4/15/93; *LRB* 11/19/92; *NYTBR* 6/27/93; *NatR* 8/23/93; *NS&S* 11/6/92; *TLS* 10/16/92; *WPBW* 5/2/93; *Yale* 10/93

Carr, Caleb (USA)

801   *Angel of Darkness* (1997); Random House 1997 (HC); Ballantine 1998 (pbk); SETTING: New York City—1897

Caleb Carr sets *Angel of Darkness*— the sequel to his best-selling *The Alienist*— in 1897 and once again features "alienist" Dr. Laszlo Kreizler (a pioneering forensic psychologist), investigative reporter John Schuyler Moor, and Moor's thirteen-year-old assistant (and narrator) Stevie "Stevepipe" Taggert. A serial killer, this one more dastardly than the last, again drives the story which makes skillful use of its Victorian setting. As the novel opens, the eighteen-month-old daughter of the Spanish ambassador has been abducted and his distraught wife seeks the assistance of Dr. Kreizler and his intrepid team.

In the view of the *L.A. Times Book Review*, "Because Carr's interest remains an era teetering on the edge of modernity — the dawning of modern consciousness in particular — this is as much a psychological detective story as it is Conan Doyle." The *Times Literary Supplement* points out that "Carr is a historian by profession, and his New York of 1897 is beautifully realized — you can practically smell the horses. The coming Spanish-American war, of 1898, is woven effortlessly into the plot.... The sureness of the historical sensibility elevates *The Angel of Darkness* above genre fiction in which modern characters potter about in historical costume." The *TLS* also concludes that "There is a good deal that is lurid — for instance, a pygmy Filipino hitman called El Nino, who lays people low with curare darts — but it is all handled with such a straight face that Carr gets away with it." According to the *Library Journal*, "Using the relatively new fields of forensics and psychoanalysis, and calling on the assistance of some well-known 'names' [Teddy Roosevelt, Franz Boas, Cornelius Vanderbilt], the team runs [a psychopath] to earth...." *Kirkus Reviews* notes that "The ambiance is convincingly thick and period-flavorful, the murderous details satisfyingly gruesome, and even the somewhat shaky central ethical question ... is quite convincingly presented." *The* (London) *Times* calls *Angel of Darkness* "a thriller so shadowed with splendid period gloom, you could almost wear it instead of sunblock on a bright modern beach."

OTHER MEDIA: Audiocassette (S&S Audio/abr); REVIEWS: *EW* 9/19/97; *KR* 9/1/97; *LATBR* 10/26/97; *LJ* 10/15/97; *LT* 3/7/98; *NYTBR* 10/12/97; *PW* 825/97; *TLS* 3/13/98; *WPBW* 11/2/97

802 *The Alienist* (1994); Random House 1994 (HC); Bantam 1995 (pbk); SETTING: New York City at the turn-of-the-century

Historian Caleb Carr's period thriller, set in the late 1890s, unfolds against the background of New York City's "Gilded Age." A serial killer (preying on boy prostitutes) prowls the streets of a city lit by gas lamps and teeming with newly arrived immigrants. Carr's protagonist, the autocratic Dr. Kreizler, is an alienist, an "expert in mental pathology." Kreizler has been brought in by a young, politically ambitious Metropolitan Police Superintendent (by the name of Theodore Roosevelt), to assist his department in tracking down the murderer.

In the view of novelist **Stephen Dobyns** *(NYTBR),* Carr "knows his history" and has produced "a pleasing entertainment ... [in which] the plot moves forward without much struggle and the events are diverting." *Time* magazine called *The Alienist* a "remarkable time-machine voyage" and praised the "brooding, detailed cityscapes and rich historical set pieces." According to the *Chicago Tribune* "It is the attention to period detail and the modernistic psychological investigation that sets apart what would otherwise be a fairly conventional murder mystery." The *Library Journal* says that Carr's "knockout" debut is "infused with intelligence, vitality, and humor" and concludes that "This novel is a highly unorthodox variant of the Holmes-Watson theme and the best since Julian Symon's *A Three Pipe Solution.*"

OTHER MEDIA: Audiocassette (S&S Audio/abr); cinematic adaptation in progress; RECOGNITION: *NYTBR* Notable Book of 1994; REVIEWS: *BL* 4/15/94; *ChiTrib* 4/17/94; *EW* 4/22/94; *LAT* 6/8/94; *LJ* 3/1/94; *LST* 7/3/94; *NY* 6/27/94; *NYT* 3/29/94; *NYTBR* 4/3/94; *PW* 2/7/94; *Time* 4/18/94; *TLS* 7/1/94; *VFair* 4/94; *WPBW* 3/27/94

Christilian, J.D. (USA)

803 *Scarlet Women* (1995); Fine 1995 (HC); NAL/Dutton 1996 (pbk); SETTING: New York City — 1871

J.D. Christilian's highly atmospheric novel is set in 1871 in a New York City of stark economic and social contrasts. When Alice Curry, prostitute, is found murdered near the East Street docks few eyebrows are raised, at least until it is learned that she was wearing the clothes of an aristocrat's missing wife. The hard-boiled private investigator Harp (himself the son of a prostitute), is called upon to take the case.

According to the *Library Journal*, *Scarlet Women*, which is less about the lives of prostitutes than the title implies, "invites readers onto the streets of Victorian New York and steeps them in vivid stories of danger, corruption, destitution, and obsession." The *New York Times Book Review* compares *Scarlet Women* favorably to E.L. Doctorow's *Waterworks* (set, interestingly enough, in the same year) and points out "Harp's world is one in which immigrants are both the cops and the robbers, lust can lead to some nasty litigation and 'governance' is a fancy word for corruption...." *Booklist* notes that the "talented Christilian (a pseudonym) provides a wonderfully evocative picture of nineteenth-century New York" complete with "gripping" plot and "fascinating" historical details but concludes that "it's the charismatic and elusive Harp who really makes the story come alive."

REVIEWS: *BL* 2/15/96; *KR* 11/15/95; *LJ* 11/1/95; *NYTBR* 5/12/96; *PW* 10/23/95

Coe, Jonathan (UK)

804 *The Winshaw Legacy: Or, What a Carve Up!* (1994); Knopf 1995 (HC); Random House 1996 (pbk); SETTING: Yorkshire, England (1940s–1990s)

The Winshaw Legacy, Jonathan Coe's 4th novel (although first to appear in the US), is set in Yorkshire, England, and concerns a large, thoroughly unscrupulous family whose fortunes were originally derived from the 17th century slave trade. Judged "intelligent, funny and important" by the *TLS,* Jonathan Coe's mordant satire combines elements of the classic horror tale, detective mystery, autobiography and political history. As the novel opens, numerous family members are still involved in questionable occupations, including illegal arms trafficking, black-market art dealing and tabloid journalism. Plot twists incorporate (among other things) the impending Gulf War, go-go finances, a haunted house, insider trading, cruelty to animals, a mad woman in the attic and a will-reading party. Into this murky family broth wades Michael Owen, a young novelist who has been commissioned to write the family's official history. Coe's novel draws rather heavily on British political history and popular culture; the subtitle, for example, is taken from a campy 1960s British comedy starring the voluptuous Shirley Eaton.

The *London Review of Books* judged Coe's novel (described as "a potted history of Thatcherism ... tucked inside some meta-textual highjunks") to be an "appealingly ambitious" novel enhanced by the author's "promiscuous intermingling of literary genres." The *Library Journal* observes that Coe has fashioned "a wildly funny" novel, which, though "occasionally didactic, is none-the-less a 'tour-de-force' and a delight to read." *The Economist* calls *The Winshaw Legacy* "a triumph ... [as] its young author has not only managed to hold [the] ingenious, sprawling plot together over more than 500 well-paced pages, but also [succeeds] in combining so many different kinds of writing so successfully."

RECOGNITION: Shortlisted for the 1994 Whitbread Prize; REVIEWS: *BL* 12/1/94; *LJ* 12/94; *Econ* 5/14/94; *LRB* 4/28/94; *LST* 5/3/95; *NS&S* 4/29/94; *NYT* 3/10/95; *PW* 12/5/94; *TLS* 4/22/94

Coetzee, J.M. (South Africa)

805   *The Master of Petersburg* (1994); Viking 1994 (HC); Viking Penguin 1995 (pbk); SETTING: Czarist Russia

In *The Master of Petersburg*, prize-winning South African novelist J.M. Coetzee weaves a fictional tale around Fyodor Dostoevsky and his stepson Pavel. In Coetzee's fabulation, Dostoevsky has returned to St. Petersburg (from self-imposed exile in Germany) in the aftermath of Pavel's death, which has been ruled a suicide by local authorities. Given Pavel's revolutionary sentiments, the anguished Dostoevsky is unconvinced that Pavel would have taken his own life, and begins his own investigation. As he moves through Pavel's world, he grapples with twin erotic obsessions (triggered by his stepson's landlady and her adolescent daughter) and uncovers a "demonic" conspiracy.

Publishers Weekly declares that Coetzee has created an "epileptic Dostoevsky ... in deepest turmoil as he mourns his stepson, tries to learn how he died ... and alternately yields to and resists his darkest erotic self" and concludes that "It's a harrowing, exhilarating performance sure to further lift Coetzee's lofty reputation." The *Chicago Tribune* observes that "Coetzee need not have been to Russia or alive in 1869 to convey with researched authority the feel of place, language and time. He moves from fact to fiction with scarcely a hitch in his stride." In the view of *The* (London) *Times*, "the figure of Dostoevsky is a perfect vehicle for what Coetzee wants to explore. And St. Petersburg, evoked here with all the crushing, claustrophobic

immensity one remembers from the Russian master's novels, is the perfect setting. Just like the South Africa of his earlier novels, the Tsarist capital provides a political predicament — one that does not need defining since it is emblematic. It may be Russia, but it is pure Coetzee territory.... We are compellingly made aware of the truth that there is no such thing as innocence in human relations." *World Literature Today* concludes that "*The Master of Petersburg* is a powerful, intelligent, and sensitive novel, exploring, in the words of the author, a quaking of the soul."

OTHER MEDIA: Audiocassette (Books-on-Tape/unabr); RECOGNITION: *NYTBR* "Editors' Choice" 1994; REVIEWS: *BL* 11/1/94; *ChiTrib* 11/27/94; *Guard* 2/22/94; *KR* 8/1/94; *LJ* 9/1/94; *LT* 3/3/94; *NYTBR* 11/20/94; *PW* 9/5/94; *Spec* 2/26/94; *TLS* 3/4/94; *WLT* Win '95; *WPBW* 11/27/94

Cook, Thomas (USA)

806   *The Chatham School Affair* (1996); Bantam 1996 (HC); 1997 (pbk); SETTING: Chatham, Massachusetts —1920s

The Chatham School Affair is the compelling account of a series of tragic events (an illicit affair, an "accidental" drowning, and a celebrated trial) which rocked the small Cape Cod town of Chatham, Massachusetts, in the mid 1920s. The story is told in the form of a fictional memoir by middle-aged attorney Henry Griswold, a former student at the Chatham School, the son of its headmaster, and witness to the unfolding tragedy.

The *Library Journal* calls Cook's novel a "well-written, genre-stretching mystery [which starts slowly] but delivers a powerful ending." According to *Booklist*, *The Chatham School Affair* is the "story of how our secrets control our destinies ... a powerful, engaging and deeply moving novel ... [and an example of] well-crafted, genre-bending crime fiction." *Kirkus Reviews* calls *The Chatham School Affair* "*The Go-Between* as reworked by Ruth Rendell" and observes that "Readers who aren't exasperated by the glacial pace will find themselves entranced."

OTHER MEDIA: Audiocassette (Recorded Books/unabr); REVIEWS: *BL* 8/96; *KR* 7/15/96; *LJ* 7/96; *NYTBR* 9/29/96; *PW* 6/24/96.

Darton, Eric (USA)

807   *Free City* (1996); W.W. Norton 1996 (HC); SETTING: 17th-Century Northern Europe

Eric Darton in his debut novel employs a narrative style that echoes, at least faintly, Edgar Allan Poe, Kafka and the darker Hawthorne. Set in a northern port city in Europe at the dawning of the Age of Enlightenment, *Free City* tells the story of a

17th century doctor/inventor (nameless throughout) who is busily at work on a number of marvelous (in the true sense of the word) projects including: anesthetics, a military airship, explosives, and a mechanical dragon. The inventor has made a kind of pact with a rich and powerful businessman by the name of Roberto. As the story progresses, it becomes clear that Roberto — sketched as a sort of prototypical crypto-fascist — has nefarious designs on the city. Add to the storyline Roberto's talking duck, Frederick (who regularly addresses the local parliament) and the whole enterprise lurches decidedly towards the offbeat. Our inventor, fortunately, is a powerful voice of reason and the historical tide is, after all, turning.

According to the *New York Times Book Review* Darton's novel "attends the stormy birth of the Enlightenment, when faith vied with reason and science threatened to replace religion in defining human destiny." *Kirkus Reviews* argues that *Free City* is "A tongue-in-cheek historical tale that's intelligent, learned, and of good cheer" but concludes that "the people [and ducks] in it remain curiously too thin to lend it the more compelling harmonies of life." *Publishers Weekly* concludes that "Published in a compact format, this short debut novel is reminiscent of Italo Calvino's work in its dashing mingling of history and fantasy."

REVIEWS: *AtlM* 10/96; *BL* 9/15/96; *KR* 7/15/96; *LJ* 4/15/97; *NYTBR* 9/22/96; *PW* 7/15/96; *SFRB* 1/97

Deane, Seamus (Ireland)

Reading in the Dark (1996); Knopf 1996 (HC); Vintage 1997 (pbk); SETTING: Derry, Northern Ireland 1948–1954); See Section 4, #355

Dexter, Pete (USA)

808 *The Paperboy* (1995); Random House 1995 (HC); Dell 1996 (pbk); SETTING: Moat County, Florida in the mid 1960s

The Paperboy is a meandering, atmospherically nuanced tale of a four-year-old murder conviction and the efforts of two investigative reporters from the *Miami Times* to reopen the case. Set in Moat County, in steamy southern Florida, the novel is distinguished by its cast of well-drawn characters including Ward James, a talented-but-conflicted Miami Times reporter, his partner the dapper and amoral Yardley Acheman, the cooly psychopathic (yet possibly innocent) death row occupant, Hilary van Wetter, and the sexy, seriously unbalanced blonde, Charlotte Bless, who works for van Wetter's release. The tale is narrated by Ward's younger brother Jack, who — having dropped out of college and at seriously loose ends — has returned to Moat County where he works for his father W.W. (World War) James, the owner/editor of the local newspaper. Jack has been hired by Ward and Yardley (both temporarily licenseless) to drive for them while they're in the neighborhood researching the death row story. Throughout, the author plumbs the depths of the Southern male psyche.

According to *Entertainment Weekly*, Pete Dexter "has turned in a deeply comic tale dramatizing the odd and troubling symbiosis between a pair of zealous Miami investigative reporters and their sources: a man perhaps wrongly sentenced to die ... an alluring death-row groupie ... and the swamp-dwelling, alligator-poaching clan from whence the condemned man came." Paul Gray, of *Time* magazine, while judging Dexter's conclusion "to be a bit hasty" assures the reader that "for much of its length, *The Paperboy* burns with the phosphorescent atmosphere of betrayal." The *Chicago Tribune* notes that "*The Paperboy* is an out-and-out yarn [full of "memorable" and "outlandish" characters], an entertaining story full of a conflicting mixture of world weariness and naiveté, told with a chip-on-the-shoulder humble pie braggadocio."

OTHER MEDIA: Audiocassette (RandomAudio/abr & Recorded Books/unabr); RECOGNITION: READING GROUP GUIDE; ALA Notable Book of 1995; *NYTBR* Notable Book of 1995; REVIEWS: *BL* 11/15/94; *ChiTrib* 1/29/95; *CSM* 2/16/95; *EW* 1/27/95; *KR* 11/1/94; *LATBR* 1/1/95; *LJ* 1/95; *NS&S* 6/30/95; *NYT* 1/14/96; *NYTBR* 1/22/95; *LST* 5/28/95; *LT* 5/20/95; *PW* 11/7/95; *Time* 1/23/95; *WPBW* 1/17/95

809 *Paris Trout* (1988); Penguin 1989 (pbk); SETTING: Faulkner country 1950s

Award-winning *Paris Trout*, Pete Dexter's first novel, explores the dark undercurrents of reflexive discrimination and racially mediated exploitation in an archetypal Southern town. The Faulkneresque story unfolds in the period just prior to the emergence of the Civil Rights movement. The eponymous Trout is a pathologically abusive shop-keeper who preys on the town's black community by lending money at exorbitant interest rates. When he shoots and kills a black woman, he is brought to trial...

In the view of *Publisher's Weekly*, *Paris Trout* is an "expertly crafted and bleakly fascinating tale of social conflict and madness in the deep South." *Newsweek* observes that "[w]ith a touch of the mastery that graces the best fiction about the South, Dexter has conjured up characters stroked broadly, voices that ring true and vignettes in miniature in a way that haunts." In the view of Richard Eder (*LATBR*), "If *Paris Trout* is about a community hamstrung by its accommodations it is also, at every moment, about the individuals caught in the accommodation. Dexter portrays them with marvelous sharpness; he knows his characters as well as God knows His, and this leaves them oddly free amid the design he has worked out for them." The *New Statesman and Society* concludes that "Without being particularly original, [*Paris Trout*] ... is a solid achievement heightened by wit and a flawless eye and ear."

OTHER MEDIA: A film version featuring Dennis Hopper as Paris Trout was released in 1991; RECOGNITION: Winner of the 1988 National Book Award; REVIEWS: *BL* 3/15/89; *LATBR* 7/24/88; *NewsWk* 9/26/88; *NS&S* 10/7/88; *NYRB* 7/24//88; *NYTBR* 7/24/88; *PW* 5/11/88; *TLS* 11/25/88; *WPBW* 7/10/88

Doctorow, E.L. (USA)

810   *The Waterworks* (1994); NAL–Dutton 1997 (pbk); SETTING: New York City—1871

E.L. Doctorow has set his sixth novel, a mystery story–cum–morality tale, in Manhattan in 1871, shortly after the end of the Civil War. New York City was filled with maimed veterans, an army of ragged street-wise newsboys, corrupt politicians and their minions, and a new unrefined monied class enriched, in no small measure, by war profiteering and shady speculation. Martin Pemberton, a young, idealistic free-lance journalist, the son of an immensely wealthy, recently deceased, slave trader and war profiteer, has disappeared. His editor, McIlvaine, one of the last to see young Martin, is uneasy. It seems that the young journalist had recently come into his office to relate a strange story having to do with a white horse-drawn omnibus which the young man claimed to have seen hurtling through the streets of Manhattan. The agitated young man was insisting that among its passengers (all elderly men dressed in black) was his own (supposedly dead) father. When Martin fails to turn up, McIlvaine enlists the aid of Edmund Donne (one of the few members of the NYC police force uncorrupted by Boss Tweed) in a search which eventually uncovers a stolen fortune, a secret laboratory, a Moriarty-like criminal genius, a deceived woman, and yes, a kidnapped orphan.

In the view of *World Literature Today*, Doctorow "has constructed ... an intriguing if implausible moral fable that is also a stylish whodunit (in the style of Arthur Conan Doyle) and a masterfully detailed evocation of Boss Tweed's New York...." Novelist **Francine Prose** (*WPBW*), claims that "the heart of the [novel's] mystery ... is nothing less than the way that greed, the hunger for power and uncontrolled scientific ambition conspire and are connected — and fueled — by our terror of aging and death." In the view of the *Times Literary Supplement*: *The Waterworks*, "like all good novels of detection, resolves its mystery through the patient investigations of freelancers and renegades: reporters and policemen out of favor with their bosses. And that's what Doctorow is too.

Though hardly out of favour with his public and hardly languishing for want of sales and literary prizes, he remains something of a renegade in his pursuit of the American historical imagination." *Publishers Weekly* observes that in *Waterworks* which is "set in the corrupt but hideously exciting New York of the decade following the Civil War ... Doctorow [achieves] a wonderfully convincing 19th-century angle of vision. *PW* concludes that "[i]t is as if Edgar Allan Poe and Henry James had somehow combined their incomparable geniuses to bring this profoundly haunting fable to life." The (London) *Sunday Times* suggests that "as the mystery begins to be solved it becomes apparent that there is no resolution possible. The setting in Boss Tweed's New York is no accident, for this novel is about corruption and its inescapable taint."

OTHER MEDIA: Audiocassette (Random Audio/abr); RECOGNITION: *NYTBR* Notable Book of 1994; *Publishers Weekly* Best Books of 1994; REVIEWS: *CSM* 6/13/94; *Econ* 8/20/94; *EW* 5/19/95; *KR* 4/1/94; *LATBR* 6/19/94; *LST* 5/22/94; *LT* 5/23/94; NY 6/27/94; *NYRB* 6/23/94; *NYTBR* 6/19/94; *PW* 4/11/94; *TLS* 5/27/94; *WLT* Win '95; *WPBW* 6/5/94

Doig, Ivan (USA)

811   *Bucking the Sun* (1996); S&S 1996 (HC); 1997 (pbk); SETTING: Depression-era Montana

Fort Peck Dam, designed to plug the massive Missouri River, was one of the most ambitious of the New Deal projects — providing thousands of Americans with steady Depression-era work. The second largest dam in the world, it took over 7 years to build. Ivan Doig uses the drama of the dam project as a backdrop for a story of murder and betrayal. The novel focuses on the Duff family (a father, three brothers and their wives) all of whom either work on the dam construction project itself, or in the boom town which grew up around it. As *Bucking the Sun* opens, two naked members of the Duff family have been discovered in a submerged pickup truck.

The *NYTBR* refers admiringly to Doig's skill at extending and deepening the original mystery. With "the guile of a ... coyote, the author [creates] a neat, excruciating Agatha Christie country-house murder set down in sprawling Montana...." The *Washington Post Book World* judges *Bucking the Sun* to be "a tour-de-force of historical fiction — no, fiction period." And concludes that "It is one of those books that takes over as you read it, invading your daydreams, lodging its cadences in your brain, summoning you back to the page." As the *Christian Science Monitor* points out: "If there is any potential problem with enjoying a contemporary writer — relishing the thought of the next book — it's that the new work will simply replow safe ground, be too predictable in style and subject matter. Or, alternatively, that there will have been a jarring departure in approach" and concludes that "With Ivan Doig's latest novel fans need not worry. All the steel and sweetness, the granite and light, the humor and sharp dialogue, in Doig's writing are here with new flair and depth."

OTHER MEDIA: Audiocassette (S&S/abr); REVIEWS: *BL* 3/16/96; *CSM* 6/27/96; *EW* 6/21/96; *LATBR* 5/12/96; *LJ* 4/1/96; *NYTBR* 6/16/96; *PW* 3/18/96; *Time* 7/1/96; *WPBW* 6/16/96

Edgerton, Clyde (USA)

Where Trouble Sleeps (1997); Algonquin 1997 (HC); Ballantine 1998 (pbk); SETTING: Rural North Carolina —1950s; See Section 4, #325

Furst, Alan (USA)

812   *The World at Night* (1996); Random House 1996 (HC); SETTING: Eastern and central Europe on the brink of World War II

Alan Furst's eighth novel is set in German-occupied Paris in 1940 — one of the 20th century's great battlegrounds of intrigue — and features Jean Casson, a Parisian film-maker, bon-vivant, and incorrigible womanizer. Casson (more than a little reluctantly) has been drawn into a complex espionage scheme which involves (among other things) passing himself off as a Nazi collaborator. As the stakes mount, the decidedly ham-fisted amateur finds himself juggling the competing demands of the Gestapo, the British Secret Service and the French Resistance. The European war-time atmosphere is highly reminiscent of the films noirs of the 1940s. "We all thought life would go on," muses a colleague of Casson, "But it won't."

Kirkus Reviews observes that "The throes of masculine existential torment are an unquestionable specialty for Furst, whose WW II fiction combines so much broad historical erudition with such genuine humanity that they ought to be made required reading" and concludes that "Furst has somehow discovered the perfect venue for uniting the European literary tragedy with the Anglo-American spy thriller. Nobody does it better." In the view of Richard Eder (*LATBR*), *The World at Night* "earns a comparison with the serious entertainments of Graham Greene and John LeCarre.... Using the pleasurable devices of its genre, it offers a lot more: an appreciation of France that is at once passionate, graceful and cold, an evocation of French virtues and vices under terrible testing and a shrewd intuition." *The* (London) *Sunday Times* points out that "Furst builds up an atmosphere of pervasive fear and hidden dangers around a hero whose humanity and style make him unforgettable."

OTHER MEDIA: Audiocassette (Isis/unabr); REVIEWS: *BL* 4/1/96; *KR* 3/1/96; *LST* 3/15/98; *LATBR* 6/2/96; *NYT* 6/5/96; *WPBW* 6/19/96

Garrett, George (USA)

813   *The King of Babylon Shall Not Come Against You* (1996); Harcourt Brace 1996 (HC); 1998 (pbk); SETTING: Paradise Springs, Florida — 1968

George Garrett's 14th work of fiction begins in the 1990s as an investigative reporter (Billy Tone) returns to his Florida hometown of Paradise Springs to take a second, admittedly retrospective, look at a series of events which occurred there in 1968. In one tragic night two men were murdered: a midget evangelist known as Little David and a local bank teller named Alpha Weatherby. On the same evening, an Episcopal minister apparently hanged himself in his attic, a local photographer was assaulted by a person or persons unknown, and Little David's revivalist's tent was burnt to the ground. That these events all occurred on April 4, 1968, the day that Martin Luther King was assassinated, resulted in a spottier than usual investigation which left the crimes unsolved and, consequently, unpunished. The lack of resolution has gnawed at Tone for more than 25 years, and he has finally come home to ask some questions. The novel reads very much like a dossier, as it is constructed out of a series of interviews, depositions, and trial transcripts. The interviewees include: the promotion manager for Little David, the preacher's obese common-law wife, a Jewish professor from the local Baptist college who supplements his meager faculty salary by writing porn, a wealthy African-American lawyer and a Bible-thumping, sex-obsessed Baptist minister.

According to novelist **James Hynes** (*WPBW*), what Garrett has produced in *The King of Babylon* is "as much a piece of social history and cultural commentary as it is a novel, but more exciting, finally, and funnier, than any straight-arrow legal thriller." In the view of the *Library Journal* "Garrett's characters speak with authentic voices, transforming local history into an American epic." *Booklist* observes that "Although this novel mimics the framework of a detective story, Garrett is after something much bigger here as he repeatedly homes in one the notion that we are rapidly becoming a nation without any real principles."

REVIEWS: *BL* 3/1/96; *LJ* 2/15/96; *NYTBR* 5/26/96; *PW* 1/22/96; *WPBW* 6/16/96

Guterson, David (USA)

814   *Snow Falling on Cedars* (1994); Harcourt Brace 1994 (HC); Random House 1995 (pbk);

SETTING: A Pacific NW island community—1954 (with flashbacks to the 1940s)

David Guterson's debut novel is set on San Pedro island in Puget Sound, home to stalwart salmon-fisherman and hard-working strawberry growers. In it he tells the story of Kabuo Miyomoto, a Japanese-American fisherman who has been accused of murdering Carl Heine, a colleague and boyhood friend. Although Miyomoto's trial provides the story's framework, its forward movement is interrupted by an intricate series of flashbacks. As the trial gets underway, the air is heavy with the threat of snow and the reality of racial tension.

According to *Booklist*: "A 1954 murder trial in an island community off the coast of Washington state broadens into an exploration of war, race, and the mysteries of human motivation." As the London *Observer* suggests that "Melancholy is a seductive current in fiction 'the slow withdrawing tug under its characters and events.' Think of Virginia Woolf's *To the Lighthouse*, with its exquisite nostalgia for a time that has gone.... David Guterson's *Snow Falling on Cedars* catches at this rich tide of melancholy...." In the view of the *Times Literary Supplement*, "Guterson's handling of the theme of racial bigotry is effectively low-keyed. In the eyes of the residents of San Pedro island, there are no hyphenated Americans. Many of the white islanders — nearly all of German or Scandinavian ancestry — are immigrants; some still speak accented English. Yet they are all 'Americans,' while second- and third-generation Japanese-Americans remain 'Japs.'" *Time* magazine concludes that *Snow Falling on Cedars* "is poised at precisely that point where an elliptical Japanese delicacy meets the woody, unmoving fiber of the Pacific Northwest. Out of that encounter, Guterson has fashioned something haunting and true."

OTHER MEDIA: Audiocassette (Random Audio/abr; Chivers/unabr; Books on Tape/unabr); READING GROUP GUIDE; RECOGNITION: Winner of the PEN/Faulkner Book Prize; *NYTBR* Notable Book of 1994; REVIEWS: *BL* 8/19/94; *CSM* 9/23/94; *LAT* 9/19/94; *LJ* 8/94; *LST* 5/28/95; *LT* 9/16/95 *NYTBR* 10/26/94; *Obs* 6/4/95; *Time* 9/26/94; *TLS* 5/26/95; *WPBW* 10/16/94

Haines, Carolyn (USA)

815   *Touched* (1996); E.F. Dutton 1996 (HC); Plume 1997 (pbk); SETTING: Jexville, Mississippi—1926

In her second novel, Carolyn Haines tells the story of Mattie Mills and her search for self and community in a hardscrabble southern community in the decades leading up to WW II. It also concerns a child "touched" by lightning (who can foretell the future), the narrow-mindedness and mean-spiritedness of closed societies, spousal abuse, revenge, and murder.

According to *Kirkus Reviews*, "Haines ladles on the pluck and grit as she limns the life of Mattie, a strong woman who comes to live in a preternaturally mean Mississippi town, where she faces down the local bigots, survives a severe spousal beating, and exacts a deadly revenge." The *New York Times Book Review* observes that *Touched* has "[l]ike the heat of a Deep South summer ... undeniable intensity" and concludes that "it's impossible to shake its brooding atmosphere."

REVIEWS: *BL* 6/1/96; *KR* 5/15/96; *LJ* 6/15/96; *NYTBR* 9/22/96; *PW* 6/3/96

Hall, Rodney (Australia)

Captivity Captive (1987); FS&G 1995 (pbk reissue); SETTING: New South Wales—1898; See Section 4, #409

Hamilton, Hugo (Ireland)

816   *The Last Shot* (1991); FS&G 1992 (HC); SETTING: Germany 1945 and 1989

Hugo Hamilton's suspense-filled second novel (after his critically well-received debut effort *Surrogate City*) is set in Germany and links two time periods and two love stories. The first takes place in 1945 and features a young Czechoslovakian woman and a German soldier, who, brought together by the havoc of war and the need to flee the Russian advance, become friends and then lovers, their union producing a son. The second is set in 1989 and follows a middle-aged American who has come to Germany to search for his missing father. While there he renews an old love affair with the German wife of an old friend.

In the view of *Publishers Weekly*, "The long-lost-wartime-father-sought-by-grown-child story is common enough to its own genre by now, but rarely is it executed with the polish and depth exhibited here." *Kirkus Reviews* notes that *The Last Shot* is "A shrewd and effective meld of adventure, pockets of dreamy romance and passion, plus a spattering of cynical comments about the 'freedom' within the united Germany — all touched with a faint dramatic melancholy." The *Times Literary Supplement* concludes that "Hamilton is a natural story teller, with poise, daring and control, and, after two books, he is already quite unmistakable."

REVIEWS: *KR* 4/1/92; *NYTBR* 9/13/92; *PW* 3/23/92; *TLS* 8/9/91

Hanna, Edward B (USA)

817   *The Whitechapel Horrors* (1992); Carroll & Graf 1993 (pbk); SETTING: Victorian London

In a novel called "intriguing and chilling" by the *New York Times Book Review* Sherlock Holmes is brought in to investigate the Whitechapel murders. Incidental characters include the Prince of Wales, Randolph Churchill, and actual employees of Scotland Yard.

According to *Publishers Weekly*, this is a "remarkably fresh and inventive integration of Holmesian lore into classic Jack the Ripper mythology [that] breathes life into two overworked topics. Hanna makes Baker Street masterfully vibrant, and paints its two most famous residents in portraits that are simultaneously reverent and startling." The *LATBR* observes that "Late 19th-century London becomes extraordinarily real, and nothing is slier about Hanna's melding of Holmes and the Ripper than his adroit resolution of a case on which history's verdict has remained open." In the view of the *Washington Post Book World*, the story is "at once romantic, mysterious, Gothic and psychological ..." The *Chicago Sun-Times* delcares that "Hanna's work will delight the legions who venerate Holmes, so convincing is the writer in rendering the rhythms of Victorian speech and the quaint oddities of the British class system."

REVIEWS: *BL* 10/1/92; *ChiSun* 10/11/92; *KR* 8/15/92; *LATBR* 11/15/92; *NYTBR* 10/18/92; *PW* 8/24/92

Hazelgrove, W.E. (USA)

818 *Tobacco Sticks* (1995); Pantonne Press 1995 (HC); Bantam 1997 (pbk); SETTING: Richmond, Virginia —1945

Tobacco Sticks is narrated by Richmond native Lee Hartwell, who looks back on his unforgettable 13th summer. In the long hot months following the end of the Second World War, Lee's family — like many others in town — was still reeling from the trauma of wounded sons and interrupted lives. To complicate matters, Lee's father, Burke Hartwell, a respected lawyer and campaign manager for a senatorial hopeful, has agreed to represent Fannie Jones, a Negro maid, in a highly controversial case. Fannie, on the basis of what appears to be purely circumstantial evidence, has been arrested and charged with the theft of a valuable heirloom from the home of her long-time employers. Fannie is a well-known "union-sympathizer" with a politically active boyfriend — and they both manage to run afoul of the most powerful man in Richmond. An emotion-charged trial in a suffocating southern courtroom (reminiscent of *To Kill a Mockingbird*) is the novel's centerpiece.

Publishers Weekly, in its starred review, notes that "Explosive racial tension, betrayal and murder, difficult ethical and social decisions, first love and a dramatic denouement in a sweaty courtroom are skillfully entwined in this haunting tale...." According to the *Library Journal*, *Tobacco Sticks* "is finally as much a coming of age story for the South as it is for the central character...." *Booklist* ob-

serves that "Hazelgrove writes with warmth and feeling, and his characters are richly drawn, but it's the love between Lee and his father that makes this novel so moving and evocative." The *School Library Journal* points out that "Despite soap-opera-like entanglements" the "plot convolutions are effective and gripping, even if occasionally melodramatic...." In the view of *People Weekly*, "Hazelgrove spices his new novel with a dash of murder, betrayal, racial tension, dirty politics and a lotta fried chicken."

REVIEWS: *BL* 7/19/95; *LJ* 7/95; *NYTBR* 8/13/95; *PeopleW* 8/14/95; *PW* 5/8/95; *SLJ* 9/95; *WPBW* 11/19/95

Hill, Carol de Chellis (USA)

819 *Henry James' Midnight Song* (1993); W.W. Norton 1994 (pbk); SETTING: fin de siècle Vienna

Ms. Hill's novel, set in Vienna at the turn of the century, begins with the delivery of a mysterious manuscript to the home of Theodore Rydewort, a scholar specializing in medieval mysticism. The manuscript, entitled *Henry James' Midnight Song* recounts a story which begins with the discovery (in Sigmund Freud's study) of a murdered woman. The woman's body subsequently disappeared, dumbfounding the local police. When reports of additional missing women begin to surface (so the story goes) and their body parts (e.g. detached toes, severed heads) begin to appear in various spots around Vienna, hysteria grips the city. Some within the profoundly anti–Semitic populace assume that the perpetrators must be Jews engaged in ritualistic murder. The Austrian Emperor is eventually consulted and he sends to Paris for the intrepid Austrian-born Jewish detective Maurice le Blanc. Ms. Hill adroitly weaves early notions of feminism, an exploration of evil, the development of psychoanalysis and the nature of anti–Semitism into her intricately constructed tale and, before the mystery is clarified, she will animate psychoanalyst Carl Jung, Viennese artist Gustav Klimt, American novelist Edith Wharton and, of course, Henry James.

Kirkus Reviews notes that "Expatriate American literati and the heavyweights of psychoanalysis collide in this spirited novel set in the dreamy streets of fin de siecle Vienna" and concludes that Ms. Hill's novel is "Rich and flavorful, with the period's ferment of ideas ably represented...." According to the *L.A. Times Book Review*, "So memorable is Hill's evocation of Wharton and James that [it is doubtful one] will ever be able to read their works again without thinking of their portrait here.... From first sentence to last there is the feeling that one [is in the hands] of an authoritative storyteller...."

RECOGNITION: *Publishers Weekly* Best Books of 1993; *NYTBR* Notable Book of 1993; REVIEWS: *BL* 7/93; *KR* 1/95; *LATBR* 11/21/93; *LJ* 8/93; *Nation* 7/17/95; *NYTBR* 9/5/93; *PW* 6/28/93; *VLS* 11/93.

Hjortsberg, William (USA)

820   *Nevermore* (1994); Tor 1996 (pbk); SETTING: New York City—1920s

In William Hjortsberg's second novel (a mixture of period pastiche, erotic thriller and madcap mystery) Harry Houdini and Arthur Conan Doyle join forces to investigate a series of gruesome murders apparently inspired by the short stories of Edgar Allan Poe. These early 20th century luminaries are drawn together by a mutual interest in the occult. The plot is further enlivened by the introduction of Opal Crosby Fletcher, a New Hampshire farm girl (and widow of a textile tycoon) who believes she is the reincarnation of the Egyptian fertility goddess Isis. The historical ambiance is well maintained throughout and the list of famous personalities of the period who have been given walk-on parts includes: Charlie Chaplin, Fanny Brice, W.C. Fields, Buster Keaton, Louis Armstrong, Jimmy Walker and Jack Dempsy.

The *Library Journal* calls *Nevermore* "an enjoyable though sometimes gruesome adventure that is much enhanced by the author's use of the many details behind Houdini's amazing escapes and magic tricks." According to novelist Tom de Haven (*NYTBR*), Hjortsberg's "intention is not to ridicule, or to play post-modernist games, but to concoct an irresistible entertainment, and so he does." As Christopher Lehman-Haupt (*NYT*) points out "If there is a more serious undercurrent in *Nevermore* it is the contest sometimes friendly, sometimes angry, waged throughout the story over the issue of spiritism, or the ability of the dead to communicate with the living which Conan Doyle strongly believes in and Houdini holds in passionate contempt.... But not too much should be made of this. What is particularly appealing about *Nevermore* is that it never grows heavy." The *San Francisco Chronicle* offers a similar observation and suggests that "no other writer has discussed [belief in the supernatural] with such wit and humor as is found in William Hjortsberg's *Nevermore*."

REVIEWS: *BL* 10/1/94; *LATBR* 12/13/94; *LJ* 7/94; *NYT* 12/22/94; *NYTBR* 10/2/94; *PW* 8/1/94; *WPBW* 10/31/94

Irwin, Robert (UK)

Exquisite Corpse (1995); Pantheon 1997 (HC); SETTING: England & Europe (1930s–1940s); See Section 3, #223

Kanon, Joseph (USA)

821   *Los Alamos* (1997); Broadway 1997 (HC); Dell 1998 (pbk); SETTING: Los Alamos, N.M., during WW II

Joseph Kanon (former head of trade publishing at Houghton Mifflin), in his debut novel, appears to have found the right balance between verisimilitude and period atmospherics. Set in Los Alamos, New Mexico (site of the U.S. Government's top secret atom bomb research & development station), during the waning months of World War II, Kanon's story revolves around the murder of a Manhattan Project security guard by the name of Karl Bruner. Civilian intelligence liaison Michael Connelly is called in to investigate — but, as Connelly soon learns, this is no routine investigation.

Salon magazine notes that "Kanon's Manhattan project setting is rendered with a good deal of authenticity ... and this allows for major historical figures to take key fictional roles. The chain- smoking Robert Oppenheimer himself, a suspect and eventual confidante of Connolly's, sets the stage when he tells the investigator, 'Officially I don't exist. None of us do. You're among ghosts now.'" According to the *Library Journal*, "Kanon seamlessly interweaves historical figures and events into an exciting, plausible scenario." The *Washington Post Book World* similarly points out that "Kanon writes with the sure hand of a veteran and does a marvelous job of portraying the various personalities involved, particularly the man at the center of everything, Robert Oppenheimer. Kanon's Oppenheimer is brilliant, charming, charismatic, and absolutely single-minded in his determination to get the 'gadget' built before the enemy does." *Publishers Weekly* observes that Kanon's use of "real-life people ... is exemplary; he has created characters who are both true to their actual selves and three-dimensional actors in a convincing fiction" and concludes that "this is a thinking person's thriller that makes wonderful use of, but never cheapens, one of history's more extraordinary moments." In the view of *Entertainment Weekly*, "The atmospherics are exactly right: *Los Alamos* brings back an era when a secret was really a secret and a lie wasn't necessarily a sin." *Newsweek* concludes that "*Los Alamos*, besides being a terrific mystery, wonderfully evokes the Southwest in the '40s, reminding us in a dozen subtle ways that life goes on even while history is being made."

OTHER MEDIA: Audiocassette (BDD/abr); RECOGNITION: *Publishers Weekly* "Best Books" 1997; REVIEWS: *BL* 3/15/97; *EW* 5/23/97; *KR* 4/1/97; *LATBR* 6/30/97; *NewsWk* 5/19/97; *NYTBR* 6/1/97; *PW* 2/10/97; *WPBW* 5/18/97; *WSJ* 6/9/97

Kennedy, William (USA)

The Flaming Corsage (1996); Viking 1996 (HC); Penguin 1997 (pbk); SETTING: Albany and Manhattan —1884 to 1912; See Section 5, #590

Landsman, Anne (South Africa)

822 *The Devil's Chimney* (1997); Soho 1997 (HC); Viking/Penguin 1999 (pbk); SETTING: South Africa —1910 through 1914

Anne Landsman has set her debut novel in the parched highlands of Oudtshoorn, South Africa, on the eve of World War I. It is narrated, retrospectively, by Connie, an aging alcoholic who recalls a dramatic series of events involving Henry and Beatrice Chapman, an upper-class English couple who had purchased (at the height of the international craze for exotic plumage as a fashion accessory) an ostrich ranch in an isolated South African community. Connie, living nearby with her abusive husband Jack, was drawn to Beatrice, a young, headstrong feminist. Exerting a kind of brooding presence was one of the region's outstanding natural wonders, the Canga Caves, which, with their eerie, convoluted subterranean passages, feature significantly in the unfolding story. Through Connie's alcoholic haze a story emerges which interweaves madness, infidelity, racial animosity and lost children. The narrator, the reader soon learns, is haunted by her memories.

In the view of South African novelist **Andre Brink**, "In *The Devil's Chimney*, South Africa is for the first time seen through a lens of magic realism. [It is] a novel which bristles with creative energy." Calling *The Devil's Chimney* "An allegory for the structure of South African society in this century," *The* (London) *Times* further observes that Anne Landsman's first novel "is an imaginative feat of the highest order. She captures the anguish and cruelty of her subject in a mist of finely wrought imagery and creates an example of the rarest form of fiction, a beautiful book about terrible things." The *Library Journal* concludes that Ms. Landsman "makes clever use of Connie not only because she sprinkles her stories liberally with Afrikaans and Xhosa words but because Connie admires Miss Beatrice so much that her admiration wonderfully embellishes an already engrossing tale." The *New Yorker* notes that the author's "hold on the crux of her story [the fate of the missing, both dead and alive] is so steady and strong that her fey, haunted characters seem to act entirely out of their own compulsions." The *Times Literary Supplement* contends that "Against a fantastic, hallucinatory background of desires and fears, Anne Landsman places a powerful allegory of the unwritten social history of twentieth- century South Africa. There is no one who is not at the peril of their own prejudices, and yet out of it all comes the hope of shared experience and integra-

tion." Kate Moses writing in *Salon* applauds Ms. Landsman for her ability to create "a dramatic setting ripe with sociopolitical undercurrents, historically accurate symbolism so rich you couldn't make it up and a parallel narrative that plays out the stillborn lives of two women from different eras" but criticizes the author's emphasis on Connie whose "disingenuous narrative" weakens the novel "significantly." The *Boston Globe* concludes that *The Devil's Chimney* is an "odd, original and atmospheric first novel."

REVIEWS: *BosGlobe* 10/29/97; *KR* 8/1/97; *LJ* 9/1/97; *LT* 5/28/98; *NY* 11/10/97; *NYTBR* 11/23/97; *PW* 7/21/97; *TLS* 7/10/98; *WPBW* 12/28/97

Libby, Lewis (USA)

823 *The Apprentice* (1996); Graywolf 1996 (HC); SETTING: Rural Japan —1903

Lewis Libby's suspenseful debut novel is set in a mountainous region of northern Japan at the turn of the century. Smallpox rages in the countryside, strangers have been reported in the nearby woods and there is talk of imminent war with surroundidng Czarist Russia. A collection of travelers (including the members of a small theatrical troupe), each curiously wary of the next, have taken refuge at a remote mountain inn as a blizzard rages outside. In the absence of the inn's owner, young Setsuo, the apprentice innkeeper, must see to the needs of the guests. Before long, Setsuo participates in a heart-stopping chase through the snowy woods, witnesses a murder, recovers a mysterious box, becomes entangled in political intrigue and falls in love with a beautiful young actress. The plot is further enlivened by patriotic samurai and the discovery of spies amidst the travelers.

As the *Library Journal* points out, "When Setsuo, an apprentice innkeeper in turn-of-the-century Japan follows a bearded man into a blizzard, he sets into motion a convoluted set of events. Robbery, murder, love, politics, mystery, and intrigue are all parts of the deadly game, but what exactly is the game?" According to *Kirkus Reviews*, *The Apprentice* "is mostly atmosphere, but it's a satisfyingly romantic atmosphere, like that of an old swashbuckling boys' novel dropped down in Japan, with a dash of Yukio Mishima for good measure." In the view of the *New York Times Book Review*, Libby "elevates the youth's narrative to the level of myth, setting his confused adolescent reactions to love at first sight against the mysterious goings-on of the other travelers." The *Washington Post Book World* observes that "Libby's cast of characters is bizarre and interesting — a 'hunched dwarf,' a pockmarked hunter, an old samurai — if not sharply delineated. His scenes are vivid and evocative, and his ear for language is wonderful.... He has a firm control of the conventions of the adventure story, the false leads and red herrings, the mystery peeled away."

REVIEWS: *KR* 7/1/96; *LJ* 7/96; *NYTBR* 11/3/96; *PW* 7/1/96; *WPBW* 10/27/96

Mailer, Norman

Harlot's Ghost (1991); Random House 1991 (HC); Ballantine 1992 (pbk); See Section 5, #606

Mantel, Hilary (UK)

824   *An Experiment in Love* (1995); H. Holt 1997 (pbk); SETTING: England in the 1960s

Hilary Mantel's 7th novel is a coming-of-age story in which Carmel McBride, the product of a working-class, Irish-Catholic family, makes the transition first from her Lancashire comprehensive school to the rather "posh" local convent school (Holy Redeemer), and thence (via scholarship) to the University of London. Carmel — bright, willing and malleable — strives to fulfill her mother's desire to see her "improve herself" in the rigidly class-stratified England of the '60s and early '70s. Ms. Mantel also tells the sometimes parallel, sometimes intersecting story of the bright but unprepossessing Karina, another scholarship student from Holy Redeemer who has also come to the University of London and resides in the same women's dorm as Carmel. It is not an easy time to be a young woman, particularly one of extremely limited means, and, as the girls' ties to family, home and community become unraveled, they search fruitlessly for replacements. Carmel, repressed and angry, frequently resorts to anorexic behavior while the increasingly unbalanced Karina eats her way to obesity. Tensions mount and the foreshadowed tragic denouement is amply realized. Ms. Mantel pays homage to her literary mentor, Muriel Spark, with a reference to *Girls of Slender Means* "whose plot Mantel proceeds to recycle, darken and adapt" (*TLS*).

According to Margaret Atwood (*NYTBR*) "The pleasures of [*An Experiment in Love*] are many. The women's-residence portions ... are as harshly delicious as those in [Mary McCarthy's] *The Group*; the childhood sections are immediate and vivid, funny and bleak, and the intricate love and love-hate relationships among the women, which, as the narrator says, have nothing to do with sex, are right on target. This is Carmel's story, but it is that of her generation as well: girls at the end of the 60s, caught between two sets of values, who had the pill but still ironed their boyfriends' shirts." Ms. Atwood concludes that Ms. Mantel's novel "with all its brilliance, its sharpness and its clear-eyed wit ... is a haunting book." *Publishers Weekly* observes that "Despite its grim subject, the writing,

replete with sharp humor and evocative details of 1960s England, is never self-indulgent. Irony prevails stoutly over sentimentality, while the finale delivers a surprising twist of horror that will shake readers to the core." The *London Review of Books* notes that Ms. Mantel has "regularly returned to the radical mysteries contemplated in her first book [*Every Day Is Mother's Day* (1985)]. Where does evil come from? Can it be overcome by human good? For all her sharp-eyed social comedy, Mantel is consistently a philosophical novelist, and often a spiritual one." The *New Statesman and Society* concludes that "'The climax of this novel is a fatal fire, possibly involving murder, but Carmel's own secret, gradually guessed at, is equally horrifying when it is eventually revealed."

OTHER MEDIA: Audiocassette (Chivers/ unabr); RECOGNITION: Winner of the Hawthorndon Award; *NYTBR* Notable Book of 1996; REVIEWS: *BL* 5/1/96; *LJ* 4/15/96; *LRB* 3/9/95; *LST* 2/26/95; *NS&S* 2/24/95; *NYTBR* 6/2/96; *PW* 4/1/96; *TLS* 2/24/95

825   *A Change in Climate* (1994); Holt 1997 (pbk); SETTING: South Africa and Botswana — mid '60s and '70s & Norfolk, England — 1980s

Anna and Ralph Eldred have recently returned to Norfolk from South Africa where, for many years, they ran a fundamentalist Christian mission outside of Pretoria. While in Africa, the Eldreds were involved in the anti-apartheid movement at a time when to do so put one at considerable risk. Police brutality was endemic and activists were routinely rounded up and imprisoned (as were the Eldreds) on the flimsiest of charges. Upon their release, the Eldreds moved to Botswana where they were the victims of a horrific crime which leaves them permanently scarred. They eventually return to England, where Ralph accepts a position with a charitable organization based in London and the couple continues to take in, at their Norfolk farmhouse, what their children call "sad cases and good souls." The African incident continues to cast a dark shadow over their lives and their faith and marriage are both severely tested.

In the view of *The* (London) *Sunday Times*, "Mantel can be relied on to produce books which are both intelligent and absorbing, and this one is no exception. Her sense of place is strong, whether writing of South Africa in the early days of apartheid or the bleak stillness of rural Norfolk." *Kirkus Review* observes that *A Change of Climate* "moving between the past and recent present, is a cautionary tale of a model family almost destroyed by its secrets" and concludes that it is both "intelligent and moving." The *Times Literary Supplement* says that "Brisk, unsentimental, unsurprised but uncynical, Hilary Mantel has previously written with rueful comedy about social workers and misfits ... with sardonic fascination about religion ... and with choking tension about personal and political nightmare.... In *A Change of Climate*, working at the peak of her powers, she clenches all these concerns together into a novel that simultaneously horrifies and heartens."

RECOGNITION: *NYTBR* Notable Book of 1997; REVIEWS: *GW* 4/24/94; *KR* 5/15/97; *LRB* 4/28/94; *LATBR* 9/14/97; *LST* 4/2/95; *NYTBR* 7/20/97; *PW* 6/23/97; *TLS* 3/25/94; *WPBW* 7/27/97; *WSJ* 9/24/97

McCabe, Patrick (Ireland)

826 *The Butcher Boy* (1992); Fromm 1993 (HC); Doubleday 1994 (pbk); SETTING: Ireland — 1960s

Patrick McCabe's raw, eerily insinuating third novel is set in the rural Ireland in the 1960s and is narrated by a seriously disturbed young man by the name of Francie Brady, son of a violent, alcoholic father and a mother who, throughout his childhood, has drifted in and out of the local mental hospital, a place Francie calls "the garage." Unhinged by his mother's suicide, Francie commits a grotesque act for which he is incarcerated. Upon his release, Francie's world view grows ever darker. McCabe's prize-winning novel was widely viewed as a macabre *tour de force*.

According to the *Times Literary Supplement*, "There is no consolation in this unashamedly horrible story but, butcher and black humor aside, it is memorable for its acid study of the Irish condition and its sensitive treatment of personal and communal nostalgia." *Kirkus Reviews* notes that "On a foundation laid by Salinger and Sillitoe, McCabe has created something all his own — an uncompromisingly bleak vision of a child who retains the pathos of a grubby urchin even as he evolves into a monster. His novel is a *tour de force*." In the view of the *Library Journal*, "The characters talk their way into your memory." Novelist **James Hynes** (*WPBW*) argues that *The Butcher Boy* "is an almost perfect novel, written with wonderful assurance and a technical skill that is as great as it is unobtrusive. It is also viciously entertaining, the sort of nasty Gothic shocker that is liable to keep you up late against your better judgment. Don't say you weren't warned."

OTHER MEDIA: Audiocassette (S&S/abr); film version released in 1998; RECOGNITION: Winner of the Irish Times-Aer Lingus Prize; shortlisted for the 1992 Booker Prize; *Publishers Weekly* Best Books 1993; *NYTBR* Notable Book of 1993; REVIEWS: *KR* 3/15/93; *LRB* 6/11/92; *NYTBR* 5/30/93; *PW* 4/5/93; *TLS* 4/24/92; *WPBW* 5/16/93

McEwan, Ian (UK)

827 *Black Dogs* (1992); Bantam 1994 (pbk); SETTING: France in 1946; England & the continent in the mid 1980s

The defining moment in McEwan's sixth novel is a tangible confrontation with evil in the mountains of northern France as experienced by a pair of idealistic young honeymooners in the summer following the end of World War II. The overarching story — an examination of the forces that brought June and Bernard Tremaine together and which eventually drove them apart — is narrated by Jeremy, the Tremaine's thoughtful son-in-law (a middle-aged British text-book publisher) who has discussed the breakup with both June and Bernard at some length. Jeremy has personally witnessed a number of key events of the late 20th century (e.g. the fall of the Berlin Wall) and he brings his own experience of the world to bear on his examination of one blighted relationship. McEwan, in telling his multi-generational tale, grapples with some very large questions having to do with the existence of evil, the possibility of redemption and the limits of love.

Publishers Weekly, in its starred review, observes that "McEwan's meticulous prose, his shaping of his material to create suspense, and his adept use of specific settings ... produce a haunting fable about the fragility of Civilization, always threatened by the cruelty latent in humankind." According to English novelist **M. John Harrison** (*TLS*), *Black Dogs* is "compassionate without resorting to sentimentality, clever without ever losing its honesty, an undisguised novel of ideas." Novelist **Bradford Morrow** suggests that *Black Dogs* is "best read in a single sitting, the novel has a brevity that belies the scope of its ambition ... It is a tender account of persistent but failed love, a bittersweet evocation of the solitudes that vex, enliven, and ultimately define marriage. It is, above all, a study of the fragile nobility of the human spirit in the face of the irrational, the terrible and the miraculous." The *New York Times Book Review* notes that "What we have [in *Black Dogs*] is a speculative ramble in the form of a cautionary fable, a brief work of fiction that explores what happens to a marriage when one partner's faith in the efficacy of political ideologies collides with the other's conviction, rooted in a sudden spiritual revelation, that evil remains alive and well in modern life, exerting its own influence on human affairs. That this exploration succeeds, and in doing so creates the tensions of good fiction, deserves applause."

RECOGNITION: Shortlisted for the 1992 Booker Prize; *NYTBR* Notable Book of 1992; REVIEWS: *LATBR* 12/20/92; *LRB* 6/25/92; *NYTBR* 11/8/92; *PW* 9/14/92; *TLS* 6/19/92; *WPBW* 10/25/92; EDITOR'S NOTE: Mr. McEwan was named by *Granta* magazine to its 1993 list of "Best Young British Novelists"

828   *The Innocent* (1990); Bantam 1995 (pbk); Anchor 1998 (pbk); SETTING: West Berlin—1955

Ian McEwan's hair-raising fifth novel is set in a post-war Berlin that is seething with subterfuge and distrust. Leonard Marnham, a shy young British communication's worker has been assigned to Operation Gold, a tunnel built by the CIA and MI6 to tap telephone lines carrying Soviet intelligence data. Before long, Marnham is seduced by Maria Eckdorf, a beautiful young German divorcée, and is too besotted to see what lurks around the corner.

According to *The* (London) *Sunday Times, The Innocent* "is a bold and bitter comment on the self-defeating cold war era." Novelist **Jonathan Carroll** (*WPBW*) observes that the story of Leonard and Maria's "courtship" and "the marvelously evocative descriptions of the city are the strongest parts of the novel. At its best, *The Innocent* has the spooky, crooked-angle, danger-around-every-corner feeling of a Carol Reed film." *Publishers Weekly* observes that "Though its plot rivals any thriller in narrative tension, this novel is also a character study—of a young man coming of age in bizarre circumstances, and of differences in national character: the gentlemanly Brits, the brash, impatient Americans; the cynical Germans." The *New York Times Book Review* suggests that McEwan "demonstrates how violence and horror can erupt from what the mind does not know about itself ... Mr. McEwan is not a genre writer. His novels are not chillers in the usual sense, for his methods are realistic and his horrors are natural rather than supernatural. they appear suddenly from human nature." English novelist James Buchan (*Spectator*) argues that with *The Innocent* "our best young, or youngish, novelist has created a new publishing category: literary slasher fiction."

OTHER MEDIA: Audiocassette (Chivers/unabr); a film version starring Anthony Hopkins and Isabella Rossellini was released in 1993; RECOGNITION: *NYTBR* Notable Book of 1990; REVIEWS: *ComW* 6/15/90; *LST* 4/28/91; *NewR* 7/23/90; *NS&S* 5/11/90; *NYRB* 12/6/90; *NYTBR* 6/3/90; *PW* 4/13/90; *Q&Q* 6/90; *Spectator* 5/12/90; *Time* 6/25/90; *TLS* 5/11/90; *WPBW* 6/3/90

McGrath, Patrick (UK)

829   *Asylum* (1997); Random House 1997 (HC); 1998 (pbk); SETTING: A British Insane Asylum—1959

In Patrick McGrath's latest gothic thriller, Stella Raphael, the beautiful, bored wife of the admittedly dull forensic psychiatrist attached to a maximum security prison for the criminally insane, falls passionately in love with young, attractive Edgar Stark, a sculptor and charming psychopath who has been incarcerated for murdering and then decapitating his wife. When Stark manages to escape from the facility, Stella abandons her husband and family and joins her "lover."

According to *Entertainment Weekly, Asylum* is "a cleverly insidious beautifully rendered thriller with just the right balance of splatter and innuendo." The *New York Times* literary critic Michiko Kakutani observes that *Asylum* "starts off as a sort of dark sendup of *Lady Chatterly's Lover*.... In McGrath's version, however, sexual love does not lead to liberation or transcendence" and further concludes that "Whereas many of McGrath's earlier books were often marred by his taste for gratuitously bizarre details ... and incredibly ornate prose, he has restrained those impulses in *Asylum* to create a taut, tension-filled narrative that derives much of its power from understatement and withheld emotion." In the view of the *New Statesman,* McGrath "pulls the tension taut until the final page and creates that rare thing, a chillingly good read." The *Times Literary Supplement* asserts that McGrath employs "the confident language of manly certainty ... to tell morbid, melodramatic stories of lust and fear and pathological consummation. This is what gives his books their heavy, disturbing power" Novelist **Joanna Scott** (*LATBR*) concludes that *Asylum* "is one of those rare pleasures, a book as absorbing as it is intelligent ... Every page is full of portent, of mystery, of the suggestion of the disasters that are about to occur. But there is an even greater thrill, the thrill of insight."

READING GROUP GUIDE; RECOGNITION: *NYTBR* Notable Book of 1997; *LATBR* "Best Books" 1997; REVIEWS: *BL* 12/1/96; *EW* 3/7/97; *LJ* 2/1/97; *LRB* 10/31/96; *NS* 9/13/96; *NY* 1/27/97; *NYT* 2/14/97; *NYTBR* 2/23/97; *PeopleW* 3/31/97; *PW* 12/16/96; *TLS* 8/23/96

830   *Dr. Haggard's Disease* (1993); Random House 1994 (pbk); SETTING: London and the south coast of England—1930s & 1940s

What is wrong with Dr. Edward Haggard? Is it a passionate love for the wife of the senior pathologist? Or is it something simpler, to do not with his broken heart but with Spike—the steel pin that holds his hip together? While a young surgical resident at a hospital in pre-war London, Dr. Haggard (sensitive and poetic by nature) became involved with (bored, sexy) Fanny Vaughan, the wife of the Chief of Pathology, Ratcliffe Vaughan. The affair ends badly, precipitated by a fist-fight between Dr. Haggard and Dr. Vaughan in which Dr. Haggard falls down a flight of stairs and is permanently injured. Hooked on morphine, Haggard eventually moves to a dark, cliff-side manse in the south of England. Here he lives a reclusive life, until, during the war, a young flier by the name of James Vaughan comes calling.

According to *The* (London) *Times Dr. Haggard's Disease* is "a tightly woven tale [which] grips the reader to its macabre end." In the view of English novelist **M. John Harrison** (*TLS*), McGrath's novel is a "rapid, elegant tour of the New Gothic sensibility, death, disease, terror, evil, and weird sexuality, each landmark given an impeccable sense of its historical niche and significance...." Novelist Katherine Dunn (*WPBW*) opines that "The reader is drawn first into sympathy and complicity and finally to a bitter judgment. This homage to Gothic murk becomes a laser vivisection of silliness so profound that it approaches tragedy, so universal that it sets the neck hairs creeping." The *New York Times Book Review* observes that McGrath's "inventory of Gothicisms is exhaustive: soaring rooftops, lancet windows, black cliffs and churning seas, ghosts, deformities, monstrosities" and concludes that "As *Dr. Haggard's Disease* demonstrates, the Gothic genre, far from being restrictive, is as capacious as the mind of the writer employing it."

RECOGNITION: *NYTBR* Notable Book of the Year 1993; REVIEWS: *BL* 4/15/93; *KR* 2/15/93; *NYTBR* 5/2/93; *PW* 3/22/93; *TLS* 5/14/93; *WPBW* 5/22/93

831 *Spider* (1990); Vintage 1991(pbk); SETTING: London's East End—1957

Patrick McGrath's second novel is narrated by Dennis "Spider" Cleg, a lonely and profoundly mentally ill young man. Spider moves into a boarding house in the East End of London after 20 years in an asylum and begins to write an account of his traumatic childhood. In a plausible and disturbing vision of psychotic illness from the inside, McGrath explores the nightmare world of schizophrenia.

According to the *Literary Review*, *Spider* (like McGrath's previous novel *The Grotesque*) "boasts a structure of weblike intricacy, an elegant precision and a power to disturb. But where *The Grotesque* gave us country house camp and literary pastiche, *Spider* enmeshes us in East End Gothic." In the view of novelist Katherine Dunn (*NYTBR*), "The tight, sharp focus of this deceptively slim volume keeps us on the track despite the speed of both the past and present plots. And the sensuous world that Mr. McGrath creates is intense in its beauty as well as its grime, a place where joy waits out in the rain and there is more murder and more mystery than even Spider can admit." *The* (London) *Sunday Times* judges *Spider* "a magnificently grim social comedy." The *Christian Science Monitor* concludes that McGrath here "transcends his already solid reputation [as a master stylist] with a powerfully realized character named Spider who simply won't let you go once you meet him in these densely evocative pages."

REVIEWS: *CSM* 1/29/91; *LATBR* 10/14/90; *LJ* 8/90; *LitRev* 3/91; *LST* 4/28/91; *LT* 10/9/90; *NYTBR* 9/23/90; *PW* 8/3/90; *TLS* 4/26/91; *WPBW* 10/14/90

Mukherjee, Bharati (India/USA)

832 *The Holder of the World* (1993); Fawcett 1994 (pbk); SETTING: Cambridge Massachusetts—1990s and Boston and India—17th century

Beige Masters, a thoughtful young Yale history graduate, is living in Cambridge, Massachusetts, with her Indian boyfriend, a computer expert. Beige is an asset investigator, that is, she tracks down rare art and jewels for wealthy clients. In the course of her work she stumbles upon historical records which shed light on what appears to be one of her own 17th Century relatives, Hannah Easton. Having survived a harrowing early New England childhood characterized by privation, Indian wars, and maternal abandonment, Hannah marries a one-eyed buccaneering Englishman by the name of Gabriel Legge. With her new husband, Hannah travels to India where she is transfixed by that country's exotic culture. While living on the Coromandel Coast, she survives a Muslim-Hindu holy war and falls in love with an Indian prince, the original owner of a jewel known as "the Emperor's tear" and the "asset" that Beige is currently investigating. The documents uncovered by Beige in the course of her research suggest a further, intriguing twist to the young girl's life in that they point to an adulterous relationship with the Raj, an illegitimate pregnancy, and a final, ignominious return to the stony shores of New England. Mukherjee playfully suggests that Hannah's life story provided Hawthorne with the impetus for his novel *The Scarlet Letter*.

According to the *New York Times Book Review*, "To sketch the plot of a book like *The Holder of the World* is to disfigure drama into melodrama. The truth is in the details, brilliantly conceived, finely written, sustained from the first to the last page." In the view of Canada's *Quill & Quire*, "Mukherjee's absorbing novel glides between continents and centuries binding together a scholarly detective thriller with an inquiry about the nature of identity, of one's place in the universe." The *Women's Review of Books*, on the other hand, asserts that "Inside the complicated apparatus of science-meta-fiction Mukherjee is, if anything, even less psychologically persuasive than in the tales of undocumented Indians. This novel feels as though it was put in place by the requirements of literary fashion."

RECOGNITION: *NYTBR* Notable Book of 1993; REVIEWS: *BellesL* Win '93/94; *BL* 9/1/93; *LJ* 10/1/93; *NYTBR* 10/10/93; *NS&S* 11/19/93; *PW* 7/26/93; *Q&Q* 10/93; *TLS* 11/12/93; *WRB* 12/93

Norfolk, Lawrence (UK)

833   *Lempriere's Dictionary* (1991); Random House 1995 (pbk); Setting: Europe 17th–18th centuries

Lawrence Norfolk's prize-winning novel is a mesmerizing (often convoluted) mix of murder, intrigue, and historical detail. Norfolk's story — which definitely takes postmodern liberties with the historical fiction genre — is constructed around three seemingly unrelated historical events: the creation of the East India Company in the early 1600s; the year-long siege (1627-1628) of La Rochelle, France, during which the city was burned to the ground and thirty thousand men, women and children were massacred; and the publication, in the late 18th century, of John Lempriere's celebrated dictionary of classical mythology. At the book's heart, however, lies a mystery having to do with "global malfeasance to put BCCI in the shade" (*Observer*).

In the view of the *London Review of Books*, *Lempriere's Dictionary* is "an astonishingly assured first novel, stretching across two centuries and much of the known world ... an engrossing and wonderfully intricate extravaganza." Michael Dirda (*WPBW*), although pointing out that the version released in the US has been "simplified [and made] leaner and faster moving" than the original, observes that *Lempriere's Dictionary* is "a further addition to that diverting sub-genre that one might call the antiquarian romance." Dirda concludes that "myriad wonders and pleasures abound in Lawrence Norfolk's superbly entertaining novel." The *London Observer* notes that "if Norfolk's eruditions lack warmth, the power of his debut epic can't be ignored. It is poised, superbly inventive and intermittently gripping. With *Lempriere's Dictionary*, the precocious author has catapulted himself into the premier league of English fiction writing."

RECOGNITION: Winner of the 1991 Somerset Maugham Award; REVIEWS: *LJ* 6/15/92; *LRB* 8/29/91; *NYTBR* 12/20/92; *Obs* 8/25/91; *PW* 8/3/92; *TLS* 8/23/91; *VLS* 9/92; *WPBW* 9/20/92

Norman, Howard (USA)

834   *The Bird Artist* (1994); FS&G 1994 (HC); Picador 1995 (pbk); SETTING: Witless Bay, Newfoundland — 1911

In his second novel, Howard Norman tells the tale of Fabian Vas, a talented artist of gentle, philosophical temperament and his interaction with a small cast of characters all residing in a strangely beautiful yet profoundly isolated coastal community in Newfoundland, Canada. On page one Vas, the narrator, reveals that he has murdered Botho August, the lighthouse keeper and his mother's lover. The rest of the novel is taken up with an exploration of the events and emotions leading up to this act and its consequences.

According to novelist **Louis B. Jones** (*NYTBR*) "an adulterous affair and murder take place. Adulterous affairs and murders are common mainsprings of fiction, of course, but *The Bird Artist* gives them a twist. In this story's community, so small and isolated, everybody knows everything: the perpetrators, their motives and passions even where the gun was purchased ... The premise Mr. Norman has taken on — that good people can be driven by passion to misdeeds is a tough one, and the bear trap tension of it is evident everywhere." Novelist **Robert Hellenga** (*WPBW*) observes that Norman's "major figures ... are as imaginative, compelling in their proud independence, as Smiley's Greenlanders and as quirky as the residents of Proulx's Killick Claw, and perhaps more finely drawn.... They surprise themselves as well as the reader as they probe the mysteries — sex, alcoholism, death and despair, on the one hand, love (and sex), nature, art, beauty on the other — that lie in the path to self-awareness." *Publishers Weekly*, in its starred review, concludes that "in weaving his compelling tale, Norman convinces you that human nature is a perennially absorbing puzzle, and that the hands of an accomplished writer can worry the solutions in fresh, surprising and altogether memorable ways." The *Times Literary Supplement* notes that "What is haunting about Norman's work is his characters' ache for transcendence. As one of [his] spirited eccentrics says [of heart attacks], 'the mystery of its way bigger than the science of it.'"

READING GROUP GUIDE; RECOGNITION: Nominated for the 1994 National Book Award; *NYTBR* Notable Book of 1994; REVIEWS: *BL* 6/19/94; *KR* 4/1/94; *NYTBR* 7/10/94; *PW* 4/25/94; *TLS* 7/29/94; *WPBW* 7/24/94

Palliser, Charles (USA/UK)

835   *The Quincunx* (1989); Ballantine 1990 (pbk); SETTING: England — Victorian era

Charles Palliser — an American professor of English living in Scotland — has woven an intricate story around an English family which is dogged by its history of wealth and murder. As the story opens, a clutch of (often unsavory) characters — all mysteriously related — are attempting to lay claim to the family's enormous fortune. The tale is narrated by John Huffam, a young man who is determined to solve the mystery of his own identity; to achieve this end he must first come into contact with some of the most unsavory elements of Victorian society. John — while uncovering unsavory real estate deals, unscrupulous business practices, and even a murder — eventually discovers that the key to the mystery lies in the pattern of the quincunx, the family's five-sided heraldic figure. Palliser's debut effort has been widely described as Dickensian (think *Bleak House*) in terms of scope and period atmospherics.

In the view of the *Library Journal*, "Palliser combines an eye for social detail and vivid descriptions of the dark side of 19th-century London with a gift for intricate plotting and sinister character development reminiscent of 19th-century novels." The *LATBR* points out that "In mood, color, atmosphere and characters, this is Charles Dickens reincarnated — the grinding poverty of the homeless in London's slums, the acrid pall of smoke from open fires, the stench of a city without sanitation ... and concludes that "The 12 years that Palliser spent researching the period pay off handsomely in a remarkable book." *Time* observes that "patient readers will find their investment of time worthwhile. The book's leisurely pace contributes to the overall effect of uncanny impersonation."

RECOGNITION: *NYTBR* Notable Book of 1990; REVIEWS: *BL* 11/1/89; *LATBR* 1/21/90; *LJ* 12/89; *NYTBR* 3/4/90; *PW* 12/15/89; *Q&Q* 4/90; *Time* 1/29/90; *TLS* 9/15/89; *WPBW* 1/28/90

Pears, Iain (UK)

836   *An Instance of the Fingerpost* (1997); Putnam 1998 (HC); Setting: Oxford, England — 1663

Iain Pears's erudite, serio-comic mystery (described by both *Time* magazine and *Kirkus Reviews* as a sort of *Rashomon* meets *The Name of the Rose*) is set in Oxford, England, in 1663. When Robert Grove, a contentious yet popular Oxford don, is found murdered the subsequent investigation begins to uncover a related web of sinister activities including witchcraft, espionage, and a plot to murder the king. Sarah Blundy, the daughter of a freethinker is quickly implicated, tried and executed for the crime. *An Instance of the Fingerpost* is constructed around a series of four first-person, eyewitness accounts of the events leading up to the crime.

According to the *Times Literary Supplement*, "As historical crime fiction, *An Instance of the Fingerpost* obviously invites comparisons with Eco's *The Name of the Rose*. In both, contemporary philosophy — here Francis rather than Roger Bacon — is brought to bear on the conventions of the whodunit with concepts such as truth, empiricism and deduction themselves investigated in a historical context which is reconstructed in an elaborately scholarly way." In the view of Michael Dirda *(WPBW)*, Pears' "mesmerizing intellectual thriller ... is a novel about deception and self-deception, about the scientific method and Jesuitical chicanery, and above all about political expedience and religious transcendence. Every sentence in the book is

as solid as brick — and as treacherous as quicksand." Henry Kisor *(Chicago Sun-Times)* observes that "There are more pleasures in this novel than can be counted. Not the least is Pears' extraordinarily readable prose style, simple and straightforward yet briskly flavored with 17th century cadences and vocabulary. Those who stumbled through Umberto Ecco or Thomas Pynchon won't falter here." *Newsweek* concludes that "Cerebral, yes, but never dull, this thriller brings not merely a huge cast of characters but a whole century vividly to life." The *Library Journal* observes that "Basing his novel loosely upon an actual case from the period, Pears pits the key minds of the day: Boyle, Locke, Wren, and others against one another as each takes a shot at gaining from the event." *Publishers Weekly* applauds Pears' "grasp of the thought of the time" and concludes that "the book boasts an overall narrative momentum that carries even an ill-informed reader along."

OTHER MEDIA: Audiocassette (AudioRenaissance/abr); RECOGNITION: *LATBR* "Best Fiction of 1998"; *NYTBR* Notable Book of 1998; *PW*'s Best '98 Fiction; REVIEWS: *BL* 12/1/97; *Chi Sun-T* 4/5/98; *EW* 3/20/98; *KR* 1/1/98; *LJ* 1/98; *NewsWk* 4/27/98; *NYTBR* 4/22/98; *PW* 12/1/97; *TLS* 8/29/97; *WPBW* 3/15/98

Phillips, Jayne Anne (USA)

837   *Shelter* (1994); Delta 1995 (pbk); SETTING: West Virginia —1963

A tale of good and evil (and the loss of innocence), Jayne Ann Philips's fifth novel is set, in the mid 1960s, in a summer camp located in the thickly wooded mountains of West Virginia. *Shelter* features two young campers (sisters Lenny and Alma) who have been emotionally damaged by their parents' bitter divorce and who are poised at the threshold between childhood and adolescence. Buddy, the son of the camp cook, also plays a significant role, as does his abusive, pathologically twisted stepfather, a former convict.

According to *Belles Lettres*, "The entire book glows with an astounding lyricism and a penetrating wisdom into the world of childhood, a place commonly associated with innocence and trust, but one that is rife with unspoken longing and secret wisdom." In the view of the *New Statesman* "Phillips makes no attempt to charm or otherwise manipulate the reader, who must immediately navigate the bewildering connections between her characters and the big themes of God, the Devil, Angels and Evil, all handled with unapologetic familiarity." The *New Statesman* concludes that "At her best, no one writing fiction in the US today comes near [Phillips] for linguistic beauty and an atavistic, almost reluctant, wisdom." The *Nation* observes that *Shelter* "builds to a fever pitch and its climax is visceral and terrifying" but concludes that "the mythic quality of the story and the accumulation of heavily weighted symbols, of snakes, caves, angels and devils, seem a pesky shorthand and a distraction from Phillip's otherwise supple storytelling." *Booklist* concludes that Jayne Anne Phillips "is a considerable talent, and people who thrive on 'literary' fiction will thrive on this."

RECOGNITION: *NYTBR* Notable Book of 1994; REVIEWS: *BL* 6/1/94; *BellesL* Spr '95; *KR* 6/1/94; *LJ* 8/94; *LRB* 4/6/95; *NYTBR* 9/18/94; *Nation* 11/14/94; *NewR* 12/26/94; *NS&S* 2/10/95; *Time* 9/19/94; *TLS* 1/20/95; *WPBW* 10/16/94; *WRB* 4/95

Priest, Christopher (UK)

838   *The Prestige* (1995); St. Martin's 1996 (HC); 1997 (pbk); SETTING: England — late 19th century

Described by its publisher as reading like *The Alienist* interpreted by Robertson Davies, *The Prestige*, by British novelist Christopher Priest, is set in Victorian England and tells the compelling tale of a bitter feud between two families of stage magicians. (The title refers to the final component of illusion which — we are told — is made up of the "setup," the "performance" and the resulting effect on the audience — the "prestige") The rival magicians, Alfred Borden and Rupert Angier, have each developed an arcane and highly intricate trick that is intensely coveted by the other. The ferocity of their rivalry (although founded on a mutual misunderstanding that occurred during a fraudulent seance) is so great that it impacts their respective families for generations.

Michael Dirda (*Washington Post Book World*) declares that *The Prestige* "is a brilliantly constructed entertainment, with a plot as simple and intricate as a nest of Chinese boxes" and concludes that "one or two loose ends aside, Christopher Priest deftly produces more than one disturbing 'prestige' in this superlative novel, a spooky diversion just right for Halloween and chilly November nights." According to the *Library Journal*, "The magicians' story is framed by that of two descendants, affected by the feud in ways they are only beginning to fathom.... Mixing elements of the psychological novel with fantasy, this is an inventive, if somewhat farfetched, British neo-Gothic." *Kirkus Reviews* concludes that *The Prestige*, characterized by "[e]lectrifying effects and a deft handling of mysteries and their explanations ... [is] an unexpectedly compelling fusion of weird science and legerdemain."

RECOGNITION: Winner of the 1995 James Tait Black Prize for Fiction and the World Fantasy Award for Best Novel; REVIEWS: *KR* 8/1/96; *LJ* 9/15/96; *PW* 7/22/96; *TLS* 10/27/96; *WPBW* 10/27/96; EDITOR'S NOTE: Mr. Priest was named by *Granta* magazine to its 1983 list of the twenty "Best Young British Novelists."

Roszak, Theodore (USA)

Memoirs of Elizabeth Frankenstein (1995); Bantam 1996 (pbk); SETTING: 18th century Europe; See Section 8, #1024

Scott, Joanna (USA)

839   *The Manikin* (1996); H. Holt 1996 (HC); 1998 (pbk); SETTING: Western New York circa 1927

Joanna Scott's fifth novel is set in a brooding, gabled mansion called Manikin (whose odd-but-apt name refers to the frames used by taxidermists to stretch animal hides). The estate, we soon learn, actually contains a famous collection of exotic stuffed animals (peacocks, crocodiles, gibbons, etc.) amassed by the late Henry Craxton, "the Henry Ford of Natural History." Manikin, as the story opens, is inhabited by Craxton's widow, Mary, and a staff of nine which includes: Ellen, the housekeeper; Peg, her restless 16-year-old daughter; and the reclusive Mr. Boggio, retired master taxidermist responsible for the house's unusual collection. As "gothic" characters will, old Mrs. Craxton has set the stage for dark disaster by disinheriting her only daughter. The author, long-admired by the literati, was the recipient of a MacArthur "genius" grant in 1987.

According to *Entertainment Weekly* the author is "a highly touted literary novelist who, though not yet 40, has already won a MacArthur Fellowship. The acclaim for her work is no doubt inspired by her uncanny ability to reimagine the intellectual climates and cultures of bygone eras." The *New York Times Book Review* observes that "what Joanna Scott has given us ... is a full-bore, old-fashioned Gothic romance, a foreboding melodrama that pulses with greed, meanspiritedness and illicit sex (decorously wrought) for about a hundred pages, all this moral rot preparing the stage for the catastrophes to come. It's an evolved, refined version, artfully fitted for our *fin-de-siecle* expectation, of the kind of story that gave novels a bad name exactly 200 years ago, when Ann Radcliffe and Monk Lewis were writing theirs." In the view of *Booklist*, "the inhabitants of the Manikin are profoundly influenced by the wild, spirit-filled forces of nature, a condition that infuses this suspenseful and erotically charged tale with cosmic grandeur." *Salon* magazine argues that "Although a fluid, believable narrative never quite emerges from under the weight of ... [the] many finely etched images, Scott has nevertheless composed a gorgeous — if cerebral — meditation on love, death and art."

RECOGNITION: Nominated for the 1997 Pulitzer Prize for Fiction; *NYTBR* Notable Book of

1996; REVIEWS: *BL* 2/1/96; *EW* 1/19/96; *LJ* 1/96; *NYTBR* 4/14/96; *PW* 11/20/95; *Salon* 1996; *WPBW* 3/24/96

Shivers, Louise (USA)

840 *Whistling Woman* (1993); Longstreet 1993 (HC); SETTING: North Carolina shortly after the Civil War

Louise Shivers's second novel is set in Tar County, N.C., in the years following the Civil War and tells the story of Georgeanna ("Georgie") Weeks, who, at the age of fourteen, is raped by John Fleeting, the son of her mother's employer, the owner of a decaying plantation. To protect her daughter's reputation (and future "prospects"), Cheney Weeks, Georgie's widowed mother, simulates a pregnancy and passes the child off as her own. Needless to say, Cheney (who had had a warm, but exceedingly platonic relationship with her minister) suffers socially. Illiterate, selfless Cheney harbors other secrets as well ... which only time will tell. Georgie, meanwhile, grows up, marries a fine man, has a family ... but cannot seem to forget John Fleeting.

The *Library Journal* observes that "Shivers' first novel *Here to Get My Baby Out of Jail* (1983), drew critical acclaim and comparisons with Flannery O'Connor and Eudora Welty. Her second assures her a place among the best of these modern writers" and concludes that her "storytelling prowess, and verbal economy are wonderful...." *Booklist* concurs, pointing out that "Shivers has the grittiness of Erskine Caldwell but the subtlety of Eudora Welty; her second novel is as delightful as her first." In the view of novelist **Richard Marius** (*NYTBR*), "just as we are readying ourselves for a Southern cliché, Ms. Shivers rips away the stereotype. Nothing turns out quite as we think it will. In a novel of crystalline details, the meaning of events dissolves into the perpetual ambiguity that blesses and curses ordinary lives." According to *Belles Lettres* "Shivers grew up in the tobacco country of eastern North Carolina, and her novel bears the authentic voices of rural women of that region."

REVIEWS: *BellesL* Wint '93/94; *BL* 8/93; *LJ* 4/1/94; *NYTBR* 11/21/93; *PW* 7/26/93; *WPBW* 10/13/93

Smith, Martin Cruz (USA)

841 *Rose* (1996); Random House 1996 (HC); Ballantine 1997 (pbk); SETTING: Lancashire England —1876

In *Rose* Martin Cruz Smith features Jonathan Blair, a young British mining engineer with a reputation for "going native." Blair, whose exploits are well-known to the tabloid-reading English public, has been recalled from Africa by his employer, the wealthy Bishop Hannay, a "coal lord" whose hobby is African exploration. (Blair, it turns out, has had the effrontery to expropriate the "Missionaries' Bible Fund" to finance part of his most recent expedition.) To make amends, Blair reluctantly (and in a malaria-induced stupor) agrees to go the Lancashire mining town of Wigan to investigate the disappearance of John Maypole, a young, idealistic curate (engaged to the Bishop's daughter) who has not been seen for almost three months. Wigan, it turns out, is a particularly insalubrious place — this being the rip-snorting epicenter of England's Industrial Revolution — especially for those associated with the local mines. Blair's search for Maypole inexplicably antagonizes the local residents — from the soot encrusted miners to the mine supervisors. When "outsider" Blair falls in love with Rose, a pit girl with a burly miner boyfriend, his problems escalate.

According to *Publishers Weekly* "Smith's extravagant talent runs the spectrum here from sparkling dialogue and tantalizing mystery to grim, graphic depictions of mining life that sear both the conscience and the imagination." *Time* magazine observes that "It is no surprise that Martin Cruz Smith, author of the Soviet-era Russian cop novel *Gorky Park*, has written the most interesting and richly textured crime story of the season. What is unexpected about *Rose* is its setting: not the disorder of present-day Russia but the rigidly stratified society of an English coal-mining town toward the end of the 19th century." The *Washington Post Book World* concludes that "in *Rose* [Martin Cruz Smith] has once again succeeded in giving us a book that brings alive a people and a place previously foreign. He's made Wigan as real as Moscow." *Booklist* similarly observes that "it is the horrific, mesmerizing portrayal of the dark, hellish Wigan, the mines themselves, and the lives of miners that makes this novel much more than a good read." Richard Bernstein (*NYT*) applauds *Rose* for providing the reader with "fun, the well-plotted, dense fun of an intelligent, shadowy, literary enigma" while concluding that Martin Cruz Smith's novel "is the kind of mystery story so thickly sown with odd circumstance that it seems almost impossible that the author will be able to extricate himself, logic intact at the end.... Smith does go to the outer limits of plausibility in *Rose* and yet, while the novel shudders like a giant, old-fashioned steam engine rumbling toward a tunnel and threatening to crash, it emerges intact and running strong on the other side." *Kirkus Reviews* concludes that "The crimes here are unremarkable, but the world evoked is memorable, glowing with life."

OTHER MEDIA: Audiocassette (AudioEditions/abr); REVIEWS: *BL* 3/15/96; *KR* 3/15/96; *LATBR* 5/19/96; *LJ* 6/1/96; *NYT* 5/1/96; *NYTBR*

6/16/96; *PW* 4/1/96; *Time* 6/3/96; *TLS* 5/31/96; *WPBW* 5/5/96

Smith, Sarah (USA)

842   *Knowledge of Water* (1996); Ballantine 1996 (HC); 1997 (pbk); Setting: Paris — 1910

Sarah Smith's *Knowledge of Water*, a sequel to *The Vanished Child* (1992) is set in Paris in 1910 — the year of the devastating flood — and features Perdita Halley, a 21-year-old American pianist who has come to Europe to further her career. Her love interest (introduced in the preceding volume) is the Baron Alexander von Reisden, a specialist in mental disturbances. As the novel opens, a prostitute has been murdered and the Baron (with a dark secret of his own) begins to receive threatening letters. Called "a sprawling baroque tale of budding early feminism, murder and art forgery" by *Publishers Weekly*, *Knowledge of Water*, while grappling with significant social issues of the day, also mines a rich (if decidedly low key) comic vein. Ms. Smith enlivens her story with sketches of such (thinly-disguised) Parisian luminaries as Gertrude Stein, Alice B. Toklas, Guillaume Appolinaire, Picasso, and Colette.

Entertainment Weekly contends that "Smith renders the rain-soaked city in dark strokes, blending fact and fiction to create a haunting tale of murderers, lovers, thieves and artists." According to the *Library Journal*, " Smith [a Harvard Ph.D.] is [once again] to be congratulated for artfully educating her readers on Victorian mores and tantalizing their minds with intrigue to the last page." In the view of *Booklist*, "Smith transports the reader back almost a century [while] her capability for posing ageless questions about love, subterfuge, and reality creates an absorbing contemporary climate." The *New York Times Book Review* declares that the author "has written a lushly erotic, feminist study of artists and lovers and killers swept up in their obsessive passions. An exquisite stylist, [Smith] observes her characters in the most intimate detail, defining them with witty precision and placing them in a rain-drenched portrait of Edwardian Paris that could hang in the Louvre." *Publishers Weekly* points out that Ms. Smith's novel is "[s]aturated with a subtle eroticism, low-key humor and luxuriant atmosphere, particularly concerning the great flood that ravaged the city of Paris early in the century." *Kirkus Reviews* concludes that despite some lulls in pacing "the thick ambiance, the forthright feminist subtext, and especially Smith's gritty and appealing heroine make for intellectual stimulation of the highest order — and should make readers impatiently eager for the completion of the trilogy."

READING GROUP GUIDE; RECOGNITION: *NYTBR* Notable Book of 1996; REVIEWS: *BL* 8/96;

EW 9/27/96; *KR* 7/15/96; *LATBR* 9/22/96; *LJ* 8/96; *NYTBR* 9/7/96; *PW* 8/5/96 *WPBW* 9/17/96

843   *The Vanished Child* (1993); Ballantine 1995 (pbk); SETTING: Boston — late 19th century

The Vanished Child, is a "stunning" (*NYTBR*) historical thriller with gothic undertones and the first volume of a projected trilogy. Set, principally, in and around Boston and a lake-side summer community in nearby New Hampshire, it tells a suspenseful story of intrigue and duplicity. In 1887 a wealthy Bostonian by the name of William Knight was brutally murdered and his young grandson, who, it was assumed, was a witness to the crime, was abducted. The story opens in 1905, some eighteen years after the murder/abduction; the missing child, if alive, would now be a young man — a very wealthy young man, to be precise — as he is the sole heir to his grandfather's massive estate.

Publishers Weekly, in its starred review, calls *The Vanished Child* "A stunning tale" wherein Ms. Smith "evokes turn-of-the-century manners and mores with style and authority." The *San Francisco Chronicle* observes that Ms. Smith "controls her characters and plot with authority. By using internal dialogue — thoughts, memories and alternative conversations that don't actually happen — to augment the plot the characters let loose details they can't say aloud." According to the *Library Journal* "Employing subtle Jamesian touches…. Smith deftly explores both the actual and the psychological mysteries surrounding" the 19-year-old case. *Kirkus Reviews* concludes that "Smith … paints a canvas reminiscent of Robert Goddard's well-upholstered period thrillers, though more tonily inconclusive at every stage."

RECOGNITION: *NYTBR* Notable Book of 1993; REVIEWS: *KR* 1/1/93; *LJ* 2/1/93; *NYTBR* 2/20/94; *PW* 11/8/93; EDITOR'S NOTE: Successful "hand-selling" by a San Francisco bookstore owner brought this above average literary thriller to the attention of a wide and enthusiastic readership, eventually outselling even the *Bridges of Madison County*.

Unsworth, Barry (UK)

844   *Morality Play* (1995); Doubleday 1996 (HC); Norton 1996 (pbk); SETTING: England — 14th Century

Barry Unsworth's ninth novel is set in the plague-ridden 14th-century, in a perpetually "wintry" England where graveyards have been turned into mass burial grounds, fields lie untilled, famine is rampant, and destitute soldiers roam the countryside in search of sustenance. Nicholas Baker, a young "insufficiently pious" cleric, has abandoned his position as subdeacon at Lincoln Cathedral. He impulsively joins up with a group of traveling actors who are journeying towards Durham — giving theatrical performances along the way. In their peregrinations the troupe comes upon a village where a young peasant boy has recently been murdered and a young woman, the beautiful, deaf-mute daughter of the local weaver, stands accused of the crime. The actors, vying for the attention of the villagers (who are clearly more interested in a rival group of rope walkers and fire-eaters) decide to stage a re-enactment of the murder. The actors quickly set out to ascertain the basic "facts" around which they spin theories and, ultimately, improvise their drama. In the process of creating a *divertissement* the troupe finds itself confronting what appears to be the truth of the matter.

In the view of the *Times Literary Supplement*, *Morality Play* is Unsworth's "best book yet ... the story itself is utterly compelling, and as a good mystery story, increasingly so up to its closing pages." The *TLS* concludes that "the lightness with which this Morality is played makes it all the more compulsive, both as a narrative and as an indictment of our own times." According to *The* (London) *Sunday Times*, Unsworth's "bleakly glittering" *Morality Play* "[s]ilhouetted against a stark background of mass graves, of the death throes of feudalism and the demise of liturgical drama ... offers freezing insights into human nature and human society." English novelist Cecilia Holland (*WPBW*), although noting that the author "raises expectations of a blockbuster finish that never materializes," further observes that "Unsworth's characters and his detail for observation save him. Time and again scenes come vibrantly to life: a market, an inn yard, a joust, the staging of the play ... *Morality Play* pleases with its wit, its clarity, its empathetic, intelligent reading of the history." The *Library Journal* concludes that "Rich in historical detail, Unsworth's well-told tale explores some timeless moral dilemmas and reads like a modern page-turner."

OTHER MEDIA: Audiocassette (Chivers/ unabr); READING GROUP GUIDE; RECOGNITION: *NYTBR* Notable Book of 1996; REVIEWS: *BL* 11/1/95; *LJ* 10/15/95; *LST* 8/27/95; *NY* 1/15/96; *NYTBR* 11/12/95; *TLS* 9/8/95; *WPBW* 11/19/95

845 *The Stone Virgin* (1985); W.W. Norton 1995 (pbk); SETTING: Contemporary, 17th and 15th Century Venice

Barry Unsworth's 6th novel — set in a sumptuously atmospheric Venice — tells the story of the creation, suppression and eventual restoration of a statue of the Madonna which has a vaguely (and disturbingly) erotic quality. The statue was long in the possession of the powerful Fornarini family, a dynasty which has always cloaked its affairs in utmost secrecy. The novel's 20th-century segments feature Simon Raikes, a frustrated artist who has been commissioned to restore the badly decayed statue. As his work progresses Simon becomes consumed with a need to solve the mystery of the stone Virgin's provenance. He also becomes involved with the wife of an Italian sculptor who — herself linked to the Fornarini family — manages to draw him into a sinister plot. Parallel stories — illuminating the tangled (possibly blasphemous) history of the work — are set in both 15th- and 17th-century Venice.

The *New Statesman* points out that "Bulging like a teardrop into its poisonous lagoon, Venice boasts a geography so graspable for purposes of art that it comes as a surprise not that so many stories are set there, but so few." *NS* concludes that *Stone Virgin* "a tale of love and death, art and decay, power and corruption and sex and drowning, has been set by Barry Unsworth ... a deft and canny teller of tales, in the best place possible to add depth and a sense of the sorrows of time to a story that otherwise might have seen marginally overblown...." In the view of English novelist Francis King (*Spectator*), "Venice is a city in which the present often seems to be no more than a contaminating accretion of the past.... . Venice is also a city in which, more than in most, one is continually aware of human mortality. What better locale then for a novel concerned with a fever to live and love at constant odds with a nagging apprehension of death? Unsworth's little jewel has its perfect setting."

REVIEWS: *LJ* 3/1/86; *NS* 8/8/86; *NYTBR* 4/6/86; *Spec* 8/24/85; *TLS* 8/30/85

Watson, Larry (USA)

846 *Montana 1948* (1993); Pocket Books 1995 (pbk); Setting: Mercer County, Montana — 1948

Haydens have lived in the small Montana town of Bentrock for generations. As Watson's story opens David Hayden — the narrator — is twelve and according to his somewhat anxious mother "is growing up wild." David's father is the local sheriff; his uncle the local doctor. When the Haydens' "Indian" housekeeper, Marie Little Soldier, accuses Dr. Hayden of sexual assault, their lives are changed forever. David, now in his early forties, looks back to a series of events which led, inexorably, to his family's repudiation and exile.

According to *Booklist*, "The action unfolds circuitously, as David remembers how he pieced together what was happening, mostly through eavesdropping.... .Yes, the novel is a kind of thriller and certainly a page turner, but, moreover, it is a quiet, almost meditative reflection on the hopelessly complex issue of doing the right thing." In the view of the *Times Literary Supplement*, "David's unpleasant discoveries about the adult world are mediated to us by the grownup he has become. Occasionally, the tone and language are so thoughtful and precise that they seem sententious.... In due course, one comes to respect this formality. The Western is, ultimately, a genre with a particular concern for justice so a certain stiff judiciousness does not come amiss." The *Christian Science Monitor* notes that "The conflict between bravado and a quieter kind of courage is seen through the eyes of the narrator, a young boy coming of age, who is a lot wiser than his years." *Kirkus* concludes that *Montana 1948* is a "literary page-turner, morally complex and satisfying in its careful accumulation of detail and in its use of landscape to reveal character."

OTHER MEDIA: Audiocassette (Recorded Bks/unabr); RECOGNITION: *Booklist* "Editors' Choice" 1993; ALA/YALSA "Best Books for Young Adults" 1994 NY Public Library "Books for the Teen Age" 1993; REVIEWS: *BL* 9/1/93; *CSM* 12/3/93; *KR* 7/1/93; *LATBR* 10/10/93; *NYTBR* 12/12/93; *TLS* 8/18/95; *WPBW* 11/7/93

West, Paul (UK/USA)

847   *The Women of Whitechapel Street* (1991); Overlook 1992 (pbk); SETTING: Victorian London

The Women of Whitechapel Street purports to be the "real" story of Jack the Ripper and his victims. In his thirteenth novel West draws on what is referred to as the "Establishment Conspiracy" which postulates that a member of the royal family was responsible for the event which, in turn, precipitated the infamous string of murders. The motivation, as elucidated in West's version, has to do with blackmail perpetrated by four prostitute/models. Also implicated in the gruesome goings-on are William Gull, Royal physician, and the painter Walter Sickert, who is shown to be a sort of Royal pimp.

According to *Publishers Weekly* "Verbal wizard West, inspired by recent journalism, imagines the infamous Jack the Ripper to have actually been a depraved trio who murdered together to cover up for a slumming duke." The *New York Times Book Review*, on the other hand, contends that in *The Women of Whitechapel Street*, "The late Victorian period, with all its charm and filth and wretchedness, is delivered up in dazzling set pieces — from frolics with a bathing machine at Yarmouth to a plague of flies descending on London — that never interferes with the story's grimly steady momentum." As the *L.A. Times Book Review* notes, *The Women of Whitechapel Street* "evokes both the prim surface of the Victorian era and its lecherous underside.... We can't help reading on...." The *New Republic* concludes that in his "superbly written and intricately choreographed" book, West "is searching for the psychology beyond the pathology."

RECOGNITION: *NYTBR* Notable Book of 1991;

REVIEWS: *AtlM* 5/91; *LJ* 3/1/91; *NewR* 5/6/91; *NYTBR* 5/12/91; *Sewanee Spr* '93; *TLS* 11/8/91; *WPBW* 4/28/91

Wharton, Thomas (Canada)

848   *Icefields* (1995); Washington Square 1996 (pbk); SETTING: Canada 1898–1923

Thomas Wharton's intensely atmospheric, decades-spanning debut novel begins in 1898 when Edward (Ned) Byrne, a young British doctor — part of an expedition to the Acturus Glacier in the Canadian Rockies — slips and falls into a crevasse. Ned, trapped in what could quite easily become an icy tomb, is transfixed by a strange sight: the body of a winged human creature caught and suspended in a wall of ice. Ned is eventually rescued but is drawn back to the Canadian icefield in an attempt to get to the bottom of the mystery. Supporting characters include an intrepid female explorer, a seductress, an industrialist intent on developing the region for tourism, and a poet who supports himself as a guide.

In the view of *Publishers Weekly*, Wharton's novel "borrows something of the mystery and icy obsessiveness of Peter Hoeg's *Smilla's Sense of Snow*, the bleak hallucinatory vision of William Vollmann's *The Ice Shirt* and a cast of haunted characters reminiscent of Josephine Hart's *Damage*." The (London) *Sunday Times* argues that *Icefields* is "a kaleidoscope of history, myth and romance ... [wherein] the story splinters off in a number of satisfying directions as a steady stream of warm prose forms an evocative portrait of a frozen wilderness." According to the *New York Times Book Review* "With careful dialogue, a steady pace and cool, subtle prose, Mr. Wharton mixes the doctor's mysterious adventures with those of the inhabitants of a nearby luxury hotel; and so, through a skillful juxtaposition of scientific observations, dialogue and journal entries and letters, fact is successfully merged with fantasy." The *Washington Post Book World* observes that "Wharton has ably captured the turn-of-the-century feel of rural Canada, complete with Boosterism, a Victorian adventuress, and teahouses in the wilderness" and concludes that Wharton has written "a slim, artful novel."

RECOGNITION: Winner of the Banff Grand National Prize for Literature, The Writers Guild of Alberta Best First Book Award, The Commonwealth Writers Best First Novel (Caribbean and Canada Region); REVIEWS: *LST* 1/25/98; *NYTBR* 10/13/96; *PW* 8/19/96; *TLS* 1/10/97; *WPBW* 10/20/96

Wilson, Jonathan (UK)

849   *The Hiding Room* (1995); Viking 1995 (HC); Penguin 1997 (pbk); SETTING: Cairo — WW II

Jonathan Wilson, in his double-stranded debut novel, tackles both a sensitive historical subject (the suppression — during WW II — by some in the Allied camp of news coming out of Eastern Europe regarding the extent of Nazi atrocities) and the more familiar (but sensitively realized) theme of the search for identity. The interrelated stories are set first in Cairo in 1941 where Archie Rawlins, a young Oxford graduate and British army intelligence officer, falls in love with Esta, a passionate Jewess (and fierce Zionist) who has managed to escape Hitler's Europe, and then, fifty years later, in Jerusalem, when Esta's middle-aged son, Daniel Weiss, comes to bury his mother. Wilson, has, in the view of a number of critics, achieved an effective mix of historical romance and political thriller.

The *Times Literary Supplement* calls *The Hiding Room* a "vividly and confidently written book" which contains "superb cameos of British squaddies and 1940s Army officers, as well as finely drawn portraits of Esta's broken father and Mendoza, the complex British Army Jewish chaplain. However, at the heart of the story lies the tortured but passionate relationship between Esta and Archie." According to the *New Yorker* "Wilson's art lies not only in each story's suspenseful telling but in the way the stories circumvent each other and ultimately collide — at a place where identity hovers just beyond the facts that should determine it...." The *Christian Science Monitor* concludes that *The Hiding Room* "is a first novel in which nothing is pure and simple, in which people find themselves making life-or-death decisions that are little more than leaps in the dark, and in which a young man loses an innocence that was little more than insularity in order to play his part in a real life drama where actions have incalculable consequences that cannot be evaded."

REVIEWS: *CSM* 11/13/95; *LJ* 7/95; *NY* 2/12/96; *NYTBR* 9/3/95; *PW* 5/22/95; *TLS* 11/17/95

Wolff, Geoffrey (USA)

850   *Age of Consent* (1995); Knopf 1995 (HC); Picador 1996 (pbk); SETTING: New York State — 1960s onward

Jinx and Anne Jenks, an idealistic couple in a decade that was just beginning to embrace "alternatives," have chosen to raise their children in Blackberry Mountain, a utopian community "'neath the balsam and within earshot of loons" in New York's Adirondak mountains. Their seemingly idyllic life is shattered when, one fateful Fourth of July, their fifteen-year-old daughter Maisie attempts suicide by diving off the top of Raven Hill gorge into a shallow pool of water. Maisie survives and Ted, her thirteen-year-old brother — and narrator of the tale — spends the rest of the novel (and

a good chunk of his life) trying to understand his sister's act.

According to *People Weekly* "Wolff, who cast an unflinching eye at his own famously dysfunctional family in [his] masterful 1970 memoir ... skillfully lays bare a world of rueful adults, even children, whose memories are rife with ache and bitterness — a place where no one can move fast or far enough from harm." In the view of *Booklist* "This is Wolff's sixth novel and possibly his best. Exquisitely paced and well timed, the book is propelled to its devastating conclusion by the pressure of something the characters refuse to discuss or acknowledge." *Kirkus Reviews* notes that "Except for the sluggish mid-section that recalls the past too lengthily and lovingly, [this is] an absorbing tale of monstrous evil with an all too human face." According to the *Washington Post Book World*, "Geoffrey Wolff's well-named new novel rises above the level of its plot, which resorts to incest, the sexual misuse of minors and the casual betrayal of friendship and principle to get and keep things moving. The regret a reader feels that a writer of Wolff's intelligence and sophistication should feel compelled ... to fashion a subtle work out of such unsubtle materials tends to be overcome by the realization that he generally succeeds."

RECOGNITION: *NYTBR* Notable Book of 1995; REVIEWS: *BL* 3/15/95; *KR* 12/15/94; *LJ* 2/1/95; *NYTBR* 2/19/95; *PeopleW* 2/20/95; *PW* 12/19/94; *TLS* 5/19/95; *WPBW* 2/27/95

Zencey, Eric (USA)

851   *Panama* (1995); FS&G 1995 (HC); Berkley 1997 (pbk); SETTING: Paris 1892

In Eric Zencey's first novel, a sophisticated mystery set in Paris, the Panama of the title refers to the Central-American canal or, more precisely, to the French scandal surrounding its construction. What had begun in 1878 as an impressive feat of engineering — and a source of intense French national pride — had deteriorated fourteen years later (from the accumulated deficit of rampant disease and inadequate funding) into a financial and technological debacle. That's the novel's background. In the foreground, Zencey (a professor of History at Goddard College) has placed the historical figure of Henry Adams (descended from two American presidents) who, while on a sojourn in France, has met and fallen in love with Miriam Talbot, a young American artist. When she later disappears, and a body identified as hers washes up on the bank of the Seine, Adams is compelled to investigate the matter. He is drawn inexorably into a very dark matter when it becomes clear to him that the corpse has been "misidentified" as (the still-missing) Miriam Talbot's. The existence of a list (supposedly in Ms. Talbot's possession) of *chequards* — French politicians who took bribes from the canal-building company — comes to light and the pursuit turns ever more deadly.

According to the *Atlantic Monthly*, *Panama* "is much more than a simple mystery story. The author draws on Adams's life and ideas for digressions on art, historical study, and the early stages of technological society." In the view of *Booklist* "Zencey's descriptions of late-nineteenth-century Paris are wonderfully detailed and atmospheric, and his dramatization of the dawn of forensic science proves quite fascinating." The *Times Literary Supplement* argues that although the "trail through a wintry nineteenth-century Paris is engagingly described and well-researched, flying into palace salons, plunging through low-life gutters" concludes that "As a mystery story ... it is rather short on thrills." An appreciative *Nation* reviewer suggests that "Zencey gets Adams exactly — mooning over the 'unity' of the Middle Ages in the face of modernity's 'chaos,' flirting with Catholicism and the idea of the Virgin, suspicious of progress as a form of moral decline, fascinated by science while deploring its advance." *Time* magazine concludes its review with the simple observation that Zencey "has provided some of the year's most cheerful literary fun."

OTHER MEDIA: Audiocassette (S&S/abr & Recorded Bks/unabr); RECOGNITION: *The (London) Sunday Times* Notable book of 1996; *NYTBR* Notable Book of 1995; REVIEWS: *AtlM* 10/95; *BL* 8/95; *EW* 9/22/95; *LJ* 9/15/95; *Nation* 10/2/95; *NYTBR* 10/1/95; *PW* 6/26/95; *Time* 10/9/95; *TLS* 2/2/96

7

Humor

This seventh section features the full gamut of comedic styles: the gently comic human dramas offered up by Karl Ackerman, Laurie Colwin, and Carol Shields; the slyly humorous works of Julian Barnes, Cathleen Schine and Fernanda Eberstadt; the socio-academic farces of David Lodge, Robert Russo, and Jane Smiley; the Generation X satire of Douglas Coupland, Gish Jen or Paul Beatty; the quirky comedies of Kate Atkinson, William Kotzwinkle or James Morrow; and the darkly comic forays into the human condition mounted by such writers as Sherman Alexie, David Gates and Tibor Fischer. As usual, what these writers have in common is talent, in copious measure.

Ackerman, Karl (USA)

852 *Patron Saint of Unmarried Women* (1994); St. Martin's 1994 (HC); 1995 (pbk)

Karl Ackerman's wryly comic debut novel is set in Washington, D.C., and features Jack Townsend, an opera-loving jock who makes his living in the decidedly un–Washingon field of landscape gardening. Jack has recently broken up with Nina Lawrence, his long-time artist girlfriend, and is beginning to realize that he has made a terrible mistake. Sundry members of Nina's large, lively Catholic family are similarly convinced, particularly her mother who prays regularly to St. Anne — the patron saint of unmarried women.

The *Washington Post Book World* judged Ackerman's novel "both rueful and funny. One of a kind." *USA Today* notes that "Ackerman leads us

deftly through the small ins and outs of love here, as well as taking us on a few cynical spins around the D.C. power loop" and concludes that occasional "minor snags [aside] ... this book is a real pleasure, a wry road map through the many sweet confusions of romance and family, politics and plain luck." The *Library Journal* calls it a "witty, modern romance, written from the male perspective ... and a very entertaining story."

RECOGNITION: *NYTBR* Notable Book of 1994; nominated for the *Library Journal*'s First Novel Award; REVIEWS: *LJ* 4/15/94; *NYTBR* 5/29/94; *PW* 4/11/94; *USA Today* 5/26/94; *WPBW* 7/23/95

Akst, Daniel (USA)

St. Burl's Obituary (1996); HB&J 1997 (pbk); See Section 6, #666

Alcorn, Alfred (USA)

Murder in the Museum of Man (1997); Zoland 1997 (HC); 1998 (pbk); See Section 6, #667

Alexie, Sherman (USA)

853 *Reservation Blues* (1995); Warner 1996 (pbk)

Reservation Blues is a first novel by short-story writer and full-blooded Spokane/Coeur d'Alene Indian Sherman Alexie. Music features prominently in Alexie's novel, which incorporates both the unquiet spirit of blues legend Robert Johnson and the decidedly corporeal "All-Indian Catholic rock band" from the Spokane reservation. Thomas Builds-the-Fire and "Junior," characters first introduced in Alexie's popular short story collection (*The Lone Ranger and Tonto Fistfight in Heaven*), are reprised here.

Booklist observes that Sherman Alexie "mixes biting black humor, a healthy dose of magic and sparkling lyricism to produce a remarkably powerful story with roots not only in Native American mythology but also in the equally potent history of rock and roll." In novelist **Leslie Marmon Silko**'s view "Alexie's talent is immense and genuine.... The power of his writing rises out of the Spokane River and the Spokane earth where it is sweetened with the music of Robert Johnson, Hank Williams, Elvis Presley, Janis Joplin and Jimi Hendrix. On this big Indian Reservation we call the US, Sherman Alexie is one of the best writers we have" (*The Nation*).

RECOGNITION: *BL* Editors Choice 1995; *Granta* magazine's Best of Young American Novelists; REVIEWS: *BL* 6/1/95; *LATBR* 6/18/95; *LJ* 6/1/95; *Nation* 6/12/95; *NYTBR* 7/16/95; *OBS* 1/28/96; *PW* 5/1/95; *WPBW* 10/18/96; *WLT* Spr '96

Allen, Edward (USA)

854   *Mustang Sally* (1992); W.W. Norton 1994 (pbk)

The "Mustang Sally" of Edward Allen's 1992 decidedly non–PC comic excursion is Sally Iverson, a hostess at a brothel called the Mustang Valley Inn; she's also a former student of Packard Schmidt, assistant professor of composition and technical writing at an undistinguished Midwestern college. When Schmidt, a self-described "liberal Republican" with an unprofessorial interest in neon motels and topless bars, flies to Las Vegas for his Christmas break, he looks Sally up.

According to the *Library Journal*, "Allen's juxtaposition of the seedy Las Vegas life with the stuffy world of academia is an original and interesting device that makes for humorous and often fast-paced, engrossing reading." The *American Book Review* finds "moments in *Mustang Sally* that are so wickedly delicious we nearly forgive Allen his excesses." The *New York Times Book Review* notes that "Much of the novel (though not all — some of its is slack and desultory), is very funny and regrettably accurate, allowing for satire's necessary selection and exaggeration."

RECOGNITION: *NYTBR* Notable Book of 1993; REVIEWS: *ABR* 10-11/93; *ChiTrib* 10/25/92; *LJ* 11/1/92; *NYTBR* 12/13/92

Amis, Kingsley (UK)

855   *The Russian Girl* (1992); Viking Penguin 1994 (pbk)

Kingsley Amis's 1992 novel, *The Russian Girl*, part academic satire and part love story, is set in the pre–Glasnost era and features Ana Danilova, an émigré Russian poet of debatable talent. London's literary and social establishment gathers round when the Russian girl arrives on a reading tour designed to raise support for her brother, a well-known Soviet dissident. Dr. Richard Vaisey, a 46-year-old scholar affiliated with the London Institute of Slavic Studies (and husband of the entrancingly appalling Cordelia) falls hard for Ana. If he could just overlook the dullness of her verse.

According to novelist Christopher Buckley (*NYTBR*), "Sex, booze and Russian intrigue have never gone as well together as they do in Kingsley Amis's brilliant, mordant and quite funny novel.... *The Russian Girl* is vintage Amis: smooth, dry and not overpriced." The *Literary Review* observes that "Amis's skill is well up to scratch" and concludes that Amis's novel contains brilliant comic set pieces, at least one unforgettable character [Cordelia], and enough of a central dilemma to give the brain a bit of exercise."

OTHER MEDIA: Audiocassette (Books-on-Tape/unabr); RECOGNITION: *NYTBR* Notable Book of 1994; REVIEWS: *ChiTrib* 6/12/94; *LATBR* 6/12/94; *LitRev* 5/92; *LRB* 5/92; *NYTBR* 5/15/94; *PW* 3/21/94; *Scotsman* 4/18/92; *TLS* 4/10/92; *WPBW* 5/94; EDITOR'S NOTE: Mr. Amis's 1954 prize-winning first novel *Lucky Jim* (re-issued by Penguin in 1993) is considered by many to be the father of all academic satires. It features Jim Dixon, a young academic who feels thoroughly out of his element among his pretentious madrigal-singing, wine savoring university colleagues.

Amis, Martin (UK)

856   *The Information* (1995); Random House 1996 (pbk)

Richard Tull, a failed novelist with marital problems, makes a living editing an obscure literary publication and composing dismissive, mean-spirited reviews. Middle-aged and counting, he becomes completely unhinged when his friend's (Gwyn Barry) simplistic "new-agey" novels begin to rocket up the best-seller charts. Martin Amis's *The Information* is an account of Richard's occasionally ingenious, often comical and generally inept attempts to damage Gwyn's career. Amis's latest offering skewers Literary London *and* the American book tour scene with equal venom. The author, a successful novelist (and himself the object of a certain amount of professional envy — generated in part by the size of his *own* pre-publication advance), is the son of the late Kingsley Amis, one of the most prodigiously talented (and thoroughly cantankerous) satirists of the mid–20th century.

English novelist and critic **Malcolm Bradbury**, writing in *The* (London) *Times*, concludes that Amis has created "a knowing *fin de notre siecle* comedy of literary degradation, cultural slippage, social and sexual humors ... male menopausal crisis ... [and] global depression." According to the *Washington Post Book World* Amis "possesses all the gifts of a first rate comic novelist — a keen eye for pretension, a deadly sense of humor and seemingly inexhaustible reservoirs of spite and bile." Novelist Christopher Buckley (son of William F. Buckley, Jr.), in his *NYTBR* review asks "Is an envious writer enough to sustain a whole novel?" and answers "Surprisingly, yes.... Richard's indignation and resentment ... and his determination to redress the cosmic imbalance makes for gorgeous, dark inventions."

OTHER MEDIA: audiocassette (Books-on-Tape/unabr); READING GROUP GUIDE: Vintage Books; RECOGNITION: *NYTBR* "Editors' Choice" 1995; REVIEWS: *BL* 4/1/95; *CSM* 5/17/95; *EW* 5/12/95; *LJ* 5/1/95; *LRB* 5/11/95; *LST* 3/26/95; *LT* 3/28/95; *NatR* 5/29/95; *NewRep* 8/14/95; *NewSci* 4/22/95; *NS&S* 3/24/95; *Time* 5/1/95; *TLS* 5/24/95; *WPBW* 5/7/95

Antrim, Donald (USA)

The Hundred Brothers (1997); Vintage 1998 (pbk); See Section 3, #167

Atkinson, Kate (UK)

857   *Human Croquet* (1997); St. Martin's 1997 (HC); 1998 (pbk)

Kate Atkinson's second novel, a lively mix of fairy tale and multigenerational saga, tells the story of the Fairfaxes who, for centuries, have lived at "Arden," their ancestral home. The Fairfaxes had once been a great family but, after four hundred years, their descendants have devolved into suburban eccentricity. Throughout their history, the Fairfaxes have struggled with a painful legacy — a curse, stemming from the mysterious disappearance of the first Lady Fairfax. *Human Croquet* is narrated by 16-year-old Isobel who, abandoned while still a child by both her parents, has been raised by her stern grandmother and her sour Aunt Vinny. As the novel opens, Isobel's father Charles has returned — seven years after walking out on his family — to Arden with a *new* wife. Ms. Atkinson does not employ a linear progression in the telling of her story; as the tale unfolds, Isobel is pulled into brief time warps which deposit her in various historical periods from the 17th century through the Roaring Twenties. Isobel gradually learns the truth about her family in a story that incorporates equal parts comedy and tragedy.

According to the *New Statesman Human Croquet* is "peppered with snatches of hilarious nonsensical suburban dialogue; big, exuberant exclamations; savvy rhetorical questions and a knuckle-crackingly morbid sense of humour....

The narrator's youthful cynicism does not descend into mannerism. Atkinson shows that it is the logical outcome of cruelty and trauma. The charms of her young-old narrators is that the worse things get, the funnier, the more wildly exuberant they become." In the view of the *Library Journal*, *Human Croquet*, "an unusual novel, concerns the nature of time, memory and most poignantly, identity.... As the fantastic and the mundane combine almost seamlessly, incest, puppy love and dysfunctional families mix to darkly comic effect." The *Literary Review* concludes that "Atkinson feeds a current appetite for the lost world of home-baked scones, funny old radios and dear ordinary life. Her twist is to backlight ordinariness with time's great glow."

RECOGNITION: *NYTBR* Notable Book of 1997; REVIEWS: *ComW* 5/9/97; *KR* 2/15/97; *LitRev* 3/97; *LJ* 3/1/97; *NS* 3/21/97; *NYTBR* 7/6/97; *Obs* 3/99/97; *PW* 2/10/97; *Spec* 3/8/97; *TLS* 3/7/97; *VV* 6/24/97

858   *Behind the Scenes at the Museum* (1995); St. Martin's 1996 (HC); Picador 1997 (pbk)

Kate Atkinson's debut novel, a picaresque, multigenerational tale of an eccentric Yorkshire family, is narrated by Ruby Lennox, youngest daughter of a philandering, pet-shop owning father and a resentful, indifferent mother. Using time-shifts and flashbacks, Ruby's chronological narration (which actually begins with the moment of her conception) is intercut with historical episodes from the lives of her mother, aunt and grandmother.

According to the *Christian Science Monitor*, *Behind the Scenes at the Museum* "marks the debut of a distinctive new voice ... [striking] a nice balance between fantasy and reality." English novelist **Hilary Mantel** (*LRB*) was impressed by Atkinson's ability to "explore the changing nature of women's lives without being either obvious or schematic, and she can do this because she respects all her characters." Ms. Mantel concludes that " Even those who seem to have no redeeming features are treated with wry humor, the book is never depressing. It is, in fact, outrageously funny on almost every page, and this is a wonder when you consider what is actually happening." The *Times Literary Supplement* observes that "This epic tale of a Yorkshire family, charted through four generations from 1888 to 1992, flirts with magic realism; the 'curious genetic whispers' and patterns which bind characters across time, the vision, allegories and impossible coincidence which prompt decisions and which both complicate and rationalize the plot" and concludes that *Behind the Scenes at the Museum*, "is too capricious, too bitingly ironic, to conform to any one genre...." The *Spectator* notes that Ms. Atkinson's novel "will give enormous pleasure to a wide range of readers: it is a coat of many colors, warm enough for the deepest winter."

OTHER MEDIA: Audiocassette (Chivers/unabr); RECOGNITION: Winner of the 1995 Whitbread "Book of the Year" Award; *NYTBR* Notable Book of 1996; *TLS* International Book of the Year; REVIEWS: *CSM* 1/10/96; *LRB* 4/4/96; *NY* 6/10/96; *NYTBR* 3/31/96; *PW* 10/30/95; Spec 11/18/95; *TLS* 4/21/95.

Baldwin, William (USA)

859   *The Fennel Family Papers* (1996); Algonquin 1996 (HC)

William Baldwin's second novel, called "raucous, funny and decidedly offbeat" by the *Library Journal* is set on the South Carolina coast and features Paul Danvers, a socially awkward yet ambitious professor of history at a local university. Professor Danvers has initiated an affair with Ginny Fennel (of the infamous Fennel family, lighthouse keepers since the American Revolution) in the hopes of gaining access to the family's cache of historically significant papers. Danvers is so eager to make the tenure track that he is willing to overlook Ginny's peculiarly menacing extended family.

Publishers Weekly found *The Fennell Family Papers* to be "a wickedly funny academic satire, grafted onto a manic plot featuring murder, madness, incest, a ghost and spirit possession." According to *Booklist* (which calls the novel "a comic gem"), Baldwin "fuels his rollicking satire with large doses of anarchic humor and totally unpredictable storytelling. And Baldwin is that rare thing — a satirist with a lot of heart."

REVIEWS: *BL* 12/1/95; *LJ* 11/1/95; *NYTBR* 2/4/96; *PW* 10/30/95; *SouthLiv* 1/96

Barnes, Julian (UK)

860   *Talking It Over* (1991); Random House 1992 (pbk)

Called a "chamber cantata of voices about adultery" by *Kirkus Reviews, Talking It Over* — incorporating elements of the classic French film *Jules et Jim* — tells the story of modern-day love triangle. As the tale begins, Stuart, a rather stuffy financial analyst, has fallen in love with and (surprising many) has married Gillian, an attractive, rather nononsense art conservator. His best friend Oliver (a free-spirited screen writer) meeting Gillian for the first time at her wedding proceeds to fall head-over-heels in love with her. He pursues her and eventually wins her away from the heartbroken Stuart. What begins as a comedy about love and misunderstanding deepens into an exploration of self-delusion, disloyalty and atonement. Told, in turn, from the perspective of each of the three main characters, *Talking It Over* examines the vagaries of memory and (through the use of dramatic monologues) "point of view."

According to the *London Review of Books*, Julian Barnes has created a tale full of cross-currents and subtle distortions ... a skein of verbal infidelities woven like a cat's cradle around the central emotional infidelity.... As in all Barnes's books, wit and readability carry the day...." In the view of novelist **Alexander Theroux** (*WPBW*), *Talking It Over* "is alternatively light and sad. What begins as a chatty, slightly preppy, seemingly not all that consequential gallery of characters — portraits really as each characters steps forth to introduce himself, chat, give us his side of things — soon turns into a bleak examination of modern love, cruelly insouciant, indeterminate, without rules or vows." The *Irish Times* observes that Barnes has "despite the sit-com dialogue and the clichés, written a readable, uncomfortably funny and wise" novel. *Publishers Weekly* calls *Talking It Over* "smart and fabulous fun ... [a] post modern *Jules et Jim*, made up only of testimonies from its [three principle] characters" and concludes that the "ingenious ending allows each of the figures to fashion his own radically different resolution, while Barnes's sly narrator leaves it to the reader to be the ultimate judge and, as such, the ultimate author."

REVIEWS: *ComW* 5/8/92; *IrTimes* 6/91; *KR* 8/1/91; *LJ* 9/1/91; *LRB* 7/25/91; *NewR* 12/16/91; *NS&S* 7/19/91; *NYRB* 12/5/91; *NYTBR* 10/13/91; *PW* 8/2/91; *TLS* 7/12/91; *VLS* 10/91; *WPBW* 10/13/91

Barthelme, Frederick (USA)

861   *Bob the Gambler* (1997); HM 1997 (HC); Mariner Bks 1998 (pbk)

Set in Barthelme's oft-limned Biloxi, Mississippi, *Bob the Gambler* tells the story of Ray Kaiser — a struggling architect — and his wife Jewel as they first oppose, and then become hopelessly addicted to, their town's latest attraction: a floating casino.

The *New York Times Book Review* observes that Barthelme's "latest dispatch from zeitgeist central, is a contemporary parable of the Garden" with Ray and June Kaiser standing in for Adam and Eve. In the view of Booklist, *Bob the Gambler* "gets off to a swift start and never loses momentum, quite a narrative feat given its extremely modest parameters. Not only is Barthelme an impeccable stylist, his crackling dialogue is hilarious...." According to novelist **Daniel Woodrell** (*WPBW*), "As we approach the millennium Barthelme seems to be saying that to have things fall apart is not necessarily so bad, if what falls apart was not so good to start with.... *Bob the Gambler* is, as ever with Barthelme, first-rate and thought-provoking and a lot of fun. Frederick Barthelme is simply one of the best we have."

RECOGNITION: *NYTBR* Notable Book of

1997; *LATBR* "Recommended Title" 1997; RE-VIEWS: *BL* 9/1/97; *KR* 9/1/97; *LATBR* 10/3/97; *NY* 11/17/97; *NYTBR* 10/12/97; *WPBW* 10/12/97

862 *Painted Desert: A Novel* (1995); Viking Penguin 1997 (pbk)

Painted Desert is a late 20th century "road" novel peopled by an appealingly quirky cast of disaffected wanderers, most notably a professor of media studies and his cyberjournalist wife who, in search of the "real" America, is determined to visit the site of all the "important American tragedies"— the Kennedy assassination, the L.A. riots, etc. Frederick Barthelme' sixth novel is also a pseudo-sequel to his *Brothers: A Novel* published in 1993.

According to novelist Tom de Haven (*NYTBR*) while the on-the-road vignettes "present some of Barthelme's best descriptive writing … they also contain his weakest, least persuasive fiction." *Booklist* notes that the "rather morbid journey is set to the beat of CNN and the Internet and [is] punctuated by some of the canniest, most cynical banter found in fiction."

RECOGNITION: *NYTBR* Notable Book of 1995; REVIEWS: *BL* 8/19/95; *LJ* 8/95; *NYMag* 10/9/95; *NYTBR* 9/24/95; *WLT* Spr '96; *WPBW* 4/6/97

863 *Brothers: A Novel* (1993); Viking Penguin 1994 (pbk)

Set in Biloxi, Mississippi, deep in the humid heart of mini-malled Dixie, Frederick Barthelme's darkly comic, characteristically off-kiltered fifth novel explores the awkward reunion of two brothers — each envious of the other's life. The recently divorced, 44-year-old Del has returned to Biloxi, home to his 50ish brother Bud (a professor of media studies and confirmed technophile) and his restless, younger wife, Margaret.

Novelist Janet Burroway (*NYTBR*) observes that Barthelme "gives us a crew of college-prof beach bums, mouthy, modern innocents: and his hero Del, stands at the wet end of the world with an exact eye and the syntax of the mall. The effect is wonderful, simultaneously vivid and bewildering." *Kirkus Reviews* calls *Brothers* "one of Barthelme's more haunting novels." Michiko Kakutani (*NYT*) argues that "Mr. Barthelme's writing is still funny and bright, but in *The Brothers* there's a new undertow of melancholy that brings with it a new depth of emotional color."

REVIEWS: *BL* 9/15/93; *KR* 7/1/93; *LJ* 8/93; *LATBR* 1/2/94; *LJ* 8/93; *NYT* 10/12/93; *NYTBR* 10/10/93; *WPBW* 4/6/97

Beatty, Paul (USA)

864 *The White Boy Shuffle* (1996); HM 1996 (HC); H. Holt 1997 (pbk)

Paul Beatty's *The White Boy Shuffle* is an MTV generation coming-of-age novel with a twist. Beatty's protagonist, Gunnar Kaufman, attends Santa Monica High School where he is widely known as the "funny, cool black guy." When Gunnar's mother, fearful that her children are losing touch with African-American culture, moves her family to West Los Angeles, Beatty's teenage hero undergoes significant culture shock. Gunnar quickly learns that "in the hood" he is not quite so cool. The text is liberally sprinkled with references to song lyrics, sound bites, films and TV and video games.

According to the *Library Journal*, Paul Beatty, "poet laureate of Generation X," has produced a first novel that "is clearly a product of our times, and many readers will enjoy his piercing, often hilarious observations on contemporary society." Richard Bernstein (*NYT*) describes *The White Boy Shuffle* as "a blast of satirical heat from the talented heart of black American life…." Bernstein further observes that the reader "may not have figured out exactly what [Beatty's novel] is striving to be — a political screed, a comedy routine, a commentary on American racism or a parody of the great American racial conundrum" and concludes that whatever it is, "Beatty is a fertile and original writer, one to watch." The *Washington Post Book World* says that "Beatty fearlessly lampoons the entire tradition of 'up from adversity' black male memoirs…."

REVIEWS: *BL* 6/1/96; *LJ* 6/1/96; *Nation* 7/8/96; *NewsWk* 7/8/96; *NYT* 5/31/96; *NYTBR* 7/28/96; *PW* 5/6/96; *WPBW* 7/20/97.

Boyle, T.C (USA)

Road to Wellville (1993); Penguin 1994 (pbk); See Section 5, #509

Bradbury, Malcolm (UK)

865 *Eating People Is Wrong* (1959); Acad Chi Press 1991 (pbk re-issue)

Malcolm Bradbury's now-classic comic novel is, in the words of *Commonweal Magazine*, "surely the funniest academic novel that has yet been written." Set at a provincial English university, *Eating People Is Wrong* takes satirical aim at the members of the English Department including: Mr. Eborebelosa, a sensitive African professor; Louis Bates, a tortured working-class genius; and the wistful Emma Fielding, hard-at-work on a thesis that examines fish imagery in Shakespeare's tragedies.

Widely viewed as a parody of Kingsley Amis's *Lucky Jim* when it was originally published in 1959, Bradbury's novel attracted mixed reviews. The *New York Times Book Review* called *Eating People Is Wrong* both "a brilliant first novel [and] … a significant social satire." In the opinion of *The (London) Times*, Bradbury's novel displayed "genuine high comedy … at once extremely funny and also tragic." The *New Yorker* asserted, however, that "there are no funny situations and the few comic episodes that occur are much too light, and perhaps, also too tired, to stand up against the predominant, tragic predicament that is [the protagonist's] life."

REVIEWS: *BL* 4/15/69; *ChiTrib* 11/15/92; *ComW* 4/22/60; *LJ* 3/1/60; *NewR* 5/2/60; *NS* 10/31/59; *NY* 7/16/60; *SatR* 4/9/60

Bradfield, Scott (USA)

What's Wrong with America (1994); St. Martin's 1995 (pbk); See Section 6, #686

Busch, Charles (USA)

866 *Whores of the Lost Atlantis* (1993); Hyperion 1993 (HC); Penguin 1995 (pbk)

Called "one of the funniest and raciest show-business books in recent memory" (*USA Today*), the title of Charles Busch's semi-autobiographical novel is also the title of a play written by his drag queen protagonist, Julian Young, during a particularly slow "office temp" assignment on Wall Street. The novel is basically the story of how Julian (and his thoroughly louche, gay buddies) subsequently manages to mount a production of this newly penned masterpiece of high camp. Bizarre and lavish productions (starring the season's reigning drag queens) are the norm in the East Village — which is about as far as a young misfit from the heartland (like Julian) can get from the conventional world. Busch knows of what he writes: he is widely known (in certain circles at least) as the author of *Vampire Lesbians of Sodom* which ran for more than 2,000 performances at a theater in Greenwich village.

According to the *Chicago Tribune*, "There are limited places in this world where a young drama student from Northwestern University can found a theater company with himself a resident 'leading lady,' write a campy play starring himself as a 2,000-year-old femme fatale vampire and go on to make a serious, if unusual, reputation for himself as an actor. Manhattan is one." The *Library Journal* asserts that "First novels are supposed to be autobiographical, and this one is blazingly so. It is often quite funny, peopled with a zany cast, most of them gay." *Kirkus Reviews* notes that "Despite a cavalier attitude to sexuality, there's much here to amuse anyone, regardless of orientation: the perfect crossover formula that's worked so well for Busch on stage."

REVIEWS: *BL* 4/15/92; *ChiTrib* 11/10/93; *KR* 9/15/93; *LATBR* 5/17/92; *LJ* 10/1/93; *NYTBR* 11/21/93; *PW* 3/16/92

Byatt, A.S. (UK)

Possession (1990); Random House 1991 (pbk); See Section 6, #691

Carkeet, David (USA)

867 *The Error of Our Ways* (1996); H. Holt 1996 (HC); 1998 (pbk)

Academician and novelist David Carkeet, in his fifth novel, has constructed a "dark, domestic" comedy of manners (and approaching middle-age) featuring a pair of linguists, Jeremy Cook and his wife, Paula Nouvelles. When Paula obtains a position at the decidedly second-rate Buford University in St. Louis, Jeremy, despite dismal job prospects, relocates with her. Jeremy is eventually hired by Ben Hudnut, wealthy owner of a gourmet nut emporium, to study (and correct) his foul-mouthed toddler's speech patterns. Jeremy and Ben Hudnut eventually strike up an unlikely friendship. An old infidelity resurfaces and Mr. Hudnut suffers financial reversals.

The *Publishers Weekly*, in its starred review, calls Carkeet's novel "a shrewd, wickedly funny delight, full of hilarious takes on rocky marriages, sexual boredom, raising kids, communication gaps — and nutty doings," and concludes that *The Error of Our Ways* "transcends the genre of academic satire and should win Carkeet a broad following." The *Library Journal* found it to be an enjoyable "comedy of errors" and "a linguistic delight."

RECOGNITION: *NYTBR* Notable Book of 1997; REVIEWS: *BL* 12/15/96; *LJ* 11/15/96; *NYTBR* 1/5/97; *PW* 10/14/96; *WPBW* 2/23/97

Chabon, Michael (USA)

868 *Wonder Boys* (1995); St. Martin's 1995 (HC); Picador 1996 (pbk)

Wonder Boys, a novel about not finishing a novel, features Grady Tripp, overweight, thrice-married, philandering academic whose novel *Wonder Boys* is seriously overdue. When his old college pal, and current editor, Terry Crabtree arrives at Grady's Pennsylvania College during WordFest Weekend the two get up to some ribald shenanigans and "mischievous capers" (*SFRB*).

According to the *San Francisco Review of Books* Chabon's "dialogue is real, as always, and the development of his plot, perfectly calibrated." *Booklist* notes that "This is a genuinely funny, laugh-out-loud novel, a sort of Fear and Loathing in Academia if you will, but infused with tenderness and a bracing skepticism about our worship of literature." The *New Statesman and Society* contends that *Wonder Boys* "is a virtuoso performance with a sequence of comprehensively visualized backdrops and enough well-rounded walk-ons to people a novel twice its length. To the mordantly luxurious prose of his first novel *The Mysteries of Pittsburgh*, he has added a memorable sequence of phrases that glitter without ever diverting our attention from the solid structure." *L.A. Times* book critic Richard Eder concludes that "There is a first-rate satirical farce in Chabon's novel but essentially it is something rarer: satirical comedy."

OTHER MEDIA: Audiocassette (Brilliance/unabr); RECOGNITION: *NYTBR* Notable Book of 1995; REVIEWS: *BL* 1/15/95; *EW* 2/2/96; *KR* 12/1/94; *LATBR* 3/26/95; *NS&S* 6/9/95; *NYTBR* 4/9/95; *PW* 5/1/95; *SFRB* 3-4/95; *Time* 4/10/95; *WPBW* 3/19/95

Childress, Mark (USA)

Crazy in Alabama; Ballantine 1994 (pbk); See Section 6, #694

Cheever, Benjamin (USA)

869 *The Plagiarist* (1992); Macmillan 1994 (pbk)

Benjamin Cheever's transparently autobiographical debut novel concerns the trials and tribulations of Arthur Prentice, a thirty-something editor faced with a "celebrity" father, a faltering marriage and a intellectually stifling work environment. Cheever fashions a highly satirical portrait of the formidable Icarus South Prentice, a gin-soaked genius based on his own father, John Cheever.

In the view of the *L.A. Times Book Review*: "There are few experiences quite so enduringly wretched as being born the son of a famous father. Benjamin Cheever [in his "wry, sad, finely crafted first novel"] may be the first novelist to capture this condition accurately in print." According to *Publishers Weekly* "Wit and pathos [are] so finely meshed [that] they become inseparable, [and] buoy the main events in this achingly funny first novel from the editor of his father's *The Letters of John Cheever*." David Gates, writing in *Newsweek* Magazine, was surprised to find how "taut and unstagy the younger Cheever's prose is by contrast to the older" and concludes that "this parody of an Olympian father by a worldly-wise son is an affectionately bemused, sometimes snarky, always engaging declaration of independence." The *Library Journal* concludes that Cheever's novel is "witty and razor sharp."

REVIEWS: *LATBR* 5/17/92; *LJ* 4/1/92; *LT* 1/20/94; *NewsWk* 6/1/92; *NYTBR* 5/17/92; *TLS* 11/27/92

Chin, Frank (USA)

870 *Gunga Din Highway* (1994); Coffee House 1994 (HC); 1995 (pbk)

Covering five decades (from the 1950s to the present), Frank Chin's expansive novel follows the changing fortunes and picaresque adventures of headstrong Ulysses Kwan, son of Hollywood actor Longman Kwan, as he makes his energetic way through a culturally evolving America. Chin's relentlessly satirical novel is divided into four parts each narrated by a single character: Longman Kwan, Ulysses Kwan, and Ulysses' two sworn blood brothers, Diego Chan and Bendict Mo.

Publishers Weekly, in its starred review, observes that "Ancient and contemporary myths of China and America propel this provocative, multilayered tale of a willful Chinese American's 50-year odyssey from black sheep to reluctant head of the family." In the view of the *L.A. Times Book Review*, *Gunga Din Highway* "is a complex and compelling work that takes us deep into the multicultural fabric of America. It is not a sellout, exotic novel for Anglos. As a hyphenated American whose life often falls between the cracks his dual identity, Chin warns: 'Chinese morality, called Confucian morality, is not built on a foundation of faith ... but on knowledge. Life is war. In war it's what you know, not what you believe, that wins battles.' In a work of the first rank, Frank Chin opens the doors to real people who happen to have an Asian ancestry." The *Library Journal* concludes that "Chin is an important writer and this new book should be added to all collections."

REVIEWS: *BL* 9/15/94; *LATBR* 12/18/94; *LJ* 10/1/94; *NYTBR* 1/29/95; *PW* 8/22/94; *VLS* 3/95; *WLT* Spr '95

Cohen, Robert (USA)

871 *The Here and Now* (1995); S&S 1995 (HC); Scribner 1997 (pbk)

Robert Cohen's second novel (his first, *The Organ Builder*, about the Manhattan Project, is out of print) is narrated by Sam, a self-absorbed 30-something editor of a quasi-trendy New York-based magazine with dwindling circulation. On the emotional front, Sam, like many of his generation, has a problem with commitment — in all its guises. The novel's precipitating event is an airplane flight on which our hero meets (and eventually becomes involved with) a Hasidic couple: the intensely engaging Aaron and his physically compelling wife, Magda. Sam, who is half-Jewish, eventually heads for Israel in search of something to believe in.

Publishers Weekly calls *The Here and Now* a "brainy comedy about what matters in life" while concluding that Cohen "writes with enough suppleness that he manages to invest Sam's spiritual yearning with both gravity and comic desperation." *Entertainment Weekly* found Cohen's novel to be "intelligent [and] searching ... with a great comedic vein running through it." *Booklist* concludes that *The Here and Now* is a "warm, philosophical comedy ... [that] has many hilarious, unexpected moments."

REVIEWS: *BL* 12/15/95; *EW* 2/16/96; *LJ* 12/95; *NYTBR* 1/28/96; *PW* 11/13/95

Colwin, Laurie (USA)

872   *A Big Storm Knocked It Over* (1993); HarpCollins 1994 (pbk)

Finished shortly before the author's untimely death in 1992, *A Big Storm Knocked It Over* explores a theme familiar to readers of Laurie Colwin's fiction: the tricky balancing act of marriage, parenthood and modern careers. Set as usual in late 20th-century Manhattan, Colwin's last novel features a group of endearingly quirky urban sophisticates who together attempt to create a kind of extended family.

Novelist **Stephen McCauley** (*NYTBR*), although arguing that *A Big Storm Knocked It Over* is "not the best introduction to Ms. Colwin's engaging talent ... the novel [does] make the idea of happy endings for decent people seem entirely plausible, almost inevitable — no small feat for a writer these days and no small pleasure for a reader." *Publishers Weekly*, in its starred review, praised Ms. Colwin's "laser-sharp eye and ... offbeat sense of humor." Novelist Kate Lehrer (*WPBW*) observes that when Ms. Colwin died "the world lost a fine writing talent, whose capacity for enchantment and comedy received all too little recognition" and concludes that "She gave us something of a cross between Noel Coward's drawing room and Jane Austen's domestic parlor, all wrapped in a most contemporary setting and sensibility."

RECOGNITION: *NYTBR* Notable Book of 1993; REVIEWS: *BL* 10/1/93; *EW* 6/10/94; *NY* 10/4/93; *NYTBR* 10/24/93; *PW* 7/19/93; *WPBW* 9/26/93

Coupland, Douglas (Canada/USA)

873   *Microserfs* (1995); HarpCollins 1996 (pbk)

Microserfs, Douglas Coupland's 3rd novel — which takes the form of a Powerbook entry — presents a comic look at the lives of a group of employees at a major West Coast software development company patterned quite good naturedly after Bill Gates' Microsoft Corporation in Redmond, Washington. In fact, the impetus for *Microserfs* was an assignment from *Wired* magazine which provided Coupland with easy access to Gates' fabled company.

The Canadian weekly *Maclean's* applauds Coupland's comedic gifts, calling the novel a "witty commentary on the mass-culture flotsam and inane diversions that distract his characters from more

profound concerns." and concludes that Coupland's "take on pop-trends is neither fetishistic nor mock reverent." According to *Booklist* "There is a new world out there, and Coupland's story grants young people their own reality, their own voice, and consequently, their own tradition."

Reviews: *BL* 5/15/95; *EW* 6/7/96; *LRB* 6/6/96; *Maclean's* 6/26/95; *NYTBR* 6/11/95; *Obs* 12/3/95; *TLS* 11/10/95; *WPBW* 12/10/95

874   *Shampoo Planet* (1992); PB 1993 (pbk)

Douglas Coupland's first novel following his ground-breaking *Generation X* is narrated by Tyler Johnson (younger brother to Andy who was featured in his previous novel), a member of the generation following Generation X. Tyler is portrayed as a tree-hugging, "global" teen, the kind of kid who maintains a "shampoo museum" in his bathroom. The plot, such as it is, concerns family friction, adolescent love and a summer spent on two continents with stops in Paris, British Columbia, the Redwood National Park and Seattle.

Booklist calls *Shampoo Planet* "contemporary self-discovery fiction at its finest." The Canadian journal *Quill & Quire* found the novel to be "funny, even moving ... and a more accomplished novel than *Generation X*" and concludes that "for all its modernity ... the book turns on themes as old as the history those characters run from: the dependability of mothers ... the romanticism of youth, the inevitable ... darkening of the soul with age, and the irresponsibility of memory." According to *Kirkus Reviews* Coupland's "TV/computer/video-savvy fiction is ... at its worst, fortune-cookies profound and, at its best, a gloss on the Zeitgeist." *Books in Canada* observes that "following [Coupland's] mind through the ethnographic, conceptual, and imagistic thickets that are his natural medium" is "demanding" and "entertaining" and concludes that "This is a good book by a brilliant writer."

Reviews: *BksCan* 10/92; *BL* 11/15/92; *CanF* 1/93; *Chi Trib* 11/8/92; *EW* 9/11/92; *Q&Q* 7/92; *LATBR* 9/13/92; *LitRev* 3/93; *PW* 6/15/92

875   *Generation X* (1991); St. Martin's 1994 (pbk)

Described by *Books in Canada* as "the story of three young refugees from the world of yuppie wannabeism," Douglas Coupland's first novel, a cult success, reads like a post-boomer's manifesto. It also introduced the term "Generation X" into the late 20th century lexicon.

According to the *New Statesman*, "*Generation X* is a surprisingly endearing read: the tale of three middle-class drifters in their late twenties ... a kind of updated *Jules et Jim* in which neither of them gets the girl: self-conscious as hell, but charming too." The *Quill & Quire* observes that "this first novel by

Douglas Coupland is what Sartre might have penned had he hung out in a shopping mall instead of Cafe Deux Maggots" and concludes that it's an "existential cri de coeur ... burst[ing] with imagination and insight." *Books in Canada* concludes that *Generation X* "is a brilliant success. Racy, colloquial, as contemporary as the depletion of the ozone layer and Benneton ads, original in voice and metaphor, this book literally sings."

RECOGNITION: Shortlisted for the 1991 Books-in-Canada "First Novel Award"; REVIEWS: *BksCan* 4/92; *LitRev* 8/92; *NS&S* 5/29/92; *PeopleW*; *PW* 2/1/91; *Q&Q* 7/91.

Crews, Harry (USA)

876 *The Mulching of America* (1995); S&S 1995 (HC); 1996 (pbk)

In his 15th work of fiction, set-once again in Florida — Harry Crews features his usual rogues' gallery of damaged misfits: Boss, the hare-lipped president of the Soap for Life company; Hickum Looney, a door-to-door soap salesman; Hickum's colleague and arch-rival "Bickle" (described by the author as "over 6 feet tall and a biscuit away from 300 pounds"); Gaye Nell O'Dell, a foul-mouthed, freckle-faced hooker; Bubba, the pit bull; and (reprised from an earlier novel) Russel Muscle, a body builder and, currently, Boss's chauffeur. The plot defies neat summarization but has something to do with harnessing the "all–American" entrepreneurial spirit.

According to the *Washington Post Book World* "Crew's wicked satire sends up corporate culture's celebration of conformity and boundless personal sacrifice. Despite the weirdness of his characters — or perhaps because of it — they have a perverse charm." Christopher Lehman-Haupt (*NYT*) offers a similar view: "What [Crews] cares most about are his proud freaks, whose sense of themselves lend them quirky passion. Crews can be sentimental in his indulgence of these people. But he still strikes sparks of colloquial poetry that make the fragments of this novel shine more brightly than the whole." The *L.A. Times Book Review* observes that *The Mulching of America* "is the funniest book ever written about a door-to-door soap salesman. Not just funny, either. Savage. Dealing hyperbole with both hands, Harry Crews bubbles to the surface again with the sort of satire that makes Swift look slow. Crews' target — an easy shot — is the excess of capitalism."

RECOGNITION: *NYTBR* Notable Book of 1995; REVIEWS: *ChiTrib* 10/11/95; *EW* 11/17/95; *KR* 8/1/95; *LATBR* 1/14/96; *LJ* 11/15/95; *NYT* 11/21/95; *NYTBR* 6/22/97; *WPBW* 2/4/96; EDITOR'S NOTE: Harry Crews's 1998 novel *Celebration* (a satirical commentary on "the American way of retirement" which garnered rather more mixed reviews) ap-

peared on the *NYTBR* Notable Books of 1998 list in December 1998.

877 *Scar Lover* (1992); S&S 1993 (pbk)

Set in Jacksonville, Florida, Harry Crews' darkly comic novel tells the story of Pete Butcher, a withdrawn, socially awkward young man who becomes romantically involved with Sarah Lemeer (an attractive young woman with a golf ball–sized lump in her breast) and her distressingly maladapted family. Pete bears the emotional scars of having grown up in his own significantly dysfunctional family.

According to the *New York Times Book Review*, Crews' depiction of Pete being "pulled kicking and screaming into the wounded bosom of the Lemeer family is pure gold, pure Harry Crews, with plenty of the grim humor and enraged charity that have become his trademark." *Time* magazine notes that "as long as Crews is taking big risks, like arranging an appallingly sentimental love scene against a backdrop of psychedelic macabre, *Scar Lover* works a kind of wacky magic," however setting the novel in the mid 1950s "for no apparent reason [lends the book] an unsettling contemporary feel that makes every detail seem anachronistic." *Publishers Weekly* concludes that "Crews' darkly comic tales gives a disturbingly accurate portrayal of characters from the rural South, each fiercely shaped by sweat, grit and cruel hardship."

RECOGNITION: *NYTBR* Notable Book of 1992; REVIEWS: *BL* 2/15/92; *KR* 12/1/91; *LJ* 2/1/92; *NYTBR* 3/15/92; *PW* 12/13/91; *Time* 3/2/92; *WPBW* 2/16/92

Davies, Robertson (Canada)

Murther & Walking Spirits (1991); Penguin 1992 (pbk); See Section 5, #526

878 *Rebel Angels* (1981); Penguin 1992 ("Cornish Trilogy"— pbk re-issue)

Rebel Angels, the first volume in Robertson Davies celebrated "Cornish" trilogy, is set for the most part on the campus of the College of St. John and the Holy Spirit (affectionately known as "Spook") in Toronto, Canada, and concerns the discovery of an unpublished manuscript by Rabelais. Davies' (characteristically) colorful cast of characters includes: a family of gypsies, a defrocked monk, a mad professor and an eccentric millionaire. Plot elements include, but are not limited to, theft, perjury, murder, scholarship and love.

The *New York Times Book Review* calls *Rebel Angels* "an amusing academic fantasy that culminates in a gratifyingly kinky murder, bye the bye providing much interesting information about gypsies, violin restoration, and filth therapy." The *Bloomsbury Good Reading Guide* points out that Davies appears to be "asking whether traditionalists (symbolized by the university fathers) or 'rebel angels' (symbolized by a riotous gypsy family) are true guardians of the human soul ... and surrounds serious philosophical inquiry with a circus-parade of jokes, lists, parodies and slapstick...." The *Canadian Forum* notes that in *Rebel Angels* Davies provides "a Bosch-like survey of doings in and about the College of St John.... What's doing is just the usual, boring academic round: paleo-psychology, gypsy legerdemain, turd analysis, and a murder committed [with] knitting needles.... Nobody gets tenure." According to *Newsweek*, "Much of [Davies'] dialectical novel is fascinating and witty, but some of it gets to be pretty heavy sledding...." Novelist and academic **David Lodge** (*New Republic*) observes that *Rebel Angels* "is one of those novels which impart a good deal of information — in this case rather esoteric information — as well as entertainment to the reader. Its flavor will be a little too gamey for some tastes...." Lodge concludes that Davies's novel "is a work of impressive vigor and vivacity which no addict of the campus novel will want to miss."

OTHER MEDIA: Audiocassette (Blackstone/unabr); REVIEWS: *BksCan* 10/81; *CanFor* 12/85; *LJ* 1/1/82; *NewR* 3/10/82; *NewsWk* 2/8/82; *NYTBR* 2/8/92; *Q&Q* 10/81

Davies, Stevie (UK)

879   *Four Dreamers and Emily* (1996); St. Martin's 1997 (HC)

An unlikely mixture of adoring fans, aficionados and contentious academics have come together at the Brontë family's Yorkshire homestead in Haworth, England, for a three-day conference on their beloved Emily Brontë. The four "dreamers" of the title are: Eileen James, a spinster in her middle 60s with full-time care of her aged mother; Marianne Pendlebury, just turning thirty, a Brontë scholar (and the leader of this particular conference) who is trying to juggle career and young children; Timothy Whitty, a shy widower convinced that he has seen Emily's ghost; and Sharon Mitchell, an overweight waitress with little use for Brontë groupies or deconstructionists.

Kirkus Reviews points out that "In a charming, comic little novel on the love literature can inspire, a motley group of Bronte enthusiasts gather for an academic conference — and end up transforming their chaste devotion into a more physical passion." According to *Booklist*, in its starred review, "With great wit and warmth, Davies shows how four people often made to feel pathetically ridiculous are, in fact, tender, stoic, and dignified. A wonderful novel." *Four Dreamers and Emily* is described by *Publishers Weekly* as "a gently satirical contemporary novel that targets academics and other devotees who worship at Emily Bronte's shrine." In the view

of the *Washington Post Book World*, "The best parts of the book capture the intimate impact of the Brontës on Davies's 'four dreamers' the moments when the skin prickles 'with a light, fluey sensation ... a sigh of recognition,' as if the character 'were reading words she herself had composed and put away to keep.'" *The* (London) *Times* concludes that *Four Dreamers and Emily* is "an immensely enjoyable novel lit by wit and wisdom."

REVIEWS: *BL* 9/1/97; *KR* 8/1/97; *LT* 4/27/96; *PW* 7/21/97; *TLS* 6/7/96; *WPBW* 12/21/97

DeLillo, Don (USA)

880   *White Noise* (1985); Penguin 1998 (pbk re-issue)

Don DeLillo's 8th novel features Jack Gladney, professor of Hitler Studies at a Midwestern University, and his very modern "blended" family. Jack and his third wife, Babette, live together with four of their children from previous marriages in a comfortable, disheveled household that includes a dog who regularly climbs the attic stairs to gaze at the stars. When a nearby industrial accident releases a cloud of highly toxic fumes, the Gladneys' small town must be evacuated.

According to *Commonweal*, "In DeLillo's truly Swiftian social satire, we're never sure what he himself believes or what he thinks of his characters. As in Swift, we're instead forced to rely on ourselves to measure literary experience against our own sense of reality." Novelist Jay McInerny (*New Republic*) calls *White Noise* "a stunning performance" and concludes that DeLillo manages to "masterfully orchestrate the idioms of pop culture, science, computer technology, advertising, politics, semiotics, espionage, and about 30 other specialized vocabularies."

RECOGNITION: Winner of the 1985 National Book Award; REVIEWS: *America* 7/13/85; *Atl* 2/85; *ComW* 4/5/85; *LJ* 2/1/85; *NYRB* 3/14/85; *NYTBR* 1/13/85; *Nation* 2/2/85; *NewR* 2/4/85; *Q&Q* 4/85; *SatR* 3-4/85; *Time* 1/21/85; EDITOR'S NOTE: Viking's re-issued (1998) edition combines the full text of the novel with extensive critical essays and a list of discussion topics.

Denton, Bradley (USA)

881   *Lunatics* (1996); St. Martin's 1996 (HC); Bantam 1997 (pbk)

Jack, still despondent over the death of his young wife, meets and falls in love with the beautiful Lily — a woman perfect in all respects save three: she has wings, clawed feet and can only meet Jack when the moon is full. To complicate matters, Jack (an engineer living in Austin, Texas) can only meet Lily "outside" and must be completely naked at the time. Lily, it turns out, is the goddess of the moon. As the novel opens, Jack has just been arrested for indecent exposure; needless to say, his friends are worried.

According to *Publishers Weekly*, Denton has written a "big-hearted, giddily plotted fantasy about the transformative power of sexual love." The *Magazine of Fantasy & Science Fiction* points out that "Denton never takes the obvious route with his books ... [and] while his plots range from whimsical to bizarre, and there is invariably an undercurrent of humor to how he tells the tale, [he] takes his characters seriously and he writes with great style and compassion." *Kirkus Reviews* concludes that "Light, eccentric, thoughtful and endearing: Planet Denton's a weird place but well worth a visit."

OTHER MEDIA: Audiocassette (Books-on-Tape/unabr); REVIEWS: *KR* 4/15/96; *LJ* 5/15/96; *MFSF* 12/96; *PW* 5/20/96; *WPBW* 7/14/96

Derbyshire, John (USA)

882 *Seeing Calvin Coolidge in a Dream* (1996); St. Martin's 1996 (HC); 1997 (pbk)

John Derbyshire's 1st novel is an offbeat domestic comedy narrated by Chai, a Chinese immigrant banker who counts Calvin Coolidge among his cultural heroes. Long years of diligent application in his adopted country, America, has enabled Chai to rise from the ranks of the lowliest messenger boy to the exalted status of a banking executive. He and his wife Ding, having achieved the elusive American dream, are enjoying a comfortable existence in an upscale Long Island community. When Chai begins to fantasize about rekindling an affair with a Hong Kong receptionist (recently relocated to Boston and with whom he had a brief affair many years ago) his wife is understandably concerned. Chai's reverence for Coolidge is used to great comic effect as Ding launches a campaign to thwart her husband's threatened infidelity.

According to *Publishers Weekly*, readers "should enjoy this debut both as a lighthearted romantic romp and as a knowing literary study of the tensions between self-discipline and determinism." Jonathan Yardley (*WPBW*) observes that "Unlike most contemporary fiction, *Seeing Calvin Coolidge in a Dream* gives no evidence of the assembly line or the confessional: it is *sui generis*" and concludes that "In more than three decades of professional book reviewing I have found perhaps a half dozen books that came out of the unknown and gave me surprise and pleasure beyond measure. *Seeing Calvin Coolidge in a Dream* most emphatically is one of these."

RECOGNITION: *NYTBR* Notable Book of 1996; REVIEWS: *KR* 1/15/96; *LJ* 3/1/96; *NY* 8/5/96; *NYTBR* 4/14/96; *PW* 1/22/96; *WPBW* 3/10/96

Dixon, Stephen

Gould (1997); H. Holt 1998 (pbk); See Section 3, #195

Djerassi, Carl (USA)

883 *Marx, Deceased* (1996); Un of Ga. Press 1996 (HC)

In *Marx, Deceased*, Carl Djerassi takes a satirical look at the contemporary world of literary publishing. Stephen Mark, a successful, prizewinning novelist, is obsessed with critical opinion. Curious to learn how the literary community would judge him posthumously, he decides to fake his own death. When a young journalist on the make gets wind of his deception, complications ensue.

According to the *Library Journal*, "In his new novel, Djerassi ... grapples with issues of literary criticism, self esteem, and the creative instinct...." *Booklist* was reminded of "the children's anatomical model, Visible Man..." and concludes that *Marx, Deceased* "may not come alive on an emotional level, but its a pleasure to watch Djerassi snap the pieces into place." In the opinion of novelist **George Garrett** (*WPBW*), *Marx, Deceased* "moves quickly and gracefully ... [becoming] a classy, easy-reading page turner, light of heart and bright of mind.... Add to this the snap, crackle and pop of some very lively dialogue and a superior sense of place ... and you have a literary novel to be reckoned with."

REVIEWS: *BL* 7/96; *KR* 6/1/96; *LJ* 7/96; *NYTBR* 11/17/96; *PW* 7/1/96; *TLS* 8/16/96; *WPBW* 9/8/96.

Dooling, Richard (USA)

884 *White Man's Grave* (1994); FS&G 1994 (HC); St. Martin's 1995 (pbk)

When Michael Killigan — an idealistic young Peace Corps volunteer stationed in Sierra Leone — disappears, his father, a wealthy lawyer (the undisputed "wizard" of the Indianapolis bankruptcy courts), sets in motion a well-financed, long-distance, ham-fisted search. Meanwhile, Michael's best friend, Boone Westfall, travels to Sierre Leone where, in the face of much good advice to the contrary, he initiates his own search for the missing volunteer. Boone's not-so-excellent West African adventure is characterized by encounters with thugs, unscrupulous businessmen, witchcraft, black magic, disgruntled ancestors, and Liberian guerrillas.

Time magazine praises Dooling's "fizz of comic energy" while David Krist (*NYTBR*) argues that "Mr. Dooling [has succeeded in his attempt] to revitalize the traditional comic novel of colonialism, steering it neatly between the Scylla of arrogance and the Charybdis of sentimentality into new and deeper waters ... [and] manages to be sharply satiric without trivializing [his] targets." The *Times Literary Supplement* asserts that *White Man's Grave* (despite the author's often "uncritical infatuation" with things African) "is a considerable achievement" further concluding that Dooling has "taken a trenchant shot at writing a modern *Heart of Darkness*...." According to *Publishers Weekly*, "Dooling's prose gifts are capacious ... [his] language similarly expands to accommodate the bizarre and mind-bending mysteries of witchcraft upon which the plot turns. In the end, the book's lush satire cleverly obscures its simple, unarguable premise: that unfathomable rituals are at the heart of any culture, even in Indiana."

OTHER MEDIA: Audiocassette (Recorded Bks/unabr); RECOGNITION: nominated for the 1994 National Book Award; *NYTBR* Notable Book of 1994; REVIEWS: *BL* 4/1/94; *KR* 3/15/94; *LATBR* 5/29/94; *LJ* 4/15/94; *NY* 9/19/94; *NYTBR* 11/13/94; *PW* 3/28/94; *Time* 7/18/94; *TLS* 10/27/95

885 *Critical Care* (1992); St. Martin's 1996 (pbk)

Richard Dooling's debut novel *Critical Care* is a deeply satirical excursion into the world of contemporary medicine. When young, overworked resident Dr. Peter Werner falls for the beautiful daughter of one of his (comatose) patients, ethical and romantic conflicts arise. Dooling, who worked in a hospital as a respiratory technician before obtaining a law degree, draws heavily on his own life experience in his first fictional effort.

In the view of *Publishers Weekly*, "Although [Dooling] sometimes overdoes attempts at sexual humor and surreal phantasmagoric fantasies, his handling of the medical satire is gut-wrenchingly accurate, authentically frightening and certainly timely." According to *Kirkus Reviews*, "Dooling's unflinching portrayal of suffering, dehumanization, and modern medical techniques is almost unbearably painful to read but near impossible to put down.... A powerhouse for those strong enough in spirit and constitution to read it." The *Washington Post Book World* concludes that *Critical Care* is a "bitter and disturbing, though often very funny first novel, with a sensibility that 'Dr. Strangelove' fans will recognize."

OTHER MEDIA: Film version released in 1997 starring James Spader; Audiocassette (Recorded Bks/unabr); REVIEWS: *BL* 2/1/92; *EW* 11/14/97; *KR* 12/1/91; *LJ* 1/92; *PW* 6/7/93; *WPBW* 2/23/92; EDITOR'S NOTE: In a review of the movie version, *Entertainment Weekly* made the following observations: "Blithely directed by Sidney Lumet, *Critical Care* takes off on the ways that law, profit, technology, and — yes — compassion have combined to create new ethical nightmares in medicine. It's the sort of clever mainstream comedy that Hollywood used to do more of, and that now arrives as an unexpected pleasure."

Drabble, Margaret (UK)

886 *Witch of Exmoor* (1996); Harcourt Brace 1996 (pbk); 1998 (pbk)

The "witch" of Exmoor is Frieda Haxby Palmer, a British academic (occasionally compared — we are told — to Simone de Beauvoir) specializing in social analysis with a decidedly socialist slant. She has raised three successful, and by her lights, overly materialistic children. Tired of the excesses of the late 20th century, Frieda has moved into a ramshackle estate in Exmoor where she holds court and terrorizes her adult children and their spouses. When, one day, she simply disappears, the children are convinced that she must be frittering away their inheritance. Numerous reviewers pointed to the Dickensian underpinnings of Ms. Drabble's preoccupation with social inequities and inheritance.

As the *New Statesman* points out, "Drabble's recurrent theme is the just society. Does it exist as a practical possibility or simply in the pieties of a failing liberal imagination? Her authorial presence is equivocal, arch, ironic, suggesting that she views the project with some skepticism ... Nevertheless, at a time when the 'political' novel often appears as either stark fable or frantic farce, her shrewd appraisals and astute observations are more than welcome." In the view of the *Wall Street Journal*, Ms. Drabble's novel is "sprightly, clever and confident. Perhaps a little too confident, but it has an infectious verve that offsets its flaws...." In the view of *Entertainment Weekly*, "Drabble offers devastating insights into the illusion of security, the perils of self-absorption, and 'family jealousy, that long-ago, ancient, fairytale hatred ... ' [and] conjures up old-fashioned literary magic." The *L.A. Times Book Review* argues that "Comic irony — what V.S. Pritchett called 'the most militant and graceful gift' — is rare in contemporary fiction, perhaps because it appeals to the head, not the heart, and because it is a difficult balancing act" and concludes that "In *The Witch of Exmoor*, Margaret Drabble gets the balance just right and proves herself a master of the art." The *New Yorker* notes that "Drabble's leisurely and mischievous novel is about the Game of Power — familial, political, fictional — and whether, various moral scruples notwithstanding, it isn't finally, the only game in town."

READING GROUP GUIDE; Harcourt Brace; RECOGNITION: *LATBR* "Best Books" 1997; REVIEWS: *BL* 5/15/97; *KR* 6/15/97; *LATBR* 9/21/97; *NS* 11/1/96; *NY* 11/3/97; *NYTBR* 10/19/97; *Salon* 9/15/97; *TLS* 10/11/96; *WPBW* 10/5/97; *WSJ* 9/24/97

Dufresne, John (USA)

Louisiana Power & Light (1994); NAL-Dutton 1995 (pbk); See Section 6, #707

Eberstadt, Fernanda (USA)

887 *When the Sons of Heaven Meet the Daughters of Earth* (1997); Knopf 1997 (HC)

In this sequel to her 1992 novel, *Isaac and His Devils*, Fernanda Eberstadt (granddaughter of Ogden Nash) again features her tormented hero, the bumbling yet immensely talented Isaac Hooker, fresh from his stint at Harvard. Set in New York's Soho art scene in the "go go" years of the 1980s, *When the Sons of Heaven Meet the Daughters of Earth* takes a bitingly satirical look at a unique era in New York City's cultural history.

Entertainment Weekly argues that "It takes a kind of genius to write about a genius, and Eberstadt's is for hyperalert metaphors that deliver information in the way it comes at you on city sidewalks … in brief, illuminating bursts…." According to *Booklist,* Eberstadt's novel "flows like a sun-spangled brook on a bright spring day" and concludes that it is an "astute, animated and funny tale about the sublime and the ridiculous in love and art." In the view of *The* (London) *Times* "Eberstadt's narrative is peppered with provoking philosophical debate, but it is her painstakingly crafted language, rich, delicate, always alive, that makes her a delight to read." *Publishers Weekly* notes that "Much in the way *The Bonfire of the Vanities* defined a certain time and place in New York's social history, this novel dissects the art scene with the intelligence of an insider who knows it well and the elan of a writer who intends to spill its dirty secrets."

RECOGNITION: *NYTBR* Notable Book of 1997; REVIEWS: *BL* 3/1/97; *EW* 3/28/97; *KR* 1/15/97; *LJ* 3/1/97; *LT* 7/11/98; *NYTBR* 3/30/97; *PW* 1/20/97; *Vogue* 3/97; EDITOR'S NOTE: Also see Benabib's *Obscene Bodies* (#680) and Lipsky's *The Art Fair* (#54) for further dissections of the Manhattan "art scene."

888 *Isaac & His Devils* (1991); Warner 1992 (pbk)

Fernanda Eberstadt's quirky second novel is set in a small New England town and features Isaac Hooker a very large, very bright, very odd young man from a modest household (headed up by his schoolteacher Dad and ambitious mother) whose intellectual ability so impresses the local math teacher that she convinces him to apply to Harvard.

According to the *Library Journal*, Ms. Eberstadt in her "rich [second] novel" has created "A memorable, brilliant, but tormented hero, reminiscent of John Kennedy O'Toole's Ignatius Reilly in *A Confederacy of Dunces*." The *San Francisco Chronicle* points out that Eberstadt's "zesty prose is crammed with descriptive gems, and she also has a knack for summing up…." In the view of the *Times Literary Supplement*, "It is in the depiction of Isaac himself, though, on which the novel's claims depend, and in the end Isaac's greatness — his genius — remains shadowy, unrealized. His 'devils', on the other hand, bode well for the future."

REVIEWS: *LJ* 3/15/91; *LATBR* 5/19/91; *NYTBR* 6/30/91; *SFCBR* 3/9/97; *TLS* 7/5/91

Edgerton, Clyde (USA)

Redeye (1995); Algonquin 1995 (HC); Viking Penguin 1996 (pbk); See Section 5, #536

Elkin, Stanley (USA)

889 *Mrs. Ted Bliss* (1995); Avon 1996 (pbk)

Stanley Elkin's final novel, published shortly before his death in 1995, is a gently comic tale featuring an octogenarian widow living alone in a condominium on Biscayne Bay. A Russian Jewish beauty who immigrated to the United States in her early teens, Dorothy Bliss met and married Ted Bliss, a steadfast butcher, to whom she remained loyally (and selflessly) married until his death more than fifty years later. In Mr. Elkin's 17th novel, the still attractive Mrs Bliss (and her affections) has become the target of a passel of more or less unscrupulous characters including a Latin drug trafficker and her husband's feckless former partner.

Publishers Weekly, in its starred review, argues that "Elkin is at his best here, blessed with the gift of one-liner insight and a definite, if reluctantly exercised, ability to tug on a reader's heart-strings." According to Michiko Kukutani (*NYT*), "In *Mrs. Ted Bliss*, [Elkin] has used [his] remarkable language to create one of the most vivid and sympathetic heroines to come along in a long time and to relate a tale that sums up all the qualities that have distinguished his fiction from the start, a tale that's sad, funny and redemptive all at once." The *New Yorker* notes that *Mrs. Ted Bliss* is all about loss; the loss of family, the deterioration of one's own body and mind" and suggests that "In this last of Mr. Elkin's books, Dorothy eventually figures out how to live a little for herself and to face what is coming. We leave her, in the end, staring down [a] hurricane."

RECOGNITION: Winner of the 1995 National Book Critics Circle Award; *NYTBR* Notable Book of 1995; REVIEWS: *America* 4/27/96; *BL* 8/95; *ChiTrib* 9/24/95; *LATBR* 9/3/95; *LJ* 9/1/95; *NY* 9/25/95; *NYT* 9/8/95; *NYTBR* 9/17/95; *PW* 5/29/95

Ellis, Alice Thomas (UK)

Fairy Tale (1996); Moyer Bell 1998 (HC); See Section 4, #357

The Summerhouse (1994); Viking Penguin 1994 (pbk); See Section 4, #358

Epstein, Leslie (American)

Pandaemonium (1997); St. Martin's 1997 (HC); See Section 5, #538

Fischer, Tibor (UK)

890   *The Collector Collector* (1997); Holt/ Metropolitan 1997 (HC); 1998 (pbk)

Inevitably, I've been talked to, more than anyone would credit. Being inanimate doesn't earn you any dispensation from being buttonholed. People prefer people, will accept pets, but failing all else they will unburden themselves to the crockery.

The voice belongs to a piece of Sumerian pottery, the garrulous narrator of Tibor Fischer's latest off-beat fictional offering, a comic story about the baseness of human nature. This multi-talented ceramic raconteur (it is capable of shape-shifting, teleprojection, and mind reading) has come into the possession of Rosa, a lonely young art appraiser. The ancient bowl has spent a millennia observing a vast array of human foibles, and finding a sympathetic ear in Rosa, is quite happy to subject the young woman to racy, Rabelesian tales, shaggy-dog stories and portentous pontifications. Rosa's new flat mate Nikki, a libidinous, kleptomaniacal trapeze artist, also comes in for some withering commentary. Rosa's personal life is not exactly under control (after all she *is* bringing food to a kidnapped advice columnist imprisoned down a well) and Nikki's questionable past is about to catch up with her in the person of "Lump," a huge woman with condor wings affixed to her white leather jacket. It might also be mentioned that the plot veers into serial killer territory near the end where the author furnishes a "handy deus ex amphora" (*GW*).

Described by *The* (London) *Sunday Times* as a "piece of super-intelligent 'pottery worth a lottery'," the novel's protagonist, a Sumerian food dish (which claims to speak more than 5,000 languages), "has seen a great deal of use and abuse ... [it seems to have changed hands frequently — aside from the 1,000 years it spent in an Egyptian tomb] ... and has a store of wacky anecdotes from various eras, regions and cultures." The *Library Journal* notes that Fischer "skillfully stitches farce, social satire, slapstick, and even a bit of romance into a crazy quilt of literary entertainment." The *Washington Post Book World* opines that "*The Collector Collector* isn't Fischer's strongest novel, but it is a likable and highly entertaining book from a writer who is gifted with formidable imagination, soul and an admirable determination not to repeat himself—or anyone else, for that matter." *The Guardian* points out that "Fischer is a wordsmith of unique, eccentric brilliance" and concludes that "*The Collector Collector* is lewd, creatively hilarious and weirdly moving: the sort of novel you'd be intrigued to find sitting on your shelf, watching you in pregnant silence."

REVIEWS: *BL* 5/1/97; *Guard* 3/13/97; *KR* 3/15/97; *LJ* 5/15/97; *LST* 3/9/97; *NS* 4/18/97; *NYTBR* 7/13/97; *PeopleW* 7/7/97; *PW* 4/7/97; *TLS* 3/7/97; *Salon* 5/6/97; *WPBW* 6/22/97; EDITOR'S NOTE: Mr. Fischer was named to *Granta* magazine's 1993 list of the twenty "Best Young British Novelists."

891   *The Thought Gang* (1995); Scribners 1997 (pbk)

In Tibor Fischer's second novel, Eddie Coffin, a middle-aged, alcoholic philosophy professor, crosses the English Channel to put some distance between himself and his unsavory past. Once ensconced in the sunny south of France, he joins forces with Hubert (a cunning, one-armed, one-legged bank robber), with whom he embarks on a spirited life of crime.

According to *Booklist*, "Fischer's new 'fin-de-millennium' novel is a rollicking good time. He puns his way through a text that manages to be as witty and erudite as the late novels of Nabokov and every bit as extreme and satirical as 'Pulp Fiction.'" English novelist Nick Hornby (*TLS*) suggests that "*The Thought Gang*, is the 'Lavender Hill Mob' rescripted by Georges Perec and Will Self, and yet Fischer somehow manages to emerge from it all with credit." *The Nation* argues that "For all its playful turns of plot, *The Thought Gang* is most notable for the effortless way Fischer integrates philosophy — pages and pages of it — into the flow of his narrative...." In the view of *Publishers Weekly* Fischer's novel is "an infectiously immoral tale about bank robbery in contemporary France.... The Juxtaposition of egghead metaphysics and juvenile gangster fantasy is summed up in the line, 'The thing about a gun is, it's like being on the right side of a Socratic dialogue.'" The *NYTBR* concludes that Fischer's novel despite occasional lapses into a kind of "Beavis & Butt-head" brand of humor, "is an intelligent, thoughtful black comedy by a writer who deserves to be taken seriously."

REVIEWS: *BL* 5/15/95; *LJ* 5/1/95; *LST* 1/8/95; *Nation* 7/10/95; *NY* 8/21/95; *NYTBR* 6/25/95; *PW* 4/10/95; *TLS* 12/9/94

892   *Under the Frog* (1992); H. Holt 1997 (pbk)

Set in post-war Hungary in the decade leading up to the October Revolution of 1956, *Under the Frog* follows a group of young Communist-era basketball players in their pursuit of casual sex and avoidance of the draft. Tibor Fischer was born in London in 1959, the son a Hungarian couple who had fled their homeland following the 1956 revolution.

According to *The (London) Times*, Tibor Fischer's "*Under the Frog* (its title is taken from a rather gnomic Hungarian proverb for the worst place in the world to be: 'under the frog's arse down a coal mine') is really a quite wonderful book ... and surely a cult in the making." *World Literature Today* calls it "a hilariously funny, bitterly sad tale of devastation during World War II, the vicissitudes of communism, the exhilaration of the revolution, and the fallacies of a basketball team" and concludes that Fischer's "phenomenal authenticity and refreshingly distinctive voice truly deserve recognition in the United States...."

RECOGNITION: Winner of the 1992 Betty Trask Award; shortlisted for the 1993 Booker Prize; *NYTBR* Notable Book of 1994; REVIEWS: *LT* 10/12/92; *NYTBR* 8/28/94; *WLT* Sum '95; *WPBW* 4/30/95

Frayn, Michael (UK)

893 *Now You Know* (1992); Penguin 1994 (pbk)

Terry is an activist running a small London-based organization dedicated to more open government. He is energetic, powerful, a tad Machiavellian — but also charming and entertaining. Around him he has collected a group of admiring helpers. The only person who can resist Terry's charm is Hilary, a serious and dedicated young civil servant in the Home Office who happens to know the truth about a big police cover-up.

As the *Times Literary Supplement* points out Frayn's "entertaining, perspicacious, funny and gently satirical" novel tells the story of "a few weeks in the life of OPEN, a freedom-of-information lobby, and the ironic gulf between this organization's aims [exposing governmental evasiveness in public issues] and the clandestine machinations of the individuals who make up its workforce." According to the *London Review of Books*, "Frayn is a consistently inventive and innovative comic talent, and though he is no Dickens he brings something more than a feather-duster to bear on the British public's hide." In Jonathan Yardley's opinion (*WPBW*) "Not merely is *Now You Know* a novel of impressive originality it is also a provocative meditation on the pitfalls of letting it all — most particularly the truth — hang out."

RECOGNITION: *NYTBR* Notable Book of 1993; REVIEWS: *BL* 1/15/93; *LATBR* 2/7/93; *LRB* 10/8/92; *NYTBR* 1/17/93; *WPBW* 1/31/93; *TLS* 8/28/92

894 *A Landing on the Sun* (1991); Penguin 1993 (pbk)

In his seventh novel, British novelist and playwright Michael Frayn spins a philosophical fable (with thriller overtones) about the nature of happiness. In 1974, Summerchild, a civil servant in a secret Strategy Unit in the new Wilson Government, falls to his death from a Whitehall rooftop. Fifteen years later, Jessel, another government functionary, is brought in to investigate the (still unresolved) case. It appears that the government researchers, in an attempt to define what determines "quality of life," had come to the revolutionary conclusion that it was not dependent on the availability of affordable housing or more efficient washing machines but, rather, on that elusive state of "happiness" which many aspire to but few actually achieve. The ill-fated Summerfield was, it appears, charged with nothing less than an investigation of happiness and how to get it.

As the *Times Literary Supplement* points out "*A Landing on the Sun* is an intelligent book about the follies of the intellect." According to the *Washington Post Book World*, "This is a marvelous novel, wise and witty, but I despair of its readerly reception in a culture that elevates *Scarlett*" and concludes that "It's been a long time since I've read a novel that was as amusing, diverting, touching, and, yes, *smart* as this one." In the view of Richard Eder (*LATBR*), "Frayn's ending is both sober and enlarging. *Landing on the Sun* is something more than a delight."

RECOGNITION: *NYTBR* Notable Book of 1992; REVIEWS: *LATBR* 2/16/92; *LJ* 1/92; *LRB* 9/12/91; *NYTBR* 2/16/92; *PW* 12/6/91; *TLS* 9/13/91; *WPBW* 2/2/92

Fry, Stephen (UK)

895 *Making History: A Novel* (1998); Random House 1998 (HC); Soho 1999 (pbk)

In his latest comic offering, Stephen Fry features Michael "Puppy" Young, a young Cambridge University doctoral student whose thesis concerns the early life of Adolf Hitler. The plot has to do with time travel and (through the use of male sterilization pills pilfered from an ex-girlfriend) a scheme to change the course of history.

According to *Kirkus Reviews*, "British TV personality and novelist Fry inflates a speculative idyll (What would have happened if Hitler had never been born?) into an overlong, glibly caustic — and often hilarious — social satire." *Booklist* notes that Fry, a "simultaneously zany and serious yarn spinner ... creates here a bizarre but skillfully controlled alternative world, with the virtuoso pacing and tension that attracts readers." The *Times Literary Supplement* points out that "Many of the plot's turns ... are surprising and effective. Many of the jokes are good, especially if you have no disquiet about the largeness of the material being recycled as gags.... Meanwhile, in the alternating chapters on Nazi history, factual and factitious ... there are passages of high seriousness and genuinely researched historical concern." The *Literary Review* asserts that Fry's novel "is packed with the author's personal enthusiams and hatreds, the former red-hot and the latter ice-black" and concludes that Fry should be "encouraged to provide us with similar entertainments." Michiko Kakutani (*NYT*) argues that "The problem is ... Fry has tried to make the death of six million people part of his joke and the joke isn't funny — it's repellent."

REVIEWS: *BL* 2/1/98; *KR* 2/1/98; *Litter* 10/96; *NYT* 4/21/98; *NYTBR* 5/3/98; *TLS* 9/27/98; *WPBW* 4/3/98

896   *The Hippopotamus* (1994); Soho 1996 (pbk)

Ted Wallace, a boozy ex–London theatre critic (who has been sacked for excessive irreverence) has also failed as a writer, father *and* husband. Nicknamed "The Hippo," Ted is a fount of politically incorrect opinions on a wide range of subjects. When offered 250,000 "fresh, fascinating" pounds (i.e. almost $500,000) for a bit of extended-family espionage, he quickly "rises from his mud-bath existence" and heads off to Swofford Hall.

According to the *Library Journal*, "Marvelous dialog enlivens a tale that is fraught with incest, bestiality, and English humor." English novelist Jonathan Keates (*TLS*) draws our attention to (among other features) the "convivial innocence of the final scene ... encapsulat[ing] the not-yet-out-of-short-trousers quality which lends charm to Fry even at his most ribald.... If he were not so adept at amusing, one might almost be tempted to urge him towards trying something more serious." *Publishers Weekly* concludes that Fry's "ruminations ... are like a combination of Evelyn Waugh and Kingsley Amis but, because Fry is such a dazzling mimic and has a splendid ear for contemporary jargon, funnier than either."

REVIEWS: *LJ* 12/94; *LST* 3/27/94; *NYTBR* 2/26/95; *PW* 10/31/94; *TLS* 4/8/94

Gaddis, William (USA)

A Frolic of his Own (1991); Simon & Schuster 1995 (pbk); See Section 3, #208

Gates, David (USA)

897   *Preston Falls* (1998); Knopf 1998 (HC)

In his first novel since his much-praised debut novel *Jernigan* (1991), David Gates tells the rueful, often bitingly comic story about a family in crisis. Willis, a PR executive rapidly approaching midlife burnout, has taken a leave of absence from his Madison Avenue firm to spend a few months renovating his country retreat in rural Preston Falls. He leaves his wife and daughter behind and before long (driven by acute ennui) falls in with a group of unsavory local characters.

In the view of *Newsweek*, *Preston Falls* is "a blistering look at a marriage in free fall ... it is also full of black humor." According to the *New York Times Book Review*, "David Gates has a superb reporter's precision, an analyst's ear, a teenager's glee in exposing deception and a moralists eye that is as unforgiving as Evelyn Waugh's." The *Boston Globe* points out that "*Preston Falls* is mesmerizing, disturbing, a brilliantly overheated monologue — the nada of a man who's been there, done that, and is out of places to go." *Newsday* points out that the book is "a mid-life crisis novel, the life in crisis, or rather, the mind, the cynical, self-conscious, late 20th-century sort — the kind that's so hip to every shade of meaning that there's just not much meaning left anymore. Willis is, as Gates puts it, living in 'the golden age of irony' when even applying a phrase like golden age to irony is itself ironic."

RECOGNITION: *NYTBR* "Editors' Choice" 1998; nominated for the 1998 National Book Critics Circle fiction prize; REVIEWS: *BosGlobe* 2/1/98; *KR* 12/1/97; *Newsday* 1/26/98; *NYT* 2/3/98; *NYTBR* 2/15/98; *WPBW* 2/1/98

Gordon, Mary (USA)

898   *Spending* (1998); S&S 1998 (HC)

Spending, Mary Gordon's excursion into social satire, features a gifted fifty-something artist by the name of Monica Szabo. After jokingly remarking to a gallery crowd in Provincetown, Massachusetts, that there is a dearth of male "muses" or patrons to stimulate — and facilitate — female creativity, Monica is approached by a sexy, wealthy commodities trader (referred to as "B") who offers to give her everything that successful male artists have come to expect. Sex and money, needless to say, play a significant role in Ms. Gordon's cheerfully uninhibited female fantasy.

Heller McAlpine, writing in the *L.A. Times Book Review*, observes that "Mary Gordon calls her fifth novel, *Spending*, a 'utopian divertimento.' I call it a lark, with more orgasms per page than anything I've read since *Portnoy's Complaint* or *A Sport and a Pastime*— but from the female point of view." *Booklist* asks "Why do novels about pleasure seem to fall into the category of fantasy rather than serious literature? Gordon, an accomplished novelist known for her keen insights into human nature, almost succeeds in rendering perfect grown-up love believable, but even in her capable hands, such happiness seems too good to be true." The *San Francisco Chronicle Book Review* calls Ms. Gordon's book "a fantasy, a fairy tale about the gratification of desire ... [that is] full of descriptions of beautiful clothes … luxurious settings and lavish meals, not to mention inventive sex" and concludes that if "this produces a bit of literary indigestion … [it's offset] by her creamy, witty prose."

OTHER MEDIA: Audiocassette (Random Audio /abr); RECOGNITION: *LATBR* "Best Fiction of 1998"; *NYTBR* Notable Book of 1998; REVIEWS: *BL* 12/1/97; *KR* 1/1/98; *LATBR* 4/26/98; *NewR* 3/2/98; *NYT* 3/1/98; *NYTBR* 3/3/98; *PW* 11/24/97; *SFCBR* 2/15/98

Gray, Alasdair (UK)

899 *Poor Things* (1992); Harcourt Brace 1993 (HC); HBK 1994 (pbk)

Purporting to be the recently discovered "memoirs" of a 19th century Scottish surgeon, *Poor Things* is set in and around Glasgow and the Mediterranean of the early 1880s. Alasdair Gray's playfully irreverent novel describes the triangle of affection between two doctors and a clever woman who has been created — not born — at the age of 25. As the novel begins, Victoria Blessington (an abused young wife) is both pregnant *and* dead as she has just succeeded in drowning herself. However, the beautiful and desperate Victoria is brought back to life by the quick action of a medical genius (and memoirist), Dr. Archibald McCandless, who removes the fetus from her womb and implants its brain in her skull. The often risqué narrative follows the unusual life of Dr. Bella Baxter (aka Victoria Blessington), a sexually emancipated woman and "female Frankenstein."

As *Newsweek* observes, *Poor Things* is "Part Gothic romance, part satire, part essay on Victorian mores and feminism … [it] also makes room for parodies of 19th-century travel writing and the mysteries of Conan Doyle." According to *Publishers Weekly Poor Things* is "a work of inspired lunacy [which] effectively skewers class snobbery, British imperialism, prudishness and the tenets of received wisdom." English novelist **Jonathan Coe** (*LRB*) calls *Poor Things* a "magnificently funny, dirty, brainy book." *Poor Things* was described as a "serio-comic political romance" by the *Washington Post Book World* which concluded that, in developing his story, Gray "offers delightful conversation, a tricksy triple ending, and some very witty writing."

RECOGNITION: Winner of the 1992 Whitbread Prize for Best Novel and winner of the 1992 *Guardian* Fiction Prize; *NYTBR* Notable Book of 1993; REVIEWS: *LATBR* 5/9/93; *LRB* 10/8/92; *NewsWk* 3/22/93; *NS&S* 9/11/92; *NYTBR* 3/28/93; *TLS* 8/28/92; *WPBW* 5/8/94

Grudin, Robert (USA)

900 *Book: A Novel* (1992?); Penguin 1993 (pbk)

In the minimally titled *Book: A Novel*, (philosopher and academic) Robert Grudin has created an extravagantly comic tale of modern academia. Not unsurprisingly, it is the English Department (with its post-modernist and post-strucuturalist literary theories) which comes in for a satirical drubbing. The cast of characters, top-heavy with oddball academic types, includes Glanda Gazza, the "amply shapely" head of the English Department and a memorable mongrel, Doppler. Plot elements include a missing professor (AWOL or murdered?), a spoof of the New York publishing scene, and the search for love.

According to *Booklist*, "Grudin has written a big, bitter, funny book that lampoons mindless academics, faddish publishers, and sheep-like literary theorists.… This is a wonderfully fun novel and may soon become … required reading on every American college campus." In the view of the *New York Times Book Review*, Grudin has "taken the genre of the academic satire … and run it through the post-structuralist dicer." *Publishers Weekly* observes that "Grudin's satire targets book people from poets to publishers to nouvelle critique freaks, and if his work is too much of an in-joke to appeal to every reader, its playful elegance wit and authority make it a gem of its type." The *LATBR* declares that "*Book* is a blast. Highly energized, intelligent and funny, it ranks almost up there with David Lodge's classic comedies *Small World* and *Changing Places*. What's more, it's satire from start to finish, a tricky form, as most folks want their literary cocktail served straight up and don't react well to ridicule — even when they're clued in to what's being ridiculed." The *Library Journal* concludes that *Book*, a "unique, well-constructed blend of truth, humor, and suspense is essential for academics: fun to read, but with real sustenance."

RECOGNITION: *NYTBR* Notable Book of 1992; REVIEWS: *BL* 8/92; *LATBR* 8/30/92; *LJ* 2/1/93; *NYTBR* 9/6/92; *PW* 7/6/92; *WPBW* 9/6/92

Hamilton-Paterson, James (UK)

901 *That Time in Malomba* (1990); Soho 1990 (HC); Sophia BKS 1992 (pbk)

Originally published in London, in 1990, as *The Bell Boy*, James Hamilton-Paterson's 5th work of fiction is set in the fictional Asian city of Malomba (a "holy city"). It features Laki, a bellboy in the decaying Hotel Nirvana and his relationship with Tessa, a young woman and seeker of spiritual knowledge who arrives in Malomba with her two youngsters in tow.

Novelist **Michael Malone** (*NYTBR*) observes that *That Time in Malomba* "is an absolutely delightful addition to the heritage of religious satire, filled with swamis as unforgettable as the om-ing guru in E.F. Benson's *Queen Lucia*" but concludes that "What makes this book more like the dark comedy of Evelyn Waugh than the spoofery of Benson is that its irony cuts all ways — faith healers are shysters *and* healers, cynics are disabused as well as confirmed, and belief— that is, the capacity for belief— is left, like life, undestroyed by all the Armageddons to which religions have for millenniums subjected it." The *Times Literary Supplement* points out that "lust, rivalry, petty obstruction and dodgy gurus all play a part in the family's relationship with the bell-boy, but the novel's beguilement is that of the watched pot: the eyes do not leave the page, yet they never see it come to the boil."

RECOGNITION: *MTBR* Notable Book of 1990; REVIEWS: *NYTBR* 10/14/90; *PW* 9/21/90; *TLS* 1/26/90

Hassler, Jon (USA)

902   *The Dean's List* (1997); Ballantine 1997 (HC); 1998 (pbk)

Jon Hassler's ninth novel (a sequel to his 1995 offering, *Rookery Blues*) is again set in the wilds of northern Minnesota at a backwater college called Rookery State. The Dean of the title, Leland Edwards, obsessed with raising academic standards at Rookery (and knee-deep in administrative hassles), is attempting to persuade an elderly Robert Frost–like poetic genius to give an historic reading at Rookery State. He is also undergoing a personal mid-life crisis, and is caring for his widowed, octogenarian mother, the formidable Lolly Leland. For sexual fulfillment, Leland, long-divorced, looks forward to the occasional tryst with his former wife.

According to novelist **David Carkeet** (*WPBW*) the "question of what exactly makes up a full life, are at the heart of this sweet, gently humorous novel." *Publishers Weekly* finds *The Dean's List* to be "as droll and charming as its prequel" and concludes that "this yarn describes campus life in the 1990s and the concerns of advancing middleage with equal skill." *Kirkus Reviews* concludes that Hassler's novel is "Enormously readable, sentimental as one might wish it to be: another dependable charmer from one of our most likable and entertaining novelists."

RECOGNITION: nominated for the 1998 Minnesota Book Award for Fiction; REVIEWS: *BL* 5/15/97; *ChiTrib* 7/8/97; *KR* 4/1/97; *NYTBR* 6/1/97; *PW* 4/14/97; *WPBW* 6/5/97

903   *Rookery Blues* (1995); Ballantine 1995 (HC); 1996 (pbk)

The "Rookery Blues" of the title refers to a jazz-quintet drawn from among the faculty of Rookery State College. Jon Hassler's eighth novel, set in the tumultuous late 1960s (when a significant portion of the male student population was pursuing higher education in an effort to avoid the draft), explores a number of themes having to do with adolescent rebellion, parochialism and community.

The *New York Times Book Review* calls Hassler "Sinclair Lewis without an attitude problem" and concludes that, although plotting isn't the author's strength, "his patient depiction of life in all its splendor and misery at 'this campus at the edge of nowhere' makes *Rookery Blues* one of his finest and funniest yet." The *Library Journal* applauds Hassler for treating "even the least attractive [characters] with bemused respect."

OTHER MEDIA: Audiocassette (Pine Curtain Audio/abr); REVIEWS: *ChiTrib* 9/5/95; *LJ* 6/1/95; *NYTBR* 10/1/95; *PW* 5/22/95

Haynes, David (USA)

904   *All-American Dream Dolls* (1997); Milkweed 1997 (HC); Harcourt Brace 1998 (pbk)

Set, like David Haynes' previous four novels in the American Midwest, *All American Dream Doll* features Deneen Wilkerson, a 37-year-old, recently jilted, advertising executive who has fled to her mother in St. Louis for a little TLC. What she actually gets is more headaches in the person of her 12-year-old half sister, Ciara, the beauty pageant princess.

The *Library Journal* says David Haynes's latest offering is "a wildly funny, realistic look at beauty pageants, sibling rivalry, self-esteem, and growing up." In the view of the *Washington Post Book World*, David Haynes is "a truly comic writer and observer of pop culture ... and although not completely successful [*All American Dream Dolls* contains] all the elements of [his] previous books, for which *Granta* magazine recognized him as one of America's best young novelists." *Kirkus Reviews* notes that "Haynes' strokes are broad, but he delivers a frequently hilarious novel, with consistently on-target punch lines and an eye for real people."

RECOGNITION: nominated for the 1998 Minnesota Book Award for Fiction; REVIEWS: *BL* 9/1/97; *LJ* 9/1/97; *PW* 8/4/97; *WPBW* 10/12/97

905   *Live at Five* (1996); Milkweed 1996 (HC); Harcourt Brace (pbk)

Set in the twin cities of St.Paul/Minneapolis, David Haynes's 4th novel is an appealing social comedy featuring Brandon Wilson, an African-American news anchor. In the face of declining ratings, Brandon's boss decides to move his five o'-clock broadcasts "into the streets" to capture the immediacy of inner city life. Brandon, whose experience with ghetto life is nil, moves his news operation to a building in the African-American Summit/University neighborhood. There he meets Nita, feisty single mother of three who provides him with a much-needed window into her world.

According to *Booklist*, *Live at Five* is a "charming, intelligent, and significant comedy regarding the gap between image and reality." The *Library Journal* observes that Haynes's "approach to the many issues [raised] in the novel, which include black-on-black as well as white-on-black racism, the role of the media in forming the public's opinion of itself, and the relationship between men and women, is never preachy but highly instructive nonetheless." *Kirkus Reviews* concludes that "Haynes's pointed little comedy relies on standard criticism of media amorality and the 'deals with the devil' we all make."

READING GROUP GUIDE: "Reading Group Choices" 1998 (Paz & Associates); RECOGNITION: nominated for the 1997 Minnesota Book Award for Fiction; David Haynes was also named one of the "Best Young American Novelists" by *Granta* magazine in 1996; REVIEWS: *BL* 2/15/96; *KR* 2/15/96; *LJ* 4/1/96; *NYTBR* 5/5/96; *PW* 2/19/96

Helprin, Mark (USA)

Memoirs from an Antproof Case (1995); HarBrace 1995 (HC); Avon 1996 (pbk); See Section 5 #576

Hope, Christopher (South African)

906 *Darkest England* (1996); Norton 1996 (HC)

South African novelist Christopher Hope's latest offering (a spoof of 19th century British explorer narratives and an attack on racist attitudes in modern Britain) is narrated by David Mungo Booi, a contemporary South African Bushman who, representing the local "Society for the Discovery of the Interior of England" (and the only member of his tribe to speak English) embarks on a journey to the court of Elizabeth II. The Bushmen, once the nomadic masters of an essentially endless veld, have been pushed further and further into the adjoining wasteland and are now in danger of extinction. David Mungo Booi's mission is to obtain the protection of the Elizabeth, the great-great granddaughter of Victoria who promised to protect the Bushmen "in perpetuity." David's subsequent adventures in pockets of high and low British society drive the novel onward to its unanticipated resolution.

In the view of the *Washington Post Book World*, Hope "walks in the footsteps of many a naif abroad; from Swift's Gulliver to Montesquieu's Usbek and Rica. But most clearly of all, he is a throwback to Candide, as the cynical savagery of modern England gradually wrings from him his abiding optimism." *Kirkus Reviews* observes that Hope "merrily turns colonialism inside out ... [and that *Darkest England* is] an oddity, ample and keen of wit, and with some wonderful moments" but concludes that

"its droll, sharp, sometimes despairing tone is only sporadically sustained." *Publishers Weekly*, on the other hand, suggests that "Hope [known more for ironic analyses of contemporary life] segues brilliantly into satire here.... When Booi finally meets HMQ, the encounter is the funniest spoof of the endangered royal species since Sue Townsend's *The Queen and I*."

REVIEWS: *BL* 9/15/96; *KR* 8/1/96; *LJ* 9/1/96; *NS&S* 3/22/96; *NYTBR* 9/29/96; *PW* 8/12/96; *TLS* 3/22/96; *WPBW* 9/15/96

Hornby, Nick (UK)

907 *High Fidelity* (1995); Putnam 1995 (HC); Berkley 1996 (pbk)

Nick Hornby's first novel, *High Fidelity*, is a social comedy that explores the psyche of Rob Fleming, record shop owner, pop music aficionado, compulsive list-maker and representative of a late 1990s "new man." Rob is in his early thirties and is stalled in a kind of extended post-adolescence. He is so obsessed with Pop Culture (of the musical variety) that he can't see beyond it in his search for meaning. He has also just broken up with his girlfriend.

According to *Time* magazine, Nick Hornby "is worshipped in Britain for his 1992 book, *Fever Pitch*, a humorous memoir about his life as a soccer fan. In this first novel, *High Fidelity*, he demonstrates his enviable talent for lucid, laconic writing.... Hornby is as fine an analyst as he is a funny man, and his book is a true original." Novelist **Suzanne Moore**, writing in the *Guardian Weekly*, observes that "in lesser hands, this tale could have become another psychobabble book about men's 'inability to commit' or 'fear of intimacy'. But Hornby is such a terrific writer that *High Fidelity* is totally charming as well as being laugh-out-loud funny." The *New Statesman* contends that Hornby "has managed to produce that rarest of products: the feel-good artifact that isn't stupid...." and concludes that " This is a wonderful read, funny and moving. It's not a novel, exactly — but who cares?" Novelist **Michele Huneven** (*L.A. Times Book Review*) points out that *High Fidelity* is as "plaintive, catchy, affecting and rollicking good fun as the best pop songs — which, according to Rob, are 'Let's Get It On,' by Marvin Gaye; 'In the U.S.A.,' by Chuck Berry; 'White Man in the Hammersmith Palais,' by the Clash; and 'Tired of Being Alone' by Al Green."

OTHER MEDIA: Audiocassette (Putnam/abr); RECOGNITION: *NYTBR* Notable Book of 1995; REVIEWS: *BL* 9/1/95; *EW* 7/12/96; *GW* 4/9/95; *LATBR* 12/24/95; *LJ* 8/95; *LRB* 5/11/95; *LST* 4/2/95; *NS&S* 4/14/95; *NY* 9/11/95; *NYTBR* 9/3/95; *Time* 10/9/95; *TLS* 3/31/95; EDITOR'S NOTE: *About a Boy*, Nick Hornby's novel about an unusual relationship between an "incompetent man and an impossible youth," was named a "Notable Book" of 1998 by the *NYTBR*.

Hynes, James (USA)
Publish and Perish (1997); Picador 1998 (pbk); See Section 6 #727

Isler, Alan (UK)
908 *Kraven Images* (1996); Bridge Works 1996 (HC); Penguin 1997 (pbk)

On one level, an enjoyable academic romp, on another, a tragi-comic look at missed opportunity, Alan Isler's second novel details the escapades of the free-wheeling, sexually voracious Nicholas Kraven, lecturer at a fourth-rate urban college. Set in the 1970s, the tale is enlivened by Kraven's encounters with blackmailing students, various and sundry college authorities, and libidinous cronies, particularly the sexually insatiable Stella. As a sideline Kraven is pursuing an original Arthurian quest — to prove that Merlin was a Jew.

According to the *New York Times Book Review*, Mr. Isler (an Englishman with many years teaching experience at a New York City college) "has produced a Restoration comedy of ill manners, circa 1974 ... [he is also] the first scholar to explain why Merlin must have been a Jew or to compose a 20-line rhymed version of 'Paradise Lost' (which begins) 'Enter vice,/Satan/Waitin'.'" *Kirkus Reviews* concludes that "This sly comedy becomes, in the end, a subtle, profoundly moving meditation on identity and responsibility: an ambitious, stirring work by a very promising young writer."

REVIEWS: *AtlM* 5/96; *KR* 2/1/96; *LATBR* 6/23/96; *LJ* 3/1/96; *NYTBR* 7/14/96; *PW* 2/5/96; *TLS* 4/12/96

909 *Prince of West End Avenue* (1994); Bridge Works 1995 (HC); Penguin 1995 (pbk)

Alan Isler's prize-winning debut novel is set in a Jewish retirement community in Manhattan where an amateur production of "Hamlet" has attracted the attention and absorbed the energy of many of the residents. The story is narrated by 83-year-old Otto Korner: poet, former critic, would-be Hamlet and compulsive chronicler (as a young man during World War I, he was sent by his family to Zurich where he fell in with a group of avant-garde writers and artists and witnessed the birth of the Dadaist movement). The plot is enlivened by the often Byzantine power struggles waged by potential cast members. Surface events, however, are kept in perspective by the fact that Korner is a Holocaust survivor who harbors long-suppressed, deeply buried secrets from that chapter of his life.

Kirkus Reviews notes that "Isler moves smoothly from war to war and to the present, with Korner moving among the memories of his youth" and concludes that *The Prince of West End Avenue* is a "delicious, evocative, gentle debut, written in prose to be savored and cherished." The *New York Times Book Review* calls Isler's novel "a paradoxical tale of how to make peace with an unbearable past and the sin of pride." According to *Choice, The Prince of West End Avenue* illuminates "the depth of the human capacity for self-deception and the responsibility of the individual to confront his own guilt."

RECOGNITION: Winner of the National Jewish Book Award; nominated for the 1994 National Book Critics Circle Award; *Library Journal* First Novel Award; REVIEWS: *ChiTrib* 6/14/94; *Choice* 11/94; *KR* 3/15/94; *LJ* 4/1/94; *NYTBR* 5/29/94; *PW* 3/14/94; *TLS* 2/10/95

Jaivan, Linda (USA/Australia)
910 *Eat Me* (1995); Broadway 1997 (HC); 1998 (pbk)

Linda Jaivan, who grew up in Connecticut, works as a journalist in Australia which is where she has set her ribald comedy of manners. *Eat Me*, a runaway bestseller in Australia, features four female friends, Philippa, Chantal, Julia and Helen, who periodically gather to eat, drink and discuss sex (real and imagined). Each woman is driven by a different set of desires and expectations although all are heavily influenced by their interest in the late-20th-century global pop culture which includes *Seinfeld* and *Absolutely Fabulous* in addition to more local fare.

Kirkus Reviews opines that if one were to: "Combine a saucy, *Waiting to Exhale* sort of girl-gossip tone with *Vox*'s lusty sexuality [you would] get this witty, sophisticated (if unfortunately titled) tale of four Australian women friends' amatory peccadilloes." According to the *LA Times Book Review*, "Although Jaivan manages to work up some moments of genuine heat ... [she] is plainly having too much fun to take any of the sex scenes very seriously ... [and] never loses sight of her self-declared goal, which is to wrench the writing of erotica from its male practitioners." In the view of the *Times Literary Supplement*, "Jaivan's book uses the framework of an erotic novel to comment on the genre of the erotic novel, as well as to examine such issues as the possibility of feminist erotica and the difficulties of wild sex in the post-AIDS era." According to the *Australian Book Review*, "*Eat Me* is a sort of erotic symposium. The novel is largely dialogue-based, magazine-slick and pacy.... However, while these friends offer one another confessions and revelations, the novel suggests that their stories may actually hide as much as they seem to disclose."

REVIEWS: *AusBkRev* 10/95; *KR* 5/10/97; *LATBR*

9/14/97; PW 5/5/97; Salon 7/17/97; TLS 8/30/96;
EDITOR'S NOTE: According to the *LATBR* "Jaivan is
an American journalist with an Asian studies degree
who ricocheted around the Pacific Rim before landing in Australia, where she has reinvented herself as
an erotic novelist."

Janowitz, Tama (USA)

911 *Male Cross-Dressing Support Group*
(1992); PB 1994 (pbk)

Tama Janowitz's 3rd work of fiction is set in
New York City and features Pamela Trowbridge a
single woman with a dead-end job and a less-than-
desirable Manhattan apartment. When a young boy
by the name of Abdhul follows her home from a
pizza parlor, and begins hanging around her apartment building, Pamela eventually takes him in. In
short order, Pamela's latent maternal impulses rise
to the fore. Further plot developments include a
frantic New England-wide search for her errant father, arson, a string of unwelcome sexual advances,
a dramatic firing, and the need to adopt a male disguise to search for the missing Abdhul.

The *San Francisco Review of Books* argues that
"The book's focus is the inadequacy of gender constructs ... [while concluding that] gender relations,
safe sex, and single motherhood have replaced yup-
piedom, nightclubbing, and hard drugs as focal
points of the urban literary landscape." According
to novelist Robert Plunket (*NYTBR*) it is "great
fun to see a first-rate comic mind tackle the issues
of the day — sexual identity, family values, the
shocking behavior of rich WASPs with enormous
trust funds.... While pretending to do no more
than entertain us, [Janowitz is] really explaining
the way the world works. And while it may not be
a pretty picture, in your heart you know she's
right." The *Times Literary Supplement* notes that
"Skeptics, unconvinced by the hype surrounding
contemporary New York fiction, should not be put
off; they will discover in this funny, disturbing anti-
Bildungsroman, something more than literary junk
food."

REVIEWS: *LATBR* 9/13/92; *LitRev* 10/92; *LJ*
6/1/92; *NYTBR* 8/30/92; *NS&S* 11/6/92; *SFRB* Fall
'92; *TLS* 10/30/92

Jen, Gish (USA)

912 *Mona in the Promised Land* (1996);
Knopf 1996 (HC); Vintage 1997 (pbk)

Gish Jen's second novel revolves around
Mona, a Chinese-American teenager growing up
in a liberal, affluent, Scarsdale-like suburb of New
York City. Jen's refreshingly comic novel explores
multiculturalism from the perspective of late '60s
teenagers comfortable with fluid definitions of ethnicity and nationality.

Publishers Weekly, in its starred review, observes that "the rich stew of ethnic differences in
America's melting pot provides robust fare in Jen's
wickedly and hilariously observant second novel."
The *Library Journal* observes that Ms. Jen "even-
handedly skewers all groups, from Jewish to black
to WASP to Chinese to Japanese, reminding each
of the shared histories that separate them," and concludes that *Mona in the Promised Land* is a "brilliantly clever, worthy successor to her first novel."
Richard Eder (*LATBR*) notes that "Hemingway invented his rhythms to create his particular American world. Gish Jen invents a percussive tempo ...
[and] creates a particular world where dim sum is
as American as apple pie."

RECOGNITION: *LA Times* "Best Books" 1996
(Top Ten); *NYTBR* Notable Book of 1996; RE-
VIEWS: *BL* 4/15/96; *CSM* 6/27/96; *KR* 3/15/96;
LATBR 5/26/96; *LJ* 3/15/96; *NYTBR* 6/9/96; *PW*
3/11/96; *WPBW* 5/12/96

Typical American (1991); NAL/Dutton 1992
(pbk); See Section 2 #122

Johnson, Diane (USA)

913 *Le Divorce* (1996); Dutton 1997 (HC);
NAL/Dutton 1997 (pbk)

Diane Johnson's 10th novel is a sophisticated
comedy of manners involving sex, money, family
power struggles and the powerful allure of Paris itself. *Le Divorce* features a pair of American sisters;
a poet, Roxeanne Walker de Persand, pregnant and
abandoned by her French husband; and her beautiful (over-sexed?), slightly gauche, younger sister,
Isabel (a Berkeley film school dropout), fresh off the
plane from L.A. The plot revolves around two
crimes: one of passion and one involving fine art.

According to *Salon*, *Le Divorce* "is thick with
frank observations about sex, manners, food,
money of the kind that illuminates all of her work,
and it lifts the novel high above those of most other
mid-career American writers." Christopher
Lehman-Haupt (*NYT*) observes that "Paranoia and
cultural disorientation are the staple ingredients of
Diane Johnson's fiction ... [and] she mixes them
well in her latest novel." In the view of *Booklist*:
"Echoes of Henry James reverberate loudly
throughout Johnson's well-written story of not-so-
innocent Americans abroad.... Johnson seems to
be having a great deal of nasty fun satirizing both
American and French cultures.... Cold and clever."
The *New York Review of Books* concludes that *Le
Divorce* is "sexy, graceful and funny." According to
Richard Eder (*LATBR*) "Isabel Walker, not Isabel
Archer, is the protagonist of Diane Johnson's *Le
Divorce*, but unquestionably the author means to
remind us of the heroine of *Portrait of a Lady*:
American innocence in the toil of European soci-

ety…. The specific gravity of Johnson's witty novel is considerably less than that of Henry James's celebrated work…. *Le Divorce* is a comedy of manners rather than a comedy of life. For James of course, manners were life, whereas for Johnson, though she is very good at them, they aren't quite." In the view of *The* (London) *Sunday Times, Le Divorce* is "a pointed comedy of manners that takes as its theme the divide between Old and New World cultures and tailors it into the literary equivalent of *haute couture*…. Perfectly executed, effortlessly classy."

READING GROUP GUIDE; RECOGNITION: *NYTBR* Notable Book of 1997; *LATBR* "Recommended Titles" 1997; nominated for the 1997 National Book Award; *Publishers Weekly* "Best Books" 1997; REVIEWS: *BL* 12/1/96; *KR* 11/1/96; *LATBR* 12/29/96; *LST* 2/22/98; *NYT* 1/23/97; *PW* 11/3/97; *Salon* 12/96

Jones, Louis B. (USA)

914   *California's Over* (1997); Pantheon 1997 (HC); Vintage 1998 (pbk)

In his third novel, Louis B. Jones tells the story of a quirky, artsy, quintessential '60s family whose patriarch, a much lauded poet, has committed suicide, leaving his not inconsiderable assets at considerable risk of being misappropriated. The tale is narrated, retrospectively, by a college professor (now middle-aged) who, at seventeen, was hired by the Farmican family to help dismantle the family homestead a crumbling old Victorian home in the coastal California town of Seawell. The narrator/professor (who once went by the name of Baelthon), first meets the Farmicans three years after the poet's suicide: his wife has found herself a new husband (a weasly psychiatrist by the name of Faro Ness), his children are floundering, and an "illegitimate" son—who had long-ago been given up for adoption—arrives on the scene seeking restitution.

According to *Kirkus Reviews*, "The struggles of a proudly eccentric family of a once-famous poet who's committed suicide lie at the heart of this kaleidoscopic comedy, which dazzlingly illuminates the exact moment when the '60s deteriorated into terminal narcissism and gave birth to today's entropic culture." *Booklist* observes that "With a delicate, complex flashback structure, luminous prose, and humor that just flows, Jones captures both the wildly inflated expectations of the '70s and the diminished expectations of the '90s." Richard Eder, writing in the *L.A. Times Book Review*, concludes that in his "thoughtfully comic novel … Jones designs his people better than his world, which can get out of hand. The people, though, are so human and written with so original a cunning that they are virtually worlds in themselves."

RECOGNITION: *LATBR* "Recommended Titles"

1997; *NYTBR* Notable Book of 1997; REVIEWS: *BL* 9/1/97; *KR* 9/15/97; *LATBR* 9/7/97; *NYT* 9/22/97; *NYTBR* 10/5/97; *PW* 7/21/97; *WPBW* 9/14/97

915   *Particles and Luck* (1993); Random 1994 (pbk)

Louis B. Jones's quirky second novel, an odd mixture of everyday life and theoretical physics, is set in and around California's Berkeley campus and features Mark Perdue, a physics professor and TV celebrity. When Mark and his radically unstable neighbor Roger join forces to protect their beloved condominium complex, each is changed in unexpected ways.

According to *Publishers Weekly*, "Jones succeeds in conveying the cluttered, perpetually analyzing mind of a scientist: Mark is obsessively compulsive about observing certain rituals, and his attention constantly wanders as he ponders the nature of time and space." Christopher Lehmann-Haupt (*NYT*) concludes that "by successfully pulling off this absurd yet oddly touching portrait of a physicist in the throes of creating, Mr. Jones has fulfilled the promise of his unusual first novel *Ordinary Money* about the real and the false in contemporary American culture…. And he has pointed the way for more good things to come." In the view of Richard Eder (*LATBR*), "Jones is writing domestic farce and social satire. His characters are innocent at heart and befuddled of mind, and they are given a radioactive high speed particle energy by the steady ticking of Mark's cogitations. At the end he has made a breakthrough. He has found a human clue to the subatomic universe … [thereby opening] a chink in the wall that separates [physics] from most of us. [Jones] has written a lovely and invigorating novel into the bargain."

RECOGNITION: *NYTBR* Notable Book of 1993; REVIEWS: *BL* 3/1/93; *KR* 2/1/93; *LATBR* 4/11/93; *LJ* 11/15/93; *NY* 4/19/93; *NYT* 4/12/93; *NYTBR* 4/18/93; *PW* 2/8/93; *WPBW* 4/14/93

Kinsella, W.P. (Canada/USA)

916   *Box Socials* (1992); Ballantine 1993 (pbk)

W.P. Kinsella, best known for his 1981 novel *Shoeless Joe*—which was made into the now classic movie *Field of Dreams*—is much admired for his baseball stories and his tales of small-town, Midwestern (US & Canadian) life. *Box Socials* is set in rural Canada in the early 1940s—the Depression years—and tells, in its inimitable, round-about way "the story of how Truckbox Al McClintock almost got a tryout with the genuine St. Louis Cardinals of the National Baseball League."

According to *Publishers Weekly*, "narrator Jamie O'Day leads the reader on a rambling tour of the rural Alberta Hamlets near which he and

Truckbox grew up, the closest being a town called Ark ... [and, with] humor and tenderness ... evokes the social rites of the Norwegian-, German-, Ukrainian- and English-speaking hillbillies, their courtship's and heartbreaks, fistfights and philandering, through a series of weddings, dances, whist drives and box socials." Stephen Jay Gould, writing in the *New York Review of Books* notes "I can't remember when a book of this genre made me laugh so much ... [Kinsella has produced] an affectionate, but never sentimentalized, portrait of life in a rough hinterland." The *Christian Science Monitor* concludes that "Taut and lyrical, at turns melancholy and hilarious, *Box Socials* continues to advance the art and the reputation of one of the most original voices in contemporary letters."

OTHER MEDIA: Audiocassette (Blackstone/unabr); REVIEWS: *CSM* 6/29/92; *KR* 5/30/92; *LJ* 3/15/92; *NYRB* 11/5/92; *NYTBR* 7/12/92; *PW* 3/2/92; *Q&Q* 12/91

Kotzwinkle, William (USA)

917 *The Bear Went Over the Mountain* (1996); Doubleday 1996 (HC); H Holt 1997 (pbk)

William Kotzwinkle's latest novel is a fable involving a depressed novelist, a missing manuscript full of fishing and sex, an enterprising bear, an unscrupulous agent and a publishing world which appears to have lost touch with even the most rudimentary definition of reality.

Publishers Weekly, in its starred review, calls *The Bear Who Went Over the Mountain* a "hilarious and sometimes touching parable ... [in which] the book industry is unmercifully skewered." Novelist Dan Wakefield (*The Nation*), while first pointing out that the last book he read that made him "laugh so hard I fell off my chair was *The Fan Man* by William Kotzwinkle, the hilarious saga of a consummate hippie" goes on to report that Kotzwinkle's newest novel "is a genuine parable for our time ... as full of truth as it is of humor." Christopher Lehman-Haupt (*NYT*) notes: "Mr. Kotzwinkle, best known for his novelization of the movie 'E.T.' [here] indulges his comic sense of quirkiness, particularly in creating the character of Hal Jam, the bear. Hal wants badly to become a person, especially when he discovers how effectively humans have hoarded the good things in life, like pies and honey."

OTHER MEDIA: Audiocassette (Audio Renaissance/abr; BKS-on-Tape/unabr); REVIEWS: *BL* 8/96; *LATBR* 11/10/96; *Nation* 11/4/96; *NYT* 10/17/96; *PW* 8/5/96; *SLJ* 12/96

Kraft, Eric (USA)

918 *At Home with the Glynns* (1995); Crown 1995 (HC); St. Martin's 1996 (pbk)

Eric Kraft's quintessentially American, perversely funny coming-of-age saga featuring Peter Leroy (and his post–World War II childhood in Babbington, New York, the "Clam Capital of America") has already achieved a cult status of sorts. In 1977 Eric Kraft, in an unusual venture in self-publishing, began sending his Peter Leroy stories to a personally selected group of readers — one which eventually expanded to include more than 200 recipients. Novellas followed, brought out by a small publishing house and, finally, a series of full-length novels, now available in hardcover and paperback from mainstream houses like Crown and Picador. Peter Kraft's fifth novel *At Home with the Glynns* continues the story of Peter Leroy, who is, in this installment, suffering his way through Jr. High School with the assistance of the enchanting Glynn twins Margot and Martha.

According to the *Washington Post Book World*, "Kraft is not Proust ... though he shares his fascination with art and time and memory. In fact, I suspect that much of the appeal of these books is that, through the genial persona of Peter Leroy, Kraft is able to raise such old and difficult literary issues in a way that is accessible and even entertaining.... Recherché Digest, if you will." *Kirkus Reviews* observes that "This gently provocative novel uses a boy's delicious dalliance with two sisters to serve up the author's true passion: Deep Questions about the nature of art and memory" and concludes that "Kraft's latest sexy-sweet novel devolves into a perfect madeleine — dissolving just as you bite into it, leaving an insatiable desire for more." *Newsweek* notes that *At Home with the Glynns* is "Charming but never sappy, droll but never cynical" and concludes that "Peter Leroy's adventures constitute one of our wittiest and most acute portraits of America at mid-century. In the bargain they are the literary equivalent of Fred Astaire's dancing: great art that looks like fun."

REVIEWS: *BL* 5/1/95; *KR* 4/1/95; *NewsWk* 7/17/95; *NYTBR* 6/4/95; *PW* 4/3/95; *WPBW* 7/30/95; EDITOR'S NOTE: In 1995 Voyager (a computer software publisher) released a three CD collection entitled *The Complete Peter Leroy (So Far)*. There is also a web site devoted exclusively to Peter Leroy entitled "Forever Babbington" at http://membrs.aol.com/elkraft.

Kureishi, Hanif (UK)

919 *The Buddha of Suburbia* (1990); Penguin 1991 (pbk)

The Buddha of Suburbia, a first novel by British screen writer (*My Beautiful Laundrette, Sammie & Rosie Get Laid*) Hanif Kureishi, takes a humorous look at the multi-racial society that has emerged in post-empire England. Its hero-narrator is Karim Amer, the British-born son of a working-class English mother and a well-borne Indian father. His parents separate and Karim moves to London with his Dad where he begins a frenetic and decidedly "alternative" urban existence. The *New York Times Book Review* points out that, "like [his] film scripts, Mr. Kureishi's novel is sexually explicit, pointedly political and highly critical of both British racism and Muslim — or, more generally, — Indian repressiveness.... The spirit is comedic, a kind of urban and immigrant 'Midsummer Night's Dream' in its determination to bring lovers together, whatever their conflicts." Mr. Blaise concludes that the "flaws and virtues [of *The Buddha of Suburbia*] are those of a [promising] first novelist." The BBC magazine *The Listener* found Kureishi's "optimistic and deeply funny" novel to be "a switchback of questions and idiosyncratic perceptions important to anyone living in this multiracial society." The *Library Journal* concludes that "The book provides a witty, satiric view of English popular culture in the '60s and '70s, but it is fairly thin on plot and character development."

OTHER MEDIA: A British TV adaptation was released in 1992; RECOGNITION: Winner of the Whitbread First Novel Award; REVIEWS: *BL* 3/1/90; *LATBR* 6/3/90; *Listener* 4/55/90; LJ 3/15/90; *LRB* 4/5/90; *NYTBR* 5/6/90; *TLS* 3/30/90; *WLT* Spr '91; *WPBW* 5/27/90; EDITOR'S NOTE: Mr. Kureishi was named by *Granta* magazine to its 1993 list of the twenty "Best Young British Novelists."

Lefcourt, Peter (USA)

920   *Abbreviating Ernie* (1997); Villard 1997 (HC)

Peter Lefcourt's wickedly comic novel features a celebrity trial that revolves around a (now-deceased) cross-dressing, bigamous urologist and his tolerant, if somewhat vacuous, wife who is accused of murder-by-castration.

According to the *Library Journal*, "After her husband suffers a fatal heart attack while they are having sex [in the kitchen, in matching pantyhose] Audrey, who is handcuffed to the stove, can find only one way to escape Ernie's dead weight...." Novelist Gary Krist (*NYTBR*) observes that Lefcourt "skillfully choreographs the ballet of exploitation surrounding the trial, shaping each grisly twist and turn of the proceedings with obvious delight" and concludes that Lefcourt "also provides us with something we don't often get in real-life celebrity trials — namely a moral center.... Leave it to Mr. Lefcourt to write a successful farce that requires no suspension of disbelief whatsoever." In the view of *Publishers Weekly*: "Daunting as the challenge might be to conceive a tale more farcical than the reality of national manias like the O.J. trial and the mutilation of John Wayne Bobbitt, Lefcourt meets it in this amusing, if uneven, satire."

RECOGNITION: *NYTBR* Notable Book of 1997; REVIEWS: *BL* 2/15/97; *LATBR* 3/17/97; *LJ* 2/1/97; *LATBR* 3/17/97; *NYTBR* 3/2/97; *PW* 12/2/96; *Salon* 4/7/97; *WPBW* 3/2/97

Lethem, Jonathan (USA)

921   *As She Climbed Across the Table* (1997); Doubleday 1997 (HC); Vintage 1998 (pbk)

Jonathan Lethem's 4th novel is set on the campus of a fictional Northern California University and concerns a screwball collection of physicists, one of whose experiments goes decidedly awry. In an attempt to replicate the origins of the universe by simulating — under laboratory conditions — the "Big Bang," Professor Soft has managed to create nothingness, a hole in the void so to speak, a vacuum, actually, which appears to function as a sort of portal into the universe. The story is narrated by Philip Engstrand — a professor of anthropology interested in "academic environments" who is in love with one of Soft's colleagues, Alice Coombs, a particle physicist. Alice is unaccountably enchanted by this "cosmic pothole" — named Lack by the physicists — which actually appears to have a personality. It definitely has a predilection for argyle socks and cats. Alice's dangerous attraction to Lack terrifies Prof. Engstrand who must devise a plan to win her back.

Publishers Weekly refers to Lethem as "a poser of warped, philosophical conundrums whose witty, genre-bending novels are set in dysfunctional worlds of the present and near future" and concludes that *As She Climbed Across the Table* is "one of the most engaging academic spoofs to emerge in the wake of Don DeLillo and David Lodge." *Entertainment Weekly* asks "Can a novel with such a goofy premise sustain our interest?" And concludes: "Amazingly, yes. Best of all, as this oddball tour de force begins to wind down, Lethem's silliness turns unexpectedly touching." In the view of *Kirkus Reviews*, "Lethem's clear-eyed prose and believably strange people ultimately make for a moving tale of narcissism and need." The *Library Journal* observes that "This is not your typically insular campus comedy; Lethem has something bigger in mind, and he succeeds admirably in skewering our pretensions, technological or not, in language that gently mocks the way we hide behind jargon." Richard Eder (*LATBR*) points out that "Lethem manages an ending that is woozy and farfetched, yet quite reasonably in line with the mind-bending properties of his story. Just as physicists borrow whimsically poetic terms such as 'charm' and 'quarks' for concepts that cannot be conceptualized, the author has pilfered the concepts as a framework for the quirks and charm of his story."

RECOGNITION: *LATBR* "Recommended Title"

1997; REVIEWS: *EW* 4/11/97; *KR* 1/15/97; *LATBR* 2/26/97; *LJ* 3/15/97; *MFSF* 8/97; *PW* 2/3/97

Leyner, Mark (USA)

922   *The Tetherballs of the Bougainville* (1997); Harmony 1997 (HC); Vintage 1998 (pbk)

In his sixth over-the-top work of fiction, Mark Leyner features a thirteen-year-old (by the name of Mark Leyner) who, as the story opens, is at the state prison attending his father's execution. The job is botched and the boy's father is condemned to an alternative fate, the "New Jersey State Discretionary Execution — which means that he can now be randomly assassinated at any time." Meanwhile, young Mark is manically trying to finish a screenplay which (if it wins the Lenore DiGiacomo/Oshimitsu Plymers America Award) will ensure the lad an annual stipend of $250,000 — for life. The plot is carried forward, loosely speaking, through the use of movie reviews, autobiographical digressions, and excerpts from the screenplay itself.

Entertainment Weekly calls *The Tetherballs of the Bougainville* a novel "about the Miracle Collar — a push-up device to enlarge men's Adam's apples; the erotic possibilities of Frank Stella paintings; a star-studded Ebola benefit; and, of course, the primal appeal of tetherball." *Kirkus Reviews* notes that "The poet laureate of the MTV generation tries to spread his wings wider with his 'first 100 percent BONA FIDE NOVEL — story, characters, everything!'" and concludes that "How well he succeeds is a question that depends on where the reader falls on the postmodern scale." *Booklist* concludes that "Combining vitriolic humor with a heightened sense of the absurd (kind of like Dave Barry on steroids), Leyner turns in his funniest, most inventive novel yet."

REVIEWS: *BL* 10/15/97; *EW* 11/7/97; *KR* 8/15/97; *LJ* 9/1/97; *NYTBR* 11/23/97; *PeopleW* 11/10/97; *PW* 7/21/97

L'Heureux, John (USA)

923   *The Handmaid of Desire* (1996); Soho 1996 (HC); 1998 (pbk)

Judged a "delectable and diabolically clever lampoon of pretension in all its forms" by *Booklist*, John L'Heureux's seventh novel is set squarely in the center of the English Department of an elite California University. The plot is driven by the growing schism between two groups: "fools" and "turks"; the former being made up of older, tenured, well-meaning, backward-looking types and the latter of younger, hipper professors devoted to the vagaries of post-modernism. Into this arena steps Olga Komen, a visiting professor and novelist with an international reputation as a theorist and feminist — she also seems to be able to divine the inner desires

of both the "turks" and the "fools" and to grant them their "deepest wishes, which she magically divines before they are aware of them" (*NYTBR*).

The *New York Times Book Review* calls *The Handmaid of Desire* a "satirical fantasy in which a motley bunch of Bartheans, deconstructionists and disciples of Foucault are wholly at the mercy of an omnnipotent novelist who rearranges their lives for them according to the requirements of her latest plot." The *Library Journal* says it's a "glorious put-down of academic pretension in today's post modern world" and concludes that it is "an [admittedly] easy target to hit ... but few writers deliver such deft punches as L'Heureux."

REVIEWS: *AtlM* 12/2/96; *BL* 8/96; *LJ* 7/96; *NYTBR* 10/20/96; *PW* 6/24/96; *WPBW* 10/13/96

Lodge, David (UK)

924   *Therapy* (1995); Penguin 1996 (pbk)

David Lodge's 10th novel is (according to Michiko Kakutani of the *New York Times*) a "quirky and enchanting" parable of mid-life crisis and the search for meaning. "Tubby" Passmore, a writer for a long-running and wildly successful British sitcom, owns a beautiful house, drives a luxury car and is married to an extremely attractive (still sensuous) wife — yet he is vaguely but persistently troubled. Slight cracks begin to appear in his well-ordered existence which eventually open up into yawning crevasses. The first half of *Therapy* consists of long excerpts from Tubby's frequently hilarious diary; the second half introduces a series of monologues (by a former girlfriend, his therapist, his wife's gay tennis coach, etc.) each of which provides a very different perspective from the one provided by Tubby.

In the view of *Newsweek*, "Lodge is as funny a writer as we have just now, but unlike many Britishers, his humor is never frivolous or bilious; something mythic is always paddling just beneath the surface of his books." According to *Booklist* "Tubby's droll accounts of his hilarious misadventures are rich amalgams of innocence and irony. With this larky novel, Lodge has proved once again that fiction can have a strong moral center and still be utterly charming." Adam Begley, writing in the *Chicago Tribune*, points out that "John Banville, a novelist who is also the literary editor of the *Irish Times*, recently remarked that it is England's so-called comic writers who best capture the anomie that haunts the English soul. There is no better way to banish spiritual malaise than to drag it out into the sunlight and whack it a bit, give it a thorough airing out. Banville's list of great English comic writers includes Lewis Carroll and Evelyn Waugh. I say add David Lodge."

OTHER MEDIA: Audiocassette (Isis/unabr); RECOGNITION: *NYTBR* Notable Book of 1995; RE-

VIEWS: *AtlM* 4/96; *BL* 6/1/95; *ChiTrib* 8/13/95; *ComW* 12/1/95; *LATBR* 7/23/95; *LT* 5/11/95; *NatR* 8/14/95; *NewsWk* 8/95; *NS&S* 5/12/95; *NYRB* 8/10/95; *NYTBR* 7/16/95; *PW* 5/1/95; *Time* 8/7/95; *TLS* 4/28/95

925   *Paradise News* (1991); Penguin 1993 (pbk)

Bernard Walsh, a middle-aged, warily celibate English priest who has lost his vocation, has escorted his father to Hawaii so as to effect a reconciliation between the old man and his estranged sister, Ursula (widow of an American G.I.) who is dying of cancer. Shortly after arriving in Honolulu, Bernard's father (failing to look right after stepping off a curb) is struck by a car, and ends up in the hospital. This unplanned release from filial duty, occurring as it does in the paradisal land of palm trees and gentle trade winds, is, for Bernard, exhilarating. It also opens up the unlooked for — possibly miraculous — possibility of late-flowering love.

As the *New York Times Book Review* points out: "Some events and relationships are possible only within the confines of a vacation; perhaps reason itself fades in the warmth of paradise. Nevertheless, with its sharp yet touching humor, *Paradise News* turns a number of lives around in speedy fashion. Travel, as they say, can be a very broadening experience." John Bayley in a review appearing in the *New York Review of Books* observes that "At once crafty but earnest, transparent but charming, the tone of the novel is that of a well-written and very up-to-date Catholic or High Anglican sermon." Bayley concludes that "The theme of helping one another is made here into a minor masterpiece, the novel soaring away from the sermon like a butterfly from its chrysalis."

OTHER MEDIA: Audiocassette (Isis/unabr); RECOGNITION: *NYTBR* Notable Book of the Year 1992; *Booklist* "Editors' Choice" 1992; REVIEWS: *ChiTrib* 3/29/92; *KR* 1/15/92; *LRB* 9/12/91; *NYRB* 4/9/92; *NYTBR* 4/5/92; *TLS* 9/27/91

926   *Nice Work* (1988); Penguin 1990 (pbk re-issue)

David Lodge, English novelist, academic and well-known literary critic, has woven a comic tale around the confrontation between an academic who steadfastly embraces both feminism and deconstructionism and a "real-world" factory director with little use for trendy academic or cultural preoccupations.. Robyn Penrose, university lecturer, and Vic Wilcox, managing director of a struggling engineering firm, are brought together by a government directive designed to help bridge the gap between the ivory tower world of academia and the "shop floor" of modern British industry. "Their meeting (and subsequent collaboration) triggers a head-on collision of life styles, ideologies, motives and methods" (*TLS*).

According to the *New York Times Book Review* "the way in which these two appealing characters are ineluctably drawn into each other's worlds is vastly entertaining…. It is also instructive. Mr. Lodge wears his learning lightly and shares it generously … [providing] a kind of crash course on structuralism, metafiction and related subjects that interest him…." In the view of the *Times Literary Supplement*, *Nice Work* "is a very enjoyable book. Lodge is accomplished at the comedy of difference, he switches perspectives like a man who can play chess with himself…." *The Spectator* argues that "Lodge wears his immense intellectual sophistication with such ease and elegance that *Nice Work* could even be recommended as a painless introduction to modern literary theory, as well as a devastating critique of it."

OTHER MEDIA: Audiocassette (Isis/unabr); RECOGNITION: Winner of the 1988 *Sunday Express* Book of the Year Award; shortlisted for the 1988 Booker Prize; REVIEWS: *CSM* 3/8/89; *NYTBR* 7/23/89; *NS* 9/23/88; *Spec* 9/24/88; *TLS* 9/23/88

927   *Small World* (1984); Penguin 1995 (pbk re-issue)

David Lodge reworks the Grail legend to great comic effect in his ingenious tale of a naive young Irish scholar. A number of characters first introduced in *Changing Places* are reprised.

According to English novelist Harriet Waugh (*The Spectator*), in *Small World* Lodge returns "to academic concerns, only this time on a global scale." English novelist and literary critic **Margaret Drabble** (writing in a British Book Trust pamphlet entitled "Twentieth Century Classics") considers *Small World* "essential reading for anyone who has ever studied English Literature, for anyone who has ever worked in a University, for anyone who has ever attended a conference, for anyone who travels much on aeroplanes — in short for most of us who read at all." Ms. Drabble concludes that Lodge's novel is "brilliantly plotted … and moves along with tremendous style and pace, and gives a satiric, comic, touching portrait of this amazing small world." The *New York Times Book Review* notes that "Despite the novel's breathless pace, profusion of incident, and geographic scope, Mr. Lodge never loses control of his material. His deliberately outrageous manipulation of character and event is entirely successful."

REVIEWS: *LT* 3/22/84; *NYRB* 8/10/95; *NYTBR* 3/17/85; *Spec* 4/7/84; *Time* 4/15/85; *TLS* 9/23/88

928   *Changing Places: A Tale of Two Campuses* (1975); Viking 1995 (pbk re-issue)

David Lodge's 5th novel is set in the tumultuous early 1970s and features Professor Philip Swallow, a lecturer at a fictional English university (strongly reminiscent of the University of Birmingham). Swallow has, through a bureaucratic snafu, become the recipient of an academic exchange fellowship with "Euphoria State," an American university (based, transparently, on UC-Berkeley) ground zero — so to speak — of the Free Speech Movement and the ideological birthplace of "the Sixties." His opposite number is the irrepressible American academic, Morris Zap, "expert at student unrest" and "utterer of some of the funniest lines Professor Lodge has invented" (British Book Trust: *20th Century Classics*).

The *Listener* argues, regarding David Lodge's cultural comparison of the US and Britain, that "No funnier or more penetrating account is likely to come your way for a long time."

OTHER MEDIA: Audiocassette (Chivers/unabr); RECOGNITION: Winner of 1975 Yorkshire Post Fiction Prize; Winner of 1975 Hawthornden Prize; REVIEWS: *GW* 2/22/75; *Listener* 2/27/75; *NS* 2/14/75; *Obs* 2/9/75; *PW* 8/13/79; *TLS* 2/14/75; *VV* 10/10/89; *Yale* 12/77

Malone, Michael (USA)

929 *Foolscap* (1991); Washington Square 1993 (pbk)

Michael Malone's fifth novel is set (for the most part) on the campus of a small, prestigious North Carolina college. Our protagonist, Professor Theo Ryan, the shy, scholarly son of a New York City–based theater couple (his mother was the former Luster Shampoo Girl, his father, famed singer of the 1950s rock 'n' roll classic "Do the Duck"), teaches Renaissance drama at Cavendish University and is secretly working on a play about the execution of Sir Walter Raleigh. Theo Ryan is also the biographer of Ford Rexford, America's most celebrated living playwright. In a moment of weakness, he gives Rexford the only copy of his play (entitled *Foolscap*). The brilliant-yet-blocked playwright, sensing a masterpiece in the rough, offers to make minor revisions. When Rexford unexpectedly leaves town with the only revised copy of the play, Ryan is justifiably outraged. Rexford eventually surfaces in London (in the company of one of Ryan's students), and Ryan flies to England in hot pursuit. There he meets up with the formidable Elizabethan scholar Dame Winifred Throckmorton.

According to *Publishers Weekly*, "Ivy-choked groves of academe and overcultivated fields of creative endeavor are pruned to riotous effect in this rollicking satire." Novelist **Richard Bausch** (*NYTBR*) observes that "Michael Malone's greatest gift as a novelist — apart from his reckless, ingenious and always exhilarating way of spinning a tale — is his ability to make distinctive substantive characters out of his comic creations." The *Atlantic Monthly* asserts that because Michael Malone "gives similar attention to every aspect of his story, this fine and funny novel should not be read in haste … [lest the reader miss] jokes, references, and even subtle but significant clues, which would be both a loss to the reader and an insult to the author's wit and skill."

REVIEWS: Atl 11/91; *BL* 9/1/91; *ComW* 2/14/92; *KR* 8/1/91; *LATBR* 3/8/92; *LJ* 10/1/91; *NYTBR* 12/8/91; *PW* 8/9/91; *SLJ* 4/92

Maupin, Armistead (USA)

930 *Maybe the Moon* (1992); HarperCollins 1993 (pbk)

The narrator of Armistead Maupin's L.A.-based novel (the first since the publication of the concluding volume of his San Francisco series *Tales of the City*) is a midget by the name of Cadence "Cady" Roth. Cady is feisty, resourceful and committed to achieving Hollywood stardom. Maupin also focuses on Cady's "star-struck" roommate Renee and her best friend Jeff, a gay activist.

Novelist **Edmund White** (*TLS*) observes that Armistead Maupin is a "consummate entertainer who has made a generation laugh with his six-volume San Francisco saga, *Tales of the City*. If this time out he's more cutting, the change in tone may be ascribed to his change of venu, from San Francisco to the much more dynamic, violent and hypocritical Los Angeles of the movies." White concludes that "Maupin has created a funny, memorable character in Candence Roth.… She is a person readers will recall long after all the topical references in this novel have faded." The *Library Journal* concludes that *Maybe the Moon* is "Both a well-told story and a subtle fable about difference.…" *Booklist* notes that Maupin follows his "fabulously funny, politically hip [six-volume] *Tales of the City* … with the story of Cady Roth, the world's shortest woman" and concludes that although *Maybe the Moon* is "[a]nimated more by keen appreciation of the different yet similar injustices little people and gays suffer than by Maupin's daffy and endearing humor … [it] is as easy to keep reading as any of the Tales."

REVIEWS: *BL* 9/15/92; *LATBR* 8/8/93; *LJ* 11/1/92; *LRB* 3/25/93; *NYTBR* 11/29/92; *TLS* 2/5/93

McCauley, Stephen (USA)

931 *The Man of the House* (1996); S&S 1996 (HC); Pocket Books 1996 (pbk)

According to novelist Kevin Allman (*WPBW*), "Stephen McCauley put the fun in dysfunctional." In his third novel, a rueful comedy, McCauley introduces us to Clyde Carmichael, a gay thirty-something stalled adult who teaches in an Adult Education Center just off Harvard Square. Clyde shares an apartment with (handsome, straight) Marcus, a 39 year old who has yet to complete his doctoral dissertation. Clyde still pines for his former lover Gordon, a self-absorbed lawyer. Meanwhile, he does his best to avoid his family, which includes his depressed single-mom sister Agnes and his bullying, hypochrondiacal homophobic Dad. Another major character, Louise, cannot seem to find a stable perch despite early literary success.

The *Washington Post Book World* observes that "Plot aside, it's McCauley's ear for incisive dialogue, for the telling bit of detail, that gives the novel its bittersweet tinge. In a time when minimum-wage slackers, lovable losers and not-so-lovable losers are all the vogue in pop culture, it's a pleasure to find an author with genuine affection for his characters." *Time* magazine notes that the author's "particular skill lies in his grasp of the bonds that link straights and gays in the maze of daily dealings. There sexual preference counts a lot less than goodwill and a hardy knack for survival."

REVIEWS: *BL* 2/1/96; *KR* 12/1/95; *LJ* 1/96; *NYTBR* 2/25/96; *Time* 3/4/96; *WPBW* 2/18/96

McCourt, James (USA)

932   *Time Remaining* (1993); Knopf 1993 (HC)

In James McCourt's mordantly funny encyclopedic tour of gay New York—both before and after the emergence of AIDS—the author reprises a number of characters introduced in his earlier novels. *Time Remaining* is structured around an extended monologue (liberally sprinkled with sometimes poignant, sometimes hilarious, and always digressive anecdotes) delivered by Odette O'Doyle, the sole remaining member of a troupe of transvestites who called themselves "Eleven Against Heaven." Odette has just returned from a memory-laden trip to Europe where she has sprinkled ashes of the "girls" over all their favorite spots and her monologue is replete with references to this memorial expedition.

The *Washington Post Book World* calls Odette "one of the great gay monologists in fiction" and argues that "Odette's is a dazzling, sometimes bewildering performance, and to keep up with her it helps if you're multilingual and up on ballet, opera, 1940s movies, Harold Bloom's *Book of J*, gay activism, James Schuyler and Jackson Pollock ... literary theory and all the arcana of New York gay life." According to the *Library Journal*, "For some, Odette's discursive, anecdotal, manic soliloquy may be off-putting. But taken together, these brilliant stories add up to a life, one full of wit and anger, courage and love." *Yale Review* concludes that Mc-

Cauley's novel is "a 'sad and beautiful elegy' for the gay old days before AIDS."

RECOGNITION: *NYTBR* Notable Book of 1993; REVIEWS: *LJ* 5/1/93; *NYTBR* 6/13/93; *WPBW* 6/20/93; *Yale* 10/93

Medwed, Mameve (USA)

933   *Mail* (1997); Warner 1997 (HC); 1998 (pbk)

Mameve Medwed's debut novel incorporates interesting aspects of both a frothy romantic-cum-academic comedy and a more acerbic take-charge-of-your-life novel. Set in Cambridge, Massachusetts, *Mail* features a 31-year-old Radcliffe graduate and struggling writer by the name of Katrinka O'-Tool. Katrinka, recently divorced from her philandering college professor husband, is currently coping with (among other things) a mother who is having an affair with a dubious academic who just happen to live in the apartment above hers. To make matters worse, the routine of her days has really started to get her down: long hours at her desk editing and re-editing her latest batch of short stories as she listens for the sound of rejected manuscripts falling through her mail slot. When Katrinka meets her new mailman, the darkly handsome Louie Capetti, she begins to look forward to her daily mail delivery.

Booklist describes *Mail* as a "touching and funny first novel [concerning] a woman struggling with love and professional success ... [that], refreshingly, never takes itself too seriously." The *New York Times Book Review* observes that "Medwed ... hones in on the rarefied, self-important atmosphere of our Ivy League institutions—and the reflected snobbishness of the people who serve them." According to *Kirkus Reviews*, "The postman doesn't have to ring twice in this wonderfully funny tale of love and lust between a struggling writer and the mailman who delivers her rejected manuscripts."

OTHER MEDIA: Audiocassette (Warner Audio/abr); REVIEWS: *BL* 4/1/97; *KR* 3/15/97; *LJ* 6/15/97; *NYTBR* 7/13/97; *PW* 3/3/97

Mordden, Ethan (USA)

934   *Some Men Are Lookers* (1997); St. Martin's 1997 (HC); 1998 (pbk)

Ethan Mordden's breezy, glibly satirical (and, at heart, deeply sentimental) novel is set in New York City and features many characters familiar to readers of the author's "Buddies" trilogy: Dennis Savage, Kiwi (his street-wise lover), Bud (the narrator) and Cosgrove his precariously balanced "ward." Mordden is often compared to Armistead Maupin (of *Tales of the City* fame) in his ability to engagingly portray the lives of a group of (mostly gay) urban eccentrics.

In the view of the *Library Journal*, "Trust, the emotional ties that bind, the fragile state of mind when a family member betrays a friendship and then wants back in, and the room given or not given to grow — these are some of the issues that Mordden explores so successfully." The *Washington Post Book Review* notes that "One of the best features of Mordden's stories is his intimate take on the alternative families in gay men's lives. Here a group of men ... become an informal family that breaks bread as well as goes to bed, together" and concludes that the novel "celebrates gay male sexuality during a time when gay sex is too often portrayed in popular culture as a dark, self-destructive act. To the narrator and his friends sex remains 'a pastime in gay life.'"

REVIEWS: *KR* 5/1/97; *LJ* 5/15/97; *NYTBR* 8/31/97; *PW* 5/12/97; *WPBW* 7/6/97

Morrow, James (USA)

935   *Blameless in Abaddon* (1996); Harcourt Brace 1997 (pbk)

In his 6th novel, James Morrow (called "Christianity's Salman Rushdie") tells the often convoluted story of Judge Martin Candle of Abaddon Township, Pennsylvania, who, after a series of devastating personal and family misfortunes, establishes the Job society, an organization dedicated to the prosecution of God at the International Court of Justice at the Hague. The charges consist of serious crimes against humanity, including, among other atrocities, the suffering of innocent children and the horrors of genocide. The defense consul is G.F. Lovett, a theologian and best-selling children's author. *Blameless in Abaddon* is a sequel to *Towing Jehovah*, which began with the discovery of God's gigantic corpse found floating face down in the Atlantic Ocean.

According to *Kirkus Reviews*, *Blameless in Abaddon* is a "clever, thought-provoking, and well-informed yarn that boldly and wittily tackles the imposing issues raised in *Towing Jehovah*...." In the view of *Booklist*, "Morrow's trenchant wit shimmers in every sentence of this keenly executed religious lampoon. Not to be missed." As the *Washington Post Book World* observes: "*Blameless in Abaddon* occupies a strangely indeterminate state between satire and realistic narrative.... This is the hallmark of Morrow's novels and his [mingling] of absurdist elements ... with grimmer ones ... maintains an unusual narrative tension."

REVIEWS: *BL* 7/19/96; *KR* 6/15/96; *NYTBR* 9/15/96; *PW* 6/10/96; *WPBW* 9/1/96

936   *Towing Jehovah* (1994); Harvest Books 1995 (pbk)

In his 5th novel, the unclassifiable James Morrow combines a number of genres (from fantasy, to sci fi, to farce) in his "satire of Western culture both sacred and profane." As the story opens, Anthony van Horne, an oil tanker captain (responsible for the biggest oil spill of the century), is visited by an angel and told not only of the death of God but of the need to tow his two-mile-long body (now floating in the sea off Africa) to the Arctic where He, according to the angel, wishes to be entombed. Needless to say, a crisis of faith ensues.

In the view of *Booklist*, "Writing a brand of masterfully understated comic prose all his own, Morrow is a genius, and this book is one of the most deliciously irreverent satirical sprees in years." The *Chicago Tribune* observes that "It's not Nietzsche but *Towing Jehovah* does explore the death-of-God theology in a great many imaginative ways." The *Washington Post Book World* declares that "Readers of Barth or Updike who haven't yet discovered Morrow's droll novels will find them very satisfying indeed."

REVIEWS: *BL* 4/1/94; *ChiTrib* 7/31/94; *KR* 3/15/94; *LATBR* 7/25/94; *LJ* 4/1/94; *PW* 4/4/94; *WPBW* 4/24/94

Narayan, Karin (Indian-American)

937   *Love, Stars and All That* (1994); PB 1995 (pbk)

Kirin Narayan paints an appealing portrait of Gita Das, a virginal young Indian graduate student who, as the novel opens, is enrolled at the University of California at Berkley. Daughter of the almost wickedly irresponsible Koo Koo Das, beloved niece of the irrepressible and whimsically eccentric Aunt Saroj, the serious, brainy Gita has journeyed from Bombay to California to pursue a coveted American degree. The cast of characters includes: Norvin Weinstein, a predatory professor (described, by the author, as the sort of man who goes through life "being short, dark, handsome and right"); Firosh, a decidedly unromantic Parsi student; Timothy Stilling, a self-absorbed poet (and love object); and Kamashree Ratnabhushitalignam-Hernadez, a deliciously irritating Camille Paglia knock-off. The action eventually moves from the West Coast to a small college town in New England.

Pakistani/American novelist **Bapsi Sidhwa** (*NYTBR*) observes that "when it is not floundering in expedient eddies, *Love, Stars and All That* presents us with an engaging portrait of a plucky young woman." In the opinion of the *Women's Review of Books*, "This post-modern [fairy tale] cheerfully patches together high and low, East and West, [and] the lingoes of three continents." The *WRB* concludes that Narayan "is a good-natured satirist, in love with life as comic spectacle." The *School Library Journal* found *Love, Stars and All That* to be a "sensual and beautifully written coming-of-age-and-beyond story."

REVIEWS: *BL* 1/1/94; *LATBR* 3/4/94; *LJ* 9/15/93; *NYTBR* 2/20/94; *PW* 12/6/93; *SLJ* 8/94; *WRB* 5/94

Nelson, Antonya (USA)

Nobody's Girl (1998); ; Scribner 1998 (HC); See Section 6, #753

Nicholson, Geoff (UK)

938   *Bleeding London* (1997); Overlook 1997 (HC); Penguin 1998 (pbk)

In a novel which interweaves three storylines, Geoff Nicholson has produced yet another savage comedy featuring contemporary London and its improbable denizens. Stuart London, an obsessive-compulsive tour guide operator, bumps up against a woman who is determined to have sex in every part of London, and Mick, a tough young fellow from Sheffield who has come to the city in search of six men who have reportedly raped his stripper girlfriend. Despite its jumped-up story line, most critics agree that, at the end of the day, Nicholson has written a eulogy to London.

According to *Kirkus Reviews*, "The plot takes a while to build up speed, and the unfiltered blizzard of facts about London is sometimes dizzying, but Nicholson's satirical eye, his obvious love of the city, and this skill at fielding odd, convincing characters overcome any problems." *KR* concludes that *Bleeding London* is: "A delightful fiction, and a wonderfully exasperated love letter to a great city." In the view of Michiko Kakutani (*NYT*), "Though many of his plot lines are ridiculously contrived, though many of his characters' antics verge on the cartoonish, Nicholson relates his story with such brio and demented charm that the reader is happy to ignore the novel's flaws, content to sit back and be entertained." *Salon* declares that *Bleeding London* "hurtles forward like few literary novels, astonishing in its reach and frenzied humor" and concludes that despite its anti-climactic denouement, Nicholson's novel, "is a wild mess of high and low, kitsch and polish and absolutely worth a visit."

REVIEWS: *KR* 8/1/97; *LJ* 8/97; *LST* 6/8/97; *LT* 5/16/98; *NYT* 12/9/97; *NYTBR* 1/4/98; *PW* 8/4/97; *TLS* 6/20/97

939   *Footsucker* (1995); Overlook 1996 (HC); 1998 (pbk)

Quirky and a bit off-putting, Nicholson's comic romp features a foot fetishist, murder and other unpleasantness. The narrator, a likable enough fellow with a penchant for women's shoes, becomes sexually involved with a freewheeling young American woman who has a decidedly darker side. Enter (before dramatically exiting) a suspicious photographer named Kramer and the plot lurches in the direction of kinky thriller.

According to *Publishers Weekly Footsucker* is not Nicholson's most ambitious book but those who aren't too grossed out will enjoy this fiendish satire of a culture obsessed with sex, power and kinky apparel." *Kirkus Reviews* observes that "While the plot is threadbare and the book slight, Nicholson once again demonstrates his biting wit and his unmatched eye for capturing modern-day compulsions" and concludes that *Footsucker* is "A darkly funny tale with a kick even for the most foot-phobic." In the view of the *Washington Post Book World*, *Footsucker* "is outrageous, but author Geoff Nicholson pulls it off. We walk more than a mile in Footsucker's shoes, laughing much of the way. We even chuckle at an ending, that might have, earlier on, made us gag. To put it simply, the book is a kick."

REVIEWS: *GW* 1/2/97; *KR* 8/1/96; *LATBR* 10/9/96; *NS&S* 12/8/95; *PW* 8/12/96; *WPBW* 12/29/96

940   *Still Life with Volkswagens* (1995); Overlook 1995 HC; 1996 (pbk)

There are probably few automobiles more identified with a period and cultural orientation than the VW "bug." In Geoff Nicholson's 1994 comic offering these much-beloved, long-discontinued "mechanical icons" are being blown up all over Great Britain and no one knows why. Barry Oglethorpe (known in the Sixties as Ishmael the Zen Warrior) a trailer park resident and current owner of one of the targeted autos, is worried. Additional plot ingredients include: a former Tory MP recently released from an insane asylum, neo-Nazis, an enigmatic weather girl, caravans of "new-agers" and an unregenerate reporter in hot pursuit of a "big story."

In the view of the *Library Journal*, *Still Life with Volkswagen* "a tale of obsession in which everyone from Adolph to Charles Manson makes a cameo appearance ... is a wickedly funny read from beginning to end ... [and one that] invites comparisons with the best of [Tom] Robbins and both Amises." According to the *New Yorker*, "Nicholson's jokey premise never loses its wit — and for this reader exploding Volkswagens and rampaging skinheads have to be handled *very* cleverly to be funny."

REVIEWS: *BL* 10/15/95; *LJ* 8/10/95; *NY* 3/18/96; *PW* 8/21/95; EDITOR'S NOTE: Geoff Nicholson's 1994 offering *Everything and More* 1994 — a comic novel set in a Harrod-like department store is currently out of print but due to be re-issued; *Hunters & Gatherers*, his mordantly funny tale of collectors and collecting, originally published in 1991, was published in paperback by Overlook in 1996.

Nordan, Lewis (USA)

Sharpshooter Blues (1995); Algonquin 1997 (pbk); See Section 6, #754;

Norman, Philip (English)

Everyone's Gone to the Moon (1996); Random House 1996 (HC); See Section 5, #632

Parks, Tim (UK)

941   *Goodness* (1991); Grove/Atl 1993 (pbk)

George Crawley, son of a missionary father and pious mother, has risen from his stiflingly dreary working class origins to become a successful computer software developer. Fiercely aesthetic and a consummate yuppie, George will not accept that life is not destined to be pleasant or that his marriage can be anything but ideal. Life progresses according to plan (with the odd sexual dalliance thrown in for good measure). Then Hilary, a deformed baby, is born. Hilary has Christenson's syndrome, characterized by severe physical deformities and mental retardation. Her parents, even her grandmother, assume some measure of blame for the tragedy. Still, as *KR* points out: "The brisk, slangy style ... is an effective antidote to the downbeat material; this is not a gloomy book."

According to the *Library Journal*, "Parks explores the nature of goodness and moral faith in this poignant, witty and disturbing novel." The *Times Literary Supplement* observes that *Goodness* "is the second work of fiction published this year ... to suggest that Thatcherite individualism may contain the seeds of murderous ruthlessness" and further points out that in George's world view, "Hilary represents a problem that must have a solution: he even draws a flow chart [which when proposed] brings the novel to a climax that is both farcical and frightening." Jonathan Yardley (*Washington Post Book World*) argues that *Goodness* is "richly deserving not merely of the usual critical applause but also of a substantial readership." He also observes that "the humor that was primarily latent in his earlier books here comes quite vigorously to the surface, the characters are drawn with a rich understanding of human contradiction, and an immensely difficult moral question is handled both head-on and with full appreciation of its ambiguity." *Publishers Weekly* concludes that "The evolution of George's moral conscience, his epiphany during a crisis he has deliberately created, and Shirley's own decision in the novel's astonishing denouement will keep readers absorbed in this mordant, thought-provoking tragicomedy."

REVIEWS: *KR* 8/1/91; *LJ* 9/15/91; *PW* 7/25/91; *TLS* 8/30/91; *WPBW* 11/20/91

942   *Family Planning* (1989); Grove/Atl 1990 (pbk)

Frank Baldwin is a hospital construction company site supervisor whose job has taken him (and his family) all over the world. As the novel opens the Baldwins are flying home to England from Frank's last assignment in Algiers. With them is Raymond, their youngest son, who happens to be schizophrenic. A very large thorn in the side of the family collective, Raymond is prone to, among other things, sending his siblings pornographic letters, assaulting his parents and volubly praising Allah. Additional characters includes Raymond's unhappy sister Lorna and her husband, a pretentious academic, as well as twin brothers — one an effeminate snob, the other a consummate mooch with high expectations and little real ambition.

According to *Publishers Weekly*, "Brilliantly original, painfully funny, sane and bawdy, this semi-epistolary novel maps the vast emotional distances that can exist between blood relations ... [and is a] tragicomic satire not to be missed." As the *Times Literary Supplement* points out: "That it all seems so uncontrollable yet bound to happen is what makes the story compelling.... Park ... avoids corniness in his nail-biting narration. He also manages to be funny, compassionate, frightening and precisely observant." The *Washington Post Book World* observes that the "characters and dilemmas are both comic and poignant ... and Raymond, who is convincingly frightening and infuriating, is also bewildered and vulnerable at the core. *Family Planning* dramatizes with wit and sensitivity the ways families unravel, and the odd loyalties that bind them despite the tatters."

REVIEWS: *BL* 8/89; *KR* 6/15/89; *NYTBR* 1/7/90; *Obs* 4/23/89; *PW* 6/23/89; *TLS* 5/26/89; *WPBW* 10/1/89

Pelletier, Cathie (USA)

943   *Beaming Sonny Home* (1996); Crown 1996 (HC); Washington Square 1997 (pbk)

Cathie Pelletier has, in *Beaming Sonny Home*, produced another wry comic novel set in the fictional town of Mattagash, Maine. Mattie, a divorced single mother, has raised three quarrelsome daughters and "Sonnie," a sweetly incompetent son. Needless to say she is devastated when Sonnie takes two women and a poodle (kidnapped from a local bank) hostage inside his ex-wife's trailer. When a media frenzy erupts and her daughters take up residence in front of the TV in her living room, Mattie ponders what went wrong.

According to *Kirkus Reviews*, "Pelletier ... is funnier than ever in this sardonic tale of an upstate Maine mother's love for her underachieving son — even as he's taking hostages in his ex-wife's trailer home and babbling to the press that John Lennon made him do it.... [She] hits just the right mix of vulnerability and humor...." *Booklist* notes that "Mattie — addicted to picture puzzles, haunted by memories of her bad marriage, regretting the way she coddled Sonny, her most loving child — is one of [Ms. Pelletier's] most sublime creations."

REVIEWS: *BL* 5/1/96; *KR* 4/1/96; *LATBR* 8/4/96; *LJ* 5/1/96; *NY* 7/22/96; *NYTBR* 8/18/96; *PW* 2/19/96

944 *A Marriage Made at Woodstock* (1994); PB 1996 (pbk)

Pelletier's 5th novel is set in Portland, Maine and concerns the breakup of the 20-year-old marriage between Chandra and Frederick Stone, a "counter-culture" couple who met at Woodstock and who had lived — more or less happily — together ever since. When Chandra Stone, a new-agey psychologist, without (apparent) prior warning, simply walks away from her marriage, her husband, Frederick, a fervent convert to entrepreneurialism and its latest technological accouterments, is thrown for a loop. This being coastal Maine, eccentric characters and picaresque situations abound, in fact, you "might describe her style as Southern Gothic with frostbite" (*NYTBR*).

According to *Kirkus Reviews*, in *A Marriage Made at Woodstock:* "Hippie/Yuppie angst [is] rendered hilarious and human by the effervescent wit of rising star Pelletier." Novelist Stephen McCauley (*NYTBR*) concludes that Ms. Pelletier "writes crowded, boisterous novels ... [which are carried along by] the vitality of [her] prose and ... keen observations." As novelist Wally Lamb observes "In *A Marriage Made at Woodstock*, Cathie Pelletier takes us to Happy Hour at the China Boat, where the disillusioned Baby Boomer is trying simultaneously to mourn the loss of his idealism and score the gal from Generation X."

REVIEWS: *BL* 5/1/94; *EW* 7/29/94; *KR* 5/1/94; *LATBR* 9/18/94; *LJ* /15/94; *NY* 10/24/94; *NYTBR* 8/7/94

Perrotta, Tom (USA)

945 *The Wishbones* (1997); Putnam 1997 (HC); Berkley 1998 (pbk)

The "Wishbones" is the name of a band comprised of Seventies rockers who, twenty years out of high school — and reduced to playing at local weddings — have not yet given up the dream of making it in the music industry. Tom Perrotta — who teaches creative writing at Harvard University–features, in his debut novel, band member Dave Raymond who, almost immediately after asking his longtime sweetheart to marry him, meets the girl of his dreams.

Kirkus Reviews observes that *The Wishbones* is "a wonderfully cacophonous celebration of life during which the tamed Dave 'already ... feels himself being transformed into a historical figure, frozen into anecdote by his unborn children and grandchildren'" and concludes that Perrotta's novel is "Pure pleasure." According to *Booklist*, *The Wishbones* "is a smart, very funny look at one man's am-

bivalence toward adulthood and commitment; it also offers a colorful cast of band mates and an obvious affection for its characters and their music." In the view of *Salon* magazine, "*The Wishbones* is a hybrid of the rhymed and the unplanned — a small-scale comedy of accommodation and unresolution that's full of loopiness and warmth ... it's a minor work but a major pleasure."

OTHER MEDIA: Audiocassette (Audio Renaissance/abr; Bks-on-Tape/unabr); RECOGNITION: *NYTBR* Notable Book of 1997; REVIEWS: *BL* 5/15/97; *KR* 3/15/97; *LJ* 4/15/97; *NYTBR* 7/27/97; *PW* 3/31/97; *Salon* 7/30/97

Peters, Daniel (USA)

946 *Rising from the Ruins* (1995); Random 1995 (HC)

Daniel Peters, author of an historical trilogy set in pre–Columbian Central America, has set *Rising from the Ruins* in contemporary Mexico — at an archaeological site near the Guatemalan border. A team of archaeologists, busily unearthing the Mayan city of Baktun, is too absorbed in the excavation to notice (among other things) the increasingly agitated local inhabitants. Harper Yates, stalled writer/academic and hectored husband (his wife is working on her doctoral dissertation), joins the dig at the insistence of one of the archaeologists, an old college friend. Yates is hoping to gather enough material for a new book.

According to the *Library Journal*, "As a novelist among academics, Harp plays court fool but gains wisdom about life and love." *Publishers Weekly* observes that the "plot, with its layers of history, has a fullness to it, as do the lively characters" and concludes that "the deeper you dig into this rewarding novel, the better it becomes." *Booklist* concludes that *Rising From the Ruins* is "[a] serious, sophisticated adventure yarn."

REVIEWS: *BL* 3/15/95; *KR* 2/1/95; *LJ* 3/15/95; *PW* 2/13/95

Phillips, Max (USA)

947 *Snakebite Sonnet;* Little, Brown 1996 (HC)

Poet Max Phillips' debut novel is a sparklingly comic coming-of-age story with a decidedly sexual focus. When one fateful summer day 10-year-old Nicky Wertheim is called upon to administer first aid to the inner thigh of Julia May Turrell, a beautiful, sexy Bennington College co-ed (nine years his senior), he is hooked for life. Julia (with whom Nick eventually develops a sporadic yet torrid sexual relationship) floats in and out of his life and is the cause of exquisite pain and pleasure. The novel spans 25 years, from Nick's childhood in New Jersey through his teenage years as a Cornell College student to his bohemian existence in Manhattan as a young adult.

In the view of *Salon, Snakebite Sonnet* "is a light, frazzled, very funny love story that swings artfully across three decades as Nicholas Wertheim, the book's protagonist, rebels against his left-wing 'weirdo family' and pursues his lifelong crush on an elusive older woman named Julia." *Booklist* observes that "Phillips is a beautiful writer, so that even when we grow impatient with Julia's erratic … behavior, and Nick's tolerance of it, the novel reminds us yet again of the dizzying rush of first love and the allure of romantic desperation." *Entertainment Weekly* concludes that "Though long bouts of unrequited love often aren't pretty, Phillip's prose is a gorgeous mesh of erotic exactitude, heaps of wit, and generous, weary wisdom."

REVIEWS: *BL* 6/1/96; *EW* 7/12/96; *LJ* 5/1/96; *NYTBR* 9/15/96; *PW* 4/22/96; *Salon* 5/96

Preston, Caroline (USA)

948 *Jackie by Josie* (1997); Scribner 1997 (HC); 1998 (pbk)

When Josie Trask, a graduate student (and a young wife and mother) is offered a summer job researching the life of Jackie Kennedy Onassis (for a Kitty Kelly–like biographer with a major book contract) she happily puts aside her stalled doctoral dissertation and heads home to Massachusetts. Her husband Peter, an up-and-coming academic with a popular book to his credit, has landed a summer position at Berkley which might lead to a permanent tenure track appointment. Meanwhile, Josie moves in with her mother, Eleanor, a divorcee with a social conscience, reconnects with her sister, Leslie, a psychologist who is fooling around with a visionary pool cleaner. Granted access to the Kennedy archives, she is soon immersed in her research. Before long, Josie is questioning her husband's fidelity, her mother's sanity and her own commitment to scholarship.

According to the *New York Times Book Review* *Jackie by Josie* is an "amiable first novel whose protagonist takes a job researching the life of Jacqueline Kennedy; soon, sure enough, her life starts running in ominous parallels to Jackie's." *Kirkus Reviews* notes that Ms. Preston's work is "so charming, wise and self-assured it's hard to believe it's a first novel" and concludes that "as first novels go, this one's a plum." In the view of *People Weekly*, the author provides us with a "deft exploration of the way we think about the famous, interpreting and reinterpreting their lives through the prism of our own experience."

RECOGNITION: *NYTBR* Notable Book of 1997; REVIEWS: *EW* 2/7/97; *KR* 12/1/96; *LJ* 12/96; *NYTBR* 2/23/97; *PeopleW* 4/7/97; *PW* 11/25/96; *SFCBR* 3/30/97; *TLS* 4/18/97

Prose, Francine (USA)

949 *Hunters and Gatherers* (1995); FS&G 1995 (HC); Owlet 1997 (pbk)

With New Age pretensions firmly in her crosshairs, Francine Prose takes aim at flabby contemporary affectations and neo-feminist flim-flammery. Her protagonist, Martha — employed by a chic women's magazine as a fact-checker — is a sort of modern Candide, who, on the rebound from a failed romance, falls in with a group of goddess worshippers, a coven, if you will, of androphobic females. Ms. Prose's satirical tale (which ranges from a well-groomed beach at Fire Island to a primitive camp in the Arizona desert) explores the "female" approach to power, sex and competition.

The *Women's Review of Books* calls *Hunters and Gatherers* a "delightful satire … [in which] Prose brilliantly captures the absurdities and hypocrisies inherent in [her material]…." According to *Booklist*, "Prose likes nothing better than portraying hypocrisy in all its tricky manifestations … [and in this novel she] is wonderfully witty and shrewd, creating vivid characters true to type and hilariously piquant dialogue." The *Atlantic Monthly* points out that Ms. Prose has "create[d] a novel that is satirically amusing but not unsympathetic. Her women are superficially silly, but their desire for a more generous ethic than society has offered them is not."

REVIEWS: *AtlM* 9/95; *BL* 7/19/95; *LATBR* 8/13/95; *LJ* 7/95; *PeopleW* 5/15/95; *PW* 5/15/95; *WRB* 12/95

950 *Primitive People* (1992); FS&G 1992 (HC)

In her seventh novel, Francine Prose weaves an offbeat tale around the character of a sophisticated Haitian au-pair and her adventures in the employ of a wildly dysfunctional upscale Hudson Valley (New York) family. When Simone, beautiful and elegant, finds it necessary to leave Haiti (thereby giving up her position as assistant to the U.S. Cultural attaché) she takes the first legitimate job on offer — and joins the Porter household. Rosemary, the matriarch is a self-absorbed potter specializing in fertility objects, while her husband, the wealthy Geoffrey Porter, is an incorrigible philanderer. Their children, George and Maisie, are innocents in need of more than a little TLC. Needless to say, the Porters are not the most representative of American families, nor are their neighbors (which include a homicidal Count). But how was Simone to know?

In the view of the *Economist*, Francine Prose's "comedy of manners has a serious purpose but it is never earnest and provides a lot of shrewd and malicious fun." The *Library Journal* (in its lukewarm review) suggests that "In Simone's adjustment to her new life, Prose's latest novel is reminiscent of

Jamaica Kincaid's *Lucy*, while its biting satire and anti-male attitude recall Fay Weldon." *Kirkus Reviews* calls *Primitive People* "social satire at its slyest" and concludes that "as always Prose's wit sparkles. Another winner by a writer who has hit her stride."

REVIEWS: *BL* 3/15/92; *KR* 2/15/92; *LJ* 3/1/92; *NY* 7/6/92; *NYTBR* 4/5/92; *PW* 2/17/92; VV 4/7/92

Proulx, Annie

The Shipping News (1993); S&S 1993 (HC); 1994 (pbk); See Section 1 #77

Reed, Ishmael (USA)

951 *Japanese by Spring* (1993); Penguin 1996 (pbk)

Benjamin "Chappie" Puttbutt is an assistant professor who longs for tenure (and the house in Oakland Hills that accompanies it) at Jack London College. However, because Chappie is black and Jack London College is overwhelmingly white, he has had some difficulty divining just what posture to adopt to ensure this outcome. Just when he thinks his faculty days are numbered, the college is bought by a group of Japanese businessmen, and his friend and ally, Dr. Yamato, becomes the new president. Chappie's fortunes are decidedly on the rise and, when he becomes head of his department, he sets out to right some old wrongs and settle some old scores (while, of course, making new enemies). Further complications ensue, including a plot to assassinate the Japanese emperor. Reed's satirical targets include: racism, parochialism, xenophobia, Japan-bashing, neo-conservatism and feminists.

According to the *Christian Science Monitor*, the author, despite his "seeming inability to comprehend the pervasive oppression of women" has written an "otherwise shrewd, funny, and instructive satire." The *Multicultural Review* calls *Japanese by Spring* a "brilliant and highly entertaining book" and Mr. Reed "the preeminent satirist of this century." The *TLS* observes that "Reed's wit, focused by four decades of literary party-crashing, is a pop-culture particle beam aimed at the nuclear cores of Right and Left orthodoxy." *TLS* concludes, however, that *Japanese by Spring* "could have been a wickedly effective vehicle to run down Japan-bashing and fear of diversity if Reed had simply put his talent in the driver's seat and his vendettas in the trunk."

RECOGNITION: *NYTBR* Notable Book of 1993; REVIEWS: *BL* 1/15/93; *ChiTrib* 4/11/93; *CSM* 3/9/93; *LJ* 1/93; *MultiCultR* 6/93; *NYTBR* 3/7/93; *TLS* 7/15/94; *VLS* 3/93; *WPBW* 3/21/93

Richler, Mordecai (Canada)

952 *Barney's Version* (1997); Knopf 1997 (HC)

The eponymous narrator of Mordecai Richler's latest novel is Barney Panofsky, a 67-year old thrice-married failed writer and wealthy owner of a "trashy" TV company: Totally Useless Productions. Barney — the presumptive murderer of his best friend Boogie (found in bed with Barney's second wife) — holds forth about his early, highly libidinous days in postwar Paris, his circle of avantgarde friends, his love for the Montreal Canadiens, and his comically skewed views of life generally.

According to John Updike (*New Yorker*), *Barney's Version* is "a rollicking novel laden with rue, a self portrait of a creative personality who never found a creative outlet that he could respect, a paen to the pleasures and perils of drink, a celebration of ice hockey and tap dancing a lament for a multicultural Montreal now torn and depressed by Quebecois separatism, a broad window into the bustle of Canadian Jewry, an extended meditation on the relationship between the sexes, even a murder mystery, with an uproarious solution." *Entertainment Weekly* found *Barney's Version* to be "Raucous but elegiac ... [a] tribute to a showbiz generation on the wane — his own." Michiko Kakutani (*NYT*) concludes that "*Barney's Version* turns out to be a fine, funny novel, often derivative, but deft, irreverent and affecting all the same."

RECOGNITION: Winner of the 1997 Giller Prize; *NYTBR* Notable Book of 1998; REVIEWS: *EW* 1/16/98; *KR* 11/1/97; *LATBR* 1/25//98; *NYT* 12/16/97; *NYTBR* 12/21/97; *TLS* 9/5/97

Rodi, Robert (USA)

953 *Kept Boy* (1996); Dutton 1996 (HC); Plume 1997 (pbk)

In his 4th novel, set mostly in the urban-chic, lakeside luxury enclaves of modern Chicago, Robert Rodi tells the farcical tale of Dennis Racine who at 31 has been a "kept boy" for more than 15 years. He's fit and trim and still a hunk, but he's worried that his "companion" (a wealthy theatrical producer in his sixties who is currently mounting an Oscar Wilde play) has begun to look longingly towards the teenage poolboy. The story (and much of the cast) eventually relocates to a Greek island where the humor turns positively manic.

According to *Booklist*, "the heterosexual 'kept' lovers of a popular male politician ('the Spanker of the House') and an aging female gossip columnist add spice to an already riotous cast that includes the likes of an actress with Tourette's syndrome and a middle-aged Greek houseboy who sings along with Maria Callas as he cleans." *Kirkus Reviews* observes that "Rodi takes a shot at being the gay Moliere and succeeds in pulling off a smart, funny and terrifically entertaining farce" and concludes that *Kept Boy* "is a high speed, at times hilarious tale."

RECOGNITION: Winner of the ALA's 1996

"Best Gay Novel" award; REVIEWS: *BL* 11/1/96; *ChiTrib* 6/8/97; *LJ* 11/1/96; *PW* 10/21/96

954   *Drag Queen* (1995); Dutton 1995 (HC); Plume 1996 (pbk)

Described by *Kirkus Reviews* as an "effervescent comedy of manners," Robert Rodi's third novel is set in Chicago and features Mitchell Sayer, a conservative gay attorney, adopted at birth, who has just learned that he has a twin brother with the stage name of "Kitten Kaboodle."

According to *Booklist*, Mitchell "thinks that drag queens hinder society's acceptance of 'normal' gay people like himself. There follows a series of misadventures...." *Kirkus Review* observes that Rodi has produced "another plateful of giddy meringue ... the humor is merciless and swift." The *Los Angeles Times Book Review* concludes that *Drag Queen* is "wildly amusing and wickedly clever."

REVIEWS: *BL* 11/15/95; *KR* 9/15/95; *LATBR* 12/24/95; *LJ* 10/1/95; *PW* 9/18/95

Roth, Philip (USA)

955   *Sabbath's Theater* (1995); Houghton 1995 (HC); Vintage 1996 (pbk)

The protagonist of Philip Roth's 21st novel is the outrageous 64-year-old Mickey Sabbath, a one-time puppeteer with an obscene street show, a former fringe theater director and failed academic whose libidinal instincts have been the guiding force of his life. When Drenka, his 52-year-old mistress, dies, Mickey is compelled to review his life.

The *Library Journal*, in its starred review, asserts that *Sabbath's Theater* is "an impressive and powerful character study beneath whose comedic structure lies a deep understanding of the ultimate pathos of life." The *Times Literary Supplement* observes that Roth's "new creation Mickey Sabbath isn't just another of the counterselves, alter egos, rivals, doubles and delinquent avatars of the author who have populated his pages for twenty years. Sabbath is a much more old-fashioned monster, a 'character' no less ... extruded from Roth's imagination like a grotesque aged baby, all incontinent appetite and regressive, stubborn spleen, stewing defiantly in his own juice" and concludes that "The whole act turns the reader into a voyeur and so a colluder. That is, you find yourself savouring the vertiginous sense that Sabbath is about to fall off the edge of his narrow stageworld." In the view of *Critic's Choice*: "After a decade or two of metaphysical tricks and postmodern identity crises, Philip has finally gotten back around to what he does best: offending people."

RECOGNITION: Winner of the 1995 National Book Award; Booklist Editors' Choice 1995; *NYTBR* "Editors' Choice" 1995: nominated for the 1996 Pulitzer Prize for fiction; REVIEWS: *BL* 7/19/95; *CC* 9/25/95; *LJ* 7/95; *NYTBR* 9/10/95; *PW* 6/12/95; *Time* 9/11/95; *TLS* 10/20/95; *WPBW* 8/27/95; *WSJ* 8/23/95

Rush, Norman (USA)

Mating (1991); Random 1992 (pbk); See Section 1 #83

Russo, Richard (USA)

956   *Straight Man* (1997); Random 1997 (HC); Vintage 1998 (pbk)

Richard Russo sets his 4th novel on the campus of the fictional — and decidedly undistinguished — West Central Pennsylvania University, and features Hank Deveraux, Jr., failed novelist and apathetic academic. When Deveraux (a "militant procedural incompetent") is voted interim chair of the English department at WCPU, his colleagues expect a continuation of the comfortable status quo. Once handed the reins of the department, however, Deveraux is suffused with a desire to shake things up. Plot complications include — in addition to the usual madcap jockeying for tenure and position — nasty and increasingly public fights with the state legislature over budgetary matters, early-morning TV talk show appearances (featuring Deveraux sporting a Groucho-style plastic nose), use of the college's famous "ducks" as hostages, numerous amatory debacles, and a confrontation with his father, a well-known academic

As the *Times Literary Supplement* points out, "Russo's portrait of the Department Wars in today's literary academy is sharp. First, there is the Old Guard, a lot of fifty-something professors who get along by doing as little as possible, and inventing reasons not to talk to one another. Then, there is the thin and stroppy Young Guard, which now consists solely of Campbell Wheemer, a specialist in French feminism, cultural studies, and postmodern American sitcoms, who is so afraid of being deemed 'logocentric' that he avoids reading books whenever possible." According to *Booklist*, "Russo has lost none of his gifts for fashioning wry comedy, endearing characters, and an artful blend of high jinks and heartache." The *L.A. Times Book Review* suggests that Russo is "a Raymond Carver without the grunge, a funny Richard Ford and, on the not-so-venerable campus of WCPU, an American Kingsley Amis." *The* (London) *Sunday Times* argues that "There are campus shenanigans of the highest order in this warm centered yet deceptively piquant account of a pushing-50 academic." *Entertainment Weekly* argues that "Russo can penetrate to the tender quick of ordinary American lives like an unpretentious John Updike." *Publishers Weekly* concludes that "Russo concocts an inspired sendup of academia's infighting and petty intrigues that ranks right up there with the best of David Lodge, as we follow Hank's progress from perverse mockery to insight and acceptance. Readers who do not laugh uncontrollably during this raucous, witty and touching work are seriously impaired."

OTHER MEDIA: Audiocassette (Random Audio/abr); READING GROUP GUIDE; RECOGNITION: *NYTBR* Notable Book of 1997; *LATBR* "Best Books" 1997; *Booklist* Editors' Choice 1997; *Chicago Sun-Times* Best Books of 1997; REVIEWS: *BL* 5/15/97; *EW* 7/18/97; *KR* 5/15/97; *LATBR* 9/21/97; *LST* 7/12/98; *NYTBR* 7/6/97; *PW* 5/12/97; *TLS* 7/25/97; *WPBW* 7/20/97

Sandlin, Tim (USA)

957   *Social Blunders* (1995); H. Holt 1995 (HC); Putnam 1997 (pbk)

Social Blunders is the third and final installment in Tim Sandlin's darkly comic series of novels which began with *Skipped Parts* (1991) and continued with *Sorrow Floats* (1992). As the story begins, lead character Sam Callahan is still recovering from the departure of his second wife Wanda, who, adding insult to injury, has run off with a youngster sporting a very bad tattoo. In an attempt to refocus his own energies Sam embarks on a madcap quest to find his father — whose identity is not known with any degree of certainty, even to his mother. Sam, it would appear, was conceived during a night of drunken debauchery involving most of the members of a high school football team. Armed with a list of possibilities, Sam sets off on his odyssey.

In the opinion of *Booklist*, *Social Blunders* "is [both] a weird, funny, raunchy novel that veers wildly from pathos to slapstick and back again [and] a loopy inquiry into the meaning of fatherhood." According to novelist Jay Gummerman (*NYTBR*) Sandlin's novel, while filled with "extravagant writing" particularly regarding the hero's sexual escapades, "is nicely comic — and more — when it settles down and allows readers a chance to catch their breath."

REVIEWS: *BL* 6/1/95; *LJ* 5/1/95; *NYTBR* 8/6/95; *PW* 5/1/95

Schine, Cathleen (USA)

958   *The Love Letter* (1995); HM 1995 (HC); Plume 1998 (pbk)

Cathleen Schine's 4th novel, a romantic comedy, is set in the idyllic New York seaside town of Pequot — home to a well-regarded (formerly female) liberal arts college, and features Helen McFarquhar, an attractive, 40-ish divorcee, incorrigible flirt, and owner of a small bookstore. When the much-admired (but always-in-control) Helen receives an anonymous love letter she becomes obsessed with uncovering the author's identity. Further plot complications include a joint visit from her stylish and relentlessly worldly mother and grandmother, and a decidedly unexpected (though gratifyingly torrid) affair with one of her college-aged summer employees.

According to the *Library Journal:* "A resort community setting, wry characters, and an off-beat plot combine elegantly into a charming novel...." In the view of *Publishers Weekly*, "Overtones of a postmodern fairy tale give added resonance to what is otherwise a very contemporary — and totally enchanting — love story." *Booklist* points out that "As Schine dissects [Helen's] passionate and utterly illogical affair, she animates a cast of deliciously piquant characters who think and say the sort of things we are taught not to, and we bask in their audacity." In the view of the *New Statesman*, *The Love Letter* is "A medley of social satire, pop fiction and grand guignol, the novel affirms that, as in life, there is a limit to how far charm can be willed." Michiko Kakutani (*NYT*) notes that *The Love Letter* "may evaporate instantly from the reader's mind, but it remains a delightful exercise in literary wit, a perfect summer screwball comedy."

RECOGNITION: *NYTBR* Notable Book of 1995; REVIEWS: *BL* 5/1/95; *EW* 8/16/96; *LATBR* 5/7/95; *LJ* 4/1/95; *NS&S* 2/2/96; *NYRB* 10/19/95; *NYT* 5/16/95; *NYTBR* 5/28/95; *PW* 2/27/95; EDITOR'S NOTE: Cathleen Schine's latest novel *The Evolution of Jane* (1998) is, according to the *New York Times Book Review* (which selected it as one of the Notable Books of 1998), "a beautifully descriptive travelogue of the Galapagos, loaded with mini-lectures on natural history, evolutionary theory and Darwiniana, wrapped around a rollicking family saga tinged with hints of sexual intrigue." The *LATBR* (which placed it on its "Top Ten Books of 1998" list) called *The Evolution of Jane* "a novel of ideas girded up with authentic if raffish emotions."

959   *Rameau's Niece* (1993); NAL-Dutton 1994 (pbk)

Cathleen Schine's 4th novel can be read both as an intellectually arch academic satire and as a romantic comedy. Margaret Nathan, brilliant but mortifyingly forgetful, is happily married to a "benevolently egotistical" Columbia University professor. Margaret has just published one of those unlikely literary works which occasionally capture the imagination of the day: a best-selling scholarly biography entitled *The Anatomy of Madame de Montigny* which has managed to delight feminists, semiologists, deconstructionists, professors of literature, and the general public alike. Margaret is emotionally fulfilled and intellectually content until, in the course of research for her next book, she discovers a decidedly lascivious — and thoroughly absorbing—18th century text masquerading as a philosophical tract. Margaret decides that her life is lacking in true passion and resolves to explore her sexual nature — with disastrous (if highly comical) results.

Rameau's Niece was described by the *L.A. Times Book Review* as "A smart, funny sendup of academia that parodies the postmodern form it imitates." According to the *Washington Post Book World*, "Comic novels about intellectuals are a flourishing subgenre: These days we need to laugh at the antics of academics, at least in part to prevent ourselves from weeping. Cathleen Schine's *Rameau's Niece* can join such small classics as Malcolm Bradbury's *The History Man*, David Lodge's *Small World*, and Randall Jarrell's *Pictures from an Institution*." *Publishers Weekly*, in its starred review, observes that "the book's greatest charm is Schine's smart and very funny observations of a postmodern 'cultural elite,' made up of those who toast 'the liberation of the signifyer', and of 40-year-olds still boasting about their SAT scores." In the opinion of novelist Carolyn See (*NYTBR*), "This lively novel compares to A.S. Byatt's *Possession*, to Alison Lurie's *Foreign Affairs*, to Rebecca Goldstein's *Strange Attractors*. These are all novels of manners in which the characters are severely impinged upon by literature, learning, the life of the mind. How minds and bodies wiggle themselves out of— and back into — appropriate alignment is a subject that bears observation...." The *Library Journal* concludes that Ms. Schine "controls her quirky plotline with the same wit and style demonstrated in her earlier novels ... [and manages] to satirize marriage, philosophy, intellectuals, sexuality, and the relentless search for self-knowledge...." In the view of novelist **Frederick Busch** *Rameau's Niece* is "Our cousinly reply to A.S. Byatt. And the sex is better."

RECOGNITION: Nominated for the *L.A. Times* Book Award; *NYTBR* Notable Book of 1993; REVIEWS: *LATBR* 9/5/93; *LJ* 3/15/93; *NYTBR* 5/9/93; *PW* 1/25/93; *WPBW* 5/15/94; *WRB* 7/93

960 *To the Birdhouse* (1990); NAL-Dutton 1996 (pbk)

The sequel to Cathleen Schine's *Alice in Bed* features a now healthy, recently married Alice, a professional photographer and art director of a small circulation "bird-watching" magazine. Her biggest concern this time out is her mother's obnoxious (psychotic?) boyfriend, Louie Scifo.

According to *Publishers Weekly*, *To the Birdhouse* is "a beguiling comedy of manners" in which Alice, who has married Peter, "an appealing, laid-back analyst of baseball statistics ... remains bemused and exasperated by her divorced, spacy, 'hideously cheerful' mother, psychologist Brenda Brody." and her romantic misadventures. The *New York Review of Books* observes that Alice's family, the

Brodys, "are as insular as the English Hons Nancy Mitford caricatured in her novels...." and concludes that "It is both uncanny and deliciously just that the spirit of Nancy Mitford, the deft satirist of xenophobia, should have reawakened in a satirist of Jewish family life, poking fun at the domestic roots of Jewish liberalism." The *Library Journal* points out that "Schine's flair for darkly humorous scenes reveal her characters at their worst and funniest."

REVIEWS: *KR* 3/1/90; *LJ* 5/15/90; *NYRB* 8/16/90; *NYTBR* 5/20/90; *PW* 2/23/90; *WPBW* 5/20/90

Shields, Carol (USA/Canada)

961 *Republic of Love* (1992); Viking 1993 (pbk)

Carol Shields has set her 6th novel in Winnipeg, Ontario, an old fashioned city with well-established neighborhoods and intertwined lives. Winnipeg native Fay McLeod, a folklorist immersed in a book on Mermaid symbolism, has, unaccountably, fallen out of love with her level-headed, professionally-accomplished, live-in-lover. As the novel progresses, Fay will be drawn inexorably towards an off-beat, thrice-divorced — and increasingly lonely — radio talk show host by the name of Tom Avery. Although sharing friends and relatives in common, their paths do not actually cross until half-way through the novel.

As Canadian novelist Rita Donovan (*Books in Canada*) observes, "Carol Shields has created a sophisticated story in the romance of Fay and Tom. And the 'happy ending,' so traditional to the romance novel, is here refurbished, updated and — most happily — earned." The *Times Literary Supplement* argues that "As if to match its intent in the urge to unite, the book marries a wide diversity of elements: mythical and modern, ironic and moving, exhilarating and melancholy. The result is a love-surveying love story that is entirely seductive." *The Age* (Australia) notes that if one were to take "the rewards and wonders of the 19th Century novel, the Balzacs and the Brontes [and] update them for a late 20th century reader ... you [would] have Carol Shields's latest novel."

RECOGNITION: Shortlisted for the 1992 *Guardian* Fiction Prize; REVIEWS: *Age* 5/9/92; *BksCan* 4/92; *KR* 12/1/91; *LATBR* 3/15/92; *LitRev* 3/92; *NYTBR* 3/1/92; *PW* 11/29/91; *TLS* 3/20/92; *WPBW* 2/18/92

962 *Small Ceremonies* (1976); Penguin 1996 (pbk)

In Carol Shields's debut novel, Judith, a biographer, is comfortably married to Martin, a Milton scholar with whom she has two teenage children. As the story opens, Judith is working on a biography of the Canadian folk hero (and quintessential "pioneer woman") Susannah Moodie. Prompted by her research, Judith begins mulling over the ultimate unknowability of even one's closest family members.

According to *Guardian Weekly* "*Small Ceremonies* is a fine novella, lucid and written with great assurance. Shields may be a superficially 'easier' read than [fellow Canadian writers] Atwood or Munro, but her wit and whimsy remain spiked." The *Times Literary Supplement* points out that Shields "gives a wry account of Canadian academic life in the mid-1970s. She describes the wedding of a colleague where the guests include 'a gentle couple [he batiks she crochets]' and the service has been written in blank verse so that Martin can speak [his] part to a familiar rhythm.' "

REVIEWS: *GW* 3/12/95; *KR* 12/15/95; *LATBR* 2/25/96; *NYTBR* 1/7/96; *PW* 12/4/95; *TLS* 2/17/95; *WRB* 4/96

Smiley, Jane (USA)

963   *Moo* (1995); Fawcett 1996 (pbk)

Jane Smiley's campus farce, *Moo*, takes an unstinting, satirical look at the bureaucracy, relentless fund-raising, and political in-fighting that — in the author's view — plague the modern American university system. Set on a Midwestern campus (familiarly called "Moo U" and highly reminiscent of Ms. Smiley's alma mater, the University of Iowa), Ms. Smiley's 6th novel is, in tone at least, a dramatic departure from her 1992 Pulitzer Prize–winning novel, *A Thousand Acres*.

Booklist observes that "Incorporating the arc of a Shakespearean comedy, Smiley skewers any number of easily recognizable campus fixtures: the grant-seeking egomaniac, bewildered freshman, the obsessive researcher." According to the *Times Literary Supplement*, "Although it is ostensibly a comic novel, *Moo* has inherited some of the concerns of *A Thousand Acres*. It is characterized by a strong distrust of men in families; and by a hatred of agribusiness, *laissez-faire* capitalism and the self-complacency of those in power." The *Library Journal* observes that in her "sharp-edged spoof of academic life.... Smiley has assembled a large, colorful group of characters who will be familiar to ivory tower dwellers...."

OTHER MEDIA: Audiocassette (Random Audio/abr); RECOGNITION: nominated for the 1995 National Book Critics Circle Award; *NYTBR* Notable Book of 1995; REVIEWS: *BellesL* 1/96; *BL* 2/1/95; *ChiTrib* 4/9/95; *CSM* 4/4/95; *LATBR* 4/2/95; *LJ* 3/15/95; *NYTBR* 4/2/95; *PW* 2/6/95; *Time* 4/17/95; *TLS* 5/19/95

Spark, Muriel (UK)

964   *Reality and Dreams* (1996); Houghton Mifflin 1997 (HC); Chapters 1998 (pbk)

In her twentieth novel Dame Muriel Spark tells the story of Tom Richards, a successful British film director, chronic womanizer, husband of an accommodating American cookie heiress, and patriarch to a haphazardly extended family. When Richards falls from a crane during the shooting of his latest film (provisionally entitled "Hamburger Girl"), he sustains multiple fractures and contusions. Facing a long recuperation period, he is forced to give up his directorial role in the film but still spends his days — at least what's left of them after his physical therapy sessions — in attempting to maintain artistic control over the project and in dealing with the increasingly dissatisfied and contentious cast. In the meantime, Marigold, one of his adult daughters (a censorious sociologist with a professional interest in the social costs of unemployment) "disappears," an event which is avidly covered by the British tabloids. When an attempt is made on his life, Richards realizes that his world is spinning badly out of control. Ms. Spark plays serio-comically with the notion of "redundancy" throughout her comedy of contemporary manners.

The *New York Times Book Review* succinctly (and accurately) describes *Reality and Dreams* as a novel in which: "A movie director who perhaps thinks to usurp the creative function of God falls into the hands of an all-knowing narrator — Muriel Spark — who visits trouble upon him." In the view of *Booklist*, *Reality and Dreams* is a "humorous, dark, imaginative novel [in which] tightness of exposition amounts to sublimity of effectiveness [and] the notion that one must never count on life really being what it seems, is cogently, beautifully articulated." According to *Kirkus Reviews*, "Spark remains in total control at all times: She can summon a world with a single gesture, a character with one seemingly artless remark." *KR* concludes that this novel represents: "Profound art disguised as a lark."

OTHER MEDIA: Audiocassette (Recorded Bks/unabr); RECOGNITION: *NYTBR* Notable Books of 1997; *TLS* "International Book of the Year" list; REVIEWS: *BL* 3/1/97; *KR* 1/15/97; *LATBR* 6/8/97; *PW* 1/27/97; *NYTBR* 5/11/97 & 12/7/97; *Salon* 4/3/97

Stead, C.K. (New Zealand)

965   *The Death of the Body* (1986); Harper-Collins 1992 (pbk re-issue)

C.K. Stead's academic farce combines two narratives: one about a philandering New Zealand professor whose wife has just converted to Sufism and whose house has been taken over by a drug squad staking out his (drug dealing?) neighbor; the other about a New Zealander in Europe who appears to be in control of the narrative.

According to *World Literature Today*, C.K. Stead "making no pretense that *The Death of the*

Body should comprise a slice of life ... sets two narratives in motion: one about a New Zealand professor entangled in academic and domestic affairs; the other about a New Zealander in Europe re-creating those same doings through 'The Story' he keeps in a blue folder and adds to while drinking coffee at an Italian cafe where a Danish diplomat's wife plays his muse." As described by *Kirkus Reviews The Death of the Body* is a "witty romp through New Zealand academe — with metafiction and mystery joining hands in the picaresque adventures of Professor Harry Butler, obsessed with the Mind/Body problem in more ways than one." In the view of the *Times Literary Supplement*, Stead's novel "is a slight work, but it's neat and enjoyable — the exact minor by-blow of an author who can hit harder."

REVIEWS: *KR* 8/15/93; *PW* 8/30/93; *TLS* 9/5/86; *WLT* Aut '87

Theroux, Alexander (USA)

966   *Darconville's Cat* (1981); H Holt 1996 (pbk re-issue)

Alexander Theroux's lengthy academic farce (called "one of the legendary books of the past 20 years" by the *Washington Post Book World*) features Alaric Darconville, a 29-year-old English instructor at Quinsy, a small Southern women's college. Darconville falls for — and is blithely rejected by — one of his students, a charming backcountry girl by the name of Isabel Rawsthorne. The bitterly broken-hearted young professor then takes a position at Harvard where he plots his revenge. In telling his tale of obsessive love, Theroux incorporates a variety of narrative forms including (but not limited to): a blank-verse play, an abecedarium, a diary, oration, a sermon, essays and numerous fables.

Novelist James Wolcott (*NYRB*) declares that "To flighty readers, the 700-plus pages of *Darconville's Cat* [a work of "imperial" fiction, which "plunders all forms of style and genre circumstance"] may seem as long as the Trojan War." Wolcott concludes, however, that Theroux's "gift for satire and abuse borders on genius." The *Christian Science Monitor* (while pointing out that *Darconville's Cat* will not appeal to everyone) concludes that "Theroux is a conjurer, a spellbinder, a master of the ironic put-down. His Quinsy College girls are as wackily done as anything in Updike; his faculty frolics as funny as Mary McCarthy's *Groves of Academe* (1952); his grotesque Harvard as hyperbolic as Thomas Wolfe's. Theroux deserves his readers — and they deserve him."

REVIEWS: *CSM* 5/11/81; *LJ* 6/1/81; *NYRB* 5/14/81; *NYTBR* 5/3/81; *NatR* 5/29/81; *NewR* 4/4/81; *Q&Q* 8/81; *WPBW* 6/2/96

Theroux, Paul (USA)

Kowloon Tong (1997); See Section 6, #781; Houghton Mifflin 1997 (HC)

967   *Millroy the Magician* (1993); Ivy 1995 (pbk)

Paul Theroux's 20th work of fiction is narrated by Jilly Farina, a sweet-natured 14-year-old naif from Marston Mills whose life is changed when she attends a performance of "Millroy the Magician" at Foskett's Funfair. Millroy, an oddly appealing character, is not only adept at magic (he once turned a girl from the audience into a glass of milk and drank her), he is also a modern-day prophet proselytizing for a healthy life built around weight control, whole foods and laxatives. Millroy and the affection-starved Jilly, sensing an immediate bond, join forces. Jilly (now a runaway) provides Millroy with inspiration and Millroy provides Jilly with warmth and security. They eventually create a successful TV show and a open a string of healthfood diners. Entanglements ensue.

In the view of novelist **Charles Johnson** (*NYTBR*), *Millroy the Magician* is an "unusual, often funny, dark satire of America's obsession with trim bodies and religious television ... [complete with a] magical transformation in the final chapter." The *New Statesman* judges *Millroy* to be "a tautly crafted exploration of that most dangerous of American pastimes, reinvention." John Updike, writing in the *New Yorker*, calls Theroux's novel "liberally and strenuously wonderful, a show case of [the author's] fluent, faintly sinister powers of vision and imagination." Updike concludes that "Millroy and his jeremiads afford the author a conduit for satire, a zestfully distasteful panorama of a bugerized America full of self-created gargoyles, doughballs and dyspeptics."

OTHER MEDIA: Audiocassette (Blackstone/ unabr); RECOGNITION: *NYTBR* Notable Book of 1994; REVIEWS: *BL* 10/15/93; *Guard* 10/12/93; *KR* 10/1/93; *LATBR* 3/20/94; *LST* 10/10/93; *NS* 10/8/93; *NY* 3/14/94; *NYTBR* 3/6/94; *WLT* Aut '95; *WPBW* 2/27/94; *WSJ* 4/11/94

Thurm, Marian (USA)

968   *The Clairvoyant* (1997); Zoland 1997 (HC)

In her fourth novel, Ms. Thurm tells the humorous tale of Victor Mackenzie, a successful Manhattan psychic with a sophisticated and well-heeled clientele. (Victor discovered his "gift" of clairvoyance at the age of eight, the year the ghost of Murray Weinbaum, one-time owner of the corner candy store, began his nocturnal visits.) When Victor falls in love with one of his clients, the gorgeous, recently divorced Katha Randall, he must convince her that romance can co-exist with second-sight.

According to novelist **Peter Lefcourt** (*NYTBR*), "As in all good love stories, Victor and Katha's future seems both perilous and ineluctable. Only Victor knows what lies ahead and he's not telling." In the view of *Publishers Weekly,* Marian Thurm "has created a wise, funny novel about seeing others better than we see ourselves." *Library Journal* observes, "This engaging book deals with the fragility of relationships both romantic and familial while posing the question 'How does a psychic manage to have a relationship without foreseeing the future?'"

RECOGNITION: *NYTBR* Notable Book of 1997; REVIEWS: *KR* 4/1/97; *LJ* 5/1/97; *NYTBR* 10/5/97; *PW* 5/12/97

Townsend, Sue (UK)

969   *The Queen and I* (1992); Soho 1993 (HC); 1994 (pbk)

I have no money; British Telecom is threatening me with disconnection; my mother thinks she is living in 1953; my husband is starving himself to death, my daughter has embarked on an affair with my carpet fitter; my son is due in court on Thursday; and my dog has fleas.

In Sue Townsend's satirical take on the British Royal family, the queen certainly has her hands full. Her troubles have, of course, just begun as, by act of Parliament, the royals have, literally overnight, been declared "commoners" and, forced to go on the dole, they find themselves living in a falling-down housing project.

According to *Kirkus Reviews,* Sue Townsend's "funny, surprisingly sweet satire" was "a big success in England. Readers on this side of the Atlantic will find it diverting, too — chaotic, silly, with no real harm meant." *Belles Lettres* argues that "*The Queen and I* really works [as social satire]: not only does Townsend give readers a sense of London life on the margins, but she peppers the story with Twain-ian flashes of insight that keep the farce going right through to the end." Michael Elliott writing in the *New York Times Book Review* declares that "This book is sui generis. I have never read anything like *The Queen and I* before. It is great fun, at least for an emigré British republican like me. As there cannot be too many of us around, I somehow doubt that it will do as well as it should here. Pity."

OTHER MEDIA: Audiocassette (Chivers/unabr); RECOGNITION: *NYTBR* Notable Book of 1992; REVIEWS: *BellesL* Sum '95; *EW* 10/8/93; *KR* 7/1/93; *LJ* 1/94; *NS&S* 9/18/92; *NYTBR* 9/12/93; *PW* 1/28/93; *WPBW* 11/1/92

Vidal, Gore (USA)

970   *The Smithsonian Institution* (1998); Random House 1998 (HC)

War clouds were gathering over Europe as T. came out of the lower school dormitory of St. Albans school and hailed a taxi. Since St. Albans was an Episcopal school, cabs — not Mary — got hailed along that part of Wisconsin Avenue.

Gore Vidal's signature style is clearly in evidence in his latest novel, a serio-comic farce set in Washington, D.C., immediately preceding the United States' entry into World War II. The "T" of the opening sentence is a thirteen-year-old math prodigy, a student at Mr. Vidal's own alma mater. Summoned (on Good Friday) to the Smithsonian by a mysterious phone call, the youngster (who, while taking an Algebra exam, has inadvertently stumbled upon a mathematical equation which could lead to a breakthrough in nuclear physics) finds himself in the strange, after-hours world of the museum. When the galleries are closed to the public, T learns, the stuffed exhibits come to life. Later developments include top-secret work on a time machine, complete with multiple journeys to "parallel pasts." T also mingles with Robert Oppenheimer, Albert Einstein, Charles Lindbergh and other historical personages and falls in love with Grover Cleveland's first-term wife, Frankie.

According to *New York Times Book Review, The Smithsonian Institution* is a "larky and thought-provoking excursion through American history." In the view of *Salon* magazine: "This is the redoubtable man of letters' 24th novel, and it is the only novel I know of to try to combine teen adventure suspense with hearty op-ed nutrition. Let's cut Vidal some slack. He is among the most interesting essayists going.... If he wants to toss off a playful trick of a novel with plot holes big enough to fly a Lockheed Elektra through, who are we to complain?" *Publishers Weekly* observes that Vidal's novel is "[p]art 'Alice in Wonderland,' part Twain's 'Mysterious Stranger,' part fictionalized autobiography ... a bagatelle [which] reintroduces many of the characters and themes already treated in Vidal's historical novels and memoirs. 'T' bears at least enough resemblance to Vidal's well-publicized great love, a St. Albans classmate who died at Iwo Jima, to explain the novelist's obvious affection for him."

OTHER MEDIA: Audiocassette (Bks-on-Tape /unabr); RECOGNITION: *NYTBR* Notable Book of 1998; REVIEWS: *BL* 2/1/98; *KR* 1/15/98; *LJ* 3/1/98; *NYTBR* 2/22/98; PeopleW 4/6/98; *PW* 2/2/98

971   *Live from Golgotha* (1992); Penguin 1993 (pbk)

Gore Vidal's lubricious religious satire is set (partly) in late 1st century Macedon and is narrated by Bishop Timothy, a confidant of St. Paul. Timothy takes a rather dim view of Paul, routinely offering up observations that are far from flattering ("all those years working as a secret agent for

Mossad had made Saint even more devious than the Big Fella in the sky had made him in the first place"). Bishop Timothy begins receiving messages from the future (they invade his dreams, appear in holograms, and eventually, in person, in the form of time travelers). As the plot progresses, lunacy prevails. At one point a time-traveling NBC-TV manages a live broadcast of the crucifixion, with Bishop Timothy as anchorman. In a separate plot development, the Bible — consigned exclusively to computer discs — is being ravaged by a virus and Bishop Timothy is drafted to write his version of the gospels before "the word" is lost forever.

Cited by *Newsday* as "an outrageous romp through the Christian era's first days," the *New Yorker* argues that *Live from Golgotha* is "basically a satire on America." The *New Yorker* further observes that the novel's "religious insights owe a debt to Jimmy Swaggert and the fabulous Bakkers, who make it a lot easier to retell the Acts of the Apostles as an elaborate con game...." The *New Yorker* concludes that "[w]hether or not an ingenious piece of fluff like *Golgotha* was worth doing at all, it's impossible to imagine its being done better." The *L.A. Times Book Review* points out that "If God exists and Jesus is His son, than Gore Vidal is going to Hell. And if God is a Jew, Vidal is no better off. There's enough to outrage everyone in this outrageous and courageous send-up of the story of Our Lord Jesus Christ...." The *Times Literary Supplement* concludes that Vidal is "particularly skillful at the farcical blending of various modes of gobbledegook: mediaspeak, econotalk, chicchat; nor does he scorn the belly laugh:

'I doubt that.' One knew immediately that the speaker was Thomas. "

REVIEWS: *BL* 9/15/92; *LATBR* 9/13/92; *Newsday* 9/27/92; *NS&S* 11/6/92; *NY* 10/26/92; *NYRB* 4/8/93; *NYTBR* 10/4/92; *Spec* 10/10/92; *TLS* 10/2/92

Vizenor, Gerald (USA)

972 *Hotline Healers: An Almost Browne Novel* (1997); Un of Nebraska 1997 (HC)

Hotline Healers is a series of 11 linked stories featuring Almost Browne (named for the fact that he was born in the back seat of a hatchback "almost" on the White Earth reservation) a "crossblooded" Indian trickster. In Vizenor's latest novel (his *Dead Voices*, published in 1992, introduced the Almost Browne character) Almost has taken a job at UC–Berkley (where Vizenor is a faculty member) as a lecturer in the "Transethnic Situations Department." As a sideline, Almost starts up a "psychic phone service" which purports to put callers in touch with authentic Native medicine men. Vizenor, a mixed blood (he's part Chippewa) Indian, writes from a wellspring of experience.

According to the *Review of Contemporary Fiction*, "Casting about to describe *Hotline Healers*, one might say it's a little postmodern, a little magical realist, a little picaresque, a lot parodic, an American Indian trickster story — or 'tricky story' as its narrator likes to say as he recounts the exploits of his cousin, Almost Browne, and the rest of the highly extended family who inhabit a fabulous barony on Minnesota's White Earth Reservation." *Publishers Weekly*, in its starred review, observes that "With wonderful fluency, and with as much passion as humor, Vizenor skewers a nation's mixture of attraction to and repulsion for its indigenous peoples and their willful ignorance about them. Further pop icons are tweaked as Ishmael Reed, Henry Louis Gates, Claude Levi-Strauss and Gloria Steinem, among others, float through the mayhem."

REVIEWS: *KR* 3/15/97; *LJ* 4/15/97; *PW* 3/31/97; *RevCF* Fall 1997

Wagner, Bruce (USA)

973 *I'm Losing You* (1996); Random House 1996 (HC); Plume 1997 (pbk)

Bruce Wagner, author of the popular (if relentlessly outré) Hollywood-insider novel *Force Majeur* (1991) as well as the television mini-series adaptation of *Wild Palms*, provides the reader of *I'm Losing You* with another jaundiced look at contemporary Hollywood. In an end-of-the-millennium Los Angeles, HIV is rampant, million-dollar watches are commonplace, and the hottest players in town have lost the ability to look at "life" as anything more than material for a new show. Mr. Wagner has inserted some real-life characters (e.g., Alec Baldwin and Richard Dreyfuss) in totally fictional cameo roles.

According to the *New York Times Book Review*, "The author's achievement is that almost every character is fascinating, no matter how hideous.... [But] since many of the characters are appalling, the things they do are sometimes physically disgusting ... [and certain] pages read like the print equivalent of a gross-out slasher movie." *Publishers Weekly* observes that in *I'm Losing You* (the title refers to the common remark made by users of car phones): "Disparate tales are partially connected through several Hollywood novels that interact as Wagner performs a ruthless and occasionally quite sharp dissection of Hollywood's caste system" and concludes that Wagner "is at his best when delineating the hierarchy and competitive paranoia of Tinseltown, and there are occasional moments of pathos in his presentation of the psychic toll of ambition." The *Library Journal* points out that although the novel is "often obscene ... [it is] more often very, very funny, although not for the fainthearted."

RECOGNITION: *NYTBR* Notable Book of 1996; REVIEWS: *KR* 5/1/96; *LATBR* 12/8/96; *LJ* 6/15/96; *NYTBR* 8/18/96; *PW* 5/6/96; *WPBW* 12/1/96

974 *Force Majeure* (1991); St. Martin's 1993 (pbk)

Bruce Wagner's debut novel features a once-hot Hollywood screenwriter, Bud Wiggins, who suddenly finds himself driving a limo and living with his mother while scrambling to line up backers for his next project. Bruce Wagner should know whereof he speaks as he makes his living in Hollywood as a screenwriter responsible for such contemporary classics as *A Nightmare on Elm Street*.

According to *Publishers Weekly*, "Wagner gleefully rips out the livid, still-beating heart of Hollywood to expose its class system, its built-in vulgarity, its shrinks, AA meetings, starlets, harlots, climbers and burn-outs. Wagner is a hip sociologist of ferocious veracity and methodical precision." The *New York Times Book Review* notes that "the novel will delight movie buffs; it's the revenge of a cynical Hollywood scribe, tickling and testing the system from within." In the view of *The Nation*, "Wagner mercilessly skewers Hollywood's insular rituals. Much like Tom Wolfe, Wagner has an unerring gift for pitch-perfect character nuances and authentic contemporary dialogue."

REVIEWS: *LJ* 8/91; *Nation* 12/23/91; *NYTBR* 9/29/91; *PW* 8/30/91

Weiss, D. (USA)

975 *The Swine's Wedding* (1996); Serpent's Tail 1996 (HC); 1999 (pbk)

Daniel Weiss has written a very dark comedy (actually "a cross between a Shakespeare Tragedy and a Philip Roth comedy with a few Stephen King horrific touches thrown in" according to the Amazon.com reviewer) about the initially unforeseen, but increasingly foreshadowed, consequences of a mixed marriage. When Solomon Beneviste, a Jew of Sephardic ancestry, becomes engaged to Allison Pennybaker, the daughter of long-time, subtly intolerant Episcopalians, Solomon's mother, Miriam Beneviste, decides to construct a family tree as a gift for the intended couple. As Miriam's research progresses, she uncovers a past which stretches back to the Spanish Inquisition. The story is narrated alternately by Allison Pennybaker and her mother-in-law to be, in the form of journal entries. The novel begins with a police report of a fatal fire of suspicious origin.

Publishers Weekly argues that "Although the supporting characters, including the bridegroom, are one-dimensional, Weiss's two narrators are complex, unselfconscious and believable. Together they provide a compelling, if grotesque, reason to remain true to one's identity." In the view of *The* (London) *Times*: "Weddings can make even the most well-adjusted families behave like later-day Montagues and Capulets, and the traditional rivalry between bride's and groom's side in Daniel Evan Weiss's funny and disquieting novel is further exacerbated by religious intolerance." *Entertainment Weekly* concludes that "*The Swine's Wedding* is a grippingly ironic account of how, in the words of Pennybaker 'religion makes normal people crazy.'"

REVIEWS: *EW* 1/29/96; *KR* 9/15/96; *LT* 5/11/97; *PW* 9/30/96

Weldon, Fay (UK)

976 *Splitting* (1995); Grove-Atlantic 1996 (pbk)

When Sir Edward Rice cavalierly divorced Lady Angelica — his wife of many years — he could not foresee the "perforating" effect this would have on his wife's personality. In the wake of her abandonment she splits "into four distinct personalities: long-suffering wife, girlish innocent, assertive career woman, and uninhibited sex pot" (*EW*). In her 20th novel, Fay Weldon explores many of her trademark themes: male chauvinism, the common female mistake of investing too much emotional capital in marriage, and the sexual battlefield.

Entertainment Weekly further observes that "Men are fools; society is misogynistic, women are their own worst enemies. From these sad truths, Weldon spins a brilliant comic fantasy on the subject of divorce, breakdown and recovery." According to the *Library Journal*, "Weldon's astringent style and sardonic view of the relationship between men and women, shown to perfection in *Life Force* (1993), are equally well demonstrated in this novel about a woman who goes to pieces when her marriage breaks up." *The* (London) *Times* points out that "The splitting of the title ... denotes more than one kind of rupture: as in split-up and split-personality, that's to say divorce and the fragmentation of self. Angelica, betrayed and abandoned by her husband, copes with this rejection by involuntarily developing a multiple personality." *The* (London) *Sunday Times* contends that *Splitting* "is a jaunty enough read; it has a definite enough, interest-awakening momentum. Even when she irritates, Weldon never bores, and there is something admirable in that confident fidelity to her own way of seeing and defining the world, the way she puts her stamp on it." *Publishers Weekly* concludes that "Weldon again proves herself one of a kind, a smart satirist whose playful exploration of psychology reveals society's fault lines and fractures."

OTHER MEDIA: Audiocassette (Recorded

Bks/unabr); REVIEWS: *BL* 5/1/95; *EW* 6/16/95; *LJ* 4/15/95; *NYTBR* 6/11/95; *LST* 4/23/95; *LT* 4/22/95; *PW* 5/1/95

977 *Trouble* (1993); Penguin 1994 (pbk)

They seem the perfect couple, Annette and Spicer, he, wide-shouldered and square-jawed, she, fair and delicately featured. They live, together with their children from previous marriages, in a lovely London home. They are literally suffused with good fortune: Annette has just published a successful novel, Spicer's business (he's a wine merchant) is thriving, and after ten years of marriage they are expecting their first child together. Life certainly feels good until the fateful day when Spicer forgets to kiss Annette goodbye, and the rock that is their marriage begins to crumble. Before long, the increasingly pregnant Annette becomes the unwitting victim of her husband's brainwashing at the hands of his "astrological psychotherapist" who also has designs on Spicer's assets.

According to the *New Statesman*, "Nothing could have prepared [Annette] for the terrors to come, not even the whole canon of Weldon's previous work. There have been callous husbands, unscrupulous rivals, children betrayed, not to mention witchcraft and extensive surgery — but nothing to match Dr. Rhea's bland delivery of evil gobbledygook." As *Publishers Weekly* observes, Ms. Weldon has marshaled "her formidable narrative talents in this characteristically acerbic domestic tragicomedy ... [and] unleashes a verbal arsenal against husbands and psychotherapists...." *The* (London) *Times* calls *Trouble* "wacky and witty and wise" and concludes that it bounds along at a crackling pace, with the reader hanging on for dear life, veering between laughter, pity and outrage, but never less than totally engaged." *Kirkus Reviews* concludes that, while "not Weldon's best ... [it's] bracing stuff nonetheless."

RECOGNITION: *SF Chronicle* "Best Books" 1993; *NYTBR* Notable Book of 1993; REVIEWS: *BL* 7/93; *KR* 10/1/94; *LATBR* 11/28/93; *Lit Rev* 5/93; *LJ* 9/1/93; *LST* 4/30/95; *NS&S* 2/11/94; *NYTBR* 10/17/93; *PW* 8/23/93; *TLS* 2/18/94; *WPBW* 11/14/93; EDITOR'S NOTE: *Trouble* was originally published in London under the title *Affliction*

Welsh, Irving (UK)

Trainspotting; (1995) Norton 1996 (pbk); See Section 3, #311

Wesley, Mary (UK)

978 *An Imaginative Experience* (1994); Bantam 1994 (HC); Penguin 1996 (pbk)

Mary Wesley's 10th novel features Julia Piper, a young London housekeeper who has recently suffered a devastating personal tragedy. The story begins with Julia pulling the emergency cord on a British Rail train (in order to rescue a hapless sheep upended in a nearby field) and opens out into a decidedly quirky comedy of manners. A series of unconventionally drawn characters are introduced including a bird watcher and aspiring writer, a racist former U.S. Senator, an urbane young book editor, and an assortment of interfering neighbors.

In the view of *Belles Lettres*, Mary Wesley's novels are characterized by a "subtle mixture of the sensual and the intellectual, Wesley's works usually include a few generously sexed older women, a handful of sensitive male or female loners, a fine garden or two, and a good measure of very dry humor" and concludes that "*An Imaginative Experience* includes all the above, plus a liberal helping of that ultimate imaginative experience, love." According to *Booklist*: "Although a tale of modern London, the novel is blessedly free of that peculiarly British sense of ennui that seems to pervade much contemporary British fiction." The *Washington Post Book World* observes that "Behind Wesley's smooth prose and quick wit is a writer who could never be mistaken for anyone but herself." English novelist Lesley Glaister (*The Spectator*) concludes that (some "contrivances" aside) Ms. Wesley "builds enough surprise and suspense into her plot to provide emotional satisfaction and there is a warm and wonderful aaah at the end."

OTHER MEDIA: Audiocassette (Chivers/ unabr); READING GROUP GUIDE; REVIEWS: *BellesL* Sum '95; *BL* 3/1/95; *KR* 2/1/95; *LJ* 2/15/95; *NYTBR* 4/30/95; *PW* 1/23/95; *Spec* 2/5/94; *TLS* 3/25/94; *WPBW* 4/19/95

979 *A Dubious Legacy* (1992); Penguin 1993 (pbk)

Mary Wesley's 9th novel (spanning the years from the early 1950s through the 1990s) features Henry Tillotson, a modern-day Mr. Rochester who, urged on by his fatally ill and excessively kindhearted father, rescues a beautiful English divorcee from perdition in Egypt (by marrying her) and brings her home to his country estate in England. Upon their arrival, Margaret takes to her bed and from that stronghold manages to thoroughly bedevil the increasingly exasperated Henry. This "misplaced act of kindness" is just one of a number of "dubious" legacies that are humorously explored in Ms. Wesley's intriguingly constructed comedy. Mary who began writing at the age of 71 is frequently compared with such masters of social comedy as **John Mortimer**, Barbara Pym, **Laurie Colwin** and Molly Keane.

In Irish novelist Aisling Foster's view *A Dubious Legacy* "is a very funny book. It stretches Larkin's warnings about man handing on misery to man into a black comedy of English manners" (TLS). *Publishers Weekly*, in its starred review, calls

A Dubious Legacy "darkly comic, wise and irresistible" while concluding that "it is in Margaret, whose monstrously selfish, malicious, eccentric behavior exceeds all rational bounds, that Wesley has created her most memorable character. Readers will root for her comeuppance, and will cheer when it arrives." *Kirkus Review* suggests that in *A Dubious Legacy* Ms. Wesley "continues her cheerful splaying out of human rottenness, eruptions of goodness, and general asininity — all with a faint brushing of enchantment."

OTHER MEDIA: Audiocassette (Chivers/unabr); REVIEWS: *KR* 8/15/92; *LRB* 3/12/92; *NYTBR* 11/8/92; *PW* 8/31/92; *Scotsman* 2/1/92; *TLS* 2/7/92

Wilcox, James

980   *Plain and Normal* (1998); Little, Brown 1998 (HC)

In his seventh novel (called a "bittersweet comedy of manners" by the *Boston Globe*) novelist James Wilcox (best known for his 1983 debut novel *Modern Baptists* — widely regarded as a modern classic) tells the story of Lloyd Norris a middle-aged, recently divorced homosexual who is just now (with his former wife's encouragement) stepping gingerly out of the closet. An employee of NyLo (a Manhattan-based firm which designs labels for personal care products), Lloyd (referred to throughout as "Mr. Norris") is half-heartedly looking for Mr. Right.

Kirkus Reviews observes that the novel "works best as a collection of riffs on sexual insanity ... with some delicious incidental comedy...." and concludes that "Almost as much of a mess as Lloyd Norris's modestly frenetic pursuit of happiness and normality [*Plain and Normal* is] ... almost as endearing and entertaining." According to novelist Karen Karbo (*NYTBR*), "James Wilcox has been hailed as a young master of the old-fashioned farce — a genre that has always been more beloved in England and France than in the United States. The traditional bedroom farce spins on mistaken identities and intentions, on who's sleeping with whom. In *Plain and Normal*, Wilcox gives the farce a face lift: the question is not who's in bed with whom — in the true modern urban manner, no one's sleeping with anyone — but who's gay and who isn't, and who's trying to pass himself off as gay in order to take advantage of a gay-friendly environment."

RECOGNITION: *NYTBR* Notable Book of 1998; REVIEWS: *BosGlobe* 9/20/98; *EW* 10/30/98; *KR* 6/15/98; *NYTBR* 9/20/98; *Salon* 9/10/98; *WPBW* 10/25/98

Willis, Connie

981   *To Say Nothing of the Dog* (1997); Bantam Books 1997 (HC)

Connie Willis's 6th novel, another clever "genre bender" (containing elements of sci fi, mystery, and comedy of manners), is filled with intriguing literary allusions and a refreshingly skewed view of history. Subtitled *How We Found the Bishop's Bird Stump at Last,* Ms. Willis's story begins in 1940 as Ned and five other time-travelers are combing a bombed-out Coventry Cathedral in search of the aforementioned stump. The tale shifts through numerous time periods including an extended stay in Victorian England. The plot is driven by a 21st century character, the powerful (unbalanced?) Lady Schrapnell who has promised to endow Oxford University's time-travel research project in return for the university's help in rebuilding Coventry Cathedral, bombed to rubble in World War II and still, in 2057, a moldering ruin.

Described by *Kirkus Reviews* as "Gleeful fun with a serious edge, set forth in an almost impeccable English accent," *To Say Nothing of the Dog* delighted the critics. As *Booklist* puts it: "Take an excursion through time, add chaos theory, romance, plenty of humor, a dollop of mystery, and a spoof of a Victorian novel, and you end up with what seems like a comedy of errors but is actually a grand scheme 'involving the entire course of history and all of time and space that, for some unfathomable reason, chose to work out its design with cats and croquet mallets and penwipers, to say nothing of the dog....'" The *New York Times Book Review* concludes that "No one mixes scientific mumbo jumbo and comedy of manners with more panache than Willis, who ... is in one of her lighter moods in this novel."

RECOGNITION: *Publishers Weekly* "Best Books" SF 1997; REVIEWS: *BL* 1/1/98; *ChiTrib* 3/8/98; *KR* 10/15/97; *NYTBR* 12/21/97; *PW* 10/27/97; EDITOR'S NOTE: Ms. Willis looks back somewhat referentially to Jerome K. Jerome's classic 1889 comic novel *Three Men and a Boat* (which was subtitled *To Say Nothing of the Dog*). described by its current publisher as concerning "all the misadventures that can befall three innocents (and a dog) on what should have been a pleasure cruise on the Thames."

Woodrell, Daniel

Give Us a Kiss: A Country Noir (1996); H. Holt 1996 (HC); See Section 6, #790

Wright, Stephen

Going Native (1994); FS&G 1994 (HC); See Section 6, #313

Zabor, Rafi

982   *The Bear Comes Home* (1997); W.W. Norton 1997 (HC), 1998 (pbk)

Rafi Zabor's picaresque debut novel about a Shakespeare-quoting, saxophone-playing circus bear — won in a card game by an endearingly shiftless man named Jones — is, by many accounts a *tour de force.*

According to the *L.A. Times Book Review,* "*The Bear Comes Home* achieves the seemingly impossible task of combining fictional and real characters, actual events, music theory, satire and fantasy with ease and panache." In the view of the *Times Literary Supplement,* "Self-conscious and distinctly self-referential, jazz is the ultimate post-modern text. In Rafi Zabor's lyrical first novel … it is a fitting backdrop for an exceedingly well-read, hyper-articulate saxophone-playing bear in deep contemplation of the existential void. Zabor, a jazz musician and critic, has composed an inspired, often hilarious portrait of the tortured artist straining towards beauty and transcendence, a novel of ideas in which Brechtian alienation is achieved by the sardonic-talking Kodiak." According to *Kirkus Reviews,* "Hip, flip, sexy and worldly-wise, with walk ons by Charlie Haden and other jazz celebrities…. [*The Bear Comes Home*] is a first novel that has the makings of a cult smash."

Recognition: Winner of the 1998 PEN/Faulkner Award; *LATBR* "Best Books" 1997; REVIEWS: *CSM* 9/15/97; *KR* 6/15/97; *LATBR* 12/14/97; *LJ* 7/97; *LST* 2/28/98; *TLS* 3/13/98; *WPBW* 8/5/97; EDITOR'S NOTE: Rafi Zabor is a professional jazz drummer and well-known music journalist.

Zigman, Laura

983   *Animal Husbandry* (1997); Dial 1998 (HC); Delta 1998 (pbk)

Laura Zigman's debut novel is set in New York City and features Jane Goodall, a young TV producer, who, on the rebound from (what was, for her, at least) a serious love affair, develops a theory, borrowed from animal science, to explain why most men are serial lovers, while most women are looking for a stable relationship.

Jonathan Yardley (*WPBW*) observes that "This clever, engaging first novel proceeds from its narrator's hypothesis that human beings of the masculine persuasion operate on bovine principles, summarized as follows: 'New Cow is short for New-Cow theory, which is short for Old-Cow, New-Cow theory, which, of course, is short for the sad, sorry truth that men leave women and never come back because all they really want is a New Cow.' " According to *Kirkus Reviews,* "Zinging along with deadeye depictions of men on the make as accurate as smart bombs, [*Animal Husbandry*] is a riot to read — and it also happens to make a great deal of sense." *Time* magazine notes that Laura Zigman's *Animal Husbandry,* a "familiar variation on the

mating dance proves fresh and hilarious…." and concludes that Zigman's "naughty vivisection of male dating rituals, should do for dumped girlfriends what Olivia Goldsmith's *The First Wives Club* and Fay Weldon's *The Life and Loves of a She-Devil* did for dumped wives: hearten, console, viciously amuse. It has already been optioned for a movie."

OTHER MEDIA: Audiocassette (Audio Renaissance/abr); film rights have been sold to Fox 2000; REVIEWS: *BL* 11/15/97; *EW* 2/13/98; *KR* 11/5/97; *LJ* 12/97; *NYTBR* 1/25/98; *PW* 10/6/97; *Time* 1/26/98; *WPBW* 1/14/98

Zuravleff, Mary Kay

984   *The Frequency of Souls* (1996); FS&G 1996 (HC); Penguin 1997 (pbk)

Mary Kay Zuravleff tells an amusing tale of a modern marriage challenged by a husband's unlikely response to a colleague's charms. In her "witty, intelligent first novel" (*TLS*), Ms. Zuravleff focuses on George Mahoney, a handsome electrical engineer — happily married for sixteen years to Judy, his attractive, efficient and sympathetic wife and mother of his two immensely appealing children — who finds himself developing a "crush" on Niagara Spence, an ungainly, untidy co-worker with a unique preoccupation. Niagara, convinced that electricity is an untapped life force, has built a contraption — made out of a satellite dish and old radios — through which she is attempting to channel the dead.

Kirkus Reviews observes that although the author "backs off from her dead souls theme just when it becomes interesting … her narrative offers a wry and original meditation on office politics, mid-life crisis, and even mortality." In the view of *Booklist,* "Although the plot veers off the map on more than one occasion, Zuravleff's endearing lead characters and inventive blending of science and mysticism make this an especially appealing book." The *Washington Post Book World* notes that *The Frequency of Souls* "is too engaging and full of promise to be dismissed as just one more wavelet in the ceaseless tide of new fiction. Yes, it's ultimately a superficial, even frivolous effort, despite all of Niagara's lofty ideas about listening for the voices of the dead. But who's to say there isn't a place for the lightweight first novel, especially one as brisk and bracing as this, on a steamy summer day?" *Salon* magazine concludes that "The humor is generally right-on despite a few sitcom moments, but the slips are rare, and like the best comic novels, this one invites you to seriously entertain its strangest inventions."

REVIEWS: *BL* 6/1/96; *Econ* 6/15/96; *KR* 4/1/96; *LJ* 5/1/96; *NYTBR* 7/28/96; *PW* 4/29/96; *Salon* 6/96; *TLS* 5/17/96; *WPBW* 8/25/96

8

Literary Extensions

Section 8 celebrates novels that draw their inspiration from a variety of literary precedents: Greek myths (Everett Percival's *Frenzy*, an iconoclastic "take" on the Dionysus/Bacchus myth); fairy tales and childrens' classics (Robert Coover's postmodern *Pinocchio in Venice* about the "delights of turning back to wood"); 16th-century dramatists (Alan Judd's *The Devil's Own Work*, a retelling of Christopher Marlowe's *Dr. Faustus*; Jane Smiley's powerful *King Lear* reworking, *A Thousand Acres*); classics of 19th-century fiction (Christopher Bigsby's "prequel" to Hawthorne's *The Scarlet Letter*, Valerie Martin's retelling of Stevenson's *Dr. Jekyll and Mr. Hyde* from the perspective of his housemaid *Mary Reilly*, Peter Carey's *Jack Maggs*, a "loving tribute" to Charles Dickens' *Great Expectations*); as well as modern classics (John Cunningham's critically acclaimed *The Hours*, an extended meditation on Virginia Woolf's *Mrs. Dalloway*; Alan Hollinghurst's *Lolita*-inspired *The Folding Star*). And for Jane Austen aficionados there are the "continuations" of *Pride and Prejudice* (Julia Barrett's *Presumption* and Emma Tennant's *An Unequal Marriage*) and *Emma* (Joan Austen-Leigh's *Later Days at Highbury*)

Readers may consult the Index under "Borrowings" for authors and works that have inspired novels in this guide.

Acker, Kathy (USA)

Pussy King of the Pirates (1996) See Section 3 #340; Grove Atlantic 1996 (HC); **Reference:** *Treasure Island* (Stevenson)

Aiken, Joan (UK)

985 *Emma Watson*: Jane Austen's unfinished novel completed (1996); St Martin's 1996 (HC); **Reference:** *The Watsons* (Austen)

Joan Aiken, in *Emma Watson*, completes Jane Austen's unfinished novel originally begun in 1804. As the story opens, Emma and Elizabeth Watson have been happily reunited after a 14 year separation. The 19-year-old Emma—who, as the youngest Watson daughter, had been adopted by her Aunt Maria upon the death of her mother—has returned home to assist her sister Elizabeth in the care of their ailing father. Elizabeth is just a year or two older than Emma, but both girls are already fearful of becoming old maids. Miss Aiken's colorful cast of characters includes: Robert, their pompous older brother, and his odious, unsympathetic wife; their shrewish sister Penelope, who has ensnared nice, elderly Dr. Harding; their next-older sister Margaret who pines for Tom Musgrave; their brother Sam, an impecunious doctor; and a clutch of suitors, all rejected. There is heartache and misunderstanding aplenty but all ends well.

According to *Kirkus Reviews* "Before the close ... there will be reversals and upheavals; a fatal accident; a destructive theft and elopement; disclosure of an old scandal; a rescue; and even a rousing horse race. As always, for those attuned to Austen, and to Aiken's imaginative, respectful variations, (*Emma Watson* is) simply charming." *Publishers Weekly* notes that "If (Aiken's) prose lacks Austen's acuity and understated wit, it's more than adequate to the task of delivering a fluid comedy of manners. Aiken is no Austen, but she's at the top of the class of the disciples."

REVIEWS: *BL* 9/15/96; *KR* 7/15/96; *LATBR* 9/15/96; *PW* 8/12/96; *TLS* 8/9/96

986   *Eliza's Daughter* (1994); St Martin's 1994 (HC); **Reference:** *Sense & Sensibility* (Austen)

Using characters from Jane Austen's *Sense & Sensibility*, Ms. Aiken weaves a tale of thwarted love, mysterious parentage and (even) some spirited international entanglements.

According to *Publishers Weekly*, "Others may try, but nobody comes close to Aiken in writing sequels to Jane Austen." In the view of *Booklist*, "Aiken's story is rich with humor and her language is compelling. Readers captivated with Elinor and Marianne Dashwood in *Sense and Sensibility* will thoroughly enjoy Aiken's crystal gazing but so will those unacquainted with Austen." *Kirkus Reviews* calls *Eliza's Daughter* an "engaging calamity filled romance rich with Aiken's shrewd retelling of Austen's people and an appreciative sense of fun."

REVIEWS: *BL* 2/15/94; *KR* 4/15/94; *LJ* 5/15/94; *PW* 5/16/94; *TLS* 8/5/94

Austen-Leigh, Joan (UK)

987   *Later Days at Highbury* (1996); St. Martin's 1996 (HC); **Reference:** *Emma* (Austen)

Mrs. Goddard, a schoolmistress in the little town of Highbury, is a keen social observer and, in a series of letters to her sister in London, describes the changes that have taken place since the death of Mr. Woodhouse. Emma and her husband had, in deference to Mr. Woodhouse, remained at Hartfield after their wedding, but have now moved to Mr. Knightly's estate. The new cast of characters includes an eligible young bachelor who has taken over Hartfield Hall, and a distant relation who is unhappily enrolled in a local girls's school. Joan Austen-Leigh, the great-great-grandniece of Jane Austen, has been called, by *Kirkus Reviews*, Austen's "heir apparent."

According to the *San Francisco Chronicle Book Review*, "Austen-Leigh captures the gossipy quality of small town life, but *Later Days at Highbury* also comments on larger political happenings...." The *New York Times Book Review* says "offers many pleasures: good humor, cleverness, and a certain spark that at moments recreates some of the surface spirit of Jane Austen." The *School Library Journal* observes that "Although the format is epistolary, there are plenty of descriptions of various balls, tea taking, and similar junkets with several romances thrown in and an elopement to engage Austen lovers anew."

REVIEWS: *LJ* 4/1/97; *NYTBR* 12/1/96; *PW* 10/21/96; *SFCBR* 2/23/97; *SLJ* 3/97

Baker, Larry (USA)

Flamingo Rising; See Section 5, #608; Knopf

1997 (HC); Ballantine 1998 (HC); **Reference:** *Romeo & Juliet* (Shakespeare) — Borrowing

Banville, John (Ireland)

Ghosts (1993); See Section 3, #213; Random House 1994 (pbk); **Reference:** *The Tempest* (Shakespeare); *Treasure Island* (Robert Louis Stevenson);

Barrett, Julia (pseudonym of English writers Julia Braun Kessler & Gabrielle Donnelly)

988   *The Third Sister* (1996); Mira Books 1998 (pbk); **Reference:** *Sense & Sensibility* (Austen)

In Julia Barrett's lively sequel to *Sense & Sensibility*, the youngest Dashwood sister takes center stage. Margaret has grown into a beautiful, strong-willed young lady who is understandably bored with life at Barton Cottage. As in all Austen novels, the search for a suitable husband drives the plot, and, as Margaret moves out into the world, she has no shortage of suitors. She is soon torn between two in particular: the kindly Mr. Osborne and the dashing Lt. William du Plessy.

According to the *New York Times Book Review* "Fans of the original novel will enjoy juicy cameo appearances by such favorites as Mrs. Ferrars and the former Lucy Steele. They'll also enjoy a good new story, tight writing and a heroine with brains and charm." In the view of *Booklist*, "Elements of (*The Third Sister*) depart from true Austen style, such as the masculine badinage over boxing and the faro table, but the dialogue is crisp and amusing and the threat of unhappy marriage compelling in this tale of Margaret Dashwood's emotional blossoming."

REVIEWS: *BL* 8/19/96; *KR* 6/15/96; *NYTBR* 8/18/96;

989   *Presumption*: An Entertainment (1993); M. Evans 1993 (HC); Un of Chi Press 1995 (pbk); **Reference:** *Pride & Prejudice* (Austen)

Julia Barrett revisits the Bennet clan and finds most of them caught up in one contretemps or another. The cast of familiar characters includes (among others) Georgina Darcy (still nursing her broken heart), Elizabeth Darcy (nee Bennet), and her nemeses Lady Catherine and Mr. Collins. New faces include the dashing Captain Heywood and a young architect Mr. James Leigh-Cooper. The plot is enlivened by another Bennett family scandal, this time involving accusations of shoplifting.

According to *Kirkus Reviews Presumption* is "A witty, amusing sequel to *Pride & Prejudice* (which will be for those) Austen lovers not affronted by the whole concept, a pleasant diversion." *KR* concludes that "Otherwise (Ms Barretts's novel is) a stylish entertainment that may lead some to the unsurpassable Jane." The *Times Literary Supplement* observes that "Jointly composed by two admirers of Jane Austen, (*Presumption*) often achieves crisp replications of her style. Abstract and concrete nouns are slyly slid together (Mrs. Bennet takes pleasure in 'safe arrival and smart livery') and … (i)rony gives sentences a mocking tone." "At its most entertaining and acute," continues the *TLS*, it "shows how sequel-writing can, like parody, be a sharp exercise in literary appreciation."

OTHER MEDIA: Audio cassette recording (unabridged); REVIEWS: *BL* 9/1/93; *CSM* 12/3/93; *KR* 8/1/93; *LJ* 9/15/93; *NYTBR* 12/12/93; *TLS* 8/5/94; *WRB* 5/94

Barthelme, Frederick (USA)

Bob the Gambler (1997); See Section 7, #1029; Houghton 1997 (HC); Mariner 1998 (pbk); **References**: Old Testament; "The Fall"

Berger, Thomas (USA)

990 *Robert Crews* (1994); Morrow 1994 (HC); **Reference**: *Robinson Crusoe*

In Thomas Berger's modern retelling of the *Robinson Crusoe* classic, Robert Crews, one of a party of men who were heading off into Canada's North Country for a fishing holiday, is the sole survivor of a plane crash. The plane went down in a remote and heavily wooded area and Crews, a sedentary, soft-about-the-middle city slicker, must live by his wits until help arrives. A number of weeks into his ordeal, he discovers a mysterious footprint…

According to the *New York Times Book Review* "Each new novel from Berger is a reason to celebrate the whole of his work, and while *Robert Crews* does not rank with his most ambitious books — a demanding standard indeed — it does share the inventiveness and the obsessions that have fueled his fiction over five decades." The *Library Journal* points out that *Robert Crews* is both "a survival tale and a story of the redemptive power of love and nature … (one that) exudes an optimism rare in contemporary fiction." *World Literature Today* notes that "Despite its (structural) problems, *Robert Crews* is immaculately written and entertaining. Berger … has always been one of America's funniest and most polished writers."

OTHER MEDIA: Audio cassette recording (Books-on-Tape/unabr); REVIEWS: *BL* 11/15/93; *ChiTrib* 2/13/94; *LJ* 1/94; *NYTBR* 3/6/94; *WLT* Spr'95

Bigsby, Christopher (UK)

991 *Pearl* (1995); Trafalgar 1996 (HC); **Reference**: *Scarlet Letter* (Hawthorne)

Christopher Bigsby, a British professor of American studies, sets his sequel to the Hawthorne classic in the 1660s and features Hester's love child, Pearl, now a beautiful young woman. As the story begins Pearl is making a transatlantic voyage back to England where she will encounter (yet another!) fatally attractive, fallen cleric as well as some unscrupulous individuals who will attempt to defraud her of her inheritance.

According to *The (London) Times* "In shifting the narrative from Boston to Norwich, the author lightens the atmosphere from brimstone and misery to intrigue and farce…." The *Times Literary Supplement* notes that "The inheritance plot (in which) a wicked local lawyer conspiring with shady Norwich businessmen and clergy to do Pearl out of her rights — is worked with some aplomb and some nice Gothic touches…."

REVIEWS: *LT* 7/28/95; *NYTBR* 10/21/94; *PW* 8/21/95; *TLS* 7/28/95

992 *Hester* (1990); Viking 1994 (HC); 1995 (pbk); **Reference**: *The Scarlet Letter* (Hawthorne)

Christopher Bigsby, in his prequel to the *Scarlet Letter*, focuses on the two years leading up to the opening of Hawthorn's classic work. In Norwich, England, a young woman by the name of Hester Prynne has made the dramatic decision to abandon her husband, the sinister and increasingly abusive, Roger Chillingworth. The frightened and conflicted young woman makes preparations to flee to the only safe place she can imagine: the New World. During the transatlantic crossing, Hester meets and falls hopelessly in love with a young minister, Arthur Dimmesdale, thereby setting in motion the tragic series of events which will, of course, lead not to sanctuary but to disgrace.

According to *Booklist*, it is "written very much in the Hawthorne tradition … a mesmerizing book which leaves one with a taste for more." *Publishers Weekly* finds the narrative voice to be "not quite of Hawthorne's time, nor of Hester's earlier century, nor of our own, leaving it curiously unanchored" but says Bigsby's labor of love offers a valiant and sometimes pleasurable attempt to complement an enduring classic." *The Voice Literary Supplement* observes that "Sequels and prequels aren't supposed to be this good" and says the book "brilliantly teaches about early colonial time."

REVIEWS: *BL* 9/1/94; *KR* 7/1/94; *LJ* 9/1/94; *PW* 8/8/94; *TLS* 5/20/94; *VLS* 9/94

Bradfield, Scott (USA)

993 *Animal Planet* (1995); St Martin's 1995 (HC); Picador 1996 (pbk); **Reference**: *Animal Farm* (Orwell)

Scott Bradfield's third novel, *Animal Planet*, is a political fable, modeled rather loosely on George Orwell's classic work of fiction, *Animal Farm*. In Bradfield's updating of the story, the "inmates" of the London Zoo have been released from their cages by animal rights activists and are being whipped into revolutionary fervor by Charlie Crow. His charismatic message is simple: "we are all different … yet somehow the same." The humans respond with tear gas and tranquilizers and an international "animal hunt" is begun for those escapees who have eluded the initial round ups.

British literary critic Eric Korn (*TLS*) suggests that in *Animal Planet* "passion and wit are (as) abundant (as in his previous novels, however) if economy and precision are less in evidence that is because the mode is what Kingsley Amis categorized as Comic Inferno." The *Library Journal* calls it "a fine, on-target satire in the tradition of Swift and Orwell." The *Washington Post Book World* concurs, pointing out that "Orwell and Bradfield … both know that revolutions go wrong and that liberty is all too easily perverted by the glib and the greedy. But different times call for different tactics; the modern world's a messy place, and Bradfield's messy narrative reflects that. Orwell had the luxury of right and wrong, Bradfield abandons himself to the sheer anarchy of it all."

REVIEWS: *BL* 10/1/95; *ChiTrib* 12/17/95; *LJ* 9/1/95; *NS&S* 4/26/96; *NYTBR* 10/1/95; *PW* 8/28/95; *TLS* 5/3/96; *WPBW* 1/21/96

Bryers, Paul (UK)

994   *In a Pig's Ear* (1996); FS&G 1996 (HC); **Reference:** *Arthurian legends*

Paul Bryer's 6th comic novel, an ironic, occasionally surreal retelling of the Arthurian legend, is narrated by Milan (aka Merlin) Kubanicek, a Czech psychotherapist, who has emigrated to California. The Camelot-like story has been transposed to Hollywood and Germany in the late 1990s. The Arthur stand-in is the fabulously successful movie director Adam Epstein. Early in the story, Adam and Milan arrive in Germany where Adam is planning to film his own version of Pendragon. As the story progresses, Bryers interjects such elements as Jungian imagery, fairy tales, Nazi archives and film lore.

Entertainment Weekly describes *In a Pig's Ear* as "fiction as magical and absorbing as the original." *Publishers Weekly* calls Bryers novel a "provocative phantasmagoria held together by the darkly funny voice of the worldly-wise Milan" and concludes that "Reveling in broad irony … (the author) tweaks the horrors of the twentieth century.…" According to *Kirkus Reviews* the "liberation of Berlin is relived — and the Nazi menace stirs again — when a powerfully idealistic American filmmaker returns

to his German roots, hoping to make the world a better place.… (*In a Pig's Ear* is) intelligent history mixed into a high complexity of entertainment — and made riveting — by a master hand." The *Times Literary Supplement* notes that "Bubbling with rare charms and full of spell-binding irony, *In a Pig's Ear* foams away like a magic potion — potent, effervescent, intoxicating. Its heady cocktail of legends past and modern grotesques forms (the *TLS* continues) a rapturous tale, rich in symbolism, disturbing in humour, with its essential joke lurking in its title."

REVIEWS: *EW* 11/8/96; *KR* 8/1/96; *LJ* 8/96; *PW* 8/12/96; *TLS* 5/3/96

Carey, Peter (Australia)

995   *Jack Maggs* (1997); Knopf 1998 (HC); Random House 1999 (pbk); **Reference:** *Great Expectations* (Charles Dickens)

Using *Great Expectations* as a springboard, Peter Carey has constructed a fast-paced, intricately plotted tale set in London in 1837 which features Jack Maggs, a prosperous former convict who was transported to — and made his fortune in — the penal colony of New South Wales. Maggs, breaking the terms of his "transportation" (he is still considered a condemned felon in his native England), has returned to London in search of the young Henry Phipps (once a penniless orphan), who has been — for many years — the recipient of Maggs's largesse. The benefactor, Maggs, given his precarious legal status must disguise his identity.

According to *Booklist* Carey's "loving tribute to Dickensian London, circa 1830 … (is filled with) vividly drawn characters (who) are in pursuit of something — wealth, fame, love — and all their obsessions come clattering together in a gripping finale that, in the classic Dickens manner, overlays broad-stroked tragedy and melodrama with a finely nuanced rendering of inner turmoil." Henry Kisor (of the *Chicago Sun-Times*) observes: "It's fun to guess at the correspondences between Carey's story and that of Dickens — and there are many — but they are really not the point of the novel.. In fact you don't have to read *Great Expectations* or be familiar with Dickens at all to enjoy this tale for its own sake. That's because Carey is after bigger game, the moral and psychic darkness of the Victorian Age — the blindness Britain displayed towards the peoples it subverted for its own ends — even so great a writer as Dickens could not perceive." The *Times Literary Supplement* points out that "ever since *The French Lieutenant's Woman* … there has been a fashion for fictional deconstructions of the great Victorian novels. But Carey's fiction is less a piece of post-modernist *Jouissance* than a mesmeric fantasy that aims to capture something of the dark psychological undertones of Dickens's world...." *Jack Maggs*, concludes the *TLS* "seems intended as the literary revenge of characters whose lives are plundered and distorted to provide the raw materials of the novelist's imagination. As such, it has something of the feeling of a conjurer's trick. As a performance, it is a *tour de force*." The *Washington Post Book World* notes that Carey's latest is, among other things, "(a) superb, free-standing work of art, with a storytelling momentum that Dickens himself would envy.... Indeed, no matter how great our expectations may have been, Carey manages to meet or surpass most of them.... His book is an advertisement for the elation, rather than the anxiety, of influence." Richard Eder (*LATBR*) argues that "Carey is doing something different and more interesting in this neo-Victorian novel. He is writing Dickens darker; the Dickens — as the late Irving Howe suggested — who may have held back, out of caution or advice, from following his darkness all the way." Meanwhile, *The* (London) *Sunday Times* concludes that "Somewhere Dickens will be applauding loudly."

RECOGNITION: Winner of *The Age* Book of the Year (fiction) 1997; Commonwealth Writers Prize 1997; Miles Franklin Literary Award 1997; *PW*'s Best '98 Fiction; *LATBR* "Best Fiction of 1998" *NYTBR* Notable Book of 1998; REVIEWS: *BL* 1/1/98; *ChiSun-Times* 2/22/98; *ChiTrib* 3/11/98; *KR* 1/1/98; *LATBR* 2/1/98; *LST* 6/7/98; *LT* 6/21/98; *NYT* 2/12/98; *NYTBR* 2/8/98; *TLS* 9/12/97; *WPBW* 3/15/98

Carson, Anne (Canada)

996   *Autobiography of Red: A Novel in Verse* (1998); Random House 1998 (HC); **Reference**: *Hercules* (Greek Myth)

In her debut novel, Canadian poet and classicist Anne Carson has chosen to update the Greek myth of Geryon (the red, winged monster) and Herakles (aka Hercules); she has also chosen to tell her story in verse. Ms. Carson's modern-day version features Geryon, a young man who, after a suffering the torment of a bullying older brother, has retreated into the fantasy world of photography. He soon becomes infatuated with a beautiful young man by the name of Herakles who, after a brief dalliance, disappears from Geryon's life — only to return, quite by accident and years later, in Buenos Aires.

According to the *New York Times Book Review* Ms. Carson's novel is "a compulsively readable hybrid work by a scholar and poet who reimagines a lost Greek poem into a destructive love affair between Hercules and an American boy who is also (somehow) a winged red monster." Given its format (it is, after all, "A Novel in Verse") more than one reviewer made the happy discovery that *Autobiography of Red* is "surprisingly readable." The Na-

tion called it "a brilliant book about desire, the ancient Greek poet Stesichorus, volcanoes, and the joyful brutalities of seeing and blindness" and concluded that "Anne Carson is a philosopher of heartbreak...." *Booklist* declares that "Narratively, philosophically, humorously, (Ms. Carson has turned in) a dazzling performance."

RECOGNITION: *NYTBR* Notable Book of 1998; REVIEWS: *BL* 4/1/98; *KR* 4/15/98; *LATBR* 5/8/98; *Nation* 6/1/98; *NYTBR* 5/3/98

Collignon, Jeff (USA)

997   *Her Monster: A Novel* (1992); Soho 1993 (pbk); **Reference**: *Beauty and the Beast*

In his debut novel, Jeff Collignon tells the story of Eddie Talbot, a best-selling sci-fi writer, who has spent his life living alone in a mountaintop cabin. He was born so hideously deformed that even his father shunned him. Eddie's mother has continued to care for him by periodically dragging provisions up the mountain path to his cabin door. When she becomes too old and lame to continue, a curious young woman with spiked orange hair takes over the task. At first, Eddie refuses to acknowledge the girl's presence, but eventually they begin to converse, separated, of course, by the cabin door. The pleasure they find in each other's company is short-lived as gun-toting townspeople eventually follow the young woman to the "monster's lair."

According to the *Library Journal* "Collignon has crafted a moving novel out of the trite beauty-and-the-beast theme, never trivializing the characters or their emotions." *Kirkus Reviews* calls *Her Monster* "a darkly modern version of *Beauty and the Beast*" and concludes that "An obviously talented Collignon makes an intriguing debut ... (despite) committing some of the typical first novel sins: awkward pacing, sketchy supporting characters and a self-conscious, too abrupt ending." The *School Library Journal* notes that "Philosophy, opposing values, warring emotions, troubling questions, and a good story all come together in this very readable and compelling book."

REVIEWS: *KR* 2/15/92; *LJ* 4/15/92; *NYTBR* 6/21/92; *PW* 2/17/92; *SLJ* 1/93

Cooke, Elizabeth (USA)

998   *Zeena* (1996); St Martin's 1996 (HC); **Reference**: *Ethan Frome* (Wharton)

Elizabeth Cooke has chosen to tell the story of Zeena, the wife of Ethan Frome so memorably (and unsympathetically) portrayed in Edith Wharton's book of the same name. As Ms. Cooke would have it, Zeena, the poor relation brought in to nurse the dying Mrs. Frome, lost her heart almost immediately to the engaging young Ethan and readily accepted Ethan's proposal of marriage. The bitter realization that Ethan had fallen in love with the carefree Mattie Silver robbed Zeena of all future happiness. When Ethan and Mattie are crippled in their futile suicide attempt, Zeena, with an icebound, but still-broken heart, must spend the rest of her life caring for them.

Kirkus points out that although "this version gains much of its resonance from a knowledge of the original text … . (Ms. Cooke presents a) successful and inventive view of Wharton's character, transcending the shrew of the original." According to the *Library Journal* "Unlike many contemporary takes on literary classics, this book is a rich and satisfying novel in its own right, as well as a fascinating twist on Edith Wharton's grim 1911 standard *Ethan Frome*." The *LA Times Book Review* concurs, pointing out that *Zeena* " is a rare case where the extrapolation from a classic novel … works well. Elizabeth Cooke succeeds in recasting one of literature's most enduring harridans … as an astonishingly sympathetic character in this 'prequel' to the classic … story."

REVIEWS: *KR* 8/15/96; *LATBR* 12/22/96; *LJ* 9/15/96; *PW* 9/2/96

Coover, Robert (USA)

999   *Briar Rose* (1997); Grove-Atlantic 1997 (HC); 1998 (pbk); **Reference:** *The Sleeping Beauty*

Robert Coover's highly irreverent retelling of the Sleeping Beauty fable incorporates a handsome young prince hacking his way through a forest of brambles (with mutilated bodies of earlier seekers strewn about him); a beautiful young woman who cannot be woken (but who dreams of princes who come to assault her); and a fairy who inhabits the young woman's dreams (and tells her endless stories of other sleeping beauties). This being Robert Coover, what is being examined, however obliquely, is the nature of human desire.

Kirkus Reviews observes that *Briar Rose* is a "tour-de-force that rings an astonishing series of changes on the familiar fairy tale of Sleeping Beauty" and concludes that "There's no doubt that Coover can do almost anything he wants. But his reluctance to finally settle for any culminating metaphor makes this unique work seem more of a collection of masterful, cerebral turns than a living, persuasive tale." According to the *New York Times Book Review* "*Briar Rose* represents a very complex novelist's intricate variations (on a fairy tale) treated with a kind of irreverent logic as sex and storytelling are seen as metaphors for each other."

RECOGNITION: *NYTBR* Notable Book of 1997; REVIEWS: *ChiTrib* 2/9/97; *KR* 12/15/96; *LATBR* 4/13/97; *LJ* 1/97; *NYTBR* 2/16/97; *PW* 11/25/96

1000   *Pinocchio in Venice;* Grove-Atlantic 1997 (pbk); **Reference:** *Pinocchio*

At the start of the Robert Coover's 9th work of fiction, Pinocchio (aka Dr. Pinenut) is now a very old man. Having made a successful career for himself as a philosopher and art historian (he has won two Nobel Prizes) he has returned to Venice, city of his "birth." It is here that he plans to complete (in final tribute to the Blue-haired Fairy) his *magnum opus*, called simply, *Mama*. Shortly after his arrival, however, Pinenut falls in with a alarming cast of characters and appears destined to re-enact the experiences of his youth.

Richard Eder *(LATBR)* notes that "In (Coover's post-structuralist) *Pinocchio in Venice* Collodi's boy/puppet has become an elderly art-critic/puppet … (and undergoes) a series of (extremely raunchy) misadventures … told in a learnedly witty logorrhea that knocks them askew" and concludes "it is 'Pinocchio' and it is utterly different." The *Times Literary Supplement* observes that, in celebration of "the centenary of the death of *Pinocchio*'s author, Carlos Lorenzini …. (Coover) has produced a hilariously phallic riposte, a carnivalesque reprise all about the agonies and delights of turning back to wood." Novelist **Salman Rushdie** *(The* London *Independent)* observes that Coover "goes at his task with an almost alarming linguistic energy, a Burgessy splatter of vocabulary, and a ferocious love of everything comic and grotesque" and concludes that *Pinocchio in Venice* "is a spectacularly scatological work…. Often erotic and frequently hilarious."

RECOGNITION: *NYTBR* Notable Book of 1991; REVIEWS: *AtlM* 2/91; *ChiTrib* 1/27/91; *Indepen* 4/28/91; LATBR 1/27/91; *LJ* 1/91; *NYTBR* 1/27/91; *TLS* 5/3/91

Cunningham, John (USA)

1001   *The Hours* (1998); FS&G 1998 (HC); **Reference:** *Mrs. Dalloway* (Virginia Woolf)

Borrowing the working title of Virginia Woolf's groundbreaking 1925 novel *Mrs. Dalloway* as well as the simple literary device found therein, Michael Cunningham has created a luminous and deeply affecting work of contemporary fiction. *The Hours*— comprised of a trio of interlocking novellas — features three women drawn from different time periods: Laura Brown an unhappily married woman living in California in 1949, Clarissa Vaughan, a young New Yorker in the 1990s who is preoccupied with the suffering (and eventual suicide) of her lover who is dying of AIDS, and Virginia Woolf, herself, as she begins work on *Mrs. Dalloway*.

In the view of Richard Eder (*L.A. Times Book Review*) John Cunningham "has fashioned a fictional instrument of intricacy and remarkable beauty. It is a kaleidoscope whose four shining and utterly unlike pieces — the lives of two fictional characters, of a real writer, and her novel — combine, separate and tumble in continually shifting and startlingly suggestive patterns." *Publishers Weekly*, in its starred review, observes that Cunningham's book "makes a reader hunger to know all about Woolf, again ... and (and this is the gargantuan accomplishment of this small book), it makes a reader believe in the possibility and depth of a communality based on great literature...." According to *Booklist* Cunningham has "reaffirmed that Woolf is of lasting significance, that the questions she asked about life remain urgent, and that, in spite of sorrow, pain and the promise of death, the simplest gestures — walking out the door on a lovely morning, setting a vase of roses on the table — can be, for one shining moment, enough." The *Washington Post Book World* declares that "Cunningham's emulation of such a revered writer as Woolf is courageous, and this is his most mature and masterful work."

RECOGNITION: *L.A. Times Book Review* "TopTen Books of 1998"; nominated for the 1998 National Book Critics Circle Award; *NYTBR* Notable Book of 1998; REVIEWS: *BL* 9/25/98; *ChiTrib* 11/15/98; *KR* 9/1/98; *LJ* 10/1/98; *LATBR* 11/15/98; *PW* 8/31/98; *WPBW* 11/22/98

Dawson, Carol (USA)

1002 *Meeting the Minotaur* (1997); Algonquin 1997 (HC); **Reference**: *Theseus and the Minotaur*

In her highly inventive re-telling of the myth of Theseus and the Minotaur, Carol Dawson sends Taylor Deeds, an engaging yet nebbishy young man of uncertain parentage, to do battle with illegal aliens, drug smugglers, the Mexican Mafia and assorted white collar criminals. The settings range from the jungles of the Yucatan to the Mexican/American border; from high-rise, high-rent Dallas to the maze-like back-streets of old Tokyo where a modern "demon" awaits.

According to *Booklist*, "If Hollywood can transport Romeo & Juliet to Miami's streets, why not bring Theseus to the seamy hinterlands of south Texas and the Minotaur to modern-day Tokyo?" *Kirkus* observes that Ms. Dawson, using her "ferocious wit" spins a "sprawling narrative that holds in a brilliant balance its winning young hero's comic insouciance and moral backbone" and concludes that given Dawson's "three terrific novels in five years.... It's time to put Dawson's name on the Contemporary Am Lit reading list."

REVIEWS: *BL* 7/19/97; *KR* 5/15/97; *LJ* 6/1/97; *PW* 5/12/97

Delbanco, Nicholas (USA)

Old Scores (1997); Warner 1997 (HC); **Reference**: *Heloise & Abelard* See Section 1, #23

Disch, Thomas M (USA)

The Priest (1995); Knopf 1995 (HC); **Reference**: *The Monk* (Matthew Lewis) See Section 6, #839

Doctorow, E.L. (USA)

1003 *Ragtime* (1975); NAL_Dutton 1997 (pbk re-issue); **Reference**: *Michael Kohlhaas* (Heinrich von Kleist)

Three families — representative of three distinct socio-cultural milieus (WASPs, black Harlem-dwellers, and recently-immigrated Jews) — are featured in E.L. Doctorow's much-admired 1975 novel *Ragtime*. The story begins in New Rochelle, N.Y., in 1906 and in it, Doctorow expertly captures the spirit and tone of its subject: a nation of limitless aspirations and seductive opportunities.

According to the *Washington Post Book World*, "E.L. Doctorow's best-seller is an act of homage, a reworking of Heinrich von Kleist's novella 'Michael Kohlhaas.' Instead of the rebellious German peasants and their warrior-leader Kohlhaas, Doctorow gives us a fictitious black man named Coalhouse Walker and a band of colleagues who react violently to extreme provocation by white bigots." As the *National Review* points out "Almost magically, Doctorow creates the atmosphere of WW I America and even if that were his only triumph — it is not — this novel would still be something to treasure." The *New York Times Book Review* observes that "*Ragtime* "incorporates the fictional realities of the era of ragtime while it rags our fiction about it. It is an anti-nostalgic novel that incorporates our nostalgia about its subject. It is cool, hard, controlled, utterly unsentimental, an art of sharp outlines and clipped phrases" and concludes that it "implies all we could ask for in the way of texture, mood, character and despair." The *Saturday Review* concludes that *Ragtime* is "a unique and beautiful work about American destiny...."

OTHER MEDIA: Audio cassette recording (Airplay/unabr): a film version of *Ragtime* was released in 1981 starring James Cagney and Elizabeth McGovern; Doctorow's novel is also the basis for the Broadway musical of the same name; REVIEWS: *AtlM* 8/75; *LJ* 7/75; *NatR* 8/15/75; *NY* 7/28/75; *NYRB* 8/7/75; *NYTBR* 7/6/75; *SatR* 7/26/75; *Time* 7/14/75; *WPBW* 10/20/91 (pbk review)

Dooling, Richard (USA)

White Man's Grave (1994); See Section 7, #1052; St. Martin's 1995 (pbk); **Reference**: *Heart of Darkness* (Conrad)

Dworkin, Susan (USA)

1004 *The Book of Candy* (1997); St Martin's 1997 (HC); **Reference:** *Old Testament* (Book of Esther)

Called a "sweet retelling of the Book of Esther" by *Entertainment Weekly*, and a "fast-paced novel of Jewish manners" by *Kirkus Reviews*, *The Book of Candy* features Candy Shapiro, a short, plump, thirty-something Long Island Jewish housewife, mother of two, and the president of her Hadassah chapter. She is also the wife of a philandering gynecologist. Propelled by the discovery of her husband's long-standing infidelities, Candy strikes out in a heretofore unforeseen direction: the gambling tables of an Atlantic City casino — owned by her father's old friend, the mobster Orpheo Pastafino — and eventually into a series of business ventures. Secondary characters include Heimlich, a Rabbi-turned-stand-up-comic, Alisette, a black rock musician and Maida Deal, Candy's mother.

According to the *Washington Post Book World* "With a seamless blend of humor and sadness, Susan Dworkin documents the transformation of Candy from hapless Jewish American princess living on Long Island to a resilient, tough-minded heroine." As the *Providence Sunday Journal* (book jacket) points out "A book that stuffs Mafiosi, white supremacists, Biblical prophecy, suicide, infanticide, gunrunners, AIDS and Haitian voodoo into the plot's thin envelope about a pampered Jewish housewife who discovers her worth shouldn't work this well." In the view of the *Library Journal* "Dworkin explores the debilitating effects of sexist and racist hate and stereotyping, perseverance in the face of such hate, and the ability of those divided by seemingly insurmountable differences to form the closest possible bonds. The result, both funny and tragic, demands rereading."

REVIEWS: *EW* 10/25/96; *KR* 8/1/96; *LJ* 9/15/96; *PW* 9/2/96; *WPBW* 1/19/97

Everett, Percival (USA)

1005 *Frenzy* (1997); Graywolf 1997 (pbk); **Reference:** *Dionysus* (Greek Myth)

Percival Everett, in his 11th novel, revisits the myth of Dionysus (also known as Bacchus), the ancient Greek god of pleasure (particularly as mediated through wine and eroticism). It is narrated by Vlepo who has been charged with observing and experiencing "all" on his ever-more curious master's behalf.

According to novelist **George Garrett** (*WPBW*) "One of the best and most original of our younger American novelists is Percival Everett ... and *Frenzy*, (an altogether indescribable accounting of the story of Dionysus and his 'mortal bookmark'

and buddy Vlepo), is like no other I know of." In the view of *Publishers Weekly* Everett, "brings his sharp eye for the mutability of identity, the clash of myth and culture, and an offbeat humor, to this iconoclastic study in Greek mythology." *Booklist* observes that Everett's "strange lyric tale of fate and hubris set in ancient Greece ... (is very) different from (his) last offering ... but no less engrossing."

REVIEWS: *BL* 1/97; *KR* 11/1/96; *LJ* 1/97; *PW* 11/18/96; *WPBW* 12/7/97

Epstein, Leslie (USA)

Pandaemonium (1997); See Section 5, #655; St Martin's 1997 (HC); **Reference:** *Paradise Lost* (Milton)

Fitzgerald, Penelope (UK)

Gate of Angels (1990); See Section 5, #659; HM 1998 (pbk); **Reference:** *classic ghost stories* (M.R. James)

Habens, Alison (UK)

1006 *Dreamhouse* (1995); Picador 1996 (HC); **Reference:** *Alice in Wonderland* (Carroll)

Prissy Celia Small has been planning her wedding since she was eight years old. When her boring banker boyfriend finally pops the question, it matters little to Celia that she doesn't actually love him. All Celia can think about is finally leaving her group house and her hateful housemates. The night of Celia's engagement party arrives and all is going exactly to plan, until that is, two of her housemates decide to throw their own parties and things begin to go seriously awry. Housemate Phoebe is hosting a last-minute surprise party for her lesbian sister, Hebe, a militant feminist filmmaker, while housemate Cath is giving a fancy-dress party where everyone must come dressed as a character from *Alice in Wonderland* and where the refreshments run to cheap beer and hallucinogenic tarts. As fate would have it, Celia manages to ingest one of Cath's tarts and embarks on a strange journey through the competing parties.

In the view of The (London) *Times*, Habens debut novel is "A truly astonishing feat of the imagination, supported by a dazzling display of wit and wordplay." The *New York Times Book Review* while noting that "Lewis Carroll's classic tale is self-parodic, merrily riffing on its own riffs' argues that, in *Dreamhouse* "Alison Habens takes on the challenge of out-wondering Wonderland. This English writer's ribald update is decidedly for grown-ups, with booze, drugs, (attempted) rape and murder thrown in for comic mayhem." According to *Entertainment Weekly* "Cleverly fusing strands from Alice in Wonderland with a psychedelic English rave, Habens' marvelous first novel crackles with wit, wordplay, and subversive underlying truths that would make Lewis Carroll proud."

REVIEWS: *EW* 3/22/96; *KR* 1/15/96; *LT* 7/28/94; *NYTBR* 4/21/96; *PW* 1/8/96; *TLS* 6/24/94

Haire-Sargeant, Lin (USA)

1007 *Heathcliff: The Return to Wuthering Heights* (1992); Pocket Books 1993 (pbk); **Reference:** *Wuthering Heights* (Bronte)

In her debut novel, Lin Haire-Sargeant, a professor of 19th-century literature at the University of Massachusetts, drawing upon her obvious fascination with *Wuthering Heights*, weaves a story around Heathcliff's missing three years. As reader's of the Bronte classic will remember, headstrong, uncouth Heathcliff fled Wuthering Heights only to return three years later as a successful gentleman. Haire-Sargeant introduces elements from *Jane Eyre*, and *Pygmalion* and even inserts Charlotte and Emily Bronte into her narrative.

Publishers Weekly, in its starred review, observes that "Embroidering the classics is a venerable literary tradition that sometimes goes awry. Here, however, Haire-Sargeant ... conjures the dark, brooding air of *Wuthering Heights* with striking authenticity." According to *Booklist*, "Haire-Sargeant has come up with a genuinely good story that offers a tantalizing mix of fact and fancy. The book begins with Charlotte Bronte returning from Brussels by train, on which she meets Mr. Lockwood, whose visit to Wuthering Heights provides the frame story for sister Emily's novel...."

Poet and writing teacher Kathy S. Coen (*WPBW*) declares that Haire-Sargeant's *Heathcliff* "cleverly explores previously unsuspected crevices and opens all the doors that seemed eternally bolted. Not only does she reinvigorate our favorite characters, but their authors join in as well." The *Chicago Tribune* while noting that "University of Massachusetts professor Lin Haire-Sargeant will ... take some critical heat for daring to tinker with Emily Bronte's" classic, doubts that " Bronte is spinning in her grave over it" and concludes that "No thoughtful reader can come away from (the author's spin-off) without concluding that Haire-Sargeant's project is all about her love of the work."

OTHER MEDIA: Audio Cassette recording (S&S Audio/abr); REVIEWS: *BL* 4/1/92; *ChiTrib* 8/3/92; *KR* 4/15/92; *LATBR* 7/16/92; *NYTBR* 7/19/92; *PW* 5/18/92; *WPBW* 7/19/92; EDITOR'S NOTE: Haire-Sargeant's novel was originally published in 1992 under the title *H: The Story of Heathcliff's Journey Back to Wuthering Heights*

Harrington, Donald (USA)

1008 *Ekaterina* (1993); Harcourt Brace 1993 (HC); 1994 (pbk); **Reference:** *Lolita* (Nabokov)

In *Ekaterina*, Donald Harrington tells the decidedly offbeat story of a beautiful Russian émigrée by the name of Ekaterina (aka V. Kilian) who has come to the United States to teach mycology (the study of mushrooms) at the Cathedral of Learning. Ekaterina, who has a definite weakness for adolescent boys, moves into Hamilton Hall, a faculty house peopled with eccentric academics, ghosts, inebriates, and the 12-year-old son of the retired professor who owns the establishment. When her first novel hits the best-seller list — thanks in no small measure to a gushing review in the *New York Review of Books*— Ekaterina succumbs to self-indulgence.

Kirkus Reviews calls *Ekaterina* "Grand entertainment from an author who's been too little known for too long: perhaps this zany homage to Nabokov (especially *Lolita*) will bring deserved attention to Harrington's impressive body of work." According to *Publishers Weekly*, "*Ekaterina* is an acknowledged homage to Nabokov, particularly to *Lolita*, and if it misses some of the Russian master's literary playfulness, it has many charms of its own...." In the view of novelist **D.M. Thomas** (*LATBR*) *Ekaterina* is "Superbly crafted, foxy, engaging, funny, joyous."

REVIEWS: *KR* 3/1/93; *LATBR* 7/18/93; *PW* 2/22/93; *WPBW* 6/9/93

Hatvary, George Egon (USA)

1009 *The Murder of Edgar Allan Poe* (1997); Carroll & Graf 1997 (HC); **Reference:** Edgar Allan Poe

When Edgar Allan Poe dies under suspicious circumstances, his attending physician alerts the French detective Auguste Dupin (Poe's fictional character who appears in both *The Murders in the Red Morgue* and *The Purloined Letter*) who immediately sets off for America determined to investigate his creator's death. Arriving in Baltimore, Dupre gets quickly to work (unofficially) exhuming Poe's body, conducting a highly revealing post mortem, and falling in love with Poe's fiancé.

In the view of *Booklist* Hatvary's "plot is an intriguing one, containing enough of the truth to satisfy history buffs while offering mystery and an entertaining and suspense-filled detective story." "According to the *Washington Post Book World* Hatvary "has done his homework. As the story races from Baltimore to Richmond to New York and back, he gives telling descriptions of the Astor Place Theater riot, the look of a 19th-century drawing room, the sounds of a 19th-century soiree. The streets of Baltimore particularly are drawn with painstaking accuracy; and he captures the feel of the New York street scene in a manner worthy of Jack

Finney's wonderful riff on history, *Time and Again*. *Publishers Weekly* notes that "The horror of Dupin's rat-infested imprisonment is as vivid as any torment created by Poe.... Hatvary does a fair imitation, too, of Poe's emotional and melodramatic style." *Kirkus Reviews*, however, contends that while "Hatvary does yeoman work tracing the literary and amatory tangle of Poe's last years ... except for despicable Griswold, none of his suspects comes to life on the page. But Edgarphiles may not be able to resist the conceit of his murder being avenged by his most famous fictional creation."

REVIEWS: *BL* 3/15/97; *KR* 1/1/97; *PW* 1/20/97; *WPBW* 2/16/97

Hill, Susan (UK)

1010 *Mrs. de Winter* (1993); Avon 1994 (pbk); **Reference:** *Rebecca* (Daphne du Maurier)

Mrs. de Winter, billed as a "completion" to Daphne du Maurier's classic novel of romantic suspense, begins ten years after the tragic fire which destroyed Manderly. Max de Winter and his second-wife (the heroine of *Rebecca* and our narrator) have come to Cornwall to attend the funeral of Max's sister Bernice. Finding a mysterious wreath at Bernice's graveside with a card marked simply "R" the couple realizes that they may not — even yet — have escaped Rebecca's reach. Whitbread Prize-winning author Susan Hill reintroduces a number of familiar characters including the vengeful Mrs. Danvers and Jack Favell who appears to have blackmail in mind.

According to the *Library Journal*, "In a voice true to the original story, Hill's *Mrs. de Winter* chronicles Rebecca's continuing shadow on their life...." The *Christian Science Monitor* observes that Ms. Hill "deftly captures the keynotes of du Maurier's style and the intense self-conscious, impressionable sensibility of the original narrator-heroine" and concludes that, on balance, this sequel is "accomplished and skillfully written."

OTHER MEDIA: Audio cassette recording (Books-on-Tape/unabr); REVIEWS: *CSM* 11/12/94; *LJ* 10/15/93; *NS&S* 11/26/93; *NYTBR* 11/7/93; *TLS* 10/15/93

Hoffman, Alice (USA)

1011 *Here on Earth* (1997); Putnam 1997 (HC); Berkley 1998 (pbk); **Reference:** *Wuthering Heights* (Brontë)

March Murray grew up in a small town in Massachusetts but now lives in California with her salt-of-the-earth husband, Richard, and her teenage daughter, Gwen. The three have returned to New England for the funeral of Judith Dale, the long-time Murray family housekeeper, who raised March and her older brother Alan. Also in attendance is Hollis, a wealthy, darkly handsome middle-aged man with an unsavory past. Hollis (once an abandoned child living on the streets of Boston) had also been raised by Ms. Dale, after being brought into their home by March's kind-hearted father. Alan disliked Hollis from the first, but March was delighted to have a playmate her age, and, inseparable as children, they eventually became lovers. When a tragic misunderstanding leads to Hollis's departure from the Murray household, March waits for him to return. But after hearing nothing for three years, she marries Richard, the boy-next-door, and moves to California. Seeing Hollis for the first time in almost twenty years, March is shocked by the knee-buckling intensity of her response and by what she is prepared to do in the name of rekindled passion.

The *Library Journal* observes that "Hoffman takes great care here to examine the many facets of love and relationships, turning them like a prism to reflect on March and Hollis" and concludes that *Here On Earth* "is a haunting tale of a woman lost in and to love." The *Times Literary Supplement*, which calls *Here on Earth* "a surprisingly successful recasting of *Wuthering Heights*, observes that "Hoffman is known for introducing flourishes of 'Yankee magic realism' into her fiction. In *Here on Earth* the magic is slight but undeniable, as delicately forceful as snow flurries. As March lingers in town and resumes her affair with Hollis, the weather turns predictably cold. *The wind wraps itself around bare trees and twists in between husbands and wives asleep in their beds. It shakes the shingles from the roofs and sifts through cracks in the plaster.* On such a night as this, Alice Hoffman's storytelling is like a hot fire being teased by an insistent, icy draught." According to novelist **Howard Frank Mosher** (*Washington Post Book World*) "Parts of *Here on Earth* are as bleakly tragic as anything you'll find in *Wuthering Heights*.... Yet Hoffman is no fatalist or doomsday crier.... She knows that here on earth, love can sometimes emerge from hatred, hope from despair, particularly for the young." Mr. Mosher concludes that "*Here on Earth* is Alice Hoffman's most powerful and moving novel to date, and one of the finest fictional explorations of family love, and all those forces that threaten to undermine it, that I've read in many years."

OTHER MEDIA: Audi cassette recording (Brilliance/abr; Bookcassette/unabr); REVIEWS: *BL* 7/97; *EW* 10/10/97; *LJ* 7/97; *NYTBR* 9/14/97; *PW* 6/16/97; *Salon* 9/9/97; *TLS* 10/10/97; *WPBW* 8/31/97

Hollinghurst, Alan (UK)

1012 *The Folding Star* (1993); Vintage 1995 (pbk); **Reference:** *Lolita* (Nabokov)

In his second novel (following the widely

praised *The Swimming-Pool Library*) Alan Holling-hurst tells another tale of homoerotic infatuation and desire. His protagonist, Edward Manners, a 33-year-old Englishman and would-be writer (seeking a "Continental experience") has come to Belgium to work as a private English tutor. In due course he takes an immigrant Moroccan as his lover, becomes romantically obsessed with one of his pupils (the 17-year-old, blonde and beautiful Luc Altidore in whose presence he can hardly catch his breath) and — while working on a catalogue for a local museum — becomes caught up in the life of an enigmatic pre-war artist by the name of Edgar Orst, a Symbolist painter who died under myste-rious circumstances during the Nazi occupation of Belgium. When Luc disappears the mood of the novel deepens and darkens.

The *Washington Post Book World* notes that *The Folding Star* "has been called a gay *Lolita*" and concludes that Hollinghurst, an editor at the *Times Literary Supplement*, writes such tesselated prose that the comparison is not to be scoffed at." Ac-cording to *Publishers Weekly* "At first events are pre-sented as clues, and Manners pursues his preoccu-pation with Luc as if unraveling a mystery…. The title, taken from Milton, refers to the first evening star; like that bright herald of night, this extraor-dinary, often darkly funny novel captures our at-tention." *The (London) SundayTimes* concludes that "The contrast between the operation of Ed-ward's lucid, fastidious mind and the urgings of his importunate lust is a hilarious irony that runs under the whole book and gives it the atmosphere of 19th-century decadence and 20th-century earthiness."

RECOGNITION: Shortlisted for the 1993 Booker Prize; nominated for the 1995 Lambda Book Award for Gay Men's Fiction; REVIEWS: *Aust-BkRev* 7/94; *KR* 7/1/94; *LJ* 10/1/94; *LRB* 6/9/94; *LST* 4/2/95; *NS&S* 6/10/94; *Obs* 5/22/94; *Spec* 5/28/94; *TLS* 5/27/94; *WPBW* 12/31/95; EDITOR'S NOTE: Mr. Hollinghurst was named by *Granta Magazine* to its 1993 list of the twenty "Best Young British Novelists"

Judd, Alan (UK)

1013   *The Devil's Own Work* (1991); Vin-tage 1995 (pbk); **Reference:** *Faust* (Marlowe)

In *The Devil's Own Work*, Alan Judd's a vari-ation on the theme of "Faust," an unnamed narra-tor recounts the rise to literary stardom of his friend, the blond-haired, blue-eyed Edward, confidante and biographer of O.M. Tyrell the reigning grand old man of English letters. Upon Tyrell's death, Edward inherits a mysterious, an-cient manuscript. Although the quality of Edward's output steadily deteriorates, his literary star con-tinues to rise leading some of his acquaintances to speculate that Edward's startling success (and his

increasingly compulsive eroticism) might have a sinister origin.

According to *Publisher's Weekly* "British nov-elist Judd's short, ambivalent fable on the hazards of creativity and fame is distinguished by a style as psychologically nuanced as that of Henry James." Merle Rubin (*WSJ*), concludes that "the secret of Mr. Judd's success … is instantly apparent; not a page longer than it needs to be, this tightly written story eloquently suggests more than it explains."

RECOGNITION: Winner of the *Guardian* Fic-tion Prize; REVIEWS: *BL* 6/1/94; *LJ* 7/94; *NYT* 6/17/94; *NYTBR* 7/31/94; *PW* 5/16/94; *TLS* 7/91; *WSJ* 8/30/94; EDITOR'S NOTE: Mr. Judd was named by *Granta Magazine* to its 1993 list of the twenty "Best Young British Novelists"

Kalpakian, Laura (USA)

1014   *Cossette: Sequel to Les Miserables* (1995); HarperCollins 1995 (HC); 1996 (pbk); **Ref-erence:** *Les Miserables* (Victor Hugo)

Laura Kalpakian was commissioned to write this sequel to Les Miserables in the aftermath of the phenomenal success of it's stage-adaptation. She appears to have acquitted herself reasonably well. Set in 1832, *Cossette* is both a retelling of the last part of Victor Hugo's classic novel and them some. As the story begins, Jean Valjean's adopted daugh-ter Cossette (now 17-years-old) has fallen in love with Maurius Pontmercy, an impoverished student and revolutionary firebrand. The story then jumps forward some 15 years: Maurius is now the much-persecuted editor of *La Lumiere*, a radical newspa-per, Cossette is his staunchest ally and the Revolu-tion of 1848 looms large.

According to the *Library Journal* "Kalpakian has written a splendid, colorful, and engrossing novel sure to amuse admirers of Hugo's master-piece." The *New York Times Book Review* calls *Cos-sette* "a tale of love and betrayal, power and op-pression, passion and illusion" and points out that even though most members of her "cast of thou-sands" belong to Victor Hugo, the author "manages to add some lively new characters of her own."

REVIEWS: *BL* 5/15/95; *EW* 7/28/95; *LJ* 7/95; *NYTBR* 7/16/95; *PW* 6/19/95

Kaplan, James (USA)

1015   *Two Guys from Verona* (1998); At-lantic Monthly 1998 (HC); **Reference:** *Two Gen-tlemen from Verona* (Shakespeare)

Set in Verona (the upscale epicenter of subur-ban New Jersey), James Kaplan's second novel fea-tures a pair of former high-school buddies whose lives have progressed along very different lines. Will, an emotionally rudderless, upwardly mobile businessman with a failing second-marriage, and

Joel, a "schizo" genius who still lives with his mother and works in the local sub-shop, experience, in the wake of their 25th high-school reunion, a series of life-altering events. As *Booklist* points out "Will expects to get richer and happier, Joel expects nothing, and both are due for some radical change."

According to *Kirkus Reviews Two Guys from Verona* is "Nervy, packed with stinging riffs on consumer rituals and passions: fiction that dares to hold up a mirror to our laughable, worrisome souls." Novelist **Tom Perrotta** (*NYTBR*) calls it "a complex and often moving meditation on the passage of time and the stubborn human urge to resist its merciless forward tug." *Booklist* concludes that "Kaplan's marvelously subtle and understated style — reminiscent of Updike, Salinger, Michael Chabon, and Ethan Canin — is the perfect vehicle for the suspense that charges this witty, sexy, and wise comedy of errors and corrections."

RECOGNITION: *NYTBR* Notable Book of 1998; REVIEWS: *BL* 11/15/97; *ChiTrib* 4/5/98; *KR* 11/1/97; *LATBR* 3/8/98; *LJ* 11/15/97; *NYTBR* 2/28/98; *PW* 10/27/97; *Time* 2/9/98

Lethem, Jonathan (USA)

As She Climbed Across the Table (1997); See under *Humor* #1089; Doubleday 1997 (HC); **Reference:** *Alice in Wonderland* (Carroll)

Martin, Valerie (USA)

1016 *Mary Reilly* (1990); PB 1995 (pbk); **References**: *Dr. Jekyll & Mr. Hyde* (Robert Louis Stevenson)

Valerie Martin's retelling of Robert Louis Stevenson's gothic chiller, *Dr. Jekyll and Mr. Hyde*, from the point of view of Mary Reilly, the devoted young housekeeper who becomes increasingly concerned that all is not right with her employer — the hard-working, increasingly distracted scientist, Henry Jekyll. She is particularly wary of Dr. Jekyll's new assistant the off-puting Mr. Hyde. Narrated in a series of journal entries, the tension is admirably heightened by a growing sense of Mary's own tormented past and continuing vulnerability.

In the view of the *Library Journal*, *Mary Reilly* "deserves praise for suspense, character creation, and historical verisimilitude.... Most compelling is a forceful consciousness about the dual propensity of human nature and the awesome power which is ours." According to the *L.A.Times Book Review* "The first thing that must be said about *Mary Reilly* ... is that it's a brilliant piece of work, a whopping good story so perfectly realized that it stands out for its honesty and beauty...." The *LATBR* concludes that the novel "deserves to become a companion of its inspiration. In fact the works fit together like

two hands whose fingers are intertwined. Part of the amazing skill of Valerie Martin is how she takes details from Stevenson's story and recasts them on the page. She fills in the blanks; she tells you the 'other' side." According to *Time* "Valerie Martin's grafting of a new novel onto Robert Louis Stevenson's (classic novel) is cleverly done. But the best part of this engaging novel is the diarist herself. Spunky, passionate, with the grinding limitations imposed by her station in life, Mary observes her employer's deterioration with a mixture of bafflement and good common sense."

OTHER MEDIA: Film version starring Julia Roberts and John Malkovich was released in 1995; REVIEWS: *ChiTrib* 2/4/90; *Econ* 12/8/90; *LATBR* 1/21/90; *LJ* 1/90; *NYTBR* 2/4/90; *PW* 12/8/89; *Time* 2/19/90; *TLS* 6/1/90; *WPBW* 1/17/90

Mathews, Harry (USA)

1017 *The Journalist* (1993); Godine 1993 (HC); Dalkey Archive 1997 (pbk); **Reference:** *Degres* (Michel Butor)

In poet and novelist Harry Mathew's *The Journalist* an unnamed resident of a college town in an undisclosed European country has been diagnosed with an ill-defined depressive condition. As a form of therapy, and as a way or re-attaching to the concrete world, the man is encouraged to keep a daily journal to record the quotidian aspects of his existence: the cost of a book, the number of pills taken each day, etc. This task, at the outset, has the desired result. The man begins to take notice of, and then an interest in, the everyday aspects of his life. However, before long, an obsessive element begins to creep into this activity and the journal begins to assume a life of its own.

According to the *New York Times Book Review*, "The complications offered up by Mr. Mathews are both daunting and funny, in a kind of psychoslapstick way.... The journal divides and replicates like a virus gone wild, until it has taken control of plot, narrative and characterization ... everything." *Kirkus Review* observes that Mathews "chronicles his diarist's dilemma with humor and gentle irony; his slide into the abyss occasions more bemusement than terror." The *Library Journal* points out that *The Journalist* (more focused and accessible than Mathews earlier works) "is essentially a reworking of Michel Butor's classic (1960) nouveau roman, *Degres*.

REVIEWS: *AtlM* 10/94; *KR* 7/1/94; *LJ* 8/94; *NY* 12/5/94; *NYTBR* 3/26/95; *PW* 8/8//94; *TLS* 3/20/98

Morley, John David (UK/USA)

1018 *Feast of Fools* (1994); St Martin's 1995 (HC); **Reference:** *Persephone* (Greek Myth)

An updating of the myth of the Greek myth Persephone, *Feast of Fools* is set in contemporary Munich and features two sisters Stephanie and Martha. The beautiful Stephanie has abandoned her husband and moved in with Max a wealthy undertaker. Martha, remains faithfully married but is pregnant and doesn't know who the father is. Morley uses the German festivals of Oktoberfest and the pre-Lenten carnival — the Feast of Fools — to frame his story.

According to the *Times Literary Supplement* "A novel which begins with a contents page, a map, a list of 'players' and a detailed calendar, complete with extensive zodiacal details, is unlikely to be easy to read, and John David Morley's *The Feast of Fools* is no exception. (However) If you skip these accouterments to launch into the more immediate pleasures of the plot you will soon regret it. The book offers certain rewards, but clarity is not among them." *World Literature Today*, after listing the section headings (e.g. "Persephone," "The King of the Rain Country" etc). asks "Oversymbolic?" and replies, "Perhaps. But also immensely intelligent, funny, learned, resourceful, satiric, affective, grotesque — yes, Pynchonesque." In the view of the *L.A. Times Book Review* "*The Feast of Fools* is a carnival of images and styles ... from the woolgathering of a Leopold Bloom canvassing through Dublin, to the complex disjunctions of a Thomas Pynchon or William Gaddis...."

RECOGNITION: Winner of the City of Munich Literary Prize; REVIEWS: *KR* 11/1/94; *LATBR* 3/27/94; *LJ* 12/94; *NYTBR* 1/22/95; *PW* 11/21/94; *TLS* 6/24/94; *WLT* Sum'95

Morrow, James (USA)

Blameless in Abaddon (1996); See under *Humor* #1103; Harcourt Brace 1996 (HC); 1997 (pbk); **Reference**: *Book of Job* (Old testament)

Murdoch, Iris (UK)

1019   *The Green Knight* (1993); Viking 1994 (pbk); **Reference**: Cain & Abel; Sir Gawain and the Green Knight

In her 25th novel, Iris Murdoch evokes the story of Cain and Abel — with a large dollop of medieval romance thrown in — in her tale of two brothers living in contemporary London. Lucas, a sourly introverted — yet renowned — academic, hates his stepbrother Clement — a charismatic actor — for being the more-favored "natural" son. Lucas, it transpires, had been adopted at birth. One dark and rainy night, in a secluded part of the city, Lucas, in a murderous rage, attempts to kill his brother. Clement's life is saved by the intervention of a mysterious stranger, Peter Mir, who deflects the blow meant for Clement. Mir is left for dead and

a trial ensues. This event, and its surprising sequelae, will impact a group of friends, bound by ties of blood and friendship, who strut their stuff across Murdoch's allegorical stage.

According to the *New Statesman and Society* *The Green Knight* "is a metaphysical mystery, a multi-layered investigation into the nature of faith, the relationship between magic and religion and, above all, the aching, desperate need to believe in a personal God." As English novelist **Patrick McGrath** *(WPBW)* points out, this "is a long novel of ideas in which a slender spine of a plot involving three male characters creates a force field into which an entire small community of friends is drawn...." McGrath concludes that Ms. Murdoch's novel is "a big, rich book (she is 'much too clever a writer ever to weary the reader') full of life, but in the end it fails to unite its diffuse motifs into a single radiant pattern, and settles instead for sentimentality." English novelist A.N. Wilson, writing in *The Spectator*, suggests that "What an outline of the plot ... fails to convey is the warmth and humor of this book, and the sheer narrative verve...." *Kirkus Reviews* concludes that *The Green Knight* is "As to be expected from Murdoch: a bracing journey through ancient mysteries and the dark pathways of the heart. And is, as always, a stimulating read."

REVIEWS: *Guard* 9/26/93; *KR* 10/15/93; *LATBR* 2/20/94; *LRB* 11/4/93; *NS&S* 9/17/93; *NYT* 12/31/93; *NYTBR* 1/9/94; *PW* 11/1/93; *Spec* 9/18/93; *WPBW* 1/9/94

Newman, Kim (UK)

1020   *The Quorum* (1994); Carroll & Graf 1995 (pbk); **Reference**: *Faust* (Goethe or Marlowe)

The Quorum, yet another "take" on the Faustian story, is set in contemporary London and features three friends who agree to inflict pain on a fourth in return for future success. The guarantor of their "pact" is the slimy Derek Leech, head of a vast media empire who, it is intimated, may have risen — fully formed — from the polluted muck of the Thames River. Additional characters include Pinnochio who — by facilitating betrayal — is still trying to earn the right to become human.

According to *Publishers Weekly*, "supernatural elements play second fiddle to social satire in this fast-paced tale." In the view of *Booklist* "Newman's sprinting intensity forces the reader to run to keep up, even as the black-comic landscape forces him to stop to appreciate the author's adroitness." The *Library Journal* concludes that "this well-told tale is peopled with a fascinating array of characters and offers much witty and sage commentary on our materialistic society."

REVIEWS: *BL* 10/1/94; *KR* 8/15/94; *LJ* 10/1/94; *NS&S* 5/6/94; *PW* 9/5/94

Noon, Jeff (UK)

1021 *Automated Alice* (1996); Crown 1996 (HC); **Reference:** *Alice in Wonderland* (Carroll)

Standing Lewis Carroll's classic on its head, Jeff Noon utilizes the inversion-of-reality theme to dazzling effect in his 3rd novel. The author's conceit is simple, he creates a future world-an "alternative" Manchester, England in 1998 — as Lewis Carroll might have imagined it. Noon peoples this world with familiar characters (e.g. Alice and her Aunt Ermintrude) as well as new ones such as "Captain Ramshackle" (replacing the Mad Hatter) and "Inspector Jack Russell" and the "policedogmen" standing in for the Queen of Hearts and her army of cards. In the courser of her adventures, Alice is exposed to a manic, yet closely argued, discourse on the completely random nature of the universe and must contend with Civil Serpents, Computermites, not to mention the "Supreme Snake" before finding her way back home. *Automated Alice* is chock full of wordplay and post-modern witticisms.

Publishers Weekly reports that "Puns, riddles, numerical puzzles and cockeyed literary references abound in this tale of Alice's trip through her great Aunt Ermintrude's clock into an unlikely alternate-universe version of Manchester, England" and concludes that although Noon's odd sense of humor (like Carroll's himself) will not appeal to everyone, he "does a fine job of imitating Carroll while adding more than a dash of his own postmodernist sensibility." According to *Booklist* "Noon's wit even includes a Quentin Tarantula, a filmmaker famous for his violent, celebratory portrayals of criminal life. Who says the classics are no longer relevant?" According to the *L.A. Times Book Review* "English novelist Noon ... propels (Alice) through the works of her great-aunt Ermintrude's grandfather clock n Manchester in 1860 and lands her, still perky and pinafored, in 1998. Only it isn't our time, exactly, its more like a future Victorians could have imagined."

REVIEWS: *BL* 10/1/96; *KR* 8/1/96; *LATBR* 12/15/96; *PW* 8/5/96

Vurt (1994); See under *Pushing the boundaries* ... #283; St Martin's 1996 (pbk); **References:** Variously: *A Clockwork Orange* (Burgess); *Alice in Wonderland* (Carroll); *Neuromancer* (Gibson); *Naked Lunch* (Burrows)

Palliser, Charles (USA/UK)

The Quincunx; See under *More Than Meets the Eye* #994; Ballantine 1990 (pbk); **Reference:** Charles Dickens

Pollack, Rachel (USA)

1022 *Godmother Night* (1996); St Martin's 1996 (HC); **Reference:** Fairy and folk tales

Borrowing liberally from myth and folklore, Rachel Pollack strings together a series of linked stories which explore themes of love, death and identity. Key players are lovers Laurie and Jacqueline, their daughter Kate, and Mother Night and her band of red-haired, motorcycle-riding harpies.

According to *Booklist, Godmother Night* is "set in an unspecified time 'when two women ... lived on the back of a turtle,' this allegorical fantasy of love and loss tells the engrossing story of Laurie and Jacqueline, star-crossed lovers whose child becomes a healer with the aid of her godmother, Mother Night." *Kirkus Reviews* observes that "While (*Godmother Night*) begins as a depiction of modern lesbian life, it grows inexorably into a magical exploration of the deepest roots of life and death.... Tender and disturbing, down-to-earth and wildly inventive, this complex novel shows Pollack to be one of our best fantasists." In the view of the *Washington Post Book World* Ms. Pollack's novel is "beautifully, even poetically written."

REVIEWS: *BL* 9/1/96; *KR* 8/1/96; *MFSF* 6/97; *PW* 8/26/96; *WPBW* 9/29/96

Powers, Richard (USA)

1023 *Galatea 2.2* (1995); FS&G 1995 (HC); HarperCollins 1996 (pbk); **Reference:** *Pygmalion* (GBS)

Richard Powers quasi-autobiographical novel, *Galatea 2.2*, is a love story incorporating failed love, artificial intelligence and the writer's gift of language. As the story opens, the narrator (Richard Powers) a humanist-in-residence at the Center for the Study of Advanced Sciences, has agreed to assist a colleague (a cognitive neurologist) in his attempt to create a "thinking machine" capable of passing a master's exam in English.

Booklist calls *Galatea 2.2* "a dazzling work of autobiography overlaid with a reinterpretation of the Pygmalion myth" and concludes that "this is a difficult, thought-provoking, and exhilarating read, electric with the power of language and, paradoxically language's ultimate inability to alleviate suffering." *Time* magazine deems Power's novel "brilliantly imaginative" and argues that it should go immediately to the top of the year's 10-best lists." *Publishers Weekly* points out that "Powers, in his mid-30s and with four well-received books under his belt ... is among our most prodigious young novelists, and without a doubt our most cerebral" and concludes that "minor flaws" aside, this is an "ingenious performance."

OTHER MEDIA: Audio cassette recording (Books-on-Tape/unabr); RECOGNITION: nominated for the 1995 National Book Critics Circle Award; *NYTBR* Notable Book of 1995; REVIEWS: *BL* 5/1/95; *LATBR* 6/18/95; *LJ* 5/15/95; *LT* 6/15/96; *Nation* 7/10/95; *NYTBR* 7/23/95; *PW* 4/17/95; *Time* 6/12/95

Roszak, Theodore (USA)

1024   *Memoirs of Elizabeth Frankenstein* (1995); Bantam 1996 (pbk);   **Reference:** *Frankenstein* (Shelley)

Theodore Roszak's exhilaratingly gothic, yet decidedly feminist, tale purports to be the memoirs of Elizabeth Frankenstein, the ill-fated "wife" of Dr. Victor Frankenstein, creator of the monster who bears his name. A minor character (and passive victim) in Mary Shelley's classic novel, Elizabeth is finally given a voice. Roszak's story follows Elizabeth from her gypsy beginnings, her adoption by Lady Caroline Frankenstein, her training as a witch, to her eventual "chymical" marriage (through a mixture of blood and semen) to Victor.

Publishers Weekly notes that Roszak "risks much and achieves all in this richly imagined, frankly erotic homage to Mary Shelley, who modeled Victor Frankenstein's murdered — and scarcely heard from — bride on herself ..." and concludes that "Passionate and lyrical, rife with period details and underpinned by a thought-provoking subtext on gender relations and the nature of modern science, this spellbinder will send readers rushing to gobble up its precursor." In the view of the *Library Journal*, Roszak (a professor who has taught *Frankenstein* for 20 years) has written a "compelling companion to Shelley's classic" which "uses the enthusiasm for science in the Age of Enlightenment as counterpoint to an alternate tradition of science as practiced by Baroness Caroline Frankenstein." According to the *New Scientist*, depictions of the "sado-masochistic games (played by Elizabeth and Victor as children), prefiguring the later experiments, and the portrayal of Elizabeth as a rebellious spirit rather than swooning victim ... act as an intriguing preamble to the encounter with the Creature." The *New York Times Book Review* observes that "Readers will remember Elizabeth ... as one of the more boring slaughtered ingenues in horror fiction.... In *The Memoirs of Elizabeth Frankenstein* ... Roszak corrects Mary Shelley by galvanizing her women into life" and concludes that Roszak's "moral design electrifies his story."

RECOGNITION: Winner of the 1995 Tiptree Award for best work of fantasy or science fiction dealing with gender; REVIEWS: *EW* 10/18/96; *LJ* 4/15/95; *NewSci* 8/12/95; *NYTBR* 6/11/95; *PW* 3/13//95

Ryman, Geoff (UK)

1025   *Was* (1992); Penguin 1993 (pbk); Reference: *Wizard of Oz* (Baum)

Englishman Geoff Ryman's re-imagining of the American classic *Wizard of Oz* tells the interwoven stories of three characters: Dorothy Gael (a sexually abused orphan who is temporarily rescued by Mr. Baum, a kindly English teacher, who later writes a story about the way he imagined her life should have been), Frances Gumm, an unhappy little girl who grew up to be the successful, yet still unhappy, movie star, Judy Garland, and Jonathan, a gay Canadian actor (who, as a child, was fixated on Oz) now dying of AIDS. Ryman's story moves from the Great Plains of the late 19th century, to Hollywood in the 1930s and 1980s.

The *London Review of Books* notes that Ryman's novel "demonstrates the linkage of lives far from each other yet deeply involved, each in each, and the involvement is a serial process or rescue or transformation" and concludes that this is "an absorbing and marvelously accomplished narrative." The *New Statesman* declares that "Ryman's imagination and his meticulous care for detail make this an extraordinarily powerful novel which should win him the mainstream critical acclaim that he so richly deserves...." *Kirkus Reviews* points out that "Science-fiction author Ryman takes a giant step forward with this mixture of history, fantasy, and cultural myth all yoked together by the question of whether you can ever really go home."

RECOGNITION: *NYTBR* Notable Book of 1992; REVIEWS: KR 3/15//92; LRB 5/14/92; NS&S 3/20/92; *NYTBR* 7/5/92; PW 3/23//92

Schine, Cathleen (USA)

Rameau's Niece (1993); Plume 1994 (pbk); References: *Rameau's Nephew* (Diderot); Locke and Kant; See Section 7, #959

Self, Will (England)

1026   *My Idea of Fun* (1993); Vintage 1995 (pbk); **Reference:** *Faust* (Goethe or Marlowe)

Will Self's outrageous, frighteningly dark first novel tells the story of Ian Wharton, a very ordinary young man who has grown up in a trailer park on the Sussex coast. There he had been taken under the insalubrious wing of a "seaside-retiree" known as Mr. Broadhurst (aka the Fat Controller). Ian eventually shows up at the University of London sporting a newly acquired photographic memory and, after a bout or two with telekinesis and teleportation, he seeks help from the resident psychiatrist, Dr. Hieronymus Gyggle. Self's post-modern take on the Faustian legend will not be to every reader's taste.

According to the *New Statesman* "The least charitable reading of this novel would be that Self is no more than an up-market Clive Barker who has stippled his Faustian horror show with intellectual credibility. Shades of Proust, Nietzsche, Bulgakov, Jonathan Carroll and other restless ghosts twist uneasily in the slipstream of his turbo-charged imagination.... [We] certainly find ourselves cheek to cheek with some very rough magic." English novelist James Buchan (*Spectator*) says that in *My Idea of Fun*, Self "introduces that stock figure of Anglo-American male highbrow fiction, the yuppie psychopath" and concludes that "the book's mixture of affectation, solemnity, offal and narrative indiscipline [described in the publisher's blurb as 'dirty magic realism'] does not flatter his talent." The *Guardian Weekly*, on the other hand, finds Self's debut novel to be [however "rickety"] "an antidote to the genteel proficiency of current British fiction...." The *New York Times Book Review* praises *My Idea of Fun* for its "intelligence and ambition, for inventiveness, comedy, heartbreak and ferocity." Jonathan Yardley, literary critic for the *Washington Post Book World* finds "nothing beneath its flash and dazzle except vast emptiness."

RECOGNITION: Will Self was named one of the "Best of Young British Novelists" by *Granta* magazine; REVIEWS: *GW* 1/15/95; *KR* 3/1/94; *LJ* 2/1/94; *LRB* 10/7/93; *NS&S* 9/10/93; *NY* 4/11/94; *NYT* 6/3/94; *NYTBR* 4/24/94; *SFRB* 4/5/94; *Spec* 9/18/93; *TLS* 1/9/93; *WPBW* 4/3/94

Simmons, Charles (USA)

1027 *Salt Water* (1998); Chronicle Books 1998 (HC); **Reference:** *First Love* (Turgenev)

Charles Simmons' *Salt Water*, a subtle retelling of Ivan Turgenev's classic story *First Love*, is set 35 years ago in a summer island community off the New England coast. The opening sentence "In the summer of 1963 I fell in love and my father drowned" sets the scene and defines the tragically elegiac tale which is to follow.

According to *Booklist*, "Simmons has written a riveting story of youthful innocence consumed by betrayal...." *BL* concludes that it is "Simply spellbinding!" *Publishers Weekly* points out that "Simmons's calm, detached telling of the tale, and the major role played by the strongly evoked ocean setting, make for an experience that seems more European than American, and it is interesting to note that the slight but telling book was first published, to enthusiastic reviews, in France." *Kirkus Reviews* suggests that Simmons has produced "a small, coherent, impeccably composed little tragicomedy whose only debility is that the ground it stakes out is well-worn." *KR* concludes, however, that *Salt Water* is "[a] little saga of adolescence that, even if not new, is a perfectly-cut gem of its kind."

RECOGNITION: *NYTBR* Notable Book of 1998; REVIEWS: *BL* 8/19/98; *KR* 7/1/98; *NYTBR* 9/6/98; *PW* 7/20/98; *WPBW* 11/22/98

Smiley, Jane (USA)

1028 *A Thousands Acres* (1991); Fawcett 1992 (pbk); **Reference:** King Lear (Shakespeare)

In Jane Smiley's prize-winning novel, set on a farm in Iowa, *King Lear* is replayed as an old farmer by the name of Larry prepares to divide his 1,000 acres among his three daughters: Ginny, Rose and Caroline. Ginny and Rose both accept their inheritance, but Caroline balks, and her father cuts her out of his will.

In the view of the *Times Literary Supplement*, "Smiley makes the silences of King Lear a metaphor for the unspeakableness of incest and rape. Her feminist re-writing of Shakespeare's plot replaces the incomprehensibly malign sisters with real women who have suffered incomprehensible malignity. In giving Goneril a voice, Smiley joins the distinguished line of women writers who have written new lines for Shakespeare's women." *Newsweek* declares that "In the end Smiley does what Shakespeare himself never did: she creates a female heroine who grows through her own anguish until she towers over the hero and conquers him." According to the *Washington Post Book World*, "While [Smiley] has written beautifully about families in all of her seven preceding books, [this] is her best: a family portrait that is also a near-epic investigation into the broad landscape, the thousand dark acres, of the human heart."

OTHER MEDIA: A film version released in 1997 stars Jessica Lange, Michelle Pfeiffer and Jennifer Jason Leigh; audiocassette (Porch Books/abr & Recorded Bks/unabr); RECOGNITION: Winner of the 1992 Pulitzer Prize for Fiction; Winner of the 1991 National Book Critics Circle Award; nominated for the 1992 *L.A. Times* Book Award; REVIEWS: *ChiTrib* 11/3/91; *LRB* 11/19/92; *NYTBR* 11/3/91; *PW* 8/23/91; *TLS* 10/30/92; *WPBW* 10/27/91

Tennant, Emma (UK)

1029 *An Unequal Marriage* (1994); St. Martin's 1994 (HC); **Reference:** *Pride & Prejudice* (Austen)

Emma Tennant's sequel to *Pemberly* which was, in turn, a sequel to *Pride & Prejudice*, features a guilt-ridden Elizabeth (kissed in the glade by an admirer), a giddy Mrs. Bennet keeping company with the shady Lady Harcourt, ex-beau Col. Fitzwilliam now engaged to young Sophia Farquhar, and a seriously wayward son.

Publishers Weekly observes that "Tennant enmeshes beautiful Elizabeth Bennet Darcy in a nicely snarled web of predicaments. Elizabeth and Darcy still blissful after 19 wedded years, have a winsome daughter, Miranda, and an unruly son, Edward, rumored to be wenching in London and dicing away his estates" and concludes that "Austenites and Tennanites should love the whole package, including the wrap-up which leaves enough loose ends to promise further sequels." In the view of

The (London) *Times*: "Only the purest Janeites could fail to enjoy such a skillful reprise."

OTHER MEDIA: Audio cassette (Chivers/unabr); REVIEWS: *BL* 11/15/94; *LJ* 11/1/94; *LT* 11/5/94; *PW* 10/10/94; *TLS* 12/2/94; EDITOR'S NOTE: Two additional titles in Ms. Tennant's Austen series, *Elinor & Marianne* and *Emma in Love*, were published in the UK in 1996 but are currently not published in the US.

1030   *Faustine* (1992); Faber & Faber 1993 (pbk re-issue); **Reference:** *Faust* (Goethe or Marlowe) *Persephone & Demeter* (Greek myths)

In her reworking of the Faust legend, set in the just-about-to-swing England of the 1960s, Emma Tennant features a 48-year-old grandmother who — while shopping for a new TV — is surprised to see her miraculously rejuvenated picture on every screen in the shop. When offered a contract promising "a lease of beauty and youth," she takes it.

According to British critic Lorna Sage, *Faustine* "is a slender, savage and wonderfully funny revamping of the old over-reaching story. Granny sells her soul in return for 'eternal' youth. Most incorrect, of course, and impeccably stylish, a worthy companion piece for her 'Jekyll and Hyde' rewrite, *Two Women of London*." In the view of the *London Review of Books*, "Beneath the surface of its very accomplished telling, the novel ponders 'the change of life.' Men grow old; women metamorphose into age by a series of disintegrating jolts. This novel is as clever, enjoyable and tactfully self-revealing as anything Tennant has written." The *Times Literary Supplement* suggests that *Faustine* "is everywoman's story of youth's short span, and this is more than a woman's Faust. It is a fascinating new spring myth in which Persephone seeks Demeter, and is not keen on hell.... This is so entertaining a tract for the times, and so piercingly clear about the failure of 'attempts at idealism and brotherhood,' that it could even be a heart-changer. The devil strips away all the possibilities of caring so adroitly that he might make some readers care."

RECOGNITION: *TLS* International Book of the Year; REVIEWS: *Lit Rev* 3/92; *LRB* 3/12/92; *Ms.* 7/93; *NS&S* 3/20/92; *Spec* 3/21/92; *TLS* 3/6/92 & 12/4/92; EDITOR'S NOTE: Emma Tennant is well-known in the UK for her unfailingly cerebral novels, many of which derive inspiration from literary classics. For example: *Tess* 1993 (*Tess of the D'Urbervilles*); *Two Women of London* 1989 (*Dr. Jekyll & Mr. Hyde*); *Queen of Stones* 1982 (*Lord of the Flies*); *Alice Fell* 1980 (*Persephone*); *The Bad Sister* 1978 (*Confessions of a Justified Sinner*)

Tharoor, Shashi (India)

1031   *The Great Indian Novel* (1990); Arcade 1992 (pbk); **Reference:** *The Mahabarata*

Shashi Tharoor's broadly satirical debut novel — while based on the ancient Hindu epic known as "The Mahabarata" — is set in 20th-century India and features a number of well-known (if barely disguised) politicians such as Ganga Data (Ghandi) and Lord and Lady Drewpad (the Mountbattens). Not limiting his satire to a retelling of the 2,000-year-old epic (although utilizing its general structure), Tharoor also pokes fun at early 20th-century British writing about India (one chapter is entitled "The Bungle Book"; Ronald Heaslop, reprised from E.M. Forster's *A Passage to India*, appears through out as a hapless civil servant) as well as contemporary Indian writing (as in the chapter entitled "Midnight's Parents").

In the view of the *Times Literary Supplement*, *The Great Indian Novel* "is a tour de force of considerable brilliance. We have here a slightly camouflaged and highly idiosyncratic version of India's political history from the Champaran satyagraha to Indira Ghandi's last election victory...." Schuyler Ingle, in a review appearing in the *L.A. Times Book Review*, while observing that "The [punning] wordplay and the drone of the narrator's voice telling me everything, explaining everything, became very wearying. But I slogged on, right to the end. Shashi Tharoor has made me look at the rise of modern India through Indian eyes. In the beginning of the book, Ved Vyas says, 'India is not an underdeveloped country but a highly developed one in an advanced state of decay.' By the end of the novel even those who never have been to India can understand those lines in an intimate way." *Kirkus Reviews* concludes that "Tharoor is one of those rare writers who felicitously combines gentle satire with an urgent concern for society's ills [in] another eloquent — and entertaining — commentary on contemporary India."

RECOGNITION: Winner of the 1990 Commonwealth Writer's Prize and the Fed. of Indian Publishers *Hindustan Times* Literary Award; REVIEWS: *ChiTrib* 6/16/91; *KR* 4/1/92; *LATBR* 7/25/91; *LJ* 3/1/91; *NYTBR* 3/24/91; *PW* 3/28/92; *TLS* 9/8/89

Updike, John (USA)

1032   *Brazil* (1994); Knopf 1994 (HC); Ballantine 1996 (pbk); **Reference:** *Tristan and Isolde*

John Updike's sixteenth novel is set in Brazil and tells the story of Tristao Rapota, the nineteen-year-old, street-hardened son of a Black Rio whore, and Isabel Leme, a pampered eighteen-year-old blonde from a wealthy neighborhood, who meet on the beach at Copacabana and fall hopelessly in love. Updike uses the romantically tragic legend of Tristan and Isolde to shape and color his story. Updike borrows liberally from the Latin American style book of magical realism.

Called "steamy" and "breathtaking" by *The New Yorker, Kirkus Reviews* took a more jaundiced view, arguing that "The Updikian intelligence and draughtsmanship and sex-awe constantly obtrude, weakening the narrative big picture, studding the book with perceptions and alertness galore but never with quite the air of exotic metaphysical enchantment the novelist seems to seek." *Booklist,* on the other hand, suggests that although the novel, given its exotic setting, sometimes has the feel of "an outsider looking in" still "is far better than most fiction writers' best efforts and deserves the attention any book by Updike is bound to receive." Michael Dirda, writing in the *Washington Post Book World,* observes that "Though there are elements in *Brazil* that irritate, like the nips of tropical insects, these are compensated for by the novel's zestful readability, by its characterizations (a deliciously epicene uncle, the jargon-perfect conversation of student radicals), by an artful use of leitmotifs (e.g. Tristao's Lone Star T-shirt and the color of Isabel's eyes), and by the depiction of a dauntless love that transcends mere passion to become a life's vocation." The (London) *Sunday Times* calls *Brazil* "an exploration of issues of colour, class, eroticism and gender in Updike's customary superb prose."

REVIEWS: *BL* 12/1/93; *ChiTrib* 1/30/94; *Guard* 4/10/94; *KR* 12/15/93; *LST* 4/10/94; *LT* 3/31/94; *NYTBR* 2/6/94; *PW* 11/22/93; *TLS* 4/1/94; *WPBW* 2/13/94

Wright, Ronald (UK/Canada)

1033 *A Scientific Romance* (1998); St. Martin's 1998 (HC); **Reference:** *The Time Machine* (H.G. Wells)

Weaving a tale which incorporates elements of H.G. Wells' classic novel *The Time Machine,* Ronald Wright tells an intriguing tale of time travel, lost love, and heroic deeds. The story begins in London in 1999 with the mysterious return of Wells' time machine — foretold, we are to learn, in a letter written by the author in 1946. Industrial archaeologist and museum curator David Lambert (the discoverer of the Time Machine) is drawn into a decidedly time-bending drama which ranges from contemporary London to a post-apocalyptic England of 2500 and includes a plot complication having to do with Creutzfeldt-Jakob — aka "Mad Cow" — disease.

According to the *New York Times Book Review,* Wright has produced a novel which achieves a "fresh take on an old formula — the dystopian postapoclypse novel — and a profound meditation on our time." *Publishers Weekly* observes that "The narrative bristles with fascinating characters, both fictional and historical, and Wright furnishes it with a rich story of enthralling scientific Victoriana. [Wright's] writing is charming, unpretentious and wonderfully literate." In the view of the *Christian Science Monitor*: "It is unfortunate that the novel's frank sexual content makes it inappropriate for younger reader who have enjoyed Orwell's *1984* and Huxley's *Brave New World,* because [Wright] has written a tale of great suspense and insight." *Macleans* asserts that Wright has presented his readers with a "brilliantly imagined debut novel" and concludes that "few writers have imagined the future with such compelling and tragic urgency." The *Guardian Weekly* notes that Wright has created "the most apocalyptic dystopia since Russell Hoban's *Ridley Walker* [achieving the same eerie fascination and consistent believability]" and concludes that "Prediction is always risky, but in 100 years time this book should be a classic, assuming, of course, civilization survives that long."

RECOGNITION: Winner of the David Higham Award for Fiction (UK); *NYTBR* Notable Book of 1998; REVIEWS: *CSM* 4/29/98; *GW* 10/2/1997; *KR* 2/1/98; *LST* 10/26/97; *Macleans* 6/2/97; *NS* 10/24/97; *NYTBR* 3/15/98; *PW* 2/23/98; *WPBW* 4/15/98

Audiocassette Recordings

Abridged

Accordion Crimes 640
  E. Annie Proulx

Alias Grace 293
  Margaret Atwood

The Alienist 802
  Caleb Carr

All The Pretty Horses 234
  Cormac McCarthy

Always Outnumbered, Always Outgunned 134
  Walter Mosely

American Pastoral 644
  Philip Roth

Angel of Darkness 801
  Caleb Carr

Animal Husbandry 983
  Laura Zigman

Babel Tower 514
  A.S. Byatt

Bastard out of Carolina 315
  Dorothy Allison

The Bear Went Over the Mountain 917
  William Kotzwinkle

Before and After 689
  Rosellen Brown

Black and Blue 78
  Anna Quindlen

Bombay Ice 709
  Forbes, Leslie

Brothers and Sisters 106
  Bebe Moore Campbell

Bucking the Sun 811
  Ivan Doig

The Butcher Boy 826
  Patrick McCabe

The Cavedweller 314
  Dorothy Allison

Charms for the Easy Life 329
  Kay Gibbons

Cities of the Plain 232
  Cormac McCarthy

Cloud Mountain 601
  Aimee Liu

Cloudsplitter 492
  Banks, Russell

Cold Mountain 550
  Charles Frazier

Crooked Little Heart 50
  Annie Lamott

The Crossing 233
  Cormack McCarthy

A Debt to Pleasure 733
  John Lanchester

Deep End of the Ocean 66
  Jacqueline Mitchard

Dreamer 584
  Charles Johnson

Enchantment of Lily Dahl 725
  Siri Hustvedt

Enduring Love 744
  Ian McEwan

The English Patient 247
  Michael Ondaatje

Fall of a Sparrow 40
  Robert Hellenga

Felix in the Underworld 750
  John Mortimer

The Fermata 172
  Nicholson Baker

A Fine Balance 471
  Rohinton Mistry

Flaming Corsage 590
  William Kennedy

Flamingo Rising 491
  Larry Baker

The Fourteen Sisters of Emilio Montez O'Brien 578
  Oscar Hijuelos

God of Small Things 474
  Roy, Arundhati

The Good Husband 33
  Gail Godwin

Gospel 678
  Wilton Barnhardt

The Gospel According to the Son 604
  Norman Mailer

Grace Notes 370
  Bernard MacLaverty

A Gracious Plenty 345
  Sheri Reynolds

Harlot's Ghost 606
  Norman Mailer

Heathcliff: The Return to Wuthering Heights 1007
Lynn Haire-Sargeant

Here on Earth 1011
Alice Hoffman

High Fidelity 907
Nick Hornby

Honor and Duty 127
Gus Lee

The House on Mango Street 21
Sandra Cisneros

I Was Amelia Earhart 235
Mendelsohn , Jane

Idoru 212
William Gibson

In the Skin of the Lion 248
Michael Ondaatje

Indian Killer 668
Sherman Alexie

An Instance of the Fingerpost 836
Pears, Ian

Katherine 133
Anchee Min

Kowloon Tong 781
Paul Theroux

Ladder of Years 92
Anne Tyler

Larry's Party 648
Carol Shields

The Last Integrationist 125
Jake Lamar

The Last Thing He Wanted 703
Joan Didion

Last Voyage of Somebody the Sailor 180
John Barth

A Lesson Before Dying 558
Earnest Gaines

Lives of the Monster Dogs 674
Kirsten Bakis

Los Alamos 821
Joseph Kanon

Mail 933
Mameve Medwed

The Mambo Kings Sing Songs of Love 579
Oscar Hijuelos

Mao II 194
Don DeLillo

Memoirs of a Geisha 564
Arthur Golden

Mistress of Spices 112
Divakaruni, Chitra

Moo 963
Jane Smiley

Moor's Last Sigh 262
Salman Rushdie

My Other Life 652
Paul Theroux

Native Speaker 126
Chang Rae Lee

Night Train 671
Martin Amis

Nobody's Fool 84
Richard Russo

Oldest Living Confederate Widow Tells All 571
Allan Gurganus

Once Were Warriors 405
Alan Duff

One True Thing 79
Anna Quindlen

Oscar & Lucinda 400
Peter Carey

Oswald's Tale 605
Norman Mailer

Paddy Clark Ha Ha Ha 356
Roddy Doyle

Panama 851
Zencey, Eric

The Paperboy 808
Pete Dexter

Paradise 241
Toni Morrison

Part of the Furniture 660
Mary Wesley

Pigs in Heaven 47
Barbara Kingsolver

Pirate's Daughter 711
Robert Girardi

Plays Well with Others 570
Allan Gurganus

Practical Magic 719
Alice Hoffman

A Promise of Rest 344
Reynolds Price

Push 141
Sapphire

A River Sutra 469
Gita Mehta

RL's Dream 68
Walter Mosely

Rookery Blues 903
Jon Hassler

Rule of the Bone 676
Russell Banks

Saint Maybe 93
Ann Tyler

School for the Blind 746
Dennis McFarland

The Secret History 780
Donna Tartt

She's Come Undone 49
Wally Lamb

The Shipping News 77
E. Annie Proulx

Sights Unseen 328
Kay Gibbons

Snow Falling on Cedars 814
Guterson, David

Son of the Circus 728
John Irving

Spending 898
Mary Gordon

Stones from the River 575
Ursula Hegi

The Straight Man 956
Richard Russo

Such a Long Journey 472
Rohinton Mistry

A Thousand Acres 1028
Jane Smiley

Tiger's Tale 734
Gus Lee

Time's Arrow 165
Martin Amis

Turtle Moon 720
Alice Hoffman

Waterworks 810
E.L. Doctorow

The Wedding 95
Dorothy West

A Widow for One Year 45
John Irving

The Wishbones 945
Tom Perrotta

The Woman Who Walked into Doors 27
Roddy Doyle

Your Blues Ain't Like Mine 515
Bebe Moore Campbell

Unabridged

Accordion Crimes 640
E. Annie Proulx

All the Pretty Horses 234
Cormac McCarthy

Altered States 12
Anita Brookner

American Pastoral 644
Phillip Roth

Animal Dreams 48
Barbara Kingsolver

Angels and Insects 800
A.S. Byatt

Atticus 717
Ron Hansen

Autobiography of My Mother 445
Jamaica Kincaid

Bailey's Cafe 244
Gloria Naylor

Bastard out of Carolina 315
Dorothy Allison

The Bear Went Over the Mountain 917
William Kotzwinkle

Before and After 689
Rosellen Brown

Behind the Scenes at the Museum 858
Kate Atkinson

Billy Bathgate 533
E.L. Doctorow

Birdsong 539
Sebastian Faulks

Black and Blue 78
Anna Quindlen

The Black Flower 488
Howard Bahr

The Blue Afternoon 799
William Boyd

Bob the Gambler 861
Frederick Barthelme

Box Socials 916
W.P. Kinsella

Brain Storm 706
Richard Dooling

Brothers and Sisters 106
Bebe Moore Campbell

Carn 371
Patrick McCabe

Carolina Moon 742
Jill McCorkle

Casting Off 580
Elizabeth Howard

The Cattle Killing 283
John Edgar Wideman

The Cavedweller 314
Dorothy Allison

Changing Places 928
David Lodge

Charming Billy 60
Alice McDermott

Chatham School Affair 806
Thomas Cook

Cloudsplitter 492
Russell Banks

Cold Mountain 550
Charles Frazier

Corelli's Mandolin 582
Louis deBernieres

Critical Care 885
Richard Dooling

Cry Me a River 766
T.R. Pearson

The Cunning Man 525
Robertson Davies

Damascus Gate 777
Robert Stone

The Distinguished Guest 64
Sue Miller

Dogs of God 681
Pinckney Benedict

A Dubious Legacy 979
Mary Wesley

Einstein's Dreams 228
Alan Lightman

Electricity 562
Victoria Glendinning

Enduring Love 744
Ian McEwan

Every Man for Himself 490
Beryl Bainbridge

An Experiment in Love 824
Hilary Mantel

An Eye in the Door 494
Pat Barker

Farewell, I'm Bound to Leave You 322
Fred Chappell

Father & Son 320
Larry Brown

Felicia's Journey 784
William Trevor

Ferris Beach 336
Jill McCorkle

Fight Club 300
Chuck Palahniuk

Flamingo Rising 491
Larry Baker

Four Letters of Love 392
Niall Williams

Fugitive Pieces 236
Anne Michaels

Galatea 2.2 1023
Richard Powers

Gate of Angels 542
Penelope Fitzgerald

The Ghost Road 493
Pat Barker

The God of Small Things 474
Arundhati Roy

The Good Husband 33
Gail Godwin

Grace Notes 370
Bernard Maclaverty

A Gracious Plenty 345
Sheri Reynolds

The Grass Dancer 256
Susan Power

The Green Man 792
Kingsley Amis

The Hand I Fan With 3
Tina McElroy Ansa

The Healing 226
Gayl Jones

Heat Wave 55
Penelope Lively

Her Own Place 645
Dori Sanders

Here on Earth 1011
Alice Hoffman

A History of the World in 10½ Chapters 178
Julian Barnes

The Hours 1001
Michael Cunningham

House of Splendid Isolation 378
Edna O'Brien

House on Mango Street 21
Sandra Cisneros

The Hundred Secret Senses 149
Amy Tan

Appendix II

Film Adaptations

Appendix III

Reading Group Guides

Bio-Bibliography

Abish, Walter (1931–)

Walter Abish was born in Vienna but in 1938 (at the age of 7) he was forced to flee with his family from the German military. They found refuge first in France, then China and finally, after the war, in Israel. In 1957 Abish moved to New York City (with his American wife) where he found work as an urban planner and began to write fiction.

Eclipse Fever 1995; *How German Is It* 1980; *Alphabetical Africa* 1974

Abraham, Pearl (1960)

Ms. Abraham grew up in a Hasidic family where Yiddish was the primary language. She currently teaches creative writing at NYU and lives in New York City.

Giving Up America 1998; ***The Romance Reader*** 1995

Acker, Kathy (1947–1997)

Kathy Acker, novelist, short story writer and essayist, was born in New York City and attended Brandeis and the University of California at San Diego. Ms. Acker, known for her relentlessly aggressive style and ultra-feminist point of view, had many admirers in contemporary literary circles. She died of breast cancer while still in her forties.

Eurydice in the Underworld (stories) 1997; ***Pussy, King of the Pirates*** 1996; ***My Mother: Demonology*** 1993; *Portrait of an Eye: Three Novels* 1992; *Hello, I'm Erica Jong* 1992; *Hannibal Lecter, My Father* 1991; *In Memorium to Identity* 1990; *Empire of the Senseless* 1988; *Literal Madness: Three Novels* 1988; *Don Quixote* 1986; *Blood & Guts in High School* 1984; *Great Expectations* 1982; *Hello, I'm Erica Jong* 1982; *New York City* 1979; *The Adult Life of Toulouse Lautrec by Henre Tououse Lautrec* 1978; *Kathie Goes to Haiti* 1978; *Florida* 1978; *I Dreamt I Was a Nymphomaniac* 1974; *The Childlike Life of the Black Tarantula* 1973; *Politics* 1972

Ackerman, Karl

Mr. Ackerman, bookseller, editor and novelist, was born in Washington, D.C., and currently lives in Charlottesville with his wife who is also a writer.

The Patron Saint of Unmarried Women 1994

Ackroyd, Peter (1949–)

Peter Ackroyd was born in London and received his university education at Cambridge. He is a writer of "cerebral" historical fiction, a biographer, a poet, respected literary journalist, a Mellon Fellow at Yale, and a former literary editor of both the *Spectator* and *The* (London) *Times*.

Milton in America 1997; ***The Trial of Elizabeth Cree*** 1994; *The House of Dr. Dee* 1993; *English Music* 1992; ***First Light*** 1989; *Chatterton* 1987; *Hawksmoor* 1985; *The Last Temptation of Oscar Wilde* 1983; *The Great Fire of London* 1982

Adams, Alice (1926–1999)

Ms. Adams was born in Virginia and was educated at Radcliffe College. She published 13 works of fiction and contributed numerous short stories to major literary periodicals. She made her home in San Francisco where she died in 1999.

Medicine Man 1997; ***A Southern Exposure*** 1995; ***Almost Perfect*** 1993; *Caroline's Daughters* 1991; *After You've Gone*—stories 1989; *Second Chances* 1988; *Return Trips*—stories 1985; *Superior Women* 1984; *Molly's Dog*—stories 1983; *To See You Again*—stories 1982; *Rich Reward* 1980; *Beautiful Girl*—stories 1979; *Listening to Billie* 1978; *Families and Survivors* 1975; *Careless Love* 1966

Adams, Glenda (1939–)

Ms. Adams, a novelist and educator, was born in Sydney, Australia, and was educated at the University of Sydney and at Columbia University in New York City. She has taught creative writing for many years and has been affiliated with Columbia University and Sarah Lawrence College. She recently returned to Australia and is teaching at the University of Technology at Sydney.

Tempest of Clemenza 1995; *Longleg* 1990; *Dancing on Coral* 1987; *Games of the Strong* 1982; *Hottest Night of the Century* 1979; *Lies and Stories* 1976

Aidoo, Ama Ata
Ms. Aidoo was born in Abeadzi Kyiakor, Ghana, and was educated in Ghana and at Stanford University. A writer, educator and lecturer, she has taught at the University of Virginia and at the University of Cape Coast, in Ghana.
Changes: A Love Story 1993; *Our Sister Killjoy* 1979; *No Sweetness Here & Other Stories* 1971

Aiken, Joan (1924–)
Ms. Aiken, a journalist and novelist who was born in Rye, England, worked for the BBC early in her career. A well-known children's author (with numerous titles to her credit), she turned her attention to writing full time in 1961.
The Youngest Miss Ward 1998; *Emma Watson* 1997; *Eliza's Daughter* 1994; *Jane Fairfax: Jane Austen's Emma Through Another's Eyes* 1991

Akst, Daniel (1956–)
Mr. Akst was born in New York City and was educated at the University of Pennsylvania and NYU.
A journalist and columnist, his work has appeared in the *New York Times* and the *L.A. Times*
St Burl's Obituary 1996

Alcala, Kathleen (1954–)
Ms. Alcala was born in California and was educated at Stanford and at the University of Washington. An Assistant Editor of *The Seattle Review*, she is also a member of "Los Nortenos" a group of Latino writers and performers with roots in the Pacific N.W.
Flower in the Skull: A Novel 1998; *Spirits of the Ordinary: A Tale of Casas Grandes* 1997; *Mrs. Vargas and the Dead Naturalist* 1992

Alcorn, Alfred (1941–)
Mr. Alcorn, director of the travel program at Harvard's Museum of Culture and Natural History, was born in England but has lived in the United States for a number of years. He makes his home in Belmont, Massachusetts.
The Long Run of Myles Mayberry 1999; *Murder in the Museum of Man* 1997; *Vestments* 1988; *The Pull of the Earth* 1986

Alexander, Meena (1951–)
Poet and novelist Meena Alexander was born in India and was educated in India, the Sudan and in England. She has lived in the U.S. since 1980 and teaches English and women's studies at Hunter College in N.Y. "Her writing deals with the sexist, racist, colonialist forces which influenced her life and which too often shape cultural identity" (*The Chronicle of Higher Education* 3/14/97).
Manhattan Music 1997; *Nampally Road* 1991

Alexie, Sherman (1966–)
Sherman Alexie, an award-winning poet, short story writer and novelist, was born in Spokane, Washington, and is a member of the Spokane/Coeur d'Alene tribe. Mr. Alexie was educated at Gonzaga University and Washington State University. He currently lives in the Seattle area.
Indian Killer 1996; *Reservation Blues* 1995; *The Lone Ranger & Tonto Fistfight in Heaven* (stories) 1994; *First Indian on the Moon* (stories) 1993; *Old Shirts and New Skins* (stories) 1993; *The Business of Fancydancing: Stories and Poems* 1992

Allen, Edward (1948–)
Mr. Allen was born in New Haven and was educated at Goddard College and Ohio State and attended the University of Iowa's Poetry Workshop. He has taught at Rhodes College and has been a free-lance writer since 1989.
Mustang Sally 1992; *Straight Through the Night* 1989

Allison, Dorothy (1949–)
Dorothy Allen, a novelist and feminist activist, was born in Greenville, South Carolina, to a 14-year-old unwed mother. She was educated at Florida Presbyterian College and the New School for Social Research in New York City.
The Cavedweller 1998; *Bastard out of Carolina* 1992; *Trash: Stories* 1988

Alvarez, Julia (1950–)
A poet, novelist and educator, Ms. Alvarez spent the first 10 years of her life in the Dominican Republic until forced to flee to the U.S. (moving to Queens) following her father's involvement in an abortive move to oust the dictator Trujillo. She was educated at Connecticut College, Middlebury College and Syracuse University. She is currently on the faculty of Middlebury College in Vermont.
Yo! 1997; *In the Time of the Butterflies* 1994; *How the Garcia Girls Lost Their Accents* 1991

Amidon, Stephen (1959–)
Born in Chicago and educated at Wake Forest University in Winston-Salem, North Carolina, Mr. Amidon currently lives in Great Britain.
The Primitive 1995; *Thirst* 1993; *Subdivision* (stories) 1992; *Splitting the Atom* 1990

Amis, Kingsley (1922–1995)
Kingsley Amis, novelist, short story writer, poet, biographer, scriptwriter and journalist, was born in London and graduated from Oxford University. Known, in the 1950s, as one of literary

England's "Angry Young Men," his most famous novel remains his first: *Lucky Jim* (1954). He won the prestigious Booker Prize for *The Old Devils* in 1986 and was knighted for his contribution to British culture. His son, Martin Amis, is also a prize-winning novelist.

Biographer's Mustache 1994; *You Can't Do Both* 1994; ***Russian Girl*** 1992; *The Folks That Lived on the Hill* 1990; *Difficulties with Girls* 1988; *Crime of the Century* 1987; *The Old Devils* 1986; *Stanley and the Women* 1984; *Jake's Thing* 1978; *The Alteration* 1976; *Ending Up* 1974; *The Riverside Villas Murders* 1973; *Girl, 20* 1971; ***The Green Man*** 1969; *I Want It Now* 1968; *Colonel Sun: A James Bond Adventure* 1968; *The Anti-Death League* 1966; *One Fat Englishman* 1964; *Take a Girl Like You* 1960; *That Uncertain Feeling* 1955; *Lucky Jim* 1954

Amis, Martin (1949–)

Novelist and essayist Martin Amis is the son of the influential postwar British satirist Kingsley Amis. He was born in Oxford, England, and received a B.A. degree with honors from Oxford University in 1971.

Heavy Water & Other Stories 1999; ***Night Train*** 1997; ***The Information*** 1995; *Visiting Mrs. Nabokov* (stories) 1993; ***Time's Arrow*** 1991; ***London Fields*** 1989; *Einstein's Monsters* 1987; *Money: A Suicide Note* 1984; *Other People: A Mystery Story* 1981; *Success* 1978; *Dead Babies* 1975; *The Rachel Papers* 1973

Anaya, Rudolfo (1937–)

Mr. Rudolfo was born in Pastura, New Mexico, and was educated at the University of New Mexico where he now teaches.

Jalamanta: A Message from the Desert 1996; *Rio Grande Fall* 1996; ***Zia Summer*** 1995; *Albuquerque* 1992; *The Legend of la Llorna: A Short Novel* 1984; *The Silence of the llano* (stories) 1982; *Tortuga* 1979; *Heart of Aztlan* 1976; *Bless Me Ultima* 1972

Anderson, Alison

A teacher, translator and novelist, Ms. Anderson grew up in New England and has lived in Greece, France, England, and Switzerland. She currently lives in California.

Hidden Latitudes 1996

Anderson, Barbara (1926–)

The House Guest 1995; *All the Nice Girls* 1994; ***Portrait of the Artist's Wife*** 1992; *Girls High* (linked stories) 1991; *I Think We Should Go into the Jungle* (stories) 1989

Ansa, Tina McElroy (1949–)

Ms. Ansa lives with her husband, a filmmaker, on St. Simon's Island off the coast of Georgia.

The Hand I Fan With 1998; *Ugly Ways* 1993; ***Baby of the Family*** 1989

Anshaw, Carol

A critic and novelist, Ms. Anshaw won the 1989-1990 national Book Critics Circle Award for excellence in reviewing. She lives and works in Chicago.

Seven Moves 1996; *Aquamarine* 1992

Antoni, Robert (1958–)

Robert Antoni was born in Detroit where his father was completing his medical residency but was brought up in the Bahamas when his father returned there to practice medicine. Mr. Antoni was educated at Duke University and Johns Hopkins University and currently teaches at the University of Miami.

Blessed Is the Fruit 1997; ***Divina Trace*** 1992

Antrim, Donald

Donald Antrim, a novelist, short story writer and essayist, was educated at Brown University and currently lives in New York City. Mr. Antrim's work has been published in *Harper's Magazine* and the *Paris Review*.

The Hundred Brothers 1997; *Elect Mr. Robinson for a Better World* 1993

Appachana, Anjana (1956–)

Ms. Appachana was born in India, and was educated there and at Penn State. She currently lives in Tempe, Arizona, where she taught at the University of Arizona before devoting herself to writing full-time.

Listening Now 1997; *Incantations and Other Stories* 1992

Askew, Rilla

Ms. Askew divides her time between the Sans Bois Mountains of Southwestern Oklahoma and Upstate New York where she has taught English at Syracuse University.

The Mercy Seat 1997; *Strange Business* (stories) 1992

Astley, Thea (1925–)

Ms. Astley, a multiple award-winning Australian novelist and short story writer, was born in Brisbane and was educated at All Hallows Convent and Queensland University. She has devoted her life to writing and teaching.

The Multiple Effects of Rain Shadows 1996; ***Coda*** 1993; *Vanishing Points* 1992; *Reaching Tin River* 1990; *It's Raining in Mango* 1987; *Beachmasters* 1985; *An Item from the Late News* 1982; *Hunting the Wild Pineapple* (stories) 1979; *A Kindness Cup* 1974; *The Acolyte* 1972; *A Boatload of Home Folk* 1968; *The Slow Natives* 1965; *The Well-dressed Explorer* 1962; *A Descant for Gossips* 1960; *Girl with a Monkey* 1958

Atkinson, Kate

Ms. Atkinson was born in York, England, but

now lives in Edinburgh, Scotland, with her two daughters.

Human Croquet 1997; **Behind the Scenes at the Museum** 1996

Atwood, Margaret (1939–)
Novelist, poet, short story writer, critic and author of books for children, Ms. Atwood was born in Ottawa and was educated at the University of Toronto and at Harvard. She published her first book of poetry at the age of 22.

Alias Grace 1996; *The Robber Bride* 1993; *Good Bones* (stories) *1992*; *Wilderness Tips* (stories) 1991; *Cat's Eye* 1989; *The Handmaid's Tale* 1985; *Bluebeard's Egg & Other Stories*; *Bodily Harm* 1981; *Life Before Man* 1979; *Dancing Girls & Other Stories* 1977; *Lady Oracle* 1976; *Surfacing* 1972; *The Edible Woman* 1969

Austen-Leigh, Joan
Jane Austen's great-great grandniece.
Later Days at Highbury 1996

Auster, Paul (1947–)
Poet, screenplay writer and novelist Paul Auster was born in Newark, New Jersey, and attended Columbia University. Mr. Auster spent a number of years living and working in France and, in addition to his own works of fiction, has translated the poetry of Mallarme.

Mr. Vertigo 1994; *Leviathan* 1992; *The Music of Chance* 1990; *Moon Palace* 1989; *In the Country of First Things* 1987; *The Locked Room* 1986; *Ghosts* 1986; *City of Glass* 1985

Bahr, Howard
A native of Oxford, Mississippi, Mr. Bahr teaches English at Matlow State Community College in Tennessee.
The Black Flower 1997

Bail, Murray (1941–)
Murray Bail, prize-winning Australian novelist, was born in Adelaide. He is considered to be one of the more accomplished members of Australia's "New Wave," a group of innovative poets and novelists. Widely traveled in Asia and Europe, he lived for a time in England where he was a regular contributor to the *Times Literary Supplement* and the *Transatlantic Review*.

Eucalyptus 1998; *Holden's Performance* 1987; *Homesickness* 1980

Bainbridge, Beryl (1934–)
Beryl Bainbridge, novelist and actress, was born in Liverpool where she attended art school. She began writing fiction at an early age (she completed her first novel *Filthy Lucre* at the age of 13) and is both known and celebrated for her distinctive, idiosyncratic style.

Master Georgie 1998; *Every Man for Him-*

self 1996; *The Birthday Boys* 1991; *An Awfully Big Adventure* 1989; *Filthy Lucre* 1986; *Mum and Mr. Armitage* 1985; *Watson's Apology* 1984; *Winter Garden* 1980; *Young Adolph* 1978; *Injury Time* 1977; *A Quiet Life* 1976; *Sweet William* 1975; *The Bottle Factory Outing* 1974; *The Dressmaker* 1973; *Harriet Said* 1972; *Another Part of the Wood* 1968; *A Weekend with Claude* 1964 (revised and reissued in 1981)

Baker, Larry (1948–)
A Southern Catholic novelist and educator.
Flamingo Rising 1997

Baker, Nicholson (1957–)
Novelist Nicholson Baker was born in New York City and attended Haverford College and the Eastman School of Music. A full-time writer since 1987, he currently lives in Berkeley, California.

The Everlasting Story of Nory 1998; *The Fermata* 1994; *Vox* 1992; *U & I: A True Story* 1991; *Room Temperature* 1990; *The Mezzanine* 1988

Bakis, Kirsten (1968–)
Ms. Bakis lives in New York City.
Lives of the Monster Dogs 1997

Baldwin, William (1944–)
A life-long resident of McClellanville, South Carolina, Mr. Baldwin is a historian and former shrimp boat builder. He was the 1991 winner of the South Carolina Arts Council fiction contest.
The Fennel Family Papers 1996; *The Hard to Catch Mercy* 1993

Banks, Iain (1954–)
Iain Banks was born in Fife, Scotland, the son of an admiralty officer and an ice-skating instructor. He was educated at Stirling University. He writes Science Fiction novels under the sobriquet Iain M. Banks.

A Song of Stone 1998; *Complicity* 1993; *The Crow Road* 1992; *Canal Dreams* 1989; *Espedair Street* 1987; *The Bridge* 1986; *Walking on Glass* 1985; *The Wasp Factory* 1984

Banks, Russell (1940–)
Russell Banks was born in Newton, Massachusetts, grew up in New Hampshire and was educated at Colgate and at the University of North Carolina–Chapel Hill. A novelist and short story writer, he has taught in colleges and universities throughout the Northeast, most recently at Princeton and Sarah Lawrence.

Cloudsplitting 1998; *Rule of the Bone* 1995; *The Sweet Hereafter* 1991; *Affliction* 1989; *Success Stories* 1986; *Continental Drift* 1985; *The Relation of My Imprisonment* 1983; *Trailerpark* (stories) 1981; *The Book of Jamaica* 1980; *Hamilton Stark* 1978; *The New World* (stories) 1978; *Searching for Survivors* (stories) 1975; *Family Life* 1975

Banville, John (1945–)

Multiple prize-winning Irish novelist John Banville was born in Wexford and has lived much of his life in Dublin where he is currently the literary editor of the *Irish Times*.

The Untouchable 1997; *Athena* 1995; **Ghosts** 1993; *Book of Evidence* 1989; *Mefisto* 1986; *Newton Letter* 1987; *Kepler* 1983; *Dr. Copernicus* 1977; *Birchwood* 1973; *Night Spawn* 1971; *Long Larkin* 1970

Baratham, Gopal

Novelist Baratham Gopal is also a leading Singapore surgeon and human rights advocate.

Moonrise, Sunset 1996; *A Candle in Sun* 1992

Barker, Pat (1943) England

Pat Barker was born and raised in a working-class neighborhood in Britain's industrial northeast but was educated at the London School of Economics. Her first novels were models of gritty, working-class realism with a strong feminist underpinning. Her widely praised "Regeneration Trilogy," which focused on the horrific realities of World War I, was a major departure for the author. Ms. Barker lives with her university professor husband in the cathedral town of Durham.

Another World 1998; **The Ghost Road** 1995; *The Eye in the Door* 1993; *Regeneration* 1991; *The Man Who Wasn't There* 1989; *The Century's Daughter* 1986; *Blow Your House Down* 1984; *Union Street* 1982

Barnes, Julian (1946–)

Julian Barnes was born in Leicester, England, was educated at Oxford University and now lives in London. Mr. Barnes also writes crime novels under the pseudonym Dan Kavanagh.

England, England 1999, *Cross Channel* (stories) 1996; *Porcupine* 1992; *Talking It Over* 1991; *A History of the World in 10 and 1/2 Chapters* 1989; *Staring at the Sun* 1986; *Flaubert's Parrot* 1984; *Before She Met Me* 1982; *Metroland* 1980

Barnhardt, Wilton (1960–)

Mr. Wilton was born in Winston-Salem, North Carolina, and received degrees from Michigan State and Oxford University.

Show World 1998; *Gospel* 1993; *Emma Who Saved My Life* 1989

Barrett, Andrea (1965–)

Ms. Barrett was raised on Cape Cod and attended Union College in Upstate New York. She and her biologist husband currently live in Rochester, New York, where she teaches in an MFA Program for writers.

Voyage of the Narwhal 1998; *Ship Fever & Other Stories* 1996; *The Forms of Water* 1993; *The Middle Kingdom* 1991; *Secret Harmonies* 1989; *Lucid Stars* 1988

Barrett, Julia

Julia Barrett is a pseudonym for Britons Julia Braun Kessler (a journalist and editor) and Gabrielle Donnelly (a novelist and critic).

The Third Sister 1998; *Presumption* 1993

Barry, Sebastian (1955–)

Poet, novelist, playwright and short story writer, Mr. Barry was born in Dublin and was educated at Trinity College, Dublin. He currently lives in Wicklow.

The Whereabouts of Enneas McNulty 1998; *The Engine of Owl Light* 1987; *Time out of Mind* (stories) 1983; *The Water-Colourist* 1983; *Macker's Garden* 1982

Barth, John (1930–) American

Novelist, short story writer and essayist, Mr. Barth was born in Cambridge, Maryland, and was educated at the Juilliard School of Music and Johns Hopkins University where he has been a long-time faculty member.

On with the Story (stories) 1996; *Once Upon a Time: A Floating Opera* 1994; *The Last Voyage of Somebody the Sailor* 1991; *The Tidewater Tales* 1987; *Sabbatical: A Romance* 1982; *Letters: A Novel* 1979; *Chimera* 1972; *Lost in the Fun House* (stories) 1968; *The Floating Opera* 1968; *Giles Goat-Boy* 1966; *The End of the Road* 1962

Barthelme, Frederick (1943–)

Mr. Barthelme was born in Houston, Texas, and attended Tulane, the University of Houston and Johns Hopkins University.

Bob the Gambler 1997; *Painted Desert* 1995; *Brothers* 1993; *Natural Selection* 1990; *Two Against One* 1988; *Chroma* (stories) 1987; *Tracer* 1985; *Second Marriage* 1984; *Moon Deluxe* 1983; *War and War* 1971; *Rangoon* (stories) 1970

Bartlett, Neil (1958–)

A biographer (of Oscar Wilde), playwright and novelist, Mr. Bartlett lives in London where he is artistic director of the Lyric Theatre.

The House on Brooke Street 1997; *Ready to Catch Him If He Falls* 1991

Bauer, Douglas

A freelance journalist, essayist, critic and novelist, Mr. Bauer was born in Iowa and attended SUNY–Albany. He has taught at Harvard and Ohio State Universities and is currently teaching creative writing at SUNY–Albany. He is also the writer-in-residence at the New York State Writer's Institute.

The Book of Famous Iowans 1997; *The Very Air* 1993; *Dexterity* 1989

Bausch, Richard (1945–)

Mr. Bausch was born in Fort Benning, Georgia; he attended George Mason University (in Virginia) and received his MFA from the University of

Iowa. He currently teaches English literature and writing at George Mason University.

In the Night Season 1998; ***Good Evening Mr. & Mrs. America and All the Ships at Sea*** 1997; *Rare and Endangered Species* (stories) 1994; ***Rebel Powers*** 1993; *Violence: A Novel* 1992; *The Fireman's Wife & Other Stories* 1990; *Mrs. Field's Daughter* 1989; *Spirits & Other Stories* 1987; *The Last Good Time* 1984; *Take Me Back* 1981; *Real Presence* 1980

Beattie, Ann (1947–)

Ms. Beattie was born in Washington, D.C. and was educated at the American University and the University of Connecticut

Convergence; New & Selected Stories 1998; ***My Life, Starring Dara Falcon*** 1997; *Another You* 1995; *What Was Mine* (stories) 1991; *Picturing Will* 1989; *Where You'll Find Me & Other Stories* 1986; *Love Always: A Novel* 1985; *The Burning House* (stories) 1982; *Falling in Place: A Novel* 1980; *Secrets and Surprises* (stories) 1978; *Chilly Scenes of Winter* 1976; *Distortions* (stories) 1976

Beatty, Paul

A poet and novelist, Mr. Beatty was born and raised in West L.A. He attended BU and received his MFA in creative writing from Brooklyn College where he studied under Alan Ginsberg.

The White Boy Shuffle 1996

Bedford, Martyn (1959–)

Mr. Bedford, a journalist and novelist, was born in Croydon, England, was educated at the University of East Anglia.

The Houdini Girl 1999; ***Acts of Revision*** 1996

Bedford, Simi

Ms. Bedford was born into a large, wealthy Nigerian family and was sent to England for her schooling.

Yoruba Girl Dancing 1992

Begley, Louis (1933–)

An attorney specializing in International Corporate Law, Mr. Begley was born in pre-war Poland to Jewish parents. At the age of fifteen, having survived the Holocaust, he immigrated to the U.S. He was educated at Harvard University.

Mistler's Exit 1998; ***About Schmidt*** 1996; *As Max Saw It* 1994; *The Man Who Was Late* 1992; ***Wartime Lies*** 1991

Behr, Mark

Mark Behr, an Afrikaner, was born — and still lives — in South Africa where he has won a number of prestigious regional prizes for his first novel.

The Smell of Apples 1994

Bell, Madison Smartt (1957–)

Born in Nashville, Tennessee, Mr. Bell at-

tended Princeton University where he won a number of literary prizes; he received his M.A. from Hollins College. Bell currently lives in Baltimore, Maryland.

Ten Indians 1996; ***All Souls Rising*** 1995; *Save Me, Joe Louis* 1993; *Dr. Sleep* 1991; *Barking Man and Other Stories* 1990; *Soldier's Joy* 1989; *Zero db & Other Stories* 1987; *The Year of Silence* 1987; *Straight Cut* 1986; *Waiting for the End of the World* 1985; *The Washington Square Ensemble* 1983

Bellow, Saul (1915–)

Mr. Bellow, a much-lauded American writer, was born in Lachine, Ontario, but soon moved to the Chicago area where he has spent most of his life. He attended the University of Chicago and Northwestern and has taught at numerous colleges and universities. Since he first began writing in the early 1940s he has produced an impressive body of work which includes novels, short stories, plays, screenplays and literary criticism.

The Actual 1997; *A Case of Love* 1992; *More Die of Heartbreak* 1987; *The Dean's December* 1982; *Humboldt's Gift* 1975; *Mr. Sammler's Planet* 1970; *Herzog* 1964; *Henderson the Rain King* 1959; *The Adventures of Augie March* 1965; *The Victim* 1947; *Dangling Man* 1944

Benabib, Kim

Mr. Benabib was born and raised in New York City.

Obscene Bodies 1996

Benedict, Pinckney (1964–)

Mr. Benedict, who grew up on a dairy farm in the mountains of S.W. Virginia, graduated from Princeton and received an MFA from the University of Iowa. He is currently an Associate Professor of English at Hollins College.

Dogs of God 1993; *The Wreaking Yard & Other Stories* 1991; *Town Smokes* (stories) 1986

Benitez, Sandra (1941–)

Ms. Benitez, a novelist and creative writing teacher, was born in Washington, D.C., and grew up in Mexico, El Salvador, and Missouri. Her father was a diplomat and her mother a translator. She currently lives and works in Minnesota.

Bitter Grounds 1997; ***A Place Where the Sea Remembers*** 1993

Berger, John (1926–)

Mr. Berger was born in London and was educated at Chelsea School of Art. In addition to writing, he has worked as an actor, a painter, an art critic and a teacher. An influential Marxist critic, he wrote for the *New Statesman* for many years. For the past 20 years he has lived in a small village in the French Alps.

King: A Street Story 1999; *Isabelle* 1998; ***To the***

Wedding 1995; *Into Their Labours Trilogy* (*Pig Earth, Once in Europa* and *Lilac & Flag*) 1991; *Lilac & Flag* 1990; *Once in Europa* 1987; *Pig Earth* 1979; *G* 1972; *Corker's Freedom* 1964; *The Foot of Clive* 1962; *A Painter of Our Time* 1958

Berger, Thomas (1924–)
Thomas Berger, a prolific novelist and screenwriter, was born in Cincinnati, Ohio, and attended Columbia University.
Suspects 1996; ***Robert Crews*** 1994; *Meeting Evil* 1992; *Orries Story* 1990; *Changing the Past* 1989; *The Houseguest* 1988; *Being Invisible* 1987; *Nowhere* 1985; *The Feud* 1983; *Reinhart's Women* 1981; *Neighbors* 1980; *Arthur Rex* 1978; *Who Is Teddy Villanova* 1977; *Sneaky People* 1975; *Regiment of Women* 1973; *Vital Parts* 1970; *Killing Time* 1967; *Little Big Man* 1964; *Reinhart in Love* 1962; *Crazy in Berlin* 1958

Berne, Suzanne
Ms. Berne, novelist, short story writer and essayist, was born in Washington, D.C., and now lives near Boston. A graduate of the University of Iowa Writer's Workshop, she has taught at Harvard and Wellesley.
A Crime in the Neighborhood 1997

Berry, Wendell (1934–)
A poet, novelist, short story writer, essayist, professor and farmer, Wendell Berry was born in Henry County Kentucky — and has lived there his entire life. He currently teaches at the University of Kentucky.
A World Lost 1996; *Watch with Me (stories)* 1994; *Fidelity (stories)* 1992; *Remembering* 1988; *The Wild Birds* (stories) 1986; *Memory of Old Jack* 1974; *A Place on Earth* 1983; *Nathan Coulter* 1960

Betts, Doris (1932–)
Ms. Betts, journalist, novelist and short story writer, was born in Statesville, North Carolina, and attended the University of North Carolina at Chapel Hill where she is currently on the faculty.
The Sharp Teeth of Love 1997; *The Gentle Insurrection & Other Stories* 1997; *The Astronomer & Other Stories* 1995; ***Souls Raised from the Dead***: *A Novel* 1994; *Heading West: A Novel* 1981; *Beasts of the Southern Woods & Other Stories* 1973; *The River to Pickle Beach* 1972

Bhattacharya, Keron
Keron Bhattacharya, novelist and journalist, was born in British India but has lived most of his life in England. Bhattacharya is a resident of Birmingham where he is a well-known business writer.
The Pearls of Coromandel 1996

Bigsby, Christopher
Christopher Bigsby is a Professor of American Literature at the University of East Anglia, England.
Pearl 1996; ***Hester*** 1994

Binstock, R. C. (1958–)
Mr. Binstock was born in Topeka, Kansas, and was educated at Harvard from which he graduated with high honors.
The Soldier 1996; ***Tree of Heaven*** 1995; *The Light of Home* 1992

Bishop, Michael (1945–)
Known for most of his career as a science fiction writer, Mr. Bishop, who was born in Lincoln, Nebraska, made the crossover to literary fiction in 1992 with *Count Geiger's Blues*
Brittle Innings 1994; *Count Geiger's Blues: A Comedy* 1992; *Unicorn Mountain* 1988; *The Secret Ascension* 1987; *Close Encounters with the Deity: Stories* 1986; *Ancient of Days* 1985; *Blooded Arachne* 1982; *Under Heaven's Bridge* 1981; *Catacomb Years* 1979; *A Little Knowledge* 1977; *Stolen Faces* 1977; *The Trees* 1976; *Stranger at Ecbatan* 1976; *A Funeral for the Eyes of Fire* 1975

Blackburn, Julia (1948–)
Ms. Blackburn, daughter of British poet Thomas Blackburn (1916–1977), lives in London with her sculptor husband.
The Leper's Companion 1999; ***The Book of Color*** 1995

Bloom, Amy (1953)
Ms. Bloom, a novelist and practicing psychotherapist, was born in New York City and was educated at Wesleyan University and Smith College.
Love Invents Us 1997; *Come to Me* (stories) 1993

Bowen, Peter
Mr. Bowen, a Native American novelist, has worked as a carpenter, a bartender, a cowboy and a wilderness guide. He also writes an "outdoor" column for *Forbes FYI* under the name of "Coyote Jack."
Thunder Horse 1998; ***Notches*** 1997; *Wolf, No Wolf* 1996; *Specimen Song* 1995; *Coyote Wind* 1994; *Imperial Kelly* 1992; *Kelly Blue* 1991; *Yellowstone Kelly: Gentleman and Scout: A Novel* 1987

Bowering, George (1935–)
George Bowering, novelist, poet and professor of English, is one of Canada's most respected contemporary writers.
Shoot! 1994; *Parents from Space* 1994; *The Rain Barrel and Other Stories* 1994; *Harry's Fragments: A Novel of International Puzzlement* 1990; *Errata* 1988; *Caprice* 1987; *Craft Slices* 1985; *Eneaux Troubles* 1982; *Burning Water* 1980; *Protective Footwear (stories)* 1978; *A Short Sad Book* 1977; *Flycatcher & Other Stories* 1974; *A Place to Die (stories)* 1973; *Mirror on the Floor* 1967

Boyd, Blanche McCrory (1945–)
Ms. Boyd was born in Charleston, South Car-

olina, and attended Duke University. She currently teaches creative writing at Connecticut College

Terminal Velocity 1997; *The Revolution of little Girls* 1991; *The Redneck Way of Knowledge* 1983; *Mourning the Death of Magic* 1977; *Nerves: A Novel* 1973

Boyd, William (1952–)

William Boyd, the son of a Scottish physician, was born in Accra, Ghana. He attended the Universities of Nice and Glasgow in addition to Oxford University. Critics often compared his early work to both Evelyn Waugh and Kingsley Amis.

Armadillo 1998; *The Destiny of Nathalie X* 1995; *The Blue Afternoon* 1993; *Brazzaville Beach* 1990; *The New Confessions* 1987; *Stars and Bars* 1984; *An Ice Cream War* 1982; *On the Yankee Station* (stories) 1982; *A Good Man in Africa* 1981

Boyle, T. C (1948–)

T.C. Boyle was born in Peekskill, New York, and studied music before turning to fiction. Like many successful writers of his generation, he did graduate work in Creative Writing at the University of Iowa. His short stories have been published in a variety of magazines including the *New Yorker*, *Esquire, Harper's, The Paris Review*, and the *Atlantic Monthly*. Mr. Boyle currently lives near Santa Barbara, California, and teaches at UCLA.

Riven Rock 1998; *The Tortilla Curtain* 1995; *Without a Hero* 1994; *The Road to Wellville* 1993; *East Is East* 1991; *If the River Was Whiskey* (stories) 1990; *World's End* 1987; *Greasy Lake & Other Stories* 1985; *Budding Prospects: A Pastoral* 1984; *Water Music* 1981; *Descent of Man* (stories) 1979

Bradbury, Malcolm (1932–)

Malcolm Bradbury was born in Sheffield, England, and was educated at the Universities of Leicester, London and Manchester. Bradbury, a well-regarded novelist, has also laboured productively in the groves of academe; his creative writing program at the University of East Anglia is arguably the finest in Great Britain (counting such luminaries as Ian McEwan, Kazuo Ishiguro, Adams Mars-Jones and Maggie Gee among its graduates).

Dr. Criminale 1992; *Cuts* 1987; *My Strange Quest for Mensonge: Structuralism's Hidden Hero* 1987; *Why Come to Slaka* 1986; *Rates of Exchange* 1983; *Who Do You Think You Are?* 1976; *The History Man* 1975; *Stepping Westward* 1965; *Eating People Is Wrong* 1959

Bradfield, Scott (1955–)

Mr. Bradfield was born in San Francisco and was educated in the University of California system. He is currently on the faculty of the University of Connecticut.

Animal Planet 1995; *What's Wrong with America?* 1994; *Greetings from Earth* (stories) 1993;

Dream of the Wolf (stories) 1990; *History of Luminous Motion* 1989; *The Secret Life of Houses* 1988

Brady, Joan (1939–)

Ms. Brady was born in San Francisco and was educated at Columbia University. Before turning to writing she danced professionally with the San Francisco Ballet and the New York City Ballet. She has lived in England for many years.

Heaven in High Gear 1997; *God on a Harley: A Spiritual Fable* 1995; *Theory of War* 1994; *The Impostor* 1979

Bram, Christopher

Mr. Bram was born in Buffalo and was educated at the College of William and Mary. He worked at various jobs (typesetter, book store clerk) before he began to write full time in 1987.

Gossip 1997; *Father of Frankenstein* 1995; *Almost History* 1992; *In Memory of Angel Clare* 1989; *Hold Tight* 1988; *Surprising Myself* 1987

Brand, Dionne (1953–)

Ms. Brand, a highly regarded poet and novelist, was born and raised in Trinidad. She immigrated to Canada as a young woman and was educated at the University of Toronto.

In Another Place Not Here 1997; *Bread Out of Stone* 1994; *Sans Souci & Other Stories* 1989

Brett, Lily (1946–)

Lily Brett was born in Germany and immigrated to Australia with her parents in 1948. In 1990 she moved with her husband and children from Melbourne to New York City. She has written five books of poetry and three of fiction. In 1987 *The Auschwitz Poems* won the Victorian Premier's Award for Poetry.

Just Like That 1994; *What God Wants* 1991; *Things Could Be Worse* 1990

Brink, Andre (1935–)

Andre Brink, one of South Africa's most revered writers, was born in Vrede, South Africa, and was educated in South Africa and at the Sorbonne. He lives in Cape Town where he teaches at Cape Town University.

Devil's Valley 1999; *Imaginings of Sand* 1996; *Cape of Storms* 1993; *On the Contrary* 1993; *An Act of Terror* 1992; *States of Emergency* 1989; *The Ambassador* 1986; *The Wall of the Plague* 1984; *A Dry White Season* 1980; *A Portrait of a Woman as a Young Girl* 1973

Brodkey, Harold (1930–1996)

Harold Brodkey, the adopted son of Joseph and Doris Brodkey, grew up in St. Louis. After graduating from Harvard University he moved to New York where he began his writing career. He taught at both Cornell University and the City

College of New York and was a staff writer at the *New Yorker*.

Profane Friendship 1994; *The Runaway Soul* 1991; *Stories in an Almost Classical Mode* 1988; *First Love & Other Sorrows* (stories) 1957

Brookner, Anita (1928–)

Novelist and art historian, Anita Brookner was born in London, and was educated at King's College, London, and received a Ph.D. from the Courtauld Institute of Art. She has taught at the University of Reading, the Courtauld Institute, and most recently, at Cambridge University.

Falling Slowly 1999; *Visitors* 1997; *Altered States* 1996; *Incidents in the Rue Laugier* 1995; *A Private View* 1994; *A Family Romance* 1993 (US title: Dolly 1994); *Fraud* 1992; *A Closed Eye* 1991; *Brief Lives* 1990; *Lewis Percy* 1989; *Latecomers* 1988; *A Friend from England* 1987; *A Misalliance* 1986; *Family and Friends* 1985; *Hotel du Lac* 1984; *Look at Me* 1983; *Providence* 1982; *A Start in Life* 1981 (U.S. title: *The Debut* 1981)

Brown, Alan (1950–)

A travel writer, journalist, and novelist, Mr. Brown was born in Scranton, Pennsylvania. He visited Japan in 1979 and later returned as a Fulbright Scholar. He lived in Japan for 7 years and taught, for part of that time, at the prestigious Keio University. *Audrey Hepburn's Neck* was winner of the first Kiriyama Pacific Rim Book Prize.

Audrey Hepburn's Neck 1996

Brown, Gita (1958–)

Ms. Brown, a novelist whose mother traced her ancestors back to the Creek Tribe and whose father came to the U.S. from the West Indies, currently lives and writes in Rhode Island.

Be I Whole 1995

Brown, John Gregory

Educated at Tulane and John Hopkins Universities (where he taught briefly), John Gregory Brown is currently on the faculty of Sweet Briar College.

The Wrecked Blessed Body of Shelton Lafleur 1996; *Decorations in a Ruined Cemetery* 1994

Brown, Larry (1951–)

Mr. Brown, the first two-time winner of the Southern Book Award for Fiction, was born in a small town near Oxford, Mississippi. A self-educated man (and the son of a farmer and the local postmistress) he worked for the Oxford Fire Department for twenty years before turning his hand to fiction writing.

Father & Son 1996; *Joe* 1991; *Big Bad Love* (stories) 1990; *Dirty Work* 1989; *Facing the Music* 1988

Brown, Linda Beatrice (1939–)

Novelist and college professor, Ms. Brown was born in Akron Ohio. She currently teaches at Bennet College.

Crossing over Jordan 1995; *Rainbow Roun Ma Shoulder* 1984; *A Love Song to Black Men* 1975

Brown, Rosellen (1939–)

Ms. Brown was born in Philadelphia and was educated at Barnard and Brandeis. She is currently on the faculty of the University of Houston.

Before and After 1993; *Street Games: Stories* 1991; *Civil Wars: A Novel* 1985; *Tender Mercies* 1978; *The Autobiography of My Mother* 1976; *Street Games* (stories) 1974

Brown, Wesley (1945–)

Wesley Brown was born in New York City and was educated at Oswego State.

Darktown Strutters 1994; *Tragic Magic* 1978

Bryers, Paul (1945–)

A journalist and novelist, Paul Bryers was born in Liverpool, England, and was educated at the University of Southampton.

Prayer of the Bone 1999; *In a Pig's Ear* 1996; *The Adultery Department* 1993; *Coming First* 1988; *The Cat Trapper* 1978; *Target Plutex* 1976

Buffong, Jean

Ms. Buffong is a Granadian novelist who has received much critical praise for her first two works of fiction.

Snow Flakes in the Sun 1995; *Under the Silk Cotton Tree* 1993; *Jump Up & Kiss Me: Two Stories from Grenada* 1992

Burgess, Anthony (1917–1993)

John Anthony Burgess Wilson was born and educated in Manchester, England, but was later stationed in the East as an education officer. This experience formed the basis for his first three novels called, collectively, The Malayan Trilogy. By the time of his death, the prolific Mr. Burgess — known for his verbal dexterity and word play — was considered by many to be one of the most ingenious writers alive. At various points in his career he taught at the University of North Carolina (Chapel Hill), Princeton, and Columbia.

Byrne 1996; *A Dead Man in Deptford* 1993; *On Mozart: A Paean for Wolfgang* 1991; *The Devil's Mode* (stories) 1989; *Any Old Iron* 1989; *The Pianoplayers* 1986; *The Kingdom of the Wicked* 1985; *Enderby's Dark Lady* 1984; *The End of the World News* 1982; *Earthly Powers* 1980; *Man of Nazareth* 1979; *1985* 1978; *Abba, Abba* 1977; *Beard's Roman Women* 1976; *Moses* 1976; *The Clockwork Testament* 1974; *The Napoleon Symphony* 1974; *MF* 1971; *Enderby Outside* 1968; *Tremor of Intent* 1966; *A Vision of Battlements* 1965; *Eve of St. Venus* 1964; *Nothing*

Like the Sun: A Novel of Shakespeare's Love Life 1964; *Inside Mr. Enderby* 1963; *Honey for the Bears* 1963; *A Clockwork Orange* 1962; *The Wanting Seed* 1962; *Devil of a State* 1961; *One Hand Clapping* 1961; *The Worm and the Ring* 1961; *Doctor Is Sick* 1960; *The Right to an Answer* 1960; *The Malayan Trilogy* 1956–1959

Busch, Charles (1954–)

Born in New York City, Mr. Busch graduated from Northwestern University in Chicago and returned to Manhattan where he embarked on a successful career as a playwright, novelist and drag queen.

Whores of the Lost Atlantis 1993

Busch, Frederick (1941–)

Busch was born in Brooklyn and was educated at Muhlenberg College and Columbia University. He is a member of the English faculty at Colgate University.

The Night Inspector 1999; **Girls** 1977; *The Children in the Wood* 1994; *Long Way from Home* 1993; *Closing Arguments* 1991; *Harry and Catherine* 1990; *War Babies* 1989; *Absent Friends* 1989; *Sometimes I Live in the Country* 1986; *Invisible Mending* 1984; *The Late American Boyhood Blues* (stories) 1984; *Take This Man* 1981; *Rounds* 1979; *Hardwater Country* 1979; *The Mutual Friend* 1978; *Domestic Particulars* 1976; *Manual Labor* 1974; *I Wanted a Year Without Fall* 1974; *Breathing Trouble* (stories)1974

Busia, Akosua

Actress, artist and novelist, Ms. Busia was born in Ghana. She currently lives in Los Angeles.

The Seasons of Beento Blackbird 1996

Butler, Robert Olen (1945–)

Journalist, teacher, actor, playwright, short story writer and novelist, Butler was born in Granite City, Illinois. He was educated at Northwestern University and the University of Iowa and currently teaches English at McNeese State University in Lake Charles, Louisiana.

The Deep Green Sea 1998; *Tabloid Dreams* (stories) 1996; **They Whisper** 1994; *A Good Scent from a Strange Mountain* (stories) 1992; *The Deuce* 1989; *Wabash* 1987; *On Distant Ground* 1985; *Countrymen of Bones* 1983; *Sun Dogs*: a novel 1982; *The Alleys of Eden* 1981

Byatt, A. S. (1936–)

A novelist and critic, Ms. Byatt was born in Sheffield, England, and was educated at Newnham College Cambridge. She is the sister of well-known novelist and editor Margaret Drabble.

Elementals: Stories of Fire and Ice 1999; **Babel Tower** 1996; *The Djinn in the Nightingale's Eye* 1994; *The Matisse Stories* 1993; **Angels and Insects** 1992;

Possession: A Romance 1990; *Sugar and Other Stories* 1987; *Still Life* 1985; *The Virgin in the Garden* 1978; *The Game* 1967; *The Shadow of the Sun* 1964

Cambor, Kathleen

Ms. Cambor graduated from the University of Pittsburgh with a degree in nursing. She eventually moved to Houston where she obtained an MFA in creating writing and began work on her first novel.

The Book of Mercy 1996

Cameron, Peter (1959–)

Born in Pompton Plains, New Jersey, Mr. Cameron graduated from Hamilton College. He has taught at Oberlin College and currently lives and writes in New York City where he works for the Lambda Legal Defense and Education Fund.

Andorra 1998; **The Weekend** 1995; *Far-Flung: Stories* 1991; *Leap Year* 1990; *One Way or Another: Stories* 1986

Campbell, Bebe Moore (1950–)

Ms. Campbell, a freelance journalist and novelist, was born in Philadelphia and graduated from the University of Pittsburgh. She currently lives in Los Angeles with her husband, Ellis Gordon, Jr., her daughter (actress Maia Campbell, from a previous marriage), and her son Ellis Gordon III.

Singing in the Comeback Choir 1998; **Brothers and Sisters** 1994; **Your Blues Ain't Like Mine** 1992

Canty, Kevin (1954–)

Kevin Canty teaches English at the University of North Carolina, Wilmington.

Nine Below Zero 1999; **Into the Great Wide Open** 1996; *A Stranger in This World* 1994

Cao, Lan (1961–)

Ms. Lan was born in Saigon and immigrated to the U.S. toward the end of the Vietnam War. She graduated from Mount Holyoke College and Yale University Law School. She is currently a law professor at the Brooklyn School of Law.

Monkey Bridge 1997

Carey, Jacqueline (1954–)

Ms. Carey, a freelance writer, was born in Cambridge, Massachusetts, and attended Swarthmore College in Pennsylvania.

The Other Family 1996; *Good Gossip* (stories) 1992

Carey, Peter (1943–)

Peter Carey was born at Bacchus Marsh, Victoria (a location celebrated in his 1985 novel, *Illywhacker*). He worked in advertising before turning his attention full time to writing. Considered to be one of Australia's leading writers, he has won numerous prizes including the Booker Prize and the Miles Franklin Literary Award (*Oscar & Lucinda*), and *The Age* Book of the Year Award (*The Unusual Life of Tristan Smith*).

Jack Maggs 1998; **The Unusual Life of Tristan Smith** 1994; **The Tax Inspector** 1991; **Oscar & Lucinda** 1988; *Illywhacker* 1985; **Bliss** 1981; *Exotic Pleasures* (stories) 1980; *War Crimes* (stories) 1979; *The Fat Man in History* (stories) 1974

Carkeet, David (1946–)

Mr. Carkeet was born in Sonora, California, and was educated at the Universities of California, Wisconsin and Indiana. He is currently on the faculty of the University of Missouri in St. Louis.

The Error of Our Ways 1997; *Quiver River* 1991; *The Full Catastrophe 1990*; *The Silent Treatment* 1988; *I Been There Before* 1985; *The Greatest Slump of All Time* 1984; *Double Negative* 1980

Carr, A.A.

Mr. Carr, a documentary filmmaker and novelist, is of Navajo and Laguna Pueblo ancestry.

The Eye Killers 1995

Carr, Caleb (1955–)

Born in New York City, Mr. Carr, a novelist and historian, attended Kenyon College and NYU

Angel of Darkness 1997; **The Alienist** 1994; *Casing the Promised Land* 1980

Carroll, Jonathan (1949–)

Mr. Carroll was born in New York City and was educated at Rutgers and the University of Virginia. His father, Sidney Carroll, was a well-known screen writer (e.g. *Hustler, Gambit*); his mother, June Carroll, was a Broadway actress and librettist. He has lived in Vienna, Austria, for many years.

Kissing the Beehive 1998; *The Panic Hand* (stories) 1995; *From the Teeth of Angels* 1993; *After Silence* 1992; *Outside the Dog Museum* 1991; *Black Cocktail* (stories) 1991; *A Child Across the Sky* 1989; *Sleeping in Flame* 1988; *Bones of the Moon* 1988; *Voice of Our Shadow* 1983; *The Land of Laughs* 1980

Carson, Anne (1950–)

A prize-winning poet and the recipient of a Rockefeller Foundation Fellowship, Ms. Carson teaches Classics at McGill University.

Autobiography of Red 1998

Cartwright, Justin

Justin Cartwright was born in South Africa and educated at Oxford University. A novelist, screenwriter and former adman, Cartwright has lived most of his adult life in London.

Leading the Cheers 1999; *In Every Face I Meet* 1995; **Masai Dreaming** 1993; *Look at It This Way* 1990; *Interior* 1988; *Freedom of the Wolves* 1983; *Horse of Darius* 1980; *The Revenge* 1978

Cary, Lorene

A novelist and teacher, Ms. Cary, as a bright

young ambitious teenager (from inner-city Philadelphia) was one of the first black and first female students at St. Paul's, an exclusive (formerly all boy) boarding school located in New Hampshire.

Pride 1998; **The Price of a Child** 1995

Casey, John (Dudley) (1939–)

A lawyer, novelist and professor of English literature, Mr. Casey graduated from Harvard University and received his MFA from the University of Iowa. He has taught at the University of Virginia for many years.

The Half-life of Happiness 1998; *Spartina 1989*; *South Country* 1988; *The Story of Breece D'J Pancake* 1983; *Testimony and Demeanor* (novellas) 1979; *An American Romance* 1977

Castedo, Elena

An educator and novelist, Ms. Castedo was born in Barcelona, Spain, and raised in Chile. She eventually moved to the U.S. where she attended UCLA and Harvard University from which she received a Ph.D. in Romance Languages and Literature.

Paradise 1990

Castillo, Ana (1953–)

Ms. Castillo was born in Chicago and attended Northern Illinois University and the University of Chicago. She has taught at a number of colleges and universities including Northwestern, the University of New Mexico and Mount Holyoke College.

Loverboys (stories) 1996; **So Far from God** 1993; *Sapogonia* 1990; *The Mixquahuala Letters* 1996

Chabon, Michael (1963–)

Novelist, short story writer and screenwriter, Michael Chabon was born in Washington, D.C., and attended the University of Pittsburgh and the University of California.

Werewolves in Their Youths (stories) 1999; **Wonder Boys** 1995; *A Model World and Other Stories* 1991; *The Mysteries of Pittsburgh* 1988

Chandra, Vikram (1961–)

A prize-winning novelist and short story writer, Vikram Chandra was educated in India and at Pomona College, Johns Hopkins University, the University of Houston and Columbia. Mr. Chandra has taught at George Washington University, Rice and Johns Hopkins. He currently lives in Washington, D.C.

Love and Longing in Bombay (stories) 1997; **Red Earth, Pouring Rain** 1995

Chao, Patricia (1955–)

Ms. Chao was born in Carmel-by-the-Sea and was educated at Brown University and NYU. A

poet, novelist and children's book author, she currently teaches at Sarah Lawrence.
Monkey King 1997

Chappell, Fred (1936–)
Mr. Chapell was born in Canton, North Carolina, and was educated at Duke University; he teaches English literature at the University of North Carolina at Greensboro.
Farewell I'm Bound to Leave You 1996; *More Shapes Than One* 1991; *Brighten the Corner Where You Are* 1989; *I'm One of You Forever* 1985; *The Gaudy Place* 1972; *Dagon* 1968; *The Inkling* 1966; *It Is Time Lord* 1963

Chavez, Denise (1948–)
Ms. Chavez was born in Las Cruces, New Mexico, and was educated at New Mexico State University and at Trinity College in Texas. She lectures widely, has taught at the University of New Mexico and is the writer-in-residence at La Compania de Teatro in Albuquerque.
Face of an Angel 1994; *The Last of the Menu Girls* (stories) 1986

Cheong, Fiona
Ms. Cheong was born and raised in Singapore. She emigrated to the U.S. where she was educated and has taught at Howard and Cornell universities. She currently teaches at the University of Pittsburgh.
The Scent of the Gods 1991

Cheever, Benjamin (1948–)
The son of John Cheever (and editor of *The Letters of John Cheever*), Benjamin Cheever is a contributing editor to the literary magazine *Archipelago*.
Famous After Death 1999; *The Partisan* 1993; ***The Plagiarist*** 1992

Childress, Mark (1951–)
Journalist and novelist, Childress was born in Monroeville, Alabama, and was educated at the University of Alabama.
Gone for Good 1998; ***Crazy in Alabama*** 1993; *Tender* 1990; *V for Victor* 1988; *A World Made of Fire* 1984

Chin, Frank
A novelist, short story writer and playwright, Mr. Chin was born in Berkeley, California, and was educated at UC–Berkeley, the State University of Iowa and UC–Santa Barbara
Gunga Din Highway 1994; ***Donald Duk*** 1990; *The Chinaman Pacific and Frisco RR CO.* (stories) 1988; *No-No Boy* 1980

Choy, Wayson (1939–)
Mr. Choy was born in Toronto where he has lived most of his life. He has taught English at Humber College for 25 years.
Jade Peony 1997

Christilian, J. D. (1924–1996)
Mr. J.D. Christilian's real name was Marvin Albert. A prolific mystery/thriller writer he wrote under the following nom de plumes: Anthony Rome, Mike Barone, Nick Quarry, Al Conroy and Ian McAlister.
Scarlet Women 1996

Christopher, Nicholas (1951–)
A poet and novelist, Mr. Christopher was born in New York City and was educated at Harvard. His poetry has won major awards and he has taught at both Columbia and NYU.
Veronica 1996; *Desperate Character* 1988; *The Soloist* 1986

Chute, Carolyn (1947–)
Ms. Chute was born in Portland, Maine, and attended the University of Southern Maine. Before devoting herself full-time to writing she worked in a shoe factory and as a social worker, tutor and teacher.
Snow Man 1999; ***Merry Men*** 1994; *Letourneau's Used Auto Parts* 1988; *The Beans of Egypt Maine* 1985

Cisneros, Sandra (1954–)
Ms. Cisneros, a poet, short story writer and novelist, was born and raised on Chicago's South Side. She was educated at Loyola University and the University of Iowa, where she attended the prestigious Writer's Workshop.
Woman Hollering Creek (stories) 1991; ***The House on Mango Street*** 1983

Clair, Maxine (1939–)
Ms. Clair grew up in Kansas City, Kansas, and was educated at the George Washington University and at American University — both located in Washington, D.C. She currently teaches writing at the George Washington University.
Rattlebone 1994

Coe, Jonathan (1961–)
Born in Birmingham, Mr. Coe was educated at Cambridge and the University of Warwick. He describes himself as a freelance writer, journalist and semi-professional musician.
House of Sleep 1998; ***The Winshaw Legacy or What a Carve Up?*** 1994; *Dwarves of Death* 1990; *A Touch of Love* 1989; *Accidental Woman* 1987

Coetzee, J. M. (1940–)
Novelist, essayist, critic, editor and translator, Mr. Coetzee was born in Cape Town, South Africa, and was educated at the University of Cape Town. He lived for a time in London, attended the University of Texas where he received his graduate degree in English and now teaches at the University of Cape Town.
The Master of Petersburg 1994; *Age of Iron* 1990; *Foe* 1986; *Life & Times of Michael K* 1983; *Waiting for the Barbarians* 1980; *In the Heart of the Country* 1977; *Dusklands* 1974

Cohen, Robert (1957–)

Mr. Cohen, a novelist, short story writer and journalist, was born in Syracuse and attended SUNY–Stony Brook, Rice and the University of Houston. He currently teaches at Middlebury College in Vermont.

The Here and Now 1996; *The Organ Builder* 1988

Cohn, Nik

Nik Cohn, a novelist, journalist, and music reviewer, was born and raised in England. His 1977 article for *New York* magazine entitled "Saturday Night Fever" became the basis for the popular film.

Need 1997; *The Heart of the World* 1992; *King Death* 1975; *Arfur: Teenage Pinball Queen* 1970

Collignon, Jeff (1953–)

A "recluse and drifter" (KR) Mr. Collignon has written one novel.

Her Monster 1992.

Collignon, Rick (1948–)

A native New Mexican, Mr. Collignon, in addition to his fiction writing, has worked as a roofer and carpenter.

Perdito 1997; *The Journal of Antonio Montoya* 1996

Colwin, Laurie (1944–1992)

Ms. Colwin, a novelist, editor and translator was born in New York City and was educated at Bard College and Columbia University.

A Big Storm Knocked It Over 1994; *Another Marvelous Thing* 1986; *Family Happiness* 1982; *The Lone Pilgrim* (stories) 1981; *Happy All the Time* 1978; *Shine On Bright and Dangerous Object* 1975; *The Dangerous French Mistress* (stories) 1975; *Passion & Affect* (stories) 1974

Connaughton, Shane

Shane Connaughton was born in Ireland and brought up along the (often violent) Cavan-Fermanagh border where his father served as a police sergeant. He now lives in London,

The Run of the Country 1991; *A Border Station* 1989

Cook, Thomas

The author of 12 novels and two "true crime" stories, Mr. Cook lives in New York City.

Blood Innocents 1999; *The Chatham School Affair* 1996; *Breakheart Hill* 1995; *Mortal Memory* 1993; *Evidence of Blood* 1991; *The City When It Rains* 1991; *Night Secrets* 1990; *Flesh and Blood* 1989; *Streets of Fire* 1989; *Sacrificial Ground* 1988; *Elena* 1986; *Tabernacle* 1983; *The Orchids* 1982

Cooke, Elizabeth

Elizabeth Cooke, a short story writer and novelist, currently teaches in the Creative Writing program at the University of Maine.

Zeena 1996; *Complicity* 1988

Cooper, Dennis (1953–)

Cooper, poet, novelist, music critic and art critic, was born in Pasadena and attended Pasadena City College and Pitzer.

Guide 1997; *Horror Hospital Unplugged* 1996; *Try* 1994; *Jerk* 1993; *Wrong* (stories) 1992; *Frisk* 1991; *Idols* 1989; *Closer* 1989; *Safe* 1984; *The Tenderness of the Wolves* 1982; *Idols* 1979

Coover, Robert (1932–)

Mr. Coover, novelist, playwright, poet, critic and educator, was born in Iowa and grew up in Indiana. He was educated at Indiana University and the University of Chicago. He has taught widely at colleges and universities throughout the U.S.

Briar Rose 1997; *John's Wife* 1996; *Pinocchio in Venice* 1991; *Whatever Happened to Gloomy Gus of the Chicago Bears?* 1989; *A Night at the Movies, or You Must Remember This* (stories) 1987; *Gerald's Party* 1986; *In Bed One Night & other Brief Encounters* (stories) 1983; *The Convention* (stories) 1981; *Spanking the Maid* 1981; *Charlie in the House of Rue* (novella) 1980; *A Political Fable* (novella) 1980; *Hair O'the Chine* (stories) 1979; *The Public Burning* 1977; *Water Pourer* 1972; *Pricksongs and Descants* (stories) 1969; *The Universal Baseball Association, Inc. J. Henry Waugh, prop* 1968; *The Origin of the Brunists* 1967

Corey, Deborah Joy (1958–)

A talented young Canadian author, Ms. Corey won the 1993 *Books in Canada* Award for Best First Novel.

Losing Eddie 1993

Coupland, Douglas (1961–)

Coupland was born on a Canadian military base in Germany but returned to Vancouver at the age of four. He studied art and design before turning his hand to writing; he divides his time between Vancouver, L.A. and Northern Scotland.

Girlfriend in a Coma 1998; *Polaroids from the Dead* 1996; *Microserfs* 1995; *Life After God* 1994; *Shampoo Planet* 1992; *Generation X* 1991

Cowan, James (1942–)

Mr. Cowan, an Australian novelist, journalist and essayist, has lived among indigenous peoples in Morocco, Libya, Tahiti and Japan and has written numerous books drawing on these experiences.

A Troubadour's Testament 1998; *A Mapmaker's Dream* 1996; *Toby's Angel* 1975

Crace, Jim (1946–)

Jim Crace was born in Brocket Hall, Lewisford, Harfordshire, and received his university degree from the Birmingham College of Commerce.

Crace has taught English in Botswana, was a volunteer writer and editor for Sudanese Educational TV, and did freelance radio and feature journalism before turning to writing full time.

Quarantine 1998; ***Signals of Distress*** *1994*; *Arcadia 1991*; *The Gift of Stones 1988*; *Continent 1986*

Crews, Harry (1935–)

Born in Bacon County, Georgia, into a hard-scrabble farm family, Crews obtained undergraduate and graduate degrees from the University of Florida. A prolific novelist, he has also taught high school and college English, most recently at the University of Florida.

Celebration 1998; ***The Mulching of America*** *1995*; ***Scar Lover*** *1992*; *Body 1990*; *The Knockout Artist 1988*; *All We Need of Hell 1987*; *A Feast of Snakes 1976*; *The Gypsy's Curse 1974*; *The Hawk Is Dying 1973*; *Car 1972*; *Karate Is a Thing of the Spirit 1971*; *This Thing Don't Lead to Heaven 1970*; *Naked in Garden Hills 1969*; *The Gospel Singer 1968*

Cunningham, Michael (1952–)

Michael Cunningham attended Stanford University and received his MFA from the University of Iowa.

The Hours *1998*; ***Flesh & Blood*** *1995*; *A Home at the End of the World 1990*; *Golden Skates 1984*

D'Aguiar, Fred (1960–)

Mr. D'Aguiar was born in London but grew up in Guyana. Educated at the University of Kent at Canterbury, he has taught at Cambridge University, Amherst College, Bates College, and the University of Miami at Coral Gables.

Feeding the Ghosts 1998; ***Dear Future*** *1996*; ***The Longest Memory*** *1994*

Danticat, Edwidge (1969–)

Ms. Danticat was born in Port-au-Prince, Haiti, and was raised by an aunt after her parents emigrated to New York. At twelve she joined her parents in Brooklyn and eventually attended Barnard College and Brown University. *Breath, Eyes, Memory* grew out of her thesis project at Brown.

The Farming of Bones 1998; *Krik Krak* (stories) *1995*; ***Breath, Eyes, Memory*** *1994*

Darton, Eric

Mr. Darton was educated at Hunter College in New York City where he currently teaches media, technology and cultural studies. He has also taught at the New School for Social Research in Manhattan.

Free City *1996*

Daugharty, Janice (1944–)

Ms. Daugharty, who began writing at the age

of 39, had her first novel published ten years later. She was born in Valdosta, Georgia, and attended Valdosta State University.

Whistle 1998; ***Earl in the Yellow Shirt*** *1997*; ***Paw Paw Patch*** *1996*; *Necessary Lies 1995*; *Going Through the Changes* (stories) *1994*; *Dark of the Moon 1994*

Davies, Robertson (1913–1995)

One of the most important North American writers of the 20th century (he was the first Canadian Honorary Member of the American Academy of Arts and Letters), Davies, a novelist, essayist, literary critic, opera aficionado and Shakespeare scholar, was born in Thomasville, Ontario, and was educated at Upper Canada College, Queen's University (Canada), and Oxford University. His prize-winning books are richly textured (he freely mixes magic, mythology and labyrinthine plots) and laced with philosophical inquiries into the nature of art and creativity.

The Cunning Man *1994*; ***Murther & Walking Spirits*** *1991*; **The Cornish Trilogy:** *The Lyre of Orpheus 1988*;; *What's Bred in the Bone 1985*; ***Rebel Angels*** *1981*; **Deptford Trilogy:** *World of Wonders 1975*; *The Manticore 1972*; *Fifth Business 1970*; **Salterton Trilogy:** *A Mixture of Frailties 1958*; *Leaven of Malice 1954*; *Tempest-Tost 1951*

Davies, Stevie (Stephanie) (1946–)

Ms. Davies was born in Salisbury, England, and was educated at Manchester University where she is currently on the faculty.

Four Dreamers and Emily *1996*; *Arms & The Girl 1992*; *Primavera 1990*; *Boy Blue 1987*

Davis, Thulani

Ms. Davis, a journalist, novelist, librettist, poet and Grammy Award–winning lyricist has written for the *Village Voice* and teaches at Barnard. She currently lives in Brooklyn.

Maker of Saints *1996*; ***1959: A Novel*** *1995*

Davison, Liam (1957–)

Mr. Davison is a prize-winning Australian novelist who is too-little known outside of the Antipodes.

The White Woman *1994*; *Soundings 1993*; *The Shipwreck Party 1989*; *The Velodrome 1988*

Dawson, Carol (1951–)

Poet, novelist, painter, jeweler, Ms. Dawson was born in Corsicana, Texas, and was educated at the University of Texas. A world traveler, she has lived in California, England, Italy, New Zealand, New Mexico and Washington. She is currently writing a history of New Zealand's Maori people.

The Mother-in-law Diaries 1999; ***Meeting of the Minotaur*** *1997*; ***Body of Knowledge*** *1994*; ***The Waking Spell*** *1992*

Deane, Seamus (1940–)

Seamus Deane, poet and novelist, was born in Derry, Northern Ireland, and was educated at Queens University (Belfast) and at Cambridge University. He has taught at a number of colleges and universities in the U.S. (including Notre Dame, Reed and Berkeley) and is currently on the faculty of the National University of Ireland.

Reading in the Dark 1997

de Bernieres, Louis (1954–)

Louis de Bernieres was born in Jordan but was raised in Surrey, England, and was educated at the Universities of Manchester and London. Before turning to writing as a career he taught school in Colombia, South America. He was named, by *Granta Magazine* in 1993 as one of the twenty "Best Young British Novelists."

Corelli's Mandolin 1994; **The Troublesome Offspring of Cardinal** 1992; **Senor Vivo and the Coca Lord** 1991; **The War of Don Emmanuel's Nether Parts** 1990

Delbanco, Nicholas

Nicholas Delbanco, novelist, short story writer, literary critic and distinguished academic, is the recipient of numerous literary awards. He is currently the director of the University of Michigan's MFA in writing program. He has taught at Columbia and Iowa universities as well as at Skidmore, Trinity, Williams and Bennington (where he founded, with John Gardner, the Bennington Writing Workshop).

Old Scores 1997; *In the Name of Mercy* 1995; *The Beaux Arts Trio* 1985; *About My Tables and Other Stories* 1983; *Stillness* 1980; *Sherbrookes* 1978; *Possession* 1977; *Small Rain* 1975; *Fathering* 1973; *In the Middle Distance* 1971; *News* 1970; *Consider Sappho Burning* 1969; *Grasse 3/22/66* 1968; *Martlet's Table* 1966

De Lillo, Don (1936–)

A preeminent, prize-winning American novelist, Mr. Delillo was born in New York City and attended Fordham University.

Underworld 1997; **Mao II** 1991; **Libra** 1988; **White Noise** 1985; *The Names* 1982; *Running Dog* 1978; *Players* 1977; *Ratner's Star* 1976; *Great Jones Street* 1973; *End Zone* 1972; *Americana* 1971

Denton, Bradley (1958–)

A novelist and short story writer, Mr. Denton was educated at the University of Kansas.

One Day Closer to Death: Eight Stabs at Immortality (stories) 1998; **Lunatics** 1996; *A Conflagration Artist* 1994; *The Calvin Coolidge Home for Dead Comedians* 1994; *Blackburn* 1993; *Buddy Holly Is Alive and Well on Ganymeade* 1991

Derbyshire, John

A freelance journalist, book critic and novelist, Mr. Derbyshire was born and raised in Great Britain and has lived in the Far East. He lives now in the U.S.

Seeing Calvin Coolidge in a Dream 1996

Desai, Anita (1937–)

Ms. Desai was born in India to a German mother and Indian father. She has taught at numerous institutions in the United States including Mount Holyoke and Smith colleges. She is currently a member of the English faculty at MIT.

Journey to Ithaca 1996; *Baumgartner's Bombay* 1988; **In Custody** 1984; *The Village by the Sea* 1982; *Clear Light of Day* 1980; *Games at Twilight & Other Stories* 1978; *Fire on the Mountain* 1977; *Bye, Bye Blackbird* 1971

Desai, Kiran

The daughter of Anita Desai, Kiran Desai was born in India but divides her time between that country, England and the U.S. She is currently a student in Columbia University's Creative Writing Program.

Hullabaloo in the Guava Orchard 1998

Dexter, Pete (1943–)

A journalist and prize-winning novelist, Pete Dexter was born in Pontiac, Michigan, but spent much of his childhood in Georgia and South Dakota; he was educated at the University of South Dakota. Mr. Dexter has worked as a truck driver, construction worker, mail sorter and as a reporter for the *West Palm Beach Post* and the *Philadelphia Daily News*. He is currently a columnist for the *Sacramento Bee*.

The Paperboy 1995; *Brotherly Love* 1993; **Paris Trout** 1988; *Deadwood* 1986; *God's Pocket* 1984

Dibdin, Michael (1947–)

Mr. Dibdin, known for his literate suspense and mystery novels, was born in Wolverhampton, England, and was educated at the University of Sussex and at the University of Alberta (Canada). Mr. Dibdin spent four years in Italy where he taught English at the University of Perugia. He now lives in Oxford.

Così Fan Tutte 1997; *Dark Specter* 1995; *Dead Lagoon* 1994; *The Dying of the Light* 1993; *Cabal* 1993; *Dirty Tricks* 1991; *Vendetta* 1991; *The Tryst* 1990; *Ratking* 1989

Dickey, James (1923–1997)

A poet, novelist and screenplay writer, Mr. Dickey was born in Buckhead, Georgia, and was educated at Vanderbilt University. He was affiliated with the University of South Carolina from 1969 until his death in 1997.

To the White Sea 1994; *Alnilam* 1987; *Deliverance* 1970

Didion, Joan (1934–)

A 6th generation Californian, Ms. Didion, novelist, essayist, screenplay writer, journalist and editor, was born in Sacramento and was educated at Berkeley. She worked for a time (1956–1963) in New York City (on the staff of *Vogue* magazine) but moved back to California with her husband, novelist and screenplay writer John Gregory Dunne, where she pursues her writing full time.

The Last Thing He Wanted 1996; *Democracy* 1984; *A Book of Common Prayer* 1977; *Play It as It Lays* 1970; *Run River* 1963

Dillard, Annie (1945–)

Ms. Dillard, Pulitzer Prize–winning essayist, poet and novelist, was born in Pittsburgh and was educated at Hollins College. She is currently adjunct Professor of English and a writer-in-residence at Wesleyan University.

For the Time Being 1999; *The Living* 1992

Disch, Thomas M.

Mr. Disch, a poet, sci-fi writer, opera librettist, theater and literary critic, anthologist, editor and novelist, was born in Des Moine, Iowa, and grew up in Minneapolis, Minnesota. He was educated at Cooper Union and NYU. He also writes under the following pseudonyms: Thom Demijohn, Leonie Hargrove, Cassandra Knye.

The Sub: A Study in Witchcraft 1999; *The Priest* 1995; *The M.D.* 1991; *The Businessman* 1984; *On Wings of Song* (sci-fi) 1979; *Getting into Death* (sci-fi stories) 1973; *334* (sci-fi) 1972; *Fun with Your New Head* (sci-fi) 1968; *Under Compulsion* (sci-fi) 1968; *Camp Concentration* (sci-fi) 1968; *The Genocides* (sci-fi) 1965

Divakaruni, Chitra (1957–)

Ms. Divakaruni was born in India and lived there until the age of nineteen when she immigrated to the U.S. She attended Wright State University and received a graduate degree from Berkeley. She currently lives in Sunnydale, California, where she teaches creative writing at Foothill College in Los Altos Hills.

Sisters of My Heart 1999; *The Mistress of Spices* 1997; *Arranged Marriages* (stories) 1995

Dixon, Melvin (1950–1992)

A novelist, poet, critic and translator, Mr. Dixon was born in Stanford, Connecticut, and was educated at Wesleyan and Brown universities. Before his death from AIDS at the age of 42, he taught at Williams College and Queens College of the City University of New York. He was also a longtime contributing editor to the literary magazine *Callaloo*.

Vanishing Rooms 1991; *Trouble the Water* 1989

Dixon, Stephen (1936–)

Mr. Dixon was born Stephen Ditchik in New York City and was educated at City College. In addition to writing and teaching, he has worked as a journalist, TV producer and a fiction consultant. He is currently on the faculty of Johns Hopkins University.

30: Pieces of a Novel 1999; *Gould: A Novel in Two Novels* 1997; *Interstate* 1995; *Long Made Short* (stories) 1993; *Frog* 1991; *Friends: More Will & Magna* (stories) 1990; *All Gone* 1990; *Love and Will* 1989; *The Play and Other Stories* 1989; *Garbage* 1988; *Fall & Rise* 1985; *Time to Go* 1984; *Movies* (stories) 1983; *14 Stories* 1980; *Quite Contrary: The Mary & Newt Story* (stories) 1979; *Too Late* 1978; *Work* 1977; *No Relief* (stories) 1976

Djerassi, Carl (1923–)

Mr. Djerassi, a poet, novelist, short story writer, academic and research chemist (who is credited with the development of oral contraceptives) was born in Vienna and was educated at Kenyon College and the University of Wisconsin. He is currently on the faculty of Stanford University.

Go 1998; *Menachem's Seed* 1997; *Marx, Deceased* 1996; *The Bourbaki Gambit* 1994; *Cantor's Dilemma* 1991; *The Futurist* (stories) 1988

Doane, Michael (1952–)

Mr. Doane, a novelist and short story writer, was born in Sioux Falls, South Dakota, and was educated at the University of South Dakota.

Bullet Heart 1994; *City of Light* 1992; *Six Miles to Roadside Business* 1990; *The Surprise of Burning* 1988; *The Legends of Jesse Dark* 1984

Dobyns, Stephen (1941–)

Mr. Dobyns was born in Orange, New Jersey, and was educated at Shimer College and Wayne State University. After receiving his MFA from the University of Iowa he taught at the University of New Hampshire and Goddard College. He is currently on the faculty of Warren Wilson College.

The Church of Dead Girls 1997; *Common Carnage* 1996; *Saratoga Fleshpot* 1995; *Saratoga Backtalk* 1994; *The Wrestler's Cruel Study* 1993; *Saratoga Hexameter* 1990; *The Two Deaths of Senora Puccini* 1988; *Saratoga Bestiary* 1988; *A Boat Off the Coast* 1987; *Saratoga Snapper* 1986; *Saratoga Headhunter* 1985; *Dancer with One Leg* 1983; *Saratoga Swimmer* 1981; *Saratoga Long Shot* 1976; *A Man of Little Evils* 1973

Doctorow, E. L. (1931–)

Doctorow, a prominent American author, was born in New York City and attended the Bronx High School of Science. He later graduated from Kenyon College and Columbia University. He has taught for many years and is currently on the faculty of NYU. He lives in New Rochelle, New York.

Waterworks 1994; *Billy Bathgate* 1989; *World's Fair* 1985; *Loon Lake* 1980; *Ragtime* 1975; *Book of Daniel* 1971; *Big as Life* 1966; *Welcome to Hard Times* 1960

Doig, Ivan (1939–)

Doig, born in White Sulphur Springs, Montana, has been a ranch hand, newspaper man and magazine editor. He graduated from Northwestern University and holds a doctorate from the University of Washington. He currently lives in Seattle.

Bucking the Sun 1996; *Ride with Me, Mariah Montana* 1990; *Dancing at the Rascal Fair* 1987; *English Creek* 1984; *The Sea Runners* 1982

Donoghue, Emma (1962–)

Ms. Donoghue, a playwright, novelist and historian, was born in Dublin and was educated at University College and at Cambridge University.

Kissing the Witch (stories) 1997; *Hood* 1996; **Stir Fry** 1994

Dooling, Richard (1954–)

An attorney and novelist, Mr. Dooling was born in Omaha, Nebraska. He was educated at the University of Nebraska and at St. Louis University. Mr. Dooling has also worked as a respiratory technician and therapist.

Brain Storm 1998; **White Man's Grave** 1994; **Critical Care** 1992

Dorris, Michael (1945–1997)

One of the most influential Native American writers of the past few decades, Mr. Dorris was educated at Georgetown and Yale and taught English and anthropology at Dartmouth. Mr. Dorris, whose marriage to novelist Louise Erdrich was foundering, committed suicide in 1997.

Cloud Chamber 1997; *Working Men* (stories) 1993; *The Crown of Columbus* (with Louise Erdrich) 1991; *A Yellow Raft in Blue Water* 1987

Dove, Rita (1952–)

Ms. Dove was born in Akron, Ohio, and was educated at Miami University (Ohio) and the University of Iowa. She has won numerous awards (including the Pulitzer Prize) for her poetry. She is currently on the faculty at the University of Virginia.

Through the Ivory Gate 1998

Doyle, Roddy (1958–)

A Dubliner by birth, Mr. Doyle, teacher, novelist, screen writer and playwright, continues to live in his old Dublin neighborhood.

The Woman Who Walked into Doors 1996; **Paddy Clarke Ha Ha Ha** 1993; *The Van* 1991; *The Snapper* 1990; *The Commitments* 1987

Drabble, Margaret (1939–)

Margaret Drabble was born in Sheffield, South Yorkshire, and was educated at the Mount

School, York and Cambridge. Ms. Drabble is well known in Great Britain as a novelist, biographer and editor of *The Oxford Companion to Literature*. She was awarded the CBE in 1980 for her many contributions to English Literature. Ms. Drabble's sister, A.S. Byatt, is also a well-known British novelist.

The Witch of Exmoor 1996; *The Gates of Ivory* 1991; *A Natural Curiosity* 1989; *The Radiant Way* 1987; *The Middle Ground* 1980; *The Ice Age* 1977; *The Realms of Gold* 1975; *The Needle's Eye* 1972; *The Waterfall* 1969; *Jerusalem the Golden* 1967; *The Millstone* 1965; *The Garrick Year* 1964; *A Summer Bird Cage* 1962

Drewe, Robert (1943–)

Mr. Drewe was born in Melbourne, Australia, where he has pursued a career as an editor, journalist, novelist and short story writer.

The Drowner 1997; *Our Sunshine* 1991; *Bay of Contented Men* 1991; *Fortune* 1987; *The Bodysurfers* (stories) 1983; *A Cry in the Jungle Bar* 1979; *The Savage Crows* 1976

Duff, Alan (1950–)

Alan Duff was born in Rotorura, New Zealand, to a Maori mother and pakeha (white) father. In addition to his novel writing, Duff is a weekly commentator for Wellington's *Evening Post*.

What Becomes of the Broken Hearted 1996; **One Night Out Stealing** 1992; **Once Were Warriors** 1990

Duffy, Bruce

Novelist and one-time correspondent of the Discovery Channel's on-line magazine.

Last Comes the Egg 1997; *The World as I Found It* 1987

Dufresne, John (1948–)

Mr. Dufresne was born in Worcester, Massachusetts, and was educated at Worcester State, the University of Arkansas and SUNY–Binghampton. He currently teaches at Florida International University and lives in Dania with his wife and son.

Love Warps the Mind a Little 1997; **Louisiana Power & Light** 1994; *The Way That Water Enters Stone* (stories) 1991

Duncker, Patricia (1951–)

Duncker teaches writing and feminist theory at the University of Wales. She was born in the West Indies, educated at Bedales, Oxford and Cambridge, and divides her time between Wales and France.

Monsieur Shoshana's Lemon Trees (stories) 1998; **Hallucinating Foucault** 1996

Dunmore, Helen (1952–)

Ms. Dunmore, a poet, novelist and nursery school teacher, was born in Yorkshire, England, and was educated at York University.

Your Blue-Eyed Boy 1998; **Talking to the Dead**

1996; A Spell of Winter 1995; Burning Bright 1994; Zennor in Darkness 1993; Going to Egypt 1992

Dworkin, Susan (1941–)

A playwright, novelist, biographer, journalist, and former *Ms. Magazine* contributing editor, Ms. Dworkin is a well-known figures in the area of Jewish and women's literature. In addition to her novels, she has written a biography of Bess Meyerson, completed a novelization of the film *Desperately Seeking Susan*, and has co-authored a biography of AIDS victim Ryan White.

The Book of Candy 1996; Stolen Goods 1987

Dyja, Tom

Mr. Dyja, an editor and novelist, was born in Chicago and was educated at Columbia University.

To Play for a Kingdom 1997

Eberstadt, Fernanda (1960–)

Ms. Eberstadt, the granddaughter of Ogdan Nash, was born in New York City and was educated at Oxford University.

When the Sons of Heaven Meet the Daughters of Earth 1997; Isaac & His Devils 1991; Low Tide 1985

Echewa, Thomas Obinkaram (1940–)

Born in Nigeria, Echewa emigrated to the U.S. in 1961. He was educated at Notre Dame, Columbia and the University of Pennsylvania.

I Saw the Sky Catch Fire 1992; The Crippled Dance 1986; The Land's Lord 1976

Edgerton, Clyde (1944–)

Mr. Edgerton, novelist, educator, and musician, was born in Durham, North Carolina, and was educated at the University of North Carolina at Chapel Hill. He has taught at North Carolina Central University, Agnes Scott College and Campbell University.

Where Trouble Sleeps 1997; Redeye 1995; In Memory of Junior 1992; Killer Diller 1991; The Floatplane Notebooks 1988; Walking Across Egypt 1987; Raney 1985

Elegant, Simon (1960–)

Mr. Elegant is the Arts and Society Editor of the *Far Eastern Economic Review.*

A Floating Life 1997

Elkin, Stanley (1930–1995)

A novelist, short story writer, playwright and screenplay writer, Mr. Elkin was born in New York City and attended the University of Illinois. He taught for much of his career at Washington University in St. Louis.

Mrs. Ted Bliss 1995; Van Gogh's Room at Arles (three novellas) *1993; The Magic Kingdom 1991; The Rabbi of Lud 1987; Early Elkin* (story collection)

1985; George Mills 1982; The First George Mills 1981; Stanly Eklin's Greatest Hits 1980; The Living End (3 novellas) *1979; The Franchiser 1976; Searches and Seizures 1973; The Making of Ashenden 1972; The Dick Gibson Show 1971; Stories from the Sixties 1971; A Bad Man 1967; Criers & Kibitzers, Kibitzers & Criers 1966; Boswell: A Modern Comedy 1964*

Ellis, Alice Thomas (1932–)

Critic, columnist, novelist and editor, Ms. Ellis (Anna Haycraft) is known for her astringent social comedies. She was born in Liverpool but spent much of her childhood in Wales. She was educated at the Liverpool College of Art. Ms. Ellis lives in London where she is an editor at Duckworth, a prominent publishing house.

Fairy Tale 1998; The Evening of Adam 1994; The Summer House trilogy (*The Clothes in the Wardrobe, The Skeleton in the Cupboard, The Fly in the Ointment*) *1994; Pillars of Gold 1992; Inn at the End of the World 1990; Fly in the Ointment 1989* (see above); *The Skeleton in the Cupboard 1988* (see above); *The Clothes in the Wardrobe 1987* (see above); *Unexplained Laughter 1985; The Other Side of the Fire 1983; The 27th Kingdom 1982; Birds of the Air 1980; The Sin Eater 1977*

Ephron, Delia

A playwright, screenplay writer, novelist and children's writer, Mr. Ephron has collaborated with her sister Nora on such films as *Sleepless in Seattle.*

Hanging Up 1995

Epstein, Leslie (1938–)

Mr. Epstein was born in Los Angeles (the son of a prominent screenwriter) and attended Yale University and Oxford. He is currently director of the Creative Writing Program at Boston University.

Pandaemonium 1997; Pinto & Sons 1992; Goldkorn Tales 1986; Regina 1982; King of the Jews 1979; Steinway's Quintet Plus Four 1976; P.D. Kemerakov 1975

Erdrich, Louise (1954–)

Ms. Erdrich was born in Little Falls, Minnesota, of a French/Ojibway mother and a German/American father. Her maternal grandfather was the tribal Chairman of the Turtle Mountain Reservation in North Dakota. She attended Dartmouth and Johns Hopkins universities and was married to Michael Dorris, well-known novelist and anthropologist, who committed suicide in 1997.

The Antelope Wife 1998; Tales of Burning Love 1996; The Bingo Palace 1994; The Crown of Columbus 1991; Tracks 1988; The Beet Queen 1986; Love Medicine 1984

Erickson, Steve (1950–)

Mr. Erickson was born in Santa Monica, California, and was educated at UCLA. A freelance writer, he has traveled extensively in Europe.

The Sea Came in at Midnight 1999; *American Nomad* 1997; *Amnesiascope* 1996; **Arc d'X** 1993; *Tour of the Black Clock* 1989; *Leap Year* 1989; *Rubicon Beech* 1986; *Days Between Stations* 1985

Eugenides, Jeffrey (1960–)

Born in Grosse Point, Michigan, Mr. Eugenides, a poet, editor and novelist, was educated at Brown and Stanford. To support his writing, he has worked at a number of jobs including cab driving. He has also worked as a volunteer with Mother Teresa in India. He currently lives in Brooklyn, New York.

The Virgin Suicides 1993

Everett, Percival (1956–)

A jazz musician, writer and educator, Mr. Everett was born in Georgia and was educated at the University of Miami, the University of Oregon and Brown University. He has taught at the University of Kentucky, Notre Dame and the University of California at Riverside.

Frenzy 1997; *Watershed* 1996; *Big Picture* (stories) 1996; *God's Country* 1994; *The Body of Martin Aquilera* 1994; *The One That Got Away* 1992; *Zulus* 1989; *For Her Dark Skin* 1989; *The Weather & Women Treat Me Fair* (stories) 1987; *Cutting Lisa* 1986; *Walk Me to the Distance* 1985; *Suder* 1983

Farah, Nuruddin (1945–)

A novelist and playwright, Mr. Farah was born in Baidoa Somalia, the son of a famous Somali poet. H was educated in Somalia, Ethiopia and India. Due to political unrest in his native country Mr. Farah has lived most of his life abroad including a brief period in the U.S. He now divides his time between Nigeria and England.

Secrets 1998; *Gifts* 1992; *Maps* 1986; *Close Sesame* 1983; *Sardines* 1981; *Sweet & Sour Milk* 1980; *A Naked Needle* 1976; *From a Crooked Rib* 1970

Faulks, Sebastian (1953–)

A journalist, teacher and novelist, Mr. Faulks was born in Newbury, England, and was educated at Cambridge University.

Charlotte Gray 1999; **Birdsong** 1993; *A Fool's Alphabet* 1992; *A Trick of the Light* 1984

Fell, Alison (1944–)

Ms. Fell, a poet and novelist, was born in Dumfries, Scotland, and was educated at the Edinburgh College of Art and at the University of London's National Film School.

The Pillow Boy of the Lady Onogoro 1994; *Serious Hysterics* 1992; *Mer de Glace* 1992; *The Bad Box* 1987; *Every Move You Make* 1984

Ferre, Rosario (1942–)

Ms. Ferre was born in Ponce, Puerto Rico, and was educated at the University of Puerto Rico and the University of Maryland.

Eccentric Neighborhood 1998; **The House on the Lagoon** 1995

Fischer, Tibor (1959–)

Tibor Fischer was born in Stockport, England, to Hungarian parents and was educated at Cambridge University. A journalist and novelist, Fischer currently lives in London. He was named by *Granta Magazine* as one of the twenty "Best Young British Novelists" in 1993.

The Collector Collector 1997; **The Thought Gang** 1994; **Under the Frog** 1992

Fitzgerald, Penelope (1916–)

Biographer and novelist, Ms. Fitzgerald was born in Lincoln, England; her father, Edmund Valpy, was a long-time editor of the English humor magazine *Punch*. Educated at Oxford, Ms. Fitzgerald began her writing career when she was in her fifties and quickly became one of Britain's most respected novelists. She once lived with her family on a Thames barge until it sank, she now divides her time between London and Somerset.

The Blue Flower 1995; **The Gate of Angels** 1990; *The Beginning of Spring* 1988; *Innocence* 1986; *At Freddies* 1982; *Human Voices* 1980; *Offshore* 1979; **The Bookshop** 1978; *The Golden Child* 1977

Flanagan, Thomas (1923–)

Mr. Flanagan, novelist and academic, was born in Greenwhich, Connecticut, and was educated at Amherst College and Columbia University. He has taught at UC–Berkeley, Columbia University and SUNY–Stonybrook

The End of the Hunt 1994; *The Tenants of Time* 1988; *The Year of the French* 1979

Fleming, John Henry (1964–)

John Henry Fleming, novelist and short story writer, was born in Detroit, Michigan, and grew up in Lake Worth, Florida. He was educated at the University of Virginia and received graduate degrees from the University of Southern Mississippi and the University of Southwestern Louisiana. He lives with his wife in Moraga, California, where he teaches in the MFA Program in Creative Writing at St. Mary's College of California. According to the author, he has recently completed a second novel, *Love Letters to the Earth*, which he describes as "an enchanting tale about a love affair between an anthropolgist and a rain forest priestess and the stories he tells her of his travels to imaginary societies."

The Legend of the Barefoot Mailman 1995

Flowers, Arthur R.

Novelist Arthur Flowers was born, and continues to live, in Memphis, Tennessee.

Another Good Lovin Blues 1993; *De Mogo Blues* 1986

Forbes, Leslie

Ms. Forbes, a broadcaster, journalist and novelist, was born in Vancouver, Canada, and now lives in London.

Bombay Ice 1998

Ford, Richard (1944–)

Mr. Ford was born in Jackson, Mississippi, and was Educated at Michigan State and at the University of California at Irvine where he received an MFA in fiction. After brief stints as a high school teacher, basketball coach and CIA employee, he turned to fiction writing. He has taught at the University of Michigan, Princeton University and Williams College. He currently lives in New Orleans where his wife is on the city planning commission.

Women with Men: Three Long Stories 1997; *Independence Day* 1995; *Wildlife* 1990; *Rock Springs* (stories) 1987; *The Sportswriter* 1986; *The Ultimate Good Luck* 1981; *A Piece of My Heart* 1976

Forrest , Leon (1937–1997)

Novelist, essayist and critic, Mr. Forrest was, at the time of his death, a Professor of African American Studies at Northwestern University.

Divine Days 1992; *Two Wings to Veil My Face* 1988; *The Bloodworth Orphans* 1977; *There Is a Tree More Ancient Than Eden* 1973

Forster, Margaret (1938–)

Ms. Forster, novelist and literary critic, was born in Carlisle, England, and was educated at Oxford University.

Shadow Baby 1996; *Mothers' Boys* 1994; *Lady's Maid* 1991; *Have the Men Had Enough?* 1989; *Private Papers* 1986; *Marital Rites* 1982; *The Bride of Lowther Fell* 1980; *Mother Can You Hear Me* 1979; *The Seduction of Mrs. Pendlebury* 1974; *Mr. Bone's Retreat* 1971; *Fenella Phizackerly* 1970; *Miss Owen-Owen Is at Home* 1969; *The Park* 1968; *The Travels of Maude Tipstaff* 1967; *Georgy Girl* 1965; *The Bogeyman* 1965; *Dame's Delight* 1964

Foster, Cecil (1954–)

Mr. Foster, journalist and novelist, was born in Bridgetown, Barbados, and was educated in Barbados and at York University in Canada. He is currently Senior Editor at Toronto's *Financial Post.*

Sleep on Beloved 1995; *No Man in the House* 1992

Fowler, Connie May (1959–)

Ms. Fowler was educated at the Universities of Kansas and Tampa.

Before Women Had Wings 1996; *River of Hidden Dreams* 1994; *Sugar Cage* 1992

Fowler, Karen Joy (1950–)

Ms. Fowler, a novelist, short story writer and winner, in 1987, of the Hugo Award for Best New Writer, was born in Bloomington, Indiana and was educated at UC–Berkeley, SUNY and UC–Davis.

Black Glass (stories) 1999; *The Sweetheart Season* 1996; *Sarah Canary* 1995; *Peripheral Vision* (stories) 1990; *Artificial Things* (stories) 1986

Frayn, Michael (1933–)

Novelist and prize-winning playwright, Mr. Frayn was born in London and was educated at Cambridge University.

Headlong 1999; *Now You Know* 1992; *A Landing on the Sun* 1991; *The Trick of It* 1989; *Sweet Dreams* 1973; *A Very Private Affair* 1968; *Towards the End of the Morning* 1967; *The Russian Interpreter* 1966; *The Tin Men* 1965

Frazier, Charles (1950–)

Charles Frazier was born in Asheville, North Carolina, and was educated at the University of North Carolina (Chapel Hill). He has taught at the University of Colorado (Boulder) and at North Carolina State University.

Cold Mountain 1997

Freed, Lynn (1945–)

Ms. Freed was born in Durban, South Africa, and emigrated to the U.S. in 1967. She was educated in South Africa and at Columbia University.

The Mirror 1997; *The Bungalow* 1993; *Home Ground* 1986

Freeman, David (1941–)

Mr. Freeman, novelist, essayist and book reviewer for the *Los Angeles Times*, lives in Los Angeles.

One of Us 1997

French, Albert (1944–)

Mr. French, a photographer, publisher and novelist, was born in raised in Pittsburgh. A former Marine who saw military service in Vietnam, he is first cousin to the well-known writer John Edgar Wideman.

Holly 1995; *Billy* 1993

Freud, Esther (1963–)

Actress and novelist, Ms. Freud is the daughter of artist Julian Freud and great-granddaughter of Sigmund Freud. Educated at the Drama Center, she is a co-founder of Norfolk Broads, a woman's theatre company.

Gaglow 1998; *Peerless Flats* 1993; *Hideous Kinky* 1992

Frucht, Abby (1957–)

Ms. Frucht, a novelist and short story writer, grew up in Hungtington, New York, and attended Washington University in St. Louis. A former recipient of a National Endowment for the Arts Fellowship, she now lives in Oberlin, Ohio, with her biologist husband.

Life Before Death 1997; *Are You Mine?* 1993; *Fruit of the Month* 1991; *Licorice* 1990; *Snap* 1988

Fry, Stephen (1957–)
Stephen Fry, an actor, comedian, novelist, poet, playwright, screenwriter and rector of Dundee University, was born in London and raised in Norwich. He attended Cambridge University where he met Hugh Laurie with whom he has collaborated on a number of successful television series including "Blackadder" and "Jeeves and Wooster." He recently starred in a film version of Oscar Wilde's life.
Making History 1998; *The Hippopotamus* 1994; *The Liar* 1991

Furst, Alan (1941–)
Mr. Furst was born in New York and was educated at Oberlin and Penn State.
Red Gold 1999; *World at Night* 1996; *Polish Officer* 1995; *Dark Stars* 1991; *Night Soldier* 1988; *Shadow Trade* 1983; *Caribbean Account* 1981; *Paris Drop* 1980; *Your Day in the Barrel* 1976

Gaddis, William (1922–1998)
William Gaddis was born in Manhattan and studied English lit at Harvard University where he wrote for the Harvard Lampoon. A member of the "Beat Generation" he counted Alan Ginsberg and Jack Kerouac among his friends.
A Frolic of His Own 1994; *Carpenter Gothic* 1974; *Jr* 1974; *The Recognition* 1955

Gaines, Ernest (1933–)
Ernest Gaines was born on a plantation in Pointe Coupee Parish, near New Roads, Louisiana. After moving with his family to San Francisco during World War II, he attended San Francisco State University and later won a Fellowship to Stanford. He currently divides his time between San Francisco and the University of Southwestern Louisiana where he is writer-in-residence.
A Lesson Before Dying 1993; *A Gathering of Old Men* 1983; *In my Father's House* 1978; *The Autobiography of Miss Jane Pitman* 1971; *A Long Day in November* 1971; *Bloodline* (stories) 1968; *of Love & Dust* 1967; *Catherine Carmier* 1964

Galloway, Janice (1956–)
Ms. Galloway, a teacher, social worker and novelist, was born in Kilwining, Scotland and was educated at Glasgow University.
Where You Find It 1996; *Foreign Parts* 1994; *Blood* 1991; *The Trick is to Keep Breathing* 1989

Ganesan, Indira
Ms. Ganesan was born in Sirangam, India and immigrated to the US while still in elementary school. She attended Vassar College and received her MFA. from the University of Iowa's Writer's Workshop. She currently teaches English at Southampton College in Long Island.
Inheritance 1998; *The Journey* 1990

Garcia, Christina (1958–)
Ms. Garcia was born in Havana, Cuba but grew up in New York City and was educated at Barnard College and at Johns Hopkins University. A past recipient of the Whiting Award and a former Guggenheim Fellow and Hodder Fellow at Princeton University, she now lives in California with her daughter Pilar.
The Aguero Sisters 1997; *Dreaming in Cuban* 1992

Gardam, Jane (1928–)
Ms Gardam was born in Yorkshire, England and was educated at Bedford College London.
Faith Fox: A Nativity 1996; *Going into a Dark House* 1994; *The Queen of the Tambourine* 1991; *Showing the Flag* 1989; *Cruse's Daughter* 1985; *The Pangs of Love* 1983; *The Sidmouth Letters* 1980; *God on the Rocks* 1978; *Bilgewater* 1977; *Pineapple Bay Hotel* 1971; *A Long Way from Verona* 1971

Garrett, George (1929–)
Mr. Garrett, novelist, short story writer and academic, was born in Orlando, Florida, and was educated at Columbia and Princeton. He has taught at Wesleyan, Rice, Hollins, and Princeton and is currently on the faculty at UVA.
The King of Babylon 1996; *The Old Army Game* (a novel & stories) 1994; *Entered from the Sun* 1990; *An Evening Performance* (stories) 1985; *The Succession: A Novel of Elizabeth and James* 1983; *Poison Pen, or Live Now & Pay Later* 1983; *To Recollect a Cloud of Ghosts* (stories) 1979; *The Magic Striptease* 1973; *Death of the Fox* 1971; *A Wreath for Garibaldi & Other Stories* 1969; *Cold Ground Was His Bed Last Night* (stories) 1964; *Which Ones Are the Enemies?* 1961; *The Finish Man* 1959; *King of the Mountain* (stories) 1958

Gass, William (1924–)
Born in Fargo, North Dakota, Mr. Gass received his doctorate from Cornell University. He is David L. May Distinguished Professor in the Humanities at Washington University in St. Louis.
Cartesian Sonata & Other Novellas 1998; *The Tunnel* 1996; *Culp* 1985; *Willie Master's Lonesome Wife* 1971; *In the Heart of the Matter* (stories) 1968; *Omensetter's Luck* 1966

Gates, David (1947–)
A native of Clinton, Connecticut, Mr. Gates was educated at Bard College and the University of Connecticut. A novelist, journalist and educator, Mr. Gates has taught at Harvard and the University of Virginia. He joined the staff of *Newsweek* in 1979 and is currently a Senior Editor at that magazine.
Preston Falls 1998; *Jernigan* 1992

Ghosh, Amitav (1956–)

Anthropologist and novelist, Mr. Ghosh was educated in Delhi, Cairo, and Oxford, England.

The Calcutta Chromosome; *a Novel of Fevers, Deliriums and Discovery* 1996; *The Shadow Lines* 1988; *The Circle of Reason* 1986

Giardina, Denise (1951–)

Born in Bluefield, West Virginia, Ms. Giardina was educated at West Virginia Wesleyan College and the Virginia Theological Seminary.

Saints and Villains 1998; *The Unquiet Earth* 1992; *Storming Heaven* 1987; *Good King Harry* 1984

Gibbons, Kaye (1960–)

Ms. Gibbons was born in Nash County, North Carolina, and was educated at the University of North Carolina at Chapel Hill. She was the youngest writer ever to receive the Chevalier de L'Ordre des Arts et des Lettres, a French Knighthood for her contribution to literature. Kaye Gibbons currently lives in Raleigh, North Carolina, with her husband, an attorney, and their three daughters.

On the Occasion of My Last Afternoon 1998; *Sights Unseen* 1995; *Charms for the Easy Life* 1993; *A Cure for Dreams* 1991; *A Virtuous Woman* 1989; *Ellen Foster 1987*

Gibson, William (1948–)

An American short story and science fiction writer who was born in Conway, South Carolina, Gibson has lived in Vancouver since 1972 and was educated at the University of British Columbia. An innovative sci-fi writer, he is credited with inventing the genre "cyberpunk" with *Neuromancer* (1984).

Idoru 1996; *Virtual Light* 1993; *The Difference Engine* 1991; *Mona Lisa Overdrive* 1988; *Count Zero* 1986; *Burning Chrome* (stories) 1986; *Neruomancer* 1984

Gifford, Barry (1946–)

Born in Chicago, Illinois, Barry Gifford, a novelist, short story writer, poet, biographer and essayist, was educated at the University of Missouri and at Cambridge, University.

The Sinaloa Story 1998; *Perdita Durango* 1996; *Baby Cat-face* 1995; *Hotel Room Trilogy* 1995; *Arise & Walk* 1994; *A Good Man to Know* 1992; *Night People* 1992; *Port Tropique* 1991; *New Mysteries of Paris* (stories) 1991; *Sailor's Holiday: The Wild Life of Sailor and Lula* 1991; *Wild at Heart: The Story of Sailor and Lula* 1990; *An Unfortunate Woman* 1984; *Francis Goes to the Seashore* 1982; *Landscape with Travelers* 1980; *A Boy's Novel* (stories) 1973

Gilb, Dagoberto (1950–)

Mr. Gilb, a Guggenheim Fellow, was born in Los Angeles and was educated in the University of California system. A carpenter and novelist, he has taught creative writing at the Universities of Arizona, Wyoming and Texas (at Austin).

The Last Known Residence of Mickey Acuna 1994; *The Magic of Blood* 1993; *Winners on the Pass Line* (stories) 1985

Gilchrist, Ellen (1935–)

Ms. Gilchrist, novelist, short story writer and journalist, was born in Vicksburg, Mississippi, and was educated at Millsaps College and the University of Arkansas.

Sarah Conley 1997; *The Courts of Love* (novella and stories) 1996; *Rhoda: A Life in Stories* 1995; *The Age of Miracles* (stories) 1995; *Starcarbon: A Meditation on Love* 1994; *Ababasis: A Journey to the Interior* 1994; *Net of Jewels* 1992; *I Cannot Get You Close Enough* (stories) 1990; *Light Can Be Both Wave and Particle* 1989; *The Anna Papers* 1988; *Two Stories* 1988; *Drunk with Love* (stories) 1986; *Victory Over Japan* (stories) 1984; *The Annunciation* 1983; *In the Land of Dreamy Dreams* (stories) 1981

Girardi, Robert

Mr. Girardi, a novelist, short story writer and essayist, has had his work published in the *New Republic*, *The Triquarterly*, and the *Washington Post*. A past recipient of a James Michener Scholarship, he lives in Washington, D.C.

Vaporetto 13 1997; *The Pirate's Daughter* 1997; *Madeleine's Ghost* 1995

Glancy, Diane (1941–)

Diane Glancy, poet, novelist, essayist and playwright, attended the University of Missouri and Central State University in Oklahoma; she received her MFA from the University of Iowa (Writer's Workshop). Part-Cherokee, she teaches Native American literature and creative writing at Macalaster College in St. Paul, Minnesota. She is also artist-in-residence for both the Oklahoma and Arkansas arts councils.

Flutie 1998; *Asylum in the Grasslands* 1998; *The West Pole* 1997; *The Only Piece of Furniture in the House* 1996; *Pushing the Bear* 1996; *Monkey Secret* 1995; *Firesticks* (stories) 1993; *Trigger Dance* (stories) 1990

Glendinning, Victoria

Ms. Glendinning, a well-known British critic and biographer of Trollope and Dame Rebecca West, was born in Sheffield, England, and was educated at Oxford and Southampton universities.

Electricity 1995; *The Grown Ups* 1990

Godden, Rumer (1907–1998)

Ms. Godden, novelist, poet, short story and prolific children's writer, was born in Sussex, England, but moved with her parents to India when she was still an infant. She lived much of her life in

India, although she was educated in England, including a stint at a Ballet Academy in London. She was appointed OBE in 1993.

Cromartie vs. The God Shiva 1997; *Pippa Passes* 1994; *Kingfishers Catch Fire* 1994; *Coromandel Sea Change* 1991; *The Dark Horse* 1981; *Five for Sorrow, Ten for Joy* 1979; *The Peacock Spring* 1975; *In the House of Brede* 1969; *The Lady and the Unicorn* 1969; *Gone: A Thread of Stories* 1968; *The Battle of Villa Fiorita* 1963; *The Greengage Summer* 1958; *An Episode of Sparrows* 1955; *Take Three Tenses: A Fugue in Time* 1945; *Chinese Puzzle* 1936

Godshalk, C. S.

Ms. Godshalk, a novelist and widely anthologized short story writer, began working on her first novel, *Kalimantaan*, while she was living in Southeast Asia. She currently lives north of Boston.

Kalimantaan 1998

Godwin, Gail (1937–)

Born in Birmingham, Alabama, but raised in Asheville, North Carolina, Ms. Godwin was educated at UNC and the University of Iowa. A former NEA grant winner and Guggenheim Fellow, she has lectured in English and creative writing at Vassar College and Columbia University. She currently lives and writes in Woodstock, New York.

Evensong (a sequel to *Father Melancholy's Daughter*) 1999; *The Good Husband* 1994; *Father Melancholy's Daughter* 1991; *A Southern Family* 1987; *The Finishing School* 1984; *Mr. Bedford and the Muses* 1983; *A Mother and Two Daughters* 1982; *Violet City* 1978; *Dream Children* (stories) 1976; *The Odd Woman* 1974; *Glass People* 1972; *The Perfectionist* 1980

Golden, Arthur (1924–)

Mr. Golden was born in New York City and was educated at Columbia University. He has taught English at the City College of the City of New York and at NYU.

Memoirs of a Geisha 1997

Goldman, Francisco (1955–)

A Guatemalan-American, Mr. Goldman was born in Boston, and grew up in Needham, Massachusetts. As a journalist, he traveled widely in Latin American and lived for five years in Guatemala, his mother's homeland. A contributing editor to *Harper's Magazine* before he turned his attention to fiction writing, he currently divides his time between New York City and Mexico City.

The Ordinary Seaman 1997; *Long Night of the White Chickens* 1992

Goldstein, Rebecca (1950–)

Ms. Goldstein was born in White Plains, New York, and was educated at Barnard and Princeton. In addition to her work as a fiction writer, she

taught philosophy at Barnard College from 1976 to 1986.

Mazel 1995; *Strange Attractors* 1993; *The Dark Sister* 1990; *The Late-Summer Passion of a Woman of Mind* 1985; *The Mind-Body Problem* 1983

Gooch, Brad (1952–)

A novelist and short story writer, Mr. Gooch was born in Kingston, Pennsylvania, and was educated at Columbia University. A free-lance writer, he lives in New York City.

The Golden Age of Promiscuity 1996; *Scary Kisses* 1988; *Jailbait & Other Stories* 1984; *The Daily News* 1977

Goodman, Allegra

Ms. Goodman was born in Brooklyn and raised in Hawaii. She was educated at Harvard and Stanford University where she received her Ph.D. in English.

Kaaterskill Falls 1998; *The Family Markowitz* 1996; *Total Immersion* (stories) 1989

Gordon, Mary (1949–)

Born on Long Island, New York, Ms. Gordon was educated at Barnard College and Syracuse University. She has taught at Dutchess Community College, Amherst College, and, since 1988, at Barnard College.

Spending: A Utopian Divertimento 1998; *The Rest of Life: Three Novellas* 1993; *The Other Side* 1990; *Temporary Shelter* 1987; *Men and Angels* 1985; *The Company of Women* 1980; *Final Payments* 1978

Gordimer, Nadine (1923–)

Nobel Prize–winning novelist and short story writer, Nadine Gordimer was born in Springs, South Africa (a mining town), and was educated at the University of Witwatersrand.

The House Gun 1998; *None to Accompany Me* 1994; *Jump & Other Stories* 1991; *My Son's Story* 1990; *A Sport of Nature* 1987; *Something Out There* 1984; *July's People* 1981; *A Soldier's Embrace* 1980; *Burgers Daughter* 1979; *The Conservationist* 1974; *Livingstone's Companions* 1971; *A Guest of Honor* 1970; *The Late Bourgeois World* 1966; *Not for Publication and Other Stories* 1965; *Occasion for Loving* 1963; *Friday's Footprint* (stories) 1960; *A World of Strangers* 1958; *Six Feet of the Country* (stories) 1956; *Lying Days* 1953; *The Soft Voice of the Serpent* (stories) 1952

Gottlieb, Eli (1956–)

Mr. Gottlieb (who was 41 when he published *The Boy Who Went Away*) was recently awarded the McKittrick Prize, a literary award given to an over-40 author who has published an outstanding debut novel.

The Boy Who Went Away 1997

Gowdy, Barbara (1950–)

Ms. Gowdy was born in Windsor, Canada,

and moved to Toronto at the age of four. A former editor at Lester and Orpen Dennys Publishers, she began writing full time in 1983. A much-lauded young writer, she was called "the future of Canadian literature" by the Canadian weekly *Saturday Night*.

The White Bone 1998; ***Mister Sandman*** 1995; *We So Seldom Look on Love* 1992; *Falling Angels* 1989; *Through the Green Valley* 1988

Grau, Shirley Ann (1929–)

Ms. Grau, Pulitzer Prize–winning novelist and short story writer, was born in New Orleans and was educated at Tulane.

The House on Colliseum Street 1996; ***Roadwalkers*** 1994; *Nine Women* (stories) 1985; *Evidence of Love* 1977; *The Wind Shifting West* 1973; *The Condor Passes* 1971; *The Keepers of the House* 1964; *The Hard Blue Sky* 1958; *The Black Prince & Other Stories* 1955

Graver, Elizabeth (1964–)

Ms. Graver, a journalist and freelance writer, was born in L.A. and was educated at Wesleyan, Washington and Cornell universities. She currently teaches creative writing at Cornell.

The Honey Thief 1999; ***Unraveling*** 1997; *Have You Seen Me?* (stories) 1991

Gray, Alasdair (1934–)

Mr. Gray, a novelist, short story writer, artist and playwright, was born in Glasgow, Scotland, and was educated at the Glasgow Art School.

Mavis Belfrage: A Romantic Tale with Five Shorter Tales 1996; *A History Maker* 1996; ***Poor Things*** 1992; *Something Leather* 1990; *The Fall of Kelvin Walker* 1986; *Unlikely Stories, Mostly* 1984; *Janine* 1984; *Lanark: A Life in Four Books* 1981

Greig, Andrew

A poet, novelist and mountaineer, Mr. Greig has written two successful non-fiction books about climbing in the Himalayas (*Summit Fever*, *Kingdoms of Experience*).

The Return of John McNab 1996; ***Electric Brae: A Modern Romance*** 1992

Grenville, Kate (1950–)

Educated in Sydney and Colorado, Grenville, a prize-winning novelist, currently pursues writing, journalism and teaching.

Albion's Story 1994; *Joan Make's History* 1988; *Dreamhouse* 1986; *Lilian's Story* 1984; *Bearded Ladies* 1984

Grimsley, Jim (1955–)

A playwright and novelist who was born in Edgecombe County, North Carolina, Mr. Grimsley was educated at the University of North Carolina at Chapel Hill. He joined the board of the Southeast Playwrights Project in 1989.

My Drowning 1997; ***Dream Boy*** 1995; ***Winter Birds*** 1994

Grudin, Robert (1938–)

Mr. Grudin, novelist, educator and Shakespeare scholar, was born in Newark and was educated at Harvard University, Trinity College and Berkeley. He has taught at the University of Oregon and at Bennington College in Vermont.

Book: A Novel 1992

Gunesekera, Romesh (1954–)

Mr. Gunesekera, novelist and short story writer, grew up in Sri Lanka and the Philippines. He currently lives in London.

The Sandglass 1998; ***Reef*** 1995; *Monkfish Moon* (stories) 1992

Gupta, Sunetra (1965–)

Born in Calcutta, Sunetra Gupta, a novelist and parasite epidemiologist, Ms. Gupta was educated at Princeton University. She grew up in Ethiopia, Ghana and Liberia and now lives and works in London.

Moonlight into Marzipan 1995; *The Glassblowers Breath* 1993; ***Memories of Rain*** 1992

Gurganus, Allan (1947–)

Mr. Gurganus was born in Rocky Mount, North Carolina, and was educated at the University of Pennsylvania, the Pennsylvania Academy of Fine Arts, Harvard, Sara Lawrence and the University of Iowa's Writer's Workshop.

Plays Well with Others 1997; *White People* 1991; ***Oldest Living Confederate Widow*** 1989

Gurnah, Abdulrazak (1948–)

A novelist and educator, Mr. Gurnah lives in England where he teaches African Literature.

Admiring Silence 1996; *Paradise* 1994; *Memory of Departure* 1987

Guterson, David (1956–)

A novelist, short story writer and contributor to various magazines, Guterson was born in Seattle, Washington. He was educated at Washington University and attended the Creative Writing Program at Brown University. He currently lives with his wife on an island in Puget Sound.

East of the Mountains 1999; ***Snow Falling on Cedars*** 1994; *The Country Ahead of Us, the Country Behind* (stories) 1989

Guy, Rosa (1928–)

Ms. Guy was born in Trinidad and immigrated to the U.S. in the 1930s. A novelist and short story writer, she was educated at NYU.

The Sun, the Sea, a Touch of the Wind 1995; *Billy the Great* 1992; *The Music of Summer* 1992; *And I Heard a Bird Sing* 1987; *My Love, My Love, or the Peasant Girl* 1985; *Paris, Pee Wee and Big Dog*

1984; *A Measure of Time* 1983; *New Guys Around the Block* 1983; *Mirror of Her Own* 1981; *The Disappearance* 1979; *Bird at My Window* 1966

Habens, Alison (1967–)
Ms. Habens lives in Portsmouth, England.
Dreamhouse 1994

Hagedorn, Jessica Tarahata (1949–)
Ms. Hagedorn, musician and novelist, was born in Manila and immigrated to the U.S. in the 1960s. She currently lives in New York City.
The Gangster of Love 1996; *Danger & Beauty* 1993; *Dogeaters* 1990

Haines, Carolyn (1953–)
A journalist and novelist, Ms. Haines was born in Hattiesburg, Mississippi, and was educated at the University of Southern Mississippi, and the University of Southern Alabama.
Touched 1996; *Summer of the Redeemers* 1994; *Summer of Fear* 1993

Haire-Sargeant, Lin
Lin Haire-Sargeant, a playwright, novelist and educator, is Professor of English Literature at Massachusetts College of Art in Boston.
Heathcliff: The Return to Wuthering Heights 1992

Hall, Brian (1959–)
Mr. Hall was born in Lexington, Massachusetts, and was educated at Harvard. He has lived with his wife in Ithaca, New York, since 1988.
The Saskiad 1997; *The Dreamers* 1989

Hall, Rodney (1935–)
Prize-winning novelist Rodney Hall was born in England but was raised — and still lives — in Australia where he was educated at the University of Queensland. In addition to writing fiction, Hall has worked in theater and television, taught, and been poetry editor of *The Australian*.
The Grisly Wife 1993; *The Second Bridegroom* 1991; *Captivity Captive* 1987; *Kisses of the Enemy* 1987; *Just Relations* 1982; *A Place Among the People* 1975; *The Ship of the Coin* 1972

Hamill, Pete (1935–)
Mr. Hamill, a journalist, columnist, editor and novelist, was born in Brooklyn, New York and attended Pratt Institute and Mexico City College.
Snow in August 1997; *Tokyo Sketches* (stories) 1993; *Loving Women: A Novel of the '50s* 1989; *The Guns of Heaven* 1983; *The Deadly* 1979; *Dirty Laundry* 1978; *Flesh and Blood* 1977; *The Gift* 1973; *A Killing for Christ* 1968

Hamilton, Hugo (1953–)
Dublin-born, Mr. Hamilton is of dual Irish and German ancestry.
Dublin Where the Palm Trees Grow (1996); *The*

Love Test 1995; *The Last Shot* 1991; *Surrogate City* 1990

Hamilton-Paterson, James (1941–)
Mr. Hamilton-Paterson is an Englishman who divides his time between Tuscany and the Philippines.
The Music (stories) 1995; *Ghosts of Manila* 1994; *Griefwork* 1993; *That Time in Malomba* (UK title: *The Bell Hop*) 1990; *Gerontius* 1989; *The View from Mount Dog* 1987; *Hostage* 1978; *Option Three* 1974

Hanna, Edward B
Broadcast journalist and novelist.
The Whitechapel Horrors 1993

Hansen, Brooks (1965–)
Mr. Hansen was born in New York City and was educated at Harvard University.
Pearlman's Ordeal 1999; *The Chess Garden* 1995; *Boone* (with Nick Davis) 1993

Hansen, Ron (1947–)
Ron Hansen was born in Omaha, Nebraska, and was educated at Creighton University and the University of Iowa. He currently lives in California where he teaches at Santa Clara University.
Hitler's Niece 1999; *Atticus* 1996; *Mexican Mystery* 1993; *Mariette in Ecstasy* 1991; *Nebraska* (stories) 1989; *The Assassination of Jesse James by the Coward Robert Ford* 1987; *Desperadoes* 1979

Harington, Donald
A novelist and educator, Mr. Harington teaches Art History at the University of Arkansas. He lives in Fayetteville with his wife. Many of his highly comic novels are set in the fictional town of Stay More, Arkansas. His one non-fiction book, *Let Us Build Us a City*, won the Porter Prize for literary excellence.
When Angels Rest 1998; *Butterfly Weed* 1996; *Ekaterina* 1993; *The Cockroaches of Stay More* 1989; *The Cherry Pit* 1988; *The Architecture of the Arkansas Ozarks* 1987; *Some Other Place, the Right Place* 1972; *Lightning Bug* 1970

Harris, Wilson (1921–)
Mr. Harris, a critic, lecturer and novelist, was born in New Amsterdam, Guyana (formerly British Guiana) and was educated at Queens College in Georgetown, Guyana.
Jonestown 1996; *Resurrection at Sorrow Hill* 1993; *The Carnival Trilogy* 1993; *The Guyana Quartet* 1985; *Carnival* 1985; *The Angel of the Gate* 1983; *The Tree of the Sun* 1978; *Da Silva da Silva's Cultivated Wilderness, and Genesis of the Clowns* 1977; *Companions of the Day and Night* 1975; *Fossil and Psyche* 1974; *The Eye of the Scarecrow* 1974; *The Whole Armour and the Secret Ladder* 1973; *Black Marsden: A Tabula Rasa Comedy* 1972; *The Age of*

the Rainmakers 1971; *The Sleepers of Roraima* 1970; *Tumatumari* 1968

Harrison, Jim (1937–)

Novelist, poet and screenwriter, Jim Harrison was born in Grayling, Michigan, and was educated at Michigan State. He currently lives on a farm in northern Michigan.

The Road Home 1998; ***Julip*** 1994; *The Woman Lit by Fireflies* 1990; *Dalva* 1988; *Sundog* 1984; *Legends of the Fall* 1979; *Farmer* 1976; *A Good Day to Die* 1973; *Wolf: A False Memoir* 1971

Harrison, Kathryn (1961–)

Ms. Harrison, novelist and former editor at Viking, was born in L.A. and was educated at Stanford and the University of Iowa (Writer's Workshop).

The Kiss 1997; ***Poison*** 1995; *Exposure* 1993; *Thicker Than Water* 1991

Hassler, Jon (1933–)

Novelist and educator, Mr. Hassler was born in Minnesota and attended St. John's University and the University of North Dakota. He currently lives in Collegeville, Minnesota, where he is on the faculty of St. John's College

The Dean's List 1997; ***Rookery Blues*** 1995; *Dear James* 1993; *North of Hope* 1990; *Grand Opening* 1987; *A Green Journey* 1985; *The Love Hunters* 1981; *Simon's Night* 1979; *Staggerford* 1977

Hatvary, George Egon

Mr. Hatvary, a novelist, short story writer, literary critic and educator, was born in Budapest, Hungary, and was educated at Northwestern University, the University of Chicago, the New School for Social Research, and NYU. He has taught at Boston University, NYU, Queens College, and, most recently, at St. Johns University.

The Murder of Edgar Alan Poe 1997

Haverty, Anne

Ms. Haverty, a poet and novelist who has also written a biography of Constance Markievich — an "Irish Revolutionary"— was born in Tipperary and currently lives in Dublin.

One Day as a Tiger (1997)

Hawkes, John (1925–)

Mr. Hawkes was born in Stanford, Connecticut, and was educated at Harvard. He has taught widely throughout the U.S. including appointments at City College, University of Virginia, Brown and M.I.T.

An Irish Eye 1997; ***The Frog*** 1996; *Sweet William* 1993; *Whistle Jacket* 1988; *Innocence in Extremis* 1985; *Adventures in the Alaskan Skin Trade* 1985; *Virginie: Her Two Lives* 1982; *The Passion Artist* 1979; *The Owl* 1977; *Travesty* 1976; *Death, Sleep and the Traveler* 1974; *The Blood Oranges* 1971;

The Second Skin 1964; *The Lime Twig* 1961; *The Goose on the Grave* 1954; *The Beetle Leg* 1951; *The Cannibal* 1949

Haynes, David (1955–)

Mr. Haynes, a children's author, editor, novelist, educator and publisher, was born in St. Louis and was educated at Macalaster College. In 1996 he was selected by *Granta Magazine* as one of the "Best Young American Novelists." Haynes has taught at Morehead State University, Mankato State, and in the Warren Wilson MFA Program.

All American Dream Dolls 1997; *Heathens* 1996; ***Live at Five*** 1996; ***Somebody Else's Mama*** 1995; *Right by My Side* 1993

Hazelgrove, William Elliott (1959–)

Mr. Hazelgrove was born in Richmond and was educated at Western Illinois University.

Mica Highways 1998; ***Tobacco Sticks*** 1995; *Ripples* 1992

Healy, Dermot (1947–)

Mr. Healy, a playwright, short story writer and novelist, was born in Westmeath, Ireland

A Goat's Song 1995; *Fighting with Shadows, or, Sciamachy* 1984

Hearon, Shelby (1931–)

Ms. Hearon was born in Marion, Kentucky, and was educated at the University of Texas. A novelist and educator, she has held visiting professorships at a number of colleges and universities including the University of Houston, UC at Irvine, Wichita State, Colgate, Clark and the University of Miami.

Footprints 1996; *Life Estates* 1994; *Hug Dancing* 1991; *Owning Joline* 1989; *Five Hundred Scorpions* 1987; *A Small Town* 1985; *Group Therapy* 1984; *Afternoon of a Faun* 1983; *Painted Dresses* 1981; *A Prince of a Fellow* 1978; *Now and Another Time* 1976; *Hannah's House* 1975; *The Second Dune* 1973; *Armadillo in the Grass* 1968

Heath, Roy (1926–)

Roy Heath was born in Georgetown, Guyana, but immigrated to England as a young man. A playwright, novelist, and language instructor (French and German), Mr. Heath was educated at the University of London and was called to the Bar, Lincolns Inn, in 1964.

The Ministry of Hope 1996; *Armstrong Trilogy* (From the Heat of the Day, One Generation, Genetha) 1996; *Shadow Bride* 1988; *Orealla* 1984; ***Kwaku, or, the Man Who Could Not Keep his Mouth Shut*** 1982; *Genetha* 1981; *One Generation* 1980; *From the Heat of the Day* 1979; *The Murderer* 1978; *A Man Come Home* 1974

Hegi, Ursula (1946–)

Ursula Hegi was born and raised in Germany

(in a small town outside of Dusseldorf) and immigrated to the U.S. in 1964, at the age of 18, where she was educated at the University of New Hampshire. A member of the faculty of Eastern Washington University, she is currently a Visiting Professor at UC-Irving.

Salt Dancers 1995; **Stones from the River** 1994; *Floating in My Mother's Palm* 1990; *Unearned Pleasures* 1988; *Intrusions* 1981

Hellenga, Robert (1941–)
Mr. Hellenga attended the University of Michigan and received his Ph.D. from Princeton University. He currently teaches at Knox College.
The Fall of a Sparrow 1998; *Sixteen Pleasures* 1994

Helprin, Mark (1947–)
Novelist, short story writer and essayist, Mr. Helprin was born in New York City and attended Harvard and Oxford universities. A contributing editor at the *Wall Street Journal*, he is also a fellow at the conservative Hudson Institute.
Memoir from an Antproof Case 1995; **A Soldier of the Great War** 1991; *Winter's Tale* 1983; *Ellis Island & Other Stories* 1981; *Refiner's Fire: The Adventures of Marshall Pearl, a Foundling* 1977; *A Dove of the East and Other Stories* 1975

Henry, Gordon
Henry, of Anishinabe heritage, is Professor of Language and Literature at Ferris State University in Michigan.
The Light People 1994

Hijuelos, Oscar (1951–)
Pulitzer Prize–winning novelist Oscar Hijuelos grew up on 118th Street in the shadow of Columbia University. A first generation Cuban-American, he was educated at City College where he was taught (and encouraged by) such literary luminaries as Joseph Heller, William Burroughs, Donald Barthelme, Susan Sontag, and Frederick Tuten.
Empress of the Splendid Season 1999; **Mr. Ives's Christmas** 1995; **The Fourteen Sisters of Emilio Montez O'Brien** 1993; **The Mambo Kings Play Songs of Love** 1989; *Our House in the Last World* 1983

Hill, Carol de Chellis (1942–)
Ms. Hill, actress, publicist, editor, playwright and novelist, was born in New Jersey and was educated at Chatham College
Henry James' Midnight Song 1993; *The Eleven Mile High Dancer* 1985; *Let's Fall in Love* 1975; *Jeremiah 8:20* 1970

Hill, Susan (1942–)
A novelist, playwright and critic, Susan Hill was born in Scarborough, Yorkshire, and was educated at King's College, University of London.
Mrs. de Winter 1993; *The Mist in the Mirror*

1992; *Air and Angels* 1991; *Lanterns Across the Snow* 1987; *Woman in Black* 1983; *In the Springtime of the Year* 1974; *A Bit of Singing and Dancing* 1973; *The Custodian* 1972; *The Bird of Night* 1972; *Strange Meeting* 1971; *The Albatross* 1971; *I'm the King of the Castle* 1970; *A Change for the Better* 1969; *Gentlemen and Ladies* 1968; *Do Me a Favor* 1963; *The Enclosure* 1961

Hitchcock, Jane Stanton
Playwright and novelist Jane Stanton Hitchcock's first novel *A Trick of the Eye* was made into a Hallmark TV movie by CBS in 1994.
The Witch's Hammer 1994; **A Trick of the Eye** 1992

Hjortsberg, William (1941–)
William Hjortsberg, a novelist, screenwriter and biographer, was born in New York City and was educated at Dartmouth, Yale and Stanford. Mr. Hjortsberg has lived in Mexico, Spain and Puerto Rico and has taught English in St. Croix, Virgin Islands. He moved to Montana in 1971
Nevermore 1994; *Tales & Fables* 1985; *Falling Angel* 1978; *Toro Toro Toro* 1974; *Symbiography* 1973; *Gray Matters* 1971; *Alps* 1969

Hoffman, Alice (1952–)
Born and raised in New York City, Ms. Hoffman was educated at Adelphi and Stanford universities. She lives in Brookline, Massachusetts, with her husband, screenwriter Tom Martin, and their two sons.
Here on Earth 1997; **Practical Magic** 1995; *Second Nature* 1994; **Turtle Moon** 1992; *Seventh Heaven* 1990; *At Risk* 1988; *Illumination Night* 1987; *Fortune's Daughter* 1985; *White Horses* 1982; *Angel Landing* 1980; *The Drowning Season* 1979; *Property Of* 1977

Hogan, Linda (1947–)
Ms. Hogan, a poet, novelist, playwright and member of the Chicksaw tribe, was born in Denver, Colorado, and was educated at the University of Colorado at Boulder where she is currently on the faculty.
Solar Storms 1995; **Mean Spirit** 1990; *That House* (stories) 1988

Holleran, Andrew (1943–)
Mr. Holleran, a pseudonym, was educated at Harvard and the University of Iowa. He is considered to be one of the foremost names in contemporary gay literature.
In September the Light Changes 1999; **The Beauty of Men** 1996; *Nights in Aruba* 1983; *Dancers from the Dance* 1978

Hollinghurst, Alan (1954–)
Poet and novelist, Mr. Hollinghurst was born in England and was educated at Oxford. He has

taught at Oxford and University College, London, and is deputy editor of the *Times Literary Supplement*

Folding Star 1994; *Swimming Pool Library* 1989

Homes, A.M.

Ms. Homes, whose 1996 novel created a firestorm of controversy upon publication (particularly in the UK), teaches creative writing at Columbia University.

Music for Burning 1999; ***The End of Alice*** 1996; ***In a Country of Mothers*** 1993; *The Safety of Objects* (stories) 1990; *Jack* 1989

Hope, Christopher (1944–)

Mr. Hope, a poet and novelist, was born in Johannesburg, South Africa, but has lived in Great Britain since 1975. He was educated at the Universities of Witwatersrand and Natal.

Darkest England 1996; *The Love Songs of Nathan J. Swirsky* 1994; *Serenity House* 1992; *My Chocolate Redeemer* 1989; *Hottentot Room* 1987; *Black Swan* 1987; *Krugers Alp* 1984; *Private Parts & Other Tales* (stories) 1981; *A Separate Development* 1981

Hornby, Nick (1960–)

A journalist and novelist, Mr. Hornby was educated at Cambridge University and lives in North London. He is a regular contributor to such publications as *The London Times, Esquire, Time Out*, etc.

About a Boy 1998; ***High Fidelity*** 1995

Hospital, Janette Turner (1942–)

Jane Turner Hospital was born in Melbourne, Australia, and grew up in Brisbane. She has lived all over the world including: India, London, Los Angeles, Boston and Kingston, Ontario. Ms. Hospital now divides her time between Canada, the U.S. and Australia.

Oyster 1998; ***The Last Magician*** 1992; *Isobars* (stories) 1990; *Charades* 1989; *Dislocations* (stories) 1986; *Borderline* 1985; *The Tiger in the Tiger Pit* 1983; *The Ivory Swing* 1982

Howard, Elizabeth Jane (1923–)

A writer, actress, model, BBC broadcaster, critic and editor, Ms. Howard was married (her third) to the late novelist Kingsley Amis, one of the most celebrated British writers of the post-war period. Ms. Howard was privately educated and trained as an actress at the London Mask Theatre School.

Casting Off 1995; ***Confusion*** 1993; ***Marking Time*** 1991; ***The Light Years*** 1990; *Getting It Right* 1982; *Mr. Wrong* 1975; *Odd Girl Out* 1972; *Something in Disguise* 1969; *After Julius* 1965; *Sea Change* 1959; *The Long View* 1956; *Beautiful Visit* 1950

Howard, Maureen (1930–)

Ms. Howard, who lives in New York City, was recently awarded the Academy Award in Literature by the American Academy of Arts and Letters.

A Lover's Almanac 1998; *Natural History* 1992; *Expensive Habits* 1986; *Grace Abounding* 1982; *Not a Word About Nightingales* 1980; *Bridgeport Bus* 1980; *Facts of Life* 1978; *Before My Time* 1975

Hughes, Glyn (1935–)

A poet, novelist, and playwright, Mr. Hughes was born in Cheshire, England, and was educated at Regional College of Art, Manchester. An committed educator, he has taught English literature at both the secondary and college level.

Bronte 1996; *Roth* 1992; *Rape of the Rose* 1987; *Antique Collector* 1990; *The Hawthorn Goddess* 1984; *Where I Used to Play on the Green* 1981

Humphreys, Josephine (1945–)

Ms. Humphreys was born in Charleston, South Carolina, and was educated at Duke, Yale and the University of Texas. A full-time writer since the late 1970s, she has taught English literature and creative writing.

Fireman's Fair 1991; *Rich in Love* 1987; *Dreams of Sleep* 1984

Huneven, Michele (1953–)

Ms. Huneven, a California-based restaurant critic, food writer, short story writer and novelist, was born in Altadena, California. She attended Grinnell College and the University of Iowa's Writers' Workshop and was awarded a GE Young Writer's Award for Fiction. She has sold the rights to her debut novel *Round Rock* to Columbia Pictures which, according to her publisher, will star Helen Hunt.

Round Rock 1997

Hustvedt, Siri (1955–)

Siri Hustvedt was born in Northfield, Minnesota, and was educated at St. Olaf's College and Columbia University. She lives in New York City with her husband, novelist Paul Auster.

The Enchantment of Lily Dahl 1996; ***The Blindfold*** 1992

Huth, Angela (1938–)

A novelist, short story writer and playwright, Ms. Huth was born in London.

Wives of the Fisherman 1998; ***Land Girls*** 1994; *An Invitation to the Married Life* 1991; *Wanting* 1984; *Infidelities* (stories) 1979; *South of the Lights* 1978; *Monday Lunch in Fairyland* 1978; *Sun Child* 1975; *Virginia Fly Is Drowning* 1972; *Somehow I Had to Find a Brass Band* 1970; *No Where Girl* 1970

Hynes, James

James Hynes, the recipient of a number of lit-

erary Awards and fellowships, lives in works in Austin, Texas. He has taught at the University of Michigan and writes TV criticism for *Mother Jones* and the *Utne Reader*.
Publish & Perish 1997; *The Wild Colonial Boy* 1990

Iida, Deborah (1956–)
A Japanese-Hawaiian novelist, Ms. Iida's first novel won the Grand Prize at the Maui Writers' Conference.
Middle Son 1996

Irving, John (1942–)
Mr. Irving was born in Exeter, New Hampshire, and was educated at the Universities of Pittsburgh and New Hampshire. He also attended the University of Vienna (for one year) and received an MFA from the University of Iowa (Writer's Workshop). He has taught at Windham and Mt. Holyoke colleges.
A Widow for One Year 1998; *Trying to Save Piggy Snead* 1996; **A Son of the Circus** 1994; *A Prayer for Owen Meany* 1989; *Cider House Rules* 1985; *Hotel New Hampshire* 1981; *The World According to Garp* 1978; *158 Pound Marriage* 1974; *The Water Method Man* 1972; *Setting Free the Bears* 1969

Irwin, Robert (1946–)
Mr. Irwin, formerly a teacher of medieval history, has turned his attention full time to writing. He currently lives in London with his family.
Exquisite Corpse 1995; *The Mysteries of Algiers* 1988; *The Arabian Nightmare* 1987

Ishiguro, Kazuo (1954–)
Kazuo Ishiguro was born in Nagasaki, Japan, in 1954 but moved to Great Britain with his family in 1960. He attended the University of Kent at Canterbury and the University of East Anglia. He now lives in London. In both 1983 and 1993 Ishiguro was named to *Granta Magazine*'s list of the twenty "Best Young British Novelists."
The Unconsoled 1995; *The Remains of the Day* 1989; *An Artist of the Floating World* 1986; *A Pale View of Hills* 1982

Isler, Alan (1934–)
Alan Isler was born in London and emigrated to the U.S. when he was 18 years old. He taught English literature in New York City for 25 years. He now lives in London.
The Bacon Fancier 1997; **Kraven Images** 1996; *The Prince of West End Avenue* 1994

Jackson, Mick
Mr. Jackson, a film director, screenwriter and novelist, was born in Great Harwood, Lancashire. He currently lives in London.
The Underground Man (1997)

Jackson-Opoku, Sandra
An award-winning poet, journalist, fiction writer and screenwriter, Ms. Jackson-Opoku lives in Chicago.
River Where Blood Is Born (1997)

Jacobs, Mark (1951–)
A career Foreign Service Officer who has been stationed in Turkey, Bolivia, Paraguay and Honduras, Mr. Jacobs has functioned as Cultural Attaché at the American Embassy in Madrid.
The Liberation of Little Heaven & Other Stories 1999; **Stone Cowboy** 1997; *A Cast of Spaniards* 1994

Jaivin, Linda
Linda Jaivin, a novelist, freelance writer and translator, is according to the *L.A. Times Book Review* "an American journalist with an Asian studies degree who ricocheted around the Pacific Rim" before landing in Australia.
Rock & Roll Babes from Outer Space 1996; **Eat Me** 1995

Janowitz, Tama (1957–)
Ms. Janowitz was born in San Francisco and was educated at Barnard, Hollins and Yale. She was a model with Vidal Sassoon International Hair salons, an actress, an art gallery director and, since 1985, a freelance journalist and novelist.
A Certain Age 1999; *By the Shores of Gitchee Gumee* 1996; **The Male Cross-Dressing Support Group** 1992; *A Cannibal in Manhattan* 1987; *Slaves in New York* (stories) 1986; *American Dad* 1991

Jen, Gish (1956–)
Ms. Jen, a first generation Chinese-American, grew up in Scarsdale and was educated at Harvard and Stanford. A Fellow at Radcliffe's Bunting Institute, she currently lives in Cambridge, Massachusetts.
Who's Irish and Other Stories 1999; **Mona in the Promised Land** 1996; **Typical American** 1991

Jennings, Kate (1948–)
Ms. Jennings, a poet, novelist and essayist, is a prominent member of the Australian feminist movement. She has lived in New York City since 1979.
Snake 1996; *Women Falling Down in the Street* (stories) 1990

Jhabvala, Ruth Prawer (1927–)
Ms. Jhabvala, novelist, short story writer, and scriptwriter (in collaboration with the producer-director team of independent filmmakers Merchant/Ivory) was born in Germany to Polish parents with whom she moved to England in 1939. She was educated at Queen Mary College, London, where she met her husband-to-be, an Indian architect. She moved with him to India in 1951.

Since 1975 she has spent most of her time in New York City.

Shards of Memory 1995; ***Poet and Dancer*** 1993; *Three Continents* 1987; *Out of India: Selected Stories* 1986; *In Search of Love and Beauty* 1983; *How I Became a Holy Mother & Other Stories* 1976; *Heat & Dust* 1975; *A New Dominion* (or *Travelers*) 1972; *An Experience of India* 1972; *A Stronger Climate: Nine Stories* 1968; *A Backward Place* 1965; *Get Ready for Battle* 1962; *The Householder* 1960

Esmond in India 1958; *The Nature of Passion* 1956; *Amrita (or To Whom She Will)* 1955

Johnson, Charles Richard (1948–)

Charles Johnson, a short story writer, playwright, scriptwriter, novelist, literary critic, historian, cartoonist, journalist and educator, was born in Evanston, Illinois, and was educated at the University of Southern Illinois. The fiction editor of the *Seattle Review*, Mr. Johnson teaches at the University of Washington in Seattle.

Dreamer 1998; ***Middle Passage*** 1990; *The Sorcerer's Apprentice* 1986; *Oxherding Tale 1982*; *Faith and the Good Thing* 1974

Johnson, Denis (1949–)

A poet, short story writer and novelist, Mr. Johnson was born in Germany but currently lives in the Western United States with his wife and two children.

Already Dead: A California Gothic 1997; *Jesus' Son* (stories) 1992; *Resuscitation of a Hanged Man* 1991; *The Stars at Noon* 1988; *Fiskadoro* 1985; *Angels* 1983

Johnson, Diane (1934–)

Ms. Johnson, novelist, short story writer, biographer, literary critic, essayist and travel writer, was born in Moline, Illinois, and was educated at the University of Utah and the University of California (M.A. & Ph.D.). She taught for a number of years at the University of California at Davis. She divides her time between San Francisco and Paris.

Le Divorce 1997; *Natural Opium: Some Travelers' Tales* 1993; *Health and Happiness* 1990; *Persian Nights* 1987; *Lying Low* 1978; *The Shadow Knows* 1975; *Burning* 1971; *Loving Hands at Home* 1968; *Fair Game* 1965

Jones, Gayl (1949–)

Born in Kentucky, Ms. Jones attended Connecticut College and Brown University. She has taught at Wellesley College and the University of Michigan.

Mosquito 1999; ***The Healing*** 1998; *White Rat: Short Stories* 1977; *Eva's Man* 1976; *Corregidora* 1975

Jones, Louis B. (1953–)

Mr. Jones, a poet and novelist, was born in Chicago and was educated at the University of Illinois.

California's Over 1997; ***Particles and Luck*** 1993; *Ordinary Money* 1991

Jones, Madison (1925–)

Mr. Jones, a former Guggenheim Fellowship recipient, was born in Nashville, Tennessee, and currently lives in Alabama. A Writer-in-Residence Emeritus at Auburn University, he is a member of the Fellowship of Southern Writers.

Nashville 1864: The Dying of the Light 1997; *To the Winds* 1996; *The Innocent* 1993; *A Buried Land* 1987; *Season of the Strangler* 1982; *A Passage Through Gehenna* 1978; *A Cry of Absence* 1971; *An Exile* 1967

Jones, Rod (1953–)

Rod Jones, a novelist and educator, was born in Melbourne, Australia, and graduated from the University of Melbourne.

Billy Sunday 1995; *Prince of the Lilies* 1991; *Julia Paradise* 1988

Jordan, Neil (1950–)

Mr. Jordan, a director, playwright, scriptwriter, novelist and short story writer, was born in Sligo, Ireland. He is best known for his films *The Crying Game* and *Mona Lisa*. He is currently directing a film version of Peter McCabe's *The Butcher Boy*.

Nightlines *1995* (published in London in 1994 as *Sunrise with Sea Monster*); *The Crying Game* 1993; *The Dream of a Beast* 1989; *Mona Lisa* 1986; *The Past* 1980; *Night in Tunisia* 1976

Jose, Nicholas (1952–)

Mr. Jose was born in London and was raised in Traralgon, Perth and Adelaide. He was educated at Oxford and the Australian National University and has traveled extensively (and resided) in Asia and Europe. He has taught at the Beijing Foreign Studies University and East China Teacher's University in Shanghai. From 1987 to 1990 he was Cultural Counselor at the Australian Embassy in Beijing.

The Custodians 1998; ***The Rose Crossing*** 1995; *Avenue of Eternal Peace* 1989; *Paper Nautilus* 1987; *Feathers or Lead* (stories) 1986; *Rowena's Field* 1984; *Possession of Amber* (stories) 1980

Judd, Alan (1946–)

Mr. Judd, biographer, book reviewer, teacher, writer, and former member of the British Foreign Office, was born in Kent and was educated at Oxford.

The Devil's Own Work 1994; *Tango* 1990; *Short of Glory* 1985; *A Breed of Heroes* 1981

Just, Ward (1935–)

Mr. Just was born in Michigan City, Indiana, and was educated at Trinity College in Hartford, Connecticut. A journalist, political reporter and novelist who has written for *Newsweek* and the *Washington Post*, he was a war correspondent in Saigon from 1965 to 1967.

Echo House 1997; *Ambition & Love* 1994; *The Translator* 1991; *In the City of Fear* 1990; *Twenty-one: Selected Stories* 1990; *Jack Gance* 1989; *The American Ambassador* 1979; *The American Blues* 1984; *In the City of Fear* 1982; *Honor, Power, Riches, Fame, and the Love of Women* 1979; *A Family Trust* 1978; *Nicholson at Large* 1975; *Stringer* 1974; *The Congressman Who Loved Flaubert & Other Stories* 1973; *A Soldier of the Revolution* 1971

Kalpakian, Laura (1945–)

Born in Long Beach, California, Ms. Kalpakian was educated at the University of California at Riverside and at the University of Delaware. A former social worker, short story writer, novelist and educator, she has taught at the University of Redlands and Western Washington University.

Cossette: The Sequel to Les Miserables 1995; *Graced Land* 1992; *Dark Continent & Other Stories* 1991; *Crescendo* 1987; *Fair Augusto and Other Stories* 1986; *These Latter Days* 1985; *Beggars and Choosers* 1978

Kanon, Joseph

Mr. Kaplan, a publishing executive (he was, at one time, the Executive V.P. for Trade and Reference Publishing at Houghton, Mifflin), was educated at Harvard and Oxford universities.

The Prodigal Spy 1998; *Los Alamos* 1997

Kaplan, James (1951–)

Mr. Kaplan, a screenwriter and freelance writer (of both fiction and non-fiction), was born in New York City and was educated at Wesleyan University.

Two Guys from Verona 1998; *Pearl's Progress* 1989

Keane, John (1928–)

Born in County Kerry, John Keane is one of Ireland's most popular humorous authors and playwrights. He has written many best-selling novels including *The Letters of an Irish Publican* and *Letter of a Matchmaker*.

The Ram of God 1996; *The Contractors* 1993; *Durango* 1992; *The Field* (screenplay) 1990; *Irish Short Stories* 1987; *The Bodhran Makers* 1986; *Owl Sandwiches* 1985; *Man of the Triple Name* 1984; *More Irish Short Stories* 1981; *Letters of an Irish Minister of State* 1978; *Letters of a Country Postman* 1977; *Death Be Not Proud & Other Stories* 1976; *Letters of a Civic Guard* 1976; *Letters of a Matchmaker* 1975; *Letters of a Love-Hungry Farmer* 1974; *Letters of a Irish Publican* 1974; *Letters of an Irish Priest* 1970; *Letters of a Successful T.D.* 1967

Kearney, Colbert

Mr. Kearney, a novelist and academic, was ed-

ucated at University College Dublin and at Cambridge University. He is on the English faculty at University College Cork, but is currently Visiting Professor of English at Colby College in Waterville, Maine.

The Consequence 1993

Keller, Nora Okjay

Ms. Keller was born in Seoul, Korea, and now lives in Hawaii where she is working on her second novel.

Comfort Woman 1997

Kelman, James (1946–)

A novelist and short story writer, Mr. Kelman was born in Glasgow where he attended the university of Strathclyde. He still lives in Glasgow.

Busted Scotch (stories) 1997; ***How Late It Was, How Late*** 1994; *The Burn* (stories) 1991; *A Disaffection* 1989; *Greyhound for Breakfast* (stories) 1987; *A Chancer* 1985

Keneally, Thomas (1935–)

Thomas Keneally, a prize-winning Australian novelist (he won the Booker Prize for *Schindler's List*), was born in Sydney and educated at St. Patrick's College. Keneally studied for the New South Wales bar; he began writing while working as a teacher in Sydney.

A River Town 1995; *Jacko the Great Intruder* 1993; ***Woman of the Inner Sea*** 1992; *Flying Hero Class* 1990; *To Amara* 1989; *The Playmaker* 1987; *A Family Madness* 1985; *Schindler's List* 1982; *Cut-Rate Kingdom* 1980; *Confederates* 1979; *Passenger* 1979; *A Victim of the Aurora* 1977; *A Season in Purgatory* 1976; *Gossip from the Forest* 1975; *Moses the Lawgiver* 1975; *Blood Red, Sister Rose* 1974; *Chant of Jimmie Blacksmith* 1972; *The Dutiful Daughter* 1971; *The Survivor* 1969; *Three Cheers for the Paraclete* 1968; *Bring Larks and Heroes* 1967; *The Fear* 1965; *The Place at Whitton* 1964

Kennedy, William (1928–)

Born in Albany and educated at Siena College, Mr. Kennedy has made a name for himself as a journalist, film critic, book editor, novelist and educator. He taught at SUNY–Albany and founded the NY State Writers Institute, where he is Professor of English.

The Flaming Corsage 1996; ***Very Old Bones*** 1992; *Quinn's Book* 1988; *Ironweed* 1983; *Billy Phelan's Greatest Game* 1978; *Legs* 1975; *The Ink Truck* 1969

Kesavan, Mukul (1957–)

Mr. Kesavan was educated at Delhi and Cambridge universities. He lives with his wife and children in Delhi where he teaches history at Jamia University.

Through the Looking Glass 1995

Kim, Patti (1970–)

Born in Pusan, Korea, in 1970, Ms. Kim immigrated to the U.S. in 1974. She currently lives in Potomac, Maryland.

A Cab Called Reliable 1997

Kincaid, Jamaica (1949–)

Ms. Kincaid was born in St. John's Antigua and came to the U.S. in her late teens to work as an au pair. She was educated at the New School for Social Research and at Franconia College and was hired as a staff writer by the *New Yorker* in 1976. She lives with her husband, composer Allen Shawn, and two children in North Bennington, Vermont.

The Autobiography of My Mother 1995; *Lucy* 1990; *Annie John* 1985; *At the Bottom of the River* 1984

King, Thomas (1943–)

A part–Cherokee novelist and chair of Native American Studies at the University of Minnesota, Mr. King's first novel, *Medicine River*, was made into a movie for Canadian TV.

One Good Story, That One (stories) 1993; *Green Grass, Running Water* 1993; *Medicine River* 1990

Kingsolver, Barbara (1955–)

Ms. Kingsolver, a journalist, science writer, human rights activist and novelist, was born and raised in Eastern Kentucky and was educated at DePauw University in Indiana and at the University of Arizona. She has written full-time since 1987.

The Poisonwood Bible 1998; *Pigs in Heaven* 1993; *Animal Dreams* 1990; *Homeland & Other Stories* 1989; *The Bean Trees* 1988

Kinsella, W.P. (1935–)

Born in Edmonton, Canada, Mr. Kinsella attended the University of Victoria and the University of Iowa. He has taught at the Universities of Calgary and Iowa but has devoted himself to writing since 1983.

The Winter Helen Dropped By 1995; *Brother Frank's Gospel Hour* 1994; *The Dixon Conbelt League & Other Baseball Stories* 1993; *Box Socials* (stories) 1992; *Red Wolf, Red Wolf* (stories) 1990; *The Further Adventure of Slugger McBatt* 1988; *The Fencespost Chronicles* 1987; *The Iowa Baseball Confederacy* 1986; *Five Stories* 1986; *The Alligator Report* (stories) 1985; *The Thrill of the Grass* 1984; *The Moccasin Telegraph & Other Indian Tales* 1983; *Shoeless Joe* 1982; *Born Indian* 1981; *Shoeless Joe Jackson Comes to Iowa* 1980; *Scars* (stories) 1978; *Dance Me Outside* (stories) 1977

Klavan, Andrew

Mr. Klavan was born in New York City and was educated at UC–Berkeley. A journalist and

novelist, he divides his time between London and Connecticut.

Hunting Down Amanda 1999; *The Uncanny* 1998; *True Crime* 1995; *The Animal Hour* 1993; *Corruption* 1993; *Don't Say a Word* 1991; *The Scarred Man* 1990; *Darling Clementine* 1988; *Face of the Earth* 1980

Koch, C.J. (1932–)

Born in Hobart, Tasmania, Australia, Koch won the prestigious Miles Franklin Literary Award for his two most recent novels: *The Doubleman* (1984) and *Highways to a War* (1994). In the view of the *Times Literary Supplement* Koch "is an honest traditional novelist bent on fulfilling his proclaimed purpose of giving to the life of his region configurations which it has not known before."

Highways to a War 1994; *The Doubleman* 1984; *The Year of Living Dangerously* 1979; *Across the Sea Wall* 1965; *The Boys in the Island* 1958

Korman, Keith (1956–)

Mr. Korman, a literary agent and novelist, was born in New York City and educated at Hobart College.

Secret Dreams 1995; *Archangel* 1983; *Swan Dive* 1980

Kotzwinkle, William (1938–)

Born in Scranton, Pennsylvania, Mr. Kotzwinkle attended Rider College and Penn State. In addition to his short stories and novels, he has written numerous books for children.

The Bear Went Over the Mountain 1996; *The Game of Thirty* 1994; *The Hot Jazz Trio* 1989; *The Midnight Examiner* 1989; *The Exile* 1987; *Hearts of Wood and Other Timeless Tales* 1986; *Jewel of the Moon* (stories) 1985; *Queen of Swords* 1983; *Trouble in Bugland* 1983; *Christmas at Fontaine's* 1982; *Jack in the Box* 1980; *Herr Nightingale & the Satin Woman* 1978; *Fata Morgana* 1977; *Doctor Rat* (sci-fi) 1976; *Swimming in the Secret Sea* 1975; *The Night-Book* 1974; *The Fat Man* 1974; *Hermes Zoo* (sci-fi) 1972; *Elephant Bangs Train* (stories) 1971

Kraft, Eric (1944–)

Born in Bayshore on Long Island, Mr. Kraft, a teacher and editorial director, was educated at Harvard. He currently lives with his family in Newburyport, Massachusetts.

At Home with the Glynns 1996; *Reservations Recommended* 1995; *What a Piece of Work I Am* 1994; *Little Follies* 1992; *Herb & Lorna* 1988; *Life on the Bolotomy* 1983; *The Static of the Spheres* 1983; *Do Clams Bite?* 1982; *My Mother Takes a Tumble* 1982

Kureishi, Hanif (1954–)

A well-known Indo-British screenplay writer, Hanif Kureishi was, on the strength of his debut novel, named to *Granta Magazine's* 1993 list of the twenty "Best Young British Novelists."

Love in a Blue Time 1997; *The Black Album* 1995; **The Buddha of Suburbia** 1990

Kurzweil, Allen
Allen Kurzweil, a Fulbright Scholar, was educated at Yale and has lived for a time in Europe. He has written for magazines both in the U.S. and in France and Italy. He currently lives in New York City with his wife, Francois Dussart, an anthropologist.
A Case of Curiosities 1992

Ladd, Florence
Ms. Ladd is director of the prestigious Bunting Institute at Radcliffe College.
Sarah's Psalm 1996

Lamar, Jake (1961–)
Mr. Lamar was born in the Bronx and was educated at Harvard. A staff writer and associate editor at *Time* magazine from 1983 to 1989, he currently lives in Europe where he is a freelance writer.
The Last Integrationist 1996

Lamb, Wally (1950–)
Mr. Lamb, both of whose novels have been chosen by Oprah Winfry for her on-air Book Club, attended the University of Connecticut and Vermont College where he received his MFA. He taught creative writing on the secondary school level for many years and is currently on the faculty of the University of Connecticut.
I Know This Much Is True 1998; **She's Come Undone** 1992

Lambkin, David (1947–)
David Lambkin is a South African novelist and book critic.
The Hanging Tree 1996

Lamott, Anne (1954–)
Ms. Lamott, a former Guggenheim Fellow, journalist, essayist and novelist, was born in San Francisco and was educated at Goucher College.
Crooked Little Heart 1997; *All New People* 1989; *Joe Jones* 1985; *Rosie* 1983; *Hard Laughter* 1980

Lanchester, John
Mr. Lanchester, novelist, journalist and food critic, was born in Hamburg; raised in Calcutta, Rangoon, Brunei, and Hong Kong. He was educated at Oxford, was married in Reno, Nevada, and currently lives in London where he has been on the editorial staff of the *Observer* and the *London Review of Books*. He is also a frequent contributor to the *New Yorker*.
A Debt to Pleasure 1996

Landsman, Anne (1959–)
Ms. Landsman was born in South Africa where she was educated at the University of Cape

Town. After immigrating to the U.S. she attended Columbia University. She currently teaches screen writing at the New School for Social Research in New York City.
The Devil's Chimney 1997

Lawrence, Starling
Mr. Lawrence, editor, novelist and short story writer, was educated at Princeton and Cambridge and currently lives in New York City where he is editor-in-chief at W.W. Norton.
Montenegro 1997; *Legacies* (stories) 1996

Law-Yone, Wendy
Ms. Law-Yone is a novelist and daughter of Law Yone, the famous Burmese journalist.
Irrawaddy Tango 1993; *The Coffin Tree* 1983

Leavitt, David (1961–)
Mr. Leavitt, an editor and novelist, was born in Pittsburgh but grew up in Palo Alto, California, where his father was a professor at Stanford University. Considered a leading light among the group of younger gay authors, he was educated at Yale and currently lives in Rome.
Arkansas (three novellas) 1997; **While England Sleeps** 1993; *A Place I've Never Been* 1990; **Equal Affections** 1989; *The Lost Language of Cranes* 1986; *Family Dancing* 1984

Lee, Chang-Rae (1965–)
Born in Seoul, Korea, Mr. Lee attended Philips-Exeter Academy and graduated from Yale and the University of Oregon where he is Professor of Creative Writing.
Native Speaker 1995

Lee, Gus (1947–)
Mr. Lee grew up in San Francisco and attended West Point. He left the military after obtaining a law degree and worked for a time as a prosecutor. He now lives in Colorado Springs where he writes full-time.
No Physical Evidence 1998; **Tiger's Tale** 1996; **Honor and Duty** 1994; **China Boy** 1991

Lee, Helen Elaine (1959–)
Ms. Lee, a lawyer and novelist, was born in Detroit, Michigan, and was educated at Harvard University. She is currently a member of the English faculty at M.I.T. and lives in Somerville, Massachusetts.
The Serpent's Gift 1994

Lefcourt, Peter (1941–)
Mr. Lefcourt, a TV producer, scriptwriter, playwright, and novelist, was born in New York City and was educated at Union College.
Abbreviating Ernie 1997; *Di & I* 1994; *The Dreyfus Affair* 1992; *The Deal* 1991

Lesley, Craig
A life-long resident of the Pacific Northwest,

Mr. Lesley lives in Portland, Oregon, with his wife and two daughters.

The Sky Fisherman 1995; *River Song* 1989; *Winterkill* 1984

Lessing, Doris (1919–)

A highly regarded novelist and short story writer, Doris Lessing was born in Persia, but moved with her British parents to a farm in Southern Rhodesia when she was five. After the breakup of her first marriage, she moved to London in 1949 where, for a time, she was seriously involved in radical left-wing politics. She has, among other topics, written about the appeals and pitfalls of Marxism, the insidiousness of racial hatred and the changing status of women in the postwar world.

Mara and Dann: An Adventure 1998; *Love, Again* 1996; *The Real Thing* 1992; *The Fifth Child* 1988; *The Good Terrorist* 1985; *The Diaries of Jane Somers* 1984; *Documents Relating to the Sentimental Agents in the Volyen Empire* 1983; *The Making of the Representative for Planet 8* 1982; *The Sirian Experiments* 1981; *The Marriage Between Zone Three, Four and Five* 1980; *Shikasta* 1979; *The Memoirs of a Survivor* 1974; *The Summer Before the Dark* 1973; *The Temptation of Jack Orkney* 1972; *Briefing for a Descent into Hell* 1971; *The Four-Gated City* 1969; *Landlocked* 1965; *African Stories* 1964; *A Man and Two Women* 1963; *The Golden Notebook* 1962; *A Ripple from the Storm* 1958; *The Habit of Loving* 1957; *A Retreat to Innocence* 1956; *A Proper Marriage* 1954; *Five: Short Novels* 1953; *Martha Quest* 1952; *This Was the Old Chief's Country* 1951; *The Grass Is Singing* 1950

Lethem, Jonathan (1964–)

Born in New York City, Mr. Lethem attended Bennington College. A novelist and short story writer, he currently lives in Brooklyn.

Girl in a Landscape 1998; *As She Climbed Across the Table* 1997; *The Wall of the Sky, the Wall of the Eye* (stories) 1996; *Amnesia Moon* 1995; *Gun with Occasional Music* 1994

Leyner, Mark (1956–)

Mark Leyner, novelist, essayist and short story writer, is a columnist for *Esquire* and *George* magazines. He lives in Hoboken, New Jersey, with his wife.

The Tetherballs of Bougainville 1997; *Tooth Imprints of a Corn Dog* 1995; *Et Tu, Babe* 1992; *My Cousin, My Gastroenterologist* (stories) 1990; *I Smell Esther Williams* (stories) 1983

L'Heureux, John (1934–)

Mr. L'Heureux, a former Jesuit priest, was born in South Hadley, Massachusetts. He was educated at Woodstock College STL, Harvard University, Holy Cross College and Boston College. He has taught at Harvard and Georgetown uni-

versities and is currently on the faculty at Stanford.

Having Everything 1999; *The Handmaid of Desire* 1996; *The Shrine at Altimara* 1992; *The Honorable Professor* 1991; *Comedians* 1990; *A Woman Run Mad* 1988; *Desires* 1987; *Jessica Fayer* 1976; *Family Affairs* 1974; *The Clang Birds* 1972; *Tight White Collar* 1972

Libby, Lewis

Mr. Lewis, a graduate of Yale University and Columbia School of Law, has spent time in Japan as an employee of the U.S. State and Defense Departments. He currently lives in the Washington, D.C., area.

The Apprentice 1996

Lightman, Alan (1940–)

Astrophysicist, novelist and educator, Mr. Lightman was born in Memphis, Tennessee, and was educated at Princeton and the California Institute of Technology. He has taught at both Cornell and Harvard and is currently a professor of science and writing and a senior lecturer in Physics at M.I.T.

Good Benito 1996; *Einstein's Dreams* 1993

Lipsky, David (1965–)

Mr. Lipsky is a short story writer, novelist, journalist and music writer. He lives in Manhattan.

The Art; Fair 1996; *Three Thousand Dollars* (stories) 1989

Liu, Aimee (1953–)

Ms. Liu was born in Connecticut and was educated at Yale. A novelist, playwright and nonfiction writer, she spent six years working as a fashion model and was, for a time, Associate Producer of NBC's *Today Show*.

Cloud Mountain 1997; *Face* 1994

Lively, Penelope (1933–)

Born in Cairo (to British parents), Ms. Lively grew up in Cairo and moved to England in the late 1940s and received a degree from Oxford University. Ms. Lively, a highly regarded novelist and short story writer, is also well known for her successful children's books.

Spiderweb 1999; *The Five Thousand and One Nights* (stories) 1997; *Heat Wave* 1996; *Cleopatra's Sister* 1993; *City of the Mind* 1991; *Passing On* 1989; *Moon Tiger* 1987; *Corruption and Other Stories* 1984; *According to Mark* 1984; *Perfect Happiness* 1983; *Next to Nature, Art* 1982; *Judgment Day* 1981; *Treasures of Time* 1980; *Nothing Missing but the Samovar & Other Stories* 1978; *The Road to Litchfield* 1977

Livesey, Margot

British novelist and short story writer, Margot Livesey divides her time between Canada, England, and the United States where she has taught

English Literature at the Carnegie Mellon University in Pittsburgh.

Criminals 1996; *Homework* 1990; *Learning by Heart* 1987

Lodge, David (1935–)

Born in South London, Mr. Lodge was educated at that city's University College. A novelist, critic, essayist, and educator, he taught for many years at Birmingham University.

Therapy 1995; **Paradise News** 1991; **Nice Work** 1988; **Small World: An Academic Romance** 1984; *Souls and Bodies* 1982; *How Far Can You Go* 1980; **Changing Places: A Tale of Two Campuses** 1975; *Out of the Shelter* 1970; *The British Museum Is Falling Down* 1967; *Ginger, You're Barmy* 1962; *The Picturegoers* 1960

Long, David (1948–)

Mr. Long was born in Boston and was educated at Albion College and the University of Montana where he received at MFA. He has taught widely at such institutions as Lewis and Clark, Arizona State, the University of Idaho and UNC at Greensboro.

The Falling Boy 1997; *Blue Spruce* (stories) 1995; *The Flood of '64* (stories) 1987; *Home Fires* (stories) 1982

Lord, Bette Bao (1938–)

Ms. Lord was born in Shanghai and was educated at Tufts and the Fletcher School of Law and Diplomacy. A writer and lecturer, she is married to Winston Lord, former U.S. Ambassador to the People's Republic of China.

Middle Heart 1996; *Spring Moon* 1981

Louis, Adrian C.

A poet, short story writer and novelist, Mr. Louis, a member of the Lovelock Pauite tribe, sets his fiction on the Oglala Lakota reservation in Pine Ridge, North Dakota.

Wild Indians and Other Creatures 1996; **Skins** 1995

Lovelace, Earl (1935–)

Mr. Lovelace, journalist, short story writer, playwright and novelist, was born in Toco, Trinidad, and was educated at Howard University and at Johns Hopkins University.

Salt 1998; *A Brief Conversion and Other Stories* 1997; *The Wine of Astonishment* 1982; **The Dragon Can't Dance** 1979; *The Schoolmaster* 1968

Lowry, Beverly (1938–)

Ms. Lowry was born in Memphis and was educated at the University off Mississippi and at Memphis State. An educator, novelist and one-time recipient of a National Endowment for the Arts Fellowship, she has taught English at the University of Houston since 1976.

The Track of Real Desire 1994; *Breaking Gentle* 1988; *The Perfect Sonya* 1987; *Daddy's Girl* 1981; *Emma Blue* 1978; *Come Back Lolly Ray* 1977

MacDonald, Ann-Marie (1958–)

Ms. MacDonald is a Toronto-based writer and actor whose play *Good Night Desdemona, Good Morning Juliet* won the Governor General's Award for Drama, the Chalmers Award for Outstanding Play and the Canadian Author's Association Award for Drama. She has also won accolades for her acting in *I've Heard the Mermaid Singing* and *Where the Spirit Lives*.

Fall on Your Knees 1996

Mackay, Shena (1944–)

A novelist and short story writer known for her distinctive brand of black humor, Shena Mackay was born and raised in Edinburgh, Scotland.

The Artist's Widow 1999; **The Orchard on Fire** 1996; *The Laughing Academy* (stories) 1993; *Dunedin* 1992; *Christmas Roses* (stories) 1988; *Dreams of a Dead Woman's Handbag* (stories) 1987; *Redhill Rococo* 1986; *A Bowl of Cherries* 1984; *Babies in Rhinestones* (stories) 1983; *Advent Calendar* 1971; *Old Crow* 1967; *Dust Falls On...* 1964; *Toddler on the Run* 1964

MacLaverty, Bernard (1942–)

A short story writer, novelist and playwright who was born in Belfast, Mr. MacLaverty has lived in Glasgow, Scotland, for many years.

Grace Notes 1997; *Walking the Dog & Other Stories* 1994; *The Great Profundo & Other Stories* 1987; *Cal* 1983; *A Time to Dance & Other Stories* 1982; *Lamb* 1980; *Secrets & Other Stories* 1977

Mailer, Norman (1923–)

Norman Mailer, novelist, journalist, essayist and political activist, graduated from Harvard University. In 1950 he co-founded the *Village Voice* and was the editor of *Dissent* from 1952 to 1963. He was awarded the Pulitzer Prize twice, in 1969 and 1980.

The Gospel According to the Son 1997; **Oswald's Tale** 1996; **Harlot's Ghost** 1991; *Tough Guys Don't Dance* 1983; *Ancient Evenings* 1983; *The Executioner's Song* 1979; *The Transit of Narcissus* 1978; *Some Honorable Men* 1976; *Maidstone* 1971; *The Armies of the Night* 1968; *The White Negro* 1957; *The Deer Park* 1955; *Barbary Shore* 1951; *The Naked and the Dead* 1948

Maitland, Sara (1950–)

Sara Maitland, a freelance academic researcher and writer since 1973, was born in London and was educated at Oxford University.

Angel Makers (stories) 1996; **Ancestral Truths** (English title was *Home Truths*) 1993; *Women Fly When Men Aren't Watching* 1993; *Three Times Table*

1990; *A Book of Spells* 1987; *Virgin Territory* 1984; *Telling Tales* 1983; *Daughter of Jerusalem* 1978

Major, Clarence (1936–)

Mr. Major was born in Atlanta, Georgia, and was educated at SUNY–Albany and at the Union for Experimenting Colleges and Universities. A lecturer, educator and novelist, he has taught at Sarah Lawrence, Queens College, Howard University, the University of Nice and UC–Davis.

Dirty Bird Blues 1995; *Fun and Games: Short Fiction* 1990; *Painted Turtle* 1988; *Such Was the Season* 1987; *My Amputations: A Novel* 1986; *Reflex and Bone Structure* 1975; *Emergency Exit* 1979

Mallon, Thomas (1951–)

Born in Glen Cove, New York, Mr. Mallon, a former Rockefeller Foundation Fellow, was educated at Brown and Harvard. An essayist, biographer and novelist, he was a Professor of English at Vassar College from 1979 to 1991.

Dewey Defeats Truman 1997; *Henry & Clara* 1994; *Aurora 7* 1991; *Arts & Sciences: A '70s Seduction* 1988

Malone, Michael (1940–)

Mr. Malone was born in North Carolina and was educated at Syracuse University, UNC and Harvard. A novelist, TV scriptwriter and playwright, he has taught at Yale, Connecticut College, the University of Pennsylvania and Swarthmore.

Foolscap (1991); *Time's Witness* (1989); *Handling Sin* (1986); *The Uncivil Season* (1983); *Dingly Falls* (1980); *The Delectable Mountains* 1976; *Painting the Roses Red* 1974

Malouf, David (1934–)

Mr. Malouf, whose father immigrated to Australia from Lebanon. was born in Brisbane and was educated at the University of Brisbane. He has traveled extensively in Europe, has taught in England and currently divides his time between Australia and Tuscany.

Conversations at Curlow Creek 1997; *Remembering Babylon* 1993; *The Great World* 1990; *Antipodes* (stories) 1985; *Harland's Half Acre* 1984; *Fly Away Peter* 1982; *Child's Play* 1982; *An Imaginary Life* 1978; *Johnno* 1975

Mantel, Hilary (1952–)

Ms. Mantel was born in Derbyshire and has lived in Africa and the Middle East. She currently lives in Berkshire, England.

The Giant, O'Brien 1998; *An Experiment in Love* 1995; *A Change in Climate* 1994; *A Place of Greater Safety* 1992; *Fludd* 1990; *Eight Months on Ghazzah Street* 1988 (1st published in the US in 1997); *Vacant Possessions* 1986; *Every Day is Mother's Day* 1985

Maraire, J. Nozipo

Dr. Maraire, a neurosurgeon, art gallery owner and novelist, was born in Zimbabwe and was educated at Harvard, Columbia and Yale. She currently divides her time between New Haven, Connecticut and Zimbabwe.

Zenzele: A Letter for My Daughter 1996

Marius, Richard (1933–)

Born in Tennessee, Mr. Marius was educated at the State University and at Yale. A newspaper reporter, novelist and educator, he has taught at Gettysburg College, the University of Tennessee, and at Harvard University where he has directed the Expository Writing Program since 1978.

After the War 1992; *Bound for the Promised Land* 1976; *The Coming of Rain* 1969

Markson, David (1927–)

Mr. Markson was born in Albany, New York, and was educated at Union College and Columbia University. A journalist, novelist, editor and academic, he has taught at Long Island University and Columbia.

Reader's Block 1996; *Wittgenstein's Mistress* 1988; *Springer's Progress* 1977; *Going Down* 1970; *The Ballad of Dingus Magee* 1966; *Miss Doll, Go Home* 1965; *Epithet for a Dead Beat* 1961; *Epithet for a Tramp* 1959

Marlowe, Stephen (1928–)

Mr. Marlowe (whose real name is Milton Lesser) was born in Brooklyn and was educated at William & Mary. A full-time writer since 1954, he has been writer-in-residence at the College of William & Mary. He also publishes under the pseudonym Jason Ridgway.

The Lighthouse at the End of the World 1995; *The Death of & Life of Miguel de Cervantes* 1991; *Memoirs of Christopher Columbus* 1987; *Deborah's Legacy* 1983; *1956* 1981; *The Valkyrie Encounter* 1978; *Translation: A Novel* 1976; *The Cawthorn Journals* 1975; *The Man with No Shadow* 1974; *Collosus: A Novel About Goya and a World Gone Mad* 1972; *The Summit* 1970; *Come Over, Red Rover: A Novel of Suspense* 1968

Marshall, Paule (1929–)

Born in Brooklyn and educated at Brooklyn College and Hunter College, Ms. Marshall (a former Guggenheim Fellow) has taught creative writing at Yale and lectured on Black Literature at Oxford University, Michigan State, Lake Forest and Cornell.

Daughters 1991; *Merle* 1985; *Reena & Other Stories* 1983; *Praissong for the Widow* 1983; *The Chosen Place* 1969; *Brown Girl, Brownstones* 1959

Martin, Valerie (1948–)

Born in Missouri and raised in New Orleans, Ms. Martin has taught at the University of New

Orleans, the University of Alabama, Mt. Holyoke and U-Mass. She currently lives in Rome.

Italian Fever 1999; **The Great Divorce** 1994; **Mary Reilly** 1990; *A Recent Martyr* 1987; *Alexandra* 1979; *Set in Motion* 1978

Maso, Carole

Ms. Maso, a recipient of the Lannan Literary Fellowship for fiction, is the director of the Creative Writing Program at Brown University.

Defiance 1999; *Aureole* (stories) 1996; **The American Woman in the Chinese Hat** 1995; *Ava* 1993; *The Art Lover* 1990; *Ghost Dance* 1986

Mason, Anita (1942–)

Ms. Mason was born in Bristol, England, and was educated at Oxford University.

Reich Angel 1995; *The Racket* 1991; *The War Against Chaos* 1988; *The Illusionist* 1984; *Bethany* 1981

Mason, Bobbie Ann (1940–)

Ms. Mason was born on a dairy farm in Mayfield, Kentucky, and was educated at SUNY-Binghampton and the University of Connecticut. In addition to writing novels, she has published short stories and critical essays in the *New Yorker*, *Redbook* and elsewhere.

Feather Crowns 1993; *Love Life* (stories) 1989; *Spence + Lila* 1988; *In Country* 1985; *Shiloh and Other Stories* 1982

Mathews, Harry (1930–)

Mathews, born in New York City, studied music at Princeton, Harvard and L'Ecole Normale de Musique in Paris. A former National Endowment for the Arts Fellow, he is a poet, novelist and translator who has taught at Bennington, Hamilton and Columbia.

The Journalist 1994; *Singular Pleasures* 1993; *The Way Home* 1988; *Cigarettes* 1987; *Selected Declarations of Dependence* 1977; *The Sinking of the Orakek Stadium & Other Novels* 1975; *The Conversions* 1962

Maupin, Armistead (1944–)

Mr. Maupin was born in Washington, D.C., and was educated at the University of North Carolina at Chapel Hill. A journalist, novelist and gay activist, he lives in San Francisco.

Maybe the Moon 1992; *Back to Barbary Lane* 1991; *28 Barbary Lane* 1990; *Sure of You* 1989; *Significant Others* 1987; *Babycakes* 1984; *Further Tales of the City* 1982; *More of the Tales of the City* 1980; *Tales of the City* 1978

Mawer, Simon (1948–)

Mr. Mawer, born in England, was raised there and in Cyprus and Malta. Educated at Oxford, he has taught in Scotland and Malta and is currently Deputy Head of St. George's English School, Rome.

Mendel's Dwarf 1998; *A Jealous God* 1996; *The Bitter Cross* 1992; *Chimera* 1989

McCabe, Patrick (1955–)

Patrick McCabe, playwright, short story writer, and novelist, was born in Ireland and currently lives and writes in London.

Breakfast on Pluto 1998; **The Dead School** 1995; **The Butcher Boy** 1992; *Carn* 1989; *Music on Clinton Street* 1986

McCarthy, Cormac (1933–)

Mr. McCarthy was born in Rhode Island, but grew up in rural Tennessee and was educated at the University of Tennessee. As a young man he traveled extensively in Europe and lived for a time at a writer's colony on the island of Ibiza. He currently lives in El Paso, Texas.

Cities of the Plain 1998; *The Crossing* 1994; **All the Pretty Horses** 1992; *Blood Meridian* 1985; *Suttree* 1979; *Child of God* 1974; *Outer Dark* 1968; *The Orchard Keeper* 1965

McCauley, Stephen

Mr. McCauley graduated from the University of Vermont in 1978.

The Man of the House 1996; **The Easy Way Out** 1992; *The Object of My Affection* 1987

McCorkle, Jill (1958–)

A short story writer, novelist and educator, Ms. McCorkle was born and raised in North Carolina. She taught at the University of North Carolina at Chapel Hill until moving to Boston. She divides her time between Bennington College and Harvard University where she is Director of the Creative Writing Program.

Final Vinyl Days (stories) 1998; **Carolina Moon** 1996; *The Cheer Leader* 1992; *Crash Diet* (stories) 1992; *Ferris Beach* 1990; *Tending to Virginia* 1987; *July 7* 1984

McCourt, James (1941–)

Mr. McCourt, a playwright, novelist, actor, teacher of Communication Arts and opera director, was born in New York City and was educated at Manhattan College, NYU and Yale.

Time Remaining 1993; *Kaye Wayfaring* 1984; *Mawrdew Czgowchwz* 1975

McCracken, Elizabeth (1966–)

Ms. McCracken was born in Boston, Massachusetts, and was educated at Boston University and the University of Iowa — from which she received her MFA. Selected as one of the "Best Young American Novelists" by *Granta Magazine* in 1996, she currently lives in Somerville, Massachusetts, where, until recently, she worked as a librarian.

The Giant's House 1996; *Here's Your Hat What's Your Hurry* (stories) 1993

McCrum, Robert (1953–)

Mr. McCrum, an editor and novelist, was born in Cambridge, England, and was educated at Cambridge University and the University of Pennsylvania. He was co-author, with Robert MacNeil, of the highly regarded *The Story of English.*

Suspicion 1997; *Jubilee* 1994; *The Psychological Moment* 1993; *Mainland* 1992; *The Fabulous Englishman* 1984; *A Loss of Heart* 1982; *In the Secret State* 1980

McDermott, Alice (1953–)

Ms. McDermott received her master's degree from the University of New Hampshire and is currently a Writers Seminar Professor at Johns Hopkins University in Baltimore. She lives in Bethesda, Maryland.

Charming Billy 1998; ***At Weddings and Wakes*** 1992; *That Night* 1988; *A Bigamist's Daughter* 1982

McEwan, Ian (1948–)

A short story writer and novelist, Mr. McEwan lives in Oxford with his wife and children.

Amsterdam 1998; ***Enduring Love*** 1997; ***Black Dog 1992***; *The Innocent* 1990; *The Child in Time* 1987; *The Comfort of Strangers* (novella) 1981; *The Imitation Game* (TV plays) 1981; *The Cement Garden* 1978; *In Between the Sheets* (stories) 1978; *First Love, Last Rites* (stories) 1975

McFarland, Dennis (1950–)

Mr. McFarland attended Brooklyn College, Goddard College, and Stanford University. He has taught at Goddard and Emerson colleges and at Stanford University.

A Face at the Window 1997; ***School for the Blind*** 1994; *The Music Room* 1990

McGahan, Andrew

Andrew McGahan, a talented young Australian novelist "with attitude," managed to capture both the Vogel Literary Award and the Commonwealth Writer's Award for his first novel *Praise* in 1993.

1988 1995; *Praise* 1993

McGahern, John (1934–)

Born in Dublin and educated at Presentation College and University College, Mr. McGahern, lecturer and novelist, has taught in the U.S. (at Colgate University) and at the British universities of New Castle and Durham.

The Collected Stories 1993; *The Power of Darkness* (stories) 1991; ***Amongst Women*** 1990; *High Ground* 1985; *Getting Through* 1980; *The Leavetaking* 1974; *Nightlines* 1970; *The Dark* 1965; *The Barracks* 1963

McGrail, Anna

Ms. McGrail was born and educated in Liverpool. An editor and novelist, she has worked in publishing and for the BBC; she currently lives in Brighton.

Mrs. Einstein 1998

McGrath, Patrick (1950–)

Mr. McGrath was born in London, England, but, as the son of a psychiatrist (and Superintendent of Broadmoor Psychiatric Hospital for the Criminally Insane), grew up on the grounds of Broadmoor. He was educated at the University of London and at Simon Fraser University in Canada. In addition to his career as a novelist, Mr. McGrath has taught (in British Columbia) and has worked in a number of psychiatric institutions in England.

Asylum 1997; ***The Grotesque*** 1996; ***Dr. Haggard's Disease*** 1993; ***Spider*** 1990; *The Grotesque* 1989; *Blood & Water & Other Tales* 1988

McIlvanney, William (1936–)

A "gifted" Scottish novelist and short story writer, McIlvanney was born in Kilmarnoch, Scotland, and was educated at the University of Glasgow. He often addresses the social and cultural condition of modern Scotland in his work, particular those novels featuring the "hardbitten" Glasgow detective Jack Laidlaw.

Strange Loyalties 1992; *Walking Wounded* (stories) 1989; *The Big Man* 1985; *The Papers of Tony Veitch* 1983; *Laidlaw* 1977; *Docherty* 1975; *A Gift from Nessus* 1968; *The Remedy Is None* 1967

McKinney-Whetstone, Diane

Ms. McKinney-Whetstone, a novelist, short story writer and educator, graduated from the University of Pennsylvania where she currently teaches fiction writing.

Tempest Rising 1998; ***Tumbling*** 1996

McLaurin, Tim

Mr. McLaurin lives in Chapel Hill, North Carolina.

The Last Great Snake Show 1997; *Cured by Fire* 1995; *Woodrow's Trumpet* 1989; *The Acorn Plan* 1988

McManus, James (1951–)

Born in New York City, Mr. McManus was educated at the University of Illinois (Chicago). He is Professor of Creative Writing at the School of the Art Institute of Chicago.

Going to the Sun 1996; *Ghost Waves* 1988; *Curtains* (stories) 1985; *Chin Music* 1985; *Out of the Blue* 1984

McNamee, Eoin (1961–)

Novelist and short story writer Mr. McNamee was born in Kilkeel County, Ireland. A popular Irish writer, a film version of his debut novel *Resurrection Man* was released in 1998.

Resurrection Man 1994; *The Last of Deeds and History* (stories) 1989

McPhee, Martha

Novelist and short story writer, Ms. McPhee has published in numerous magazines including the *New Yorker* and *Red Book*. She lives in New York City.

Bright Angel Time 1997

Medwed, Mameve

Born in Bangor, Maine, and educated at Simmons College, Ms. Medwed currently teaches a fiction workshop at the Cambridge Center for Adult Education in Cambridge, Massachusetts.

Mail 1997

Meer, Ameena

A short story writer, journalist and novelist, Ms. Meer was born in Boston, Massachusetts.

Bombay Talkie 1994

Mehta, Gita

Ms Mehta was born in India into a politically active (i.e. pro–Independence) family and was educated in India and at Cambridge University. She currently lives in London with her husband, a prominent publisher.

A River Sutra 1993; **Raj** 1989

Melville, Pauline

Ms. Melville, a former stand up comic and occasional actress (*The Black Adder, The Young Ones*) was born in Guyana but has lived in England for many years.

The Ventriloquist 1998; *Shape Shifter* (stories) 1990

Mendelsohn, Jane

Novelist and critic Jane Mendelsohn was educated at Yale University and lives with her husband in New York City.

I Was Amelia Earhart 1996

Merlis, Mark

Mr. Merlis is an extraordinarily talented young novelist who writes about contemporary gay culture.

An Arrow's Flight 1998; **American Studies** 1994

Messud, Claire (1966–)

Born in the U.S. and educated at Yale and Oxford, Ms. Messud, a novelist and book critic, currently lives in London.

When the World Was Steady 1994

Michaels, Anne (1958–)

Ms. Michaels was born in Toronto and was educated at the University of Toronto. A poet and novelist, she teaches creative writing in Toronto.

Fugitive Pieces 1994

Miller, Andrew (1958–)

Mr. Miller, who has worked as a martial arts instructor, waiter and tour guide, lives and writes in Bath, England.

Casanova in Love 1998; **Ingenious Pain** 1997

Miller, Sue (1943–)

Sue Miller, a novelist, short story writer and creative writing teacher, was educated at Radcliffe, Harvard, Brown and Wesleyan.

While I Was Gone 1999; **The Distinguished Guest** 1995; **For Love** 1993; *Family Pictures* 1990; *Inventing the Abbots & Other Stories* 1987; *The Good Mother* 1986

Millhauser, Steven (1943–)

Mr. Millhauser was born in New York City and was educated at Columbia and Brown. He has taught at Williams College and is currently Associate Professor of English at Skidmore College.

The Knife Thrower & Other Stories 1998; **Martin Dressler: The Tale of an American Dreamer** 1996; **Little Kingdoms** 1993; *The Barnum Museum* 1990; *From the Realm of Orpheus* 1986; *In the Penny Arcade* 1986; *Portrait of a Romantic* 1977; *Edwin Mullhouse: The Life & Death of an American Writer, 1934–1954* 1972

Min, Anchee (1957–)

Ms. Min, an artist and writer, was born in Shanghai and grew up during the Cultural Revolution. She immigrated to the U.S. where she attended the School of the Art Institute of Chicago and received a BA and MFA.

Katherine 1995; *Red Azalea* (a memoir) 1994

Minot, Susan (1956–)

Born in Manchester, Massachusetts, and educated at Boston University, Brown and Columbia, Ms. Minot, a short story writer, editor, novelist and screenplay writer (*Stealing Beauty*) has taught at Columbia and NYU.

Evening 1998; **Folly** 1992; *Lust & Other Stories* 1989; *Monkey* 1986

Mistry, Rohinton (1952–)

Rohinton Mistry, novelist and short story writer, was born in Bombay and emigrated to Canada in 1975. He worked as a bank teller while pursuing a joint degree in English and philosophy at the University of Toronto.

A Fine Balance 1996; **Such a Long Journey** 1992

Mitchard, Jacqueline

A journalist and novelist, Ms. Mitchard lives in Madison, Wisconsin, with her five children. She is a frequent contributor to *Ladies Home Journal* and other publications.

The Most Wanted 1998; **Deep End of the Ocean** 1996

Moody, Rick (Hiram F. III) (1961–)

A novelist, editor and educator, Mr. Millhauser was born in New York City and was educated at Brown and Columbia. He currently teaches Creative Writing at Bennington College.

Purple America 1998; *Garden State* 1997; *The Ice Storm* 1995; *The Ring of Brightest Angels Around Heaven* (novella and stories) 1995

Moore, Brian (1921–1999)

Mr. Moore, a highly respected novelist, was born in Belfast, Northern Ireland, but immigrated to Canada in 1948. He was educated at St. Malachy's College. He eventually moved to California where he was living at the time of his death in 1999.

The Magician's Wife 1998; *The Statement* 1996; *My Other Life* 1993; *Lies of Silence* 1990; *The Color of Blood* 1987; *Black Robe* 1985; *Cold Heaven* 1983; *The Temptation of Eileen Hughes* 1981; *Two Stories* 1979; *The Mangan Inheritance* 1979; *The Doctor's Wife* 1976; *The Great Victorian Collection* 1975; *Catholics* 1972; *The Revolution Script* 1971; *Fergus* 1970; *I Am Mary Dunne* 1968; *The Emperor of Ice Cream* 1965; *An Answer from Limbo* 1962; *The Luck of Ginger Coffey* 1960; *Feast of Lupercal* 1957; *Judith Hearne* 1955

Moore, Lorrie (1957–)

Born in Glens Falls, New York, Ms. Moore was educated at St. Lawrence College and Cornell University and currently teaches at the University of Wisconsin at Madison.

Birds of America (stories) 1998; *Who Will Run the Frog Hospital?* 1994; *Like Life* (stories) 1990; *Anagrams* 1986; *Self-Help* (stories) 1985

Moore, Susanna (1948–)

Ms. Moore grew up in Hawaii and now lives in New York City.

In the Cut 1995; *Sleeping Beauties* 1993; *The Whiteness of Bones* 1989; *My Old Sweetheart* 1982

Moorhouse, Frank (1938–)

Frank Moorhouse was born in Nowra, a small Australian coastal town. A highly regarded novelist, short story writer and essayist, he traveled extensively in Europe and the Middle East before returning to live and write in Australia.

Grand Days 1993; *Lateshows* ("pieces") 1990; *Forty-Seventeen* 1988; *Room Service* 1985; *The Everlasting Family Secret* (stories) 1980; *Tales of Mystery and Romance* 1977; *Futility and Other Animals* (stories) 1969; *Confernce-ville* 1976; *The Electrical Experience* 1974; *The Americans, Baby* 1972; *Futility and Other Animals* 1969

Mordden, Ethan (1947–)

Born near Wilkes Barre, Pennsylvania, Mr. Mordden was educated at the University of Pennsylvania. In addition to novel writing, he is an opera critic and journalist.

The Venice Adriana 1998; *Some Men Are Lookers* 1997; *How Long Has This Been Going On?* 1995; *Everybody Loves You: Further Adventures in Gay Manhattan* 1988; *Ones Last Waltz* 1986; *Buddies* 1986; *I've a Feeling We're Not in Kansas Anymore: Tales from Gay Manhattan* 1985

Morgan, Robert (1944–)

Born in Hendersonville, North Carolina, Robert Morgan was educated at the University of North Carolina at Chapel Hill and at Greensboro. A poet and novelist, he has taught for many years at Cornell University.

The Truest Pleasure 1995; *The Hinterlands* 1994; *The Mountains Won't Remember Us & Other Stories* 1992

Morley, John David (1948–)

Mr. Morley was born in Singapore was educated at Oxford and has lived in Japan. A freelance writer, interpreter and translator (who has also worked for the Japan Broadcasting Corporation) he currently lives in Munich, Germany.

The Feast of Fools 1995; *The Anatomy Lesson* 1995; *The Case of Thomas N* 1987; *In the Labyrinth* 1986; *Pictures from the Water Trade: Adventures of a Westerner in Japan* 1985

Morris, Bill (1952–)

Bill Morris grew up in Detroit and currently lives in North Carolina.

All Souls Day 1997; *Motor City* 1992

Morrison, Toni (1931–)

A Pulitzer Prize–winning novelist, Ms. Morrison was born in Lorain, Ohio and was educated at Harvard and Cornell. She has taught at Yale, Cambridge and SUNY–Albany. She is currently Goheen Professor of the Humanities at Princeton University.

Paradise 1998; *Jazz* 1992; *Beloved* 1987; *Tar Baby* 1981; *Song of Solomon* 1977; *Sula* 1974; *The Bluest Eye* 1970

Morrissy, Mary (1957–)

Ms. Morrissy, a novelist and short story writer, a native of Dublin, is a literary critic for the *Irish Times*. She received a Lannan Foundation Award in 1995.

A Lazy Eye (stories) 1996; *Mother of Pearl* 1995

Morrow, Bradford (1951–)

Mr. Morrow, a jazz musician and novelist, was born in Baltimore, Maryland, and was educated at the Liceo Scientifico in Turin, Italy, at the University of Colorado (Boulder) and at Yale University. A Bard Center Fellow at Bard College (who has also taught at Brown and Temple universities), he divides his time between New York City and Upstate New York.

The Unquiet Country 1997; *Giovanni's Gift*

1997; *Trinity Fields* 1995; *The Almanac Branch* 1991; *Come Sunday* 1988

Morrow, James (1947–)
Born and educated in Philadelphia (he attended the University of Pennsylvania), Morrow has received the Nebula Fantasy Award and the World Fantasy Awards twice each. A freelance writer, he has taught at both the secondary and college level and lives in State College, Pennsylvania.
The Eternal Footman 1999; ***Blameless in Abadon*** 1996; ***Towing Jehovah*** 1994; *City of Truth* 1993; *Only Begotten Daughter* 1990; *This Is the Way the World Ends* 1986; *The Continent of Lies* 1984; *The Wine of Violence* 1981

Mortimer, John (1923–)
John Mortimer was born in London and was educated at Oxford. A novelist, playwright, drama critic and barrister he is best known for his *Rumpole of the Bailey* series. Three of his novels (*Summer's Lease*, *Paradise Postponed*, and *Titmuss Regained*) were made into successful TV series in Great Britain.
The Sound of Trumpets (Volume III of the Rapstone Chronicles) 1999; ***Felix in the Underworld*** 1997; *Dunster* 1993; ***Summer's Lease*** 1991; *Titmuss Regained* (Volume II of the Rapstone Chronicles) 1991; *Paradise Postponed* (Volume I of the Rapstone Chronicles) 1985; *The Narrowing Stream* 1956; *Three Winters* 1956; *Like Men Betrayed* 1954; *Answers Yes or No* 1950; *Rumming Park* 1949; *Charade* 1948

Morton, Brian (1955–)
Mr. Morton, the executive editor of *Dissent* magazine, lives in New York City,
Starting Out in the Evening 1998; *The Dylanist* 1991

Mosher, Howard Frank (1943–)
Mr. Mosher was educated at Syracuse University, the University of Vermont and the University of California. He lives in Vermont near the Canadian border with his wife and their son and daughter.
Northern Borders 1994; *A Stranger in the Kingdom* 1989; *Marie Blythe* 1983; *Where the Rivers Flow North* (stories) 1978; *Disappearances* 1977

Mosley, Nicholas (1923–)
Mr. Mosley, the son of Oswald Mosley, founder of the British Union of Fascists, was educated at Oxford and inherited his father's baronetcy in 1966. A left-leaning, innovative writer best known for his Catastrophe Practice Series, he has won a number of literary prizes.
Hopeful Monsters 1990; *Judith* 1986; *Serpent* 1981; *Imago Bird* 1980; *Catastrophe Practice* 1979; **Other Novels:** *Children of Darkness & Light* 1996; *Natalie Natalia* 1971; *Impossible Object* 1968; *Assas-*

sins 1966; *Accident* 1965; *Meeting Place* 1962; *Corruption* 1957; *Rainbearers* 1955; *Spaces of the Dark* 1951

Mosley, Walter (1952–)
Walter Mosley attended college in Vermont (Goddard and Johnson State) and participated in City College's Creative Writing Program. A past president of the Mystery Writers of America (he is best known for his mysteries featuring Easy Rawlins), he currently lives in New York City.
Blue Light 1998; *Gone Fishing* 1997; ***Always Outnumbered*** 1997; *A Little Yellow Dog* 1996; ***Rls Dream*** 1995; *Black Betty* 1994; *White Butterfly* 1992; *A Red Death* 1991; *Devil in a Blue Dress* 1990

Mukherjee, Bharati (1940–)
Ms. Mukherjee was born in Calcutta but moved to Canada in 1961. She was educated in India and at the University of Iowa. A professor of English at UC–Berkeley, she moved permanently to the U.S. in 1980.
Leave It to Me 1997; ***Holder of the World*** 1993; *Jasmine* 1989; *The Middleman & Other Stories* 1988; *Darkness* (stories) 1985; *Wife* 1975; *The Tiger's Daughter* 1972

Murdoch, Iris (1919–)
Dame Iris Murdoch was born in Dublin, Ireland, into an Anglo-Irish family. She was educated at Oxford and Cambridge and, in addition to her career as a novelist, she taught philosophy at Oxford University. Recently diagnosed with Alzheimer's, she lives in Oxford with her husband, John Bayly, a literary critic.
Jackson's Dilemma 1996; ***The Green Knight*** 1993; *The Message to the Planet* 1990; *The Book and the Brotherhood* 1988; *The Good Apprentice* 1986; *The Philosopher's Pupil* 1983; *Nuns and Soldiers* 1981; *The Sea the Sea* 1978; *Henry and Cato* 1977; *A Word Child* 1975; *The Sacred & Profane Love Machine* 1974; *The Black Prince* 1973; *An Accidental Man* 1971; *A Fairly Honorable Defeat* 1970; *Bruno's Dream* 1969; *The Nice and the Good* 1968; *The Time of the Angels* 1956; *The Red and the Green* 1965; *The Italian Girl* 1964; *The Unicorn* 1963; *An Unofficial Rose* 1962; *A Severed Head* 1961; *The Bell* 1958; *The Sandcastle* 1857; *The Flight from the Enchanter* 1956; *Under the Net* 1954

Murphy, Yannick
Ms. Murphy, a novelist and screenwriter and past recipient of a Whiting Award and a National Endowment for the Arts Fellowship, lives in Pasadena with her husband and son.
The Sea of Trees 1997

Murray, Albert (1916–)
"Albert Murray is one of the best-kept secrets in contemporary American literature. He is our

premier writer about jazz and the blues, an incisive literary critic, a social commentator of wide-ranging vision, and a fictional tale spinner in the grand Southern tradition of William Faulkner, Joel Chandler Harris, Walker Percy, Reynolds Price, Eudora Welty and Flannery O'Connor. An Alabama native and graduate of Tuskegee, Murray entered the Air Force in World War II and retired with the rank of major. He then settled in Harlem and began a prodigious literary career, which he has mixed with periods as a teacher, holding visiting academic posts and lecturing at leading universities" (WPBW 11/3/91).

The Seven League Boots 1995; *The Spyglass Tree* 1991; *Train Whistle Guitar* 1974

Muske Dukes, Carol (1945–)
Award-winning poet and novelist Carol Muske Dukes teaches creative writing at the University of Southern California. She lives in Los Angeles with her husband and daughter.
Saving St. Germ 1993; *Dear Digby* 1989

Naipaul, V.S. (1932–)
V.S. Naipaul was born in Trinidad and was educated at University College, Oxford. In addition to writing highly acclaimed novels and short stories he has worked as a BBC radio producer. Mr. Naipaul has lived in Britain since 1950 and was recently knighted for his service to British letters.
A Way in the World 1994; *The Enigma of Arrival* 1987; *A Bend in the River* 1979; *Guerillas* 1975; *In a Free State* 1971; *A Flag on the Island* 1967; *The Mimic Men* 1967; *Mr. Stone and the Knight's Companion* 1963; *A House for Mr. Biswas* 1961; *Miguel Street* 1959; *The Suffrage of Elvira* 1958; *The Mystic Masseur* 1957

Narayan, Karin
Ms. Narayan, an anthropologist and novelist, received her Ph.D. from UC–Berkeley and is currently an assistant professor of Anthropology at the University of Wisconsin.
Love Stars & All That 1994

Naumoff, Lawrence (1946–)
Born in Charlotte, North Carolina, Mr. Naumoff was educated at the University of North Carolina. A freelance writer since 1988, he also writes under the pseudonym of Peter Nesovich.
A Plan for Women 1997; *Silk Hope, N.C* 1994; *Taller Women: A Cautionary Tale* 1992; *Rootie Kazootie* 1990; *The Night of the Weeping Women* 1988

Naylor, Gloria (1950–)
A graduate of Brooklyn College and Yale University, Ms. Naylor, an award-winning novelist, was born and raised in Queens. A former Guggenheim Fellow, she currently lives and writes in New York City.

The Men of Brewster Place 1998; *Bailey's Cafe* 1992; *Mama Day* 1988; *Linden Hills* 1985; *The Women of Brewster Place* 1982

Neihart, Ben (1965–)
Mr. Neihart grew up in Florida and was educated at George Washington University, the University of Southern Mississippi and Johns Hopkins University (where he obtained an MA). He currently lives in Baltimore.
Burning Girl 1999; *Hey Joe* 1996

Nelson, Antonya (1961–)
Ms. Nelson was born in Wichita, Kansas, and was educated at the University of Kansas and the University of Arizona. She lives in New Mexico (where she teaches at New Mexico State) and Colorado with her novelist husband, Robert Boswell.
Nobody's Girl 1998; *Talking in Bed* 1996; *Family Terrorists: A Novel & 7 Stories* 1994; *In the Land of Men* (stories) 1992

Newman, Kim James (1959–)
Mr. Newman was born in London and attended the University of Sussex. A playwright, novelist, musician, broadcaster, film critic, editor and Director of the Peace and Love Corporation, Mr. Newman also writes under the pseudonym Addison DeWitt.
The Bloody Red Baron 1995; *The Quorum* 1994; *Ano-Dracula* 1993; *Jago* 1993; *Bad Dreams* 1991; *The Night Mayor* 1990

Ng, Fae Myenne (1956–)
Ms. Ng was born in San Francisco and was educated at UC–Berkeley and at Columbia University where she received her MFA. A widely published short story writer, she lives in New York City with her husband, novelist Mark Coovelis.
Bone 1993

Ng, Mei (1966–)
A talented young novelist whose debut novel was reviewed widely and well.
Eating Chinese Food Naked 1998

Nicholson, Geoff (1953–)
Mr. Nicholson was born in Sheffield, England, and was educated at Cambridge and the University of Sussex.
Bleeding London 1997; *Footsucker* 1995; *Still Life with Volkswagens* 1995; *The Errol Flynn Novel* 1994; *Hunters and Gatherers* 1994; *The Food Chain* 1992; *Street Sleeper* 1987

Nigam, Sanjay
Sanjay Nigam, a novelist and short story writer, was born and raised in India and is currently a medical researcher at Harvard University and a Professor of Medicine at Brigham and Women's Hospital in Boston.

The Snake Charmer 1998; *The Non-resident Indian & Other Stories* 1996

Noon, Jeff (1957–)

Born in Manchester, England, and educated at the University of Manchester, prize-winning novelist Noon (a former member of a punk rock band) has turned his hand, variously, to bookselling, art, music, and play writing.

Pixel Juice 1998; *Nymphomation* 1997; **Automated Alice** 1996; **Pollen** 1995; **Vurt** 1993

Nordan, Lewis (1939–)

Mr. Nordan was born in Jackson, Mississippi, and was educated at Millsaps College, Mississippi State, and Auburn University. He is currently on the faculty at the University of Pittsburgh.

Lightning Song 1997; *Sugar Among the Freaks* (stories) 1996; **The Sharpshooter Blues** 1995; *Wolf Whistle* 1993; *Music of the Swamp* 1991; *The All-Girl Football Team* 1986; *Welcome to Arrow-Catcher Fair* (stories) 1983

Norfolk, Lawrence (1963–)

A poetry reviewer for the *Times Literary Supplement*, Mr. Norfolk was born in London and was educated at King's College, London.

The Pope's Rhinoceros 1996; **Lempriere's Dictionary** 1991

Norman, Howard

Mr. Norman divides his time between Washington, D.C., and Vermont and teaches at the University of Maryland.

The Museum Guard 1998; **The Bird Artist** 1994; *Kiss in the Hotel Joseph Conrad* (stories) 1989

Norman, Philip (1943–)

Mr. Norman is a London-based journalist and novelist who has written extensively about the British Rock "scene."

Everyone's Gone to the Moon 1996; *Tilt the Hourglass and Begin Again* 1985; *The Skaters' Waltz* 1985; *Plumridge* 1971; *Slip on a Fat Lady* 1970

Nova, Craig (1945–)

Craig Nova was born and raised in Hollywood and was educated at UC–Berkeley and at Columbia University (where he received his MFA). He now lives in Vermont with his wife and two daughters.

The Universal Donor 1997; *The Book of Dreams* 1994; *Trombone* 1992; *Tornado Alley* 1989; *The Congressman's Daughter* 1986; *The Good Son* 1982; *Incandescence* 1979; *The Geek* 1975; *Turkey Hash* 1972

Oates, Joyce Carol (1938–)

Ms. Oates, a prolific novelist, short story writer and essayist, was born in Lockport, New York, and studied at Syracuse University and the University of Wisconsin. She has taught at the University of Windsor (in Toronto) and at Princeton.

She also publishes mysteries under the name of Rosamund Smith.

Broke Heart Blues 1999; *My Heart Laid Bare* 1998; **Man Crazy** 1997; **We Were the Mulvaneys** 1996; *First Love; A Gothic Tale* 1996; *Will You Always Love Me?* 1996; **Zombie** 1995; **What I Lived For** 1994; *Haunted Tales of the Grotesque* 1994; *Foxfire: Confessions of a Girl Gang* 1993; *Where Is Here?* 1992; *Black Water* 1992; *The Rise of Life on Earth* 1991; *Heat & Other Stories* 1991; *I Lock My Door Upon Myself* 1990; *Because It Is Bitter, and Because It Is My Heart* 1990; *American Appetites* 1989; *The Assignation* 1988; *You Must Remember This* 1987; *Raven's Wing* 1986; *Marya; A Life* 1986; *Solstice* 1985; *Last Days* 1984; *Mysteries of Winterthur* 1984; *A Bloodsmoor Romance* 1982; *Angel of Light* 1981; *A Sentimental Education* 1980; *Bellefleur* 1980; *Unholy Loves* 1979; *Son of the Morning* 1978; *Night-Side* 1977; *Crossing the Border* 1976; *Childwold* 1976; *The Assassins: A Book of Hours* 1975; *The Poisoned Kiss & Other Stories from the Portuguese* 1975; *Where Are You Going, Where Have You Been? Stories of Young America* 1974; *The Goddess & Other Women* 1974; *The Hungry Ghosts: Seven Allusive Comedies* 1974; *Do with Me What You Will* 1973; *Marriages and Infidelities* 1972; *Wonderland* 1971; *The Wheel of Love* 1970; *Them* 1969; *Expensive People* 1968; *A Garden of Earthly Delights* 1967; *Upon the Sleeping Flood* 1966; *With Shuddering Fall* 1964; *By the North Gate* 1963

Obejas, Achy (1956–)

A novelist, short story writer, columnist and journalist (her work appears frequently in the *Chicago Tribune* and *Chicago Reader*), Ms. Obejas received her MFA from Warren Wilson College. A former NEA Creative Writing Fellow, she teaches at Columbia College in Chicago.

Memory Mambo 1996; *We Came All the Way from Cuba So You Could Dress Like That?* (stories) 1994

O'Brien, Edna (1932–)

Ms. O'Brien was born in County Clare, Ireland, and attended the Pharmaceutical College of Ireland. A novelist, playwright, short story writer and screenwriter, she has taught creative writing at City College in New York City since 1986.

Down by the River 1997; **House of Splendid Isolation** 1994; *Time and Tide* 1992; *Lantern Slides* 1990; *The High Road* 1988; *The Country Girls Trilogy* 1986; *A Fanatic Heart* 1984; *Returning* 1982; *A Rose in the Heart* 1979; *Mrs. Reinhardt & Other Stories* 1978; *Johnny I Hardly Knew You* 1977; *A Scandalous Woman & Other Stories* 1974; *Night* 1973; *Zee & Co.* 1971; *A Pagan Place* 1970; *The Love Object* 1968; *Casualties of Peace* 1966; *August Is a Wicked Month* 1965; *Girls in Their Married Bliss* 1964; *The Lonely Girl* 1962; *The Country Girls* 1960

O'Donnell, Mark (1954–)

    Born in Cleveland, Ohio, Mr. O'Donnell attended the Academy of the Dramatic Arts and graduated (magna cum laude) from Harvard University. A freelance writer and cartoonist since 1978, he lives in New York City.

    Let Nothing You Dismay 1998; **Getting Over Homer** 1996; *Vertigo Park & Other Tall Tales* 1993

Offutt, Chris (1958–)

    Mr. Offutt, a former Guggenheim Fellow and winner of a Whiting Award, grew up in the Appalachian Mountains of Kentucky. He now lives in Montana.

    Out of the Woods (Stories) 1999; **The Good Brother** 1997; *Kentucky Straight* 1992

Okri, Ben (1959–)

    Born in Minna, Nigeria, and educated in that country and at the University of Essex, England, Mr. Okri, a poet, journalist, short story writer and novelist, lives and writes in London. He has worked as a broadcaster with the BBC and as the poetry editor for *West Africa Magazine*.

    Dangerous Love 1996; *Astonishing the Gods* 1995; **Songs of Enchantment** 1993; **The Famished Road** 1991; *Stars of the New Curfew* 1985; *Incidents at the Shrine (stories)* 1986; *The Landscapes Within* 1981; *Flowers and Shadows* 1980

Olds, Bruce (1951–)

    Mr. Olds was born in Milwaukee and was educated at the University of Wisconsin.

    Raising Holy Hell 1995

O'Nan, Stewart (1961–)

    Mr. O'Nan was born in Pittsburgh and attended Boston University and Cornell University (where he received his MFA). A test engineer from 1984 to 1988, he currently teaches English at Trinity College in Hartford, Connecticut.

    A World Away 1998; **The Speed Queen** 1997; **The Names of the Dead** 1996; **Snow Angels** 1994; *In the Walled City* 1993

Ondaatje, Michael (1943–)

    Highly acclaimed poet and novelist Michael Ondaatje was born in Sri Lanka and emigrated to England as a young man. He attended Dulwich College in London and, in 1962, emigrated to Canada where he attended Bishops University, the University of Toronto, and Queen's University. He currently lives in Toronto.

    The English Patient 1992; **In the Skin of a Lion** 1987; *Coming Through Slaughter* 1976

Owen, Howard (1949–)

    Mr. Owen, a journalist and novelist, was educated at the University of North Carolina at Chapel Hill.

    The Measured Man 1997; **Answers to Lucky** 1996; *Fat Lightning* 1994; *Little John* 1992

Owens, Louis (1948–)

    Mr. Owens (of mixed Irish/American and Chocktaw/Cherokee lineage) was born in Lampoc, California. He was educated within the University of California system. He is currently on the faculty of the University of California at Santa Cruz.

    Dark River 1999; **Nightland** 1996; **Bone Game** 1994; **Sharpest Sight** 1992; *Wolfsong* 1991

Ozick, Cynthia (1928–)

    Ms. Ozick was born in New York City and was educated at NYU and at Ohio State. A writer, translator and lecturer, she has taught English at City College and NYU.

    The Puttermesser Papers 1997; *The Shawl* 1989; *The Messiah of Stockholm* 1987; *Trust: A Novel* 1983; *The Cannibal Galaxy* 1983; *Levitations: Five Fictions* 1982; *Bloodshed* 1976; *The Pagan Rabbi & Other Stories* 1976

Palahniuk, Chuck

    Chuck Palahniuk is a graduate of the University of Oregon. He debut novel is currently being filmed (starring Brad Pitt and Edward Norton)

    Survivor 1999; **The Fight Club** 1996

Palliser, Charles (1947–)

    Palliser, an American who has taught in England and the U.S., currently lives in London.

    Betrayals 1995; *The Sensationist* 1991; **The Quincunx** 1990

Parini, Jay (1948–)

    Jay Parini, a professor of English at Middlebury College, was educated at Lafayette College and the University of St. Andrews, Scotland. A highly acclaimed poet, novelist, essayist and biographer (of Robert Frost and John Steinbeck), he is a former Guggenheim Fellow and a visiting Fellow at Christ Church, Oxford.

    Benjamin's Crossing 1996; *Bay of Arrows* 1992; *The Last Station* 1990; *The Patch Boys* 1986; *The Love Run* 1980

Park, Jacqueline

    Ms. Park was born and educated in Canada and currently divides her time between New York City, Toronto and Miami Beach. She is the founding chairman of the Dramatic Writing Program and Professor Emerita at NYU's Tisch School of the Arts.

    The Secret Book of Grazia dei Rossi 1997

Parker, Gwendolyn

    Ms. Parker grew up in (still-segregated) Durham, North Carolina, in the 1950s. The daughter of a pharmacist and a teacher she attended a boarding school in Connecticut, Radcliffe College and NYU (where she received her law degree). She has also written a well-regarded memoir called *Trespassing*.

    These Same Long Bones 1994

Parks, Tim

Mr. Parks was born in Manchester and was educated at Cambridge. He currently lives in Verona where he teaches at the University of Verona.

Europa 1997; ***Shear*** 1994; ***Goodness*** 1991; *Juggling the Stars* 1990; ***Family Planning*** 1989; *Loving Roger* 1987; *Home Thoughts* 1986; *Tongues of Flame* 1985

Patchett, Ann (1963–)

Ms. Patchett was born in Nashville, Tennessee, and lived for a number of years in Los Angeles. She was educated at Sarah Lawrence and was a Fellow at Radcliffe's Bunting Institute. She currently is the Tennessee Williams Fellow in Creative Writing at the University of the South (Sewanee).

The Magician's Assistant 1997; *Taft* 1994; *The Patron Saint of Liars* 1992

Pate, Alexs (1950–)

Alexs Pate teaches creative writing and literature at Macalester College.

Finding Makeba 1996; ***Losing Absalom*** 1994

Paul, Jim (1950–)

Jim Paul, poet, novelist, translator and former recipient of a Wallace Stegner Creative Writing Fellowship and former Guggenheim Fellow, currently lives in San Francisco.

Medieval in L.A. 1996; *Called Love* 1993; *Catapult: Harry and I Build a Siege Weapon* 1991

Pears, Iain (1955–)

Mr. Pears, journalist, art historian and novelist, was born in Coventry, England, and was educated at Oxford and Yale. Although he has traveled widely in Europe and the U.S., he currently lives in London.

An Instance of the Fingerpost 1998; *Death & Restoration* 1998; *Giotto's Hand* 1997; *The Titian Committee* 1993; *The Last Judgment* 1993; *The Bernini Bust* 1994; *The Raphael Affair* 1992

Pears, Tim (1954–)

Born in Tonbridge Wells, England, Mr. Pears was educated at the National Film and Television School in London. He currently lives and writes in Oxford.

In a Land of Plenty 1998; ***In the Place of Falling Leaves*** 1993

Pearson, T.R. (1956–)

Mr. Pearson, who began writing at the age of twenty-five, was born and raised in North Carolina.

Cry Me a River 1993; *Gospel Hour* 1991; *Call & Response* 1989; *The Last of How It Was* 1986; *Off for the Sweet Hereafter* 1986; *A Short History of a Small Place* 1985

Peck, Dale (1967–)

Dale Peck was born on Long Island and raised in Kansas. He lives in New York City.

Now It's Time to Say Goodbye 1998; ***The Law of Enclosures*** 1996; ***Martin & John*** 1995

Peery, Janet

Ms. Peery was educated at Wichita State University and is currently Assistant Professor of English and Fiction writing at Old Dominion University.

The River Beyond the World 1996; *Alligator Dance* (stories) 1993

Pelletier, Cathie (1953–)

Ms. Pelletier, novelist and songwriter, was born and raised in Maine where she attended the State University. She curently divides her time between Tennessee and Toronto, Canada.

Beaming Sonny Home 1996; ***A Marriage Made at Woodstock*** 1994; *The Bubble Reputation* 1993; *The Weight of Winter* 1991; *Once upon a Time on the Banks* 1989; *The Funeral Makers* 1986

Penn, W.S. (1949–)

W.S. Penn was educated at UC–Davis and at Syracuse University. He currently teaches at Michigan State University and has been, since 1992, Regional Coordinator of Wordcraft Circle of Native American Writers. He also consults widely on ethnic studies.

In the Absence of Angels 1994

Perrotta, Tom (1961–)

Mr. Perrotta grew up in Garwood, New Jersey, and was educated at Yale. He currently teaches creative writing at Harvard University.

Election 1998; ***The Wishbones*** 1997; *Bad Haircut: Stories of the '70s* 1994

Peters, Daniel (1948–)

Born in Milwaukee and educated at Yale, Mr. Peters currently lives in Tucson, Arizona.

Rising from the Ruins 1995; *The Incas* 1991; *Tikal: A Novel About the Maya* 1983; *The Luck of Huemac: A Novel About the Aztecs* 1981; *Border Crossings* 1978

Phillips, Caryl (1958–)

Playwright and novelist Caryl Phillips was born on the island of St. Kitts but soon after moved to England where he attended Oxford University. Mr. Phillips has lived for many years in the U.S. where he is a Professor of English at Amherst College in Massachusetts.

The Nature of Blood 1997; ***Crossing the River*** 1994; ***Cambridge*** 1992; *Higher Ground* 1989; *A State of Independence* 1986; *The Final Passage* 1985; *The Shelter* 1984

Phillips, Jayne Ann (1952–)

Ms. Phillips, a recipient of Guggenheim and

National Endowment for the Arts Fellowship, lives near Boston with her husband and sons.

Shelter 1994; *Fast Lanes* 1987; *Machine Dreams* 1984; *How Mickey Made It* 1981; *Black Tickets* 1979

Phillips, Max

A poet and novelist, Max Philips' debut novel was greeted enthusiastically by the critics.

Snakebite Sonnet 1996

Picano, Felice (1944–)

Mr. Picano was born in New York City and was educated at Queens College. He is co-founder of the Gay Presses of New York. He has also taught creative writing at the West Side Y Writer's Voice Workshop since 1982.

Looking Glass Lives 1998; **Like People in History** 1995; *Dryland's End* 1995; *Men Who Loved Me* 1989; *To the 7th Power* 1989; *Ambidextrous: The Secret Lives of Children* 1985; *House of Cards* 1984; *Late in the Season* 1981; *The Lure* 1979; *The Mesmerist* 1977; *Eyes* 1975; *Smart as the Devil* 1975

Pinckney, Darryl (1953–)

Born in Indianapolis into prominent African-American family, he was educated at Columbia and Princeton. A critic, essayist and novelist, he teaches at Columbia University.

High Cotton 1992

Ping, Wang

Wang Ping, who was born and raised in China, is a poet, novelist, short story writer and translator.

Foreign Devil 1996; *American Visa* (stories) 1994

Pollack, Rachel

Ms. Pollack, a poet, novelist, comic book writer and expert at the Tarot, was born in Poughkeepsie, New York, but moved to Europe in the early 1970s. She returned to the U.S. in the 1990s and currently lives and writes in Rhineland, New York.

Godmother Night 1996; **Temporary Agency** 1994; **Unquenchable Fire** 1992; *Alqua Dreams* 1987; *Golden Variety* 1984

Porter, Dorothy (1954–)

"Dorothy Porter has been called an audacious poet...a sexy read...[and] an exuberant and perceptive purveyor of passion. With the publication of her latest book, *The Monkey's Mask* Porter's reputation stands firm." (Australian Book Review)

The Monkey's Mask 1994

Powell, Padgett (1952–)

Born in Gainesville, Florida, and educated at the College of Charleston and the University of Houston, Mr. Powell currently teaches at the University of Florida at Gainesville.

Aliens of Affection (stories) 1998; **Edisto Revisited** 1996; *Typical* 1991; *A Woman Named Drown* 1987; *Edisto* 1984

Power, Susan (1961–)

Susan Power, a novelist, attorney and member of the Standing Rock Sioux tribe, was born in Chicago and was educated at Harvard University and the University of Iowa where she received her MFA. She has been a Fellow at the Bunting Institute in Cambridge, Massachusetts.

The Grass Dancer 1994

Powers, Charles T. (1943–1996)

Charles Powers was a highly respected journalist for the *New York Times* for more than 20 years. A former Nieman Fellow at Harvard, he served as the *Times* East European chief. He moved to Burlington, Vermont, in 1991 and died there in 1996.

In the Memory of the Forest 1997

Powers, Richard (1957–)

Mr. Powers, a recipient of a MacArthur "genius grant" and reclusive by nature, lived in the Netherlands for most of the 1980s. A self-educated polymath, he has strong interests in music and computer technology.

Gain 1998; **Galatea 2.2** 1995; **Operation Wandering Soul** 1993; *The Gold Bug Variations* 1991; *Prisoner's Dilemma* 1988; *Three Farmers on Their Way to a Dance* 1985

Preston, Caroline

Ms. Preston lives and works outside of Boston with her writer husband, Christopher Tilghman, and their three sons.

Jackie by Josie 1997

Price, Reynolds (1933–)

The estimable Reynolds Price was born in Macon, North Carolina, and was educated at Duke and Oxford universities. He has long been the James B. Duke professor of English at Duke.

Roxanna Slade 1998; **The Promise of Rest** 1995; *Blue Calhoun* 1992; *The Foreseeable Future* 1991; *The Tongues of Angels* 1990; *Good Hearts* 1988; *Kate Vaidan* 1986; *The Source of Light* 1981; *The Surface of Earth* 1975; *Permanent Errors* 1970; *Love and Work* 1968; *A Generous Man* 1966; *The Names and Faces of Heroes* 1963; *A Long and Happy Life* 1962

Priest, Christopher (1943–)

Mr. Priest, who was born near Manchester, England, was a successful writer of romantic science fiction before he turned his hand to literary fiction. He lives in England with his wife, novelist Leigh Kennedy, and their two children.

The Extremes 1999; **The Prestige** 1995; *The Glamour* 1989; *The Affirmation* 1981; *An Infinite Summer* 1979; *A Dream of Wessex* 1977; *The Perfect Lover* 1977; *The Space Machine: A Scientific Romance* 1976; *Real-Time World* 1974; *The Inverted World* 1974; *Darkening Island* 1972; *Indoctrinaire* 1970

Prose, Francine (1947–)

A Fulbright winner, Guggenheim Fellow, novelist and educator, Ms. Prose currently lives in Upstate New York. She has taught at Harvard, the University of Arizona, the Breadloaf Writer's Conference, Sara Lawrence and the Iowa Writer's Workshop. She is currently affiliated with Warren Wilson College's MFA in Creative Writing program.

Guided Tours of Hell (novellas)1997; **Hunters & Gatherers** 1995; *The Peaceable Kingdom* (stories) 1993; **Primitive People** 1992; *Women and Children First* (stories) 1988; *Bigfoot Dreams* 1987; *Hungry Hearts* 1983; *Household Saints* 1981; *Animal Magnetism* 1978; *Marie Levau* 1977; *The Glorious Ones* 1974; *Judah the Pious* 1973

Proulx, E. Annie (1935–)

Pulitzer Prize–winning novelist Annie Proulx, a novelist, editor and reviewer, was born in Norwich, Connecticut, and was educated at Colby College, the University of Vermont and Concordia College. She currently divides her time between Vermont and Newfoundland.

Accordion Crimes 1996; **The Shipping News** 1993; *Postcards* 1992, *Heart Songs and Other Stories* 1988

Pye, Michael (1946–)

Michael Pye, a journalist, novelist, broadcaster and historian, was born in Manchester and was educated at Oxford University. He currently divides his time between New York City (about which he has written extensively) and Portugal.

Taking Lives 1999; **The Drowning Room** 1995

Pynchon, Thomas (1937–)

Mr. Pynchon, a notorious recluse, was educated at Cornell University. He is thought to live in New York City with his wife and son.

Mason & Dixon 1997; **Vineland** 1990; *Slow Learner* 1984; *Gravity's Rainbow 1973*; *The Crying of Lot 49* 1966

Quindlen, Anna (1953–)

A Pulitzer Prize–winning columnist for the *New York Times*, Ms. Quindlen was born in Philadelphia and was educated at Barnard.

Black & Blue 1998; **One True Thing** 1994; *Object Lesson* 1988

Rainey, John Calvin (1951–)

Born in Miami, Mr. Rainey was raised in the Bahamas by his grandmother.

That Thang That Ate My Granddaddy's Dog 1997

Raymond, Linda (1952–)

Ms. Raymond was educated at the American River College and San Francisco State University at Sacramento. She received her M.A. in Creative Writing from the University of California at Davis.

Rocking the Babies 1994

Read, Piers Paul (1941–)

Mr. Read was brought up in Yorkshire and was educated at Cambridge University. He has traveled extensively in Eastern Europe and Israel and currently lives in London.

The Patriot 1995; *On the Third Day* 1990; *A Season in the West* 1988; *The Free Frenchman* 1986; *The Villa Golitsyn* 1981; *A Married Man* 1979; *Polonaise* 1976; *The Upstart* 1973; *Professors's Daughter* 1971; *Monk Dawson* 1969; *The Junkers* 1968; *Game in Heaven with Tussy Marx* 1966

Reed, Ishmael (1938–)

Mr. Reed, novelist, poet and essayist, was born in Chattanooga, Tennessee, but grew up in Buffalo, New York. He attended the University of Buffalo and eventually moved to New York City where he founded the *East Village Other*.

Japanese by Spring 1993; *Airing Dirty Laundry* 1993; *The Terrible Threes* 1989; *Cab Calloway Stands In for the Moon* 1986; *Reckless Eyeballing* 1986; *The Terrible Twos* 1982; *Flight to Canada* 1976; *The Last Days of Louisiana Red* 1974; *Mumbo Jumbo* 1972; *19 Necromancers from Now Yellow Back Radio Broke-down* 1969; *The Freelance Pallbearers* 1867

Reidy, Sue

Ms. Reidy, a recipient of a Katherine Mansfield short story award, lives in Auckland, New Zealand.

The Visitation 1996; *Modettes* 1988

Reuss, Frederick (1960–)

Mr. Reuss lives and writes in Washington, D.C., where he lives with his wife and two children.

Horace Afoot 1997

Revoyr, Nina

Ms. Revoyr was born in Japan and moved to southern California at the age of six. A high school basketball star, she later attended Yale and Cornell universities. She currently teaches literature and writing classes at Cornell.

The Necessary Hunger 1997

Reynolds, Sheri (1967–)

Ms. Reynolds was born in Conway, South Carolina, and was educated at Davidson and at Virginia Commonwealth University where she has taught since 1992.

A Gracious Plenty 1997; *The Rapture of Canaan* 1995; *Bitterrot Landing* 1994

Ricci, Nino (1959–)

Mr. Ricci, who holds dual Canadian and Italian citizenship, was born in Leamington, Ontario. He currently lives in Toronto.

Where She Has Gone 1998; *In a Glass House* 1993; *The Book of Saints* 1990 (original Canadian title: *The Lives of the Saints* 1990)

Richler, Mordecai (1931–)

Mordecai Richler was born in Montreal and was educated at Sir George Williams University. He has lived in both Paris and London and currently divides his time between Canada and Great Britain.

Barney's Version 1998; *Solomon Gursky Was Here* 1989; *Joshua Then and Now* 1980; *A Choice of Enemies* 1977; *A Choice of Enemies* 1973; *Shoveling Trouble* 1972; *St. Urbain's Horseman* 1971; *The Apprenticeship of Duddy Kravitz* 1969; *The Street* 1969; *Cocksure* 1968; *Son of a Smaller Hero* 1966; *The Incomparable Atuk* 1963

Ridgway, Keith

A poet, short story writer (he has been published in a number of anthologies of Irish writing) and novelist, Mr. Ridgway lives in Dublin.

The Long Falling 1998

Robson, Ruthann (1956–)

Ms. Robson, an attorney, professor of law, and novelist, was educated at Ramapo College and at Stetson University (where she received her law degree).

A K/A 1997; *Another Mother* 1995; *Cecile* (stories) 1991; *Eye of a Hurricane* 1989

Rodi, Robert

Mr. Rodi lives and works in Chicago.

Kept Boy 1996; *The Bird Cage* (a novelization of the stage play) 1996; *Drag Queen* 1995; *What They Did to Princess Paragon* 1994; *Closet Case* 1993; *Fag Hag* 1992

Rogers, Jane (1952–)

Ms. Rogers was born in London and was educated at Cambridge University. A novelist and television screen writer, she has taught writing at Northern College and Sheffield Polytechnic. She currently lives in Lancashire.

Promised Land 1995; *Mr. Wroe's Virgins* 1991; *The Ice Is Singing* 1987; *Her Living Image* 1986; *Separate Tracks* 1985

Roszak, Theodore (1933–)

Theodore Roszak was born in Chicago and was educated at UCLA and Princeton. He teaches English at the California State University at Hayward.

Memoirs of Elizabeth Frankenstein 1995; *Flicker* 1991; *Dreamwatcher* 1985; *Bugs* 1981

Roth, Henry (1906–1995)

Mr. Roth was born in Austria-Hungary and moved as an adolescent to New York City where he attended City College. A writer, schoolteacher, tutor, chicken farmer and machinist, Mr. Roth found early success with his debut novel *Some Call It Sleep* but was unable to concentrate fully on his writing until the end of his life when he worked assiduously on a quartet of novels (beginning with *A Star Shines Over Mt. Morris Park*) which have the collective title "Mercies of a Rude Stream." The last two volumes were published posthumously.

Requiem for Harlem 1997 (posthumously); *From Bondage* 1996 (posthumously); *A Diving Rock in the Hudson* 1995; *A Star Shines Over Mt. Morris Park* 1994; *Shifting Landscapes* (stories) 1994; *Boundaries of Love* 1990; *Some Call It Sleep* 1934

Roth, Philip (1933–)

Born in Newark, New Jersey, Mr. Roth was educated at Rutgers, Bucknell and the University of Chicago. A prolific writer, he has taught at SUNY–Stony Brook, Princeton and the University of Pennsylvania.

American Pastoral 1997; *Sabbath's Theater* 1995; *Operation Shylock: A Confession* 1993; *Deception* 1990; *The Counterlife* 1986; *Zuckerman Bound: A Trilogy and Epilogue* 1985; *The Anatomy Lesson* 1983; *Zuckerman Unbound* 1981; *The Ghost Writer* 1979; *The Professor of Desire* 1977; *My Life as a Man* 1974; *The Great American Novel* 1973; *The Breast* 1972; *Our Gang* 1971; *Portnoy's Complaint* 1969; *When She Was Good* 1967; *Letting Go* 1962

Roy, Arundhati

Ms. Roy, Booker Prize–winning novelist, was born in Bengal and grew up in Kerala, India. After studying architecture in Delhi she turned her hand to acting and screenwriting. Known as something of a rebel in India (she once lived in a squatters colony on the outskirts of Delhi) she has been both widely praised and widely reviled for her seemingly "overnight" success as a novelist.

The God of Small Things 1997

Rush, Norman (1933–)

Born and raised in the San Francisco area, Rush was educated at Swarthmore. He has worked as an antiquarian book dealer and a college instructor. He lived and worked in Africa from 1978 to 1983.

Mating 1991; *Whites* (stories) 1986

Rushdie, Salman (1947–)

Salman Rushdie grew up in a Muslim family in Bombay but was educated in England (at Rugby — an elite preparatory school — and Cambridge University). Mr. Rushdie is well known as the object of numerous death threats including the issuing of a *fatwa* by Ayatollah Khomeini — all prompted by the publication in 1988 of his controversial novel *The Satanic Verses*. Rushdie — with the assistance of the British government — has spent much of the past 10 years in hiding.

The Ground Beneath Her Feet 1999; **The Moor's Last Sigh** 1995; *East, West* 1994; **The Satanic Verses** 1988; *Shame* 1983; **Midnight's Children** 1981; *Grimus* 1979

Russo, Richard (1949–)
Mr. Russo grew up in upstate New York in a small town that serves at the model for his fictional town of Mohawk. He was educated at the University of Arizona and currently teaches writing at Colby College in Waterville, Maine.

The Straight Man 1997; **Nobody's Fool** 1993; *The Risk Pool* 1988; *Mohawk* 1986

Ryan, Hugh Fitzgerald (1941–)
Mr. Ryan is an established Irish novelist who has recently found an American publisher.

Ancestral Voices 1994; **On Borrowed Ground** 1991; *Reprisal* 1989; *The Kybe* 1983

Ryman, Geoff (1951–)
Mr. Ryman was born in Ontario and was educated at UCLA. A novelist, short story writer, critic and editor, he currently lives in London.

253! The Print Remix 1998; *Unconquered Country* 1994; *Was; A Novel* 1992; *The Child Garden: A Low Comedy* 1990

Sahgal, Nayantara (1927–)
"Ms. Sahgal is the niece of Nehru and as both novelist and journalist she writes about India's political and social elites with the insight born of first-hand knowledge. She has written nine novels, two volumes of autobiography and the widely acclaimed biography *Indira Ghandi: Her Road to Power*" (TLS).

Mistaken Identity 1988; **Rich Like Us** 1985; *Plans for Departure* 1985; *A Voice for Freedom* 1977; *The Day in Shadow* 1971; *Storm in Chandigarh* 1969

Sanders, Dori (1934–)
Ms. Sanders was born and raised on a farm in York County, South Carolina. She was educated at community colleges in Montgomery and Prince George's Counties (Maryland). She still helps out with her family's peach harvest.

Her Own Place 1993; *Clover* 1990

Sandlin, Tim (1950–)
Tim Sandlin, novelist and columnist, lives in Jackson Hole, Wyoming. He is best known for his darkly comic Gro-Vont trilogy (*Skipped Parts, Sorrow Floats* and *Social Blunders*).

Social Blunders 1995; *Sorrow Floats* 1992; *Skipped Parts* 1991; *Western Swing* 1988; *Sex & Sunsets* 1987

Sapphire (1950–)
A performance poet and novelist, Sapphire (Ramona Lofton) grew up on Army bases. She was educated at City College and received her MFA from Brooklyn College.

Push 1996

Sarris, Greg
Mr. Sarris was born in Santa Rosa, California. His father, a well-known college athlete, was part Miwok, Pomo and Filipino. His mother was German Jewish and Irish. Mr. Sarris attended UCLA where he played football. He also attended Stanford University where he received his MFA and Ph.D. The Chief of the Federated Coast Miwok tribe, he has taught at UCLA and is a consultant to the Turner Broadcasting Company.

Watermelon Nights 1998; **Grand Avenue** 1994

Sayers, Valerie (1952–)
Born and raised in Beaufort, South Carolina, Ms. Sayers received her MFA from Columbia University. She is currently Director of the Creative Writing Program at Notre Dame.

Brain Fever 1996; *The Distance Between Us* 1994; *Who Do You Love?* 1991; *How I Got Him Back* 1989; *Due East* 1987

Schine, Cathleen
Ms. Schine was born in Connecticut and was educated at Barnard and at the University of Chicago (Medieval Studies). A novelist and widely published short story writer, she currently lives in New York City with her husband David Denby and her two sons.

The Evolution of Jane 1998; **The Love Letter** 1995; **Rameau's Niece** 1993; **To the Birdhouse** 1990; *Alice in Bed* 1983

Schulman, Sarah (1958–)
Ms. Schulman, a playwright, novelist, social activist and former Fulbright fellow, was born (and still lives) in New York City.

Shimmer 1998; **Rat Bohemia** 1995; *Empathy* 1992; *People in Trouble* 1989; *After Delores* 1988; *Girls, Visions, and Everything* 1986; *Sophie Horowitz's Story* 1984

Schumacher, Julie
An Explanation for Chaos (stories) 1998; **The Body Is Water** 1995

Schweidel, David
With his debut novel, *Confidence of the Heart*, Mr. Schweidel won the 1994 Milkweed National Fiction Prize.

Confidence of the Heart 1994

Scott, Joanna (1960–)
Born in Greenwich, Connecticut, Ms. Scott was educated at Trinity College and Brown University. An educator, novelist and recipient of a MacArthur "genius" grant, she currently lives in

Rochester, New York, where she teaches at the University of Rochester.

The Manikin 1996; *Various Antidotes* (stories) 1994; *Arrogance* 1990; *The Closest Possible Union* 1988; *Fading, My Parmacheene Belle* 1987

Self, Will (1961–)

Will Self was born in London and educated at Oxford. A full-time writer, he was voted one of the "Best Young British Novelists" by *Granta* magazine in 1993.

Tough, Tough Toys, for Tough, Tough Boys (stories) 1999; **Great Apes** 1997; *Gray Area* (stories) 1994; **My Idea of Fun** 1993; **Cock & Bull** 1992; *Quantity Theory of Insanity* (stories) 1991

Selvadurai, Shyam (1965–)

Mr. Selvadurai, a prize-winning novelist, television scriptwriter, essayist and short story writer, was born in Sri Lanka but immigrated to Canada as a young man. He graduated from York University in Canada and currently lives in Toronto.

Cinnamon Gardens 1999; **Funny Boy** 1996

Seth, Vikram (1952–)

Vikram Seth was born in Calcutta and has studied Demography and Economics at Oxford University, at Stanford, and in Nanking. A writer of both fiction and non-fiction, he currently divides his time between Delhi and Great Britain.

A Suitable Boy 1993; *The Golden Gate* 1986

Shacochis, Bob (1951–)

Mr. Shacochis, an editor, short story writer, novelist and columnist (for *GQ*), currently lives in Florida. He recently published a non-fiction book about the recent U.S. intervention in Haiti (Operation Uphold Democracy).

Swimming in the Volcano 1993; *The Next New World* 1989; *Easy in the Island* 1985

Shadbolt, Maurice (1932–)

A novelist and short story writer, Mr. Shadbolt was born in Auckland, New Zealand and has lived in London, Spain and New Zealand. According to the *Cambridge Guide to Literature in English*: "His fiction is characterized by complex plot structures which are often ingeniously handled."

House of Strife 1993; **Monday's Warrior's** 1990; *Season of the Jew* 1986; *The Lovelock Version* 1980; *Danger Zone* 1975; *A Touch of Clay* 1974; *Strangers and Journeys* 1972; *An Ear of the Dragon* 1971; *This Summer's Dolphin* 1969; *The Presence of Music* 1967; *Among the Cinders* 1965; *Summer Fires and Winter Country* 1963

Shakespeare, Nicholas (1957–)

Mr. Shakespeare was born in England and was educated at Cambridge and the University of London. After living and working (as a gaucho among other things) in South America for almost twenty years, he now lives in London where he is the literary editor of the *Daily Telegraph*.

The Dancer Upstairs 1995; *The High Flyer* 1993; *The Vision of Elena Silves* 1989

Shange, Ntzoke (1948–)

A highly-acclaimed playwright, poet and novelist, Ms. Shange lives in Philadelphia with her family.

Liliane: Resurrection of the Daughter 1994; *Betsey Brown* 1985; *Sassafrass, Cypress and Indigo* 1982

Shea, Lisa

A novelist and freelance journalist whose work has appeared in such publications as *Esquire*, the *New York Times Book Review*, and *People*. Ms. Shea is a past recipient of the prestigious Whiting Award.

Hula 1994

Shepard, Jim (1956–)

Born in Bridgeport, Connecticut, Mr. Shepard was educated at Trinity College and Brown University. He has taught at the University of Michigan and is currently on the faculty of Williams College.

Nosferatu 1998; *Batting Against Castro* (stories) 1996; *Kiss of the Wolf* 1994; *Lights Out in the Reptile House* 1990; *Paper Doll* 1986; *Flights* 1983

Sherman, Charlotte Watson (1958–)

Born in Seattle, Washington, and educated at Seattle University, Ms. Watson, in addition to her fiction writing, has worked as a social worker and writing instructor.

Touch 1996; **One Dark Body** 1993; *Killing Color* (stories) 1992

Sherwood, Frances (1940–)

Ms. Sherwood was born in Washington, D.C., and was educated at Howard University, Brooklyn College, NYU and Johns Hopkins University. She has been a professor of creative writing and journalism at Indiana University since 1986.

Green 1995; **Vindication** 1993; *Everything You've Heard Is True* 1989

Shields, Carol (1936–)

Carol Shields was born and raised in Oak Park, Illinois, and was educated at Hanover College and the University of Ottawa. She has lived in Canada — almost without interruption — since 1957 and holds dual U.S. and Canadian citizenships. She is currently chancellor of the University of Manitoba where she taught English for a number of years. She and her husband, dean of the Engineering Department at the University of Manitoba, spend each summer in France.

Larry's Party 1997; **The Stone Diaries** 1994; *Republic of Love* 1992; *A Celibate Season* 1991; *The*

Orange Fish (stories) 1989; *Swann: A Mystery* 1987 (Canadian title: *Mary Swann*); *Various Miracles* (stories) 1985; *Happenstance* 1980; *Box Gardens* 1977; **Small Ceremonies** 1976

Shigekuni, Julie

Ms. Shigekuni, a fifth-generation Japanese-American, was raised in Los Angeles and attended Hunter College in New York City. She currently lives in New Mexico and is professor of Creative Writing at the Institute of American Indian Arts.

A Bridge Between Us 1995

Shivers, Louise (1929–)

Ms. Shivers was born in Stantonsburg, North Carolina, and was educated at Atlantic Christian College and Augusta College. She is a professor of Creative Writing and a writer-in-residence at Augusta College.

Whistling Woman 1993; *Here to Get My Baby out of Jail* 1983

Shreve, Anita (1947–)

Novelist Anita Shreve lives and writes in Massachusetts.

The Pilot's Wife 1998; **The Weight of Water** 1997; *Resistance* 1995; *Strange Fits of Passion Eden Close* 1990

Sidhwa, Bapsi

Ms. Sidhwa was born into a Parsee family in what is now Pakistan. She was educated at home and at a university in the Punjab. She has taught in numerous colleges and universities in the U.S. (including Columbia, Rice, and the University of Houston) and is currently writer-in-residence at Mt. Holyoke College.

An American Brat 1993; **Cracking India** 1991; *The Bride* 1983; **The Crow Eaters** 1978

Silko, Leslie Marmon (1949–)

Born in Albuquerque, New Mexico, Ms. Silko, a member of the Laguna Pueblo, was educated at the University of New Mexico. In 1981, Silko received a five-year MacArthur "genius grant" which allowed her to devote herself to fiction writing. She has taught at the University of Arizona and the University of New Mexico.

Gardens in the Dunes 1999; **Almanac of the Dead** 1991; *Storyteller* 1981; *Ceremony* 1977

Simmons, Charles

A former editor at the *New York Times Book Review*, Mr. Simmons was born in New York City and was educated at Columbia University. According to *Publishers Weekly* Simmons "made a name for himself— in the late 60s and early 70s — with a series of surreal comic novels, including *Powdered Eggs* and *Wrinkles*."

Salt Water 1998; *Wrinkles* 1978; *An Old Fashioned Darling* 1971; *Powdered Eggs*

Sinclair, April

A community organizer, novelist and educator, April Sinclair grew up in Chicago where she has taught reading and creative writing to inner-city children and youth. She currently lives in the San Francisco Bay area where she devotes herself to writing full-time.

I Left My Back Door Open 1999; **Ain't Gonna Be the Same Fool Twice** 1996; *Coffee Will Make You Black* 1994

Sinclair, Iain (1943–)

A lecturer, poet, filmmaker, book dealer and writer, Mr. Sinclair was born in Cardiff, Wales, and was educated at the London School of Film Techniques and at Trinity College, Dublin.

Radon Daughters 1994; **Downriver** 1991; *White Chappell, Scarlet Tracings* 1987; *Lud Heat: A Book of the Dead Hamlets* 1975

Skibell, Joseph

Mr. Skibell received an MFA from the University of Texas Center for Writers and currently teaches at the University of Wisconsin where he was the 1996–97 Halls Fellow in fiction.

Blessing on the Moon 1997

Skinner, Margaret (1942–)

Ms. Skinner was born in Memphis, Tennessee, and was educated at the University of Memphis (where she currently teaches creative writing).

Molly Flanagan & the Holy Ghost 1995; *Old Jim Canaan* 1990

Smiley, Jane (1949–)

Ms. Smiley, a Pulitzer Prize–winning novelist, was educated at Vassar and at the University of Iowa. She also spent a year in Iceland on a Fulbright Scholarship. For many years a Distinguished Professor of Liberal Arts at Iowa State University, she is now living and writing in Northern California.

The All-True Travels and Adventures of Lidie Newton 1998; **Moo** 1995; **A Thousand Acres** 1991; *Ordinary Love & Goodwill: Two Novellas* 1989; *The Greenlanders* 1988; *The Age of Grief: A Novella & Stories* 1987; *Duplicate Keys* 1984; *At Paradise Gate* 1981; *Barn Blind* 1980

Smith, Dinitia (1945–)

Ms. Smith, a journalist and novelist, lives in New York City.

The Illusionist 1997; *Remember This* 1989; *The Hard Rain* 1980

Smith, Faye McDonald

A native of Washington, D.C., Ms. Smith, a journalist, novelist, and scriptwriter, currently lives in Atlanta, Georgia.

Flight of the Blackbird 1996

Smith, Lee (1944–)

Ms. Smith, a novelist and educator, teaches at

North Carolina State in Raleigh, North Carolina. She currently lives in Chapel Hill, N.C.

News of the Spirit 1997; *The Christmas Letters* 1996; ***Saving Grace*** 1995; *The Devil's Dream* 1993; *Me & My Babies View the Eclipse* 1990; *Fair & Tender Ladies* 1988; *Family Linen* 1985; *Oral History* 1983; *Cakewalk* 1981; *Black Mountain Breakdown* 1980; *Fancy Strut* 1973; *Something in the Wind* 1971; *The Last Day the Dogbushes Bloomed* 1968

Smith, Martin Cruz (1942–)

Born in Reading, Pennsylvania, Smith was educated at the University of Pennsylvania. His mother, a jazz singer, was active in the Native American rights movement. He also writes under the pseudonyms of Jake Logan and Simon Quinn.

Havana Bay 1999; ***Rose*** 1996; *Red Square* 1993; *Polar Star* 1989; *Stallion Gate* 1986; *Gorky Park* 1981; *Nightwing* 1977; *Canto for a Gypsy* 197?; *Gypsy in Amber* 1971

Smith, Sarah (1947–)

Ms. Smith was born in Boston and was educated at Radcliffe, University College (London), and Harvard University. An editor, short story writer, novelist and Independent Media Consultant, she has taught at Northeastern and Tufts universities.

Knowledge of Water 1996; ***The Vanished Child*** 1992

Sontag, Susan (1933–)

Ms. Sontag, essayist, critic, and novelist, was born in New York City but grew up in Arizona and California. She graduated from high school at the age of fifteen, and was educated at the University of Chicago, Harvard and Oxford University.

The Volcano Lover: A Romance 1992; *I, Etcetera* (stories) 1978; *Death Kit* 1967; *The Benefactor* 1963

Spark, Muriel (1918–)

An editor, critic, poet, short story writer and novelist, Ms. Spark was born and educated in Edinburgh. She lived in Rhodesia for a number of years (in the late 1930s and early 1940s) and worked in London as a Propaganda Officer for the British Foreign Office during World War II. She has lived in Italy for many years and, for her service to English letters, was made a "Dame" in 1993.

Open to the Public (Stories) 1997; ***Reality and Dreams*** 1997; *Symposium* 1990; *A Far Cry from Kensington* 1988; *The Stories of Muriel Spark* 1985; *The Only Problem* 1984; *Bang Bang You're Dead and Other Stories* 1982; *Loitering with Intent* 1981; *Territorial Rights* 1979; *The Takeover* 1976; *The Abbess of Crewe* 1974; *The Hothouse on the East River* 1973; *Not to Disturb* 1971; *The Driver's Seat*; *The Public Image*; *Collected Stories*; *The Mandelbaum Gate* 1965; *The Girls of Slender Means* 1963; *The Prime*

of Miss Jean Brodie 1961; *Voices at Play* 1961; *The Bachelors* 1960; *The Ballad of Peckham Rye* 1960; *Memento Mori* 1959; *The Go-Away Bird & Other Stories* 1958; *Robinson* 1958; *The Comforters* 1957

Stead, C.K. (1932–)

C.K. Stead, critic, poet and novelist, enjoys an international reputation. His most well-known work is *The Death of the Body*, a metafictional tale of murder set in New Zealand and Europe.

The Singing Whakapapa 1995; *The End of the Century at the End of the World* 1992; *Sister Hollywood* 1989; ***The Death of the Body*** 1986; *All Visitors Ashore* (stories) 1984; *Five for the Symbol* (stories) 1981; *Smith's Dream* 1971

Stevens, April (1963–)

Ms. Stevens was educated at Bennington College and the New School for Social Research in New York City. She divides her time between Manhattan and Cornwall, Connecticut.

Angel, Angel 1995

Stone, Robert (1937–)

Mr. Stone, a journalist and novelist, was born in Brooklyn, New York, and, after a stint in the Navy, studied at NYU and Stanford. He has taught at Amherst College and Stanford and Princeton universities. He and his wife divide their time between Westport, Connecticut, Block Island and Key West, Florida.

Damascus Gate 1998; *Bear and His Daughter* 1997; *Outerbridge Reach* 1992; *Children of Light* 1986; *A Flag for Sunrise* 1981; *Dog Soldiers* 1974; *A Hall of Mirrors* 1967

Straight, Susan (1960–)

Born in Riverside California, Ms. Straight was educated at the University of Southern California and the University of Massachusetts. She has taught in programs involving gang members, dropouts, refugees and juvenile offenders and has been on the faculty of UC–Irvine since 1988.

The Gettin Place 1996; *Blacker Than a Thousand Midnights* 1994; *I Been in Sorrow's Kitchen & Licked Out All the Pots* 1992; *Aquaboogie: A Novel in Stories* 1991

Strong, Albertine

Ms. Strong, an Ojibwa Cherokee novelist, was raised in the Minneapolis and St. Paul area and on the White Earth and Red Lake reservations. In addition to writing, she has worked as a rodeo clown, a cosmetologist, and an organic farmer. She currently lives in Kansas.

Deluge 1997

Swan, Susan (1944–)

A journalist, short story writer and novelist, Ms. Swan is Assistant Professor of Humanities at York University in Toronto.

Stupid Boys Are Good to Relax With (stories) 1999; **The Wives of Bath** 1993; *The Last of the Golden Girls* 1989; *The Biggest Modern Woman in the World* 1983

Sweeney, Eamonn (1968–)
A freelance journalist, short story writer and novelist, Mr. Sweeney is a frequent contributor to (among others) the Irish Times. He currently lives in Dublin.
Waiting for the Healer 1998

Swick, Marly (1949–)
A former winner of the Iowa "Short Fiction Award," Ms. Swick lives and teaches in Nebraska.
Evening News 1999; **Paper Wings** 1996; *The Summer Before the Summer of Love* (stories) 1995; *Monogamy* (stories) 1992; *A Hole in the Language* 1990

Swift, Graham (1949–)
Mr. Swift was born in London and was educated at Cambridge and York universities. He taught English literature before turning his attention full-time to writing.
Last Orders 1996; *Ever After* 1992; *Out of This World* 1988; *Waterland* 1983; *Learning to Swim & Other Stories* 1982; *Shuttlecock* 1981; *The Sweet-shop Owner* 1980

Syal, Meera
Ms. Syal, a popular comedienne, actress, screenplay writer and novelist, was born in a mining community in the English midlands. Her parents immigrated to Great Britain from India.
Anita & Me 1996

Tan, Amy (1952–)
Ms. Tan was born in Oakland, California, and was educated at San Jose State and UC–Berkeley.
The Hundred Secret Senses 1995; *The Kitchen God's Wife* 1991; *The Joy Luck Club* 1989

Tartt, Donna (1964–)
Born in Greenwood, Mississippi, Ms. Tartt attended the University of Mississippi for one year and then transferred to Bennington College in Vermont where she was a classmate of Brett Easton Ellis. She currently lives in Manhattan.
The Secret History 1992

Taylor, Peter (1917–1994)
Pulitzer Prize–winning novelist, short story writer, Fulbright scholar and playwright, Mr. Taylor was born in Trenton, Tennessee, and was educated at Vanderbilt and Southwestern universities and at Kenyon College. He taught for over twenty years at the University of North Carolina and has been the recipient of numerous literary awards and fellowships.
In the Tennessee Country 1994; *The Oracle at*

Stoneleigh Court (stories) 1993; *A Summons to Memphis* 1986; *The Old Forest & Other Stories* 1985; *In the Miro District & Other Stories* 1977; *The Collected Stories of Peter Taylor* 1969; *Miss Lenna When Last Seen & Other Stories* 1963; *Happy Families Are All Alike* 1959; *The Widow of Thornton* 1954; *A Woman of Means* 1950; *A Long Fourth & Other Stories* 1948

Tennant, Emma (1937–)
Ms. Tennant was born in London and was educated at St. Paul's Girls' School. A critic and editor, she has written fiction full-time since 1973.
Emma in Love 1996; **An Unequal Marriage** 1994; *Pemberly* 1993; *Tess* 1993; **Faustine** 1992; *Sisters and Strangers* 1990; *Two Women of London* 1989; *The Magic Drum* 1989; *A Wedding of Cousins* 1988; *The House of Hospitalities* 1988; *The Adventures of Robena by Herself* 1988; *Black Marina* 1985; *Women Beware Women* 1983; *Queen of Stones* 1982; *Alice Fell* 1980; *Wild Nights* 1979; *The Bad Sister* 1978; *Hotel de Dream* 1976; *The Last of the Country House Murders* 1974; *The Time of the Crack* 1973; *The Colour of Rain* 1963

Tharoor, Shashi (1956–)
Mr. Tharoor was born London and grew up in Bombay and Calcutta. He was educated at St. Stephen's College (India) and received a doctorate from the Fletcher School of Law and Diplomacy at Tufts University. In addition to his fiction writing, he has worked for the U.N. since 1987.
Show Business 1992; *Five Dollar Smile* (stories) 1991; **The Great Indian Novel** 1989

Theroux, Alexander (1939–)
Mr. Theroux was born in Medford, Massachusetts, and was educated at St. Francis College, the University of Virginia and Oxford University. A former member of a Trappist Monastery (where he observed a vow of silence for two years), he has been a visiting artist at MIT since 1983. He is the older brother of novelist Paul Theroux (see below).
An Adultery 1987; **Darconville's Cat** 1981; *Three Wogs* 1972

Theroux, Paul (1941–)
Mr. Theroux was born and raised in Medford, Massachusetts, and was educated at the University of Massachusetts and Syracuse. A inveterate traveler and former Peace Corps volunteer in Malawi, he taught for at time at the University of Singapore. After many years living in England, he currently divides his time between Hawaii and Cape Cod.
Kowloon Tong 1997; *The Collected Stories* 1997; **My Other Life** 1996; **Millroy the Magician** 1994; *Chicago Loop* 1991; *My Secret Life* 1989; *O-Zone* 1986; *Half Moon Street* 1984; *Doctor Slaughter* 1984; *The London Embassy* (stories) 1982; *World's End and Other Stories* 1980; *Picture Palace* 1978;

The Consul's Fire (stories) 1977; *The Family Arsenal* 1976; *The Black House* 1974; *Saint Jack 1973*; *Sinning with Annie and Other Stories* 1972; *Jungle Lovers* 1971; *Girls at Play* 1969; *Fong and the Indians* 1968; *Waldo* 1967

Thomas, D. M. (1935–)

British novelist, biographer (of Solzhenitsyn) and academic with a background in Russian studies, D.M. Thomas is the author of one of the most controversial novels of the 1980s, *The White Hotel*, which is now considered by many to be a contemporary classic.

Lady with a Laptop 1996; ***Eating Pavlova*** 1994; ***Pictures at an Exhibition*** 1993; *Flying into Love* 1992; *Lying Together* 1990; *Memories and Hallucinations* 1988; *Summit* 1987; *Sphinx* 1986; *Swallow* 1984; *Ararat* 1983; ***The White Hotel*** 1981; *The Birthstone* 1980; *The Flute Player* 1979

Thomson, Rupert (1955–)

Rupert Thomson was born in Eastbourne, England, and was educated at Christ's Hospital School and Cambridge.

The Insult 1996; ***Air and Fire*** 1993; *The Five Gates of Hell* 1991; *Dreams of Leaving* 1987

Thornton, Lawrence (1937–)

A native of California and a former Guggenheim Fellow, Mr. Thornton has lived in England, France and Spain. He currently lives in Claremont, California.

Tales from the Blue Archives 1998; ***Naming the Spirit*** 1995; *Ghost Woman* 1992; *Under the Gypsy Moon* 1990; *Imagining Argentina* 1988

Thurm, Marian

A novelist and short story writer, Ms. Thurm is known for her lighthearted urban comedies.

The Clairvoyant 1997; *The Way We Live Now* 1991; *Henry in Love* 1990; *These Things Happen* 1988; *Walking Distance* 1987; *Floating* (stories) 1984

Tilghman, Christopher (1948–)

Mr. Tilghman, a novelist and short story writer, was educated at Yale and currently lives outside of Boston with his wife, novelist Caroline Preston, and their three sons.

Mason's Retreat 1996; *In Another Place* 1990

Toibin, Colm (1955–)

Mr. Toibin was born in Enniscothy, County Wexford. A novelist and non-fiction writer, he currently lives in Dublin.

The Story of the Night 1997; ***The Heather Blazing*** 1992; ***The South*** 1990

Torrington, Jeff (1935–)

Jeff Torrington was born in Scotland and has worked in a banana warehouse and in an automobile plant and as a whiskey crate packer and a postal clerk. It took him thirty years to write his first novel which went on to win the prestigious Whitbread Award for best first novel of 1993.

Devil's Carousel 1996; ***Swing Hammer Swing*** 1992

Townsend, Sue (1946–)

A highly successful British novelist, Ms. Townsend did not attend university. In addition to writing, she has held a number of jobs including garage attendant, dress shop worker, factory hand and community worker.

Ghost Children 1998; *Adrian Mole, the Lost Years* 1994; *Adrian Mole in the Wilderness* Years 1993; ***The Queen & I*** 1993; *Rebuilding Coventry* 1990; *Mr. Bevan's Dream* 1989; *The Adrian Mole Diaries* 1986; *The Secret Diary of Adrian Mole* 1985; *The Great Celestial Cow* 1984

Trapido, Barbara (1941–)

Ms. Trapido was born and raised in South Africa and moved to England in 1963 at the age of 22. She currently lives in Oxford, England.

The Traveling Horn Player 1999; ***Temples of Delight*** 1990; *Noah's Ark 1984*; *Brother of the More Famous Jack* 1982

Tremain, Rose (1943–)

Ms. Tremain, a much-acclaimed short story writer and novelist (she was voted one of the Best Young British Novelists in 1983), has also written plays for radio and television. A Fellow of the Royal Society of Literature, she currently lives in Norwich and teaches Creative Writing at the University of East Anglia.

The Way I Found Her 1998; *Evangelista's Fan* 1994; ***Sacred Country*** 1992; ***Restoration*** 1989; *The Garden of the Villa Molini* 1987; *The Swimming Pool Season* 1985; *The Colonel's Daughter* 1984; *The Cupboard* 1981; *Letter to Sister Benedicta* 1978; *Sadler's Birthday* 1973

Treuer, David

A member of the Ojibwe, Mr. Treuer grew up on the Leech Lake Reservation in Northern Minnesota. He was educated at Princeton.

Little 1995

Trevor, William (1928–)

William Trevor, a much-recognized short story writer, novelist and former history and art teacher, was born in Mitchelstown, County Cork, Ireland, and was educated at Trinity College, Dublin.

Death in Summer 1998; *After Rain* 1996; ***Felicia's Journey*** 1994; *Two Lives (two novellas)* 1991; *Family Sins* 1990; *The Silence in the Garden* 1988; *The News from Ireland* (stories) 1986; *Fools of Fortune* 1983; *Beyond the Pale* (stories) 1981; *Other People's Worlds* 1980; *Lovers of Their Time (stories)* 1978;

The Children of Dynmouth 1976; *Angels at the Ritz (stories)* 1975; *Elizabeth Alone* 1973; *The Ballroom of Romance (stories)* 1972; *Miss Gomez and the Brethern* 1971; *Mrs. Eckdorf in O'Neill's Hotel* 1969; *The Day We Got Drunk on Cake* (stories) 1967; *The Love Department* 1966; *The Boarding House* 1965; *The Old Boys* 1964; *A Standard of Behavior* 1958

Trice, Dawn Turner

A novelist and editor, Ms Trice — who attended the prestigious Iowa Writers Workshop — is on the editorial staff of the *Chicago Tribune*.
Only Twice I've Wished for Heaven 1997

Trollope, Joanna (1943–)

Born in England, Ms. Trollope was educated Oxford University. A freelance writer for most of her career, she has taught English and was, for a time, associated with the British Foreign Office.
Next of Kin 1996; *The Best of Friends* 1995; **A Spanish Lover** 1993; *The Choir* 1992; **The Men & the Girls** 1992; *The Rector's Wife* 1991; *A Passionate Man* 1990; *A Village Affair* 1989; *The Taverner's Place* 1986; *The Steps of the Sun* 1984; *Leaves from the Valley* 1980; *Mistaken Virtues* 1980; *Parson Harding's Daughter* 1978; *Eliza Stanhope* 1978

Troy, Judy (1951–)

Born in Chicago, Illinois, Ms. Troy was educated at the University of Illinois at Chicago and Indiana University. She currently teaches English at Auburn University.
From the Black Hills 1999; **West of Venus** 1997; *Mourning Doves* (stories) 1993

Tuck, Lily (1938–)

Ms. Tuck divides her time between New York City and Maine.
The Woman Who Walked on Water 1996; *Interviewing Matisse or the Woman Who Died Standing Up* 1991

Tyau, Kathleen

Ms. Tyau grew up on the island of Oahu in a large Chinese-American family. A former NEA Fellowship winner, she currently lives in Oregon.
Makai 1999; **A Little Too Much Is Enough** 1995

Tyler, Anne (1941–)

Ms. Tyler was born in Minneapolis, Minnesota, and was educated at Duke University. She worked as a Russian bibliographer (at Duke) and as a Library Assistant (at McGill University in Montreal) before moving to Baltimore, Maryland, with her psychiatrist husband and starting her writing career.
A Patchwork Planet 1998; **Ladder of Years** 1995; **Saint Maybe** 1991; *Breathing Lessons* 1988; *The Accidental Tourist* 1985; *Dinner at the Homesick Restaurant* 1982; *Morgan's Passing* 1980; *Earthly Possessions* 1977; *Searching for Caleb* 1976; *Celestial*

Navigation 1974; *The Clock Winder* 1972; *A Slipping-down Life* 1970; *The Tin Can Tree* 1965; *If Morning Ever Comes* 1964

Unsworth, Barry (1930–)

Mr. Unsworth was born in Durham, England, and was educated at the University of Manchester. He has lived in Italy for many years.
After Hannibal 1997; **Morality Play** 1995; *Sacred Hunger* 1992; *Sugar & Rum* 1988; *Stone Virgin* 1985; *The Rage of the Vulture* 1982; *Pascali's Island* 1980; *The Big Day* 1976; *Mooncranker's Gift* 1973; *The Hide* 1970; *The Greek's Have a Word for It* 1967; *The Partnership* 1966

Updike, John (1932–)

John Updike was born in Shillington, Pennsylvania, and was educated at Harvard and at the Ruskin School of Drawing and Fine Arts, Oxford. A novelist, short story writer, critic and essayist, he has been associated with the *New Yorker* for much of his career.
Bech at Bay: A Quasi-novel 1998; **Toward the End of Time** 1997; **In the Beauty of the Lilies** 1996; **Brazil** 1994; *The Afterlife & Other Stories* 1994; **Memories of the Ford Administration** 1992; *Rabbit at Rest* 1990; *S.* 1988; *Trust Me* (stories) 1997; *Roger's Version* (1986); *The Witches of Eastwick* (1984); *Bech Is Back* 1982; *Rabbit Is Rich* 1981; *Problems* (stories) 1979; *Too Far to Go* (stories) 1979; *The Coup* 1978; *Marry Me* 1976; *A Month of Sundays*; *Museums and Women* (stories) 1972; *Rabbit Redux* 1971; *Bech: A Book* (stories) 1970; *Couples* 1968; *The Music School* (stories) 1966; *Of the Farm* 1965; *The Centaur* 1963; *Pigeon Feathers* (stories) 1962; *Rabbit Run* 1960; *The Poorhouse Fair* 1959; *The Same Door* (stories) 1959

Urquhart, Jane (1949–)

Jane Urquhart, an art historian, poet and novelist, was born in Ontario and was educated at the University of Guelph. Ms. Urquhart has served as a writer-in-residence at a number of Canadian universities.
The Underpainter 1998; **Away** 1994; *Changing Heaven* 1990; *Storm Glass* 1987; *The Whirlpool* 1986

Uyemoto, Holly

Ms. Uyemoto grew up in California and, after dropping out of high school worked at a variety of jobs (while writing her first novel), eventually ending up in Japan. She returned to the U.S. and enrolled at Wellesley College.
Go 1995; *Rebel Without a Clue* 1989

Vakil, Ardashir

Mr. Ardashir, born in Bombay, currently teaches English at the Pimlico Comprehensive School in London.
Beach Boy 1998

Vanderhaeghe, Guy (1951–)

Mr. Vanderhaeghe, novelist, short story writer, playwright and professional archivist, was born in Saskatchewan and was educated at the University of Saskatchewan and at the University of Regina. He still lives in Saskatchewan where he is Visiting Professor of English at S.T. M. College.

The Englishman's Boy 1997; *Things as They Are* 1992; *Homesick* 1989; *My Present Age* 1984; *The Trouble with Heroes & Other Stories* 1983; *Man Descending* (stories) 1982

Vassanji, M.G. (1950–)

An award-winning Canadian novelist of East Indian descent, Mr. Vassanji was born in Kenya and raised in Tanzania. After immigrating to Canada, he received degrees in physics from MIT and the University of Pennsylvania. He was a research associate and lecturer in physics at the University of Toronto from 1980 to 1989. He lives in Toronto and has been a full-time writer since 1989.

Book of Secrets 1996; *Uhuru Street* 1992; *No New Land* 1991; *The Gunny Sack* 1989

Vea, Alfredo

Mr. Vea, the son of migrant workers, was born in Arizona. After serving in Vietnam, he received a law degree and, in addition to fiction writing, practices a form of public interest law in the Mission District of San Francisco.

God Go Begging 1999; *The Silver Cloud Cafe* 1996; *La Maravilla* 1993

Veciana-Suarez, Ana

Ana Veciana-Suarez was born in Cuba and now lives in Miami with her five children where she writes a column for the *Miami Herald*.

The Chin Kiss King (1997)

Vidal, Gore (1925–)

Mr. Vidal, short story writer, essayist, novelist and script writer, was born at West Point. He attended St. Albans School in Washington, D.C., and graduated from Philips Exeter. A grandson of the Oklahoma Senator, Thomas P. Gore, he inherited an intense interest in politics and ran (unsuccessfully) for Congress from New York State and for the Senate from California. He writes mysteries under the pseudonym Edgar Box and lives in Italy.

The Smithsonian Institution 1998; *Live from Golgotha* 1992; *Hollywood* 1990; *Empire* 1987; *Lincoln* 1984; *Duluth* 1983; *Kalki* 1978; *1876* 1976; *Myron* 1974; *Burr* 1973; *Two Sisters* 1970; *Myra Breckinridge* 1968; *Washington, D.C.* 1967; *Julian* 1964; *Messiah* 1954; *The Judgment of Paris* 1952; *Dark Green, Bright Red* 1950; *A Search for the King—A Twentieth Century Legend* 1950; *The Season of Comfort* 1949; *The City and the Pillar* 1948; *In a Yellow Wood* 1947; *Williwaw* 1946

Vilmure, Daniel

A novelist and playwright, Mr. Vilmure was educated at Harvard and Stanford. His plays have been well-received in both the U.S. and the U.K.

Toby's Lie 1995; *Life in the Land of the Living* 1987

Vizenor, Gerald (1934–)

Gerald Vizenor, a member of the Chippewa tribe, was born in Minneapolis and was educated at NYU, the University of Minnesota and Harvard. A poet, novelist, and editor, he currently teaches at UC–Berkeley.

Hotline Healers 1997; *Dead Voices* 1994; *The Heirs of Columbus* 1991; *Landfill Meditations* (stories) 1991; *Bearheart: the Heirship Chronicles* 1990; *Griever, an American Monkey King in China* 1987; *Woodarrows* 1981; *Darkness in St. Louis: Bearheart* 1978

Vollmann, William T. (1959–)

Mr. Vollmann, a writer and publisher, was born in Santa Monica, California, and was educated at Deep Spring College, Cornell and UC–Berkeley.

The Atlas 1996; *Butterfly Stories* 1993; *The Rifles* 1994 (Part III — Seven Dream Series); *Fathers & Crows* 1992 (Part II — Seven Dream Series); *Thirteen Stories & Thirteen Epithets* 1991; *Whores for Gloria* 1991; *The Ice Shirt* 1990 (Part I — Seven Dream Series); *The Rainbow Stories* 1989; *You Bright & Risen Angels* 1987

Wagner, Bruce (1954–)

A novelist, TV scriptwriter and producer (he created *Wild Palms*), Mr. Wagner has been a long-time Hollywood habitué and L.A. resident.

I'm Losing You 1996; *Force Majeur* 1991

Walker, Alice (1944–)

Prize-winning novelist Alice Walker was born in Eatonton, Georgia, and was educated at Spellman College and at Sarah Lawrence. A former Guggenheim Fellow, she worked briefly for *Ms.* magazine and taught at Wellesley College before turning her attention to fiction writing. She currently lives in Northern California.

By the Light of My Father's Smile 1998; *Possessing the Secret of Joy* 1992; *The Temple of My Familiar* 1989; *The Color Purple* 1982; *You Can't Keep a Good Woman Down* (stories) 1981; *Meridian* 1976; *In Love & Trouble: Stories of Black Women* 1973; *The Third Life of Grange Copeland* 1970

Wallace, David Foster (1962–)

Mr. Wallace, short story writer, novelist and educator, was born in Ithaca, New York, and was educated at Amherst College and the University of Arizona where he received an MFA.

Infinite Jest 1996; *The Girl with Curious Hair* 1988; *The Broom of the System* 1987

Walsh, Jill (Gilian) Paton (1937–)

A novelist and children's author, Ms. Walsh was born in London and was educated at Oxford. She currently lives in Cambridge, England, where she runs a small specialist publishing house called Green Bay Publishers.

The Serpentine Cave 1997; *Knowledge of Angels* 1994; *Lapsing* 1986; *Five Tides* (stories) 1986; *Farewell, Great King* 1972

Warlick, Ashley

Ms. Warlick was born in Salt Lake City, Utah, and was educated at Dickenson College. She was awarded a Houghton Mifflin Literary Fellowship in 1995.

The Summer After June 1999; **Distance from the Heart of Things** 1996

Warner, Alan (1964–)

A short story writer and novelist, Mr. Warner was born in Oban, Scotland, and now lives in Ireland. His first novel, *Morvern Caller* has been televised by the BBC.

The Sopranos 1999; **These Demented Lands** 1997; **Morvern Caller** 1995

Watson, Larry

Mr. Watson, a poet, novelist and educator, was born in Rugby, North Dakota, and raised in Bismark. He teaches English at the University of Wisconsin at Stevens Point.

White Crosses 1997; *Justice* 1996; **Montana 1948** 1993; *In a Dark Time* 1980

Weiss, Daniel Ethan (1953–)

A novelist and non-fiction writer, Mr. Weiss was born in New York City and was educated at Harvard.

The Swine's Wedding 1996; *The Roaches Have No King* 1994; *Hell on Wheels* 1991

Welch, James (1940–)

James Welch, a poet and novelist who grew up on a Blackfoot-Gros reservation in Montana, was educated at the University of Montana. His nonfiction book, *Killing Custer*, is a treatment of the Battle of Little Bighorn from the perspective of the Indians.

The Indian Lawyer 1990; *Fools Crow* 1986; *The Death of Jim Loney* 1979; *Winter in the Blood* 1974

Welch, Robert (1947–)

A poet, critic and novelist, Robert Welch is the editor of the *Oxford Companion to Irish Literature*.

Groundwork 1997; *Muskerry* 1991

Weldon, Fay (1933–)

Ms. Weldon was born in Alvechurch, England, was raised in an all-female household in New Zealand. She returned to England with her mother at the age of 14 and was educated at St. Andrews University in Scotland. She eventually moved to London where she began a successful career as an advertising copywriter. She soon began to write radio and television scripts and then turned her hand to fiction writing.

Big Girl's Don't Cry 1998; *Wicked Women* 1997; **Worst Fears** 1996; **Splitting** 1995; **Trouble** 1993; *Life Force* 1992; *Growing Rich* 1992; *The Moon Over Minneapolis* 1991; *Darcy's Utopia* 1990; *The Cloning of Joanna May* 1989; *The Leader of the Band* 1988; *The Heart of the Country* 1987; *The Rules of Life* 1987; *The Hearts and Lives of Men* 1987; *The Shrapnel Academy* 1986; *Polaris and Other Stories* 1989; *Letters to Alice on First Reading Jane Austen* 1984; *The Life and Loves of A She-Devil* 1983; *The President's Child* 1982; *Watching Me, Watching You* (stories) 1981; *Puffball* 1980; *Praxis* 1978; *Little Sisters* (U.S. title: *Words of Advice*) 1977; *Remember Me* 1976; *Female Friends* 1974; *Down Among the Women* 1971; *The Fat Woman's Joke* 1967

Weller, Anthony

An award-winning poet, travel writer, foreign correspondent, and novelist, Weller's work has appeared in *GQ*, *National Geographic*, and *Paris Review*. *The Polish Lover* 1997; **The Garden of the Peacocks** 1996

Wells, Rebecca

Ms. Wells, a Louisiana native, is a successful novelist, actor and playwright. She lives on an island near Seattle, Washington.

Divine Secrets of the Ya Ya Sisterhood 1996; *Little Altars Everywhere* 1992

Welsh, Irvine

Mr. Welsh was born in Glasgow and currently divides his time between Scotland, London and Amsterdam.

Filth 1998; **Marabou Stork Nightmare** 1996; *Ecstasy* (stories) 1996; *The Acid House* (stories) 1995; **Trainspotting** 1994

Wesley, Mary (1912–)

Mary Wesley, a novelist, published her first work of fiction at the age of 71. She worked for the War Office during World War II and has lived in Italy, France and Germany. She lives in Devon.

Part of the Furniture 1997; **An Imaginative Experience** 1994; **A Dubious Legacy** 1992; *A Sensible Life* 1990; *Second Fiddle* 1988; *Not That Sort of Girl* 1987; *The Vacillations of Poppy Carew* 1986; *Harnessing Peacocks* 1985; *The Camomile Lawn* 1984; *Jumping the Queue* 1983

West, Dorothy (1909–)

Ms. West, an original member of the "Harlem Renaissance," was born in Boston and was educated at Columbia and Boston University. A short story writer, novelist and editor, she founded the literary magazine *Challenge* in the 1930s.

The Richer, The Poorer 1995; ***The Wedding*** 1995; *The Living Is Easy* 1948

West, Paul (1930–)

Paul West was born in Derbyshire, England, and was educated at the University of Birmingham, Oxford University and Columbia University. A novelist, short story writer, essayist and literary critic, he has been on the English faculty at Penn State for more than three decades.

Life with Swan 1999; *Terrestrials* 1997; ***Sporting with Amaryllis*** 1996; ***The Tent of Orange Mist*** 1995; *Love's Mansion* 1992; *The Women of Whitechapel and Jack the Ripper* 1991; *Lord Byron's Doctor* 1989; *The Place in Flowers Where Pollen Rests* 1989; *The Universe and Other Fictions* 1988; *Rat Man of Paris* 1986; *The Very Rich Hours of Count von Stauffenberg* 1980; *Gala* 1976; *Bela Lugosi's White Christmas* 1972; *Colonel Mint* 1972; *Caliban's Filibuster* 1971; *I'm Expecting to Live Quite Soon* 1970; *Alley Jiggers* 1966; *Tenements of Clay* 1965; *A Quality of Mercy* 1961

Westlake, Donald (1933–)

A novelist and script writer, Mr. Westlake attended Champlain College and SUNY–Binghampton. He also writes under the following pseudonyms: Richard Stark, John B. Allen and Tucker Coe.

The Ax 1997; *What's the Worst That Could Happen?* 1996; *Smoke* 1995; *Baby, Would I Lie: A Romance of the Ozarks* 1994; *Don't Ask* 1993; *Humans* 1992; *Drowned Hopes* 1990; *Tomorrow's Crimes* 1989; *Sacred Monster* 1989; *Trust Me on This* 1988; *Good Behavior* 1987; *Good Behavior* 1985; *Levine* 1984; *Why Me* 1983; *Kahawa* 1981; *Castle in the Air* 1980; *Enough* 1977; *Nobody's Perfect* 1977; *Dancing Aztecs* 1976; *Brothers Keepers* 1975; *Two Much* 1975; *Help, I'm Being Held Prisoner* 1974; *Jimmy the Kid* 1974; *Gangway* 1973; *Cops and Robbers* 1972; *Under an English Heaven* 1972; *Bank Shot* 1972; *I Gave at the Office* 1971; *The Mercenaries* 1970; *Adios, Scheherezade* 1970; *The Hot Rock* 1970; *Who Stole Sassi Manoon* 1969; *Somebody Owes Me Money* 1969; *Up Your Banners* 1969; *The Curious Facts Preceding My Execution & Other Fictions* 1968; *God Save the Mark* 1967; *Philip* 1967; *The Spy in the Ointment* 1966; *The Busy Body* 1966; *The Fugitive Pigeon* 1965; *Pity Him Afterwards* 1964; *Kelly* 1963; *361* 1962; *Killing Time* 1961; *The Mercenaries* 1960

Wharton, Thomas (1963–)

Mr. Wharton was born in Alberta, Canada, and was educated at the University of Alberta. He currently lives in Peace River. He was the Grant McEwan writer-in-residence for 1999.

Icefields 1995

White, Edmund (Valentine III) (1940–)

Playwright, novelist and short story writer, Mr. White was born in Cincinnati, Ohio, and was educated at the University of Michigan. He has taught widely including stints at Johns Hopkins, Columbia, Yale and George Mason.

Farewell Symphony 1997; *Skinned Alive* 1995; *The Beautiful Room* 1988; *Darker Proof: Stories from a Crisis* 1988; *Caracole* 1985; *Aphrodesiac* (stories) 1984; *A Boy's Own Story* 1982; *Nocturnes for the King of Naples* 1978; *Forgetting Elena* 1973

Wideman, John Edgar (1941–)

Mr. Wideman, a prominent African-American writer and musician, was born in Washington, D.C., and was educated at the University of Pennsylvania and at Oxford University. He has worked in publishing in New York City and has taught at a number of colleges and universities (including the University of Massachusetts, Howard University and the University of Pennsylvania) and was awarded a MacArthur Fellowship in 1993.

The Cattle Killing 1996; *The Stories of John Edgar Wideman* 1992; ***Philadelphia Fire*** 1990; *Fever* (stories) 1989; *Reuben* 1987; *Sent for You Yesterday* 1983; *Hiding Place* 1981; *Damballah* 1981; *The Lynchers* 1973; *Hurry Home* 1970; *A Glance Away* 1967

Wilcox, James (1949–)

Mr. Wilcox was born in Hammon, Louisiana, and was educated at Yale. He worked in the publishing industry in New York City from 1971 to 1978. He has written full-time since 1978.

Plain & Normal 1998; *Guest & Sinner* 1993; *Polite Sex* 1991; *Sort of Rich* 1989; *Miss Undine's Living Room* 1987; *North Gladiola* 1985; *Modern Baptists* 1983

Wilkins, Damien (1963–) New Zealand

Damien Wilkins was born and raised in lower Hutt, New Zealand; he also spent two years as a creative writing student in the U.S.

Little Masters 1997; *The Miserables* 1993; *The Veteran Peril* 1990

Williams, Niall (1958–)

Born in Dublin, Mr. Williams, a novelist and playwright, has also written — in collaboration with his wife, Christine Breen — a number of successful non-fiction books about life in Ireland.

Four Letters of Love 1997

Willis, Connie (1945–)

Ms. Willis, the winner of six (record-breaking) Nebula Awards, lives in Greely, Colorado.

To Say Nothing of the Dog, or, How We Found the Bishop's Bird Stump at Last 1998; *Promised Land* (with Cynthia Felice) 1997; *Bellwether* 1996; *Futures Imput* (stories) 1996; *Remake,*

Locus (novellas) 1995; *Uncharted Territory* 1994; *Impossible Things* (stories) 1993; *Doomsday Book* 1992; *Light Raid* (with Cynthia Felice) 1989; *Lincoln's Dreams* 1987; *Fire Watch* (stories) 1985; *Water Witch* (with Cynthia Felice) 1982

Wilson, Jonathan (1950–)
A novelist and short story writer, Mr. Wilson was born in England but immigrated to the U.S. in 1983.
The Hiding Room 1995; *Schoom* (stories) 1995

Wilson, Robert McLiam (1964–)
Mr. Wilson, a novelist who has won both the Rooney Prize and the Irish Book Award, was born in Belfast, Northern Ireland.
Eureka Street 1996; *Manfred's Pain* 1992; *Ripley Bogle* 1989

Winegardner, Mark (1961–)
Mr. Winegardner was educated at Miami University and George Mason University where he is currently on the faculty. He is also affiliated with the Writer's Center in Bethesda, Maryland.
The Veracruz Blues 1966

Winterson, Jeannette (1959–)
Ms. Winterson, a playwright, novelist and short story writer, was born in Manchester, England, and was educated at Oxford.
World & Other Places 1999; *Gut Symmetries* 1997; *Art & Lies* 1994; *Written on the Body* 1992; *The Passion* 1987; *Sexing the Cherry* 1987; *Boating for Beginners* 1985; *Oranges Are Not the Only Fruit* 1985

Winton, Tim (1960–)
Prize-winning Australian novelist Tim Winton was born and educated in Perth Australia. In addition to capturing the 1984 Miles Franklin Literary Award, Winton was also the recipient of a senior fellowship from the Literature Board of the Australian Council.
The Riders 1994; *Cloudstreet* 1991; *In the Winter Dark* 1988; *Minimum of Two* (stories) 1987; *That Eye, That Sky* 1986; *Scissons* (stories) 1984; *Shallows* 1984; *An Open Swimmer* 1981

Wolff, Geoffrey (1937–)
Geoffrey Wolff, novelist and author of the successful memoir *Duke of Deception* , was born in L.A. A former Fulbright Scholar, he was educated at Princeton University.
The Age of Consent 1996; *The Final Club* 1990; *Providence* 1986; *Inklings* 1977; *The Sightseer* 1974; *Bad Debts* 1969

Womack, Jack (1956–)
Born in Lexington, Kentucky, Mr. Womack, an editor and novelist, lives in New York City.
Let's Put the Future Behind Us 1996; *Random*

Acts of Senseless Violence 1994; *Elvissey* 1993; *Heathern* 1990; *Terraplane* 1988; *Ambient* 1987

Wong, Norman (1963–)
Norman Wong grew up in Honolulu and was educated at the University of Chicago and Johns Hopkins University (where he earned an M.A. in the Creative Writing program). He currently lives in New York City.
Cultural Revolution 1994

Woodrell, Daniel (1953–)
Daniel Woodrell, whose descendants settled in the Ozarks in the years preceding the Civil War, was raised in Missouri and Kansas. After a stint in the Marines he enrolled at the University of Kansas. He currently lives in West Plains, Missouri.
Tomato Red 1998; *Give Us a Kiss* 1996; *The Ones You Do* 1992; *Muscle for the Wing* 1988; *Woe to Live On* 1987; *Under the Bright Lights* 1986

Wright, Ronald (1948–)
Mr. Wright was born in Weybridg, England, and immigrated to Canada in 1970. He was educated at Cambridge University and the University of Calgary. A freelance journalist, lecturer, travel writer and novelist, Mr. Wright has long studied and written about the indigenous peoples of both North and South America.
A Scientific Romance 1998

Wright, Stephen (1943–)
Novelist Stephen Wright has studied at the (highly regarded) University of Iowa's Writers Workshop.
Going Native 1994; *M31, A Family Romance* 1988; *Meditation in Green* 1983

Yamaguchi, Yoji (1963–)
Mr. Yamaguchi, a book and editor and novelist, was educated at Johns Hopkins University. He lives in New York City.
The Face of a Stranger 1995

Yamanaka, Lois-Ann (1961)
Born in Molokoi, Hawaii, Ms. Yamanaka attended the University of Hawaii at Manoa. In addition to fiction writing she is an English and Language Resource teacher for Hawaii's Department of Education.
Blu's Hanging 1997; *Wild Meat & Bully Burgers* 1996; *Saturday Night at the Pahala Theater* 1993

Yamashita, Karen Tei (1951–)
Ms. Yamashita was born in California and lived in Brazil for nine years (where she met and married her architect husband). She now lives in Seto, Japan.
Tropic of Orange 1997; *Brazil-Maru* 1992; *Through the Arc of the Rain Forest* 1990

Youmans, Marly

A published poet, short story writer and novelist, Ms. Youmans is a native of South Carolina.
Catherwood 1996; *Little Jordan* 1995

Young Bear, Ray (1950–)

A poet, short story writer, novelist and member of the Mesquake tribe, Ray Young Bear was educated at Claremont College, Grinnell College and the University of Iowa. He was born in Iowa and grew up on the Mesquakie Tribal Settlement.
Remnants of the First Earth 1996; *Black Eagle Child: The Facepaint Narratives* 1992

Youngblood, Shay

Ms. Youngblood, playwright and novelist, was born in Columbus, Georgia, and was educated at Brown University. She is currently writer-in-residence at the New School for Social Research in New York City.
Soul Kiss 1997; *Big Mama Stories* 1989

Zabor, Rafi (1946–)

A well respected music journalist and some-time jazz drummer, Mr. Zabor was born in Brooklyn and was educated at Brooklyn College.
The Bear Comes Home 1977

Zencey, Eric

Eric Zencey is a professor or History at Goddard College in Vermont.
Panama 1996

Zigman, Laura

Ms. Zigman grew up in Newtonville, Massachusetts, and was educated at the University of Massachusetts at Amherst. She worked in the New York publishing world for ten years and currently lives in Washington, D.C.
Animal Husbandry 1998

Zuravleff, Mary Kay

Mary Kay Zuravleff, a native of Oklahoma, was a recipient of the American Academy's Rosenthal Foundation Award. She currently lives in the Washington, D.C., area.
The Frequency of Souls 1996

Author and Title Index

References are to entry numbers

Subject Index

References are to entry numbers